**Volume I**

# Constitutional Structure and Political Power

D1284083

# AMERICAN CONSTITUTIONAL LAW: POWER AND POLITICS

## Volume I

# Constitutional Structure and Political Power

**Gregg Ivers**
*American University*

Houghton Mifflin Company     Boston • New York

**Editor-in-Chief:** Jean L. Woy
**Sponsoring Editor:** Mary Dougherty
**Development Editor:** Katherine Meisenheimer
**Editorial Assistant:** Tonya Lobato
**Project Editor:** Tracy Patruno
**Manufacturing Manager:** Florence Cadran
**Marketing Manager:** Jay Hu

**Cover design:** Diana Coe/ko Design Studio
**Cover image:** *Daniel Ellsberg and Wife Walk from Courthouse,* © Bettmann/CORBIS.

**Copyright © 2001 by Houghton Mifflin Company. All rights reserved.**

No part of this work may be reproduced or transmitted in any form or by any means, electronic or mechanical, including photocopying and recording, or by any information storage or retrieval system without the prior written permission of Houghton Mifflin Company unless such copying is expressly permitted by federal copyright law. Address inquiries to College Permissions, Houghton Mifflin Company, 222 Berkeley Street, Boston, MA 02116–3764.

Printed in the U.S.A.

Library of Congress Catalog Card Number: 00-133890

ISBN: 0-395-88983-9

1 2 3 4 5 6 7 8 9 - CRS - 04 03 02 01 00

For my family,
past, present, and future

# Contents

Each semester when I teach Constitutional Law and Civil Liberties, I always tell my undergraduates that no one is going to learn anything, including myself, if we cannot make the subject come alive. And what makes the study of the Constitution fun is the human drama behind the cases that have resulted in many of the landmark decisions by the United States Supreme Court. In *American Constitutional Law,* I have emphasized the relationship between law and society, with a special focus on the people and organized interests that turned their personal disputes with the law into cases of monumental importance that resulted in constitutional change.

## How the Book Is Organized

Like most professors, I have a certain point of view about the subjects I teach and write about. One point I want my students to understand is that the Constitution was not handed to the American people as God is said to have handed Moses the Ten Commandments on Mount Sinai. The Constitution was the result of an intense political battle between bitterly divided foes over how to organize the nation's social and economic life, how to distribute political power to govern a new nation, and how to secure individual rights while maintaining an orderly society. In the introductory chapter, I explain the theoretical and political roots of the Framers' decisions on these issues. I also introduce in Chapter 1 the concept of law as an instrument of social and political change, and describe the important role that organized interests play in the litigation process.

In Chapter 2, I offer an in-depth discussion of constitutional theory and why it matters. Here, I do not follow the path of some of my colleagues in emphasizing the attitudinal model of judicial behavior, or focus solely on modes of judicial review or emphasize the Court's decision-making process independent of concurrent social and political forces. Instead, I take the student through various theories of constitutional interpretation and explain the choices that the justices and the parties involved in litigation face in trying to articulate and defend what they believe the Constitution means. While

I offer a balanced discussion of the strengths and weaknesses of different approaches to interpreting the Constitution, I also want the student to understand that constitutional theory has its roots in what Justice Oliver Wendell Holmes, Jr. called the "felt necessities" of our time. In other words, the societal arrangements that law protects do not just exist; they are the product of political choices. I emphasize this theme beyond this one chapter on constitutional interpretation to give it prominent weight throughout the casebook.

Volume I is subtitled *Constitutional Structure and Political Power,* and the themes I explore include the separation of powers, federalism, congressional and state commerce power, and the protection of private property and ownership rights. Although the emphasis in Volume I is on the social organization of American political power, I go beyond just a dry recitation of the traditional cases that define the authority of the different branches of government and the distribution of power between the national government and the states. I also infuse constitutional development with commentary on the social and political dynamics of the era. Supreme Court justices, like everybody else, are products of their time. How a justice in the late 1800s, for example, understood private property rights had a great deal to do with the nation's rapid move toward an industrialized society, the influence that such titans of American industry as the Rockefeller and Carnegie families had on attitudes toward government regulation, and the legal and economic theories being advanced by leading intellectuals in support of property rights. Likewise, in the late 1930s, the Great Depression and the panic that gripped the nation during this time inevitably shaped what a growing number of justices believed about the power of Congress to regulate the economy.

## Features of the Book

Each chapter begins with an opening story that is designed to illustrate the complexities involved in that particular area of constitutional law and how the law affects the lives of ordinary American citizens. I then offer an essay that leads students into the cases and, from that point forward, interweave commentary and narrative with excerpts from Supreme Court opinions. In almost every case, I include concurring and dissenting opinions so that students can see the range of views among the justices on important constitutional questions. Each case excerpt is preceded by a headnote that emphasizes the social and political dimension of the litigation and, when appropriate, the role of organized interests. Starting with Chapter 2, each chapter includes several SIDEBARs, short pieces that highlight the human origins and real-world consequences of particularly critical cases. I also include suggested readings at the end of each chapter to assist students writing research papers or who simply want to know more about the subject.

Houghton Mifflin will provide instructors and students comprehensive support for *American Constitutional Law.* The award-winning CD-ROM *The Supreme Court's Greatest Hits* is available with new copies of the text. This CD contains more than seventy hours of Supreme Court oral arguments and opinion pronouncements from fifty of the most important cases decided in the last forty years. Cases on the CD that are excerpted in the text are marked with a CD icon; this cross-referencing will help students easily locate the multimedia resources that correspond to their assigned readings.

There is also a Web site (accessible via the College Division homepage at http://www.college.hmco.com) that will provide hypothetical problems to use in conjunction with each chapter; ACE self-tests that students can use to test their comprehension of the readings; a Guide to Legal Reports and Periodicals to help students with their research; and links to organizations that frequently participate in Supreme Court litigation. Each year, Houghton Mifflin will publish an annual supplement to *American Constitutional Law* to keep instructors and students abreast of the Court's most recent decisions and other related developments.

## Acknowledgments

I never had the slightest illusion I could undertake this book without research support and assistance from my students, who remain a teacher's greatest resource. I would like to thank the following students for all their hard work: Dan Weiss, Kristen Eastlick, Chris Donovan, Erika Schlachter, Eric Eikenberg, Mari Strydom, Meredith Mecca, Scott Shoreman, Kyle Cruley, Kim Horn, Meg Streff, Kristen Murray, Nicole Goodrich, Kara Ruzicka, Carey Ng, Jennie Tucker, Jarrett Alexander, Erin Ackerman, Reuben Ackerman, Gina Connell, Jay Liotta, Stephanie Lenner, Michelle Moyer, Dominique Fanizza, Shannon Thornton, and Jeremy Gauld. Several other students helped make my life easier in many other ways, and they, too, deserve thanks: Lisa Loftin, Amy Hannah, Eva Rallis, Allison Viscardi, Michael Wilkosz, Ethan Rosenzweig, Sarah Simmons, Bridget McGuire, Fred Turner, Chris Canavan, Tim Titus, Jon Liebman, Damon Manetta, Shawn Bates, Kim Nelson, Meg Scully, Carla Cerino, and Melanie Auerbach. These are all special people who are destined for great things. It was a privilege to work with all of you.

Scott Diener, Bruce Field, John Reteneller, Scott Stephenson, and Jim Verhoff are not political scientists, but they are great friends and always a necessary source of laughter, error-correction, and support. Jon Kaplan and Scott Aronson, two great friends and talented musicians, were my partners in Available Jones, one of Washington's great bar and party bands. Thanks for helping me not think about the Constitution while we were cranking out the hits! And you're welcome for learning that drummer's rule.

My colleagues at American University have provided support, advice, and inspiration along the way, and a special group deserves my thanks: Ron Shaiko, Diane Singerman, Saul Newman, Joe Soss, Karen O'Connor, Bill LeoGrande, David Rosenbloom, Richard Bennett, Christine DeGregorio, and Jim Thurber. I am especially grateful for the support of my former Dean in the School of Public Affairs, Neil Kerwin, who has always encouraged me to pursue my interests on my own terms. I also appreciate the support of my current Dean, Walter Broadnax, who gave me the time I needed to bring this casebook to fruition.

Several colleagues from other colleges and universities provided first-rate criticism and suggestions during the development of this casebook. These reviewers helped me articulate my own ideas, even if they did not necessarily agree with them. Thanks to: James Brent, San Jose State University; Susan Burgess, University of Wisconsin–

Milwaukee; Robert A. Carp, University of Houston; Cornell W. Clayton, Washington State University; Sue Davis, University of Delaware; John P. Forren, Miami University; Martin Gruberg, University of Wisconsin–Oshkosh; Christine Harrington, New York University; Stacia L. Haynie, Louisiana State University; Beth Henschen, Eastern Michigan University; William Lasser, Clemson University; John A. Maltese, University of Georgia; Kevin T. McGuire, University of North Carolina–Chapel Hill; Richard Pacelle, University of Missouri–St. Louis; Bill Swinford, University of Richmond; Howard Tolley, Jr., University of Cincinnati; and Michael C. Tolley, Northeastern University.

I would like to extend my special gratitude to Bette Novit Evans of Creighton University and her Fall 1999 constitutional law students: Khader Abou-Nasr, Adam Astley, Christine Delgado, Jennifer Glaser, Scott Hahn, Jessalyn Haluza, Jeremy Hix, Kelly Johnstone, David Lutz, Daniel Moore, Jason Nickla, Marty Palmer, William Semple, and Thomas Volberg, for testing this material while it was still in progress. Professor Evans and her students offered thoughtful and detailed commentary on the draft manuscript that was extremely useful in helping shape the final version.

Three people deserve a special mention all of their own: Sarah Becker, who agreed to work with me her senior year in college on this project when it was still getting off the ground. You gave me the gift of your maturity, intelligence, and persistence. Thank you for believing in me. Michael Palermo, who has shared his endless smile with my family for almost ten years, thank you for the gifts you have given all of us, and especially my children. David Kaib has been much more than my graduate assistant for the past three years. He has been, quite literally, my lifeline, without whom this book never would have seen the light of day. Dave read every word of this casebook, from the photo captions to the opinions, tracked down every missing citation and, in

the spirit of full disclosure, saved me from screwing up on a daily basis. He is "Uncle Dave" to my children, and, in the eyes of my wife, a candidate for sainthood. As my son, Max, once told a playmate in the sandbox, "Uncle Dave is my dad's assistant. My dad's a professor and when he doesn't know what to do he calls Uncle Dave and Uncle Dave fixes it. He's one of our best friends."

Former Sponsoring Editor Melissa Mashburn is many things—witty, charming, endlessly optimistic, persistent, and a first-rate connoisseur of barbeque and donuts—but most of all endlessly supportive and marvelously inspirational. Melissa gave me the confidence to move forward with this casebook. After I reached the initial wall, Melissa told me, "Don't worry! I'm going to get you a great development editor! Just wait! You'll love her!" And, lo and behold, Katherine Meisenheimer came along, and sure enough, whipped this project into shape and kept me going, offering just the perfect blend of support, encouragement, and "that's great, Gregg, but when am I going to see Chapter 5" reminders that every author needs. Faced with Katherine's powerful intelligence and acute sense of purpose, I was left with little choice but to listen to this amazing woman. Nancy Benjamin managed the production process with ease and skill. June Waldman turned frequently unintelligible prose bearing only a remote kinship to the English language into coherent sentences. Martha Friedman took my less-than-specific ideas for photographs and illustrations and managed to find exactly what I wanted. Jean Woy, Editor-in-Chief, is legendary in political science publishing circles, and after working with her on *American Constitutional Law,* I understand why. Finally, thanks to Jay Hu, Marketing Manager, and the Houghton Mifflin sales representatives for believing in and selling my book.

For Janet, still sweet and lovely after all these years, and Max, who makes every day a fun day, and Claire, the wonderwaif of Maplewood Park, you make me feel all right, and that is better than I can say.

**Volume I**

# Constitutional Structure and Political Power

# Law and Constitutional Structure

A student preparing to study American constitutional law for the first time usually experiences a mix of emotions. First, the big, fat casebook—like this one—that goes with the course immediately suggests to the student that a lot of reading will be involved, inviting fear. Professors think that reading is a good thing. In fact, some even take pride in believing that their constitutional law course will require students to read more than any other course the student ever takes. Second, after flipping through this clean, unhighlighted, new casebook, the student notices that phrases such as *ipso facto, ex post facto, subpoena duces tecum, in toto,* and *stare decisis* appear—repeatedly—throughout the opinions, leaving him or her to wonder in just what language constitutional law is taught. Third, as if this newly discovered need to brush up on Latin is not enough to cause anguish, the student then discovers that familiar topics such as congressional committees, majority leaders, cabinet secretaries, and political parties have been replaced by obscure subjects: appellants filing writs of *certiorari, amici curiae* briefs, jurisdictional claims, and equitable remedies. The result? Bewilderment, confusion or maybe a little of each!

So, is it possible for the uninitiated student to learn about constitutional law and, as only a professor could dare ask, love it at the same time?

Indeed it is, for constitutional law is about far more than dry legal rules and their application to what seem like distant abstract disputes. Constitutional law is about how the most critical and important questions involving government power, social and political organization, and individual rights evolved from disputes between citizens and their government—or between and among the different branches and levels of government—into legal rules. Concurrent with this theme is the other critical component in understanding American constitutional law: how the Supreme Court has interpreted the United States Constitution and what the Court's interpretations mean for the relationship between law and society. This casebook has two purposes: (1) to help you understand the social and political context of modern American constitutional law and (2) to encourage you to think about the Court not only as an institution that creates constitutional doctrine based on iron-clad rules of legal jurisprudence but also as one whose decisions are intertwined with social and political forces.

Students of the Court and the Constitution need to know more than just the chronological development of constitutional law. This casebook includes materials that tell you who the clients were in these cases and how they were selected; the role organized interests play in the dynamics of the litigation process; the historical and social context in which particularly controversial cases were decided; and how the Court's decisions affect the real world. The Court most often has the last word on what the Constitution means. But after the Court hands down an opinion, responsibility shifts to government agencies, large corporations, small businesses, college admissions directors, farmers, police departments, and public schools, to name just a few of the people and institutions that must apply judicial decisions to everyday life.

## Law as Constitutional Foundation

Constitutional law is more than just a body of rules that organize our social and political institutions, protect individual rights, and establish government power. Law serves as the "connective tissue" that binds the structure, substance, and culture of American constitutionalism together.[1] Law is the foundation upon which government and social organization rests. Think for a moment about the use of the adjective *constitutional* to describe the rule of law. The Constitution created our current government structure and established, in principle, the balance between liberty and authority. But the decision of the Framers to create a written constitution also represented the decision to create, or *constitute,* a government. Although the American model of government is often described as representative and democratic, it is above all a constitutional government because it depends on the consent of the governed for its legitimacy. A government that derives its authority from sources other than the people is not, under this definition, properly constituted.

Our Constitution, then, creates the legal structure for our political institutions. The decision of the Framers to create a political system in which the legislature, the executive branch, and the courts served independent purposes and were accountable to different societal interests reflected a *political theory* about the possibilities and limits of popular government. That government should represent the wishes and aspirations of the people held out the more optimistic side of the Framers. That the sources of political power and the motives that drove its exercise were, in the view of James Madison, a pernicious threat to the operation of representative democracy represented their own experience with popular government. "The accumulation of all powers, legislative, executive, and judiciary, in the same hands," wrote Madison in *Federalist* 47, "whether of one, a few, or many, and whether hereditary, self-appointed, or elective, may justly be pronounced the very definition of tyranny."[2]

Here, well before Alexander Hamilton's more explicit description of judicial power in *Federalist* 78, Madison also hints of the important functional role the courts will have in the American form of constitutional government. To defend his model of popular government based on the separation of powers, Madison drew heavily from the French philosopher Baron de Montesquieu's classic 1784 work of political theory, *The Spirit of the Laws.* Noting Montesquieu's argument on behalf of an independent judicial branch in an otherwise elected popular government, Madison wrote that "he did not mean that these departments ought to have no partial agency in, or no control over, the acts of each other. [W]here the whole power of one department is exercised by the same hands which possess the whole power of another department, the fundamental principles of a free constitution are subverted."[3]

Madison, and the Framers in general, believed that a proper constitutional structure was necessary to limit government power and protect individual rights. In a perfect world no constitution would be needed because no government would be necessary to organize and channel social and political currents. But, as Madison wrote in *Federalist* 51, his most famous defense of the new constitutional order: "In framing a government which is to be administered by men over men, the great difficulty lies in this: you must first enable the government to control the governed; and in the next place oblige it to control itself. A dependence on the people is, no doubt, the primary control on the government; but experience has taught mankind the necessity of auxiliary precautions."[4] What were—and remain—those "auxiliary precautions" of which Madison spoke? A constitutional government that called for separation of powers, checks and balances, federalism, and protections for individual rights against reckless majority rule.

In 1789 the nation ratified its new Constitution and with it "A New Order for the Ages," or *Novus Ordo Seclorum,* the Latin phrase embossed on the great seal of the United States. These core principles of American constitutionalism remain vibrant and timeless. But, as you will see over the course of this book, the transformation of those principles into constitutional law has created new issues and questions that continue to confront the participants in our constitutional system. The next section examines the basic structure of the Constitution, the government it created, and the political theory underlying American popular government.

## Constitutional Structure

In *Federalist* 1, Alexander Hamilton made clear that nothing less than the survival of the United States as a democratic republic was at stake in the ratification process over the new Constitution. Indeed, in the first paragraph of the first of eighty-five papers that he, Madison, and John Jay, writing under the pseudonym of *Publius,* Latin for "Public Man," Hamilton implored the nation to consider the historical significance of the Constitution's ratification. "The subject speaks its own importance; comprehending in its consequences nothing less than the existence of the UNION," Hamilton wrote, "[f]or it has been frequently remarked that it seems to have been reserved to the people of this country, by their conduct and example, to decide the important question, *whether societies of men are really capable of good government through reflection and choice, or whether they are forever destined to depend for their political constitutions on accident and force.*"[5]

Could popular government, rooted in consent—a word mentioned no less than forty-eight times in the *Federalist Papers*—and dependent upon the power of reason rather than the power of force survive the factional disputes that would be inevitable among a people characterized by social, economic, religious, and political differences? For *Publius,* the answer was yes if the nation was willing to embrace a constitution that created a strong national government, separated and divided the sources of government power, gave each branch of government partial control over the other, allowed states to retain jurisdiction over matters of law and public policy closest to the people, and kept tyrannical majorities from usurping individual rights.

Here, let us remember that the Constitution is much more than a suggestion box for good government. It is the foundation for the rule of law. Even early opponents of the Constitution could agree with the assessment of one Boston newspaper, not long after the Constitution's ratification, that "that which is not regulated by law must depend on the arbitrary will of the rulers, which would put an end to civil society."[6] The Constitution is also *public* law in that it creates the rules that govern the relationship between our public institutions and the people. All laws made by our legal and political institutions must be consistent with its meaning. What the Constitution means or, better phrased, *should* mean, is open to debate. How and where to ascribe meaning to the Constitution, what it means from generation to generation, and who should have ultimate authority in constitutional interpretation are questions that have been at the center of constitutional litigation since the establishment of the Republic.

Creating the constitutional structure of public law was the problem that confronted the state representatives to the Constitutional Convention held in Philadelphia during the summer of 1787. Consensus existed among the delegates over the inadequacies of the Articles of Confederation, but opinion over the extent to which the Articles should be revised was far from settled. When the Constitution was completed and presented to the public later that September, its language reflected the textual ambiguities that are an essential feature in the art of political compromise. Convention delegates and numerous others involved in the drafting of the Constitution held widely divergent views on what it was supposed to mean. Several delegates left the convention confused over the meaning of key sections of the Constitution even after it was completed. Some of the more prominent Framers, including Madison and Hamilton, changed their original views on the Constitution's meaning during their lifetimes. Notable opponents of ratification, such as George Mason, who refused to sign the Constitution and actively campaigned against its ratification, later became more hopeful of its possibilities. If the Framers resolved their political differences through textual ambiguities and, in some cases, deliberate exclusion, should it come as any great surprise that subsequent generations continue to disagree over what the Constitution means?[7]

The Constitution that emerged from the convention in September 1787 created a legal and political structure radically different from the Articles of Confederation. No nation had ever devised a constitutional framework that centralized power in an elected national government to the extent the United States Constitution did. No nation had created an elaborate federal structure to protect the domain of state governments from national intrusion. No nation had ever developed such an imaginative and complex series of constitutional safeguards against the improper use of institutional power. No nation steeped in the culture and language of popular rule had ever created a judicial branch unaccountable to electoral will to declare acts and laws of political majorities unconstitutional. And, in the Bill of Rights, no nation had ever deemed civil and political liberties so fundamental that their protection was not dependent on the sentiments and prejudices of popular

*George Washington presiding over the Constitutional Convention in 1787.*
Bettman/CORBIS.

majorities. That women, African Americans, Native Americans, and poor whites were not, in different degrees, the beneficiaries of the Constitution's majestic promises raised troublesome questions then—and even now—about the democratic intentions of the constitutional Framers. We will deal with these important issues throughout this casebook. For now, let us consider the four major and interlocking components of our constitutional structure: national government, separation of powers, federalism, and civil and constitutional rights.

### National Government

Complaints directed at the Constitution's decided emphasis on national power by the Anti-Federalists, as the various opponents of ratification were better known, were quite legitimate if we consider how the new consti-

tutional structure altered the sources and distribution of government power established by the Articles of Confederation. In place of the loose, lateral framework that characterized the Articles, one in which the states retained their primacy, the Constitution delegated supreme legislative, executive, and judicial authority to the national government. Moreover, the Constitution provided comprehensive and specific powers to each branch that the Articles did not. Among the most dramatic changes that illustrated the Constitution's emphasis on national power were the following:

• Congress, in Article I, now had the exclusive power to regulate interstate commerce; to authorize and collect taxes; to create federal courts and establish their jurisdiction; and the general authority to make all laws necessary and proper to exercise its legislative responsibilities. Throughout this volume you will see how, since the early nineteenth century, the Court's interpretation of the Necessary and Proper Clause, the Commerce Clause, and the power of Congress to tax and spend has been instrumental in the expansion of legislative power at the national level.

- The executive branch, created by Article II, now consisted of a single, elected president, and not, as some Anti-Federalists had wanted, a plural council. Article II also delegated to the president the power to make judicial and cabinet appointments. In language that first appeared to be an afterthought but has proven to be critical in the constitutional expansion of executive power, Article II reserved to the president the power to faithfully execute the laws of the United States. This book also explores how the growth of presidential power based on the "implied powers" of the executive has been enormous and extraordinarily consequential for the balance of constitutional power.

- Concurrent with the exercise of the judicial power by the Supreme Court, the sole court created by Article III of the Constitution, was the implied power of judicial review. Judicial review remains controversial for this reason alone. However, the Court's use of judicial review to advance dramatic new concepts of government power and individual rights, often in the face of popular opposition, has generated additional controversy.

- Article VI made all laws and treaties enacted under the "Authority of the United States . . . the supreme Law of the Land," and bound the state governments to the laws created under national power. Disagreement continues, however, over the scope of power retained by the states in areas such as commercial and police power regulation.

Criticism of the Constitution, which came in a series of written responses to the *Federalist Papers,* was swift and severe. *Brutus,* the pseudonym of one of most vociferous and articulate Anti-Federalists, charged:

This government is to possess absolute and uncontroulable power, legislative, executive and judicial, with respect to every object to which it extends, for by the last clause of section 8th, article 1st, it is declared 'that the Congress shall have power to make all laws which shall be necessary and proper for carrying into execution the foregoing powers, and all other powers vested by this constitution, in the government of the United States; or in any department or office thereof.' And by the 6th article, it is declared 'that this constitution, and the laws of the United States . . . shall be the supreme law of the land; and the judges in every state shall be bound thereby, any thing in the constitution, or law of any state to the contrary notwithstanding.'

This government then, so far as it extends, is a complete one, and not a confederation. It [has] . . . absolute and perfect powers to make and execute all laws, to appoint all officers, institute courts, declare offences, and annex penalties, with respect to every object to which it extends, as any other in the world. So far therefore as its powers reach, all ideas of confederation are given up and lost. It is true this government is limited to certain objects, or to speak more properly, some small degree of power is still left to the states, but a little attention to the powers vested in the general government, will convince every candid man, that if it is capable of being executed, all that is reserved for the individual states must very soon be annihilated, except so far as they are barely necessary to the organization of the general government.[8]

Although several influential opponents of the Constitution acknowledged the need for a more efficient and cohesive national government, they never anticipated the wholesale transfer of legal and political power from the states to the national level.[9] But the inherent contradiction of the Anti-Federalists' desires to retain the advantages of a small, state-centered republic while granting to the national government the necessary power to forge and maintain the bonds of union left the Constitution's opponents vulnerable to the scornful criticism of *Publius:*

For the absurdity must continually stare us in the face of confiding to a government the direction of the most essential national interests, without daring to trust it to the authorities which are indispensable to their proper and efficient management. Let us not attempt to reconcile contradictions, but firmly embrace a rational alternative.[10]

*Publius* had a powerful point here, "given the Anti-Federalists' own desire for a Union government powerful enough to secure common interests, especially defense."[11] By itself *Publius's* argument that the proposed

T H E

FEDERALIST:

ADDRESSED TO THE

PEOPLE OF THE STATE OF
NEW-YORK.

N U M B E R  I.

*Introduction.*

AFTER an unequivocal experience of the ineffi-
cacy of the subsisting federal government, you
are called upon to deliberate on a new constitution for
the United States of America. The subject speaks its
own importance; comprehending in its consequences,
nothing less than the existence of the UNION, the
safety and welfare of the parts of which it is composed, the fate of an empire, in many respects, the
most interesting in the world. It has been frequently
remarked, that it seems to have been reserved to the
people of this country, by their conduct and example,
to decide the important question, whether societies of
men are really capable or not, of establishing good
government from reflection and choice, or whether
they are forever destined to depend, for their political
constitutions, on accident and force. If there be any
truth in the remark, the crisis, at which we are arrived,
may with propriety be regarded as the æra in which
                    A                              that

*The* Federalist Papers, *written by Alexander Hamilton, John
Jay, and James Madison in support of the ratification of the
Constitution, originally were published in New York City
newspapers from October 1787 to August 1788.*
North Wind Picture Archives.

Constitution at least presented the kind of "rational
alternative" to the Articles of Confederation was one
that the Anti-Federalists could not answer. They were
unable to reconcile their own wants and aspirations into
a new governmental structure.[12] National power as the
thread that would bind the states into a union became

the baseline for the Federalists' argument on behalf of
the Constitution. *Publius* said as much in *Federalist 44,*
where he commented that without strong and substantive national power, "the whole Constitution would be a
dead letter."[13]

Here, it is important to understand that what the
opponents of the Constitution, such as *Brutus,* feared
from national power—that, for example, the scheme of
representation proposed for Congress would result in a
"heterogeneous" and chaotic composition of interests—
the Federalists viewed as its great strength.[14] To secure
the political and economic stability of a large, commercial republic and protect the rights of its citizens from
unreasonable majority rule, Madison believed the Constitution had to quell three major threats. The first was
disunion, the second was the "mischiefs of faction," and
the third was the threat to the rights and liberties of individuals and political minorities regardless of whether
those threats came from majorities or other minorities.[15]
Madison's solution was to establish first a strong, vibrant
national government, complete with the appropriate
powers to allow the branches to pursue their respective
ends. Such "energetic" government, *Publius* confessed,
would need constitutional constraints to promote both
the "public good and private rights." Separation of powers, as you will see, became the most important of those
constraints.

## Separation of Powers

Before the Federalists could turn their attention to how
the Constitution's positive features would attract virtuous leaders dedicated to the promotion of good government, they had to persuade the public that it was, above
all, a safe government. In *Federalist 47,* Madison conceded the point that the "accumulation" of all legislative, executive and judicial power in a single branch
of government could "*justly* be pronounced the very
definition of tyranny." To sooth the suspicions of the
Constitution's opponents, Madison asserted his agreement with their "objection" that governments that fail to
adhere to the principle of separation of powers *do*
endanger the liberties of the people.

One of the principal objections inculcated by the more
respectable adversaries to the Constitution is its supposed

violation of the *political maxim that the legislative, executive, and judiciary departments ought to be separate and distinct. In the structure of the federal government no regard, it is said, seems to have been paid to this essential precaution in favor of liberty.*[16]

Madison makes two fundamental points here in defense of the constitutional arrangement of the separation of powers. The first is that Madison admits as "truth" the notion that the accumulation of all powers in the "same hands" is the "very definition" of tyranny. With that truth established, Madison states that the "maxim" deduced from it is that separation of powers is necessary to protect a constitutional government. If the Constitution really accumulates or tends to accumulate power in the same hands, then "no further arguments would be necessary to inspire a universal reprobation of the system."[17]

A steadfast belief in limited government based on separation of powers also reinforced the commitment of the Framers to the rule of law. Because the Constitution announces the division of legislative, executive, and judicial functions among the three branches, each is required to exercise its respective power by what one of the most influential Enlightenment philosophers on the Framers, John Locke, referred to as "declared Laws."[18] Rule by "declared," or public, law, constrained the abilities of the three branches to act against their enumerated, limited powers. Laws enacted and enforced under popular government were known in advance and thus generally applicable to all cases in which such laws applied. Rule by law is possible without a government formed on the separation of powers principle. But the conception of separation of powers, as applied to our constitutional structure, *requires* government by the rule of law. The Constitution, because it is "declared" law that defines the duties and limits of its various powers, meets this requirement.[19]

Separation of powers, designed to quell the concerns of the public and allow it to guard against the false exercise of government power, could not function without each branch having the constitutional means to resist the potential intrusions of another. Of course, the Constitution creates three separate branches of the national government, each with distinct powers and responsibilities, and divides levels of government power along a federal structure, allowing state and local governments to retain appropriate legal jurisdiction and political power. These lines of division, however, are not strict. The constitutional structure outlined by the Framers can be more accurately described as one in which separate government institutions share in the exercise of their responsibilities. Each branch, as Madison states in *Federalist* 51, "should have a will of its own." But the constitutional structure envisioned by *Publius* also included an interest of each branch in the operation of another. As Madison argued:

> [T]he great security against a gradual concentration of the several powers in the same department consists in giving to those who administer each department the necessary constitutional means and personal motives to resist encroachments of the others.
>
> The provision for [each branch's] defense must in this, as in all other cases, be made commensurate to the danger of attack. *Ambition must be made to counteract ambition. The interest of the man must be connected to the constitutional rights of the place.*[20]

The assignment of different powers to different branches is intended to do more than just prevent the rise of a zealous national government. A major objective of the Framers was to promote equilibrium among the branches. That meant paying as much attention to the "balances" component of the "checks and balances" principle as to the "checks." For *Publius*, the degree to which one branch can check the actions of another depends on the nature of the power exercised. The "constitutional rights" of each branch must have enough substantive power to attract worthwhile occupants, who, in turn, must have the personal and public motive to both exercise and defend its powers.

Notice here how *Publius* uses a circular path of reasoning to create an interdependent relationship between strong national government and separation of powers. "Energetic" national government is essential to preserve the Union. Separation of powers creates an institutional safeguard against oppressive, tyrannical government. Checks and balances ensure that each branch, while having a "will of its own," remains bound by law to its constitutional powers. Finally, only strong, coequal branches will have the personal and public incentives to defend their constitutional prerogatives.

How and where does the Constitution put this principle into practice? Here are a few examples:

- Article I provides Congress the power to declare war, but the president, in Article II, is made commander in chief of the armed forces.
- Article III creates the Supreme Court and vests it with jurisdiction over all cases arising under "law and equity." Article I leaves to Congress the power to create inferior courts. Congress is also given the power to establish the jurisdiction of the lower courts by Article III. Congress also decides how much money the federal judiciary receives each year to operate. Who appoints judges to the federal courts? The president. Who confirms them? The Senate.
- Article II says nothing about the president's power to make laws, but the president's constitutional responsibility to address the state of the union and recommend measures "he shall judge necessary and expedient" gives the office a considerable role in the congressional lawmaking function that is for Congress.
- Article II places the power to veto legislation in the hands of the president, but Congress, in Article I, has the power to override presidential vetoes with the support of two-thirds majorities of each chamber.

Difficult questions emerge from these examples. Does Article I allow Congress to create a "legislative veto" over rules made by administrative agencies it created to carry out federal law? Does the Constitution permit one branch of government to delegate its power to another? For example, may Congress delegate to agencies under the control of the judicial branch the power to create and enforce sentencing guidelines for federal judges? Suppose majorities in both the House and Senate believe that the Supreme Court has erred on a major constitutional question, such as one that involves abortion rights, school prayer, or affirmative action. Does the Exceptions and Regulations Clause of Article III, which leaves to Congress the responsibility to establish federal court jurisdiction, mean that it has the right to remove the Court's authority to hear cases involving those issues? Or does congressional authority to establish federal court jurisdiction mean something more general and less intrusive as it applies to courts' core functions?

These are hard questions, indeed. They are not just tough for students encountering constitutional law for the first time but, as you will see, for the Supreme Court as well.

### Federalism

Madison's conception of separation of powers was not the only departure from the established principles of popular government. The Constitution, *Publius* argued, created a republic that was a mixture of national and federal principles. Federalism, as we understand its most basic form, creates a multilevel government that permits the national and various state governments to operate in parallel fashion. But, as James Monroe, who later served as the nation's fifth president, wrote in opposition to the Constitution's proposed federal structure:

> To mark the precise point at which the powers of the general government shall cease, and that from whence those of the states shall commence, to poise them in such manner as to prevent either destroying the other, will require the utmost force of human wisdom and ingenuity. No possible ground of variance or even interference should be left, for there would the conflict commence, that might prove fatal to both.[21]

Monroe's complaint was that the Constitution avoided the specific assignment of power along federal lines. He is on solid ground here, for the character of the Constitution, as Madison claimed in *Federalist* 39, was "mixed," a combination of national and federal principles. "The proposed Constitution," Madison wrote, "therefore is in strictness neither a national nor federal constitution; but a composition of both. In its foundation, it is federal, not national; in the sources from which the ordinary powers of the Government are drawn, it is partly federal and partly national; in the operation of these powers, it is national not federal."[22]

It is difficult to know even now, as it was during the founding period, how these generalities apply to specific problems that arise between the forces of state and national power. However, the "new" federal structure that Madison envisioned undoubtedly represented a dramatic departure from the "old" federalism of the Articles of Confederation. Madison might not have been clear about the line separating national from state responsibilities, but he did confess that the federal structure proposed in the Constitution left the states in a subordinate position to the national government. For the Constitution's supporters, a confederate structure in which the states retained sovereign power against the national government was out of the question. The failure of the Articles, as Madison reminded the "adversaries" of the Constitution, assured that much:

> The difference between a federal and national government, as it relates to the *operation of government,* is by the adversaries of the plan of the convention supposed to consist in this, that in the former the powers operate on the political bodies composing the Confederacy in their political capacities; in the latter, on the individual citizens composing the nation in their individual capacities. On trying the Constitution by this criterion, it falls under the *national* not the *federal* character; though perhaps not so completely as has been understood.[23]

Federalism, like the separation of powers, was essential to the equilibrium that Madison believed was the basis for the Constitution's success. Placing power where it did not belong, whether on the national or state level, could doom the Constitution. This concern is similar to Madison's in *Federalist* 51, where he emphasized the need to diffuse the sources of unrest in the administration of government by "supplying" each branch of the national government with "opposite and rival interests."[24] Federalism allows the national and state governments to retain control over their respective spheres of influence. States retain explicit constitutional guarantees for the right to exist and to administer their respective governments. Those guarantees include the following:

- The Tenth Amendment, which states that "the powers not delegated to the United States by the Constitution, nor prohibited by it to the states, are reserved to the states respectively, or to the people." Remember the phrase "powers not delegated to the United States" as you encounter the Court's opinions on federal structure. Supporters of more state independence from federal rules and judicial decisions have pointed to those words as supportive of their position. Are they?
- Article V requires that all proposed amendments to the Constitution must be ratified, upon approval of

two-thirds of the Senate and the House of Representatives, by three-fourths of the states. Although this process gives the states the ultimate power to amend the Constitution, the Framers' decision to create a nonunanimous decision rule represented a "mixed" approach somewhere between supreme national power—congressional approval only—and state supremacy—a unanimous rule would permit one state to determine ratification or rejection. In whose favor does the balance of constitutional power over the Constitution tip, the national government or the states?

In the end, the Constitution's federal structure emphasizes the need for union through national government. Several other key constitutional provisions support the national character of the federal structure. Article IV, for example, requires each state to give "Full Faith and Credit" to the public laws of another state. It also affords citizens of other states the "Privileges and Immunities" provided to its own and empowers the United States to "guarantee" each state a republican form of government.

THE FUGITIVE SLAVE LAW IN OPERATION.

*Article IV, Section 2, of the Constitution originally permitted slave owners to capture fugitive slaves who had escaped into free states. This provision was later nullified by the Thirteenth Amendment, ratified in 1865.*
North Wind Picture Archives.

Despite the national features of the federal structure created by the Constitution, the states have continued to press for more power and independence. On more than one occasion, the states have prevailed in their efforts to retain control over matters that have ranged from civil rights protection to gun control to commercial regulation. Federalism continues to remain a vibrant constitutional principle.

## Civil and Constitutional Rights

Most Americans believe the chief purpose of the Constitution is to protect the fundamental rights of individuals and minorities from harsh majority rule. Thus it is remarkable to learn that the proposal for a bill of rights in the Constitutional Convention was considered and rejected with little more than a snap of the fingers. Debate over the inclusion of a bill of rights was limited to the morning of September 12, 1787, less than a week before the convention completed the Constitution and adjourned. Each state present when the proposal for the Bill of Rights was submitted to the floor of the convention, including Virginia, which counted James Madison, Thomas Jefferson, George Washington, and George Mason among its more famous residents, voted against the document. What little debate took place centered on George Mason's comments that he wished the Constitution "had been prefaced with a bill of rights. It would give great quiet to the people." Mason added that the convention could put together a bill of rights in no time; it would simply adopt the language of the eight states that had bills of rights of their own.[25]

The issue that concerned Mason, and later the Anti-Federalist writers in their subsequent fight against ratification, was the potential of the national government to use its "supreme" power to declare certain rights, such as freedom of speech and religion, that were included in various state constitutions as incompatible with national objectives. To the Constitution's opponents, the broad powers granted to Congress under the Necessary and Proper Clause, and to the national government more generally under the Supremacy Clause, did nothing to guarantee that state constitutions would be respected. If the states were no longer sovereign, but now political subdivisions of the national government with limited rights and powers, some constitutional

assurance was needed, as the Anti-Federalist tract written by the *Federal Farmer* claimed, to ensure the "people [that they] may never lose their liberties by construction" of the new government.[26] *Aristocrotis* put the matter in even more direct terms:

> [T]his Constitution is much better and gives more scope to the rulers than they [might] safely take if there was no constitution at all; for then the people might contend that the power was inherent in them; and that they had made some implied reserves in the original grant; but now they cannot, for every thing is expressly given away to government in this plan. No one [could stop Congress] unless we had a bill of rights to which we might appeal; and under which we might contend against any assumption of undue power and appeal to the judicial branch of the government to protect us by their judgements.[27]

Even upon submission of the Constitution to the states for ratification, the Federalists refused to concede that the absence of a bill of rights posed a potential problem in the protection of individual rights and liberties. Hamilton, in *Federalist* 84, wrote that the Constitution itself was, "in every rational sense, and to every useful purpose, A BILL OF RIGHTS." Furthermore, wrote Hamilton:

> I go further, and affirm that bills of rights, in the sense and in the extent in which they are contended for, are not only unnecessary in the proposed constitution, but would even be dangerous. They would contain various exceptions to powers which are not granted; and on this very account, would afford a colourable pretext to claim more than were granted. For why declare that things shall not be done which there is no power to do? Why for instance, should it be said, that the liberty of the press shall not be restrained, when no power is given by which restrictions may be imposed?[28]

Hamilton's last point here exemplifies the Federalists' initial position against the Bill of Rights. Because the Constitution vested each branch of government with no more than its textually defined power, all other rights and liberties were, therefore, reserved by the people and, where appropriate, the states. The Constitution permitted the government to exercise only those powers expressly granted in the text. James Wilson, a Federalist proponent of the Constitution who had considerable influence on the ideas of *Publius,* summarized this position in language somewhat less argumentative than Hamilton's in *Federalist* 84:

> [T]he congressional power is to be collected, not from tacit implication, but from the positive grant expressed in the instrument of the union. Thus, it would have been superfluous and absurd to have stipulated with a federal body of our own creation, that we should enjoy those privileges of which we are not divested, either by the intention or the act that has brought the body into existence.

To admit the need for a bill of rights, wrote Wilson, "would imply that whatever is not expressed [in the Constitution] was given, which is not the principle of the proposed Constitution."[29]

Wilson and Hamilton also pressed a second point, one that was more utilitarian than structural, on the question of whether a bill of rights was necessary. Could a bill of rights competently enumerate all the rights of man? What about the "natural rights" that people retained under the principles of "natural law?"[30] Does the failure of the constitutional text to enumerate "natural rights" mean that the government has seized them, or at least subjugated them to political order? No bill of rights could provide all the rights the people retained under constitutional government, especially one whose existence depended on the sovereignty of the people. Under the proposed American constitutional structure, the Federalists maintained, the people could lose their rights in only two ways: either by their own choosing (consent) or through the illegitimate exercise of government power (tyranny). Because of the enumerated, limited nature of government power under the Constitution, the people are not disposed to return their rights. The Constitution's structural design, as *Publius* made clear throughout the *Federalist Papers,* prevented the formation of tyrannical government.

What is wrong with this argument, at least from the perspective of the Constitution's opponents? First, although the Constitution does enumerate specific grants of power to all three branches, it offers no insight as to what the "necessary and proper" exercise of congressional power might be. Such latent, broad power vested in the national government was, to the Anti-Federalists, a sleeping giant. Even now, the constitutional definition of this clause, as well as other provisions of Article I such as the Commerce Clause, continues to evolve. The Supreme Court often becomes the arbiter of these intra- and intergovernmental disputes over what powers belong to which levels and branches of American government.

Second, the Constitution does, in fact, include several provisions that pertain to the concerns of the Anti-Federalists, such as the writ of *habeas corpus,* included in Article I, and the prohibition against religious oaths to hold public office, included in Article IV. Their inclusion in the original Constitution contradicted the Federalists' position that it was a self-executing bill of rights. Nothing in the Constitution permitted the government to suspend writs of *habeas corpus,* compel religious obedience to serve as a public official, or, perhaps most obvious, declare that the criminally accused were entitled to a trial by jury, included in Article III.

Such rights, the Anti-Federalists contended, were assumed even before the Constitutional Convention began. If their inclusion in the Constitution was simply to reinforce their importance, then the Federalists had just made the Anti-Federalists' point for them: Bills of rights are essential tools in the moral and civic education of a free people. Points such as these, hammered home in the opposition pamphlets and articles of such Anti-Federalists as *Brutus,* George Mason, and the *Federal Farmer,* gradually took hold among a public skeptical of Hamilton's position that constitutional silences equaled individual rights and liberties retained by the people. Wasn't a nation willing to experiment with a radical new constitutional structure and the political institutions it created entitled to know whether the most basic rights were independent of legislative control and political whim? Wrote the *Federal Farmer:*

> We do not by declarations change the nature of things, or create new truths, but we give existence, or at least establish in the minds of the people truths and principles which they might never otherwise have thought of, or soon forgot. If a nation means its systems, religious or political shall have duration, it ought to recognize the leading principles of them in the front page of every family book.[31]

James Madison recognized that ratification would be a much smoother process if the Constitution's proponents promised to consider the inclusion of a bill of rights upon approval of the original document. It is also fair to say that Madison was not unsympathetic to the Anti-Federalists' objections over the Constitution's lack of a bill of rights. Over time, Madison, prodded by his friend Thomas Jefferson, became a firm proponent of a bill of rights. He agreed with Jefferson that "a bill of rights is what the people are entitled to against every government on earth, general or particular, and what no just government should refuse, or rest on inference."[32] Perhaps a bill of rights would contribute to the public education of the people and reassure them that the Constitution did more than just authorize what the national government was allowed to do: By attaching an absolute negative on the exercise of government power, as the command throughout the First Amendment that "Congress shall make no law . . . abridging the freedom of speech," a bill of rights would declare what government could not do to its people.

In the process the inclusion of a bill of rights further reinforced the institutional safeguards created by the original Constitution and strengthened the rights of individuals and minorities against the possibilities of foolish, oppressive, and expedient government rule. In return for ratification of the original Constitution, Madison agreed to introduce a bill of rights in the opening session of the First Congress. In December 1791, Rhode Island became the final state to ratify the ten amendments written largely by Madison. He received considerable conceptual and intellectual guidance from fellow Virginians Thomas Jefferson and George Mason, who authored the Virginia constitution's Declaration of Rights in 1776.

In light of this historical backdrop, it might seem strange that the modern construction and application of the majestic promises contained in the Bill of Rights has been a twentieth-century phenomenon, and a rather late one at that. Our perception of the Supreme Court's counter-majoritarian role in defending fundamental rights from the clutches of powerful political majorities is a development that dates from the Great Depression. Prior to the 1930s the Court decided only a handful of cases involving claims brought under the Bill of Rights. You will see throughout both volumes of this casebook that as the Court began to assert its authority over the Bill of Rights, aggrieved individuals and institutions redirected their resources toward the legal resolution of problems once thought to be the province of the politi-

cal branches of government. Seen in this light, law is much more than our constitutional foundation. Law, in the form of litigation, is also an instrument of social and political reform.

## Legal Instrumentalism and Constitutional Development

The other prominent theme of this casebook is the importance of litigation, or the resolution of legal conflicts through the judicial process, in constitutional development. The litigation process attracts organizations that represent public and private interests; elite law firms; and various government actors, such as the Department of Justice, states attorneys general, and public defenders. Political scientist Richard C. Cortner, writing in 1968, noted that great constitutional cases do not arrive on the "Supreme Court's doorsteps like orphans in the night."[33] He was right. In the cases and materials presented in this casebook, note how often the Court's resolution of landmark cases began with the deliberate decision of an interest group, a public interest law firm, a trade association, or an elite private firm to use a particular case to challenge the legal status quo. Public law litigation, because it deals with constitutional provisions, federal statutes, or state laws that raise federal constitutional questions, is about much more than the resolution of an individual claim or grievance. In a single judicial stroke, the Court can affect the lives of people on a national scale and redraw the boundaries in which our political institutions make public policy.

The American constitutional arrangement offers multiple points of access to organized interests and individuals seeking to influence the various branches of government. Organized influence in the political process is something we all learn in American government. Often, in the same course, we are also taught to consider the courts, and the judicial process more generally, as the neutral and independent branch of government where legal, not political, disputes are resolved. Judges should make decisions in accordance with what a law or constitutional provision means. They should not introduce their biases, personal experience, or other nonlegal factors into the decision-making calculus. Judicial appointments should be based on merit, not politics; competence, not ideological leanings; and so on.

But the fact is that judges are people, not computers, whose constitutional vision is the sum of a constellation of values rooted in their life experience, their education, their professional socialization, and numerous other factors more difficult to pin down. The process of judicial selection and confirmation is a political one, with the president, who is the figurative leader of a political party, in the position to nominate someone who can extend the interests of the executive branch in the courts. Presidents, however, are not always successful. Sometimes they guess wrong. Other times their nominees are rejected, forcing them to turn to someone less controversial. In truth, judicial appointments represent a mixture of politics and merit.[34]

Whatever the case, one is hard-pressed to escape the conclusion that the courts, and the Supreme Court in particular, are an integral part of the American political process. Former Justice William Brennan, who served on the Court from 1956 to 1990, acknowledged the partisan nature of constitutional litigation in *NAACP* v. *Button* (1963), an important case involving freedom of association. Brennan wrote in *Button* that litigation is "a form of political expression, [which] may well be the sole practicable avenue open to a minority to petition for redress of grievances."[35] Litigants before the Supreme Court that have failed to secure redress for their constitutional grievances in the elected branches of government have included corporations and labor unions, slaveholders and abolitionists, abortion rights advocates and pro-life opponents, civil rights organizations and state governments opposing their claims, newspapers and public officials, and religious activists and civil libertarians. This list is far from exhaustive. Litigation, as you will discover, is a powerful tool of political advocacy and, in some cases, social reform.

Law as constitutional foundation. Law as constitutional structure. Law and litigation as instruments of social and political reform. These three themes serve as the collective undercurrent for our approach to the study of constitutional law. Rules are important. The Court's most important decisions affecting our constitutional order are all included here. But you will also see how the development and adjudication of constitutional law occurs within a set of social and political processes. As such, litigation affects society as a whole.

## FOR FURTHER READING

Ackerman, Bruce. *We the People: Foundations.* Cambridge, Mass.: Harvard University Press, 1991.

———. *We The People: Transformations.* Cambridge, Mass.: Harvard University Press, 1998.

Bowen, Catherine Drinker. *Miracle at Philadelphia.* New York: Little, Brown and Co., 1986.

Epstein, David F. *The Political Theory of the Federalist.* Chicago: University of Chicago Press, 1984.

Hall, Kermit L. *The Magic Mirror: Law in American History.* New York: Oxford University Press, 1989.

Hamilton, Alexander, John Jay, and James Madison. *The Federalist Papers.* Clinton Rossiter, ed. New York: Mentor Books, 1961.

Horwitz, Morton. *The Transformation of American Law, 1780–1860.* Cambridge, Mass.: Harvard University Press, 1977.

———. *The Transformation of American Law, 1870–1960.* New York: Oxford University Press, 1994.

Irons, Peter. *A People's History of the Supreme Court.* New York: Viking, 1999.

Kammen, Michael. *A Machine That Would Go of Itself: The Constitution in American Culture.* New York: Vintage Books, 1987.

O'Brien, David. *Storm Center: The Supreme Court in American Politics.* New York: W. W. Norton, 1993.

Rakove, Jack N. *Original Meanings: Politics and Ideas in the Making of the Constitution.* New York: Alfred A. Knopf, 1997.

Rosenberg, Gerald. *The Hollow Hope.* Chicago: University of Chicago Press, 1991.

Storing, Herbert J. *What the AntiFederalists Were For.* Chicago: University of Chicago Press, 1981.

Vose, Clement E. *Caucasians Only: The Supreme Court, the NAACP, and the Restrictive Covenant Cases.* Berkeley: University of California Press, 1959.

Wills, Garry. *A Necessary Evil: A History of American Distrust of Government.* New York: Simon & Schuster, 1999.

Wood, Gordon S. *The Creation of the American Republic, 1776–1787.* Chapel Hill: University of North Carolina Press, 1969.

# 2  Interpreting the Constitution

When the Beatles released their second album, *With the Beatles,* in late 1963, William Mann, the classical music critic for the London newspaper, the *Times,* referred to songwriters John Lennon and Paul McCartney as "the outstanding English composers of 1963." Enamored in particular with the melodic and harmonic structure of one Lennon-McCartney composition, "Not a Second Time," Mann congratulated the songwriters for their use of "Aeolian cadences" and noted that the song featured the same chord progression that ended Mahler's "Song of the Earth." Curious that a classical musicologist could find such sophisticated musical technique in a self-professed primitive rock 'n' roll song, John Lennon remarked years later that "it was just chords like any other chords. To this day, I have no idea what Aeolian cadences are. They sound like exotic birds."[1]

Musicians are not alone in having others outside the walls of their creative process take it upon themselves to assign to their words and ideas an intent that, in their own minds, never existed. From almost the moment the Constitution was ratified, each subsequent generation of Americans has argued over the document's meaning and application. The range of opinions, whether of scholars or Supreme Court justices, on what the clauses and provisions of the Constitution mean, how it divides and allocates power among the branches of government, and the limits it creates on the exercise of government power over individual rights is so wide that one unfamiliar with this debate would be stunned to discover that almost all of its participants claim to speak on behalf of the Framers' intent.

The debate over the Constitution's meaning is remarkable for the emphasis it places on original meaning, intent, and historical context. But the idea that it is possible to recover and discern the Constitution's "true" meaning obscures the larger point of this enterprise: the need for participants in this debate—judges, lawyers, scholars, and so on—to find a "usable past" to defend their interpretation of the Constitution.[2] The emphasis on historical and theoretical precision sometimes leads us to forget that the Constitution was the work of statesmen and politicians, not philosophers and theorists.[3] Still, the Framers were more than just political pragmatists in search of a constitutional structure to defend their social, economic, and political preferences. They also had clear moral goals that they believed the Constitution's republican form of government could best promote.[4]

The purpose of this chapter is to explore the various approaches and theories to interpreting the Constitution. Since even those who believe that the Constitution means and requires different things agree that the Constitution is the authoritative source of law in the United States, the Court's decisions must have legitimacy. Because the Supreme Court is so often the last word on what the Constitution means, constitutional theory is often bound together with the process of judicial review. For constitutional adjudication to have power and resonance, the Court must explain how and why it has reached its decision. Its decisions cannot stand if they are viewed as nothing more than raw exercises in political power. Even if the justices, regardless of their assertions to the contrary, cannot help but infuse their constitutional philosophies with their own policy preferences, those choices must bear some relationship to the more general, abstract principles of the Constitution.

What should judges emphasize in interpreting the Constitution? Some theories suggest that the Court should minimize the role of judicial review and allow legislatures and other democratic institutions wide latitude in their policy choices. Other theories suggest that the Court must remain aware of the prevailing social and political sentiments and interpret the Constitution in light of modern societal norms. Still, two broad and interrelated sets of ideas are pervasive throughout all constitutional theories. One is that theories of constitutional interpretation often differ about the certainty of the constitutional text's meaning and the appropriate methods for discovering its meaning. The second involves beliefs about the allocation of institutional responsibilities and roles between the courts and the elected branches of government.[5]

*"As a matter of fact, I have read the Constitution, and, frankly, I don't get it."*

© The New Yorker Collection 1988, Robert Weber from cartoonbank.com. All Rights Reserved.

Keep in mind as well another important question that pervades the debate over constitutional interpretation as you think through the ideas presented in this chapter: Is it possible to separate constitutional theory from the outcomes it produces? How the Court decides, for example, to interpret the power of Congress to regulate interstate commerce will do more than just address an important theoretical question about the separation of powers. It will mean that Congress will have more or less power to regulate the environment or the sale and ownership of handguns. The same is true for the Free Speech Clause of the First Amendment. The Court's decision to interpret free speech rights broadly will, on a much more specific level, affect our rights to engage in public protest, our rights to use the public schools for religious purposes, and the rights of homeowners to place objectionable signs on their lawns. In sum, the enterprise of constitutional interpretation has real consequences for our public institutions and the lives of the most common of citizens. With this background in mind, consider whether it is possible to separate the rules that should govern constitutional interpretation from their real-world consequences.

## Methods and Approaches

The categorization of complex, sometimes overlapping ideas in an effort to emphasize differences in approaches and methods to constitutional interpretation is hard to avoid. Although text, intent, and structure often provide the basic foundation for theories of constitutional interpretation, the emphasis of one factor over another results in a particular approach being labeled as interpretivist or noninterpretivist; literalist or indeterminist; activist or strict constructionist; traditionalist or postmodernist; and so on. Some scholars discount the effort to root constitutional interpretation in legal theories and instead insist that judicial behavior is an expression of ideological and policy-based values. Supreme Court outcomes can and should be understood as reflective of strategic choices made by the justices to advance these interests.[6]

The discussion here resists the lure of seeing constitutional interpretation as the result of mutually exclusive legal and nonlegal influences. It is true that a "system of interpretation that disregards the constitutional text cannot deserve support."[7] That said, legal theories have risen, fallen, and risen again that have emphasized different blends of legal, political, social, and economic considerations, largely because of the persuasiveness, or lack thereof, of the principles used to justify them.

Categorization, despite its risks and drawbacks, does have certain advantages. We have created three broad categories that draw the sharpest distinctions between competing approaches to constitutional interpretation: legal formalism, alternatives to formalism, and natural law. On the most general level, the differences between these approaches are greater than their similarities. A clear view of these visible differences will allow you to see the different weight accorded to constitutional text, Framers' intent, and other sources used to support different theories of constitutional interpretation. But also note the differences that exist within a particular school of thought as well as the similarities between what superficially appear to be separate categories.

We will return to summarize and synthesize the questions and problems generated by this discussion after we examine these three categories.

## Legal Formalism

*Legal formalism* rests largely on the assumption that the Constitution can be understood as having a specific and true meaning. The sole task of those charged with interpreting the Constitution is to uncover the historical intent of its creators. Judges should not take it upon themselves to decide what the Constitution *should* mean, but instead uncover the facts and historical intent that informs the language of the Constitution. To suggest that the Constitution does not impart clear commands risks putting judges in the position of "creating" and not "discovering" constitutional values. Personal biases must be constrained in favor of a neutral approach to constitutional interpretation. If the Constitution no longer stands apart from politics, then it becomes just another instrument for the advancement of a social and political agenda.

Perhaps the most stark and dramatic expression of legal formalism is found in the interpretive method called *originalism*. Advocates of originalism (or, as it is also called, *original intent*), argue that the Constitution (and the Bill of Rights) must be interpreted in a manner consistent with those who wrote and ratified it. Originalists claim that judges who favor approaches inconsistent with the intent of the Framers are legislators in disguise, creating and bending the law to suit their own version of the Constitution.

Originalism has always been part of the debate over constitutional interpretation, but the publication of former U.S. Court of Appeals judge Robert H. Bork's *The Tempting of America* in 1990 gave the issue a renewed prominence.[8] For reasons that were as much about politics as they were about ideas, *The Tempting of America* created quite a stir. In 1987 the Senate defeated Judge Bork's nomination to replace Justice Lewis F. Powell, a far more moderate jurist, on the Supreme Court. Judge Bork was defeated, in part, because his views were considered eccentric in light of contemporary constitutional values. But what tipped the scales against Bork was the powerful and unparalleled media campaign on the part of civil rights and civil liberties groups to defeat his nomination. Washington, D.C., advocacy groups such as People for the American Way, the NAACP, the National Organization for Women, and the Alliance for Justice succeeded in painting Bork's views as hostile to women, racial minorities, First Amendment freedoms, and the rights of criminal defendants.[9] They produced television commercials, including a memorable one featuring Gregory Peck, an actor famous for his portrayal of Abraham Lincoln, reducing the complexity of Bork's views to cartoonlike snapshots. Negative ads appeared in newspapers around the country. These strategies were continually updated and refined in light of constant public opinion polls to gauge their success.[10]

Bork was also hurt by charges that he was a Trojan horse for the conservative political agenda of the Reagan administration. This charge stemmed from the similarities between the constitutional philosophy of Judge Bork and Edwin Meese, who served as attorney general under President Ronald Reagan from 1985 to 1988. In a 1985 address to the American Bar Association, Attorney General Meese called for the Court to return to "a jurisprudence of original intention." He stated in no uncertain terms that several of the Court's recent and more well-known decisions involving abortion rights, school prayer, affirmative action, federalism, and criminal due process were wrong as matters of constitutional law.[11]

*Robert Bork's nomination to the Supreme Court in 1987 drew opposition in the streets as well as in the corridors of power in Washington, D.C.*
AP/Wide World Photos.

During the Reagan presidency (1981–1989), the Department of Justice, with full support from the White House, urged the Supreme Court to overrule several of these cases, which together painted over the broad canvas of American constitutional law. As strange as it was for a sitting attorney general to question the worth of the Court's constitutional jurisprudence in full public view, even more unusual was the response that Meese's comments generated from a sitting justice, William J. Brennan. In a public address to the Georgetown Law School in Washington, D.C., Justice Brennan replied that it was "arrogant to pretend that from our vantage we can gauge accurately the intent of the Framers. . . . *Those who would restrict claims of right to the values of 1789 specifically articulated in the Constitution, turn a blind eye to social progress and eschew adaptation of overarching principles to changes of social circumstances.*"[12] Justice Brennan was often cited by originalists as the evil spirit behind the modern Court's entrance into policy questions properly left with political branches, explained in part his candid response to Attorney General Meese's remarks.[13]

Caught in the crossfire of this political firestorm was Judge Bork. Although he continued to insist that his support for originalism bore no relationship to his own personal views, and defended his theories as "apolitical" and based on "neutral legal principles," his opponents continued to attack Bork and attack him hard. By the end more than three hundred organized interests were on record as opposing Bork's nomination to the Court, a standing army with resources that far exceeded his supporters, including his White House patrons.[14] Bork was unable to explain how originalism stood apart from the conservative political agenda and unwilling to retract his criticism of Supreme Court cases such as *Brown* v. *Board of Education* (1954), the landmark school desegregation case, and *Roe* v. *Wade* (1973), which established a legal right to abortion. He was defeated in his nomination to serve on the Court by a Senate vote of 58–42.[15]

Judge Bork used *The Tempting of America* to explain originalism outside the political vortex of his confirmation hearings. Originalism, wrote Judge Bork, "is the only method that can preserve the Constitution, the separation of powers, and the liberties of the people." To the claim that the original intent of the Constitution's Framers is unknowable, Judge Bork writes that the sources for discerning their original intent are "abundant." These include the *Federalist Papers* and the collected Anti-Federalist commentaries; congressional debates; early, seminal Supreme Court decisions such as *Marbury* v. *Madison* (1803); and authoritative judicial commentaries such as Justice Joseph Story's (1812–1845) *Commentaries on the Constitution of the United States* (1833). Concluded Judge Bork, "About much of the Constitution, therefore, we know a good deal; about other parts less; and, in a few cases, very little or nothing."[16]

On those rare occasions when a judge cannot make out a constitutional provision, "the judge should refrain from working. A provision whose meaning cannot be ascertained is precisely like a provision that is written in Sanskrit or is obliterated past deciphering by an ink blot. No judge is entitled to interpret an ink blot on the grounds that there might be something under it." Adherence to neutral principles, defined as the Framers' choices and not the judge's, absolves a judge from making unguided value judgments better left to the political branches. Originalism "is capable of supplying neutrality in all three respects—in deriving, defining, and applying principle."[17]

Criticism of originalism comes from several angles. The most obvious question comes first: Who were the "Framers" and how do we know they were of one mind? Few dispute the intellectual force that Thomas Jefferson brought to the constitutional design of American government and his oceanic influence over what later became the First Amendment. But Jefferson was in Paris during the four-year period when the Constitution and the Bill of Rights were written and ratified. Moreover, in correspondence with James Madison, Jefferson, while pleased with the basic constitutional structure of the government, was disturbed at "the omission of a bill of rights," a defect he insisted must be remedied before the Constitution could be complete.[18] John Adams, who succeeded George Washington as president and was another monumental figure in the founding of the Republic, was in London serving the nation as an emissary to Great Britain while Jefferson was in Paris. Should the ideas of these two pivotal figures be dismissed because of their absence during the Constitutional Convention and ratification period?

Should George Mason, a prominent Virginian who attended the convention and vigorously debated its provisions, but refused to sign the Constitution because the delegates failed to include a bill of rights, which he proposed, be considered a Framer? If not for the decision of the Federalists, especially James Madison, to agree to the submission of a Bill of Rights during the First Congress, the Constitution may have never been ratified. Do we include the Anti-Federalist pamphleteers as Framers, since the final version of the Constitution would have been far different without them? Originalism, despite its promises, provides no clear answer to the larger question of who framed the Constitution and whether consensus existed among those so designated as Framers.

Moreover, it is important to remember that the historical materials favored by originalists were also manipulated to serve the partisan political agendas of the Framers and, later, its ratifiers. Those who would rely upon convention records should be "warn[ed] that there are problems with most of them and that some have been compromised—perhaps fatally—by the editorial interventions of hirelings and partisans. . . . To recover original intent from these records may be an impossible . . . assignment."[19] For example, James Madi-

son's notes and commentaries on the Constitutional Convention, although reliable, are incomplete. Madison also did not permit the release of his notes in full form until after his death. Thus the American public did not have Madison's notes on the convention or his other constitutional commentaries until 1840. Problems such as these raise the question of whether an incomplete and sometimes unreliable historical record compromise the originalist enterprise beyond repair.

Second, is originalism a truly "value free," or "neutral" approach to constitutional interpretation? Bork admits the Constitution embodies partisan political values but argues that because those choices were "made long ago by those who designed and enacted the Constitution" they form the starting point of discussions of its meaning.[20] Judges should honor the Framers' choices, not disturb them. One critic has argued that Bork's claim is an assertion on behalf of originalism, not a defense of it:

> On this view, the original understanding is binding because the original understanding was that the original understanding is binding. The historical claim itself is debatable. The breadth of the words of the Constitution invites the view that its meaning is capable of change over time. There is evidence that the framers did not believe that their original understanding would control the future. But we should put that point to one side. Bork's claim is that the binding character of the original understanding is settled by the original understanding. This is not an argument at all; it is circular, or a rallying cry. To those who believe it is necessary to defend the view that the original understanding is binding, it cannot be persuasive.[21]

In other words, originalism treats the limits on government power and protections for individual rights created by the Constitution as prepolitical and presocial. These conditions are not a product of law, but a reflection of "nature." Originalists argue that no substantive defense or theoretical justification is necessary to explain the Constitution because the Constitution explains itself. This viewpoint raises two important questions: Is it possible to interpret the Constitution without taking into account the social and political context of law and litigation? Is it possible to interpret the admittedly abstract and vague provisions of the Constitution in neutral fashion?

Third, critics of originalism claim that it understates and misreads the Framers' intent. Indeed, the Constitution is quite specific in some parts—no one, for example, can dispute the constitutional requirement that one must be thirty-five years old to serve as president or that Congress possesses the sole power to establish the "Post Office and post Roads." It is, however, also ill-defined, open-ended, abstract, and anything but self-evident in its meaning and application. For courts to interpret the freedom of speech guarantee in an age of instantaneous communication through the Internet; criminal due-process rights in light of modern, wholly unimagined electronic and computerized surveillance and evasion techniques; or the nature of interstate commerce without going beyond the text assumes that constitutional choices are self-evident. Constitutional scholar H. Jefferson Powell describes this problem well:

> It is commonly assumed that the "interpretive intention" of the Constitution's framers was that the Constitution would be construed in accordance with what future interpreters could gather of the framers' own purposes, expectations, and intentions. Inquiry shows that assumption to be incorrect. Of the numerous . . . options that were available in the framers' day . . . none corresponds to the modern notion of [originalism]. . . . In defending their claim that the "original understanding at Philadelphia" should control constitutional interpretation, modern intentionalists usually argue that other interpretive strategies undermine or even deny the possibility of subjectivity and consistency in constitutional law. Critics of this position typically respond with a battery of practical and theoretical objections to the attempt to construe the nation's fundamental law in accord with historical reconstructions of the purposes of the framers. There may well be grounds to support either of these positions. This debate cannot be resolved, however, and should not be affected, by the claim or assumption that modern [original] intentionalism was the original presupposition of American constitutional discourse. Such a claim is historically mistaken.[22]

## Wallace v. Jaffree
### 472 U.S. 38 (1985)

In 1978 the Alabama legislature enacted a law requiring elementary school teachers to establish a moment of silence before school started for student meditation, reflection, or prayer. In 1981 Alabama enacted another law

that gave teachers the discretion to provide a one-minute period of silence for meditation or "voluntary" prayer. A year later the legislature passed another law, this time giving "any teacher or professor . . . in any public educational institution within the state of Alabama" the right to lead "willing students" in specifically worded prayer that expressly recognized "God . . . Creator and Supreme Judge of the World."

The 1981 law eventually reached the Supreme Court after Ishmael Jaffree, a legal services lawyer, challenged its constitutionality on behalf of his three children in the Mobile school system. Jaffree was raised a Baptist, although later became an agnostic in college. His wife, Mozelle, was a devout Bahai, but she agreed with her husband that religious practices had no place in public schools. Jaffree had tried to settle with school authorities outside of court. Support, however, from Alabama's political establishment for the prayer laws was overwhelming, thus making any chance to resolve the issue impossible.

The Court, 6-3, struck down the 1981 law (the 1978 and 1982 laws were invalidated in lower courts and not appealed). *Wallace* was notable not only for raising the school prayer issue almost twenty years to the day that such practices were declared unconstitutional but also for Justice Rehnquist's dissent. In a thirty-page dissent that demonstrated remarkable historical range and facility, Justice Rehnquist offered a powerful critique of the Court's religion decisions. His reliance on Framers' intent and historical sources offers an excellent example of the originalist approach to constitutional interpretation.

▼▲▼

JUSTICE REHNQUIST, dissenting.

Thirty-eight years ago this Court, in *Everson v. Board of Education*, 330 U.S. 1 (1947), summarized its exegesis of the Establishment Clause doctrine thus:

> In the words of Jefferson, the clause against establishment of religion by law was intended to erect "a wall of separation between church and State."

This language from *Reynolds*, a case involving the Free Exercise Clause of the First Amendment, rather than the Establishment Clause, quoted from Thomas Jefferson's letter to the Danbury Baptist Association the phrase

> I contemplate with sovereign reverence that act of the whole American people which declared that their legislature should "make no law respecting an establishment of religion, or prohibiting the free exercise thereof," thus building a wall of separation between church and State.

It is impossible to build sound constitutional doctrine upon a mistaken understanding of constitutional history, but unfortunately the Establishment Clause has been expressly freighted with Jefferson's misleading metaphor for nearly 40 years. Thomas Jefferson was, of course, in France at the time the constitutional Amendments known as the Bill of Rights were passed by Congress and ratified by the States. His letter to the Danbury Baptist Association was a short note of courtesy, written 14 years after the Amendments were passed by Congress. He would seem to any detached observer as a less than ideal source of contemporary history as to the meaning of the Religion Clauses of the First Amendment.

Jefferson's fellow Virginian, James Madison, with whom he was joined in the battle for the enactment of the Virginia Statute of Religious Liberty of 1786, did play as large a part as anyone in the drafting of the Bill of Rights. He had two advantages over Jefferson in this regard: he was present in the United States, and he was a leading Member of the First Congress. But when we turn to the record of the proceedings in the First Congress leading up to the adoption of the Establishment Clause of the Constitution, including Madison's significant contributions thereto, we see a far different picture of its purpose than the highly simplified "wall of separation between church and State." . . .

On the basis of the record of these proceedings in the House of Representatives, James Madison was undoubtedly the most important architect among the Members of the House of the Amendments which became the Bill of Rights, but it was James Madison speaking as an advocate of sensible legislative compromise, not as an advocate of incorporating the Virginia Statute of Religious Liberty into the United States Constitution. During the ratification debate in the Virginia Convention, Madison had actually opposed the idea of any Bill of Rights. His sponsorship of the Amendments in the House was obviously not that of a zealous believer in the necessity of the Religion Clauses, but of one who felt it might do some good, could do no harm, and would satisfy those who had ratified the Constitution on the condition that Congress propose a Bill of Rights. His original language "nor shall any national religion be established" obviously does not conform to the "wall of separation" between church and State idea which latter-day commentators have ascribed to him. His explanation on the floor of the meaning of his language—"that Congress should not establish a religion, and enforce the legal observation of it by law"—is of the same ilk. When he replied to Huntington in the debate over the proposal which came from the Select Committee of the House, he urged that the language "no religion shall be established by law" should be amended by inserting the word "national" in front of the word "religion."

It seems indisputable from these glimpses of Madison's thinking, as reflected by actions on the floor of the House in 1789, that he saw the Amendment as designed to prohibit the establishment of a national religion, and perhaps to prevent discrimination among sects. He did not see it as requiring neutrality on the part of government between religion and irreligion. Thus the Court's opinion in *Everson*—while correct in bracketing Madison and Jefferson together in their exertions in their home State leading to the enactment of the Virginia Statute of Religious Liberty—is totally incorrect in suggesting that Madison carried these views onto the floor of the United States House of Representatives when he proposed the language which would ultimately become the Bill of Rights. . . .

The actions of the First Congress, which reenacted the Northwest Ordinance for the governance of the Northwest Territory in 1789, confirm the view that Congress did not mean that the Government should be neutral between religion and irreligion. The House of Representatives took up the Northwest Ordinance on the same day as Madison introduced his proposed amendments which became the Bill of Rights; while at that time the Federal Government was, of course, not bound by draft amendments to the Constitution which had not yet been proposed by Congress, say nothing of ratified by the States, it seems highly unlikely that the House of Representatives would simultaneously consider proposed amendments to the Constitution and enact an important piece of territorial legislation which conflicted with the intent of those proposals. The Northwest Ordinance, 1 Stat. 50, reenacted the Northwest Ordinance of 1787 and provided that "[r]eligion, morality, and knowledge, being necessary to good government and the happiness of mankind, schools and the means of education shall forever be encouraged." . . .

It would seem from this [and other] evidence [discussed by Justice Rehnquist in his dissent, omitted here] that the Establishment Clause of the First Amendment had acquired a well-accepted meaning: it forbade establishment of a national religion, and forbade preference among religious sects or denominations. Indeed, the first American dictionary defined the word "establishment" as "the act of establishing, founding, ratifying or ordaining," such as in "[t]he episcopal form of religion, so called, in England." The Establishment Clause did not require government neutrality between religion and irreligion, nor did it prohibit the Federal Government from providing nondiscriminatory aid to religion. There is simply no historical

*Ishmael Jaffree, left, who challenged Alabama's school prayer law in the early 1980s, with his attorney, Ronnie L. Williams, on the steps of the U.S. Supreme Court.*
AP/Wide World Photos.

foundation for the proposition that the Framers intended to build the "wall of separation" that was constitutionalized in *Everson*.

Notwithstanding the absence of a historical basis for this theory of rigid separation, the wall idea might well have served as a useful, albeit misguided, analytical concept, had it led this Court to unified and principled results in Establishment Clause cases. The opposite, unfortunately, has been true; in the 38 years since *Everson*, our Establishment Clause cases have been neither principled nor unified. Our recent opinions, many of them hopelessly divided pluralities, have with embarrassing candor conceded that the "wall of separation" is merely a "blurred, indistinct, and variable barrier," which "is not wholly accurate" and can only be "dimly perceived."

Whether due to its lack of historical support or its practical unworkability, the *Everson* "wall" has proved all but useless as a guide to sound constitutional adjudication. It illustrates only too well the wisdom of Benjamin Cardozo's observation that "[m]etaphors in law are to be narrowly watched, for starting as devices to liberate thought, they end often by enslaving it."

But the greatest injury of the "wall" notion is its mischievous diversion of judges from the actual intentions of the drafters of the Bill of Rights. The "crucible of litigation" is well adapted to adjudicating factual disputes on the basis of testimony presented in court, but no amount of repetition of historical errors in judicial opinions can make the errors true. The "wall of separation between church and State" is a metaphor based on bad history, a metaphor which has proved useless as a guide to judging. It should be frankly and explicitly abandoned. . . .

The true meaning of the Establishment Clause can only be seen in its history. As drafters of our Bill of Rights, the Framers inscribed the principles that control today. Any deviation from their intentions frustrates the permanence of that Charter, and will only lead to the type of unprincipled decisionmaking that has plagued our Establishment Clause cases since *Everson*.

The Framers intended the Establishment Clause to prohibit the designation of any church as a "national" one. The Clause was also designed to stop the Federal Government from asserting a preference for one religious denomination or sect over others. Given the "incorporation" of the Establishment Clause as against the States via the Fourteenth Amendment in *Everson*, States are prohibited as well from establishing a religion or discriminating between sects. As its history abundantly shows, however, nothing in the Establishment Clause requires government to be strictly neutral between religion and irreligion, nor does that Clause prohibit Congress or the States from pursuing legitimate secular ends through nondiscriminatory sectarian means. . . .

It would come as much of a shock to those who drafted the Bill of Rights as it will to a large number of thoughtful Americans today to learn that the Constitution, as construed by the majority, prohibits the Alabama Legislature from "endorsing" prayer. George Washington himself, at the request of the very Congress which passed the Bill of Rights, proclaimed a day of "public thanksgiving and prayer, to be observed by acknowledging with grateful hearts the many and signal favors of Almighty God." History must judge whether it was the Father of his Country in 1789, or a majority of the Court today, which has strayed from the meaning of the Establishment Clause.

▼▲▼

Legal formalism also finds a visible and prominent place in *literalism*. Constitutional literalists, like originalists, argue that the Constitution, as written, settles the need to go beyond the text to understand its meaning. Literalism and originalism also share similarities in their acceptance, but fundamental distrust, of judicial review. Each approach emphasizes the need for courts to defer to the laws created by democratic majorities—especially when the Constitution is silent on a particular question or when dealing with one of its more open-ended clauses. Judges that stray from the text of the Constitution and the intent of the Framers, properly understood, have granted themselves a license to impose their own values through judicial review.

Literalism and originalism do share the trait of legal authoritarianism, or a belief that judicial choices are self-evident, but their similarities end there.[23] It is far more difficult to tie literalism to a specific set of political outcomes than to do so with originalism. Another important difference between the two approaches is the role that each assigns to the Court to use judicial review to defend the clear and absolute commands of the Constitution. No individual better exemplifies the literalist approach to constitutional interpretation and its differences with originalism than former Supreme Court justice Hugo L. Black.

A giant of twentieth-century American law and jurisprudence, Justice Black served on the Supreme Court for thirty-four years (1937–1971), under five chief justices and six U.S. presidents. Prior to his appointment by President Franklin D. Roosevelt, Justice Black represented Alabama in the U.S. Senate, where he developed a justified reputation as one of the staunchest supporters of the New Deal. Unlike most justices when they come to the Court, Justice Black arrived almost fully formed in his approach to constitutional interpretation. He believed that courts should not interfere with the right of Congress and the state legislatures to regulate the nation's economic and business affairs unless a clear violation of due process had occurred. His most succinct description of this view is captured in his opinion for the Court in *Ferguson* v. *Skrupa* (1963) in which he wrote, "[w]e refuse to sit as a 'super-legislature to weigh the wisdom of legislation.' Whether the legislature takes for its textbook Adam Smith, Herbert Spencer, Lord Keynes, or some other is no concern of ours."[24]

Justice Black also adhered to a rigid conception of the separation of powers, rejecting even the slightest suggestion that one branch had the power to assume the functions of another. *Youngstown Sheet & Tube Co.* v. *Sawyer* (1952), which involved President Harry S. Truman's famous effort to seize the nation's steel mills, provided "the setting for the most clear-cut expression" of Justice Black's constitutional literalism outside the context of the Bill of Rights.[25] President Truman invoked his presidential authority to end a strike at the nation's steel mills and force production to assure a steady supply of materials to the armed forces at the height of the Korean War. In the *Youngstown* opinion, which halted President Truman's action, note the emphasis that Justice Black places on the formal construction of the separation of powers:

> In the framework of our Constitution, the President's power to see that the laws are faithfully executed refutes the idea that he is to be a lawmaker. The Constitution limits his functions in the lawmaking process to the recommending of laws he thinks wise and the vetoing of laws he thinks bad. *And the Constitution is neither silent nor equivocal about who shall make the laws which the President is to execute. The first section of [Article I] says that "All legislative Powers herein granted shall be vested in a Congress of the United States. . . .* It is said that other Presidents without congressional authority have taken possession of private business enterprises in order to settle labor disputes. But even if this is true, Congress has not thereby lost its exclusive constitutional authority to make laws necessary and proper to carry out the powers vested by the Constitution.[26]

But where Justice Black receives the most attention for his constitutional literalism is for his position on the First Amendment. Here, Justice Black took the phrase "Congress shall make no law . . ." as it applied to all the guarantees of the First Amendment—speech, press, assembly, and religious freedom—at its word. No plausible argument was possible in defense of a law that touched upon the guarantees of the First Amendment. Historical evidence to the contrary—and there is much—did not dissuade Justice Black from his position that the Framers intended for the absolute protection of the First Amendment to apply absolutely.[27] Otherwise, Black claimed, they would have used different phrasing. Justice Black's own words capture his position on the First Amendment best:

My view is, without deviation, without exception, without any if's, but's, or whereases, that freedom of speech means that government shall not do anything to people . . . either for the views they have or the views they express or the words they speak or write. Some people would have you believe that this is a very radical position, and maybe it is. But all I am doing is following what to me is the clear wording of the First Amendment. . . .

As I have said innumerable times before I simply believe that "Congress shall make no law" means Congress shall make no law . . . abridging freedom of speech or the press.[28]

Note here the difference in how Justice Black's literalism and Judge Bork's originalism interpret the freedom-of-speech guarantee. Justice Black, with his emphasis on the absolute phrasing of the First Amendment, believed the originalist interpretation of the First Amendment—that it protects little more than political speech—was simply wrong. In Justice Black's view, obscenity is protected without the need to weigh or balance "competing" government interests, libel and slander laws are unconstitutional per se, and political speech that advocates the violent overthrow of the government is beyond the power of majorities to control. Originalists, on the other hand, reach the opposite conclusion based on their historical understanding of the First Amendment, not its linguistic commands.[29]

Although literalism and originalism in constitutional interpretation have their differences, each adheres to the fundamental tenets of legal formalism. Constitutional interpretation does not require one to go beyond the Constitution because its clauses and provisions define themselves. To wander in search of legal and theoretical sources "outside" the Constitution is to risk the imposition of value judgments that compromise the authority and integrity of its majestic commands. Our discussion of originalism and literalism has questioned whether either approach provides a sufficient baseline from which to interpret the Constitution. But what are the alternatives, and are they any better?

## Alternatives to Formalism

Formalism dominated the Court's approach to constitutional interpretation from the founding period until the early part of the twentieth century, when the first serious challenge emerged to this long-held consensus in American law and jurisprudence. Parallel to the larger "progressive" movement underfoot in American politics, legal scholars, jurists, and social scientists began to question the legal foundation upon which the current economic, social, and political arrangements rested. Unlike formalists, who stressed the predetermined nature of legal rights, *legal realists* argued that law was the creation of a political process, one in which ever-changing social and economic forces competed for control of the public interest. Existing law reflected the triumph of private interests that used the legislative process to assert their place in the social and political order, not "discoveries" of the Framers' intent or rights self-evident in the "natural" law. Law determined the social order; it did not reflect a natural or predetermined state of affairs and thus could not have a meaning independent of the environment in which it was created.[30]

Legal realism, because of its association with the Progressive Era and the challenge to the status quo, attracted some of the most prominent intellectuals in American public life. Several of the most influential Progressive writers offered perspectives outside the law. Individuals such as Robert Hale, Morris Cohen, John Dewey, Thorstein Veblen, William James, and Jane Addams, none of whom was a lawyer, influenced the idea championed by the legal realists of law as instrumental in nature. Legal realists questioned several orthodox assumptions about the organization and distribution of social, economic, and political power in American society. They argued that law not only created the status quo but also could and should be used to change it.

Front and center in the legal realist movement were two of the most eminent figures in the history of American law, Oliver Wendell Holmes Jr. and Louis D. Brandeis. Their association with legal realism added luster to its strength as a counterpoint to formalism. Although scholars consider Holmes (1902–1932) and Brandeis (1916–1939) among the greatest justices to serve on the Supreme Court, each had left an indelible mark on American constitutional development before entering what, for each man, was the final stage of his career. In 1881, Holmes, while still in private practice, published *The Common Law,* which rejected the natural law tradition. Holmes argued in the clearest and most comprehensive terms to date that law reflected the deliberate choices made by people in response to perceived social and economic needs.[31] Holmes's central thesis, that law embodied policy preferences and that such preferences should be allowed to stand in absence of a clear constitutional mistake on the part of the legislature, had little influence on the Court but reverberated throughout some of the nation's most elite law schools. Harvard, Yale, and Columbia embraced Holmes's legal theories and a subsequent generation of legal scholars, advocates, and judges, including Brandeis and, later, Felix Frankfurter (1939–1962), absorbed Holmes's often-quoted lesson that "[t]he life of the law has not been logic: it has been experience."[32]

Because law, in addition to being a product of experience, was a social creation, Holmes believed that the Constitution permitted legislatures to make laws designed to meet evolving societal challenges. Such laws were entitled to a presumption of constitutionality unless a legislature could demonstrate no reasonable relationship of a law to its body's policy objectives. Holmes believed that using natural rights theories to reject legal change "w[as] simply [a] 'pontifical or imperial way of forbidding discussion.' Policy was no longer derivable from customary norms but was a coercive imposition of the state."[33]

Holmes did not share the reform-minded goals of the Progressives. If legislatures had chosen not to respond to the economic consequences of industrialization and other social crises that pervaded American life in the late nineteenth and early twentieth centuries, he would not have insisted that courts do their work for them. Brandeis, however, was a true believer in the Progressive cause. Before he joined the Court, Brandeis was the most famous "public interest" lawyer in America, having labored on behalf of reform causes almost his entire career. Unlike Holmes, who believed that legislatures should be permitted to experiment free from judicial supervision as part of the democratic nature of American politics, Brandeis believed that judges should evaluate the reasonableness of legislation through an assessment of the "facts" that formed the basis of legislation. Brandeis advocated a jurisprudence that enabled judges to differentiate between reform-minded legislation and laws that simply reflected the struggles between powerful private interests, the more classic Madisonian vision to which Holmes subscribed.

Brandeis's experience in pushing public interest legislation through state legislatures had "taught him that what appeared to be a reasonable piece of legislation might be no more than a giveaway to vested interests."[34] Although Holmes offered the first comprehensive argument for legal realism, Brandeis introduced "sociological jurisprudence" to American law. Brandeis believed that facts should preface legislative purpose and that courts should weigh the impact that laws would have on social betterment. Holmes recognized law's dynamic qualities and insisted that they should be allowed to flourish independent of a mythical attachment to a natural order. But Brandeis believed that legislatures and courts should use their knowledge of modern social science to improve the world, an approach he first brought to the Court's attention with stunning success in *Muller v. Oregon* (1908).[35]

*Muller* involved a challenge to a maximum-work-hour law for women who worked in commercial laundries. Brandeis submitted a brief of about one hundred pages, only two of which dealt with questions of law. The rest consisted of evidence collected from around the country on the public health consequences for women and their families who worked longer than ten hours per day in such demanding conditions. So impressed was the Court that it directly referred to the "very copious" body of information provided by Brandeis as the basis for its decision. The "Brandeis Brief" became a model for subsequent generations of reform-minded lawyers attacking a wide range of established government practices, from racial discrimination to public education expenditures.

Although Holmes and Brandeis are often grouped as twins in discussions of legal realism's place in American law, other than their mutual disdain for formalism and natural law, they held very different conceptions of law's potential to transform the conditions of American life. Holmes's skepticism of law as the protector of "natural" truths formed the basis for his views. Brandeis, on the other hand, believed that law and litigation could be positive forces in altering the balance of social and economic power between worker and owner, dissident and majority, and rich and poor.

## OLIVER WENDELL HOLMES JR. AND THE COMMON LAW

Perhaps the most revered figure in the history of American law, Oliver Wendell Holmes Jr. enjoyed a remarkable legal career, one that began as the Civil War came to a close and ended shortly after Franklin Roosevelt won his first presidential campaign in 1932. A Harvard law graduate, Holmes spent only a limited part of his career in private practice. His intellectual gifts were evident as far back as his freshman year in college, and he impressed many of his college professors as a literary stylist. Indeed, Holmes's judicial opinions are remembered as much for their well-crafted language as for their legal thought.

But the importance of Holmes's contribution to the development of legal theory is unmistakable. His opinions in *Schenck* v. *United States* (1919) and *Abrams* v. *United States* (1919) established

the "clear and present danger" test and the "marketplace of ideas" concept, which together established the constitutional baseline for the boundaries of modern free speech law. In addition, Holmes argued that legislatures should be free to experiment with solutions to social and economic problems without judicial interference, but he placed tight reigns on their ability to interfere with more "fundamental" rights, such as freedom of speech, religion, and assembly.

*Oliver Wendell Holmes enjoying an afternoon in the garden—with, of course, a little reading.*
Courtesy of the Harvard University Archives.

### The Common Law

The object of this book is to present a general view of the Common Law. To accomplish the task, other tools are needed besides logic. It is something to show that the consistency of a system requires a particular result, but it is not all. The life of the law has not been logic: it has been experience. The felt necessities of the time, the prevalent moral and political theories, intuitions of public policy, avowed or unconscious, even the prejudices which judges share with their fellow-men, have had a good deal more to do than the syllogism in determining the rules by which men should be

**25**

governed. The law embodies the story of a nation's development through many centuries, and it cannot be dealt with as if it contained only the axioms and corollaries of a book of mathematics. In order to know what it is, we must know what it has been, and what it tends to become. We must alternately consult history and existing theories of legislation. But the most difficult labor will be to understand the combination of the two into new products at every stage. The substance of the law at any given time pretty nearly corresponds, so far as it goes, with what is then understood to be convenient; but its form and machinery, and the degree to which it is able to work out desired results, depend very much upon its past.

In Massachusetts today, while, on the one hand, there are a great many rules which are quite sufficiently accounted for by their manifest good sense, on the other, there are some which can only be understood by reference to the infancy of procedure among the German tribes, or to the social condition of Rome under the Decemvirs.

I shall use the history of our law so far as it is necessary to explain a conception or to interpret a rule, but no further. In doing so there are two errors equally to be avoided both by writer and reader. One is that of supposing, because an idea seems very familiar and natural to us, that it has always been so. Many things which we take for granted had to be laboriously fought out or thought out in past times. The other mistake is the opposite one of asking too much of history. We start with man full grown. It may be assumed that the earliest barbarian whose practices are to be considered had a good many of the same feelings and passions as ourselves.

Legal realism came to dominate the Court's jurisprudence immediately after the Constitutional Revolution of 1937, a term often used to describe the Court's sudden rejection of formalism. But legal realism, while an influence in the modern Court's approach to constitutional interpretation, soon came in for harsh criticism. Even constitutional theorists who acknowledged that the Court makes social and political value choices when it interprets the Constitution suggested that a more principled, less political justification was required to defend the Court's decisions. Accordingly, in the first major challenge to legal realism in the post–New Deal era, Herbert Wechsler argued that the Court must make its decisions based on *neutral principles* of law, not on contextual or policy-based considerations.[36]

Wechsler's conception of neutral principles differed from the formalist model in several crucial aspects. Wechsler did not contest the proposition that the Constitution authorized judicial review. Nor did he dispute the central contention of the legal realists that constitutional interpretation and the exercise of judicial review required the Court to make value choices. But Wechsler argued that constitutional interpretation should not be rooted in a contextual, case-specific examination of a particular set of facts. Instead, constitutional interpretation should be a neutral principle of law that applied equally to all parties. To illustrate his point, Wechsler argued that the Court should have decided the historic *Brown* case on freedom of association grounds, not under the Equal Protection Clause. The National Association for the Advancement of Colored People, which represented the African American families in *Brown*, not only argued that mandated school segregation fostered unequal educational opportunities for blacks, created a racial stigma, and lessened their future economic opportunities but also introduced social science data to support these arguments.[37]

Wechsler argued that the Court should have ruled that school segregation violated the freedom-of-association rights of African American students to attend the schools of their choice. Wechsler believed the Court had interpreted the Fourteenth Amendment to favor African Americans based on their disadvantaged position in public education, a decision that amounted to a partisan choice. Freedom of association was a "race neutral" principle applicable in such cases that avoided the "sociological jurisprudence" of the actual *Brown* decision. Wechsler commented that segregation laws penalized whites and African Americans to an equal degree because members of both races were denied the lawful opportunity to free association based on race.

Putting aside for the moment the unusual notion that racial segregation harmed whites and African Americans to an equal degree, are neutral principles really possible in American constitutional law? In some ways, Wechsler could not have picked a worse case to use as the basis for his neutral-principles argument. Segregation was a condition created by a political system steeped in racial prejudice, one that excluded African Americans from meaningful participation and representation until the mid-1960s. It was not a condition of nature. Segregation was precisely the sort of problem pointed out by the legal realists.

Still, Wechsler's effort to offer an alternative to legal realism was an important contribution to constitutional theory. Neutral principles, as an idea, was an attempt to reconcile the consequences of the Constitutional Revolution of 1937 with the position of legal formalists that the Constitution should have a meaning independent of what the justices think it should mean at a given point in time.[38] The same concerns that motivated Wechsler were also evident in the subsequent contribution of another exceptionally influential theorist, John Hart Ely, who, in *Democracy and Distrust* (1981), argued that courts should refrain from using their power to create rights through the "open textured" clauses of the Constitution. Ely claimed the Court in the post–New Deal era had done just that. Instead, the Court should limit judicial review to laws that prevented the political process from functioning in a fair and open manner. Ely agreed with critics of legal formalism that a "clause bound" approach to constitutional interpretation was impossible, but he was also suspicious of grandiose legal theories that granted excessive power to the courts to "discover" the Constitution's fundamental values.

Ely laid out three specific instances when the courts should strike down laws: (1) when laws violated specific substantive constitutional guarantees (e.g., free speech, criminal due-process protections); (2) when laws operated to disadvantage "discrete and insular" minorities in the political process (e.g., voting rights,

political participation); and (3) when laws created procedural obstacles that created unreasonable barriers to political and social reform through the political process. Courts should defer to the political process in disputes involving the open-ended provisions of the Constitution. Ely believed that such cases presented dangerous vehicles for the courts to impose their value choices on the general population, a practice he believed had no defense in constitutional theory.[39]

Constitutional scholars and political scientists have found much to admire in Ely's studied and ambitious effort to construct a generally applicable theory of judicial review. But critics have pointed out that his ideas offer little guidance on how to interpret the substance of the Constitution. *Democracy and Distrust* denied one of the central lessons of the legal realist movement: that constitutional choices involve moral and substantive value choices, not just determinations of procedural fairness. For example, a court's conclusion that the political process is "malfunctioning," to use Ely's term, calls for a value choice.[40] Moreover, Ely believes that courts have the obligation to strike down legislation that violates free speech or religious rights, but he notes that the content of those rights is not necessarily defined by text of the Constitution.[41] Thus, is it really possible for the courts to avoid discretionary value choices even when they confront the "specific" clauses of the Constitution? Chief among those flaws is the need to use substantive values. Eli relies on the very "value-oriented" approach that he seeks, through a process-based theory, to avoid.[42]

Process-oriented approaches to constitutional law emphasize the need to understand the limits and possibilities of judicial review in the American system of government rather than the value choices made by the courts. Perhaps, then, it is only natural that a resurgence of *rights-oriented* theories has emerged to challenge the central premises of the process-oriented *and* originalist approaches. Rights-oriented theories of constitutional interpretation place a decided emphasis on the value choices involved in constitutional interpretation, with judicial review, viewed here as a means to accomplish particular policy goals, given secondary attention. Although such theories have their historical antecedent in legal realism, modern rights-oriented theories are much more concerned with questions involving, for example, affirmative action, abortion rights, obscenity, and sexual privacy—questions that never concerned Holmes, Brandeis, and the Progressives influenced by them.

For some time, rights-oriented theories of constitutional interpretation were developed in support of liberal political objectives that stood little chance of success in the political branches. Scholars such as Ronald Dworkin and Laurence Tribe argued that the courts were best suited to make principled decisions about the substance and scope of protected rights, in contrast to the "interest based" outcomes that were characteristic of the push and pull of legislative politics.[43] Guided by reason and unaccountable to the political impulses of majorities, the courts should use their special position and special competence to examine the moral and political components of rights-based claims. The courts should make decisions that best enforce the abstract principles of the Constitution, which include concepts such as human dignity, equality, and fairness.

More so than any other liberal rights-oriented scholar, Dworkin has argued for sweeping judicial power to determine the rights inherent in these constitutional concepts on the assumption that the Supreme Court, and by extension the lower federal courts, is a "forum of principle."[44] On first glance Dworkin's approach might appear to give judges the broad discretion to create any suitable "concept" of constitutional theory. But he does insist that the courts are constrained by legal norms, including the Constitution, judicial precedent, and common law principles. In the end, however, Dworkin, indicative of most rights-oriented constitutional theorists, offers little institutional assurance to constrain judicial discretion. His hope is that judges will make the correct moral choices.

Recent conservative constitutional theorists have used the language of rights, rather than appeals to originalism, to mount provocative challenges to legal scholars in search of liberal political outcomes. Two major tenets of liberal theories of rights have come under close scrutiny. The first is the belief that the right to make individual choices is more important than the moral consequences of what those choices entail; the second is the idea that majorities should not make moral judgments about whether certain choices are better than others.[45] For example, the law should not allow the majority's conceptions of abortion, gay rights, or obscenity to interfere with an individual's basic right to lead an independent life. Majorities usually do a pretty good job of protecting their own rights and interests, but individuals looked down upon for their political or religious views, their sexual orientation, or their interest in sexually explicit materials have to fight much harder for their legal rights. Rights theories should be concerned with the protection of minorities who cannot protect themselves.

Conservative rights theorists do not suggest that constitutional interpretation should or can be value neutral. Instead, they argue that rights and their purpose in the larger moral universe should be considered in another fashion. Rights should be assigned based on whether their exercise allows individuals to do or accomplish something that is good. Rights are a means to achieve some productive or useful moral end. Rights should recognize that some choices are morally superior to others. Constitutional law should not treat a woman's decision to choose an abortion over childbirth as morally indistinguishable; churches and religious individuals should, in some cases, receive preferential treatment over atheists and skeptics; and homosexual love weighs differently in the minds of the public than heterosexual love, thus raising different questions about the value of extending legal recognition to same-sex marriages. For their constitutional status, rights depend on the consequences that permitting such choices will have on the moral and political fabric of society.

Conservative and liberal constitutional theorists might want very different things from the law, but these rights-oriented approaches to constitutional law share certain similarities. Interpretive principles and the substance of rights receive a heavy and unapologetic injection of moral and political philosophy. When making their decisions, judges should not attempt to reconcile rights claims with the Framers' intent or similar fixed poles in the legal universe, but should consider the moral sensibilities of communities as well as the individual. Constitutional interpretation should take place at a very abstract level that allows for an open, evolving dialogue over the substance and range of rights and power. Judicial discretion to define and impose value choices is not an inherent evil. One is hard-pressed to find such a deliberative discussion over the future direction of our constitutional culture unattractive. But do rights-oriented theories provide a better and more defensible theory of constitutional interpretation and judicial power than any of the other theories discussed thus far?

## *Furman v. Georgia*
### 408 U.S. 238 (1972)

Disturbed by patterns of racial discrimination and arbitrariness in capital sentencing, as well as a general sense that society had evolved to the point where it no longer considered capital punishment constitutional, the National Association for the Advancement of Colored People Legal Defense Fund (LDF) and the American Civil Liberties Union (ACLU) joined forces in the mid-1960s to develop a litigation campaign to end the death penalty. Encouragement for the LDF's and the ACLU's legal efforts came from a dissent issued by Justice Arthur Goldberg from the Supreme Court's denial of *certiorari* in a 1963 case, *Rudolph v. Alabama,* in which the defendant was sentenced to death for rape. Goldberg believed that the Court should have taken the case to consider whether "evolving standards of decency" had made the death penalty no longer consistent with the Eighth Amendment's prohibition on cruel and unusual punishments.

The LDF targeted death-penalty appeals all over the country that would highlight various objections to capital punishment. By 1971 the Court had agreed to consolidate three capital cases out of Georgia and Texas and decide them together. Of the three only *Furman* involved murder; the other two were rape cases.

By a 5-4 vote, the Court invalidated the death penalty as violative of the Eighth Amendment ban on cruel and unusual punishment. Each justice in the majority, however, wrote a separate decision to explain his objection to the death penalty as it was currently administered in the United States. Only two justices, William Brennan and Thurgood Marshall, believed that the death penalty was unconstitutional under any circumstance. The three other justices cited due-process concerns and racial discrimination as their reasons for holding the death penalty unconstitutional.

Justice Brennan's opinion offers an excellent counterpoint to the originalism of Justice Rehnquist's *Wallace* dissent. Compared with Rehnquist, Justice Brennan believes that history is far less exact and the Framers' far more ambiguous about their intentions.

▼▲▼

MR. JUSTICE BRENNAN, concurring.

We have very little evidence of the Framers' intent in including the Cruel and Unusual Punishments Clause. . . .

[Little] evidence of the Framers' intent appears from the debates in the First Congress on the adoption of the Bill of Rights. As the Court noted in (1910), the Cruel and Unusual Punishments Clause "received very little debate." The extent of the discussion, by two opponents of the Clause in the House of Representatives, was this:

> Mr. SMITH, of South Carolina, objected to the words "nor cruel and unusual punishments," the import of them being too indefinite.
> Mr. LIVERMORE.—The [Eighth Amendment] seems to express a great deal of humanity, on which account I have no objection to it; but as it seems to have no meaning in it, I do not think it necessary. . . . No cruel and unusual punishment is to be inflicted; it is sometimes necessary to hang a man, villains often deserve whipping, and perhaps having their ears cut off; but are we in future to be prevented from inflicting these punishments because they are cruel? If a more lenient mode of correcting vice and deterring others from the commission of it could be invented, it would be very prudent in the Legislature to adopt it; but until we have some security that this will be done, we ought not to be restrained from making necessary laws by any declaration of this kind.
> The question was put on the [Eighth Amendment], and it was agreed to by a considerable majority.

Several conclusions thus emerge from the history of the adoption of the Clause. We know that the Framers' concern was directed specifically at the exercise of legislative power. They included in the Bill of Rights a prohibition upon "cruel and unusual punishments" precisely because the legislature would otherwise have had the unfettered power to prescribe punishments for crimes. Yet we cannot now know exactly what the Framers thought "cruel and unusual punishments" were. Certainly they intended to ban torturous punishments, but the available evidence does not support the further conclusion that only torturous punishments were to be outlawed. As Livermore's comments demonstrate, the Framers were well aware that the reach of the Clause was not limited to the proscription of unspeakable atrocities. Nor did they intend simply to forbid punishments considered "cruel and unusual" at the time. The "import" of the Clause is, indeed, "indefinite," and for good reason. . . .

In short, this Court [has] adopted the Framers' view of the Clause as a "constitutional check" to ensure that, "when we come to punishments, no latitude ought to be left, nor dependence put on the virtue of representatives." That, indeed, is the only view consonant with our constitutional form of government. . . .

Judicial enforcement of the Clause, then, cannot be evaded by invoking the obvious truth that legislatures have the power to prescribe punishments for crimes. That is precisely the reason the Clause appears in the Bill of Rights. The difficulty arises, rather, in formulating the "legal principles to be applied by the courts" when a legislatively prescribed punishment is challenged as "cruel and unusual." In formulating those constitutional principles, we must avoid the insertion of "judicial conception[s] of . . . wisdom or propriety," yet we must not, in the guise of "judicial restraint," abdicate our fundamental responsibility to enforce the Bill of Rights. Were we to do so, the "constitution would indeed be as easy of application as it would be deficient in efficacy and power. Its general principles would have little value and be converted by precedent into impotent and lifeless formulas. Rights declared in words might be lost in reality." The Cruel and Unusual Punishments Clause would become, in short, "little more than good advice." . . .

> Ours would indeed be a simple task were we required merely to measure a challenged punishment against those that history has long condemned. That narrow and unwarranted view of the Clause, however, was left behind with the 19th century. Our task today is more complex. We know "that the words of the [Clause] are not precise, and that their scope is not static." We know, therefore, that the Clause "must draw its meaning from the evolving standards of decency that mark the progress of a maturing society." That knowledge, of course, is but the beginning of the inquiry.

In *Trop* v. *Dulles* it was said that "[t]he question is whether [a] penalty subjects the individual to a fate forbidden by the principle of civilized treatment guaranteed by the [Clause]." It was also said that a challenged punishment must be examined "in light of the basic prohibition against inhuman treatment" embodied in the Clause. It was said, finally, that:

> The basic concept underlying the [Clause] is nothing less than the dignity of man. While the State has the power to punish, the [Clause] stands to assure that this power be exercised within the limits of civilized standards.

At bottom, then, the Cruel and Unusual Punishments Clause prohibits the infliction of uncivilized and inhuman punishments. The State, even as it punishes, must treat its members with respect for their intrinsic worth as human beings. A punishment is "cruel and unusual," therefore, if it does not comport with human dignity.

This formulation, of course, does not, of itself, yield principles for assessing the constitutional validity of particular punishments. Nevertheless, even though "[t]his Court has had little occasion to give precise content to the [Clause]," *ibid.,* there are principles recognized in our cases and inherent in the Clause sufficient to permit a judicial determination whether a challenged punishment comports with human dignity. . . .

More than the presence of pain, however, is comprehended in the judgment that the extreme severity of a punishment makes it degrading to the dignity of human beings. The barbaric punishments condemned by history, "punishments which inflict torture, such as the rack, the thumbscrew, the iron boot, the stretching of limbs and the like," are, of course, "attended with acute pain and suffering." When we consider why they have been condemned, however, we realize that the pain involved is not the only reason. The true significance of these punishments is that they treat members of the human race as nonhumans, as objects to be toyed with and discarded. They are thus inconsistent with the fundamental premise of the Clause that even the vilest criminal remains a human being possessed of common human dignity.

In determining whether a punishment comports with human dignity, we are aided also by a second principle inherent in the Clause—that the State must not arbitrarily inflict a severe punishment. This principle derives from the notion that the State does not respect human dignity when, without reason, it inflicts upon some people a severe punishment that it does not inflict upon others. Indeed, the very words "cruel and unusual punishments" imply condemnation of the arbitrary infliction of severe punishments. . . .

A third principle inherent in the Clause is that a severe punishment must not be unacceptable to contemporary society. Rejection by society, of course, is a strong indication that a severe punishment does not comport with human dignity.

The question under this principle, then, is whether there are objective indicators from which a court can conclude that contemporary society considers a severe punishment unacceptable. Accordingly, the judicial task is to review the history of a challenged punishment and to examine society's present practices with respect to its use. Legislative authorization, of course, does not establish acceptance. The acceptability of a severe punishment is measured not by its availability, for it might become so offensive to society as never to be inflicted, but by its use.

The final principle inherent in the Clause is that a severe punishment must not be excessive. A punishment is excessive under this principle if it is unnecessary: the infliction of a severe punishment by the State cannot comport with human dignity when it is nothing more than the pointless infliction of suffering. If there is a significantly less severe punishment adequate to achieve the purposes for which the punishment is inflicted, the punishment inflicted is unnecessary, and therefore excessive. . . .

Since the Bill of Rights was adopted, this Court has adjudged only three punishments to be within the prohibition of the Clause. *Weems* v. *United States,* (1910) (12 years in chains at hard and painful labor); *Trop* v. *Dulles,* (1958) (expatriation); *Robinson* v. *California,* (1962) (imprisonment for narcotics addiction). Each punishment, of course, was degrading to human dignity, but of none could it be said conclusively that it was fatally offensive under one or the other of the principles. Rather, these "cruel and unusual punishments" seriously implicated several of the principles, and it was the application of the principles in combination that supported the judgment. That, indeed, is not surprising. The function of these principles, after all, is simply to provide means by which a court can determine whether a challenged punishment comports with human dignity. They are, therefore, interrelated, and, in most cases, it will be their convergence that will justify the conclusion that a punishment is "cruel and unusual." The test, then, will ordinarily be a cumulative one: if a punishment is unusually severe, if there is a strong probability that it is inflicted arbitrarily, if it is substantially rejected by contemporary society, and if there is no reason to believe that it serves any penal purpose more effectively than some less severe punishment, then the continued infliction of that punishment violates the command of the Clause that the State may not inflict inhuman and uncivilized punishments upon those convicted of crimes. . . .

In comparison to all other punishments today, then, the deliberate extinguishment of human life by the State is uniquely degrading to human dignity. I would not hesitate to hold, on that ground alone, that death is today a "cruel and unusual" punishment, were it not that death is a punishment of longstanding usage and acceptance in this country. I therefore turn to the second principle—that the State may not arbitrarily inflict an unusually severe punishment. . . .

[Justice Brennan then provided an analysis of the infrequency of executions in the United States in the twentieth century, concluding that the odds of execution for capital crimes was so remote as to make such punishment arbitrary and "freakish."]

There is, then, no substantial reason to believe that the punishment of death, as currently administered, is necessary for the protection of society. The only other purpose suggested, one that is independent of protection for society, is retribution. Shortly stated, retribution in this context means that criminals are put to death because they deserve it. . . .

In sum, the punishment of death is inconsistent with [the] four principles [described here]: death is an unusually severe and degrading punishment; there is a strong probability that it is inflicted arbitrarily; its rejection by contemporary society is virtually total; and there is no reason to believe that it serves any penal purpose more effectively than the less severe punishment of imprisonment. The function of these principles is to enable a court to determine whether a punishment comports with human dignity. Death, quite simply, does not.

▼▲▼

## Natural Law

Our discussion thus far leaves us with two certainties. First, the Constitution creates certain rights and freedoms that deserve protection from the exercise of "naked" majoritarian preferences. That is, majorities must have solid grounds for treating certain individuals or groups within society differently, other than for reasons of raw political power.[46] Today, the rational basis of practices such as slavery, Jim Crow, sex-based discrimination, zoning restrictions designed to disadvantage unpopular religious movements, or the exploitation of child labor is difficult to understand. We have come to associate these practices with prejudice and greed, not public value. Conservative and liberals, legal formalists and their critics, and constitutional theorists who see the Constitution and the legal culture in very different terms agree in far more cases than not that laws must, at minimum, further some rational public objective. Indeed, much of the intricate design of the Constitution is premised on the rationale that the governmental branches possess the power to veto public policies that do not serve interests beyond those of powerful, self-interested majorities. Second, and obvious by now, is that constitutional scholars cannot agree on what the Constitution means; how to enforce its substantive and procedural provisions; and who, or which branch of government, should possess the preeminent power to undertake these responsibilities.

Do certainties, then, exist in constitutional interpretation and the exercise of judicial power? If we accept the premises of *natural law and natural rights* theorists, that certain rights exist independent of those established by artificial legal rules, then the answer is yes. Natural law theories presuppose certain unalienable truths about individuals and the rights they retain when they enter civil and political society. If the phrase "unalienable truths" sounds familiar, it should. Thomas Jefferson alluded to the natural rights tradition in the Declaration of Independence, writing that "the Laws of Nature and of Nature's God" endowed men with "certain unalienable rights," among which were "Life, Liberty and the Pursuit of Happiness." Historian Forrest McDonald has noted that the American colonies' invocation of natural law as the basis for rebellion made the British constitution irrelevant. American independence largely owes its intellectual justification to the decision of the revolution's leaders "to go outside the forms and norms of English law" and claim their rights on the basis of natural law.[47] On an abstract level natural law has great appeal, for it posits that universal truths, absolute in their moral goodness, exist outside the relativist framework of *positive law,* or the legal rules that society chooses to create. Natural law theorists contend that laws enacted by civil societies, even if done through open and democratic processes, are invalid if they violate these universal principles. Edward Corwin, whose work in the early twentieth century was quite influential in how political scientists thought about the relationship between law and society, wrote that the Constitution was conceived against the "higher" background of natural law and deserved an appropriate place in constitutional adjudication.[48]

But the application of natural law theories to the Constitution raises serious problems. Political scientist Benjamin F. Wright, in an early appraisal of the use of natural law as a source of interpretive principles, noted:

> [N]atural law has had as its content whatever the individual in question desired to advocate. This has varied from a defense of theocracy to a defense of the complete separation of church and state, from revolutionary rights in 1776 to liberty of contract in recent judicial opinions, from the advocacy of universal adult suffrage to a defense of rigid limitations upon the voting power . . . from the advocacy

of the inalienable right to succession to the assertion of the natural law of national supremacy, from the right of majority rule to the rights of vested interests.[49]

Wright wrote in 1931 but neglected to mention that natural law principles were prominent in three of the Court's less luminous nineteenth-century opinions. In all three cases the Court rejected individual rights claims on grounds now thoroughly discredited in modern constitutional law: *Dred Scott v. Sandford* (1857), in which the Court ruled that African Americans were bound by the laws of nature to their status as property;[50] *Bradwell v. Illinois* (1872), where the Court held that state law could bar women from becoming lawyers on the grounds that "the civil law, as well as nature herself, has always recognized a wide difference in the respective spheres and destinies of man and woman. . . . The paramount destiny and mission of women are to fulfill the noble and benign offices of wife and mother [because] this is the law of the Creator";[51] and *Plessy v. Ferguson* (1896), in which the Court upheld state-enforced racial segregation as a legitimate exercise of "the established usages, customs and traditions of the people."[52] To enfold this latter phrase into natural law theories of rights creates an unstoppable double helix of constitutional possibilities, as "custom and tradition" are malleable terms that can mean almost anything, depending upon whose customs and traditions are in question. Garry Wills is succinct on this point, noting that "[r]unning men out of town on a rail is as much an American tradition as declaring unalienable rights."[53]

In modern times natural law principles have been used to defend and attack abortion rights, affirmative action, conscientious objector status, capital punishment, the minimum wage, gun control, gay rights, and the rights of terminally ill or comatose patients.[54] This ambiguity leads one to ask what should be an obvious question: If natural law recognizes the existence of universal rights that can be derived from moral absolutes, why have legal scholars, philosophers, theologians, and constitutional scholars been unable to agree on what those universal rights are? One reason is that almost no one agrees on the sources of natural rights. Do natural rights have a divine origin as Jefferson's rhetoric in the Declaration of Independence suggests? Are they derived from the ancient Greek philosophers? If so, how were the Greeks able to distinguish natural from positive rights? Another reason for the lack of agreement on the specifics of universal rights is that although the constitutional founders were certainly influenced by natural rights theories, we have no indication that the founders intended a place for such theories in the Constitution. Ely has noted that because revolutionaries are unlikely to have positive law on their side, appeals to natural law and natural rights, or whatever will help justify their cause, are inevitable.[55]

The Constitution quite clearly is the product of legal positivism. It is also intended to govern. References, explicit or otherwise, to natural law are absent from the Constitution. Given the abstract nature and uncertain origins of natural law, is it unreasonable to conclude that the enactment of the Constitution and the Bill of Rights, the two most enduring acts of written legal positivism in Western civilization, reflect the Framers' deliberate refutation of such theories? On the other hand, are natural law theories implicit in some of the other approaches to constitutional interpretation discussed thus far? What similarities and differences do you see when natural law theories are compared with other theories of constitutional interpretation?

## Griswold v. Connecticut
### 381 U.S. 479 (1965)

Estelle Griswold served as the executive director of the Connecticut office of Planned Parenthood. An advocate of low-cost access to birth control and other materials to assist in family planning, Griswold spent more than twenty years attempting to overturn an 1879 Connecticut law prohibiting such services before the Supreme Court agreed to hear her case.

In 1961, Griswold, along with physician C. Lee Buxton, opened a family-planning clinic in New Haven fully expecting—and hoping—to be arrested. Their wish was quickly granted, and Griswold and Buxton were charged with violating the 1879 law. A legal team, led by Yale law professor Thomas Emerson, had been assembled to defend Griswold and Buxton. The lawyers rooted their argument in the "liberty" component of the Due Process Clause of the Fourteenth Amendment, claiming that the clause was broad enough to encompass a right to privacy that permitted married couples to receive information about birth control and use it.

The Court, 7-2, struck down the Connecticut law, agreeing with Griswold's lawyers that it violated a marital right of privacy protected by the Constitution. Griswold prompted several strong opinions, with two of the most notable being Justice Arthur Goldberg's concurrence and Justice Hugo Black's dissent. Goldberg alludes to the idea that certain rights and liberties exist outside the constitutional text. Black offers a classic statement of his literalist approach to constitutional interpretation, including a pointed criticism of Goldberg's opinion as founded in a "mysterious and uncertain natural law" concept.

▼▲▼

MR. JUSTICE GOLDBERG, whom THE CHIEF JUSTICE and MR. JUSTICE BRENNAN join, concurring.

I agree with the Court that Connecticut's birth control law unconstitutionally intrudes upon the right of marital privacy, and I join in its opinion and judgment. Although I have not accepted the view that "due process," as used in the Fourteenth Amendment, incorporates all of the first eight Amendments, I do agree that the concept of liberty protects those personal rights that are fundamental, and is not confined to the specific terms of the Bill of Rights. My conclusion that the concept of liberty is not so restricted, and that it embraces the right of marital privacy, though that right is not mentioned explicitly in the Constitution, is supported both by numerous decisions of this Court, referred to in the Court's opinion, and by the language and history of the Ninth Amendment. In reaching the conclusion that the right of marital privacy is protected as being within the protected penumbra of specific guarantees of the Bill of Rights, the Court refers to the Ninth Amendment. I add these words to emphasize the relevance of that Amendment to the Court's holding. . . .

The language and history of the Ninth Amendment reveal that the Framers of the Constitution believed that there are additional fundamental rights, protected from governmental infringement, which exist alongside those fundamental rights specifically mentioned in the first eight constitutional amendments. The Ninth Amendment reads, "The enumeration in the Constitution, of certain rights, shall not be construed to deny or disparage others retained by the people." The Amendment is almost entirely the work of James Madison. It was introduced in Congress by him, and passed the House and Senate with little or no debate and virtually no change in language. It was proffered to quiet expressed fears that a bill of specifically enumerated rights could not be sufficiently broad to cover all essential rights, and that the specific mention of certain rights would be interpreted as a denial that others were protected. . . .

While this Court has had little occasion to interpret the Ninth Amendment, "[i]t cannot be presumed that any clause in the constitution is intended to be without effect." *Marbury v. Madison*, (1803). In interpreting the Constitution, "real effect should be given to all the words it uses." The Ninth Amendment to the Constitution may be regarded by some as a recent discovery, and may be forgotten by others, but, since 1791, it has been a basic part of the Constitution which we are sworn to uphold. To hold that a right so basic and fundamental and so deep-rooted in our society as the right of privacy in marriage may be infringed because that right is not guaranteed in so many words by the first eight amendments to the Constitution is to ignore the Ninth Amendment, and to give it no effect whatsoever. Moreover, a judicial construction that this fundamental right is not protected by the Constitution because it is not mentioned in explicit terms by one of the first eight amendments or elsewhere in the Constitution would violate the Ninth Amendment, which specifically states that "[t]he enumeration in the Constitution, of certain rights, shall not be *construed* to deny or disparage others retained by the people." . . .

In determining which rights are fundamental, judges are not left at large to decide cases in light of their personal and private notions. Rather, they must look to the "traditions and [collective] conscience of our people" to determine whether a principle is "so rooted [there] . . . as to be ranked as fundamental." . . .

Although the Constitution does not speak in so many words of the right of privacy in marriage, I cannot believe that it offers these fundamental rights no protection. The fact that no particular provision of the Constitution explicitly forbids the State from disrupting the traditional relation of the family—a relation as old and as fundamental as our entire civilization—surely does not show that the Government was meant to have the power to do so. Rather, as the Ninth Amendment expressly recognizes, there are fundamental personal rights such as this one, which are protected from abridgment by the Government, though not specifically mentioned in the Constitution. . . .

In sum, I believe that the right of privacy in the marital relation is fundamental and basic—a personal right "retained by the people" within the meaning of the Ninth Amendment. Connecticut cannot constitutionally abridge this fundamental right, which is protected by the Fourteenth Amendment from infringement by the States. I agree with the Court that petitioners' convictions must therefore be reversed.

MR. JUSTICE BLACK, with whom MR. JUSTICE STEWART joins, dissenting.

In order that there may be no room at all to doubt why I vote as I do, I feel constrained to add that the law is every bit as offensive to me as it is to my Brethren of the majority and my Brothers HARLAN, WHITE and GOLDBERG, who, reciting reasons why it is offensive to them, hold it unconstitutional. There is no single one of the graphic and eloquent strictures and criticisms fired at the policy of this Connecticut law either by the Court's opinion or by those of my concurring Brethren to which I cannot subscribe—except their conclusion that the evil qualities they see in the law make it unconstitutional. . . .

One of the most effective ways of diluting or expanding a constitutionally guaranteed right is to substitute for the crucial word or words of a constitutional guarantee another word or words, more or less flexible and more or less restricted in meaning. This fact is well illustrated by the use of the term "right of privacy" as a comprehensive substitute for the Fourth Amendment's guarantee against "unreasonable searches and seizures." "Privacy" is a broad, abstract and ambiguous concept which can easily be shrunken in meaning but which can also, on the other hand, easily be interpreted as a constitutional ban against many things other than searches and seizures. I have expressed the view many times that First Amendment freedoms, for example, have suffered from a failure of the courts to stick to the simple language of the First Amendment in construing it, instead of invoking multitudes of words substituted for those the Framers used. For these reasons, I get nowhere in this case by talk about a constitutional "right of privacy" as an emanation from one or more constitutional provisions. I like my privacy as well as the next one, but I am nevertheless compelled to admit that government has a right to invade it unless prohibited by some specific constitutional provision. For these reasons, I cannot agree with the Court's judgment and the reasons it gives for holding this Connecticut law unconstitutional. . . .

My Brother GOLDBERG has adopted the recent discovery that the Ninth Amendment as well as the Due Process Clause can be used by this Court as authority to strike down all state legislation which this Court thinks violates "fundamental principles of liberty and justice," or is contrary to the "traditions and [collective] conscience of our people." He also states, without proof satisfactory to me, that, in making decisions on this basis, judges will not consider "their personal and private notions." One may ask

*Estelle Griswold, left, and Mrs. Ernest Jahncke, president of the Planned Parenthood League of Connecticut, are all smiles as they read about the Supreme Court's decision striking down Connecticut's anti–birth control law.*
UPI/Bettmann–CORBIS.

how they can avoid considering them. Our Court certainly has no machinery with which to take a Gallup Poll. And the scientific miracles of this age have not yet produced a gadget which the Court can use to determine what traditions are rooted in the "[collective] conscience of our people." . . .

I realize that many good and able men have eloquently spoken and written, sometimes in rhapsodical strains, about the duty of this Court to keep the Constitution in tune with the times. The idea is that the Constitution must be changed from time to time, and that this Court is charged with a duty to make those changes. For myself, I must, with all deference, reject that philosophy. The Constitution makers knew the need for change, and provided for it. Amendments suggested by the people's elected representatives can be submitted to the people or their selected agents for ratification. That method of change was good for our Fathers, and, being somewhat old-fashioned, I must add it is good enough for me. And so I cannot rely on the Due Process Clause or the Ninth Amendment or any mysterious and uncertain natural law concept as a reason for striking down this state law. The Due Process Clause, with an "arbitrary and capricious" or "shocking to the conscience" formula, was liberally used by this Court to strike down economic legislation in the early decades of this century, threatening, many people thought, the tranquility and stability of the Nation. That

formula, based on subjective considerations of "natural justice," is no less dangerous when used to enforce this Court's views about personal rights than those about economic rights. I had thought that we had laid that formula, as a means for striking down state legislation, to rest once and for all in cases such as *West Coast Hotel Co.* v. *Parrish* (1937).

▼▲▼

## In Search of Constitutional Meaning

Do not be disappointed as we leave this chapter without a clear answer to the question posed at the outset: How should we interpret the Constitution? Does that mean we have no preference in how you choose to think about constitutional interpretation and the other questions it raises? Not at all. We have deliberately offered a diverse palette of theoretical choices that have their intellectual roots in the law-based theories of how the courts—and the other branches of government as well—should approach constitutional interpretation. Although disputing the notion that social and political forces influence constitutional law and litigation—whether from the vantage point of the justices, elected officials, or aggrieved individuals in search of their rights and liberties—makes little sense, we believe that thinking about the Constitution in law-based terms is important. The cases, narrative commentaries, and Court's opinions that make up this casebook include threads of all the approaches discussed here. The purpose of this chapter has been twofold: to provide you with the tools to understand the sources of the justices' approaches to constitutional interpretation and to encourage you to develop a theoretical rationale of your own to assist in the explanation and defense of the constitutional choices you will make.

Notice that phrases or descriptions of judicial review and constitutional interpretation that you might have encountered before, such as judicial activism, judicial restraint, the "living Constitution," and strict construction, are absent from this chapter. This omission is no accident. Our concern here is with the substance of constitutional interpretation because the search for constitutional values is part of a larger debate over which societal values deserve protection. To reduce this complex enterprise to a handful of simplistic and often inaccurate descriptions of how the Court interprets the Constitution is to forget, as one prominent legal scholar has summarized it, that "much of what looks like a difference in approach is really a disagreement over substantive goals."[56] Consider these two questions as you go forward: Does any singular, universal theory of constitutional interpretation best capture the spirit and intent of the Constitution? Is it possible to create a theoretical approach to constitutional interpretation independent of the substantive values that one understands the Constitution to protect?

## FOR FURTHER READING

Amar, Akhil Reed. *The Bill of Rights: Creation and Reconstruction.* New Haven, Conn.: Yale University Press, 1998.

Bickel, Alexander. *The Least Dangerous Branch.* New Haven, Conn.: Yale University Press, 1962.

Black, Hugo L. *A Constitutional Faith.* New York: Alfred A. Knopf, 1969.

Bork, Robert H. *The Tempting of America.* New York: The Free Press, 1990.

Brigham, John. *The Constitution of Interests.* New York: New York University Press, 1996.

Bronner, Ethan. *Battle for Justice.* New York: W. W. Norton, 1989.

Dworkin, Ronald. *Law's Empire.* Cambridge, Mass.: Harvard University Press, 1986.

Ely, John Hart. *Democracy and Distrust.* Cambridge, Mass.: Harvard University Press, 1980.

Garvey, John H. *What Are Freedoms For?* Cambridge, Mass.: Harvard University Press, 1996.

Kahn, Ronald. *The Supreme Court and Constitutional Theory, 1953–1993.* Lawrence: University Press of Kansas, 1994.

Levy, Leonard W. *The Emergence of a Free Press.* New York: Oxford University Press, 1985.

———. *Original Intent and the Framers' Constitution.* New York: Oxford University Press, 1988.

McDonald, Forrest. *Novus Ordo Seclorum: The Intellectual Origins of the Constitution.* Lawrence: University Press of Kansas, 1985.

Savage, David G. *Turning Right: The Making of the Rehnquist Supreme Court.* New York: John Wiley & Sons, 1992.

Scalia, Antonin. *A Matter of Interpretation: Federal Courts and the Law.* Princeton, N.J.: Princeton University Press, 1997.

Segal, Jeffrey A. and Harold J. Spaeth. *The Supreme Court and the Attitudinal Model.* New York: Cambridge University Press, 1993.

Simon, James F. *The Center Holds: The Power Struggle inside the Rehnquist Court.* New York: Simon & Schuster, 1995.

Strum, Phillipa. *Louis D. Brandeis: Justice for the People.* New York: Schoken, 1984.

Sunstein, Cass R. *One Case at a Time: Judicial Minimalism and the Supreme Court.* Cambridge, Mass.: Harvard University Press, 1993.

Tushnet, Mark. *Taking the Constitution Away from the Courts.* Princeton, N.J.: Princeton University Press, 1999.

Walker, Samuel. *The Rights Revolution: Rights and Community in Modern America.* New York: Oxford University Press, 1998.

Wright, Benjamin F. *American Interpretations of Natural Law.* Cambridge, Mass.: Harvard University Press, 1931.

Yarbrough, Tinsley E. *Mr. Justice Black and His Critics.* Durham, N.C.: Duke University Press, 1988.

# 3 Judicial Power

When *Sports Illustrated* anointed Curt Flood as major league baseball's premier center fielder by featuring him on the cover during the height of the 1968 season, it could never have known that, just one year later, this three-time All-Star and seven-time Gold Glove winner would be making another kind of news. Flood's refusal to accept a trade from the St. Louis Cardinals, for whom he had played for twelve seasons, to the Philadelphia Phillies would shake the rafters of the national pastime's business structure with an earthquakelike force. Beginning in 1880, professional baseball had incorporated what later became known as the "reserve clause" into the standard contracts that each major league team issued to its players. The reserve clause permitted the owners to retain exclusive rights to the services of the players of their respective teams by forbidding the players to negotiate with other teams after the expiration of their annual contracts for a period of one year. The practical result of the reserve clause was to bind a player to the team that first signed him into perpetuity, since refusing to sign an annual contract meant that a player would have to sit out a year before he could offer his services to other teams. Previous attempts by players to test the reserve clause's operation had resulted in their banishment from the game, the illegal but uncontested response of the owners to anyone who dared to challenge a system so favorable to their business interests.

Observers of Flood's career were surprised that this quiet man, a skilled portrait artist whose work hung in the offices of August Busch, owner of the Cardinals, would challenge the ancient business practices of the sport that, by his own admission, had paid him well. But Flood's reticence concealed a powerful intelligence and evolving social conscience, one whose values were shaped by the tumultuous events of the era in which he came of age. A self-professed "child of the sixties," Flood decided he could not accept a business arrangement that denied him what he believed were basic civil rights in his own profession.[1]

Determined not to accept the trade, Flood contacted Marvin Miller, the chief counsel and negotiator for the Players Association, the union that represents major league baseball players in labor and contract matters with the owners, to inquire about a lawsuit attacking the reserve clause on antitrust grounds. Miller advised Flood that two previous such lawsuits had reached the United States Supreme Court and had been unsuccessful. The first, *Federal Baseball Club* v. *The National League* (1922), involved a challenge by a start-up professional baseball league to attract players from the established National and American Leagues. Federal League owners claimed that the reserve clause allowed the National and American Leagues to restrain trade in violation of the Sherman Antitrust Act of 1890, the first major congressional effort to prohibit and punish monopolistic business practices and price fixing. A unanimous Court rejected the Federal League's argument, holding, in an opinion written by Justice Oliver Wendell Holmes, that professional baseball was not, in fact, a business beholden to federal antitrust laws, but a series of exhibitions played for the public's enjoyment.[2] In other words, baseball was a game, not a business, and thus escaped the reach of federal antitrust law.

*In 1968, Curt Flood was major league baseball's best center fielder. A year later, his refusal to accept a trade to another team led to a Supreme Court decision on the sport's labor practices.*
© Sports Illustrated.

Justice Holmes's ruling established a judicially created exemption to the Sherman Act that Congress had never contemplated when it passed the legislation. The Court refused to disturb this exemption when it addressed the reserve clause for the second time in *Toolson v. New York Yankees* (1953). In *Toolson* the Court addressed the question of player mobility under the reserve clause, holding that as a "game," federal antitrust law did not reach labor disputes in baseball. Despite declaring that horse racing, boxing, and football were interstate businesses covered by federal antitrust laws, the Court chose to exempt baseball once again on the grounds that, as the "national pastime," it was "different." Moreover, baseball had prospered without inter-

ference from the government. *Toolson* offered no compelling reason to change that policy.[3]

As illogical as the Court's decisions in *Federal Baseball* and *Toolson* appeared to those who understood the economics of professional baseball, Miller advised Flood that the Court was unlikely to reverse either decision on the principle of *stare decisis,* or the established judicial tradition of adhering to past precedent. Courts were reluctant to reverse prior holdings, even those that were considered flawed, because of the legal and societal disruption it would cause. Clear and unequivocal legal error was one thing, Miller said, but bad antitrust policy that did not raise substantial constitutional questions was another. Undaunted, Flood, with the support of the Players Association, pressed ahead. He informed the commissioner of major league baseball, Bowie Kuhn, in a letter addressed Christmas Eve of 1969, that he would not accept his trade to the Philadelphia Phillies. Wrote Flood: "After twelve years in the Major Leagues, I do not feel that I am a piece of property to be bought and sold irrespective of my wishes. I believe that any system that produces that result violates my basic rights as a citizen and is inconsistent with the laws of the United States."[4]

Flood also asked Kuhn to inform all the other major league teams that his services were available. Kuhn's response was that he would not honor Flood's request because of the reserve clause. Flood then filed a lawsuit in federal court, naming the commissioner as the defendant, and charged that the Court's decisions in *Federal Baseball* and *Toolson* exempting major league baseball from federal antitrust law were erroneous and should be reversed. To reinforce the seriousness with which the Players Association viewed this case and in anticipation that *Flood v. Kuhn* would reach the Supreme Court, Miller was able to persuade a former justice of the Supreme Court, Arthur Goldberg (1962–1965), to represent Flood. Before entering public service in 1961 as President John F. Kennedy's secretary of labor, Goldberg had risen to legal prominence as a labor lawyer for the nation's largest automobile and industrial unions. Miller had an edge when he approached Goldberg—the two had worked together for more than ten years representing the United Steelworkers union.

Two lower federal courts rejected Flood's arguments. And not even the logic of the law and a former justice arguing his case could help Flood's chances before the

Court. Although it found that professional baseball was in fact interstate commerce and called its exemption from the federal antitrust laws an "aberration," the Court relied upon *stare decisis* and ruled that Congress, not "this Court," should take appropriate corrective action.[5] Dissenting, Justice Thurgood Marshall wrote that, since it was the Court through its prior rulings that made the players "impotent" to confront the settled power structure of professional baseball, it was "this Court [that] should correct its errors."[6] But Justice Marshall's voice was not powerful enough to carry the day. Thus, in the spring of 1972, just as the sights, sounds, and smells of another baseball season were back in the public's consciousness, Curt Flood, a center fielder so good that his defensive skills were often mentioned in the same breath as Hall of Famer Willie Mays, would watch from afar, his career over.

But Flood's decision to pursue his grievance with the economics of professional baseball all the way to the Supreme Court provided an excellent example of how litigation, even if unsuccessful, can raise public awareness and spur reform through channels outside the nation's courtrooms. *Flood* v. *Kuhn* resulted in a much more aggressive and educated players union. Exposed to the economic and legal arrangements of their sport as never before, the union was able, through more sophisticated negotiating strategies and strikes, to convince the owners to change the reserve clause to allow greater player mobility. This development led to unparalleled increases in salary and compensation, since players were now free to entertain competitive bids from all major league teams after a certain period of service with one team. Change would have come about at some point, but it would have happened much later had Curt Flood followed traditional business practices and simply packed his bags and reported to the Philadelphia Phillies.

But the *Flood* case is also important because it demonstrates the extent to which conflicts from the most unlikely corners of American society ultimately find their way to the Supreme Court. Could the Framers possibly have envisioned a professional athlete, almost two hundred years later, taking an employment dispute to the nation's highest constitutional court? Or, for that matter, could they have envisioned lawsuits asserting that the Constitution includes a right to abortion, to own and operate a nightclub featuring nude dancing, to engage in consensual sexual conduct with a person of the same sex, or to allow a citizen to sue a sitting president for sexual harassment? These questions and many more that were most likely beyond the comprehension of the Framers have reached the Court, whose decisions have transformed almost every conceivable aspect of American society, often in ways decidedly at odds with public opinion. The Court's involvement in the intricacies of the social, political, and economic forces that shape the lives of American citizens and their institutions can be traced to its assertion and use of *judicial review,* or the power to decide whether federal, state, and local laws violate the Constitution. Although the Court has no affirmative power to initiate legal action, it has encouraged a more litigious society through its willingness to accept and decide cases that raise questions once thought to be private or political in nature.

How did the Court, the branch of government that Alexander Hamilton famously described in *Federalist 78* as the "least dangerous to the political rights of the Constitution," become the most powerful court of law in the world?[7] The answer lies in the Court's exercise of judicial review as the source of its "extraordinary" power over American politics and government. To describe the power of judicial review as "extraordinary" does not risk overstatement. The power of the courts to declare laws enacted through the democratic channels of government unconstitutional is indeed a formidable weapon. Judicial review enables the Court, in a single judicial stroke, to replace the customs, approaches, and rules of various regions, states, and localities with national constitutional standards. From the sheer volume of scholarship on the controversies involving the origins, boundaries, and legitimacy of judicial review, one would think that the Court strikes down federal, state, and local laws with great regularity. Quite the opposite is, in fact, the case. Since the Court, in *Marbury* v. *Madison* (1803), first declared an act of Congress unconstitutional, the Court has upheld federal, state, and local laws against constitutional challenges much more often than it has not.

If the Court tends to affirm rather than disturb the legal and political choices of the democratic process, what accounts for the disproportionate emphasis that judicial review receives in any discussion of federal judicial power? Three major reasons come to mind. One is that judicial review, as a component of judicial power, is nowhere mentioned in the Constitution. Ample evidence exists that the Framers intended the courts to have some sort of power to control the unconstitutional excesses of majority rule. Still, the Constitution offers no guidance on the source and scope of judicial review. This paradox of constitutional construction—the creation of a judicial branch with undefined powers and responsibilities—offers a stark contrast to the detail that defines the powers of the legislative and executive branches of government. We will discuss the theoretical and political rationales that have been offered on behalf of both a limited and expansive conception of judicial review as we discuss the cases that have defined the Court's assumption and use of this power. For now, it is reasonable to conclude that the absence of a textual definition "is not to say that the power of judicial review cannot be placed in the Constitution; merely that it cannot be found there."[8]

Second, judicial review, in the purest sense, is a profoundly anti-democratic exercise. Unlike the political branches of government, which are responsive and accountable to the electorate, the courts are not bound by such temporal concerns. The justices are appointed for life terms and are not required to subject their decisions to political constituencies that will determine their fitness for reelection. The Constitution's opponents during the ratification debates expressed fear that the placement of such power in the federal courts would enable judges to dominate the government. Of judicial review the Anti-Federalist *Brutus* wrote:

> There is no authority that can remove them, and they cannot be controlled by the laws of the legislature. In short, they are independent of the people, of the legislature, and of every power under heaven. . . . And in their decisions they will not confine themselves to any fixed or established rules, but will determine, according to what appears to them, the reason and spirit of the constitution. The opinions of the supreme court, whatever they may be, will have the force of law; because there is no power provided in the constitution, that can correct their errors, or control their adjudications. From this court there is no appeal.
>
> This power in the judicial will enable them to mold the government, into almost any shape they please.[9]

Even today *Brutus's* complaints are representative of those who view judicial review as lacking a democratic foundation. How can the power of the courts to strike down popularly enacted laws be reconciled with the democratic aspirations of the Constitution? On the most basic level, the answer is that it cannot. But this reply assumes that the Framers, or more accurately, the triumphant Federalists, equated the democratic republic created by the Constitution with unchecked majority rule. James Madison dispelled this notion in *Federalist* 47. He clearly stated that the Constitution's intricate and complex structure was designed to place strategic controls on the power of the political branches. Madison wrote: "The accumulation of all powers, legislative, executive and judiciary, in the same hands, whether of one, a few, or many . . . may justly be pronounced the very definition of tyranny."[10] To leave the courts without meaningful, independent power in the separation of powers design would be to withdraw a vital check on the power of political majorities. Alexander Hamilton, in *Federalist* 78, was even more direct in pointing to the need and virtues on an independent judiciary, writing that "in a republic it is a no less excellent barrier to the encroachments and oppressions of the representative body."[11]

Moreover, some constitutional historians have argued that the central question concerning the courts in the early Republic was not whether they possessed the power of judicial review, which was taken as a given component of judicial power, but how to protect them from the political pressure of the elected branches. For the founding generation, the solution was to reserve matters of law, especially those involving individual rights claims, to the courts while allowing the elected branches to control political affairs.[12] Even so, legitimate questions attach to the exercise of judicial review if only because it does deviate from the basic democratic principle of consent of the governed. These questions and their related controversies are explored in more detail later in this chapter.

Third, in the absence of a constitutional directive, the Court's assumption of the *power* of judicial review also created the parallel responsibility to create a *theory* of judicial review. Since Chief Justice John Marshall first expounded the constitutional basis for judicial review in *Marbury*, scholars have offered numerous theories to guide the courts on the use of that power. Political scientists Louis Fisher and Susan R. Burgess have argued, for example, that constitutional interpretation should not be viewed as the sole province of the courts, but as a collaborative process among the different levels and branches of government.[13] Although this approach certainly has a great deal of merit, the truth is that, for better or worse, most modern theories of constitutional interpretation are intertwined with the role of judicial review.

The Court, as we discussed in Chapter 2, has been criticized and praised for its approach to judicial review and constitutional interpretation for reasons that often depend on the results of a particular case. Some constitutional theorists have argued that firm and objective rules to govern judicial review are possible, whereas others have suggested that such theories are rooted in the substantive values that one believes the Constitution should protect. On this latter point, disagreement is inevitable. It is entirely possible to believe that the Constitution's failure to articulate the rules on judicial review reflected an understood consensus of the courts' responsibilities in this regard. It is also equally possible to believe that the Framers fully anticipated that the Court would ultimately call up and define, out of the constitutional vapors, the role of the judiciary in the American political system. Either way, we can reasonably conclude that theoretical precision is not something we are prepared to associate with judicial review.[14] For the courts to retain possession of such a powerful force with no clear-cut rules conditioning its use cannot be anything but controversial.

Judicial review, while the most potent instrument of judicial power, is not the sole instrument that defines the constitutional responsibilities of the federal courts. Several other features of judicial power have emerged after protracted constitutional battles. Before a court can even hear an argument, that court must have *jurisdiction,* or the power to hear and determine a case, over the contested matter. Once a court determines jurisdiction over a case, the process of litigation must comport with *federal judicial procedure,* or the rules that govern the mechanics of the legal process. Although federal judicial procedure entails the actual conduct of litigation and access to the judicial process, legal evolution in this area has come about from critical constitutional conflicts. The gradual expansion of federal judicial authority, much of which has come at the expense of power once held by the legislative and executive branches, has raised questions over whether the courts have supreme power to interpret the Constitution. Article VI of the Constitution does make federal law "supreme Law of the Land." Does this language, however, create what some scholars have called the *judicial supremacy* theory of judicial power? Or, in the elegant phrasing of Justice Robert H. Jackson, is the Supreme Court "final because it is infallible or infallible because it is final?"[15] The Court's resolution of these critical questions of constitutional law has brought enormous change to the substance and process of American government, as well as to the social and political dynamics that have shaped them.

## The Constitutional and Legal Structure of the Federal Judiciary

Before we can discuss the rise and constitutional development of judicial review, we must first examine the powers the Constitution does and does not grant to the federal courts. One of the more instructive elements of this discussion will be the extent to which Congress has defined the power and jurisdiction of the federal courts, particularly the Supreme Court. The result is a federal court system that is a delicate blend of political accountability and judicial independence.

### Constitutional Formation

In contrast to the constitutional design and political expectations of the legislative and executive branches, the Framers' intent for the structure and substantive responsibilities of the judicial branch was rather tenuous and unclear. Some scholars have argued that the general and undefined nature of Article III of the Constitution, which established the judicial branch, can be traced to the relative unimportance the Framers attached to the courts in the constitutional architecture of the separation of powers. The more persuasive explanation is that the delegates to the Constitutional Convention, well aware of the courts' potential power and influence, were unable to reach a consensus on its role and relationship to the political branches. Rather than risk the

Constitution's ratification on the intricacies of law and the judicial process, the Framers chose to leave the most controversial aspects of the federal courts' powers and jurisdictional responsibilities to Congress for resolution. The Framers also believed that much of the established powers and responsibilities of the federal courts would develop through the legal expertise of judicial appointees and the subsequent practice of the adjudication process.[16]

Even though the Framers offered little specific instruction or guidance to Congress on their expectations for a federal judicial system, Article III settled several key points of contention that arose between the Federalists and Anti-Federalists during the Constitutional Convention. These disputes centered around four main concerns: *judicial federalism, federal jurisdiction, judicial independence,* and *political control.*

In calling for the "judicial Power of the United States [to] be vested in one supreme Court, and in such inferior Courts as the Congress may from time to time ordain and establish," the Framers handed victories to both the Federalists and Anti-Federalists. The consensus of the delegates was that one appellate court positioned at the pinnacle of the nation's judicial system was essential to ensure uniformity among the various federal and state courts. Still, the delegates differed greatly as to the extent the Constitution should spell out the responsibilities of the interior federal courts. The delegates eventually agreed to the constitutional establishment of a single "Supreme Court," but left to Congress the responsibility of creating the federal judicial system. Anti-Federalists believed that they could persuade Congress to allow the states to retain considerable responsibility for the administration of civil and criminal justice

**KEY LEGISLATION ESTABLISHING AND REGULATING THE JURISDICTION OF THE SUPREME COURT**

|  |  |
| --- | --- |
| Judiciary Act of 1789 | Provided basic appellate jurisdiction; created a three-tier judicial system staffed by district judges and justices; required circuit riding. Permitted jurisdiction over cases on appeal from state supreme courts when such courts declared a federal law or treaty unconstitutional; ruled against a claim of federal constitutional right or privilege; or upheld a state law that had been challenged as unconstitutional or illegal under the laws of the United States. |
| Acts of 1866, 1867, 1869, and 1871 | Expanded federal jurisdiction over civil rights; reorganized country into nine circuits and reduced the number of justices to seven, later fixed number at nine; expanded jurisdiction over habeas corpus and state court decisions. |
| Act of 1875 | Expanded jurisdiction over civil disputes and gave power to review writs of error; granted full federal question review from state courts. |
| Act of 1892 | Provided for *in forma pauperis* filings. |
| Judiciary Act of 1925 | Replaced mandatory appeals with petitions for *certiorari* in many cases. |
| Voting Rights Act of 1965 | Provided direct appeal over decisions of three-judge court requirement in area of voting rights. |
| Act to Improve the Administration of Justice of 1988 | Eliminated almost all of the Court's nondiscretionary appellate jurisdiction except for appeals in reapportionment cases, cases arising under the Civil Rights Act of 1964, and Voting Rights Act of 1965, antitrust laws, and the Presidential Election Campaign Fund Act of 1971. |

through their own judicial systems. The Federalists, however, agreed to this provision of Article III because they believed that Congress, as the national legislature, would vest the federal courts with the power and jurisdiction required to emphasize their interests in constitutional nationalism.[17]

Both sides proved to have accurate foresight. The First Congress made passage of the Judiciary Act of 1789 among its highest legislative priorities. But the speed with which Congress undertook to create the federal judiciary should not be confused with haste, as the law laid out in meticulous detail the organization and jurisdictional responsibilities of the courts. Congress created a multi-tiered federal system of lower district and circuit courts, spelled out in even greater detail the original and appellate jurisdiction of the federal courts described in Article III, and authorized the Supreme Court to hear appeals from these courts. The law also authorized appeals from state supreme courts if the claims involved federal constitutional questions. Congressional passage of this latter provision of the 1789 law, Section 25, was perhaps the most important statement the Federalists were able to make on behalf of the nationalist side of judicial federalism. The limited jurisdiction of the lower federal courts made clear that most criminal and civil cases would be resolved in state courts, a feature designed to placate the Anti-Federalists. But Section 25 cemented the Federalists' wish to secure judicial enforcement of the Supremacy Clause of the Constitution by allowing federal courts to hear appeals from state supreme courts in cases that involved challenges to federal constitutional law.

Section 25 permitted the Supreme Court to hear cases on appeal from state supreme courts when such courts (1) declared a federal law or treaty unconstitutional, (2) ruled against an assertion of a federal constitutional claim of right or privilege, or (3) upheld a state law that had been challenged as unconstitutional or illegal under the laws of the United States.[18] The language of Section 25 also addressed another important question of the still-evolving power of the federal courts. By allowing the federal courts to hear claims arising from state courts that satisfied the above-mentioned criteria, the 1789 law acknowledged the importance of judicial review to the exercise of judicial power. The law, however, said nothing in Section 25 or anywhere else about the power of the federal courts to review congressional laws or executive actions. The power of the federal courts to review federal laws, long assumed as implicit to the exercise of judicial power, was assumed by the Court, after more than a decade of silence, in *Marbury* v. *Madison*.

The 1789 law also established the initial boundaries of lower federal court jurisdiction. It created two separate categories of jurisdictional responsibilities. The first involved subject matter and was derived directly from Article III's command that "the judicial Power shall extend to all Cases, in Law and Equity, arising under this Constitution, the Laws of the United States, and Treaties made, or which shall be made, under their Authority." In addition, the lower federal courts were authorized to hear maritime and admiralty disputes as well as cases involving crimes against the United States, the substance of which was defined by federal criminal law. Although the jurisdiction afforded to the federal courts by the 1789 law appears, on first blush, quite expansive, the fact is that Congress, in this provision, placed a severe constraint on the scope of their power to hear and decide cases involving federal questions. Section 9 established concurrent federal and state court jurisdiction in cases that involved most federal questions and required such lawsuits, with rare exception, to commence in state courts with appeals subject to the criteria set out in Section 25.

Original jurisdiction, or the authority to hear cases in their first instance, was limited to admiralty and maritime cases and "all crimes and offences that shall be cognizable under the authority of the United States." In 1875, as part of its Reconstruction-era reform efforts to expand federal supervision of Southern legal and political institutions, Congress enacted legislation that granted the lower federal courts jurisdiction over almost all federal questions outlined in Article III. Until then Section 9 of the 1789 law had operated as a states' rights counterpoint to Section 25 in the equation of judicial federalism.

The 1875 law reconfigured the once-overlapping jurisdictional lines that had existed between the federal and state courts. It also marked the first time that Congress had altered the jurisdiction of the federal courts in any real sense. Although Congress has passed several important laws that have increased the Supreme Court's power and discretion over its appellate docket, no subsequent statute has affected the substantive jurisdiction of the lower federal courts as the Judiciary Act of 1875 did.[19] Felix Frankfurter, while still a professor at Harvard Law School, and his colleague James M. Landis, commented that the 1875 law initiated a "revolution" in the function of the federal courts. Prior to the law:

> . . . the lower federal courts were, in the main, designed as protection to citizens litigating outside of their own states and thereby exposed to the threatened prejudice of unfriendly tribunals. Barring admiralty jurisdiction, the federal courts were subsidiary courts. [After] [t]he Act of 1875 . . . [t]hese courts ceased to be restricted tribunals of fair dealing between citizens of different states and became the primary and powerful reliance for vindicating every right given by the Constitution, the laws and treaties of the United States.[20]

Apart from jurisdiction over subject matter, Congress also established the rules that governed which parties were entitled to have their cases heard in federal court. Here the 1789 law simply codified the jurisdictional mandate of Article III.

Even though Congress has made several changes in how the federal courts are structured and staffed, the foundation established by the 1789 law still serves as the cornerstone of federal judicial organization. A single judge still presides over district courts, designed to serve as the point of entry for federal claims, and those courts hold jury trials as required by criminal and civil law. In a nod to judicial federalism, Congress agreed to place one district court in each state, with one additional such court assigned to Virginia and Massachusetts.[21] Innovative in the congressional design was the organization of the federal appeals courts. Rather than place appeals courts in each state, as it had done with trial courts, Congress divided the states, based on geographic proximity, into regional circuits. The 1789 law required two Supreme Court justices and a district court judge to serve as three-judge panels on these circuit courts of appeals. Historian Kermit L. Hall has noted that the presence of Supreme Court justices on the circuit courts and the requirements that the circuit courts convene twice yearly in the states from which an appeal originated made the justices "into republican schoolmasters whose presence in the circuits symbolized the

authority of the remote national government."[22] Circuit courts of appeals and district courts have expanded in number as the nation has grown, and jurisdictional requirements have been eliminated or modified. But the various levels of the lower federal courts, with only a few important exceptions, retain the essence of the original purpose set out for them by the Judiciary Act of 1789.

## Judicial Independence Within a Political Process

The Federalists insisted that the Constitution secure the independence of the federal courts and protect them from the pressure of temporal political majorities. At the same time, the principal Federalist architects of the American constitutional design recognized that the more general concern for equilibrium among the branches of government required some mechanism of political control over the courts. Moreover, the Federalists, to secure ratification, had to assure the Anti-Federalists that the creation of a federal court system did not render either state courts or state constitutions irrelevant. How, then, did the Framers attempt to negotiate these delicate constitutional and political interests?

To safeguard judicial independence and establish some modicum of distinction between the spheres of law and politics, Article III declared that the "Judges, both of the supreme and inferior Courts, shall hold their Offices during Good Behavior . . ." Moreover, Article II stated that the president "shall have Power . . . [to] nominate, and by and with the Advice and Consent of the Senate . . . Judges of the Supreme Court," a power that was extended to lower federal court appointments as well. Evident here is the Framers' need to establish some level of political accountability for the federal courts by vesting the appointment and confirmation powers in the political branches of government. Federal judges would not be directly responsible to the electorate, but their nomination and confirmation to the federal bench would allow open debate on their qualifications and fitness to hold such a specialized public office. This latter feature was considered especially important in light of the possible permanence of their appointment. Although, in a literal sense, the life-tenured appointment rather than election of federal judges deviates from the otherwise democratic features of the Amer-

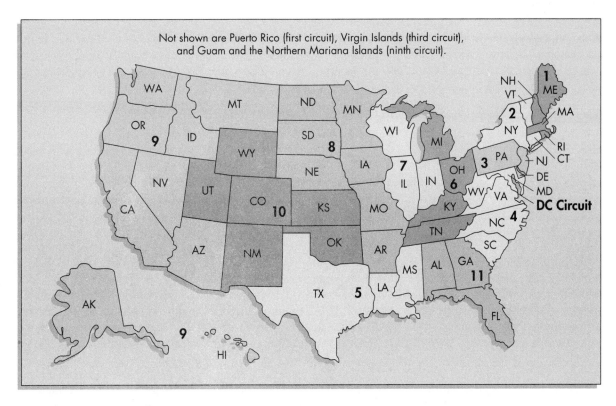

*The federal courts are divided into eleven geographic circuits, plus the District of Columbia*

ican constitutional design, a judicial branch insulated from the insurgencies of partisan politics was regarded as indispensable to the Framers' vision of constitutional government. Wrote Alexander Hamilton in *Federalist* 78:

> If, then, the courts of justice are to be considered as the bulwarks of a limited Constitution against legislative encroachments, this consideration will afford a strong argument for the permanent tenure of judicial offices, since nothing will contribute so much as this to that independent spirit in the judges which must be essential to the faithful performance of so arduous a duty.
>
> This independence of the judges is equally requisite to guard the Constitution and the rights of individuals from the effects of those ill humors which the arts of designing men, or the influence of particular conjunctures, sometimes disseminate among the people themselves, and which, though they speedily give place to better information, and

more deliberate reflection, have a tendency, in the meantime, to occasion dangerous innovations in the government, and serious oppressions of the minor party in the community.[23]

Although the theoretical basis upon which this institutional arrangement rests appears to respect the narrow tightrope that separates the spheres of law and politics, the political environment into which the courts were plunged after the passage of the 1789 law cast a guarded eye on the exercise of judicial power. Aware that Congress also possessed the constitutional prerogative under Article III to make exceptions to their appellate jurisdiction, the federal courts avoided sensitive, politically charged cases and generally deferred to state courts on more controversial matters of law. Indicative of how insignificant the role of the federal judiciary was during the formative years of the Republic, the Supreme Court did not hear a case during its first three years and seldom even convened to discuss current or pending judicial matters. The lower federal courts were busier but behaved with great restraint toward the political process, deciding cases on the narrowest of possible grounds. Not until the Court decided *Chisholm v. Georgia* (1793) did it generate a political backlash by crossing the established border between law and politics to an unacceptable degree.

In *Chisholm* the Court held that two South Carolina citizens were entitled to enter federal court to recover a debt against the state of Georgia, rebutting the state's claim that it was permitted, as a sovereign entity, to choose the appropriate judicial forum in which to defend itself. To compound the outrage, the opinions of Chief Justice John Jay and Justice James Wilson, two prominent advocates of the Federalist cause during the ratification debates, sent shivers down the spines of the emerging ranks of the Jeffersonian opposition. "As to the purposes of the Union," wrote Justice Wilson, "Georgia is not a sovereign state."[24] Chief Justice Jay, reiterating an important theme from *The Federalist Papers,* wrote that the people, not the states, established "a constitution by which it was their will, that the state governments should be bound, and to which the state constitutions should be made to conform."[25] Response among the states, which, for the most part, supported Georgia's decision not to comply with the Court's ruling, was to introduce the Eleventh Amendment. Ratified in 1798, the Eleventh Amendment narrowed federal court jurisdiction to prohibit exactly the type of lawsuits the Court approved in *Chisholm*. Although subsequent constitutional amendments have overruled prior Supreme Court decisions, the enactment of the Eleventh Amendment is the only instance in which the amending process has been used to withdraw jurisdiction from the federal courts.

*Chisholm* underscored two problems facing the federal judiciary as it sought to establish a forceful presence in the American constitutional system. The first was the judiciary's visible institutional weakness, a flaw that the *Chisholm* debacle had exposed in full public view. For much of the 1790s, any effort to exercise federal judicial power was characterized by tepidness for fear of noncompliance. Decisions that did exhibit some forcefulness were frequently seen as Federalist attacks against the states and often ignored.[26] Second, the Jeffersonians,

in their rise to power, had placed the federal judiciary squarely within the cross hairs of their partisan sights, claiming that the Federalists were using the courts to accomplish what was no longer possible through the political process.

Upon taking office in 1801, President Thomas Jefferson and the Democratic Republicans who took power in Congress immediately set out to weaken the authority of the federal judiciary, passing several laws in quick succession that made it easier for Congress to impeach federal judges and limit jurisdiction. Congress also reduced the number of circuit court judges and ordered the Supreme Court not to reconvene until February 1803 so that Republican legislation could go into effect without the risk of it being declared unconstitutional. Worst of all, Congress restored circuit riding to the justices' duties, something they despised to no end.[27] Unlike the 1789 law, which placed the institutional concerns of the federal courts first, passage of the 1802 and 1803 Judiciary Acts by the Republican Congress was nothing more than calculated retribution for the Federalists' perceived abuse of the federal courts to promote political goals adverse to their opponents' interests.

Lackluster leadership within the Court, combined with the sustained political offensive of the Jeffersonian Republicans, reduced the judicial branch to a state of constitutional limbo. Its independence was increasingly under attack, and its role in the separation of powers was uncertain. But if the Court was ever to achieve some semblance of real independence and emerge as a coequal branch in the constitutional scheme, the enactment of the 1802 law showed that the political branches were not prepared to offer their assistance. The task of articulating the Court's defense against legislative and executive dominance fell to Chief Justice John Marshall, who President John Adams appointed to the Court in 1801 before his successor, Thomas Jefferson, was inaugurated. Marshall's response came in the form of judicial review.

## Judicial Review

Almost two centuries after John Marshall explained and defended judicial review on behalf of a unanimous Supreme Court in *Marbury v. Madison,* scholars continue to debate the power that this landmark decision gave the Court to declare unconstitutional laws enacted by the political branches. Did Marshall's opinion declare that the Court was the ultimate and supreme expositor of the Constitution? Did Marshall's opinion have a legitimate foundation, since judicial review is neither mentioned or explained anywhere in the Constitution? Did Marshall's opinion serve as a sophisticated Trojan horse to advance Federalist political interests through judicial subterfuge? Did Marshall's opinion, as sensitive as it was to the charged partisan atmosphere that surrounded *Marbury,* demonstrate that the Court, despite its professed concern for judicial independence, had to impose self-restraint on its power to exercise judicial review?

Like any good story that gets told one too many times, an accurate assessment of Chief Justice Marshall's motives in the case and the legal and political import of his opinion has suffered at the hands of scholarly and popular storytellers. Too many have attributed to the chief justice an agenda he did not possess and a constitutional vision for the judicial role to which he did not subscribe. For one, the chief justice did not believe nor did he write that the Court possessed supreme and unyielding authority over the meaning of the Constitution. True, Chief Justice Marshall did write in the clearest possible terms that it was "emphatically the province and duty of the judicial department to say what the law is," and it was the "very essence of judicial duty" to strike down laws it believed were unconstitutional. But Chief Justice Marshall also tempered the reach of his opinion, and thus the power of judicial review, concluding that the "*courts,* as well as other departments, are bound" by the requirements of the Constitution.[28] Legal folklore aside, John Marshall used *Marbury* as the instrument through which to achieve equality rather than supremacy for the Court in the American constitutional system.[29]

Critics have accused Marshall of using *Marbury* to manufacture the doctrine of judicial review, flouting the intent of the Framers and turning the settled understanding of judicial power on its head. Such a view is persuasive only if we disregard the theoretical framework, historical background, and political context against which Marshall placed the theory of judicial review into practice. First, Marshall's conception of judicial review bears a remarkable similarity to that set forth by Hamilton in *Federalist* 78. Compare, for example, Hamilton in *Federalist* 78:

The complete independence of the courts of justice is peculiarly essential in a limited Constitution. By a limited Constitution, I understand one which contains certain specified exceptions to the legislative authority; such, for instance, as that it shall pass no bills of attainder, no ex post facto laws, and the like. Limitations of this kind can be preserved in practice no other way than through the medium of courts of justice, whose duty it must be to declare all acts contrary to the manifest tenor of the Constitution void. Without this, all the reservations of particular rights or privileges would amount to nothing.

[A]ccordingly, whenever a particular statute contravenes the Constitution, it will be the duty of the judicial tribunals to adhere to the latter and disregard the former.[30]

with Marshall's discourse on judicial review in *Marbury:*

If an act of the legislature, repugnant to the constitution, is void, does it, notwithstanding its invalidity, bind the courts, and oblige them to give it effect? Or, in other words, though it be no law, does it constitute a rule as operative as if it was a law? This would be to overthrow in fact what was established in theory; and would seem at first view, an absurdity too gross to be insisted on . . .

It is emphatically the province and duty of the judicial department to say what the law is. Those who apply the rule to particular cases, must of necessity expound and interpret that rule. If two laws conflict with each other, the courts must decide on the operation of each. . . . This is the very essence of judicial duty.[31]

Hamilton, and Madison as well, had argued in *The Federalist* for an equal, coordinate yet independent role for the federal courts. Does Marshall's opinion, in how it conceives of judicial review and the scope of the Court's power to invoke it against the political branches, exceed the theoretical and political boundaries of *Federalist* 78?

Second, Chief Justice Marshall's critics are hard-pressed to explain the deviant nature of judicial review. After all, of the seventeen states in the Republic when *Marbury* was decided, eight had given positive expression to the power of their courts to declare laws unconstitutional, a trend that continued with little resistance. Political scientist Benjamin F. Wright has commented that judicial review was understood, as far back as the Constitutional Convention, as an integral part of judicial power and thus was not considered in need of express constitutional sanction.[32] Agreement over the proper exercise of judicial review, then as now, was elusive. But the notion that the courts ought to possess the power to strike down legislation that violates the Constitution rests upon a firm theoretical and historical foundation.

Did Chief Justice Marshall construct an opinion ripe with intellectual weaknesses and borderline dishonesty in order to serve the political interests of his Federalist patrons? He certainly went out of his way in *Marbury* to rebuke President Jefferson's handling of the administrative appointments, the issue that spurred the lawsuit. Balanced against the chief justice's reprimand to President Jefferson, however, was the final decision not to authorize the commission of William Marbury, an appointee of Federalist President John Adams, to assume his federal judgeship. Chief Justice Marshall struck down Section 13 of the Judiciary Act of 1789 as violative of Article III, which Marbury had relied upon to support his claim that the court had authority to order his appointment. But his ruling not to compel President Jefferson to order Marbury's appointment averted a sure-fire political showdown between the Federalist-dominated Court and the Republican administration.

To acknowledge that Chief Justice Marshall was aware of and sensitive to the political environment of the moment does not mean that he disregarded legal and judicial principle in *Marbury*. Just two weeks after it announced *Marbury*, the Court, in *Stuart* v. *Laird* (1803), upheld the Judiciary Act of 1802 against a constitutional challenge. The 1802 law, as we discussed earlier, was a partisan detonation from the Republican Congress designed to weaken the Federalist control of the federal courts. If Chief Justice Marshall had been a true cold-blooded political partisan out to preserve Federalist political power, as some scholars have suggested, how then do we explain the Court's unanimous decision in *Laird*? Whatever political squabbles may or may not have been settled in Marbury, it seems fair to conclude that Chief Justice Marshall's foremost concern was to establish the independence and legitimacy of the Court in the American constitutional system. To accomplish that objective, he took a well-known and accepted principle of judicial power—the doctrine of judicial review—and gave it constitutional life.

For all the hoopla surrounding *Marbury*, five decades passed before the Court declared another federal law unconstitutional. That came in the infamous decision in *Dred Scott* v. *Sanford* (1857). Far more important in the Court's assertion of judicial review was the potential force of that instrument to alter the balance of power between the national government and the states. Sec-

*President John Adams signing the "midnight commissions," the act touching off the political firestorm that resulted in* Marbury v. Madison.

Lisa Biganzoli/NGS Image Collection.

tion 25 of the Judiciary Act of 1789 authorized the Supreme Court to hear federal constitutional challenges brought against state laws. Enormous changes had taken place in American politics since passage of the 1789 law, namely, the recession of Federalist power and the rise of Jefferson-inspired states' rights rebellion against centralized national power. Whether states would actually comply with Section 25 when put to the test or simply ignore it was uncertain. More than a decade after the Court had asserted its authority over the constitutional trespasses of the national government in *Marbury,* such a challenge arose. In *Martin* v. *Hunter's Lessee* (1816), the Virginia supreme court refused to abide by an earlier Supreme Court decision declaring a Virginia law unconstitutional on the grounds that it conflicted with a provision of the 1783 Treaty of Paris.

Justice Joseph Story, appointed to the Court by President James Madison in 1812, assembled a unanimous Court in *Martin* and authored an opinion that resonated with a constitutional nationalism almost indistinguishable from that of the chief justice. As Marshall had in *Marbury,* Justice Story, along with the four other Jeffersonian Republicans now sitting on the Court, placed partisan considerations in remission and underscored the need to respect the rule of law. Sovereign power, noted Justice Story, did not rest with the states, but with the people of the United States. If state courts were free to disregard the constitutional decisions of the Supreme Court, chaos would ensue upon the power of the national government to enforce uniform standards of law on matters that fell squarely under federal jurisdiction. Thus, in the first major confrontation over the concurrent jurisdiction of federal and state courts, the Court asserted in resolute terms both its implied power under the Supremacy Clause of Article VI and the authority under Section 25 of the Judiciary Act of 1789 to exercise judicial review over state court judgments.[33]

Justice Story's unqualified defense in *Martin* of the Court's power to harmonize the often conflicting judgments of state courts into a coherent, uniform body of federal law did not dissuade Virginia from mounting another challenge to the Court's jurisdiction to review state court decisions. In *Cohens* v. *Virginia* (1821), the Court, with Chief Justice John Marshall back in the center chair, settled the question about its power to hear appeals from state courts that raised questions under

Section 25. For a unanimous Court, the chief justice left no doubt about its power to review such matters:

> The constitutions and laws of a state, so far as they are repugnant to the constitution and laws of a state, so far as they are repugnant to the constitution and laws of the United States, are absolutely void. These states are constituent parts of the United States. They are members of one great empire—for some purposes sovereign, for some purposes subordinate.
>
> In a government so constituted, is it unreasonable that the judicial power should be competent to give efficacy to the constitutional laws of the legislature? That department can decide on the validity of the constitution or law of a state, if it be repugnant to the constitution or to a law of the United States. Is it unreasonable that it should also be empowered to decide on the judgement of a state tribunal enforcing such constitutional law? . . . We think it is not.[34]

*Cohens,* coming as it did on the heels of *Martin,* laid to rest any question over the Court's power to hear civil and criminal cases arising from all inferior courts, whether state or federal. It also marked a major defeat for one of Marshall's major political opponents, Judge Spencer Roane, whose court had declared Section 25 unconstitutional. Jefferson, for one, never could get over the Court's assumption of judicial review, calling it an instrument on behalf of a "subtle corps of sappers and miners constantly working underground to undermine the foundations of our confederated fabric." The courts, he said, were "construing our Constitution from coordination of a general and special government to a general and supreme one alone."[35] Marshall, the recipient of most of Jefferson's tirades, responded that his fellow Virginians were motivated by reasons other than good government:

> For Mr. Jefferson's opinion as respects this department, it is not difficult to assign the cause. He is among the most ambitious, and I suspect among the most unforgiving of men. His great power is over the mass of the people, and this power is chiefly acquired by professions of democracy. Every check on the wild impulse of democracy is a check on his own power, and he is unfriendly to the source from which it flows. He looks, of course, with ill will at an independent Judiciary.[36]

Jefferson and Marshall continued their feud over the doctrine of judicial review, the constitutional nationalism it encouraged and solidified, and the extent to which the courts were empowered to "control" the political branches. Little question existed, however, about whose views carried the historical moment. John Marshall served as chief justice for thirty-four years (1801–1835), thirty-two of them after he delivered his *Marbury* opinion; never again, however, would the Marshall Court declare a federal law unconstitutional. Moreover, the chief justice himself authored numerous opinions that expanded the scope of congressional power over the states as well as within the national governmental structure. Several of those cases remain good law and form the constitutional foundation for the modern exercise of federal legislative power.[37]

Despite the incomparable influence that John Marshall had on the development of American constitutional law, the *Marbury* decision and Marshall's defense of judicial review will forever remain instantly synonymous with his name.

## Marbury v. Madison

### 5 U.S. 137 (1803)

*Marbury* v. *Madison* is best known as the case in which Chief Justice John Marshall explains the constitutional basis for judicial review, but it also offers a splendid example of the political nature of constitutional law and litigation. Neither the Court's rationale for its power to strike down laws nor the social and political currents that run beneath law and litigation have changed much since *Marbury*.

After his defeat for reelection in November 1800, President John Adams teamed with his Federalist allies in Congress to establish more than two hundred new administrative appointments, including dozens of federal judgeships, to protect their political interests from Thomas Jefferson and his supporters, who had won a majority of congressional seats. Adams continued to make appointments until midnight of his last day in office. Adams's thinly disguised use of presidential appointment power to maintain a Federalist foothold in national politics infuriated Jefferson, who vowed upon taking office not to carry out the commissions assigned by his rival.

Adams had appointed John Marshall, his secretary of state, to be the chief justice of the Supreme Court. One of Marshall's last acts as secretary of state was to deliver Adams's commissions to the appointees. Marshall was able to deliver all but seventeen commissions, which he left to his successor in the Jefferson administration, James Madison, to handle. On Jefferson's orders, Madison refused to deliver the remaining commissions.

William Marbury was one of the Federalists who was denied his commission. He had been appointed for the position of justice of the peace for the county of Washington, in the District of Columbia. Marbury and three others sued to have the Supreme Court issue a writ of mandamus to direct Jefferson's secretary of state, James Madison, to deliver the commissions. Section 13 of the Judiciary Act of 1789 had authorized the Court to issue such a writ. When the case was heard, Marshall had taken his seat as chief justice and failed to recuse himself despite his personal involvement in the case.

Although Marshall's opinion has been criticized as lacking in textual authority, the flawless manner in which he reconciled the different political interests at work attests to a more basic truism about constitutional interpretation: that "apolitical" theories of judicial review are impossible in a system of constitutional government that is a product of political choices.

The Court's decision was unanimous. Chief Justice Marshall delivered the opinion of the Court.

▼▲▼

MR. CHIEF JUSTICE MARSHALL delivered the opinion of the Court.

At the last term, on the affidavits then read and filed with the clerk, a rule was granted in this case requiring the Secretary of State to show cause why a mandamus should not issue directing him to deliver to William Marbury his commission as a justice of the peace for the county of Washington, in the District of Columbia.

No cause has been shown, and the present motion is for a mandamus. The peculiar delicacy of this case, the novelty of some of its circumstances, and the real difficulty attending the points which occur in it require a complete exposition of the principles on which the opinion to be given by the Court is founded.

These principles have been, on the side of the applicant, very ably argued at the bar. In rendering the opinion of the Court, there will be some departure in form, though not in substance, from the points stated in that argument.

In the order in which the Court has viewed this subject, the following questions have been considered and decided.

1. Has the applicant a right to the commission he demands?
2. If he has a right, and that right has been violated, do the laws of his country afford him a remedy?
3. If they do afford him a remedy, is it a mandamus issuing from this court?

The first object of inquiry is:

1. Has the applicant a right to the commission he demands?

His right originates in an act of Congress passed in February, 1801, concerning the District of Columbia. . . .

In order to determine whether he is entitled to this commission, it becomes necessary to inquire whether he has been appointed to the office. For if he has been appointed, the law continues him in office for five years, and he is entitled to the possession of those evidences of office, which, being completed, became his property.

The second section of the second article of the Constitution declares, [that] "The President shall nominate, and, by and with the advice and consent of the Senate, shall appoint ambassadors, other public ministers and consuls, and all other officers of the United States, whose appointments are not otherwise provided for." The third section declares, that "He shall commission all the officers of the United States." . . .

These are the clauses of the Constitution and laws of the United States which affect this part of the case. They seem to contemplate three distinct operations:

1. The nomination. This is the sole act of the President, and is completely voluntary.
2. The appointment. This is also the act of the President, and is also a voluntary act, though it can only be performed by and with the advice and consent of the Senate.
3. The commission. To grant a commission to a person appointed might perhaps be deemed a duty enjoined by the Constitution. "He shall," says that instrument, "commission all the officers of the United States." . . .

It is . . . decidedly the opinion of the Court that, when a commission has been signed by the President, the appointment is made, and that the commission is complete when the seal of the United States has been affixed to it by the Secretary of State.

Where an officer is removable at the will of the Executive, the circumstance which completes his appointment is of no concern, because the act is at any time revocable, and the commission may be arrested if still in the office. But when the officer is not removable at the will of the Executive, the appointment is not revocable, and cannot be annulled. It has conferred legal rights which cannot be resumed.

The discretion of the Executive is to be exercised until the appointment has been made. But having once made the appointment, his power over the office is terminated in all cases, where by law the officer is not removable by him. The right to the office is then in the person appointed, and he has the absolute, unconditional power of accepting or rejecting it.

Mr. Marbury, then, since his commission was signed by the President and sealed by the Secretary of State, was appointed, and as the law creating the office gave the officer a right to hold for five years independent of the Executive, the appointment was not revocable, but vested in the officer legal rights which are protected by the laws of his country.

To withhold the commission, therefore, is an act deemed by the Court not warranted by law, but violative of a vested legal right.

This brings us to the second inquiry, which is:

2. If he has a right, and that right has been violated, do the laws of his country afford him a remedy?

The very essence of civil liberty certainly consists in the right of every individual to claim the protection of the laws whenever he receives an injury. One of the first duties of government is to afford that protection. In Great Britain, the King himself is sued in the respectful form of a petition, and he never fails to comply with the judgment of his court. . . .

By the Constitution of the United States, the President is invested with certain important political powers, in the exercise of which he is to use his own discretion, and is accountable only to his country in his political character and to his own conscience. To aid him in the performance of these duties, he is authorized to appoint certain officers, who act by his authority and in conformity with his orders.

In such cases, their acts are his acts; and whatever opinion may be entertained of the manner in which executive discretion may be used, still there exists, and can exist, no power to control that discretion. The subjects are political. They respect the nation, not individual rights, and, being entrusted to the Executive, the decision of the Executive is conclusive. The application of this remark will be perceived by adverting to the act of Congress for establishing the Department of Foreign Affairs. This officer, as his duties were prescribed by that act, is to conform precisely to the will of the President. He is the mere organ by whom that will is communicated. The acts of such an officer, as an officer, can never be examinable by the Courts.

But when the Legislature proceeds to impose on that officer other duties; when he is directed peremptorily to perform certain acts; when the rights of individuals are dependent on the performance of those acts; he is so far the officer of the law, is amenable to the laws for his conduct, and cannot at his discretion, sport away the vested rights of others.

The conclusion from this reasoning is that, where the heads of departments are the political or confidential agents of the Executive, merely to execute the will of the President, or rather to act in cases in which the Executive possesses a constitutional or legal discretion, nothing can be more perfectly clear than that their acts are only politically examinable. But where a specific duty is assigned by law, and individual rights depend upon the performance of that duty, it seems equally clear that the individual who considers himself injured has a right to resort to the laws of his country for a remedy.

If this be the rule, let us inquire how it applies to the case under the consideration of the Court. . . .

The question whether a right has vested or not is, in its nature, judicial, and must be tried by the judicial authority. If, for example, Mr. Marbury had taken the oaths of a magistrate and proceeded to act as one, in consequence of which a suit had been instituted against him in which his defence had depended on his being a magistrate; the validity of his appointment must have been determined by judicial authority.

So, if he conceives that, by virtue of his appointment, he has a legal right either to the commission which has been made out for him or to a copy of that commission, it is equally a question examinable in a court, and the decision of the Court upon it must depend on the opinion entertained of his appointment. . . .

It is then the opinion of the Court:

1. That, by signing the commission of Mr. Marbury, the President of the United States appointed him a justice of peace for the County of Washington in the District of Columbia, and that the seal of the United States, affixed thereto by the Secretary of State, is conclusive testimony of the verity of the signature, and of the completion of the appointment, and that the appointment conferred on him a legal right to the office for the space of five years.

2. That, having this legal title to the office, he has a consequent right to the commission, a refusal to deliver which is a plain violation of that right, for which the laws of his country afford him a remedy.

It remains to be inquired whether,

3. He is entitled to the remedy for which he applies. This depends on:

1. The nature of the writ applied for, and
2. The power of this court.

1. The nature of the writ.

This writ, if awarded, would be directed to an officer of government, and its mandate to him would be, to use the words of Blackstone, "to do a particular thing therein specified, which appertains to his office and duty and which the Court has previously determined or at least supposes to be consonant to right and justice."

Or, in the words of Lord Mansfield, the applicant, in this case, has a right to execute an office of public concern, and is kept out of possession of that right. These circumstances certainly concur in this case.

Still, to render the mandamus a proper remedy, the officer to whom it is to be directed must be one to whom, on legal principles, such writ may be directed, and the person applying for it must be without any other specific and legal remedy.

1. With respect to the officer to whom it would be directed. The intimate political relation, subsisting between the President of the United States and the heads of departments, necessarily renders any legal investigation of the acts of one of those high officers peculiarly irksome, as well as delicate, and excites some hesitation with respect to the propriety of entering into such investigation. Impressions are often received without much reflection or examination, and it is not wonderful that, in such a case as this, the assertion by an individual of his legal claims in a court of justice, to which claims it is the duty of that court to attend, should, at first view, be considered by some as an attempt to intrude into the cabinet and to intermeddle with the prerogatives of the Executive.

It is scarcely necessary for the Court to disclaim all pretensions to such a jurisdiction. An extravagance so absurd and excessive could not have been entertained for a moment. The province of the Court is solely to decide on the rights of individuals, not to inquire how the Executive or Executive officers perform duties in which they have a discretion. Questions, in their nature political or which are, by the Constitution and laws, submitted to the Executive, can never be made in this court. . . .

But where he is directed by law to do a certain act affecting the absolute rights of individuals, in the performance of which he is not placed under the particular direction of the President, and the performance of which the President cannot lawfully forbid, and therefore is never presumed to have forbidden—as for example, to record a commission, or a patent for land, which has received all the legal solemnities; or to give a copy of such record—in such cases, it is not perceived on what ground the Courts of the country are further excused from the duty of giving judgment that right to be done to an injured individual than if the same services were to be performed by a person not the head of a department. . . .

This, then, is a plain case of a mandamus, either to deliver the commission or a copy of it from the record, and it only remains to be inquired:

Whether it can issue from this Court.

The act [Judiciary Act of 1789] to establish the judicial courts of the United States authorizes the Supreme Court "to issue writs of mandamus, in cases warranted by the principles and usages of law, to any courts appointed, or persons holding office, under the authority of the United States."

The Secretary of State, being a person, holding an office under the authority of the United States, is precisely within the letter of the description, and if this Court is not authorized to issue a writ of mandamus to such an officer, it must be because the law is unconstitutional, and therefore absolutely incapable of conferring the authority and assigning the duties which its words purport to confer and assign.

The Constitution vests the whole judicial power of the United States in one Supreme Court, and such inferior courts as Congress shall, from time to time, ordain and establish. This power is expressly extended to all cases arising under the laws of the United States; and consequently, in some form, may be exercised over the present case, because the right claimed is given by a law of the United States.

In the distribution of this power, it is declared that "The Supreme Court shall have original jurisdiction in all cases affecting ambassadors, other public ministers and consuls, and those in which a state shall be a party. In all other cases, the Supreme Court shall have appellate jurisdiction."

It has been insisted at the bar, that, as the original grant of jurisdiction to the Supreme and inferior courts is general, and the clause assigning original jurisdiction to the Supreme Court contains no negative or restrictive words, the power remains to the Legislature to assign original jurisdiction to that Court in other cases than those specified in the article which has been recited, provided those cases belong to the judicial power of the United States.

If it had been intended to leave it in the discretion of the Legislature to apportion the judicial power between the Supreme and inferior courts according to the will of that body, it would certainly have been useless to have proceeded further than to have defined the judicial power and the tribunals in which it should be vested. The subsequent part of the section is mere surplusage—is entirely without meaning—if such is to be the construction. If Congress remains at liberty to give this court appellate jurisdiction where the Constitution has declared their jurisdiction shall be original, and original jurisdiction where the Constitution has declared it shall be appellate, the distribution of jurisdiction made in the Constitution, is form without substance.

Affirmative words are often, in their operation, negative of other objects than those affirmed, and, in this case, a negative or exclusive sense must be given to them or they have no operation at all.

It cannot be presumed that any clause in the Constitution is intended to be without effect, and therefore such construction is inadmissible unless the words require it.

If the solicitude of the Convention respecting our peace with foreign powers induced a provision that the Supreme Court should take original jurisdiction in cases which might be supposed to affect them, yet the clause would have proceeded no further than to provide for such cases if no further restriction on the powers of Congress had been intended. That they should have appellate jurisdiction in all other cases, with such exceptions as Congress might make, is no restriction unless the words be deemed exclusive of original jurisdiction.

When an instrument organizing fundamentally a judicial system divides it into one Supreme and so many inferior courts as the Legislature may ordain and establish, then enumerates its powers, and proceeds so far to distribute them as to define the jurisdiction of the Supreme Court by declaring the cases in which it shall take original jurisdiction, and that in others it shall take appellate jurisdiction, the plain import of the words seems to be that, in one class of cases, its jurisdiction is original, and not appellate; in the other, it is appellate, and not original. If any other construction would render the clause inoperative, that is an additional reason for rejecting such other construction, and for adhering to the obvious meaning.

To enable this court then to issue a mandamus, it must be shown to be an exercise of appellate jurisdiction, or to be necessary to enable them to exercise appellate jurisdiction.

It has been stated at the bar that the appellate jurisdiction may be exercised in a variety of forms, and that, if it be the will of the Legislature that a mandamus should be used for that purpose, that will must be obeyed. This is true; yet the jurisdiction must be appellate, not original.

It is the essential criterion of appellate jurisdiction that it revises and corrects the proceedings in a cause already instituted, and does not create that case. Although, therefore, a mandamus may be directed to courts, yet to issue such a writ to an officer for the delivery of a paper is, in effect, the same as to sustain an original action for that paper, and therefore seems not to belong to appellate, but to original jurisdiction. Neither is it necessary in such a case as this to enable the Court to exercise its appellate jurisdiction.

The authority, therefore, given to the Supreme Court by the act establishing the judicial courts of the United States to issue writs of mandamus to public officers appears not to be warranted by the Constitution, and it becomes necessary to inquire whether a jurisdiction so conferred can be exercised.

The question whether an act repugnant to the Constitution can become the law of the land is a question deeply interesting to the United States, but, happily, not of an intricacy proportioned to its interest. It seems only necessary to recognise certain principles, supposed to have been long and well established, to decide it.

That the people have an original right to establish for their future government such principles as, in their opinion, shall most conduce to their own happiness is the basis on which the whole American fabric has been erected. The exercise of this original right is a very great exertion; nor can it nor ought it to be frequently repeated. The principles, therefore, so established are deemed fundamental. And as the authority from which they proceed, is supreme, and can seldom act, they are designed to be permanent.

This original and supreme will organizes the government and assigns to different departments their respective powers. It may either stop here or establish certain limits not to be transcended by those departments.

The Government of the United States is of the latter description. The powers of the Legislature are defined and limited; and that those limits may not be mistaken or forgotten, the Constitution is written. To what purpose are powers limited, and to what purpose is that limitation committed to writing, if these limits may at any time be passed by those intended to be restrained? The distinction between a government with limited and unlimited powers is abolished if those limits do not confine the persons on whom they are imposed, and if acts prohibited and acts allowed are of equal obligation. It is a proposition too plain to be contested that the Constitution controls any legislative act repugnant to it, or that the Legislature may alter the Constitution by an ordinary act.

Between these alternatives there is no middle ground. The Constitution is either a superior, paramount law, unchangeable by ordinary means, or it is on a level with ordinary legislative acts, and, like other acts, is alterable when the legislature shall please to alter it.

If the former part of the alternative be true, then a legislative act contrary to the Constitution is not law; if the latter part be true, then written Constitutions are absurd attempts on the part of the people to limit a power in its own nature illimitable.

Certainly all those who have framed written Constitutions contemplate them as forming the fundamental and paramount law of the nation, and consequently the theory of every such government must be that an act of the Legislature repugnant to the Constitution is void.

This theory is essentially attached to a written Constitution, and is consequently to be considered by this Court as one of the fundamental principles of our society. It is not, therefore, to be lost sight of in the further consideration of this subject.

If an act of the Legislature repugnant to the Constitution is void, does it, notwithstanding its invalidity, bind the Courts and oblige them to give it effect? Or, in other words, though it be not law, does it constitute a rule as operative as if it was a law? This would be to overthrow in fact what was established in theory, and would seem, at first view, an absurdity too gross to be insisted on. It shall, however, receive a more attentive consideration.

It is emphatically the province and duty of the Judicial Department to say what the law is. Those who apply the rule to particular cases must, of necessity, expound and interpret that rule. If two laws conflict with each other, the Courts must decide on the operation of each.

So, if a law be in opposition to the Constitution, if both the law and the Constitution apply to a particular case, so that the Court must either decide that case conformably to the law, disregarding the Constitution, or conformably to the Constitution, disregarding the law, the Court must determine which of these conflicting rules governs the case. This is of the very essence of judicial duty.

If, then, the Courts are to regard the Constitution, and the Constitution is superior to any ordinary act of the Legislature, the Constitution, and not such ordinary act, must govern the case to which they both apply.

Those, then, who controvert the principle that the Constitution is to be considered in court as a paramount law are reduced to the necessity of maintaining that courts must close their eyes on the Constitution, and see only the law.

This doctrine would subvert the very foundation of all written Constitutions. It would declare that an act which, according to the principles and theory of our government, is entirely void, is yet, in practice, completely obligatory. It would declare that, if the Legislature shall do what is expressly forbidden, such act, notwithstanding the express prohibition, is in reality effectual. It would be giving to the Legislature a practical and real omnipotence with the same breath which professes to restrict their powers within narrow limits. It is prescribing limits, and declaring that those limits may be passed at pleasure.

That it thus reduces to nothing what we have deemed the greatest improvement on political institutions—a written Constitution, would of itself be sufficient, in America where written Constitutions have been viewed with so much reverence, for rejecting the construction. But the peculiar expressions of the Constitution of the United States furnish additional arguments in favour of its rejection.

The judicial power of the United States is extended to all cases arising under the Constitution. Could it be the intention of those who gave this power to say that, in using it, the Constitution should not be looked into? That a case arising under the Constitution should be decided without examining the instrument under which it arises?

This is too extravagant to be maintained.

In some cases then, the Constitution must be looked into by the judges. And if they can open it at all, what part of it are they forbidden to read or to obey?

There are many other parts of the Constitution which serve to illustrate this subject.

It is declared that "no tax or duty shall be laid on articles exported from any State." Suppose a duty on the export of cotton, of tobacco, or of flour, and a suit instituted to recover it. Ought judgment to be rendered in such a case? ought the judges to close their eyes on the Constitution, and only see the law?

The Constitution declares that "no bill of attainder or *ex post facto* law shall be passed."

If, however, such a bill should be passed and a person should be prosecuted under it, must the Court condemn to death those victims whom the Constitution endeavours to preserve?

"No person," says the Constitution, "shall be convicted of treason unless on the testimony of two witnesses to the same overt act, or on confession in open court."

Here, the language of the Constitution is addressed especially to the Courts. It prescribes, directly for them, a rule of evidence not to be departed from. If the Legislature should change that rule, and declare one witness, or a confession out of court, sufficient for conviction, must the constitutional principle yield to the legislative act?

From these and many other selections which might be made, it is apparent that the framers of the Constitution contemplated that instrument as a rule for the government of courts, as well as of the Legislature.

Why otherwise does it direct the judges to take an oath to support it? This oath certainly applies in an especial manner to their conduct in their official character. How immoral to impose it on them if they were to be used as the instruments, and the knowing instruments, for violating what they swear to support!

The oath of office, too, imposed by the Legislature, is completely demonstrative of the legislative opinion on this subject. It is in these words:

> I do solemnly swear that I will administer justice without respect to persons, and do equal right to the poor and to the rich; and that I will faithfully and impartially discharge all the duties incumbent on me as according to the best of my abilities and understanding, agreeably to the Constitution and laws of the United States.

Why does a judge swear to discharge his duties agreeably to the Constitution of the United States if that Constitution forms no rule for his government? if it is closed upon him and cannot be inspected by him?

If such be the real state of things, this is worse than solemn mockery. To prescribe or to take this oath becomes equally a crime.

It is also not entirely unworthy of observation that, in declaring what shall be the supreme law of the land, the Constitution itself is first mentioned, and not the laws of the United States generally, but those only which shall be made in pursuance of the Constitution, have that rank.

Thus, the particular phraseology of the Constitution of the United States confirms and strengthens the principle, supposed to be essential to all written Constitutions, that a law repugnant to the Constitution is void, and that courts, as well as other departments, are bound by that instrument.

The rule must be discharged.

▼▲▼

## *Martin* v. *Hunter's Lessee*
### 14 U.S. 304 (1816)

Lord Fairfax, a British loyalist who owned property in Virginia and also lived there, died in 1781. Fairfax left the property to his nephew, Denny Martin, a British subject living in England at the time. A 1781 Virginia law stipulated that no "enemy" could inherit land, and the state accordingly confiscated the property. John Marshall, the future chief justice, who was then serving in the Virginia legislature, attempted to negotiate a settlement between the state and Martin. After a number of years, negotiations broke down, and both parties began to sell pieces of the property.

The dispute, which had originally been heard in a Virginia trial court, was then appealed to Virginia's highest court, which denied Martin's claim. Martin had argued that his rights to the property were secured by the Treaty of Peace that had ended the Revolutionary War. He appealed to the Supreme Court, which reversed the Virginia court's ruling. In a separate matter, the Virginia court then ruled that the portion of Section 25 of the Judiciary Act of 1789 extending federal jurisdiction over state supreme courts was unconstitutional. Martin appealed this ruling to the Supreme Court. Because Marshall, now chief justice, and his brother James were attempting to buy some of the property from Martin, he did not participate in the case.

The Supreme Court's decision was unanimous. Justice Story delivered the opinion of the Court.

▼▲▼

. . . The questions involved in this judgment are of great importance and delicacy. Perhaps it is not too much to affirm that, upon their right decision rest some of the most solid principles which have hitherto been supposed to sustain and protect the Constitution itself. The great respectability, too, of the Court whose decisions we are called upon to review, and the entire deference which we entertain for the learning and ability of that Court, add much to the difficulty of the task which has so unwelcomely fallen upon us. . . .

Before proceeding to the principal questions, it may not be unfit to dispose of some preliminary considerations which have grown out of the arguments at the bar.

The Constitution of the United States was ordained and established not by the States in their sovereign capacities, but emphatically, as the preamble of the Constitution declares, by "the people of the United States." There can be no doubt that it was competent to the people to invest the general government with all the powers which they might deem proper and necessary, to extend or restrain these powers according to their own good pleasure, and to give them a paramount and supreme authority. As little doubt can there be that the people had a right to prohibit to the States the exercise of any powers which were, in their judgment, incompatible with the objects of the general compact, to make the powers of the State governments, in given cases, subordinate to those of the nation, or to reserve to themselves those sovereign authorities which they might not choose to delegate to either. The Constitution was not, therefore, necessarily carved out of existing State sovereignties, nor a surrender of powers already existing in State institutions, for the powers of the States depend upon their own Constitutions, and the people of every State had the right to modify and restrain them according to their own views of the policy or principle. On the other hand, it is perfectly clear that the sovereign powers vested in the State governments by their respective Constitutions remained unaltered and unimpaired except so far as they were granted to the Government of the United States.

These deductions do not rest upon general reasoning, plain and obvious as they seem to be. They have been positively recognised by one of the articles in amendment of the Constitution, which declares that "The powers not delegated to the United States by the Constitution, nor prohibited by it to the States, are reserved to the States respectively, or to the people."

The government, then, of the United States can claim no powers which are not granted to it by the Constitution, and the powers actually granted, must be such as are expressly given, or given by necessary implication. On the other hand, this instrument, like every other grant, is to have a reasonable construction, according to the import of its terms, and where a power is expressly given in general terms, it is not to be restrained to particular cases unless that construction grow out of the context expressly or by necessary implication. The words are to be taken in their natural and obvious sense, and not in a sense unreasonably restricted or enlarged.

The Constitution unavoidably deals in general language. It did not suit the purposes of the people, in framing this great charter of our liberties, to provide for minute specifications of its powers or to declare the means by which those powers should be carried into execution. It was foreseen that this would be a perilous and difficult, if not an impracticable, task. The instrument was not intended to provide merely for the exigencies of a few years, but was to endure through a long lapse of ages, the events of which were locked up in the inscrutable purposes of Providence. It could not be foreseen what new changes and modifications of power might be indispensable to effectuate the general objects of the charter, and restrictions and specifications which at the present might seem salutary might in the end prove the overthrow of the system itself. Hence its powers are expressed in general terms, leaving to the legislature from time to time to adopt its own means to effectuate legitimate objects and to mould and model the exercise of its powers as its own wisdom and the public interests, should require.

With these principles in view, principles in respect to which no difference of opinion ought to be indulged, let us now proceed to the interpretation of the Constitution so far as regards the great points in controversy. . . .

This leads us to the consideration of the great question as to the nature and extent of the appellate jurisdiction of the United States. We have already seen that appellate jurisdiction is given by the Constitution to the Supreme Court in all cases where it has not original jurisdiction, subject, however, to such exceptions and regulations as Congress may prescribe. It is therefore capable of embracing every case enumerated in the Constitution which is not exclusively to be decided by way of original jurisdiction. But the exercise of appellate jurisdiction is far from being limited by the terms of the Constitution to the Supreme Court. There can be no doubt that Congress may create a succession of inferior tribunals, in each of which it may vest appellate as well as original jurisdiction. The judicial power is delegated by the Constitution in the most general terms, and may therefore be exercised by Congress under every variety of form of appellate or original jurisdiction. And as there is nothing in the Constitution which restrains or limits this power, it must therefore, in all other cases, subsist in the utmost latitude of which, in its own nature, it is susceptible.

As, then, by the terms of the Constitution, the appellate jurisdiction is not limited as to the Supreme Court, and as to this Court it may be exercised in all other cases than those of which it has original cognizance, what is there to restrain its exercise over State tribunals in the enumerated cases? The appellate power is not limited by the terms of the third article to any particular Courts. The words are, "the judicial power (which includes appellate power) shall extend to all cases," &c., and "in all other cases before mentioned, the Supreme Court shall have appellate jurisdiction." It is the case, then, and not the court, that gives the jurisdiction. If the judicial power

extends to the case, it will be in vain to search in the letter of the Constitution for any qualification as to the tribunal where it depends. It is incumbent, then, upon those who assert such a qualification to show its existence by necessary implication. If the text be clear and distinct, no restriction upon its plain and obvious import ought to be admitted, unless the inference be irresistible.

If the Constitution meant to limit the appellate jurisdiction to cases pending in the Courts of the United States, it would necessarily follow that the jurisdiction of these Courts would, in all the cases enumerated in the Constitution, be exclusive of State tribunals. How otherwise could the jurisdiction extend to all cases arising under the Constitution, laws, and treaties of the United States, or to all cases of admiralty and maritime jurisdiction? If some of these cases might be entertained by State tribunals, and no appellate jurisdiction as to them should exist, then the appellate power would not extend to all, but to some, cases. If State tribunals might exercise concurrent jurisdiction over all or some of the other classes of cases in the Constitution without control, then the appellate jurisdiction of the United States might, as to such cases, have no real existence, contrary to the manifest intent of the Constitution. Under such circumstances, to give effect to the judicial power, it must be construed to be exclusive, and this not only when the *casus foederis* should arise directly, but when it should arise incidentally in cases pending in State courts. This construction would abridge the jurisdiction of such Court far more than has been ever contemplated in any act of Congress.

On the other hand, if, as has been contended, a discretion be vested in Congress to establish or not to establish inferior Courts, at their own pleasure, and Congress should not establish such Courts, the appellate jurisdiction of the Supreme Court would have nothing to act upon unless it could act upon cases pending in the State courts. Under such circumstances it must be held that the appellate power would extend to State courts, for the Constitution is peremptory that it shall extend to certain enumerated cases, which cases could exist in no other Courts. Any other construction, upon this supposition, would involve this strange contradiction that a discretionary power vested in Congress, and which they might rightfully omit to exercise, would defeat the absolute injunctions of the Constitution in relation to the whole appellate power.

But it is plain that the framers of the Constitution did contemplate that cases within the judicial cognizance of the United States not only might, but would, arise in the State courts in the exercise of their ordinary jurisdiction. . . .

It is obvious that this obligation is imperative upon the State judges in their official, and not merely in their private, capacities. From the very nature of their judicial duties, they would be called upon to pronounce the law applicable to the case in judgment. They were not to decide merely according to the laws or Constitution of the State, but according to the Constitution, laws and treaties of the United States—"the supreme law of the land." . . .

It must therefore be conceded that the Constitution not only contemplated, but meant to provide for, cases within the scope of the judicial power of the United States which might yet depend before State tribunals. It was foreseen that, in the exercise of their ordinary jurisdiction, State courts would incidentally take cognizance of cases arising under the Constitution, the laws, and treaties of the United States. Yet to all these cases the judicial power, by the very terms of the Constitution, is to extend. It cannot extend by original jurisdiction if that was already rightfully and exclusively attached in the State courts, which (as has been already shown) may occur; it must therefore extend by appellate jurisdiction, or not at all. It would seem to follow that the appellate power of the United States must, in such cases, extend to State tribunals; and if in such cases, there is no reason why it should not equally attach upon all others within the purview of the Constitution.

It has been argued that such an appellate jurisdiction over State courts is inconsistent with the genius of our Governments, and the spirit of the Constitution. That the latter was never designed to act upon State sovereignties, but only upon the people, and that, if the power exists, it will materially impair the sovereignty of the States, and the independence of their courts. We cannot yield to the force of this reasoning; it assumes principles which we cannot admit, and draws conclusions to which we do not yield our assent.

It is a mistake that the Constitution was not designed to operate upon States in their corporate capacities. It is crowded with provisions which restrain or annul the sovereignty of the States in some of the highest branches of their prerogatives. The tenth section of the first article contains a long list of disabilities and prohibitions imposed upon the States. Surely, when such essential portions of State sovereignty are taken away or prohibited to be exercised, it cannot be correctly asserted that the Constitution does not act upon the States. The language of the Constitution is also imperative upon the States as to the performance of many duties. . . . When therefore the States are stripped of some of the highest attributes of sovereignty, and the same are given to the United States; when the leg-

islatures of the States are, in some respects, under the control of Congress, and in every case are, under the Constitution, bound by the paramount authority of the United States, it is certainly difficult to support the argument that the appellate power over the decisions of State courts is contrary to the genius of our institutions. The courts of the United States can, without question, revise the proceedings of the executive and legislative authorities of the States, and if they are found to be contrary to the Constitution, may declare them to be of no legal validity. Surely the exercise of the same right over judicial tribunals is not a higher or more dangerous act of sovereign power.

Nor can such a right be deemed to impair the independence of State judges. It is assuming the very ground in controversy to assert that they possess an absolute independence of the United States. In respect to the powers granted to the United States, they are not independent; they are expressly bound to obedience by the letter of the Constitution, and if they should unintentionally transcend their authority or misconstrue the Constitution, there is no more reason for giving their judgments an absolute and irresistible force than for giving it to the acts of the other coordinate departments of State sovereignty. . . .

It is further argued that no great public mischief can result from a construction which shall limit the appellate power of the United States to cases in their own Courts, first because State judges are bound by an oath to support the Constitution of the United States, and must be presumed to be men of learning and integrity, and secondly because Congress must have an unquestionable right to remove all cases within the scope of the judicial power from the State courts to the courts of the United States at any time before final judgment, though not after final judgment. As to the first reason—admitting that the judges of the State courts are, and always will be, of as much learning, integrity, and wisdom as those of the courts of the United States (which we very cheerfully admit), it does not aid the argument. It is manifest that the Constitution has proceeded upon a theory of its own, and given or withheld powers according to the judgment of the American people, by whom it was adopted. We can only construe its powers, and cannot inquire into the policy or principles which induced the grant of them. The Constitution has presumed (whether rightly or wrongly we do not inquire) that State attachments, State prejudices, State jealousies, and State interests might sometimes obstruct or control, or be supposed to obstruct or control, the regular administration of justice. Hence, in controversies between States, between citizens of different States, between citizens claiming grants under different States, between a State and its citizens, or foreigners, and between citizens and foreigners, it enables the parties, under the authority of Congress, to have the controversies heard, tried, and determined before the national tribunals. No other reason than that which has been stated can be assigned why some, at least, of those cases should not have been left to the cognizance of the State courts. . . .

This is not all. A motive of another kind, perfectly compatible with the most sincere respect for State tribunals, might induce the grant of appellate power over their decisions. That motive is the importance, and even necessity, of uniformity of decisions throughout the whole United States upon all subjects within the purview of the Constitution. Judges of equal learning and integrity in different States might differently interpret a statute or a treaty of the United States, or even the Constitution itself; if there were no revising authority to control these jarring and discordant judgments and harmonize them into uniformity, the laws, the treaties, and the Constitution of the United States would be different in different States, and might perhaps never have precisely the same construction, obligation, or efficacy in any two States. The public mischiefs that would attend such a State of things would be truly deplorable, and it cannot be believed that they could have escaped the enlightened convention which formed the Constitution. What, indeed, might then have been only prophecy has now become fact, and the appellate jurisdiction must continue to be the only adequate remedy for such evils. . . .

On the whole, the Court are of opinion that the appellate power of the United States does extend to cases pending in the State courts, and that the 25th section of the judiciary act, which authorizes the exercise of this jurisdiction in the specified cases by a writ of error, is supported by the letter and spirit of the Constitution. We find no clause in that instrument which limits this power, and we dare not interpose a limitation where the people have not been disposed to create one.

Strong as this conclusion stands upon the general language of the Constitution, it may still derive support from other sources. It is an historical fact that this exposition of the Constitution, extending its appellate power to State courts, was, previous to its adoption, uniformly and publicly avowed by its friends and admitted by its enemies as the basis of their respective reasonings, both in and out of the State conventions. It is an historical fact that, at the time when the Judiciary Act was submitted to the deliberations of the first Congress, composed, as it was, not only of men of great learning and ability but of men who had acted a principal part in framing, supporting, or opposing that Constitution, the same exposition was explicitly declared and admitted by the friends and by the opponents of that system. It is an historical fact that the Supreme Court of the United States have, from time to time, sustained this appellate jurisdiction in a great variety of cases brought from the tribunals of many of the most important States in the Union, and that no State tribunal has ever breathed a judicial doubt on the subject, or declined to obey the mandate of the Supreme Court until the present occasion. This weight of contemporaneous exposition by all parties, this acquiescence of enlightened State courts, and these judicial decisions of the Supreme Court through so long a period do, as we think, place the doctrine upon a foundation of authority which cannot be shaken without delivering over the subject to perpetual and irremediable doubts. . . .

It is the opinion of the whole Court that the judgment of the Court of Appeals of Virginia, rendered on the mandate in this cause, be reversed, and the judgment of the District Court, held at Winchester, be, and the same is hereby affirmed.

## Judicial Supremacy

The Marshall Court's decisions establishing and reinforcing the doctrine of judicial review had the unforeseen and unintended consequence of creating the "*Marbury* myth," or the view that Marshall's opinion in *Marbury* vindicated the Court as the final, infallible interpreter of the Constitution.[38] This conclusion does not square with the conception of judicial review embraced by either Madison or Hamilton, or that of Chief Justice Marshall. Madison's opposition to the proposed (and defeated) Council of Revision during the Constitutional Convention (which would have enabled the Court to rule upon the constitutionality of legislation before it was forwarded to the president), his subsequent alliance with Jefferson, and his commentaries on *Marbury* all suggest his opposition to judicial review. Furthermore, Madison accepted the federal review of state court decisions. The exercise of such power at the national level was the subject of his doubts.[39] Even Hamilton, the unrepentant nationalist, did not subscribe to a theory of judicial dominance over constitutional interpretation. And a careful parsing of *Marbury*, divorced from the hype and mythology that have come to surround it, makes clear that John Marshall never asserted nor inferred that the Court reigned supreme over the Constitution. Marshall believed that the Court possessed only the authority to interpret and, because of the function inherent in the judicial power, strike down unconstitutional legislation.

The widely held perception that the Court has supreme power over the Constitution derives, then, not from the Framers' or the Marshall Court's views, but from the assumption of such authority by the post–New Deal era Court. In an opinion that far exceeds even the most imaginative conception of judicial power envisioned by John Marshall, the Court, in *Cooper v. Aaron* (1958), announced "the basic principle that the federal judiciary is supreme in the exposition of the law of the Constitution, and that principle has ever since been respected by this Court and the country as a permanent and indispensable feature of constitutional system." From what source did this "basic principle" originate? According to the Court, the "notable case of *Marbury v. Madison*," in which Chief Justice Marshall referred to the Constitution as "the fundamental and paramount law of the nation."[40] Note here how the Court, in *Cooper,* wraps two separate arguments—that the Constitution is the supreme law of the land and that the Court is the final, supreme expositor of the Constitution—into one inseparable package. To doubt the Court's authoritative power to interpret and foreclose a constitutional question is to defy the Constitution itself. Is this conception of judicial power correct? Is it what Marshall argued for in *Marbury?*

*Cooper* cannot be understood, however, independent of the political forces that propelled it before the Court. The SIDEBAR on *Cooper* describes the social and political context that infused the Court's urgent sense of purpose to lay claim to what it insisted was its exclusive authority over the meaning of the Constitution. For now, note the pains the Court took to defend this proposition: In addition to grounding its authority in the Supremacy Clause of Article VI, *Marbury,* and four prior unanimous Court opinions asserting the judicial supremacy theory, the Court even invoked an opinion of Chief Justice Roger Taney defending *Dred Scott* against an abolitionist state court. The Court thus appeared to insist on unquestioning obedience by every government official, as well as the public, to even those

decisions that future generations might find morally repugnant.[41]

Unusual as well in *Cooper* was the Court's unprecedented decision, at the suggestion of Justice Frankfurter, to have each justice sign the opinion. This step was taken to underscore the Court's authority as the constitutional apex of the American governmental system and reaffirm the Court's commitment to its historic *Brown v. Board of Education* ruling. Did this symbolic gesture strengthen the Court's opinion in *Cooper,* or did it expose the Court's insecurity as the authoritative voice of the American constitution by going to such great strides to insist upon obedience to a decision that was only four years old? Did the fact that *Cooper* made a point of mentioning that the three justices who had joined the Court since *Brown* all agreed with the "correctness" of that opinion also suggest a self-consciousness about the scope of that institution's authority? Or, given the political environment in which *Cooper* was decided, was the Court's opinion here as much about the nation's commitment to the revolution in civil rights law sparked in *Brown* as it was about the Court's correct role in the American constitutional system?

Since *Cooper,* the Court, even in the wake of continued criticism from scholars and elected officials of its claim as the ultimate interpreter of the Constitution, has refused to budge from this position. In *City of Boerne v. Flores* (1997), the Court struck down the Religious Freedom Restoration Act (RFRA) of 1993, a law passed with near unanimous bipartisan support in Congress and signed into law with great enthusiasm by President Bill Clinton. RFRA's basic purpose was to protect religious practices from the unintended consequences of government regulation, a right that Congress believed the Court's decision seven years earlier in *Employment Division of Oregon v. Smith* (1990) had substantially compromised. In *Smith* the Court held that laws that did not target religion, but still infringed upon religious practices, did not have to advance an important or compelling governmental interest. All the government had to demonstrate was that the law promoted a rational objective. Congress, in response to a broad coalition of religious and civil liberties organizations, enacted RFRA to require federal courts to evaluate such laws, regardless of the level at which they were enacted, under the compelling interest standard. This standard holds that a law that would deprive religious individuals or institutions of their constitutional rights cannot stand unless the government can demonstrate that enforcement of the law is necessary to achieve a public policy interest of the highest order.[42]

Justice Anthony M. Kennedy, in a 6-3 opinion that RFRA's supporters claimed "staked out a claim to judicial supremacy that exceed[ed] anything" any previous Court had claimed, held that Congress had far surpassed the limits of its constitutional authority when it passed legislation to curtail the impact of *Smith*.[43] Does Justice Kennedy's opinion deprive Congress of what RFRA's supporters have called its legitimate power to protect the substantive nature of constitutional rights?[44] Or is the Court correct in claiming for itself the final, exclusive, and authoritative power to interpret the Constitution? As you consider the implications of *Cooper* and *Flores*, consider this question: Is there a workable alternative to the judicial supremacy theory of constitutional interpretation?

## *Cooper* v. *Aaron*
### 358 U.S. 1 (1958)

In 1957 a federal district court in Arkansas, citing community disruption and the threat of violence, granted the Little Rock school board's request to delay the desegregation plan that it had approved two years earlier. A court of appeals reversed. For more information on the facts and background of this case, see the accompanying SIDEBAR.

The Supreme Court's decision was unanimous. Justice Frankfurter filed a concurring opinion.

Opinion of the Court by THE CHIEF JUSTICE, MR. JUSTICE BLACK, MR. JUSTICE FRANKFURTER, MR. JUSTICE DOUGLAS, MR. JUSTICE BURTON, MR. JUSTICE CLARK, MR. JUSTICE HARLAN, MR. JUSTICE BRENNAN, and MR. JUSTICE WHITTAKER.

As this case reaches us, it raises questions of the highest importance to the maintenance of our federal system of government. It necessarily involves a claim by the Governor and Legislature of a State that there is no duty on state officials to obey federal court orders resting on this Court's considered interpretation of the United States Constitution. Specifically, it involves actions by the Governor and Legislature of Arkansas upon the premise that they are not bound by our holding in *Brown* v. *Board of Education* (1954). That holding was that the Fourteenth Amendment forbids States to use their governmental powers to bar children on racial grounds from attending schools where there is state participation through any arrangement, management, funds or property. We are urged to uphold a suspension of the Little Rock School Board's plan to do away with segregated public schools in Little Rock until state laws and efforts to upset and nullify our holding in *Brown* v. *Board of Education* have been further challenged and tested in the courts. We reject these contentions. . . .

In affirming the judgment of the Court of Appeals which reversed the District Court, we have accepted without reservation the position of the School Board, the Superintendent of Schools, and their counsel that they displayed entire good faith in the conduct of these proceedings and in dealing with the unfortunate and distressing sequence of events which has been outlined. We likewise have accepted the findings of the District Court as to the conditions at Central High School during the 1957–1958 school year, and also the findings that the educational progress of all the students, white and colored, of that school has suffered, and will continue to suffer if the conditions which prevailed last year are permitted to continue.

The significance of these findings, however, is to be considered in light of the fact, indisputably revealed by the record before us, that the conditions they depict are directly traceable to the actions of legislators and executive officials of the State of Arkansas, taken in their official capacities, which reflect their own determination to resist this Court's decision in the *Brown* case and which have brought about violent resistance to that decision in Arkansas. In its petition for certiorari filed in this Court, the School Board itself describes the situation in this language: "The legislative, executive, and judicial departments of the state government opposed the desegregation of Little Rock schools by enacting laws, calling out troops, making statements vilifying federal law and federal courts, and failing to utilize state law enforcement agencies and judicial processes to maintain public peace."

One may well sympathize with the position of the Board in the face of the frustrating conditions which have confronted it, but, regardless of the Board's good faith, the actions of the other state agencies responsible for those conditions compel us to reject the Board's legal position. Had Central High School been under the direct management of the State itself, it could hardly be suggested that those immediately in charge of the school should be heard to assert their own good faith as a legal excuse for delay in implementing the constitutional rights of these respondents, when vindication of those rights was rendered difficult of impossible by the actions of other state officials. The situation here is in no different posture because the members of the School Board and the Superintendent of Schools are local officials; from the point of view of the Fourteenth Amendment, they stand in this litigation as the agents of the State.

The constitutional rights of respondents are not to be sacrificed or yielded to the violence and disorder which have followed upon the actions of the Governor and Legislature. . . . Thus, law and order are not here to be preserved by depriving the Negro children of their constitutional rights. The record before us clearly establishes that the growth of the Board's difficulties to a magnitude beyond its unaided power to control is the product of state action. Those difficulties, as counsel for the Board forthrightly conceded on the oral argument in this Court, can also be brought under control by state action.

The controlling legal principles are plain. The command of the Fourteenth Amendment is that no "State" shall deny to any person within its jurisdiction the equal protection of the laws. "A State acts by its legislative, its executive, or its judicial authorities. It can act in no other way. The constitutional provision, therefore, must mean that no agency of the State, or of the officers or agents by whom its powers are exerted, shall deny to any person within its jurisdiction the equal protection of the laws. Whoever, by virtue of public position under a State government, . . . denies or takes away the equal protection of the laws violates the constitutional inhibition; and, as he acts in the name and for the State, and is clothed with the State's power, his act is that of the State. This must be so, or the constitutional prohibition has no meaning." *Ex parte Virginia* (1880). Thus, the prohibitions of the Fourteenth Amendment extend to all action of the State denying equal protection of the laws; whatever the agency of the State taking the action, or whatever the guise in which it is taken. In short, the constitutional rights of children not to be discriminated against in school admission on grounds of race or color declared by this Court in the *Brown* case can neither be nullified openly and directly by state legislators or state executive or judicial officers nor nullified indirectly by them through evasive schemes for segregation whether attempted "ingeniously or ingenuously." *Smith* v. *Texas* (1940).

What has been said, in the light of the facts developed, is enough to dispose of the case. However, we should answer the premise of the actions of the Governor and Legislature that they are not bound by our holding in the *Brown* case. It is necessary only to recall some basic constitutional propositions which are settled doctrine.

Article VI of the Constitution makes the Constitution the "supreme Law of the Land." In 1803, Chief Justice Marshall, speaking for a unanimous Court, referring to the Constitution as "the fundamental and paramount law of the nation," declared in the notable case of *Marbury* v. *Madison,* that "It is emphatically the province and duty of the judicial department to say what the law is." This decision declared the basic principle that the federal judiciary is supreme in the exposition of the law of the Constitution, and that principle has ever since been respected by this Court and the Country as a permanent and indispensable feature of our constitutional system. It follows that the interpretation of the Fourteenth Amendment enunciated by this Court in the *Brown* case is the supreme law of the land, and Article VI of the Constitution makes it of binding effect on the States "any Thing in the Constitution or Laws of any State to the Contrary notwithstanding." Every state legislator and executive and judicial officer is solemnly committed by oath taken pursuant to Article VI, clause 3 "to support this Constitution." . . .

No state legislator or executive or judicial officer can war against the Constitution without violating his undertaking to support it. Chief Justice Marshall spoke for a unanimous Court in saying that, "If the legislatures of the several states may at will, annul the judgments of the courts of the United States, and destroy the rights acquired under those judgments, the constitution itself becomes a solemn mockery . . . ." *United States* v. *Peters* (1809). A Governor who asserts a power to nullify a federal court order is similarly restrained. If he had such power, said Chief Justice Hughes, in 1932, also for a unanimous Court, "it is manifest that the fiat of a state Governor, and not the Constitution of the United States, would be the supreme law of the land; that the restrictions of the Federal Constitution upon the exercise of state power would be but impotent phrases. . . ." *Sterling* v. *Constantin* (1932).

It is, of course, quite true that the responsibility for public education is primarily the concern of the States, but it is equally true that such responsibilities, like all other state activity, must be exercised consistently with federal constitutional requirements as they apply to state action. The Constitution created a government dedicated to equal justice under law. The Fourteenth Amendment embodied and emphasized that ideal. State support of segregated schools through any arrangement, management, funds, or property cannot be squared with the Amendment's command that no State shall deny to any person within its jurisdiction the equal protection of the laws. The right of a student not to be segregated on racial grounds in schools so maintained is indeed so fundamental and pervasive that it is embraced in the concept of due process of law. *Bolling* v. *Sharpe* (1954). The basic decision in *Brown* was unanimously reached by this Court only after the case had been briefed and twice argued and the issues had been given the most serious consideration. Since the first *Brown* opinion, three new Justices have come to the Court. They are at one with the Justices still on the Court who participated in that basic decision as to its correctness, and that decision is now unanimously reaffirmed. The principles announced in that decision and the obedience of the States to them, according to the command of the Constitution, are indispensable for the protection of the freedoms guaranteed by our fundamental charter for all of us. Our constitutional ideal of equal justice under law is thus made a living truth.

Concurring opinion of MR. JUSTICE FRANKFURTER.

While unreservedly participating with my brethren in our joint opinion, I deem it appropriate also to deal individually with the great issue here at stake. . . .

We are now asked to hold that the illegal, forcible interference by the State of Arkansas with the continuance of what the Constitution commands, and the consequences in disorder that it entrained, should be recognized as justification for undoing what the School Board had formulated, what the District Court in 1955 had directed to be carried out, and what was in process of obedience. No explanation that may be offered in support of such a request can obscure the inescapable meaning that law should bow to force. To yield to such a claim would be to enthrone official lawlessness, and lawlessness, if not checked, is the precursor of anarchy. On the few tragic occasions in the history of the Nation, North and South, when law was forcibly resisted or systematically evaded, it has signaled the breakdown of constitutional processes of government on which ultimately rest the liberties of all. Violent resistance to law cannot be made a legal reason for its suspension without loosening the fabric of our society. What could this mean but to acknowledge that disorder under the aegis of a State has moral superiority over the law of the Constitution? For those in authority thus to defy the law of the land is profoundly subversive not only of our constitutional system, but of the presuppositions of a democratic society. . . .

When defiance of law, judicially pronounced, was last sought to be justified before this Court, views were expressed which are now especially relevant:

The historic phrase "a government of laws, and not of men" epitomizes the distinguishing character of our political society. When John Adams put that phrase into the Massachusetts Declaration of Rights, he was not indulging in a rhetorical flourish. He was expressing the aim of those who, with him, framed the Declaration of Independence and founded the Republic. "A government of laws, and not of men," was the rejection in positive terms of rule by fiat, whether by the fiat of governmental or private power. Every act of government may be challenged by an appeal to law, as finally pronounced by this Court. Even this Court has the last say only for a time. Being composed of fallible men, it may err. But revision of its errors must be by orderly process of law. The Court may be asked to reconsider its decisions, and this has been done successfully again and again throughout our history. Or what this Court has deemed its duty to decide may be changed by legislation, as it often has been, and, on occasion, by constitutional amendment.

But, from their own experience and their deep reading in history, the Founders knew that Law alone saves a society from being rent by internecine strife or ruled by mere brute power however disguised. . . . The conception of a government by laws dominated the thoughts of those who founded this Nation and designed its Constitution, although they knew as well as the belittlers of the conception that laws have to be made, interpreted and enforced by men. To that end, they set apart a body of men who were to be the depositories of law, who, by their disciplined training and character and by withdrawal from the usual temptations of private interest, may reasonably be expected to be "as free, impartial, and independent as the lot of humanity will admit." So strongly were the framers of the Constitution bent on securing a reign of law that they endowed the judicial office with extraordinary safeguards and prestige. No one, no matter how exalted his public office or how righteous his private motive, can be judge in his own case. That is what courts are for. *United States* v. *United Mine Workers* (1947)

The duty to abstain from resistance to "the supreme Law of the Land," U.S. Const., Art. VI, Section 2, as declared by the organ of our Government for ascertaining it, does not require immediate approval of it, nor does it deny the right of dissent. Criticism need not be stilled.

## COOPER V. AARON

### *The Constitution in Crisis*

Shortly after the Court announced its historic decision in *Brown v. Board of Education* (1954) outlawing segregated public schools, the superintendent of the Little Rock public schools, Virgil T. Blossom, began work on a draft desegregation plan to comply with the ruling at the earliest possible date. Blossom's ambitious plan calling for the integration of all Little Rock schools by 1958 was quickly watered down by the local school board, which eventually limited desegregation to just one of its secondary schools, Central High. Initial implementation of Blossom's plan was delayed until September 1957. School board officials were concerned about the potential violence that lurked if change came about too fast. As Juan Williams, the author of *Eyes on the Prize,* the great documentary of the civil rights movement, describes it:

> There was reason to believe that the Little Rock school board's decision was made with the best of intentions. Arkansas had been one of only two Southern states—Texas was the other—to integrate a school district in the fall after *Brown* was decided. African-Americans had been eligible for admission into the University of Arkansas law school since 1948, a policy that came about voluntarily. In stark contrast to other Southern states, roughly thirty-three percent of all eligible blacks in Arkansas were registered to vote. In Little Rock, African-Americans had even been permitted to join the police force, something simply unheard of in the pre–Civil Rights era Deep South. Even before the Court issued its desegregation order in *Brown II* (1955), the Little Rock school board had issued a statement that said, "It is our responsibility to comply with federal constitutional requirements, and we intend to do so when the Supreme Court of the United States outlines the methods to be followed."

In May 1955 the Court handed down *Brown II,* which, in an effort to accommodate the South, said only that desegregation must take place "with all deliberate speed." This phrase, soon to become the bane of civil rights organizations in their efforts to promote integrated schools, gave Southern obstructionists all the room they needed to avoid swift compliance. In Arkansas, James Johnson, an emerging young politician with strong ties to the state's southern plantation region, announced he would lead a campaign to pass a state constitutional amendment designed to avoid the Court's ruling. His sudden gain in statewide popularity disturbed the first-term Arkansas governor, Orval Faubus. Until the Little Rock showdown, Faubus had cultivated a reputation as a populist

reformer, showing little interest in racial issues one way or the other. Unnerved by his potential rival's broad support, Faubus, who faced reelection in 1956, decided to jump on the segregationist bandwagon with the zeal that only a convert can muster.

In January 1956, Governor Faubus announced that "Arkansas [was] not ready for complete and sudden mixing of races in public schools." He issued public support for statements such as those from the segregationist Little Rock Capital Citizens Council opposing "race mixing at school dances and social functions" and "love scenes in class plays featuring students of different races." Faubus supported and signed legislation authorizing a separate budget to defend school desegregation suits, making school attendance voluntary, and creating a state "sovereignty" commission to protect Arkansas from federal encroachment.

African American parents who had anticipated enrolling their children at Central High in September 1957 soon realized that local forces, now backed by the governor, were not going to yield without legal pressure. In February a group of black parents enlisted the support of the Arkansas National Association for the Advancement of Colored People (NAACP), which filed an unsuccessful suit in federal court demanding compliance with the desegregation order. An appeals court affirmed in April, a loss that prompted NAACP legal director Thurgood Marshall to counsel delay until desegregation began in September.

In late August, just days before Central High would open its doors to black students for the first time, Governor Faubus persuaded a local prosegregation parents group to file suit in county court to halt the desegregation plan. The suit claimed, despite all evidence to the contrary, that black and white students were buying guns and knives in preparation for gang warfare. The governor also testified in court, even though he was unable to provide such information to U.S. Department of Justice officials, who had recently visited Little Rock to investigate that very issue. The judge agreed to grant the injunction, but a federal judge, at the request of the NAACP, nullified the ruling. Desegregation was scheduled to proceed.

Now Governor Faubus went on television to announce that he would order the Arkansas National Guard to surround Central High to turn away any black student who attempted to enter. White students were told to stay home until this "problem" had been resolved. Faubus's decision stunned NAACP leaders. Wiley Branton, the lead attorney on behalf of the Little Rock students, later said, "When the governor couldn't block us in court . . . everybody thought he was going to say that he'd done his best, and that the law is the law and everybody ought to be patient and tolerant and cooperative and this, that, and the other. . . ."

One student who did not get the message to stay home was Elizabeth Eckford, who, on the day school was scheduled to begin, rode the public bus to Central High, got off, and started to walk toward the main entrance. Followed by a jeering mob of white students, she headed toward the National Guardsmen posted by the door. When a guard raised his bayonet toward her as she tried to enter the school, Eckford turned around to the shouting and spitting of the white students who had followed her. Terrified by calls to "Lynch the nigger bitch," Eckford ran toward a bus stop, where she was met by a reporter and a

The "Little Rock Nine" being escorted into Central High School by soldiers from the 101st Airborne Division of the U.S. Army. Once safely inside the school, each black student was assigned a bodyguard.
AP/Wide World Photos.

sympathetic white woman whose husband taught at the local black college. They accompanied her back home.

President Dwight D. Eisenhower, who had still not issued a public statement in support of *Brown*, was furious at the chaos that Faubus had caused. Eisenhower had been patient up until this point with Faubus. The president had believed a previous assurance from the governor that the Eckford incident would not be repeated. Now, Eisenhower's anger boiled over as the governor defied federal court orders compelling desegregation on state sovereignty grounds, challenging the very notion of the Constitution as supreme law of the land. In late September, Eisenhower federalized the Arkansas National Guard and sent 1,000 additional paratroopers to Little Rock to maintain order. The troops and the students remained at Central High for the rest of the school year. In a television address to the nation to explain his action in the Little Rock crisis, Eisenhower said:

> [I]n speaking from the house of Lincoln, of Jackson, and of Wilson, my words would better convey both the sadness I feel in the action I was compelled today to take and the firmness with which I intend to pursue this course until the orders at Little Rock can be executed without unlawful interference. . . . I have today issued an executive order directing the use of troops under federal authority to aid in the execution of federal law at Little Rock. Our personal opinions on the decision have no bearing on matters of en-

forcement. . . . Mob rule cannot be allowed to override the decisions of our courts.

Daisy Bates, president of the Arkansas NAACP and publisher of the *Arkansas State Press,* a weekly black newspaper with a circulation of 20,000, played an instrumental role in the desegregation of Central High, acting as a surrogate parent for the Little Rock Nine and as an intermediary between the city's African American and white leadership. When the federal troops arrived to supervise the protection of the black students, a young reporter ran up to Bates and said, "Daisy, they're here! The soldiers are here! Aren't you excited? Aren't you happy?" Bates replied, "Excited, yes, but not happy. Any time it takes eleven thousand five hundred soldiers to assure nine Negro children their constitutional right in a democratic society, I can't be happy."

### References

Bates, Daisy. *The Long Shadow of Little Rock: A Memoir.* New York: David McKay, 1962.
Williams, Juan. *Eyes on the Prize.* New York: Viking Press, 1987.

---

Active obstruction or defiance is barred. Our kind of society cannot endure if the controlling authority of the Law as derived from the Constitution is not to be the tribunal specially charged with the duty of ascertaining and declaring what is "the supreme Law of the Land." Particularly is this so where the declaration of what "the supreme Law" commands on an underlying moral issue is not the dubious pronouncement of a gravely divided Court, but is the unanimous conclusion of a long-matured deliberative process. The Constitution is not the formulation of the merely personal views of the members of this Court, nor can its authority be reduced to the claim that state officials are its controlling interpreters. Local customs, however hardened by time, are not decreed in heaven. Habits and feelings they engender may be counteracted and moderated. Experience attests that such local habits and feelings will yield, gradually though this be, to law and education. And educational influences are exerted not only by explicit teaching. They vigorously flow from the fruitful exercise of the responsibility of

those charged with political official power, and from the almost unconsciously transforming actualities of living under law. . . .

That the responsibility of those who exercise power in a democratic government is not to reflect inflamed public feeling, but to help form its understanding, is especially true when they are confronted with a problem like a racially discriminating public school system. This is the lesson to be drawn from the heartening experience in ending enforced racial segregation in the public schools in cities with Negro populations of large proportions. Compliance with decisions of this Court, as the constitutional organ of the supreme Law of the Land, has often, throughout our history, depended on active support by state and local authorities. It presupposes such support. To withhold it, and indeed to use political power to try to paralyze the supreme Law, precludes the maintenance of our federal system as we have known and cherished it for one hundred and seventy years.

▼▲▼

# City of Boerne v. Flores, Archbishop of San Antonio

## 521 U.S. 507 (1997)

Soon after the Supreme Court's decision in *Employment Division, Dept. of Human Resources of Oregon* v. *Smith* (1990), a diverse coalition of religious, civic, educational, and civil liberties organizations came together to persuade Congress to pass legislation that would require federal courts to adhere to a more exacting standard of judicial review. The coalition was remarkable for the strange political bedfellows it kept. Liberal to moderate groups such as the American Jewish Congress, the American Civil Liberties Union, Americans United for Separation of Church and State, and the Baptist Joint Committee joined forces with the more conservative Christian Legal Society, National Association of Evangelicals, and Concerned Women for America to point out the dangers of *Smith* for religious liberty. By the time Congress passed the Religious Freedom Restoration Act of 1993 (RFRA), more than forty-five groups had signed on as part of the Coalition to Preserve Religious Liberty.

An early and expected challenge to the law came when the zoning board of the city of Boerne refused to issue a building permit to permit a Catholic church to expand its facilities. The city claimed that the St. Peter Catholic Church, built in 1923, was bound by a local law governing historic preservation in a district that included the church. The decision was challenged under RFRA. A federal district court ruled that Congress exceeded the scope of its enforcement power under Section 5 of the Fourteenth Amendment when it enacted RFRA. The lower court was reversed by the United States Court of Appeals for the Fifth Circuit, one of the nation's most influential appeals courts.

The Supreme Court's decision was 6 to 3. Justice Kennedy delivered the opinion of the Court. Justices Stevens and Scalia, who wrote the Court's opinion in *Smith*, concurred. Justices O'Connor and Souter, who have both written elsewhere that *Smith* was wrongly decided, also concurred. Justice Breyer also filed a concurring opinion.

JUSTICE KENNEDY delivered the opinion of the Court.

A decision by local zoning authorities to deny a church a building permit was challenged under the Religious Freedom Restoration Act of 1993 (RFRA). The case calls into question the authority of Congress to enact RFRA. We conclude the statute exceeds Congress' power. . . .

Congress enacted RFRA in direct response to the Court's decision in *Employment Div., Dept. of Human Resources of Ore.* v. *Smith* (1990). There, we considered a Free Exercise Clause claim brought by members of the Native American Church who were denied unemployment benefits when they lost their jobs because they had used peyote. Their practice was to ingest peyote for sacramental purposes, and they challenged an Oregon statute of general applicability which made use of the drug criminal. In evaluating the claim, we declined to apply the balancing test set forth in *Sherbert* v. *Verner* (1963), under which we would have asked whether Oregon's prohibition substantially burdened a religious practice and, if it did, whether the burden was justified by a compelling government interest. . . .

Four Members of the Court disagreed. They argued the law placed a substantial burden on the Native American Church members so that it could be upheld only if the law served a compelling state interest and was narrowly tailored to achieve that end. . . .

These points of constitutional interpretation were debated by Members of Congress in hearings and floor debates. Many criticized the Court's reasoning, and this disagreement resulted in the passage of RFRA. Congress announced:

1. [T]he framers of the Constitution, recognizing free exercise of religion as an unalienable right, secured its protection in the First Amendment to the Constitution;
2. laws 'neutral' toward religion may burden religious exercise as surely as laws intended to interfere with religious exercise;
3. governments should not substantially burden religious exercise without compelling justification;
4. in *Employment Division* v. *Smith* (1990), the Supreme Court virtually eliminated the requirement that the government justify burdens on religious exercise imposed by laws neutral toward religion; and
5. the compelling interest test as set forth in prior Federal court rulings is a workable test for striking sensible balances between religious liberty and competing prior governmental interests.

RFRA prohibits "[g]overnment" from "substantially burden[ing]" a person's exercise of religion even if the burden results from a rule of general applicability unless the government can demonstrate the burden, "(1) is in furtherance of a compelling governmental interest; and (2) is the least restrictive means of furthering that compelling governmental interest." The Act's mandate applies to any "branch, department, agency, instrumentality, and official (or other person acting under color of law) of the United States," as well as to any "State, or . . . subdivision of a State." The Act's universal coverage is confirmed in Section 2000bb-3(a), under which RFRA, "applies to all Federal and State law, and the implementation of that law, whether statutory or otherwise, and whether adopted before or after [RFRA's enactment]." In accordance with RFRA's usage of the term, we shall use "state law" to include local and municipal ordinances.

Under our Constitution, the Federal Government is one of enumerated powers. The judicial authority to determine the constitutionality of laws, in cases and controversies, is based on the premise that the "powers of the legislature are defined and limited, and that those limits may not be mistaken, or forgotten, the constitution is written." *Marbury* v. *Madison* (1803).

Congress relied on its Fourteenth Amendment enforcement power in enacting the most far reaching and substantial of RFRA's provisions, those which impose its requirements on the States. . . .

The parties disagree over whether RFRA is a proper exercise of Congress' Section 5 power "to enforce" by "appropriate legislation" the constitutional guarantee that no State shall deprive any person of "life, liberty, or property, without due process of law" nor deny any person "equal protection of the laws."

[The] respondent contends, with support from the United States as *amicus,* that RFRA is permissible enforcement legislation. Congress, it is said, is only protecting by legislation one of the liberties guaranteed by the Fourteenth Amendment's Due Process Clause, the free exercise of religion, beyond what is necessary under *Smith.* It is said the congressional decision to dispense with proof of deliberate or overt discrimination and instead concentrate on a law's effects accords with the settled understanding that Section 5 includes the power to enact legislation designed to prevent as well as remedy constitutional violations. It is further contended that Congress' Section 5 power is not limited to remedial or preventive legislation.

All must acknowledge that Section 5 is "a positive grant of legislative power" to Congress. *Katzenbach* v. *Morgan* (1966). . . . Legislation which deters or remedies constitutional violations can fall within the sweep of Congress' enforcement power even if in the process it prohibits conduct which is not itself unconstitutional and intrudes into "legislative spheres of autonomy previously reserved to the States." *Fitzpatrick* v. *Bitzer* (1976). For example, the Court upheld a suspension of literacy tests and similar voting requirements under Congress' parallel

power to enforce the provisions of the Fifteenth Amendment, as a measure to combat racial discrimination in voting. . . . We have also concluded that other measures protecting voting rights are within Congress' power to enforce the Fourteenth and Fifteenth Amendments, despite the burdens those measures placed on the States.

It is also true, however, that, "[a]s broad as the congressional enforcement power is, it is not unlimited." *Oregon* v. *Mitchell* (1970). In assessing the breadth of Section 5's enforcement power, we begin with its text. Congress has been given the power "to enforce" the "provisions of this article." We agree with respondent, of course, that Congress can enact legislation under Section 5 enforcing the constitutional right to the free exercise of religion. The "provisions of this article," to which Section 5 refers, include the Due Process Clause of the Fourteenth Amendment. . . .

Congress' power under Section 5, however, extends only to "enforc[ing]" the provisions of the Fourteenth Amendment. The Court has described this power as "remedial." The design of the Amendment and the text of Section 5 are inconsistent with the suggestion that Congress has the power to decree the substance of the Fourteenth Amendment's restrictions on the States. Legislation which alters the meaning of the Free Exercise Clause cannot be said to be enforcing the Clause. Congress does not enforce a constitutional right by changing what the right is. It has been given the power "to enforce," not the power to determine what constitutes a constitutional violation. Were it not so, what Congress would be enforcing would no longer be, in any meaningful sense, the "provisions of [the Fourteenth Amendment]."

While the line between measures that remedy or prevent unconstitutional actions and measures that make a substantive change in the governing law is not easy to discern, and Congress must have wide latitude in determining where it lies, the distinction exists and must be observed. There must be a congruence and proportionality between the injury to be prevented or remedied and the means adopted to that end. Lacking such a connection, legislation may become substantive in operation and effect. History and our case law support drawing the distinction, one apparent from the text of the Amendment. . . .

There is language in our opinion in *Katzenbach* v. *Morgan* (1966), which could be interpreted as acknowledging a power in Congress to enact legislation that expands the rights contained in Section 1 of the Fourteenth Amendment. This is not a necessary interpretation, however, or even the best one. In *Morgan*, the Court considered the constitutionality of Section 4(e) of the Voting Rights Act of 1965, which provided that no person who had successfully completed the sixth primary grade in a public school in, or a private school accredited by, the Commonwealth of Puerto Rico in which the language of instruction was other than English could be denied the right to vote because of an inability to read or write English. New York's Constitution, on the other hand, required voters to be able to read and write English. The Court provided two related rationales for its conclusion that Section 4(e) could "be viewed as a measure to secure for the Puerto Rican community residing in New York nondiscriminatory treatment by government." Under the first rationale, Congress could prohibit New York from denying the right to vote to large segments of its Puerto Rican community, in order to give Puerto Ricans "enhanced political power" that would be "helpful in gaining nondiscriminatory treatment in public services for the entire Puerto Rican community." Section 4(e) thus could be justified as a remedial measure to deal with "discrimination in governmental services." The second rationale, an alternative holding, did not address discrimination in the provision of public services but "discrimination in establishing voter qualifications." The Court perceived a factual basis on which Congress could have concluded that New York's literacy requirement "constituted an invidious discrimination in violation of the Equal Protection Clause." Both rationales for upholding Section 4(e) rested on unconstitutional discrimination by New York and Congress' reasonable attempt to combat it. As Justice Stewart explained in *Oregon* v. *Mitchell,* interpreting *Morgan* to give Congress the power to interpret the Constitution "would require an enormous extension of that decision's rationale."

If Congress could define its own powers by altering the Fourteenth Amendment's meaning, no longer would the Constitution be "superior paramount law, unchangeable by ordinary means." It would be "on a level with ordinary legislative acts, and, like other acts, . . . alterable when the legislature shall please to alter it." *Marbury* v. *Madison.* Under this approach, it is difficult to conceive of a principle that would limit congressional power. Shifting legislative majorities could change the Constitution and effectively circumvent the difficult and detailed amendment process contained in Article V.

We now turn to consider whether RFRA can be considered enforcement legislation under Section 5 of the Fourteenth Amendment.

Respondent contends that RFRA is a proper exercise of Congress' remedial or preventive power. The Act, it is said, is a reasonable means of protecting the free exercise of religion as defined by *Smith*. It prevents and remedies laws which are enacted with the unconstitutional object of targeting religious beliefs and practices. To avoid the difficulty of proving such violations, it is said, Congress can simply invalidate any law which imposes a substantial burden on a religious practice unless it is justified by a compelling interest and is the least restrictive means of accomplishing that interest. If Congress can prohibit laws with discriminatory effects in order to prevent racial discrimination in violation of the Equal Protection Clause, then it can do the same, respondent argues, to promote religious liberty.

While preventive rules are sometimes appropriate remedial measures, there must be a congruence between the means used and the ends to be achieved. The appropriateness of remedial measures must be considered in light of the evil presented. Strong measures appropriate to address one harm may be an unwarranted response to another, lesser one.

A comparison between RFRA and the Voting Rights Act is instructive. In contrast to the record which confronted Congress and the judiciary in the voting rights cases, RFRA's legislative record lacks examples of modern instances of generally applicable laws passed because of religious bigotry. The history of persecution in this country detailed in the hearings mentions no episodes occurring in the past 40 years.

The absence of more recent episodes stems from the fact that . . . , "deliberate persecution is not the usual problem in this country." Rather, the emphasis of the hearings was on laws of general applicability which place incidental burdens on religion. Much of the discussion centered upon anecdotal evidence of autopsies performed on Jewish individuals and Hmong immigrants in violation of their religious beliefs, and on zoning regulations and historic preservation laws (like the one at issue here), which as an incident of their normal operation, have adverse effects on churches and synagogues. It is difficult to maintain that they are examples of legislation enacted or enforced due to animus or hostility to the burdened religious practices or that they indicate some widespread pattern of religious discrimination in this country. Congress' concern was with the incidental burdens imposed, not the object or purpose of the legislation. This lack of support in the legislative record, however, is not RFRA's most serious shortcoming. . . .

Regardless of the state of the legislative record, RFRA cannot be considered remedial, preventive legislation, if those terms are to have any meaning. RFRA is so out of proportion to a supposed remedial or preventive object that it cannot be understood as responsive to, or designed to prevent, unconstitutional behavior. It appears, instead, to attempt a substantive change in constitutional protections. Preventive measures prohibiting certain types of laws may be appropriate when there is reason to believe that many of the laws affected by the congressional enactment have a significant likelihood of being unconstitutional.

RFRA is not so confined. Sweeping coverage ensures its intrusion at every level of government, displacing laws and prohibiting official actions of almost every description and regardless of subject matter. RFRA's restrictions apply to every agency and official of the Federal, State, and local Governments. RFRA applies to all federal and state law, statutory or otherwise, whether adopted before or after its enactment. RFRA has no termination date or termination mechanism. Any law is subject to challenge at any time by any individual who alleges a substantial burden on his or her free exercise of religion. . . .

When Congress acts within its sphere of power and responsibilities, it has not just the right but the duty to make its own informed judgment on the meaning and force of the Constitution. This has been clear from the early days of the Republic. In 1789, when a Member of the House of Representatives objected to a debate on the constitutionality of legislation based on the theory that "it would be officious" to consider the constitutionality of a measure that did not affect the House, James Madison explained that, "it is incontrovertibly of as much importance to this branch of the Government as to any other, that the constitution should be preserved entire. It is our duty." Were it otherwise, we would not afford Congress the presumption of validity its enactments now enjoy.

Our national experience teaches that the Constitution is preserved best when each part of the government respects both the Constitution and the proper actions and determinations of the other branches. When the Court has interpreted the Constitution, it has acted within the province of the Judicial Branch, which embraces the duty to say what the law is. *Marbury* v. *Madison.* When the political branches of the Government act against the background of a judicial interpretation of the Constitution already issued, it must be understood that, in later cases and controversies, the Court will treat its precedents with the respect due them under settled principles, including *stare decisis*, and contrary expectations must be disappointed. RFRA was designed to control cases and controversies, such as the one before us; but, as the provisions of the federal statute here invoked are beyond congressional

authority, it is this Court's precedent, not RFRA, which must control.

It is for Congress in the first instance to "determin[e] whether and what legislation is needed to secure the guarantees of the Fourteenth Amendment," and its conclusions are entitled to much deference. *Katzenbach* v. *Morgan.* Congress' discretion is not unlimited, however, and the courts retain the power, as they have since *Marbury* v. *Madison,* to determine if Congress has exceeded its authority under the Constitution. Broad as the power of Congress is under the Enforcement Clause of the Fourteenth Amendment, RFRA contradicts vital principles necessary to maintain separation of powers and the federal balance. The judgment of the Court of Appeals sustaining the Act's constitutionality is reversed.

*It is so ordered.*

## Federal Court Jurisdiction

Jurisdiction refers to the ability of a court to hear a case based on procedural criteria. The box on page 71 describes the constitutional source of the Supreme Court's original and appellate jurisdiction, the original and appellate jurisdiction of the lower federal courts, and the division of their jurisdictional mandate over disputes between subject matter and individual parties (see page 42 for key legislation establishing the Court's jurisdiction). This brief review will help you understand the difference between the affirmative power vested in the federal courts by the Constitution and Congress to decide cases and the restraints that each places on the courts' jurisdiction and their power to exercise judicial review.

Our concern here is the extent of congressional power to restrict or withdraw the appellate jurisdiction of the Supreme Court and the lower federal courts under the Exceptions and Regulations Clause of Article III. This question is not as simple as the language makes it seem—several theories exist on the scope of legislative power to withdraw the appellate jurisdiction of the federal courts after it has been established. Political scientist Edward Keynes has pointed to three major such theories: the *plenary* view, the *mandatory* view, and the *broad but limited* view of congressional power to regulate and limit federal court jurisdiction.[45] Let us now turn to a brief discussion of these approaches.

## ARTICLE III JURISDICTION OF THE SUPREME COURT

Original Jurisdiction
- Cases affecting ambassadors, public ministers, and consuls
- Cases in which a state is a party

Appellate Jurisdiction
- Cases falling under the jurisdiction of the lower federal courts (those arising under the Constitution or the laws and treaties of the United States) "with such Exceptions and such Regulations as the Congress shall make"

Amended by the Eleventh Amendment
- Removed federal jurisdiction over cases in which a person who is not a citizen of a state can bring suit against the state

Advocates of the plenary view contend that neither the Exceptions and Regulations Clause nor the Ordain and Establish Clause imposes any constraint on the power of Congress to establish or withdraw the Court's appellate jurisdiction or to abolish the lower federal courts altogether. The Framers intended for Congress to have the necessary constitutional tools to prevent the judicial usurpation of legislative and executive power at both the federal and state level. Scholars have sometimes pointed to the opinion of Chief Justice Salmon Chase in *Ex parte McCardle* as evidence that the Court accepted its complete dependence upon Congress for jurisdictional authority. Wrote Chase:

> We are not at liberty to inquire into the motives of the Legislature. We can only examine into its power under the Constitution; and the power to make exceptions to the appellate jurisdiction of this court is given by express words.
>
> What then, is the effect of the repealing Act upon the case before us? We cannot doubt as to this. Without jurisdiction the court cannot proceed at all in any cause . . . judicial duty is not less fitly performed by declining ungranted jurisdiction than in exercising firmly that which the Constitution and the laws confer.[46]

Two important points should be made here. First, *McCardle* is *sui generis,* or one of a kind, in American constitutional law. Never before or since has the Court considered a constitutional challenge under the Exceptions and Regulations Clause to the power of Congress to withdraw its appellate jurisdiction. Equally significant is that Congress, since *McCardle,* has never succeeded in stripping the Court of its appellate jurisdiction to hear and decide a case involving a constitutional claim. Second, when placed in the historical and political context of the case, one is left to doubt whether Chief Justice Chase subscribed to the plenary view of congressional power over federal court jurisdiction that its supporters have often attributed to him. In *Ex parte Yerger* (1869), decided just months after *McCardle,* the Court implied that Congress could not limit access to writs of habeas corpus except under the most "imperious of public emergencies." The Court pointed to Article I, Section 9, of the Constitution, which states, "The Privilege of the Writ of Habeas Corpus shall not be suspended, unless when in Cases of Rebellion or Invasion the public Safety may require it."[47] Does the Court's opinion in *Yerger* mean, as Keynes suggests, that Congress may regulate but not eliminate access to the federal courts when a question involving a fundamental constitutional right is at stake?

Supporters of the mandatory view of congressional power under the Exceptions and Regulations Clause contend that the Framers intended to create a federal court system that was coequal with Congress and the president, with full authority to enforce national constitutional supremacy against national and state abuses of power. The mandatory view is perhaps most prominently associated with Justice Joseph Story, whose scholarly knowledge of the Constitution—he wrote nine books, including the seminal *Commentaries on the Constitution,* while an associate justice—is considered without equal among justices who have served on the Court. Justice Story's opinion in *Martin v. Hunter's Lessee* observed that the Constitution vested all three branches of the national government with exclusive power over their core functions. Thus Congress, as a constitutional imperative, is required to vest "the Judicial power of the United States" in the Supreme Court and the inferior courts it chooses to establish. Congress may regulate and distribute jurisdictional responsibilities among the different levels of the federal judiciary. But what Congress may not do is to interfere with the federal courts' ability to carry out their constitutional responsibilities.

Proponents of the broad but limited view of congressional authority over federal court jurisdiction attempt to combine features from both the plenary and mandatory approaches into a workable accommodation of judicial power within the separation of powers design. This view contends that granting plenary power to Congress to restrict and withdraw specific elements of federal court jurisdiction cannot be reconciled with the Framers' decision to create a judicial branch and imply powers of judicial review. Such an arrangement would give Congress the power to enfeeble the Supreme Court and the entire federal judiciary and alter the basic structure of the American governmental system. On the other hand, shouldn't Congress have some means to check the Court's exercise of judicial review? Advocates of the broad but limited view suggest that congressional power over federal court jurisdiction extends slightly further than the mandatory approach is willing to concede but is largely limited to the appeals process and does not reach substantive areas of constitutional law. Do *McCardle* and *Yerger* suggest that the Court's view of congressional power over its appellate jurisdiction is informed by the broad but limited approach? Or does the gradual expansion of the Court's appellate jurisdiction since the Reconstruction Era suggest that it would view those cases today from a much different perspective?

Since *McCardle*, Congress has considered but failed to pass legislation designed to restrict or eliminate the Court's appellate jurisdiction over specific federal constitutional questions. With one exception, Congress did not invoke the Exceptions and Regulations Clause as an affirmative grant of power to alter or abolish a substantive area of the Court's appellate jurisdiction. That came in the 1950s when Congress passed a jurisdictional bill designed to limit the reach of Supreme Court decision that prohibited the legal profession from probing for subversive applicants to the bar. Then, beginning in the late 1960s and continuing into the early 1980s, Congress introduced dozens of bills that, if passed, would have eliminated the Court's appellate jurisdiction, and that of the lower federal courts as well, in abortion, school prayer, and school desegregation cases. Because

Congress had failed to muster the necessary two-thirds majority in the House and Senate to overturn the Court's controversial decisions in these areas, it sought to circumvent the amendment process by eliminating access to the federal courts to consider the merits of any subsequent constitutional claims.[48]

Suppose Congress had succeeded in passing a law that revoked the Court's appellate jurisdiction over federal constitutional claims. Would such legislation constitute an unconstitutional interference with the Court's ability to exercise the judicial power vested in it by the Constitution? Does the Exceptions and Regulations Clause permit Congress to seal off access to the federal courts to individuals who allege violations of their constitutional rights?

## Ex Parte McCardle
### 74 U.S. 506 (1868)

In 1867, Congress passed the Habeas Corpus Act, which gave federal district courts the power to grant writs of habeas corpus "in all cases where any person may be restrained of his or her liberty in violation of the Constitution or any of its treaties or law of the United States." This action was taken to protect individuals in the former Confederate states, especially African Americans, Republicans, and federal government officials who were engaged in registering black voters. One month later Congress passed the Enforcement Act, a key element of the Radical Republicans' plan to promote post–Civil War reconstruction in the South. The law divided the former Confederacy into five military districts and gave complete control over their internal affairs to the Union officers appointed to govern them.

William McCardle was a journalist who wrote editorials urging Southerners to resist military rule. As a result, he was arrested and held for trial before a military tribunal. McCardle claimed that he was being held illegally because of his status as a civilian. He petitioned unsuccessfully for a writ of habeas corpus in federal district court. McCardle then appealed directly to the Supreme Court, as Congress had authorized under the Habeas Corpus Act. That the Court sympathized with McCardle was apparent to observers during the oral argument. The Radical Republicans moved immediately to have Congress repeal the Habeas Corpus Act, which it did. President Johnson, an opponent of the Radical Republicans' plan for reconstruction, vetoed the law. Congress quickly overrode the president's veto.

The Court's decision was unanimous. Chief Justice Chase delivered the opinion of the Court.

▼▲▼

THE CHIEF JUSTICE delivered the opinion of the Court.

The first question necessarily is that of jurisdiction, for if the act of March, 1868, takes away the jurisdiction defined by the act of February, 1867, it is useless, if not improper, to enter into any discussion of other questions. . . .

It is unnecessary to consider whether, if Congress had made no exceptions and no regulations, this court might not have exercised general appellate jurisdiction under rules prescribed by itself. For among the earliest acts of the first Congress, at its first session, was the act of September 24th, 1789, to establish the judicial courts of the United States. That act provided for the organization of this court, and prescribed regulations for the exercise of its jurisdiction. . . .

The exception to appellate jurisdiction in the case before us . . . is not an inference from the affirmation of other appellate jurisdiction. It is made in terms. The provision of the act of 1867 affirming the appellate jurisdiction of this court in cases of habeas corpus is expressly repealed. It is hardly possible to imagine a plainer instance of positive exception.

We are not at liberty to inquire into the motives of the legislature. We can only examine into its power under the Constitution, and the power to make exceptions to the appellate jurisdiction of this court is given by express words.

What, then, is the effect of the repealing act upon the case before us? We cannot doubt as to this. Without jurisdiction, the court cannot proceed at all in any cause. Jurisdiction is power to declare the law, and, when it ceases to exist, the only function remaining to the court is that of announcing the fact and dismissing the cause. And this is not less clear upon authority than upon principle. . . .

[T]he general rule, supported by the best elementary writers is that "when an act of the legislature is repealed, it must be considered, except as to transactions past and closed, as if it never existed." And the effect of repealing acts upon suits under acts repealed has been determined by the adjudications of this court. . . . In . . . these cases, it was held that no judgment could be rendered in a suit after the repeal of the act under which it was brought and prosecuted.

It is quite clear, therefore, that this court cannot proceed to pronounce judgment in this case, for it has no longer jurisdiction of the appeal, and judicial duty is not less fitly performed by declining ungranted jurisdiction than in exercising firmly that which the Constitution and the laws confer.

Counsel seem to have supposed, if effect be given to the repealing act in question, that the whole appellate power of the court, in cases of habeas corpus, is denied. But this is an error. The act of 1868 does not except from that jurisdiction any cases but appeals from Circuit Courts under the act of 1867. It does not affect the jurisdiction which was previously exercised.

The appeal of the petitioner in this case must be DISMISSED FOR WANT OF JURISDICTION.

▼▲▼

## Federal Judicial Procedure

Federal courts are limited in the exercise of their power and in the scope of their jurisdiction over legal disputes by the constitutional requirements of Article III and the terms established by Congress under the Exceptions and Regulations Clause. These constraints on federal court jurisdiction, however, are but one form of procedural control over the exercise of judicial power. In addition to restraints on its jurisdiction, the Court is constrained by several informal and formal rules from deciding all the prospective cases that come before it. Some of these rules are derived from constitutional commands, but the Court has created most of them. Several scholars have suggested that the Court would rather create the rules to restrain its own power than have another branch of government do so.[49]

The Court has developed several rules to help it decide whether a legal dispute is *justiciable* in a court of law. For a case to be justiciable in federal court, or suitable for judicial resolution, it must present, as Article III specifies, a "Case or Controversy." The Court has interpreted the Case or Controversy requirement to mean that a case must meet several, often interrelated, procedural criteria before it is permitted to address the substance of the legal questions before it. Because Article III does not define what constitutes an actual "case" or "controversy," the Court has accepted that responsibility for itself. These rules are designed to narrow the range of the Court's reach into areas of dispute that are more political and policy oriented in nature. Even when the Court agrees to decide a case that has satisfied the threshold requirements of justiciability, it still professes a concern to minimize the scope of its rulings except in the most compelling of circumstances. Chief Justice Earl Warren acknowledged the difficulties the Court faced in trying to enforce its self-imposed rules of restraint, noting that "justiciability is itself a concept of uncertain meaning and scope."[50] Warren also pointed to several broader factors that the Court must consider in weighing the threshold requirements of justiciability. We consider four of those factors here: adverseness, mootness and ripeness, standing to sue, and the "political questions" doctrine.

## Adverseness

From the first time it was called upon to do so, the Court has refused to issue opinions in lawsuits that do not involve adversarial parties. From the Court's vantage point, the absence of real, as opposed to abstract, and adversarial, as opposed to friendly, parties from a case means there is no case or controversy under Article III to consider. Although the Justices have often disagreed over the dismissal of cases on mootness, standing, or "political questions" grounds, there has been no dissent from the Court's policy on the adverseness requirement. In keeping with this rule, the Court has refused to issue advisory opinions, or opinions that serve as advice upon a question of law submitted by legislative bodies, government officials, or other interested parties.

The Court's rule on adverseness dates to 1793, when it refused, upon the request of Secretary of State Thomas Jefferson, to provide an advisory opinion on several questions of international law and provide an interpretation of the major treaties between the United States and France. Chief Justice John Jay, on behalf of the Court, declined. In a letter to President George Washington, Jay wrote:

> We exceedingly regret every event that may cause embarrassment to your administration, but we derive consolation from the reflection that your judgement will discern what is right, and that your usual prudence, decision, and firmness will surmount every obstacle to the preservation of the rights, peace, and dignity of the United States.[51]

In *Muskrat v. United States* (1911), the Court reaffirmed its unwillingness to issue advisory opinions. In *Muskrat* the Court dismissed a case brought by a class of Native Americans for the sole purpose of obtaining an advisory opinion on the constitutionality of a federal statute. The Court concluded that the lawsuit was "collusive," that is, it presented no adverseness between the parties, and that it sought "advice concerning legislative action, a function never conferred upon it by the Constitution and against the exercise of which this court has steadily set its face from the beginning."[52] While the Court continues to adhere to *Muskrat*, it has managed to circumvent its internal rules against giving formal advice through the use of *obiter dicta*, or statements made in its opinions that are not necessary to the disposition of the case. Examples of *dicta* in the Court's, or, more often, an individual justice's, opinions, abound.

One such example is *Wallace v. Jaffree* (1985) in which the Court declared three separate Alabama laws intended to permit state-sponsored and -assisted prayer in its public schools unconstitutional. Concurring, Justice Sandra Day O'Connor, while agreeing with the Court that laws intended to introduce sectarian prayer into the public schools were unconstitutional, wrote that "moment-of-silence laws in many States should pass Establishment Clause scrutiny because they do not favor the child who chooses to meditate or reflect."[53] Concurring separately, Justice Lewis Powell "agree[d] fully with Justice O'Connor's assertion that some moment-of-silence statutes may be constitutional, a suggestion set forth in the Court's opinion as well."[54] Since *Wallace*, numerous states have passed moment-of-silence laws drafted in accord with Justice O'Connor's concurring opinion.

## Mootness and Ripeness

In addition to adversarial parties, the Court must be presented with a case that is "live," that is, one in which the parties stand to be affected by a judicial decision. If litigation no longer meets this requirement by the time it reaches the Court, then it can be dismissed as "moot." Causes of mootness vary, but in general they render any practical effect a judicial decision might have purely hypothetical. Mootness and adverseness, as the Court's opinion in *Mills v. Green* (1895) makes clear, are strongly interrelated. Because it is a court of law and not an advisory body, the Court's purpose is to "decide actual controversies by a judgement which can be carried into effect, and not to give opinions upon moot questions or abstract propositions, or to declare principles or rules of law which cannot affect the matter in issue in the case before it."[55] Conversely, *ripeness* is the legal term to describe a case that has met all the criteria for judicial resolution.

*DeFunis* v. *Odegard* (1974) provides the classic illustration of the Court's exposition and use of the mootness doctrine. In 1973, Marcos DeFunis Jr., a white male, brought suit against the University of Washington law school, having been rejected earlier that year despite the fact that thrity-six minority students with lower LSAT scores and poorer undergraduate academic records were admitted. Applicants who ranked in the top third of their class were admitted regardless of their racial or ethnic affiliation. DeFunis discovered, however, that the minority applicants who did not meet this criterion were admitted under a process separate from that for "nonminority track" applicants. Students whose applications were sorted into these two separate tracks were never compared. The state trial court in which DeFunis filed his claim found in his favor and ordered him admitted into law school. On appeal, the Washington state supreme court reversed the lower court and upheld the law school's admissions policies as constitutional under the Equal Protection Clause of the Fourteenth Amendment.

DeFunis appealed to the Supreme Court, which refused to consider the merits of his constitutional claim on the grounds that it was moot. The Court reasoned that because DeFunis was in his final semester he would not stand to benefit from a decision on the merits of the law school's admissions program. Prior to oral argument in *DeFunis*, the university had provided a letter to the Court, stipulating that DeFunis, regardless of the outcome of the case, would be permitted to complete his final semester and graduate from law school. Despite the information on DeFunis's status, most of the Court's conference on the case was devoted to the constitutionality of the law school's minority admissions program. Later the Court chose to dispose of the case on mootness grounds. Justice Potter Stewart wrote that *DeFunis* was "not a class action and not remotely akin to *Roe* [v. *Wade*] or *Doe* [v. *Bolton*]," the two abortion cases the Court had decided the previous term despite a request

from the Georgia and Texas attorney generals to void them on mootness grounds.[56]

Dissenting, Justice Brennan strongly suggested that the Court was using the mootness doctrine to avoid a difficult decision on the merits of DeFunis's equal protection claim, noting that "[f]ew constitutional questions in recent history have stirred as much debate, and they will not disappear. They will inevitably return to the federal courts and ultimately again to the Court."[57] On this point Justice Brennan was absolutely correct. Minority admissions programs have been at the front and center of the affirmative action debate since the Court decided the landmark case of *Regents, University of California* v. *Bakke* (1978), which raised the same issues presented four years earlier in *DeFunis*.

The criteria for mootness are not carved in stone. In *Weinstein* v. *Bradford* (1975), the Court explained that exceptions to the mootness rule could be granted whenever two conditions were satisfied: (1) the challenged action was too short in duration to be litigated fully prior to its cessation or expiration, and (2) there was a reasonable expectation that the same complaining party would be subjected to the same action again. Sometimes referred to as the "repetition" exception, the Court reasoned in *Roe* that no litigation involving pregnancy could ever survive beyond the trial stage because of the condition's terminal nature. "Pregnancy," wrote Justice Harry Blackmun in *Roe*, "provides a classic justification for a conclusion of nonmootness. It truly could be 'capable of repetition, yet evading review.'"[58] Does Justice Blackmun's logic square with the Court's rationale in *DeFunis* for refusing to address the affirmative action issue, or does it suggest that the Court will sometimes invoke procedural requirements to avoid confronting a controversial public policy question?

## Standing to Sue

To discourage third parties from using litigation to advance interests that are political, and not judicial or legal in character, the Court has developed an intricate series of rules to determine whether the parties engaged in a lawsuit have standing to sue. Bound together with the threshold criteria of adverseness and ripeness, the standing-to-sue rule requires parties engaged in litigation to have a clear and definitive stake in its outcome.

On the most basic level, this requirement appears guided by common sense. For a lawsuit to proceed, the complaining parties must be able to demonstrate actual harm or injury as a result of the defendant's actions or behavior. Our concern here, however, is not with civil litigation over injuries resulting from a breach in the legal obligation of one private party to another, but with public law litigation intended to challenge the laws that violate the constitutional rights of entire classes of citizens.

Prior to the ascent of the administrative welfare state that arrived with the New Deal, individuals could not easily demonstrate that, in their capacity as federal taxpayers, a general public expenditure violated their constitutional rights. Proving that such expenditure caused actual harm was difficult. The Court said as much, in *Frothingham* v. *Mellon* (1923), when it dismissed a Massachusetts woman's claim that the congressional Maternity Act of 1921 violated her constitutional rights. The law authorized the federal government to make conditional grants to states that wished to supplement their prenatal and infant care programs. Mary Frothingham claimed that the law violated her constitutional rights as a taxpayer because it increased her tax burden without due process of law. Without dissent, the Court dismissed the complaint because the plaintiff had failed to demonstrate either that the federal statute in question was invalid or that its administration had resulted in an injury or affliction sufficient to sustain her claim. For the plaintiff to allege that "he suffers in some indefinite way in common with people generally," wrote Justice George Sutherland, would not suffice for a showing of harm.[59]

*Frothingham* held such lawsuits in check for more than forty years, until a carefully orchestrated lawsuit organized by the American Jewish Congress persuaded the Court to revise the *Frothingham* rules on the standing of taxpayers to sue. In *Flast* v. *Cohen* (1968), the Court modified, but did not overturn, *Frothingham,* holding that when taxpayers could satisfy the new "double nexus" requirement they possessed legal standing to bring lawsuits in federal court.

*Flast* opened the courthouse door to the numerous organized interests that viewed litigation as an instrument of social and political reform, but were unable, under *Frothingham,* to demonstrate direct personal or financial harm. Chief Justice Warren recognized as much when, in his opinion, he commented on the need to create alternative rules for individuals and the "private attorneys general" who represented them to initiate taxpayer lawsuits against unconstitutional government action. The SIDEBAR to this case provides an in-depth discussion of the interest-group politics behind *Flast,* describing how and why the Elementary and Secondary Education Act (ESEA) of 1965 became the vehicle with which to challenge the Court's rules on taxpayer lawsuits.

But, as the Court's subsequent decisions on the standing of taxpayers to sue have made clear, *Flast* was not without its limits. For example, the Court has ruled that taxpayers do not have standing to compel the U.S. Central Intelligence Agency to release classified information or to challenge the power of Congress to declare and conduct war.[60] Moreover, the Court has limited the ability of organized interests to obtain standing to challenge government action, holding that plaintiffs in such cases must be able to demonstrate a "personal" and "imminent" injury.[61] In *Lujan* v. *Defenders of Wildlife* (1992), the Court ruled that an environmental group lacked standing under the Endangered Species Act of 1973 to challenge the changes the Department of Interior had made to its regulations enforcing the law overseas. How does Justice Scalia's interpretation of the "double nexus" requirement of *Flast* compare with that of the original *Flast* opinion itself? In retrospect, was *Flast* a clear departure from *Frothingham?* Or has *Flast* proven to be little more than a narrow exception to the Court's otherwise restrictive posture toward taxpayer lawsuits?

## *Flast* v. *Cohen*
### 392 U.S. 83 (1968)

The facts and background of this case are set out in the accompanying SIDEBAR.

The Court's decision was 8 to 1. Chief Justice Warren delivered the opinion of the Court. Justices Douglas, Stewart, and Fortas filed concurring opinions. Justice Harlan dissented.

▼▲▼

Mr. Chief Justice Warren delivered the opinion of the Court.

In *Frothingham v. Mellon,* this Court ruled that a federal taxpayer is without standing to challenge the constitutionality of a federal statute. That ruling has stood for 45 years as an impenetrable barrier to suits against Acts of Congress brought by individuals who can assert only the interest of federal taxpayers. In this case, we must decide whether the *Frothingham* barrier should be lowered when a taxpayer attacks a federal statute on the ground that it violates the Establishment and Free Exercise Clauses of the First Amendment. . . .

This Court first faced squarely the question whether a litigant asserting only his status as a taxpayer has standing to maintain a suit in a federal court in *Frothingham v. Mellon, supra,* and that decision must be the starting point for analysis in this case. The taxpayer in *Frothingham* attacked as unconstitutional the Maternity Act of 1921, which established a federal program of grants to those States which would undertake programs to reduce maternal and infant mortality. The taxpayer alleged that Congress, in enacting the challenged statute, had exceeded the powers delegated to it under Article I of the Constitution and had invaded the legislative province reserved to the several States by the Tenth Amendment. The taxpayer complained that the result of the allegedly unconstitutional enactment would be to increase her future federal tax liability, and "thereby take her property without due process of law." The Court noted that a federal taxpayer's "interest in the moneys of the Treasury . . . is comparatively minute and indeterminable," and that "the effect upon future taxation, of any payment out of the [Treasury's] funds, . . . [is] remote, fluctuating and uncertain." As a result, the Court ruled that the taxpayer had failed to allege the type of "direct injury" necessary to confer standing.

Although the barrier *Frothingham* erected against federal taxpayer suits has never been breached, the decision has been the source of some confusion, and the object of considerable criticism. The confusion has developed as commentators have tried to determine whether *Frothingham* establishes a constitutional bar to taxpayer suits or whether the Court was simply imposing a rule of self-restraint which was not constitutionally compelled. The conflicting viewpoints are reflected in the arguments made to this Court by the parties in this case. The Government has pressed upon us the view that *Frothingham* announced a constitutional rule, compelled by the Article III limitations on federal court jurisdiction and grounded in

considerations of the doctrine of separation of powers. Appellants, however, insist that *Frothingham* expressed no more than a policy of judicial self-restraint which can be disregarded when compelling reasons for assuming jurisdiction over a taxpayer's suit exist. The opinion delivered in *Frothingham* can be read to support either position. The concluding sentence of the opinion states that to take jurisdiction of the taxpayer's suit, "would be not to decide a judicial controversy, but to assume a position of authority over the governmental acts of another and coequal department, an authority which plainly we do not possess." Yet the concrete reasons given for denying standing to a federal taxpayer suggest that the Court's holding rests on something less than a constitutional foundation. For example, the Court conceded that standing had previously been conferred on municipal taxpayers to sue in that capacity. However, the Court viewed the interest of a federal taxpayer in total federal tax revenues as "comparatively minute and indeterminable" when measured against a municipal taxpayer's interest in a smaller city treasury. This suggests that the petitioner in *Frothingham* was denied standing not because she was a taxpayer, but because her tax bill was not large enough. In addition, the Court spoke of the "attendant inconveniences" of entertaining that taxpayer's suit because it might open the door of federal courts to countless such suits, "in respect of every other appropriation act and statute whose administration requires the outlay of public money, and whose validity may be questioned." Such a statement suggests pure policy considerations.

To the extent that *Frothingham* has been viewed as resting on policy considerations, it has been criticized as depending on assumptions not consistent with modern conditions. . . . Whatever the merits of the current debate over *Frothingham,* its very existence suggests that we should undertake a fresh examination of the limitations upon standing to sue in a federal court and the application of those limitations to taxpayer suits. . . .

Justiciability is itself a concept of uncertain meaning and scope. Its reach is illustrated by the various grounds upon which questions sought to be adjudicated in federal courts have been held not to be justiciable. Thus, no justiciable controversy is presented when the parties seek adjudication of only a political question, when the parties are asking for an advisory opinion, when the question sought to be adjudicated has been mooted by subsequent developments, and when there is no standing to maintain the action. Yet it remains true that, "[j]usticiability is . . . not a legal concept with a fixed content or susceptible of scientific verification. Its utilization is the resultant of many subtle pressures. . . ." *Poe* v. *Ullman* (1961). . . .

Additional uncertainty exists in the doctrine of justiciability because that doctrine has become a blend of constitutional requirements and policy considerations. And a policy limitation is "not always clearly distinguished from the constitutional limitation." For example, in his concurring opinion in *Ashwander* v. *Tennessee Valley Authority* (1936), Mr. Justice Brandeis listed seven rules developed by this Court "for its own governance" to avoid passing prematurely on constitutional questions. Because the rules operate in "cases confessedly within [the Court's] jurisdiction," they find their source in policy, rather than purely constitutional, considerations. However, several of the cases cited by Mr. Justice Brandeis in illustrating the rules of self-governance articulated purely constitutional grounds for decision. The "many subtle pressures" which cause policy considerations to blend into the constitutional limitations of Article III make the justiciability doctrine one of uncertain and shifting contours.

It is in this context that the standing question presented by this case must be viewed and that the Government's argument on that question must be evaluated. As we understand it, the Government's position is that the constitutional scheme of separation of powers, and the deference owed by the federal judiciary to the other two branches of government within that scheme, present an absolute bar to taxpayer suits challenging the validity of federal spending programs. The Government views such suits as involving no more than the mere disagreement by the taxpayer "with the uses to which tax money is put." According to the Government, the resolution of such disagreements is committed to other branches of the Federal Government, and not to the judiciary. Consequently, the Government contends that under no circumstances should standing be conferred on federal taxpayers to challenge a federal taxing or spending program. An analysis of the function served by standing limitations compels a rejection of the Government's position.

Standing is an aspect of justiciability, and, as such, the problem of standing is surrounded by the same complexities and vagaries that inhere in justiciability. Standing has been called one of "the most amorphous [concepts] in the entire domain of public law." Some of the complexities peculiar to standing problems result because standing "serves, on occasion, as a shorthand expression for all the various elements of justiciability." . . .

Despite the complexities and uncertainties, some meaningful form can be given to the jurisdictional limitations placed on federal court power by the concept of standing. The fundamental aspect of standing is that it focuses on the party seeking to get his complaint before a federal court, and not on the issues he wishes to have adjudicated. The "gist of the question of standing" is whether the party seeking relief has, "alleged such a personal stake in the outcome of the controversy as to assure that concrete adverseness which sharpens the presentation of issues upon which the court so largely depends for illumination of difficult constitutional questions." *Baker* v. *Carr* (1962). In other words, when standing is placed in issue in a case, the question is whether the person whose standing is challenged is a proper party to request an adjudication of a particular issue, and not whether the issue itself is justiciable. Thus, a party may have standing in a particular case, but the federal court may nevertheless decline to pass on the merits of the case because, for example, it presents a political question. A proper party is demanded so that federal courts will not be asked to decide "ill-defined controversies over constitutional issues," or a case which is of "a hypothetical or abstract character." So stated, the standing requirement is closely related to, although more general than, the rule that federal courts will not entertain friendly suits, or those which are feigned or collusive in nature.

When the emphasis in the standing problem is placed on whether the person invoking a federal court's jurisdiction is a proper party to maintain the action, the weakness of the Government's argument in this case becomes apparent. The question whether a particular person is a proper party to maintain the action does not, by its own force, raise separation of powers problems related to improper judicial interference in areas committed to other branches of the Federal Government. . . .

A taxpayer may or may not have the requisite personal stake in the outcome, depending upon the circumstances of the particular case. Therefore, we find no absolute bar in Article III to suits by federal taxpayers challenging allegedly unconstitutional federal taxing and spending programs. There remains, however, the problem of determining the circumstances under which a federal taxpayer will be deemed to have the personal stake and interest that impart the necessary concrete adverseness to such litigation so that standing can be conferred on the taxpayer *qua* taxpayer consistent with the constitutional limitations of Article III.

The various rules of standing applied by federal courts have not been developed in the abstract. Rather, they have been fashioned with specific reference to the status asserted by the party whose standing is challenged and to the type of question he wishes to have adjudicated. We have noted that, in deciding the question of standing, it is not relevant that the substantive issues in the litigation might be nonjusticiable. However, our decisions establish that, in ruling on standing, it is both appropriate and necessary to look to the substantive issues for another purpose, namely, to determine whether there is a logical nexus between the status asserted and the claim sought to be adjudicated. For example, standing requirements will vary in First Amendment religion cases depending upon whether the party raises an Establishment Clause claim or a claim under the Free Exercise Clause. Such inquiries into the nexus between the status asserted by the litigant and the claim he presents are essential to assure that he is a proper and appropriate party to invoke federal judicial power. Thus, our point of reference in this case is the standing of individuals who assert only the status of federal taxpayers and who challenge the constitutionality of a federal spending program. Whether such individuals have standing to maintain that form of action turns on whether they can demonstrate the necessary stake as taxpayers in the outcome of the litigation to satisfy Article III requirements.

The nexus demanded of federal taxpayers has two aspects to it. First, the taxpayer must establish a logical link between that status and the type of legislative enactment attacked. Thus, a taxpayer will be a proper party to allege the unconstitutionality only of exercises of congressional power under the taxing and spending clause of Article I, Section 8, of the Constitution. It will not be sufficient to allege an incidental expenditure of tax funds in the administration of an essentially regulatory statute. This requirement is consistent with the limitation imposed upon state-taxpayer standing in federal courts in *Doremus* v. *Board of Education* (1952). Secondly, the taxpayer must establish a nexus between that status and the precise nature of the constitutional infringement alleged. Under this requirement, the taxpayer must show that the challenged enactment exceeds specific constitutional limitations imposed upon the exercise of the congressional taxing and spending power, and not simply that the enactment is generally beyond the powers delegated to Congress by Article I, Section 8. When both nexuses are established, the litigant will have shown a taxpayer's stake in the outcome of the controversy, and will be a proper and appropriate party to invoke a federal court's jurisdiction.

The taxpayer appellants in this case have satisfied both nexuses to support their claim of standing under the test we announce today. Their constitutional challenge is made to an exercise by Congress of its power under Article I, Section 8, to spend for the general welfare, and the challenged program involves a substantial expenditure of federal tax funds. In addition, appellants have alleged that the challenged expenditures violate the Establishment and Free Exercise Clauses of the First Amendment. Our history vividly illustrates that one of the specific evils feared by those who drafted the Establishment Clause and fought for its adoption was that the taxing and spending power would be used to favor one religion over another or to support religion in general. James Madison, who is generally recognized as the leading architect of the religion clauses of the First Amendment, observed in his famous Memorial and Remonstrance Against Religious Assessments that, "the same authority which can force a citizen to contribute three pence only of his property for the support of any one establishment may force him to conform to any other establishment in all cases whatsoever." The concern of Madison and his supporters was quite clearly that religious liberty ultimately would be the victim if government could employ its taxing and spending powers to aid one religion over another or to aid religion in general. The Establishment Clause was designed as a specific bulwark against such potential abuses of governmental power, and that clause of the First Amendment operates as a specific constitutional limitation upon the exercise by Congress of the taxing and spending power conferred by Article I, Section 8.

The allegations of the taxpayer in *Frothingham* v. *Mellon*, were quite different from those made in this case, and the result in *Frothingham* is consistent with the test of taxpayer standing announced today. The taxpayer in *Frothingham* attacked a federal spending program, and she, therefore, established the first nexus required. However, she lacked standing because her constitutional attack was not based on an allegation that Congress, in enacting the Maternity Act of 1921, had breached a specific limitation upon its taxing and spending power. The taxpayer in *Frothingham* alleged essentially that Congress, by enacting the challenged statute, had exceeded the general powers delegated to it by Article I, Section 8, and that Congress had thereby invaded the legislative province reserved to the States by the Tenth Amendment. To be sure, Mrs. Frothingham made the additional allegation that her tax liability would be increased as a result of the allegedly unconstitutional enactment, and she framed that allegation in terms of a deprivation of property without due process of law. However, the Due Process Clause of the Fifth Amendment does not protect taxpayers against increases in tax liability, and the taxpayer in *Frothingham* failed to make any additional claim that the harm she alleged resulted from a breach by Congress of the specific constitutional limitations imposed upon an exercise of the taxing and spending power. In essence, Mrs. Frothingham was attempting to assert the States' interest in their legislative prerogatives, and not a federal taxpayer's interest in being free of taxing and spending in contravention of specific constitutional limitations imposed upon Congress' taxing and spending power.

We have noted that the Establishment Clause of the First Amendment does specifically limit the taxing and spending power conferred by Article I, Section 8. Whether the Constitution contains other specific limitations can be determined only in the context of future cases. However, whenever such specific limitations are found, we believe a taxpayer will have a clear stake as a taxpayer in assuring that they are not breached by Congress. Consequently, we hold that a taxpayer will have standing consistent with Article III to invoke federal judicial power when he alleges that congressional action under the taxing and spending clause is in derogation of those constitutional provisions which operate to restrict the exercise of the taxing and spending power. The taxpayer's allegation in such cases would be that his tax money is being extracted and spent in violation of specific constitutional protections against such abuses of legislative power. Such an injury is appropriate for judicial redress, and the taxpayer has established the necessary nexus between his status and the nature of the allegedly unconstitutional action to support his claim of standing to secure judicial review. Under such circumstances, we feel confident that the questions will be framed with the necessary specificity, that the issues will be contested with the necessary adverseness, and that the litigation will be pursued with the necessary vigor to assure that the constitutional challenge will be made in a form traditionally thought to be capable of judicial resolution. We lack that confidence in cases, such as *Frothingham*, where a taxpayer seeks to employ a federal court as a forum in which to air his generalized grievances about the conduct of government or the allocation of power in the Federal System.

While we express no view at all on the merits of appellants' claims in this case, their complaint contains sufficient allegations under the criteria we have outlined to give them standing to invoke a federal court's jurisdiction for an adjudication on the merits.

*Reversed.*

MR. JUSTICE DOUGLAS, concurring.

While I have joined the opinion of the Court, I . . . think . . . it . . . would therefore be the part of wisdom, as I see the problem, to be rid of *Frothingham* here and now.

I do not view with alarm, as does my Brother HARLAN, the consequences of that course. *Frothingham,* decided in 1923, was in the heyday of substantive due process, when courts were sitting in judgment on the wisdom or reasonableness of legislation. The claim in *Frothingham* was that a federal regulatory Act dealing with maternity deprived the plaintiff of property without due process of law. When the Court used substantive due process to determine the wisdom or reasonableness of legislation, it was indeed transforming itself into the Council of Revision which was rejected by the Constitutional Convention. It was that judicial attitude, not the theory of standing to sue rejected in *Frothingham,* that involved "important hazards for the continued effectiveness of the federal judiciary," to borrow a phrase from my Brother HARLAN. A contrary result in *Frothingham* in that setting might well have accentuated an ominous trend to judicial supremacy.

But we no longer undertake to exercise that kind of power. Today's problem is in a different setting.

Most laws passed by Congress do not contain even a ghost of a constitutional question. The "political" decisions, as distinguished from the "justiciable" ones, occupy most of the spectrum of congressional action. The case or controversy requirement comes into play only when the Federal Government does something that affects a person's life, his liberty, or his property. The wrong may be slight or it may be grievous. Madison, in denouncing state support of churches, said the principle was violated when even "three pence" was appropriated to that cause by the Government. It therefore does not do to talk about taxpayers' interest as "infinitesimal." The restraint on "liberty" may be fleeting and passing, and still violate a fundamental constitutional guarantee. The "three pence" mentioned by Madison may signal a monstrous invasion by the Government into church affairs, and so on. . . .

Taxpayers can be vigilant private attorneys general. Their stake in the outcome of litigation may be *de minimis* by financial standards, yet very great when measured by a particular constitutional mandate. My Brother HARLAN's opinion reflects the British, not the American, tradition of constitutionalism. We have a written Constitution, and it is full of "thou shalt nots" directed at Congress and the President, as well as at the courts. And the role of the federal courts is not only to serve as referee between the States and the center, but also to protect the individual against prohibited conduct by the other two branches of the Federal Government. . . .

I would not be niggardly, therefore, in giving private attorneys general standing to sue. I would certainly not wait for Congress to give its blessing to our deciding cases clearly within our Article III jurisdiction. To wait for a sign from Congress is to allow important constitutional questions to go undecided and personal liberty unprotected.

There need be no inundation of the federal courts if taxpayers' suits are allowed. There is a wise judicial discretion that usually can distinguish between the frivolous question and the substantial question, between cases ripe for decision and cases that need prior administrative processing, and the like.

MR. JUSTICE FORTAS, concurring.

I would confine the ruling in this case to the proposition that a taxpayer may maintain a suit to challenge the validity of a federal expenditure on the ground that the expenditure violates the Establishment Clause. As the Court's opinion recites, there is enough in the constitutional history of the Establishment Clause to support the thesis that this Clause includes a specific prohibition upon the use of the power to tax to support an establishment of religion. There is no reason to suggest, and no basis in the logic of this decision for implying, that there may be other types of congressional expenditures which may be attacked by a litigant solely on the basis of his status as a taxpayer. . . .

[T]he urgent necessities of this case and the precarious opening through which we find our way to confront it, do not demand that we open the door to a general assault upon exercises of the spending power. The status of taxpayer should not be accepted as a launching pad for an attack upon any target other than legislation affecting the Establishment Clause.

MR. JUSTICE HARLAN, dissenting.

The problems presented by this case are narrow and relatively abstract, but the principles by which they must be resolved involve nothing less than the proper functioning of the federal courts, and so run to the roots of our constitutional system. The nub of my view is that the end result of *Frothingham*, was correct, even though, like others, I do not subscribe to all of its reasoning and premises. Although I therefore agree with certain of the conclusions reached today by the Court, I cannot accept the standing doctrine that it substitutes for *Frothingham*, for it seems to me that this new doctrine rests on premises that do not withstand analysis. Accordingly, I respectfully dissent. . . .

The lawsuits here and in *Frothingham* are fundamentally different. They present the question whether federal taxpayers *qua* taxpayers may, in suits in which they do not contest the validity of their previous or existing tax obligations, challenge the constitutionality of the uses for which Congress has authorized the expenditure of public funds. These differences in the purposes of the cases are reflected in differences in the litigants' interests. An action brought to contest the validity of tax liabilities assessed to the plaintiff is designed to vindicate interests that are personal and proprietary. The wrongs alleged and the relief sought by such a plaintiff are unmistakably private; only secondarily are his interests representative of those of the general population. I take it that the Court, although it does not pause to examine the question, believes that the interests of those who as taxpayers challenge the constitutionality of public expenditures may, at least in certain circumstances, be similar. Yet this assumption is surely mistaken. . . .

It is surely clear that a plaintiff's interest in the outcome of a suit in which he challenges the constitutionality of a federal expenditure is not made greater or smaller by the unconnected fact that the expenditure is, or is not, "incidental" to an "essentially regulatory" program. An example will illustrate the point. Assume that two independent federal programs are authorized by Congress, that the first is designed to encourage a specified religious group by the provision to it of direct grants in aid, and that the second is designed to discourage all other religious groups by the imposition of various forms of discriminatory regulation. Equal amounts are appropriated by Congress for the two programs. If a taxpayer challenges their constitutionality in separate suits, are we to suppose, as evidently does the Court, that his "personal stake" in the suit involving the second is necessarily smaller than it is in the suit involving the first, and that he should therefore have standing in one, but not the other?

Presumably the Court does not believe that regulatory programs are necessarily less destructive of First Amendment rights, or that regulatory programs are necessarily less prodigal of public funds than are grants in aid, for both these general propositions are demonstrably false. The Court's disregard of regulatory expenditures is not even a logical consequence of its apparent assumption that taxpayer plaintiffs assert essentially monetary interests, for it surely cannot matter to a taxpayer *qua* taxpayer whether an unconstitutional expenditure is used to hire the services of regulatory personnel or is distributed among private and local governmental agencies as grants in aid. His interest as taxpayer arises, if at all, from the fact of an unlawful expenditure, and not as a consequence of the expenditure's form. Apparently the Court has repudiated the emphasis in *Frothingham* upon the amount of the plaintiff's tax bill, only to substitute an equally irrelevant emphasis upon the form of the challenged expenditure. . . .

It seems to me clear that public actions, whatever the constitutional provisions on which they are premised, may involve important hazards for the continued effectiveness of the federal judiciary. Although I believe such actions to be within the jurisdiction conferred upon the federal

## FLAST V. COHEN

### Litigation as Political Action

Upon witnessing the almost universal faith that common citizens held in the power of private, voluntary organizations to promote effective participation in their young democratic nation, Alexis de Tocqueville wrote that "better use had been made of association in [the United States] than anywhere else in the world." The French aristocrat, whose analysis of the social, economic, and political fabric of early-nineteenth-century America remains as fresh and vibrant today as it was in the 1830s, marveled at the skill with which these citizens groups applied their resources to an almost endless number of social aims. Having also noted how controversial political questions sooner or later turn into judicial ones, Tocqueville would hardly blink an eye at the prominent role that organized interests have played in shaping and defining the use of litigation to achieve their social and political objectives.

In the modern context, the role of interest groups in the litigation process is well summarized by political scientist Richard Cortner's phrase that "[c]ases do not arrive at the doorsteps of the Supreme Court like orphans in the night." Indeed, they do not. Interest groups routinely seek out cases not so much to settle a dispute between two parties, but to accomplish broader, more long-term goals. Sometimes interest groups turn to litigation to reinforce victories won in the political branches of government, or, as is often the case, to accomplish through the courts what they have been unable to achieve elsewhere. Interest group use of the courts is now the norm rather than the exception, especially in cases that raise issues of great public significance.

Organized interests have always attempted to influence the nomination and confirmation of judges to the federal judiciary. But until the NAACP decided in the late 1920s to mount a judicial campaign to dis-mantle the law of racial segregation, no organization committed to traditional forms of lobbying had placed its full weight behind litigation as an instrument of reform. That campaign resulted in a stunning series of victories beginning in the late 1930s that culminated in *Brown v. Board of Education* (1954), the Court's landmark decision that declared segregated public schools unconstitutional and initiated a revolution in the law of equal protection. Among the NAACP lawyers who traveled throughout the hostile courtrooms of the South and the Jim Crow states of middle and southwest America in search of justice for African Americans was Thurgood Marshall, who later became a household name after his successful argument before the Court in *Brown*. In 1967, President Lyndon Johnson named Marshall to the Court.

The NAACP's success in *Brown* inspired a number of other public interest organizations to consider the prospect of litigation as an instrument of reform, especially organizations that found themselves in a disadvantaged position in the elected branches of government. One admiring student of the NAACP's litigation campaign was Leo Pfeffer, who, in 1945, had just joined the American Jewish Congress (AJCongress) as a staff attorney. Pfeffer had watched the NAACP accumulate important legal victories that never would been possible in the political arena. Buoyed by the NACCP's success, Pfeffer began to encourage the AJCongress to emphasize legal rather than social action to address what, for most American Jews, was a problematic issue—government support for religion in public schools.

Over the next two decades, Leo Pfeffer and the AJCongress developed and led a litigation campaign to declare as unconstitutional several state-supported religious practices in the public schools that enjoyed the firm support of political majorities. Among Pfeffer's most important victories were *McCollum* v. *Board of Education* (1948), which struck down released-time programs permitting religious education in public schools; *Torcaso* v. *Watkins* (1961), which struck down the use of religious oaths to hold public office; and most critically, *Engel* v. *Vitale* (1962) and *Abington* v. *Schempp* (1963), which together made illegal the state support for prayer and Bible reading exercises in public schools. In these cases, Pfeffer asked for and received the support of the American Civil Liberties Union (ACLU), several mainline Protestant groups, and other Jewish organizations to assist with the selection of plaintiffs, the coordination of amicus curiae briefs, and financial expenses.

But the historic cases of *Engel* and *Schempp* did not represent the end of the line for Pfeffer. By that time his peers considered Pfeffer as the foremost scholar, legal advocate, and strategist working in the field of church and state. Having won several crucial cases limiting state support for religious doctrine, Pfeffer turned his attention to an issue that had bothered him as far back as 1947, when the Court upheld the use of public funds to pay for the transportation of parochial school students. In 1965, Congress passed the Elementary and Secondary Education Act, as of then the most comprehensive federal legislation ever conceived to bolster the financial resources of public schools. The general purpose of the law was to supplement low-income school districts whose resources were inferior to their wealthier neighbors. But for the first time, the federal government also made parochial schools eligible for public funds. Pfeffer had tried to persuade his traditional allies on church-state matters to lobby Congress to defeat the bill, but they refused because they did not want to lose the massive federal aid that was earmarked for the public schools.

Litigation, of course, seemed the appropriate recourse. But a formidable barrier stood between Pfeffer and any reasonable chance to challenge federal parochial aid in court. That barrier was a 1923 procedural rule developed by the Court in *Frothingham* v. *Mellon* that limited the scope of taxpayer standing to sue in federal court. For forty years that rule had stood unchallenged. Pfeffer, better than anyone else involved in the church-state reform movement, knew that no meaningful attack on parochial aid could go forward until the Court modified its standing rules for taxpayer lawsuits. Since *Frothingham,* several Justices had expressed concern that the Court's standing rules narrowed to the point of unfairness a taxpayer's ability to seek redress in the federal courts.

MEMORANDUM

American Jewish Congress
15 East Sixth Street
New York, N.Y.

November 14, 1966

To:
From: Haskell Lazere, Director, N.Y. Metropolitan Council

I am enclosing for your information, comment and participation a copy of the complaint drafted by Leo Pfeffer which we propose to file in the state court challenging various aspects of the Federal Title I program under the ESEA. You will notice from reading the complaint that much of it is based on information and belief. Some of the information is already public—a lot of it isn't. It is essential, therefore, that all of us pool our resources in assembling as much of the pertinent information as possible to support the allegations in the complaint. To that end, Lester Greenberg of our staff will shortly be calling you for your help in preparing the facts necessary for trial.

I need not tell you how urgent this litigation has become in view of what has been happening at the Board of Education and in view of what lies ahead in regard to the Constitutional Convention.

We invite you to participate as a co-sponsor of this litigation both by way of either being or furnishing a key member of your organization as a plaintiff and by lending the name of your organization to the sponsorship of the suit. Leo Pfeffer will be the general counsel in the litigation representing plaintiff.

I hope that we may hear from you in the next few days about your participation.

enc.

Following that lead, Pfeffer decided to use the 1965 law as the lever with which to pry open the courthouse door for taxpayers who believed that federal expenditures violated their constitutional rights.

Pfeffer persuaded the United Parents Association, the New York Civil Liberties Union, and the United Federation of Teachers to serve as co-plaintiffs in *Flast v. Cohen,* a lawsuit directed by the AJCongress and so named for Florence Flast, the president of the teachers association. Although Pfeffer had raised questions at trial about the constitutionality of the federal parochial aid program, the Court, upon accepting the case, announced it would limit briefing and oral argument solely to the standing issue. That was fine with Pfeffer. If the Court relaxed the *Frothingham* rule, the justices would most likely remand the case to federal district court, where the Establishment Clause issues would be briefed and argued in full.

Important as well to Pfeffer was the need to persuade other public interest groups to submit amicus briefs to the Court in support of his position. In addition to an amicus brief signed by more than thirty major Jewish organizations, Pfeffer secured the support of the National Council of Churches, Americans United for the Separation of Church and State, and several other public school lobbies. The purpose of such broad and extensive support was to show the Court that taxpayer access to the federal courts was not particular to church-state matters, but a constitutional question that transcended the special interests of specific communities. In contrast, only the AFL-CIO and the National Commission on Law and Public Affairs, an Orthodox Jewish group that favors government support for its parochial school system, submitted a joint brief opposing more expansive standing rules.

Chief Justice Earl Warren's opinion for an 8-1 Court in *Flast* made direct reference to Pfeffer's stated desire of democratizing access to the federal courts for public interest organizations. *Frothingham,* wrote the chief justice, "announced only a nonconstitutional rule of self-restraint" and posed no barrier to litigants and "the private attorneys general" representing them if they could satisfy the new conditions set forth in *Flast.* Chief Justice Warren's reference to "private attorneys general" was a direct acknowledgement of the value that organizations such as the ACLU, the NAACP, and the AJCongress, whose positions were often unpopular in the political branches, placed on litigation as an instrument of constitutional reform.

In his brief, Pfeffer had offered the Court three alternatives to Frothingham, each of which would allow taxpayers greater latitude to bring lawsuits against federal expenditures: (1) the Court could overrule *Frothingham* and create new rules from scratch; (2) the Court could rule that *Frothingham* did not apply in First Amendment cases, the idea being that individuals challenging government infringements of their civil liberties should have greater latitude to challenge them in court; or (3) the Court could rule that *Frothingham* did not apply in Establishment or Free Exercise Clause cases. For Pfeffer this strategy was designed to give the Court a menu of choices from which to choose an alternative to *Frothingham.* Although Pfeffer and his supporting amici cannot claim sole credit for the Court's new "double nexus" rule announced in *Flast,* it is worth considering whether the parallels between Chief Justice Warren's opinion and their meticulously coordinated briefs are more than coincidental.

*Flast* permitted Pfeffer and the AJCongress to launch the next step of their litigation campaign to reform the law of church and state. From the 1960s until the mid-1980s, the Court struck down almost every single parochial aid program administered by federal and state authorities. Leo Pfeffer served as lead counsel or submitted an amicus brief in every such case the Court decided from 1967 to 1980. He appeared either on behalf of the Committee on Public Education and Religious Liberty (PEARL), which he formed while *Flast* was in progress to handle only parochial aid cases, or the AJCongress. That campaign resulted in significant limits being placed on the ability of government to fund parochial schools and related programs.

*Flast* eventually became an invitation to all litigation-oriented groups to vindicate their constitutional grievances in the courts without first having to demonstrate personal harm or injury. Although narrowed somewhat by decisions such as *Valley Forge* and

*Lujan,* the expanded access for "private attorneys general" to the federal courts created by *Flast* has allowed lawsuits that never would have seen the inside of a courtroom to proceed. Leo Pfeffer is best remembered for his scholarship and advocacy in the church-state arena, but his victory in *Flast* forever changed the practice of public interest law and deserves an equally important place in the annals of constitutional development.

## References

Cortner, Richard C. *The Supreme Court and Civil Liberties Policy.* Palo Alto, Calif.: Mayfield Publishing Co., 1975.

Ivers, Gregg. *To Build a Wall: American Jews and the Separation of Church and State.* Charlottesville, Va.: University Press of Virginia, 1995.

courts by Article III of the Constitution, there surely can be little doubt that they strain the judicial function and press to the limit judicial authority. There is every reason to fear that unrestricted public actions might well alter the allocation of authority among the three branches of the Federal Government. It is not, I submit, enough to say that the present members of the Court would not seize these opportunities for abuse, for such actions would, even without conscious abuse, go far toward the final transformation of this Court into the Council of Revision which, despite Madison's support, was rejected by the Constitutional Convention. I do not doubt that there must be "some effectual power in the government to restrain or correct the infractions" of the Constitution's several commands, but neither can I suppose that such power resides only in the federal courts. The powers of the federal judiciary will be adequate for the great burdens placed upon them only if they are employed prudently, with recognition of the strengths as well as the hazards that go with our kind of representative government.

Presumably the Court recognizes at least certain of these hazards, else it would not have troubled to impose limitations upon the situations in which, and purposes for which, such suits may be brought. Nonetheless, the limitations adopted by the Court are, as I have endeavored to indicate, wholly untenable. This is the more unfortunate because there is available a resolution of this problem that entirely satisfies the demands of the principle of separation of powers. This Court has previously held that individual litigants have standing to represent the public interest, despite their lack of economic or other personal interests, if Congress has appropriately authorized such suits. I would adhere to that principle. Any hazards to the proper allocation of authority among the three branches of the Government would be substantially diminished if public actions had been pertinently authorized by Congress and the President. I appreciate that this Court does not ordinarily await the mandate of other branches of the Government, but it seems to me that the extraordinary character of public actions, and of the mischievous, if not dangerous, consequences they involve for the proper functioning of our constitutional system, and in particular of the federal courts, makes such judicial forbearance the part of wisdom. It must be emphasized that the implications of these questions of judicial policy are of fundamental significance for the other branches of the Federal Government.

Such a rule could readily be applied to this case. Although various efforts have been made in Congress to authorize public actions to contest the validity of federal expenditures in aid of religiously affiliated schools and other institutions, no such authorization has yet been given.

This does not mean that we would, under such a rule, be enabled to avoid our constitutional responsibilities, or that we would confine to limbo the First Amendment or any other constitutional command. The question here is not, despite the Court's unarticulated premise, whether the religious clauses of the First Amendment are hereafter to be enforced by the federal courts; the issue is simply whether plaintiffs of an additional category, heretofore excluded from those courts, are to be permitted to maintain suits. The recent history of this Court is replete with illustrations, including even one announced today, that questions involving the religious clauses will not, if federal taxpayers are prevented from contesting federal expenditures, be left "unacknowledged, unresolved, and undecided."

Accordingly, for the reasons contained in this opinion, I would affirm the judgment of the District Court.

## Lujan v. Defenders of Wildlife
### 504 U.S. 555 (1992)

The Endangered Species Act of 1973 requires federal agencies to consult with either the secretary of the interior or the secretary of commerce to ensure that any action funded by the agency is not likely to jeopardize the continued existence or habitat of any endangered or threatened species. When the law was enacted, the secretaries of both departments issued a joint regulation that applied this provision to projects in foreign nations. The Reagan administration limited the provision to domestic projects and to projects on the high seas. Defenders of Wildlife and other environmental groups sued, arguing that the new rule misinterpreted the statute, and asked the court to require the secretaries to restore the previous rule. The D.C. court of appeals reversed the lower court's dismissal of the suit for lack of standing and ordered it to hear the case. The district court then ordered the secretary to publish a new rule. By then the Bush administration had taken up the case. It sought an appeal, which the D.C. circuit court rejected.

The Supreme Court's decision was 7 to 2. Justice Scalia delivered the opinion of the Court. Justice Kennedy filed a concurrence joined by Justice Souter. Justice Stevens filed a concurrence. Justice Blackmun filed a dissent that was joined by Justice O'Connor.

▼▲▼

JUSTICE SCALIA delivered the opinion of the Court.

. . . Over the years, our cases have established that the irreducible constitutional minimum of standing contains three elements: first, the plaintiff must have suffered an "injury in fact"—an invasion of a legally-protected interest which is (a) concrete and particularized, and (b) "actual or imminent, not 'conjectural' or 'hypothetical.'" Second, there must be a causal connection between the injury and the conduct complained of—the injury has to be fairly . . . trace[able] to the challenged action of the defendant, and not . . . th[e] result [of] the independent action of some third party not before the court. Third, it must be "likely," as opposed to merely "speculative," that the injury will be "redressed by a favorable decision." . . .

When the suit is one challenging the legality of government action or inaction, the nature and extent of facts that must be averred (at the summary judgment stage) or proved (at the trial stage) in order to establish standing depend considerably upon whether the plaintiff is himself an object of the action (or forgone action) at issue. If he is, there is ordinarily little question that the action or inaction has caused him injury, and that a judgment preventing or requiring the action will redress it. When, however, as in this case, a plaintiff's asserted injury arises from the government's allegedly unlawful regulation (or lack of regulation) of *someone else*, much more is needed. In that circumstance, causation and redressability ordinarily hinge on the response of the regulated (or regulable) third party to the government action or inaction—and perhaps on the response of others as well. The existence of one or more of the essential elements of standing, depends on the unfettered choices made by independent actors not before the courts and whose exercise of broad and legitimate discretion the courts cannot presume either to control or to predict. . . .

We think the Court of Appeals failed to apply the foregoing principles. . . .

Besides failing to show injury, respondents failed to demonstrate redressability. Instead of attacking the separate decisions to fund particular projects allegedly causing them harm, the respondents chose to challenge a more generalized level of government action (rules regarding consultation), the invalidation of which would affect all overseas projects. This programmatic approach has obvious practical advantages, but also obvious difficulties insofar as proof of causation or redressability is concerned. As we have said in another context, "suits challenging, not specifically identifiable Government violations of law, but the particular programs agencies establish to carry out their legal obligations . . . [are], even when premised on allegations of several instances of violations of law, . . . rarely if ever appropriate for federal court adjudication." . . .

We have consistently held that a plaintiff raising only a generally available grievance about government—claiming only harm to his and every citizen's interest in proper application of the Constitution and laws, and seeking relief that no more directly and tangibly benefits him than it does the public at large—does not state an Article III case or controversy. For example, in *Fairchild* v. *Hughes* (1922), we dismissed a suit challenging the propriety of the process by which the Nineteenth Amendment was ratified. Justice Brandeis wrote for the Court:

> [This is] not a case within the meaning of . . . Article III. . . . Plaintiff has [asserted] only the right, possessed by every citizen, to require that the Government be administered according to law and that the public moneys be not wasted. Obviously this general right does not entitle a private citizen to institute in the federal courts a suit. . . .

In *Frothingham* v. *Mellon* (1923), we dismissed for lack of Article III standing a taxpayer suit challenging the propriety of certain federal expenditures. . . .

More recent cases are to the same effect. In *United States* v. *Richardson* (1974), we dismissed for lack of standing a taxpayer suit challenging the Government's failure to disclose the expenditures of the Central Intelligence Agency, in alleged violation of the constitutional requirement, Article I, Section 9, clause 7, that "a regular Statement and Account of the Receipts and Expenditures of all public Money shall be published from time to time." We held that such a suit rested upon an impermissible "generalized grievance," and was inconsistent with "the framework of Article III" because "the impact on [plaintiff] is plainly undifferentiated and common to all members of the public." And in *Schlesinger* v. *Reservists Committee to Stop the War* (1974), we dismissed for the same reasons a citizen-taxpayer suit contending that it was a violation of the Incompatibility Clause, Article I, Section 6, clause 2, for Members of Congress to hold commissions in the military Reserves. We said that the challenged action, "standing alone, would adversely affect only the generalized interest of all citizens in constitutional governance. . . . We reaffirm *Levitt* in holding that standing to sue may not be predicated upon an interest of th[is] kind. . . ." Since *Schlesinger,* we have on two occasions held that an injury amounting only to the alleged violation of a right to have the Government act in accordance with law was not judicially cognizable, because, "assertion of a right to a particular kind of Government conduct, which the Government has violated by acting differently, cannot alone satisfy the requirements of Article III without draining those requirements of meaning." And only two Terms ago, we rejected the notion that Article III permits a citizen-suit to prevent a condemned criminal's execution on the basis of "the public interest protections of the Eighth Amendment"; once again, "[t]his allegation raise[d] only the generalized interest of all citizens in constitutional governance . . . , and [was] an inadequate basis on which to grant . . . standing."

To be sure, our generalized-grievance cases have typically involved Government violation of procedures assertedly ordained by the Constitution, rather than the Congress. But there is absolutely no basis for making the Article III inquiry turn on the source of the asserted right. Whether the courts were to act on their own, or at the invitation of Congress, in ignoring the concrete injury requirement described in our cases, they would be discarding a principle fundamental to the separate and distinct constitutional role of the Third Branch—one of the essential elements that identifies those "Cases" and "Controversies" that are the business of the courts, rather than of the political branches. . . . Vindicating the *public* interest (including the public interest in government observance of the Constitution and laws) is the function of Congress and the Chief Executive. The question presented here is whether the public interest in proper administration of the laws (specifically, in agencies' observance of a particular, statutorily prescribed procedure) can be converted into an individual right by a statute that denominates it as such, and that permits all citizens (or, for that matter, a subclass of citizens who suffer no distinctive concrete harm) to sue. If the concrete injury requirement has the separation of powers significance we have always said, the answer must be obvious: to permit Congress to convert the undifferentiated public interest in executive officers' compliance with the law into an "individual right" vindicable in the courts is to permit Congress to transfer from the President to the courts the Chief Executive's most important constitutional duty, to "take Care that the Laws be faithfully executed," Article II, Section 3. It would enable the courts, with the permission of Congress, "to assume a position of authority over the governmental acts of another and coequal department," and to become "'virtually continuing monitors of the wisdom and soundness of Executive action.'" We have always rejected that vision of our role.

---

## The "Political Questions" Doctrine

Although the political questions doctrine is not found in the Constitution, the Court has also invoked that doctrine to avoid the judicial resolution of a legal dispute. Like the other threshold requirements we have discussed, the political questions doctrine is a Court-created instrument designed to constrain the use of judicial power. But whereas adverseness, mootness, and standing-to-sue requirements all deal with questions of judicial procedure, the Court will invoke the political questions doctrine on the grounds that the dispute before it is "political," not "legal" in nature. Although the Court did not fully articulate and refine the political questions doctrine until the mid-twentieth century, Chief Justice John Marshall first alluded to the distinctions between questions of law and those that were political in nature in *Marbury* v. *Madison*, writing that "[t]he province of the court is, solely, to decide on the rights of individuals, not to inquire how the executive, or executive officers, perform duties in which they have a discretion. Questions in their nature political . . . can never be made in this court."[62]

Given the political nature of much constitutional litigation, how does the Court distinguish between legal and political questions? In general, the Court will invoke the political questions doctrine when it believes that a legal dispute involves political or policy differences between the parties rather than questions of law. For example, the Court has abstained from most questions involving foreign affairs, such as border disputes, military power, and the power to negotiate and terminate treaties, holding that the political branches, not the courts, are best suited to resolve conflicts over such matters.[63] The Court also has held that, as a general matter, the federal courts have no jurisdiction to review questions of legislative governance or internal procedure.[64]

On the other hand, the Court's refusal to invoke the political questions doctrine in cases involving similar questions and the exceptions it has carved out on matters once considered nonjusticiable on political grounds suggests a judicial sleight-of-hand at work. No better area of American constitutional law illustrates the fluid nature of the Court's use of the political questions doctrine than the interrelated issues of electioneering, voting rights, and legislative malapportionment. In *Luther v. Borden* (1849), the Court first invoked the political questions doctrine to avoid considering the substance of a constitutional claim. *Luther* involved a political scenario that is unthinkable in modern times. Unable to persuade Rhode Island to call a state constitutional convention for the purpose of reconsidering its voting-eligibility requirements, a rival political faction decided to form a separate government, complete with its own militia. Several leaders of Rhode Island's political opposition argued that the existing charter—Rhode Island had no written constitution—denied them their right to a "republican government" under Article IV of the Constitution. Article IV reads:

> The United States shall guarantee to every State in this Union a Republican Form of Government, and shall protect each of them against Invasion; and on application of the Legislature, or of the Executive (when the Legislature cannot be convened) against domestic Violence.

For an 8-1 Court, Chief Justice Taney held that responsibility for enforcing the Guarantee Clause of Article IV rested with Congress, not the courts, writing that "Congress must necessarily decide what government it is established in the State before it can determine whether it is republican or not . . . [a]nd its decision is binding on every other department of the government, and could not be questioned in a judicial tribunal." Further eluciding the Court's limits to review "political" disputes, Taney wrote:

> Much of the argument on the part of the plaintiff turned upon political rights and political questions, upon which the court has been urged to express an opinion. We decline. . . . This tribunal . . . should be the last to overstep the boundaries which limit its own jurisdiction. And while it should always be ready to meet any question confided to it by the Constitution, it is equally its duty not to pass beyond its appropriate sphere of action.[65]

For more than one hundred years, the Court continued to invoke the political questions doctrine to explain the justice's refusal to decide constitutional claims brought under the Guarantee Clause. In *Colegrove v. Green* (1946), Justice Felix Frankfurter, in a classic explanation of the "legal process" method of constitutional interpretation, explained that the Court was powerless to intervene in a case involving legislative malapportionment. Frankfurter did not contest the evidence presented at trial demonstrating the gross inequities that existed in the electoral representation of state residents in the Illinois legislature. Nor did he suggest that the disproportionate power wielded by sparsely populated rural districts in legislative politics was desirable or even defensible, nor that Illinois had even made an effort to redress these inequities. Instead, the issue that concerned Frankfurter was the power of the Court to enter the "political thicket":

> We are of the opinion that the petitioners ask of this Court what is beyond its competence to grant. This is one of those demands on judicial power which cannot be met by verbal fencing about "jurisdiction." It must be resolved by considerations on the basis of which this Court, from time to time, has refused to intervene in controversies. It has refused to do so because due regard for the effective working of our Government revealed this issue to be of a pecu-

liarly political nature and therefore not meet for judicial determination.

Nothing is clearer than that this controversy concerns matters that bring courts into immediate and active relations with party contests. From the determination of such issues this Court has traditionally held aloof. It is hostile to the democratic system to involve the judiciary in the politics of the people. And it is not less pernicious if such judicial intervention is an essentially political contest dressed up in the abstract phrases of the law.[66]

Sixteen years later, in a stunning reversal, the Court retreated from its position in Colegrove. In Baker v. Carr (1962), the Court held that when individuals have exhausted all possible remedies available through the political process, the federal courts have jurisdiction to decide whether a state legislative apportionment plan violates the Equal Protection Clause of the Fourteenth Amendment. Justice Brennan's opinion for the Court poses a direct counterpoint to Justice Frankfurter's Colegrove opinion, one that he revisited and reaffirmed in his Baker dissent. The SIDEBAR offers a more in-depth look at the behind-the-scenes politics within the Court over Baker, as well as an opportunity to examine the contrasts in Justice Hugo Black's fundamental rights approach to constitutional claims, one that was quite influential on Justice Brennan's opinion, with Justice Frankfurter's adherence to the legal process method. Which approach offers the best explanation of the Court's role in such matters? Do you believe that the social and political forces of the time influenced the Court's decision to reconsider the political questions doctrine?

Since Baker, the Court has entered the political thicket to decide far more than jurisdictional questions involving legislative malapportionment. The Court has since held that states must draw their legislative districts on the basis of population, ensuring that the "one person, one vote" rule is enforced in state legislatures and Congress.[67] The Court has also held that constitutional challenges to legislative districts deliberately drawn to favor the incumbent political party in power, even if they satisfy the "one person, one vote" requirement, present justiciable questions.[68]

Outside the realm of malapportionment and political participation, the Court has stretched the once-narrow boundaries of its jurisdiction to decide matters previ-ously thought properly left to the political branches. For example, the Court, in Missouri v. Jenkins (1990), ruled that a lower federal appeals court did not exceed its jurisdictional authority by ordering a local school district to raise taxes to satisfy a government-imposed school desegregation order.[69] The justices divided sharply on their reading of the facts and subsequent judicial commands in Jenkins. A bare five-member majority concluding that the lower court's order was within its power under Article III to order equitable remedies for constitutional violations. But compare Justice Kennedy's separate opinion in Jenkins, which views the lower court's order as an intrusion into the legislature's sole power to control the "purse," with the Court majority's. What explains the dramatic divergence of views on this exercise of judicial power and conception of federal court jurisdiction?

Although the Court has expanded its jurisdictional domain over political questions far beyond the confines it announced in Baker, the Court still recognizes the need to impose restraints on the exercise of its power. In Nixon v. United States (1993), a unanimous Court ruled that the Senate's decision to substitute an expedited impeachment rule in place of its traditional process in such matters presented a nonjusticiable question.[70] Chief Justice William H. Rehnquist, you will note, relied on the express constitutional authority of the Senate to retain "sole power" over "all Impeachments" to conclude that the federal courts possessed no jurisdiction over this question. Chief Justice Rehnquist's dictionary-like, almost literal analysis of the relevant constitutional provisions contested in Nixon stands in sharp contrast with the Court's much more open-ended approach to the language of Article IV and constraints on justiciable questions in Baker. Is it possible that the Court's willingness to invoke the political questions doctrine is related to what it believes is the gravity of the constitutional right at stake?

## Baker v. Carr
### 369 U.S. 186 (1962)

Charles Baker and a number of Tennessee voters challenged the state's apportionment of representation in the General Assembly, as a violation of the Equal Protection

Clause of the Fourteenth Amendment. Baker's chief complaint was that Tennessee's apportionment plan denied urban areas and other more densely populated communities fair representation in the state legislature. A federal district court agreed that Tennessee's apportionment plan denied those communities effective representation, but ruled that, under the political questions doctrine, the district court could not offer them a remedy for the state's violation. Accordingly, the court dismissed the suit for lack of a justiciable issue.

For more details, see the accompanying SIDEBAR.

The decision was 6 to 2. Justice Brennan delivered the opinion of the Court. Justices Douglas, Clark, and Stewart filed concurring opinions. Justices Frankfurter and Harlan filed dissents. *Baker* also featured Justice Frankfurter's last great dissent. Justice Whittaker did not participate.

▼▲▼

Mr. Justice Brennan delivered the opinion of the Court.

. . . Between 1901 and 1961, Tennessee . . . experienced substantial growth and redistribution of her population. In 1901, the population was 2,020,616, of whom 487,380 were eligible to vote. The 1960 Federal Census reports the State's population at 3,567,089, of whom 2,092,891 are eligible to vote. The relative standings of the counties in terms of qualified voters have changed significantly. It is primarily the continued application of the 1901 Apportionment Act to this shifted and enlarged voting population which gives rise to the present controversy.

Indeed, the complaint alleges that the 1901 statute, even as of the time of its passage, "made no apportionment of Representatives and Senators in accordance with the constitutional formula . . . , but instead arbitrarily and capriciously apportioned representatives in the Senate and House without reference . . . to any logical or reasonable formula whatever." It is further alleged that, "because of the population changes since 1900, and the failure of the Legislature to reapportion itself since 1901," the 1901 statute became "unconstitutional and obsolete." Appellants also argue that, because of the composition of the legislature effected by the 1901 Apportionment Act, redress in the form of a state constitutional amendment to change the entire mechanism for reapportioning, or any other change short of that, is difficult or impossible. The complaint concludes that "these plaintiffs and others similarly situated, are denied the equal protection of the laws accorded them by the Fourteenth Amendment to the

Constitution of the United States by virtue of the debasement of their votes." . . .

[W]e hold today only (a) that the court possessed jurisdiction of the subject matter; (b) that a justiciable cause of action is stated upon which appellants would be entitled to appropriate relief, and (c) because appellees raise the issue before this Court, that the appellants have standing to challenge the Tennessee apportionment statutes. Beyond noting that we have no cause at this stage to doubt the District Court will be able to fashion relief if violations of constitutional rights are found, it is improper now to consider what remedy would be most appropriate if appellants prevail at the trial.

## Jurisdiction of the Subject Matter

The District Court was uncertain whether our cases withholding federal judicial relief rested upon a lack of federal jurisdiction or upon the inappropriateness of the subject matter for judicial consideration—what we have designated "nonjusticiability." The distinction between the two grounds is significant. In the instance of nonjusticiability, consideration of the cause is not wholly and immediately foreclosed; rather, the Court's inquiry necessarily proceeds to the point of deciding whether the duty asserted can be judicially identified and its breach judicially determined, and whether protection for the right asserted can be judicially molded. In the instance of lack of jurisdiction, the cause either does not "arise under" the Federal Constitution, laws or treaties (or fall within one of the other enumerated categories of Article III, Section 2); or is not a "case or controversy" within the meaning of that section; or the cause is not one described by any jurisdictional statute. Our conclusion, that this cause presents no nonjusticiable "political question" settles the only possible doubt that it is a case or controversy. . . .

The appellees refer to *Colegrove* v. *Green* (1946), as authority that the District Court lacked jurisdiction of the subject matter. Appellees misconceive the holding of that case. The holding was precisely contrary to their reading of it. Seven members of the Court participated in the decision. Unlike many other cases in this field which have assumed without discussion that there was jurisdiction, all three opinions filed in *Colegrove* discussed the question. Two of the opinions expressing the views of four of the Justices, a majority, flatly held that there was jurisdiction of the subject matter. Mr. Justice Black, joined by Mr. Justice Douglas and Mr. Justice Murphy, stated: "It is my judgment that the District Court had jurisdiction. . . ." Mr. Justice Rutledge, writing separately, expressed agreement with this conclusion. Indeed, it is even questionable that the opinion of MR. JUSTICE FRANKFURTER, joined by Justices Reed and Burton, doubted jurisdiction of the subject matter. . . .

We hold that the District Court has jurisdiction of the subject matter of the federal claim asserted in the complaint. . . .

## Justiciability

In holding that the subject matter of this suit was not justiciable, the District Court relied on *Colegrove*, and subsequent per curiam cases. The court stated, "From a review of these decisions, there can be no doubt that the federal rule . . . is that the federal courts . . . will not intervene in cases of this type to compel legislative reapportionment." We understand the District Court to have read the cited cases as compelling the conclusion that, since the appellants sought to have a legislative apportionment held unconstitutional, their suit presented a "political question," and was therefore nonjusticiable. We hold that this challenge to an apportionment presents no nonjusticiable "political question." . . .

Of course, the mere fact that the suit seeks protection of a political right does not mean it presents a political question. Such an objection "is little more than a play upon words." Rather, it is argued that apportionment cases, whatever the actual wording of the complaint, can involve no federal constitutional right except one resting on the guaranty of a republican form of government, and that complaints based on that clause have been held to present political questions which are nonjusticiable.

We hold that the claim pleaded here neither rests upon nor implicates the Guaranty Clause, and that its justiciability is therefore not foreclosed by our decisions of cases involving that clause. To show why we reject the argument based on the Guaranty Clause, we must examine the authorities under it. But because there appears to be some uncertainty as to why those cases did present political questions, and specifically as to whether this apportionment case is like those cases, we deem it necessary first to consider the contours of the "political question" doctrine.

Our discussion, even at the price of extending this opinion, requires review of a number of political question cases, in order to expose the attributes of the doctrine—attributes which, in various settings, diverge, combine, appear, and disappear in seeming disorderliness. Since that review is undertaken solely to demonstrate that neither singly nor collectively do these cases support a con-

clusion that this apportionment case is nonjusticiable, we, of course, do not explore their implications in other contexts. That review reveals that, in the Guaranty Clause cases and in the other "political question" cases, it is the relationship between the judiciary and the coordinate branches of the Federal Government, and not the federal judiciary's relationship to the States, which gives rise to the "political question."

We have said that, "In determining whether a question falls within [the political question] category, the appropriateness under our system of government of attributing finality to the action of the political departments and also the lack of satisfactory criteria for a judicial determination are dominant considerations." The nonjusticiability of a political question is primarily a function of the separation of powers. Much confusion results from the capacity of the "political question" label to obscure the need for case-by-case inquiry. Deciding whether a matter has in any measure been committed by the Constitution to another branch of government, or whether the action of that branch exceeds whatever authority has been committed, is itself a delicate exercise in constitutional interpretation, and is a responsibility of this Court as ultimate interpreter of the Constitution. To demonstrate this requires no less than to analyze representative cases and to infer from them the analytical threads that make up the political question doctrine. We shall then show that none of those threads catches this case.

**Foreign Relations** There are sweeping statements to the effect that all questions touching foreign relations are political questions. Not only does resolution of such issues frequently turn on standards that defy judicial application, or involve the exercise of a discretion demonstrably committed to the executive or legislature, but many such questions uniquely demand single-voiced statement of the Government's views. Yet it is error to suppose that every case or controversy which touches foreign relations lies beyond judicial cognizance. Our cases in this field seem invariably to show a discriminating analysis of the particular question posed, in terms of the history of its management by the political branches, of its susceptibility to judicial handling in the light of its nature and posture in the specific case, and of the possible consequences of judicial action. . . .

**Dates of Duration of Hostilities** Though it has been stated broadly that "the power which declared the necessity is the power to declare its cessation, and what the cessation requires," here too analysis reveals isolable reasons for the presence of political questions, underlying this Court's refusal to review the political departments' determination of when or whether a war has ended. Dominant is the need for finality in the political determination, for emergency's nature demands "[a] prompt and unhesitating obedience," . . .

**Validity of Enactments** In *Coleman v. Miller* (1939), this Court held that the questions of how long a proposed amendment to the Federal Constitution remained open to ratification, and what effect a prior rejection had on a subsequent ratification, were committed to congressional resolution and involved criteria of decision that necessarily escaped the judicial grasp. Similar considerations apply to the enacting process: "[t]he respect due to coequal and independent departments," and the need for finality and certainty about the status of a statute contribute to judicial reluctance to inquire whether, as passed, it complied with all requisite formalities. But it is not true that courts will never delve into a legislature's records upon such a quest: if the enrolled statute lacks an effective date, a court will not hesitate to seek it in the legislative journals in order to preserve the enactment. The political question doctrine, a tool for maintenance of governmental order, will not be so applied as to promote only disorder. . . .

**Republican Form of Government** *Luther* v. *Borden* (1848), though in form simply an action for damages for trespass was, as Daniel Webster said in opening the argument for the defense, "an unusual case." The defendants, admitting an otherwise tortious breaking and entering, sought to justify their action on the ground that they were agents of the established lawful government of Rhode Island, which State was then under martial law to defend itself from active insurrection; that the plaintiff was engaged in that insurrection, and that they entered under orders to arrest the plaintiff. . . .

The plaintiff's right to recover depended upon which of the two groups was entitled to such recognition; but the lower court's refusal to receive evidence or hear argument on that issue, its charge to the jury that the earlier established or "charter" government was lawful, and the verdict for the defendants were affirmed upon appeal to this Court. . . .

Clearly, several factors were thought by the Court in *Luther* to make the question there "political": the commitment to the other branches of the decision as to which is the lawful state government; the unambiguous action by the President in recognizing the charter government as the lawful authority; the need for finality in the executive's decision, and the lack of criteria by which a court could determine which form of government was republican.

But the only significance that *Luther* could have for our immediate purposes is in its holding that the Guaranty Clause is not a repository of judicially manageable standards which a court could utilize independently in order to identify a State's lawful government. The Court has since refused to resort to the Guaranty Clause—which alone had been invoked for the purpose as the source of a constitutional standard for invalidating state action. . . .

We come, finally, to the ultimate inquiry whether our precedents as to what constitutes a nonjusticiable "political question" bring the case before us under the umbrella of that doctrine. A natural beginning is to note whether any of the common characteristics which we have been able to identify and label descriptively are present. We find none: the question here is the consistency of state action with the Federal Constitution. We have no question decided, or to be decided, by a political branch of government coequal with this Court. Nor do we risk embarrassment of our government abroad, or grave disturbance at home if we take issue with Tennessee as to the constitutionality of her action here challenged. Nor need the appellants, in order to succeed in this action, ask the Court to enter upon policy determinations for which judicially manageable standards are lacking. Judicial standards under the Equal Protection Clause are well developed and familiar, and it has been open to courts since the enactment of the Fourteenth Amendment to determine, if, on the particular facts, they must, that a discrimination reflects no policy, but simply arbitrary and capricious action.

This case does, in one sense, involve the allocation of political power within a State, and the appellants might conceivably have added a claim under the Guaranty Clause. Of course, as we have seen, any reliance on that clause would be futile. But because any reliance on the Guaranty Clause could not have succeeded, it does not follow that appellants may not be heard on the equal protection claim which, in fact, they tender. True, it must be clear that the Fourteenth Amendment claim is not so enmeshed with those political question elements which render Guaranty Clause claims nonjusticiable as actually to present a political question itself. But we have found that not to be the case here. . . .

We conclude, then, that the nonjusticiability of claims resting on the Guaranty Clause, which arises from their embodiment of questions that were thought "political," can have no bearing upon the justiciability of the equal protection claim presented in this case. Finally, we emphasize that it is the involvement in Guaranty Clause claims of the elements thought to define "political questions," and no other feature, which could render them nonjusticiable. . . .

We conclude that the complaint's allegations of a denial of equal protection present a justiciable constitutional cause of action upon which appellants are entitled to a trial and a decision. The right asserted is within the reach of judicial protection under the Fourteenth Amendment. . . .

*Reversed and remanded.*

Mr. Justice Douglas, concurring.

While I join the opinion of the Court and, like the Court, do not reach the merits, a word of explanation is necessary. I put to one side the problems of "political" questions involving the distribution of power between this Court, the Congress, and the Chief Executive. We have here a phase of the recurring problem of the relation of the federal courts to state agencies. More particularly, the question is the extent to which a State may weight one person's vote more heavily than it does another's.

So far as voting rights are concerned, there are large gaps in the Constitution. Yet the right to vote is inherent in the republican form of government envisaged by Article IV, Section 4 of the Constitution. The House—and now the Senate—are chosen by the people. The time, manner, and place of elections of Senators and Representatives are left to the States subject to the regulatory power of Congress. Yet, those who vote for members of Congress do not "owe their right to vote to the State law in any sense which makes the exercise of the right to depend exclusively on the law of the State." The power of Congress to prescribe the qualifications for voters, and thus override state law, is not in issue here. It is, however, clear that, by reason of the commands of the Constitution, there are several qualifications that a State may not require.

Race, color, or previous condition of servitude is an impermissible standard by reason of the Fifteenth Amendment. . . .

Sex is another impermissible standard by reason of the Nineteenth Amendment.

There is a third barrier to a State's freedom in prescribing qualifications of voters, and that is the Equal Protection Clause of the Fourteenth Amendment, the provision invoked here. And so the question is, may a State weight the vote of one county or one district more heavily than it weights the vote in another?

The traditional test under the Equal Protection Clause has been whether a State has made "an invidious discrimination," as it does when it selects "a particular race or nationality for oppressive treatment." *Skinner* v. *Oklahoma* (1942). Universal equality is not the test; there is room for weighting. . . .

I agree with my Brother Clark that, if the allegations in the complaint can be sustained, a case for relief is established. We are told that a single vote in Moore County, Tennessee, is worth 19 votes in Hamilton County, that one vote in Stewart or in Chester County is worth nearly eight times a single vote in Shelby or Knox County. The opportunity to prove that an "invidious discrimination" exists should therefore be given the appellants.

It is said that any decision in cases of this kind is beyond the competence of courts. Some make the same point as regards the problem of equal protection in cases involving racial segregation. Yet the legality of claims and conduct is a traditional subject for judicial determination. Adjudication is often perplexing and complicated. . . . The constitutional guide is often vague, as the decisions under the Due Process and Commerce Clauses show. The problem under the Equal Protection Clause is no more intricate. . . .

There are, of course, some questions beyond judicial competence. Where the performance of a "duty" is left to the discretion and good judgment of an executive officer, the judiciary will not compel the exercise of his discretion one way or the other for to do so would be to take over the office. . . .

With the exceptions of *Colegrove* and the decisions [it] spawned, the Court has never thought that protection of voting rights was beyond judicial cognizance. Today's treatment of those cases removes the only impediment to judicial cognizance of the claims stated in the present complaint.

Mr. Justice Clark, concurring.

One emerging from the rash of opinions with their accompanying clashing of views may well find himself suffering a mental blindness. The Court holds that the appellants have alleged a cause of action. However, it refuses to award relief here—although the facts are undisputed—and fails to give the District Court any guidance whatever. One dissenting opinion, bursting with words that go through so much and conclude with so little, contemns the majority action as "a massive repudiation of the experience of our whole past." Another describes the complaint as merely asserting conclusory allegations that Tennessee's apportionment is "incorrect," "arbitrary," "obsolete," and "unconstitutional." I believe it can be shown that this case is distinguishable from earlier cases dealing with the distribution of political power by a State, that a patent violation of the Equal Protection Clause of the United States Constitution has been shown, and that an appropriate remedy may be formulated.

## BAKER V. CARR

### *The Relationship Between Justices Black and Frankfurter*

Students of the Court and the Constitution are often surprised to learn that Chief Justice Earl Warren (1953–1969) considered *Baker* v. *Carr* the most important decision of his tenure. Coming from the man who presided over a Court that declared an end to segregated public education, banned state-sponsored religious exercises from public schools, revolutionized the rights of criminal defendants, and erected a near-impenetrable barrier on behalf of the news media against libel suits, this statement is remarkable. So why *Baker?*

Chief Justice Warren believed that the Court's decision to permit challenges under the Equal Protection Clause to malapportioned state legislative districts cleared the way for the "one person, one vote" principle announced a year later in *Reynolds v. Sims* (1964). The Court ruled that same year in *Wesberry* v. *Sanders* (1964) that the one person, one vote principle also applied to malapportioned congressional districts. *Baker* was the critical first step toward redistributing political power in the American electoral process. By 1965, Congress passed the historic Voting Rights Act of 1965, which eliminated long-standing barriers to voter registration and required states to guarantee the effective representation of racial minorities.

But for those who had watched the Court's increased intervention in the nation's most controversial social and political problems since Earl Warren's arrival also saw another drama that had gone on behind the scenes for nearly twenty-five years reach its final curtain call. Raising such a clear-cut question on the scope of judicial power in a matter that had long been considered a political problem also brought to light the powerful contrast in the judicial philosophies of Justices Hugo Black and Felix Frankfurter.

The relationship between these two undisputed giants of American constitutional law has sometimes been portrayed as one of unrelenting antagonism. Given the stark contrasts of their personal and professional backgrounds, this characterization would seem accurate. Black was a Southerner and ex–Ku Klux Klansman.

March 10, 1962

MEMORANDUM TO: The Chief Justice
Mr. Justice Black
Mr. Justice Douglas

RE: No. 6 – Baker v. Carr

  The changes represent the maximum to which Potter will subscribe. We discussed much more elaborate changes which would have taken over a substantial part of Tom Clark's opinion. Potter felt that if they were made it would be necessary for him to dissent from that much of the revised opinion. I therefore decided it was best not to press for the changes but to hope that Tom will be willing to join the Court opinion but say he would go further as per his separate opinion.

W.J.B.

Frankfurter was a European Jew whose family left Vienna for New York City when he was twelve years old. Black received his legal education at the University of Alabama and soon established himself as a trial lawyer on behalf of plaintiffs challenging the business practices of large corporations. Frankfurter went to Harvard Law School, where his brilliance was so overwhelming that he was rewarded after graduation with a place on its faculty. From this rarified perch, Frankfurter became active in the American Civil Liberties Union. He sent his best students to Washington to clerk for his close friends on the Court, Oliver Wendell Holmes and Louis Brandeis, and to staff the New Deal agencies of Franklin Roosevelt. Black, on the other hand, took the path of elected office, winning a seat to the Senate in 1927, where he soon developed a reputation as one its most ardent New Dealers and civil libertarians. His only prior judicial experience came as an Alabama police court judge.

A combination of political loyalty, irrepressible ambition, and accident of birth resulted in Black's appointment to the Court in 1937. For Frankfurter, the heir apparent to Holmes, Cardozo, and Brandeis as the professor-in-residence on the Court, that long-expected call came in 1939. Soon after Frankfurter arrived, he attempted to bring Black under his influence through a series of informal "tutorials" designed to school him in the legal process approach to constitutional law that had long been associated with Harvard. This approach stressed judicial deference to legislative lawmaking, with intervention justified only when a law violated a fundamental constitutional right. Black proved a stubborn student. He not only ignored Frankfurter's overtures, but soon embarked on an effort of his own to win over his colleagues with his own novel theories of constitutional law and judicial power. Black's success in pushing the Court toward a more aggressive defense of civil rights and liberties infuriated Frankfurter, who complained incessantly about the Alabaman's tactics:

> Every time we have that which should be merely an intellectual difference it gets into a championship by

February 6, 1962

MEMORANDUM FOR THE CONFERENCE

No. 6 - <u>Baker</u> v. <u>Carr</u>.

At the appropriate place on page 2 of the circulated dissent, the following will be inserted:

For this Court to direct a district court to enforce a claim to which the Court has over the years consistently found itself required to deny legal enforcement and at the same time to find it necessary to withhold any guidance to lower courts how to enforce this turnabout, new legal claim, manifests an odd -- indeed an esoteric -- conception of judicial propriety.

F.F.

The Chief Justice
Mr. Justice Black
Mr. Justice Douglas
Mr. Justice Clark
Mr. Justice Harlan
Mr. Justice Brennan
Mr. Justice Whittaker
Mr. Justice Stewart

Black of justice and right and decency and everything, and those who take the other view are . . . always made out to be the oppressors of the people and the supporters of some exploiting interest.

From the moment Black rejected Frankfurter's guidance, the two men engaged in a running private and sometimes public feud that ceased fire only during times of personal and family crisis. Here was the other component of their complex relationship: a personal warmth that each shared with the other's families and, as time went by, with each other. When Black's wife, Josephine, died in 1951, and later when he suffered through a terrible bout of shingles, Frankfurter was his most steadfast friend and a source of great comfort to Black's only daughter, Jo-Jo. After Frankfurter suffered the debilitating stroke in 1962 that ended his career, Black was a constant bedside companion, reading to him and keeping him abreast of the issues before the Court. On the Court, however, they circled each other like warring gladiators, working in secret within their respective spheres of influence to mold the Court's opinions.

Black, in fact, had written the biting dissent to Frankfurter's opinion for the Court in *Colegrove,* one that came to have great bearing on Justice Brennan's majority opinion in *Baker.* Politics within the Court prevented Chief Justice Warren from assigning *Baker* to Black, who would have taken the opinion much further than Brennan. Brennan's views were closest to the fragile fifth vote of Potter Stewart, who had indicated at conference that he viewed the Tennessee malapportionment case as one involving the jurisdictional issue and nothing else. Black's willingness to defer to the chief justice's judgment as compared with Frankfurter's open condemnation of the motives and intellectual veracity of his colleagues provides a clear example of the differences in their political skills as justices.

Frankfurter's memo after the *Baker* conference, which detailed the "problems in this case, the disposition of which has such far-reaching implications for the well-being of the Court," illustrated the depth of his anger over the forthcoming eclipse of his *Colegrove* opinion. In response, Brennan, guided by Black, wrote his colleagues to emphasize that "there was no reason for the disparate treatment, and that maybe the Legislature could justify it but [the state's lawyers] could not. . . . Tennessee should be required to justify if it is to avoid the conclusion that the 1901 Act applied to today's facts, is simple caprice." Later, in a memo to his colleagues in the *Baker* majority, which now included Justice Tom Clark who had defected from Frankfurter's dissent, Brennan wrote, "I believe that the full discussion of 'political question,' and its bearing on apportionment suits, is required if we are effectively and finally to dispel the fog of another day produced by Felix's opinion in *Colegrove.*"

Frankfurter, knowing that the assembled majority was going to hold, at minimum, that plaintiffs in malapportioned legislative districts were now entitled to judicial review, sought to minimize the damage to the political questions doctrine by issuing one draft dissent after another. The decibel levels of his dissents rose with each successive draft, warning his colleagues of the dangers of a broad opinion. His persistence was rewarded with a small concession by Brennan to confine the holding in *Baker* to the jurisdictional questions and not reach the issues raised by Justices Douglas and Clark in their concurrences. But that victory was short-lived, as the Court, during the 1963–1964 term, decided seventeen reapportionment cases that affected the composition of legislative districts in forty-eight states.

January 27, 1962

MEMORANDUM TO: The Chief Justice
Mr. Justice Black
Mr. Justice Douglas

Enclosed is the proposed opinion in Baker v. Carr, which Potter Stewart tells me entirely satisfies him. Contrary to his tentative reaction at conference, Potter now agrees with me that we should not pass on any issues except the three actually requiring decision at this time. I doubt that Felix's dissent will deal with any others but even if he does, I think that a response that no other questions are before us would be all that was required. I should say further that, after much thought, I believe that the full discussion of "political question", and its bearing on apportionment suits, is required if we are effectively and finally to dispel the fog of another day produced by Felix's opinion in Colegrove v. Green.

I'll be leaving Thursday night, February 1, for ten days but will be here every day until then and will welcome your suggestions. I shall not make a general circulation until I have heard from you.

W.J.B.

*Felix Frankfurter, left, and Hugo Black, right, were polar opposites in personality and judicial philosophy. Here, they share pleasant conversation at a 1943 Bar Association lunch.* Photo by Bill Klemm © 1943 The Washington Post. Reprinted with permission.

Black was a pivotal force in the Court's drive to democratize legislative apportionment. Few issues so deeply touched his populist instincts as those involving the right to equal participation in the electoral process. In Black's view courts existed to protect the fundamental rights of individuals who could not count on the entrenched majorities in the legislature. Black had been a legislator; he knew how the system worked; and the one thing legislators did not do was give away their power. This fact of political life was something he always believed that his more professorial colleague never understood.

In fairness, Frankfurter's commitment to the legal process school did not stem from some professorial abstraction. It came from his own experience as a public interest lawyer who worked alongside Louis Brandeis to reform the bleak social and economic conditions of early-twentieth-century America through progressive legislation. The Court, in its heyday as the guardian of American corporate and property interests, routinely struck down such legislation as inconsistent with the natural order of the economic marketplace. Principled judicial restraint, in Frankfurter's view, prevented the Court from stemming the reform impulses of the legislative process, one in which he had always held the highest hopes.

Unbound by traditional categories, the relationship between Hugo Black and Felix Frankfurter was characterized by a dynamic tension that brought out the best in each justice and greatly strengthened the Court during one of the most tumultuous periods in its history.

### References

Simon, James F. *The Antagonists: Hugo Black, Felix Frankfurter and Civil Liberties in Modern America.* New York: Simon & Schuster, 1989.

Papers of Earl Warren, Library of Congress.

Papers of William J. Brennan, Library of Congress.

Papers of William O. Douglas, Library of Congress.

Although I find the Tennessee apportionment statute offends the Equal Protection Clause, I would not consider intervention by this Court into so delicate a field if there were any other relief available to the people of Tennessee. But the majority of the people of Tennessee have no "practical opportunities for exerting their political weight at the polls" to correct the existing "invidious discrimination." Tennessee has no initiative and referendum. I have searched diligently for other "practical opportunities" present under the law. I find none other than through the federal courts. The majority of the voters have been caught up in a legislative strait jacket. Tennessee has an "informed, civically militant electorate" and "an aroused popular conscience," but it does not sear "the conscience of the people's representatives." This is because the legislative policy has riveted the present seats in the Assembly to their respective constituencies, and by the votes of their incumbents a reapportionment of any kind is prevented. The people have been rebuffed at the hands of the Assembly; they have tried the constitutional convention route, but since the call must originate in the Assembly it, too, has been fruitless. They have tried Tennessee courts with the same result, and

Governors have fought the tide only to flounder. It is said that there is recourse in Congress, and perhaps that may be, but, from a practical standpoint, this is without substance. To date, Congress has never undertaken such a task in any State. We therefore must conclude that the people of Tennessee are stymied, and, without judicial intervention, will be saddled with the present discrimination in the affairs of their state government. . . .

As John Rutledge (later Chief Justice) said 175 years ago in the course of the Constitutional Convention, a chief function of the Court is to secure the national rights. Its decision today supports the proposition for which our forebears fought and many died, namely that, to be fully conformable to the principle of right, the form of government must be representative. That is the keystone upon which our government was founded and lacking which no republic can survive. It is well for this Court to practice self-restraint and discipline in constitutional adjudication, but never in its history have those principles received sanction where the national rights of so many have been so clearly infringed for so long a time. National respect for the courts is more enhanced through the forthright enforcement of those rights, rather than by rendering them nugatory through the interposition of subterfuges. In my view, the ultimate decision today is in the greatest tradition of this Court.

Mr. Justice Stewart, concurring.

The separate writings of my dissenting and concurring Brothers stray so far from the subject of today's decision as to convey, I think, a distressingly inaccurate impression of what the Court decides. For that reason, I think it appropriate, in joining the opinion of the Court, to emphasize in a few words what the opinion does and does not say.

The Court today decides three things, and no more. "(a) that the court possessed jurisdiction of the subject matter; (b) that a justiciable cause of action is stated upon which appellants would be entitled to appropriate relief, and (c) . . . that the appellants have standing to challenge the Tennessee apportionment statutes."

Mr. Justice Frankfurter, whom Mr. Justice Harlan joins, dissenting.

The Court today reverses a uniform course of decision established by a dozen cases, including one by which the very claim now sustained was unanimously rejected only five years ago. The impressive body of rulings thus cast aside reflected the equally uniform course of our political history regarding the relationship between population and legislative representation—a wholly different matter from denial of the franchise to individuals because of race, color, religion or sex. Such a massive repudiation of the experience of our whole past in asserting destructively novel judicial power demands a detailed analysis of the role of this Court in our constitutional scheme. Disregard of inherent limits in the effective exercise of the Court's "judicial Power" not only presages the futility of judicial intervention in the essentially political conflict of forces by which the relation between population and representation has time out of mind been, and now is, determined. It may well impair the Court's position as the ultimate organ of "the supreme Law of the Land" in that vast range of legal problems, often strongly entangled in popular feeling, on which this Court must pronounce. The Court's authority—possessed of neither the purse nor the sword—ultimately rests on sustained public confidence in its moral sanction. Such feeling must be nourished by the Court's complete detachment, in fact and in appearance, from political entanglements and by abstention from injecting itself into the clash of political forces in political settlements.

A hypothetical claim resting on abstract assumptions is now for the first time made the basis for affording illusory relief for a particular evil even though it foreshadows deeper and more pervasive difficulties in consequence. The claim is hypothetical, and the assumptions are abstract, because the Court does not vouchsafe the lower courts—state and federal—guidelines for formulating specific, definite, wholly unprecedented remedies for the inevitable litigations that today's umbrageous disposition is bound to stimulate in connection with politically motivated reapportionments in so many States. In such a setting, to promulgate jurisdiction in the abstract is meaningless. It is as devoid of reality as "a brooding omnipresence in the sky," for it conveys no intimation what relief, if any, a District Court is capable of affording that would not invite legislatures to play ducks and drakes with the judiciary. For this Court to direct the District Court to enforce a claim to which the Court has over the years consistently found itself required to deny legal enforcement and, at the same time, to find it necessary to withhold any guidance to the lower court how to enforce this turnabout, new legal claim, manifests an odd—indeed an esoteric—conception of judicial propriety. One of the Court's supporting opinions, as elucidated by commentary, unwittingly affords a disheartening preview of the mathematical quagmire (apart from divers judicially inappropriate and elusive determinants) into which this Court today catapults the lower courts of the country without so much as adumbrating the basis for a legal calculus as a means of extrication. Even assuming the indispensable intellectual disinterestedness on the part of judges in such matters, they do not have accepted legal standards or criteria or even reliable analogies to draw upon for making judicial judgments. To charge courts with the task of accommodating the incommensurable factors of policy that underlie these mathematical puzzles is to attribute, however flatteringly, omnicompetence to judges. The Framers of the Constitution persistently rejected a proposal that embodied this assumption, and Thomas Jefferson never entertained it. . . .

We were soothingly told at the bar of this Court that we need not worry about the kind of remedy a court could effectively fashion once the abstract constitutional right to have courts pass on a statewide system of electoral districting is recognized as a matter of judicial rhetoric, because legislatures would heed the Court's admonition. This is not only a euphoric hope. It implies a sorry confession of judicial impotence in place of a frank acknowledgment that there is not under our Constitution a judicial remedy for every political mischief, for every undesirable exercise of legislative power. The Framers, carefully and with deliberate forethought, refused so to enthrone the judiciary. In this situation, as in others of like nature, appeal for relief does not belong here. Appeal must be to an informed, civically militant electorate. In a democratic society like ours, relief must come through an aroused popular conscience that sears the conscience of the people's representatives. In any event, there is nothing judicially more unseemly nor more self-defeating than for this Court to make *in terrorem* pronouncements, to indulge in merely empty rhetoric, sounding a word of promise to the ear sure to be disappointing to the hope. . . .

The *Colegrove* doctrine, in the form in which repeated decisions have settled it, was not an innovation. It represents long judicial thought and experience. From its earliest opinions, this Court has consistently recognized a class of controversies which do not lend themselves to judicial standards and judicial remedies. To classify the various instances as "political questions" is, rather, a form of stating this conclusion than revealing of analysis. Some of the cases so labelled have no relevance here. But from others emerge unifying considerations that are compelling.

1. The cases concerning war or foreign affairs, for example, are usually explained by the necessity of the country's speaking with one voice in such matters. While this concern alone undoubtedly accounts for many of the decisions, others do not fit the pattern. It would hardly embarrass the conduct of war were this Court to determine, in connection with private transactions between litigants, the date upon which war is to be deemed terminated. But the Court has refused to do so. . . .

2. The Court has been particularly unwilling to intervene in matters concerning the structure and organization of the political institutions of the States. The abstention from judicial entry into such areas has been greater even than that which marks the Court's ordinary approach to issues of state power challenged under broad federal guarantees. . . .

3. The cases involving Negro disfranchisement are no exception to the principle of avoiding federal judicial intervention into matters of state government in the absence of an explicit and clear constitutional imperative. For here the controlling command of Supreme Law is plain and unequivocal. An end of discrimination against the Negro was the compelling motive of the Civil War Amendments. The Fifteenth expresses this in terms, and it is no less true of the Equal Protecting Clause of the Fourteenth. Thus, the Court, in cases involving discrimination against the Negro's right to vote, has recognized not only the action at law for damages, but, in appropriate circumstances, the extraordinary remedy of declaratory or injunctive relief. Injunctions in these cases, it should be noted, would not have restrained statewide general elections.

4. The Court has refused to exercise its jurisdiction to pass on "abstract questions of political power, of sovereignty, of government." *Massachusetts v. Mellon* (1923). The "political question" doctrine, in this aspect, reflects the policies underlying the requirement of "standing": that the litigant who would challenge official action must claim infringement of an interest particular and personal to himself, as distinguished from a cause of dissatisfaction with the general frame and functioning of government—a complaint that the political institutions are awry. What renders cases of this kind nonjusticiable is not necessarily the nature of the parties to them, for the Court has resolved other issues between similar parties; nor is it the nature of the legal question involved, for the same type of question has been adjudicated when presented in other forms of controversy. The crux of the matter is that courts are not fit instruments of decision where what is essentially at stake is the composition of those large contests of policy traditionally fought out in nonjudicial forums, by which governments and the actions of governments are made and unmade. . . .

5. The influence of these converging considerations—the caution not to undertake decision where standards meet for judicial judgment are lacking, the reluctance to interfere with matters of state government in the absence of an unquestionable and effectively enforceable mandate, the unwillingness to make courts arbiters

of the broad issues of political organization historically committed to other institutions and for whose adjustment the judicial process is ill-adapted—has been decisive of the settled line of cases, reaching back more than a century, which holds that Art. IV, § 4, of the Constitution, guaranteeing to the States "a Republican Form of Government," is not enforceable through the courts. . . .

The present case involves all of the elements that have made the Guarantee Clause cases nonjusticiable. It is, in effect, a Guarantee Clause claim masquerading under a different label. But it cannot make the case more fit for judicial action that appellants invoke the Fourteenth Amendment, rather than Art. IV, § 4, where, in fact, the gist of their complaint is the same—unless it can be found that the Fourteenth Amendment speaks with greater particularity to their situation. We have been admonished to avoid "the tyranny of labels." Art. IV, § 4, is not committed by express constitutional terms to Congress. It is the nature of the controversies arising under it, nothing else, which has made it judicially unenforceable. . . .

What, then, is this question of legislative apportionment? Appellants invoke the right to vote and to have their votes counted. But they are permitted to vote, and their votes are counted. They go to the polls, they cast their ballots, they send their representatives to the state councils. Their complaint is simply that the representatives are not sufficiently numerous or powerful—in short, that Tennessee has adopted a basis of representation with which they are dissatisfied. Talk of "debasement" or "dilution" is circular talk. One cannot speak of "debasement" or "dilution" of the value of a vote until there is first defined a standard of reference as to what a vote should be worth. What is actually asked of the Court in this case is to choose among competing bases of representation—ultimately, really, among competing theories of political philosophy—in order to establish an appropriate frame of government for the State of Tennessee, and thereby for all the States of the Union.

In such a matter, abstract analogies which ignore the facts of history deal in unrealities; they betray reason. This is not a case in which a State has, through a device however oblique and sophisticated, denied Negroes or Jews or redheaded persons a vote, or given them only a third or a sixth of a vote. . . . What Tennessee illustrates is an old and still widespread method of representation—representation by local geographical division, only in part respective of population—in preference to others, others, forsooth, more appealing. Appellants contest this choice, and seek to make this Court the arbiter of the disagree-

ment. They would make the Equal Protection Clause the charter of adjudication, asserting that the equality which it guarantees comports, if not the assurance of equal weight to every voter's vote, at least the basic conception that representation ought to be proportionate to population, a standard by reference to which the reasonableness of apportionment plans may be judged.

To find such a political conception legally enforceable in the broad and unspecific guarantee of equal protection is to rewrite the Constitution. Certainly "equal protection" is no more secure a foundation for judicial judgment of the permissibility of varying forms of representative government than is "Republican Form." Indeed, since "equal protection of the laws" can only mean an equality of persons standing in the same relation to whatever governmental action is challenged, the determination whether treatment is equal presupposes a determination concerning the nature of the relationship. . . .

The notion that representation proportioned to the geographic spread of population is so universally accepted as a necessary element of equality between man and man that it must be taken to be the standard of a political equality preserved by the Fourteenth Amendment—that it is, in appellants' words "the basic principle of representative government"—is, to put it bluntly, not true. However desirable and however desired by some among the great political thinkers and framers of our government, it has never been generally practiced, today or in the past. It was not the English system, it was not the colonial system, it was not the system chosen for the national government by the Constitution, it was not the system exclusively or even predominantly practiced by the States at the time of adoption of the Fourteenth Amendment, it is not predominantly practiced by the States today. Unless judges, the judges of this Court, are to make their private views of political wisdom the measure of the Constitution—views which, in all honesty, cannot but give the appearance, if not reflect the reality, of involvement with the business of partisan politics so inescapably a part of apportionment controversies—the Fourteenth Amendment, "itself a historical product," provides no guide for judicial oversight of the representation problem.

Manifestly, the Equal Protection Clause supplies no clearer guide for judicial examination of apportionment methods than would the Guarantee Clause itself. Apportionment, by its character, is a subject of extraordinary complexity, involving—even after the fundamental theoretical issues concerning what is to be represented in a representative legislature have been fought out or compromised—considerations of geography, demography, electoral convenience, economic and social cohesions or divergencies among particular local groups, communications, the practical effects of political institutions like the lobby and the city machine, ancient traditions and ties of settled usage, respect for proven incumbents of long experience and senior status, mathematical mechanics, censuses compiling relevant data, and a host of others. Legislative responses throughout the country to the reapportionment demands of the 1960 Census have glaringly confirmed that these are not factors that lend themselves to evaluations of a nature that are the staple of judicial determinations or for which judges are equipped to adjudicate by legal training or experience or native wit. And this is the more so true because, in every strand of this complicated, intricate web of values meet the contending forces of partisan politics. The practical significance of apportionment is that the next election results may differ because of it. Apportionment battles are overwhelmingly party or intra-party contests. It will add a virulent source of friction and tension in federal-state relations to embroil the federal judiciary in them. . . .

Although the District Court had jurisdiction in the very restricted sense of power to determine whether it could adjudicate the claim, the case is of that class of political controversy which, by the nature of its subject, is unfit for federal judicial action. The judgment of the District Court . . . should therefore be affirmed.

## *Missouri v. Jenkins*
### 495 U.S. 33 (1990)

In 1977, students in the Kansas City School District filed suit in federal district court charging that the school district and the State of Missouri operated a segregated school system. The litigation dragged on for years. Finally, in 1984, the court found in favor of students' claim and issued an order detailing a desegregation remedy and the financing necessary to implement it. The original estimate of the remedy's cost was $88 million, leaving the school district to claim that it did not have the revenue to satisfy the order. Because Missouri voters firmly opposed tax increases and state law already restricted the school district's power to raise revenue, the school district was left in a legal and political dilemma.

A district court agreed to enjoin the state's laws that prevented the district from paying its share of the desegregation order, but even that decision still left the school dis-

trict substantially short of funds. Citing its power to order equitable remedies for violations to the federal Constitution, the district court held that it was within its power to order an increase in the school district's property tax rate. The court of appeals affirmed the lower court's ruling, but warned that future tax increases must come from the school district.

The Supreme Court's judgment was unanimous, but the opinion was not. Justice White delivered the opinion of the Court. A concurrence was filed by Justice Kennedy, which was joined by Chief Justice Rehnquist and Justices O'Connor and Scalia.

JUSTICE WHITE delivered the opinion of the Court.

The United States District Court for the Western District of Missouri imposed an increase in the property taxes levied by the Kansas City, Missouri, School District (KCMSD) to ensure funding for the desegregation of KCMSD's public schools. For the reasons given below, we hold that the District Court abused its discretion in imposing the tax increase. We also hold, however, that the modifications of the District Court's order made by the Court of Appeals do satisfy equitable and constitutional principles governing the District Court's power. . . .

We turn to the tax increase imposed by the District Court. . . .

It is accepted by all the parties, as it was by the courts below, that the imposition of a tax increase by a federal court was an extraordinary event. In assuming for itself the fundamental and delicate power of taxation, the District Court not only intruded on local authority but circumvented it altogether. Before taking such a drastic step, the District Court was obliged to assure itself that no permissible alternative would have accomplished the required task. We have emphasized that, although the "remedial powers of an equity court must be adequate to the task, . . . they are not unlimited," *Whitcomb* v. *Chavis* (1971), and one of the most important considerations governing the exercise of equitable power is a proper respect for the integrity and function of local government institutions. Especially is this true where, as here, those institutions are ready, willing, and—but for the operation of state law curtailing their powers—able to remedy the deprivation of constitutional rights themselves.

The District Court believed that it had no alternative to imposing a tax increase. But there was an alternative: it could have authorized or required KCMSD to levy property taxes at a rate adequate to fund the desegregation remedy, and could have enjoined the operation of state laws that would have prevented KCMSD from exercising this power. The difference between the two approaches is far more than a matter of form. Authorizing and directing local government institutions to devise and implement remedies not only protects the function of those institutions but, to the extent possible, also places the responsibility for solutions to the problems of segregation upon those who have themselves created the problems.

As *Brown* II (1955), observed, local authorities have the "primary responsibility for elucidating, assessing, and solving" the problems of desegregation. This is true as well of the problems of financing desegregation, for no matter has been more consistently placed upon the shoulders of local government than that of financing public schools. As was said in another context, "[t]he very complexity of the problems of financing and managing a . . . public school system suggests that 'there will be more than one constitutionally permissible method of solving them,' and that . . . 'the legislature's efforts to tackle the problems' should be entitled to respect." *San Antonio Independent School District v. Rodriguez* (1973). By no means should a district court grant local government *carte blanche*, but local officials should at least have the opportunity to devise their own solutions to these problems. . . .

We stand on different ground when we review the modifications to the District Court's order made by the Court of Appeals. [T]he Court of Appeals held that the District Court in the future should authorize KCMSD to submit a levy to the state tax collection authorities adequate to fund its budget, and should enjoin the operation of state laws that would limit or reduce the levy below that amount.

The State argues that the funding ordered by the District Court violates principles of equity and comity because the remedial order itself was excessive. As the State puts it, "[t]he only reason that the court below needed to consider an unprecedented tax increase was the equally unprecedented cost of its remedial programs." We think this argument aims at the scope of the remedy, rather than the manner in which the remedy is to be funded, and thus falls outside our limited grant of certiorari in this case. We accept, without approving or disapproving, the Court of Appeals' conclusion that the District Court's remedy was proper.

The State has argued here that the District Court, having found the State and KCMSD jointly and severally liable, should have allowed any monetary obligations that KCMSD could not meet to fall on the State rather than interfere with state law to permit KCMSD to meet them. Under the circumstances of this case, we cannot say it was an abuse of discretion for the District Court to rule that

KCMSD should be responsible for funding its share of the remedy. The State strenuously opposed efforts by respondents to make it responsible for the cost of implementing the order, and had secured a reversal of the District Court's earlier decision placing on it all of the cost of substantial portions of the order. The District Court declined to require the State to pay for KCMSD's obligations because it believed that the Court of Appeals had ordered it to allocate the costs between the two governmental entities. Furthermore, if the District Court had chosen the route now suggested by the State, implementation of the remedial order might have been delayed if the State resisted efforts by KCMSD to obtain contribution. . . .

We turn [now] to the constitutional issues. The modifications ordered by the Court of Appeals cannot be assailed as invalid under the Tenth Amendment. "The Tenth Amendment's reservation of nondelegated powers to the States is not implicated by a federal court judgment enforcing the express prohibitions of unlawful state conduct enacted by the Fourteenth Amendment." "The Fourteenth Amendment . . . was avowedly directed against the power of the States," *Pennsylvania v. Union Gas Co.* (1989), and so permits a federal court to disestablish local government institutions that interfere with its commands. . . .

Finally, the State argues that an order to increase taxes cannot be sustained under the judicial power of Article III. Whatever the merits of this argument when applied to the District Court's own order increasing taxes, a point we have not reached, a court order directing a local government body to levy its own taxes is plainly a judicial act within the power of a federal court. We held as much in *Griffin v. Prince Edward County School Bd.* (1964), where we stated that a District Court, faced with a county's attempt to avoid desegregation of the public schools by refusing to operate those schools, could, "require the [County] Supervisors to exercise the power that is theirs to levy taxes to raise funds adequate to reopen, operate, and maintain without racial discrimination a public school system. . . ." *Griffin* followed a long and venerable line of cases in which this Court held that federal courts could compel local governmental bodies to levy taxes adequate to satisfy their debt obligations. . . .

The State maintains, however, that, even under these cases, the federal judicial power can go no further than to require local governments to levy taxes *as authorized under state law*. In other words, the State argues that federal courts cannot set aside state-imposed limitations on local taxing authority, because to do so is to do more than to require the local government "to exercise the power *that is theirs*." We disagree. . . .

It is therefore clear that a local government with taxing authority may be ordered to levy taxes in excess of the limit set by state statute where there is reason based in the Constitution for not observing the statutory limitation. Here the KCMSD may be ordered to levy taxes despite the statutory limitations on its authority in order to compel the discharge of an obligation imposed on KCMSD by the Fourteenth Amendment. To hold otherwise would fail to take account of the obligations of local governments, under the Supremacy Clause, to fulfill the requirements that the Constitution imposes on them. However wide the discretion of local authorities in fashioning desegregation remedies may be, "if a state-imposed limitation on a school authority's discretion operates to inhibit or obstruct the operation of a unitary school system or impede the disestablishing of a dual school system, it must fall; state policy must give way when it operates to hinder vindication of federal constitutional guarantees." *North Carolina State Bd. of Education v. Swann* (1971). Even though a particular remedy may not be required in every case to vindicate constitutional guarantees, where (as here) it has been found that a particular remedy is required, the State cannot hinder the process by preventing a local government from implementing that remedy.

Accordingly, the judgment of the Court of Appeals is affirmed insofar as it required the District Court to modify its funding order, and reversed insofar as it allowed the tax increase imposed by the District Court to stand. . . .

*It is so ordered.*

Justice Kennedy, with whom The Chief Justice, Justice O'Connor, and Justice Scalia join, concurring in part and concurring in the judgment.

I agree that the District Court exceeded its authority by attempting to impose a tax. The Court is unanimous in its holding that the Court of Appeals' judgment affirming "the actions that the [district] court has taken to this point," must be reversed. This is consistent with our precedents and the basic principles defining judicial power.

In my view, however, the Court transgresses these same principles when it goes further, much further, to embrace by broad dictum an expansion of power in the federal judiciary beyond all precedent. Today's casual embrace of taxation imposed by the unelected, life-tenured Federal Judiciary disregards fundamental precepts for the democratic control of public institutions. I cannot acquiesce in the majority's statements on this point, and, should there arise an actual dispute over the collection of taxes as here contemplated in a case that is not, like this one, premature, we should not confirm the outcome of premises adopted with so little constitutional justification. The Court's statements, in my view, cannot be seen as necessary for its judgment, or as precedent for the future. . . .

Article III of the Constitution states that, "[t]he judicial Power of the United States, shall be vested in one supreme Court, and in such inferior Courts as the Congress may from time to time ordain and establish." The description of the judicial power nowhere includes the word "tax," or anything that resembles it. This reflects the Framers' understanding that taxation was not a proper area for judicial involvement. "The judiciary . . . has no influence over either the sword or the purse, no direction either of the strength or of the wealth of the society, and can take no active resolution whatever." Federalist 78. . . .

The nature of the District Court's order here reveals that it is not a proper exercise of the judicial power. The exercise of judicial power involves adjudication of controversies and imposition of burdens on those who are parties before the Court. The order at issue here is not of this character. It binds the broad class of all KCMSD taxpayers. It has the purpose and direct effect of extracting money from persons who have had no presence or representation in the suit. For this reason, the District Court's direct order imposing a tax was more than an abuse of discretion, for any attempt to collect the taxes from the citizens would have been a blatant denial of due process.

Taxation by a legislature raises no due process concerns, for the citizens, "rights are protected in the only way that they can be in a complex society, by their power, immediate or remote, over those who make the rule." The citizens who are taxed are given notice and a hearing through their representatives, whose power is a direct manifestation of the citizens' consent. A true exercise of judicial power provides due process of another sort. Where money is extracted from parties by a court's judgment, the adjudication itself provides the notice and opportunity to be heard that due process demands before a citizen may be deprived of property.

The order here provides neither of these protections. Where a tax is imposed by a governmental body other than the legislature, even an administrative agency to which the legislature has delegated taxing authority, due process requires notice to the citizens to be taxed and some opportunity to be heard. The citizens whose tax bills would have been doubled under the District Court's direct tax order would not have had these protections. The taxes were imposed by a District Court that was not "representative" in any sense, and the individual citizens of the

KCMSD whose property (they later learned) was at stake were neither served with process nor heard in court. The method of taxation endorsed by today's dicta suffers the same flaw, for a district court order that overrides the citizens' state law protection against taxation without referendum approval can in no sense provide representational due process. No one suggests the KCMSD taxpayers are parties.

A judicial taxation order is but an attempt to exercise a power that always has been thought legislative in nature. The location of the federal taxing power sheds light on today's attempt to approve judicial taxation at the local level. Article I, Section 1 states that" *[a]ll* legislative Powers herein granted shall be vested in a Congress of the United States, which shall consist of a Senate and House of Representatives. . . ." (Emphasis added.) The list of legislative powers in Article I, Section 8, clause 1 begins with the statement that "[t]he Congress shall have Power To lay and collect Taxes. . . ."

True, today's case is not an instance of one branch of the Federal Government invading the province of another. It is instead one that brings the weight of federal authority upon a local government and a State. This does not detract, however, from the fundamental point that the judiciary is not free to exercise all federal power; it may exercise only the judicial power. And the important effects of the taxation order discussed here raise additional federalism concerns that counsel against the Court's analysis.

The confinement of taxation to the legislative branches, both in our Federal and State Governments, was not random. It reflected our ideal that the power of taxation must be under the control of those who are taxed. This truth animated all our colonial and revolutionary history.

> Your Memorialists conceive it to be a fundamental Principle . . . without which Freedom can no Where exist, that the People are not subject to any Taxes but such as are laid on them by their own Consent, or by those who are legally appointed to represent them: Property must become too precarious for the Genius of a free People which can be taken from them at the Will of others, who cannot know what Taxes such people can bear, or the easiest Mode of raising them; and who are not under that Restraint, which is the greatest Security against a burthensome Taxation, when the Representatives themselves must be affected by every tax imposed on the People. Virginia Petitions to King and Parliament, December 18, 1764.

The power of taxation is one that the federal judiciary does not possess. In our system "the legislative department alone has access to the pockets of the people," Federalist 48, for it is the legislature that is accountable to them and represents their will. The authority that would levy the tax at issue here shares none of these qualities. Our federal judiciary, by design, is not representative or responsible to the people in a political sense; it is independent. Federal judges do not depend on the popular will for their office. They may not even share the burden of taxes they attempt to impose, for they may live outside the jurisdiction their orders affect. And federal judges have no fear that the competition for scarce public resources could result in a diminution of their salaries. It is not surprising that imposition of taxes by an authority so insulated from public communication or control can lead to deep feelings of frustration, powerlessness, and anger on the part of taxpaying citizens. . . .

One of the most troubling aspects of the Court's opinion is that discussion of the important constitutional issues of judicial authority to tax need never have been undertaken to decide this case. Even were I willing to accept the Court's proposition that a federal court might in some extreme case authorize taxation, this case is not the one. The suggestion that failure to approve judicial taxation here would leave constitutional rights unvindicated rests on a presumption that the District Court's remedy is the *only* possible cure for the constitutional violations it found. Neither our precedents nor the record support this view. In fact, the taxation power is sought here on behalf of a remedial order unlike any before seen. . . .

Perhaps it is good educational policy to provide a school district with the items included in the KCMSD capital improvement plan, for example: high schools in which every classroom will have air conditioning, an alarm system, and 15 microcomputers; a 2,000-square-foot planetarium; greenhouses and vivariums; a 25-acre farm with an air-conditioned meeting room for 104 people; a Model United Nations wired for language translation; broadcast capable radio and television studios with an editing and animation lab; a temperature controlled art gallery; movie editing and screening rooms; a 3,500-square-foot dust-free diesel mechanics room; 1,875-square-foot elementary school animal rooms for use in a Zoo Project; swimming pools; and numerous other facilities. But these items are a part of legitimate political debate over educational policy and spending priorities, not the Constitution's command of racial equality. Indeed, it may be that a mere 12-acre petting farm, or other corresponding reductions in court-ordered spending, might satisfy constitutional requirements while preserving scarce public funds for legislative allocation to other public needs, such as paving streets, feeding the poor, building prisons, or housing the homeless. Perhaps the KCMSD's Classical Greek theme schools emphasizing forensics and self-government will provide exemplary training in participatory democracy. But if today's dicta become law, such lessons will be of little use to students who grow up to become taxpayers in the KCMSD.

This case is a stark illustration of the ever-present question whether ends justify means. Few ends are more important than enforcing the guarantee of equal educational opportunity for our Nation's children. But rules of taxation that override state political strictures not themselves subject to any constitutional infirmity raise serious questions of federal authority, questions compounded by the odd posture of a case in which the Court assumes the validity of a novel conception of desegregation remedies we never before have approved. The historical record of voluntary compliance with the decree of *Brown* v. *Board of Education* is not a proud chapter in our constitutional history, and the judges of the District Courts and Courts of Appeals have been courageous and skillful in implementing its mandate. But courage and skill must be exercised with due regard for the proper and historic role of the courts.

I do not acknowledge the troubling departures in today's majority opinion as either necessary or appropriate to ensure full compliance with the Equal Protection Clause and its mandate to eliminate the cause and effects of racial discrimination in the schools. Indeed, while this case happens to arise in the compelling context of school desegregation, the principles involved are not limited to that context. There is no obvious limit to today's discussion that would prevent judicial taxation in cases involving prisons, hospitals, or other public institutions, or indeed to pay a large damages award levied against a municipality under 42 U.S.C. 1983. This assertion of judicial power in one of the most sensitive of policy areas, that involving taxation, begins a process that, over time, could threaten fundamental alteration of the form of government our Constitution embodies.

▼▲▼

## Nixon v. United States
### 506 U.S. 224 (1993)

Walter L. Nixon, chief judge of a federal district court, was investigated in 1989 by federal prosecutors who believed he had accepted a bribe to influence a criminal investigation of a friend's son. Judge Nixon denied these charges and was not charged for his alleged involvement. He was, however, charged with lying to the grand jury investigating the case and was sentenced to five years in prison. Still asserting his innocence, Judge Nixon refused to resign and thus continued to collect his judicial salary from his jail cell. Other than his resignation, only impeachment would remove him from the bench and terminate his salary. The House of Representatives adopted articles of impeachment against him and presented them to the Senate. Following a Senate rule permitting a committee to hear evidence against an impeached individual and to report that evidence to the full Senate, the Senate voted to convict Nixon. The presiding officer entered judgment removing him from office.

Nixon brought suit asking for reinstatement to his judgeship, but the district court hearing his case ruled that his claim involved a nonjusticiable "political question." An appeals court affirmed.

The Supreme Court's decision was unanimous. Chief Justice Rehnquist delivered the opinion of the Court. Justices White and Souter filed concurrences.

CHIEF JUSTICE REHNQUIST delivered the opinion of the Court.

Petitioner Walter L. Nixon, Jr., asks this court to decide whether Senate Rule XI, which allows a committee of Senators to hear evidence against an individual who has been impeached and to report that evidence to the full Senate, violates the Impeachment Trial Clause, Article I, Section 3, clause 6. That Clause provides that the "Senate shall have the sole Power to try all Impeachments." But before we reach the merits of such a claim, we must decide whether it is "justiciable," that is, whether it is a claim that may be resolved by the courts. We conclude that it is not. . . .

A controversy is nonjusticiable—*i.e.*, involves a political question—where there is, "a textually demonstrable constitutional commitment of the issue to a coordinate political department; or a lack of judicially discoverable and manageable standards for resolving it. . . ." *Baker* v. *Carr* (1962). But the courts must, in the first instance, interpret the text in question and determine whether and to what extent the issue is textually committed. As the discussion that follows makes clear, the concept of a textual commitment to a coordinate political department is not completely separate from the concept of a lack of judicially discoverable and manageable standards for resolving it; the lack of judicially manageable standards may strengthen the conclusion that there is a textually demonstrable commitment to a coordinate branch.

In this case, we must examine Article I, Section 3, clause 6, to determine the scope of authority conferred upon the Senate by the Framers regarding impeachment. It provides:

> The Senate shall have the sole Power to try all Impeachments. When sitting for that Purpose, they shall be on Oath or Affirmation. When the President of the United States is tried, the Chief Justice shall preside: And no Person shall be convicted without the Concurrence of two thirds of the Members present.

The language and structure of this Clause are revealing. The first sentence is a grant of authority to the Senate, and the word "sole" indicates that this authority is reposed in the Senate, and nowhere else. . . .

Petitioner argues that the word "try" in the first sentence imposes by implication an additional requirement on the Senate, in that the proceedings must be in the nature of a judicial trial. From there petitioner goes on to argue that this limitation precludes the Senate from delegating to a select committee the task of hearing the testimony of witnesses, as was done pursuant to Senate Rule XI. " '[T]ry' means more than simply 'vote on' or 'review' or 'judge.' In 1787 and today, trying a case means hearing the evidence, not scanning a cold record." Petitioner concludes from this that courts may review whether or not the Senate "tried" him before convicting him.

There are several difficulties with this position which lead us ultimately to reject it. The word "try," both in 1787 and later, has considerably broader meanings than those to which petitioner would limit it. Older dictionaries define try as "[t]o examine" or "[t]o examine as a judge." In more modern usage, the term has various meanings. For example, try can mean "to examine or investigate judicially," "to conduct the trial of," or "to put to the test by experiment, investigation, or trial." Petitioner submits that "try," as contained in T. Sheridan, Dictionary of the English Language (1796), means "to examine as a judge; to bring before a judicial tribunal." Based on the variety of definitions, however, we cannot say that the Framers used the word "try" as an implied limitation on the method by which the Senate might proceed in trying impeachments. "As a rule the Constitution speaks in general terms, leaving Congress to deal with subsidiary matters of detail as the public interests and changing conditions may require. . . ."

The conclusion that the use of the word "try" in the first sentence of the Impeachment Trial Clause lacks sufficient precision to afford any judicially manageable standard of review of the Senate's actions is fortified by the existence of the three very specific requirements that the Constitution does impose on the Senate when trying impeachments: the members must be under oath, a two-thirds vote is required to convict, and the Chief Justice presides when the President is tried. These limitations are quite precise, and their nature suggests that the Framers did not intend to impose additional limitations on the form of the Senate proceedings by the use of the word "try" in the first sentence. . . .

The history and contemporary understanding of the impeachment provisions support our reading of the constitutional language. The parties do not offer evidence of a single word in the history of the Constitutional Convention or in contemporary commentary that even alludes to the possibility of judicial review in the context of the impeachment powers. This silence is quite meaningful in light of the several explicit references to the availability of judicial review as a check on the Legislature's power with respect to bills of attainder, *ex post facto* laws, and statutes.

The Framers labored over the question of where the impeachment power should lie. Significantly, in at least two considered scenarios, the power was placed with the Federal Judiciary. Indeed, Madison and the Committee of Detail proposed that the Supreme Court should have the power to determine impeachments. Despite these proposals, the Convention ultimately decided that the Senate would have "the sole Power to Try all Impeachments." According to Alexander Hamilton, the Senate was the "most fit depositary of this important trust" because its members are representatives of the people. The Supreme Court was not the proper body, because the Framers, "doubted whether the members of that tribunal would, at all times, be endowed with so eminent a portion of fortitude as would be called for in the execution of so difficult a task" or whether the Court "would possess the degree of credit and authority" to carry out its judgment if it conflicted with the accusation brought by the Legislature—the people's representative. In addition, the Framers believed the Court was too small in number: "The awful discretion, which a court of impeachments must necessarily have, to doom to honor or to infamy the most confidential and the most distinguished characters of the community, forbids the commitment of the trust to a small number of persons."

There are two additional reasons why the Judiciary, and the Supreme Court in particular, were not chosen to have any role in impeachments. First, the Framers recognized that most likely there would be two sets of proceedings for individuals who commit impeachable offenses—the impeachment trial and a separate criminal trial. In fact, the Constitution explicitly provides for two separate proceedings. The Framers deliberately separated the two forums to avoid raising the specter of bias and to ensure independent judgments. . . .

Certainly judicial review of the Senate's "trial" would introduce the same risk of bias as would participation in the trial itself.

Second, judicial review would be inconsistent with the Framers' insistence that our system be one of checks and balances. In our constitutional system, impeachment was designed to be the *only* check on the Judicial Branch by the Legislature. . . .

Judicial involvement in impeachment proceedings, even if only for purposes of judicial review, is counterintuitive, because it would eviscerate the "important constitutional check" placed on the Judiciary by the Framers. Nixon's argument would place final reviewing authority with respect to impeachments in the hands of the same body that the impeachment process is meant to regulate.

Nevertheless, Nixon argues that judicial review is necessary in order to place a check on the Legislature. Nixon fears that, if the Senate is given unreviewable authority to interpret the Impeachment Trial Clause, there is a grave risk that the Senate will usurp judicial power. The Framers anticipated this objection and created two constitutional safeguards to keep the Senate in check. The first safeguard is that the whole of the impeachment power is divided between the two legislative bodies, with the House given the right to accuse and the Senate given the right to judge. This split of authority, "avoids the inconvenience of making the same persons both accusers and judges; and guards against the danger of persecution from the prevalency of a factious spirit in either of those branches." The second safeguard is the two-thirds supermajority vote requirement. Hamilton explained that, "[a]s the concurrence of two-thirds of the senate will be requisite to a condemnation, the security to innocence, from this additional circumstance, will be as complete as itself can desire."

In addition to the textual commitment argument, we are persuaded that the lack of finality and the difficulty of fashioning relief counsel against justiciability. We agree with the Court of Appeals that opening the door of judicial review to the procedures used by the Senate in trying impeachments would "expose the political life of the country to months, or perhaps years, of chaos." This lack of finality would manifest itself most dramatically if the President were impeached. The legitimacy of any successor, and hence his effectiveness, would be impaired severely, not merely while the judicial process was running its course, but during any retrial that a differently constituted Senate might conduct if its first judgment of conviction were invalidated. Equally uncertain is the question of what relief a court may give other than simply setting aside the judgment of conviction. Could it order the reinstatement of a convicted federal judge, or order Congress to create an additional judgeship if the seat had been filled in the interim? . . .

In the case before us, there is no separate provision of the Constitution which could be defeated by allowing the Senate final authority to determine the meaning of the word "try" in the Impeachment Trial Clause. We agree with Nixon that courts possess power to review either legislative or executive action that transgresses identifiable textual limits. As we have made clear, "whether the action of [either the Legislative or Executive Branch] exceeds whatever authority has been committed is itself a delicate exercise in constitutional interpretation, and is a responsibility of this Court as ultimate interpreter of the Constitution." But we conclude, after exercising that delicate responsibility, that the word "try" in the Impeachment Clause does not provide an identifiable textual limit on the authority which is committed to the Senate.

For the foregoing reasons, the judgment of the Court of Appeals is

*Affirmed.*

JUSTICE STEVENS, concurring.

For me, the debate about the strength of the inferences to be drawn from the use of the words "sole" and "try" is far less significant than the central fact that the Framers decided to assign the impeachment power to the Legislative Branch. The disposition of the impeachment of Samuel Chase in 1805 demonstrated that the Senate is fully conscious of the profound importance of that assignment, and nothing in the subsequent history of the Senate's exercise of this extraordinary power suggests otherwise. . . . Accordingly, the wise policy of judicial restraint, coupled with the potential anomalies associated with a contrary view, provide a sufficient justification for my agreement with the views of THE CHIEF JUSTICE.

One theme is consistent in the formulation of the Court's "nonconstitutional rules of restraint," as Chief Justice Warren described them in *Flast v. Cohen:* the

notion that the rules of judicial procedure operate as an institutional constraint on the power of the federal judiciary and are unrelated to the substance of the Court's work. When we consider the flexible nature of the Court's approach to these self-imposed restraints on the exercise of judicial power, is there a stronger relationship between the substance and process of law than the Court is willing to acknowledge? Or do you believe that the Court's rules to guide the exercise of federal judicial power are motivated less by substantive concerns and more by the need to respect the position and prestige of the courts in the separation of powers?

## FOR FURTHER READING

Bickel, Alexander. *The Least Dangerous Branch*. New Haven, Conn.: Yale University Press, 1962.

Burgess, Susan R. *Contest for Constitutional Authority*. Lawrence: University Press of Kansas, 1992.

Burt, Robert A. *The Constitution in Conflict*. Cambridge, Mass.: Harvard University Press, 1992.

Clinton, Robert Lowery. *Marbury v. Madison and Judicial Review*. Lawrence: University Press of Kansas, 1989.

Fisher, Louis. *Constitutional Dialogues*. Princeton, N.J.: Princeton University Press, 1988.

Frankfurter, Felix and James M. Landis. *The Business of the Supreme Court: A Study in the Federal Judicial System*. New York: Macmillan, 1928.

Gillman, Howard and Cornell W. Clayton. *The Supreme Court in American Politics*. Lawrence: University Press of Kansas, 1999.

Keynes, Edward and Randall K. Miller. *The Court v. Congress*. Durham, N.C.: Duke University Press, 1989.

Lasser, William. *The Limits of Judicial Power: The Supreme Court in American Politics*. Chapel Hill, N.C.: University of North Carolina Press, 1988.

O'Brien, David. *Storm Center: The Supreme Court in American Politics*. New York: W. W. Norton, 1996.

Schwartz, Bernard. *The Ascent of Pragmatism: The Burger Court in Action*. Reading, Mass.: Addison-Wesley, 1990.

Sunstein, Cass R. *One Case at a Time: Judicial Minimalism and the Supreme Court*. Cambridge, Mass.: Harvard University Press, 1999.

Warren, Charles. *The Supreme Court in United States History*. Boston: Little, Brown, 1935.

Wolfe, Christopher. *The Rise of Modern Judicial Review*. New York: Basic Books, 1986.

Wright, Benjamin F. *The Growth of American Constitutional Law*. New York: Holt, 1942.

# 4 Legislative Power

In October 1997 the Government Reform and Oversight Committee of the House of Representatives launched an investigation into the fund-raising practices of President Bill Clinton's successful 1996 reelection campaign. Based on evidence it had received suggesting that much of President Clinton's $113-million reelection fund came from illegal sources—including foreign governments, tax-exempt organizations, and "paper" corporations designed to channel funds otherwise barred by federal campaign finance law—the committee claimed that a full-scale congressional investigation was warranted to expose a fund-raising scandal that it alleged was unparalleled in the history of American presidential campaigns. Over time the investigation expanded to include charges that President Clinton's campaign managers paid "hush" money to former administration officials in exchange for their silence on the committee's inquires.

Congress later broadened the investigation to inquire whether the president, while governor of Arkansas, and his wife, Hillary Rodham Clinton, then a partner in a prominent Little Rock law firm, used their power to secure a series of questionable loans to engage in real estate speculation. Finally, Congress took up the most controversial investigation of them all, the one that resulted in President Clinton's impeachment by the House in December 1998: Did the president have a sexual relationship with a White House intern and then violate federal law by encouraging her to lie about it?

By the time Congress had concluded its impeachment inquiry of President Clinton in January 1999, including his Senate acquittal on all charges, more than forty committees in the House and Senate had con-

ducted inquiries into the alleged improprieties of his administration. The results, however, paled in comparison to the time, money, and effort that had gone into them. The president remained in office, amid record job-approval ratings. His wife's popularity surged right along with her husband's, so much so that she was encouraged to run for the Senate as the Democratic candidate from New York—and did! Meanwhile, two of the Clintons' most outspoken congressional critics, Representatives Dan Burton (R–Ind.) and Robert Livingston (R–La.), were mired in their own sex scandals. Livingston resigned from the House, even though he had been designated its new Speaker; Burton kept his seat but quietly faded into the background.

But while the Clintons could revel in their opponents' public embarrassment and insist that the entire episode was motivated by the Republican leadership's desire to smear the president, there was nothing, from a constitutional perspective, they could have done about it. The Constitution does not expressly authorize Congress to conduct investigations into governmental or public affairs, but the Supreme Court has recognized such a power since 1881 and expanded upon it ever since. The Court considers Congress's power "of inquiry—with process to enforce it—[as] an essential and auxiliary to the legislative function" and thus implied by the very nature of the legislature's role in the separation of powers. Moreover, although a congressional investigation must have some legislative purpose, the investigation need only demonstrate the "potential" for corrective legislation on the matter under review, with no need to specify a "predictable end result."[1]

A congressional committee can conduct an investigation that is motivated more by electoral or political concerns than policy goals and remain squarely within its constitutional prerogative. During the second term of the Reagan administration (1985–1989) and first term of the Bush administration (1989–1993), Republicans accused the Democratic-controlled House of "criminalizing political differences" in their conduct of the Iran-Contra hearings. That inquiry stemmed from a scandal involving a series of alleged criminal violations by executive branch officials that ranged from illegal arms sales to foreign countries to covert assistance for rebel forces—the *Contras*—attempting to topple the Nicaraguan government. As partisan as many Republicans considered this investigation, they were nonetheless left with no constitutional defense against it.[2]

The Constitution also protects the rights of members of Congress to engage in vigorous speechmaking and public debate without fear of legal reprisal, as long as their statements bear some tangential relationship to legislative business. Members are thus free to say, quite literally, anything they want in floor speeches, committee hearings, or public statements for inclusion into the Congressional Record without running afoul of the Court's interpretation of the Speech or Debate Clause of Article I. Whatever members choose to say about each other, the president, executive branch officials, or private citizens in the context of legislative business is protected from legal action.

The power of Congress to investigate a vast range of issues and concerns in the name of the public interest represents just a fraction of the enormous power and influence it wields in its function as the legislative branch of government. And legislative power—the power to make and enact laws—is the most basic and essential feature of democratic government. The Constitution vested in Congress, the most politically responsive and publicly accountable branch of the national government, far more direct power over the lives of American citizens than it gave to the executive and judicial branches. Article I grants to Congress, in seventeen separate clauses, specific legislative authority that is sweeping in its scope. These powers include, for example, the power to tax and spend, to regulate commerce, to declare war, to establish federal courts, to confer patents, to borrow money, and to raise and maintain standing armies. Moreover, Congress is permitted to make all laws "necessary and proper" to carry out its legislative function, an expansive grant of authority it has used with great effect to extend the reach of its power and influence in the American constitutional design.

To emphasize the democratic roots of the new Constitution, the Framers made the House of Representatives, whose members' two-year terms were—and remain—the shortest for any elected federal officeholders, the only division of the national government directly elected by the general population. Until the ratification of the Seventeenth Amendment in 1913, which made Senate elections direct but did not change the six-year term, state legislatures, not the people, nominated and elected senators. The Framers' decision to create a bicameral legislature further reflects the intricate constitutional architecture in which the separation of powers emerges as the lead instrument with which to guard against the concentration of excessive authority in any one branch of government. The choice to create separate election rules and terms of service for each chamber of Congress reflects both the trust and suspicion the Framers placed in the concept of majority rule. The Framers believed that the distribution of different responsibilities and commensurate powers to the House and the Senate would provide an internal check on the exercise of legislative power, with the Senate—"the great anchor of the Government," in James Madison's words—positioned to curb the potential excesses of the more democratic House.[3]

The constitutional foundation of legislative power thus rests upon a paradox. The Framers granted more sheer political power to Congress than to the other branches of government but divided the responsibilities of the House and Senate so as to reflect their different constituent obligations and to promote the balance of interests. Fresh from the disaster of the Articles of Confederation, the Framers envisioned Congress as the institutional centerpiece of a strong national government and vested that body with the appropriate legislative power. On the other hand, the need to constrain the power of Congress, both to ensure the Constitution's ratification and to promote the objective of constitutional equilibrium, led the Framers to limit legislative authority by enumerating in unparalleled detail both its substance and scope. The insertion of the Necessary and

Proper Clause into Article I, Section 8, suggests that the Framers intended for congressional power to extend far as well as wide. But the Convention's rejection of a similar but even broader clause intimates that this most democratic and powerful branch of government needed firm constitutional limits.[4]

Consider, too, the nature of Congress's relationship to the other branches of government. Unlike either the executive or judicial branches, Congress alone is responsible for its staffing, internal affairs, and management. Contrast that with, for example, the dependence of the executive on Congress to approve federal judicial appointees, cabinet-level officers, and foreign ambassadors. Congress also has the sole power to create the laws governing the impeachment, judgment, and punishment of all government officials, including federal judges. The Court has held that these rules are not subject to judicial review.[5] Congress thus enjoys a degree of institutional independence and control over the other branches that is nowhere reciprocated in the Constitution.

But as the Framers also intended, the executive and judicial branches have real and substantial power to check the core function of legislative power—the power to enact laws. In addition to the power to veto congressional legislation, the president is authorized to enforce federal law through the issuance of regulations and executive orders, many of which do not require legislative approval. In recent years the Court has increased the president's role in the lawmaking process by declaring unconstitutional "legislative vetoes." The legislative veto is a rule of nonconstitutional origin that permitted Congress to negate the enactment and enforcement of some form of congressional power it had delegated to the executive branch that was often included in congressional legislation.[6]

The courts, of course, have the power to restrain Congress through their power of judicial review, an instrument it has used with great success to alter the balance of policymaking within the American constitutional design. And in what is perhaps the most express limitation placed on the exercise of legislative power, the Bill of Rights prohibits Congress from passing laws that establish religion or limit the rights of religious conscience; seize property for the public domain without just compensation; take life or liberty without due

process of law; require individuals to testify against themselves in federal criminal proceedings; and suppress the freedom of speech, press, and assembly. Subsequent judicial decisions would bring alive the parchment promises of the Bill of Rights, as the Court, since the early 1960s, has interpreted these limits on popular rule in terms stricter than the Framers might ever have imagined.

Congress also has assumed the singular responsibility to enforce civil and constitutional rights once denied or ignored by the executive and judicial branches, as well as the various states, through several amendments added to the Constitution since the passage of the Bill of Rights. The most well-known examples of the modern use of legislative power to enforce constitutional rights previously denied or abridged are the Thirteenth, Fourteenth, and Fifteenth Amendments. Ratified in the aftermath of the Civil War, these three amendments, which the former Confederate states were required to approve for readmission into the Union, abolished slavery and extended civil and political rights to African Americans. By giving Congress the authority to enforce substantive provisions against the recalcitrant states, the authors of the Civil War amendments further tipped the federal balance in favor of national power. Since then, several amendments have given Congress the power to enforce a range of constitutional rights established through the amendment process, including the Nineteenth (establishing the right of women to vote), the Twenty-fourth (abolishing the poll tax), and the Twenty-sixth (lowering the voting age to eighteen) Amendments. That the Constitution both limits and empowers Congress on matters of such foundational social and political import demonstrates the search for equilibrium that remains a constant theme in the American constitutional design.

Our discussion thus far should make clear the fact that legislative power derives from multiple sources within the constitutional framework. It is important to summarize here the different forms of legislative power granted to Congress and the constitutional sources from which these powers are derived. Doing so will help us correct the common misperception that Congress is permitted, within the constitutional limits established by the Court, to enact all reasonable rules that command the support of popular majorities. For Congress to remain true to its position in the American constitutional structure, that branch must demonstrate how its decision to act is rooted in the four basic forms of legislative power established in Article I. These include powers that are expressly *enumerated,* powers that are *implied,* powers that derive from Congress's responsibility to *enforce constitutional amendments,* and powers that are *inherent* in congressional authority.

The preceding discussion of judicial power (see Chapter 3) pointed out the struggle of the Court to define the essence of its own power and that which it possesses over the other branches of government, a task that requires the Court to balance numerous and often opposing constitutional and political concerns. Determining the water's edge of legislative power is fraught with similar difficulties. Just as the Court's recognition and exercise of the power of judicial review have altered the balance of power between the branches and levels of the American governmental system, so have its efforts to interpret and define the power of Congress under Article I. Decisions that affect the balance of power within the national government or alter the existing allocation of responsibilities within the federal structure have important consequences for the organization and operation of American government because the Constitution creates a zero-sum distribution of power among the government's constituent parts.

The remainder of this chapter examines the constitutional development of Article I legislative power on two major fronts: the extent to which the congressional exercise of this power has conformed to its recognized sources of constitutional authority and the power of Congress to organize and manage its internal affairs. The feature that separates our examination of legislative power from our discussion of judicial and executive power is the degree to which the Constitution clarifies in remarkable detail the rights and powers of Congress. Even so, Congress, from the early nineteenth century forward, has found both its power and independence tested in crucial litigation before the Court. Some of these cases have involved challenges to the boundaries of Congress's power to legislate under its Article I, Section 8, mandate. Others have centered on the baseline of its implied power under the Necessary and Proper Clause. Still others have focused on Congress's power to define and enforce the substantive provisions of constitutional amendments. Regardless of the arena of conflict, the Court's decisions on the numerous dimensions of legislative power have had a far-reaching impact on both the form and function of American government.

## The Foundation and Scope of Legislative Power

Article I states that "[a]ll legislative Powers herein granted shall be vested in a Congress of the United States." Here, as elsewhere in the Constitution, this authoritative command is not self-executing. However tempted one is to suggest that some facets of legislative power are easier to understand than others, the struggle between the Court and Congress over the substance and exercise of this power demonstrates otherwise. Even when the Constitution is clear that certain powers belong to Congress and no one else, the debate continues over the substance of those powers and whether they have been carried out in a constitutional manner. Similarly, the exercise of certain legislative power may well be implied or inherent in congressional authority. Still, determining the nature and definition of the extent of this power requires an act of constitutional interpretation. How the Court has interpreted the power of Congress to exercise the Constitution's grant of legislative power is the focus of the remainder of this section.

### Enumerated and Implied Powers

Constitutional law casebooks, as a general rule, distinguish between those rights and powers specifically set out in the Constitution (enumerated) and those that have no such textual anchor (unenumerated or implied) but are thought to exist as a matter of custom, tradition, or intent. In our discussion of the different approaches to constitutional interpretation in Chapter 2, we saw that two of the major points of disagreement centered on whether the Constitution confers or recognizes "unenumerated" rights and whether the Court is authoritatively positioned to identify and protect these rights. The thread of that discussion goes something like this: We know that the Constitution recognizes, for example, freedom of speech, freedom of religion, and the right to counsel because the text makes explicit reference to these rights. On the other hand, the right to abortion, sexual privacy, freedom from unwanted medical treatment, and "home schooling" for elementary and secondary-level children are often treated as unenumerated rights because they cannot be located in the constitutional text. This distinction suggests that enumerated rights are more genuine because of their stated nature, whereas unenumerated rights often reflect the policy preferences of judges using their power to impose rights rejected by political and social majorities.[7]

But numerous constitutional scholars have also argued that the supposed distinction between enumerated and unenumerated rights is, in fact, a fictitious one. All constitutional rights, privileges, and powers are the result of a process of interpretation that requires the use of principles external to the Constitution. This view stands in contrast to that of legal formalists, who argue that the answers to constitutional questions can be found in the text of the Constitution. Certainly, the Constitution never mentions a general right of privacy, much less the right to abortion or the right to purchase and use birth control. But the Constitution also never mentions the right to engage in ritualistic animal sacrifice, the right to burn the American flag, or the right to a state-funded insanity defense. Nevertheless, the Court has ruled that the Constitution protects all these rights.[8]

How we determine which rights the Constitution protects may well depend on the rights and liberties we believe the Constitution ought to protect. Here it is important to understand, as legal philosopher Ronald Dworkin points out, the difference between making *references* to the Constitution and *interpreting* the Constitution.[9] Defending or attacking the existence of a constitutional right or power simply by pointing to a clause or provision that appears to have a suitable linguistic or contextual reference is not the same thing as locating a right or power through the process of constitutional interpretation. A similar challenge is posed in the interpretation of Article I legislative power. To say that Congress is authorized to legislate in those areas specified by the seventeen specific clauses of Article I, Section 8, is, on the surface, indisputable. Does Article I alone allow us to conclude that the Constitution is clearer on the meaning of the congressional exercise of power under the Commerce Clause than it is on the power of Congress to legislate under the Necessary and Proper Clause? Or does Article I require us to acknowledge that the scope of legislative power under both

clauses has derived from the Court's interpretation of those clauses and not from the text alone.

Over the course of American constitutional development, the Court has enumerated the legislative powers of Congress through the interpretation of both its specific and general clauses. That the Commerce Clause permits Congress to forbid racial discrimination by private businesses, establish a minimum-wage requirement, outlaw child labor, and regulate occupational health and safety standards is not because such authorization leaps from the constitutional text. Rather, such power is the result of abstract principles and political considerations applied to the Constitution through the process of constitutional interpretation.

Such has also been the case in the Court's interpretation of the Necessary and Proper Clause. Even the premise that all constitutional rights and powers, regardless of their textual origin, are enumerated does not mean that certain provisions and clauses do not pose greater challenges in their interpretation than do others. From the moment it was proposed in the convention, the Necessary and Proper Clause generated a level of debate that certainly ranks among the most contentious of the founding era. Federalists and advocates of broad national power, such as Alexander Hamilton, maintained that the Necessary and Proper Clause was essential to the exercise of legislative power. The clause would allow Congress to retain those "resultant" and "implied" powers that were as much a component of its authority as the powers enumerated in Article I, Section 8. Resultant powers are derived from the general grants of power the Constitution made to the national government, such as the right to assert control over conquered territories. Far more important, in Hamilton's view, was the belief that Congress needed to retain a broad grant of authority to execute both its express and implied legislative power. Such was the purpose of the Necessary and Proper Clause. Hamilton admitted that it was difficult to identify the precise origin and stopping point of this broad, unstated grant of congressional power. He offered the following rationale as the basis for a constitutional test:

> This criterion is the *end,* to which the measure [of Congress] relates as a *mean.* If the *end* be clearly comprehended within any of the specified powers, and if the measure have

an obvious relation to that *end,* and is not forbidden by any particular provision of the Constitution, it may safely be deemed to come within the compass of the national authority.[10]

James Madison and Thomas Jefferson did not share Hamilton's interpretation of the Necessary and Proper Clause. In the first major flash point over the meaning of the clause, Madison contended that Hamilton's proposal in 1790 to charter a national bank was unconstitutional because it had no textual source of authority. Madison believed that if the Constitution were meant to authorize such power, the Framers would have granted it to Congress in specific terms. Madison noted that the convention had rejected his proposal that Congress be given this power. In light of that experience, he argued that the Necessary and Proper Clause could not confer upon Congress a power that the convention had rejected just three years before.

Jefferson also opposed Hamilton's bill and offered a criticism even more trenchant than that of Madison, who had once been allied with his former Federalist compatriot on many of the key components of constitutional nationalism. Jefferson believed that Congress had absolutely no constitutional power to charter a bank. Such a claim was nowhere provided in the enumerated powers granted to Congress and could not be inferred from any resultant or implied power derived from the Necessary and Proper Clause. Moreover, Jefferson argued, neither the Necessary and Proper Clause nor any other provision of the Constitution conferred any legislative power upon Congress not specifically set out in Article I, Section 8. To do anything under the Necessary and Proper Clause, Congress had to demonstrate that the enactment of a law was truly "necessary" to the execution of the branch's enumerated responsibilities. Only then, and assuming that such a law was "indispensable" to enable Congress to carry out its understood responsibilities, did the Necessary and Proper Clause provide a constitutional basis for the exercise of congressional power.[11]

In 1791, Congress voted to incorporate the First National Bank of the United States. President George Washington, who had commissioned the opinions of Jefferson and Hamilton to assist him in determining the constitutionality of such an act, signed the law authoriz-

ing its twenty-year charter shortly thereafter. Controversy over the bank faded from the front and focus of national political debate after the initial confrontation between the Hamiltonian nationalists and the Jefferson-led advocates of decentralization and states' rights. The controversy soon reemerged, however, upon the expiration of the bank's charter in 1811. This time, Congress, dominated by Democratic-Republicans loyal to now-President Madison and Jefferson and under pressure from private banking interests, voted not to recharter the bank. This decision, however, proved to be disastrous, as the United States entered the War of 1812 without a central banking system. The nation learned the hard way that state banks were poorly positioned to distribute funds between and among different banks and regions. The sheer number of state banks, the number of which had grown from 3 to 143 by 1812, also prevented central management of the nation's debts. Lessons learned from a disorganized banking structure in a time of crisis led Congress to reauthorize the Second National Bank of the United States in 1815.[12]

After their initial opposition to Hamilton's 1790 proposal, neither Madison nor Jefferson challenged the constitutional authority of Congress to establish a national banking system. In fact, President Madison signed the 1815 congressional act into law, extending the Second National Bank's charter for another twenty years. Opposition to the reminted central banking system nonetheless continued among members of Madison and Jefferson's own Democratic-Republican party, as well as within several states. Individuals such as Virginia's Spencer Roane persisted in their criticism and outright defiance of the 1815 law, which they viewed as a cover for the aggrandizement of national power by Congress and the Court. This atmosphere of distrust between nationalists and states' rights advocates was exacerbated when public reports alleged that the Second Bank's operations were rife with fraud, embezzlement, and mismanagement. Several states, determined to build additional support for a return to a decentralized banking system, attempted to drive the local branches of the national bank out of business by imposing taxes on their operations.

Maryland was among the more aggressive of the mid-Atlantic and Southern states that chafed at the Second National Bank's existence and sought to bring it down by any means. In February 1818 the Maryland Assembly had enacted a law that required the Baltimore branch of the national bank to purchase stamped paper from the state, on which the bank's notes were printed, or pay the state a $15,000 fee to remain in business. James W. McCulloch, the cashier, refused to either buy the stamped paper or pay the fee, which he knew was not an instrument for the state to raise revenue, but part of a well-designed plan to force the bank to leave the state. As transparent as the Maryland law was, it was less punitive than similar measures passed by Tennessee, Georgia, North Carolina, Kentucky, and Ohio, whose fees to operate within the state ran upward of $60,000. Indiana and Illinois refused to permit the national bank to establish local offices.[13]

McCulloch's response was exactly what Maryland authorities had anticipated. It filed suit against the Second National Bank, naming McCulloch as the defendant, in Baltimore County Court. The court entered a judgment on behalf of Maryland, which was confirmed on appeal to the state supreme court. The Court's recent decision in *Hunter* v. *Martin's Lessee* (1816), which upheld Section 25 of the 1789 Judiciary Act giving the federal courts the power of judicial review in cases involving state laws that raised federal constitutional questions, combined with the importance of the constitutional questions presented in the bank dispute, guaranteed that the Court would agree to hear McCulloch's appeal. In late February and early March 1819, the Court entertained almost two weeks of oral arguments, with Daniel Webster and William Pinkney, two of the greatest lawyers of the nineteenth century, representing the federal bank and the state, respectively.

Three days after it concluded oral arguments, the Court handed down *McCulloch* v. *Maryland* (1819). In a unanimous opinion, which included five members appointed by Democratic-Republican Presidents Jefferson and Madison, Chief Justice Marshall settled two of the most important questions concerning the still-fledgling nation's constitutional and political structure. First, in direct homage to Hamilton's arguments on behalf of the national bank's constitutionality, Marshall ruled that the Constitution conferred upon Congress the discretion that permitted it to make laws that were "necessary" and "proper" to allow it to carry out its "great" powers and responsibilities. Creation of a national bank-

ing system was firmly within the scope of congressional power. In a passage that ranks with any Marshall—or any other justice—ever wrote for clarity, importance, and constitutional legacy, the chief justice wrote of Congress's lawmaking power:

> Let the end be legitimate, let it be within the scope of the constitution, and all means which are appropriate, which are plainly adapted to that end, which are not prohibited, but consist with the letter and spirit of the constitution, are constitutional.[14]

Compare the logic and phrasing of Marshall's opinion here with Hamilton's earlier statement on the relationship between legislative means and ends. Is the similarity more than coincidental?

In addition to his unequivocal endorsement of the Federalist theory of the Necessary and Proper Clause's conferral of "implied power" to Congress, Marshall awarded a second, and equally important, victory to the advocates of constitutional nationalism. To uphold Maryland's tax on the national bank would, in the chief justice's view, invert the constitutional design of American federalism, which made the national government supreme over the states. "[T]here is a plain repugnance," he wrote, "in conferring on one government a power to control the constitutional measures of another, which other, with respect to those very measures, is declared to be supreme."[15] In *McCulloch* the Court built upon the foundation laid down in *Marbury* v. *Madison* (1803) and *Martin's* that articulated a precise vision of a strong national government, with Congress as the centrifugal force, as a fundamental principle of the American constitutional structure.

Since *McCulloch* the Court has rarely invalidated the exercise of congressional power under the Necessary and Proper Clause. To offer just a handful of examples, Congress has relied upon its implied powers to enter and assume control over national fiscal and monetary policies, establish the basis for its eminent domain power, enact remedial legislation expanding federal constitutional and civil rights, and create the military draft.[16] Congress has exercised its power under the Necessary and Proper Clause in a decidedly Hamiltonian fashion. It has used the clause as a source of constitutional authority to engage in a wide range of lawmaking activity that often bears little more than a tangential relationship to the enumerated sources of its Article I, Section 8, legislative power.

*McCulloch,* though, settled just one side of the question on the foundation and scope of congressional power. Still unanswered even after Chief Justice Marshall's landmark opinion was the substance and breadth of one of the most important express powers conferred upon Congress by the Constitution: the power to regulate commerce. The Framers considered the Articles of Confederation's omission of an effective grant of national power to Congress to regulate interstate and foreign commerce a major flaw that needed firm correction in the Constitution. Regulation of such commerce was among the least divisive issues introduced during the convention and debated in the immediate ratification period. Prior to the convention, James Madison had written Thomas Jefferson that "[m]ost of our political evils may be traced to our commercial ones."[17] Madison, along with Alexander Hamilton, later built upon that theme in *The Federalist Papers.* Each noted, in different papers, the economic and political stability that several European countries had achieved by centralizing the "superintending authority" over reciprocal trade arrangements between domestic and foreign "sovereignties" and the need to correct such deficiencies under the Constitution.[18]

Consensus on the need to establish national control over interstate and foreign commerce did not resolve the extent to which the Constitution authorized Congress to regulate commercial matters that the states considered as intrastate or to offer a precise definition on what constituted "interstate commerce." The Anti-Federalists had offered little opposition to the need for a national commerce power. Nonetheless, that stance did not eliminate the suspicion still residual among their Democratic-Republican successors of a Congress and Supreme Court hell-bent on dissolving the borders between national and state lines of authority, with the former poised to triumph over the latter. Acknowledging that Congress ought to have the power to create uniform commerce and trade rules that prevented state interference with legitimate national needs was one thing. But assuming that this power permitted Congress to interfere with intrastate commercial matters was another issue. These concerns ranged, on the one hand, from the regulation of production and distribution in local

manufacturing to, in the case of the Southern states, the fear of Northern-led efforts to eliminate slavery.

In *Gibbons* v. *Ogden* (1824), the Court, as in *McCulloch,* was confronted with the confluence of two great constitutional issues. The first was the substance and scope of congressional power to regulate interstate and foreign commerce; the second was the power of the states to make laws in the new American federal structure on matters deemed intrastate and local in nature. Having established a broad constitutional domain for Congress in which to legislate under the Necessary and Proper Clause, the Court, in *Gibbons,* was now positioned to complete the explication of the nature of congressional power under Article I, Section 8, to carry out its legislative function. Here again, as in *Marbury, Martin's,* and *McCulloch,* Chief Justice Marshall was well aware that "he stood at another major constitutional crossroad."[19] How the Court interpreted the power of Congress to regulate commerce would have a profound and substantial impact on the social, economic, and political development of the Republic for generations to come. In what is perhaps his last great opinion, Chief Justice Marshall entered another landmark triumph for the vision of constitutional nationalism he had begun with *Marbury.*

But Marshall alone did not solidify the power of Congress to define and regulate interstate commerce in the broadest possible terms. The stakes were without precedent. How the Court ruled would determine the economic and political framework within which the next generation of American business, particularly communications and transportation, would begin its aggressive commercial expansion into under-served states and the still-undeveloped territories. The ruling would also affect the international trading position of American business. The Court was unanimous in its support for Marshall's broad nationalist interpretation of congressional power to regulate commerce, an outcome that surprised most of the parties involved in *Gibbons* because the case involved a challenge to the monopoly rights awarded to former New York Governor Robert R. Livingston and Robert Fulton, an inventor, who together launched the first reliable and successful commercial steamboat in the United States. Theirs was a fortuitous partnership of social privilege, political power, and scientific brilliance.

Fulton had acquired two United States patents to protect this revolutionary enterprise. Rather than seek refuge in science for their innovation, though, he and Livingston secured monopoly rights from the New York legislature that permitted them to bar from state waterways all steamboats whose owners had not obtained a license from Fulton and Livingston to operate. A powerful band of Republican legislators, who enjoyed close political ties with the Democratic-Republican majority on the Court, was instrumental in helping the partners secure their monopoly. Moreover, Congress had not passed comprehensive legislation that enjoined states from granting monopolistic licenses over activities such as navigation. The only legislation on the books was an obscure 1793 law that permitted Congress to grant federal licenses to operate on coastal waterways. This situation raised the question of whether the Court was prepared to issue a landmark definition of congressional commerce power in a case where Congress had not really asserted that power in earnest.[20]

The Court stunned those constitutional nationalists who feared that Marshall would be unable to persuade his colleagues to endorse a broad conception of congressional commerce power. For the Court, Marshall endorsed an interpretation of the Commerce Clause that gave Congress near-exclusive control over all interstate commerce, writing that "[t]his power, like all others vested in [C]ongress, is complete in itself, may be exercised to its utmost extent, and acknowledges no limitations, other than are prescribed in the constitution."[21] The Court held that the federal Coastal Licensing Act of 1793, upon which Thomas Gibbons had relied to skirt the monopolistic terms of the New York law and operate his steamboat between New York City and the New Jersey coast, superseded all state laws to the contrary. "Commerce among the states," wrote Marshall, "cannot stop at the external boundary line of each state, but may be introduced into the interior."[22]

The Court did not rule that Congress possessed "complete and entire" control over all commerce that originated within state boundaries, a position for which Gibbons's lawyer, the great Daniel Webster, had argued, but just that found within the stream of interstate commerce. Even though Thomas Jefferson later bemoaned Gibbons as another step toward the "federal usurpation of all the rights reserved to the states,"[23] Marshall, as

much for prudent political reasons as for constitutional logic, left room for the state regulation of commerce that did "not extend to or affect other states."[24] Still, *Gibbons* was an undisputed triumph for the forces of constitutional nationalism in general and congressional power in particular. Together, *McCulloch* and *Gibbons* form the classic exposition of congressional legislative power under Article I in the American constitutional structure.

## McCulloch v. Maryland
### 17 U.S. 316 (1819)

*McCulloch* ranks with *Marbury* v. *Madison* (1803), which established the power of judicial review, and *Gibbons* v. *Ogden* (1824), which outlined the baseline of congressional power to regulate commerce, as one of John Marshall's greatest opinions as chief justice. Some even consider Marshall's opinion his most important, as it had an enormous impact on the future of national power and illustrated the chief justice's singular talent for stately political argument cloaked in the language of law.

The Court's opinion was unanimous. Chief Justice Marshall delivered the opinion of the Court. Justice Todd did not participate.

▼▲▼

MARSHALL, CHIEF JUSTICE, delivered the opinion of the Court.

In the case now to be determined, the defendant, a sovereign State, denies the obligation of a law enacted by the legislature of the Union, and the plaintiff, on his part, contests the validity of an act which has been passed by the legislature of that State. The Constitution of our country, in its most interesting and vital parts, is to be considered, the conflicting powers of the Government of the Union and of its members, as marked in that Constitution, are to be discussed, and an opinion given which may essentially influence the great operations of the Government. No tribunal can approach such a question without a deep sense of its importance, and of the awful responsibility involved in its decision. . . . On the Supreme Court of the United States has the Constitution of our country devolved this important duty.

The first question made in the cause is—has Congress power to incorporate a bank? . . .

The government proceeds directly from the people; is "ordained and established" in the name of the people, and is declared to be ordained, "in order to form a more perfect union, establish justice, insure domestic tranquillity, and secure the blessings of liberty to themselves and to their posterity." The assent of the States in their sovereign capacity is implied in calling a convention, and thus submitting that instrument to the people. But the people were at perfect liberty to accept or reject it, and their act was final. It required not the affirmance, and could not be negatived, by the State Governments. The Constitution, when thus adopted, was of complete obligation, and bound the State sovereignties. . . .

The Government of the Union then (whatever may be the influence of this fact on the case) is, emphatically and truly, a Government of the people. In form and in substance, it emanates from them. Its powers are granted by them, and are to be exercised directly on them, and for their benefit.

This Government is acknowledged by all to be one of enumerated powers. The principle that it can exercise only the powers granted to it would seem too apparent to have required to be enforced by all those arguments which its enlightened friends, while it was depending before the people, found it necessary to urge; that principle is now universally admitted. But the question respecting the extent of the powers actually granted is perpetually arising, and will probably continue to arise so long as our system shall exist.

In discussing these questions, the conflicting powers of the General and State Governments must be brought into view, and the supremacy of their respective laws, when they are in opposition, must be settled.

If any one proposition could command the universal assent of mankind, we might expect it would be this—that the Government of the Union, though limited in its powers, is supreme within its sphere of action. This would seem to result necessarily from its nature. It is the Government of all; its powers are delegated by all; it represents all, and acts for all. Though any one State may be willing to control its operations, no State is willing to allow others to control them. The nation, on those subjects on which it can act, must necessarily bind its component parts. But this question is not left to mere reason; the people have, in express terms, decided it by saying, "this Constitution, and the laws of the United States, which shall be made in pursuance thereof," "shall be the supreme law of the land," and by requiring that the members of the State legislatures and the officers of the executive and judicial departments of the States shall take the oath of fidelity to it. The Government of the United States, then, though limited in its powers, is supreme, and its laws, when made in pursuance of the Constitution, form the supreme law of the land, "anything in the Constitution or laws of any State to the contrary notwithstanding."

Among the enumerated powers, we do not find that of establishing a bank or creating a corporation. But there is no phrase in the instrument which, like the Articles of Confederation, excludes incidental or implied powers and which requires that everything granted shall be expressly and minutely described. Even the 10th Amendment, which was framed for the purpose of quieting the excessive jealousies which had been excited, omits the word "expressly," and declares only that the powers "not delegated to the United States, nor prohibited to the States, are reserved to the States or to the people," thus leaving the question whether the particular power which may become the subject of contest has been delegated to the one Government, or prohibited to the other, to depend on a fair construction of the whole instrument. The men who drew and adopted this amendment had experienced the embarrassments resulting from the insertion of this word in the Articles of Confederation, and probably omitted it to avoid those embarrassments. A Constitution, to contain an accurate detail of all the subdivisions of which its great powers will admit, and of all the means by which they may be carried into execution, would partake of the prolixity of a legal code, and could scarcely be embraced by the human mind. It would probably never be understood by the public. Its nature, therefore, requires that only its great outlines should be marked, its important objects designated, and the minor ingredients which compose those objects be deduced from the nature of the objects themselves. That this idea was entertained by the framers of the American Constitution is not only to be inferred from the nature of the instrument, but from the language. Why else were some of the limitations found in the 9th section of the 1st article introduced? It is also in some degree warranted by their having omitted to use any restrictive term which might prevent its receiving a fair and just interpretation. In considering this question, then, we must never forget that it is a *Constitution* we are expounding.

Although, among the enumerated powers of Government, we do not find the word "bank" or "incorporation," we find the great powers, to lay and collect taxes; to borrow money; to regulate commerce; to declare and conduct a war; and to raise and support armies and navies. The sword and the purse, all the external relations, and no inconsiderable portion of the industry of the nation are intrusted to its Government. It can never be pretended that these vast powers draw after them others of inferior importance merely because they are inferior. Such an idea can never be advanced. But it may with great reason be contended that a Government intrusted with such ample powers, on the due execution of which the happiness and prosperity of the Nation so vitally depends, must also be intrusted with ample means for their execution. The power being given, it is the interest of the Nation to facilitate its execution. It can never be their interest, and cannot be presumed to have been their intention, to clog and embarrass its execution by withholding the most appropriate means. . . .

On what foundation does this argument rest? On this alone: the power of creating a corporation is one appertaining to sovereignty, and is not expressly conferred on Congress. This is true. But all legislative powers appertain to sovereignty. The original power of giving the law on any subject whatever is a sovereign power, and if the Government of the Union is restrained from creating a corporation as a means for performing its functions, on the single reason that the creation of a corporation is an act of sovereignty, if the sufficiency of this reason be acknowledged, there would be some difficulty in sustaining the authority of Congress to pass other laws for the accomplishment of the same objects. The Government which has a right to do an act and has imposed on it the duty of performing that act must, according to the dictates of reason, be allowed to select the means, and those who contend that it may not select any appropriate means that one particular mode of effecting the object is excepted take upon themselves the burden of establishing that exception. . . .

But the Constitution of the United States has not left the right of Congress to employ the necessary means for the execution of the powers conferred on the Government to general reasoning. To its enumeration of powers is added that of making, "all laws which shall be necessary and proper for carrying into execution the foregoing powers, and all other powers vested by this Constitution in the Government of the United States or in any department thereof."

The counsel for the State of Maryland have urged various arguments to prove that this clause, though in terms a grant of power, is not so in effect, but is really restrictive of the general right which might otherwise be implied of selecting means for executing the enumerated powers . . .

[T]he argument on which most reliance is placed is drawn from that peculiar language of this clause. Congress is not empowered by it to make all laws which may have relation to the powers conferred on the Government, but such only as may be "necessary and proper" for carrying them into execution. The word "necessary" is considered as controlling the whole sentence, and as limiting the right to pass laws for the execution of the granted

powers to such as are indispensable, and without which the power would be nugatory. That it excludes the choice of means, and leaves to Congress in each case that only which is most direct and simple.

Is it true that this is the sense in which the word "necessary" is always used? Does it always import an absolute physical necessity so strong that one thing to which another may be termed necessary cannot exist without that other? We think it does not. If reference be had to its use in the common affairs of the world or in approved authors, we find that it frequently imports no more than that one thing is convenient, or useful, or essential to another. To employ the means necessary to an end is generally understood as employing any means calculated to produce the end, and not as being confined to those single means without which the end would be entirely unattainable. Such is the character of human language that no word conveys to the mind in all situations one single definite idea, and nothing is more common than to use words in a figurative sense. Almost all compositions contain words which, taken in their rigorous sense, would convey a meaning different from that which is obviously intended. It is essential to just construction that many words which import something excessive should be understood in a more mitigated sense—in that sense which common usage justifies. The word "necessary" is of this description. It has not a fixed character peculiar to itself. It admits of all degrees of comparison, and is often connected with other words which increase or diminish the impression the mind receives of the urgency it imports. . . . This word, then, like others, is used in various senses, and, in its construction, the subject, the context, the intention of the person using them are all to be taken into view.

Let this be done in the case under consideration. The subject is the execution of those great powers on which the welfare of a Nation essentially depends. It must have been the intention of those who gave these powers to insure, so far as human prudence could insure, their beneficial execution. This could not be done by confiding the choice of means to such narrow limits as not to leave it in the power of Congress to adopt any which might be appropriate, and which were conducive to the end. This provision is made in a Constitution intended to endure for ages to come, and consequently to be adapted to the various crises of human affairs. To have prescribed the means by which Government should, in all future time, execute its powers would have been to change entirely the character of the instrument and give it the properties of a legal code. It would have been an unwise attempt to provide by immutable rules for exigencies which, if foreseen at all, must have been seen dimly, and which can be best provided for as they occur. To have declared that the best means shall not be used, but those alone without which the power given would be nugatory, would have been to deprive the legislature of the capacity to avail itself of experience, to exercise its reason, and to accommodate its legislation to circumstances. . . .

Take, for example, the power "to establish post-offices and post-roads." This power is executed by the single act of making the establishment. But from this has been inferred the power and duty of carrying the mail along the post road from one post office to another. And from this implied power has again been inferred the right to punish those who steal letters from the post office, or rob the mail. It may be said with some plausibility that the right to carry the mail, and to punish those who rob it, is not indispensably necessary to the establishment of a post office and post road. This right is indeed essential to the beneficial exercise of the power, but not indispensably necessary to its existence. . . .

The baneful influence of this narrow construction on all the operations of the Government, and the absolute impracticability of maintaining it without rendering the Government incompetent to its great objects, might be illustrated by numerous examples drawn from the Constitution and from our laws. The good sense of the public has pronounced without hesitation that the power of punishment appertains to sovereignty, and may be exercised, whenever the sovereign has a right to act, as incidental to his Constitutional powers. It is a means for carrying into execution all sovereign powers, and may be used although not indispensably necessary. It is a right incidental to the power, and conducive to its beneficial exercise.

If this limited construction of the word "necessary" must be abandoned in order to punish, whence is derived the rule which would reinstate it when the Government would carry its powers into execution by means not vindictive in their nature? If the word "necessary" means "needful," "requisite," "essential," "conducive to," in order to let in the power of punishment for the infraction of law, why is it not equally comprehensive when required to authorize the use of means which facilitate the execution of the powers of Government, without the infliction of punishment?

In ascertaining the sense in which the word "necessary" is used in this clause of the Constitution, we may derive some aid from that with which it is associated. Congress shall have power "to make all laws which shall be necessary and proper to carry into execution" the powers of the Government. If the word "necessary" was used

in that strict and rigorous sense for which the counsel for the State of Maryland contend, it would be an extraordinary departure from the usual course of the human mind, as exhibited in composition, to add a word the only possible effect of which is to qualify that strict and rigorous meaning, to present to the mind the idea of some choice of means of legislation not strained and compressed within the narrow limits for which gentlemen contend.

But the argument which most conclusively demonstrates the error of the construction contended for by the counsel for the State of Maryland is founded on the intention of the convention as manifested in the whole clause. To waste time and argument in proving that, without it, Congress might carry its powers into execution would be not much less idle than to hold a lighted taper to the sun. As little can it be required to prove that, in the absence of this clause, Congress would have some choice of means. That it might employ those which, in its judgment, would most advantageously effect the object to be accomplished. That any means adapted to the end, any means which tended directly to the execution of the Constitutional powers of the Government, were in themselves Constitutional. This clause, as construed by the State of Maryland, would abridge, and almost annihilate, this useful and necessary right of the legislature to select its means. That this could not be intended is, we should think, had it not been already controverted, too apparent for controversy.

We think so for the following reasons:

1st. The clause is placed among the powers of Congress, not among the limitations on those powers.

2d. Its terms purport to enlarge, not to diminish, the powers vested in the Government. It purports to be an additional power, not a restriction on those already granted. No reason has been or can be assigned for thus concealing an intention to narrow the discretion of the National Legislature under words which purport to enlarge it. The framers of the Constitution wished its adoption, and well knew that it would be endangered by its strength, not by its weakness. . . .

The result of the most careful and attentive consideration bestowed upon this clause is that, if it does not enlarge, it cannot be construed to restrain, the powers of Congress, or to impair the right of the legislature to exercise its best judgment in the selection of measures to carry into execution the Constitutional powers of the Government. If no other motive for its insertion can be suggested, a sufficient one is found in the desire to remove all doubts respecting the right to legislate on that vast mass of incidental powers which must be involved in the Constitution if that instrument be not a splendid bauble.

We admit, as all must admit, that the powers of the Government are limited, and that its limits are not to be transcended. But we think the sound construction of the Constitution must allow to the national legislature that discretion with respect to the means by which the powers it confers are to be carried into execution which will enable that body to perform the high duties assigned to it in the manner most beneficial to the people. Let the end be legitimate, let it be within the scope of the Constitution, and all means which are appropriate, which are plainly adapted to that end, which are not prohibited, but consist with the letter and spirit of the Constitution, are Constitutional. . . .

But were its necessity less apparent, none can deny its being an appropriate measure; and if it is, the decree of its necessity, as has been very justly observed, is to be discussed in another place. Should Congress, in the execution of its powers, adopt measures which are prohibited by the Constitution, or should Congress, under the pretext of executing its powers, pass laws for the accomplishment of objects not intrusted to the Government, it would become the painful duty of this tribunal, should a case requiring such a decision come before it, to say that such an act was not the law of the land. But where the law is not prohibited, and is really calculated to effect any of the objects intrusted to the Government, to undertake here to inquire into the decree of its necessity would be to pass the line which circumscribes the judicial department and to tread on legislative ground. This Court disclaims all pretensions to such a power. . . .

After the most deliberate consideration, it is the unanimous and decided opinion of this Court that the act to incorporate the Bank of the United States is a law made in pursuance of the Constitution, and is a part of the supreme law of the land.

It being the opinion of the Court that the act incorporating the bank is constitutional, and that the power of establishing a branch in the State of Maryland might be properly exercised by the bank itself, we proceed to inquire:

. . . Whether the State of Maryland may, without violating the Constitution, tax that branch?

That the power of taxation is one of vital importance; that it is retained by the States; that it is not abridged by the grant of a similar power to the Government of the Union; that it is to be concurrently exercised by the two Governments—are truths which have never been denied.

But such is the paramount character of the Constitution that its capacity to withdraw any subject from the action of even this power is admitted. The States are expressly forbidden to lay any duties on imports or exports except what may be absolutely necessary for executing their inspection laws. If the obligation of this prohibition must be conceded—if it may restrain a State from the exercise of its taxing power on imports and exports—the same paramount character would seem to restrain, as it certainly may restrain, a State from such other exercise of this power as is in its nature incompatible with, and repugnant to, the constitutional laws of the Union. A law absolutely repugnant to another as entirely repeals that other as if express terms of repeal were used. . . .

This great principle is that the Constitution and the laws made in pursuance thereof are supreme; that they control the Constitution and laws of the respective States, and cannot be controlled by them. From this, which may be almost termed an axiom, other propositions are deduced as corollaries, on the truth or error of which, and on their application to this case, the cause has been supposed to depend. These are, 1st. That a power to create implies a power to preserve; 2d. That a power to destroy, if wielded by a different hand, is hostile to, and incompatible with these powers to create and to preserve; 3d. That, where this repugnancy exists, that authority which is supreme must control, not yield to that over which it is supreme. . . .

That the power of taxing it by the States may be exercised so as to destroy it is too obvious to be denied. But taxation is said to be an absolute power which acknowledges no other limits than those expressly prescribed in the Constitution, and, like sovereign power of every other description, is intrusted to the discretion of those who use it. But the very terms of this argument admit that the sovereignty of the State, in the article of taxation itself, is subordinate to, and may be controlled by, the Constitution of the United States. How far it has been controlled by that instrument must be a question of construction. In making this construction, no principle, not declared, can be admissible which would defeat the legitimate operations of a supreme Government. It is of the very essence of supremacy to remove all obstacles to its action within its own sphere, and so to modify every power vested in subordinate governments as to exempt its own operations from their own influence. This effect need not be stated in terms. It is so involved in the declaration of supremacy, so necessarily implied in it, that the expression of it could not make it more certain. We must, therefore, keep it in view while construing the Constitution.

The argument on the part of the State of Maryland is not that the States may directly resist a law of Congress, but that they may exercise their acknowledged powers upon it, and that the Constitution leaves them this right, in the confidence that they will not abuse it. . . .

The sovereignty of a State extends to everything which exists by its own authority or is introduced by its permission, but does it extend to those means which are employed by Congress to carry into execution powers conferred on that body by the people of the United States? We think it demonstrable that it does not. Those powers are not given by the people of a single State. They are given by the people of the United States, to a Government whose laws, made in pursuance of the Constitution, are declared to be supreme. Consequently, the people of a single State cannot confer a sovereignty which will extend over them.

If we measure the power of taxation residing in a State by the extent of sovereignty which the people of a single State possess and can confer on its Government, we have an intelligible standard, applicable to every case to which the power may be applied. We have a principle which leaves the power of taxing the people and property of a State unimpaired; which leaves to a State the command of all its resources, and which places beyond its reach all those powers which are conferred by the people of the United States on the Government of the Union, and all those means which are given for the purpose of carrying those powers into execution. We have a principle which is safe for the States and safe for the Union. We are relieved, as we ought to be, from clashing sovereignty; from interfering powers; from a repugnancy between a right in one Government to pull down what there is an acknowledged right in another to build up; from the incompatibility of a right in one Government to destroy what there is a right in another to preserve. We are not driven to the perplexing inquiry, so unfit for the judicial department, what degree of taxation is the legitimate use and what degree may amount to the abuse of the power. The attempt to use it on the means employed by the Government of the Union, in pursuance of the Constitution, is itself an abuse because it is the usurpation of a power which the people of a single State cannot give. . . .

That the power to tax involves the power to destroy; that the power to destroy may defeat and render useless the power to create; that there is a plain repugnance in conferring on one Government a power to control the constitutional measures of another, which other, with respect to those very measures, is declared to be supreme over that which exerts the control, are propositions not to be denied. But all inconsistencies are to be reconciled by the magic of the word CONFIDENCE. Taxation, it is said, does not necessarily and unavoidably destroy. To carry it to the excess of destruction would be an abuse, to presume which would banish that confidence which is essential to all Government. . . .

If we apply the principle for which the State of Maryland contends, to the Constitution generally, we shall find it capable of changing totally the character of that instrument. We shall find it capable of arresting all the measures of the Government, and of prostrating it at the foot of the States. The American people have declared their Constitution and the laws made in pursuance thereof to be supreme, but this principle would transfer the supremacy, in fact, to the States. . . .

If the States may tax one instrument, employed by the Government in the execution of its powers, they may tax any and every other instrument. They may tax the mail; they may tax the mint; they may tax patent rights; they may tax the papers of the custom house; they may tax judicial process; they may tax all the means employed by the Government to an excess which would defeat all the ends of Government. This was not intended by the American people. They did not design to make their Government dependent on the States. . . .

It has also been insisted that, as the power of taxation in the General and State Governments is acknowledged to be concurrent, every argument which would sustain the right of the General Government to tax banks chartered by the States, will equally sustain the right of the States to tax banks chartered by the General Government.

But the two cases are not on the same reason. The people of all the States have created the General Government, and have conferred upon it the general power of taxation. The people of all the States, and the States themselves, are represented in Congress, and, by their representatives, exercise this power. When they tax the chartered institutions of the States, they tax their constituents, and these taxes must be uniform. But when a State taxes the operations of the Government of the United States, it acts upon institutions created not by their own constituents, but by people over whom they claim no control. It acts upon the measures of a Government created by others as well as themselves, for the benefit of others in common with themselves. The difference is that which always exists, and always must exist, between the action of the whole on a part, and the action of a part on the whole—between the laws of a Government declared to be supreme, and those of a Government which, when in opposition to those laws, is not supreme. . . .

We are unanimously of opinion that the law passed by the Legislature of Maryland, imposing a tax on the Bank of the United States is unconstitutional and void.

This opinion does not deprive the States of any resources which they originally possessed. It does not extend to a tax paid by the real property of the bank, in common with the other real property within the State, nor to a tax imposed on the interest which the citizens of Maryland may hold in this institution, in common with other property of the same description throughout the State. But this is a tax on the operations of the bank, and is, consequently, a tax on the operation of an instrument employed by the Government of the Union to carry its powers into execution. Such a tax must be unconstitutional. . . .

## Gibbons v. Ogden
### 22 U.S. 1 (1824)

By 1815, Robert Livingston and Robert Fulton had died, leaving their exclusive rights to operate steamboats in New York waters to their heirs. Two years later, Aaron Ogden, a former governor of New Jersey and prominent Federalist politician, and Thomas Gibbons, a Georgia-born wealthy lawyer with a shady political background, formed a partnership and purchased a share of the monopoly rights to run steamboats. Gibbons and Ogden soon clashed over how to run their steamboat business, broke off their relationship, and formed rival companies. They continued to sue each other over improper business practices, with Gibbons operating in New York waters whenever the moment suited him, as much for spite as for money. Ogden sued Gibbons in New York state court and won a judgment that halted his steamboat expeditions. But the judge in that case, Chancellor James Kent, well respected for his scholarly approach to legal questions, raised the issue of whether the New York law interfered with the 1793 coastal Licensing Act passed by Congress.

Gibbons retaliated against Ogden, ultimately persuading the New Jersey legislature to pass a law making it illegal for "any nonresident" to navigate a steamboat in any of the waters along the New Jersey shore. John K. Livingston, the heir to his father's monopoly, soon found his steamboat, the *Olive Branch*, detained in New Brunswick for operating in violation of the New Jersey law. That was

Ogden's political punishment. The question that Gibbons raised on appeal was whether the 1793 law superceded state power over commerce.

The Court's decision was unanimous. Chief Justice Marshall delivered the opinion of the Court. Justice Johnson concurred. Justice Thompson did not participate.

Mr. Chief Justice Marshall delivered the opinion of the Court.

The appellant contends that this decree is erroneous because the laws which purport to give the exclusive privilege it sustains are repugnant to the Constitution and laws of the United States.

They are said to be repugnant:

1st. To that clause in the Constitution which authorizes Congress to regulate commerce. . . .

[The Constitution] contains an enumeration of powers expressly granted by the people to their government. It has been said that these powers ought to be construed strictly. But why ought they to be so construed? Is there one sentence in the Constitution which gives countenance to this rule? In the last of the enumerated powers, that which grants expressly the means for carrying all others into execution, Congress is authorized "to make all laws which shall be necessary and proper" for the purpose. . . .

What do gentlemen mean by a "strict construction"? If they contend only against that enlarged construction, which would extend words beyond their natural and obvious import, we might question the application of the term, but should not controvert the principle. If they contend for that narrow construction which, in support or some theory not to be found in the Constitution, would deny to the government those powers which the words of the grant, as usually understood, import, and which are consistent with the general views and objects of the instrument; for that narrow construction which would cripple the government and render it unequal to the object for which it is declared to be instituted, and to which the powers given, as fairly understood, render it competent; then we cannot perceive the propriety of this strict construction, nor adopt it as the rule by which the Constitution is to be expounded. . . .

If, from the imperfection of human language, there should be serious doubts respecting the extent of any given power, it is a well settled rule that the objects for which it was given, especially when those objects are expressed in the instrument itself, should have great influence in the construction. We know of no reason for excluding this rule from the present case. The grant does not convey power which might be beneficial to the grantor if retained by himself, or which can enure solely to the benefit of the grantee, but is an investment of power for the general advantage, in the hands of agents selected for that purpose, which power can never be exercised by the people themselves, but must be placed in the hands of agents or lie dormant. We know of no rule for construing the extent of such powers other than is given by the language of the instrument which confers them, taken in connexion with the purposes for which they were conferred.

The words are, "Congress shall have power to regulate commerce with foreign nations, and among the several States, and with the Indian tribes."

The subject to be regulated is commerce, and our Constitution being . . . one of enumeration, and not of definition, to ascertain the extent of the power, it becomes necessary to settle the meaning of the word. The counsel for the appellee would limit it to traffic, to buying and selling, or the interchange of commodities, and do not admit that it comprehends navigation. This would restrict a general term, applicable to many objects, to one of its significations. Commerce, undoubtedly, is traffic, but it is something more: it is intercourse. It describes the commercial intercourse between nations, and parts of nations, in all its branches, and is regulated by prescribing rules for carrying on that intercourse. The mind can scarcely conceive a system for regulating commerce between nations which shall exclude all laws concerning navigation, which shall be silent on the admission of the vessels of the one nation into the ports of the other, and be confined to prescribing rules for the conduct of individuals in the actual employment of buying and selling or of barter.

If commerce does not include navigation, the government of the Union has no direct power over that subject, and can make no law prescribing what shall constitute American vessels or requiring that they shall be navigated by American seamen. Yet this power has been exercised from the commencement of the government, has been exercised with the consent of all, and has been understood by all to be a commercial regulation. All America understands, and has uniformly understood, the word "commerce" to comprehend navigation. It was so understood, and must have been so understood, when the Constitution was framed. The power over commerce, including navigation, was one of the primary objects for which the people of America adopted their government, and must have been contemplated in forming it. The convention must have used the word in that sense, because all

have understood it in that sense, and the attempt to restrict it comes too late.

If the opinion that "commerce," as the word is used in the Constitution, comprehends navigation also, requires any additional confirmation, that additional confirmation is, we think, furnished by the words of the instrument itself. . . .

The word used in the Constitution, then, comprehends, and has been always understood to comprehend, navigation within its meaning, and a power to regulate navigation is as expressly granted as if that term had been added to the word "commerce."

To what commerce does this power extend? The Constitution informs us, to commerce "with foreign nations, and among the several States, and with the Indian tribes."

It has, we believe, been universally admitted that these words comprehend every species of commercial intercourse between the United States and foreign nations. No sort of trade can be carried on between this country and any other to which this power does not extend. It has been truly said that "commerce," as the word is used in the Constitution, is a unit every part of which is indicated by the term.

If this be the admitted meaning of the word in its application to foreign nations, it must carry the same meaning throughout the sentence, and remain a unit, unless there be some plain intelligible cause which alters it.

The subject to which the power is next applied is to commerce "among the several States." The word "among" means intermingled with. A thing which is among others is intermingled with them. Commerce among the States cannot stop at the external boundary line of each State, but may be introduced into the interior.

It is not intended to say that these words comprehend that commerce which is completely internal, which is carried on between man and man in a State, or between different parts of the same State, and which does not extend to or affect other States. Such a power would be inconvenient, and is certainly unnecessary.

Comprehensive as the word "among" is, it may very properly be restricted to that commerce which concerns more States than one. The phrase is not one which would probably have been selected to indicate the completely interior traffic of a State, because it is not an apt phrase for that purpose, and the enumeration of the particular classes of commerce to which the power was to be extended would not have been made had the intention been to extend the power to every description. The enumeration presupposes something not enumerated, and that something, if we regard the language or the subject of the sentence, must be the exclusively internal commerce of a State. The genius and character of the whole government seem to be that its action is to be applied to all the external concerns of the nation, and to those internal concerns which affect the States generally, but not to those which are completely within a particular State, which do not affect other States, and with which it is not necessary to interfere for the purpose of executing some of the general powers of the government. The completely internal commerce of a State, then, may be considered as reserved for the State itself.

But, in regulating commerce with foreign nations, the power of Congress does not stop at the jurisdictional lines of the several States. It would be a very useless power if it could not pass those lines. The commerce of the United States with foreign nations is that of the whole United States. Every district has a right to participate in it. The deep streams which penetrate our country in every direction pass through the interior of almost every State in the Union, and furnish the means of exercising this right. If Congress has the power to regulate it, that power must be exercised whenever the subject exists. If it exists within the States, if a foreign voyage may commence or terminate at a port within a State, then the power of Congress may be exercised within a State.

This principle is, if possible, still more clear, when applied to commerce "among the several States." They either join each other, in which case they are separated by a mathematical line, or they are remote from each other, in which case other States lie between them. What is commerce "among" them, and how is it to be conducted? Can a trading expedition between two adjoining States, commence and terminate outside of each? And if the trading intercourse be between two States remote from each other, must it not commence in one, terminate in the other, and probably pass through a third? Commerce among the States must, of necessity, be commerce with the States. In the regulation of trade with the Indian tribes, the action of the law, especially when the Constitution was made, was chiefly within a State. The power of Congress, then, whatever it may be, must be exercised within the territorial jurisdiction of the several States. . . .

We are now arrived at the inquiry—What is this power?

It is the power to regulate, that is, to prescribe the rule by which commerce is to be governed. This power, like all others vested in Congress, is complete in itself, may be exercised to its utmost extent, and acknowledges no limitations other than are prescribed in the Constitution. These are expressed in plain terms, and do not affect the

questions which arise in this case, or which have been discussed at the bar. If, as has always been understood, the sovereignty of Congress, though limited to specified objects, is plenary as to those objects, the power over commerce with foreign nations, and among the several States, is vested in Congress as absolutely as it would be in a single government, having in its Constitution the same restrictions on the exercise of the power as are found in the Constitution of the United States. The wisdom and the discretion of Congress, their identity with the people, and the influence which their constituents possess at elections are, in this, as in many other instances, as that, for example, of declaring war, the sole restraints on which they have relied, to secure them from its abuse. They are the restraints on which the people must often solely rely, in all representative governments.

The power of Congress, then, comprehends navigation, within the limits of every State in the Union, so far as that navigation may be in any manner connected with "commerce with foreign nations, or among the several States, or with the Indian tribes." It may, of consequence, pass the jurisdictional line of New York and act upon the very waters to which the prohibition now under consideration applies.

But it has been urged with great earnestness that, although the power of Congress to regulate commerce with foreign nations and among the several States be coextensive with the subject itself, and have no other limits than are prescribed in the Constitution, yet the States may severally exercise the same power, within their respective jurisdictions. In support of this argument, it is said that they possessed it as an inseparable attribute of sovereignty, before the formation of the Constitution, and still retain it except so far as they have surrendered it by that instrument; that this principle results from the nature of the government, and is secured by the tenth amendment; that an affirmative grant of power is not exclusive unless in its own nature it be such that the continued exercise of it by the former possessor is inconsistent with the grant, and that this is not of that description.

The appellant, conceding these postulates except the last, contends that full power to regulate a particular subject implies the whole power, and leaves no residuum; that a grant of the whole is incompatible with the existence of a right in another to any part of it. . . .

The grant of the power to lay and collect taxes is, like the power to regulate commerce, made in general terms, and has never been understood to interfere with the exercise of the same power by the State, and hence has been drawn an argument which has been applied to the question under consideration. But the two grants are not, it is conceived, similar in their terms or their nature. Although many of the powers formerly exercised by the States are transferred to the government of the Union, yet the State governments remain, and constitute a most important part of our system. The power of taxation is indispensable to their existence, and is a power which, in its own nature, is capable of residing in, and being exercised by, different authorities at the same time. . . . Congress is authorized to lay and collect taxes, &c. to pay the debts and provide for the common defence and general welfare of the United States. This does not interfere with the power of the States to tax for the support of their own governments, nor is the exercise of that power by the States an exercise of any portion of the power that is granted to the United States. In imposing taxes for State purposes, they are not doing what Congress is empowered to do. Congress is not empowered to tax for those purposes which are within the exclusive province of the States. When, then, each government exercises the power of taxation, neither is exercising the power of the other. But, when a State proceeds to regulate commerce with foreign nations, or among the several States, it is exercising the very power that is granted to Congress, and is doing the very thing which Congress is authorized to do. There is no analogy, then, between the power of taxation and the power of regulating commerce.

In discussing the question whether this power is still in the States, in the case under consideration, we may dismiss from it the inquiry whether it is surrendered by the mere grant to Congress, or is retained until Congress shall exercise the power. We may dismiss that inquiry because it has been exercised, and the regulations which Congress deemed it proper to make are now in full operation. The sole question is can a State regulate commerce with foreign nations and among the States while Congress is regulating it? . . .

It has been contended by the counsel for the appellant that, as the word "to regulate" implies in its nature full power over the thing to be regulated, it excludes necessarily the action of all others that would perform the same operation on the same thing. That regulation is designed for the entire result, applying to those parts which remain as they were, as well as to those which are altered. It produces a uniform whole which is as much disturbed and deranged by changing what the regulating power designs to leave untouched as that on which it has operated.

There is great force in this argument, and the Court is not satisfied that it has been refuted.

Since, however, in exercising the power of regulating their own purely internal affairs, whether of trading or police, the States may sometimes enact laws the validity of which depends on their interfering with, and being contrary to, an act of Congress passed in pursuance of the Constitution, the Court will enter upon the inquiry whether the laws of New York, as expounded by the highest tribunal of that State, have, in their application to this case, come into collision with an act of Congress and deprived a citizen of a right to which that act entitles him. Should this collision exist, it will be immaterial whether those laws were passed in virtue of a concurrent power "to regulate commerce with foreign nations and among the several States" or in virtue of a power to regulate their domestic trade and police. In one case and the other, the acts of New York must yield to the law of Congress, and the decision sustaining the privilege they confer against a right given by a law of the Union must be erroneous.

This opinion has been frequently expressed in this Court, and is founded as well on the nature of the government as on the words of the Constitution. In argument, however, it has been contended that, if a law passed by a State, in the exercise of its acknowledged sovereignty, comes into conflict with a law passed by Congress in pursuance of the Constitution, they affect the subject and each other like equal opposing powers.

But the framers of our Constitution foresaw this state of things, and provided for it by declaring the supremacy not only of itself, but of the laws made in pursuance of it. The nullity of any act inconsistent with the Constitution is produced by the declaration that the Constitution is the supreme law. The appropriate application of that part of the clause which confers the same supremacy on laws and treaties is to such acts of the State Legislatures as do not transcend their powers, but, though enacted in the execution of acknowledged State powers, interfere with, or are contrary to, the laws of Congress made in pursuance of the Constitution or some treaty made under the authority of the United States. In every such case, the act of Congress or the treaty is supreme, and the law of the State, though enacted in the exercise of powers not controverted, must yield to it. . . .

[A]ll inquiry into this subject seems to the Court to be put completely at rest by the act already mentioned, entitled, "An act for the enrolling and licensing of steamboats."

[The 1793 coastal licensing] act authorizes a steamboat employed, or intended to be employed, only in a river or bay of the United States, owned wholly or in part by an alien, resident within the United States, to be enrolled and licensed as if the same belonged to a citizen of the United States.

This act demonstrates the opinion of Congress that steamboats may be enrolled and licensed, in common with vessels using sails. They are, of course, entitled to the same privileges, and can no more be restrained from navigating waters and entering ports which are free to such vessels than if they were wafted on their voyage by the winds, instead of being propelled by the agency of fire. The one element may be as legitimately used as the other for every commercial purpose authorized by the laws of the Union, and the act of a State inhibiting the use of either to any vessel having a license under the act of Congress comes, we think, in direct collision with that act. . . .

Powerful and ingenious minds, taking as postulates that the powers expressly granted to the government of the Union are to be contracted by construction into the narrowest possible compass and that the original powers of the States are retained if any possible construction will retain them may, by a course of well digested but refined and metaphysical reasoning founded on these premises, explain away the Constitution of our country and leave it a magnificent structure indeed to look at, but totally unfit for use. They may so entangle and perplex the understanding as to obscure principles which were before thought quite plain, and induce doubts where, if the mind were to pursue its own course, none would be perceived. In such a case, it is peculiarly necessary to recur to safe and fundamental principles to sustain those principles, and when sustained, to make them the tests of the arguments to be examined. . . .

MR. JUSTICE JOHNSON, concurring.

The judgment entered by the Court in this cause, has my entire approbation, but, having adopted my conclusions on views of the subject materially different from those of my brethren, I feel it incumbent on me to exhibit those views. I have also another inducement: in questions of great importance and great delicacy, I feel my duty to the public best discharged by an effort to maintain my opinions in my own way.

In attempts to construe the Constitution, I have never found much benefit resulting from the inquiry whether the whole or any part of it is to be construed strictly or literally. The simple, classical, precise, yet comprehensive language in which it is couched leaves, at most, but very little latitude for construction, and when its intent and meaning is discovered, nothing remains but to execute the will of those who made it in the best manner to effect the purposes intended. The great and paramount purpose was to unite this mass of wealth and power, for the protection of the humblest individual, his rights, civil and political, his interests and prosperity, are the sole end; the rest are nothing but the means. But the principal of those means, one so essential as to approach nearer the characteristics of an end, was the independence and harmony of the States that they may the better subserve the purposes of cherishing and protecting the respective families of this great republic.

The strong sympathies, rather than the feeble government, which bound the States together during a common war dissolved on the return of peace, and the very principles which gave rise to the war of the revolution began to threaten the Confederacy with anarchy and ruin. The States had resisted a tax imposed by the parent State, and now reluctantly submitted to, or altogether rejected, the moderate demands of the Confederation. Everyone recollects the painful and threatening discussions which arose on the subject of the five percent. duty. Some States rejected it altogether; others insisted on collecting it themselves; scarcely any acquiesced without reservations, which deprived it altogether of the character of a national measure; and at length, some repealed the laws by which they had signified their acquiescence.

For a century, the States had submitted, with murmurs, to the commercial restrictions imposed by the parent State; and now, finding themselves in the unlimited possession of those powers over their own commerce which they had so long been deprived of and so earnestly coveted, that selfish principle which, well controlled, is so salutary, and which, unrestricted, is so unjust and tyrannical, guided by inexperience and jealousy, began to show itself in iniquitous laws and impolitic measures from which grew up a conflict of commercial regulations destructive to the harmony of the States and fatal to their commercial interests abroad. . . .

The history of the times will therefore sustain the opinion that the grant of power over commerce, if intended to be commensurate with the evils existing and the purpose of remedying those evils, could be only commensurate with the power of the States over the subject. And this opinion is supported by a very remarkable evidence of the general understanding of the whole American people when the grant was made.

There was not a State in the Union in which there did not at that time exist a variety of commercial regulations; concerning which it is too much to suppose that the whole ground covered by those regulations was immediately assumed by actual legislation under the authority of the Union. But where was the existing statute on this subject that a State attempted to execute? or by what State was it ever thought necessary to repeal those statutes? By common consent, those laws dropped lifeless from their statute books for want of the sustaining power that had been relinquished to Congress.

And the plain and direct import of the words of the grant is consistent with this general understanding. . . .

The "power to regulate commerce" here meant to be granted was that power to regulate commerce which previously existed in the States. But what was that power? The States were unquestionably supreme, and each possessed that power over commerce which is acknowledged to reside in every sovereign State. The definition and limits of that power are to be sought among the features of international law, and, as it was not only admitted but insisted on by both parties in argument that, "unaffected by a state of war, by treaties, or by municipal regulations, all commerce among independent States was legitimate," there is no necessity to appeal to the oracles of the jus commune for the correctness of that doctrine. The law of nations, regarding man as a social animal, pronounces all commerce legitimate in a state of peace until prohibited by positive law. The power of a sovereign state over commerce therefore amounts to nothing more than a power to limit and restrain it at pleasure. And since the power to prescribe the limits to its freedom necessarily implies the power to determine what shall remain unrestrained, it follows that the power must be exclusive; it can reside but in one potentate, and hence the grant of this power carries with it the whole subject, leaving nothing for the State to act upon.

And such has been the practical construction of the act. Were every law on the subject of commerce repealed tomorrow, all commerce would be lawful, and, in practice, merchants never inquire what is permitted, but what is forbidden commerce. Of all the endless variety of branches of foreign commerce now carried on to every quarter of the world, I know of no one that is permitted by act of Congress any otherwise than by not being forbidden. No statute of the United States that I know of was ever passed to permit a commerce unless in consequence of its having been prohibited by some previous statute. . . .

It has been contended that the grants of power to the United States over any subject do not necessarily paralyze the arm of the States or deprive them of the capacity to act on the same subject. [T]his can be the effect only of prohibitory provisions in their own Constitutions, or in that of the General Government. The vis vitae of power is still existing in the States, if not extinguished by the Constitution of the United States. That, although as to all those grants of power which may be called aboriginal, with relation to the Government, brought into existence by the Constitution, they, of course, are out of the reach of State power, yet, as to all concessions of powers which previously existed in the States, it was otherwise. The practice of our Government certainly has been, on many subjects, to occupy so much only of the field opened to them as they think the public interests require. . . .

It would be in vain to deny the possibility of a clashing and collision between the measures of the two governments. The line cannot be drawn with sufficient distinctness between the municipal powers of the one and the commercial powers of the other. In some points, they meet and blend so as scarcely to admit of separation. Hitherto, the only remedy has been applied which the case admits of—that of a frank and candid cooperation for the general good. Witness the laws of Congress requiring its officers to respect the inspection laws of the States and to aid in enforcing their health laws, that which surrenders to the States the superintendence of pilotage, and the many laws passed to permit a tonnage duty to be levied for the use of their ports. Other instances could be cited abundantly to prove that collision must be sought to be produced, and when it does arise, the question must be decided how far the powers of Congress are adequate to put it down. Wherever the powers of the respective governments are frankly exercised, with a distinct view to the ends of such powers, they may act upon the same object, or use the same means, and yet the powers be kept perfectly distinct. A resort to the same means therefore is no argument to prove the identity of their respective powers.

▼▲▼

## The Power to Investigate

In contrast to the Necessary and Proper Clause, the Framers never seriously debated the power of Congress to hold public hearings and investigate matters of public concern. Derived from Article I, Section I, of the Constitution, which assigns to Congress "all legislative powers herein granted," the congressional exercise of investigative power has its historical roots in the practices of the British House of Commons. As far back as the sixteenth century, the House of Commons used this power to support its lawmaking function, conduct inquiries into public malfeasance, and oversee the executive branch. State legislatures, the Continental Congress under the Articles of Confederation, and even colonial legislatures prior to the Declaration of Independence followed the

British model. By the time of the Constitution's ratification, the assumption of a broad investigative power by Congress was considered a fundamental component of its legislative responsibilities.[25]

Congress wasted no time in asserting this power. In reaction to an Indian attack on American soldiers engaged in a late 1791 expedition in the Northwest Territories that left hundreds dead, Congress convened a special committee the following legislative session to investigate what went wrong. It ordered Major General Arthur St. Clair, who commanded the expedition, Secretary of War Henry Knox, and Secretary of Treasury Alexander Hamilton to appear in person before the committee to explain what led to the disaster. Using its subpoena power, Congress ordered President Washington to turn over all relevant papers from the White House and executive branch agencies that dealt with the St. Clair investigation. President Washington agreed but added the following qualifier:

> [T]he Executive ought to communicate such papers as the public good would permit, *and ought to refuse those, the disclosure of which would injure the public.*[26]

Political scientist Marc J. Rozell has noted that President Washington's action in the St. Clair investigation, while deferential to Congress, marked the first presidential claim of "executive privilege." Rozell defines executive privilege as "the right of the president and important executive branch officials to withhold information from Congress, the courts, and, ultimately, the public."[27] President Washington's response to the Senate's demand for information established the baseline for future claims of executive privilege: Information damaging to the "public interest" could and should be withheld from Congress. Not long after the St. Clair affair, President Washington refused to submit executive branch papers to Congress in its investigation of his administration's negotiation of the Jay Treaty, which resolved several unsettled issues from the Revolutionary War. Congress opposed President Washington's assertion of executive privilege, but other than passing two nonbinding resolutions expressing its disagreement with the president's decision, did nothing about it.[28]

The St. Clair investigation underscored the first and perhaps most basic function of the power of Congress in this regard: to provide the public with information through Congress's unique position as the sovereign representative of the people. President Woodrow Wilson, while still a doctoral student at Princeton, observed that "[i]t is the proper duty of a representative body to look diligently into every affair of government and to talk much about what it sees. It is meant to be the eyes and the voice, and to embody the wisdom and will of its constituents. . . . The informing function of Congress should be preferred even to its legislative function."[29] Wilson argued that Congress was authorized to use its power to investigate to oversee the executive branch. Information gathering is not the sole purpose of a congressional investigation. Information is, however, an important precursor to legislative action intended to address public policy deficiencies and improve the administration of current programs.

Constitutional controversies over the investigative power of Congress have derived from how it has exercised its power, not from the assertion of power. Because the Constitution is silent on how Congress is to conduct public inquiries, the legal development of its power to investigate has come about through a trial and error process of legislative initiatives and judicial decisions interpreting its constitutional boundaries of operation. For the most part, the Court has deferred to Congress on questions involving the right of investigating committees to establish broad jurisdiction over their inquiries, call witnesses, and issue contempt orders against those who refuse to testify. But the Court has also ruled that Congress does not have free reign over the exercise of its investigative power. Likewise, witnesses who are called before congressional committees do not sacrifice their constitutional rights upon entering the hearing room.

The Court has never challenged either the constitutional basis of the power of Congress to investigate or the legal means it has used to enforce compliance with its proceedings. In 1821 the Court held that Congress had full use of the contempt power to punish witnesses who refused to answer a summons to appear before a committee. The Court, however, qualified the potential reach of this ruling, holding that Congress was restricted to "the least power adequate to the end proposed."[30] Later, in *Kilbourn v. Thompson* (1881), the Court continued to carve out a middle ground between the legitimate need of Congress to retain effective investigatory powers and the rights of witnesses to some recourse of due process in such matters. In *Kilbourn* the Court held that a witness in a congressional inquiry into a real estate scandal was not required to produce documents demanded by a House committee because the materials bore no relationship to a legitimate public inquiry. Because Congress had exceeded its proper scope of inquiry, it was without the power to issue a contempt order against the witness, Hallet Kilbourn, who refused to provide his private papers to the committee.

*Kilbourn* stood as the constitutional baseline of congressional investigative power for almost fifty years. Then, in 1922, the Teapot Dome scandal broke open during the presidency of Warren G. Harding (1921–1923). The scandal compelled Congress to investigate a staggering series of bribery and corruption charges against high government officials and their ties to powerful real estate and financial interests. Congress set its sights on two key participants in the scandal: Attorney General Harry M. Daugherty, who came under suspicion for his refusal to prosecute several alleged participants in Teapot Dome, and his brother, Mally S. Daugherty, a bank president, who Congress believed had entered into a series of government-assisted fraudulent land deals aided and abetted by his brother. When Mally refused to appear before the Senate committee investigating the Teapot Dome scandal, he was arrested and charged with contempt. Mally claimed that *Kilbourn* prohibited Congress from ordering him, a private individual, to testify on a matter unrelated to its scope of public inquiry.

In *McGrain v. Daugherty* (1927), a unanimous Court held that Mally Daugherty's claim held no defense against the legitimate legislative interest of Congress in investigating public corruption. For the Court, Justice Willis Van Devanter wrote that Congress, while possessed of no "general power to inquire into private matters," had broad power to compel private individuals to testify in matters that are related to its legislative function.[31] Note, in *McGrain,* how careful the Court was to affirm the core of *Kilbourn*—that a congressional inquiry must bear a relationship to a legislative end—while making clear that Congress had full constitutional authority to order private individuals to testify in congressional inquiries. That authority included the power of Congress to issue contempt orders and impose fines

and punishment for the refusal of witnesses to appear. Important as well in *McGrain* was the Court's first substantial explication of the implied constitutional basis of congressional investigative power.

For most of the 1920s, congressional inquiries focused on alleged executive branch misbehavior; related charges of government mismanagement and corruption; and, after the stock market crash of 1929, efforts to alleviate the social and economic dislocation touched off by the Great Depression. With the parallel rise of communism in Soviet Russia; fascist ideologies in Western Europe; and most ominous and threatening of all, the ascension of Nazi Germany, Congress began to turn its investigative powers on what it perceived were internal threats to America's security at home. Fearful that the communist takeover of Russia in 1919 would encourage similar workers' revolts at home, American law-enforcement agencies at the state and federal levels launched routine raids on labor unions. For the first time, unions had begun to wield genuine economic and political clout in their negotiations with industry. Thousands of individuals, a great number of whom were recent European immigrants, were arrested on suspicion of harboring sympathies for foreign ideologies such as anarchism, communism, and socialism and supporting the violent overthrow of the American government.[32]

Congress supported this effort by opening investigations of its own around the same time on subversive elements in the American labor movement. Later, as Adolf Hitler's rise to power in Nazi Germany made anti-Semitism in that country no longer a prominent cultural strain but a requirement of political faith and the Soviet revolution in Russia collapsed into the authoritarian control of Joseph Stalin, Congress expanded the scope of its investigation to question the political beliefs and associational ties of American citizens whose national origin now made their patriotism suspect. What began as an effort to root out potential threats to domestic security in a time when the world was entering one of the darkest periods in modern history soon dissipated into a series of congressional inquisitions that would ruin the lives of thousands of innocent citizens and plunge the nation into a era of unprecedented political repression.

# McGrain v. Daugherty
## 273 U.S. 135 (1927)

In 1922, Congress began investigating accusations that several well-positioned public officials in President Warren Harding's administration had given leasing rights to government-held oil reserves to private companies in exchange for bribes. This scandal became known as Teapot Dome, an area in Wyoming where the government held large oil reserves. The investigation began by targeting officials in the Department of the Interior but soon moved to Attorney General Harry M. Daugherty. Daugherty attracted the notice of congressional investigators because he failed to prosecute several officials against whom significant evidence had been compiled.

A Senate committee ordered Mally S. Daugherty, Harry's brother, to appear before it and produce certain documents that it believed would incriminate the attorney general. Harry resigned rather than face his accusers, and his brother refused to appear before the Senate committee. The Senate then ordered the sergeant at arms, John J. McGrain, to arrest Mally Daugherty. He was subsequently imprisoned while awaiting trial. Daugherty was successful in persuading a federal district court to grant him a writ of habeas corpus. McGrain appealed directly to the Supreme Court.

The Supreme Court's decision was unanimous. Justice Van Devanter delivered the opinion of the Court. Justice Stone did not participate, as he had written the federal government's brief when the case was argued in the lower court.

▼▲▼

MR. JUSTICE VAN DEVANTER delivered the opinion of the Court.

. . . We have given the case earnest and prolonged consideration because the principal questions involved are of unusual importance and delicacy. They are (a) whether the Senate—or the House of Representatives . . . has power, through its own process, to compel a private individual to appear before it or one of its committees and give testimony needed to enable it efficiently to exercise a legislative function belonging to it under the Constitution; and (b) whether it sufficiently appears that the process was being employed in this instance to obtain testimony for that purpose. . . .

The Constitution provides for a Congress, consisting of a Senate and House of Representatives, and invests it with 'all legislative powers' granted to the United States, and with power 'to make all laws which shall be necessary and proper' for carrying into execution these powers and 'all other powers' vested by the Constitution in the United States or in any department or officer thereof . . . there is no provision expressly investing either house with power to make investigations and exact testimony, to the end that it may exercise its legislative function advisedly and effectively. So the question arises whether this power is so far incidental to the legislative function as to be implied.

In actual legislative practice, power to secure needed information by such means has long been treated as an attribute of the power to legislate. It was so regarded in the British Parliament and in the colonial Legislatures before the American Revolution, and a like view has prevailed and been carried into effect in both houses of Congress and in most of the state Legislatures. . . .

The state courts quite generally have held that the power to legislate carries with it by necessary implication ample authority to obtain information needed in the rightful exercise of that power, and to employ compulsory process for the purpose. . . .

We have referred to the practice of the two houses of Congress, and we now shall notice some significant congressional enactments. May 3, 1798, Congress provided that oaths or affirmations might be administered to witnesses by the President of the Senate, the Speaker of the House of Representatives, the chairman of a committee of the whole, or the chairman of a select committee, 'in any case under their examination.' February 8, 1817, it enlarged that provision so as to include the chairman of a standing committee. January 24, 1857, it passed 'An act more effectually to enforce the attendance of witnesses on the summons of either house of Congress, and to compel them to discover testimony.' This act provided, first, that any person summoned as a witness to give testimony or produce papers in any matter under inquiry before either house of Congress, or any committee of either house, who should wilfully make default, or, if appearing, should refuse to answer any question pertinent to the inquiry, should, in addition to the pains and penalties then existing, be deemed guilty of a misdemeanor and be subject to indictment as there prescribed; and, secondly, that no person should be excused from giving evidence in such an inquiry on the ground that it might tend to incriminate or disgrace him, nor be held to answer criminally, or be subjected to any penalty or forfeiture, for any fact or act as to which he was required to testify excepting that he might be subjected to prosecution for perjury committed while so testifying. January 24, 1862, Congress modified the immunity provision in particulars not material here . . . They show very plainly that Congress intended thereby (a) to recognize the power of either house to institute inquiries and exact evidence touching subjects within its jurisdiction and on which it was disposed to act; (b) to recognize that such inquiries may be conducted through committees; (c) to subject defaulting and contumacious witnesses to indictment and punishment in the courts, and thereby to enable either house to exert the power of inquiry 'more effectually'; and (d) to open the way for obtaining evidence in such an inquiry, which otherwise could not be obtained, by exempting witnesses required to give evidence therein from criminal and penal prosecutions in respect of matters disclosed by their evidence.

Four decisions of this court . . . definitely settle two propositions which we recognize as entirely sound and having a bearing on its solution: One, that the two houses of Congress, in their separate relations, possess, not only such powers as are expressly granted to them by the Constitution, but such auxiliary powers as are necessary and appropriate to make the express powers effective; and the other, that neither house is invested with 'general' power to inquire into private affairs and compel disclosures, but only with such limited power of inquiry as is shown to exist when the rule of constitutional interpretation just stated is rightly applied. . . .

With this review of the legislative practice, congressional enactments, and court decisions, we proceed to a statement of our conclusions on the question.

We are of opinion that the power of inquiry with process to enforce it is an essential and appropriate auxiliary to the legislative function. . . . A legislative body cannot legislate wisely or effectively in the absence of information respecting the conditions which the legislation is intended to affect or change; and where the legislative body does not itself possess the requisite information—which not infrequently is true—recourse must be had to others who do possess it. Experience has taught that mere requests for such information often are unavailing, and also that information which is volunteered is not always accurate or complete; so some means of compulsion are essential to obtain what is needed. All this was true before and when the Constitution was framed and adopted. In that period the power of inquiry, with enforcing process, was regarded and employed as a necessary and appropriate attribute of the power to legislate—indeed, was treated as inhering in it. Thus there is ample warrant for thinking, as we do, that

the constitutional provisions which commit the legislative function to the two houses are intended to include this attribute to the end that the function may be effectively exercised.

The contention is earnestly made on behalf of the witness that this power of inquiry, if sustained, may be abusively and oppressively exerted. If this be so, it affords no ground for denying the power. The same contention might be directed against the power to legislate, and of course would be unavailing. We must assume, for present purposes, that neither houses will be disposed to exert the power beyond its proper bounds, or without due regard to the rights of witnesses. But if, contrary to this assumption, controlling limitations or restrictions are disregarded, the decisions in *Kilbourn v. Thompson* point to admissible measures of relief. And it is a necessary deduction from the decisions in *Kilbourn* that a witness rightfully may refuse to answer where the bounds of the power are exceeded or the questions are not pertinent to the matter under inquiry.

We come now to the question whether it sufficiently appears that the purpose for which the witness' testimony was sought was to obtain information in aid of the legislative function. . . .

It is quite true that the resolution directing the investigation does not in terms avow that it is intended to be in aid of legislation; but it does show that the subject to be investigated was the administration of the Department of Justice whether its functions were being properly discharged or were being neglected or misdirected, and particularly whether the Attorney General and his assistants were performing or neglecting their duties in respect of the institution and prosecution of proceedings to punish crimes and enforce appropriate remedies against the wrongdoers; specific instances of alleged neglect being recited. Plainly the subject was one on which legislation could be had and would be materially aided by the information which the investigation was calculated to elicit. This becomes manifest when it is reflected that the functions of the Department of Justice, the powers and duties of the Attorney General, and the duties of his assistants are all subject to regulation by congressional legislation, and that the department is maintained and its activities are carried on under such appropriations as in the judgment of Congress are needed from year to year.

The only legitimate object the Senate could have in ordering the investigation was to aid it in legislating, and we think the subject matter was such that the presumption should be indulged that this was the real object. An express avowal of the object would have been better; but in view of the particular subject matter was not indispensable. . . .

We conclude that the investigation was ordered for a legitimate object; that the witness wrongfully refused to appear and testify before the committee and was lawfully attached; [and] that the Senate is entitled to have him give testimony pertinent to the inquiry, either at its bar or before the committee; and that the district court erred in discharging him from custody under the attachment. . . .

### "Are You Now, Or Have You Ever Been . . .": Congress Confronts the Red Scare

In May 1930, Representative Hamilton Fish (R–N.Y.) introduced a proposal to form a temporary committee to investigate communist activities and domestic subversion. By a vote of 210 to 18, Congress established the House Special Committee to Investigate Communist Activities in the United States. Representative Fish assured his colleagues that the committee was not intended to "interfere with any group except the Communists in the United States." After another member suggested during debate on the resolution that Congress ought to spend its time figuring out ways to combat the social and economic ills brought about by the Great Depression, Fish responded that the deportation of "alien Communists" would create job opportunities for honest, loyal, but unemployed Americans.[33]

After six months of investigation, Fish's committee produced a report that credited the Communist Party with around twelve thousand dues-paying members and five hundred thousand more sympathizers. How it arrived at the latter figure was not clear. Of greater importance, though, was the relative impotence of Congress to legislate on membership in a political party. Congress could rant and rave about the dangers of communism but could do little about it, other than expose what members believed were sources of potential domestic unrest. In January 1934, Representative Samuel Dickstein (D–N.Y.) formed a Special Committee on Un-American Activities. Chaired by Rep. John W. McCormack (D–Mass.), the committee focused less on domestic communism and more on the activities of Nazi sympathizers. A year later the Dickstein-McCormack committee submitted a report that yielded little new information. It

documented the presence of pro-Hitler political parties and the existence of anti-Semitic organizations, as well as efforts by the German government to distribute Nazi propaganda in the United States.

Congress subsequently enacted two laws designed to counteract such activities. The first required foreign agents distributing information and propaganda in the United States to register with the American government. The other authorized Congress to use its subpoena power in investigations undertaken outside of Washington, D.C. The lack of any real legislative legacy from these investigations led to considerable criticism that Congress was motivated more by the advantages to be reaped from the political moment than by any true legislative concern. Nonetheless, Congress was pursuing, whether for good reason or for show, its informing function, one that President Wilson declared was more important than its legislative function.[34]

Representative Martin Dies Jr. (D–Tex.), an outspoken anticommunist; fervent opponent of the New Deal; and as his predecessor, Representative Dickstein, would soon realize, a rabid anti-Semite, was undaunted by the apparent lack of congressional power to outlaw foreign ideologies that exhibited no genuine threat to domestic tranquility. In August 1938 Dies and Dickstein succeeded in forming another special committee to investigate "subversive and un-American propaganda." Previous committees had limited their mandates to communism and Nazi sympathizers; the Dies resolution, a modified form of an earlier, unsuccessful resolution introduced by Dickstein, expanded the investigative scope to include all "subversive" activities, a category so broad that it was impossible to discern its limits. Enamored with the possibilities that a congressional investigation offered to elevate his own national political profile, Dies subpoenaed hundreds of individuals with real and alleged ties to Nazi and communist causes before his committee within the first month of its existence.

More so than any previous committee investigating un-American activities, the work of the Dies committee splashed across the headlines of the nation's most important newspapers. In the first month alone, this committee's investigation, which focused primarily on organized labor, generated more front-page coverage in the *New York Times* than the work of the previous special un-American activities committees combined.[35] Some members of

Congress continued to view these efforts as a diversion from the Great Depression. A Wisconsin congressman, for example, noted that "[w]henever a parliamentary body in any country of the world has found itself unable to deal with the economic problems that face the people they go on a witch hunt." Nonetheless, the Dies committee reaped an extraordinary amount of favorable publicity in Congress and support in American public opinion. Representative Sam Rayburn (D–Tex.), the legendary Speaker of the House, commented that "Dies could beat me right now in my own district," a statement whose accuracy was matched only by his disdain for his fellow Texan.[36]

The Dies committee continued to press ahead with its investigation, but the entrance of the United States into World War II in December 1941 swept congressional inquiries into domestic subversion off the front pages. After World War II ended in August 1945, Congress evidenced no real desire to renew the Dies committee's special standing. That is, until Representative John E. Rankin (D–Miss.), an outspoken anticommunist, as well as racist and anti-Semite, defied the House leadership and persisted in his efforts to make the House Committee on Un-American Activities (HUAC) a permanent, standing committee. His concern was not with Nazi and fascist ideologies, but with communist infiltration into American government, the media, and other powerful industries. After his initial resolution failed, Rankin insisted on a roll call vote. Fearful that opposition to HUAC would brand them as communist sympathizers, a solid majority voted to create permanent status for HUAC.[37] Thus were the seeds sown for what later became known as "McCarthyism," a period that one historian has described as "one of the most severe episodes of political repression the United States ever experienced."[38]

McCarthyism took its name from Senator Joseph McCarthy (D–Wisc.), who, more so than any other individual, dominated the post–World War II red scare. Senator McCarthy did not emerge as a visible leader in the congressional inquiries into the American communist movement until well after HUAC had launched its investigation into alleged communist influence in the U.S. Department of State and, to even greater effect, the Hollywood entertainment industry. In need of a reelection issue to shore up a faltering campaign, McCarthy gave a speech in February 1950 before a Wheeling,

West Virginia, women's club that ranks as one of the great moments in American political theatre. After decrying the communist influence in American government, McCarthy reached in his pocket, held up a piece of paper, and charged that it contained a list of 205 "card carrying" communists who worked in the State Department. In fact, McCarthy had no such list, but the lack of evidence was secondary to the possibility that, to a public fearful of Soviet-inspired threats to American domestic security, one could exist.[39]

Buoyed by an extraordinary media reaction, McCarthy returned to Washington. He used the Senate Permanent Investigations Subcommittee as the springboard for his ascent to the first tier of congressional inquisitors into American communism. For the next two years, McCarthy accused countless high government officials, including President Harry S. Truman and Secretary of State Dean Acheson, of either direct involvement with or unwitting assistance to communist infiltrators. Historian William L. O'Neill has commented that McCarthy soon discovered, "to his own amazement, that he could say almost anything with impunity. Millions of people, frightened and confused by cold war reverses, were prepared to swallow any charge McCarthy made, however ridiculous. They did not care if he had any evidence himself and were singularly unmoved by evidence to the contrary."[40]

By June 1954, McCarthy was ultimately undone by his own personal and political excesses, his downfall played out before millions of Americans in the first congressional investigation broadcast on national television, the Army-McCarthy hearings. Called to investigate possible Soviet espionage in the U.S. Army, the hearings were really an opportunity for McCarthy to showboat before an unprecedented American television audience. This time, however, the public was put off by his intemperate behavior, lack of consideration for witnesses and his Senate colleagues, and baseless smears against people unconnected to the matter under investigation. Public support for the Wisconsin senator fell through the bottom after the Army-McCarthy hearings, as did tolerance by the Senate. In December 1954, by a 67-22 margin, his colleagues voted to censure him for conduct unbecoming a member of the Senate. He served out the remainder of his term. Hobbled by health problems, personal disgrace, and alcoholism, he died in May 1957.[41]

**"I HAVE HERE IN MY HAND--"**

From *Herblock: A Cartoonist's Life* (Times Books, 1998).

For his personal style and unbridled aggressiveness, Joseph McCarthy remains the best-remembered self-appointed communist investigator of the period that bears his name. The number of people whose lives he and his committee ruined pales in comparison with those who suffered at the hands of HUAC. True, the phrase "Fifth Amendment Communist" was born with McCarthy, a testament to his willingness to accuse witnesses who refused to testify as guilty by their very presence before his committee. But witnesses called before HUAC fared no better, as the suspicion aroused by their refusal to offer testimony about their political activities was often compounded by their unwillingness to name individuals who were active in the American communist movement. Perhaps the episode that illustrates this dilemma best was HUAC's investigation of Hollywood, which the committee believed was the most receptive portal to Soviet influence because of the community's perceived sympathies for radical politics.

HUAC terrified the Hollywood entertainment establishment. Some of the most respected writers, actors, and directors in the nation offered to "name names," out of fear that their refusal to cooperate would result in the loss of their jobs and permanent banishment from the industry. Witnesses who refused to appear before HUAC or answer questions about their current and past political activities almost always found themselves "blacklisted" soon afterward. A group of Hollywood figures with current or past ties to the Communist Party, known as the "Hollywood Ten," tried to invoke the First Amendment as a defense against a congressional subpoena. As individuals, they did not make sympathetic witnesses and failed to receive support in the courts or in public opinion. The result was that HUAC was able to secure greater cooperation from witnesses.

The most famous of the cooperating Hollywood witnesses was Academy Award–winning director Elia Kazan, who offered HUAC riveting testimony of his own brief flirtation with communism in the 1930s. Kazan warned of the need for contemporary liberals to speak out against the ever-present Soviet-sponsored effort to use American entertainment as a propaganda tool.[42] Most people in the entertainment industry, however, continued to resist. If and when entertainment figures were called before HUAC, their decision to invoke the Fifth Amendment offered no plausible escape route. Doing so suggested they had something to hide. HUAC soon expanded the scope of its investigation to include television, radio, popular music, public schools, state and local government, and universities. Scholars have never been able to pinpoint the exact number of writers, professors, and government officials who lost their jobs during the McCarthy era. The best estimates place the figure at around twenty thousand, the vast majority of whom had done nothing to suggest subversion.[43] And no figure comes close to capturing the number of people who found their reputations irreparably damaged as a result of just being considered a communist sympathizer.

It was within and against these social and political forces that the Court again took up the question of the congressional power to investigate. But the current moment was far different from what it had been in *McGrain,* and the Court was not indifferent to the tenor of the times. In *Dennis v. United States* (1951), the Court upheld the Smith Act, a 1940 law passed by Congress that made it illegal to teach or advocate the overthrow of the United States government by force or violence, against a First Amendment challenge. Although the defendants in *Dennis* did not engage in any violent behavior, they did teach what the Smith Act banned. The Court ruled that such teachings posed an "imminent and probable" danger to public order that justified their suppression, an opinion from which only Justices Black and Douglas dissented.[44] *Dennis* did not address the rights of witnesses to assert their constitutional rights in congressional inquiries, but it did signal that the Court was very much a partner in the American government's larger effort to contain domestic communist influence.

Distance from the worst excesses of McCarthyism allowed the Court to weigh the assertion of one's constitutional rights by a witness in a congressional proceeding with the government's need to compel testimony that was regarded as essential to exposing domestic subversion. The different approaches the justices took to *Watkins* v. *United States* (1957)[45] and *Barenblatt* v. *United States* (1959)[46] illustrate the severe tension within the Court over the need to balance the First Amendment rights of private citizens with what it believed was the legitimate need of government to protect itself from the grave threat posed by communism. These were the two most important decisions the Court handed down during the height of the Cold War involving the rights of witnesses called to appear before Congress.

Both cases involved efforts by HUAC to compel private citizens alleged to have ties to the American communist movement to testify about the extent of their personal involvement and that of other parties. In other words, both John T. Watkins, a labor organizer, and Lloyd Barenblatt, a college professor, were asked to name names of other Communist Party activists. Both refused, but only Watkins was successful in persuading the Court that HUAC's demands violated his constitutional rights. Even then, the Court did not find in favor of Watkins on the basis of his First Amendment defense. What did the Court ultimately say in *Watkins* about the relevance of the First Amendment in congressional inquiries? Just what in *Barenblatt* was so different that led Justices Frankfurter and John Marshall Harlan to defect from the *Watkins* majority? Consider the rationale of Justice Harlan's opinion for the Court in *Barenblatt* and whether such an analysis could withstand First Amendment analysis in the post–Cold War era.

*Barenblatt* inspired Justice Black to write one of his most passionate dissents on what he believed was the absolute prohibition on government power to infringe upon "speech, writings, thoughts and public assemblies, against the unequivocal command of the First Amendment." For Justice Black, as we discussed in Chapter 2, this guarantee was unimpeachable regardless of the content of the speech in question. He rejected Justice Harlan's "balancing test," which placed the importance of the government's interest against the purpose of the First Amendment rights in question. For Black, this approach left "all persons to guess just what the law really means to cover, and fear of a wrong guess inevitably leads people to forego the very rights the Constitution sought to protect above all others."[47]

But Justice Black's emphasis on principle was merely dust in the wind during a time when freedom of conscience was under close watch by Congress. The Court, sensitive to political weapons at the disposal of Congress to limit judicial power and in need of public support for the justices' controversial decision in *Brown* v. *Board of Education,* decided not to push its luck. Since *Brown,* Congress had, in fact, introduced numerous bills to reverse specific decisions and alter the structure and function of the Court, including its jurisdiction to hear cases involving loyalty-security programs.[48] Careful to tread the line between constitutional principle and the place of the judiciary within the American political process, the Court, rather than risk further attacks on its institutional integrity, erred on the side of caution during the tumultuous years when the Cold War intensified by the moment.

By the early 1960s the Court signaled that its decisions involving both the power of Congress to compel testimony from witnesses that involved matters of political association and conscience and the conditional nature of First Amendment free speech rights would not necessarily control future such cases. In *Gibson* v. *Florida Legislative Investigation Committee* (1963), the Court held that a state court had erred when it upheld the contempt conviction of the president of the Miami branch of the National Association for the Advancement of Colored People (NAACP). The NAACP refused to make its lists available to a state legislative committee investigating alleged communist influence in the civil rights movement. For a 5-4 Court, the same margin that had upheld Lloyd Barenblatt's conviction, Justice Arthur Goldberg reversed Theodore Gibson's conviction on the grounds that the legislative committee had violated his First Amendment rights to freedom of association. Justice Goldberg noted, first, that the NAACP differed from Communist Party–affiliated organizations in that the NAACP was lawful and, second, that the evidence produced by the legislative committee "disclose[d] the utter failure to demonstrate the existence of any substantial relationship between the NAACP and subversive or communist activities."[49]

Around the same time, the Court reversed several other contempt convictions involving the rights of witnesses called before congressional investigating committees, holding that the broad right of Congress to investigate did not mean that it was free to disregard the rules of due process and the rights of witnesses.[50] One scholar has commented that the "First Amendment's great renaissance came in the 1960s," when it began to uphold the rights of unpopular speakers to articulate unpopular causes within a much firmer constitutional framework than during the height of the red scare. Rather than uphold government suppression of political speech based on the potential threat it held for social and political order, the Court began to formulate a standard that required *actual harm*, a position that crystallized by the end of the decade in *Brandenburg* v. *Ohio* (1968). Furthermore, notes First Amendment scholar Rodney A. Smolla:

> In virtually every freedom of speech case involving political dissent that has ever reached the Supreme Court for resolution, *no palpable harm has ever in fact occurred* . . . It is not the irrationality, passion, or paranoia of speakers that society should fear, but of censors. When [Justice] Brandeis emphasized that freedom of speech served to vindicate the triumph of the deliberative processes, he should not be understood as requiring that speakers be sober and intellectual in order to qualify for First Amendment protection, but rather that *governments* not be permitted to enact their paranoias into law. It cannot be said often enough: "Men feared witches and burned women."[51]

But the high drama produced by Watergate in the 1970s, Iran-Contra in the 1980s, and the seemingly endless inquiries into the Clinton administration's political and financial dealings in the 1990s indicate that the constitutional boundaries of the congressional power to investigate are far from established. Even if McCarthyism and its consequences are now an anachronism in American constitutional law, the Court faces numerous other questions involving the substance and scope of the power of Congress to compel uncooperative witnesses to appear before its investigating committees. One such area pertains to the rights of public officials to protect their off-the-record conversations with reporters, a question that we touch upon in Volume II of this casebook. Of more immediate interest is the question of executive privilege, which emerged in full public bloom in the early 1970s when President Richard M. Nixon attempted to quash the publication of the Pentagon Papers by the *New York Times*. Later, Nixon also refused to submit subpoenaed documents to the House and Senate committees investigating the Watergate scandal. The latter is an issue that we revisit in full in Chapter 5, when we begin our discussion of executive power.

## *Watkins* v. *United States*
### 354 U.S. 178 (1957)

John T. Watkins stood out from most of the other witnesses called to testify before the HUAC and Senator Joe McCarthy's Senate committee in the 1950s. Watkins neither offered oblique denials of his communist associations nor offered up any of his past or present colleagues in the communist movement. Subpoenaed in April 1954 after two witnesses previously called before HUAC named him as an active member of the Communist Party, Watkins admitted that

> For a period of time from approximately 1942 to 1947 I cooperated with the Communist Party and participated in Communist activities to such a degree that some persons may honestly believe that I was a member of the party. I have made contributions on occasions to Communist causes. I have signed petitions for Communist causes. I attended caucuses at [a] . . . convention at which Communist officials were present.

The statement that got Watkins into trouble follows.

> I refuse to answer certain questions that I believe are outside the proper scope of your committee's activities. I will answer any questions which this committee

puts to me about myself. [But] I will not . . . answer any questions with respect to others with whom I associated in the past. I do not believe that any law in this country requires me to testify about persons who may in the past have been Communist Party members or otherwise engaged in Communist Party activity but who to my best knowledge and belief have long since removed themselves from the Communist movement.

Watkins was held in contempt and convicted by a federal district court for violating a federal law making it a misdemeanor for any person summoned as a witness by either house of Congress or any committee thereof to refuse to answer any question "pertinent to the question under inquiry." His conviction was upheld on appeal.

The Court's decision was 6 to 1. Chief Justice Warren delivered the opinion of the Court. Justice Frankfurter filed a concurrence. Justice Clark dissented. Justices Burton and Whittaker took no part in the consideration or decision of this case.

▼▲▼

Mr. Chief Justice Warren delivered the opinion of the Court.

. . . We start with several basic premises on which there is general agreement. The power of the Congress to conduct investigations is inherent in the legislative process. That power is broad. It encompasses inquiries concerning the administration of existing laws, as well as proposed or possibly needed statutes. It includes surveys of defects in our social, economic or political system for the purpose of enabling the Congress to remedy them. It comprehends probes into departments of the Federal Government to expose corruption, inefficiency or waste. But, broad as is this power of inquiry, it is not unlimited. There is no general authority to expose the private affairs of individuals without justification in terms of the functions of the Congress. This was freely conceded by the Solicitor General in his argument of this case. Nor is the Congress a law enforcement or trial agency. These are functions of the executive and judicial departments of government. No inquiry is an end in itself; it must be related to, and in furtherance of, a legitimate task of the Congress. Investigations conducted solely for the personal aggrandizement of the investigators or to "punish" those investigated are indefensible.

It is unquestionably the duty of all citizens to cooperate with the Congress in its efforts to obtain the facts needed for intelligent legislative action. It is their unremitting obligation to respond to subpoenas, to respect the dignity of the Congress and its committees, and to testify fully with respect to matters within the province of proper investigation. This, of course, assumes that the constitutional rights of witnesses will be respected by the Congress as they are in a court of justice. The Bill of Rights is applicable to investigations as to all forms of governmental action. Witnesses cannot be compelled to give evidence against themselves. They cannot be subjected to unreasonable search and seizure. Nor can the First Amendment freedoms of speech, press, religion, or political belief and association be abridged. . . .

In the decade following World War II, there appeared a new kind of congressional inquiry unknown in prior periods of American history. Principally this was the result of the various investigations into the threat of subversion of the United States Government, but other subjects of congressional interest also contributed to the changed scene. This new phase of legislative inquiry involved a broad-scale intrusion into the lives and affairs of private citizens. It brought before the courts novel questions of the appropriate limits of congressional inquiry. Prior cases, like *Kilbourn*, *McGrain* and *Sinclair* had defined the scope of investigative power in terms of the inherent limitations of the sources of that power. In the more recent cases, the emphasis shifted to problems of accommodating the interest of the Government with the rights and privileges of individuals. The central theme was the application of the Bill of Rights as a restraint upon the assertion of governmental power in this form.

It was during this period that the Fifth Amendment privilege against self-incrimination was frequently invoked and recognized as a legal limit upon the authority of a committee to require that a witness answer its questions. Some early doubts as to the applicability of that privilege before a legislative committee never matured. When the matter reached this Court, the Government did not challenge in any way that the Fifth Amendment protection was available to the witness, and such a challenge could not have prevailed. It confined its argument to the character of the answers sought and to the adequacy of the claim of privilege.

A far more difficult task evolved from the claim by witnesses that the committees' interrogations were infringements upon the freedoms of the First Amendment. Clearly, an investigation is subject to the command that the Congress shall make no law abridging freedom of speech or press or assembly. While it is true that there is no statute to be reviewed, and that an investigation is not a law, nevertheless an investigation is part of law-making. It is justified solely as an adjunct to the legislative process. The First Amendment may be invoked against infringement of the protected freedoms by law or by law-making.

Abuses of the investigative process may imperceptibly lead to abridgment of protected freedoms. The mere summoning of a witness and compelling him to testify, against his will, about his beliefs, expressions or associations is a measure of governmental interference. And when those forced revelations concern matters that are unorthodox, unpopular, or even hateful to the general public, the reaction in the life of the witness may be disastrous. This effect is even more harsh when it is past beliefs, expressions or associations that are disclosed and judged by current standards, rather than those contemporary with the matters exposed. Nor does the witness alone suffer the consequences. Those who are identified by witnesses, and thereby placed in the same glare of publicity, are equally subject to public stigma, scorn and obloquy. Beyond that, there is the more subtle and immeasurable effect upon those who tend to adhere to the most orthodox and uncontroversial views and associations in order to avoid a similar fate at some future time. That this impact is partly the result of nongovernmental activity by private persons cannot relieve the investigators of their responsibility for initiating the reaction. . . .

Accommodation of the congressional need for particular information with the individual and personal interest in privacy is an arduous and delicate task for any court. We do not underestimate the difficulties that would attend such an undertaking. It is manifest that, despite the adverse effects which follow upon compelled disclosure of private matters, not all such inquiries are barred. *Kilbourn* teaches that such an investigation into individual affairs is invalid if unrelated to any legislative purpose. That is beyond the powers conferred upon the Congress in the Constitution. . . . The critical element is the existence of, and the weight to be ascribed to, the interest of the Congress in demanding disclosures from an unwilling witness. We cannot simply assume, however, that every congressional investigation is justified by a public need that overbalances any private rights affected. To do so would be to abdicate the responsibility placed by the Constitution upon the judiciary to insure that the Congress does not unjustifiably encroach upon an individual's right to privacy nor abridge his liberty of speech, press, religion or assembly.

Petitioner has earnestly suggested that the difficult questions of protecting these rights from infringement by legislative inquiries can be surmounted in this case because there was no public purpose served in his interrogation. His conclusion is based upon the thesis that the Subcommittee was engaged in a program of exposure for the sake of exposure. The sole purpose of the inquiry, he contends, was to bring down upon himself and others the violence of public reaction because of their past beliefs, expressions and associations. In support of this argument, petitioner has marshalled an impressive array of evidence that some Congressmen have believed that such was their duty, or part of it.

We have no doubt that there is no congressional power to expose for the sake of exposure. The public is, of course, entitled to be informed concerning the workings of its government. That cannot be inflated into a general power to expose where the predominant result can only be an invasion of the private rights of individuals. But a solution to our problem is not to be found in testing the motives of committee members for this purpose. Such is not our function. Their motives alone would not vitiate an investigation which had been instituted by a House of Congress if that assembly's legislative purpose is being served.

Petitioner's contentions do point to a situation of particular significance from the standpoint of the constitutional limitations upon congressional investigations. The theory of a committee inquiry is that the committee members are serving as the representatives of the parent assembly in collecting information for a legislative purpose. Their function is to act as the eyes and ears of the Congress in obtaining facts upon which the full legislature can act. To carry out this mission, committees and subcommittees, sometimes one Congressman, are endowed with the full power of the Congress to compel testimony. In this case, only two men exercised that authority in demanding information over petitioner's protest.

An essential premise in this situation is that the House or Senate shall have instructed the committee members on what they are to do with the power delegated to them. It is the responsibility of the Congress, in the first instance, to insure that compulsory process is used only in furtherance of a legislative purpose. That requires that the instructions to an investigating committee spell out that group's jurisdiction and purpose with sufficient particularity. Those instructions are embodied in the authorizing resolution. That document is the committee's charter. Broadly drafted and loosely worded, however, such resolutions can leave tremendous latitude to the discretion of the investigators. The more vague the committee's charter is, the greater becomes the possibility that the committee's specific actions are not in conformity with the will of the parent House of Congress.

The authorizing resolution of the Un-American Activities Committee was adopted in 1938, when a select committee, under the chairmanship of Representative Dies, was created. Several years later, the Committee was made a standing organ of the House with the same mandate. It defines the Committee's authority as follows:

> The Committee on Un-American Activities, as a whole or by subcommittee, is authorized to make from time to time investigations of (1) the extent, character, and objects of un-American propaganda activities in the United States, (2) the diffusion within the United States of subversive and un-American propaganda that is instigated from foreign countries or of a domestic origin and attacks the principle of the form of government as guaranteed by our Constitution, and (3) all other questions in relation thereto that would aid Congress in any necessary remedial legislation.

It would be difficult to imagine a less explicit authorizing resolution. Who can define the meaning of "un-American"? What is that single, solitary "principle of the form of government as guaranteed by our Constitution"? There is no need to dwell upon the language, however. At one time, perhaps, the resolution might have been read narrowly to confine the Committee to the subject of propaganda. The events that have transpired in the fifteen years before the interrogation of petitioner make such a construction impossible at this date. . . .

The Government contends that the public interest at the core of the investigations of the Un-American Activities Committee is the need by the Congress to be informed of efforts to overthrow the Government by force and violence, so that adequate legislative safeguards can be erected. From this core, however, the Committee can radiate outward infinitely to any topic thought to be related in some way to armed insurrection. The outer reaches of this domain are known only by the content of "un-American activities." Remoteness of subject can be aggravated by a probe for a depth of detail even farther removed from any basis of legislative action. A third dimension is added when the investigators turn their attention to the past to collect minutiae on remote topics, on the hypothesis that the past may reflect upon the present. . . .

Absence of the qualitative consideration of petitioner's questioning by the House of Representatives aggravates a serious problem, revealed in this case, in the relationship of congressional investigating committees and the witnesses who appear before them. Plainly, these committees are restricted to the missions delegated to them, *i.e.*, to acquire certain data to be used by the House or the Senate in coping with a problem that falls within its legislative sphere. No witness can be compelled to make disclosures on matters outside that area. This is a jurisdictional concept of pertinency drawn from the nature of a congressional committee's source of authority. It is not wholly different from nor unrelated to the element of pertinency embodied in the criminal statute under which petitioner was prosecuted. When the definition of jurisdictional pertinency is as uncertain and wavering as in the case of the Un-American Activities Committee, it becomes extremely difficult for the Committee to limit its inquiries to statutory pertinency. . . .

The problem attains proportion when viewed from the standpoint of the witness who appears before a congressional committee. He must decide at the time the questions are propounded whether or not to answer. As the Court said in *Sinclair* v. *United States,* the witness acts at his peril. He is ". . . bound rightly to construe the statute." An erroneous determination on his part, even if made in the utmost good faith, does not exculpate him if the court should later rule that the questions were pertinent to the question under inquiry.

It is obvious that a person compelled to make this choice is entitled to have knowledge of the subject to which the interrogation is deemed pertinent. That knowledge must be available with the same degree of explicitness and clarity that the Due Process Clause requires in the expression of any element of a criminal offense. The "vice of vagueness" must be avoided here, as in all other crimes. There are several sources that can outline the "question under inquiry" in such a way that the rules against vagueness are satisfied. The authorizing resolution, the remarks of the chairman or members of the committee, or even the nature of the proceedings themselves, might sometimes make the topic clear. This case demonstrates, however, that these sources often leave the matter in grave doubt. . . .

The statement of the Committee Chairman in this case, in response to petitioner's protest, was woefully inadequate to convey sufficient information as to the pertinency of the questions to the subject under inquiry. Petitioner was thus not accorded a fair opportunity to determine whether he was within his rights in refusing to answer, and his conviction is necessarily invalid under the Due Process Clause of the Fifth Amendment.

We are mindful of the complexities of modern government and the ample scope that must be left to the Congress as the sole constitutional depository of legislative power. Equally mindful are we of the indispensable function, in the exercise of that power, of congressional investigations. The conclusions we have reached in this case will not prevent the Congress, through its committees, from obtaining any information it needs for the proper fulfillment of its role in our scheme of government. The legislature is free to determine the kinds of data that should be collected. It is only those investigations that are conducted by use of compulsory process that give rise to a need to protect the rights of individuals against illegal encroachment. That protection can be readily achieved through procedures which prevent the separation of power from responsibility and which provide the constitutional requisites of fairness for witnesses. A measure of added care on the part of the House and the Senate in authorizing the use of compulsory process and by their committees in exercising that power would suffice. That is a small price to pay if it serves to uphold the principles of limited, constitutional government without constricting the power of the Congress to inform itself.

Mr. Justice Frankfurter, concurring.

I deem it important to state what I understand to be the Court's holding. Agreeing with its holding, I join its opinion. . . .

To turn to the immediate problem before us, the scope of inquiry that a committee is authorized to pursue must be defined with sufficiently unambiguous clarity to safeguard a witness from the hazards of vagueness in the enforcement of the criminal process against which the Due Process Clause protects. The questions must be put with relevance and definiteness sufficient to enable the witness to know whether his refusal to answer may lead to conviction for criminal contempt and to enable both the trial and the appellate courts readily to determine whether the particular circumstances justify a finding of guilt.

While implied authority for the questioning by the Committee, sweeping as was its inquiry, may be squeezed out of the repeated acquiescence by Congress in the Committee's inquiries, the basis for determining petitioner's guilt is not thereby laid. Prosecution for contempt of Congress presupposes an adequate opportunity for the defendant to have awareness of the pertinency of the information that he has denied to Congress. And the basis of such awareness must be contemporaneous with the witness' refusal to answer and not at the trial for it. Accordingly, the actual scope of the inquiry that the Committee was authorized to conduct and the relevance of the questions to that inquiry must be shown to have been luminous at the time when asked and not left, at best, in cloudiness. The circumstances of this case were wanting in these essentials.

Mr. Justice Clark, dissenting.

As I see it, the chief fault in the majority opinion is its mischievous curbing of the informing function of the Congress. While I am not versed in its procedures, my experience in the Executive Branch of the Government leads me to believe that the requirements laid down in the opinion for the operation of the committee system of inquiry are both unnecessary and unworkable. . . .

It may be that, at times the House Committee on Un-American Activities has, as the Court says, "conceived of its task in the grand view of its name." And, perhaps, as the Court indicates, the rules of conduct placed upon the Committee by the House admit of individual abuse and unfairness. But that is none of our affair. So long as the object of a legislative inquiry is legitimate and the questions propounded are pertinent thereto, it is not for the courts to interfere with the committee system of inquiry. To hold otherwise would be an infringement on the power given the Congress to inform itself, and thus a trespass upon the fundamental American principle of separation of powers. The majority has substituted the judiciary as the grand inquisitor and supervisor of congressional investigations. It has never been so. . . .

The Court indicates that, in this case, the source of the trouble lies in the "tremendous latitude" given the Un-American Activities Committee in the Legislative Reorganization Act. It finds that the Committee "is allowed, in essence, to define its own authority, [and] to choose the direction and focus of its activities." This, of course, is largely true of all committees within their respective spheres. And, while it is necessary that the "charter," as the opinion calls the enabling resolution, "spell out [its] jurisdiction and purpose," that must necessarily be in more or less general terms. An examination of the enabling resolutions of other committees reveals the extent to which this is true. . . .

The Court finds fault with the use made of compulsory process, power for the use of which is granted the Committee in the Reorganization Act. While the Court finds that the Congress is free "to determine the kinds of data" it wishes its committees to collect, this has led the Court says, to an encroachment on individual rights through the abuse of process. To my mind, this indicates a lack of understanding of the problems facing such committees. I am sure that the committees would welcome voluntary disclosure. It would simplify and relieve their burden considerably if the parties involved in investigations would come forward with a frank willingness to cooperate. But everyday experience shows this just does not happen. One needs only to read the newspapers to know that the Congress could gather little "data" unless its committees had, unfettered, the power of subpoena. In fact, Watkins himself could not be found for appearance at the first hearing, and it was only by subpoena that he attended the second. The Court generalizes on this crucial problem, saying, "added care on the part of the House and the Senate in authorizing the use of compulsory process and by their committees in exercising that power would suffice." It does not say how this "added care" could be applied in practice; however, there are many implications, since the opinion warns that "procedures which prevent the separation of power from responsibility" would be necessary along with "constitutional requisites of fairness for witnesses." The "power" and "responsibility" for the investigations are, of course, in the House where the proceeding is initiated. But the investigating job itself can only be done through the use of committees. They must have the "power" to force compliance with their requirements. If the rule requires that this power be retained in the full House, then investigations will be so cumbrous that their conduct will be a practical impossibility. As to "fairness for witnesses," there is nothing in the record showing any abuse of Watkins. If anything, the Committee was abused by his recalcitrance. . . .

Coming to the merits of Watkins' case, the Court reverses the judgment because: (1) The subject matter of the inquiry was not "made to appear with undisputable clarity" either through its "charter" or by the Chairman at the time of the hearing and, therefore, Watkins was deprived of a clear understanding of "the manner in which the propounded questions [were] pertinent thereto," and (2) the present committee system of inquiry of the House, as practiced by the Un-American Activities Committee, does not provide adequate safeguards for the protection of the constitutional right of free speech. I subscribe to neither conclusion.

Watkins had been an active leader in the labor movement for many years, and had been identified by two previous witnesses at the Committee's hearing in Chicago as a member of the Communist Party. There can be no question that he was fully informed of the subject matter of the inquiry. His testimony reveals a complete knowledge and understanding of the hearings at Chicago. There, the Chairman had announced that the Committee had been

directed, "to ascertain the extent and success of subversive activities directed against these United States [and] on the basis of these investigations and hearings . . . [report] its findings to the Congress and [make] recommendations . . . for new legislation." He pointed to the various laws that had been enacted as a result of Committee recommendations. He stated that, "The Congress has also referred to the House Committee on Un-American Activities a bill which would amend the National Security Act of 1950," which, if made law, would restrict the availability of the Labor Act to unions not "in fact Communist controlled action groups." The Chairman went on to say that, "It cannot be said that subversive infiltration has had a greater nor a lesser success in infiltrating this important area. The hearings today are the culmination of an investigation. . . . Every witness who has been subpoenaed to appear before the committee here in Chicago . . . [is] known to possess information which will assist the Committee in performing its directed function to the Congress of the United States." . . .

I think the Committee here was acting entirely within its scope, and that the purpose of its inquiry was set out with "undisputable clarity." In the first place, the authorizing language of the Reorganization Act must be read as a whole, not dissected. It authorized investigation into subversive activity, its extent, character, objects, and diffusion. While the language might have been more explicit than using such words as "un-American," or phrases like "principle of the form of government," still, these are fairly well understood terms. We must construe them to give them meaning if we can. Our cases indicate that, rather than finding fault with the use of words or phrases, we are bound to presume that the action of the legislative body in granting authority to the Committee was with a legitimate object "if [the action] is *capable* of being so construed." Before we can deny the authority, "it must be obvious that" the Committee has "exceeded the bounds of legislative power." The fact that the Committee has often been attacked has caused close scrutiny of its acts by the House as a whole, and the House has repeatedly given the Committee its approval. "Power" and "responsibility" have not been separated. But the record in this case does not stop here. It shows that, at the hearings involving Watkins, the Chairman made statements explaining the functions of the Committee. And, furthermore, Watkins' action at the hearing clearly reveals that he was well acquainted with the purpose of the hearing. It was to investigate Communist infiltration into his union. This certainly falls within the grant of authority from the Reorganization Act, and the House has had ample opportunity to limit the investigative scope of the Committee if it feels that the Committee has exceeded its legitimate bounds.

The Court makes much of petitioner's claim of "exposure for exposure's sake," and strikes at the purposes of the Committee through this catch phrase. But we are bound to accept as the purpose of the Committee that stated in the Reorganization Act, together with the statements of the Chairman at the hearings involved here. Nothing was said of exposure. The statements of a single Congressman cannot transform the real purpose of the Committee into something not authorized by the parent resolution. The Court indicates that the questions propounded were asked for exposure's sake, and had no pertinency to the inquiry. It appears to me that they were entirely pertinent to the announced purpose of the Committee's inquiry. Undoubtedly Congress has the power to inquire into the subjects of communism and the Communist Party. As a corollary of the congressional power to inquire into such subject matter, the Congress, through its committees, can legitimately seek to identify individual members of the Party.

The pertinency of the questions is highlighted by the need for the Congress to know the extent of infiltration of communism in labor unions. This technique of infiltration was that used in bringing the downfall of countries formerly free but now still remaining behind the Iron Curtain. . . . Association with its officials is not an ordinary association. Nor does it matter that the questions related to the past. Influences of past associations often linger on, as was clearly shown in the instance of the witness Matusow and others. The techniques used in the infiltration which admittedly existed here might well be used again in the future. If the parties about whom Watkins was interrogated were Communists and collaborated with him, as a prior witness indicated, an entirely new area of investigation might have been opened up. Watkins' silence prevented the Committee from learning this information which could have been vital to its future investigation. The Committee was likewise entitled to elicit testimony showing the truth or falsity of the prior testimony of the witnesses who had involved Watkins and the union with collaboration with the Party. If the testimony was untrue, a false picture of the relationship between the union and the Party leaders would have resulted. For these reasons, there were ample indications of the pertinency of the questions.

The Court condemns the long-established and long-recognized committee system of inquiry of the House because it raises serious questions concerning the protection it affords to constitutional rights. It concludes that compelling a witness to reveal his "beliefs, expressions or associations" impinges upon First Amendment rights. The system of inquiry, it says, must, "insure that the Congress does not unjustifiably encroach upon an individual's right to privacy, nor abridge his liberty of speech, press, religion or assembly." In effect, the Court honors Watkins' claim of a "right to silence" which brings all inquiries, as we know, to a "dead end." I do not see how any First Amendment rights were endangered here. There is nothing in the First Amendment that provides the guarantees Watkins claims. That Amendment was designed to prevent attempts by law to curtail freedom of speech. It forbids Congress from making any law "abridging the freedom of speech, or of the press." It guarantees Watkins' right to join any organization and make any speech that does not have an intent to incite to crime. But Watkins was asked whether he knew named individuals and whether they were Communists. He refused to answer on the ground that his rights were being abridged. What he was actually seeking to do was to protect his former associates, not himself, from embarrassment. He had already admitted his own involvement. He sought to vindicate the rights, if any, of his associates. It is settled that one cannot invoke the constitutional rights of another. . . .

We do not have in this case unauthorized, arbitrary, or unreasonable inquiries and disclosures with respect to a witness' personal and private affairs. . . . It involves new faces and new issues brought about by new situations which the Congress feels it is necessary to control in the public interest. The difficulties of getting information are identical, if not greater. Like authority to that always used by the Congress is employed here, and in the same manner so far as congressional procedures are concerned. We should afford to Congress the presumption that it takes every precaution possible to avoid unnecessary damage to reputations. Some committees have codes of procedure, and others use the executive hearing technique to this end. The record in this case shows no conduct on the part of the Un-American Activities Committee that justifies condemnation. That there may have been such occasions is not for us to consider here. Nor should we permit its past transgressions, if any, to lead to the rigid restraint of all congressional committees. To carry on its heavy responsibility, the compulsion of truth that does not incriminate is not only necessary to the Congress, but is permitted within the limits of the Constitution.

▼▲▼

## *Barenblatt* v. *United States*
### 360 U.S. 109 (1959)

In February 1953 a HUAC subcommittee began investigating communist activities in the field of education, with "subversion" in colleges and universities as its primary target. A former University of Michigan graduate student, Francis Crowley, testified that for a short time in 1950 he belonged to a club with communist sympathies. He told HUAC investigators that another graduate student, Lloyd Barenblatt, had been involved with the club as well. Crowley's testimony was certainly heard in the president's office of Vassar College, where Barenblatt taught psychology. His contract was terminated after the 1953 academic year ended.

Barenblatt was called before the same subcommittee in June 1954, where, unlike Watkins, he refused to provide any information about his or anyone else's association with the Communist Party. He had no idea why he had been called before HUAC, because he did not know anyone who would provide the committee with such information about him. Barenblatt was stunned to find out that Crowley, his ex-roommate, had exposed him. Not until Barenblatt appeared before the committee did he learn that it was Crowley—he appeared on a stage with his back turned to the witnesses called to testify.

Barenblatt's refusal to testify landed him in prison. He had difficulties finding an attorney to represent him—so intimidating was HUAC that not even the American Civil Liberties Union would touch his original case nor his initial appeal. With the support of the American Friends Service Committee, a Quaker group, Barenblatt was able to secure a lawyer. The appeals court ordered his case reargued. From that point on, Barenblatt became a celebrity among free speech advocates. The ACLU did handle Barenblatt's appeal to the Supreme Court.

Barenblatt served time in four federal prisons. After his release he was never able to get another university-level teaching job.

The Court's decision was 5 to 4. Justice Harlan delivered the opinion of the Court. Justice Black, joined by Justices Warren and Douglas, dissented. Justice Brennan also filed a dissent.

▼▲▼

Mr. Justice Harlan delivered the opinion of the Court.

Once more the Court is required to resolve the conflicting constitutional claims of congressional power, and of an individual's right to resist its exercise. The congressional power in question concerns the internal process of Congress in moving within its legislative domain; it involves the utilization of its committees to secure "testimony needed to enable it efficiently to exercise a legislative function belonging to it under the Constitution." *McGrain v. Daugherty* (1927). . . . The scope of the power of inquiry, in short, is as penetrating and far-reaching as the potential power to enact and appropriate under the Constitution.

Broad as it is, the power is not, however, without limitations. Since Congress may only investigate into those areas in which it may potentially legislate or appropriate, it cannot inquire into matters which are within the exclusive province of one of the other branches of the Government. Lacking the judicial power given to the Judiciary, it cannot inquire into matters that are exclusively the concern of the Judiciary. Neither can it supplant the Executive in what exclusively belongs to the Executive. And the Congress, in common with all branches of the Government, must exercise its powers subject to the limitations placed by the Constitution on governmental action, more particularly, in the context of this case, the relevant limitations of the Bill of Rights. . . .

Pursuant to a subpoena, and accompanied by counsel, petitioner, on June 28, 1954, appeared as a witness before this congressional Subcommittee. After answering a few preliminary questions and testifying that he had been a graduate student and teaching fellow at the University of Michigan from 1947 to 1950 and an instructor in psychology at Vassar College from 1950 to shortly before his appearance before the Subcommittee, petitioner objected generally to the right of the Subcommittee to inquire into his "political" and "religious" beliefs or any "other personal and private affairs" or "associational activities," upon grounds set forth in a previously prepared memorandum which he was allowed to file with the Subcommittee. Thereafter, petitioner specifically declined to answer each of the following five questions:

Are you now a member of the Communist Party? [Count One.]

Have you ever been a member of the Communist Party? [Count Two.]

Now, you have stated that you knew Francis Crowley. Did you know Francis Crowley as a member of the Communist Party? [Count Three.]

Were you ever a member of the Haldane Club of the Communist Party while at the University of Michigan? [Count Four.]

Were you a member while a student of the University of Michigan Council of Arts, Sciences, and Professions? [Count Five.]

In each instance the grounds of refusal were those set forth in the prepared statement. Petitioner expressly disclaimed reliance upon "the Fifth Amendment." . . .

Petitioner's various contentions resolve themselves into three propositions: first, the compelling of testimony by the Subcommittee was neither legislatively authorized nor constitutionally permissible because of the vagueness of Rule XI of the House of Representatives, Eighty-third Congress, the charter of authority of the parent Committee. Second, petitioner was not adequately apprised of the pertinency of the Subcommittee's questions to the subject matter of the inquiry. Third, the questions petitioner refused to answer infringed rights protected by the First Amendment.

## Subcommittee's Authority to Compel Testimony

At the outset, it should be noted that Rule XI authorized this Subcommittee to compel testimony within the framework of the investigative authority conferred on the Un-American Activities Committee. Petitioner contends that *Watkins v. United States*, nevertheless held the grant of this power in all circumstances ineffective because of the vagueness of Rule XI in delineating the Committee jurisdiction to which its exercise was to be appurtenant. . . .

The *Watkins* case cannot properly be read as standing for such a proposition. A principal contention in *Watkins* was that the refusals to answer were justified because the requirement that the questions asked be "pertinent to the question under inquiry" had not been satisfied. This Court reversed the conviction solely on that ground, holding that Watkins had not been adequately apprised of the subject matter of the Subcommittee's investigation or the pertinency thereto of the questions he refused to answer. . . .

Petitioner also contends, independently of *Watkins*, that the vagueness of Rule XI deprived the Subcommittee of the right to compel testimony in this investigation into Communist activity. We cannot agree with this contention, which, in its furthest reach, would mean that the House Un-American Activities Committee under its existing authority has no right to compel testimony in any circumstances. Granting the vagueness of the Rule, we may not read it in isolation from its long history in the House of Representatives. Just as legislation is often given meaning by the gloss of legislative reports, administrative interpretation, and long usage, so the proper meaning of an authorization to a congressional committee is not to be derived alone from its abstract terms unrelated to the definite content furnished them by the course of congressional actions. The Rule comes to us with a "persuasive gloss of legislative history," which shows beyond doubt that, in pursuance of its legislative concerns in the domain of "national security," the House has clothed the Un-American Activities Committee with pervasive authority to investigate Communist activities in this country. . . .

In the context of these unremitting pursuits, the House has steadily continued the life of the Committee at the commencement of each new Congress; it has never narrowed the powers of the Committee, whose authority has remained throughout identical with that contained in Rule XI, and it has continuingly supported the Committee's activities with substantial appropriations. Beyond this, the Committee was raised to the level of a standing committee of the House in 1945, it having been but a special committee prior to that time.

In light of this long and illuminating history, it can hardly be seriously argued that the investigation of Communist activities generally, and the attendant use of compulsory process, was beyond the purview of the Committee's intended authority under Rule XI. . . .

In this framework of the Committee's history, we must conclude that its legislative authority to conduct the inquiry presently under consideration is unassailable, and that, independently of whatever bearing the broad scope of Rule XI may have on the issue of "pertinency" in a given investigation into Communist activities, as in *Watkins*, the Rule cannot be said to be constitutionally infirm on the score of vagueness. The constitutional permissibility of that authority otherwise is a matter to be discussed later.

## Pertinency Claim

Undeniably, a conviction for contempt cannot stand unless the questions asked are pertinent to the subject matter of the investigation. But the factors which led us to rest decision on this ground in *Watkins* were very different from those involved here.

In *Watkins*, the petitioner had made specific objection to the Subcommittee's questions on the ground of pertinency; the question under inquiry had not been disclosed in any illuminating manner, and the questions asked the petitioner were not only amorphous on their face, but, in some instances, clearly foreign to the alleged subject matter of the investigation—"Communism in labor."

In contrast, petitioner in the case before us raised no objections on the ground of pertinency at the time any of the questions were put to him. It is true that the memorandum which petitioner brought with him to the Subcommittee hearing contained the statement, "to ask me whether I am or have been a member of the Communist Party may have dire consequences. I might wish to . . . challenge the pertinency of the question to the investigation." . . . [This statement] cannot, however, be accepted as the equivalent of a pertinency objection. At best, [it] constituted but a contemplated objection to questions still unasked, and, buried as they were in the context of petitioner's general challenge to the power of the Subcommittee, they can hardly be considered adequate, within the meaning of what was said in *Watkins*, to trigger what would have been the Subcommittee's reciprocal obligation had it been faced with a pertinency objection.

We need not, however, rest decision on petitioner's failure to object on this score, for here "pertinency" was made to appear "with undisputable clarity." First of all, it goes without saying that the scope of the Committee's authority was for the House, not a witness, to determine, subject to the ultimate reviewing responsibility of this Court. What we deal with here is whether petitioner was sufficiently apprised of "the topic under inquiry" thus authorized "and the connective reasoning whereby the precise questions asked relate[d] to it." In light of his prepared memorandum of constitutional objections, there can be no doubt that this petitioner was well aware of the Subcommittee's authority and purpose to question him as it did. In addition, the other sources of this information which we recognized in *Watkins*, leave no room for a "pertinency" objection on this record. The subject matter of the inquiry had been identified at the commencement of the investigation as Communist infiltration into the field of education. Just prior to petitioner's appearance before the Subcommittee, the scope of the day's hearings had been announced as, "in the main, communism in education and the experiences and background in the party by Francis X. T. Crowley. It will deal with activities in Michigan, Boston, and, in some small degree, New York." Petitioner had heard the Subcommittee interrogate the witness Crowley along the same lines as he, petitioner, was evidently to be questioned, and had listened to Crowley's testimony identifying him as a former member of an alleged Communist student organization at the University of Michigan while they both were in attendance there. Further, petitioner had stood mute in the face of the Chair-

man's statement as to why he had been called as a witness by the Subcommittee. And, lastly, unlike *Watkins*, petitioner refused to answer questions as to his own Communist Party affiliations, whose pertinency, of course, was clear beyond doubt. . . .

## Constitutional Contentions

. . . The precise constitutional issue confronting us is whether the Subcommittee's inquiry into petitioner's past or present membership in the Communist Party transgressed the provisions of the First Amendment, which, of course, reach and limit congressional investigations.

The Court's past cases establish sure guides to decision. Undeniably, the First Amendment in some circumstances protects an individual from being compelled to disclose his associational relationships. However, the protections of the First Amendment, unlike a proper claim of the privilege against self-incrimination under the Fifth Amendment, do not afford a witness the right to resist inquiry in all circumstances. Where First Amendment rights are asserted to bar governmental interrogation, resolution of the issue always involves a balancing by the courts of the competing private and public interests at stake in the particular circumstances shown. These principles were recognized in the *Watkins* case, where, in speaking of the First Amendment in relation to congressional inquiries, we said: "It is manifest that, despite the adverse effects which follow upon compelled disclosure of private matters, not all such inquiries are barred. . . . The critical element is the existence of, and the weight to be ascribed to, the interest of the Congress in demanding disclosures from an unwilling witness."

More recently, in *National Association for the Advancement of Colored People* v. *Alabama*, we applied the same principles in judging state action claimed to infringe rights of association assured by the Due Process Clause of the Fourteenth Amendment, and stated that the "'subordinating interest of the State must be compelling'" in order to overcome the individual constitutional rights at stake. In light of these principles, we now consider petitioner's First Amendment claims.

The first question is whether this investigation was related to a valid legislative purpose, for Congress may not constitutionally require an individual to disclose his political relationships or other private affairs except in relation to such a purpose.

That Congress has wide power to legislate in the field of Communist activity in this Country, and to conduct appropriate investigations in aid thereof, is hardly debatable. The existence of such power has never been questioned by this Court, and it is sufficient to say, without particularization, that Congress has enacted or considered in this field a wide range of legislative measures, not a few of which have stemmed from recommendations of the very Committee whose actions have been drawn in question here. In the last analysis, this power rests on the right of self-preservation, "the ultimate value of any society." Justification for its exercise, in turn, rests on the long and widely accepted view that the tenets of the Communist Party include the ultimate overthrow of the Government of the United States by force and violence, a view which has been given formal expression by the Congress. . . .

To suggest that, because the Communist Party may also sponsor peaceable political reforms, the constitutional issues before us should now be judged as if that Party were just an ordinary political party from the standpoint of national security, is to ask this Court to blind itself to world affairs which have determined the whole course of our national policy since the close of World War II . . . and to the vast burdens which these conditions have entailed for the entire Nation.

Indeed, we do not understand petitioner here to suggest that Congress in no circumstances may inquire into Communist activity in the field of education. Rather, his position is, in effect, that this particular investigation was aimed not at the revolutionary aspects, but at the theoretical classroom discussion of communism.

In our opinion, this position rests on a too constricted view of the nature of the investigatory process, and is not supported by a fair assessment of the record before us. An investigation of advocacy of or preparation for overthrow certainly embraces the right to identify a witness as a member of the Communist Party, and to inquire into the various manifestations of the Party's tenets. The strict requirements of a prosecution under the Smith Act, are not the measure of the permissible scope of a congressional investigation into "overthrow," for, of necessity, the investigatory process must proceed step by step. Nor can it fairly be concluded that this investigation was directed at controlling what is being taught at our universities, rather than at overthrow. The statement of the Subcommittee Chairman at the opening of the investigation evinces no such intention, and, so far as this record reveals nothing thereafter transpired which would justify our holding that the thrust of the investigation later changed. The record discloses considerable testimony concerning the foreign domination and revolutionary purposes and efforts of the Communist Party. That there was also testimony on

the abstract philosophical level does not detract from the dominant theme of this investigation—Communist infiltration furthering the alleged ultimate purpose of overthrow. And certainly the conclusion would not be justified that the questioning of petitioner would have exceeded permissible bounds had he not shut off the Subcommittee at the threshold.

Nor can we accept the further contention that this investigation should not be deemed to have been in furtherance of a legislative purpose because the true objective of the Committee and of the Congress was purely "exposure." So long as Congress acts in pursuance of its constitutional power, the Judiciary lacks authority to intervene on the basis of the motives which spurred the exercise of that power. . . . These principles, of course, apply as well to committee investigations into the need for legislation as to the enactments which such investigations may produce. Thus, in stating in the *Watkins* case, that "there is no congressional power to expose for the sake of exposure," we at the same time declined to inquire into the "motives of committee members," and recognized that their, "motives alone would not vitiate an investigation which had been instituted by a House of Congress if that assembly's legislative purpose is being served." Having scrutinized this record, we cannot say that the unanimous panel of the Court of Appeals which first considered this case was wrong in concluding that "the primary purposes of the inquiry were in aid of legislative processes." Certainly this is not a case like *Kilbourn*, where, "the House of Representatives not only exceeded the limit of its own authority, but assumed a power which could only be properly exercised by another branch of the government, because it was in its nature clearly judicial." The constitutional legislative power of Congress in this instance is beyond question.

Finally, the record is barren of other factors which, in themselves, might sometimes lead to the conclusion that the individual interests at stake were not subordinate to those of the state. There is no indication in this record that the Subcommittee was attempting to pillory witnesses. Nor did petitioner's appearance as a witness follow from indiscriminate dragnet procedures, lacking in probable cause for belief that he possessed information which might be helpful to the Subcommittee. And the relevancy of the questions put to him by the Subcommittee is not open to doubt.

We conclude that the balance between the individual and the governmental interests here at stake must be struck in favor of the latter, and that, therefore, the provisions of the First Amendment have not been offended. . . .

MR. JUSTICE BLACK, with whom THE CHIEF JUSTICE and MR. JUSTICE DOUGLAS concur, dissenting.

. . . It goes without saying that a law, to be valid, must be clear enough to make its commands understandable. For obvious reasons, the standard of certainty required in criminal statutes is more exacting than in noncriminal statutes. This is simply because it would be unthinkable to convict a man for violating a law he could not understand. This Court has recognized that the stricter standard is as much required in criminal contempt cases as in all other criminal cases, and has emphasized that the "vice of vagueness" is especially pernicious where legislative power over an area involving speech, press, petition and assembly is involved. In this area, the statement that a statute is void if it "attempts to cover so much that it effectively covers nothing," takes on double significance. For a statute broad enough to support infringement of speech, writings, thoughts and public assemblies against the unequivocal command of the First Amendment necessarily leaves all persons to guess just what the law really means to cover, and fear of a wrong guess inevitably leads people to forego the very rights the Constitution sought to protect above all others. Vagueness becomes even more intolerable in this area if one accepts, as the Court today does, a balancing test to decide if First Amendment rights shall be protected. It is difficult, at best, to make a man guess—at the penalty of imprisonment—whether a court will consider the State's need for certain information superior to society's interest in unfettered freedom. It is unconscionable to make him choose between the right to keep silent and the need to speak when the statute supposedly establishing the "state's interest" is too vague to give him guidance. . . .

The First Amendment says in no equivocal language that Congress shall pass no law abridging freedom of speech, press, assembly or petition. The activities of this Committee, authorized by Congress, do precisely that through exposure, obloquy and public scorn. The Court does not really deny this fact, but relies on a combination of three reasons for permitting the infringement: (A) the notion that, despite the First Amendment's command, Congress can abridge speech and association if this Court decides that the governmental interest in abridging speech is greater than an individual's interest in exercising that freedom, (B) the Government's right to "preserve itself," (C) the fact that the Committee is only after Communists or suspected Communists in this investigation. . . .

To apply the Court's balancing test under such circumstances is to read the First Amendment to say, "Congress shall pass no law abridging freedom of speech, press, assembly and petition, unless Congress and the Supreme Court reach the joint conclusion that, on balance, the interest of the Government in stifling these freedoms is greater than the interest of the people in having them exercised." This is closely akin to the notion that neither the First Amendment nor any other provision of the Bill of Rights should be enforced unless the Court believes it is *reasonable* to do so. Not only does this violate the genius of our *written* Constitution, but it runs expressly counter to the injunction to Court and Congress made by Madison when he introduced the Bill of Rights. "If they [the first ten amendments] are incorporated into the Constitution, independent tribunals of justice will consider themselves in a peculiar manner the guardians of those rights; they will be an impenetrable bulwark against *every* assumption of power in the Legislative or Executive; they will be naturally led to resist *every* encroachment upon rights expressly stipulated for in the Constitution by the declaration of rights." Unless we return to this view of our judicial function, unless we once again accept the notion that the Bill of Rights means what it says and that this Court must enforce that meaning, I am of the opinion that our great charter of liberty will be more honored in the breach than in the observance.

But even assuming what I cannot assume, that some balancing is proper in this case, I feel that the Court after stating the test ignores it completely. At most, it balances the right of the Government to preserve itself, against Barenblatt's right to refrain from revealing Communist affiliations. Such a balance, however, mistakes the factors to be weighed. In the first place, it completely leaves out the real interest in Barenblatt's silence, the interest of the people as a whole in being able to join organizations, advocate causes and make political "mistakes" without later being subjected to governmental penalties for having dared to think for themselves. It is this right, the right to err politically, which keeps us strong as a Nation. For no number of laws against communism can have as much effect as the personal conviction which comes from having heard its arguments and rejected them, or from having once accepted its tenets and later recognized their worthlessness. Instead, the obloquy which results from investigations such as this not only stifles "mistakes," but prevents all but the most courageous from hazarding any views which might at some later time become disfavored. This result, whose importance cannot be overestimated, is doubly crucial when it affects the universities, on which we must largely rely for the experimentation and development of new ideas essential to our country's welfare. It is these interests of society, rather than Barenblatt's own right to silence, which I think the Court should put on the balance against the demands of the Government, if any balancing process is to be tolerated. Instead they are not mentioned, while, on the other side, the demands of the Government are vastly overstated, and called "self-preservation." It is admitted that this Committee can only seek information for the purpose of suggesting laws, and that Congress' power to make laws in the realm of speech and association is quite limited, even on the Court's test. Its interest in making such laws in the field of education, primarily a state function, is clearly narrower still. Yet the Court styles this attenuated interest self-preservation, and allows it to overcome the need our country has to let us all think, speak, and associate politically as we like, and without fear of reprisal. Such a result reduces "balancing" to a mere play on words, and is completely inconsistent with the rules this Court has previously given for applying a "balancing test," where it is proper: "[T]he courts should be *astute* to examine the effect of the challenged legislation. Mere *legislative preferences or beliefs* . . . may well support regulation directed at other personal activities, but be insufficient to justify such as diminishes the exercise of rights so vital to the maintenance of democratic institutions."

(B) Moreover, I cannot agree with the Court's notion that First Amendment freedoms must be abridged in order to "preserve" our country. That notion rests on the unarticulated premise that this Nation's security hangs upon its power to punish people because of what they think, speak or write about, or because of those with whom they associate for political purposes. The Government, in its brief, virtually admits this position when it speaks of the "communication of unlawful ideas." I challenge this premise, and deny that ideas can be proscribed under our Constitution. I agree that despotic governments cannot exist without stifling the voice of opposition to their oppressive practices. The First Amendment means to me, however, that the only constitutional way our Government can preserve itself is to leave its people the fullest possible freedom to praise, criticize or discuss, as they see fit, all governmental policies and to suggest, if they desire, that even its most fundamental postulates are bad, and should be changed. . . . To say that our patriotism must be protected against false ideas by means other than these is, I think, to make a baseless charge. Unless we can rely on these qualities—if, in short, we begin to punish speech—we cannot honestly proclaim ourselves to be a free Nation, and we have lost what the Founders of this land risked their lives and their sacred honor to defend.

The fact is that, once we allow any group which has some political aims or ideas to be driven from the ballot and from the battle for men's minds because some of its members are bad and some of its tenets are illegal, no group is safe. Today we deal with Communists or suspected Communists. In 1920, instead, the New York Assembly suspended duly elected legislators on the ground that, being Socialists, they were disloyal to the country's principles. In the 1830s, the Masons were hunted as outlaws and subversives, and abolitionists were considered revolutionaries of the most dangerous kind in both North and South. Earlier still, at the time of the universally unlamented alien and sedition laws, Thomas Jefferson's party was attacked and its members were derisively called "Jacobins." Fisher Ames described the party as a "French faction" guilty of "subversion" and "officered, regimented and formed to subordination." Its members, he claimed, intended to "take arms against the laws as soon as they dare." History should teach us then, that, in times of high emotional excitement, minority parties and groups which advocate extremely unpopular social or governmental innovations will always be typed as criminal gangs, and attempts will always be made to drive them out. It was knowledge of this fact, and of its great dangers, that caused the Founders of our land to enact the First Amendment as a guarantee that neither Congress nor the people would do anything to hinder or destroy the capacity of individuals and groups to seek converts and votes for any cause, however radical or unpalatable their principles might seem under the accepted notions of the time. Whatever the States were left free to do, the First Amendment sought to leave Congress devoid of any kind or quality of power to direct any type of national laws against the freedom of individuals to think what they please, advocate whatever policy they choose, and join with others to bring about the social, religious, political and governmental changes which seem best to them. Today's holding, in my judgment, marks another major step in the progressively increasing retreat from the safeguards of the First Amendment. . . .

Finally, I think Barenblatt's conviction violates the Constitution because the chief aim, purpose and practice of the House Un-American Activities Committee, as disclosed by its many reports, is to try witnesses and punish them because they are or have been Communists or because they refuse to admit or deny Communist affiliations. The punishment imposed is generally punishment by humiliation and public shame. There is nothing strange or novel about this kind of punishment. It is, in fact, one of the oldest forms of governmental punishment known to mankind; branding, the pillory, ostracism and subjection to public hatred being but a few examples of it. Nor is there anything strange about a court's reviewing the power of a congressional committee to inflict punishment. In 1880, this Court nullified the action of the House of Representatives in sentencing a witness to jail for failing to answer questions of a congressional committee. The Court held that the Committee, in its investigation of the Jay Cooke bankruptcy, was seeking to exercise judicial power, and this, it emphatically said, no committee could do. It seems to me that the proof that the Un-American Activities Committee is here undertaking a purely judicial function is overwhelming, far stronger, in fact, than it was in the Jay Cooke investigation which, moreover, concerned only business transactions, not freedom of association. . . .

The same intent to expose and punish is manifest in the Committee's investigation which led to Barenblatt's conviction. The declared purpose of the investigation was to identify to the people of Michigan the individuals responsible for the, alleged, Communist success there. The Committee claimed that its investigation "uncovered" members of the Communist Party holding positions in the school systems in Michigan; that most of the teachers subpoenaed before the Committee refused to answer questions on the ground that to do so might result in self-incrimination, and that most of these teachers had lost their jobs. It then stated that "the Committee on Un-American Activities approves of this action." Similarly, as a result of its Michigan investigation, the Committee called upon American labor unions to amend their constitutions, if necessary, in order to deny membership to any Communist Party member. This would, of course, prevent many workers from getting or holding the only kind of jobs their particular skills qualified them for. The Court, today, barely mentions these statements, which, especially when read in the context of past reports by the Committee, show unmistakably what the Committee was doing. I cannot understand why these reports are deemed relevant to a determination of a congressional intent to investigate communism in education, but irrelevant to any finding of congressional intent to bring about exposure for its own sake or for the purposes of punishment.

I do not question the Committee's patriotism and sincerity in doing all this. I merely feel that it cannot be done by Congress under our Constitution. For, even assuming that the Federal Government can compel witnesses to testify as to Communist affiliations in order to subject them to ridicule and social and economic retaliation, I cannot agree that this is a legislative function. Such publicity is

clearly punishment, and the Constitution allows only one way in which people can be convicted and punished. . . . Thus, if communism is to be made a crime, and Communists are to be subjected to "pains and penalties," I would still hold this conviction bad, for the crime of communism, like all others, can be punished only by court and jury, after a trial with all judicial safeguards. . . .

Ultimately, all the questions in this case really boil down to one—whether we as a people will try fearfully and futilely to preserve democracy by adopting totalitarian methods or whether, in accordance with our traditions and our Constitution, we will have the confidence and courage to be free.

▼▲▼

## The Power to Enforce Constitutional Amendments

After the Civil War, Congress passed the Thirteenth, Fourteenth, and Fifteenth Amendments, which provided it with another important constitutional source of legislative power. This new grant of legislative power to Congress to enforce the rights created by the Civil War amendments, intended to serve as the cornerstone of Reconstruction, was considered by Southern Democrats the most revolutionary measure ever to receive congressional approval. The amendments served as the crowning achievement of the Radical Republicans to assimilate the former slaves into American life and promote African American equality. From a structural perspective, opponents of Reconstruction considered the Civil War amendments the ultimate shot across the bow in the Radical Republican effort to transform the United States from a confederation of sovereign states to a centralized nation.[52]

The Civil War amendments, for the first time, gave Congress the affirmative power to enforce fundamental rights against intrusion by state and local authorities. Prior to the enactment of the Thirteenth Amendment in 1865, the Constitution and the Bill of Rights had sought to protect fundamental constitutional rights from the exercise of congressional power. But the persistence of slavery and the failure of the states—including those outside of the Confederacy—to guarantee the civil and political rights of African Americans led Congress to create a broad new form of legislative power to enforce rights denied or abridged by states and localities. Since the passage of the Fifteenth Amendment in 1870,

## CONSTITUTIONAL AMENDMENTS GRANTING CONGRESS ENFORCEMENT POWER

Thirteenth Amendment (1865) abolished slavery and involuntary servitude.

Fourteenth Amendment (1868) established national citizenship; created an explicit guarantee to due process, equal protection and privileges, and immunities rights against state abridgement. Overturned *Dred Scott* v. *Sandford* (1857) in which the Court held that African Americans were not citizens under the Constitution, regardless of their status.

Fifteenth Amendment (1870) extended the vote without regard to race, color, or previous condition of servitude.

Eighteenth Amendment (1919) prohibited the manufacture, sale, or transportation of intoxicating liquors.*

Nineteenth Amendment (1920) extended the vote regardless of sex .

Twenty- third Amendment (1961) secured votes in the Electoral College for the District of Columbia.

Twenty-fourth Amendment (1964) outlawed the poll tax and all other taxes in national elections.

Twenty-sixth Amendment (1971) lowered the voting age in all elections to eighteen.

*(Later repealed in 1933 by the Twenty-first Amendment.)

---

four additional constitutional amendments have granted Congress enforcement power through appropriate legislation.

The Court and Congress have differed on what constitutes "appropriate" legislative power to enforce its constitutional responsibilities authorized by these amendments. In one of the earliest and most ambitious efforts to enforce the Civil War amendments, Congress passed the Civil Rights Act of 1875, which outlawed discrimination on the basis of "race or color" in restaurants, hotels, inns, and places of public accommodation. Republicans who spearheaded the drive for the passage of the Fourteenth Amendment believed that its equal protection guarantee included protection from private discrimination as well as by the government. In their view the Civil Rights Act of 1875 was a proper exercise of legislative power to enforce the Equal Protection Clause.

This law, which represented an unprecedented exercise of congressional legislative power, inverted American federalism more so than any other piece of Reconstruction legislation.[53] But it accomplished very little, as it placed the burden for enforcement on African American litigants, whose efforts to secure Southern compliance with the law received little to no political support from Northern Republicans. The gradual withdrawal of Republican support for Reconstruction and the rise in influence of Southern Democrats, especially the "Redeemers" whose mission was to recapture the social and political order of the Old South, meant that the "Civil Rights Act of 1875 was a dead letter from the day of its enactment."[54]

In the *Civil Rights Cases of 1883*, the Court affirmed the collapse of Reconstruction, striking down the 1875 law as an unconstitutional exercise of congressional power under Section 5 of the Fourteenth Amendment to enforce the Equal Protection Clause against the states. Justice Joseph P. Bradley, writing for an 8-1 majority, held that "civil rights, such as are guaranteed by the Constitution, against State aggression, cannot be impaired by the wrongful acts of individuals, unsupported by State authority in the shape of laws, customs, or judicial or executive proceedings. The wrongful act of an individual, unsupported by any such authority, is simply a private wrong," one that Congress has no power to redress through corrective legislation.[55] Justice Bradley did offer, however, that "Congress, in the exercise of its power to regulate commerce amongst the several States, might or might not pass a law regulating rights in public conveyances passing from one State to another."[56] The commerce power did, in fact, become the constitutional source of congressional authority to enact the landmark Civil Rights Act of 1964, which, among other things, banned discrimination in public accommodations. For now the Court's decision in the *Civil Rights Cases* limited congressional enforcement power to official acts of state-sponsored discrimination, a position it has never overruled.

That said, the Court has dramatically expanded the concept of state action since the *Civil Rights Cases* to include private conduct undertaken under the color, or sanction, of state law.[57] The first major turnaround in the Court's approach to the state action doctrine came in *Shelley v. Kraemer* (1948). In *Shelley* the Court held that the Civil Rights Act of 1866, a Reconstruction statute which extends to all persons the "same right . . . as is enjoyed by white citizens . . . to inherit, purchase, lease, sell, hold, and convey real and personal property," prohibited the use of racially restrictive covenants in real estate transactions. The Court ruled that state court enforcement of restrictive covenants amounted to state action, and concluded that the 1866 law was a valid exercise of congressional power to enforce the Equal Protection Clause of the Fourteenth Amendment.[58]

Legislation enacted under the enforcement provisions of the Thirteenth and Fifteenth Amendments continued to find a more receptive audience within the Court. In the *Civil Rights Cases,* the Court held that congressional power to enforce the Thirteenth Amendment reached private as well as state action, although, in the spirit of the times, the Court placed severe constraints on the exercise of such power. In 1968, in *Jones v. Alfred H. Mayer Co.,* the Court modified that definition substantially, affording a broad latitude of power for Congress under the Thirteenth Amendment to eradicate the "badges and incidents" of slavery in the private sphere.

In *Jones* the Court held that the Civil Rights Act of 1866 was meant to secure the right to buy, own, and sell property "against interference from any source whatever, whether governmental or private." *Jones* differed from *Shelley* in that the disputed transaction (in *Jones*) involved two private actors, not (as in *Shelley*) a challenge to the state enforcement of a discriminatory real estate agreement. Nonetheless, the Court ruled (1) that the Thirteenth Amendment prohibited any form of racial discrimination that restricted the free exercise of the basic right to own property and (2) that Congress had power to remove such "relics of slavery" by appropriate legislation.[59] The Court went even further in *Runyon v. McCreary* (1976) when it ruled that private schools that refused to admit African Americans solely on the basis of their race were prohibited from doing so under the Thirteenth Amendment. The Court held that the 1866 law was an appropriate use of congressional power to achieve this objective.[60]

The area in which the Court has interpreted congressional enforcement power of new guarantees created through the process of constitutional amendment involves the Voting Rights Act of 1965. President Johnson presented the law to Congress just after the events of "Bloody Sunday" in Selma, Alabama, brought the struggle for voting rights into full public view. The Voting Rights Act of 1965 was the most comprehensive congressional legislation to date designed to enforce the Fifteenth Amendment's guarantee that "the right of citizens . . . to vote shall not be denied or abridged by the United States or by any State on account of race, color, or previous condition of servitude." The Voting Rights Act went where no previous congressional legislation to enforce the Fifteenth Amendment had dared to tread. The act eliminated poll taxes, literacy tests, grandfather clauses, residency requirements, and other such legal subterfuges historically used to deny African Americans—and in some cases, Hispanics, non-English-speaking minorities, and even poor whites—access to the ballot.[61] Unprecedented as well was the degree of power the law granted to the federal government to supervise and enforce the law in states that had long discriminated against racial minorities in their efforts to vote. Provisions to enforce compliance with the law included the federal government's authority to send examiners into states and congressional districts covered by the Voting Rights Act to supervise registration efforts and elections. The law included an even more controversial section that required affected states to submit their apportionment plans to the Justice Department for "preclearance" before they could go into effect. This provision meant that the federal government would have to approve any state legislative reapportionment plan before it could go into effect.

South Carolina challenged the Voting Rights Act immediately upon its passage by Congress. Illustrative of the gravity of the issues involved in *South Carolina v. Katzenbach* (1966) was the Court's decision to assume original jurisdiction in the case, only the fifteenth time it had done so. For all the attention centered on *Katzenbach,* the Court easily sustained all the challenged provisions of the 1965 law. Note the emphasis that Chief Justice Warren's opinion placed on the phrase "appropriate legislation" in its interpretation of congressional power to enforce the Fifteenth Amendment.

*John Lewis, chairman of the Student Non-Violent Coordinating Committee, lower left, under assault by Alabama state troopers after leading a march across the Edmund Pettus bridge in Selma to encourage African American voter registration. Twenty-one years later, Lewis was elected to Congress.*
UPI/Bettmann–CORBIS.

Compare also the Court's opinions in *Katzenbach* and *Katzenbach v. Morgan* (1966) in which the justices upheld another, perhaps even more aggressive assertion of congressional power to enforce the guarantees of the Fourteenth and Fifteenth Amendments. In *Morgan* the Court ruled that Congress had the power to define and even expand the "substance" of Court-created constitutional guarantees, as long as such legislation was "remedial" in nature. Some commentators, however, believe that Justice Brennan's opinion in *Morgan* went much further than the judicial endorsement of broad congressional power to enforce remedial constitutional rights. In this view Brennan's opinion suggested that Congress was permitted to address constitutional violations absent a previous determination by the Court.[62] Do you agree? Should Congress have the power to define the substance of constitutional rights when it believes the Court has limited their proper scope?

*Morgan* and *Runyon,* in retrospect, represent the Court's most deferential posture toward the power of Congress to enforce the substantive provisions of constitutional amendments. In *Patterson v. McClean Credit Union* (1989), the Court, in granting certiorari, had asked the litigants to consider whether it should overrule *Runyon,* a decision that, along with *Mayer,* several justices believed was wrong for extending the Civil Rights of 1866 beyond immediate state action.[63] The Court's initial action in *Patterson* resulted in widespread criticism from on and off the Court. Ultimately, it decided not to disturb *Runyon.*[64] Since *Patterson,* however, the Court has interpreted the reach of federal civil rights laws designed to enforce the Civil War amendments rather narrowly.

In *City of Borene v. Flores* (1997), the Court sent an even stronger message to Congress about the limits of *Morgan* as a baseline for the exercise of congressional amendment-enforcement power. There, as we discussed in Chapter 3, the Court struck down the Religious Freedom Restoration Act of 1993 (RFRA) as an unconstitutional exercise of Section 5 power under the Fourteenth Amendment. In language that reaffirmed but placed firm limits on the reach of *Morgan*, Justice Anthony Kennedy wrote that the Voting Rights Act of 1965 was an appropriate legislative response to the "persisting deprivation of constitutional rights resulting from this country's history of racial discrimination." RFRA, on the other hand, "lacked proportionality or congruence between the means adopted and the legitimate end to be achieved" and addressed no remedial purpose.[65] Until *Flores* the Court had left open the definition of what constituted "appropriate" power under the Fourteenth Amendment. By requiring it to demonstrate a "proportional" relationship between a law's objective and the constitutional deprivation it is intended to redress, the Court has announced an important new limitation on the power of Congress to enforce constitutional amendments.

## Runyon v. McCrary
### 427 U.S. 160 (1976)

The Southern states' determination to resist the Court's landmark desegregation ruling in *Brown* v. *Board of Education* (1954) was evident from the moment it was handed down. *Brown II*, decided the following year, ordered illegal school districts to desegregate "with all deliberate speed." The all-deliberate-speed idea was Justice Felix Frankfurter's, who believed judges in the South, many of whom he knew, would respect the Court's sensitivity to the social and political concerns and proceed reasonably. As it turned out, Frankfurter was dead wrong.

Southern schools remained segregated well into the 1960s, as federal judges, with the exception of a notable group of judges who served on what was then the United States Court of Appeals for the Fifth Circuit, which covered Alabama, Georgia, Florida, Mississippi, Louisiana, and Texas, refused to carry out *Brown*. Passage of the Civil Rights Act of 1964, in addition to barring discrimination in employment and public accommodations, prohibited any institution receiving federal funds from discriminating on the basis of race. This provision affected elementary and secondary public schools, which were the beneficiaries of congressional spending to improve education.

The response of the more determined segregationists in the South was to form private schools that were not bound by federal civil rights laws, informally called "segregation academies." Some schools claimed a religious affiliation, making them exempt from the 1964 law. Other schools simply refused to entertain federal assistance, allowing them to continue to discriminate. State legislatures often offered vouchers and other forms of financial assistance to students attending private schools. For this reason, many civil rights organizations, such as the NAACP, still oppose federal and state voucher plans for parents whose children attend parochial schools.

Michael McCrary and Colin Gonzales were denied admission into a private Virginia school. They relied on the Civil Rights Act of 1866, a Reconstruction-era law that gave "all persons within the jurisdiction of the United States . . . [the] same right in every State . . . to make and enforce contracts." McCrary and Gonzales claimed that racial discrimination in this context constituted a "badge of slavery," thus making the 1866 law a proper instrument to enforce the Thirteenth Amendment.

The Court's decision was 7 to 2. Justice Stewart delivered the opinion of the Court. Justices Powell and Stevens filed separate concurring opinions. Justice White, joined by Justice Rehnquist, dissented.

▼▲▼

MR. JUSTICE STEWART delivered the opinion of the Court.

The principal issue presented by these consolidated cases is whether a federal law, namely 42 U.S.C. 1981, prohibits private schools from excluding qualified children solely because they are Negroes. . . .

It is worth noting at the outset some of the questions that these cases do not present. They do not present any question of the right of a private social organization to limit its membership on racial or any other grounds. They do not present any question of the right of a private school to limit its student body to boys, to girls, or to adherents of a particular religious faith, since 42 U.S.C. 1981 is in no way addressed to such categories of selectivity. They do not even present the application of 1981 to private sectarian schools that practice racial exclusion on religious grounds. Rather, these cases present only two basic questions: whether 1981 prohibits private, commercially operated, nonsectarian schools from denying admission to prospective students because they are Negroes, and, if so, whether that federal law is constitutional as so applied.

It is now well established that Section 1 of the Civil Rights Act of 1866, or 42 U.S.C. 1981, prohibits racial discrimination in the making and enforcement of private contracts. *Jones v. Alfred E. Mayer Co.* (1968). . . .

It is apparent that the racial exclusion practiced by the Fairfax-Brewster School and Bobbe's Private School amounts to a classic violation of 1981. The parents of Colin Gonzales and Michael McCrary sought to enter into contractual relationships with Bobbe's School for educational services. Colin Gonzales' parents sought to enter into a similar relationship with the Fairfax-Brewster School. Under those contractual relationships, the schools would have received payments for services rendered, and the prospective students would have received instruction in return for those payments. The educational services of Bobbe's School and the Fairfax-Brewster School were advertised and offered to members of the general public. But neither school offered services on an equal basis to white and nonwhite students. As the Court of Appeals held, "there is ample evidence in the record to support the trial judge's factual determinations . . . [that] Colin [Gonzales] and Michael [McCrary] were denied admission to the schools because of their race." The Court of Appeals' conclusion that 1981 was thereby violated follows inexorably from the language of that statute, as construed in *Jones, Tillman,* and *Johnson.*

The petitioning schools and school association argue principally that 1981 does not reach private acts of racial discrimination. That view is wholly inconsistent with *Jones'* interpretation of the legislative history of Section 1 of the Civil Rights Act of 1866. . . . And this consistent interpretation of the law necessarily requires the conclusion that 1981 reaches private conduct.

It is noteworthy that Congress in enacting the Equal Employment Opportunity Act of 1972, specifically considered and rejected an amendment that would have repealed the Civil Rights Act of 1866, as interpreted by this Court in *Jones,* insofar as it affords private sector employees a right of action based on racial discrimination in employment. *See Johnson v. Railway Express Agency.* There could hardly be a clearer indication of congressional agreement with the view that 1981 does reach private acts of racial discrimination. In these circumstances, there is no basis for deviating from the well settled principles of *stare decisis* applicable to this Court's construction of federal statutes. . . .

The Court has repeatedly stressed that while parents have a constitutional right to send their children to private schools and a constitutional right to select private schools that offer specialized instruction, they have no constitutional right to provide their children with private school education unfettered by reasonable government regulation. *See Wisconsin v. Yoder; Pierce v. Society of Sisters; Meyer v. Nebraska.* Indeed, the Court in *Pierce* expressly acknowledged "the power of the State reasonably to regulate all schools, to inspect, supervise and examine them, their teachers and pupils. . . . "

Section 1981, as applied to the conduct at issue here, constitutes an exercise of federal legislative power under Section 2 of the Thirteenth Amendment fully consistent with *Meyer, Pierce,* and the cases that followed in their wake. As the Court held in *Jones v. Alfred H. Mayer Co.:* "It has never been doubted . . . that the power vested in Congress to enforce [the Thirteenth Amendment] by appropriate legislation" . . . includes the power to enact laws "direct and primary, operating upon the acts of individuals, whether sanctioned by State legislation or not." The prohibition of racial discrimination that interferes with the making and enforcement of contracts for private educational services furthers goals closely analogous to those served by 1981's elimination of racial discrimination in the making of private employment contracts and, more generally, by 1982's guarantee that "a dollar in the hands of a Negro will purchase the same thing as a dollar in the hands of a white man."

MR. JUSTICE WHITE, with whom MR. JUSTICE REHNQUIST joins, dissenting.

We are urged here to extend the meaning and reach of 42 U.S.C. 1981 so as to establish a general prohibition against a private individual's or institution's refusing to enter into a contract with another person because of that person's race. Section 1981 has been on the books since 1870, and to so hold for the first time would be contrary to the language of the section, to its legislative history, and to the clear dictum of this Court in the *Civil Rights Cases* (1883), almost contemporaneously with the passage of the statute, that the section reaches only discriminations imposed by state law. The majority's belated discovery of a congressional purpose which escaped this Court only a decade after the statute was passed and which escaped all other federal courts for almost 100 years is singularly unpersuasive. I therefore respectfully dissent. . . . The majority seeks to avoid the construction of 42 U.S.C. 1981 arrived at above by arguing that it . . . is a reenactment *both* of the Voting Rights Act of 1870—the Fourteenth Amendment statute—*and* of part of Section 1 of the Civil Rights Act of 1866—the Thirteenth Amendment statute. The majority argues from this that 1981 does limit *private* contractual choices, because Congress may, under its Thirteenth

Amendment powers, proscribe certain kinds of private conduct thought to perpetuate "'badges and incidents of slavery,'" *Jones* v. *Alfred H. Mayer Co.* (1968); and because this Court has already construed the language "[a]ll citizens of the United States shall have the same right . . . as is enjoyed by white citizens . . . to . . . *purchase . . . real . . . property*" (emphasis added), contained in the Thirteenth Amendment statute, to proscribe a refusal by a private individual to sell real estate to a Negro because of his race. The majority's position is untenable.

First of all, as noted above, [1981] of the Revised Statutes was passed by Congress with the Revisers' unambiguous note before it that the section derived solely from the Fourteenth Amendment statute, accompanied by the confirmatory sidenote "Equal rights under the law." Second and more importantly, the majority's argument is logically impossible, because it has the effect of construing the language "*the same rights to make . . . contracts . . . as is enjoyed by white citizens,*" contained in [1981] of the Revised Statutes, to mean one thing with respect to one class of "persons" and another thing with respect to another class of "persons." If [1981] is held to be a reenactment of the Thirteenth Amendment statute aimed at private discrimination against "citizens" *and* the Fourteenth Amendment statute aimed at state law-created legal disabilities for "all persons," including aliens, then one class of "persons"—Negro citizens—would, under the majority's theory, have a right not to be discriminated against by private individuals and another class—aliens—would be given *by the same language* no such right. The statute draws no such distinction among classes of persons. It logically must be construed either to give "all persons" a right not to be discriminated against by private parties in the making of contracts or to give no persons such a right. Aliens clearly never had such a right under the Fourteenth Amendment statute (or any other statute); [1981] is concededly derived solely from the Fourteenth Amendment statute so far as coverage of aliens is concerned; and there is absolutely no indication that aliens' rights were expanded by the reenactment of the Fourteenth Amendment statute. . . . Accordingly, the statute gives *no* class of persons the right not to be discriminated against by private parties in the making of contracts. . . .

Second, the majority's argument may well rest on a false assumption that the repeal of part of the Thirteenth Amendment statute changed the law. The repealed portion of the Thirteenth Amendment statute may well never have had any effect other than that of removing certain legal disabilities. First, as noted above, some of the rights granted under the Thirteenth Amendment statute—the rights to sue, be parties, give evidence, enforce contracts—could not possibly accomplish anything other than the removal of *legal* disabilities. Thus, the question is whether the right to "make contracts" in the repealed part of the Thirteenth Amendment statute would have been construed in the same vein as these other rights (later included in the Fourteenth Amendment statute), or rather in the same vein as the right to "purchase, etc., real and personal property." The fact that one of the leaders of the efforts to pass the Thirteenth Amendment statute—Senator Stewart—included the right to "make contracts," but not the right to "purchase, etc., real and personal property" in the Fourteenth Amendment statute providing for equal rights under the laws which he sponsored four years later is strong evidence of the fact that Congress always viewed the right to "make contracts" as simply granting equal legal capacity to contract. Plainly that is the only effect of such language in the Fourteenth Amendment statute. It is reasonable to suppose Congress intended the identical language to accomplish the same result when included in a different statute four years earlier. Indeed Senator Stewart specifically drew a distinction between the rights enumerated in the Fourteenth Amendment statute including the right to "make contracts" and the real and personal property rights not so included. . . .

Finally, as a matter of common sense, it would seem extremely unlikely that Congress would have intended—without a word in the legislative history addressed to the precise issue—to pass a statute prohibiting every racially motivated refusal to contract by a private individual. It is doubtful that all such refusals could be considered badges or incidents of slavery within Congress' proscriptive power under the Thirteenth Amendment. A racially motivated refusal to hire a Negro or a white babysitter or to admit a Negro or a white to a private association cannot be called a badge of slavery—and yet the construction given by the majority to the Thirteenth Amendment statute attributes to Congress an intent to proscribe them. . . .

The majority's holding that 42 U.S.C. 1981 prohibits all racially motivated contractual decisions . . . threatens to embark the Judiciary on a treacherous course. Whether such conduct should be condoned or not, whites and blacks will undoubtedly choose to form a variety of associational relationships pursuant to contracts which exclude members of the other race. Social clubs, black and white, and associations designed to further the interests of blacks or whites are but two examples. Lawsuits by members of the other race attempting to gain admittance to such an association are not pleasant to contemplate. As the associational or contractual relationships become more private, the pressures to hold 1981 inapplicable to them will increase. Imaginative judicial construction of the word "contract" is foreseeable; Thirteenth Amendment limitations on Congress' power to ban "badges and incidents of slavery" may be discovered; the doctrine of the right to association may be bent to cover a given situation. In any event, courts will be called upon to balance sensitive policy considerations against each other—considerations which have never been addressed by any Congress—all under the guise of "construing" a statute. This is a task appropriate for the Legislature, not for the Judiciary.

## *South Carolina* v. *Katzenbach*
### 383 U.S. 301 (1966)

*I am sixty-five years old, I own one hundred acres of land that is paid for, I am a taxpayer and I have six children. All of them is teachin', workin'. . . . If what I done ain't enough to be a registered voter . . . the Lord have mercy on America.*

> —An African American man in Selma, attempting to register to vote in the early 1960s

Of all the great civil rights struggles of the late 1950s and early 1960s, none was more important to the future of African American equality than the right to vote. Led by organizers from the Student Non-Violent Coordinating Committee (SNCC), such as John Lewis and Hosea Williams, and the Southern Christian Leadership Conference, such as Martin Luther King Jr., Ralph Abernathy, and Andrew Young, civil rights marchers engaged in demonstrations all over the South. The dramatic high point between Southern authorities determined to resist the peaceful demands of African Americans for the right to vote came on March 7, 1965, when police officers used tear gas, dogs, and clubs to assault civil rights marchers who were crossing the Edmund Pettus bridge in Selma, Alabama, to register to vote at the courthouse. Known as "Bloody Sunday," the violence was captured by television cameras and broadcast on the evening news reports. Leading newspapers and magazines prominently featured the story, which shook the nation's conscience.

A week later, President Lyndon Johnson appeared before Congress to announce his support for the Voting Rights Act of 1965. The address was also televised, reaching an estimated 70 million people. He concluded his address by quoting the old Negro spiritual, "We Shall Overcome," which had become an anthem of the civil rights movement, and called for "no delay, no hesitation, no compromise with our purpose."

Invoking the Supreme Court's original jurisdiction under Article III, Section 2, of the Constitution, South Carolina, one of the seven states covered under its provisions, challenged the act as unconstitutional on a host of grounds. The state asked the Court to enjoin Attorney General Nicholas Katzenbach from enforcing the statute. Katzenbach was a notable figure in the civil rights movement as well, confronting Alabama Governor George Wallace in 1963 after he refused to allow black students to register and attend the University of Alabama.

The Court's decision was unanimous. Chief Justice Warren delivered the opinion of the Court. Justice Black concurred in part and dissented in part.

MR. CHIEF JUSTICE WARREN delivered the opinion of the Court.

. . . The Voting Rights Act was designed by Congress to banish the blight of racial discrimination in voting, which has infected the electoral process in parts of our country for nearly a century. The Act creates stringent new remedies for voting discrimination where it persists on a pervasive scale, and, in addition, the statute strengthens existing remedies for pockets of voting discrimination elsewhere in the country. Congress assumed the power to prescribe these remedies from Section 2 of the Fifteenth Amendment, which authorizes the National Legislature to effectuate by "appropriate" measures the constitutional prohibition against racial discrimination in voting. We hold that the sections of the Act which are properly before us, are an appropriate means for carrying out Congress' constitutional responsibilities, and are consonant with all other provisions of the Constitution. We therefore deny South Carolina's request that enforcement of these sections of the Act be enjoined.

The constitutional propriety of the Voting Rights Act of 1965 must be judged with reference to the historical experience which it reflects. Before enacting the measure, Congress explored with great care the problem of racial discrimination in voting. The House and Senate

Committees on the Judiciary each held hearings for nine days and received testimony from a total of 67 witnesses. More than three full days were consumed discussing the bill on the floor of the House, while the debate in the Senate covered 26 days in all. At the close of these deliberations, the verdict of both chambers was overwhelming. The House approved the bill by a vote of 328-74, and the measure passed the Senate by a margin of 79-18.

Two points emerge vividly from the voluminous legislative history of the Act contained in the committee hearings and floor debates. First: Congress felt itself confronted by an insidious and pervasive evil which had been perpetuated in certain parts of our country through unremitting and ingenious defiance of the Constitution. Second: Congress concluded that the unsuccessful remedies which it had prescribed in the past would have to be replaced by sterner and more elaborate measures in order to satisfy the clear commands of the Fifteenth Amendment. We pause here to summarize the majority reports of the House and Senate Committees, which document in considerable detail the factual basis for these reactions by Congress. . . .

The Fifteenth Amendment to the Constitution was ratified in 1870. Promptly thereafter, Congress passed the Enforcement Act of 1870, which made it a crime for public officers and private persons to obstruct exercise of the right to vote. The statute was amended in the following year to provide for detailed federal supervision of the electoral process, from registration to the certification of returns. As the years passed and fervor for racial equality waned, enforcement of the laws became spotty and ineffective, and most of their provisions were repealed in 1894. The remnants have had little significance in the recently renewed battle against voting discrimination.

Meanwhile, beginning in 1890, the States of Alabama, Georgia, Louisiana, Mississippi, North Carolina, South Carolina, and Virginia enacted tests still in use which were specifically designed to prevent Negroes from voting. Typically, they made the ability to read and write a registration qualification and also required completion of a registration form. These laws were based on the fact that, as of 1890, in each of the named States, more than two-thirds of the adult Negroes were illiterate, while less than one-quarter of the adult whites were unable to read or write. At the same time, alternate tests were prescribed in all of the named States to assure that white illiterates would not be deprived of the franchise. These included grandfather clauses, property qualifications, "good character" tests, and the requirement that registrants "understand" or "interpret" certain matter.

The course of subsequent Fifteenth Amendment litigation in this Court demonstrates the variety and persistence of these and similar institutions designed to deprive Negroes of the right to vote. Grandfather clauses were invalidated in *Guinn* v. *United States* (1915). The white primary was outlawed in *Smith* v. *Allwright* (1944), and *Terry* v. *Adams*, (1953). Improper challenges were nullified in *United States* v. *Thomas* (1960). Racial gerrymandering was forbidden in *Gomillion* v. *Lightfoot* (1960). Finally, discriminatory application of voting tests was condemned in *Schnell* v. *Davis* (1949). . . .

According to the evidence in recent Justice Department voting suits, the latter stratagem is now the principal method used to bar Negroes from the polls. Discriminatory administration of voting qualifications has been found in all eight Alabama cases, in all nine Louisiana cases, and in all nine Mississippi cases which have gone to final judgment. Moreover, in almost all of these cases, the courts have held that the discrimination was pursuant to a widespread "pattern or practice." White applicants for registration have often been excused altogether from the literacy and understanding tests, or have been given easy versions, have received extensive help from voting officials, and have been registered despite serious errors in their answers. Negroes, on the other hand, have typically been required to pass difficult versions of all the tests, without any outside assistance and without the slightest error. The good-morals requirement is so vague and subjective that it has constituted an open invitation to abuse at the hands of voting officials. Negroes obliged to obtain vouchers from registered voters have found it virtually impossible to comply in areas where almost no Negroes are on the rolls.

In recent years, Congress has repeatedly tried to cope with the problem by facilitating case-by-case litigation against voting discrimination. The Civil Rights Act of 1957 authorized the Attorney General to seek injunctions against public and private interference with the right to vote on racial grounds. Perfecting amendments in the Civil Rights Act of 1960 permitted the joinder of States as parties defendant, gave the Attorney General access to local voting records, and authorized courts to register voters in areas of systematic discrimination. . . .

Despite the earnest efforts of the Justice Department and of many federal judges, these new laws have done little to cure the problem of voting discrimination. According to estimates by the Attorney General during hearings on the Act, registration of voting-age Negroes in Alabama rose only from 14.2% to 19.4% between 1958 and 1964; in Louisiana, it barely inched ahead from 31.7% to 31.8%

between 1956 and 1965, and in Mississippi it increased only from 4.4% to 6.4% between 1954 and 1964. In each instance, registration of voting-age whites ran roughly 50 percentage points or more ahead of Negro registration. . . .

The Voting Rights Act of 1965 reflects Congress' firm intention to rid the country of racial discrimination in voting. The heart of the Act is a complex scheme of stringent remedies aimed at areas where voting discrimination has been most flagrant. Section 4(a)-(d) lays down a formula defining the States and political subdivisions to which these new remedies apply. The first of the remedies, contained in §4(a), is the suspension of literacy tests and similar voting qualifications for a period of five years from the last occurrence of substantial voting discrimination. Section 5 prescribes a second remedy, the suspension of all new voting regulations pending review by federal authorities to determine whether their use would perpetuate voting discrimination. The third remedy, is the assignment of federal examiners on certification by the Attorney General to list qualified applicants who are thereafter entitled to vote in all elections.

Other provisions of the Act prescribe subsidiary cures for persistent voting discrimination. Section 8 authorizes the appointment of federal poll-watchers in places to which federal examiners have already been assigned. Section 10(d) excuses those made eligible to vote in sections of the country covered by Section 4(b) of the Act from paying accumulated past poll taxes for state and local elections. Section 12(e) provides for balloting by persons denied access to the polls in areas where federal examiners have been appointed.

The remaining remedial portions of the Act are aimed at voting discrimination in any area of the country where it may occur. Section 2 broadly prohibits the use of voting rules to abridge exercise of the franchise on racial grounds. Sections 3, 6(a), and 13(b) strengthen existing procedures for attacking voting discrimination by means of litigation. Section 4(e) excuses citizens educated in American schools conducted in a foreign language from passing English language literacy tests. Section 10(a)-(c) facilitates constitutional litigation challenging the imposition of all poll taxes for state and local elections. Sections 11 and 12(a)-(d) authorize civil and criminal sanctions against interference with the exercise of rights guaranteed by the Act. . . .

These provisions of the Voting Rights Act of 1965 are challenged on the fundamental ground that they exceed the powers of Congress and encroach on an area reserved to the States by the Constitution. . . .

The ground rules for resolving this question are clear. The language and purpose of the Fifteenth Amendment, the prior decisions construing its several provisions, and the general doctrines of constitutional interpretation all point to one fundamental principle. As against the reserved powers of the States, Congress may use any rational means to effectuate the constitutional prohibition of racial discrimination in voting. We turn now to a more detailed description of the standards which govern our review of the Act.

Section 1 of the Fifteenth Amendment declares that, "[t]he right of citizens of the United States to vote shall not be denied or abridged by the United States or by any State on account of race, color, or previous condition of servitude." This declaration has always been treated as self-executing, and has repeatedly been construed, without further legislative specification, to invalidate state voting qualifications or procedures which are discriminatory on their face or in practice. . . . The gist of the matter is that the Fifteenth Amendment supersedes contrary exertions of state power. "When a State exercises power wholly within the domain of state interest, it is insulated from federal judicial review. But such insulation is not carried over when state power is used as an instrument for circumventing a federally protected right."

South Carolina contends that . . . to allow an exercise of this authority by Congress would be to rob the courts of their rightful constitutional role. On the contrary, Section 2 of the Fifteenth Amendment expressly declares that "Congress shall have power to enforce this article by appropriate legislation." By adding this authorization, the Framers indicated that Congress was to be chiefly responsible for implementing the rights created in Section 1. "It is the power of Congress which has been enlarged. Congress is authorized to enforce the prohibitions by appropriate legislation. Some legislation is contemplated to make the [Civil War] amendments fully effective." Accordingly, in addition to the courts, Congress has full remedial powers to effectuate the constitutional prohibition against racial discrimination in voting. . . .

After enduring nearly a century of widespread resistance to the Fifteenth Amendment, Congress has marshalled an array of potent weapons against the evil, with authority in the Attorney General to employ them effectively. Many of the areas directly affected by this development have indicated their willingness to abide by any restraints legitimately imposed upon them. We here hold that the portions of the Voting Rights Act properly before us are a valid means for carrying out the commands of the Fifteenth Amendment. Hopefully, millions of non-white

Americans will now be able to participate for the first time on an equal basis in the government under which they live. We may finally look forward to the day when truly, "[t]he right of citizens of the United States to vote shall not be denied or abridged by the United States or by any State on account of race, color, or previous condition of servitude."

The bill of complaint is [d]ismissed.

## Katzenbach v. Morgan
### 384 U.S. 641 (1966)

*Katzenbach* v. *Morgan* was an important follow-up to the Court's decision in *South Carolina* v. *Katzenbach* upholding the constitutionality of the Voting Rights Act of 1965. The case involved a conflict with a New York state law that required its citizens to meet a literacy requirement to register to vote. Section 4(e) of the Voting Rights Act prohibited New York from denying a large segment of its Puerto Rican community the right to vote. The conflict centered on whether Congress was within its authority under Section 5 to enforce the Equal Protection Clause against a state law that effectively limited the franchise. How the case was resolved would determine just how broad congressional power was to enforce the Voting Rights Act.

Justice Brennan's opinion in *Morgan* stands in notable contrast to the Court's opinion in *Cooper* v. *Aaron* (1958), the Court's decision upholding the federal government's right to enforce school desegregation over Arkansas's objection on states' rights grounds. In *Cooper* the Court offered a ringing endorsement of judicial supremacy, concluding that it possessed the sole authority to determine the final meaning of the Constitution. In *Morgan* Justice Brennan offers a very different conclusion about the shared nature of constitutional interpretation among the branches of government.

The Court's decision was 7 to 2. Justice Brennan delivered the opinion of the Court. Justice Douglas filed a concurrence. Justice Harlan, joined by Justice Stewart, dissented.

▼▲▼

MR. JUSTICE BRENNAN delivered the opinion of the Court.

These cases concern the constitutionality of Section 4(e) of the Voting Rights Act of 1965. That law . . . provides that no person who has successfully completed the sixth primary grade in a public school in, or a private school accredited by, the Commonwealth of Puerto Rico in which the language of instruction was other than English shall be denied the right to vote in any election because of his inability to read or write English. Appellees, registered voters in New York City, brought this suit to challenge the constitutionality of Section 4(e) insofar as it prohibits the enforcement of the election laws of New York requiring an ability to read and write English as a condition of voting. Under these laws, many of the several hundred thousand New York City residents who have migrated there from the Commonwealth of Puerto Rico had previously been denied the right to vote, and appellees attack Section 4(e) insofar as it would enable many of these citizens to vote. . . . We hold that, in the application challenged in these cases, §4(e) is a proper exercise of the powers granted to Congress by Section 5 of the Fourteenth Amendment, and that, by force of the Supremacy Clause, Article VI, the New York English literacy requirement cannot be enforced to the extent that it is inconsistent with Section 4(e).

Under the distribution of powers effected by the Constitution, the States establish qualifications for voting for state officers, and the qualifications established by the States for voting for members of the most numerous branch of the state legislature also determine who may vote for United States Representatives and Senators. But, of course, the States have no power to grant or withhold the franchise on conditions that are forbidden by the Fourteenth Amendment, or any other provision of the Constitution. Such exercises of state power are no more immune to the limitations of the Fourteenth Amendment than any other state action. The Equal Protection Clause itself has been held to forbid some state laws that restrict the right to vote.

[T]he State of New York argues that an exercise of congressional power under Section 5 of the Fourteenth Amendment that prohibits the enforcement of a state law can only be sustained if the judicial branch determines that the state law is prohibited by the provisions of the Amendment that Congress sought to enforce. More specifically, he urges that Section 4(e) cannot be sustained as appropriate legislation to enforce the Equal Protection Clause unless the judiciary decides—even with the guidance of a congressional judgment—that the application of the English literacy requirement prohibited by Section 4(e) is forbidden by the Equal Protection Clause itself. We disagree. Neither the language nor history of Section 5 supports such a construction. As was said with regard to Section 5 in *Ex parte Virginia* (1880), "It is the power of Congress which has been enlarged. Congress is authorized to enforce the prohibitions by appropriate legislation. Some legislation is contemplated to make the amendments fully effective." A construction of Section 5 that would require a judicial determination that the enforcement of the state law precluded by Congress violated the Amendment, as a condition of sustaining the congressional enactment, would depreciate both congressional resourcefulness and congressional responsibility for implementing the Amendment. It would confine the legislative power in this context to the insignificant role of abrogating only those state laws that the judicial branch was prepared to adjudge unconstitutional, or of merely informing the judgment of the judiciary by particularizing the "majestic generalities" of Section 1 of the Amendment.

Thus, our task in this case is not to determine whether the New York English literacy requirement, as applied to deny the right to vote to a person who successfully completed the sixth grade in a Puerto Rican school, violates the Equal Protection Clause. . . . [Rather] our task is limited to determining whether such legislation is, as required by Section 5, appropriate legislation to enforce the Equal Protection Clause.

By including Section 5, the draftsmen sought to grant to Congress, by a specific provision applicable to the Fourteenth Amendment, the same broad powers expressed in the Necessary and Proper Clause. The classic formulation of the reach of those powers was established by Chief Justice Marshall in *McCulloch* v. *Maryland* (1819):

Let the end be legitimate, let it be within the scope of the constitution, and all means which are appropriate, which are plainly adapted to that end, which are not prohibited, but consist with the letter and spirit of the constitution, are constitutional. . . .

We therefore proceed to the consideration whether Section 4(e) is "appropriate legislation" to enforce the Equal Protection Clause, that is, under the *McCulloch* v. *Maryland* standard, whether Section 4(e) may be regarded as an enactment to enforce the Equal Protection Clause, whether it is "plainly adapted to that end," and whether it is not prohibited by, but is consistent with, "the letter and spirit of the constitution."

There can be no doubt that Section 4(e) may be regarded as an enactment to enforce the Equal Protection Clause. Congress explicitly declared that it enacted Section 4(e), "to secure the rights under the fourteenth amendment of persons educated in American-flag schools in which the predominant classroom language was other than English." The persons referred to include those who have migrated from the Commonwealth of Puerto Rico to New York and who have been denied the right to vote because of their inability to read and write English, and the Fourteenth Amendment rights referred to include those emanating from the Equal Protection Clause. More specifically, Section 4(e) may be viewed as a measure to secure for the Puerto Rican community residing in New York nondiscriminatory treatment by government—both in the imposition of voting qualifications and the provision or administration of governmental services, such as public schools, public housing and law enforcement.

Section 4(e) may be readily seen as "plainly adapted" to furthering these aims of the Equal Protection Clause. The practical effect of Section 4(e) is to prohibit New York from denying the right to vote to large segments of its Puerto Rican community. Congress has thus prohibited the State from denying to that community the right that is "preservative of all rights." This enhanced political power will be helpful in gaining nondiscriminatory treatment in public services for the entire Puerto Rican community. Section 4(e) thereby enables the Puerto Rican minority better to obtain "perfect equality of civil rights and the equal protection of the laws." It was well within congressional authority to say that this need of the Puerto Rican minority for the vote warranted federal intrusion upon any state interests served by the English literacy requirement. It was for Congress, as the branch that made this judgment, to assess and weigh the various conflicting considerations—the risk or pervasiveness of the discrimination in governmental services, the effectiveness of eliminating the state restriction on the right to vote as a means of dealing with the evil, the adequacy or availability of alternative remedies, and the nature and significance of the state interests that would be affected by the nullification of the English literacy requirement as applied to residents who have successfully completed the sixth grade in a Puerto Rican school. It is not for us to review the congressional resolution of these factors. It is enough that we be able to perceive a basis upon which the Congress might resolve the conflict as it did. There plainly was such a basis to support Section 4(e) in the application in question in this case. Any contrary conclusion would require us to be blind to the realities familiar to the legislators. . . .

Section 4(e) does not restrict or deny the franchise, but, in effect, extends the franchise to persons who otherwise would be denied it by state law. Thus, we need not decide whether a state literacy law conditioning the right to vote on achieving a certain level of education in an American-flag school (regardless of the language of instruction) discriminates invidiously against those educated in non-American-flag schools. We need only decide whether the challenged limitation on the relief effected in § 4(e) was permissible. In deciding that question, the principle that calls for the closest scrutiny of distinctions in laws denying fundamental rights, is inapplicable; for the distinction challenged by appellees is presented only as a limitation on a reform measure aimed at eliminating an existing barrier to the exercise of the franchise. Rather, in deciding the constitutional propriety of the limitations in such a reform measure, we are guided by the familiar principles that a "statute is not invalid under the Constitution because it might have gone farther than it did," that a legislature need not "strike at all evils at the same time," and that "reform may take one step at a time, addressing itself to the phase of the problem which seems most acute to the legislative mind."

Guided by these principles, we are satisfied that appellees' challenge to this limitation in Section 4(e) is without merit. In the context of the case before us, the congressional choice to limit the relief effected in Section 4(e) may, for example, reflect Congress' greater familiarity with the quality of instruction in American-flag schools, a recognition of the unique historic relationship between the Congress and the Commonwealth of Puerto Rico, an awareness of the Federal Government's acceptance of the desirability of the use of Spanish as the language of instruction in Commonwealth schools, and the fact that Congress has fostered policies encouraging migration from the Commonwealth to the States. We have no occasion to determine in this case whether such factors would justify a similar distinction embodied in a voting qualification law that denied the franchise to persons educated in non-American-flag schools. We hold only that the limitation on relief effected in Section 4(e) does not constitute a forbidden discrimination, since these factors might well have been the basis for the decision of Congress to go "no farther than it did."

We therefore conclude that Section 4(e), in the application challenged in this case, is appropriate legislation to enforce the Equal Protection Clause.

MR. JUSTICE HARLAN, whom MR. JUSTICE STEWART joins, dissenting.

Worthy as its purposes may be thought by many, I do not see how Section 4(e) of the Voting Rights Act of 1965, can be sustained except at the sacrifice of fundamentals in the American constitutional system—the separation between the legislative and judicial function and the boundaries between federal and state political authority. . . .

The Court declares that, since Section 5 of the Fourteenth Amendment gives to the Congress power to "enforce" the prohibitions of the Amendment by "appropriate" legislation, the test for judicial review of any congressional determination in this area is simply one of rationality; that is, in effect, was Congress acting rationally in declaring that the New York statute is irrational? Although Section 5 most certainly does give to the Congress wide powers in the field of devising remedial legislation to effectuate the Amendment's prohibition on arbitrary state action, I believe the Court has confused the issue of how much enforcement power Congress possesses under §5 with the distinct issue of what questions are appropriate for congressional determination and what questions are essentially judicial in nature.

When recognized state violations of federal constitutional standards have occurred, Congress is, of course, empowered by Section 5 to take appropriate remedial measures to redress and prevent the wrongs. But it is a judicial question whether the condition with which Congress has thus sought to deal is, in truth, an infringement of the Constitution, something that is the necessary prerequisite to bringing the Section 5 power into play at all. . . .

A more recent Fifteenth Amendment case also serves to illustrate this distinction. In *South Carolina* v. *Katzenbach* (1966) decided earlier this Term, we held certain remedial sections of this Voting Rights Act of 1965 constitutional under the Fifteenth Amendment, which is directed against deprivations of the right to vote on account of race. In enacting those sections of the Voting Rights Act, the Congress made a detailed investigation of various state practices that had been used to deprive Negroes of the franchise. In passing upon the remedial provisions, we reviewed first the "voluminous legislative history," as well as judicial precedents supporting the basic congressional finding that the clear commands of the Fifteenth Amendment had been infringed by various state subterfuges. Given the existence of the evil, we held the remedial steps taken by the legislature under the Enforcement Clause of the Fifteenth Amendment to be a justifiable exercise of congressional initiative.

Section 4(e), however, presents a significantly different type of congressional enactment. The question here is not whether the statute is appropriate remedial legislation to cure an established violation of a constitutional command, but whether there has, in fact, been an infringement of that constitutional command, that is, whether a particular state practice, or, as here, a statute, is so arbitrary or irrational as to offend the command of the Equal Protection Clause of the Fourteenth Amendment. That question is one for the judicial branch ultimately to determine. Were the rule otherwise, Congress would be able to qualify this Court's constitutional decisions under the Fourteenth and Fifteenth Amendments, let alone those under other provisions of the Constitution, by resorting to congressional power under the Necessary and Proper Clause. . . .

In effect, the Court reads Section 5 of the Fourteenth Amendment as giving Congress the power to define the substantive scope of the Amendment. If that indeed be the true reach of Section 5, then I do not see why Congress should not be able as well to exercise its Section 5 "discretion" by enacting statutes so as, in effect, to dilute equal protection and due process decisions of this Court. In all such cases, there is room for reasonable men to differ as to whether or not a denial of equal protection or due process has occurred, and the final decision is one of judgment. Until today, this judgment has always been one for the judiciary to resolve. . . .

Thus, we have here not a matter of giving deference to a congressional estimate, based on its determination of legislative facts, bearing upon the validity *vel non* of a statute, but rather what can, at most, be called a legislative announcement that Congress believes a state law to entail an unconstitutional deprivation of equal protection. Although this kind of declaration is, of course, entitled to the most respectful consideration, coming as it does from a concurrent branch and one that is knowledgeable in matters of popular political participation, I do not believe it lessens our responsibility to decide the fundamental issue of whether, in fact, the state enactment violates federal constitutional rights.

In assessing the deference we should give to this kind of congressional expression of policy, it is relevant that the judiciary has always given to congressional enactments a presumption of validity. . . . Whichever way this case is decided, one statute will be rendered inoperative in whole or in part, and, although it has been suggested that this Court should give somewhat more deference to Congress than to a state legislature, such a simple weighing of presumptions is hardly a satisfying way of resolving a matter that touches the distribution of state and federal power in an area so sensitive as that of the regulation of the franchise. Rather, it should be recognized that, while the Fourteenth Amendment is a "brooding omnipresence" over all state legislation, the substantive matters which it touches are all within the primary legislative competence of the States. Federal authority, legislative no less than judicial, does not intrude unless there has been a denial by state action of Fourteenth Amendment limitations, in this instance, a denial of equal protection. At least in the area of primary state concern, a state statute that passes constitutional muster under the judicial standard of rationality should not be permitted to be set at naught by a mere contrary congressional pronouncement unsupported by a legislative record justifying that conclusion.

To deny the effectiveness of this congressional enactment is not, of course, to disparage Congress' exertion of authority in the field of civil rights; it is simply to recognize that the Legislative Branch, like the other branches of federal authority, is subject to the governmental boundaries set by the Constitution. To hold, on this record, that Section 4(e) overrides the New York literacy requirement seems to me tantamount to allowing the Fourteenth Amendment to swallow the State's constitutionally ordained primary authority in this field. For if Congress . . . can set that otherwise permissible requirement partially at naught, I see no reason why it could not also substitute its judgment for that of the States in other fields of their exclusive primary competence as well

▼▲▼

## The Delegation of Legislative Power

The issue that best illustrates political scientist Richard Neustadt's classic description of the separation of powers as a system that features separate institutions sharing power is the delegation of legislative power by Congress to the executive or judicial branches.[66] On first glance the notion that Congress can delegate its legislative power to another branch seems to fly in the face of James Madison's admonition in *Federalist* 47. There, Madison wrote: "[T]he accumulation of all powers, legislative, executive, or judiciary, in the same hands, whether of one, a few or many, and whether self-appointed, or elective, may justly be pronounced the very definition of tyranny." But Madison, quoting the "celebrated Montesquieu," from whom much of the Framers' conception of separation of powers doctrine was derived, noted that while

> "There can be no liberty where the legislative and executive powers are united in the same person, or body of magistrates," . . . he did not mean that these departments ought to have no partial agency in or no control over, the acts of each other. His meaning . . . can amount to no more than this, that where the whole power of one department is exercised by the same hands which possess the whole power of another department, the fundamental principles of a free constitution are subverted.[67]

Some commentators have taken the explicit delegation in Article I of all legislative power to Congress as confirmation of Madison's maxim in *Federalist* 47 that each branch is forbidden from intruding upon the constitutional duties of another. Moreover, the rule of nondelegation, one derived from the ancient legal principle of *delegata potestas non potests delegari,* the Latin phrase for "a power once delegated cannot be redelegated," posits that the Constitution prohibits Congress from delegating its powers to the other branches of government. Nonetheless, the Constitution is silent on whether Congress is permitted to delegate its powers, leaving the doctrine of nondelegation essentially one that has been defined by the courts. As such, the courts have interpreted the nondelegation doctrine to restrain Congress from transferring wholesale legislative responsibilities to other branches or, as you will see in the upcoming discussion of one of the Court's most important constitutional decisions of the New Deal, *Schechter Poultry Corporation v. United States* (1935), nongovernmental organizations. This restriction has proven to be the exception. The Court has permitted Congress to delegate its powers to the executive and judicial branches as long as it does so for the purpose of exercising its own legislative power.[68]

For the most part, debate over the rule of nondelegation has been academic, as Congress has delegated its power to the executive and judicial branches since the formative years of the Republic. In fact, the first such test to the nondelegation rule came in 1825, a time in which the Court, under Chief Justice John Marshall, was giving shape to the American constitutional design through one foundational decision after another. Just one term after it had given broad definition to the power of Congress to regulate commerce and handed constitutional nationalists their most important victory to date, the Court, in *Wayman v. Southard,* endorsed Congress's decision to allow the federal courts to develop their rules of practice and administration. Congress could not, the Court held, delegate responsibility for those "important subjects, which must be entirely regulated by the legislature itself," but it could authorize another branch to "fill up the details" to assist in the implementation of legislation.[69]

For a brief but critical moment during the New Deal period, the Court rebuffed a plan drafted by congressional Democrats to delegate expansive legislative power to President Franklin D. Roosevelt. The National Industrial Recovery Act (NIRA), a centerpiece of the New Deal legislative agenda and a law that numerous scholars have described as the most extraordinary ever passed by Congress, granted near complete control of domestic economic policy to the president. The law allowed the president to create and enforce rules setting the terms and conditions of competition for several large industries. Even more controversial was an NIRA provision that permitted private trade associations to approve or reject executive branch regulation of their particular industry. Cooperation between the private and public sectors has never been an uncommon practice in drafting laws or the rules developed by the executive agencies responsible for their enforcement. With the NIRA, Congress exceeded any previous delegation of legislative power, especially the nearly unfettered authority it gave private trade groups over the rules that affected their respective industries.[70]

The following SIDEBAR describes in greater detail the events that led to *Schechter Poultry,* a decision that was one the Court's most authoritative rejections of the New Deal and one that would ultimately set in motion the series of political maneuverings that culminated in FDR's Court-packing plan of 1937 (see Chapter 6). This overt attempt to manipulate the Court by challenging its independence, as you will see in subsequent chapters, never came to fruition because of the Court's sudden embrace that same year of the New Deal agenda it had once scorned. The Court has not enforced the rule of nondelegation since *Schechter* and *Panama Refining Co.* v. *Ryan* (1935), a case decided a few months before that struck down another ambitious effort by Congress to delegate power under the NIRA. Still, these two decisions teach important lessons about the exercise of legislative power in the modern administrative welfare state.

Those lessons are on view in a more recent decision involving the delegation of legislative power, *Mistretta* v. *United States* (1989), in which the Court upheld a challenge to the federal Sentencing Reform Act of 1984. In the first major test to the nondelegation rule since the New Deal, the Court considered whether Congress had delegated "core" legislative power to the judicial branch by creating the U.S. Sentencing Commission and authorizing it to establish sentencing guidelines for use in the lower federal courts. Judges, in turn, were required to follow the guidelines established by the commission. For reasons set out in the facts and background of *Mistretta*, the Court found itself revisiting the rules and principles created in *Schechter* and *Panama Refining Co.* that governed the delegation of legislative power. The Court had little trouble with the delegation of power at issue in *Mistretta*, upholding the law by an 8-1 margin. But the Court's lone dissenter, Justice Antonin Scalia, raises some interesting points in his dissent, one that offers a powerful critique of the majority's consideration of the question. What does Justice Scalia's opinion say about the Court's prior decisions on the rule of nondelegation and about the nature of modern interbranch cooperation?

Questions involving the delegation of power are not limited to the exercise of power by the executive and judicial branches to assist in carrying out the legislative purpose of a statute. In response to political demands, Congress has enacted laws enabling the president to veto individual provisions of legislation presented for his signature and authorized an officer of a federal agency created by the legislative branch to enforce mandatory budget reductions stipulated by legislation. On a related but nonetheless quite different separation of powers question, Congress has seen its unstated but traditional use of the "legislative veto," a rule often inserted into legislation that permits either the House or Senate, or one of its committees, to cancel the rules created by executive branch agencies responsible for enforcing a law declared unconstitutional. We will consider each of these issues in turn.

## A.L.A. Schechter Poultry Corporation v. United States
### 295 U.S. 495 (1935)

The facts and background of this case are set out in the accompanying SIDEBAR on this case.

The Court's decision was unanimous. Chief Justice Hughes delivered the opinion of the Court. Justice Cardozo, joined by Justice Stone, concurred.

▼▲▼

MR. CHIEF JUSTICE HUGHES delivered the opinion of the Court.

. . . *The question of the delegation of legislative power.* We recently had occasion to review the pertinent decisions and the general principles which govern the deter-

mination of this question. *Panama Refining Co. v. Ryan* (1935). The Constitution provides that, "All legislative powers herein granted shall be vested in a Congress of the United States, which shall consist of a Senate and House of Representatives." And the Congress is authorized "To make all laws which shall be necessary and proper for carrying into execution" its general powers. Article I, Section 8. The Congress is not permitted to abdicate or to transfer to others the essential legislative functions with which it is thus vested. We have repeatedly recognized the necessity of adapting legislation to complex conditions involving a host of details with which the national legislature cannot deal directly. We pointed out in the *Panama Company* case that the Constitution has never been regarded as denying to Congress the necessary resources of flexibility and practicality which will enable it to perform its function in laying down policies and establishing standards while leaving to selected instrumentalities the making of subordinate rules within prescribed limits, and the determination of facts to which the policy, as declared by the legislature, is to apply. But we said that the constant recognition of the necessity and validity of such provisions, and the wide range of administrative authority which has been developed by means of them, cannot be allowed to obscure the limitations of the authority to delegate, if our constitutional system is to be maintained.

[W]e look to the statute to see whether Congress has overstepped these limitations—whether Congress, in authorizing "codes of fair competition," has itself established the standards of legal obligation, thus performing its essential legislative function, or, by the failure to enact such standards, has attempted to transfer that function to others.

The aspect in which the question is now presented is distinct from that which was before us in the case of the *Panama Company*. . . . That subject was the transportation in interstate and foreign commerce of petroleum and petroleum products which are produced or withdrawn from storage in excess of the amount permitted by State authority. The question was with respect to the range of discretion given to the President in prohibiting that transportation. As to the "codes of fair competition," under section 3 of the Act, the question is more fundamental. It is whether there is any adequate definition of the subject to which the codes are to be addressed.

What is meant by "fair competition" as the term is used in the Act? Does it refer to a category established in the law, and is the authority to make codes limited accordingly? Or is it used as a convenient designation for whatever set of laws the formulators of a code for a particular trade or industry may propose and the President may approve (subject to certain restrictions), or the President may himself prescribe, as being wise and beneficent provisions for the government of the trade or industry in order to accomplish the broad purposes of rehabilitation, correction and expansion which are stated in the first section of Title I? . . .

[W]e turn to the Recovery Act to ascertain what limits have been set to the exercise of the President's discretion. *First*, the President, as a condition of approval, is required to find that the trade or industrial associations or groups which propose a code, "impose no inequitable restrictions on admission to membership," and are "truly representative." That condition, however, relates only to the status of the initiators of the new laws, and not to the permissible scope of such laws. *Second*, the President is required to find that the code is not "designed to promote monopolies or to eliminate or oppress small enterprises, and will not operate to discriminate against them." And to this is added a proviso that the code "shall not permit monopolies or monopolistic practices." But these restrictions leave virtually untouched the field of policy envisaged by section one, and, in that wide field of legislative possibilities, the proponents of a code, refraining from monopolistic designs, may roam at will, and the President may approve or disapprove their proposals as he may see fit. That is the precise effect of the further finding that the President is to make—that the code "will tend to effectuate the policy of this title." While this is called a finding, it is really but a statement of an opinion as to the general effect upon the promotion of trade or industry of a scheme of laws. These are the only findings which Congress has made essential in order to put into operation a legislative code having the aims described in the "Declaration of Policy."

Nor is the breadth of the President's discretion left to the necessary implication of this limited requirement as to his findings. As already noted, the President, in approving a code, may impose his own conditions, adding to or taking from what is proposed as, "in his discretion," he thinks necessary "to effectuate the policy" declared by the Act. Of course, he has no less liberty when he prescribes a code on his own motion or on complaint, and he is free to prescribe one if a code has not been approved. The Act provides for the creation by the President of administrative agencies to assist him, but the action or reports of such agencies, or of his other assistants—their recommendations and findings in relation to the making of codes— have no sanction beyond the will of the President, who may accept, modify, or reject them as he pleases. Such recommendations or findings in no way limit the authority which Section 3 undertakes to vest in the President with no other conditions than those there specified. And this authority relates to a host of different trades and industries, thus extending the President's discretion to all the varieties of laws which he may deem to be beneficial in dealing with the vast array of commercial and industrial activities throughout the country.

Such a sweeping delegation of legislative power finds no support in the decisions upon which the Government especially relies. By the Interstate Commerce Act, Congress has itself provided a code of laws regulating the activities of the common carriers subject to the Act in order to assure the performance of their services upon just and reasonable terms, with adequate facilities and without unjust discrimination. Congress, from time to time, has elaborated its requirements as needs have been disclosed. To facilitate the application of the standards prescribed by the Act, Congress has provided an expert body. That administrative agency, in dealing with particular cases, is required to act upon notice and hearing, and its orders must be supported by findings of fact which, in turn, are sustained by evidence. When the Commission is authorized to issue, for the construction, extension or abandonment of lines, a certificate of "public convenience and necessity," or to permit the acquisition by one carrier of the control of another, if that is found to be "in the public interest," we have pointed out that these provisions are not left without standards to guide determination. The authority conferred has direct relation to the standards prescribed for the service of common carriers, and can be exercised only upon findings, based upon evidence, with respect to particular conditions of transportation. . . .

To summarize and conclude upon this point: Section 3 of the Recovery Act is without precedent. It supplies no standards for any trade, industry or activity. It does not undertake to prescribe rules of conduct to be applied to particular states of fact determined by appropriate administrative procedure. Instead of prescribing rules of conduct, it authorizes the making of codes to prescribe them. For that legislative undertaking, §3 sets up no standards, aside from the statement of the general aims of rehabilitation, correction and expansion described in section one. In view of the scope of that broad declaration, and of the nature of the few restrictions that are imposed, the discretion of the President in approving or prescribing codes, and thus enacting laws for the government of trade and industry throughout the country, is virtually unfettered. We think that the code-making authority this conferred is an unconstitutional delegation of legislative power. . . .

MR. JUSTICE CARDOZO, concurring.

The delegated power of legislation which has found expression in this code is not canalized within banks that keep it from overflowing. It is unconfined and vagrant, if I may borrow my own words in an earlier opinion. *Panama Refining Co.* v. *Ryan* (1935). . . .

[T]here is another conception of codes of fair competition, their significance and function, which leads to very different consequences, though it is one that is struggling now for recognition and acceptance. By this other conception, a code is not to be restricted to the elimination of business practices that would be characterized by general acceptance as oppressive or unfair. It is to include whatever ordinances may be desirable or helpful for the well-being or prosperity of the industry affected. In that view, the function of its adoption is not merely negative, but positive—the planning of improvements as well as the extirpation of abuses. What is fair, as thus conceived, is not something to be contrasted with what is unfair or fraudulent or tricky. The extension becomes as wide as the field of industrial regulation. If that conception shall prevail, anything that Congress may do within the limits of the commerce clause for the betterment of business may be done by the President upon the recommendation of a trade association by calling it a code. This is delegation running riot. No such plenitude of power is susceptible of transfer. The statute, however, aims at nothing less, as one can learn both from its terms and from the administrative practice under it. Nothing less is aimed at by the code now submitted to our scrutiny.

The code does not confine itself to the suppression of methods of competition that would be classified as unfair according to accepted business standards or accepted norm of ethics. It sets up a comprehensive body of rules to promote the welfare of the industry, if not the welfare of the nation, without reference to standards, ethical or commercial, that could be known or predicted in advance of its adoption. One of the new rules, the source of ten counts in the indictment, is aimed at an established practice, not unethical or oppressive, the practice of selective buying. Many others could be instanced as open to the same objection if the sections of the code were to be examined one by one. The process of dissection will not be traced in all its details. Enough at this time to state what it reveals. Even if the statute itself had fixed the meaning of fair competition by way of contrast with practices that are oppressive or unfair, the code outruns the bounds of the authority conferred. What is excessive is not sporadic or superficial. It is deep-seated and pervasive. The licit and illicit sections are so combined and welded as to be incapable of severance without destructive mutilation.

▼▲▼

**The Legislative Veto.** Until 1933, Congress had never included in a law a "legislative veto," permitting it to exercise control over executive enforcement of that law. Then, as part of the Legislative Appropriations Act of 1932, which gave the president near unprecedented power to reorganize and consolidate federal agencies and issue executive orders, Congress inserted a legislative veto to allow it to retain some control over the exercise of this broad and untested delegation of legislative power. President Herbert Hoover claimed that such broad power was necessary to allow him to respond to the social and economic exigencies caused by the Great Depression. But Congress, controlled by Democrats, rejected all eleven of the reorganization plans that Hoover submitted under the 1932 law. Congress soon abandoned the legislative veto, perhaps in response to the Hoover administration's argument that the veto was unconstitutional. A more likely explanation is that Franklin Roosevelt had just been elected and the Democratic Congress was more willing, in the spirit of the New Deal, to encourage presidential experimentation.[71]

By 1939, however, Congress returned to the legislative veto to control presidential discretion under the Legislative Appropriations Act. Soon, Congress began inserting veto power with increasing regularity into federal laws that touched upon areas in which the legislative branch had long-standing political and policy interests, such as foreign affairs, immigration, and domestic military base operations. Although presidents from Roosevelt to Clinton have found the legislative veto an occasional obstacle to their ability to shape the enforcement of legislation through the rule-making process, most have accepted this admittedly quirky device as a necessary tradeoff to benefit from the delegation of legislative power to executive agencies. Political scientist Louis Fisher has called the legislative veto a successful attempt to "reconcile the interests of both the executive and legislative branches: the desire of agencies for greater discretionary authority and the need of Congress to maintain control short of passing another public law."[72]

This arrangement between Congress and the president stood until 1983. That year the Court, in *Immigration and Naturalization Service v. Chadha,* invalidated the legislative veto as an unconstitutional intrusion on the traditional relationship between the legislative and executive branches in the formulation and execution of legislation. Chief Justice Warren E. Burger, writing for a 7-2 Court, held that Congress could not use the legislative veto to control the rule-making responsibilities of the executive branch. Instead, Congress must exercise its legislative power "with a single, finely wrought and exhaustively considered, procedure," one characterized by a "step-by-step, deliberate and deliberative process."[73] The Court's opinion drew a long and blistering dissent from Justice Byron E. White, in which he accused the majority, more or less, of being painfully out of touch with the practical realities of the give-and-take that exists in the relationship between Congress and the president in the legislative process.

Since *Chadha,* Congress has inserted the legislative veto into more than two hundred laws that involve the congressional delegation of power to the executive branch. Thus, Justice White's dissent appears to support the observation that Chadha is one of the most important but least followed separation of powers decisions in the Court's history.[74] What is Justice White's central complaint in his *Chadha* dissent? Does he raise important questions about the congruence between constitutional theory and the realities of the American governmental process?

**Federal Agencies in the Tug of Constitutional War.**
In 1980, Ronald Reagan was elected president in no small part because he promised to improve the economic life of the nation. During his successful campaign, Reagan, a Republican, criticized his predecessor, Jimmy Carter, a Democrat, for endorsing a failed economic policy that emphasized increased taxes to support greater government spending, which in turn ran up federal budget deficits. President Reagan countered that the nation's economic prosperity would improve if Congress would cut taxes, increase defense spending, decrease nondefense federal expenditures, and balance the budget.

Suffice it to say that President Reagan's objective proved more difficult in fact than in theory. When President Carter left office in January 1980, he left a budget deficit of $73.8 billion. By the end of President Reagan's first term in 1984, the nation's budget deficit stood at $185.3 billion, with projections for 1985 and 1986 that ranged from $212.3 billion to $221.2 billion. These estimates were provided by the Office of Management and Budget (OMB) of the executive branch; the Congressional Budget Office (CBO), the congressional agency responsible for providing economic analysis to members of Congress; and the General Accounting Office (GAO), an agency created by Congress that audits and evaluates government programs and operations, but whose chief officer is appointed by the president and subject to Senate approval.

In response to political pressure to bring down the budget deficit and restrain federal spending, Congress, in 1985, enacted the Balanced Budget and Emergency Deficit Control Act, otherwise known as the Gramm-Rudman-Hollings Act, so named for three of the twenty-four senators who cosponsored the legislation. The law, which Justice White later called "one of the most novel and far-reaching legislative responses to a national crisis since the New Deal," was a last-ditch effort to place some mandatory limits on federal spending after the 1982 defeat of a constitutional amendment requiring a balanced budget. Indeed, Justice White's description is no hyperbole, as Gramm-Rudman-Hollings involved a number of complex arrangements between the executive and legislative branches that dealt with budget enforcement issues, some of which had little or no precedent in American constitutional law.

Among the most strongly contested provisions of the law was one that authorized broad discretion to the GAO's chief officer, the comptroller general, to make factual determinations in preparing a report that analyzed budget and deficit estimates provided by the OMB and the CBO. The comptroller's report then had to detail the reductions required for Congress to meet its deficit-reduction targets under Gramm-Rudman-Hollings. This requirement, as well as a provision from the 1921 law creating the GAO that permitted Congress to remove the comptroller, led Rep. Mike Synar (D–Okla.) and several other representatives to have Gramm-Rudman-Hollings declared unconstitutional. They charged that the law vested the comptroller general, a legislative branch officer, with the power to execute the fundamental budget-reduction requirements of the law. This, the plaintiffs claimed, granted the comptroller the equivalent of executive branch power, an outcome prohibited by Article I.

In *Bowsher* v. *Synar* (1986), the Court declared that provision of Gramm-Rudman-Hollings, as well as several others, unconstitutional. Note the similarities of the Court's approach in *Bowsher* and *Chadha*. In both cases the Court relies greatly on a formal interpretation of the separation of powers doctrine and the respective roles of Congress and the president in the lawmaking process. Again, Justice White dissents, adhering to his position in *Chadha* that the Court's adherence to a rigid theoretical conception of the separation of powers misreads and makes more cumbersome the give-and-take that characterizes the relationship between Congress and the president.

Of historical note is the fact that Justice Antonin Scalia, just months before he was nominated and confirmed to the Court, wrote the opinion for the D.C. circuit court of appeals in *Bowsher*. He found the power granted to the comptroller general to violate the separation of powers doctrine. Earlier in his career, Justice Scalia served as the assistant attorney general in the Office of Legal Counsel in the Department of Justice during the Ford administration. During his tenure at the Justice Department, Scalia developed an influential set of arguments on the legislative veto's unconstitutionality. He criticized the legislative veto in testimony before Congress and in several published articles. Scalia's views, cultivated over a long period of time, ultimately carried great influence in the Court's opinions in *Chadha* and *Bowsher*.[75]

**The Presidential Line-Item Veto.** Congress has always been willing to experiment with innovative legislation to control federal expenditures and reduce what it and often the public perceive as tax dollars spent on wasteful programs. Public opinion, when consulted, is almost always in favor of balancing the federal budget, reducing the size and scope of the federal government, and eliminating programs that serve no useful purpose. Although such suggestions make intuitive sense, Congress often stops short of taking decisive action because few members are willing to eliminate federal programs that are popular in their own district.

Tobacco subsidies, for example, may not make sense to members who live in states without farmers and related businesses that depend on good prices and political support for tobacco products in the economic marketplace. But such federal support means a lot to areas that depend on tobacco for their livelihoods and thus makes a lot of sense, whereas increased public funds to support mass transit in large cities might be viewed as a pointless use of tax dollars. Because members need each other to support pet projects important to powerful political constituencies, legislative tradeoffs are part and parcel of the business of Congress. Thus members from tobacco states support legislation that contains increased funds for mass transit and public road maintenance. In return, they receive support for their pet programs. Congressional rhetoric over wasteful spending can sometimes reach ear-piercing levels, but it rarely solves this age-old problem: How do you convince senators and representatives to vote against their electoral interests?

Presidents as far back as George Washington have responded that Congress is incapable of reining in its power of the purse and have, in turn, requested discretionary authority over the appropriation of funds designated for federal programs. While Congress, on occasion, has granted the president such power, more often than not it has sought to retain a firm hand on the funding of its programs. President George Bush summarized more recent presidential frustration with congressional expenditures when he claimed, in his 1992 State of the Union speech, "[t]he Press has a field day making fun of outrageous examples [of wasteful federal programs]: A Lawrence Welk museum, research grants for Belgian endive. . . . Maybe you need someone to help you say no. I know how to say it, and I know what I need to make it stick. Give me . . . the line-item veto."[76]

In 1996, Congress enacted the Line Item Veto Act, giving the president, for the first time, the authority to veto specific expenditures and programs in legislation waiting to be signed. Like the enactment of Gramm-Rudman in 1985, passage of the Line Item Veto Act came after Congress, in March 1995, had failed to muster the two-thirds majority necessary to approve a constitutional amendment that would have required a balanced budget. It should come as no surprise that President Clinton had barely replaced the cap on his

## SCHECHTER POULTRY CORP. V. UNITED STATES

### *"Sick Chickens" and Free Markets*

Almost no trade or profession was immune from the effects of the Great Depression, but some ways to earn a living during the worst economic crisis in American history were tougher than others. Few, however, equaled New York City's wholesale poultry trade for corruption and the squalor of its working conditions. Despite these odds, Joseph, Alex, Martin, and Aaron Schechter managed to beat the gangsters and the Depression. They built the largest poultry businesses in Brooklyn, the A.L.A. Schechter Corp. and the Schechter Live Poultry Co. In fact, Joe Schechter stood up to mob henchmen during the early 1930s by refusing to pay the exorbitant rental fees for chicken coops used by members of the poultry trade. Schechter's reward was to have two cups of emery powder dumped in the crankcase of his truck. From that point on, however, the mob left the Schechter brothers alone.

Although the Schechters refused to enter a relationship with organized crime, they had few qualms about systematically evading the complex legislation that Congress passed in 1933 to control competition and level prices in several unstable American industries, including the poultry business. Conceived by lawyers scattered about the new federal agencies created to oversee President Roosevelt's New Deal, the National Industrial Recovery Act (NIRA) authorized various industries to devise their own regulatory codes. Those codes, in turn, were submitted to the National Recovery Administration (NRA), which was responsible for their industrywide enforcement. The NIRA included the Live Poultry Code, which created specific maximum work hours and minimum wage requirements for poultry industry workers and created workplace safety and health rules.

In one sense the NRA was extremely successful. It helped stabilize the chaotic economic state of numerous national industries, averted costly and politically charged labor disputes, and instilled confidence in an American public shaken by the catastrophic consequences of the Great Depression. On the other hand, the novelty of the federal government's new central position in the regulation of the nation's economic life

challenged even the brightest lawyers of Roosevelt's elite "brain trust" of New Deal lawyers, many of whom were learning their antitrust and business law as they went. This ad hoc approach to litigation and enforcement often drew the ire of industries that did not welcome federal control. As more and more industries regained their economic health, a mood of resistance set in toward the NIRA. Local inspectors began to report that even the display of the Blue Eagle, the NRA's official emblem, in the window of a poultry or fish shop no longer meant that its owner was complying with the act. As turf battles between the Justice Department and the NRA over enforcement responsibilities for the NIRA led to ineffective compliance by industries, the New Deal legal brain trust decided that it needed to select and litigate a test case to rejuvenate the NIRA and save the NRA.

Because New York City housed more than 96 percent of the nation's live poultry market, and because the Schechters' companies were among its largest and most profitable, the NRA turned its investigative sights on their business practices. It found that the Schechters had violated nineteen separate counts of the Live Poultry Code, including wage and hour rules and separate provisions governing unfair trade practices. Witnesses testified that the Schechters had even sold thousands of pounds of diseased chickens at below market rates to boost sales.

But these violations would not have encouraged the government to press ahead with its case against the Schechters had it not also learned that hundreds of the diseased chickens sold suffered from tuberculosis, which humans could contract by eating them. According to one witness who testified at the Schechters' trial, almost forty people had contracted tuberculosis from chickens sold by the brothers' companies. The Schechters were ultimately found guilty of violating the NIRA codes on seventeen counts, given brief jail sentences, and fined approximately $7,500.

A federal appeals court reversed, however, on two crucial points. First, it ruled that Congress had unconstitutionally delegated its legislative power to an unusual alliance of private trade associations and executive branch agencies. Second, the appeals court held that Congress had exceeded its power under the Commerce Clause to impose such regulations on business that were fundamentally intrastate in nature. The Supreme Court agreed.

Roosevelt was incensed by the Court's decision, but he didn't show his anger in public. Instead, he waited to gauge the public reaction, which was equally negative, before he held a press conference. "The implications of this decision," said Roosevelt to more than 250 reporters, "are much more important than any decision probably since the *Dred Scott* case . . . [and] the big issue is this: Does this decision mean that the United States Government has no control over any national economic problem?" He castigated business executives for their short-sighted efforts to limit federal regulation by pointing to their involvement in funding the Schechters' defense, which was provided by the Liberty League, an anti–New Deal group that promoted laissez-faire economics, and the

Iron and Steel Institute. Indeed, the Liberty League had been able to enlist Frederick J. Wood, an experienced Supreme Court advocate, to join the Schechters' original attorney, Joseph Heller, who had no such experience.

Then Roosevelt heightened the drama, pointing to a stack of telegrams that he had received from small business owners. The president said that the

*A poultry market owner in 1930s New York City proudly displays his wares.*
The Museum of the City of New York.

telegrams proved that the average businessman was suffering at the hands of the *Schechter* decision. "We are the only nation in the world that has not solved that problem [of economic regulation]. We thought we were solving it, and now it has been thrown right straight in our faces and we have been relegated to the horse-and-buggy definition of interstate commerce."

Newspapers across the nation reprinted Roosevelt's remarks and featured his "horse and buggy" remark in their headlines. *Schechter* also served as the launch point for Roosevelt's continued attacks on the Court for the next two years, which struck down numerous key provisions of his New Deal agenda and placed handcuffs on state efforts to regulate their own Depression-affected economic and social conditions. This pattern continued until the Court's self-imposed shift in 1937 that led to the validation of the New Deal welfare state.

After their moment in the national spotlight, the Schechters returned to Brooklyn and picked up where they had left off. Their prosperity was short-lived, though, as a year later the brothers lost their business and were forced to sell their homes. It was a sad ending for a successful business whose warehouses and storefronts had once proudly displayed the Blue Eagle emblem.

"The Liberty Leaguers sent us a lot of swell letters saying they appreciated what we had done," Aaron Schechter later said, "but they didn't put any money in those letters."

### References

Freidel, Frank. "The Sick Chicken Case," in John A. Garraty, ed., *Quarrels That Have Shaped the Constitution.* New York: Harper & Row, 1987, pp. 233–252.

Irons, Peter H. *The New Deal Lawyers* Princeton, N.J.: Princeton University Press, 1982.

signature pen when Senator Robert C. Byrd (D–W.Va.) and several other members of Congress filed suit to have the line-item veto declared unconstitutional. The Court dismissed *Raines* v. *Byrd* (1997) on standing grounds, claiming that the members could not show direct injury from President Clinton's use of the line-item veto.

Other plaintiffs that were able to clear the Court's threshold requirements on standing to sue soon emerged to challenge the statute. The path to the Court's decision in *Clinton* v. *City of New York* (1998), in which it struck down the law as violative of the Presentment Clause of Article I, offers a rare window into the complex mix of legal and political considerations that go into a constitutional decision. For the 6-3 Court, Justice Kennedy's opinion seems as much a civics lesson on the need for Congress to exercise the necessary discipline and restraint to control federal expenditures as it is an analysis of this complex constitutional issue. Is Justice Kennedy's approach to the separation of powers doctrine similar to or different from the majorities in *Chadha* and *Bowsher?* How so?

In *City of New York,* Justice Scalia dissents, writing that "[t]here is not a dime's worth of difference between Congress's authorizing the president to cancel a spending item, and Congress's authorizing money to be spent on a particular item at the president's discretion." Compare the Court's opinions and lead dissents in *Bowsher* and *City of New York.* In particular, do you believe that

Justice Scalia's *City of New York* dissent is inconsistent with his position on Gramm-Rudman?

Some scholars have criticized *Chadha* and *Bowsher* as failed exercises by the Court in constitutional literalism. Rather than understand the separation of powers doctrine as one that encourages and depends on the shared, consensual distribution of crucial functions, the Court ignored Madison's distinction between the branches of government having partial agency in, as opposed to control over, the acts of each other. Indeed, the Court's decisions discussed in this section illustrate the difficulties inherent in balancing theories of constitutional government with the actual process of governing. We will return to the complexities of the separation of powers doctrine in Chapter 5, this time from the vantage point of the executive branch.

## *Mistretta* v. *United States*
### 488 U.S. 361 (1989)

A sure-fire winner in any congressional reelection campaign is a promise to have the federal government "get tough on crime." Since the 1960s, when the Supreme Court decided several landmark cases revolutionizing the rights of criminal defendants, Congress had made persistent noises about broadening federal jurisdiction to prosecute cases involving drugs and gun violence, expanding the range of death penalty offenses, and eliminating the sentencing discretion of federal judges. Members of Congress with self-proclaimed "law and order" orientations were particularly angered by what they saw as lenient sentencing from liberal federal judges.

In 1984, Congress passed the Sentencing Reform Act, a comprehensive effort to mandate sentences for federal offenses. The law created the United States Sentencing Commission, described as "an independent [body] in the Judicial Branch" with the authority to determine binding prison sentences for all federal offenses." The commission consisted of seven members, who were nominated by the president and confirmed by the Senate. The law required three members to be federal judges. No more than four members could belong to the same political party.

Many federal judges openly expressed their disdain for sentencing laws, believing them to be motivated less by a concern to mandate appropriate punishment than a desire to score political points with the public. Mandatory sentencing meant more prisoners, which meant that the federal government would need to build more jails, as space to house inmates began to rapidly dwindle. In fact, prison construction was one the fastest growing federal spending programs of the 1980s and 1990s. With many states enacting tougher sentencing laws as well, building prisons and housing and transporting prisoners became a growth industry nationwide. More important, these laws required judges to issue lengthy sentences for sometimes petty offenses, raising questions of appropriate justice. An example of such a law was the "three strikes and you're out" approach taken by the federal government (and the states) in many drug cases. After a third offense, a defendant, depending upon the statute, could be sentenced to life for an offense no greater than simple possession of marijuana.

The federal courts split on the constitutionality of the 1984 law. John Mistretta had been sentenced to eighteen months in prison for cocaine possession with the intent to distribute. He challenged the law as an unconstitutional delegation of power. The Supreme Court granted his petition and agreed to consider the federal government's request for a determination on the constitutionality of the sentencing guidelines.

The Court's decision was 8 to 1. Justice Blackmun delivered the opinion of the Court. Justice Scalia dissented.

▼▲▼

JUSTICE BLACKMUN delivered the opinion of the Court.

. . . Petitioner argues that, in delegating the power to promulgate sentencing guidelines for every federal criminal offense to an independent Sentencing Commission, Congress has granted the Commission excessive legislative discretion in violation of the constitutionally based nondelegation doctrine. We do not agree.

The nondelegation doctrine is rooted in the principle of separation of powers that underlies our tripartite system of Government. The Constitution provides that "[a]ll legislative Powers herein granted shall be vested in a Congress of the United States," Article I, Section 1, and we long have insisted that "the integrity and maintenance of the system of government ordained by the Constitution" mandate that Congress generally cannot delegate its legislative power to another Branch. We also have recognized, however, that the separation of powers principle, and the nondelegation doctrine in particular, do not prevent Congress from obtaining the assistance of its coordinate Branches. In a passage now enshrined in our jurisprudence, Chief Justice Taft, writing for the Court, explained our approach to such cooperative ventures: "In determining what [Congress] may do in seeking assistance from another branch, the extent and character of that assistance must be fixed according to common sense and the inherent necessities of the government coordination." So long as Congress, "shall lay down by legislative act an intelligible principle to which the person or body authorized to [exercise the delegated authority] is directed to conform, such legislative action is not a forbidden delegation of legislative power."

Applying this "intelligible principle" test to congressional delegations, our jurisprudence has been driven by a practical understanding that, in our increasingly complex society, replete with ever-changing and more technical problems, Congress simply cannot do its job absent an ability to delegate power under broad general directives. . . .

Until 1935, this Court never struck down a challenged statute on delegation grounds. After invalidating in 1935 two statutes as excessive delegations, *Schechter Poultry Corp.* v. *United States* (1935), and *Panama Refining Co.* v. *Ryan* (1935), we have upheld, again without deviation, Congress' ability to delegate power under broad standards. . . .

In light of our approval of these broad delegations, we harbor no doubt that Congress' delegation of authority to the Sentencing Commission is sufficiently specific and detailed to meet constitutional requirements. Congress charged the Commission with three goals: to "assure the meeting of the purposes of sentencing as set forth" in the Act; to, "provide certainty and fairness in meeting the purposes of sentencing, avoiding unwarranted sentencing disparities among defendants with similar records . . . while maintaining sufficient flexibility to permit individualized sentences," where appropriate; and to "reflect, to the extent practicable, advancement in knowledge of human behavior as it relates to the criminal justice process." Congress further specified four "purposes" of sentencing that the Commission must pursue in carrying out its mandate: "to reflect the seriousness of the offense, to promote respect for the law, and to provide just punishment for the offense"; "to afford adequate deterrence to criminal conduct"; "to protect the public from further crimes of the defendant"; and "to provide the defendant with needed . . . correctional treatment."

In addition, Congress prescribed the specific tool—the guidelines system—for the Commission to use in regulating sentencing. More particularly, Congress directed the Commission to develop a system of "sentencing ranges" applicable "for each category of offense involving each category of defendant." Congress instructed the Commission that these sentencing ranges must be consistent with pertinent provisions of Title 18 of the United States Code, and could not include sentences in excess of the statutory maxima. Congress also required that, for sentences of imprisonment, "the maximum of the range established for such a term shall not exceed the minimum of that range by more than the greater of 25 percent or 6 months, except that, if the minimum term of the range is 30 years or more, the maximum may be life imprisonment." Moreover, Congress directed the Commission to use current average sentences "as a starting point" for its structuring of the sentencing ranges.

To guide the Commission in its formulation of offense categories, Congress directed it to consider seven factors: the grade of the offense; the aggravating and mitigating circumstances of the crime; the nature and degree of the harm caused by the crime; the community view of the gravity of the offense; the public concern generated by the crime; the deterrent effect that a particular sentence may have on others; and the current incidence of the offense. Congress set forth 11 factors for the Commission to consider in establishing categories of defendants. These include the offender's age, education, vocational skills, mental and emotional condition, physical condition (including drug dependence), previous employment record, family ties and responsibilities, community ties, role in the offense, criminal history, and degree of dependence upon crime for a livelihood. Congress also prohib-

ited the Commission from considering the "race, sex, national origin, creed, and socioeconomic status of offenders," and instructed that the guidelines should reflect the "general inappropriateness" of considering certain other factors, such as current unemployment, that might serve as proxies for forbidden factors.

In addition to these overarching constraints, Congress provided even more detailed guidance to the Commission about categories of offenses and offender characteristics. Congress directed that guidelines require a term of confinement at or near the statutory maximum for certain crimes of violence and for drug offenses, particularly when committed by recidivists. Congress further directed that the Commission assure a substantial term of imprisonment for an offense constituting a third felony conviction, for a career felon, for one convicted of a managerial role in a racketeering enterprise, for a crime of violence by an offender on release from a prior felony conviction, and for an offense involving a substantial quantity of narcotics. Congress also instructed "that the guidelines reflect . . . the general appropriateness of imposing a term of imprisonment" for a crime of violence that resulted in serious bodily injury. On the other hand, Congress directed that guidelines reflect the general inappropriateness of imposing a sentence of imprisonment, "in cases in which the defendant is a first offender who has not been convicted of a crime of violence or an otherwise serious offense." Congress also enumerated various aggravating and mitigating circumstances, such as, respectively, multiple offenses or substantial assistance to the Government, to be reflected in the guidelines. In other words, although Congress granted the Commission substantial discretion in formulating guidelines, in actuality it legislated a full hierarchy of punishment—from near maximum imprisonment, to substantial imprisonment, to some imprisonment, to alternatives—and stipulated the most important offense and offender characteristics to place defendants within these categories.

We cannot dispute petitioner's contention that the Commission enjoys significant discretion in formulating guidelines. The Commission does have discretionary authority to determine the relative severity of federal crimes and to assess the relative weight of the offender characteristics that Congress listed for the Commission to consider. The Commission also has significant discretion to determine which crimes have been punished too leniently, and which too severely. Congress has called upon the Commission to exercise its judgment about which types of crimes and which types of criminals are to be considered similar for the purposes of sentencing. . . .

But our cases do not at all suggest that delegations of this type may not carry with them the need to exercise judgment on matters of policy. . . .

We conclude that, in creating the Sentencing Commission—an unusual hybrid in structure and authority—Congress neither delegated excessive legislative power nor upset the constitutionally mandated balance of powers among the coordinate Branches. The Constitution's structural protections do not prohibit Congress from delegating to an expert body located within the Judicial Branch the intricate task of formulating sentencing guidelines consistent with such significant statutory direction as is present here. Nor does our system of checked and balanced authority prohibit Congress from calling upon the accumulated wisdom and experience of the Judicial Branch in creating policy on a matter uniquely within the ken of judges. Accordingly, we hold that the Act is constitutional.

JUSTICE SCALIA, dissenting.

While the products of the Sentencing Commission's labors have been given the modest name "Guidelines," they have the force and effect of laws, prescribing the sentences criminal defendants are to receive. A judge who disregards them will be reversed. I dissent from today's decision because I can find no place within our constitutional system for an agency created by Congress to exercise no governmental power other than the making of laws. . . .

Precisely because the scope of delegation is largely uncontrollable by the courts, we must be particularly rigorous in preserving the Constitution's structural restrictions that deter excessive delegation. The major one, it seems to me, is that the power to make law cannot be exercised by anyone other than Congress, except in conjunction with the lawful exercise of executive or judicial power.

The whole theory of *lawful* congressional "delegation" is not that Congress is sometimes too busy or too divided, and can therefore assign its responsibility of making law to someone else, but rather that a certain degree of discretion, and thus of lawmaking, *inheres* in most executive or judicial action, and it is up to Congress, by the relative specificity or generality of its statutory commands, to determine—up to a point—how small or how large that degree shall be. Thus, the courts could be given the power to say precisely what constitutes a "restraint of trade," or to adopt rules of procedure, or to prescribe by rule the manner in which their officers shall execute their judgments, because that "lawmaking" was ancillary to their

exercise of judicial powers. And the Executive could be given the power to adopt policies and rules specifying in detail what radio and television licenses will be in the "public interest, convenience or necessity," because that was ancillary to the exercise of its executive powers in granting and policing licenses and making a "fair and equitable allocation" of the electromagnetic spectrum. Or, to take examples closer to the case before us: Trial judges could be given the power to determine what factors justify a greater or lesser sentence within the statutorily prescribed limits, because that was ancillary to their exercise of the judicial power of pronouncing sentence upon individual defendants. And the President, through the Parole Commission subject to his appointment and removal, could be given the power to issue Guidelines specifying when parole would be available, because that was ancillary to the President's exercise of the executive power to hold and release federal prisoners. . . .

The focus of controversy, in the long line of our so-called excessive delegation cases, has been whether the *degree* of generality contained in the authorization for exercise of executive or judicial powers in a particular field is so unacceptably high as to *amount* to a delegation of legislative powers. I say "so-called excessive delegation" because, although that convenient terminology is often used, what is really at issue is whether there has been *any* delegation of legislative power, which occurs (rarely) when Congress authorizes the exercise of executive or judicial power without adequate standards. Strictly speaking, there is *no* acceptable delegation of legislative power. As John Locke put it almost 300 years ago, "[t]he power of the *legislative*, being derived from the people by a positive voluntary grant and institution, can be no other than what the positive grant conveyed, which, being only to make *laws*, and not to make *legislators*, the *legislative* can have no power to transfer their authority of making laws, and place it in other hands." . . . In the present case, however, a pure delegation of legislative power is precisely what we have before us. It is irrelevant whether the standards are adequate, because they are not standards related to the exercise of executive or judicial powers; they are, plainly and simply, standards for further legislation. . . .

The delegation of lawmaking authority to the Commission is, in short, unsupported by any legitimating theory to explain why it is not a delegation of legislative power. To disregard structural legitimacy is wrong in itself—but since structure has purpose, the disregard also has adverse practical consequences. In this case, as suggested earlier, the consequence is to facilitate and encourage judicially uncontrollable delegation. Until our decision last Term in *Morrison* v. *Olson* (1988), it could have been said that Congress could delegate lawmaking authority only at the expense of increasing the power of either the President or the courts. Most often, as a practical matter, it would be the President, since the judicial process is unable to conduct the investigations and make the political assessments essential for most policymaking. Thus, the need for delegation would have to be important enough to induce Congress to aggrandize its primary competitor for political power, and the recipient of the policymaking authority, while not Congress itself, would at least be politically accountable. But even after it has been accepted, pursuant to *Morrison*, that those exercising executive power need not be subject to the control of the President, Congress would still be more reluctant to augment the power of even an independent executive agency than to create an otherwise powerless repository for its delegation. Moreover, assembling the full-time senior personnel for an agency exercising executive powers is more difficult than borrowing other officials (or employing new officers on a short-term basis) to head an organization such as the Sentencing Commission.

By reason of today's decision, I anticipate that Congress will find delegation of its lawmaking powers much more attractive in the future. If rulemaking can be entirely unrelated to the exercise of judicial or executive powers, I foresee all manner of "expert" bodies, insulated from the political process, to which Congress will delegate various portions of its lawmaking responsibility. How tempting to create an expert Medical Commission (mostly M.D.'s, with perhaps a few Ph.D.'s in moral philosophy) to dispose of such thorny, "now-in" political issues as the withholding of life-support systems in federally funded hospitals, or the use of fetal tissue for research. This is an undemocratic precedent that we set—not because of the scope of the delegated power, but because its recipient is not one of the three Branches of Government. The only governmental power the Commission possesses is the power to make law; and it is not the Congress. . . .

Today's decision follows the regrettable tendency of our recent separation of powers jurisprudence, to treat the Constitution as though it were no more than a generalized prescription that the functions of the Branches should not be commingled too much—how much is too much to be determined, case-by-case, by this Court. The Constitution is not that. Rather, as its name suggests, it is a prescribed structure, a framework, for the conduct of Government. In designing that structure, the Framers *themselves* considered how much commingling was, in the generality of things, acceptable, and set forth their conclusions in the document. That is the meaning of the statements concerning acceptable commingling made by Madison in defense of the proposed Constitution, and now routinely used as an excuse for disregarding it. When he said, as the Court correctly quotes, that separation of powers " 'd[oes] not mean that these [three] departments ought to have no *partial agency* in, or no *controul* over, the acts of each other,'" *Federalist 47*, his point was that the commingling specifically provided for in the structure that he and his colleagues had designed—the Presidential veto over legislation, the Senate's confirmation of executive and judicial officers, the Senate's ratification of treaties, the Congress' power to impeach and remove executive and judicial officers—did not violate a proper understanding of separation of powers. He would be aghast, I think, to hear those words used as justification for ignoring that carefully designed structure so long as, in the changing view of the Supreme Court from time to time, "too much commingling" does not occur. Consideration of the degree of commingling that a particular disposition produces may be appropriate at the margins, where the outline of the framework itself is not clear; but it seems to me far from a marginal question whether our constitutional structure allows for a body which is not the Congress, and yet exercises no governmental powers except the making of rules that have the effect of laws.

I think the Court errs, in other words, not so much because it mistakes the degree of commingling, but because it fails to recognize that this case is not about commingling, but about the creation of a new Branch altogether, a sort of junior varsity Congress. It may well be that, in some circumstances, such a Branch would be desirable; perhaps the agency before us here will prove to be so. But there are many desirable dispositions that do not accord with the constitutional structure we live under. And, in the long run, the improvisation of a constitutional structure on the basis of currently perceived utility will be disastrous.

## *INS* v. *Chadha*
462 U.S. 919 (1983)

After the expiration of his visa, Jagdish Rai Chadha was ordered by the Immigration and Naturalization Service (INS) to show why he should not be deported. Chadha agreed that he met the criteria for deportation but filed for a suspension, pending a hearing before an immigration judge. The United States attorney general granted Chadha the suspension, as authorized by federal law. That same law required the attorney general to report all such suspensions to Congress, which may then veto the order. The House of Representatives passed a resolution opposing the grant of the suspension to Chadha and five others. When the deportation hearings were subsequently reopened, Chadha challenged the legislative veto in the court of appeals. The court of appeals held that 244(c)(2) violated the constitutional doctrine of separation of powers and accordingly directed the attorney general to cease taking any steps to deport Chadha based upon the House resolution. The government appealed to the Supreme Court.

The Court's decision was 7 to 2. Chief Justice Burger delivered the opinion of the Court. Justice Powell concurred. Justice Rehnquist filed a dissent, which was joined by Justice White.

▼▲▼

CHIEF JUSTICE BURGER delivered the opinion of the Court.

[This case] presents a challenge to the constitutionality of the provision in Section 244(c)(2) of the Immigration and Nationality Act, authorizing one House of Congress, by resolution, to invalidate the decision of the Executive Branch, pursuant to authority delegated by Congress to the Attorney General of the United States, to allow a particular deportable alien to remain in the United States. . . .

We begin, of course, with the presumption that the challenged statute is valid. Its wisdom is not the concern of the courts; if a challenged action does not violate the Constitution, it must be sustained. . . .

By the same token, the fact that a given law or procedure is efficient, convenient, and useful in facilitating functions of government, standing alone, will not save it if it is contrary to the Constitution. Convenience and efficiency are not the primary objectives—or the hallmarks—of democratic government and our inquiry is sharpened rather than blunted by the fact that congressional veto provisions are appearing with increasing frequency in statutes which delegate authority to executive and independent agencies. . . .

JUSTICE WHITE undertakes to make a case for the proposition that the one-House veto is a useful "political invention," and we need not challenge that assertion. We can even concede this utilitarian argument, although the long-range political wisdom of this "invention" is arguable.

It has been vigorously debated, and it is instructive to compare the views of the protagonists. But policy arguments supporting even useful "political inventions" are subject to the demands of the Constitution, which defines powers and, with respect to this subject, sets out just how those powers are to be exercised.

Explicit and unambiguous provisions of the Constitution prescribe and define the respective functions of the Congress and of the Executive in the legislative process. . . .

The records of the Constitutional Convention reveal that the requirement that all legislation be presented to the President before becoming law was uniformly accepted by the Framers. Presentment to the President and the Presidential veto were considered so imperative that the draftsmen took special pains to assure that these requirements could not be circumvented. . . .

The decision to provide the President with a limited and qualified power to nullify proposed legislation by veto was based on the profound conviction of the Framers that the powers conferred on Congress were the powers to be most carefully circumscribed. It is beyond doubt that lawmaking was a power to be shared by both Houses and the President. In *Federalist* 73, Hamilton focused on the President's role in making laws:

> If even no propensity had ever discovered itself in the legislative body to invade the rights of the Executive, the rules of just reasoning and theoretic propriety would of themselves teach us that the one ought not to be left to the mercy of the other, but ought to possess a constitutional and effectual power of self-defence.

The President's role in the lawmaking process also reflects the Framers' careful efforts to check whatever propensity a particular Congress might have to enact oppressive, improvident, or ill-considered measures. The President's veto role in the legislative process was described later during public debate on ratification:

> It establishes a salutary check upon the legislative body, calculated to guard the community against the effects of faction, precipitancy, or of any impulse unfriendly to the public good, which may happen to influence a majority of that body. . . .
>
> The primary inducement to conferring the power in question upon the Executive is to enable him to defend himself; the secondary one is to increase the chances in favor of the community against the passing of bad laws, through haste, inadvertence, or design. *Federalist* 73. . . .

The bicameral requirement of Article I, Section 1, Clause 7, was of scarcely less concern to the Framers than was the Presidential veto, and indeed the two concepts are interdependent. By providing that no law could take effect without the concurrence of the prescribed majority of the Members of both Houses, the Framers reemphasized their belief, already remarked upon in connection with the Presentment Clauses, that legislation should not be enacted unless it has been carefully and fully considered by the Nation's elected officials. . . .

We see therefore that the Framers were acutely conscious that the bicameral requirement and the Presentment Clauses would serve essential constitutional functions. The President's participation in the legislative process was to protect the Executive Branch from Congress and to protect the whole people from improvident laws. The division of the Congress into two distinctive bodies assures that the legislative power would be exercised only after opportunity for full study and debate in separate settings. The President's unilateral veto power, in turn, was limited by the power of two-thirds of both Houses of Congress to overrule a veto, thereby precluding final arbitrary action of one person. It emerges clearly that the prescription for legislative action in Article I, Section 1, Clause 7, represents the Framers' decision that the legislative power of the Federal Government be exercised in accord with a single, finely wrought and exhaustively considered, procedure.

The Constitution sought to divide the delegated powers of the new Federal Government into three defined categories, Legislative, Executive, and Judicial, to assure, as nearly as possible, that each branch of government would confine itself to its assigned responsibility. The hydraulic pressure inherent within each of the separate Branches to exceed the outer limits of its power, even to accomplish desirable objectives, must be resisted.

Although not "hermetically" sealed from one another, the powers delegated to the three Branches are functionally identifiable. When any Branch acts, it is presumptively exercising the power the Constitution has delegated to it. When the Executive acts, he presumptively acts in an executive or administrative capacity as defined in Article II. And when, as here, one House of Congress purports to act, it is presumptively acting within its assigned sphere. . . .

Examination of the action taken here by one House . . . reveals that it was essentially legislative in purpose and effect. In purporting to exercise power defined in Article I, Section 8, clause 4, to "establish an uniform Rule of Naturalization," the House took action that had the purpose and effect of altering the legal rights, duties, and relations of persons, including the Attorney General, Executive Branch officials and Chadha, all outside the Legislative Branch. . . .

The legislative character of the one-House veto in these cases is confirmed by the character of the congressional action it supplants. Neither the House of Representatives nor the Senate contends that, absent the veto provision, either of them, or both of them acting together, could effectively require the Attorney General to deport an alien once the Attorney General, in the exercise of legislatively delegated authority, had determined the alien should remain in the United States. Without the challenged provision, this could have been achieved, if at all, only by legislation requiring deportation. Similarly, a veto by one House of Congress cannot be justified. . . .

The nature of the decision implemented by the one-House veto in these cases further manifests its legislative character. After long experience with the clumsy, time-consuming private bill procedure, Congress made a deliberate choice to delegate to the Executive Branch, and specifically to the Attorney General, the authority to allow deportable aliens to remain in this country in certain specified circumstances. It is not disputed that this choice to delegate authority is precisely the kind of decision that can be implemented only in accordance with the procedures set out in Article I. Disagreement with the Attorney General's decision on Chadha's deportation—that is, Congress' decision to deport Chadha—no less than Congress' original choice to delegate to the Attorney General the authority to make that decision, involves determinations of policy that Congress can implement in only one way; bicameral passage followed by presentment to the President. Congress must abide by its delegation of authority until that delegation is legislatively altered or revoked.

Finally, we see that, when the Framers intended to authorize either House of Congress to act alone and outside of its prescribed bicameral legislative role, they narrowly and precisely defined the procedure for such action. There are four provisions in the Constitution, explicit and unambiguous, by which one House may act alone with the unreviewable force of law, not subject to the President's veto:

a. The House of Representatives alone was given the power to initiate impeachments. Article I, Section 2, clause 5;
b. The Senate alone was given the power to conduct trials following impeachment on charges initiated by the House, and to convict following trial. Article I, Section 3, clause 6;
c. The Senate alone was given final unreviewable power to approve or to disapprove Presidential appointments. Article II, Section 2, clause 2;

d. The Senate alone was given unreviewable power to ratify treaties negotiated by the President. Article II, Section 2, clause 2.

Clearly, when the Draftsmen sought to confer special powers on one House, independent of the other House, or of the President, they did so in explicit, unambiguous terms. These carefully defined exceptions from presentment and bicameralism underscore the difference between the legislative functions of Congress and other unilateral but important and binding one-House acts provided for in the Constitution. These exceptions are narrow, explicit, and separately justified; none of them authorize the action challenged here. On the contrary, they provide further support for the conclusion that congressional authority is not to be implied, and for the conclusion that the veto provided for is not authorized by the constitutional design of the powers of the Legislative Branch. . . .

The veto . . . doubtless has been in many respects a convenient shortcut; the "sharing" with the Executive by Congress of its authority over aliens in this manner is, on its face, an appealing compromise. In purely practical terms, it is obviously easier for action to be taken by one House without submission to the President; but it is crystal clear from the records of the Convention, contemporaneous writings, and debates that the Framers ranked other values higher than efficiency. The records of the Convention and debates in the states preceding ratification underscore the common desire to define and limit the exercise of the newly created federal powers affecting the states and the people. There is unmistakable expression of a determination that legislation by the national Congress be a step-by-step, deliberate and deliberative process.

The choices we discern as having been made in the Constitutional Convention impose burdens on governmental processes that often seem clumsy, inefficient, even unworkable, but those hard choices were consciously made by men who had lived under a form of government that permitted arbitrary governmental acts to go unchecked. There is no support in the Constitution or decisions of this Court for the proposition that the cumbersomeness and delays often encountered in complying with explicit constitutional standards may be avoided, either by the Congress or by the President. With all the obvious flaws of delay, untidiness, and potential for abuse, we have not yet found a better way to preserve freedom than by making the exercise of power subject to the carefully crafted restraints spelled out in the Constitution.

JUSTICE WHITE, dissenting.

Today the Court not only invalidates Section 244(c)(2) of the Immigration and Nationality Act, but also sounds the death knell for nearly 200 other statutory provisions in which Congress has reserved a "legislative veto." For this reason, the Court's decision is of surpassing importance. And it is for this reason that the Court would have been well advised to decide the cases, if possible, on the narrower grounds of separation of powers, leaving for full consideration the constitutionality of other congressional review statutes operating on such varied matters as war powers and agency rulemaking, some of which concern the independent regulatory agencies.

The prominence of the legislative veto mechanism in our contemporary political system and its importance to Congress can hardly be overstated. It has become a central means by which Congress secures the accountability of executive and independent agencies. Without the legislative veto, Congress is faced with a Hobson's choice: either to refrain from delegating the necessary authority, leaving itself with a hopeless task of writing laws with the requisite specificity to cover endless special circumstances across the entire policy landscape, or, in the alternative, to abdicate its lawmaking function to the Executive Branch and independent agencies. To choose the former leaves major national problems unresolved; to opt for the latter risks unaccountable policymaking by those not elected to fill that role. Accordingly, over the past five decades, the legislative veto has been placed in nearly 200 statutes. The device is known in every field of governmental concern: reorganization, budgets, foreign affairs, war powers, and regulation of trade, safety, energy, the environment, and the economy. . . .

[T]he apparent sweep of the Court's decision today is regrettable. The Court's Article I analysis appears to invalidate all legislative vetoes, irrespective of form or subject. Because the legislative veto is commonly found as a check upon rulemaking by administrative agencies and upon broad-based policy decisions of the Executive Branch, it is particularly unfortunate that the Court reaches its decision in cases involving the exercise of a veto over deportation decisions regarding particular individuals. Courts should always be wary of striking statutes as unconstitutional; to strike an entire class of statutes based on consideration of a somewhat atypical and more readily indictable exemplar of the class is irresponsible. . . .

If the legislative veto were as plainly unconstitutional as the Court strives to suggest, its broad ruling today would be more comprehensible. But the constitutionality of the legislative veto is anything but clear-cut. The issue divides scholars, courts, Attorneys General, and the two other branches of the National Government. If the veto devices so flagrantly disregarded the requirements of Art. I as the Court today suggests, I find it incomprehensible that Congress, whose Members are bound by oath to uphold the Constitution, would have placed these mechanisms in nearly 200 separate laws over a period of 50 years.

The reality of the situation is that the constitutional question posed today is one of immense difficulty over which the Executive and Legislative Branches—as well as scholars and judges—have understandably disagreed. That disagreement stems from the silence of the Constitution on the precise question: the Constitution does not directly authorize or prohibit the legislative veto. Thus, our task should be to determine whether the legislative veto is consistent with the purposes of Art. I and the principles of separation of powers which are reflected in that Article and throughout the Constitution. We should not find the lack of a specific constitutional authorization for the legislative veto surprising, and I would not infer disapproval of the mechanism from its absence. From the summer of 1787 to the present, the Government of the United States has become an endeavor far beyond the contemplation of the Framers. Only within the last half century has the complexity and size of the Federal Government's responsibilities grown so greatly that the Congress must rely on the legislative veto as the most effective, if not the only, means to insure its role as the Nation's lawmaker. But the wisdom of the Framers was to anticipate that the Nation would grow and new problems of governance would require different solutions. Accordingly, our Federal Government was intentionally chartered with the flexibility to respond to contemporary needs without losing sight of fundamental democratic principles. This was the spirit in which Justice Jackson penned his influential concurrence in the *Steel Seizure Case:*

> The actual art of governing under our Constitution does not and cannot conform to judicial definitions of the power of any of its branches based on isolated clauses or even single Articles torn from context. While the Constitution diffuses power the better to secure liberty, it also contemplates that practice will integrate the dispersed powers into a workable government. *Youngstown Sheet & Tube Co.* v. *Sawyer* (1952).

This is the perspective from which we should approach the novel constitutional questions presented by the legislative veto. In my view, neither Article I of the Constitution nor the doctrine of separation of powers is violated by this mechanism by which our elected Representatives preserve their voice in the governance of the Nation. . . .

I do not suggest that all legislative vetoes are necessarily consistent with separation of powers principles. A legislative check on an inherently executive function, for example, that of initiating prosecutions, poses an entirely different question. But the legislative veto device here—and in many other settings—is far from an instance of legislative tyranny over the Executive. It is a necessary check on the unavoidably expanding power of the agencies, both Executive and independent, as they engage in exercising authority delegated by Congress.

I regret that I am in disagreement with my colleagues on the fundamental questions that these cases present. But even more I regret the destructive scope of the Court's holding. It reflects a profoundly different conception of the Constitution than that held by the courts which sanctioned the modern administrative state. Today's decision strikes down in one fell swoop provisions in more laws enacted by Congress than the Court has cumulatively invalidated in its history. I fear it will now be more difficult to, "insur[e] that the fundamental policy decisions in our society will be made not by an appointed official, but by the body immediately responsible to the people." I must dissent.

## Bowsher v. Synar

478 U.S. 714 (1986)

Representative Mike Synar and other U.S. representatives, as well as the National Treasury Employees Union, challenged the Balanced Budget and Emergency Deficit Control Act of 1985, popularly known as the Gramm-Rudman-Hollings Act. A three-judge panel held that the act was unconstitutional. Comptroller General Bowsher appealed to the Supreme Court.

The facts of the case are set out in the opinion below.

The Court's decision was 7 to 2. Chief Justice Burger delivered the opinion of the Court. Justice Stevens filed a concurring opinion, which was joined by Justice Marshall. Justices White and Blackmun each filed dissenting opinions.

CHIEF JUSTICE BURGER delivered the opinion of the Court.

The question presented by these appeals is whether the assignment by Congress to the Comptroller General of the United States of certain functions under the Balanced Budget and Emergency Deficit Control Act of 1985 violates the doctrine of separation of powers. . . .

On December 12, 1985, the President signed into law the Balanced Budget and Emergency Deficit Control Act of 1985, popularly known as the "Gramm-Rudman-Hollings Act." The purpose of the Act is to eliminate the federal budget deficit. To that end, the Act sets a "maximum deficit amount" for federal spending for each of fiscal years 1986 through 1991. The size of that maximum deficit amount progressively reduces to zero in fiscal year 1991. If in any fiscal year the federal budget deficit exceeds the maximum deficit amount by more than a specified sum, the Act requires across-the-board cuts in federal spending to reach the targeted deficit level, with half of the cuts made to defense programs and the other half made to nondefense programs. The Act exempts certain priority programs from these cuts.

These "automatic" reductions are accomplished through a rather complicated procedure. . . . Each year, the Directors of the Office of Management and Budget (OMB) and the Congressional Budget Office (CBO) independently estimate the amount of the federal budget deficit for the upcoming fiscal year. If that deficit exceeds the maximum targeted deficit amount for that fiscal year by more than a specified amount, the Directors of OMB and CBO independently calculate, on a program-by-program basis, the budget reductions necessary to ensure that the deficit does not exceed the maximum deficit amount. The Act then requires the Directors to report jointly their deficit estimates and budget reduction calculations to the Comptroller General.

The Comptroller General, after reviewing the Directors' reports, then reports his conclusions to the President. The President, in turn, must issue a "sequestration" order mandating the spending reductions specified by the Comptroller General. There follows a period during which Congress may by legislation reduce spending to obviate, in whole or in part, the need for the sequestration order. If such reductions are not enacted, the sequestration order becomes effective and the spending reductions included in that order are made.

Anticipating constitutional challenge to these procedures, the Act also contains a "fallback" deficit reduction process to take effect "[i]n the event that any of the reporting procedures described are invalidated." Under these provisions, the report prepared by the Directors of OMB and the CBO is submitted directly to a specially created Temporary Joint Committee on Deficit Reduction, which must report in five days to both Houses a joint resolution setting forth the content of the Directors' report. Congress then must vote on the resolution under special rules, which render amendments out of order. If the resolution is passed and signed by the President, it

then serves as the basis for a Presidential sequestration order. . . .

[W]e conclude that Congress cannot reserve for itself the power of removal of an officer charged with the execution of the laws except by impeachment. To permit the execution of the laws to be vested in an officer answerable only to Congress would, in practical terms, reserve in Congress control over the execution of the laws. As the District Court observed: "Once an officer is appointed, it is only the authority that can remove him, and not the authority that appointed him, that he must fear and, in the performance of his functions, obey." The structure of the Constitution does not permit Congress to execute the laws; it follows that Congress cannot grant to an officer under its control what it does not possess.

Our decision in *INS* v. *Chadha* (1983) supports this conclusion. In *Chadha*, we struck down a one-House "legislative veto" provision by which each House of Congress retained the power to reverse a decision Congress had expressly authorized the Attorney General to make. . . .

To permit an officer controlled by Congress to execute the laws would be, in essence, to permit a congressional veto. Congress could simply remove, or threaten to remove, an officer for executing the laws in any fashion found to be unsatisfactory to Congress. This kind of congressional control over the execution of the laws, *Chadha* makes clear, is constitutionally impermissible.

The dangers of congressional usurpation of Executive Branch functions have long been recognized. "[T]he debates of the Constitutional Convention, and the Federalist Papers, are replete with expressions of fear that the Legislative Branch of the National Government will aggrandize itself at the expense of the other two branches." *Buckley* v. *Valeo* (1976). Indeed, we also have observed only recently that, "[t]he hydraulic pressure inherent within each of the separate Branches to exceed the outer limits of its power, even to accomplish desirable objectives, must be resisted." With these principles in mind, we turn to consideration of whether the Comptroller General is controlled by Congress.

Appellants urge that the Comptroller General performs his duties independently and is not subservient to Congress. We agree with the District Court that this contention does not bear close scrutiny.

The critical factor lies in the provisions of the statute defining the Comptroller General's office relating to removability. Although the Comptroller General is nominated by the President from a list of three individuals recommended by the Speaker of the House of Representatives and the President *pro tempore* of the Senate, and confirmed by the Senate, he is removable only at the initiative of Congress. He may be removed not only by impeachment, but also by joint resolution of Congress "at any time" resting on any one of the following bases:

i.   permanent disability;
ii.  inefficiency;
iii. neglect of duty;
iv.  malfeasance; or
v.   a felony or conduct involving moral turpitude.

This provision was included, as one Congressman explained in urging passage of the Act, because Congress, "felt that [the Comptroller General] should be brought under the sole control of Congress, so that Congress, at any moment when it found he was inefficient and was not carrying on the duties of his office as he should and as the Congress expected, could remove him without the long tedious process of a trial by impeachment."

The removal provision was an important part of the legislative scheme, as a number of Congressmen recognized. Representative Hawley commented: "[H]e is our officer, in a measure, getting information for us. . . . If he does not do his work properly, we, as practically his employers, ought to be able to discharge him from his office." Representative Sisson observed that the removal provisions would give "[t]he Congress of the United States . . . absolute control of the man's destiny in office." The ultimate design was to "give the legislative branch of the Government control of the audit not through the power of appointment, but through the power of removal." . . .

It is clear that Congress has consistently viewed the Comptroller General as an officer of the Legislative Branch. The Reorganization Acts of 1945 and 1949, for example, both stated that the Comptroller General and the GAO are "a part of the legislative branch of the Government." Similarly, in the Accounting and Auditing Act of 1950, Congress required the Comptroller General to conduct audits "as an agent of the Congress."

Over the years, the Comptrollers General have also viewed themselves as part of the Legislative Branch. In one of the early Annual Reports of Comptroller General, the official seal of his office was described as reflecting:

the independence of judgment to be exercised by the General Accounting Office, subject to the control of the legislative branch. . . . The combination represents an agency of the Congress independent of other authority auditing and checking the expenditures of the Government as required by law and subjecting any questions arising in that connection to quasi-judicial determination.

Later, Comptroller General Warren, who had been a Member of Congress for 15 years before being appointed Comptroller General, testified: "During most of my public life, . . . I have been a member of the legislative branch. Even now, although heading a great agency, it is an agency of the Congress, and *I am an agent of the Congress.*" . . .

Against this background, we see no escape from the conclusion that, because Congress has retained removal authority over the Comptroller General, he may not be entrusted with executive powers. The remaining question is whether the Comptroller General has been assigned such powers in the Balanced Budget and Emergency Deficit Control Act of 1985.

The primary responsibility of the Comptroller General under the instant Act is the preparation of a "report." This report must contain detailed estimates of projected federal revenues and expenditures. The report must also specify the reductions, if any, necessary to reduce the deficit to the target for the appropriate fiscal year. The reductions must be set forth on a program-by-program basis. . . .

Appellants suggest that the duties assigned to the Comptroller General in the Act are essentially ministerial and mechanical, so that their performance does not constitute "execution of the law" in a meaningful sense. On the contrary, we view these functions as plainly entailing execution of the law in constitutional terms. Interpreting a law enacted by Congress to implement the legislative mandate is the very essence of "execution" of the law. Under [the law], the Comptroller General must exercise judgment concerning facts that affect the application of the Act. He must also interpret the provisions of the Act to determine precisely what budgetary calculations are required. Decisions of that kind are typically made by officers charged with executing a statute.

The executive nature of the Comptroller General's functions under the Act is revealed [by the provision] which gives the Comptroller General the ultimate authority to determine the budget cuts to be made. Indeed, the Comptroller General commands the President himself to carry out, without the slightest variation (with exceptions not relevant to the constitutional issues presented), the directive of the Comptroller General as to the budget reductions. . . .

Congress, of course, initially determined the content of the Balanced Budget and Emergency Deficit Control Act, and undoubtedly the content of the Act determines the nature of the executive duty. However, as *Chadha* makes clear, once Congress makes its choice in enacting legislation, its participation ends. Congress can thereafter control the execution of its enactment only indirectly—by passing new legislation. By placing the responsibility for execution of the Balanced Budget and Emergency Deficit Control Act in the hands of an officer who is subject to removal only by itself, Congress, in effect, has retained control over the execution of the Act, and has intruded into the executive function. The Constitution does not permit such intrusion. . . .

No one can doubt that Congress and the President are confronted with fiscal and economic problems of unprecedented magnitude, but, "the fact that a given law or procedure is efficient, convenient, and useful in facilitating functions of government, standing alone, will not save it if it is contrary to the Constitution. Convenience and efficiency are not the primary objectives—or the hallmarks—of democratic government. . . . " [*I.N.S.* v. *Chadha* (1983).]

We conclude that the District Court correctly held that the powers vested in the Comptroller General violate the command of the Constitution that the Congress play no direct role in the execution of the laws. . . .

JUSTICE WHITE, dissenting.

The Court, acting in the name of separation of powers, takes upon itself to strike down the Gramm-Rudman-Hollings Act, one of the most novel and far-reaching legislative responses to a national crisis since the New Deal. The basis of the Court's action is a solitary provision of another statute that was passed over 60 years ago and has lain dormant since that time. I cannot concur in the Court's action. Like the Court, I will not purport to speak to the wisdom of the policies incorporated in the legislation the Court invalidates; that is a matter for the Congress and the Executive, both of which expressed their assent to the statute barely half a year ago. I will, however, address the wisdom of the Court's willingness to interpose its distressingly formalistic view of separation of powers as a bar to the attainment of governmental objectives through the means chosen by the Congress and the President in the legislative process established by the Constitution. Twice in the past four years I have expressed my view that the Court's recent efforts to police the separation of powers have rested on untenable constitutional propositions leading to regrettable results. *Northern Pipeline Construction Co.* v. *Marathon Pipe Line Co.* (1982); *INS* v. *Chadha* (1983). Today's result is even more misguided. As I will explain, the Court's decision rests on a feature of the legislative scheme that is of minimal practical significance and that presents no substantial threat to the basic scheme of separation of powers. In attaching dispositive

significance to what should be regarded as a triviality, the Court neglects what has in the past been recognized as a fundamental principle governing consideration of disputes over separation of powers:

> The actual art of governing under our Constitution does not and cannot conform to judicial definitions of the power of any of its branches based on isolated clauses or even single Articles torn from context. While the Constitution diffuses power the better to secure liberty, it also contemplates that practice will integrate the dispersed powers into a workable government. *Youngstown Sheet & Tube Co.* v. *Sawyer* (1952) (Jackson, J. concurring). . . .

It is evident (and nothing in the Court's opinion is to the contrary) that the powers exercised by the Comptroller General under the Gramm-Rudman-Hollings Act are not such that vesting them in an officer not subject to removal at will by the President would in itself improperly interfere with Presidential powers. Determining the level of spending by the Federal Government is not, by nature, a function central either to the exercise of the President's enumerated powers or to his general duty to ensure execution of the laws; rather, appropriating funds is a peculiarly legislative function, and one expressly committed to Congress by Article I, Section 9, which provides that "No Money shall be drawn from the Treasury, but in Consequence of Appropriations made by Law." In enacting Gramm-Rudman-Hollings, Congress has chosen to exercise this legislative power to establish the level of federal spending by providing a detailed set of criteria for reducing expenditures below the level of appropriations in the event that certain conditions are met. Delegating the execution of this legislation—that is, the power to apply the Act's criteria and make the required calculations—to an officer independent of the President's will does not deprive the President of any power that he would otherwise have or that is essential to the performance of the duties of his office. Rather, the result of such a delegation, from the standpoint of the President, is no different from the result of more traditional forms of appropriation: under either system, the level of funds available to the Executive Branch to carry out its duties is not within the President's discretionary control. To be sure, if the budget-cutting mechanism required the responsible officer to exercise a great deal of policymaking discretion, one might argue that, having created such broad discretion, Congress had some obligation based upon Article II to vest it in the Chief Executive or his agents. In Gramm-Rudman-Hollings, however, Congress has done no such thing;

instead, it has created a precise and articulated set of criteria designed to minimize the degree of policy choice exercised by the officer executing the statute, and to ensure that the relative spending priorities established by Congress in the appropriations it passes into law remain unaltered. Given that the exercise of policy choice by the officer executing the statute would be inimical to Congress' goal in enacting "automatic" budget-cutting measures, it is eminently reasonable and proper for Congress to vest the budget-cutting authority in an officer who is, to the greatest degree possible, nonpartisan and independent of the President and his political agenda, and who therefore may be relied upon not to allow his calculations to be colored by political considerations. Such a delegation deprives the President of no authority that is rightfully his.

## Clinton v. City of New York
### 523 U.S. 1071 (1998)

The facts and background of this case are set out in the accompanying SIDEBAR.

The Court's decision was 6 to 3. Justice Scalia, joined by Justice O'Connor, concurred in part and dissented in part. Justice Breyer also dissented.

JUSTICE STEVENS delivered the opinion of the Court.

. . . The Line Item Veto Act gives the President the power to "cancel in whole" three types of provisions that have been signed into law: "(1) any dollar amount of discretionary budget authority; (2) any item of new direct spending; or (3) any limited tax benefit." It is undisputed that the New York case involves an "item of new direct spending" and that the Snake River case involves a "limited tax benefit" as those terms are defined in the Act. It is also undisputed that each of those provisions had been signed into law pursuant to Article I, Section 7, of the Constitution before it was canceled.

The Act requires the President to adhere to precise procedures whenever he exercises his cancellation authority. In identifying items for cancellation he must consider the legislative history, the purposes, and other relevant information about the items. He must determine, with respect to each cancellation, that it will "(i) reduce the Federal budget deficit; (ii) not impair any essential Government functions; and (iii) not harm the national interest."

Moreover, he must transmit a special message to Congress notifying it of each cancellation within five calendar days (excluding Sundays) after the enactment of the canceled provision. It is undisputed that the President meticulously followed these procedures in these cases.

A cancellation takes effect upon receipt by Congress of the special message from the President. If, however, a "disapproval bill" pertaining to a special message is enacted into law, the cancellations set forth in that message become "null and void." The Act sets forth a detailed expedited procedure for the consideration of a "disapproval bill," but no such bill was passed for either of the cancellations involved in these cases.

A majority vote of both Houses is sufficient to enact a disapproval bill. The Act does not grant the President the authority to cancel a disapproval bill, but he does, of course, retain his constitutional authority to veto such a bill.

The effect of a cancellation is plainly stated . . . . With respect to both an item of new direct spending and a limited tax benefit, the cancellation prevents the item "from having legal force or effect."

Thus, under the plain text of the statute, the two actions of the President that are challenged in these cases prevented one section of the Balanced Budget Act of 1997 and one section of the Taxpayer Relief Act of 1997 "from having legal force or effect." The remaining provisions of those statutes, with the exception of the second canceled item in the latter, continue to have the same force and effect as they had when signed into law.

In both legal and practical effect, the President has amended two Acts of Congress by repealing a portion of each. "[R]epeal of statutes, no less than enactment, must conform with Art. I." *INS* v. *Chadha*, (1983). There is no provision in the Constitution that authorizes the President to enact, to amend, or to repeal statutes. Both Article I and Article II assign responsibilities to the President that directly relate to the lawmaking process, but neither addresses the issue presented by these cases. The President "shall from time to time give to the Congress Information on the State of the Union, and recommend to their Consideration such Measures as he shall judge necessary and expedient . . . ." Art. II, Section 3. Thus, he may initiate and influence legislative proposals. Moreover, after a bill has passed both Houses of Congress, but "before it become[s] a Law," it must be presented to the President. If he approves it, "he shall sign it, but if not he shall return it, with his Objections to that House in which it shall have originated, who shall enter the Objections at large on their Journal, and proceed to reconsider it." His "return" of a bill, which is usually described as a "veto," is subject to being overridden by a twothirds vote in each House.

There are important differences between the President's "return" of a bill pursuant to Article I, Section 7, and the exercise of the President's cancellation authority pursuant to the Line Item Veto Act. The constitutional return takes place before the bill becomes law; the statutory cancellation occurs after the bill becomes law. The constitutional return is of the entire bill; the statutory cancellation is of only a part. Although the Constitution expressly authorizes the President to play a role in the process of enacting statutes, it is silent on the subject of unilateral Presidential action that either repeals or amends parts of duly enacted statutes.

There are powerful reasons for construing constitutional silence on this profoundly important issue as equivalent to an express prohibition. The procedures governing the enactment of statutes set forth in the text of Article I were the product of the great debates and compromises that produced the Constitution itself. Familiar historical materials provide abundant support for the conclusion that the power to enact statutes may only "be exercised in accord with a single, finely wrought and exhaustively considered, procedure." Our first President understood the text of the Presentment Clause as requiring that he either "approve all the parts of a Bill, or reject it in toto."

What has emerged in these cases from the President's exercise of his statutory cancellation powers, however, are truncated versions of two bills that passed both Houses of Congress. They are not the product of the "finely wrought" procedure that the Framers designed. At oral argument, the Government suggested that the cancellations at issue in these cases do not effect a "repeal" of the canceled items because under the special "lockbox" provisions of the Act, a canceled item "retain[s] real, legal budgetary effect" insofar as it prevents Congress and the President from spending the savings that result from the cancellation. The text of the Act expressly provides, however, that a cancellation prevents a direct spending or tax benefit provision "from having legal force or effect." That a canceled item may have "real, legal budgetary effect" as a result of the lockbox procedure does not change the fact that by canceling the items at issue in these cases, the President made them entirely inoperative as to appellees. . . Such significant changes do not lose their character simply because the canceled provisions may have some continuing financial effect on the Government. The cancellation of one section of a statute may be the functional equivalent of a partial repeal even if a portion of the section is not canceled.

The Government advances two related arguments to support its position that despite the unambiguous provisions of the Act, cancellations do not amend or repeal properly enacted statutes in violation of the Presentment Clause. First . . . the Government contends that the cancellations were merely exercises of discretionary authority granted to the President by the Balanced Budget Act and the Taxpayer Relief Act read in light of the previously enacted Line Item Veto Act. Second, the Government submits that the substance of the authority to cancel tax and spending items "is, in practical effect, no more and no less than the power to 'decline to spend' specified sums of money, or to 'decline to implement' specified tax measures." Neither argument is persuasive.

In *Field* v. *Clark* (1892), the Court upheld the constitutionality of the Tariff Act of 1890. That statute contained a "free list" of almost 300 specific articles that were exempted from import duties "unless otherwise specially provided for in this act." Section 3 was a special provision that directed the President to suspend that exemption for sugar, molasses, coffee, tea, and hides "whenever, and so often" as he should be satisfied that any country producing and exporting those products imposed duties on the agricultural products of the United States that he deemed to be "reciprocally unequal and unreasonable. . . ." The section then specified the duties to be imposed on those products during any such suspension. The Court provided this explanation for its conclusion that Section 3 had not delegated legislative power to the President:

> Nothing involving the expediency or the just operation of such legislation was left to the determination of the President. . . . [W]hen he ascertained the fact that duties and exactions, reciprocally unequal and unreasonable, were imposed upon the agricultural or other products of the United States by a country producing and exporting sugar, molasses, coffee, tea or hides, it became his duty to issue a proclamation declaring the suspension, as to that country, which Congress had determined should occur. He had no discretion in the premises except in respect to the duration of the suspension so ordered. But that related only to the enforcement of the policy established by Congress. As the suspension was absolutely required when the President ascertained the existence of a particular fact, it cannot be said that in ascertaining that fact and in issuing his proclamation, in obedience to the legislative will, he exercised the function of making laws. . . . It was a part of the law itself as it left the hands of Congress that the provisions, full and complete in themselves, permitting the free

introduction of sugars, molasses, coffee, tea and hides, from particular countries, should be suspended, in a given contingency, and that in case of such suspensions certain duties should be imposed.

This passage identifies three critical differences between the power to suspend the exemption from import duties and the power to cancel portions of a duly enacted statute. First, the exercise of the suspension power was contingent upon a condition that did not exist when the Tariff Act was passed: the imposition of "reciprocally unequal and unreasonable" import duties by other countries. In contrast, the exercise of the cancellation power within five days after the enactment of the Balanced Budget and Tax Reform Acts necessarily was based on the same conditions that Congress evaluated when it passed those statutes. Second, under the Tariff Act, when the President determined that the contingency had arisen, he had a duty to suspend; in contrast, while it is true that the President was required by the Act to make three determinations before he canceled a provision, those determinations did not qualify his discretion to cancel or not to cancel. Finally, whenever the President suspended an exemption under the Tariff Act, he was executing the policy that Congress had embodied in the statute. In contrast, whenever the President cancels an item of new direct spending or a limited tax benefit he is rejecting the policy judgment made by Congress and relying on his own policy judgment.

Thus, the conclusion in *Field* v. *Clark* that the suspensions mandated by the Tariff Act were not exercises of legislative power does not undermine our opinion that cancellations pursuant to the Line Item Veto Act are the functional equivalent of partial repeals of Acts of Congress that fail to satisfy Article I, Section 7. . . .

The Line Item Veto Act authorizes the President himself to effect the repeal of laws, for his own policy reasons, without observing the procedures set out in Article I, Section 7. The fact that Congress intended such a result is of no moment. Although Congress presumably anticipated that the President might cancel some of the items in the Balanced Budget Act and in the Taxpayer Relief Act, Congress cannot alter the procedures set out in Article I, Section 7, without amending the Constitution.

Neither are we persuaded by the Government's contention that the President's authority to cancel new direct spending and tax benefit items is no greater than his traditional authority to decline to spend appropriated funds. The Government has reviewed in some detail the series of statutes in which Congress has given the Executive broad discretion over the expenditure of appropriated funds. For example, the First Congress appropriated "sum[s] not exceeding" specified amounts to be spent on various Government operations. In those statutes, as in later years, the President was given wide discretion with respect to both the amounts to be spent and how the money would be allocated among different functions. It is argued that the Line Item Veto Act merely confers comparable discretionary authority over the expenditure of appropriated funds. The critical difference between this statute and all of its predecessors, however, is that unlike any of them, this Act gives the President the unilateral power to change the text of duly enacted statutes. None of the Act's predecessors could even arguably have been construed to authorize such a change.

Although they are implicit in what we have already written, the profound importance of these cases makes it appropriate to emphasize three points.

First, we express no opinion about the wisdom of the procedures authorized by the Line Item Veto Act. Many members of both major political parties who have served in the Legislative and the Executive Branches have long advocated the enactment of such procedures for the purpose of "ensur[ing] greater fiscal accountability in Washington."

The text of the Act was itself the product of much debate and deliberation in both Houses of Congress and that precise text was signed into law by the President. We do not lightly conclude that their action was unauthorized by the Constitution.

We have, however, twice had full argument and briefing on the question and have concluded that our duty is clear.

Second, although appellees challenge the validity of the Act on alternative grounds, the only issue we address concerns the "finely wrought" procedure commanded by the Constitution. We have been favored with extensive debate about the scope of Congress' power to delegate lawmaking authority, or its functional equivalent, to the President. The excellent briefs filed by the parties and their amici curiae have provided us with valuable historical information that illuminates the delegation issue but does not really bear on the narrow issue that is dispositive of these cases. Thus, because we conclude that the Act's cancellation provisions violate Article I, Section 7, of the Constitution, we find it unnecessary to consider the District Court's alternative holding that the Act "impermissibly disrupts the balance of powers among the three branches of government."

Third, our decision rests on the narrow ground that the procedures authorized by the Line Item Veto Act are not authorized by the Constitution. The Balanced Budget Act of 1997 is a 500-page document that became "Public Law 105-33" after three procedural steps were taken: (1) a bill containing its exact text was approved by a majority of the Members of the House of Representatives; (2) the Senate approved precisely the same text; and (3) that text was signed into law by the President. The Constitution explicitly requires that each of those three steps be taken before a bill may "become a law." If one paragraph of that text had been omitted at any one of those three stages, Public Law 105-33 would not have been validly enacted. If the Line Item Veto Act were valid, it would authorize the President to create a different law, one whose text was not voted on by either House of Congress or presented to the President for signature. Something that might be known as "Public Law 105-33 as modified by the President" may or may not be desirable, but it is surely not a document that may "become a law" pursuant to the procedures designed by the Framers of Article I, Section 7, of the Constitution.

If there is to be a new procedure in which the President will play a different role in determining the final text of what may "become a law," such change must come not by legislation but through the amendment procedures set forth in Article V of the Constitution.

JUSTICE KENNEDY, concurring.

A nation cannot plunder its own treasury without putting its Constitution and its survival in peril. The statute before us, then, is of first importance, for it seems undeniable the Act will tend to restrain persistent excessive spending. Nevertheless, for the reasons given by JUSTICE STEVENS in the opinion for the Court, the statute must be found invalid. Failure of political will does not justify unconstitutional remedies. . . .

Separation of powers helps to ensure the ability of each branch to be vigorous in asserting its proper authority. In this respect the device operates on a horizontal axis to secure a proper balance of legislative, executive, and judicial authority. Separation of powers operates on a vertical axis as well, between each branch and the citizens in whose interest powers must be exercised. The citizen has a vital interest in the regularity of the exercise of governmental power. If this point was not clear before *Chadha*, it should have been so afterwards. Though *Chadha* involved the deportation of a person, while the case before us involves the expenditure of money or the grant of a tax exemption, this circumstance does not mean that the vertical operation of the separation of powers is irrelevant here. By increasing the power of the President beyond what the Framers envisioned, the statute compromises the political liberty of our citizens, liberty which the separation of powers seeks to secure.

The Constitution is not bereft of controls over improvident spending. Federalism is one safeguard, for political accountability is easier to enforce within the States than nationwide. The other principal mechanism, of course, is control of the political branches by an informed and responsible electorate. Whether or not federalism and control by the electorate are adequate for the problem at hand, they are two of the structures the Framers designed for the problem the statute strives to confront. The Framers of the Constitution could not command statesmanship. They could simply provide structures from which it might emerge. The fact that these mechanisms, plus the proper functioning of the separation of powers itself, are not employed, or that they prove insufficient, cannot validate an otherwise unconstitutional device. With these observations, I join the opinion of the Court.

JUSTICE SCALIA . . . concurring in part and dissenting in part.

. . . I turn, then, to the crux of the matter: whether Congress's authorizing the President to cancel an item of spending gives him a power that our history and traditions show must reside exclusively in the Legislative Branch. I may note, to begin with, that the Line Item Veto Act is not the first statute to authorize the President to "cancel" spending items. In *Bowsher v. Synar*, (1986), we addressed the constitutionality of the Balanced Budget and Emergency Deficit Control Act of 1985, which required the President, if the federal budget deficit exceeded a certain amount, to issue a "sequestration" order mandating spending reductions specified by the Comptroller General. The effect of sequestration was that "amounts sequestered . . . shall be permanently cancelled." We held that the Act was unconstitutional, not because it impermissibly gave the Executive legislative power, but because it gave the Comptroller General, an officer of the Legislative Branch over whom Congress retained removal power, "the ultimate authority to determine the budget cuts to be made," "functions . . . plainly entailing execution of the law in constitutional terms." The President's discretion under the Line Item Veto Act is certainly broader than the Comptroller General's discretion was under the 1985 Act, but it is no broader than the discretion traditionally granted the President in his execution of spending laws. Insofar as the degree of political, "lawmaking" power conferred upon the Executive is concerned, there is not a dime's worth of difference between Congress's authorizing the President to cancel a spending item, and

# CLINTON V. CITY OF NEW YORK

## *Fighting Over the Family Checkbook*

Much like the recent, unsuccessful movement to impose term limits on members of Congress, proposals to grant the president line-item veto power over federal laws have been debated since the earliest years of the Republic. In 1789, Congress gave President Washington, in certain cases, the discretion to determine how much of an appropriate sum of money would be spent on its authorized uses. This pattern continued throughout the presidencies of Washington, Adams, Jefferson, and Madison. In 1809, Congress passed legislation that permitted President Madison "to direct . . . that a portion of the monies appropriated for a particular branch of expenditure in [a] department, be applied to another branch of expenditure in the same department." In 1873, Ulysses S. Grant issued the first presidential request for a constitutional amendment to grant the president more comprehensive line-item veto authority.

Economic crises of the early twentieth century and later the Great Depression persuaded Congress to delegate more informal line-item veto power to the president. In 1905 and 1906, Congress passed separate measures permitting the president "to waive spending appropriations in the event of emergencies of unusual circumstances." In 1933, Congress granted President Roosevelt broad discretion to refrain from spending appropriated funds, and even authorized him to impound all unused funds and return them to the Treasury Department. Legislative arrangements such as these continued as standard practice between Congress and the president even after the emergency conditions prompting the enactment of such laws had ended. Between 1873 and 1996, when it finally passed the Line Item Veto Act giving the president formal power to delete particular items from federal legislation, Congress had introduced and defeated more than 150 similar resolutions.

Prior to and even after the passage of the 1996 law, Congress exhibited mixed feelings about granting the president such specific control over the appropriations process, a power that lies at the core of legislative power and distinguishes it from the other branches of government. Alexander Hamilton, in fact, pointed to Congress's power of the "purse" in *Federalist* 78 to highlight the differences in strength between the legislative and judicial branches. Delegating veto power to the president shifts political responsibility for government spending and thereby permits senators and representatives to pass the blame at election time for the wayward spending of the federal government. On the other hand, the transfer of veto power to the president also requires Congress to give up its most jealously guarded powers.

In the wake of the Great Society and Vietnam, Congress had enacted two major pieces of legislation intended to reduce the federal budget and reorient spending priorities. The first, the Congressional Budget Impoundment Control Act, came in 1974. That law sought to return greater control over the federal budget to Congress from the president. At bottom, the law was a response to President Nixon's frequent impoundment of the pet programs of his political enemies in Congress. By 1973, as Nixon was reeling from the Watergate crisis, Congress wanted to strip as much power as it could from the president's recision authority. The law required the president to submit a proposal before he could impound congressionally appropriated funds, a mechanism that prohibited him from acting unilaterally. In practice, however, the law was scarcely effective.

In 1985, Congress passed the Gramm-Rudman-Hollings law mandating cuts in federal spending to comply with reduced budget deficit targets. Whatever hope Gramm-Rudman-Hollings held out for bringing federal spending into line quickly vanished when the Court declared the statute's key provisions unconstitutional in *Bowsher* v. *Synar* (1986).

Congress then turned to the Line Item Veto Act to control the federal budget deficit, but this time with the president along for the ride. Supporters of the line-item veto pointed to its widespread use on the state level. As of 1998, forty-three governors had such recision authority over their legislatures. Moreover, if Congress was going to grant the president such power, it should do so through statute rather than constitutional amendment. A constitutional amendment, Senator Joe Biden (D–Del.) testified during hearings on the line-item veto, would "commit the citizens and the government of the United States to an unknown and practically unalterable course and fundamentally shift the balance of power in a way that could not, absent of another amendment, be changed back." In other words, if Congress believed the president had assumed too much control over the legislative process, it could correct its mistake much more easily through a law than a constitutional amendment.

The line-item veto enjoyed the support of such prominent senators as Bob Dole (R–Kan.), who was also running for president that year. But it also drew heated opposition from some of the Senate's most respected students of the Constitution, such as Robert C. Byrd (D–W.Va.) and Pat Moynihan (D–N.Y.), who argued that the presidential line-item veto violated the principle of separation of powers. Some long-time Washington political observers suggested that Congress was less interested in balancing the budget than it was in letting the president take the heat for the federal budget deficit. Presidents from Truman to Clinton, with the exception of Kennedy and Carter, supported the line-item veto. Congress now had the chance to teach the president to be careful what he wished for.

Senator Byrd filed suit in federal court to have the law declared unconstitutional. A lower court agreed, but the Supreme Court reversed, ruling in *Byrd* v. *Raines* (1997) that Senator Byrd and the members who had joined his lawsuit lacked standing to bring such a suit. The Court ruled that they were unable to demonstrate direct harm or establish a particular injury as a result of the law's enforcement.

Shortly thereafter, the Snake River Potato Growers, a trade association representing the public affairs interests of Idaho potato growers, filed suit against President Clinton after he canceled a federal provision that would have allowed its members to defer paying almost $100 million in taxes over five years. Around the same time, New York City also filed suit against the president for canceling a program that would have reduced its tax liability under a health care financing scheme. The Court consolidated the suits and, on June 28, 1998, struck down the presidential line-item veto as unconstitutional.

Undeterred, several members announced a plan to get around the Court's decision by introducing legislation that would break each appropriations bill into individual items. This approach would permit Congress to pass each bill separately and send them up together to the president for signature or veto. But as *Clinton* faded from the headlines, so did congressional enthusiasm for the line-item veto. In January 1998, President Clinton claimed the political advantage of the moment by introducing a legislative package to balance the budget by the year 2000, with surpluses projected for several years after. Of course, the potential elimination of some members' favorite programs—and subsequent chances for reelection—might also have had something to do with Congress's change of heart.

Congress's authorizing money to be spent on a particular item at the President's discretion. And the latter has been done since the Founding of the Nation. From 1789–1791, the First Congress made lumpsum appropriations for the entire Government "sum[s] not exceeding" specified amounts for broad purposes. From a very early date Congress also made permissive individual appropriations, leaving the decision whether to spend the money to the President's unfettered discretion. In 1803, it appropriated $50,000 for the President to build "not exceeding fifteen gun boats, to be armed, manned and fitted out, and employed for such purposes as in his opinion the public service may require." President Jefferson reported that "[t]he sum of fifty thousand dollars appropriated by Congress for providing gun boats remains unexpended. The favorable and peaceable turn of affairs on the Mississippi rendered an immediate execution of that law unnecessary." Examples of appropriations committed to the discretion of the President abound in our history. During the Civil War, an Act appropriated over $76 million to be divided among various items "as the exigencies of the service may require." During the Great Depression, Congress appropriated $950 million "for such projects and/or purposes and under such rules and regulations as the President in his discretion may prescribe," and $4 billion for general classes of projects, the money to be spent "in the discretion and under the direction of the President." The constitutionality of such appropriations has never seriously been questioned. Rather, "[t]hat Congress has wide discretion in the matter of prescribing details of expenditures for which it appropriates must, of course, be plain. Appropriations and other acts of Congress are replete with instances of general appropriations of large amounts, to be allotted and expended as directed by designated government agencies." . . .

The short of the matter is this: Had the Line Item Veto Act authorized the President to "decline to spend" any item of spending contained in the Balanced Budget Act of 1997, there is not the slightest doubt that authorization would have been constitutional. What the Line Item Veto Act does instead—authorizing the President to "cancel" an item of spending—is technically different. But the technical difference does not relate to the technicalities of the Presentment Clause, which have been fully complied with; and the doctrine of unconstitutional delegation, which is at issue here, is preeminently not a doctrine of technicalities. The title of the Line Item Veto Act, which was perhaps designed to simplify for public comprehension, or perhaps merely to comply with the terms of a campaign pledge, has succeeded in faking out the Supreme Court. The Pres-

ident's action it authorizes in fact is not a line item veto and thus does not offend Art. I, Section 7; and insofar as the substance of that action is concerned, it is no different from what Congress has permitted the President to do since the formation of the Union. . . .

## Internal Affairs: Membership and Its Privileges

### The Qualifications Clause

Before it sets out the nature and scope of legislative power, Article I describes the prerequisites that all individuals who want to serve in Congress must meet. Some of these conditions are incontestable as matters of constitutional interpretation, such as the citizenship, residence, and age requirements to serve in the House and Senate or the stipulation that no member of Congress may serve while holding any other office of the United States. Congress has modified the qualifications for congressional membership only once since 1789, when it attached a provision to the Fourteenth Amendment, ratified in 1868, that prohibited any member from continuing service who had engaged in or supported rebellion against the United States. Prior to the Fourteenth Amendment, Congress, in 1862, had enacted separation legislation that required all members to swear under oath that they had never engaged in seditious activities against the United States.

Through 2000, Congress has convened 106 times since 1789 and has excluded only thirteen duly elected members to the House and Senate. The Senate has excluded three senators-elect—one under the Test Oath Act of 1862 and two others for failing to meet the citizenship requirements. Ten representatives-elect have been refused their seats—four for disloyalty during the Civil War; another, Victor L. Berger (Socialist Party–Wisc.), was excluded twice for sedition; one for malfeasance; and another, Brigham H. Roberts (D–Utah), for a prior conviction under a polygamy law.[77] This latter case, in particular, raised a question that went unanswered until *Powell v. McCormack* (1969): Does Congress have the power to exclude members for reasons other than those set out in Article I or the Fourteenth Amendment?

*Powell* divided the Court after it heard oral arguments. Chief Justice Warren believed that Representative Powell was entitled to his seat because he met all the constitutional qualifications. How Congress wanted to punish a sitting congressman was separate from its power to exclude a representative-elect for reasons not authorized by the Constitution. Several other justices believed that the House might have grounds to formulate an expulsion argument but were later persuaded by the chief justice to find in favor of Powell.[78]

*Powell* was the last constitutional decision of import handed down by the Warren Court, as one week later the chief justice would swear in his successor, Warren E. Burger. Of note here is that the Court's 8-1 decision in *Powell* reversed then–D.C. court of appeals judge Burger, who dismissed Powell's claim on the grounds that it constituted a political question and thus was not subject to judicial review. Chief Justice Warren's opinion appears guided by a concern for the Framers' intent and textual literalism, two approaches to constitutional interpretation that are rarely associated with his jurisprudential legacy. How closely does his opinion tread the line of the political questions doctrine without crossing that trip wire?

*Powell* served as the constitutional baseline for the Court's most important and high-profile decision since then, *U.S. Term Limits, Inc.* v. *Thornton* (1995), on the power of Congress to attach additional rules on membership in Congress not set in the Qualifications Clause.[79] Although the idea of term limits has its roots in Anti-Federalist opposition to the Constitution, it did not emerge as a national, front-burner political issue until the early 1990s.[80] *Thornton,* as the next SIDEBAR describes, culminated in the first major political movement to limit the number of terms senators and representatives were eligible to serve in Congress. The Court divided 5 to 4 on the term limits question, holding that neither the states nor Congress possessed the power to alter the "exclusive" terms of the Qualifications Clause. Such modifications could be accomplished only through a constitutional amendment.

But the opinion of Justice John Paul Stevens took *Powell* an important step further, holding that the states cannot claim the Tenth Amendment "reserves" to them power they did not have prior to the ratification of the Constitution. Comparing Justice Stevens's opinion with the dissent of Justice Clarence Thomas, a casual observer of American politics might not think the justices in *Thornton* were talking about the same Constitution. Justice Stevens and Justice Thomas both advance compelling theories of the Framers' intent to strike down and support, respectively, the constitutionality of legislatively imposed term limits. Outside the merits of their respective arguments, what do the opinions in *Thornton* say about the difficulties of using Framers' intent as a method of constitutional interpretation?

That Congress cannot exclude individuals who meet the criteria of the Qualifications Clause absent a constitutional amendment does not mean that Congress is without power to discipline and punish members who violate its rules or federal laws. Since 1789, Congress has expelled nineteen members, all of whom but one were found guilty of rebellion or providing aid and comfort to the enemy. More frequent but still rare are congressional punishments such as censure, reprimand, and removal from committee and leadership positions. Censure is the most severe of these measures, allowing a member to continue service but attaching such a personal stigma that resignation is often the result of this process. Such was the case in 1989, when Jim Wright (D–Tex.), the Speaker of the House, was censured on corruption charges and resigned from Congress rather than simply accept the loss of his position.[81]

The Court has never interfered with the right of Congress to invoke these measures. In *In re Thompson* (1897), the Court held that the "right to expel extends to all cases where the offense is such as in the judgement of the Senate is inconsistent with the trust and duty of a member."[82]

## Congressional Immunity: The Speech or Debate Clause

In our earlier section on the congressional power to investigate, we discussed how the Court's 1881 decision in *Kilbourn* v. *Thompson* recognized the right of Congress to conduct hearings and compel witnesses to come before its committees, as long as the request bore some relationship to a legislative end. Of equal significance in *Kilbourn* was that it also provided the Court's first major interpretation of the Speech or Debate Clause. Found in Article I, Section 6, this provision states, in part, that members "shall in all Cases, except Treason, Felony and Breach of the Peace, be privileged from Arrest during their Attendance at the Session of their respective Houses, and in going to and returning from the same; and for any Speech or Debate in either House, they shall not be questioned in any other *Place*."

*Kilbourn* is taught and understood as a case about congressional investigative power; the Court, however, used its opinion to declare an expansive interpretation of the protection afforded to senators and representatives under the Speech or Debate Clause for anything they said or wrote in their capacity as legislators. Holding that the Speech or Debate Clause covered "[i]n short, those things generally done in a session of the house by one of its members in relation to the business before it," the Court affirmed the notion of independence from political and legal reprisals of the other branches that concerned the Framers enough to adopt this constitutional provision without opposition or debate.[83] Ironically, the Court framed a much broader initial right of members to remain immune from the legal repercussions of their speechmaking and related conduct as legislators than it did for Congress to use its investigative power.

*Kilbourn* remained undisturbed until 1972 when the Court, in *Gravel v. United States* (1972), was asked to consider whether the Speech or Debate Clause protected legislative aides from legal action if their behavior otherwise warranted criminal prosecution. *Gravel* was one of several cases in the early 1970s related to the release of the Pentagon Papers, a series of classified documents that detailed the involvement of the United States in the Vietnam War. What distinguished *Gravel* from prior cases involving the Speech or Debate Clause was that it centered on whether a legislative aide should be considered the functional equivalent of a legislator. The aide was working with his boss, Senator Mike Gravel (D–Alaska), to prepare the Pentagon Papers for publication with a press affiliated with the Unitarian Universalist Church.

The Court divided on the scope of the Speech or Debate Clause's application to legislative aides. On the one hand, Justice White's opinion for the five-member majority extends *Kilbourn* by ruling that the Speech or Debate Clause applies when a legislative aide acts as a surrogate for the member, but no further. Justice Douglas's dissent views the Speech or Debate Clause from a very different perspective and pulls no punches in its criticism of the Court. Keep *Gravel* in mind when you read *New York Times v. United States* (1971), a landmark case involving the Pentagon Papers in which the Court dealt with conflicting assertions of executive privilege and freedom of the press, ahead in our discussion of executive power in Chapter 5.

In *Hutchinson v. Proxmire* (1979), the Court extended the inside-outside application of the Speech or Debate Clause to members who have engaged in activity under the pretext of the legislative process. That is, the Court continued to hold to the rule it created in *Gravel* that congressional immunity did not extend to a member's actions that took place beyond the floor of the House or Senate. In *Proxmire* the Court, quite literally, drew a line between the statements made on the Senate floor by Senator William Proxmire (D–Wisc.) about a recipient of federal research grants and the excerpts that were included in press releases and constituent news releases. The Court held that the Speech or Debate Clause protected the comments made on the floor, but not the press releases and materials for distribution outside the legislative chamber. *Proxmire* offers a good place to consider the following question: Do you believe the Speech or Debate Clause should protect all legislative activities, including those undertaken in *Gravel* and *Proxmire*, or just those in the context of the legislative forum?

## Powell v. McCormack
### 395 U.S. 486 (1969)

Adam Clayton Powell Jr. (D–N.Y.) surely stands out as one of the most memorable individuals ever to serve in Congress, no mean feat for an institution that has seen more than its fair share of characters come and go. First elected to the House in 1944, Powell continued to represent his Harlem district until 1971. Powell, one of the few African Americans to serve in the House between Reconstruction and the passage of the Voting Rights Act of 1965, cut a controversial figure in Congress from the moment he was elected. An ordained Baptist minister who inherited the pulpit of the Abyssinian Baptist Church from his father, one of the largest congregations in the nation, Powell shunned the cleric's vow of poverty. He dressed well, maintained an extravagant lifestyle, had one of the highest absentee rates in Congress, and was often seen, both at home and on government "fact finding" trips abroad, in the company of women who were not his wife.

From 1961 to 1967, Powell served as the chairman of the House Committee on Education and Labor. This position was a remarkable accomplishment considering that on two occasions just prior to his elevation to this powerful post he had been indicted on tax-evasion charges and convicted of libel. Powell was acquitted of tax charges, and he paid the libel judgment only after four contempt citations and a separate guilty verdict on charges of hiding personal assets to avoid paying the damages. Powell's antics infuriated other members, but not his constituents, who rejoiced in his willingness to provoke the staid, conservative Washington establishment. He was serious one moment—he was known as "Mr. Civil Rights" before most Americans had heard of Martin Luther King Jr.—and outrageous and unpredictable the next. His libel suit, in fact, stemmed from his calling a Harlem woman a "bag lady." Somehow, Powell managed to skirt above congressional reproach until 1965, when Congress formed a special committee to investigate several alleged improprieties of House rules.

In March 1967, Congress decided to exclude Powell, even though he had been reelected the previous November. His exclusion came after Congress found that he had used federal funds to take two women with him on a congressional junket to Europe and to pay his ex-wife a $20,000 yearly salary as a staff assistant for work she did not perform. Powell contested his exclusion, claiming that Congress had no power other than that set out in Article I to refuse him his seat. Congress relied upon its enactment of the Test Oath Act of 1862 to support the argument that the body had internal power to exclude a representative-elect for ethical and possibly criminal violations.

The Court's decision was 8 to 1. Chief Justice Warren delivered the opinion of the Court. Justice Douglas concurred. Justice Stewart dissented.

▼▲▼

Mr. Chief Justice Warren delivered the opinion of the Court.

In November, 1966, petitioner Adam Clayton Powell, Jr., was duly elected from the 18th Congressional District of New York to serve in the United States House of Representatives for the 90th Congress. However, pursuant to a House resolution, he was not permitted to take his seat. Powell (and some of the voters of his district) then filed suit in Federal District Court, claiming that the House could exclude him only if it found he failed to meet the standing requirements of age, citizenship, and residence contained in Article I, Section 2, of the Constitution—requirements the House specifically found Powell met—and thus had excluded him unconstitutionally. The District Court dismissed petitioners' complaint "for want of jurisdiction of the subject matter." A panel of the Court of Appeals affirmed the dismissal, although on somewhat different grounds, each judge filing a separate opinion. We have determined that it was error to dismiss the complaint, and that petitioner Powell is entitled to a declaratory judgment that he was unlawfully excluded from the 90th Congress. . . .

## Speech or Debate Clause

The Speech or Debate Clause, adopted by the Constitutional Convention without debate or opposition, finds its roots in the conflict between Parliament and the Crown culminating in the Glorious Revolution of 1688 and the English Bill of Rights of 1689. [T]he purpose of this clause was "to prevent intimidation [of legislators] by the executive and accountability before a possibly hostile Judiciary." Although the clause sprang from a fear of seditious libel actions instituted by the Crown to punish unfavorable speeches made in Parliament, we have held that it would be a "narrow view" to confine the protection of the Speech or Debate Clause to words spoken in debate. Committee reports, resolutions, and the act of voting are equally covered, as are "things generally done in a session of the House by one of its members in relation to the business before it." Furthermore, the clause not only provides a defense on the merits, but also protects a legislator from the burden of defending himself. . . .

Legislative immunity does not, of course, bar all judicial review of legislative acts. That issue was settled by implication as early as 1803 [in] *Marbury* v. *Madison*, and expressly in *Kilbourn* v. *Thompson* (1881), the first of this Court's cases interpreting the reach of the Speech or Debate Clause. . . .

## Exclusion or Expulsion

The resolution excluding petitioner Powell was adopted by a vote in excess of two-thirds of the 434 Members of Congress, 307 to 116. Respondents assert that the House may expel a member for any reason whatsoever, and that, since a two-thirds vote was obtained, the procedure by which Powell was denied his seat in the 90th Congress should be regarded as an expulsion, not an exclusion. . . .

Relying heavily on Charles Warren's analysis of the Convention debates, petitioners argue that the proceedings manifest the Framers' unequivocal intention to deny either branch of Congress the authority to add to or otherwise vary the membership qualifications expressly set forth in the Constitution. We do not completely agree, for the debates are subject to other interpretations. However, we have concluded that the records of the debates, viewed in the context of the bitter struggle for the right to freely choose representatives which had recently concluded in England and in light of the distinction the Framers made between the power to expel and the power to exclude, indicate that petitioners' ultimate conclusion is correct.

The Convention opened in late May, 1787. By the end of July, the delegates adopted, with a minimum of debate, age requirements for membership in both the Senate and the House. The Convention then appointed a Committee of Detail to draft a constitution incorporating these and other resolutions adopted during the preceding months. Two days after the Committee was appointed, George Mason, of Virginia, moved that the Committee consider a clause "'requiring certain qualifications of landed property & citizenship'" and disqualifying from membership in Congress persons who had unsettled accounts or who were indebted to the United States. A vigorous debate ensued. Charles Pinckney and General Charles C. Pinckney, both of South Carolina, moved to extend these incapacities to both the judicial and executive branches of the new government. But John Dickinson, of Delaware, opposed the inclusion of any statement of qualifications in the Constitution. He argued that it would be, "impossible to make a compleat one, and a partial one would, by implication, tie up the hands of the Legislature from supplying the omissions." Dickinson's argument was rejected, and, after eliminating the disqualification of debtors and the limitation to "landed" property, the Convention adopted Mason's proposal to instruct the Committee of Detail to draft a property qualification.

The Committee reported in early August, proposing no change in the age requirement; however, it did recommend adding citizenship and residency requirements for membership. After first debating what the precise requirements should be, on August 8, 1787, the delegates unanimously adopted the three qualifications embodied in Article I, Section 2.

On August 10, the Convention considered the Committee of Detail's proposal that the, "Legislature of the United States shall have authority to establish such uni-form qualifications of the members of each House, with regard to property, as to the said Legislature shall seem expedient." The debate on this proposal discloses much about the views of the Framers on the issue of qualifications. For example, James Madison urged its rejection, stating that the proposal would vest:

> an improper & dangerous power in the Legislature. The qualifications of electors and elected were fundamental articles in a Republican Govt., and ought to be fixed by the Constitution. If the Legislature could regulate those of either, it can by degrees subvert the Constitution. A Republic may be converted into an aristocracy or oligarchy as well by limiting the number capable of being elected as the number authorised to elect. . . . It was a power also which might be made subservient to the views of one faction agst. another. Qualifications founded on artificial distinctions may be devised by the stronger in order to keep out partizans of [a weaker] faction.

Significantly, Madison's argument was not aimed at the imposition of a property qualification as such, but rather at the delegation to the Congress of the discretionary power to establish any qualifications. . . .

The debates at the state conventions also demonstrate the Framers' understanding that the qualifications for members of Congress had been fixed in the Constitution. Before the New York convention, for example, Hamilton emphasized: "[T]he true principle of a republic is that the people should choose whom they please to govern them. Representation is imperfect in proportion as the current of popular favor is checked. This great source of free government, popular election, should be perfectly pure, and the most unbounded liberty allowed." In Virginia, where the Federalists faced powerful opposition by advocates of popular democracy, Wilson Carey Nicholas, a future member of both the House and Senate and later Governor of the State, met the arguments that the new Constitution violated democratic principles with the following interpretation of Article I, Section 2, clause 2, as it respects the qualifications of the elected: "It has ever been considered a great security to liberty that very few should be excluded from the right of being chosen to the legislature. This Constitution has amply attended to this idea. We find no qualifications required except those of age and residence, which create a certainty of their judgment being matured, and of being attached to their state."

Mr. Justice Douglas, concurring.

While I join the opinion of the Court, I add a few words. As the Court says, the important constitutional question is whether the Congress has the power to deviate from or alter the qualifications for membership as a Representative contained in Article I, 2, clause 2, of the Constitution. Up to now the understanding has been quite clear to the effect that such authority does not exist. To be sure, Article I, 5, provides that: "Each House shall be the Judge of the Elections, Returns and Qualifications of its own Members . . . ." Contests may arise over whether an elected official meets the "qualifications" of the Constitution, in which event the House is the sole judge. But the House is not the sole judge when "qualifications" are added which are not specified in the Constitution.

A man is not seated because he is a Socialist or a Communist.

Another is not seated because in his district members of a minority are systematically excluded from voting.

Another is not seated because he has spoken out in opposition to the war in Vietnam.

The possible list is long. Some cases will have the racist overtones of the present one.

Others may reflect religious or ideological clashes.

At the root of all these cases, however, is the basic integrity of the electoral process. Today we proclaim the constitutional principle of "one man, one vote." When that principle is followed and the electors choose a person who is repulsive to the Establishment in Congress, by what constitutional authority can that group of electors be disenfranchised?

By Article I, 5, the House may "expel a Member" by a vote of two-thirds. And if this were an expulsion case I would think that no justiciable controversy would be presented, the vote of the House being two-thirds or more. But it is not an expulsion case. Whether it could have been won as an expulsion case, no one knows. Expulsion for "misconduct" may well raise different questions, different considerations. Policing the conduct of members, a recurring problem in the Senate and House as well, is quite different from the initial decision whether an elected official should be seated. It well might be easier to bar admission than to expel one already seated.

MR. JUSTICE STEWART, dissenting.

I believe that events which have taken place since certiorari was granted in this case on November 18, 1968, have rendered it moot, and that the Court should therefore refrain from deciding the novel, difficult, and delicate constitutional questions which the case presented at its inception.

The essential purpose of this lawsuit by Congressman Powell and members of his constituency was to regain the seat from which he was barred by the 90th Congress. That purpose, however, became impossible of attainment on January 3, 1969, when the 90th Congress passed into history and the 91st Congress came into being. On that date, the petitioners' prayer for a judicial decree restraining enforcement of House Resolution No. 278 and commanding the respondents to admit Congressman Powell to membership in the 90th Congress became incontestably moot.

The petitioners assert that actions of the House of Representatives of the 91st Congress have prolonged the controversy raised by Powell's exclusion and preserved the need for a judicial declaration in this case. I believe, to the contrary, that the conduct of the present House of Representatives confirms the mootness of the petitioners' suit against the 90th Congress. Had Powell been excluded from the 91st Congress, he might argue that there was a "continuing controversy" concerning the exclusion attacked in this case. And such an argument might be sound even though the present House of Representatives is a distinct legislative body, rather than a continuation of its predecessor, and though any grievance caused by conduct of the 91st Congress is not redressable in this action. But on January 3, 1969, the House of Representatives of the 91st Congress admitted Congressman Powell to membership, and he now sits as the Representative of the 18th Congressional District of New York. With the 90th Congress terminated and Powell now a member of the 91st, it cannot seriously be contended that there remains a judicial controversy between these parties over the power of the House of Representatives to exclude Powell and the power of a court to order him reseated.

▼▲▼

## U.S. Term Limits, Inc. v. Thornton
### 514 U.S. 779 (1995)

In 1992, Arkansas voters approved Amendment 73 to the state constitution, which limited the number of consecutive terms an incumbent candidate's name could appear on the ballot. Representative Ray Thornton, a one-term Democrat who represented Arkansas's second congressional district, challenged Amendment 73 as unconstitutional.

The state trial court ruled that Amendment 73 was unconstitutional. The Arkansas Supreme Court affirmed, after which U.S. Term Limits, Inc., a nonprofit group formed to promote term-limit amendments nationwide, appealed to the U.S. Supreme Court.

For more information on the rise and fall of the term-limits movement, see the accompanying SIDEBAR.

The Court's decision was 5 to 4. Justice Stevens delivered the opinion of the Court. Justice Kennedy filed a concurring opinion. Justice Thomas, joined by Chief Justice Rehnquist and Justices O'Connor and Scalia, dissented.

▼▲▼

JUSTICE STEVENS delivered the opinion of the Court.

The Constitution sets forth qualifications for membership in the Congress of the United States. Article I, Section 2, clause 2, which applies to the House of Representatives, provides:

> No Person shall be a Representative who shall not have attained to the Age of twenty five Years, and been seven Years a Citizen of the United States, and who shall not, when elected, be an Inhabitant of that State in which he shall be chosen.

Article I, Section 3, clause 3, which applies to the Senate, similarly provides:

> No Person shall be a Senator who shall not have attained to the Age of thirty Years, and been nine Years a Citizen of the United States, and who shall not, when elected, be an Inhabitant of that State for which he shall be chosen.

Today's cases present a challenge to an amendment to the Arkansas State Constitution that prohibits the name of an otherwise eligible candidate for Congress from appearing on the general election ballot if that candidate has already served three terms in the House of Representatives or two terms in the Senate. The Arkansas Supreme Court held that the amendment violates the Federal Constitution. We agree with that holding. Such a state-imposed restriction is contrary to the "fundamental principle of our representative democracy," embodied in the Constitution, that "the people should choose whom they please to govern them." *Powell v. McCormack* (1969). Allowing individual States to adopt their own qualifications for congressional service would be inconsistent with the Framers' vision of a uniform National Legislature representing the people of the United States. If the qualifications set forth in the text of the Constitution are to be changed, that text must be amended. . . .

Twenty-six years ago, in *Powell v. McCormack*, we reviewed the history and text of the Qualifications Clauses in a case involving an attempted exclusion of a duly elected Member of Congress. The principal issue was whether the power granted to each House . . . to judge the "Qualifications of its own Members" includes the power to impose qualifications other than those set forth in the text of the Constitution. In an opinion by CHIEF JUSTICE WARREN for eight Members of the Court, we held that it does not. . . .

[In *Powell*,] we viewed the Convention debates as manifesting the Framers' intent that the qualifications in the Constitution be fixed and exclusive. We found particularly revealing the debate concerning a proposal made by the Committee of Detail that would have given Congress the power to add property qualifications. James Madison argued that such a power would vest "'an improper & dangerous power in the Legislature,'" by which the Legislature "'can by degrees subvert the Constitution.'" Madison continued: "A Republic may be converted into an aristocracy or oligarchy as well by limiting the number capable of being elected as the number authorised to elect."

The Framers further revealed their concerns about congressional abuse of power when Gouverneur Morris suggested modifying the proposal of the Committee of Detail to grant Congress unfettered power to add qualifications. We noted that Hugh Williamson, expressed concern that if a majority of the legislature should happen to be "composed of any particular description of men, of lawyers for example, . . . the future elections might be secured to their own body." We noted too that Madison emphasized the British Parliament's attempts to regulate qualifications, and that he observed: "'[T]he abuse they had made of it was a lesson worthy of our attention.'" We found significant that the Convention rejected both Morris' modification and the Committee's proposal.

We also recognized in *Powell* that the post-Convention ratification debates confirmed that the Framers understood the qualifications in the Constitution to be fixed and unalterable by Congress. For example, we noted that in response to the anti-federalist charge that the new Constitution favored the wealthy and well-born, Alexander Hamilton wrote:

> The truth is that there is no method of securing to the rich the preference apprehended but by prescribing qualifications of property either for those who may elect or be elected. But this forms no part of the power to be conferred upon the national government. . . . *The qualifications of the persons who may choose or be chosen, as has been remarked upon other occasions, are*

*defined and fixed in the Constitution, and are unalterable by the legislature.*

We thus attached special significance to "Hamilton's express reliance on the immutability of the qualifications set forth in the Constitution." Moreover, we reviewed the debates at the state conventions and found that they "also demonstrate the Framers' understanding that the qualifications for members of Congress had been fixed in the Constitution."

The exercise by Congress of its power to judge the qualifications of its Members further confirmed this understanding. We concluded that, during the first 100 years of its existence, "Congress strictly limited its power to judge the qualifications of its members to those enumerated in the Constitution."

As this elaborate summary reveals, our historical analysis in *Powell* was both detailed and persuasive. We thus conclude now, as we did in *Powell*, that history shows that, with respect to Congress, the Framers intended the Constitution to establish fixed qualifications. . . .

*Powell* thus establishes two important propositions: first, that the "relevant historical materials" compel the conclusion that, at least with respect to qualifications imposed by Congress, the Framers intended the qualifications listed in the Constitution to be exclusive; and second, that that conclusion is equally compelled by an understanding of the "fundamental principle of our representative democracy . . . 'that the people should choose whom they please to govern them.'"

In sum, after examining *Powell*'s historical analysis and its articulation of the "basic principles of our democratic system," we reaffirm that the qualifications for service in Congress set forth in the text of the Constitution are "fixed," at least in the sense that they may not be supplemented by Congress.

Our reaffirmation of *Powell*, does not necessarily resolve the specific questions presented in these cases. For petitioners argue that, whatever the constitutionality of additional qualifications for membership imposed by Congress, the historical and textual materials discussed in *Powell* do not support the conclusion that the Constitution prohibits additional qualifications imposed by States. In the absence of such a constitutional prohibition, petitioners argue, the Tenth Amendment and the principle of reserved powers require that States be allowed to add such qualifications. . . .

Contrary to petitioners' assertions, the power to add qualifications is not part of the original powers of sovereignty that the Tenth Amendment reserved to the States. Petitioners' Tenth Amendment argument misconceives the nature of the right at issue because that Amendment could only "reserve" that which existed before. As Justice Story recognized, "the states can exercise no powers whatsoever, which exclusively spring out of the existence of the national government, which the constitution does not delegate to them. . . . No state can say, that it has reserved, what it never possessed."

Justice Story's position thus echoes that of Chief Justice Marshall in *McCulloch v. Maryland* (1819). In *McCulloch*, the Court rejected the argument that the Constitution's silence on the subject of state power to tax corporations chartered by Congress implies that the States have "reserved" power to tax such federal instrumentalities. As Chief Justice Marshall pointed out, an "original right to tax" such federal entities "never existed, and the question whether it has been surrendered, cannot arise." In language that presaged Justice Story's argument, Chief Justice Marshall concluded: "This opinion does not deprive the States of any resources which they originally possessed."

With respect to setting qualifications for service in Congress, no such right existed before the Constitution was ratified. The contrary argument overlooks the revolutionary character of the government that the Framers conceived. Prior to the adoption of the Constitution, the States had joined together under the Articles of Confederation. In that system, "the States retained most of their sovereignty, like independent nations bound together only by treaties." *Wesberry v. Sanders* (1964). After the Constitutional Convention convened, the Framers were presented with, and eventually adopted a variation of, "a plan not merely to amend the Articles of Confederation, but to create an entirely new National Government with a National Executive, National Judiciary, and a National Legislature." In adopting that plan, the Framers envisioned a uniform national system, rejecting the notion that the Nation was a collection of States, and instead creating a direct link between the National Government and the people of the United States. In that National Government, representatives owe primary allegiance not to the people of a State, but to the people of the Nation. . . .

Two other sections of the Constitution further support our view of the Framers' vision. First, consistent with Story's view, the Constitution provides that the salaries of representatives should "be ascertained by Law, and paid out of the Treasury of the United States," rather than by individual States. The salary provisions reflect the view that representatives owe their allegiance to the people, and not to States. Second, the provisions governing elections reveal the Framers' understanding that powers over the election of federal officers had to be delegated to, rather than reserved by, the States. It is surely no coincidence that the context of federal elections provides one of the few areas in which the Constitution expressly requires action by the States, namely that, "[t]he Times, Places and Manner of holding Elections for Senators and Representatives, shall be prescribed in each State by the legislature thereof." This duty parallels the duty under Article II that "Each State shall appoint, in such Manner as the Legislature thereof may direct, a Number of Electors." These Clauses are express delegations of power to the States to act with respect to federal elections. This conclusion is consistent with our previous recognition that, in certain limited contexts, the power to regulate the incidents of the federal system is not a reserved power of the States, but rather is delegated by the Constitution.

In short, as the Framers recognized, electing representatives to the National Legislature was a new right, arising from the Constitution itself. The Tenth Amendment thus provides no basis for concluding that the States possess reserved power to add qualifications to those that are fixed in the Constitution. Instead, any state power to set the qualifications for membership in Congress must derive not from the reserved powers of state sovereignty, but rather from the delegated powers of national sovereignty. In the absence of any constitutional delegation to the States of power to add qualifications to those enumerated in the Constitution, such a power does not exist. . . .

We find further evidence of the Framers' intent in Article 1, Section 5, clause 1, which provides: "Each House shall be the Judge of the Elections, Returns and Qualifications of its own Members." That Article I, Section 5 vests a federal tribunal with ultimate authority to judge a Member's qualifications is fully consistent with the understanding that those qualifications are fixed in the Federal Constitution, but not with the understanding that they can be altered by the States. If the States had the right to prescribe additional qualifications such as property, educational, or professional qualifications for their own representatives, state law would provide the standard for judging a Member's eligibility. As we concluded in *Murdock* v. *Memphis* (1875), federal questions are generally answered finally by federal tribunals because rights which depend on federal law "should be the same everywhere," and "their construction should be uniform." The judging of questions concerning rights which depend on state law is not, however, normally assigned to federal tribunals. The Constitution's provision for each House to be the

judge of its own qualifications thus provides further evidence that the Framers believed that the primary source of those qualifications would be federal law.

We also find compelling the complete absence in the ratification debates of any assertion that States had the power to add qualifications. In those debates, the question whether to require term limits, or "rotation," was a major source of controversy. The draft of the Constitution that was submitted for ratification contained no provision for rotation. In arguments that echo in the preamble to Arkansas' Amendment 73, opponents of ratification condemned the absence of a rotation requirement, noting that, "there is no doubt that senators will hold their office perpetually; and in this situation, they must of necessity lose their dependence, and their attachments to the people." Even proponents of ratification expressed concern about the "abandonment in every instance of the necessity of rotation in office." At several ratification conventions, participants proposed amendments that would have required rotation. . . .

[W]e believe that state-imposed qualifications, as much as congressionally imposed qualifications, would undermine the second critical idea recognized in *Powell*: that an aspect of sovereignty is the right of the people to vote for whom they wish. Again, the source of the qualification is of little moment in assessing the qualification's restrictive impact.

Finally, state-imposed restrictions, unlike the congressionally imposed restrictions at issue in *Powell*, violate a third idea central to this basic principle: that the right to choose representatives belongs not to the States, but to the people. From the start, the Framers recognized that the "great and radical vice" of the Articles of Confederation was, "the principle of LEGISLATION for STATES or GOVERNMENTS, in their CORPORATE or COLLECTIVE CAPACITIES, and as contradistinguished from the INDIVIDUALS of whom they consist." *Federalist* 15. Thus, the Framers, in perhaps their most important contribution, conceived of a Federal Government directly responsible to the people, possessed of direct power over the people, and chosen directly, not by States, but by the people. The Framers implemented this ideal most clearly in the provision, extant from the beginning of the Republic, that calls for the Members of the House of Representatives to be "chosen every second Year by the People of the several States." Following the adoption of the 17th Amendment in 1913, this ideal was extended to elections for the Senate. The Congress of the United States, therefore, is not a confederation of nations in which separate sovereigns are represented by appointed delegates, but is instead a body composed of representatives of the people. As Chief Justice John Marshall observed: "The government of the union, then, . . . is, emphatically, and truly, a government of the people. In form and in substance, it emanates from them. Its powers are granted by them, and are to be exercised directly on them, and for their benefit." *McCulloch* v. *Maryland* (1819). . . .

Permitting individual States to formulate diverse qualifications for their representatives would result in a patchwork of state qualifications, undermining the uniformity and the national character that the Framers envisioned and sought to ensure. Such a patchwork would also sever the direct link that the Framers found so critical between the National Government and the people of the United States.

Petitioners attempt to overcome this formidable array of evidence against the States' power to impose qualifications by arguing that the practice of the States immediately after the adoption of the Constitution demonstrates their understanding that they possessed such power. One may properly question the extent to which the States' own practice is a reliable indicator of the contours of restrictions that the Constitution imposed on States, especially when no court has ever upheld a state-imposed qualification of any sort. But petitioners' argument is unpersuasive even on its own terms. At the time of the Convention, "[a]lmost all the State Constitutions required members of their Legislatures to possess considerable property." Despite this near uniformity, only one State, Virginia, placed similar restrictions on members of Congress, requiring that a representative be, *inter alia*, a "freeholder." Just 15 years after imposing a property qualification, Virginia replaced that requirement with a provision requiring that representatives be only "qualified according to the constitution of the United States." Moreover, several States, including New Hampshire, Georgia, Delaware, and South Carolina, revised their Constitutions at around the time of the Federal Constitution. In the revised Constitutions, each State retained property qualifications for its own state elected officials, yet placed no property qualification on its congressional representatives.

The contemporaneous state practice with respect to term limits is similar. At the time of the Convention, States widely supported term limits in at least some circumstances. The Articles of Confederation contained a provision for term limits. As we have noted, some members of the Convention had sought to impose term limits for Members of Congress. In addition, many States imposed term limits on state officers, four placed limits on delegates to the Continental Congress, and several States

voiced support for term limits for Members of Congress. Despite this widespread support, no State sought to impose any term limits on its own federal representatives. Thus, a proper assessment of contemporaneous state practice provides further persuasive evidence of a general understanding that the qualifications in the Constitution were unalterable by the States.

In sum, the available historical and textual evidence, read in light of the basic principles of democracy underlying the Constitution and recognized by this Court in *Powell*, reveal the Framers' intent that neither Congress nor the States should possess the power to supplement the exclusive qualifications set forth in the text of the Constitution. . . .

In our view, Amendment 73 is an indirect attempt to accomplish what the Constitution prohibits Arkansas from accomplishing directly. As the plurality opinion of the Arkansas Supreme Court recognized, Amendment 73 is an "effort to dress eligibility to stand for Congress in ballot access clothing," because the "intent and the effect of Amendment 73 are to disqualify congressional incumbents from further service." We must, of course, accept the State Court's view of the purpose of its own law: we are thus authoritatively informed that the sole purpose of Amendment 73 was to attempt to achieve a result that is forbidden by the Federal Constitution. Indeed, it cannot be seriously contended that the intent behind Amendment 73 is other than to prevent the election of incumbents. The preamble of Amendment 73 states explicitly: "[T]he people of Arkansas . . . herein limit the terms of elected officials." . . .

The merits of term limits, or "rotation," have been the subject of debate since the formation of our Constitution, when the Framers unanimously rejected a proposal to add such limits to the Constitution. The cogent arguments on both sides of the question that were articulated during the process of ratification largely retain their force today. Over half the States have adopted measures that impose such limits on some offices either directly or indirectly, and the Nation as a whole, notably by constitutional amendment, has imposed a limit on the number of terms that the President may serve. Term limits, like any other qualification for office, unquestionably restrict the ability of voters to vote for whom they wish. On the other hand, such limits may provide for the infusion of fresh ideas and new perspectives, and may decrease the likelihood that representatives will lose touch with their constituents. It is not our province to resolve this longstanding debate.

We are, however, firmly convinced that allowing the several States to adopt term limits for congressional service would effect a fundamental change in the constitutional framework. Any such change must come not by legislation adopted either by Congress or by an individual State, but rather—as have other important changes in the electoral process—through the Amendment procedures set forth in Article V. The Framers decided that the qualifications for service in the Congress of the United States be fixed in the Constitution and be uniform throughout the Nation. That decision reflects the Framers' understanding that Members of Congress are chosen by separate constituencies, but that they become, when elected, servants of the people of the United States. They are not merely delegates appointed by separate, sovereign States; they occupy offices that are integral and essential components of a single National Government. In the absence of a properly passed constitutional amendment, allowing individual States to craft their own qualifications for Congress would thus erode the structure envisioned by the Framers, a structure that was designed, in the words of the Preamble to our Constitution, to form a "more perfect Union."

The judgment is affirmed.

JUSTICE THOMAS, with whom THE CHIEF JUSTICE, JUSTICE O'CONNOR, and JUSTICE SCALIA join, dissenting.

It is ironic that the Court bases today's decision on the right of the people to "choose whom they please to govern them." Under our Constitution, there is only one State whose people have the right to "choose whom they please" to represent Arkansas in Congress. The Court holds, however, that neither the elected legislature of that State nor the people themselves (acting by ballot initiative) may prescribe any qualifications for those representatives. The majority therefore defends the right of the people of Arkansas to "choose whom they please to govern them" by invalidating a provision that won nearly 60% of the votes cast in a direct election and that carried every congressional district in the State.

I dissent. Nothing in the Constitution deprives the people of each State of the power to prescribe eligibility requirements for the candidates who seek to represent them in Congress. The Constitution is simply silent on this question. And where the Constitution is silent, it raises no bar to action by the States or the people. . . .

Our system of government rests on one overriding principle: all power stems from the consent of the people. To phrase the principle in this way, however, is to be imprecise about something important to the notion of "reserved" powers. The ultimate source of the Constitution's authority is the consent of the people of each individual State, not the consent of the undifferentiated people of the Nation as a whole.

The ratification procedure erected by Article VII makes this point clear. The Constitution took effect once it had been ratified by the people gathered in convention in nine different States. But the Constitution went into effect only "between the States so ratifying the same," Art. VII; it did not bind the people of North Carolina until they had accepted it. In Madison's words, the popular consent upon which the Constitution's authority rests was, "given by the people, not as individuals composing one entire nation, but as composing the distinct and independent States to which they respectively belong." *Federalist* 39.

When they adopted the Federal Constitution, of course, the people of each State surrendered some of their authority to the United States (and hence to entities accountable to the people of other States as well as to themselves). They affirmatively deprived their States of certain powers, and they affirmatively conferred certain powers upon the Federal Government. Because the people of the several States are the only true source of power, however, the Federal Government enjoys no authority beyond what the Constitution confers: the Federal Government's powers are limited and enumerated. In the words of Justice Black, "[t]he United States is entirely a creature of the Constitution. Its power and authority have no other source." *Reid* v. *Covert* (1957).

In each State, the remainder of the people's powers—"[t]he powers not delegated to the United States by the Constitution, nor prohibited by it to the States,"—are either delegated to the state government or retained by the people. The Federal Constitution does not specify which of these two possibilities obtains; it is up to the various state constitutions to declare which powers the people of each State have delegated to their state government. As far as the Federal Constitution is concerned, then, the States can exercise all powers that the Constitution does not withhold from them. The Federal Government and the States thus face different default rules: where the Constitution is silent about the exercise of a particular power—that is, where the Constitution does not speak either expressly or by necessary implication—the Federal Government lacks that power and the States enjoy it.

These basic principles are enshrined in the Tenth Amendment, which declares that all powers neither delegated to the Federal Government nor prohibited to the States "are reserved to the States respectively, or to the people." With this careful last phrase, the Amendment avoids taking any position on the division of power between the state governments and the people of the States: it is up to the people of each State to determine which "reserved" powers their state government may exercise. But the Amendment does make clear that powers reside at the state level except where the Constitution removes them from that level. All powers that the Constitution neither delegates to the Federal Government nor prohibits to the States are controlled by the people of each State.

In short, the notion of popular sovereignty that undergirds the Constitution does not erase state boundaries, but rather tracks them. The people of each State obviously did trust their fate to the people of the several States when they consented to the Constitution; not only did they empower the governmental institutions of the United States, but they also agreed to be bound by constitutional amendments that they themselves refused to ratify. At the same time, however, the people of each State retained their separate political identities. As Chief Justice Marshall put it, "[n]o political dreamer was ever wild enough to think of breaking down the lines which separate the States, and of compounding the American people into one common mass." *McCulloch* v. *Maryland* (1819).

The majority is . . . quite wrong to conclude that the people of the States cannot authorize their state governments to exercise any powers that were unknown to the States when the Federal Constitution was drafted. Indeed, the majority's position frustrates the apparent purpose of the Amendment's final phrase. The Amendment does not preempt any limitations on state power found in the state constitutions, as it might have done if it simply had said that the powers not delegated to the Federal Government are reserved to the States. But the Amendment also does not prevent the people of the States from amending their state constitutions to remove limitations that were in effect when the Federal Constitution and the Bill of Rights were ratified. . . .

The majority settles on "the Qualifications Clauses" as the constitutional provisions that Amendment 73 violates. Because I do not read those provisions to impose any unstated prohibitions on the States, it is unnecessary for me to decide whether the majority is correct to identify Arkansas' ballot access restriction with laws fixing true term limits or otherwise prescribing "qualifications" for congressional office. . . . [T]he Qualifications Clauses are merely straightforward recitations of the minimum eligibility requirements that the Framers thought it essential for every Member of Congress to meet. They restrict state power only in that they prevent the States from *abolishing* all eligibility requirements for membership in Congress. . . .

Although the Qualifications Clauses neither state nor imply the prohibition that it finds in them, the majority infers from the Framers' "democratic principles" that the Clauses must have been generally understood to preclude the people of the States and their state legislatures from prescribing any additional qualifications for their representatives in Congress. But the majority's evidence on this point establishes only two more modest propositions: (1) the Framers did not want the Federal Constitution itself to impose a broad set of disqualifications for congressional office, and (2) the Framers did not want the Federal Congress to be able to supplement the few disqualifications that the Constitution does set forth. The logical conclusion is simply that the Framers did not want the people of the States and their state legislatures to be constrained by too many qualifications imposed at the national level. The evidence does not support the majority's more sweeping conclusion that the Framers intended to bar the people of the States and their state legislatures from adopting additional eligibility requirements to help narrow their own choices.

I agree with the majority that Congress has no power to prescribe qualifications for its own Members. This fact, however, does not show that the Qualifications Clauses contain a hidden exclusivity provision. The reason for Congress' incapacity is not that the Qualifications Clauses deprive Congress of the authority to set qualifications, but rather that nothing in the Constitution grants Congress this power. In the absence of such a grant, Congress may not act. But deciding whether the Constitution denies the qualification-setting power to the States and the people of the States requires a fundamentally different legal analysis. . . .

The fact that the Framers did not grant a qualification-setting power to Congress does not imply that they wanted to bar its exercise at the state level. One reason why the Framers decided not to let Congress prescribe the qualifications of its own members was that incumbents could have used this power to perpetuate themselves or their ilk in office. As Madison pointed out at the Philadelphia Convention, Members of Congress would have an obvious conflict of interest if they could determine who may run against them. But neither the people of the States nor the state legislatures would labor under the same conflict of interest when prescribing qualifications for Members of Congress, and so the Framers would have had to use a different calculus in determining whether to deprive them of this power.

As the majority argues, democratic principles also contributed to the Framers' decision to withhold the qualification-setting power from Congress. But the majority is wrong to suggest that the same principles must also have led the Framers to deny this power to the people of the States and the state legislatures. In particular, it simply is

## U.S. TERM LIMITS, INC. V. THORNTON

### The Devil You Know

Like so many other important questions involving the intersection of law and policy, the raucous debate that emerged in the early 1990s over whether to limit the number of consecutive terms that elected officials should be permitted to serve reduced a complex constitutional question to the lowest common denominator. Such are the demands of the sound-bite culture of contemporary American politics. Challengers and incumbents alike, along with the standing army of Washington reporters and commentators ready to offer their expertise on this as well as any other topic on a moment's notice, often phrased term limits as a "for or against" question. This vastly oversimplified the issue. The Constitution already limits presidents to two consecutive terms. The issue this time was about term limits for members of Congress.

Long before the Republican leadership in Congress made term limits a hot-button issue during the 1994 campaign season, the Framers debated whether the Constitution should continue the "rotation in office" of its elected officials required by the Articles of Confederation. Drawing upon the practices of the ancient republics of Rome and Greece, the Framers of the Articles of Confederation limited members of the Continental Congress to serving only "three years in any term of six years." By 1784 the idea of rotation in office was severely tested when several delegates exceeded their terms and insisted on continuing to serve. The ugliness surrounding their expulsion was such that James Madison was compelled to remark that he had "never [seen] more indecent conduct in any assembly before."

Madison, too, was later required to leave the Continental Congress, leading some prominent Framers to suggest upon arriving in Philadelphia in 1787 for the convention to amend the Articles that ending rotation in office should be among the highest of reform priorities. Proposals to limit the terms of members of the executive and legislative branches were rejected on the belief that "rotation" would take care of itself. Moreover, as Madison explained in *Federalist* 62, term limits would constrict the ability of elected officials, particularly legislators, to develop "a knowledge of the means

by which the object [of government] can best be obtained." And there term limits stood until 1951, when the Twenty-second Amendment limiting the president to no more than two 4-year terms was ratified.

Congress, however, exempted itself from the limits it imposed on the president. Congressional Republicans, who had assumed control of the House for the first time since 1954, viewed this move as a partisan shot. Upset that President Franklin Roosevelt had defied the self-imposed two-term limit established by President Washington by seeking third and fourth terms in 1940 and 1944, respectively, House Republicans introduced the Twenty-second Amendment shortly after the start of the 1947 legislative session. It quickly won approval in the House and Senate and was then sent to the states for ratification. After seventeen states ratified the amendment within ninety days, it languished for four years before securing the necessary two-thirds majority for approval.

Congressional term limits had been introduced at various points in the House and Senate between the founding period and the passage of the Twenty-second Amendment, specifically in 1896, 1904, and 1906, but had never come to a floor vote. Beginning in 1975, in the spirit of post-Watergate reform, one proposal or another to limit the terms of senators and

A *Doonesbury* cartoon captures some of the skepticism that many experienced political observers felt about the term limits movement.

DOONESBURY © G. B. Trudeau. Reprinted with permission of UNIVERSAL PRESS SYNDICATE. All rights reserved.

representatives was introduced every year up until the House Republicans brought term limits to a floor vote in 1995. Popular for a while as well during the 1970s were proposals to limit the president to a single six-year term. None of these proposals, however, made it past the academic conferences and op-ed pages where they were most often discussed.

In early 1994 extensive polling by the Republican campaign apparatus had found a deep antipathy within public opinion toward what it perceived as a permanent political class entrenched on Capitol Hill. Subsequently, three hundred House Republican candidates, both challengers and incumbents, declared their intent to vote on congressional term limits during the first one hundred days of Congress. Fueling the anti-incumbent fever that had spread through all levels of American politics that year was an embarrassing check-bouncing scandal involving dozens of representatives' abuse of their in-house banking privileges. This focus on the special privileges afforded to members of Congress led to high-decibel campaign tirades against discount haircuts in the House barbershop, reserved airport parking, and other such stately perks of political office.

Rather than face the voters, forty-eight representatives resigned or retired. Several senators also declined to seek reelection rather than face similar political embarrassment. This rather comical sequence of charges and countercharges over member privileges combined with the more serious failure of the Clinton administration to pass a national health care reform plan earlier in the year to produce the first Republican majority in the House of Representatives since 1952. For the first time since the passage of the Seventeenth Amendment in 1913, every single newly elected senator was Republican. But the mood of 1994 was best summarized by the following note: Every incumbent Democratic representative, senator, and governor who ran in a contested election was defeated.

Even though the 1994 election returns seemed to suggest that public disgust was still the best available method to remove incumbents, grassroots activism for a formal mechanism to guard against an entrenched political class continued even after the Republican sweep of Congress. Between 1990 and 1994, when the Court upheld the constitutionality of state-imposed term limits for state-level offices, more than twenty states had passed laws to limit the terms of their elected officials. By 1995, when the Court handed down *U.S. Term Limits, Inc. v. Thornton,* 75 percent of the American public supported term limits for members of Congress. That support, moreover, was exceptionally broad based, with little variance among various demographic categories, including sex, age, race, and education.

The Court's decision in *Thornton,* however, derailed whatever slim hope congressional Republicans held for passing a federal term-limits provision. By declaring unconstitutional an Arkansas constitutional amendment limiting the number of times an incumbent's name could appear on the ballot, the Court left Congress with no choice but to enact a federal constitutional amendment. The Court, as it did in *Powell v. McCormack,* interpreted the Qualifications Clause of Article I to bar a simple legislative alteration of the stated constitutional requirements to run for Congress. If Congress wanted to limit the terms of federal lawmakers, then it would have to follow the path that led to the enactment of the Twenty-second Amendment in 1951. Four separate constitutional amendments to limit the terms of senators and representatives from six to twelve years fell substantially short when they came to the floor for a vote in 1995.

By that time, however, enthusiasm for term limits in Congress had begun to wane. Some of the enthusiastic new members who touted themselves as foot soldiers in the "Republican Revolution" had come to believe Madison's arguments in *Federalist* 53 that legislative experience had its advantages. "A few members," wrote Madison, "as it happens in all such assemblies, will possess superior talents; will, by frequent reelections, become members of long standing; will be thoroughly masters of public business, and perhaps, not unwilling to avail themselves of those advantages." Others no doubt had simply fallen sway to "Potomac fever," that mysterious pull of nautical forces that keeps more than 90 percent of incumbent members of Congress returning year after year. As Representative Bob Ingles (R–S.C.) summarized the transformed mood, getting Congress to move on term limits would be like asking chickens to get out the vote for Colonel Sanders.

By 1996, several firebrand challengers who had campaigned on term limits and against the Washington establishment two years before had begun to emphasize experience and professionalism in their reelection literature, suggesting that the complexities of American politics demanded wise, tested legislators to see the nation through its tough challenges. Perhaps then, even in the post-five-dollar-haircut and free-airport-parking era of Congress, the possibility exists that the former proponents of term limits had discovered a secret that their predecessors knew well: that there are far worse jobs out there than serving as a member of Congress.

## References

O'Connor, Karen and Larry J. Sabato. *American Government: Continuity and Change.* Boston: Allyn and Bacon, 1997.

Rakove, Jack N. *The Beginning of National Politics: An Interpretive History of the Continental Congress.* Boston: Allyn and Bacon, 1979.

not true that "the source of the qualification is of little moment in assessing the qualification's restrictive impact." There is a world of difference between a self-imposed constraint and a constraint imposed from above. . . .

It is radical enough for the majority to hold that the Constitution implicitly precludes the people of the States from prescribing any eligibility requirements for the congressional candidates who seek their votes. This holding, after all, does not stop with negating the term limits that many States have seen fit to impose on their Senators and Representatives. Today's decision also means that no State may disqualify congressional candidates whom a court has found to be mentally incompetent, or who have past vote-fraud convictions. Likewise, after today's decision, the people of each State must leave open the possibility that they will trust someone with their vote in Congress even though they do not trust him with a vote in the election for Congress. . . .

No matter how narrowly construed, however, today's decision reads the Qualifications Clauses to impose substantial implicit prohibitions on the States and the people of the States. I would not draw such an expansive negative inference from the fact that the Constitution requires Members of Congress to be a certain age, to be inhabitants of the States that they represent, and to have been United States citizens for a specified period. Rather, I would read the Qualifications Clauses to do no more than what they say. I respectfully dissent.

## *Gravel v. United States*
### 408 U.S. 606 (1972)

Mike Gravel, a Democratic senator from Alaska, was an outspoken opponent of the Vietnam War. He had been negotiating with several publishing companies for some time to publish the Pentagon Papers but decided to wait until the evening of June 29, 1971, to announce his intentions. Earlier in the day, the Supreme Court, in *New York Times* v. *United States,* had ruled that the Nixon administration could not enjoin the publication of the papers. Senator Gravel held an open meeting of his subcommittee, the committee on Buildings and Grounds; read from the papers; and then placed them into the public record. The press in attendance reported that Gravel had reached an agreement with Beacon Press, the publishing arm of the Unitarian Church, for the publication of the papers. A grand jury investigating the release of the Pentagon Papers subpoenaed Leonard Rodberg, an aide to Gravel who had helped the senator prepare the papers for publication. The United States claimed that the Speech or Debate Clause did not protect Gravel or Rodberg in their release of what was then classified information on the floor of the Senate and points beyond.

The lower courts ruled that congressional aides and other persons may not be questioned regarding legislative acts. That rule did not apply to the Beacon Press, however. What had protected Gravel and his aide under the Speech or Debate Clause was the understanding that a common-

law privilege similar to the privilege of protecting executive officials from liability for libel also prohibited questioning the aide concerning the publication of the Pentagon Papers.

The Court's decision was 5 to 4. Justice White delivered the opinion of the Court. Justices Douglas and Stewart each filed dissents. Justice Brennan, joined by Justice Marshall, also dissented.

Opinion of the Court by Mr. Justice White.

. . . [T]he claim [before us] is that a Member's aide shares the Member's constitutional privilege, [so] we consider first whether and to what extent Senator Gravel himself is exempt from process or inquiry by a grand jury investigating the commission of a crime. . . .

[The Speech or Debate] Clause provides Members of Congress with two distinct privileges. Except in cases of "Treason, Felony and Breach of the Peace," the Clause shields Members from arrest while attending or traveling to and from a session of their House. History reveals, and prior cases so hold, that this part of the Clause exempts Members from arrest in civil cases only. . . . Nor does freedom from arrest confer immunity on a Member from service of process as a defendant in civil matters, or as a witness in a criminal case. . . . It is, therefore, sufficiently plain that the constitutional freedom from arrest does not exempt Members of Congress from the operation of the ordinary criminal laws, even though imprisonment may prevent or interfere with the performance of their duties as Members. Indeed, implicit in the narrow scope of the privilege of freedom from arrest is, as Jefferson noted, the judgment that legislators ought not to stand above the law they create but ought generally to be bound by it as are ordinary persons.

In recognition, no doubt, [of this history] Senator Gravel disavows any assertion of general immunity from the criminal law. But he points out that the last portion of [the Clause] affords Members of Congress another vital privilege they may not be questioned in any other place for any speech or debate in either House. The claim is not that while one part of [the Clause] generally permits prosecutions for treason, felony, and breach of the peace, another part nevertheless broadly forbids them. Rather, his insistence is that the Speech or Debate Clause, at the very least, protects him from criminal or civil liability and from questioning elsewhere than in the Senate, with respect to the events occurring at the subcommittee hearing at which the Pentagon Papers were introduced into the public record. To us this claim is incontrovertible. The

Speech or Debate Clause was designed to assure a co-equal branch of the government wide freedom of speech, debate, and deliberation without intimidation or threats from the Executive Branch. It thus protects Members against prosecutions that directly impinge upon or threaten the legislative process. We have no doubt that Senator Gravel may not be made to answer either in terms of questions or in terms of defending himself from prosecution—for the events that occurred at the subcommittee meeting. Our decision is made easier by the fact that the United States appears to have abandoned whatever position it took to the contrary in the lower court.

Even so, the United States strongly urges that, because the Speech or Debate Clause confers a privilege only upon "Senators and Representatives," Rodberg himself has no valid claim to constitutional immunity from grand jury inquiry. In our view, both courts below correctly rejected this position. We agree that, for the purpose of construing the privilege a Member and his aide are to be "treated as one." Both courts recognized what the Senate of the United States urgently presses here: that it is literally impossible, in view of the complexities of the modern legislative process, with Congress almost constantly in session and matters of legislative concern constantly proliferating, for Members of Congress to perform their legislative tasks without the help of aides and assistants; that the day-to-day work of such aides is so critical to the Members' performance that they must be treated as the latter's alter egos; and that, if they are not so recognized, the central role of the Speech or Debate Clause—to prevent intimidation of legislators by the Executive and accountability before a possibly hostile judiciary—will inevitably be diminished and frustrated. . . .

The United States fears the abuses that history reveals have occurred when legislators are invested with the power to relieve others from the operation of otherwise valid civil and criminal laws. But these abuses, it seems to us, are for the most part obviated if the privilege applicable to the aide is viewed, as it must be, as the privilege of the Senator, and invocable only by the Senator or by the aide on the Senator's behalf, and if, in all events, the privilege available to the aide is confined to those services that would be immune legislative conduct if performed by the Senator himself. This view places beyond the Speech or Debate Clause a variety of services characteristically performed by aides for Members of Congress, even though within the scope of their employment. It likewise provides no protection for criminal conduct threatening the security of the person or property of others, whether performed at the direction of the Senator in preparation for or in execu-tion of a legislative act or done without his knowledge or direction. Neither does it immunize Senator or aide from testifying at trials or grand jury proceedings involving third-party crimes where the questions do not require testimony about or impugn a legislative act. Thus, our refusal to distinguish between Senator and aide in applying the Speech or Debate Clause does not mean that Rodberg is for all purposes exempt from grand jury questioning.

We are convinced also that the Court of Appeals correctly determined that Senator Gravel's alleged arrangement with Beacon Press to publish the Pentagon Papers was not protected speech or debate. . . .

Legislative acts are not all-encompassing. The heart of the Clause is speech or debate in either House. Insofar as the Clause is construed to reach other matters, they must be an integral part of the deliberative and communicative processes by which Members participate in committee and House proceedings with respect to the consideration and passage or rejection of proposed legislation or with respect to other matters which the Constitution places within the jurisdiction of either House. As the Court of Appeals put it, the courts have extended the privilege to matters beyond pure speech or debate in either House, but "only when necessary to prevent indirect impairment of such deliberations."

Here, private publication by Senator Gravel through the cooperation of Beacon Press was in no way essential to the deliberations of the Senate; nor does questioning as to private publication threaten the integrity or independence of the Senate by impermissibly exposing its deliberations to executive influence. The Senator had conducted his hearings; the record and any report that was forthcoming were available both to his committee and the Senate. Insofar as we are advised, neither Congress nor the full committee ordered or authorized the publications. We cannot but conclude that the Senator's arrangements with Beacon Press were not part and parcel of the legislative process.

There are additional considerations. . . . While the Speech or Debate Clause recognizes speech, voting, and other legislative acts as exempt from liability that might otherwise attach, it does not privilege either Senator or aide to violate an otherwise valid criminal law in preparing for or implementing legislative acts. If republication of these classified papers would be a crime under an Act of Congress, it would not be entitled to immunity under the Speech or Debate Clause. It also appears that the grand jury was pursuing this very subject in the normal course of a valid investigation. The Speech or Debate Clause does not, in our view, extend immunity to Rodberg, as a Senator's aide, from testifying before the grand jury about the arrangement between Senator Gravel and Beacon Press or about his own participation, if any, in the alleged transaction, so long as legislative acts of the Senator are not impugned. . . .

Because the Speech or Debate Clause privilege applies both to Senator and aide, it appears to us that paragraph one of the order, alone, would afford ample protection for the privilege if it forbade questioning any witness, including Rodberg: (1) concerning the Senator's conduct, or the conduct of his aides at the June 29, 1971, meeting of the subcommittee; (2) concerning the motives and purposes behind the Senator's conduct, or that of his aides, at that meeting; (3) concerning communications between the Senator and his aides during the term of their employment and related to said meeting or any other legislative act of the Senator; (4) except as it proves relevant to investigating possible third-party crime, concerning any act, in itself, not criminal, performed by the Senator, or by his aides in the course of their employment, in preparation for the subcommittee hearing. We leave the final form of such an order to the Court of Appeals in the first instance, or, if that court prefers, to the District Court.

Mr. Justice Douglas, dissenting.

I would construe the Speech or Debate Clause to insulate Senator Gravel and his aides from inquiry concerning the Pentagon Papers, and Beacon Press from inquiry concerning publication of them, for that publication was but another way of informing the public as to what had gone on in the privacy of the Executive Branch concerning the conception and pursuit of the so-called "war" in Vietnam. Alternatively, I would hold that Beacon Press is protected by the First Amendment from prosecution or investigations for publishing or undertaking to publish the Pentagon Papers. . . .

The secrecy of documents in the Executive Department has been a bone of contention between it and Congress from the beginning. Most discussions have centered on the scope of the executive privilege in stamping documents as "secret," "top secret," "confidential," and so on, thus withholding them from the eyes of Congress and the press. The practice has reached large proportions, it being estimated that

1. Over 30,000 people in the Executive Branch have the power to wield the classification stamp.
2. The Department of State, the Department of Defense, and the Atomic Energy Commission have over 20 million classified documents in their files.

3. Congress appropriates approximately $15 billion annually without most of its members or the public or the press knowing for what purposes the money is to be used. . . .

Classification of documents is a concern of the Congress. It is, however, no concern of the courts, as I see it, how a document is stamped in an Executive Department or whether a committee of Congress can obtain the use of it. The federal courts do not sit as an ombudsman refereeing the disputes between the other two branches. The federal courts do become vitally involved whenever their power is sought to be invoked either to protect the press against censorship as in *New York Times Co.* v. *United States* (1971), or to protect the press against punishment for publishing "secret" documents or to protect an individual against his disclosure of their contents for any of the purposes of the First Amendment.

Forcing the press to become the Government's coconspirator in maintaining state secrets is at war with the objectives of the First Amendment. That guarantee was designed in part to ensure a meaningful version of self-government by immersing the people in a "steady, robust, unimpeded, and uncensored flow of opinion and reporting which are continuously subjected to critique, rebuttal, and reexamination." As I have said . . . elsewhere, that Amendment is aimed at protecting not only speakers and writers but also listeners and readers. The essence of our form of governing was at the heart of Mr. Justice Black's reminder in the Pentagon Papers case that "[t]he press was protected so that it could bare the secrets of government and inform the people." Similarly, Senator Sam Ervin has observed: "When the people do not know what their government is doing, those who govern are not accountable for their actions—and accountability is basic to the democratic system. By using devices of secrecy, the government attains the power to "manage" the news, and, through it, to manipulate public opinion." Ramsey Clark, as Attorney General, expressed a similar sentiment: "If government is to be truly of, by, and for the people, the people must know in detail the activities of government. Nothing so diminishes democracy as secrecy."

Yet, as has been revealed by such exposes as the Pentagon Papers, the My Lai massacres, the Gulf of Tonkin "incident," and the Bay of Pigs invasion, the Government usually suppresses damaging news but highlights favorable news. In this filtering process, the secrecy stamp is the officials' tool of suppression, and it has been used to withhold information which in "99 1/2%" of the cases would present no danger to national security. To refuse to publish "classified" reports would at times relegate a publisher to distributing only the press releases of Government or remaining silent; if he printed only the press releases or "leaks," he would become an arm of officialdom, not its critic. Rather, in my view, when a publisher obtains a classified document, he should be free to print it without fear of retribution unless it contains material directly bearing on future, sensitive planning of the Government. By that test, Beacon Press could with impunity reproduce the Pentagon Papers inasmuch as their content "is all history, not future events. None of it is more recent than 1968." . . .

The story of the Pentagon Papers is a chronicle of suppression of vital decisions to protect the reputations and political hides of men who worked an amazingly successful scheme of deception on the American people. They were successful not because they were astute, but because the press had become a frightened, regimented, submissive instrument, fattening on favors from those in power and forgetting the great tradition of reporting. To allow the press further to be cowed by grand jury inquiries and prosecution is to carry the concept of "abridging" the press to frightening proportions.

What would be permissible if Beacon Press "stole" the Pentagon Papers is irrelevant to today's decision. What Beacon Press plans to publish is matter introduced into a public record by a Senator acting under the full protection of the Speech or Debate Clause. In light of the command of the First Amendment, we have no choice but to rule that here, government, not the press, is lawless. . . .

MR. JUSTICE BRENNAN, with whom MR. JUSTICE DOUGLAS and MR. JUSTICE MARSHALL join, dissenting.

. . . In holding that Senator Gravel's alleged arrangement with Beacon Press to publish the Pentagon Papers is not shielded from extra-senatorial inquiry by the Speech or Debate Clause, the Court adopts what for me is a far too narrow view of the legislative function. The Court seems to assume that words spoken in debate or written in congressional reports are protected by the Clause, so that, if Senator Gravel had recited part of the Pentagon Papers on the Senate floor or copied them into a Senate report, those acts could not be questioned "in any other Place." Yet because he sought a wider audience, to publicize information deemed relevant to matters pending before his own committee, the Senator suddenly loses his immunity and is exposed to grand jury investigation and possible prosecution for the republication. The explanation for this anomalous result is the Court's belief that "Speech or Debate" encompasses only acts necessary to the internal deliberations of Congress concerning proposed legislation. "Here," according to the Court, "private publication by Senator Gravel through the cooperation of Beacon Press was in no way essential to the deliberations of the Senate." Therefore, "the Senator's arrangements with Beacon Press were not part and parcel of the legislative process."

Thus, the Court excludes from the sphere of protected legislative activity a function that I had supposed lay at the heart of our democratic system. I speak, of course, of the legislator's duty to inform the public about matters affecting the administration of government. That this "informing function" fall into the class of thing "generally done in a session of the House by one of its members in relation to the business before it," *Kilbourn v. Thompson* (1881), was explicitly acknowledged by the Court in *Watkins v. United States* (1957). In speaking of the "power of the Congress to inquire into and publicize corruption, maladministration or inefficiency in agencies of the Government," the Court noted that, "[f]rom the earliest times in its history, the Congress has assiduously performed an 'informing function' of this nature." . . .

Whether the Speech or Debate Clause extends to the informing function is an issue whose importance goes beyond the fate of a single Senator or Congressman. What is at stake is the right of an elected representative to inform, and the public to be informed, about matters relating directly to the workings of our Government. The dialogue between Congress and people has been recognized, from the days of our founding, as one of the necessary elements of a representative system. We should not retreat from that view merely because, in the course of that dialogue, information may be revealed that is embarrassing to the other branches of government or violates their notions of necessary secrecy. A Member of Congress who exceeds the bounds of propriety in performing this official task may be called to answer by the other Members of his chamber. We do violence to the fundamental concepts of privilege, however, when we subject that same conduct to judicial scrutiny at the instance of the Executive. The threat of "prosecution by an unfriendly executive and conviction by a hostile judiciary," that the Clause was designed to avoid, can only lead to timidity in the performance of this vital function. The Nation as a whole benefits from the congressional investigation and exposure of official corruption and deceit. It likewise suffers when that exposure is replaced by muted criticism, carefully hushed behind congressional walls.

▼▲▼

# Hutchinson v. Proxmire
## 443 U.S. 111 (1979)

Dennis Hutchinson was a behavioral research scientist who received a grant from the federal government to investigate aggressive behavior in animals. Hutchinson ultimately sued Senator William Proxmire, a Wisconsin Democrat, for libel after the senator held up Hutchinson's research as an example of wasteful government spending. The lower courts rejected his libel argument.

The remainder of the facts and background of the case are set out in the opinion below.

The Court's decision was 7 to 2. Chief Justice Burger delivered the opinion of the Court. Justice Brennan filed a dissent. Justice Stewart filed a statement concurring in part and dissenting in part.

▼▲▼

MR. CHIEF JUSTICE BURGER delivered the opinion of the Court.

. . . [William] Proxmire is a United States Senator from Wisconsin. In March, 1975, he initiated the "Golden Fleece of the Month Award" to publicize what he perceived to be the most egregious examples of wasteful governmental spending. The second such award, in April, 1975, went to the National Science Foundation, the National Aeronautics and Space Administration, and the Office of Naval Research, for spending almost half a million dollars during the preceding seven years to fund Hutchinson's research. . . .

[As] Proxmire described the federal grants for Hutchinson's research:

> "The funding of this nonsense makes me almost angry enough to scream and kick or even clench my jaw. It seems to me it is outrageous."

> "Dr. Hutchinson's studies should make the taxpayers as well as his monkeys grind their teeth. In fact, the good doctor has made a fortune from his monkeys, and, in the process, made a monkey out of the American taxpayer."

> "It is time for the Federal Government to get out of this "monkey business." In view of the transparent worthlessness of Hutchinson's study of jaw-grinding and biting by angry or hard-drinking monkeys, it is time we put a stop to the bite Hutchinson and the bureaucrats who fund him have been taking of the taxpayer."

In May 1975, Proxmire referred to his Golden Fleece Awards in a newsletter sent to about 100,000 people whose names were on a mailing list that included constituents in Wisconsin as well as persons in other states. The newsletter repeated the essence of the speech and the press release. Later in 1975, Proxmire appeared on a television interview program where he referred to Hutchinson's research, though he did not mention Hutchinson by name.

The final reference to the research came in a newsletter in February, 1976. In that letter, Proxmire summarized his Golden Fleece Awards of 1975. The letter did not mention Hutchinson's name, but it did report:

> The NSF, the Space Agency, and the Office of Naval Research won the "Golden Fleece" for spending jointly $500,000 to determine why monkeys clench their jaws
>
> . . . .
>
> All the studies on why monkeys clench their jaws were dropped. No more monkey business.

The Speech or Debate Clause has been directly passed on by this Court relatively few times in 190 years. . . . Literal reading of the Clause would, of course, confine its protection narrowly to a "Speech or Debate in either House." But the Court has given the Clause a practical, rather than a strictly literal, reading which would limit the protection to utterances made within the four walls of either Chamber. Thus, we have held that committee hearings are protected, even if held outside the Chambers; committee reports are also protected. The gloss going beyond a strictly literal reading of the Clause has not, however, departed from the objective of protecting only legislative activities. . . .

Whatever imprecision there may be in the term "legislative activities," it is clear that nothing in history or in the explicit language of the Clause suggests any intention to create an absolute privilege from liability or suit for defamatory statements made outside the Chamber. . . .

Claims under the Clause going beyond what is needed to protect legislative independence are to be closely scrutinized. . . . Indeed, the precedents abundantly support the conclusion that a Member may be held liable for republishing defamatory statements originally made in either House. We perceive no basis for departing from that long-established rule.

MR. JUSTICE STORY, in his Commentaries, for example, explained that there was no immunity for republication of a speech first delivered in Congress:

> Therefore, although a speech delivered in the house of commons is privileged, and the member cannot be

questioned respecting it elsewhere, *yet, if he publishes his speech, and it contains libelous matter, he is liable to an action and prosecution therefor, as in common cases of libel.* And the same principles seem applicable to the privilege of debate and speech in congress. No man ought to have a right to defame others under colour of a performance of the duties of his office. And if he does so *in the actual discharge of his duties in congress, that furnishes no reason why he should be enabled, through the medium of the press, to destroy the reputation, and invade the repose of other citizens.* It is neither within the scope of his duty nor in furtherance of public rights or public policy. Every citizen has as good a right to be protected by the laws from malignant scandal, and false charges, and defamatory imputations, as a member of congress has to utter them in his seat. J. Story, *Commentaries on the Constitution* (1833). . . .

We reaffirmed that principle in *Doe* v. *McMillan* (1973):

A Member of Congress may not with impunity publish a libel from the speaker's stand in his home district, and clearly the Speech or Debate Clause would not protect such an act even though the libel was read from an official committee report. The reason is that republishing a libel under such circumstances is not an essential part of the legislative process, and is not part of that deliberative process "by which Members participate in committee and House proceedings."

We reach a similar conclusion here. A speech by Proxmire in the Senate would be wholly immune, and would be available to other Members of Congress and the public in the Congressional Record. But neither the newsletters nor the press release was "essential to the deliberations of the Senate," and neither was part of the deliberative process.

▼▲▼

## FOR FURTHER READING

Craig, Barbara Hinkson. *Chadha: The Story of an Epic Constitutional Struggle.* New York: Oxford University Press, 1988.

Fisher, Louis. *Constitutional Dialogues: Interpretation as a Political Process.* Princeton, N.J.: Princeton University Press, 1988.

Foner, Eric. *Reconstruction: America's Unfinished Revolution, 1863–1877.* New York: Harper & Row, 1988.

Franklin, John Hope. *Reconstruction after the Civil War.* Chicago: University of Chicago Press, 1994.

Garraty, John A., ed. *Quarrels That Have Shaped the Constitution.* New York: Harper & Row, 1987.

Garrow, David J. *Protest at Selma: Martin Luther King, Jr. and the Voting Rights Acts of 1965.* New Haven, Conn.: Yale University Press, 1978.

Goodman, Walter. *The Committee: The Extraordinary Career of the House Committee on Un-American Activities.* New York: Farrar, Straus & Giroux, 1968.

Hamilton, Charles V. *Adam Clayton Powell, Jr.: The Biography of an American Dilemma.* New York: Atheneum, 1991.

Korn, Jessica. *The Power of Separation: American Constitutionalism and the Myth of the Legislative Veto.* Princeton, N.J.: Princeton University Press, 1996.

Lublin, David. *The Paradox of Representation.* Princeton, N.J.: Princeton University Press, 1997.

Miller, John C. *The Federalist Era, 1789–1801.* New York: Harper & Row, 1960.

Navasky, Victor S. *Naming Names.* New York: Viking Press, 1980.

Paulson, Ross Evans. *Liberty, Equality and Justice: Civil Rights, Women's Rights, and the Regulation of Business, 1865–1932.* Durham, N.C.: Duke University Press, 1997.

Rovere, Richard H. *Senator Joe McCarthy.* New York: Harper Books, 1959.

Schrecker, Ellen W. *No Ivory Tower: McCarthyism and the Universities.* New York: Oxford University Press, 1986.

Schwartz, Bernard. *Super Chief: Earl Warren and His Supreme Court.* New York: New York University Press, 1983.

Smolla, Rodney A. *Free Speech in an Open Society.* New York: Alfred A. Knopf, 1992.

Sunstein, Cass. *After the Rights Revolution: Reconceiving the Regulatory State.* Cambridge, Mass.: Harvard University Press, 1990.

Thompson, Dennis. *Ethics in Congress.* Washington, D.C.: The Brookings Institution, 1995.

# 5 Executive Power

Contemplating the difficulties that his potential successor would have, President Harry S. Truman, speaking of General Dwight D. Eisenhower, would often remark to aides, "He'll sit here [tapping his Oval Office desk for emphasis], and he'll say, 'Do this! Do that!' *And nothing will happen.* Poor Ike—it won't be a bit like the Army. He'll find it very frustrating." Previously, President Truman had spoken of the continual problems he faced in trying to carry out the powers of his office: "I'll sit here all day trying to persuade people to the things they ought to have sense enough to do without my persuading them. . . . That's all the powers of the President amount to."[1]

The "power" to which President Truman referred was the power of persuasion. And the contradiction he offers is quite telling. After all, here was the president of the United States, the elected occupant of an office often described by presidential scholars and journalists as the most powerful in the world, unable to exercise the vast range of power assigned to him by the Constitution because of the political demands made from Congress, the bureaucracy, public opinion, foreign nations, and the news media. The dilemma of the president, as political scientist Richard E. Neustadt explained in his classic book, *Presidential Power,* was that "despite his status he does not get action without an argument." In other words, the formal powers of the executive provided by Article II are without substance if the president is unable to persuade the major constituencies in and beyond the government that their interests are mutual. Command was subordinate to persuasion in the exercise of presidential power.[2]

Even though Neustadt's focus was on the president's exercise of personal power, he did not discount the importance of the formal constitutional powers of the American presidency. Indeed, the president's need to acquire and maintain the power to persuade is essential to make the powers set out in Article II come alive in the service of the office. Occasionally, special, crisis-centered circumstances offer the president the opportunity to enforce the law of the land through command. More often than not, however, to exercise the formal powers of the office, the president is required to negotiate with Congress, cultivate public opinion, mobilize federal agencies, and win over partisan opposition. Personal power is the factor that transforms Article II from parchment promise to actual performance.

The need for the president to concentrate on the acquisition and effective use of personal power might not appear to be an especially brilliant or original insight into the nature of executive power. But *Presidential Power,* when it appeared in 1960, was nothing short of revolutionary. Up until then, scholarship on presidential power was confined to the interpretation and analysis of the constitutional delegation of power in Article II. Neustadt also emphasized another important fundamental principle of the American constitutional design: the notion that the Madisonian conception of the separation of powers rested on the assumption of shared powers. This principle, in turn, led to a more fluid, less partitioned relationship among the branches of government. With rare exception, the president cannot command the other branches with which he shares certain powers to take action.[3] This "realism" of the separation of powers relationship, combined with the emphasis on personal power, has left its imprint on a subsequent generation of presidential scholars.

Nonetheless, the most effective and persuasive of presidents cannot exercise their power independent of constitutional means. Theories on the nature of presidential power have their roots in the decision of the delegates to the Constitutional Convention to recast the executive branch from a weak, codependent institution to one that was singular, vested with substantive powers, and elected separately from Congress. Since Alexander Hamilton first issued his clarion call in *Federalist* 70 for an "energetic" executive, scholars have debated the exercise of presidential power in emergency situations and wartime, the president's role as diplomat in chief, and the balance of power that ought to exist between Congress and the president in foreign affairs. Part of the problem in interpreting the constitutional limits of presidential power derives from the different perceptions that scholars, elected officials, and the courts have assigned to the role of the executive branch in the American governmental process.[4] But our concern here is with the other dimension of presidential power: What do the broad, yet vague, grants of power in Article II mean for the actual exercise of executive power?

Unlike Article I, which spells out legislative power in near-exhaustive detail, Article II provides very few specific powers to the executive branch. Section 1 is devoted to electoral rules and procedures; qualification for office; compensation; and presidential succession in the event of removal, death, or resignation. Section 2 gives the president the sole power to pardon officials convicted of crimes against the United States and to appoint "Ambassadors, other public Ministers and Consuls, Judges of the Supreme Court, and all other Officers of the United States, whose Appointments are otherwise not provided for." Section 3 gives the president no specific power independent of or over the other branches, other than to "Commission all the Officers of the United States."

But the executive branch, and the president in particular, is much bigger and more powerful than these provisions suggest. Formal presidential power, much like similar assignments of legislative power exercised by Congress, derives from shared responsibilities with the other branches. The formal constitutional role of the executive branch in the legislative process is, as Chief Justice William H. Taft wrote in *Myers* v. *United States* (1926) "essentially a grant of the power to execute the laws." As a practical matter, the president's participation in the modern legislative arena extends far beyond the power to veto legislation, a power found in Article I, and to convene Congress for the purpose of assessing and providing information on the state of the Union.[5]

In the modern media age of instant, mass communication, the president now uses the State of the Union address to set the legislative agenda for the upcoming session of Congress. Or, as President Franklin D. Roosevelt, who is most often credited for recasting the position of the president in the legislative process, described it: "It is the duty of the President to propose and it is the privilege of the Congress to dispose."[6] Clearly, some presidents have been more successful than others in moving their legislative agenda through Congress, but none, since FDR, has shied away from the president's modern role of "legislator in chief."

Another example of shared legislative power between Congress and the executive branch is the qualified nature of the presidential veto. Hamilton, for one, wanted the president to have absolute veto power over Congress but found himself virtually alone in that view. His proposal at the Constitutional Convention for such a grant of power to the executive did not receive approval from a single state. But Hamilton prevailed on the larger question of whether the president should have a limited veto. James Madison, who believed that the president needed some form of veto power to protect the nation from bad laws, whether "through haste, inadvertence, or design," supported Hamilton. Wrote Hamilton in *Federalist* 73:

The propensity of the legislative department to intrude upon the rights, and to absorb the powers, of the other departments has been already more than once suggested . . . Without the [veto], the former would be absolutely unable to defend himself against the depredations of the latter. . . .

But the power in question has a further use. It not only serves as a shield to the executive, but it furnishes an additional security against the enaction of improper laws. It establishes a salutary check upon the legislative body, calculated to guard the community against the effects of faction, precipitancy, or of any impulse unfriendly to the public good, which may happen to influence a majority of that body.[7]

In the end, however, the qualified nature of the presidential veto buttresses another of feature of the Madisonian conception of separation of powers: Each branch must have a "partial agency" in the affairs of the other.[8] Article I authorizes Congress to invalidate an executive veto if two-thirds of each chamber vote to override the president's decision. The Framers' decision to allow each branch veto power over the other was simply a historical continuation of the general role the veto has placed in governmental administration, from the era of the Roman tribunes to the Articles of Confederation. This position on the veto amounted to a flat rejection of the Anti-Federalists' view that such power encroached upon the constitutional rights of the legislature.[9]

That the Framers viewed the veto as a vital instrument of good government is evident from its placement throughout the Constitution. Either through specific language or through judicial interpretation, the Constitution authorizes more than just the executive veto and provisions for its cancellation. Courts, through the power of judicial review, exercise veto power over the political branches. Congress still utilizes a "legislative veto" over executive branch implementation of legislative directives, even though the Court declared that type of veto unconstitutional in *INS* v. *Chadha* (1983), a decision the justices have chosen to all but ignore. Another powerful veto available to Congress is the power to overturn judicial decisions through constitutional amendment. Congress has used this mechanism just one time. The Fourteenth Amendment, ratified in 1868, invalidated the Court's notorious decision in *Dred Scott* v. *Sandford* (1857), which held that African Americans were not persons entitled to full citizenship under the Constitution.[10]

The executive branch has few specific powers and is constrained by the "shared responsibilities" that entail the exercise of power in the Madisonian design. So what explains the growth and development of presidential power? The rise of executive power has come through the efforts of presidents to trace their justification of certain actions to the broad provisions of Article II. In some ways the development of presidential power is similar to the Court's use of the general clauses of Article I, such as

the Necessary and Proper Clause, to expand congressional power. In fact, most of the seminal decisions involving the formal powers of the president have required the Court to define the three broad provisions of Article II.

Those provisions read: "The executive Power shall be vested in a President"; that "he shall take Care that the Law be faithfully executed"; and that "[t]he President shall be Commander in Chief of the Army and Navy of the United States. . . ." While there is nothing vague about who is authorized to act as commander in chief of the nation's armed forces, the Court has often defined the substance and scope of the president's power after confrontations with Congress, which has institutional interests of its own in the conduct of foreign policy and war. For the most part, the Court's interpretation of these three provisions of Article II are responsible for the evolution of presidential power.

Constitutional scholar Edward S. Corwin has summarized the dilemma created by the language of Article II quite well:

> Article II is the most loosely drawn chapter of the Constitution. To those who think that a constitution ought to settle everything beforehand, it should be a nightmare; by the same token, to those who think that constitution-makers ought to leave considerable leeway for the future play of political forces, it should be a vision realized.[11]

## Constitutional Theories of Presidential Power

Two main theories, the stewardship approach and the limited or traditional approach, have emerged to describe presidential power under Article II. These theories derive from two questions that should be familiar from our earlier discussions of judicial and legislative power, since each involves determining the relationship between the exercise of power and the intent and text of the Constitution. First, do the abstract provisions of Article II, coupled with the absence of specific constraints, endow the president with broad powers? Second, do the few express and affirmative clauses in Article II limit the power of the president to that which is described and defined in the constitutional text? The remainder of this section examines and compares these two theories of executive power.

## The Stewardship Theory

The notion that the Framers intended the executive to have power beyond that which is formally specified in the Constitution received its earliest and most articulate voicing from President Theodore Roosevelt (1901–1909), who believed that the office demanded an activist determined to provide leadership on important national issues. Roosevelt was among the leaders of the early-twentieth-century political movement known as Progressivism, which took aim at the economic and social conditions that had resulted from the Industrial Revolution and the unheeded consequences of laissez-faire capitalism. In contrast to his recent predecessors, Roosevelt did not believe the government's role was to clear the obstacles that stood in the path of the economic and political agenda of American corporations. Instead, Roosevelt viewed the presidency as a "bully pulpit" from which to encourage support for programs in the public interest and the national government as an instrument of positive reform.[12]

Roosevelt's clearest statement on executive power came after his retirement from public life, when, in his autobiography, he wrote that the president was not constrained by the powers and restrictions enumerated by the Constitution. If Congress, as the Court had found, has implied and inherent powers not specifically spelled out in the Constitution, the president should have such powers as well. Roosevelt described the nation's chief executive this way:

> [A] *steward* of the people bound actively and affirmatively to do all he could for the people and to content himself with the negative merit of keeping his talents undamaged in a napkin. My belief that it was not only his right but his duty to do anything that the needs of the nation demanded unless such action was forbidden by the Constitution or by the laws.[13]

President Woodrow Wilson (1913–1921), another vanguard leader of the Progressive movement, became an ardent supporter of the stewardship theory upon taking office. Wilson's embrace of presidential power is all the more interesting when we consider that he had championed legislative dominance in the separation of powers and minimized the role of the executive office

in his book, *Congressional Government*, which he wrote while a graduate student at Princeton during the 1880s.[14] Wilson believed the president's election by the nation and not a small, particular constituency made him the sole national political spokesman. As such, the president was obligated to discern and define the public interest. Whether to push for domestic reform or defend America's interests abroad or in war, Wilson believed that the president was fully authorized by Article II as the representative of "the whole people" to fuse the office with bold powers.[15]

Presidents prior to Roosevelt and Wilson summoned up the powers of the office when necessary to accomplish a national interest of the highest order. Jefferson's unilateral decision to go ahead with the Louisiana Purchase in 1803 and Abraham Lincoln's often unauthorized actions on behalf of the Union during the Civil War are perhaps the best early examples of presidents pushing the constitutional edge of executive power. Still, Roosevelt and Wilson were the first to engage their power on behalf of a sustained, activist agenda. Their vision of the president's role was notable more for the new expectations it placed on the office for political leadership than as a radical reconception of formal constitutional power. Constitutional transformation of the executive office would come with the election of Franklin D. Roosevelt (1933–1945), who is responsible for the birth and development of the modern presidency. No president before or since has tested the powers of the executive in domestic and foreign affairs with such success, whether in response to crisis or out of desire to improve existing conditions.[16]

Roosevelt's bold and unprecedented exercise of presidential power had its roots in the Framers' conception of the executive office. In *Federalist 70*, Hamilton dismissed the idea that a "vigorous executive [was] inconsistent with the genius of republican government:

> Energy in the executive is a leading character in the definition of good government. It is essential to the protection of the community against foreign attacks; it is not less essential to the steady administration of the laws; to the protection of property against those irregular and high-handed combinations which sometimes interrupt the ordinary course of justice; to the security of liberty against the

enterprises and assaults of ambition, of faction, and of anarchy. . . .

A feeble executive implies a feeble execution of the government. A feeble execution is but another phrase for a bad execution; and a government ill executed, whatever it may be in theory, must be, in practice, a bad government. . . .

The ingredients which constitute energy in the executive are unity, duration, an adequate provision for its support; and competent powers.

The ingredients which constitute safety in the republican sense are a due dependence on the people, and a due responsibility.[17]

Many American government textbooks (and constitutional law casebooks) begin their discussion of the executive branch by commenting on how surprised the Framers would be at the power wielded by modern presidents. But wouldn't almost every aspect of the structure and practice of modern American government surprise the Framers? A more accurate assessment of the Framers' response to the growth of the executive office and the exercise of presidential power is that we cannot be quite sure what they would think. Not every Framer was as enamored with the strong presidency as Hamilton was or as hostile to its need for strength and independence to guard "against an authoritarian leader in the style of Napoleon."[18]

Moreover, John Locke, a leading Enlightenment-era philosopher whose ideas are found throughout the Declaration of Independence and the Constitution, heavily influenced the Framers' conception of presidential power. Drawn to Montesquieu's separation of powers argument as the foundation for liberal, democratic government, Locke believed the executive, as the national political figure, possessed the "prerogative" to take action beyond the enumerated confines of constitutional power. Locke, whose vision was never truly realized until Franklin Roosevelt asserted that extraordinary times demand extraordinary measures by the president, wrote: "The strict obedience of the law by the executive may at times be harmful to the community and therefore there should be reserved to the executive the power to act according to discretion, for the public good, without the prescription of the law and sometimes even against it."[19]

## The Limited or Traditional Theory

Some presidents have found themselves under the microscope of congressional inquiries, special prosecutors, and public opinion for their efforts, in President John F. Kennedy's words, to "exercise the fullest powers of [the] office—all that are specified and some that are not."[20] Nonetheless, the stewardship theory of presidential leadership is now the foundation for the exercise of presidential power, as no president since Franklin D. Roosevelt has questioned the underlying assumptions of this approach. The presidency's development in the twentieth century has eclipsed what political scientist Richard Rose has called the "traditional" conception of the office, one that was clearly considered inferior to Congress in both power and prestige.[21]

The traditional presidency lasted as long as it did "because there was very little that the White House needed or was expected to do; the prevailing doctrine was the best government governed least." Even Lincoln, considered the most exceptional of the nation's presidents prior to Franklin Roosevelt for his exercise of executive power during the Civil War, still respected the doctrines of the traditional presidency. Until Roosevelt and Wilson challenged the traditional presidency, the office did not attract individuals of great consequence because there was so little for the president to do.[22] After a shattered and demoralized Wilson left the presidency in 1921 and before Roosevelt took office in 1933, Warren Harding, Calvin Coolidge, and Herbert Hoover served as president, none of whom were as popular—or as well-paid—as Al Capone, Babe Ruth, or Louis Armstrong.

The theory of the traditional presidency is based on an interpretation of Article II that is limited and formal in approach. William H. Taft, the only person ever to serve as both president (1909–1913) and chief justice of the United States Supreme Court (1921–1930), provides the most articulate and famous expression of this approach to executive power. In 1916, Taft wrote:

The true view of the Executive function is, as I conceive it, that the President can exercise no power which cannot be fairly and reasonably traced to some specific grant of power or justly implied and included within such express grant as proper and necessary to its exercise. Such specific grant must be either in the Federal Constitution or in an act of Congress passed in pursuance thereof. There is no undefined residium of power which he can exercise because it seems to him to be in the public interest.[23]

Indeed, the title of Taft's book on the presidency, *Our Chief Magistrate and His Powers,* suggests that he did not view the office as one that commanded prestige and power on a plane equal to Congress. Perhaps Taft's ultimate opinion of the presidency rests with his decision to serve on the Court *after* having held the office. Can you imagine any president from the contemporary era serving in *any* elected or appointed capacity upon leaving office, much less one that depends on the approval of the political branches of government? Each era brings with it a new set of expectations.

Few presidential or constitutional scholars any longer subscribe to or endorse the limited theory of executive power. Only when presidents, in the eyes of Congress and public opinion, have careened out of control to assume "imperial" powers that bear no relationship to the public interest has the modern conception of executive power been challenged. Examples of such behavior include President Truman's ill-fated attempt to seize control of the nation's steel mills during the Korean War, the escalation of the undeclared war in Vietnam by Presidents Kennedy and Johnson, and President Nixon's actions leading up to the Watergate scandal. These episodes all drew legislative responses from Congress, which, encouraged by the public, attempted to devise proper restraints to control a presidency it viewed as out of control. In each case disagreement between Congress and the president over the proper boundaries of executive power resulted in decisions of great historical import from the Court.

Political scientists Joseph Bessette and Jeffrey Tulis have suggested that presidential power is most suited to "a constitutional arrangement that allows for a substantial degree of executive initiative and discretion within a framework of political checks." Such an arrangement "is more effective and less dangerous than a set of arrangements that so constrains and restricts the executive power that it renders it incapable of carrying out its proper tasks." This approach reduces the likelihood that the president will need "to set aside the Constitution to do what the good of the community requires."[24] How

the Court has sought to balance the interests of the executive office in the constitutional order in both domestic and foreign affairs is the focus of the remainder of this chapter.

## The President as Chief Executive

The president derives power and status as the chief executive of the United States from Article II, specifically the provisions that vest "the executive power . . . in a President" and require the president to "take Care that the Laws be faithfully executed." Our discussion of the theories of presidential power makes clear that the broad language of Article II is open to interpretation. The Court has left no doubt that Article II confers broad administrative and enforcement power on the president to carry out the executive function of the office. That is, the president is more than just the titular head of state. As you will see, the Court has ruled that some of that power derives from the sweeping grants of power from Article II. In other cases, the Court has contributed to the expansion of presidential power by upholding congressional laws that delegate quasi-legislative responsibilities to the executive branch.

The rise of the administrative welfare state and the emergence of the United States as an international military and economic superpower in the twentieth century have resulted in an expansive, institutionalized executive branch. This development has led to conflicts between the president and Congress over the power to appoint and remove federal officers who carry out the law-enforcement responsibilities of the executive branch. Presidents since Franklin Roosevelt have argued that the appropriate presidential response to problems of great domestic and international magnitude requires a broad interpretation of the discretion afforded the executive under the Execution Clause.

Although no president until Theodore Roosevelt challenged the traditional approach to presidential power under the Constitution, the Court first recognized a broad right to enforce the interests and responsibilities of the executive office that extended beyond the letter of the law in *In re Neagle* (1890). In *Neagle* the Court was asked to decide whether the "inherent" power of the president as chief executive authorized him to appoint, in the absence of a congressional statute, a federal marshal to protect a sitting federal judge. The facts were indeed peculiar. Federal marshal David Neagle had killed former California supreme court judge David S. Terry after Terry had threatened his former colleague and now United States Supreme Court Justice Stephen Field with death. The Court, 7-2, ruled that the president's power to faithfully execute the law was not limited to the enforcement of federal statutes and international treaties. Rather, it grew out of the "rights, duties and obligations . . . of the Constitution itself . . . and all the protection implied by the nature of government under the Constitution."[25]

*Neagle* established a constitutional baseline for the broad exercise of presidential power. By ruling that such power was inherent in the very nature of the Framers' design for the executive office, the Court endorsed the view that a president without power to enforce the law cannot perform the function assigned to the office as the chief executive of the United States. It is critical, the Court ruled, to vest the president with the power to deal adequately with problems that come within the orbit of the national interest. Presidents have subsequently relied upon the broad discretion granted by *Neagle* to assert the power of the executive branch on behalf of the general public interest and also in times of crisis. But executive discretion has its limits, whether in the service of the spectacular or the mundane, as the Court has ruled on several occasions since *Neagle*.

## The Power of Appointment and Removal

"To the victor go the spoils" is a phrase often used to describe the power of elected officials to staff their administration with the personnel of their choice through the power of appointment and removal. However sweeping the power of political patronage may be for America's governors, mayors, and county commissioners, it does not extend to the president's power to appoint executive branch officials. Indeed, the power of the president to name executive branch officials without Senate confirmation is very limited. It is only one of four methods of the appointment power specified by Article II, Section 2. This provision authorizes the president to:

[N]ominate, and by, and with the Advice and Consent of the Senate . . . appoint Ambassadors, other public Minis-

ters and Consuls, Judges of the supreme Court, and all other Officers of the United States, whose Appointments are not herein otherwise provided for, and which shall be established by Law; but the Congress may by Law vest the Appointment of such inferior Officers, as they think proper, in the Presidents alone, in the Courts of Law, or in the Heads of Departments.

In addition to patronage appointments, the Appointments Clause permits the president to make appointments with Senate approval. Congress, however, retains the power to authorize the other two methods of appointment—by courts of law or by the heads of executive departments. Congress is also permitted to create specific requirements for the offices that it creates. These include, but are not limited to, citizenship, age, residence, professional qualification, and political affiliation. Moreover, the Civil Service Act of 1883 restricts the patronage power of the president to the highest grades of the federal agencies within executive branch authority, or about 10 percent of the federal bureaucracy.[26]

For the most part, constitutional controversies over presidential appointment power have been few and far between. Although the Court, in *Marbury* v. *Madison* (1803), held that the power to appoint executive officials resides solely with the president, the exercise of this power has evolved through a combination of informal custom, constitutional mandates, and laws passed by Congress. As a result, the Senate has developed a large degree of informal power to suggest nominees to the president to serve in federal district courts, the U.S. attorney's office, and other executive branch offices located in the states of respective members. Failure of the president to respect this arrangement, better known as "senatorial courtesy," can often mean rejection of nominees to serve as cabinet secretaries, federal commissioners, and Supreme Court justices. Ideological and political subterfuge—not concerns over the encroachment of constitutional power—have largely driven conflict between Congress and the president over the appointment process.[27]

On occasion, however, partisan politics have combined with serious and unresolved constitutional issues of power and authority between Congress and the president to produce hurricane force winds of great moment. For both its impact on American politics and the constitutional law of separation of powers, few cases in the modern era rival *Morrison v. Olson* (1988). This case brought to its head the long-simmering dispute over the Ethics in Government Act of 1978, the federal statute that created the office of the independent counsel.[28]

Of the congressional motive behind the law's passage, political scientist Katy J. Harriger has noted that it was "firmly rooted in the Watergate experience. Special prosecutors had been employed in the Teapot Dome scandal, but it was the central role played by the Watergate Special Prosecution Force in the resolution of that scandal that laid the groundwork for the creation of the [new] statutory arrangement."[29] If any one event in particular persuaded Congress that reform of the federal special prosecutor's role was necessary, it was President Richard Nixon's decision to fire Watergate special prosecutor Archibald Cox, renowned constitutional scholar and a former solicitor general (1961–1965). Under heavy congressional pressure, Nixon had appointed Cox to investigate the Watergate scandal. Cox's firing offense was his demand for access to presidential tapes and other confidential White House documents. His dismissal culminated in one the darkest moments in the Watergate crisis. Less than twenty-four hours earlier, Attorney General Elliot Richardson and Deputy Attorney General William Ruckelshaus had resigned rather than carry out President Nixon's order to fire Cox.

The "Saturday Night Massacre," so named because Cox was fired on Saturday, October 20, 1973, was etched in the memories of the reform-minded and overwhelmingly liberal Democratic class of representatives elected to Congress in 1974. Determined to reassert legislative dominance in the American political process and institute controls on the "imperial presidency," Congress passed the Ethics in Government Act to correct the deficiencies of the Watergate model. The law made the special prosecutor independent of the executive branch it was appointed to investigate. The law also required the attorney general to conduct an initial investigation into the allegation of criminal activity by a high-ranking executive branch official. If the attorney general's office concluded that further investigation or prosecution was appropriate, it was required to file a report with the D.C. circuit court of appeals requesting the appointment of a special prosecutor. The statute then required a special division of the court, consisting of three senior or retired judges, to appoint a special prosecutor and define the scope of the investigation. Balance with the executive branch was sought by allowing the attorney general to remove a special prosecutor for "extraordinary impropriety."

With the exception of a two-year period between 1992 and 1994, when the Republican-controlled Congress refused to renew the original law because of what it perceived as abusive behavior by the independent counsel's office in its prosecution of the Reagan and Bush administrations over the Iran-Contra scandal, the law remained in effect until 1999. In June of that year, Congress, after extensive hearings, decided not to reauthorize the 1978 law. That decision stemmed largely from the negative public reaction to Independent Counsel Kenneth Starr's high-profile investigation of President Bill Clinton's extramarital affair with former White House intern Monica Lewinsky. Starr claimed that Clinton had not only encouraged Lewinsky to lie about their affair to federal prosecutors but also lied himself in a deposition he gave in the Paula Jones sexual harassment case, which we discuss later in this chapter. Starr's team of lawyers and investigators spent four years and more than $50 million investigating President Clinton. The investigation began in 1994, when Starr was appointed to investigate whether the president and his wife, Hillary Rodham Clinton, violated federal laws when they invested in a failed Arkansas land deal, better known as Whitewater, during the 1980s. Starr's investigation ultimately turned up nothing on the Whitewater charges; his investigation of the president's affair with Lewinsky ultimately led to Clinton's impeachment in December 1998. The Senate, after a month-long trial in January 1999, acquitted Clinton of all the impeachment charges recommended by Starr and approved by the House of Representatives.

Ironically, Clinton the presidential candidate had pledged to seek renewal of the special prosecutor law. As president, he encouraged Congress to reauthorize the law and, in 1994, signed the Independent Counsel Act. By the end of the Clinton administration, the Office of the Independent Counsel had spent more than $100 million and conducted dozens of separate investigations on alleged executive branch criminal misconduct that extended to several cabinet members and White House appointees.

*"Sorry we're late, but Kenneth Starr subpoenaed our regular babysitter."*

© The New Yorker Collection 1998 Danny Shanahan from cartoonbank.com. All Right Reserved.

Shortly before the act was allowed to expire in June 1999, legal scholar Cass Sunstein criticized the Independent Counsel Act as one of the most "ill conceived pieces of legislation" in the post–Watergate era. The law provided the special prosecutor with great and unchecked discretionary power, left the executive branch with no effective means of defense, and encouraged wasteful tax expenditures on investigations of little or no significant consequence. Special prosecutors, under pressure to produce results, tend to expand the scope of their inquiries into areas previously thought irrelevant to the original charges, since ending their investigation without a successful criminal conviction or plea will brand them a failure. Sunstein also suggested that the law encouraged the news media to devote a disproportionate amount of time to the alleged travails of a high-level public official while neglecting important policy questions. From late 1978 to late 1997, the *New York Times* and *Washington Post* devoted 3 stories on executive branch investigations during the one-term Carter presidency; 275 over the two-term Reagan presidency; 63 during the one-term Bush presidency; 220 during President Clinton's first term; and 100 through November 1997 of his second term.[30]

What was once a permanent state of investigation by federal special prosecutors of alleged executive branch improprieties was made possible by the Court's decision in *Morrison* upholding the 1978 independent counsel law. Against the lone dissent of Justice Antonin Scalia, the Court found that the institutional arrangement created by the Ethics in Government Act did not violate the Appointments Clause of Article II. Crucial in Chief Justice Rehnquist's opinion was whether the special prosecutor was properly defined as an "inferior" or "principal" officer under the Appointments Clause. Remember, Congress has the power to appoint "inferior" officials free from executive approval, whereas the power to appoint "principal" officers rests with the president. Do you believe that the chief justice makes a persuasive case on this point?

Justice Scalia's dissent questioning the constitutional and political fitness of the law assumed a central position in the debate over whether to renew the Independent Counsel Act. Writing that the Court's decision to uphold the law was no less than an act of "constitutional revolution," Justice Scalia warned that *Morrison* had dire political consequences as well:

> The institutional design of the Independent Counsel is designed to heighten, not to check, all of the institutional hazards of the dedicated prosecutor; the danger of too narrow a focus, of the loss of perspective, of preoccupation with the pursuit of one alleged suspect to the exclusion of other interests.

Compare the arguments on both the constitutionality and political desirability of the Independent Counsel Act with Justice Scalia's dissent in *Morrison*. Do you believe that *Morrison* is, as one former Court law clerk involved with the case has claimed, "one of the most important cases in all of constitutional jurisprudence [because] [i]t says that none of the three branches can ever again claim to be the absolute arbiter of anything"? Consider as well how *Morrison* fits into the court's current architecture of separation of powers law, with *Chadha*, *Mistretta*, and *Bowsher* as the context for your thinking.

As controversial as *Morrison* remains, the most contested provision of the Appointments Clause has been the power of the president to *remove* executive branch officials. Unlike presidential appointment power, the Constitution is silent on the right on the removal of *all* public officials, except those subject to impeachment and subsequent dismissal. Hamilton argued in *Federalist* 77 that the Senate would possess ample restraints over the potential abuse of presidential appointment *and* removal power, writing that its consent "would be necessary to displace as well as to appoint."[31]

In 1789 the First Congress rejected Hamilton's view when it created the Departments of Foreign Affairs (now State), War (now Defense), and Treasury to serve under President George Washington. This innovation came, ironically, at the behest of Hamilton's *Federalist Papers* coauthor, James Madison. In introducing the proposal for these cabinet agencies, Representative Madison suggested that the president have sole removal power over Foreign Affairs and War, with Senate confirmation required for the removal of the Treasury comptroller. After a complex series of legislative maneuvers that required Vice President John Adams to break a deadlocked Senate, President Washington signed legislation giving the president the uncontested power to remove the heads of all three executive departments.[32]

Although the question of presidential control over the removal power arose briefly during the administration of Andrew Jackson (1829–1837), Congress kept to its unspoken arrangement with the executive branch permitting the president to exercise such power without restraint. The president's removal power did not face a serious challenge until 1867, when Congress passed the Tenure in Office Act, which subjected the removal of any executive branch department head to Senate approval. The law's passage was a measure of spite aimed at President Andrew Johnson (1865–1869) by pro-Reconstruction, Radical Republicans in Congress, who wanted to protect President Lincoln's cabinet from removal by his more conservative successor. President Johnson's willingness to flout the 1867 law was, in fact, one of the charges in his impeachment, for which he was ultimately acquitted. After Johnson left office, Congress modified the law to return removal power to the president. In 1887, Congress repealed the Tenure in Office Act.[33]

The question of the president's power to remove executive branch officers finally reached the Court in 1926. In *Myers v. United States* (1926), the Court declared unconstitutional an 1876 congressional law that required the Senate to approve all first-, second-, and third-class postmasters removed by the president.[34] The case stemmed from President Wilson's decision to remove Frank Myers without Senate approval from his position as a first-class postmaster after his term expired. Wilson intended to replace Myers with another patronage appointment, a condition that had been the basis for Myers's original appointment. But what appeared to be a minor scuffle between the president and an insignificant federal bureaucrat produced a Supreme Court decision of great importance for the exercise of this crucial aspect of executive power. Of even greater historical irony is that Chief Justice Taft wrote the Court's 6-3 opinion, which placed the removal power solely with the president. Recall that Taft, while president, had advanced one the earliest and most articulate pleas on behalf of limited executive power in the constitutional order.

In *Myers*, Chief Justice Taft wrote one of the longest and most elaborate opinions in the Court's history. In the opinion he offers a comprehensive analysis of the legislative history of the First Congress's decision to vest the president with the sole removal power. Taft also included a discussion of the partisan basis for the aberrational Tenure in Office Act of 1867 and a lesson in constitutional formalism with his interpretation of the language of Article II, which he argued gave the president unrestricted power over the executive function. Does Chief Justice Taft make a persuasive case that the president has unlimited power to exercise the limited grants of authority created by Article II? Is Justice Brandeis, who dissented, correct in saying that for Congress to create an office and an officer to fill it, but to retain no removal power, did not make much sense? Note also in *Myers* the disagreement between Chief Justice Taft and Justice Brandeis over who and what constitutes "inferior" and "principal" executive branch officials, a point of disagreement that assumed center stage in *Morrison*.

But in *Humphrey's Executor v. United States* (1935), the Court, taking a giant step back from the sweeping rhetoric and holding in *Myers*, ruled that unqualified presidential removal power did not extend to those offices that were "quasi-legislative" or "quasi-judicial" in origin.[35] The Roosevelt administration argued that *Myers* gave the president complete control over the removal of executive officers. That view did not prevail. A unanimous Court, in fact, went out of its way to mark the lines between those officials over whom the president has complete control and those within the power of Congress to restrict. *Humphrey* continues as good law today. Do you believe that *Myers* and *Humphrey* are irreconcilable because they offer different opinions of the same question, or that each offers a plausible explanation of the president's power to remove public officers who fall into different categories of constitutional definition?

## Morrison v. Olson
### 487 U.S. 654 (1988)

In 1986, Alexia Morrison, a special prosecutor in the Office of the Independent Counsel, was assigned to investigate a Justice Department official, Theodore Olson, an assistant attorney general in the Land and Natural Resources Division of the Justice Department. Two house subcommittees had begun investigating whether the division and the Environmental Protection Agency had purposely withheld documents that the subcommittees had requested. Olson refused to cooperate on the grounds that the Ethics in Government Act of 1978 violated the separation of powers doctrine. Olson's decision received the full support of the Department of Justice, whose political appointees reflected the conservative philosophy of the Reagan administration. Many in the administration believed that Democrats were using the special prosecutor provision to paint a criminal stamp on activities of executive branch officials that were fundamentally political in nature.

By the time Morrison was appointed to prosecute Olson, several other parallel investigations were taking place against high-level Reagan administration officials. The most visible investigations were the Iran-Contra affair, which involved allegations of illegal arms sales to foreign countries by White House and military officials, and the Wedtech scandal, in which Attorney General Edwin Meese was accused of making special financial arrangements for a defense contractor. Such were the politics of these scandals that if either came to trial the administration would certainly lose, so key Reagan officials nixed the idea of using either investigation to challenge the constitutionality of the independent counsel. Any challenge to the law, Reagan officials knew, would just look like a way to protect the criminal misdeeds of the administration. Using a fairly low-visibility case on the political radar screen to test the law suggested purer motives.

A trial court upheld the law, but the D.C. circuit court of appeals reversed.

The Court's decision was 7 to 1. Chief Justice Rehnquist delivered the opinion of the Court. Justice Scalia, who served on the D.C. appeals court until 1986, filed a dissenting opinion. Justice Kennedy, who had just joined the Court, did not participate.

▼▲▼

CHIEF JUSTICE REHNQUIST delivered the opinion of the Court.

. . . The parties do not dispute that "[t]he Constitution for purposes of appointment . . . divides all its officers into two classes." As we stated in *Buckley* v. *Valeo* (1976): "Principal officers are selected by the President with the advice and consent of the Senate. Inferior officers Congress may allow to be appointed by the President alone, by the heads of departments, or by the Judiciary." The initial question is, accordingly, whether appellant is an "inferior" or a "principal" officer. If she is the latter, as the Court of Appeals concluded, then the Act is in violation of the Appointments Clause.

The line between "inferior" and "principal" officers is one that is far from clear, and the Framers provided little guidance into where it should be drawn. . . . We need not attempt here to decide exactly where the line falls between the two types of officers, because, in our view, appellant clearly falls on the "inferior officer" side of that line. Several factors lead to this conclusion.

First, [Morrison] is subject to removal by a higher Executive Branch official. . . . Second, [Morrison] is empowered by the Act to perform only certain, limited duties. An independent counsel's role is restricted primarily to investigation and, if appropriate, prosecution for certain federal crimes. . . . Third, appellant's office is limited in jurisdiction. Not only is the Act itself restricted in applicability to certain federal officials suspected of certain serious federal crimes, but an independent counsel can only act within the scope of the jurisdiction that has been granted by the Special Division pursuant to a request by the Attorney General. Finally, appellant's office is limited in tenure. There is concededly no time limit on the appointment of a particular counsel. Nonetheless, the office of independent counsel is "temporary" in the sense that an independent counsel is appointed essentially to accomplish a single task, and when that task is over, the office is terminated, either by the counsel herself or by action of the Special Division. Unlike other prosecutors, appellant has no ongoing responsibilities that extend beyond the accomplishment of the mission that she was appointed for and authorized by the Special Division to undertake. In our view, these factors relating to the "ideas of tenure, duration . . . and duties" of the independent counsel, are sufficient to establish that appellant is an "inferior" officer in the constitutional sense. . . .

This does not, however, end our inquiry under the Appointments Clause. Appellees argue that, even if appellant is an "inferior" officer, the Clause does not empower Congress to place the power to appoint such an officer outside the Executive Branch. They contend that the Clause does not contemplate congressional authorization of "interbranch appointments," in which an officer of one branch is appointed by officers of another branch. The relevant language of the Appointments Clause is worth repeating. It reads: ". . . but the Congress may by Law vest the Appointment of such inferior Officers, as they think proper, in the President alone, in the courts of Law, or in the Heads of Departments." On its face, the language of this "excepting clause" admits of no limitation on interbranch appointments. Indeed, the inclusion of "as they think proper" seems clearly to give Congress significant discretion to determine whether it is "proper" to vest the appointment of, for example, executive officials in the "courts of Law." . . .

We do not mean to say that Congress' power to provide for interbranch appointments of "inferior officers" is unlimited. In addition to separation of powers concerns, which would arise if such provisions for appointment had the potential to impair the constitutional functions assigned to one of the branches. . . . Congress' decision to vest the appointment power in the courts would be improper if there was some "incongruity" between the functions normally performed by the courts and the performance of their duty to appoint. . . . Congress of course was concerned when it created the office of independent counsel with the conflicts of interest that could arise in situations when the Executive Branch is called upon to investigate its own high-ranking officers. If it were to remove the appointing authority from the Executive Branch, the most logical place to put it was in the Judicial Branch. In the light of the Act's provision making the judges of the Special Division ineligible to participate in any matters relating to an independent counsel they have appointed, we do not think that appointment of the independent counsel by the court runs afoul of the constitutional limitation on "incongruous" interbranch appointments.

Appellees next contend that the powers vested in the Special Division by the Act conflict with Article III of the Constitution. We have long recognized that by the express provision of Article III, the judicial power of the United States is limited to "Cases" and "Controversies." . . . With this in mind, we address in turn the various duties given to the Special Division by the Act.

Most importantly, the Act vests in the Special Division the power to choose who will serve as independent counsel and the power to define his or her jurisdiction. Clearly, once it is accepted that the Appointments Clause gives Congress the power to vest the appointment of officials such as the independent counsel in the "courts of Law," there can be no Article III objection to the Special Division's exercise of that power, as the power itself derives from the Appointments Clause, a source of authority for judicial action that is independent of Article III. Appellees contend, however, that the Division's Appointments Clause powers do not encompass the power to define the independent counsel's jurisdiction. We disagree. In our view, Congress' power under the Clause to vest the "Appointment" of inferior officers in the courts may, in certain circumstances, allow Congress to give the courts some discretion in defining the nature and scope of the appointed official's authority. Particularly when, as here, Congress creates a temporary "office" the nature and duties of which will by necessity vary with the factual circumstances giving rise to the need for an appointment in the first place, it may vest the power to define the scope of the office in the court as an incident to the appointment of the officer pursuant to the Appointments Clause. This said, we do not think that Congress may give the Division unlimited discretion to determine the independent counsel's jurisdiction. In order for the Division's definition of the counsel's jurisdiction to be truly "incidental" to its power to appoint, the jurisdiction that the court decides upon must be demonstrably related to the factual circumstances that gave rise to the Attorney General's investigation and request for the appointment of the independent counsel in the particular case. . . .

We now turn to consider whether the Act is invalid under the constitutional principle of separation of powers. Two related issues must be addressed: the first is whether the provision of the Act restricting the Attorney General's power to remove the independent counsel to only those instances in which he can show "good cause," taken by itself, impermissibly interferes with the President's exercise of his constitutionally appointed functions. The second is whether, taken as a whole, the Act violates the separation of powers by reducing the President's ability to control the prosecutorial powers wielded by the independent counsel.

Two Terms ago, we had occasion to consider whether it was consistent with the separation of powers for Congress to pass a statute that authorized a Government official who is removable only by Congress to participate in what we found to be "executive powers." *Bowsher* v. *Synar* (1986). We held in *Bowsher* that "Congress cannot reserve for itself the power of removal of an officer charged with the execution of the laws except by impeachment." A primary antecedent for this ruling was our 1926 decision in *Myers* v. *United States* (1926). *Myers* had considered the propriety of a federal statute by which certain postmasters of the United States could be removed by the President only "by and with the advice and consent of the Senate." There too, Congress' attempt to involve itself in the removal of an executive official was found to be sufficient grounds to render the statute invalid. As we observed in *Bowsher*, the essence of the decision in *Myers* was the judgment that the Constitution prevents Congress from, "draw[ing] to itself . . . the power to remove or the right to participate in the exercise of that power. To do this would be to go beyond the words and implications of the [Appointments Clause] and to infringe the constitutional principle of the separation of governmental powers."

Unlike both *Bowsher* and *Myers*, this case does not involve an attempt by Congress itself to gain a role in the removal of executive officials other than its established powers of impeachment and conviction. The Act instead puts the removal power squarely in the hands of the Executive Branch; an independent counsel may be removed from office, "only by the personal action of the Attorney General, and only for good cause." There is no requirement of congressional approval of the Attorney General's removal decision, though the decision is subject to judicial review. In our view, the removal provisions of the Act make this case more analogous to *Humphrey's Executor* v. *United States* (1935), than to *Myers* or *Bowsher*. . . .

Considering for the moment the "good cause" removal provision in isolation from the other parts of the Act at issue in this case, we cannot say that the imposition of a "good cause" standard for removal by itself unduly trammels on executive authority. There is no real dispute that the functions performed by the independent counsel are "executive" in the sense that they are law enforcement functions that typically have been undertaken by officials within the Executive Branch. . . .

Nor do we think that the "good cause" removal provision at issue here impermissibly burdens the President's power to control or supervise the independent counsel, as an executive official, in the execution of his or her duties under the Act. This is not a case in which the power to remove an executive official has been completely stripped from the President, thus providing no means for the President to ensure the "faithful execution" of the laws. Rather,

because the independent counsel may be terminated for "good cause," the Executive, through the Attorney General, retains ample authority to assure that the counsel is competently performing his or her statutory responsibilities in a manner that comports with the provisions of the Act. . . .

The final question to be addressed is whether the Act, taken as a whole, violates the principle of separation of powers by unduly interfering with the role of the Executive Branch. Time and again we have reaffirmed the importance in our constitutional scheme of the separation of governmental powers into the three coordinate branches. . . . We have not hesitated to invalidate provisions of law which violate this principle. On the other hand, we have never held that the Constitution requires that the three Branches of Government "operate with absolute independence." . . .

We observe first that this case does not involve an attempt by Congress to increase its own powers at the expense of the Executive Branch. Unlike some of our previous cases, most recently *Bowsher* v. *Synar*, this case simply does not pose a "dange[r] of congressional usurpation of Executive Branch functions." Indeed, with the exception of the power of impeachment—which applies to all officers of the United States—Congress retained for itself no powers of control or supervision over an independent counsel. The Act does empower certain Members of Congress to request the Attorney General to apply for the appointment of an independent counsel, but the Attorney General has no duty to comply with the request, although he must respond within a certain time limit. Other than that, Congress' role under the Act is limited to receiving reports or other information and oversight of the independent counsel's activities, functions that we have recognized generally as being incidental to the legislative function of Congress.

Similarly, we do not think that the Act works any judicial usurpation of properly executive functions. As should be apparent from our discussion of the Appointments Clause above, the power to appoint inferior officers such as independent counsel is not, in itself, an "executive" function in the constitutional sense, at least when Congress has exercised its power to vest the appointment of an inferior office in the "courts of Law." We note nonetheless that, under the Act, the Special Division has no power to appoint an independent counsel *sua sponte*; it may only do so upon the specific request of the Attorney General, and the courts are specifically prevented from reviewing the Attorney General's decision not to seek appointment. In addition, once the court has appointed a counsel and defined his or her jurisdiction, it has no power to supervise or control the activities of the counsel. As we pointed out in our discussion of the Special Division in relation to Article III, the various powers delegated by the statute to the Division are not supervisory or administrative, nor are they functions that the Constitution requires be performed by officials within the Executive Branch. The Act does give a federal court the power to review the Attorney General's decision to remove an independent counsel, but in our view this is a function that is well within the traditional power of the judiciary.

Finally, we do not think that the Act "impermissibly undermine[s]" the powers of the Executive Branch, or, "disrupts the proper balance between the coordinate branches [by] prevent[ing] the Executive Branch from accomplishing its constitutionally assigned functions. It is undeniable that the Act reduces the amount of control or supervision that the Attorney General and, through him, the President exercises over the investigation and prosecution of a certain class of alleged criminal activity. The Attorney General is not allowed to appoint the individual of his choice; he does not determine the counsel's jurisdiction; and his power to remove a counsel is limited. Nonetheless, the Act does give the Attorney General several means of supervising or controlling the prosecutorial powers that may be wielded by an independent counsel. Most importantly, the Attorney General retains the power to remove the counsel for "good cause," a power that we have already concluded provides the Executive with substantial ability to ensure that the laws are "faithfully executed" by an independent counsel. . . .

In sum, we conclude today that it does not violate the Appointments Clause for Congress to vest the appointment of independent counsel in the Special Division; that the powers exercised by the Special Division under the Act do not violate Article III; and that the Act does not violate the separation of powers principle by impermissibly interfering with the functions of the Executive Branch.

JUSTICE SCALIA, dissenting.

. . . [T]his suit is about . . . [p]ower. The allocation of power among Congress, the President, and the courts in such fashion as to preserve the equilibrium the Constitution sought to establish—so that "a gradual concentration of the several powers in the same department," can effectively be resisted. Frequently an issue of this sort will come before the Court clad, so to speak, in sheep's clothing: the potential of the asserted principle to effect important change in the equilibrium of power is not immediately evident, and must be discerned by a careful and perceptive analysis. But this wolf comes as a wolf.

The present case began when the Legislative and Executive Branches became "embroiled in a dispute concerning the scope of the congressional investigatory power," which—as is often the case with such interbranch conflicts—became quite acrimonious. . . .

Thus, by the application of this statute in the present case, Congress has effectively compelled a criminal investigation of a high-level appointee of the President in connection with his actions arising out of a bitter power dispute between the President and the Legislative Branch. Mr. Olson may or may not be guilty of a crime; we do not know. But we do know that the investigation of him has been commenced, not necessarily because the President or his authorized subordinates believe it is in the interest of the United States, in the sense that it warrants the diversion of resources from other efforts and is worth the cost in money and in possible damage to other governmental interests; and not even, leaving aside those normally considered factors, because the President or his authorized subordinates necessarily believe that an investigation is likely to unearth a violation worth prosecuting; but only because the Attorney General cannot affirm, as Congress demands, that there are *no reasonable grounds* to believe that further investigation is warranted. The decisions regarding the scope of that further investigation, its duration, and, finally, whether or not prosecution should ensue, are likewise beyond the control of the President and his subordinates.

If to describe this case is not to decide it, the concept of a government of separate and coordinate powers no longer has meaning. The Court devotes most of its attention to such relatively technical details as the Appointments Clause and the removal power, addressing briefly and only at the end of its opinion the separation of powers. As my prologue suggests, I think that has it backwards. . . .

First, however, I think it well to call to mind an important and unusual premise that underlies our deliberations, a premise not expressly contradicted by the Court's opinion, but in my view not faithfully observed. It is rare in a case dealing, as this one does, with the constitutionality of a statute passed by the Congress of the United States, not to find anywhere in the Court's opinion the usual, almost formulary caution that we owe great deference to Congress' view that what it has done is constitutional. . . . That caution is not recited by the Court in the present case, *because it does not apply.* Where a private citizen challenges action of the Government on grounds unrelated to separation of powers, harmonious functioning of the system demands that we ordinarily give some deference, or a presumption of validity, to the actions of the political branches in what is agreed, between themselves at least, to be within their respective spheres. But where the issue pertains to separation of powers, and the political branches are (as here) in disagreement, neither can be presumed correct. The reason is stated concisely by Madison: "The several departments being perfectly co-ordinate by the terms of their common commission, neither of them, it is evident, can pretend to an exclusive or superior right of settling the boundaries between their respective powers. . . . " Federalist 49. The playing field for the present case, in other words, is a level one. As one of the interested and coordinate parties to the underlying constitutional dispute, Congress, no more than the President, is entitled to the benefit of the doubt.

To repeat, Article II, Section 1, clause 1, of the Constitution provides: "The executive Power shall be vested in a President of the United States." [T]his does not mean *some* of the executive power, but *all* of the executive power. It seems to me, therefore, that the decision of the Court of Appeals invalidating the present statute must be upheld on fundamental separation of powers principles if the following two questions are answered affirmatively: (1) Is the conduct of a criminal prosecution (and of an investigation to decide whether to prosecute) the exercise of purely executive power? (2) Does the statute deprive the President of the United States of exclusive control over the exercise of that power? Surprising to say, the Court appears to concede an affirmative answer to both questions, but seeks to avoid the inevitable conclusion that, since the statute vests some purely executive power in a person who is not the President of the United States, it is void.

The Court concedes that "[t]here is no real dispute that the functions performed by the independent counsel are 'executive'," though it qualifies that concession by adding "in the sense that they are 'law enforcement' functions that typically have been undertaken by officials within the Executive Branch." The qualifier adds nothing but atmosphere. In what *other* sense can one identify "the executive Power" that is supposed to be vested in the President (unless it includes everything the Executive Branch is given to do) *except* by reference to what has always and everywhere—if conducted by government at all—been conducted never by the legislature, never by the courts, and always by the executive. There is no possible doubt that the independent counsel's functions fit this description. She is vested with the, "full power and independent authority to exercise all *investigative and prosecutorial* functions and powers of the Department of Justice [and] the Attorney General."

As for the second question, whether the statute before us deprives the President of exclusive control over that quintessentially executive activity: the Court does not, and could not possibly, assert that it does not. That is indeed the whole object of the statute. Instead, the Court points out that the President, through his Attorney General, has at least *some* control. That concession is alone enough to invalidate the statute, but I cannot refrain from pointing out that the Court greatly exaggerates the extent of that "some" Presidential control. "Most impor-tan[t]" among these controls, the Court asserts, is the Attorney General's "power to remove the counsel for 'good cause.'" This is somewhat like referring to shackles as an effective means of locomotion. As we recognized in *Humphrey's Executor* v. *United States* (1935)—indeed, what *Humphrey's Executor* was all about—limiting removal power to "good cause" is an impediment to, not an effective grant of, Presidential control. . . .

[I]t is ultimately irrelevant *how much* the statute reduces Presidential control. The case is over when the Court acknowledges, as it must, that, "[i]t is undeniable that the Act reduces the amount of control or supervision that the Attorney General and, through him, the President exercises over the investigation and prosecution of a certain class of alleged criminal activity." It effects a revolution in our constitutional jurisprudence for the Court, once it has determined that (1) purely executive functions are at issue here, and (2) those functions have been given to a person whose actions are not fully within the supervision and control of the President, nonetheless to proceed further to sit in judgment of whether, "the President's need to control the exercise of [the independent counsel's] discretion is *so central* to the functioning of the Executive Branch" as to require complete control, whether the conferral of his powers upon someone else, "*sufficiently* deprives the President of control over the independent counsel to interfere impermissibly with [his] constitutional obligation to ensure the faithful execution of the laws," and whether, "the Act give[s] the Executive Branch *sufficient* control over the independent counsel to ensure that the President is able to perform his constitutionally assigned duties." It is not for us to determine, and we have never presumed to determine, how much of the purely executive powers of government must be within the full control of the President. The Constitution prescribes that they *all* are. . . .

Is it unthinkable that the President should have such exclusive power, even when alleged crimes by him or his close associates are at issue? No more so than that Congress should have the exclusive power of legislation, even when what is at issue is its own exemption from the burdens of certain laws. No more so than that this Court should have the exclusive power to pronounce the final decision on justiciable cases and controversies, even those pertaining to the constitutionality of a statute reducing the salaries of the Justices. A system of separate and coordinate powers necessarily involves an acceptance of exclusive power that can theoretically be abused. As we reiterate this very day, "[i]t is a truism that constitutional protections have costs." While the separation of powers may prevent us from righting every wrong, it does so in order to ensure that we do not lose liberty. The checks against any branch's abuse of its exclusive powers are twofold: first, retaliation by one of the other branch's use of *its* exclusive powers: Congress, for example, can impeach the executive who willfully fails to enforce the laws; the executive can decline to prosecute under unconstitutional statutes, and the courts can dismiss malicious prosecutions. Second, and ultimately, there is the political check that the people will replace those in the political branches. . . . Political pressures produced special prosecutors—for Teapot Dome and for Watergate, for example—long before this statute created the independent counsel.

The Court has, nonetheless, replaced the clear constitutional prescription that the executive power belongs to the President with a "balancing test." What are the standards to determine how the balance is to be struck, that is, how much removal of Presidential power is too much? Many countries of the world get along with an executive that is much weaker than ours—in fact, entirely dependent upon the continued support of the legislature. Once we depart from the text of the Constitution, just where short of that do we stop? The most amazing feature of the Court's opinion is that it does not even purport to give an answer. It simply *announces*, with no analysis, that the ability to control the decision whether to investigate and prosecute the President's closest advisers, and indeed the President himself, is not "so central to the functioning of the Executive Branch" as to be constitutionally required to be within the President's control. Apparently that is so because we say it is so. . . . This is not only not the government of laws that the Constitution established; it is not a government of laws at all. . . .

In sum, this statute does deprive the President of substantial control over the prosecutory functions performed by the independent counsel, and it does substantially affect the balance of powers. That the Court could possibly conclude otherwise demonstrates both the wisdom of our former constitutional system, in which the degree of reduced control and political impairment were irrelevant, since all purely executive power had to be in the President, and the folly of the new system of standardless judicial allocation of powers we adopt today. . . .

The purpose of the separation and equilibration of powers in general, and of the unitary Executive in particular, was not merely to assure effective government but to preserve individual freedom. Those who hold or have held offices covered by the Ethics in Government Act are entitled to that protection as much as the rest of us, and I conclude my discussion by considering the effect of the Act upon the fairness of the process they receive. . . .

Under our system of government, the primary check against prosecutorial abuse is a political one. The prosecutors who exercise this awesome discretion are selected, and can be removed, by a President whom the people have trusted enough to elect. Moreover, when crimes are not investigated and prosecuted fairly, nonselectively, with a reasonable sense of proportion, the President pays the cost in political damage to his administration. If federal prosecutors "pick people that [they] thin[k] [they] should get, rather than cases that need to be prosecuted," if they amass many more resources against a particular prominent individual, or against a particular class of political protesters, or against members of a particular political party, than the gravity of the alleged offenses or the record of successful prosecutions seems to warrant, the unfairness will come home to roost in the Oval Office. I leave it to the reader to recall the examples of this in recent years. That result, of course, was precisely what the Founders had in mind when they provided that all executive powers would be exercised by a *single* Chief Executive. As Hamilton put it, "[t]he ingredients which constitute safety in the republican sense are a due dependence on the people, and a due responsibility." *Federalist* 70. The President is directly dependent on the people, and, since there is only *one* President, *he* is responsible. The people know whom to blame, whereas "one of the weightiest objections to a plurality in the executive . . . is that it tends to conceal faults and destroy responsibility."

That is the system of justice the rest of us are entitled to, but what of that select class consisting of present or former high-level Executive-Branch officials? If an allegation is made against them of any violation of any federal criminal law (except Class B or C misdemeanors or infractions), the Attorney General must give it his attention. That in itself is not objectionable. But if, after a 90-day investigation without the benefit of normal investigatory tools, the Attorney General is unable to say that there are "no reasonable grounds to believe" that further investigation is warranted, a process is set in motion that is *not* in the full control of persons "dependent on the people," and whose flaws cannot be blamed on the President. An independent counsel is selected, and the scope of his or her authority prescribed, by a panel of judges. What if they are politically partisan, as judges have been known to be, and select a prosecutor antagonistic to the administration, or even to the particular individual who has been selected for this special treatment? There is no remedy for that, not even a political one. Judges, after all, have life tenure, and appointing a sure-fire enthusiastic prosecutor could hardly be considered an impeachable offense. So if there is anything wrong with the selection, there is effectively no one to blame. The independent counsel thus selected proceeds to assemble a staff. As I observed earlier, in the nature of things, this has to be done by finding lawyers who are willing to lay aside their current careers for an indeterminate amount of time, to take on a job that has no prospect of permanence and little prospect for promotion. One thing is certain, however: it involves investigating and perhaps prosecuting a particular individual. Can one imagine a less equitable manner of fulfilling the Executive responsibility to investigate and prosecute? What would be the reaction if, in an area not covered by this statute, the Justice Department posted a public notice inviting applicants to assist in an investigation and possible prosecution of a certain prominent person? Does this not invite what Justice Jackson described as "picking the man and then searching the law books, or putting investigators to work, to pin some offense on him"? To be sure, the investigation must relate to the area of criminal offense specified by the life-tenured judges. But that has often been (and nothing prevents it from being) very broad—and should the independent counsel or his or her staff come up with something beyond that scope, nothing prevents him or her from asking the judges to expand his or her authority or, if that does not work, referring it to the Attorney General, whereupon the whole process would recommence and, if there was "reasonable basis to believe" that further investigation was warranted, that new offense would be referred to the Special Division, which would in all likelihood assign it to the same independent counsel. It seems to me not conducive to fairness. But even if it were entirely evident that unfairness was in fact the result—the judges hostile to the administration, the independent counsel an old foe of the President, the staff refugees from the recently defeated administration—*there would be no one accountable to the public to whom the blame could be assigned.* . . . The notion that every violation of law should be prosecuted, including—indeed, *especially*—every violation by those in high places, is an attractive one, and it would be risky to argue in an election campaign that that is not an absolutely overriding value. *Fiat justitia, ruat coelum.* Let justice be done, though the heavens may fall. The reality is, however, that it is not an absolutely overriding value, and it was with the hope that we would be able to acknowledge and apply such realities that the Constitution spared us, by life tenure, the necessity of election campaigns. I cannot imagine that there are not many thoughtful men and women in Congress who realize that the benefits of this legislation are far outweighed by its harmful effect upon our system of government, and even upon the nature of justice received by those men and women who agree to serve in the Executive Branch. But it is difficult to vote not to enact, and even more difficult to vote to repeal, a statute called, appropriately enough, the Ethics in Government Act. If Congress is controlled by the party other than the one to which the President belongs, it has little incentive to repeal it; if it is controlled by the same party, it dare not. By its shortsighted action today, I fear the Court has permanently encumbered the Republic with an institution that will do it great harm.

Worse than what it has done, however, is the manner in which it has done it. A government of laws means a government of rules. Today's decision on the basic issue of fragmentation of executive power is ungoverned by rule, and hence ungoverned by law. It extends into the very heart of our most significant constitutional function the "totality of the circumstances" mode of analysis that this Court has in recent years become fond of. Taking all things into account, we conclude that the power taken away from the President here is not really too much. The next time executive power is assigned to someone other than the President, we may conclude, taking all things into account, that it *is* too much. That opinion, like this one, will not be confined by any rule. We will describe, as we have today (though I hope more accurately) the effects of the provision in question, and will authoritatively announce: "The President's need to control the exercise of the [subject officer's] discretion is so central to the functioning of the Executive Branch as to require complete control." This is not analysis; it is *ad hoc* judgment. And it fails to explain why it is not true that—as the text of the Constitution seems to require, as the Founders seemed to expect, and as our past cases have uniformly assumed—all purely executive power must be under the control of the President.

▼▲▼

## Myers v. United States
### 272 U.S. 52 (1926)

In 1917, President Woodrow Wilson appointed Frank S. Myers to the position of first-class postmaster. Myers was to serve his four-year term in Portland, Oregon. In 1920, Wilson wanted to replace Myers and asked him to resign. Patronage politics has always been a key element of the electoral reward structure, and the post office, for many years, was considered one the major landing spots for loyal political supporters. Wilson assumed that Myers, being a patronage appointment, would understand that political appointees serve at the pleasure of the president.

After Myers refused to step down, Wilson ordered the postmaster general to fire Myers. Myers claimed his removal was illegal, since he was appointed, with the approval of the Senate, to serve a four-year term. The president could not remove him without Senate approval. The argument before the Supreme Court centered on the constitutionality of an 1876 congressional law requiring that first-, second-, and third-class postmasters to receive the consent of the Senate before the president could remove them.

By the time *Myers* reached the Court, Frank Myers had died. The executor of his estate carried out the lawsuit, as Myers was owed almost $10,000 in back salary.

The Court's decision was 6 to 3. Chief Justice Taft delivered the opinion of the Court. Justices McReynolds, Brandeis, and Holmes dissented.

▼▲▼

Mr. Chief Justice Taft delivered the opinion of the Court.

This case presents the question whether, under the Constitution, the President has the exclusive power of removing executive officers of the United States whom he has appointed by and with the advice and consent of the Senate. . . .

The debates in the Constitutional Convention indicated an intention to create a strong Executive, and, after a controversial discussion, the executive power of the Government was vested in one person and many of his important functions were specified so as to avoid the humiliating weakness of the Congress during the Revolution and under the Articles of Confederation.

Mr. Madison and his associates in the discussion in the House dwelt at length upon the necessity there was for construing Article II to give the President the sole power of removal in his responsibility for the conduct of the executive branch, and enforced this by emphasizing his duty expressly declared in the third section of the Article to "take care that the laws be faithfully executed."

The vesting of the executive power in the President was essentially a grant of the power to execute the laws. But the President, alone and unaided, could not execute the laws. He must execute them by the assistance of subordinates. This view has since been repeatedly affirmed by this Court. As he is charged specifically to take care that they be faithfully executed, the reasonable implication, even in the absence of express words, was that, as part of his executive power, he should select those who were to act for him under his direction in the execution of the laws. The further implication must be, in the absence of any express limitation respecting removals, that, as his selection of administrative officers is essential to the execution of the laws by him, so must be his power of removing those for whom he cannot continue to be responsible. It was urged that the natural meaning of the term "executive power" granted the President included the appointment and removal of executive subordinates. If such appointments and removals were not an exercise of the executive power, what were they? They certainly were not the exercise of legislative or judicial power in government as usually understood. . . .

The power to prevent the removal of an officer who has served under the President is different from the authority to consent to or reject his appointment. When a nomination is made, it may be presumed that the Senate is, or may become, as well advised as to the fitness of the nominee as the President, but, in the nature of things, the defects in ability or intelligence or loyalty in the administration of the laws of one who has served as an officer under the President are facts as to which the President, or his trusted subordinates, must be better informed than the Senate, and the power to remove him may, therefore, be regarded as confined, for very sound and practical reasons, to the governmental authority which has administrative control. The power of removal is incident to the power of appointment, not to the power of advising and consenting to appointment, and when the grant of the executive power is enforced by the express mandate to take care that the laws be faithfully executed, it emphasizes the necessity for including within the executive power as conferred the exclusive power of removal. . . .

The constitutional construction that excludes Congress from legislative power to provide for the removal of superior officers finds support in the second section of Article II. By it, the appointment of all officers, whether superior or inferior, by the President is declared to be subject to the advice and consent of the Senate. In the absence of any specific provision to the contrary, the power of appointment to executive office carries with it, as a necessary incident, the power of removal. Whether the Senate must concur in the removal is aside from the point we now are considering. That point is that, by the specific constitutional provision for appointment of executive officers, with its necessary incident of removal, the power of appointment and removal is clearly provided for the Constitution, and the legislative power of Congress in respect to both is excluded save by the specific exception as to inferior offices in the clause that follows, *viz.*, "but the Congress may by law vest the appointment of such inferior officers, as they think proper, in the President alone, in the Courts of Law, or in the Heads of Departments." These words, it has been held by this Court, give to Congress the power to limit and regulate removal of such inferior officers by heads of departments when it exercises its constitutional power to lodge the power of appointment with them. Here, then, is an express provision, introduced in words of exception, for the exercise by Congress of legislative power in the matter of appointments and removals in the case of inferior executive officers. The phrase "But Congress may by law vest" is equivalent to "excepting that Congress may by law vest." By the plainest implication, it excludes Congressional dealing with appointments or removals of executive officers not falling within the exception, and leaves unaffected the executive power of the President to appoint and remove them.

A reference of the whole power of removal to general legislation by Congress is quite out of keeping with the plan of government devised by the framers of the Constitution. It could never have been intended to leave to Congress unlimited discretion to vary fundamentally the operation of the great independent executive branch of government, and thus most seriously to weaken it. It would be a delegation by the Convention to Congress of the function of defining the primary boundaries of another of the three great divisions of government. The inclusion of removals of executive officers in the executive power vested in the President by Article II, according to its usual definition, and the implication of his power of removal of such officers from the provision of section 2 expressly recognizing in him the power of their appointment, are a much more natural and appropriate source of the removing power.

It is reasonable to suppose also that, had it been intended to give to Congress power to regulate or control removals in the manner suggested, it would have been included among the specifically enumerated legislative powers in Article I, or in the specified limitations on the executive power in Article II. The difference between the grant of legislative power under Article I to Congress, which is limited to powers therein enumerated, and the more general grant of the executive power to the President under Article II, is significant. The fact that the executive power is given in general terms, strengthened by specific terms where emphasis is appropriate, and limited by direct expressions where limitation is needed, and that no express limit is placed on the power of removal by the executive, is a convincing indication that none was intended. . . .

An argument in favor of full Congressional power to make or withhold provision for removals of all appointed by the President is sought to be found in an asserted analogy between such a power in Congress and its power in the establishment of inferior federal courts. By Article III, the judicial power of the United States is vested in one Supreme Court and in such inferior courts as the Congress may from time to time establish. By section 8 of Article I, also, Congress is given power to constitute tribunals inferior to the Supreme Court. By the second section, the judicial power is extended to all cases in law and equity under this Constitution and to a substantial number of other classes of cases. Under the accepted construction, the cases mentioned in this section are treated as a description and reservoir of the judicial power of the United States and a boundary of that federal power as between the United States and the States, and the field of jurisdiction within the limits of which Congress may vest particular jurisdiction in any one inferior federal court which it may constitute. It is clear that the mere establishment of a federal inferior court does not vest that court with all the judicial power of the United States as conferred in the second section of Article III, but only that conferred by Congress specifically on the particular court. It must be limited territorially and in the classes of cases to be heard, and the mere creation of the court does not confer jurisdiction except as it is conferred in the law of its creation or its amendments. It is said that, similarly, in the case of the executive power which is "vested in the President," the power of appointment and removal cannot arise until Congress creates the office and its duties and powers, and must accordingly be exercised and limited only as Congress shall, in the creation of the office, prescribe.

We think there is little or no analogy between the two legislative functions of Congress in the cases suggested. The judicial power described in the second section of Article III is vested in the courts collectively, but is manifestly to be distributed to different courts and conferred or withheld as Congress shall, in its discretion, provide their respective jurisdictions, and is not all to be vested in one particular court. Any other construction would be impracticable. The duty of Congress, therefore, to make provision for the vesting of the whole federal judicial power in federal courts, were it held to exist, would be one of imperfect obligation, and unenforceable. On the other hand, the moment an office and its powers and duties are created, the power of appointment and removal, as limited by the Constitution, vests in the Executive. The functions of distributing jurisdiction to courts, and the exercise of it when distributed and vested, are not at all parallel to the creation of an office, and the mere right of appointment to, and of removal from, the office, which at once attaches to the Executive by virtue of the Constitution. . . .

Made responsible under the Constitution for the effective enforcement of the law, the President needs as an indispensable aid to meet it the disciplinary influence upon those who act under him of a reserve power of removal. But it is contended that executive officers appointed by the President with the consent of the Senate are bound by the statutory law, and are not his servants to do his will, and that his obligation to care for the faithful execution of the laws does not authorize him to treat them as such. The degree of guidance in the discharge of their duties that the President may exercise over executive officers varies with the character of their service as prescribed in the law under which they act. The highest and most important duties which his subordinates perform are those in which they act for him. In such cases, they are exercising not their own, but his, discretion. This field is a very large one. It is sometimes described as political. Each head of a department is and must be the President's alter ego in the matters of that department where the President is required by law to exercise authority. . . .

The duties of the heads of departments and bureaus in which the discretion of the President is exercised and which we have described are the most important in the whole field of executive action of the Government. There is nothing in the Constitution which permits a distinction between the removal of the head of a department or a bureau, when he discharges a political duty of the President or exercises his discretion, and the removal of executive officers engaged in the discharge of their other normal duties. The imperative reasons requiring an unrestricted power to remove the most important of his subordinates in their most important duties must, therefore, control the interpretation of the Constitution as to all appointed by him.

But this is not to say that there are not strong reasons why the President should have a like power to remove his appointees charged with other duties than those above described. The ordinary duties of officers prescribed by statute come under the general administrative control of the President by virtue of the general grant to him of the executive power, and he may properly supervise and guide their construction of the statutes under which they act in order to secure that unitary and uniform execution of the laws which Article II of the Constitution evidently contemplated in vesting general executive power in the President alone. Laws are often passed with specific provision for the adoption of regulations by a department or bureau head to make the law workable and effective. The ability and judgment manifested by the official thus empowered, as well as his energy and stimulation of his subordinates, are subjects which the President must consider and supervise in his administrative control. Finding such officers to be negligent and inefficient, the President should have the power to remove them. Of course, there may be duties so peculiarly and specifically committed to the discretion of a particular officer as to raise a question whether the President may overrule or revise the officer's interpretation of his statutory duty in a particular instance. Then there may be duties of a *quasi*-judicial character imposed on executive officers and members of executive tribunals whose decisions after hearing affect interests of individuals, the discharge of which the President cannot in a particular case properly influence or control. But even in such a case, he may consider the decision after its rendition as a reason for removing the officer, on the ground that the discretion regularly entrusted to that officer by statute has not been, on the whole, intelligently or wisely exercised. Otherwise, he does not discharge his own constitutional duty of seeing that the laws be faithfully executed.

We have devoted much space to this discussion and decision of the question of the Presidential power of removal in the First Congress, not because a Congressional conclusion on a constitutional issue is conclusive, but, first, because of our agreement with the reasons upon which it was avowedly based; second, because this was the decision of the First Congress, on a question of primary importance in the organization of the Government, made within two years after the Constitutional Convention and within a much shorter time after its ratification; and, third, because that Congress numbered among its leaders those who had been members of the Convention. It must necessarily constitute a precedent upon which many future laws supplying the machinery of the new Government would be based, and, if erroneous, it would be likely to evoke dissent and departure in future Congresses. It would come at once before the executive branch of the Government for compliance, and might well be brought before the judicial branch for a test of its validity. As we shall see, it was soon accepted as a final decision of the question by all branches of the Government. . . .

We come now to consider an argument advanced and strongly pressed on behalf of the complainant, that this case concerns only the removal of a postmaster; that a postmaster is an inferior officer; that such an office was not included within the legislative decision of 1789, which related only to superior officers to be appointed by the President by and with the advice and consent of the Senate. This, it is said, is the distinction which Chief Justice Marshall had in mind in *Marbury v. Madison* in the language already discussed in respect of the President's power to remove a District of Columbia justice of the peace appointed and confirmed for a term of years. We find nothing in *Marbury* to indicate any such distinction. . . . In view of the doubt as to what was really the basis of the remarks relied on, and their *obiter dictum* character, they can certainly not be used to give weight to the argument that the 1789 decision only related to superior officers. . . .

The power to remove inferior executive officers, like that to remove superior executive officers, is an incident of the power to appoint them, and is in its nature an executive power. The authority of Congress given by the excepting clause to vest the appointment of such inferior officers in the heads of departments carries with it authority incidentally to invest the heads of departments with power to remove. It has been the practice of Congress to do so and this Court has recognized that power. . . . But the Court never has held, nor reasonably could hold, although it is argued to the contrary on behalf of the appellant, that the excepting clause enables Congress to draw to itself, or to either branch of it, the power to remove or the right to participate in the exercise of that power. To do this would be to go beyond the words and implications of that clause and to infringe the constitutional principle of the separation of governmental powers.

Assuming then the power of Congress to regulate removals as incidental to the exercise of its constitutional power to vest appointments of inferior officers in the heads of departments, certainly so long as Congress does not exercise that power, the power of removal must remain where the Constitution places it, with the President, as part of the executive power, in accordance with

the legislative decision of 1789 which we have been considering. . . .

Our conclusion on the merits, sustained by the arguments before stated, is that Article II grants to the President the executive power of the Government, *i.e.*, the general administrative control of those executing the laws, including the power of appointment and removal of executive officers—a conclusion confirmed by his obligation to take care that the laws be faithfully executed; that Article II excludes the exercise of legislative power by Congress to provide for appointments and removals, except only as granted therein to Congress in the matter of inferior offices; that Congress is only given power to provide for appointments and removals of inferior officers after it has vested, and on condition that it does vest, their appointment in other authority than the President with the Senate's consent; that the provisions of the second section of Article II, which blend action by the legislative branch, or by part of it, in the work of the executive are limitations to be strictly construed, and not to be extended by implication; that the President's power of removal is further established as an incident to his specifically enumerated function of appointment by and with the advice of the Senate, but that such incident does not, by implication, extend to removals the Senate's power of checking appointments, and finally that to hold otherwise would make it impossible for the President, in case of political or other differences with the Senate or Congress, to take care that the laws be faithfully executed.

Mr. Justice Brandeis, dissenting.

. . . May the President, having acted under the statute insofar as it creates the office and authorizes the appointment, ignore, while the Senate is in session, the provision which prescribes the condition under which a removal may take place?

It is this narrow question, and this only, which we are required to decide. We need not consider what power the President, being Commander in Chief, has over officers in the Army and the Navy. We need not determine whether the President, acting alone, may remove high political officers. We need not even determine whether, acting alone, he may remove inferior civil officers when the Senate is not in session. It was in session when the President purported to remove Myers, and for a long time thereafter. All questions of statutory construction have been eliminated by the language of the Act. It is settled that, in the absence of a provision expressly providing for the consent of the Senate to a removal, the clause fixing the tenure will be construed as a limitation, not as a grant, and that, under such legislation, the President, acting alone, has the power of removal. But, in defining the tenure, this statute used words of grant. Congress clearly intended to preclude a removal without the consent of the Senate. . . .

The practice of Congress to control the exercise of the executive power of removal from inferior offices is evidenced by many statutes which restrict it in many ways besides the removal clause here in question. Each of these restrictive statutes became law with the approval of the President. Every President who had held office since 1861, except President Garfield, approved one or more of such statutes. Some of these statutes, prescribing a fixed term, provide that removal shall be made only for one of several specified causes. Some provide a fixed term, subject generally to removal for cause. Some provide for removal only after hearing. Some provide a fixed term, subject to removal for reasons to be communicated by the President to the Senate. Some impose the restriction in still other ways.

The historical data submitted present a legislative practice, established by concurrent affirmative action of Congress and the President, to make consent of the Senate a condition of removal from statutory inferior, civil, executive offices to which the appointment is made for a fixed term by the President with such consent. They show that the practice has existed, without interruption, continuously for the last fifty-eight years; that, throughout this period, it has governed a great majority of all such offices; that the legislation applying the removal clause specifically to the office of postmaster was enacted more than half a century ago, and that recently the practice has, with the President's approval, been extended to several newly created offices. The data show further that the insertion of the removal clause in acts creating inferior civil offices with fixed tenure is part of the broader legislative practice, which has prevailed since the formation of our Government, to restrict or regulate in many ways both removal from and nomination to such offices. A persistent legislative practice which involves a delimitation of the respective powers of Congress and the President, and which has been so established and maintained, should be deemed tantamount to judicial construction in the absence of any decision by any court to the contrary.

The persuasive effect of this legislative practice is strengthened by the fact that no instance has been found, even in the earlier period of our history, of concurrent affirmative action of Congress and the President which is inconsistent with the legislative practice of the last fifty-eight years to impose the removal clause. Nor has any instance been found of action by Congress which involves

recognition in any other way of the alleged uncontrollable executive power to remove an inferior civil officer. The action taken by Congress in 1789 after the great debate does not present such an instance. The vote then taken did not involve a decision that the President had uncontrollable power. It did not involve a decision of the question whether Congress could confer upon the Senate the right, and impose upon it the duty, to participate in removals. It involved merely the decision that the Senate does not, in the absence of legislative grant thereof, have the right to share in the removal of an officer appointed with its consent, and that the President has, in the absence of restrictive legislation, the constitutional power of removal without such consent. Moreover, as Chief Justice Marshall recognized, the debate and the decision related to a high political office, not to inferior ones. . . .

The separation of the powers of government did not make each branch completely autonomous. It left each in some measure dependent upon the others, as it left to each power to exercise, in some respects, functions in their nature executive, legislative and judicial. Obviously the President cannot secure full execution of the laws, if Congress denies to him adequate means of doing so. Full execution may be defeated because Congress declines to create offices indispensable for that purpose. Or because Congress, having created the office, declines to make the indispensable appropriation. Or because Congress, having both created the office and made the appropriation, prevents, by restrictions which it imposes, the appointment of officials who in quality and character are indispensable to the efficient execution of the law. If, in any such way, adequate means are denied to the President, the fault will lie with Congress. The President performs his full constitutional duty if, with the means and instruments provided by Congress and within the limitations prescribed by it, he uses his best endeavors to secure the faithful execution of the laws enacted.

Checks and balances were established in order that this should be "a government of laws, and not of men." As White said in the House in 1789, an uncontrollable power of removal in the Chief Executive "is a doctrine not to be learned in American governments." Such power had been denied in Colonial Charters, and even under Proprietary Grants and Royal Commissions. It had been denied in the thirteen States before the framing of the Federal Constitution. The doctrine of the separation of powers was adopted by the convention of 1787 not to promote efficiency, but to preclude the exercise of arbitrary power. The purpose was not to avoid friction but, by means of the inevitable friction incident to the distribution of the governmental powers among three departments, to save the people from autocracy. In order to prevent arbitrary executive action, the Constitution provided in terms that presidential appointments be made with the consent of the Senate, unless Congress should otherwise provide, and this clause was construed by Alexander Hamilton in *Federalist* 77, as requiring like consent to removals. Limiting further executive prerogatives customary in monarchies, the Constitution empowered Congress to vest the appointment of inferior officers, "as they think proper, in the President alone, in the Courts of Law, or in the Heads of Departments." Nothing in support of the claim of uncontrollable power can be inferred from the silence of the Convention of 1787 on the subject of removal. For the outstanding fact remains that every specific proposal to confer such uncontrollable power upon the President was rejected. In America, as in England, the conviction prevailed then that the people must look to representative assemblies for the protection of their liberties. And protection of the individual, even if he be an official, from the arbitrary or capricious exercise of power was then believed to be an essential of free government.

▾▲▾

## Humphrey's Executor v. United States
### 295 U.S. 602 (1935)

In 1914, Congress created the Federal Trade Commission (FTC), an independent regulatory agency charged with enforcing antitrust laws and preventing unfair competition. The FTC was one of several independent agencies created to run in accordance with the modern principles of public administration. Around this time, many reform-minded political scientists and management experts believed that federal agencies should become more professional and less political. Agencies should reflect "administrative expertise," and not serve as dumping grounds for political patrons.

The law also stated that the president could remove FTC commissioners only for reasons of "inefficiency, neglect of duty, or malfeasance in office." In 1931, President Hoover had reappointed William E. Humphrey, appointed to the FTC in 1924 by President Coolidge, for a second seven-year term. After President Roosevelt took office in 1933, he requested Humphrey's resignation on political grounds. Roosevelt wrote to Humphrey: "I do not feel that your mind and my mind go along together on either the poli-

cies or the administering of the Federal Trade Commission, and, frankly, I think it's best for the people of this country that I should have full confidence." When Humphrey refused to resign, President Roosevelt removed him.

Like Frank Myers, Humphrey did not live to see his case make it to the Supreme Court. His executor carried out the original lawsuit, the original purpose of which was to recover lost wages and compensation for his improper dismissal. The Roosevelt administration argued that Myers gave the president complete control over the removal of executive officers. That view did not prevail.

The Court's decision was unanimous. Justice Sutherland delivered the opinion of the Court.

▾▲▾

Mr. Justice Sutherland delivered the opinion of the Court.

... The question first to be considered is whether, by the provisions of Section 1 of the Federal Trade Commission Act ... the President's power is limited to removal for the specific causes enumerated therein. ...

The commission is to be nonpartisan, and it must, from the very nature of its duties, act with entire impartiality. It is charged with the enforcement of no policy except the policy of the law. Its duties are neither political nor executive, but predominantly *quasi*-judicial and *quasi*-legislative. Like the Interstate Commerce Commission, its members are called upon to exercise the trained judgment of a body of experts "appointed by law and informed by experience."

The legislative reports in both houses of Congress clearly reflect the view that a fixed term was necessary to the effective and fair administration of the law. In the report to the Senate, the Senate Committee on Interstate Commerce, in support of the bill which afterwards became the act in question, after referring to the provision fixing the term of office at seven years, so arranged that the membership would not be subject to complete change at any one time. ...

The debates in both houses demonstrate that the prevailing view was that the commission was not to be "subject to anybody in the government, but ... only to the people of the United States"; free from "political domination or control" or the "probability or possibility of such a thing"; to be "separate and apart from any existing department of the government—not subject to the orders of the President."

More to the same effect appears in the debates, which were long and thorough, and contain nothing to the contrary. While the general rule precludes the use of these debates to explain the meaning of the words of the statute, they may be considered as reflecting light upon its general purposes and the evils which it sought to remedy.

Thus, the language of the act, the legislative reports, and the general purposes of the legislation as reflected by the debates all combine to demonstrate the Congressional intent to create a body of experts who shall gain experience by length of service—a body which shall be independent of executive authority *except in its selection,* and free to exercise its judgment without the leave or hindrance of any other official or any department of the government. To the accomplishment of these purposes it is clear that Congress was of opinion that length and certainty of tenure would vitally contribute. And to hold that, nevertheless, the members of the commission continue in office at the mere will of the President might be to thwart, in large measure, the very ends which Congress sought to realize by definitely fixing the term of office.

We conclude that the intent of the act is to limit the executive power of removal to the causes enumerated, the existence of none of which is claimed here, and we pass to the second question.

To support its contention that the removal provision of Section 1, as we have just construed it, is an unconstitutional interference with the executive power of the President, the government's chief reliance is *Myers* v. *United States* (1926). That case has been so recently decided, and the prevailing and dissenting opinions so fully review the general subject of the power of executive removal, that further discussion would add little of value to the wealth of material there collected. These opinions examine at length the historical, legislative and judicial data bearing upon the question, beginning with what is called "the decision of 1789" in the first Congress and coming down almost to the day when the opinions were delivered. . . . Nevertheless, the narrow point actually decided was only that the President had power to remove a postmaster of the first class without the advice and consent of the Senate as required by act of Congress. In the course of the opinion of the court, expressions occur which tend to sustain the government's contention, but these are beyond the point involved, and, therefore do not come within the rule of *stare decisis.* Insofar as they are out of harmony with the views here set forth, these expressions are disapproved. . . .

The office of a postmaster is so essentially unlike the office now involved that the decision in the *Myers* case cannot be accepted as controlling our decision here. A postmaster is an executive officer restricted to the performance of executive functions. He is charged with no duty at all related to either the legislative or judicial power. The actual decision in the *Myers* case finds support in the theory that such an officer is merely one of the units in the executive department, and, hence, inherently subject to the exclusive and illimitable power of removal by the Chief Executive, whose subordinate and aid he is. Putting aside dicta, which may be followed if sufficiently persuasive but which are not controlling, the necessary reach of the decision goes far enough to include all purely executive officers. It goes no farther; much less does it include an officer who occupies no place in the executive department, and who exercises no part of the executive power vested by the Constitution in the President.

The Federal Trade Commission is an administrative body created by Congress to carry into effect legislative policies embodied in the statute in accordance with the legislative standard therein prescribed, and to perform other specified duties as a legislative or as a judicial aid. Such a body cannot in any proper sense be characterized as an arm or an eye of the executive. Its duties are performed without executive leave, and, in the contemplation of the statute, must be free from executive control. In administering the provisions of the statute in respect of "unfair methods of competition"—that is to say, in filling in and administering the details embodied by that general standard—the commission acts in part *quasi*-legislatively and in part *quasi*-judicially. In making investigations and reports thereon for the information of Congress under 6, in aid of the legislative power, it acts as a legislative agency. Under Section 7, which authorizes the commission to act as a master in chancery under rules prescribed by the court, it acts as an agency of the judiciary. To the extent that it exercises any executive function—as distinguished from executive power in the constitutional sense—it does so in the discharge and effectuation of its *quasi*-legislative or *quasi*-judicial powers, or as an agency of the legislative or judicial departments of the government.

If Congress is without authority to prescribe causes for removal of members of the trade commission and limit executive power of removal accordingly, that power at once becomes practically all-inclusive in respect of civil officers with the exception of the judiciary provided for by the Constitution. The Solicitor General, at the bar, apparently recognizing this to be true, with commendable candor, agreed that his view in respect of the removability of members of the Federal Trade Commission necessitated a like view in respect of the Interstate Commerce Commission and the Court of Claims. We are thus confronted with the serious question whether not only the members of these *quasi*-legislative and *quasi*-judicial bodies, but the judges of the legislative Court of Claims, exercising judicial power, continue in office only at the pleasure of the President.

We think it plain under the Constitution that illimitable power of removal is not possessed by the President in respect of officers of the character of those just named. The authority of Congress, in creating *quasi*-legislative or *quasi*-judicial agencies, to require them to act in discharge of their duties independently of executive control cannot well be doubted, and that authority includes, as an appropriate incident, power to fix the period during which they shall continue in office, and to forbid their removal except for cause in the meantime. For it is quite evident that one who holds his office only during the pleasure of another cannot be depended upon to maintain an attitude of independence against the latter's will.

The fundamental necessity of maintaining each of the three general departments of government entirely free from the control or coercive influence, direct or indirect, of either of the others has often been stressed, and is hardly open to serious question. So much is implied in the very fact of the separation of the powers of these departments by the Constitution, and in the rule which recognizes their essential coequality. The sound application of a principle that makes one master in his own house precludes him from imposing his control in the house of another who is master there. . . .

The power of removal here claimed for the President falls within this principle, since its coercive influence threatens the independence of a commission which is not only wholly disconnected from the executive department, but which, as already fully appears, was created by Congress as a means of carrying into operation legislative and judicial powers, and as an agency of the legislative and judicial departments. . . .

The result of what we now have said is this: whether the power of the President to remove an officer shall prevail over the authority of Congress to condition the power by fixing a definite term and precluding a removal except for cause will depend upon the character of the office; the *Myers* decision, affirming the power of the President alone to make the removal, is confined to purely executive officers, and, as to officers of the kind here under consideration, we hold that no removal can be made during the prescribed term for which the officer is appointed except for one or more of the causes named in the applicable statute.

To the extent that, between the decision in the *Myers* case, which sustains the unrestrictable power of the President to remove purely executive officers, and our present

decision that such power does not extend to an office such as that here involved, there shall remain a field of doubt, we leave such cases as may fall within it for future consideration and determination as they may arise. . . .

▼▲▼

## Emergency Power

Our discussion of executive power in this section involves one central question: To what extent is the president authorized to act on behalf of the national interest in times of foreign and domestic emergencies in the absence of law, or in defiance of law? This question requires us once again to consider the influence that Locke's doctrine of executive prerogative had in the Framers' understanding of presidential power. Locke believed that executive prerogative included the power to act against the law. Executive prerogative also covered situations where laws do not yet exist, where they do exist but must be ignored, and where there can be no law. Without such power, the president could not serve the public interest as the Constitution required.[36]

Just how influential was Locke's notion of executive prerogative on the Framers' conception of presidential power in times of exigent circumstances? Some might argue that the Framers chose the language of Article II with care, instructing the president to "take care" that the nation's laws be "faithfully executed." Political scientist Donald L. Robinson has noted that such "emphatic phrasing . . . bears eloquent witness that the convention, dominated by lawyers, intended to brook no nonsense to the effect that the chief executive would have the power to suspend, ignore, or transcend the rule of law." Prerogative might be fine for monarchs, but the American president was to obey and carry out the laws strictly and faithfully.[37]

On the other hand, presidential action in times of crisis from the earliest days of the Republic belies the view that the Framers rejected Locke's notion of prerogative as a component of executive power. President Washington, considered the model for presidential adherence to the rule of law, combined a liberal interpretation of his power as commander in chief with the unstated but understood constitutional prerogative of his office to quell domestic insurrection by using force, if necessary, against the Indian tribes. Thomas Jefferson, long a critic of broad executive power, nonetheless stretched the outer boundaries of his office in his successful campaign to purchase Louisiana from France in 1803. He feared that less than immediate and decisive action would result in a lost historical opportunity. A less well-known but equally important testament to Jefferson's willingness to bend the stated powers of Article II came in 1807, when he ordered military purchases without congressional approval to respond to a naval attack by the British on an American ship. President Jefferson reported his response to Congress, and justified it by arguing that "[t]o have awaited a previous and special sanction by law would have lost occasions which might not be retrieved." On the question of whether the president was obligated to uphold only the written laws of the nation, Jefferson wrote, "[t]o lose our country by a scrupulous adherence to written law, would be to lose the law itself, with life, liberty, property and all those who are enjoying them with us; thus absurdly sacrificing the end to the means."[38]

The responses of Washington and Jefferson reflect a careful if often controversial blend of constitutional idealism and political realism that, for the most part, has since guided executive discretion in times of perceived emergencies. Until the Civil War the presidential exercise of emergency power was confined largely to matters involving external military threats to the United States. In the spring of 1846, President James J. Polk authorized American troops deployed in Texas, which had been annexed the year before, to use military force against Mexican soldiers. After a series of especially bloody battles, Polk requested a declaration of war from Congress, which he received shortly thereafter. Of historical note here is that Abraham Lincoln, then a representative from Illinois, objected to Polk's request, claiming that *no one man* should hold the power" to lead the nation into war.[39] In fact, Lincoln was instrumental in persuading the House of Representatives to censure President Polk for initiating an "unnecessary and unconstitutional" war.[40]

The Mexican War of 1846 was the second war, after the War of 1812 (against Great Britain), to be declared by Congress. It was by no means, however, the second armed conflict into which the United States had entered since 1789. Several presidents had authorized the worldwide deployment of naval forces throughout the early nineteenth century to secure American commercial interests and engaged American troops to fight what have been called "quasi-wars," or wars never approved by Congress.[41] The first such quasi-war came during the presidency of John Adams (1797–1801), who ordered American naval forces into an undeclared war with France from 1798 to 1800 to resolve a dispute between the two countries over the Jay Treaty of 1795. President Adams's power to engage in such sustained military action was challenged in court by political opponents in Congress as a violation of his Article II authority. This confrontation reached the Supreme Court. In two separate decisions, *Bas v. Tingy* (1800) and *Talbot* v. *Seeman* (1801), the Court recognized the existence of such limited warfare as a condition of relations between nations and declared presidential conduct in these matters constitutional.[42] The Court, in these decisions, also established the constitutional credence for another, often ignored facet of the relationship between Congress and the president in times of war: Congress is capable and willing to support presidential initiatives in military conflicts through means other than a declaration of war.

Since the first quasi-war between the United States and France, the United States has engaged in more than 125 such conflicts. These have included high-profile, full-scale undeclared wars such as the Korean War (1950–1953), the Vietnam War (1954–1973), and the Persian Gulf War (1991) and lesser but still substantial exertions of military force to secure American interests in Cuba (1962), Grenada (1983), Libya (1986), Lebanon (1982–1984), Panama (1989–1990), Somalia (1993), Haiti (1993–1994), Bosnia (1994), and Yugoslavia (1999).[43] Congress has issued an official declaration of war in only three instances since the Mexican War of 1845: in the Spanish-American War of 1898, World War I (1914–1918), and World War II (1939–1945). President McKinley precipitated the 1898 war by sending an American battleship into Havana, Cuba, to confront Spain over Cuban independence. America entered World War I in April 1917 and World War II in December 1941. In each case the United States had been indirectly involved as a supplier of equipment, munitions, and money to its allies well before the president asked for and Congress passed an official declaration of war.

President Lincoln's broad and bold use of executive power during the Civil War recast the debate over presidential prerogative. For the first time an American president defended the prerogative of the executive to go beyond what either the Court or Congress had recognized as the written law governing the president's role as commander in chief. No president prior to Lincoln stretched the boundaries of executive power or duties as commander in chief as he had. Then again, no president had been faced with an internal crisis that was remotely comparable to that of the Civil War. Thus it was no surprise that the Court was soon called upon to decide whether Lincoln's invocation of executive power to conduct and manage the Civil War violated the Constitution. The Court, in the *Prize Cases* (1863), was presented with the question of whether President Lincoln's command to impose a naval blockade of Southern ports usurped the power of Congress to declare war.[44] This case was the first of several that the Court decided during the Civil War and in the ensuing Reconstruction period that involved challenges to the crisis-driven exercise of presidential or legislative power.

Whereas Article II, Section 2, reserves to the president the power to command the armed and naval forces of the United States and the militias of the "several States, when called into the actual Service of the United States," Article I, Section 8, gives Congress the power to:

[D]eclare War, grant Letters of Marque and Reprisal, and make Rules concerning the Captures on Land and Water; To raise and support Armies. . . . To provide and maintain a Navy; to make Rules for the Government and Regulation of the land and naval Forces; To provide for calling forth the Militia to execute the Laws of the Union, suppress Insurrections, and repel Invasions.

The *Prize Cases* required the Court to wrestle with the absolute versus shared nature of constitutional power between Congress and the president. Note how the Court conceded the plaintiffs' assertions that President Lincoln's decision to order the blockade of Southern ports was the equivalent of an act of war and that Congress alone, not the president, possessed the power the declare war. Even so, a 5-4 majority upheld Lincoln's actions as consistent with his obligation as commander in chief to suppress an insurrection. Although Congress did not recognize the "insurrection" against

the United States by the "sovereign" states of the Confederacy until July 1861, the Court concluded that the hostilities that commenced with Fort Sumter placed the nation in a state of war, thus triggering the president's power as commander in chief. Justice Samuel Nelson, writing on behalf of the Court's four dissenters, insisted that Lincoln's orders violated the "sole" power of Congress to "declare war or recognize its existence."[45]

The Court's opinion in the *Prize Cases* provided Lincoln with the constitutional foundation upon which to conduct his aggressive prosecution of the Civil War and validated several of his most controversial decisions. Before the *Prize Cases* had even been decided, President Lincoln had instituted a draft, ordered the arrest and imprisonment of countless civilians for alleged conspiracies against the United States, and commanded low-level officials throughout the nation to monitor dissent in the newspapers (and, if necessary, arrest their editors and publishers). Congress usually followed suit with legislation authorizing the president to take such action, but Lincoln's indiscriminate willingness to violate the civil liberties of American civilians led his opponents in Congress and the press—and even some supporters—to label him a "dictator, (for that and nothing less than it does)."[46] The Court's holding that the president was authorized to take all appropriate action to defend the nation when war was forced upon it "without waiting for any special legislative authority" also amounted to indirect approval of Lincoln's decision to suspend the writ of habeas corpus privilege.[47]

But three years later, in *Ex parte Milligan* (1866), the Court trimmed the sails of the president's expansive power to take emergency measures during times of war and insurrection. In *Milligan* the Court ruled that the conviction of a civilian by a military commission in an area where civil courts continued to function was unconstitutional.[48] A unanimous Court made clear that a genuine crisis must be actual and present for the president to activate his emergency powers, especially when the action undertaken violates the rights of civilians otherwise protected by the Constitution. *Milligan* involved the arrest of an Indiana attorney on charges of plotting to secure the release of Confederate prisoners held in border states such as his own, Ohio, and Illinois and to provide them with arms to take up their cause. Indiana, especially the southern region where L. P. Milligan lived, had been settled by Southerners making their way up the Ohio river or through Kentucky and was generally sympathetic to slave interests and the secession of the Confederate states. For his fanaticism on behalf of the Southern crusade, Milligan had become quite well-known to Union military authorities who patrolled the border states for traitors and signs of insurrection.[49]

In October 1864 military authorities arrested Milligan, along with several other "Copperheads," as Northern and border-state sympathizers active in support of the Confederate states were known, and charged him with treason. Such power derived from President Lincoln's September 1862 proclamation announcing that "all Rebels and Insurgents, their aiders and abettors within the United States, and all persons discouraging volunteer enlistments, resisting militia drafts, or guilty of any disloyal practice . . . shall be subject to martial law and liable to trial and punishment by Courts Martial or Military Commission." One prominent historian has commented that Lincoln's order here went too far, "indeed, in overriding the civil courts. Moreover, as it came two days after the Emancipation Proclamation, it seemed to offer a threat of overcoming all opposition to that measure by harsh punitive arrests."[50]

The Court did not hear and decide *Milligan* until April 1866. By then the Civil War had ended, as had President Lincoln's life at the hands of his assassin, John Wilkes Booth. In the interim, Milligan had remained imprisoned, his death sentence commuted by President Andrew Johnson in 1865. Eased from the exigencies that the Civil War had created for American constitutionalism, the Court made clear that presidential power to suspend the constitutional rights of civilians and exercise executive prerogative as President Lincoln had did not extend beyond wartime emergencies. For the Court, Justice David Davis, a Lincoln appointee, wrote:

> The Constitution . . . is a law for rulers and people, equally in war and in peace, and covers with the shield of its protection all classes of men, at all times and under all circumstances. No doctrine, involving more pernicious consequences, was ever invented by the wit of man than that any of its provisions can be suspended during any of the great exigencies of government. . . .

> Martial law cannot arise from a threatened invasion. The necessity must be actual and present; the invasion real, such as effectually closes the courts. . . .

> Martial rule can never exist where the courts are open, and in the proper and unobstructed exercise of their jurisdiction. It is also confined to the locality of actual war.[51]

Radical Republicans in Congress, who believed the decision would impede the federal government's authority to enforce the military occupation of the South during Reconstruction and disciplinary measures against potential seditionists, denounced *Milligan*. Nonetheless, most historians believe that the Court's decision drew the correct line between what it recognized as the need for the "extra-constitutional" exercise of presidential power in wartime and the supremacy of civilian institutions over the military in nonexigent circumstances.

Woodrow Wilson exercised considerable discretionary power over the nation's public and private interests upon the entrance of the United States into World War I. He did so with congressional approval, thus avoiding a major showdown in the Supreme Court. Moreover, Congress delegated almost complete power to President Wilson to manage the war effort through a law authorizing him to impose whatever emergency measures he deemed appropriate. With this broad mandate, Wilson created several commissions, such as the Council of National Defense and the War Industries Board, to manage the nation's economic affairs. The council regulated everything from food production and distribution to transportation and communication. To assist him with complex issues in budgetary and financial management, Wilson appointed to these boards several Wall Street titans and business tycoons, who, in turn, often exercised "dictator-like" control over the nation's economy. Congress did not grant or require any statutory authority for the president's decisions. Instead, Wilson relied upon his inherent powers as the nation's chief executive and commander in chief to engage in emergency-related presidential action of a magnitude unseen since Lincoln's management of the Civil War.[52]

With the encouragement and approval of President Wilson, Congress also enacted several laws during World War I (and also in response to the 1918 Communist revolution in Russia) that, in retrospect, clearly violated the civil liberties of American citizens. The foremost of these, the Espionage Act of 1917, was intended to compel obedience to the wartime draft. The law's real effect was to constrict the rights of political dissenters. The Court upheld numerous convictions under the law, even though the accused individuals were often guilty of nothing more than expressing their vigorous opposition to the dominant political climate. Civil liberties violations in the three best-known cases of this period, *Schenck v. United States* (1919), *Debs v. United States* (1919), and *Abrams v. United States* (1919), were casualties of the wartime atmosphere.[53]

*Debs,* in particular, is notable for the stain it left on the Court's First Amendment jurisprudence and for the crisis of conscience it appeared to arouse in Justice Oliver Wendell Holmes. For a unanimous Court, Justice Holmes had written the opinion that sent Eugene Debs, a well-known political activist and labor organizer, to prison for speaking out against World War I and on behalf of economic socialism. In upholding Deb's conviction under the Espionage Act, Holmes wrote that "one purpose of speech, whether incidental or not does not matter, was to oppose not only war in general but this war." This opposition was so expressed "that its natural and intended effect would be to obstruct recruiting" into the draft. Although Holmes sent Debs to prison with "cryptic dispatch," the case led the justice to doubt the premises of his thoughts on free speech. As one First Amendment scholar has commented: "In the course of a few short months, [Holmes] underwent a spectacular conversion experience. It was if some angel of free speech had appeared to Holmes in the night."[54] In *Abrams,* the next major protest case to reach the Court, Holmes penned one of the most famous of his great dissents, the one that introduced the metaphor of the "marketplace of ideas" into the lexicon of free speech thought.[55]

Nonetheless, the action of Congress and President Wilson, upheld by a Court sensitive to stated emergency needs of the American government in wartime and domestic crisis, eased the path for the spectacular assertion of such powers by President Franklin Roosevelt during World War II. Using his first inaugural speech in March 1933, Roosevelt asked Congress for emergency

power to combat the Great Depression. He claimed that such power was "the one remaining instrument to meet the crisis—broad Executive power to wage a war against the emergency as great as the power that would be given me if we were in fact invaded by a foreign foe."[56] Democratic majorities in the House and Senate embraced Roosevelt's assertion of executive discretion to institute emergency measures to relieve the Depression. The Court, however, resisted the New Deal legislative agenda with an air of spectacular defiance. The confrontation between the Court and Roosevelt produced a constitutional crisis, one that was not resolved until the Court's self-imposed revolution of 1937, an event that we discuss in considerable detail in Chapters 6 and 9.

By the time the United States entered into World War II, the Court had given President Roosevelt full and complete power to impose emergency domestic measures in the service of national security interests, whether economic or political in nature, regardless of their impact on the civil liberties of American citizens. As an exercise in raw executive power, few presidential orders compare to President Roosevelt's decision in February 1942 to order the evacuation of Japanese Americans from the West Coast and intern them indefinitely into makeshift prison camps. This decision came just six weeks after Japan's attack in December 1941 on American air bases in Pearl Harbor, Hawaii. Japanese Americans awaiting notification of their evacuation were subjected to government-imposed curfews, general in nature and without regard to suspicion of alleged seditious activities.[57]

In *Hirabayashi v. United States* (1943), the Court ruled in the first of three cases decided within the next two years that challenged President Roosevelt's executive orders directed at Japanese Americans. Rather than assess whether the president alone possessed the authority to order a curfew for Japanese Americans, a unanimous Court ruled that Congress *and* the president had acted lawfully in their joint exercise of "wartime" power. Chief Justice Harlan Fiske Stone, keenly aware of the ironies involved in the Court's decision, went to great pains to point out that the government's order was not motivated by racial discrimination, which he stated was "odious to a free people." Instead, Stone emphasized the need to monitor the threat posed by Japanese

Americans, who had demonstrated no real interest in becoming "an integral part of the white population." Japanese immigrants, the chief justice noted, maintained strong "attachments to Japan and its institutions" and sent their children to Japanese-language schools to maintain ties to their cultural heritage.[58]

In conference, Justice Frank Murphy expressed outrage that Stone could justify such an obvious display of racial bigotry. That same year, Stone had been instrumental in persuading the Court to reverse a 1940 decision upholding the expulsion of Jehovah's Witnesses from the public schools for their refusal to salute the flag. In *West Virginia* v. *Barnette* (1943), the chief justice had encouraged the Court to put aside the nation's suspicion of the unfamiliar, especially during a time of war, and insist that civil liberties were not subject to the pendulum of war and peace.[59] Now, Stone was capable of writing that a curfew on "residents having ethnic affiliations with an invading enemy" was a reasonable exercise of government power during wartime. Several other justices appealed to Murphy to withdraw his dissent, arguing that anything less than a unanimous opinion on the curfew order would play into the hands of the enemy. In the end, he agreed.

*Hirabayashi,* however, is where Murphy drew the line. In *Korematsu* v. *United States* (1944), the Court upheld President Roosevelt's evacuation and internment order as a valid exercise of wartime power.[60] Justice Hugo Black's opinion on behalf of the 6-3 majority to provide the federal government with all requisite power to protect American shores from hostile forces offers a vivid contrast to the fears expressed in the separate dissents of Justice Murphy and Justice Robert Jackson. Murphy and Jackson argued that the Court had cleared a path for Congress and the president to run rampant over the civil liberties of American citizens at the slightest provocation. Justice Jackson wrote that the federal government's action was "a military expedient that has no place in law under the Constitution." Justice Murphy castigated the Court for exceeding the "brink of constitutional power" that he believed the Court in *Hirabayashi* had established for presidential authority in wartime. In Murphy's view the Court's opinion amounted to the "legalization of racism."[61] The related SIDEBAR provides a much richer description of the social and historical context of the Court's decision to exclude more than 112,000 persons of Japanese descent, 70,000 of whom were American citizens.

Presidents Wilson and Roosevelt both used their executive discretion and commander-in-chief powers to exercise substantial controls over all aspects of the national economy during wartime. That discretion extended to presidential intervention in labor strikes when such disputes threatened industrial production in areas believed necessary to promote American foreign policy. In June 1941, seven months prior to America's entrance into World War II, President Roosevelt sent two thousand Army soldiers to a Los Angeles aircraft plant to maintain order while labor and management, at his request, negotiated a settlement to a labor dispute. Congress had provided no express authority for the president to seize control of industrial production. Rather, the legislative branch simply accepted Roosevelt's assumption that the president possessed the inherent power to respond to emergencies created by wartime necessity as the nation's chief foreign policy architect and decision maker. The Court had validated this inherent power in *United States* v. *Curtiss-Wright Export Corp.* (1936), a case of stunning consequence that we will discuss later in this chapter.[62]

It was against this legal and political background that President Harry S. Truman issued an executive order in April 1952 compelling the secretary of commerce to seize control of the nation's steel plants in anticipation of an industrywide strike by the United Steelworkers Union. Unlike President Roosevelt's action in the Japanese American curfew and internment cases, Truman's order did not coincide with a congressional resolution or statute authorizing such action. Since June 1950, when President Truman first authorized American air and naval strikes to defend South Korea from an invasion by North Korea, the United States had been steadfastly committed to the containment of Soviet and Chinese aggression in the East Asian region. President Truman never asked Congress for a declaration of war against North Korea to justify American military intervention there because circumstances did not require it. Congress reflected the post–World War II consensus in American public opinion that tacitly accepted the need for the president to do what was necessary to defend American economic and territorial interests abroad against the perceived expansionist threat of Soviet and

Chinese Communism, even if such action came at the expense of congressional authority in foreign affairs.[63]

President Truman initially justified his seizure order as commensurate with his wartime responsibilities as commander in chief and consistent with his obligation to faithfully execute the laws as president of the United States. By this time, Truman had sent American ground troops to Korea as part of a United Nations effort to contain the North Korean invasion. Like the order to commence air and naval bombardment in June 1950, the president's decision later that December to lend American support to the ground war came without congressional authorization. The steel-seizure directive was the latest in a line of executive orders by President Truman that drew their justification from his earlier declaration that the Korean War had created a national state of emergency and therefore supported bold presidential action.

But what made *Youngstown Sheet & Tube Co.* v. *Sawyer* (1952) an even more dramatic showdown over President's Truman assertion of near limitless presidential power was the argument put forth by the Justice Department to defend the steel-seizure order. Rather than follow the historical precedent set by Wilson and Roosevelt, Assistant Attorney General Homer Balbridge argued that president's inherent power allowed him to take any action necessary as long as it was directed toward emergency conditions. The courts, moreover, were powerless to control the exercise of such power. Indeed, when asked at a press conference if his seizure of the steel mills meant he could also "seize the newspapers and/or the radio stations," President Truman replied that "under similar circumstances the president of the United States [could] act for whatever is for the best of the country." His response did not receive a positive response in Congress. While deferential to presidential power in times of war and domestic crisis, Congress was not willing to abdicate completely its foreign policy role to the executive. By the time Truman backtracked from his original assertion, a federal court judge had issued a decisive and pointed rejection of the administration's analysis of emergency presidential power.[64]

The Court affirmed the lower court ruling, but divided five ways on why the president's inherent power to take emergency action on behalf of the nation had its limits. Only Justice Black, who wrote the Court's opin-ion, and Justice Douglas concluded that the president needed specific constitutional or statutory authority to seize private property in exigent circumstances. Four other justices concluded that such authority was not always required, but agreed that Truman's action had pushed the limits of presidential power. Because Justice Robert H. Jackson's concurrence emphasized the importance of the exercise of concurrent power by Congress and the president in emergency situations, most scholars consider Jackson's opinion to be the most influential of those produced by the *Youngstown Sheet & Tube* case. Does Jackson's opinion hold up in light of the techniques of modern warfare, which often require a rapid response inconceivable in 1952?

Chief Justice Fred Vinson dissented, claiming that the Court's emphasis on the concurrent exercise of power in times of crisis amounted to a "messenger-boy concept of the [executive] Office." This view, Vinson believed, did not vest the president with the appropriate power to enforce legislative programs or save them from their "destruction so that Congress will have something left to act." Rather than point to his commander-in-chief authority to justify such prerogative action, Vinson emphasized the president's broad power as the nation's chief executive. Of interest here is the much more pragmatic quality of Vinson's dissent when compared with Jackson's scholarly approach. Could Chief Justice Vinson's experience prior to his appointment to the Court in 1946—first as director of the Office of Economic Stabilization under Roosevelt during World War II and then as secretary of the treasury under President Truman—have had anything to do with his decision to view the steel-seizure order as one of political expediency?

Constitutional scholar John Hart Ely has commented that the Cold War, which began the moment that Franklin Roosevelt; the prime minister of England, Winston Churchill; and the president of the Soviet Union, Joseph Stalin, shook hands after signing the Yalta treaty of 1945 (the document that divided up control of the defeated and conquered European continent), bequeathed the United States a number of unfortunate legacies. These included a sense of permanent emergency, a consequent condition of continuous large-scale military preparation, and an "infectious attitude of secrecy" to guard against foreign and domestic knowledge of the national security state.[65] The Court, in

*Youngstown Sheet & Tube,* drew a firm line on the exercise of executive prerogative in the domestic sphere. Nevertheless, presidents from Dwight D. Eisenhower to Richard Nixon continued to cite the Cold War and the sense of permanent crisis that existed between the United States and its enemies and to use executive power in the military, national security, and foreign policy arenas with little or no resistance from Congress. Congressional acquiescence permitted President Lyndon Johnson (1963–1969) to escalate United States involvement in Vietnam to a level far beyond that of any of his predecessors. This included President John F. Kennedy (1961–1963), who had stepped up the American presence in Vietnam to a much greater degree than it had been under President Eisenhower (1953–1961).

The true turning point for presidential power to conduct "undeclared" war came in 1964, when President Johnson sought and received congressional authorization to increase American military involvement in Vietnam to warlike levels. The Gulf of Tonkin Resolution, which did not have the force of law, authorized the "President . . . to take all necessary steps, including the use of armed force, to assist any member or protocol state of the Southeast Asia Collective Defense Treaty requesting defense of its freedom." Antiwar activists brought suit on several occasions in the late 1960s and early 1970s asking the Court to declare the American presence in Vietnam unconstitutional because of the absence of a congressional war declaration. The Court refused to consider these requests on the grounds that the relationship between Congress and president in the conduct of war was a political question.[66]

By the late 1960s domestic support for American involvement in Vietnam began to deteriorate, in large part because of the widening gap between what Americans were reading in their newspapers and seeing on the nightly television news and the government's continued insistence on the war's success. To restore public confidence in the war effort, Secretary of Defense Robert McNamara commissioned the Rand Corporation, a nongovernmental research organization, to collect top-secret government materials related to the war and produce a comprehensive analysis of American involvement in Vietnam. McNamara had expressed his own private doubts about the war; he believed, however, that the report would vindicate the American war effort. But

the forty-seven-volume report, referred to within the government as the Pentagon Papers, proved so critical and damning to the government's position that plans for its eventual public release were immediately canceled.

The Pentagon Papers, in the words of Pulitzer Prize–winning journalist Sanford J. Ungar, "illustrated the Orwellian vocabulary of Vietnam policymaking, a bizarre combination of frontier talk and show business jargon" used to discuss the business of war. Such language troubled several members of the Vietnam History Task Force, created by McNamara and without the knowledge of President Johnson after the commission of the Pentagon Papers, to further study America's worsening position in the war. Said one member:

> To talk about the use of bombing as if it were an orchestral score—you know, heavy on the brass, a bit of tympani, and that sort of thing—when you're talking about the use of napalm and high explosives and terrible devices . . . was very dangerous.[67]

Only fifteen copies of the Pentagon Papers were distributed to McNamara and other high-level officials involved with the Vietnam War. Embarrassed by their contents, Pentagon officials gave the Pentagon Papers a "top-secret-sensitive" classification and buried them to ensure that no one within the government would have access to make them public. This strategy enabled the Pentagon Papers to remain secret for almost four years. But in March 1971, after months of careful negotiation, Daniel Ellsberg, one of the lead authors on the project, agreed to provide copies to *New York Times* reporter and former Vietnam correspondent Neil Sheehan. After his work on the Pentagon Papers, Ellsberg's opposition to America's involvement in the war intensified to the point that he viewed his decision to release all but the final four volumes of the report as a way to help stop "the bombing and killing."[68]

The *New York Times,* after having debated the legal and journalistic issues involved in publishing classified government materials, began running excerpts from the Pentagon Papers in June 1971. By this time Ellsberg had also made copies of the Pentagon Papers available to the *Washington Post,* which had held the same internal debate. Two days after the *New York Times* ran its first installment, the Nixon administration requested a federal court to enjoin the paper, along with the *Washington*

*Post,* from publishing further excerpts. The lower court refused, but an appeals court granted President Nixon's request. On June 25 the Court agreed to hear the Pentagon Papers case and set arguments for the next day. In the interim, the Court upheld the appeals court's decision to enjoin publication of the Pentagon Papers until it ruled on the case.

Within a week, the Court announced its historic ruling in *New York Times Co. v. United States* (1971), holding that the president possessed no inherent power to order the prior restraint of the Pentagon Papers from publication by either the *New York Times* or the *Washington Post.*[69] So divided was the Court's 6-3 decision that the justices were left to issue an unsigned, *per curiam* opinion on behalf of the majority and issue individual concurring opinions. The Court's three dissenters issued separate opinions as well. As dramatic as the Court's decision was for its firm rejection of the most significant crisis-based claim of presidential power since *Youngstown Sheet & Tube,* only two justices, Black and Douglas, believed that such prior restraint, with or without congressional authorization, was always unconstitutional. The remaining justices who signed the Court's opinion concluded that the president possessed the power to quash the dissemination of information whose publication could cause irreparable damage to national security. Congressional authorization and the individual merits of the government's claim, however, bolstered the constitutionality of such action.[70]

In dissent, Justice John Harlan suggested the Court had been "irresponsibly feverish in dealing" with the Pentagon Papers case. Do you believe that the Court was motivated, in part, by the need to dispose of the injunction that was restraining the publication of the Pentagon Papers as much as by the need to resolve an unprecedented question involving presidential power in a wartime environment? Suppose that Ellsberg had given the Pentagon Papers to a small, radical antiwar publication instead of two titans of the mainstream American news media, whose respective editors deliberated the propriety of publishing the papers for months before they finally went ahead. Do you believe the Court might have ruled in favor of the government?

By the time the Pentagon Papers were published, public opposition to the Vietnam War had increased to the point where such opinion now reflected the domi-

nant mood of Congress. Put off by what it believed was an intentional campaign of deceit and disinformation by the Nixon administration with regard to American involvement in Vietnam, Congress, for the first time in the post–World War II era, sought to reclaim its constitutional role in the conduct and management of war.[71] In 1973, Congress, over the veto of President Nixon, passed the War Powers Resolution, which requires the president to consult Congress when possible before committing American forces to imminent hostilities. The resolution also requires the president to inform Congress within forty-eight hours of sending American military forces into hostilities of the purpose and intent of his order. Finally, the resolution authorizes Congress, after a period of sixty days, to recall armed forces in the absence of an additional resolution approving the president's stated mission, or to pass a declaration of war.

Over time, however, the War Powers Resolution has been little more than a paper tiger. Each president since Nixon has committed American armed forces to foreign hostilities with almost no invocation of its provisions. For example, prior to the American-led invasion of United Nations forces into Iraq in January 1991, President Bush had committed thousands of American troops and air and naval power, of a level unseen since Vietnam, as far back as August 1990 in preparation for the Persian Gulf War. Yet Bush did not consult with Congress until after the fact. Although the United States accomplished its objectives in the Gulf War in a swift and impressive fashion, Congress never really injected itself into the decision-making process, making the "portrait of a passive, quiescent Congress in the face of unilateral presidential military actions painfully familiar."[72] In sum, the War Powers Resolution has had no real impact on presidential power to conduct war and has failed in its initial objective to promote joint executive-legislative consultation in such matters.

Presidential conduct in times of war and foreign policy–related crises often straddles the line between the domestic and international spheres of influence. Our final case in this section illustrates, in a somewhat novel context, how intertwined domestic and foreign interests can be in the exercise of emergency presidential power. In December 1979, two months after Iranian militants seized the American embassy in Teheran, Iran, and took as hostages American diplomatic personnel, President

Jimmy Carter, with congressional authorization, froze all Iranian assets held within the United States. In a series of executive orders, President Carter barred parties whose assets had been affected by his decision from seeking their release in court. In January 1981, President Carter secured the release of the hostages through a complex agreement that also terminated the freeze on Iranian assets and agreed to the resolution of related claims by a joint Iranian-American tribunal.

In *Dames & Moore* v. *Regan* (1981), the Court revisited a question that had occupied center stage in *Youngstown Sheet & Tube:* To what extent was it permissible for the president to seize private property in the service of an American foreign policy emergency?[73] But *Dames & Moore* involved one critical fact that distinguished it from President Truman's 1951 order seizing control of the nation's steel mills: President Carter's action was permissible under federal law. For an 8-1 Court, Justice Rehnquist upheld the president's order as a valid exercise of presidential power in a time of crisis. Compare Rehnquist's opinion with the separate opinions of Justices Black and Jackson in *Youngstown Sheet & Tube.* Which one do you believe was more influential?

## The Prize Cases
### 67 U.S. 935 (1863)

After a bitterly fought and tightly contested battle, Republican candidate Abraham Lincoln was elected president in 1860. Before his inauguration in March 1861, seven Southern states seceded from the United States in response to Lincoln's victory. In April 1861, just moments after Confederate forces fired on Fort Sumter, near the coast of South Carolina, Lincoln declared an insurrection against the Union, called forth state militias to suppress the rebellion, suspended the writ of habeas corpus, and ordered a blockade of Southern ports. One month later, Lincoln authorized millions of dollars in federal expenditures on behalf of the war, increased the size of the Union's armed and naval forces, and amassed a debt of $250 million, an amount unheard of during this time.

President Lincoln executed all these orders while Congress was in recess. Not until July 1861 did Congress convene in a special session to hear the president explain his

unilateral decisions and debate their constitutional fitness. President Lincoln justified his unprecedented decisions as appropriate not just in his role as the commander in chief, but in his capacity as the nation's chief executive to faithfully enforce and carry out the law. After some debate, Congress passed a resolution approving the president's decisions as having the same force and power as if they had been done under the previous express authority and direction of Congress.

The Court's decision was 5 to 4. Justice Grier delivered the opinion of the Court. Justice Nelson, joined by Chief Justice Taney and Justices Catron and Clifford, dissented.

▼▲▼

MR. JUSTICE GRIER delivered the opinion of the Court.

There are certain propositions of law which must necessarily affect the ultimate decision of these cases, and many others which it will be proper to discuss and decide before we notice the special facts peculiar to each.

They are, 1st. Had the President a right to institute a blockade of ports in possession of persons in armed rebellion against the Government, on the principles of international law, as known and acknowledged among civilized States? . . .

That a blockade *de facto* actually existed, and was formally declared and notified by the President on the 27th and 30th of April, 1861, is an admitted fact in these cases.

That the President, as the Executive Chief of the Government and Commander-in-chief of the Army and Navy, was the proper person to make such notification has not been, and cannot be disputed.

The right of prize and capture has its origin in the "*jus belli*" [laws of war], and is governed and adjudged under the law of nations. To legitimate the capture of a neutral vessel or property on the high seas, a war must exist *de facto*, and the neutral must have knowledge or notice of the intention of one of the parties belligerent to use this mode of coercion against a port, city, or territory, in possession of the other.

Let us enquire whether, at the time this blockade was instituted, a state of war existed which would justify a resort to these means of subduing the hostile force.

War has been well defined to be, "That state in which a nation prosecutes its right by force."

The parties belligerent in a public war are independent nations. But it is not necessary, to constitute war, that both parties should be acknowledged as independent nations or sovereign States. A war may exist where one of the belligerents claims sovereign rights as against the other.

Insurrection against a government may or may not culminate in an organized rebellion, but a civil war always begins by insurrection against the lawful authority of the Government. A civil war is never solemnly declared; it becomes such by its accidents—the number, power, and organization of the persons who originate and carry it on. When the party in rebellion occupy and hold in a hostile manner a certain portion of territory, have declared their independence, have cast off their allegiance, have organized armies, have commenced hostilities against their former sovereign, the world acknowledges them as belligerents, and the contest a war. They claim to be in arms to establish their liberty and independence, in order to become a sovereign State, while the sovereign party treats them as insurgents and rebels who owe allegiance, and who should be punished with death for their treason.

The laws of war, as established among nations, have their foundation in reason, and all tend to mitigate the cruelties and misery produced by the scourge of war. Hence the parties to a civil war usually concede to each other belligerent rights. They exchange prisoners, and adopt the other courtesies and rules common to public or national wars. . . .

As a civil war is never publicly proclaimed, *eo nomine*, against insurgents, its actual existence is a fact in our domestic history which the Court is bound to notice and to know.

The true test of its existence, as found in the writings of the sages of the common law, may be thus summarily stated: "When the regular course of justice is interrupted by revolt, rebellion, or insurrection, so that the Courts of Justice cannot be kept open, *civil war exists*, and hostilities may be prosecuted on the same footing as if those opposing the Government were foreign enemies invading the land."

By the Constitution, Congress alone has the power to declare a national or foreign war. It cannot declare war against a State, or any number of States, by virtue of any clause in the Constitution. The Constitution confers on the President the whole Executive power. He is bound to take care that the laws be faithfully executed. He is Commander-in-chief of the Army and Navy of the United States, and of the militia of the several States when called into the actual service of the United States. He has no power to initiate or declare a war either against a foreign nation or a domestic State. But, by the Acts of Congress of February 28th, 1795, and 3d of March, 1807, he is authorized to call out the militia and use the military and naval forces of the United States in case of invasion by foreign nations and to suppress insurrection against the government of a State or of the United States.

If a war be made by invasion of a foreign nation, the President is not only authorized but bound to resist force by force. He does not initiate the war, but is bound to accept the challenge without waiting for any special legislative authority. And whether the hostile party be a foreign invader or States organized in rebellion, it is nonetheless a war although the declaration of it be "unilateral." Lord Stowell observes, "It is not the less a war on that account, for war may exist without a declaration on either side. It is so laid down by the best writers on the law of nations. A declaration of war by one country only is not a mere challenge to be accepted or refused at pleasure by the other." . . .

It is not the less a civil war, with belligerent parties in hostile array, because it may be called an "insurrection" by one side, and the insurgents be considered as rebels or traitors. It is not necessary that the independence of the revolted province or State be acknowledged in order to constitute it a party belligerent in a war according to the law of nations. Foreign nations acknowledge it as war by a declaration of neutrality. The condition of neutrality cannot exist unless there be two belligerent parties. . . .

Whether the President, in fulfilling his duties as Commander-in-chief in suppressing an insurrection, has met with such armed hostile resistance and a civil war of such alarming proportions as will compel him to accord to them the character of belligerents is a question to be decided by him, and this Court must be governed by the decisions and acts of the political department of the Government to which this power was entrusted. "He must determine what degree of force the crisis demands." The proclamation of blockade is itself official and conclusive evidence to the Court that a state of war existed which demanded and authorized a recourse to such a measure under the circumstances peculiar to the case.

MR. JUSTICE NELSON, dissenting.

. . . In the case of a rebellion or resistance of a portion of the people of a country against the established government, there is no doubt, if in its progress and enlargement the government thus sought to be overthrown sees fit, it may by the competent power recognize or declare the existence of a state of civil war, which will draw after it all the consequences and rights of war between the contending parties as in the case of a public war. Mr. Wheaton observes, speaking of civil war, "But the general usage of nations regards such a war as entitling both the contending parties to all the rights of war as against each other, and even as respects neutral nations." It is not to be denied, therefore, that if a civil war existed between that portion of the people in organized insurrection to overthrow this Government at the time this vessel and cargo were seized, and if she was guilty of a violation of the blockade, she would be lawful prize of war. But before this insurrection against the established Government can be dealt with on the footing of a civil war, within the meaning of the law of nations and the Constitution of the United States, and which will draw after it belligerent rights, it must be recognized or declared by the war-making power of the Government. No power short of this can change the legal status of the Government or the relations of its citizens from that of peace to a state of war, or bring into existence all those duties and obligations of neutral third parties growing out of a state of war. The war power of the Government must be exercised before this changed condition of the Government and people and of neutral third parties can be admitted. There is no difference in this respect between a civil or a public war. . . .

An idea seemed to be entertained that all that was necessary to constitute a war was organized hostility in the district of a country in a state of rebellion—that conflicts on land and on sea—the taking of towns and capture of fleets—in fine, the magnitude and dimensions of the resistance against the Government—constituted war with all the belligerent rights belonging to civil war. With a view to enforce this idea, we had, during the argument, an imposing historical detail of the several measures adopted by the Confederate States to enable them to resist the authority of the general Government, and of many bold and daring acts of resistance and of conflict. It was said that war was to be ascertained by looking at the armies and navies or public force of the contending parties, and the battles lost and won—that, in the language of one of the learned counsel, "Whenever the situation of opposing hostilities has assumed the proportions and pursued the methods of war, then peace is driven out, the ordinary authority and administration of law are suspended, and war in fact and by necessity is the status of the nation until peace is restored and the laws resumed their dominion."

Now, in one sense, no doubt this is war, and may be a war of the most extensive and threatening dimensions and effects, but it is a statement simply of its existence in a material sense, and has no relevancy or weight when the question is what constitutes war in a legal sense, in the sense of the law of nations, and of the Constitution of the United States? For it must be a war in this sense to attach to it all the consequences that belong to belligerent rights. Instead, therefore, of inquiring after armies and

navies, and victories lost and won, or organized rebellion against the general Government, the inquiry should be into the law of nations and into the municipal fundamental laws of the Government. For we find there that to constitute a civil war in the sense in which we are speaking, before it can exist in contemplation of law, it must be recognized or declared by the sovereign power of the State, and which sovereign power by our Constitution is lodged in the Congress of the United States—civil war, therefore, under our system of government, can exist only by an act of Congress, which requires the assent of two of the great departments of the Government, the Executive and Legislative. . . .

Upon the whole, after the most careful consideration of this case which the pressure of other duties has admitted, I am compelled to the conclusion that no civil war existed between this Government and the States in insurrection till recognized by the Act of Congress 13th of July, 1861; that the President does not possess the power under the Constitution to declare war or recognize its existence within the meaning of the law of nations, which carries with it belligerent rights, and thus change the country and all its citizens from a state of peace to a state of war; that this power belongs exclusively to the Congress of the United States, and, consequently, that the President had no power to set on foot a blockade under the law of nations, and that the capture of the vessel and cargo in this case, and in all cases before us in which the capture occurred before the 13th of July, 1861, for breach of blockade, or as enemies' property, are illegal and void, and that the decrees of condemnation should be reversed, and the vessel and cargo restored.

## Korematsu v. United States
### 323 U.S. 214 (1944)

In *Plessy* v. *Ferguson* (1896), Homer Plessy was arrested for violating a Louisiana law making it illegal for members of the "colored race" to ride in the same train cars as whites. Segregation on rail systems was one the originating points of "Jim Crow," the name given to the system of racial apartheid that dominated the South from the collapse of Reconstruction until the early 1960s. One of the ironies of *Plessy* was that its protagonist had often passed as white in the diverse Creole community of late-1800s New Orleans. His deliberate effort to flout the segregation law was supported by one of the city's leading civil liberties lawyers, Rudolph Desdunes, who headed the New Orleans branch of the American Citizens' Equal Rights Association. Desdunes had recruited Plessy to test the rail car law in large part because of his "white" features. But according to the Southern system, any person who possessed one drop of "colored" blood was considered a member of the "colored race." If he had not proclaimed his mixed heritage, Homer Plessy would have continued to pass as white.

Toyosaburo Korematsu was born and raised in the United States and grew up in San Francisco, the son of Japanese Americans. In 1942, Korematsu was arrested for violating the Roosevelt administration's evacuation and relocation order. Much like Homer Plessy, few people outside Korematsu's immediate circle of friends knew that he was Japanese American. Toyosaburo was known as Fred to his American friends. He had undergone plastic surgery to hide his Japanese features, for fear that anti-Japanese prejudice would limit his ability to find employment and move freely in white social circles. He was also engaged to an Italian American woman; the surgery was also an effort to placate reaction to an "interracial" marriage.

But unlike Plessy, Korematsu did not deliberately challenge the law. When the police approached him on a suburban San Francisco street, he told them his name was Clyde Sarah and that he was of Spanish-Hawaiian origin. After a clerk at the police station recognized Korematsu, he told the police his real name and ancestry.

After Korematsu's arrest made news, the American Civil Liberties Union contacted him with an offer to handle his case.

For more background, see the accompanying SIDEBAR.

The Supreme Court's decision was 6 to 3. Justice Black delivered the opinion of the Court. Justice Frankfurter concurred. Justices Roberts, Murphy, and Jackson dissented.

▼▲▼

MR. JUSTICE BLACK delivered the opinion of the Court.

. . . It should be noted, to begin with, that all legal restrictions which curtail the civil rights of a single racial group are immediately suspect. That is not to say that all such restrictions are unconstitutional. It is to say that courts must subject them to the most rigid scrutiny. Pressing public necessity may sometimes justify the existence of such restrictions; racial antagonism never can. . . .

In *Hirabayashi* v. *United States* (1942), we sustained a conviction obtained for violation of the curfew order. The Hirabayashi conviction and this one thus rest on the same 1942 Congressional Act and the same basic executive and military orders, all of which orders were aimed at the twin dangers of espionage and sabotage.

The 1942 Act was attacked in the *Hirabayashi* case as an unconstitutional delegation of power; it was contended that the curfew order and other orders on which it rested were beyond the war powers of the Congress, the military authorities, and of the President, as Commander in Chief of the Army, and, finally, that to apply the curfew order against none but citizens of Japanese ancestry amounted to a constitutionally prohibited discrimination solely on account of race. To these questions, we gave the serious consideration which their importance justified. We upheld the curfew order as an exercise of the power of the government to take steps necessary to prevent espionage and sabotage in an area threatened by Japanese attack.

In the light of the principles we announced in the *Hirabayashi* case, we are unable to conclude that it was beyond the war power of Congress and the Executive to exclude those of Japanese ancestry from the West Coast war area at the time they did. True, exclusion from the area in which one's home is located is a far greater deprivation than constant confinement to the home from 8 P.M. to 6 A.M. Nothing short of apprehension by the proper military authorities of the gravest imminent danger to the public safety can constitutionally justify either. But exclusion from a threatened area, no less than curfew, has a definite and close relationship to the prevention of espionage and sabotage. The military authorities, charged with the primary responsibility of defending our shores, concluded that curfew provided inadequate protection and ordered exclusion. They did so, as pointed out in our *Hirabayashi* opinion, in accordance with Congressional authority to the military to say who should, and who should not, remain in the threatened areas.

In this case, the petitioner challenges the assumptions upon which we rested our conclusions in the *Hirabayashi* case. He also urges that, by May, 1942, when Order No. 34 was promulgated, all danger of Japanese invasion of the West Coast had disappeared. After careful consideration of these contentions, we are compelled to reject them.

Here, as in the *Hirabayashi* case, ". . . we cannot reject as unfounded the judgment of the military authorities and of Congress that there were disloyal members of that population, whose number and strength could not be precisely and quickly ascertained. We cannot say that the war-making branches of the Government did not have ground for believing that, in a critical hour, such persons could not readily be isolated and separately dealt with, and constituted a menace to the national defense and safety which demanded that prompt and adequate measures be taken to guard against it."

Like curfew, exclusion of those of Japanese origin was deemed necessary because of the presence of an unascertained number of disloyal members of the group, most of whom we have no doubt were loyal to this country. It was because we could not reject the finding of the military authorities that it was impossible to bring about an immediate segregation of the disloyal from the loyal that we sustained the validity of the curfew order as applying to the whole group. In the instant case, temporary exclusion of the entire group was rested by the military on the same ground. The judgment that exclusion of the whole group was, for the same reason, a military imperative answers the contention that the exclusion was in the nature of group punishment based on antagonism to those of Japanese origin. That there were members of the group who retained loyalties to Japan has been confirmed by investigations made subsequent to the exclusion. Approximately five thousand American citizens of Japanese ancestry refused to swear unqualified allegiance to the United States and to renounce allegiance to the Japanese Emperor, and several thousand evacuees requested repatriation to Japan.

We uphold the exclusion order as of the time it was made and when the petitioner violated it. In doing so, we are not unmindful of the hardships imposed by it upon a large group of American citizens. But hardships are part of war, and war is an aggregation of hardships. All citizens alike, both in and out of uniform, feel the impact of war in greater or lesser measure. Citizenship has its responsibilities, as well as its privileges, and, in time of war, the burden is always heavier. Compulsory exclusion of large groups of citizens from their homes, except under circumstances of direst emergency and peril, is inconsistent with our basic governmental institutions. But when, under conditions of modern warfare, our shores are threatened by hostile forces, the power to protect must be commensurate with the threatened danger. . . .

We are thus being asked to pass at this time upon the whole subsequent detention program in both assembly and relocation centers, although the only issues framed at the trial related to petitioner's remaining in the prohibited area in violation of the exclusion order. Had petitioner here left the prohibited area and gone to an assembly center, we cannot say, either as a matter of fact or law, that his presence in that center would have resulted in his detention in a relocation center. Some who did report to the assembly center were not sent to relocation centers, but were released upon condition that they remain outside the prohibited zone until the military orders were modified or lifted. This illustrates that they pose different problems, and may be governed by different principles. The lawfulness of one does not necessarily determine the lawfulness of the others. This is made clear when we analyze the requirements of the separate provisions of the separate orders. These separate requirements were that those of Japanese ancestry (1) depart from the area; (2) report to and temporarily remain in an assembly center; (3) go under military control to a relocation center, there to remain for an indeterminate period until released conditionally or unconditionally by the military authorities. Each of these requirements, it will be noted, imposed distinct duties in connection with the separate steps in a complete evacuation program. Had Congress directly incorporated into one Act the language of these separate orders, and provided sanctions for their violations, disobedience of any one would have constituted a separate offense. There is no reason why violations of these orders, insofar as they were promulgated pursuant to Congressional enactment, should not be treated as separate offenses. . . .

Since the petitioner has not been convicted of failing to report or to remain in an assembly or relocation center, we cannot in this case determine the validity of those separate provisions of the order. It is sufficient here for us to pass upon the order which petitioner violated. To do more would be to go beyond the issues raised, and to decide momentous questions not contained within the framework of the pleadings or the evidence in this case. It will be time enough to decide the serious constitutional issues which petitioner seeks to raise when an assembly or relocation order is applied or is certain to be applied to him, and we have its terms before us.

Some of the members of the Court are of the view that evacuation and detention in an Assembly Center were inseparable. After May 3, 1942, the date of Exclusion Order No. 34, Korematsu was under compulsion to leave the area not as he would choose, but via an Assembly Center. The Assembly Center was conceived as a part of the machinery for group evacuation. The power to exclude includes the power to do it by force if necessary. And any forcible measure must necessarily entail some degree of detention or restraint, whatever method of removal is selected. But whichever view is taken, it results in holding that the order under which petitioner was convicted was valid.

It is said that we are dealing here with the case of imprisonment of a citizen in a concentration camp solely because of his ancestry, without evidence or inquiry concerning his loyalty and good disposition towards the United States. Our task would be simple, our duty clear, were this a case involving the imprisonment of a loyal citizen in a concentration camp because of racial prejudice. Regardless of the true nature of the assembly and relocation centers—and we deem it unjustifiable to call them concentration camps, with all the ugly connotations that term implies—we are dealing specifically with nothing but an exclusion order. To cast this case into outlines of racial prejudice, without reference to the real military dangers which were presented, merely confuses the issue. Korematsu was not excluded from the Military Area because of hostility to him or his race. He was excluded because we are at war with the Japanese Empire, because the properly constituted military authorities feared an invasion of our West Coast and felt constrained to take proper security measures, because they decided that the military urgency of the situation demanded that all citizens of Japanese ancestry be segregated from the West Coast temporarily, and, finally, because Congress, reposing its confidence in this time of war in our military leaders—as inevitably it must—determined that they should have the power to do just this. There was evidence of disloyalty on the part of some, the military authorities considered that the need for action was great, and time was short. We cannot—by availing ourselves of the calm perspective of hindsight—now say that, at that time, these actions were unjustified.

Mr. Justice Roberts, dissenting.

I dissent, because I think the indisputable facts exhibit a clear violation of Constitutional rights.

This is not a case of keeping people off the streets at night, as was *Hirabayashi* v. *United States*, nor a case of temporary exclusion of a citizen from an area for his own safety or that of the community, nor a case of offering him an opportunity to go temporarily out of an area where his presence might cause danger to himself or to his fellows. On the contrary, it is the case of convicting a citizen as a punishment for not submitting to imprisonment in a concentration camp, based on his ancestry, and solely because of his ancestry, without evidence or inquiry concerning his loyalty and good disposition towards the United States. If this be a correct statement of the facts disclosed by this record, and facts of which we take judicial notice, I need hardly labor the conclusion that Constitutional rights have been violated.

The Government's argument, and the opinion of the court, in my judgment, erroneously divide that which is single and indivisible, and thus make the case appear as if the petitioner violated a Military Order, sanctioned by Act of Congress, which excluded him from his home by refusing voluntarily to leave, and so knowingly and intentionally defying the order and the Act of Congress. . . .

[I]t is lawful to compel an American citizen to submit to illegal imprisonment on the assumption that he might, after going to the Assembly Center, apply for his discharge by suing out a writ of habeas corpus. . . . The answer, of course, is that, where he was subject to two conflicting laws, he was not bound, in order to escape violation of one or the other, to surrender his liberty for any period. Nor will it do to say that the detention was a necessary part of the process of evacuation, and so we are here concerned only with the validity of the latter.

Again, it is a new doctrine of constitutional law that one indicted for disobedience to an unconstitutional statute may not defend on the ground of the invalidity of the statute, but must obey it though he knows it is no law, and, after he has suffered the disgrace of conviction and lost his liberty by sentence, then, and not before, seek, from within prison walls, to test the validity of the law.

Moreover, it is beside the point to rest decision in part on the fact that the petitioner, for his own reasons, wished to remain in his home. If, as is the fact, he was constrained so to do, it is indeed a narrow application of constitutional rights to ignore the order which constrained him in order to sustain his conviction for violation of another contradictory order. . . .

Mr. Justice Murphy, dissenting.

This exclusion of "all persons of Japanese ancestry, both alien and non-alien," from the Pacific Coast area on a plea of military necessity in the absence of martial law ought not to be approved. Such exclusion goes over "the very brink of constitutional power," and falls into the ugly abyss of racism.

In dealing with matters relating to the prosecution and progress of a war, we must accord great respect and consideration to the judgments of the military authorities who are on the scene and who have full knowledge of the military facts. The scope of their discretion must, as a matter of necessity and common sense, be wide. And their judgments ought not to be overruled lightly by those whose training and duties ill-equip them to deal intelligently with matters so vital to the physical security of the nation.

At the same time, however, it is essential that there be definite limits to military discretion, especially where martial law has not been declared. Individuals must not be left impoverished of their constitutional rights on a plea of military necessity that has neither substance nor support.

Thus, like other claims conflicting with the asserted constitutional rights of the individual, the military claim must subject itself to the judicial process of having its reasonableness determined and its conflicts with other interests reconciled. . . .

The judicial test of whether the Government, on a plea of military necessity, can validly deprive an individual of any of his constitutional rights is whether the deprivation is reasonably related to a public danger that is so "immediate, imminent, and impending" as not to admit of delay and not to permit the intervention of ordinary constitutional processes to alleviate the danger. Civilian Exclusion Order No. 34, banishing from a prescribed area of the Pacific Coast "all persons of Japanese ancestry, both alien and non-alien," clearly does not meet that test. Being an obvious racial discrimination, the order deprives all those within its scope of the equal protection of the laws as guaranteed by the Fifth Amendment. It further deprives these individuals of their constitutional rights to live and work where they will, to establish a home where they choose and to move about freely. In excommunicating them without benefit of hearings, this order also deprives them of all their constitutional rights to procedural due process. Yet no reasonable relation to an "immediate, imminent, and impending" public danger is evident to support this racial restriction, which is one of the most sweeping and complete deprivations of constitutional rights in the history of this nation in the absence of martial law.

It must be conceded that the military and naval situation in the spring of 1942 was such as to generate a very real fear of invasion of the Pacific Coast, accompanied by fears of sabotage and espionage in that area. The military command was therefore justified in adopting all reasonable means necessary to combat these dangers. In adjudging the military action taken in light of the then apparent dangers, we must not erect too high or too meticulous standards; it is necessary only that the action have some reasonable relation to the removal of the dangers of invasion, sabotage and espionage. But the exclusion, either temporarily or permanently, of all persons with Japanese blood in their veins has no such reasonable relation. And that relation is lacking because the exclusion order necessarily must rely for its reasonableness upon the assumption that all persons of Japanese ancestry may have a dangerous tendency to commit sabotage and espionage and to aid our Japanese enemy in other ways. It is difficult to believe that reason, logic, or experience could be marshalled in support of such an assumption.

That this forced exclusion was the result in good measure of this erroneous assumption of racial guilt, rather than *bona fide* military necessity is evidenced by the Commanding General's Final Report on the evacuation from the Pacific Coast area. In it, he refers to all individuals of Japanese descent as "subversive," as belonging to "an enemy race" whose "racial strains are undiluted," and as constituting "over 112,000 potential enemies . . . at large today" along the Pacific Coast. In support of this blanket condemnation of all persons of Japanese descent, however, no reliable evidence is cited to show that such individuals were generally disloyal, or had generally so conducted themselves in this area as to constitute a special menace to defense installations or war industries, or had otherwise, by their behavior, furnished reasonable ground for their exclusion as a group.

Justification for the exclusion is sought, instead, mainly upon questionable racial and sociological grounds not ordinarily within the realm of expert military judgment, supplemented by certain semi-military conclusions drawn from an unwarranted use of circumstantial evidence. Individuals of Japanese ancestry are condemned because they are said to be "a large, unassimilated, tightly knit racial group, bound to an enemy nation by strong ties of race, culture, custom and religion." They are claimed to be given to "emperor worshipping ceremonies," and to "dual citizenship." Japanese language schools and allegedly pro-Japanese organizations are cited as evidence of possible group disloyalty, together with facts as to certain persons being educated and residing at length in Japan. It is intimated that many of these individuals deliberately resided "adjacent to strategic points," thus enabling them, "to carry into execution a tremendous program of sabotage on a mass scale should any considerable number of them have been inclined to do so." The need for protective custody is also asserted. The report refers, without identity, to "numerous incidents of violence," as well as to other admittedly unverified or cumulative incidents. From this, plus certain other events not shown to have been connected with the Japanese Americans, it is concluded that the "situation was fraught with danger to the Japanese population itself," and that the general public "was ready to take matters into its own hands." Finally, it is intimated, though not directly charged or proved, that persons of Japanese ancestry were responsible for three minor isolated shellings and bombings of the Pacific Coast area, as well as for unidentified radio transmissions and night signaling.

The main reasons relied upon by those responsible for the forced evacuation, therefore, do not prove a reasonable relation between the group characteristics of Japanese Americans and the dangers of invasion, sabotage and espionage. The reasons appear, instead, to be largely an accumulation of much of the misinformation, half-truths and insinuations that for years have been directed against Japanese Americans by people with racial and economic prejudices—the same people who have been among the foremost advocates of the evacuation. A military judgment based upon such racial and sociological considerations is not entitled to the great weight ordinarily given the judgments based upon strictly military considerations. Especially is this so when every charge relative to race, religion, culture, geographical location, and legal and economic status has been substantially discredited by independent studies made by experts in these matters.

The military necessity which is essential to the validity of the evacuation order thus resolves itself into a few intimations that certain individuals actively aided the enemy, from which it is inferred that the entire group of Japanese Americans could not be trusted to be or remain loyal to the United States. No one denies, of course, that there were some disloyal persons of Japanese descent on the Pacific Coast who did all in their power to aid their ancestral land. Similar disloyal activities have been engaged in by many persons of German, Italian and even more pioneer stock in our country. But to infer that examples of individual disloyalty prove group disloyalty and justify discriminatory action against the entire group is to deny that, under our system of law, individual guilt is the sole basis for deprivation of rights. Moreover, this inference, which is at the very heart of the evacuation orders, has been used in support of the abhorrent and despicable treatment of minority groups by the dictatorial tyrannies which this nation is now pledged to destroy. To give constitutional sanction to that inference in this case, however well intentioned may have been the military command on the Pacific Coast, is to adopt one of the cruelest of the rationales used by our enemies to destroy the dignity of the individual and to encourage and open the door to discriminatory actions against other minority groups in the passions of tomorrow.

No adequate reason is given for the failure to treat these Japanese Americans on an individual basis by holding investigations and hearings to separate the loyal from the disloyal, as was done in the case of persons of German and Italian ancestry. It is asserted merely that the loyalties of this group "were unknown and time was of the essence." Yet nearly four months elapsed after Pearl Harbor before the first exclusion order was issued; nearly eight months went by until the last order was issued, and the last of these "subversive" persons was not actually removed until almost eleven months had elapsed. Leisure

and deliberation seem to have been more of the essence than speed. And the fact that conditions were not such as to warrant a declaration of martial law adds strength to the belief that the factors of time and military necessity were not as urgent as they have been represented to be.

Moreover, there was no adequate proof that the Federal Bureau of Investigation and the military and naval intelligence services did not have the espionage and sabotage situation well in hand during this long period. Nor is there any denial of the fact that not one person of Japanese ancestry was accused or convicted of espionage or sabotage after Pearl Harbor while they were still free, a fact which is some evidence of the loyalty of the vast majority of these individuals and of the effectiveness of the established methods of combatting these evils. It seems incredible that, under these circumstances, it would have been impossible to hold loyalty hearings for the mere 112,000 persons involved—or at least for the 70,000 American citizens—especially when a large part of this number represented children and elderly men and women. Any inconvenience that may have accompanied an attempt to conform to procedural due process cannot be said to justify violations of constitutional rights of individuals.

I dissent, therefore, from this legalization of racism. Racial discrimination in any form and in any degree has no justifiable part whatever in our democratic way of life. It is unattractive in any setting, but it is utterly revolting among a free people who have embraced the principles set forth in the Constitution of the United States. All residents of this nation are kin in some way by blood or culture to a foreign land. Yet they are primarily and necessarily a part of the new and distinct civilization of the United States. They must, accordingly, be treated at all times as the heirs of the American experiment, and as entitled to all the rights and freedoms guaranteed by the Constitution.

Mr. Justice Jackson, dissenting.

Korematsu was born on our soil, of parents born in Japan. The Constitution makes him a citizen of the United States by nativity, and a citizen of California by residence. No claim is made that he is not loyal to this country. There is no suggestion that, apart from the matter involved here, he is not law-abiding and well disposed. Korematsu, however, has been convicted of an act not commonly a crime. It consists merely of being present in the state whereof he is a citizen, near the place where he was born, and where all his life he has lived.

## KOREMATSU V. UNITED STATES

### "I Was Conscience Stricken"

By the time Japanese warplanes had returned to the aircraft carriers that had brought them to within 275 miles of the Hawaiian island of Oahu on December 7, 1941, to launch their stunning early morning air raid on the major American naval and air force installation located at Pearl Harbor, American intelligence agencies in Washington were already hard at work. One popular theory speculated that the dozens of commercial ships owned and operated by Japanese American fishermen and sitting off the northern California coastline were really sending secret signals to enemy military officials. The theory made perfect sense. After all, so the stereotype went, Japanese immigrants had never bothered to learn the culture and values of mainstream America. They continued to publish Japanese-language newspapers and speak their native tongue at home and to live in geographically dense, tightly knit neighborhoods. Moreover, their West Coast location served as a perfect beachhead for espionage. These were people who could not be trusted. Never mind that much the same could be said for the millions of German, Polish, and Italian immigrants living in East Coast cities such as New York, Boston, and Philadelphia whose European countries of origin were preparing to go to war against the United States.

The Japanese had been viewed with distrust and suspicion ever since their arrival in the late nineteenth century at the behest of American industrialists to work the lush California fruit and vegetable farms. That fear grew as more and more Japanese left menial agricultural jobs to become entrepreneurs, farm and business owners, lawyers, doctors, and scientists. Their success was rewarded with legislation such as the California Alien Land Law of 1913, which made immigrants from Asian countries ineligible for naturalization and forbade them from holding property for more than three years, and the federal Japanese Exclusion Act of 1924, which barred the Japanese, the Issei, and Japanese born outside Japan and the United States from immigrating to America. Quotas to limit Japanese immigration were finally lifted by Congress in 1965.

A report commissioned by American naval intelligence *prior* to the attack on Pearl Harbor turned up no evidence that Japanese Americans posed a threat to national security. A separate inquiry conducted by the Federal Bureau of Investigation reached the same conclusion. In fact, during the entire course of World War II, ten people were convicted of spying for Japan, all of whom were Caucasians. Nonetheless, the American government was convinced that the approximately 112,000 Japanese Americans living on the West Coast posed a serious security threat. In cooperation with elected officials and law-enforcement officials in California, Washington, and Oregon, federal authorities began the process that forced 70,000 Japanese Americans to leave their homes for the government internment camps that were scattered across several inland states. One of the states chosen to participate in the relocation program was Minnesota, where Earl Warren's successor as chief justice, Warren Burger, who was then still in private practice but active in local civil rights causes, formed a special committee to assist detained Japanese Americans find adequate housing.

One of the great ironies of the Japanese American evacuation and internment during World War II was the unrelenting commitment of Earl Warren to the program, who was attorney general of California when it began and governor when it ended. Neither his attitudes toward the Japanese nor his wholesale support for their exclusion bore any relationship to his liberal record on the Court. Warren implemented Roosevelt's executive orders mandating curfew and then evacuation without question and backed in full the call for military authorities to supervise the proceedings. In 1943, during his first gubernatorial term, Warren addressed a national governor's conference as a spokesman for the program, commenting that "We don't propose to have the Japs back in California during the war if there is any lawful means of preventing it." Warren never actually gave any direct orders to evacuate Japanese Americans—those came from the federal government—but he was a tireless advocate on behalf of their evacuation and internment. As the chief law-enforcement officer and later governor of the state with the greatest number of Japanese American citizens and alien residents, his compliance and support for the program carried great weight among his peers.

Warren later admitted that his enthusiasm for the Japanese American internment program was a product of wartime fear and prejudice. This popular California politician, who once belonged to the anti-Asian Native Sons of the Golden West, rarely spoke of this tragic chapter in American history once the last Japanese detainees had been allowed to return to their homes. In his memoirs, he wrote:

The federal government's internment of Japanese Americans in crude, makeshift camps during World War II often separated families, including young children from their parents. Reproduced from the Collections of the Library of Congress. Neg. # lc-usf 33-13289-M5.

> Whenever I thought of the innocent little children who were torn from their home, school, friends, and congenial surroundings, I was conscience stricken. . . .
>
> At about the same time we were considering their removal for military reasons, I wrote a formal opinion to the State Personnel Board, telling its members that they could not constitutionally take away Japanese Americans' Civil Service rights to their state jobs as the commission directed. I know that it seems ambivalent to protect their constitutional rights in this regard with one hand and deprive them of other rights by removing them from their homes. However, I consoled myself with the thought that the latter was occasioned by my obligation to keep the security of the state.

It is impossible to know what, if any, impact Warren's crucial role in the internment program had on his subsequent transformation from a nativist who harbored prejudicial views against Asian Americans to the leading force behind the great civil right decisions handed down during his tenure as chief justice; from a proponent of a state loyalty oaths to an ardent defender of academic freedom for Communists; and from a crusading law-enforcement official to an architect of new constitutional rights on behalf of criminal defendants. But some of Warren's biographers have suggested that the chief justice's experience with the program forever changed his views on law and the Constitution. In an interview shortly before his death, Warren had to dry the tears from his eyes when he was read some of the comments he had made about Japanese Americans. He offered little in defense of himself and acknowledged he had made a "mistake." In contrast, Justices Hugo Black and William Douglas, considered among the greatest civil libertarians to serve on the Court, never publicly recanted their votes to uphold the government's program in *Korematsu*.

The federal government closed the War Relocation Authority in June 1946. Almost forty years later, in 1983, Gordon Hirabayashi and Fred Korematsu, whose names will remain forever enshrined in the law books, filed appeals asking to have their convictions overturned for refusing to comply with their respective curfew and evacuation orders. Both were successful. The government did not appeal either decision. In 1988, President Ronald Reagan signed congressional legislation that offered an official apology for the relocation and internment of all Japanese Americans during World War II and provided a payment of $20,000 to the families of each camp survivor. To date the Justice Department has paid out more than $1 billion in compensation.

February 19 is recognized as the Day of Remembrance in San Francisco. It includes a public commemoration of the Japanese American internment and a public school holiday to promote awareness of the human and social costs that went with it. In Washington, D.C., the Smithsonian Museum of American History has developed a special exhibit on the causes and consequences of the internment program. This exhibit includes a rich selection of books, films, photographs, and artifacts that provides a powerful look at a shameful episode in America's not-too-distant past.

## References

Warren, Earl. *The Memoirs of Earl Warren.* New York: Doubleday, 1977.

White, G. Edward. *Earl Warren: A Public Life.* New York: Oxford University Press, 1982.

Even more unusual is the series of military orders which made this conduct a crime. They forbid such a one to remain, and they also forbid him to leave. They were so drawn that the only way Korematsu could avoid violation was to give himself up to the military authority. This meant submission to custody, examination, and transportation out of the territory, to be followed by indeterminate confinement in detention camps.

A citizen's presence in the locality, however, was made a crime only if his parents were of Japanese birth. Had Korematsu been one of four—the others being, say, a German alien enemy, an Italian alien enemy, and a citizen of American-born ancestors, convicted of treason but out on parole—only Korematsu's presence would have violated the order. The difference between their innocence and his crime would result, not from anything he did, said, or thought, different than they, but only in that he was born of different racial stock.

Now, if any fundamental assumption underlies our system, it is that guilt is personal and not inheritable. Even if all of one's antecedents had been convicted of treason, the Constitution forbids its penalties to be visited upon him, for it provides that "no attainder of treason shall work corruption of blood, or forfeiture except during the life of the person attainted." But here is an attempt to make an otherwise innocent act a crime merely because this prisoner is the son of parents as to whom he had no choice, and belongs to a race from which there is no way to resign. If Congress, in peacetime legislation, should enact such a criminal law, I should suppose this Court would refuse to enforce it.

But the "law" which this prisoner is convicted of disregarding is not found in an act of Congress, but in a military order. Neither the Act of Congress nor the Executive Order of the President, nor both together, would afford a basis for this conviction. . . . And it is said that, if the military commander had reasonable military grounds for promulgating the orders, they are constitutional, and become law, and the Court is required to enforce them. There are several reasons why I cannot subscribe to this doctrine. . . .

In the very nature of things, military decisions are not susceptible of intelligent judicial appraisal. They do not pretend to rest on evidence, but are made on information that often would not be admissible and on assumptions that could not be proved. Information in support of an order could not be disclosed to courts without danger that it would reach the enemy. Neither can courts act on communications made in confidence. Hence, courts can never have any real alternative to accepting the mere declaration of the authority that issued the order that it was reasonably necessary from a military viewpoint.

Much is said of the danger to liberty from the Army program for deporting and detaining these citizens of Japanese extraction. But a judicial construction of the due process clause that will sustain this order is a far more subtle blow to liberty than the promulgation of the order itself. A military order, however unconstitutional, is not apt to last longer than the military emergency. Even during that period, a succeeding commander may revoke it all. But once a judicial opinion rationalizes such an order to show that it conforms to the Constitution, or rather rationalizes the Constitution to show that the Constitution sanctions such an order, the Court for all time has validated the principle of racial discrimination in criminal procedure and of transplanting American citizens. The principle then lies about like a loaded weapon, ready for the hand of any authority that can bring forward a plausible claim of an urgent need. Every repetition imbeds that principle more deeply in our law and thinking and expands it to new purposes. All who observe the work of courts are familiar with what Judge Cardozo described as "the tendency of a principle to expand itself to the limit of its logic." A military commander may overstep the bounds of constitutionality, and it is an incident. But if we review and approve, that passing incident becomes the doctrine of the Constitution. There it has a generative power of its own, and all that it creates will be in its own image. Nothing better illustrates this danger than does the Court's opinion in this case.

It argues that we are bound to uphold the conviction of Korematsu because we upheld one in *Hirabayashi* v. *United States* (1942), when we sustained these orders insofar as they applied a curfew requirement to a citizen of Japanese ancestry. I think we should learn something from that experience.

In that case, we were urged to consider only the curfew feature, that being all that technically was involved, because it was the only count necessary to sustain Hirabayashi's conviction and sentence. We yielded, and the Chief Justice guarded the opinion as carefully as language will do. He said: "Our investigation here does not go beyond the inquiry whether, in the light of all the relevant circumstances preceding and attending their promulgation, the challenged orders and statute *afforded a reasonable basis for the action taken in imposing the curfew*." "We decide only the issue as we have defined it—we decide only that the *curfew order,* as applied, and at the time it was applied, was within the boundaries of the war power." And again: "It is unnecessary to consider whether or to what extent *such findings would support orders differing from the curfew order*." However, in spite of our limiting words, we did validate a discrimination on the basis of ancestry for mild and temporary deprivation of liberty. Now the principle of racial discrimination is pushed from support of mild measures to very harsh ones, and from temporary deprivations to indeterminate ones. And the precedent which it is said requires us to do so is *Hirabayashi*. The Court is now saying that, in *Hirabayashi*, we did decide the very things we there said we were not deciding. Because we said that these citizens could be made to stay in their homes during the hours of dark, it is said we must require them to leave home entirely, and if that, we are told they may also be taken into custody for deportation, and, if that, it is argued, they may also be held for some undetermined time in detention camps. How far the principle of this case would be extended before plausible reasons would play out, I do not know.

I should hold that a civil court cannot be made to enforce an order which violates constitutional limitations even if it is a reasonable exercise of military authority. The courts can exercise only the judicial power, can apply only law, and must abide by the Constitution, or they cease to be civil courts and become instruments of military policy.

▼▲▼

## *Youngstown Sheet & Tube Co.* v. *Sawyer*
### 343 U.S. 579 (1952)

In 1946, Congress, over President Harry S. Truman's veto, passed the Taft-Hartley Act, which authorized the president to impose a cooling-off period of eighty days to avoid a strike that seriously threatened the public interest. *Youngstown Sheet & Tube*, often called the *Steel Seizure Case*, came about after Truman, in April 1952, disregarded Taft-Hartley and ordered his secretary of commerce, Charles Sawyer, to seize the nation's steel mills in order to force production. Truman claimed that the nation could ill afford any disruption to the flow of military supplies to Korea. Mill owners were furious. They went along with the order but filed suit in federal court contesting the president's action as unconstitutional.

The Court's decision was 6 to 3. Justice Black delivered the opinion of the Court. Justices Jackson, Burton, Clark, Douglas, and Frankfurter each filed concurring opinions. Chief Justice Vinson, joined by Justices Reed and Minton, dissented.

MR. JUSTICE BLACK delivered the opinion of the Court.

We are asked to decide whether the President was acting within his constitutional power when he issued an order directing the Secretary of Commerce to take possession of and operate most of the Nation's steel mills. The mill owners argue that the President's order amounts to lawmaking, a legislative function which the Constitution has expressly confided to the Congress, and not to the President. The Government's position is that the order was made on findings of the President that his action was necessary to avert a national catastrophe which would inevitably result from a stoppage of steel production, and that, in meeting this grave emergency, the President was acting within the aggregate of his constitutional powers as the Nation's Chief Executive and the Commander in Chief of the Armed Forces of the United States. . . .

The President's power, if any, to issue the order must stem either from an act of Congress or from the Constitution itself. There is no statute that expressly authorizes the President to take possession of property as he did here. Nor is there any act of Congress to which our attention has been directed from which such a power can fairly be implied. Indeed, we do not understand the Government to rely on statutory authorization for this seizure. There are two statutes which do authorize the President to take both personal and real property under certain conditions. However, the Government admits that these conditions were not met, and that the President's order was not rooted in either of the statutes. . . .

Moreover, the use of the seizure technique to solve labor disputes in order to prevent work stoppages was not only unauthorized by any congressional enactment; prior to this controversy, Congress had refused to adopt that method of settling labor disputes. When the Taft-Hartley Act was under consideration in 1947, Congress rejected an amendment which would have authorized such governmental seizures in cases of emergency. Apparently it was thought that the technique of seizure, like that of compulsory arbitration, would interfere with the process of collective bargaining. Consequently, the plan Congress adopted in that Act did not provide for seizure under any circumstances. Instead, the plan sought to bring about settlements by use of the customary devices of mediation, conciliation, investigation by boards of inquiry, and public reports. In some instances, temporary injunctions were authorized to provide cooling-off periods. All this failing, unions were left free to strike after a secret vote by employees as to whether they wished to accept their employers' final settlement offer.

It is clear that, if the President had authority to issue the order he did, it must be found in some provision of the Constitution. And it is not claimed that express constitutional language grants this power to the President. The contention is that presidential power should be implied from the aggregate of his powers under the Constitution. Particular reliance is placed on provisions in Article II which say that "The executive Power shall be vested in a President . . . "; that "he shall take Care that the Laws be faithfully executed", and that he "shall be Commander in Chief of the Army and Navy of the United States."

The order cannot properly be sustained as an exercise of the President's military power as Commander in Chief of the Armed Forces. The Government attempts to do so by citing a number of cases upholding broad powers in military commanders engaged in day-to-day fighting in a theater of war. Such cases need not concern us here. Even though "theater of war" be an expanding concept, we cannot with faithfulness to our constitutional system hold that the Commander in Chief of the Armed Forces has the ultimate power as such to take possession of private property in order to keep labor disputes from stopping production. This is a job for the Nation's lawmakers, not for its military authorities.

Nor can the seizure order be sustained because of the several constitutional provisions that grant executive power to the President. In the framework of our Constitution, the President's power to see that the laws are faithfully executed refutes the idea that he is to be a lawmaker. The Constitution limits his functions in the lawmaking process to the recommending of laws he thinks wise and the vetoing of laws he thinks bad. And the Constitution is neither silent nor equivocal about who shall make laws which the President is to execute. The first section of the first article says that "All legislative Powers herein granted shall be vested in a Congress of the United States. . . . " After granting many powers to the Congress, Article I goes on to provide that Congress may, "make all Laws which shall be necessary and proper for carrying into Execution the foregoing Powers, and all other Powers vested by this Constitution in the Government of the United States, or in any Department or Officer thereof."

The President's order does not direct that a congressional policy be executed in a manner prescribed by Congress—it directs that a presidential policy be executed in a manner prescribed by the President. The preamble of the order itself, like that of many statutes, sets out reasons why the President believes certain policies should be adopted, proclaims these policies as rules of conduct to be followed, and again, like a statute, authorizes a government official to promulgate additional rules and regulations consistent with the policy proclaimed and needed to carry that policy into execution. The power of Congress to adopt such public policies as those proclaimed by the order is beyond question. It can authorize the taking of private property for public use. It can make laws regulating the relationships between employers and employees, prescribing rules designed to settle labor disputes, and fixing wages and working conditions in certain fields of our economy. The Constitution does not subject this lawmaking power of Congress to presidential or military supervision or control.

It is said that other Presidents, without congressional authority, have taken possession of private business enterprises in order to settle labor disputes. But even if this be true, Congress has not thereby lost its exclusive constitutional authority to make laws necessary and proper to carry out the powers vested by the Constitution "in the Government of the United States, or any Department or Officer thereof."

The Founders of this Nation entrusted the lawmaking power to the Congress alone in both good and bad times. It would do no good to recall the historical events, the fears of power, and the hopes for freedom that lay behind their choice. Such a review would but confirm our holding that this seizure order cannot stand.

MR. JUSTICE JACKSON, concurring in the judgment and opinion of the Court.

That comprehensive and undefined presidential powers hold both practical advantages and grave dangers for the country will impress anyone who has served as legal adviser to a President in time of transition and public anxiety. While an interval of detached reflection may temper teachings of that experience, they probably are a more realistic influence on my views than the conventional materials of judicial decision which seem unduly to accentuate doctrine and legal fiction. But, as we approach the question of presidential power, we half overcome mental hazards by recognizing them. The opinions of judges, no less than executives and publicists, often suffer the infirmity of confusing the issue of a power's validity with the cause it is invoked to promote, of confounding the permanent executive office with its temporary occupant. The tendency is strong to emphasize transient results upon policies—such as wages or stabilization—and lose sight of enduring consequences upon the balanced power structure of our Republic.

A judge, like an executive adviser, may be surprised at the poverty of really useful and unambiguous authority applicable to concrete problems of executive power as they actually present themselves. Just what our forefathers did envision, or would have envisioned had they foreseen modern conditions, must be divined from materials almost as enigmatic as the dreams Joseph was called upon to interpret for Pharaoh. A century and a half of partisan debate and scholarly speculation yields no net result, but only supplies more or less apt quotations from respected sources on each side of any question. They largely cancel each other. And court decisions are indecisive because of the judicial practice of dealing with the largest questions in the most narrow way.

The actual art of governing under our Constitution does not, and cannot, conform to judicial definitions of the power of any of its branches based on isolated clauses, or even single Articles torn from context. While the Constitution diffuses power the better to secure liberty, it also contemplates that practice will integrate the dispersed powers into a workable government. It enjoins upon its branches separateness but interdependence, autonomy but reciprocity. Presidential powers are not fixed but fluctuate depending upon their disjunction or conjunction with those of Congress. We may well begin by a somewhat over-simplified grouping of practical situations in which a President may doubt, or others may challenge, his powers, and by distinguishing roughly the legal consequences of this factor of relativity.

1. When the President acts pursuant to an express or implied authorization of Congress, his authority is at its maximum, for it includes all that he possesses in his own right plus all that Congress can delegate. In these circumstances, and in these only, may he be said

*President Truman's decision to seize the steel mills was viewed by many as heavy-handed.*
Reproduced from the Collections of the Library of Congress. Neg. # 213511 Z62.90269.

(for what it may be worth) to personify the federal sovereignty. If his act is held unconstitutional under these circumstances, it usually means that the Federal Government, as an undivided whole, lacks power. A seizure executed by the President pursuant to an Act of Congress would be supported by the strongest of presumptions and the widest latitude of judicial interpretation, and the burden of persuasion would rest heavily upon any who might attack it.

2. When the President acts in absence of either a congressional grant or denial of authority, he can only rely upon his own independent powers, but there is a zone of twilight in which he and Congress may have concurrent authority, or in which its distribution is uncertain. Therefore, congressional inertia, indifference or quiescence may sometimes, at least, as a practical matter, enable, if not invite, measures on independent presi-

dential responsibility. In this area, any actual test of power is likely to depend on the imperatives of events and contemporary imponderables, rather than on abstract theories of law.

3. When the President takes measures incompatible with the expressed or implied will of Congress, his power is at its lowest ebb, for then he can rely only upon his own constitutional powers minus any constitutional powers of Congress over the matter. Courts can sustain exclusive presidential control in such a case only by disabling the Congress from acting upon the subject. Presidential claim to a power at once so conclusive and preclusive must be scrutinized with caution, for what is at stake is the equilibrium established by our constitutional system.

Into which of these classifications does this executive seizure of the steel industry fit? It is eliminated from the first by admission, for it is conceded that no congressional authorization exists for this seizure. That takes away also the support of the many precedents and declarations which were made in relation, and must be confined, to this category.

Can it then be defended under flexible tests available to the second category? It seems clearly eliminated from that class, because Congress has not left seizure of private property an open field, but has covered it by three statutory policies inconsistent with this seizure. In cases where the purpose is to supply needs of the Government itself, two courses are provided: one, seizure of a plant which fails to comply with obligatory orders placed by the Government; another, condemnation of facilities, including temporary use under the power of eminent domain. The third is applicable where it is the general economy of the country that is to be protected, rather than exclusive governmental interests. None of these were invoked. . . .

This leaves the current seizure to be justified only by the severe tests under the third grouping, where it can be supported only by any remainder of executive power after subtraction of such powers as Congress may have over the subject. In short, we can sustain the President only by holding that seizure of such strike-bound industries is within his domain and beyond control by Congress. Thus, this Court's first review of such seizures occurs under circumstances which leave presidential power most vulnerable to attack and in the least favorable of possible constitutional postures. . . .

The Solicitor General seeks the power of seizure in three clauses of the Executive Article, the first reading, "The executive Power shall be vested in a President of the United States of America." Lest I be thought to exaggerate, I quote the interpretation which his brief puts upon it:

"In our view, this clause constitutes a grant of all the executive powers of which the Government is capable." If that be true, it is difficult to see why the forefathers bothered to add several specific items, including some trifling ones.

The example of such unlimited executive power that must have most impressed the forefathers was the prerogative exercised by George III, and the description of its evils in the Declaration of Independence leads me to doubt that they were creating their new Executive in his image. Continental European examples were no more appealing. And, if we seek instruction from our own times, we can match it only from the executive powers in those governments we disparagingly describe as totalitarian. I cannot accept the view that this clause is a grant in bulk of all conceivable executive power, but regard it as an allocation to the presidential office of the generic powers thereafter stated. . . .

That seems to be the logic of an argument tendered at our bar—that the President having, on his own responsibility, sent American troops abroad derives from that act "affirmative power" to seize the means of producing a supply of steel for them. To quote, "Perhaps the most forceful illustration of the scope of Presidential power in this connection is the fact that American troops in Korea, whose safety and effectiveness are so directly involved here, were sent to the field by an exercise of the President's constitutional powers." Thus, it is said, he has invested himself with "war powers."

I cannot foresee all that it might entail if the Court should endorse this argument. Nothing in our Constitution is plainer than that declaration of a war is entrusted only to Congress. Of course, a state of war may, in fact, exist without a formal declaration. But no doctrine that the Court could promulgate would seem to me more sinister and alarming than that a President whose conduct of foreign affairs is so largely uncontrolled, and often even is unknown, can vastly enlarge his mastery over the internal affairs of the country by his own commitment of the Nation's armed forces to some foreign venture. I do not, however, find it necessary or appropriate to consider the legal status of the Korean enterprise to discountenance argument based on it. . . .

The appeal, however, that we declare the existence of inherent powers *ex necessitate* to meet an emergency asks us to do what many think would be wise, although it is something the forefathers omitted. They knew what emergencies were, knew the pressures they engender for authoritative action, knew, too, how they afford a ready pretext for usurpation. We may also suspect that they suspected that emergency powers would tend to kindle emergencies. Aside from suspension of the privilege of the writ of habeas corpus in time of rebellion or invasion, when the public safety may require it, they made no express provision for exercise of extraordinary authority because of a crisis. I do not think we rightfully may so amend their work, and, if we could, I am not convinced it would be wise to do so, although many modern nations have forthrightly recognized that war and economic crises may upset the normal balance between liberty and authority. Their experience with emergency powers may not be irrelevant to the argument here that we should say that the Executive, of his own volition, can invest himself with undefined emergency powers. . . .

I have no illusion that any decision by this Court can keep power in the hands of Congress if it is not wise and timely in meeting its problems. A crisis that challenges the President equally, or perhaps primarily, challenges Congress. If not good law, there was worldly wisdom in the maxim attributed to Napoleon that "The tools belong to the man who can use them." We may say that power to legislate for emergencies belongs in the hands of Congress, but only Congress itself can prevent power from slipping through its fingers.

The essence of our free Government is "leave to live by no man's leave, underneath the law"—to be governed by those impersonal forces which we call law. Our Government is fashioned to fulfill this concept so far as humanly possible. The Executive, except for recommendation and veto, has no legislative power. The executive action we have here originates in the individual will of the President, and represents an exercise of authority without law. No one, perhaps not even the President, knows the limits of the power he may seek to exert in this instance, and the parties affected cannot learn the limit of their rights. We do not know today what powers over labor or property would be claimed to flow from Government possession if we should legalize it, what rights to compensation would be claimed or recognized, or on what contingency it would end. With all its defects, delays and inconveniences, men have discovered no technique for long preserving free government except that the Executive be under the law, and that the law be made by parliamentary deliberations.

Such institutions may be destined to pass away. But it is the duty of the Court to be last, not first, to give them up.

MR. CHIEF JUSTICE VINSON, with whom MR. JUSTICE REED and MR. JUSTICE MINTON join, dissenting.

. . . Some members of the Court are of the view that the President is without power to act in time of crisis in the absence of express statutory authorization. Other members of the Court affirm on the basis of their reading of certain statutes. Because we cannot agree that affirmance is proper on any ground, and because of the transcending importance of the questions presented not only in this critical litigation, but also to the powers of the President and of future Presidents to act in time of crisis, we are compelled to register this dissent.

In passing upon the question of Presidential powers in this case, we must first consider the context in which those powers were exercised.

Those who suggest that this is a case involving extraordinary powers should be mindful that these are extraordinary times. A world not yet recovered from the devastation of World War II has been forced to face the threat of another and more terrifying global conflict.

Accepting in full measure its responsibility in the world community, the United States was instrumental in securing adoption of the United Nations Charter, approved by the Senate by a vote of 89 to 2. The first purpose of the United Nations is to, "maintain international peace and security, and, to that end, to take effective collective measures for the prevention and removal of threats to the peace, and for the suppression of acts of aggression or other breaches of the peace...." In 1950, when the United Nations called upon member nations "to render every assistance" to repel aggression in Korea, the United States furnished its vigorous support. For almost two full years, our armed forces have been fighting in Korea, suffering casualties of over 108,000 men. Hostilities have not abated. The "determination of the United Nations to continue its action in Korea to meet the aggression" has been reaffirmed. Congressional support of the action in Korea has been manifested by provisions for increased military manpower and equipment and for economic stabilization, as hereinafter described....

The steel mills were seized for a public use. The power of eminent domain, invoked in this case, is an essential attribute of sovereignty, and has long been recognized as a power of the Federal Government. Plaintiffs cannot complain that any provision in the Constitution prohibits the exercise of the power of eminent domain in this case. The Fifth Amendment provides: "nor shall private property be taken for public use, without just compensation." It is no bar to this seizure for, if the taking is not otherwise unlawful, plaintiffs are assured of receiving the required just compensation.

Admitting that the Government could seize the mills, plaintiffs claim that the implied power of eminent domain can be exercised only under an Act of Congress; under no circumstances, they say, can that power be exercised by the President unless he can point to an express provision in enabling legislation. This was the view adopted by the District Judge when he granted the preliminary injunction. Without an answer, without hearing evidence, he determined the issue on the basis of his "fixed conclusion . . . that defendant's acts are illegal" because the President's only course in the face of an emergency is to present the matter to Congress and await the final passage of legislation which will enable the Government to cope with threatened disaster.

Under this view, the President is left powerless at the very moment when the need for action may be most pressing and when no one, other than he, is immediately capable of action. Under this view, he is left powerless because a power not expressly given to Congress is nevertheless found to rest exclusively with Congress. . . .

A review of executive action demonstrates that our Presidents have on many occasions exhibited the leadership contemplated by the Framers when they made the President Commander in Chief, and imposed upon him the trust to "take Care that the Laws be faithfully executed." With or without explicit statutory authorization, Presidents have at such times dealt with national emergencies by acting promptly and resolutely to enforce legislative programs, at least to save those programs until Congress could act. Congress and the courts have responded to such executive initiative with consistent approval. . . .

The diversity of views expressed in the six opinions of the majority, the lack of reference to authoritative precedent, the repeated reliance upon prior dissenting opinions, the complete disregard of the uncontroverted facts showing the gravity of the emergency, and the temporary nature of the taking all serve to demonstrate how far afield one must go to affirm the order of the District Court.

The broad executive power granted by Article II to an officer on duty 365 days a year cannot, it is said, be invoked to avert disaster. Instead, the President must confine himself to sending a message to Congress recommending action. Under this messenger-boy concept of the Office, the President cannot even act to preserve legislative programs from destruction so that Congress will have something left to act upon. There is no judicial finding that the executive action was unwarranted because there was, in fact, no basis for the President's finding of the existence of an emergency for, under this view, the gravity of the emergency and the immediacy of the threatened disaster are considered irrelevant as a matter of law.

Seizure of plaintiffs' property is not a pleasant undertaking. Similarly unpleasant to a free country are the draft which disrupts the home and military procurement which causes economic dislocation and compels adoption of price controls, wage stabilization and allocation of materials. The President informed Congress that even a temporary Government operation of plaintiffs' properties was "thoroughly distasteful" to him, but was necessary to prevent immediate paralysis of the mobilization program. Presidents have been in the past, and any man worthy of the Office should be in the future, free to take at least interim action necessary to execute legislative programs essential to survival of the Nation. A sturdy judiciary should not be swayed by the unpleasantness or unpopularity of necessary executive action, but must independently determine for itself whether the President was acting, as required by the Constitution, to "take Care that the Laws be faithfully executed." . . .

## *New York Times Co. v. United States*
### 403 U.S. 713 (1971)

The facts and background of this case are set out on pp. 242–243.

The Court's *per curiam* decision was 6 to 3. Justices Black, Douglas, Brennan, Stewart, White, and Marshall each filed concurring opinions. Chief Justice Burger and Justices Harlan and Blackmun each filed dissenting opinions.

### Per Curiam

We granted certiorari in these cases in which the United States seeks to enjoin the New York Times and the Washington Post from publishing the contents of a classified study entitled "History of U.S. Decision-Making Process on Viet Nam Policy." [The Pentagon Papers]

"Any system of prior restraints of expression comes to this Court bearing a heavy presumption against its constitutional validity." *Bantam Books, Inc. v. Sullivan,* (1963); *Near v. Minnesota* (1931). The Government "thus carries a heavy burden of showing justification for the imposition of such a restraint." *Organization for a Better Austin v. Keefe* (1971). The District Court for the Southern District of New York, in the *New York Times* case, and the District Court for the District of Columbia and the Court of Appeals for the District of Columbia

Circuit, in the *Washington Post* case, held that the Government had not met that burden. We agree.

The judgment of the Court of Appeals for the District of Columbia Circuit is therefore affirmed. The order of the Court of Appeals for the Second Circuit is reversed, and the case is remanded with directions to enter a judgment affirming the judgment of the District Court for the Southern District of New York. The stays entered June 25, 1971, by the Court are vacated. The judgments shall issue forthwith.

*So ordered.*

MR. JUSTICE BLACK, with whom MR. JUSTICE DOUGLAS joins, concurring.

I adhere to the view that the Government's case against the Washington Post should have been dismissed, and that the injunction against the New York Times should have been vacated without oral argument when the cases were first presented to this Court. I believe that every moment's continuance of the injunctions against these newspapers amounts to a flagrant, indefensible, and continuing violation of the First Amendment. . . . In my view, it is unfortunate that some of my Brethren are apparently willing to hold that the publication of news may sometimes be enjoined. Such a holding would make a shambles of the First Amendment.

Our Government was launched in 1789 with the adoption of the Constitution. The Bill of Rights, including the First Amendment, followed in 1791. Now, for the first time in the 182 years since the founding of the Republic, the federal courts are asked to hold that the First Amendment does not mean what it says, but rather means that the Government can halt the publication of current news of vital importance to the people of this country.

In seeking injunctions against these newspapers, and in its presentation to the Court, the Executive Branch seems to have forgotten the essential purpose and history of the First Amendment. When the Constitution was adopted, many people strongly opposed it because the document contained no Bill of Rights to safeguard certain basic freedoms. They especially feared that the new powers granted to a central government might be interpreted to permit the government to curtail freedom of religion, press, assembly, and speech. In response to an overwhelming public clamor, James Madison offered a series of amendments to satisfy citizens that these great liberties would remain safe and beyond the power of government to abridge. Madison proposed what later became the First Amendment in three parts, two of which are set out

**LATE CITY EDITION**

VOL. CXX .. No 41,431          © 1971 The New York Times Company          NEW YORK, THURSDAY, JULY 1, 1971          15 CENTS

# SUPREME COURT, 6-3, UPHOLDS NEWSPAPERS ON PUBLICATION OF THE PENTAGON REPORT; TIMES RESUMES ITS SERIES, HALTED 15 DAYS

*A New York Times banner headline celebrates the Court's decision prohibiting the Nixon administration from enjoining the publication of the Pentagon Papers. The decision permitted the Times and the Washington Post to resume publication of the Pentagon-sponsored study of the Vietnam War. The Pentagon Papers exposed far more weaknesses in the United States' war effort than the government had publicly acknowledged.*

© The New York Times.

below, and one of which proclaimed: "The people shall not be deprived or abridged of their right to speak, to write, or to publish their sentiments, *and the freedom of the press, as one of the great bulwarks of liberty, shall be inviolable.*" The amendments were offered to curtail and restrict the general powers granted to the Executive, Legislative, and Judicial Branches two years before in the original Constitution. The Bill of Rights changed the original Constitution into a new charter under which no branch of government could abridge the people's freedoms of press, speech, religion, and assembly. Yet the Solicitor General argues and some members of the Court appear to agree that the general powers of the Government adopted in the original Constitution should be interpreted to limit and restrict the specific and emphatic guarantees of the Bill of Rights adopted later. I can imagine no greater perversion of history. Madison and the other Framers of the First Amendment, able men that they were, wrote in language they earnestly believed could never be misunderstood: "Congress shall make no law . . . abridging the freedom . . . of the press. . . ." Both the history and language of the First Amendment support the view that the press must be left free to publish news, whatever the source, without censorship, injunctions, or prior restraints.

In the First Amendment, the Founding Fathers gave the free press the protection it must have to fulfill its essential role in our democracy. The press was to serve the governed, not the governors. The Government's power to censor the press was abolished so that the press would remain forever free to censure the Government. The press was protected so that it could bare the secrets of govern-

ment and inform the people. Only a free and unrestrained press can effectively expose deception in government. And paramount among the responsibilities of a free press is the duty to prevent any part of the government from deceiving the people and sending them off to distant lands to die of foreign fevers and foreign shot and shell. In my view, far from deserving condemnation for their courageous reporting, the New York Times, the Washington Post, and other newspapers should be commended for serving the purpose that the Founding Fathers saw so clearly. In revealing the workings of government that led to the Vietnam war, the newspapers nobly did precisely that which the Founders hoped and trusted they would do. . . .

In other words, we are asked to hold that, despite the First Amendment's emphatic command, the Executive Branch, the Congress, and the Judiciary can make laws enjoining publication of current news and abridging freedom of the press in the name of "national security." The Government does not even attempt to rely on any act of Congress. Instead, it makes the bold and dangerously far-reaching contention that the courts should take it upon themselves to "make" a law abridging freedom of the press in the name of equity, presidential power and national security, even when the representatives of the people in Congress have adhered to the command of the First Amendment and refused to make such a law. To find that the President has "inherent power" to halt the publication of news by resort to the courts would wipe out the First Amendment and destroy the fundamental liberty and security of the very people the Government hopes to make "secure." No one can read the history of the adoption of the First Amendment without being convinced beyond any doubt that it was injunctions like those sought here that Madison and his collaborators intended to outlaw in this Nation for all time.

The word "security" is a broad, vague generality whose contours should not be invoked to abrogate the fundamental law embodied in the First Amendment. The guarding of military and diplomatic secrets at the expense of informed representative government provides no real security for our Republic. The Framers of the First Amendment, fully aware of both the need to defend a new nation and the abuses of the English and Colonial governments, sought to give this new society strength and security by providing that freedom of speech, press, religion, and assembly should not be abridged.

Mr. Justice Douglas, with whom Mr. Justice Black joins, concurring.

. . . The Government says that it has inherent powers to go into court and obtain an injunction to protect the national interest, which, in this case, is alleged to be national security. . . .

The dominant purpose of the First Amendment was to prohibit the widespread practice of governmental suppression of embarrassing information. It is common knowledge that the First Amendment was adopted against the widespread use of the common law of seditious libel to punish the dissemination of material that is embarrassing to the powers-that-be. Z. Chafee, *Free Speech in the United States*, (1941). The present cases will, I think, go down in history as the most dramatic illustration of that principle. A debate of large proportions goes on in the Nation over our posture in Vietnam. That debate antedated the disclosure of the contents of the present documents. The latter are highly relevant to the debate in progress. Secrecy in government is fundamentally antidemocratic, perpetuating bureaucratic errors. Open debate and discussion of public issues are vital to our national health. On public questions, there should be "uninhibited, robust, and wide-open" debate.

Mr. Justice Brennan, concurring.

I write separately in these cases only to emphasize what should be apparent: that our judgments in the present cases may not be taken to indicate the propriety, in the future, of issuing temporary stays and restraining orders to block the publication of material sought to be suppressed by the Government. So far as I can determine, never before has the United States sought to enjoin a newspaper from publishing information in its possession.

The relative novelty of the questions presented, the necessary haste with which decisions were reached, the magnitude of the interests asserted, and the fact that all the parties have concentrated their arguments upon the question whether permanent restraints were proper may have justified at least some of the restraints heretofore imposed in these cases. Certainly it is difficult to fault the several courts below for seeking to assure that the issues here involved were preserved for ultimate review by this Court. But even if it be assumed that some of the interim restraints were proper in the two cases before us, that assumption has no bearing upon the propriety of similar judicial action in the future. To begin with, there has now been ample time for reflection and judgment; whatever values there may be in the preservation of novel questions for appellate review may not support any restraints in the future. More important, the First Amendment stands as an absolute bar to the imposition of judicial restraints in circumstances of the kind presented by these cases.

Mr. Justice Stewart, with whom Mr. Justice White joins, concurring.

In the governmental structure created by our Constitution, the Executive is endowed with enormous power in the two related areas of national defense and international relations. This power, largely unchecked by the Legislative and Judicial branches, has been pressed to the very hilt since the advent of the nuclear missile age. For better or for worse, the simple fact is that a President of the United States possesses vastly greater constitutional independence in these two vital areas of power than does, say, a prime minister of a country with a parliamentary form of government.

In the absence of the governmental checks and balances present in other areas of our national life, the only effective restraint upon executive policy and power in the areas of national defense and international affairs may lie in an enlightened citizenry—in an informed and critical public opinion which alone can here protect the values of democratic government. For this reason, it is perhaps here that a press that is alert, aware, and free most vitally serves the basic purpose of the First Amendment. For, without an informed and free press, there cannot be an enlightened people.

Yet it is elementary that the successful conduct of international diplomacy and the maintenance of an effective national defense require both confidentiality and secrecy. Other nations can hardly deal with this Nation in an atmosphere of mutual trust unless they can be assured that their confidences will be kept. And, within our own executive departments, the development of considered and intelligent international policies would be impossible if those charged with their formulation could not communicate with each other freely, frankly, and in confidence. In the area of basic national defense, the frequent need for absolute secrecy is, of course, self-evident. I think there can be but one answer to this dilemma, if dilemma it be. The responsibility must be where the power is. If the Constitution gives the Executive a large degree of unshared power in the conduct of foreign affairs and the maintenance of our national defense, then, under the Constitution, the Executive must have the largely unshared duty to determine and preserve the degree of internal security necessary to exercise that power successfully. It is an awesome responsibility, requiring judgment and wisdom of a high order. I should suppose that moral, political, and practical considerations would dictate that a very first principle of that wisdom would be an insistence upon avoiding secrecy for its own sake. For when everything is classified, then nothing is classified, and the system becomes one to be disregarded by the cynical or the careless, and to be manipulated by those intent on self-protection or self-promotion. I should suppose, in short, that the hallmark of a truly effective internal security system would be the maximum possible disclosure, recognizing that secrecy can best be preserved only when credibility is truly maintained. But, be that as it may, it is clear to me that it is the constitutional duty of the Executive—as a matter of sovereign prerogative, and not as a matter of law as the courts know law—through the promulgation and enforcement of executive regulations, to protect the confidentiality necessary to carry out its responsibilities in the fields of international relations and national defense.

This is not to say that Congress and the courts have no role to play. Undoubtedly, Congress has the power to enact specific and appropriate criminal laws to protect government property and preserve government secrets. Congress has passed such laws, and several of them are of very colorable relevance to the apparent circumstances of these cases. And if a criminal prosecution is instituted, it will be the responsibility of the courts to decide the applicability of the criminal law under which the charge is brought. Moreover, if Congress should pass a specific law authorizing civil proceedings in this field, the courts would likewise have the duty to decide the constitutionality of such a law, as well as its applicability to the facts proved.

But in the cases before us, we are asked neither to construe specific regulations nor to apply specific laws. We are asked, instead, to perform a function that the Constitution gave to the Executive, not the Judiciary. We are asked, quite simply, to prevent the publication by two newspapers of material that the Executive Branch insists should not, in the national interest, be published. I am convinced that the Executive is correct with respect to some of the documents involved. But I cannot say that disclosure of any of them will surely result in direct, immediate, and irreparable damage to our Nation or its people. That being so, there can under the First Amendment be but one judicial resolution of the issues before us.

MR. JUSTICE WHITE, with whom MR. JUSTICE STEWART joins, concurring.

I concur in today's judgments, but only because of the concededly extraordinary protection against prior restraints enjoyed by the press under our constitutional system. I do not say that in no circumstances would the First Amendment permit an injunction against publishing information about government plans or operations. Nor, after examining the materials the Government characterizes as the most sensitive and destructive, can I deny that revelation of these documents will do substantial damage to public interests. Indeed, I am confident that their disclosure will have that result. But I nevertheless agree that the United States has not satisfied the very heavy burden that it must meet to warrant an injunction against publication in these cases, at least in the absence of express and appropriately limited congressional authorization for prior restraints in circumstances such as these.

The Government's position is simply stated: the responsibility of the Executive for the conduct of the foreign affairs and for the security of the Nation is so basic that the President is entitled to an injunction against publication of a newspaper story whenever he can convince a court that the information to be revealed threatens "grave and irreparable" injury to the public interest; and the injunction should issue whether or not the material to be published is classified, whether or not publication would be lawful under relevant criminal statutes enacted by Congress, and regardless of the circumstances by which the newspaper came into possession of the information. At least in the absence of legislation by Congress, based on its own investigations and findings, I am quite unable to agree that the inherent powers of the Executive and the courts reach so far as to authorize remedies having such sweeping potential for inhibiting publications by the press. Much of the difficulty inheres in the "grave and irreparable danger" standard suggested by the United States. If the United States were to have judgment under such a standard in these cases, our decision would be of little guidance to other courts in other cases, for the material at issue here would not be available from the Court's opinion or from public records, nor would it be published by the press. Indeed, even today, where we hold that the United States has not met its burden, the material remains sealed in court records and it is properly not discussed in today's opinions. Moreover, because the material poses substantial dangers to national interests, and because of the hazards of criminal sanctions, a responsible press may choose never to publish the more sensitive materials. To sustain the Government in these cases would start the courts down a long and hazardous road that I am not willing to travel, at least without congressional guidance and direction.

It is not easy to reject the proposition urged by the United States, and to deny relief on its good faith claims in these cases that publication will work serious damage to the country. But that discomfiture is considerably dispelled by the infrequency of prior-restraint cases. Normally, publication will occur and the damage be done before the Government has either opportunity or grounds for suppression. So here, publication has already begun, and a substantial part of the threatened damage has already occurred. The fact of a massive breakdown in security is known, access to the documents by many unauthorized people is undeniable, and the efficacy of equitable relief against these or other newspapers to avert anticipated damage is doubtful, at best.

Mr. Justice Marshall, concurring.

The Government contends that the only issue in these cases is whether, in a suit by the United States, "the First Amendment bars a court from prohibiting a newspaper from publishing material whose disclosure would pose a 'grave and immediate danger to the security of the United States.'" With all due respect, I believe the ultimate issue in these cases is even more basic than the one posed by the Solicitor General. The issue is whether this Court or the Congress has the power to make law. The problem here is whether, in these particular cases, the Executive Branch has authority to invoke the equity jurisdiction of the courts to protect what it believes to be the national interest. The Government argues that, in addition to the inherent power of any government to protect itself, the President's power to conduct foreign affairs and his position as Commander in Chief give him authority to impose censorship on the press to protect his ability to deal effectively with foreign nations and to conduct the military affairs of the country. Of course, it is beyond cavil that the President has broad powers by virtue of his primary responsibility for the conduct of our foreign affairs and his position as Commander in Chief. And, in some situa-

tions, it may be that, under whatever inherent powers the Government may have, as well as the implicit authority derived from the President's mandate to conduct foreign affairs and to act as Commander in Chief, there is a basis for the invocation of the equity jurisdiction of this Court as an aid to prevent the publication of material damaging to "national security," however that term may be defined.

It would, however, be utterly inconsistent with the concept of separation of powers for this Court to use its power of contempt to prevent behavior that Congress has specifically declined to prohibit. There would be a similar damage to the basic concept of these co-equal branches of Government if, when the Executive Branch has adequate authority granted by Congress to protect "national security," it can choose, instead, to invoke the contempt power of a court to enjoin the threatened conduct. The Constitution provides that Congress shall make laws, the President execute laws, and courts interpret laws. *Youngstown Sheet & Tube Co. v. Sawyer* (1952). It did not provide for government by injunction in which the courts and the Executive Branch can "make law" without regard to the action of Congress. It may be more convenient for the Executive Branch if it need only convince a judge to prohibit conduct, rather than ask the Congress to pass a law, and it may be more convenient to enforce a contempt order than to seek a criminal conviction in a jury trial. Moreover, it may be considered politically wise to get a court to share the responsibility for arresting those who the Executive Branch has probable cause to believe are violating the law. But convenience and political considerations of the moment do not justify a basic departure from the principles of our system of government.

Mr. Justice Harlan, with whom The Chief Justice and Mr. Justice Blackmun join, dissenting.

These cases forcefully call to mind the wise admonition of Mr. Justice Holmes. . . .

> Great cases, like hard cases, make bad law. For great cases are called great not by reason of their real importance in shaping the law of the future, but because of some accident of immediate overwhelming interest which appeals to the feelings and distorts the judgment. These immediate interests exercise a kind of hydraulic pressure which makes what previously was clear seem doubtful, and before which even well settled principles of law will bend.

With all respect, I consider that the Court has been almost irresponsibly feverish in dealing with these cases.

This frenzied train of events took place in the name of the presumption against prior restraints created by the First Amendment. Due regard for the extraordinarily important and difficult questions involved in these litigations should have led the Court to shun such a precipitate timetable. In order to decide the merits of these cases properly, some or all of the following questions should have been faced:

1. Whether the Attorney General is authorized to bring these suits in the name of the United States.
2. Whether the First Amendment permits the federal courts to enjoin publication of stories which would present a serious threat to national security.
3. Whether the threat to publish highly secret documents is of itself a sufficient implication of national security to justify an injunction on the theory that, regardless of the contents of the documents, harm enough results simply from the demonstration of such a breach of secrecy.
4. Whether the unauthorized disclosure of any of these particular documents would seriously impair the national security.
5. What weight should be given to the opinion of high officers in the Executive Branch of the Government with respect to questions 3 and 4.
6. Whether the newspapers are entitled to retain and use the documents notwithstanding the seemingly uncontested facts that the documents, or the originals of which they are duplicates, were purloined from the Government's possession, and that the newspapers received them with knowledge that they had been feloniously acquired.
7. Whether the threatened harm to the national security or the Government's possessory interest in the documents justifies the issuance of an injunction against publication in light of—
   a. The strong First Amendment policy against prior restraints on publication;
   b. The doctrine against enjoining conduct in violation of criminal statutes; and
   c. The extent to which the materials at issue have apparently already been otherwise disseminated.

These are difficult questions of fact, of law, and of judgment; the potential consequences of erroneous decision are enormous. The time which has been available to us, to the lower courts, and to the parties has been wholly inadequate for giving these cases the kind of consideration they deserve. It is a reflection on the stability of the judicial process that these great issues—as important as any that

have arisen during my time on the Court—should have been decided under the pressures engendered by the torrent of publicity that has attended these litigations from their inception.

Forced as I am to reach the merits of these cases, I dissent from the opinion and judgments of the Court. Within the severe limitations imposed by the time constraints under which I have been required to operate, I can only state my reasons in telescoped form, even though, in different circumstances, I would have felt constrained to deal with the cases in the fuller sweep indicated above. . . .

In a speech on the floor of the House of Representatives, Chief Justice John Marshall, then a member of that body, stated [in 1800]: "The President is the sole organ of the nation in its external relations, and its sole representative with foreign nations." From that time, shortly after the founding of the Nation, to this, there has been no substantial challenge to this description of the scope of executive power. *United States* v. *Curtiss-Wright Corp.* (1936).

From this constitutional primacy in the field of foreign affairs, it seems to me that certain conclusions necessarily follow. Some of these were stated concisely by President Washington, declining the request of the House of Representatives for the papers leading up to the negotiation of the Jay Treaty:

> The nature of foreign negotiations requires caution, and their success must often depend on secrecy; and even when brought to a conclusion, a full disclosure of all the measures, demands, or eventual concessions which may have been proposed or contemplated would be extremely impolitic; for this might have a pernicious influence on future negotiations, or produce immediate inconveniences, perhaps danger and mischief, in relation to other powers.

. . . Pending further hearings in each case conducted under the appropriate ground rules, I would continue the restraints on publication. I cannot believe that the doctrine prohibiting prior restraints reaches to the point of preventing courts from maintaining the *status quo* long enough to act responsibly in matters of such national importance as those involved here.

MR. JUSTICE BLACKMUN, dissenting.

. . . The First Amendment . . . is only one part of an entire Constitution. Article II of the great document vests in the Executive Branch primary power over the conduct of foreign affairs, and places in that branch the responsibility for the Nation's safety. Each provision of the Constitution is important, and I cannot subscribe to a doctrine of unlimited absolutism for the First Amendment at the cost of downgrading other provisions. First Amendment absolutism has never commanded a majority of this Court. *Near* v. *Minnesota* (1931), and *Schenck* v. *United States* (1919). What is needed here is a weighing, upon properly developed standards, of the broad right of the press to print and of the very narrow right of the Government to prevent. Such standards are not yet developed. The parties here are in disagreement as to what those standards should be. But even the newspapers concede that there are situations where restraint is in order and is constitutional. . . .

It may well be that, if these cases were allowed to develop as they should be developed, and to be tried as lawyers should try them and as courts should hear them, free of pressure and panic and sensationalism, other light would be shed on the situation, and contrary considerations, for me, might prevail. But that is not the present posture of the litigation. . . .

I hope that damage has not already been done. If, however, damage has been done, and if, with the Court's action today, these newspapers proceed to publish the critical documents and there results therefrom "the death of soldiers, the destruction of alliances, the greatly increased difficulty of negotiation with our enemies, the inability of our diplomats to negotiate," to which list I might add the factors of prolongation of the war and of further delay in the freeing of United States prisoners, then the Nation's people will know where the responsibility for these sad consequences rests.

## *Dames & Moore* v. *Regan*

453 U.S. 654 (1981)

In February 1979, Iranian revolutionaries aligned with Shiite Muslim leader Ayatollah Ruholla Khomeni overthrew the United States-backed government led by Shah Mohammed Reza Pahlevi. The Shah had governed Iran since the early 1950s and had enjoyed a fruitful financial and military relationship with several American presidents. By the late 1970s, opposition to the Shah's regime, especially among the radical Shiites, had reached a fever pitch. In November 1979, Shiite students seized the American embassy in Teheran and took over fifty-three persons hostage, including persons who did not serve in diplomatic capacities. The embassy's seizure was motivated in

large part by the decision of the United States to permit the Shah to enter for cancer treatment, a decision that the American ambassador in Teheran warned would have dire consequences. In October 1980 the United States had attempted a military operation to rescue the hostages, but it failed after planes and other equipment broke down in the desert. Photos in newspapers and magazines of the botched American raid symbolized the nation's paralysis in handling the hostage crisis.

Until the failed rescue effort, the United States had relied upon economic measures to squeeze the Khomeni government's position. The most severe sanction imposed by the American government came when President Jimmy Carter invoked the International Emergency Economic Powers Act, which mandated a freeze on Iranian assets in the United States. On January 20, 1981, just as President Carter's successor, Ronald Reagan, was being sworn into office, Iran released the hostages. In the days leading up to the release of the hostages, President Carter had issued several orders putting into effect an agreement reached by the American and Iranian governments. Under the arrangement the United States agreed to "terminate all legal proceedings in the United States courts involving claims of the United States persons and institutions against Iran and its state enterprises."

Dames & Moore attempted to recover several millions of dollars it was owed by the Iranian government and several Iranian banks. The lower courts rejected their arguments.

The defendant is this case is Donald Regan, who, at the time, was treasury secretary under President Reagan. Reagan had continued to issue executive orders as necessary to carry out the agreement reached between the Carter administration and the Iranians. The Treasury Department also was responsible for enforcing regulations relevant to the agreement; hence the decision of Dames & Moore to sue Regan.

The Court's decision was unanimous. Justice Rehnquist delivered the opinion of the Court. Justice Stevens filed a concurring opinion. Justice Powell concurred in part and dissented in part.

JUSTICE REHNQUIST delivered the opinion of the Court.

The questions presented by this case touch fundamentally upon the manner in which our Republic is to be governed. Throughout the nearly two centuries of our Nation's existence under the Constitution, this subject has generated considerable debate. We have had the benefit of commentators such as John Jay, Alexander Hamilton, and James Madison writing in *The Federalist Papers* at the Nation's very inception, the benefit of astute foreign observers of our system such as Alexis de Tocqueville and James Bryce writing during the first century of the Nation's existence, and the benefit of many other treatises, as well as more than 400 volumes of reports of decisions of this Court. As these writings reveal, it is doubtless both futile and perhaps dangerous to find any epigrammatical explanation of how this country has been governed. Indeed, as Justice Jackson noted, "[a] judge . . . may be surprised at the poverty of really useful and unambiguous authority applicable to concrete problems of executive power as they actually present themselves." *Youngstown Sheet & Tube Co.* v. *Sawyer* (1952). . . .

We are confined to a resolution of the dispute presented to us. That dispute involves various Executive Orders and regulations by which the President nullified attachments and liens on Iranian assets in the United States, directed that these assets be transferred to Iran, and suspended claims against Iran that may be presented to an International Claims Tribunal. This action was taken in an effort to comply with an Executive Agreement between the United States and Iran. . . .

[W]e freely confess that we are obviously deciding only one more episode in the never-ending tension between the President exercising the executive authority in a world that presents each day some new challenge with which he must deal, and the Constitution under which we all live and which no one disputes embodies some sort of system of checks and balances. . . .

The parties and the lower courts . . . have all agreed that much relevant analysis is contained in *Youngstown Sheet & Tube Co.* v. *Sawyer* (1952). Justice Black's opinion for the Court in that case, involving the validity of President Truman's effort to seize the country's steel mills in the wake of a nationwide strike, recognized that "[t]he President's power, if any, to issue the order must stem either from an act of Congress or from the Constitution itself." Justice Jackson's concurring opinion elaborated in a general way the consequences of different types of interaction between the two democratic branches in assessing Presidential authority to act in any given case. When the President acts pursuant to an express or implied authorization from Congress, he exercises not only his powers but also those delegated by Congress. In such a case, the executive action "would be supported by the strongest of presumptions and the widest latitude of judicial interpre-

tation, and the burden of persuasion would rest heavily upon any who might attack it." When the President acts in the absence of congressional authorization, he may enter "a zone of twilight in which he and Congress may have concurrent authority, or in which its distribution is uncertain." In such a case, the analysis becomes more complicated, and the validity of the President's action, at least so far as separation of powers principles are concerned, hinges on a consideration of all the circumstances which might shed light on the views of the Legislative Branch toward such action, including "congressional inertia, indifference or quiescence." Finally, when the President acts in contravention of the will of Congress, "his power is at its lowest ebb," and the Court can sustain his actions "only by disabling the Congress from acting upon the subject."

Although we have in the past found, and do today find, Justice Jackson's classification of executive actions into three general categories analytically useful, we should be mindful of Justice Holmes' admonition . . . that "[t]he great ordinances of the Constitution do not establish and divide fields of black and white." Justice Jackson himself recognized that his three categories represented "a somewhat over-simplified grouping," and it is doubtless the case that executive action in any particular instance falls not neatly in one of three pigeonholes, but rather at some point along a spectrum running from explicit congressional authorization to explicit congressional prohibition. This is particularly true as respects cases such as the one before us, involving responses to international crises the nature of which Congress can hardly have been expected to anticipate in any detail. . . .

This Court has previously recognized that the congressional purpose in authorizing blocking orders is "to put control of foreign assets in the hands of the President. . . ." *Propper* v. *Clark* (1949). Such orders permit the President to maintain the foreign assets at his disposal for use in negotiating the resolution of a declared national emergency. The frozen assets serve as a "bargaining chip" to be used by the President when dealing with a hostile country. Accordingly, it is difficult to accept petitioner's argument, because the practical effect of it is to allow individual claimants throughout the country to minimize or wholly eliminate this "bargaining chip" through attachments, garnishments, or similar encumbrances on property. Neither the purpose the statute was enacted to serve nor its plain language supports such a result.

Because the President's action in nullifying the attachments and ordering the transfer of the assets was taken pursuant to specific congressional authorization, it is, "supported by the strongest of presumptions and the widest latitude of judicial interpretation, and the burden of persuasion would rest heavily upon any who might attack it." *Youngstown.* Under the circumstances of this case, we cannot say that petitioner has sustained that heavy burden. A contrary ruling would mean that the Federal Government as a whole lacked the power exercised by the President, and that we are not prepared to say.

Although we have concluded that the IEEPA constitutes specific congressional authorization to the President to nullify the attachments and order the transfer of Iranian assets, there remains the question of the President's authority to suspend claims pending in American courts. Such claims have, of course, an existence apart from the attachments which accompanied them. . . .

We conclude that, although the IEEPA authorized the nullification of the attachments, it cannot be read to authorize the suspension of the claims. The claims of American citizens against Iran are not, in themselves, transactions involving Iranian property or efforts to exercise any rights with respect to such property. An *in personam* lawsuit, although it might eventually be reduced to judgment and that judgment might be executed upon, is an effort to establish liability and fix damages, and does not focus on any particular property within the jurisdiction. The terms of the IEEPA therefore do not authorize the President to suspend claims in American courts. . . .

Not infrequently in affairs between nations, outstanding claims by nationals of one country against the government of another country are "sources of friction" between the two sovereigns. *United States v. Pink* (1942). To resolve these difficulties, nations have often entered into agreements settling the claims of their respective nationals. . . . Consistent with that principle, the United States has repeatedly exercised its sovereign authority to settle the claims of its nationals against foreign countries. Though those settlements have sometimes been made by treaty, there has also been a longstanding practice of settling such claims by executive agreement, without the advice and consent of the Senate. Under such agreements, the President has agreed to renounce or extinguish claims of United States nationals against foreign governments in return for lump-sum payments or the establishment of arbitration procedures. To be sure, many of these settlements were encouraged by the United States claimants themselves, since a claimant's only hope of obtaining any payment at all might lie in having his Government negotiate a diplomatic settlement on his behalf. But it is also undisputed that the "United States has sometimes disposed of the claims of its citizens without their consent, or even without consultation with them, usually

without exclusive regard for their interests, as distinguished from those of the nation as a whole." . . . It is clear that the practice of settling claims continues today. Since 1952, the President has entered into at least 10 binding settlements with foreign nations, including an $80 million settlement with the People's Republic of China.

Crucial to our decision today is the conclusion that Congress has implicitly approved the practice of claim settlement by executive agreement. This is best demonstrated by Congress' enactment of the International Claims Settlement Act of 1949. The Act had two purposes: (1) to allocate to United States nationals funds received in the course of an executive claims settlement with Yugoslavia, and (2) to provide a procedure whereby funds resulting from future settlements could be distributed. To achieve these ends Congress created the International Claims Commission, now the Foreign Claims Settlement Commission, and gave it jurisdiction to make final and binding decisions with respect to claims by United States nationals against settlement funds. By creating a procedure to implement future settlement agreements, Congress placed its stamp of approval on such agreements. Indeed, the legislative history of the Act observed that the United States was seeking settlements with countries other than Yugoslavia, and that the bill contemplated settlements of a similar nature in the future. . . .

In addition to congressional acquiescence in the President's power to settle claims, prior cases of this Court have also recognized that the President does have some measure of power to enter into executive agreements without obtaining the advice and consent of the Senate. In *United States v. Pink* (1942), for example, the Court upheld the validity of the Litvinov Assignment, which was part of an Executive Agreement whereby the Soviet Union assigned to the United States amounts owed to it by American nationals so that outstanding claims of other American nationals could be paid. . . .

In light of all of the foregoing—the inferences to be drawn from the character of the legislation Congress has enacted in the area, such as the IEEPA and the Hostage Act, and from the history of acquiescence in executive claims settlement—we conclude that the President was authorized to suspend pending claims pursuant to Executive Order No. 12294. . . .

Our conclusion is buttressed by the fact that the means chosen by the President to settle the claims of American nationals provided an alternative forum, the Claims Tribunal which is capable of providing meaningful relief. . . . The fact that the President has provided such a forum here means that the claimants are receiving something in return for the suspension of their claims, namely, access to an international tribunal before which they may well recover something on their claims. Because there does appear to be a real "settlement" here, this case is more easily analogized to the more traditional claim settlement cases of the past.

Just as importantly, Congress has not disapproved of the action taken here. Though Congress has held hearings on the Iranian Agreement itself, Congress has not enacted legislation, or even passed a resolution, indicating its displeasure with the Agreement. Quite the contrary, the relevant Senate Committee has stated that the establishment of the Tribunal is "of vital importance to the United States." We are thus clearly not confronted with a situation in which Congress has in some way resisted the exercise of Presidential authority.

Finally, we reemphasize the narrowness of our decision. We do not decide that the President possesses plenary power to settle claims, even as against foreign governmental entities. . . . But where, as here, the settlement of claims has been determined to be a necessary incident to the resolution of a major foreign policy dispute between our country and another, and where, as here, we can conclude that Congress acquiesced in the President's action, we are not prepared to say that the President lacks the power to settle such claims.

▼▲▼

## The President as Diplomat-in-Chief

Our discussion of presidential power in times of emergencies and war-related crises makes clear that the Court has been exceedingly generous to the claims of presidents since Thomas Jefferson that the power to conduct foreign affairs, including war and diplomacy, should rest with the executive branch. But the now-accepted notion that the president should be the "nation's sole organ for foreign affairs" has little foundation in the text and design of the Constitution.[74] Rather, the basis for presidential supremacy in foreign affairs rests with the assumption that such power is inherent in the role of the executive office. The Framers inherited this feature from political philosophers such as Locke and Montesquieu, whose views on executive power influenced American constitutional design. This notion of "inherent" presidential power, along with the gradual transfer of power from Congress to the president in war and foreign affairs, more so than a particular constitutional provision or combination of provisions, accounts for the Court's deference to the wishes of the political branches.[75]

In fact, the Court's opinion in *United States* v. *Curtiss-Wright Corp.* (1936), which gave the first comprehensive constitutional expression to the "sole organ" theory of presidential power in foreign relations, makes very little reference to the Constitution. George Sutherland's historic opinion reads much more like the labor of a historian than it does a Supreme Court justice. For sure, Sutherland discusses the pivotal constitutional question presented by *Curtiss-Wright* of whether Congress could delegate to the president the power to ban arms sales to foreign countries. But Sutherland relies on a much more abstract concept of constitutional interpretation to support his ultimate conclusion: The "inherent power of the president" allows him to conduct foreign relations as the "sole negotiator" on behalf of the United States. Note the emphasis that Sutherland places on the distinction between the constitutional limits of presidential power in the domestic sphere and in foreign relations. The justice even confesses that the congressional delegation of power under review would have been unconstitutional had it not been directed toward a foreign policy objective.

It is impossible to overestimate the importance of Justice Sutherland's opinion in *Curtiss-Wright* for the subsequent independence of presidents to conduct foreign policy. Much of President Roosevelt's legal authority to exercise the power that Congress continued to delegate to the executive branch during World War II was made possible by Justice Sutherland.[76] Indeed, no other decision has given the president such singular power to carry out the aspirations of Alexander Hamilton, who, in *Federalist* 70, had called the executive the "bulwark of the national security."[77]

Another crucial area of foreign policy in which the Court has interpreted executive power as supreme involves the power of the president to make and enforce international treaties on behalf of the United States. Article II, Section 2, authorizes the president to have "Power, by and with the Advice and Consent of the Senate, to make Treaties, provided two thirds of the Senators present concur." Once ratified, treaties have the same force as federal law. Moreover, their unique application in the international context—the fact that treaties create rules between nations and not merely states—often result in the use of executive agreements to enforce treaty provisions. Executive agreements are the foreign policy equivalent of executive orders used by the president to enforce federal statutes in the domestic context. They are as binding as any other federal law.[78]

Presidents have made ample use of this authority granted to them to make treaties since the Court's first important statement on the scope of such power in *Missouri v. Holland* (1920). Strange as it may seem now, *Holland* involved a lawsuit brought by the state of Missouri that challenged the president's power to make treaties with foreign nations. The issue was whether President Wilson had usurped the police powers reserved to the states by the Constitution by entering into a 1918 treaty with Canada to protect migratory birds from hunters during their annual passage through the United States. Missouri claimed that it, not the federal government, possessed the power to enact laws regulating the hunting of wild game and other important animal and bird species within the state's borders. This complaint also extended to Congress, which had enacted a law to enforce the provisions of the treaty.

Some constitutional scholars have commented that Justice Holmes's opinion for a 7-2 Court recognizing and upholding the president's treaty power in *Holland* is not among Holmes's better efforts. Political scientist C. Herman Pritchett has written of Holmes's opinion: "There is at first glance something startling about a situation whereby ratification of a treaty gives Congress constitutional powers it did not possess in the absence of the treaty. But this result is an inevitable consequence of the plenary nature of federal power over foreign affairs."[79] Consider two questions here: Is Justice Holmes's opinion startling in the assumption it makes for the supremacy of federal power in the absence of text in the Constitution to the contrary? Based on our discussion of *Holland, Curtiss-Wright,* and the cases preceding them that dealt with presidential emergency power, is the "plenary nature" of federal power, and presidential power in particular, over foreign affairs a positive development in American constitutional law?

## United States v. Curtiss-Wright Export Corp.

### 299 U.S. 304 (1936)

In 1932, Bolivia and Paraguay entered an undeclared war for control over the Chaco region, an area east of Bolivia that provided access to the Atlantic Ocean. Curtiss-Wright, an American aircraft company, began a lucrative business selling planes to the Bolivian government. Like most other businesses during the Great Depression, Curtiss-Wright's fortunes had taken a huge tumble, having lost $13 million by 1931. Plain and simple, the Chaco War was enabling Curtiss-Wright to survive the Depression.

Journalists and other commentators, after having discovered Curtiss-Wright's relationship with the Bolivian government, were highly critical of the airplane company's activities. One critic described Curtiss-Wright and other arms manufacturers as "the greatest and most profitable secret international [organization] of our time—the international of bloodshed and profits." In May 1934, President Roosevelt, sensitive to the tide of public opinion that was running against the involvement of American companies in other nation's wars, urged Congress to pass a resolution authorizing the president to ban arms sales to countries in armed conflict. Congress quickly delivered, and the president wasted no time in imposing an arms embargo.

Curtiss-Wright Export Corporation attempted to evade the president's order by disguising the bombers it was selling to Bolivia as passenger aircraft. In June 1934, Justice Department officials seized $600,000 worth of arms, weapons, and warplanes off a New York pier, all of which were destined for Bolivia. Curtiss-Wright challenged the embargo as an unconstitutional exercise of executive power, claiming that Congress had delegated to the president authority reserved to itself under the Constitution.

The Court's decision was 7 to 1. Justice Sutherland delivered the opinion of the Court. Justice McReynolds dissented. Justice Stone did not participate.

▼▲▼

MR. JUSTICE SUTHERLAND delivered the opinion of the Court.

. . . It will contribute to the elucidation of the question if we first consider the differences between the powers of the federal government in respect of foreign or external affairs and those in respect of domestic or internal affairs. That there are differences between them, and that these differences are fundamental, may not be doubted.

The two classes of powers are different both in respect of their origin and their nature. The broad statement that the federal government can exercise no powers except those specifically enumerated in the Constitution, and such implied powers as are necessary and proper to carry into effect the enumerated powers, is categorically true only in respect of our internal affairs. In that field, the primary purpose of the Constitution was to carve from the general mass of legislative powers then possessed by the states such portions as it was thought desirable to vest in the federal government, leaving those not included in the enumeration still in the states. That this doctrine applies only to powers which the states had is self-evident. And since the states severally never possessed international powers, such powers could not have been carved from the mass of state powers, but obviously were transmitted to the United States from some other source. . . .

Not only, as we have shown, is the federal power over external affairs in origin and essential character different from that over internal affairs, but participation in the exercise of the power is significantly limited. In this vast external realm, with its important, complicated, delicate and manifold problems, the President alone has the power to speak or listen as a representative of the nation. He makes treaties with the advice and consent of the Senate; but he alone negotiates. Into the field of negotiation the Senate cannot intrude, and Congress itself is powerless to invade it. As Marshall said in his great argument of March 7, 1800, in the House of Representatives, "The President is the sole organ of the nation in its external relations, and its sole representative with foreign nations." The Senate Committee on Foreign Relations, at a very early day in our history [February 1816], reported to the Senate, among other things, as follows:

> The President is the constitutional representative of the United States with regard to foreign nations. He manages our concerns with foreign nations, and must necessarily be most competent to determine when, how, and upon what subjects negotiation may be urged with the greatest prospect of success. For his conduct, he is responsible to the Constitution. The committee consider this responsibility the surest pledge for the faithful discharge of his duty. They think the interference of the Senate in the direction of foreign negotiations calculated to diminish that responsibility, and thereby to impair the best security for the national safety. The nature of transactions with foreign nations, moreover, requires caution and unity of design, and their success frequently depends on secrecy and dispatch.

It is important to bear in mind that we are here dealing not alone with an authority vested in the President by an exertion of legislative power, but with such an authority plus the very delicate, plenary and exclusive power of the President as the sole organ of the federal government in the field of international relations—a power which does not require as a basis for its exercise an act of Congress but which, of course, like every other governmental power, must be exercised in subordination to the applicable provisions of the Constitution. It is quite apparent that if, in the maintenance of our international relations, embarrassment—perhaps serious embarrassment—is to be avoided and success for our aims achieved, congressional legislation which is to be made effective through negotiation and inquiry within the international field must often accord to the President a degree of discretion and freedom from statutory restriction which would not be admissible were domestic affairs alone involved. Moreover, he, not Congress, has the better opportunity of knowing the conditions which prevail in foreign countries, and especially is this true in time of war. He has his confidential sources of information. He has his agents in the form of diplomatic, consular and other officials. Secrecy in respect of information gathered by them may be highly necessary, and the premature disclosure of it productive of harmful results. Indeed, so clearly is this true that the first President refused to accede to a request to lay before the House of Representatives the instructions, correspondence and documents relating to the negotiation of the Jay Treaty—a refusal the wisdom of which was recognized by the House itself, and has never since been doubted. In his reply to the request, President Washington said:

> The nature of foreign negotiations requires caution, and their success must often depend on secrecy, and even when brought to a conclusion, a full disclosure of all the measures, demands, or eventual concessions which may have been proposed or contemplated would be extremely impolitic, for this might have a pernicious influence on future negotiations or produce immediate inconveniences, perhaps danger and mischief, in relation to other powers. The necessity of such caution and secrecy was one cogent reason for vesting the power of making treaties in the President, with the advice and consent of the Senate, the principle on which that body was formed confining it to a small number of members. To admit, then, a right in the House of Representatives to demand and to have as a matter of course all the papers respecting a negotiation with a foreign power would be to establish a dangerous precedent.

The marked difference between foreign affairs and domestic affairs in this respect is recognized by both houses of Congress in the very form of their requisitions for information from the executive departments. In the case of every department except the Department of State, the resolution directs the official to furnish the information. In the case of the State Department, dealing with foreign affairs, the President is requested to furnish the information "if not incompatible with the public interest." A statement that to furnish the information is not compatible with the public interest rarely, if ever, is questioned.

When the President is to be authorized by legislation to act in respect of a matter intended to affect a situation in foreign territory, the legislator properly bears in mind the important consideration that the form of the President's action or, indeed, whether he shall act at all—may well depend, among other things, upon the nature of the confidential information which he has or may thereafter receive, or upon the effect which his action may have upon our foreign relations. This consideration, in connection with what we have already said on the subject, discloses the unwisdom of requiring Congress in this field of governmental power to lay down narrowly definite standards by which the President is to be governed. . . .

The result of holding that the joint resolution here under attack is void and unenforceable as constituting an unlawful delegation of legislative power would be to stamp this multitude of comparable acts and resolutions as likewise invalid. And while this court may not, and should not, hesitate to declare acts of Congress, however many times repeated, to be unconstitutional if beyond all rational doubt it finds them to be so, an impressive array of legislation such as we have just set forth, enacted by nearly every Congress from the beginning of our national existence to the present day, must be given unusual weight in the process of reaching a correct determination of the problem. A legislative practice such as we have here, evidenced not by only occasional instances but marked by the movement of a steady stream for a century and a half of time, goes a long way in the direction of proving the presence of unassailable ground for the constitutionality of the practice, to be found in the origin and history of the power involved, or in its nature, or in both combined. . . .

The uniform, long-continued and undisputed legislative practice just disclosed rests upon an admissible view of the Constitution which, even if the practice found far less support in principle than we think it does, we should not feel at liberty at this late day to disturb. . . .

▼▲▼

## Missouri v. Holland
### 252 U.S. 416 (1920)

In response to conservationist pressure, Congress, under its power to regulate interstate and foreign commerce, passed the Migratory Bird Act of 1913 to protect certain species of birds in danger of extinction. Two separate federal trial courts declared the law an unconstitutional use of such power. Several years later, President Woodrow Wilson negotiated a treaty with Great Britain to protect endangered species of migratory birds in the United States and Canada. Wilson included a provision in the treaty that their respective "law-making" bodies should enact laws to enforce its provisions.

In 1918, Congress passed the Migratory Bird Treaty Act. The law banned the hunting, killing, sale, or shipment of protected birds, granting to the secretary of agriculture the power to make exceptions to the law as appropriate. Like many other states, Missouri was prevented by the act from setting the hunting season outside the provisions of the federal law. The state brought suit in federal court against U.S. game warden Ray P. Holland to enjoin him from enforcing the regulations. The district court dismissed the suit. The state appealed to the Supreme Court.

The Court's decision was 7 to 2. Justice Holmes delivered the opinion of the Court. Justices Van Devanter and Pitney dissented, but did not write opinions to explain their positions.

MR. JUSTICE HOLMES delivered the opinion of the court.

. . . On December 8, 1916, a treaty between the United States and Great Britain was proclaimed by the President. It recited that many species of birds in their annual migrations traversed certain parts of the United States and of Canada, that they were of great value as a source of food and in destroying insects injurious to vegetation, but were in danger of extermination through lack of adequate protection. It therefore provided for specified close seasons and protection in other forms, and agreed that the two powers would take or propose to their lawmaking bodies the necessary measures for carrying the treaty out. The above mentioned Act of July 3, 1918, entitled an act to give effect to the convention, prohibited the killing, capturing or selling any of the migratory birds included in the terms of the treaty except as permitted by regulations compatible with those terms, to be made by the Secretary of Agriculture. It is unnecessary to go into any details because, as we have said, the question raised is the general one whether the treaty and statute are void as an interference with the rights reserved to the States.

To answer this question, it is not enough to refer to the Tenth Amendment, reserving the powers not delegated to the United States, because, by Article II, Section 2, the power to make treaties is delegated expressly, and by Article VI treaties made under the authority of the United States, along with the Constitution and laws of the United States made in pursuance thereof, are declared the supreme law of the land. If the treaty is valid, there can be no dispute about the validity of the statute under Article I, Section 8, as a necessary and proper means to execute the powers of the Government. The language of the Constitution as to the supremacy of treaties being general, the question before us is narrowed to an inquiry into the ground upon which the present supposed exception is placed.

It is said that a treaty cannot be valid if it infringes the Constitution, that there are limits, therefore, to the treaty-making power, and that one such limit is that what an act of Congress could not do unaided, in derogation of the powers reserved to the States, a treaty cannot do. An earlier act of Congress that attempted by itself and not in pursuance of a treaty to regulate the killing of migratory birds within the States had been held bad in the District Court. Those decisions were supported by arguments that migratory birds were owned by the States in their sovereign capacity for the benefit of their people, and . . . this control was one that Congress had no power to displace. The same argument is supposed to apply now with equal force.

Whether the two cases cited were decided rightly or not, they cannot be accepted as a test of the treaty power. Acts of Congress are the supreme law of the land only when made in pursuance of the Constitution, while treaties are declared to be so when made under the authority of the United States. It is open to question whether the authority of the United States means more than the formal acts prescribed to make the convention. We do not mean to imply that there are no qualifications to the treaty-making power, but they must be ascertained in a different way. It is obvious that there may be matters of the sharpest exigency for the national wellbeing that an act of Congress could not deal with, but that a treaty followed by such an act could, and it is not lightly to be assumed that, in matters requiring national action, "a power which must belong to and somewhere reside in every civilized government" is not to be found. What was said in that case with regard to the powers of the States applies with equal force to the powers of the nation in cases where the States individually are incompetent to act. We are not yet discussing the particular case before us, but only are considering the validity of the test proposed. With regard to that we may add that, when we are dealing with words that also are a constituent act, like the Constitution of the United States, we must realize that they have called into life a being the development of which could not have been foreseen completely by the most gifted of its begetters. It was enough for them to realize or to hope that they had created an organism; it has taken a century and has cost their successors much sweat and blood to prove that they created a nation. The case before us must be considered in the light of our whole experience, and not merely in that of what was said a hundred years ago. The treaty in question does not contravene any prohibitory words to be found in the Constitution. The only question is whether it is forbidden by some invisible radiation from the general terms of the Tenth Amendment. We must consider what this country has become in deciding what that Amendment has reserved.

The State, as we have intimated, founds its claim of exclusive authority upon an assertion of title to migratory birds, an assertion that is embodied in statute. No doubt it is true that, as between a State and its inhabitants, the State may regulate the killing and sale of such birds, but it does not follow that its authority is exclusive of paramount powers. To put the claim of the State upon title is to lean upon a slender reed. Wild birds are not in the possession of anyone, and possession is the beginning of ownership. The whole foundation of the State's rights is the presence within their jurisdiction of birds that yesterday had not arrived, tomorrow may be in another State, and, in a week, a thousand miles away. If we are to be accurate, we cannot put the case of the State upon higher ground than that the treaty deals with creatures that, for the moment are within the state borders, that it must be carried out by officers of the United States within the same territory, and that, but for the treaty, the State would be free to regulate this subject itself.

As most of the laws of the United States are carried out within the States and as many of them deal with matters which, in the silence of such laws, the State might regulate, such general grounds are not enough to support Missouri's claim. Valid treaties, of course, "are as binding within the territorial limits of the States as they are elsewhere throughout the dominion of the United States." No doubt the great body of private relations usually fall within the control of the State, but a treaty may override its power. . . .

Here, a national interest of very nearly the first magnitude is involved. It can be protected only by national action in concert with that of another power. The subject matter is only transitorily within the State, and has no permanent habitat therein. But for the treaty and the statute, there soon might be no birds for any powers to deal with.

We see nothing in the Constitution that compels the Government to sit by while a food supply is cut off and the protectors of our forests and our crops are destroyed. It is not sufficient to rely upon the States. The reliance is vain, and were it otherwise, the question is whether the United States is forbidden to act. We are of opinion that the treaty and statute must be upheld.

## Executive Independence

The Framers designed each branch to have the necessary "constitutional means and personal motives" to defend itself against the assaults of ambition by the others. "The provision for defense must in this, as in all other cases," James Madison wrote in *Federalist* 51, "be made commensurate to the danger of attack. Ambition must be made to counteract ambition. The interest of man must be connected to the constitutional rights of the place."[80] The Constitution affords specific protection in this regard both to Congress (Speech or Debate Clause, "political questions" doctrine) and to the federal courts (life tenure for judges, jurisdictional and justiciability doctrines, judicial review) but offers no such defense to the president. Still, the Court has never rejected the notion put forth by the president that the office is entitled to certain constitutional privileges and immunities. We close this chapter and our discussion of the separation of powers in the American constitutional design by focusing on a theme familiar from the preceding chapters on judicial and legislative power: How has the Court permitted the executive branch to defend itself against political and judicial interference from the other branches?

Presidents since George Washington have asserted that the office carries with it two major constitutional lines of defense against legal and political intervention from the other branches. The first is *executive immunity,* a claim that the president should remain immune from (1) judicial interference in the execution of presidential policy decisions and (2) private criminal and civil lawsuits while in office. The second is *executive privilege,* a prerogative that allows the president to withhold information from Congress and the public on the grounds that the release of such information would compromise sensitive national security interests. The Court has ruled that the Constitution confers certain privileges and immunities upon the president but has been careful to point out that such claims are the exception rather than the rule.

## Executive Immunity

Just as the Court has ruled that courts may not interfere in the internal processes of Congress, it has also ruled that the president cannot be enjoined from enforcing a federal law that is alleged to be unconstitutional. Even prominent critics of executive privilege have conceded this point. One has even written that "[i]t is a startling notion that the President, who by terms of Article II, Section 3, 'shall take care that the Laws be faithfully executed,' may refuse to execute a law on the ground that it is unconstitutional. To wring from a duty faithfully to execute the laws a power to defy them would appear to be a feat of splendid illogic."[81] But in *Mississippi* v. *Johnson* (1867), the Court was confronted with just that question, one that arose out of President Andrew Johnson's decision to enforce several laws passed by Congress after the Civil War as part of its Reconstruction program.[82]

President Johnson, a former Democratic senator from Tennessee, did not share President Lincoln's sympathies for the massive intervention in and military occupation of the defeated Southern states after the Civil War. Johnson opposed the civil rights laws spearheaded by Radical Republicans in Congress but agreed to enforce them until the Court declared them unconstitutional. For example, even after Congress dealt Johnson one of his most embarrassing defeats when it overrode his veto of the Civil Rights Act of 1866, the first time Congress had passed legislation over presidential objection, the president carried out its enforcement.[83] Such was also the case when Congress again overrode President Johnson's veto of the Reconstruction Acts of 1867. Those laws set out the conditions for the provisional military governments under federal authority in the South until the readmitted Confederate states could prove their loyalty.

In April 1867, the provisional governor of Mississippi announced that he would file suit in federal court to enjoin the president from enforcing the Reconstruction Acts. Mississippi's action was one of several early efforts by the former Confederate states to obstruct federal enforcement of Reconstruction. Georgia's provisional governor soon followed with a similar complaint, but the Court, in *Georgia v. Stanton* (1868), refused, on jurisdictional grounds, to hear the case.[84] And in *Ex parte McCardle,* the Court avoided handing another defeat to the South by holding that the Court had no jurisdiction to decide a case involving a Reconstruction measure that was repealed after it had decided to hear the lawsuit.[85] The decision of the Southern provisional governments to use the courts as a means of "orderly obstruction" was a brief exception to resistance otherwise characterized by violence and corruption.[86]

A unanimous Court rejected Mississippi's claim that presidential action in the political arena is subject to judicial review. In *Johnson,* Chief Justice Salmon Chase held that "an attempt on the part of the Judicial Department of the Government to enforce the performance of such duties by the President might be justly characterized, in the language of Chief Justice [John] Marshall, as 'an absurd and excessive extravagance.'"[87] Here, Chase was referring to the former chief justice's opinion in *Marbury v. Madison. Marbury* ruled that the federal courts could order the president to perform a legal obligation over which the president had no discretion, but could not interfere with the president's discretionary authority to carry out the responsibilities of the office.

*Johnson* settled the question of whether presidents may be held legally accountable for the execution of their constitutional responsibilities while in office. But not until *Nixon v. Fitzgerald* (1982) did the Court consider whether this grant of executive immunity extended to presidential decisions that result in personal harm to private individuals. Here a 5-4 Court clarified and extended the general principle of executive immunity that it had announced in *Johnson,* holding that the president is entitled to absolute immunity from civil lawsuits for official acts undertaken while in office. *Fitzgerald* involved a lawsuit by a former civil service employee, who, in congressional testimony, criticized the cost estimates of several pet defense projects of the Nixon administration and openly questioned their technical and engineering feasibility. Even though his appearance before Congress came in the final days of Lyndon Johnson's presidency, high-level officials within the Nixon administration were sufficiently disturbed by Fitzger-

ald's loyalty to fire him. After the Civil Service Commission determined that Fitzgerald's dismissal was not performance related, the former Pentagon analyst filed suit against former President Nixon and several of his key advisors.

Writing for the Court, Justice Lewis Powell rejected Fitzgerald's claim that the president should be held liable and subject to damage awards for what amounted to a wrongful termination suit. Holding that the "President's unique status under the Constitution distinguishes him from other executive officials," Justice Powell wrote that absolute presidential immunity for official conduct is "a functionally mandated incident of the President's unique office, rooted in the constitutional tradition of the separation of powers and supported by our history." In language that proved especially prescient in light of the Court's decision in *Clinton v. Jones* (1997), Powell noted:

> Because of the singular importance of the President's duties, diversion of his energies by concern with private lawsuits would raise unique risks to the effective functioning of government. As is the case with prosecutors and judges—for whom absolute immunity now is established—a President must concern himself with matters likely to 'arouse the most intense feelings'. . . . Yet, as our decisions have recognized, it is in precisely such cases that there exists the greatest public interest in providing an official 'the maximum ability to deal fearlessly and impartially with' the duties of his office . . . In view of the visibility of his office and the effect of his actions on countless people, the President would be an easily identifiable target for suits for civil damages. Cognizance of this personal vulnerability frequently could distract a President from his public duties, to the detriment of not only the President and his office but also the Nation that the Presidency was designed to serve.[88]

Concurring, Chief Justice Burger emphasized that Justice Powell's opinion did not place the president "above the law." Noting that the Court's decision dealt only with the issue of absolute immunity from civil damage claims for official acts, Burger wrote that "a President, like Members of Congress, judges, prosecutors, or congressional aides—all having absolute immunity—are not immune for acts outside official duties."[89]

Precisely the question of whether the president's immunity from civil lawsuits extended to unofficial acts or acts alleged to have occurred before assuming the presidency was before the Court in *Clinton v. Jones* (1997). In a case that proved to have consequences for the presidency that few could have imagined, the Court held that President Bill Clinton was not immune from a civil lawsuit brought by Paula Jones, a former Arkansas state employee. Jones alleged that the president sexually harassed her in 1991 while he was still governor of Arkansas. The accompanying SIDEBAR describes the highly charged political atmosphere of the *Jones* case.

The Court's unanimous opinion, which was not insensitive to the consequences of allowing a civil lawsuit to go forward against a sitting president, rejected President Clinton's contention that *Fitzgerald* applied to the charges brought against him. Note how John Paul Stevens referred to both *Fitzgerald* and *United States v. Nixon* (1974) in his *Jones* opinion, writing that "it is . . . settled that the president is subject to judicial process in appropriate circumstances." This conclusion flows directly from the post-Watergate skepticism of the "imperial," unaccountable presidency in which assertions of executive immunity and privilege are thought to be synonymous with secrecy and lies. Concurring, Justice Stephen Breyer raised several concerns about the unintended consequences of the Court's decision, specifically whether it would encourage frivolous lawsuits that would drain the president's time from the nation's business. Several political commentators seized upon Breyer's concurrence as an unheeded warning in light of President Clinton's subsequent travails in the *Jones* sexual harassment suit. In light of the events described in the *Jones* SIDEBAR, do you believe the Court's opinion was shortsighted or correct in holding that presidents should be held legally accountable for unofficial acts?

## Nixon v. Fitzgerald
### 457 U.S. 731 (1982)

A. Ernest Fitzgerald was a civilian employee of the U.S. Air Force. Fitzgerald testified before a congressional committee in 1968 concerning cost overruns on a plane the Air Force was purchasing as well as on technical problems encountered in producing the aircraft. His testimony was embarrassing for the Defense Department and military contractors. Thirteen months later after Richard Nixon had replaced Lyndon Johnson in the White House, Fitzgerald was fired. This action was justified as part of a department reorganization requiring a reduction in staff. Fitzgerald charged that his dismissal was in retaliation for his testimony before Congress. He filed suit in federal district court challenging his dismissal. The court rejected Nixon's claim of absolute presidential immunity. The court of appeals affirmed.

The Supreme Court's decision was 5 to 4. Justice Powell delivered the opinion of the Court. Chief Justice Burger filed a concurrence. Justices Blackmun and White filed dissents.

▼▲▼

JUSTICE POWELL delivered the opinion of the Court.

. . . Our decisions concerning the immunity of government officials from civil damages liability have been guided by the Constitution, federal statutes, and history. Additionally, at least in the absence of explicit constitutional or congressional guidance, our immunity decisions have been informed by the common law. This Court necessarily also has weighed concerns of public policy, especially as illuminated by our history and the structure of our government.

This case now presents the claim that the President of the United States is shielded by absolute immunity from civil damages liability. In the case of the President the inquiries into history and policy, though mandated independently by our cases, tend to converge. Because the Presidency did not exist through most of the development of common law, any historical analysis must draw its evidence primarily from our constitutional heritage and structure. Historical inquiry thus merges almost at its inception with the kind of "public policy" analysis appropriately undertaken by a federal court. This inquiry involves policies and principles that may be considered implicit in the nature of the President's office in a system structured to achieve effective government under a constitutionally mandated separation of powers.

Here a former President asserts his immunity from civil damages claims of two kinds. He stands named as a defendant in a direct action under the Constitution and in two statutory actions under federal laws of general applicability. In neither case has Congress taken express legislative action to subject the President to civil liability for his official acts.

Applying the principles of our cases to claims of this kind, we hold that petitioner, as a former President of the United States, is entitled to absolute immunity from damages liability predicated on his official acts. We consider this immunity a functionally mandated incident of the President's unique office, rooted in the constitutional tradition of the separation of powers and supported by our history. Justice Story's analysis remains persuasive:

> There are . . . incidental powers belonging to the executive department which are necessarily implied from the nature of the functions which are confided to it. Among these must necessarily be included the power to perform them. . . . The president cannot, therefore, be liable to arrest, imprisonment, or detention, while he is in the discharge of the duties of his office, and, for this purpose, his person must be deemed, in civil cases at least, to possess an official inviolability.

The President occupies a unique position in the constitutional scheme. Article II, Section 1, of the Constitution provides that "[t]he executive Power shall be vested in a President of the United States. . . . " This grant of authority establishes the President as the chief constitutional officer of the Executive Branch, entrusted with supervisory and policy responsibilities of utmost discretion and sensitivity. These include the enforcement of federal law—it is the President who is charged constitutionally to "take Care that the Laws be faithfully executed"; the conduct of foreign affairs—a realm in which the Court has recognized that, "[i]t would be intolerable that courts, without the relevant information, should review and perhaps nullify actions of the Executive taken on information properly held secret," and management of the Executive Branch— a task for which, "imperative reasons requir[e] an unrestricted power [in the President] to remove the most important of his subordinates in their most important duties."

In arguing that the President is entitled only to qualified immunity, the respondent relies on cases in which we have recognized immunity of this scope for governors and cabinet officers. We find these cases to be inapposite. The President's unique status under the Constitution distinguishes him from other executive officials.

Because of the singular importance of the President's duties, diversion of his energies by concern with private lawsuits would raise unique risks to the effective functioning of government. As is the case with prosecutors and judges—for whom absolute immunity now is established—a President must concern himself with matters likely to "arouse the most intense feelings." Yet, as our

decisions have recognized, it is in precisely such cases that there exists the greatest public interest in providing an official "the maximum ability to deal fearlessly and impartially with" the duties of his office. This concern is compelling where the officeholder must make the most sensitive and far-reaching decisions entrusted to any official under our constitutional system. Nor can the sheer prominence of the President's office be ignored. In view of the visibility of his office and the effect of his actions on countless people, the President would be an easily identifiable target for suits for civil damages. Cognizance of this personal vulnerability frequently could distract a President from his public duties, to the detriment of not only the President and his office but also the Nation that the Presidency was designed to serve.

Courts traditionally have recognized the President's constitutional responsibilities and status as factors counseling judicial deference and restraint. For example, while courts generally have looked to the common law to determine the scope of an official's evidentiary privilege, we have recognized that the Presidential privilege is "rooted in the separation of powers under the Constitution." It is settled law that the separation of powers doctrine does not bar every exercise of jurisdiction over the President of the United States. But our cases also have established that a court, before exercising jurisdiction, must balance the constitutional weight of the interest to be served against the dangers of intrusion on the authority and functions of the Executive Branch. When judicial action is needed to serve broad public interests—as when the Court acts not in derogation of the separation of powers, but to maintain their proper balance, or to vindicate the public interest in an ongoing criminal prosecution—the exercise of jurisdiction has been held warranted. In the case of this merely private suit for damages based on a President's official acts, we hold it is not.

In defining the scope of an official's absolute privilege, this Court has recognized that the sphere of protected action must be related closely to the immunity's justifying purposes. Frequently our decisions have held that an official's absolute immunity should extend only to acts in performance of particular functions of his office. But the Court also has refused to draw functional lines finer than history and reason would support. . . . In view of the special nature of the President's constitutional office and functions, we think it appropriate to recognize absolute Presidential immunity from damages liability for acts within the "outer perimeter" of his official responsibility.

Under the Constitution and laws of the United States, the President has discretionary responsibilities in a broad variety of areas, many of them highly sensitive. In many cases, it would be difficult to determine which of the President's innumerable "functions" encompassed a particular action. In this case, for example, respondent argues that he was dismissed in retaliation for his testimony to Congress. . . . The Air Force, however, has claimed that the underlying reorganization was undertaken to promote efficiency. Assuming that petitioner Nixon ordered the reorganization in which respondent lost his job, an inquiry into the President's motives could not be avoided under the kind of "functional" theory asserted both by respondent and the dissent. Inquiries of this kind could be highly intrusive.

Here, respondent argues that petitioner Nixon would have acted outside the outer perimeter of his duties by ordering the discharge of an employee who was lawfully entitled to retain his job in the absence of "'such cause as will promote the efficiency of the service.'" Because Congress has granted this legislative protection, respondent argues, no federal official could, within the outer perimeter of his duties of office, cause Fitzgerald to be dismissed without satisfying this standard in prescribed statutory proceedings.

This construction would subject the President to trial on virtually every allegation that an action was unlawful, or was taken for a forbidden purpose. Adoption of this construction thus would deprive absolute immunity of its intended effect. It clearly is within the President's constitutional and statutory authority to prescribe the manner in which the Secretary will conduct the business of the Air Force. Because this mandate of office must include the authority to prescribe reorganizations and reductions in force, we conclude that petitioner's alleged wrongful acts lay well within the outer perimeter of his authority.

A rule of absolute immunity for the President will not leave the Nation without sufficient protection against misconduct on the part of the Chief Executive. There remains the constitutional remedy of impeachment. In addition, there are formal and informal checks on Presidential action that do not apply with equal force to other executive officials. The President is subjected to constant scrutiny by the press. Vigilant oversight by Congress also may serve to deter Presidential abuses of office, as well as to make credible the threat of impeachment. Other incentives to avoid misconduct may include a desire to earn reelection, the need to maintain prestige as an element of Presidential influence, and a President's traditional concern for his historical stature.

The existence of alternative remedies and deterrents establishes that absolute immunity will not place the President "above the law." For the President, as for judges and prosecutors, absolute immunity merely precludes a particular private remedy for alleged misconduct in order to advance compelling public ends.

JUSTICE WHITE, with whom JUSTICE BRENNAN, JUSTICE MARSHALL, and JUSTICE BLACKMUN join, dissenting.

The four dissenting Members of the Court in *Butz v. Economu* (1978) argued that all federal officials are entitled to absolute immunity from suit for any action they take in connection with their official duties. That immunity would extend even to actions taken with express knowledge that the conduct was clearly contrary to the controlling statute or clearly violative of the Constitution. Fortunately, the majority of the Court rejected that approach: we held that, although public officials perform certain functions that entitle them to absolute immunity, the immunity attaches to particular functions—not to particular offices. Officials performing functions for which immunity is not absolute enjoy qualified immunity; they are liable in damages only if their conduct violated well-established law and if they should have realized that their conduct was illegal.

The Court now applies [this] dissenting view . . . to the Office of the President: a President, acting within the outer boundaries of what Presidents normally do, may, without liability, deliberately cause serious injury to any number of citizens even though he knows his conduct violates a statute or tramples on the constitutional rights of those who are injured. Even if the President in this case ordered Fitzgerald fired by means of a trumped-up reduction in force, knowing that such a discharge was contrary to the civil service laws, he would be absolutely immune from suit. By the same token, if a President, without following the statutory procedures which he knows apply to himself as well as to other federal officials, orders his subordinates to wiretap or break into a home for the purpose of installing a listening device, and the officers comply with his request, the President would be absolutely immune from suit. He would be immune regardless of the damage he inflicts, regardless of how violative of the statute and of the Constitution he knew his conduct to be, and regardless of his purpose.

The Court intimates that its decision is grounded in the Constitution. If that is the case, Congress cannot provide a remedy against Presidential misconduct, and the criminal laws of the United States are wholly inapplicable to the President. I find this approach completely unacceptable. I do not agree that, if the Office of President is to operate effectively, the holder of that Office must be permitted, without fear of liability and regardless of the function he is performing, deliberately to inflict injury on others by conduct that he knows violates the law. . . .

In declaring the President to be absolutely immune from suit for any deliberate and knowing violation of the Constitution or of a federal statute, the Court asserts that the immunity is "rooted in the constitutional tradition of the separation of powers and supported by our history." The decision thus has all the earmarks of a constitutional pronouncement—absolute immunity for the President's office is mandated by the Constitution. Although the Court appears to disclaim this, it is difficult to read the opinion coherently as standing for any narrower proposition: attempts to subject the President to liability either by Congress through a statutory action or by the courts through [such a] proceeding would violate the separation of powers. Such a generalized absolute immunity cannot be sustained when examined in the traditional manner and in light of the traditional judicial sources. . . .

No bright line can be drawn between arguments for absolute immunity based on the constitutional principle of separation of powers and arguments based on what the Court refers to as "public policy." This necessarily follows from the Court's functional interpretation of the separation of powers doctrine:

> [I]n determining whether the Act disrupts the proper balance between the coordinate branches, the proper inquiry focuses on the extent to which it prevents the Executive Branch from accomplishing its constitutionally assigned functions. *Nixon* v. *Administrator of General Services* (1977). . . .

The functional approach to the separation of powers doctrine and the Court's more recent immunity decisions converge on the following principle: the scope of immunity is determined by function, not office. The wholesale claim that the President is entitled to absolute immunity in all of his actions stands on no firmer ground than did the claim that all Presidential communications are entitled to an absolute privilege, which was rejected in favor of a functional analysis, by a unanimous Court in *United States* v. *Nixon* (1974). Therefore, whatever may be true of the necessity of such a broad immunity in certain areas of executive responsibility, the only question that must be answered here is whether the dismissal of employees falls within a constitutionally assigned executive function, the performance of which would be substantially impaired by the possibility of a private action for damages. I believe it does not.

▼▲▼

## Clinton v. Jones
### 520 U.S. 681 (1997)

The facts and background are set out in the accompanying SIDEBAR.

The Supreme Court's decision was unanimous. Justice Stevens delivered the opinion of the Court. Justice Breyer filed a concurring opinion.

▼▲▼

JUSTICE STEVENS delivered the opinion of the Court.

This case raises a constitutional and a prudential question concerning the Office of the President of the United States. Respondent, a private citizen, seeks to recover damages from the current occupant of that office based on actions allegedly taken before his term began. The President submits that in all but the most exceptional cases the Constitution requires federal courts to defer such litigation until his term ends and that, in any event, respect for the office warrants such a stay. Despite the force of the arguments supporting the President's submissions, we conclude that they must be rejected. . . .

Only three sitting Presidents have been defendants in civil litigation involving their actions prior to taking office. Complaints against Theodore Roosevelt and Harry Truman had been dismissed before they took office; the dismissals were affirmed after their respective inaugurations. Two companion cases arising out of an automobile accident were filed against John F. Kennedy in 1960 during the Presidential campaign. After taking office, he unsuccessfully argued that his status as Commander in Chief gave him a right to a stay under the Soldiers' and Sailors' Civil Relief Act of 1940. The motion for a stay was denied by the District Court, and the matter was settled out of court. Thus, none of those cases sheds any light on the constitutional issue before us.

The principal rationale for affording certain public servants immunity from suits for money damages arising out of their official acts is inapplicable to unofficial conduct. In cases involving prosecutors, legislators, and judges we have repeatedly explained that the immunity serves the public interest in enabling such officials to perform their designated functions effectively without fear that a particular decision may give rise to personal liability. . . .

That rationale provided the principal basis for our holding that a former President of the United States was "entitled to absolute immunity from damages liability predicated on his official acts." *Nixon* v. *Fitzgerald* (1981).

Our central concern was to avoid rendering the President "unduly cautious in the discharge of his official duties."

This reasoning provides no support for an immunity for unofficial conduct. As we explained in Fitzgerald, "the sphere of protected action must be related closely to the immunity's justifying purposes." Because of the President's broad responsibilities, we recognized in that case an immunity from damages claims arising out of official acts extending to the "outer perimeter of his authority." But we have never suggested that the President, or any other official, has an immunity that extends beyond the scope of any action taken in an official capacity. . . .

Moreover, when defining the scope of an immunity for acts clearly taken within an official capacity, we have applied a functional approach. "Frequently our decisions have held that an official's absolute immunity should extend only to acts in performance of particular functions of his office." Hence, for example, a judge's absolute immunity does not extend to actions performed in a purely administrative capacity. As our opinions have made clear, immunities are grounded in "the nature of the function performed, not the identity of the actor who performed it."

Petitioner's effort to construct an immunity from suit for unofficial acts grounded purely in the identity of his office is unsupported by precedent.

We are also unpersuaded by the evidence from the historical record to which petitioner has called our attention. He points to a comment by Thomas Jefferson protesting the subpoena duces tecum Chief Justice Marshall directed to him in the Burr trial, a statement in the diaries kept by Senator William Maclay of the first Senate debates, in which then Vice President John Adams and Senator Oliver Ellsworth are recorded as having said that "the President personally [is] not . . . subject to any process whatever," lest it be "put . . . in the power of a common Justice to exercise any Authority over him and Stop the Whole Machine of Government," and to a quotation from Justice Story's Commentaries on the Constitution. None of these sources sheds much light on the question at hand.

Respondent, in turn, has called our attention to conflicting historical evidence. Speaking in favor of the Constitution's adoption at the Pennsylvania Convention, James Wilson—who had participated in the Philadelphia Convention at which the document was drafted—explained that, although the President "is placed [on] high," "not a single privilege is annexed to his character; far from being above the laws, he is amenable to them in his private character as a citizen, and in his public character by impeachment." This description is consistent with both the doctrine of presidential immunity as set forth in Fitzgerald, and rejection of the immunity claim in this case. With respect to acts taken in his "public character"— that is official acts—the President may be disciplined principally by impeachment, not by private lawsuits for damages. But he is otherwise subject to the laws for his purely private acts.

In the end, as applied to the particular question before us, we reach the same conclusion about these historical materials that Justice Jackson described when confronted with an issue concerning the dimensions of the President's power. "Just what our forefathers did envision, or would have envisioned had they foreseen modern conditions, must be divined from materials almost as enigmatic as the dreams Joseph was called upon to interpret for Pharoah. A century and a half of partisan debate and scholarly speculation yields no net result but only supplies more or less apt quotations from respected sources on each side. . . . They largely cancel each other." *Youngstown Sheet & Tube Co. v. Sawyer* (1952).

Petitioner's strongest argument supporting his immunity claim is based on the text and structure of the Constitution. He does not contend that the occupant of the Office of the President is "above the law," in the sense that his conduct is entirely immune from judicial scrutiny. The President argues merely for a postponement of the judicial proceedings that will determine whether he violated any law. His argument is grounded in the character of the office that was created by Article II of the Constitution, and relies on separation of powers principles that have structured our constitutional arrangement since the founding.

As a starting premise, petitioner contends that he occupies a unique office with powers and responsibilities so vast and important that the public interest demands that he devote his undivided time and attention to his public duties. He submits that—given the nature of the office—the doctrine of separation of powers places limits on the authority of the Federal Judiciary to interfere with the Executive Branch that would be transgressed by allowing this action to proceed.

We have no dispute with the initial premise of the argument. Former presidents, from George Washington to George Bush, have consistently endorsed petitioner's characterization of the office. After serving his term, Lyndon Johnson observed: "Of all the 1,886 nights I was President, there were not many when I got to sleep before 1 or 2 A.M., and there were few mornings when I didn't wake up by 6 or 6:30." In 1967, the Twenty fifth Amendment to the Constitution was adopted to ensure continuity in the

## CLINTON V. JONES

*Sex and Lies in the White House*

In May 1994, Paula Corbin Jones, a former low-level Arkansas state employee, held a press conference in Washington, D.C., to announce that she was going to file a sexual harassment lawsuit against President Bill Clinton. She claimed that Clinton had made an unwelcome sexual advance toward her while he was still governor of Arkansas. Jones claimed that, in May 1991, Clinton dispatched an Arkansas state trooper who served as his personal bodyguard, Danny Ferguson, to invite her up to his suite at the Excelsior Hotel in Little Rock. The governor was there speaking at a state industrial conference, and she was working the reception desk. Ferguson, she claimed, slipped her a piece of paper that said: "Bill would like to meet with you in his room." Uncertain of the governor's intent, Jones accompanied Ferguson up to Clinton's hotel room. Standing in shirt sleeves, Governor Clinton greeted her at the door and showed her in to his room. Ferguson remained outside.

Jones later explained what happened next:

> He [Clinton] was leaning up against the back of a wingback chair, and I was standing a little ways off from him, and we were talking. Well, he leaned up and, well, he tried to pull me over, and he put his hand up my leg. I mean, he just, you know, it was real quick. And he tried to kiss on my neck. And he told me how he liked the way my curves were and liked the way my hair went down to the middle of my back. And then I said, you know, "Don't do this," you know? I rejected it.

Jones then claimed the governor pulled down his pants and requested that she perform oral sex. "I was just shocked," she later said. "I jumped, and I said, 'No, I'm not this kind of girl. I'm not that kind of girl.' And he said, 'Well, I don't want to make you do something you don't want to do.'" Jones then left the room and went back down to her post at the registration desk. She immediately confided in a coworker but kept her alleged encounter with the governor secret until her extraordinary announcement three years later. In her suit, Jones asked for a public apology from President Clinton and $700,000 in damages.

President Clinton's inner circle of political advisors winced as they read the transcripts of Jones's press conference but were hardly thrown into a panic. Since early stages of the 1992 presidential campaign, a special team of consultants, media advisors, and public relations professionals had been created to deal with what Betsey Wright, a long-time aide to Clinton from his Arkansas days, had termed "bimbo eruptions." As governor, Clinton had been dogged by accusations of womanizing from his political opponents. In what soon became a practiced method of political counter-attack, Clinton's staff would usually find information to undermine his accusers' credibility. This "rapid response" to charges made against Clinton had always managed to confine these problems to the category of rumor rather than fact.

But Jones's charges were different from the start. First, she had secured the legal services of a northern Virginia-based conservative public interest law firm, the Rutherford Institute, to assist with the funding of her case. Gilbert K. Davis, a Virginia Republican who was preparing to run for governor of Virginia, and several other politically savvy and experienced lawyers agreed to serve as Jones's counsel. Second, Jones brought her charges against a popular Democratic president who had carried the women's vote in 1992. Clinton supported abortion rights, federally mandated family leave, and strong legislative measures to combat sex discrimination and harassment in the workplace. Finally, her charges against Clinton came after he had admitted in an interview on the nation's most watched newsmagazine program, *60 Minutes,* broadcast during the heat of the 1992 presidential primaries, that he had "caused pain" in his marriage by previous infidelities. During that same interview, Clinton, while holding his wife's hand, categorically denied an accusation by a former Arkansas lounge singer and television reporter, Gennifer Flowers, that he had maintained a twelve-year adulterous relationship with her. Hillary Clinton characterized Flowers's charges as nonsense and claimed they were the work of her husband's political opponents.

President Clinton issued an immediate denial of Jones's charges. Attorneys for the president claimed that Jones had become an unwitting pawn in another of the persistent efforts of his "right wing" enemies to discredit him personally. Hillary Clinton, on the popular morning television program *Today,* went so far as to suggest that a "vast right wing conspiracy" existed to bring down the president. Again, she dismissed the accusations against her husband. James Carville, who had earned a deserved reputation as President Clinton's most colorful and quotable campaign strategist during the 1992 election, referred to Jones as "trailer park trash" and claimed she was out to make some quick cash. But Jones pressed ahead with her suit, an uncharacteristic response to previous efforts by Clinton's aides to discredit his accusers. She filed suit in an Arkansas federal district court. Judge Susan Webber Wright, a student of Clinton when he taught constitutional law at the University of Arkansas law school, ruled in favor of the president's claim that the doctrine of executive immunity protected him from civil lawsuits that were unrelated to the discharge of his office. Ironically, President George Bush, who Clinton had defeated in 1992, had appointed Wright to the federal bench. She did, however, rule that pretrial discovery could move forward.

The U.S. Court of Appeals for the Eighth Circuit reversed Judge Wright. The president's lawyers then appealed to the Supreme Court, which ruled in May 1997 that Jones could proceed with her sexual harassment suit during the president's term of office. The Court remanded the *Jones* case back to Judge Wright's court and ordered the parties to prepare for trial.

In January 1998, President Clinton, along with his lawyers, met with Jones's legal team to give his deposition. During a line of questioning intended to establish a "prior pattern of conduct" of alleged unwanted sexual advances and covered-up affairs by the president, the public learned two important pieces of information. The first was that the president did have a sexual relationship with Gennifer Flowers, albeit one that Clinton claimed was limited to one such encounter. That admission came as no real surprise to a public that never really believed his denial on *60 Minutes.* But the other disclosure revealed a previously secret eighteen-month sexual relationship between President Clinton and a twenty-one-year-old former White House intern. President Clinton was asked if he knew Monica Lewinsky, whether he had ever been alone with her in the Oval Office, and whether he had ever had "sexual relations" with her. President Clinton acknowledged his acquaintance with Lewinsky but answered no to the other questions.

His denial of a sexual relationship with Lewinsky prompted special prosecutor Kenneth Starr to investigate whether Clinton had lied under oath during his deposition in the Jones case. Starr's aggressive tactics included the use of a former coworker of Lewinsky, Linda Tripp, to secretly record her conversations with Lewinsky about the intern's relationship with the president. Starr also subpoenaed several other women who had charged that the president sexually harassed them or with whom he had allegedly had affairs. President Clinton continued to issue categorical denials of all these charges. He went on television shortly after his deposition had been leaked to the news media to deny, with his wife standing alongside of him, that he ever had "sexual relations with that woman, Miss Lewinsky." The bad feelings that had simmered between Starr's office and the Clinton administration over the handling of the Whitewater investigation boiled over into a blood feud and led to a seven-month standoff between the special prosecutor's office and the White House. It ended with the president's televised confession in August that he had indeed had an "inappropriate relationship" with the former intern. During his speech the president referred to the Jones lawsuit, which he claimed was a "politically inspired" effort to undermine his presidency.

In the interim, Judge Wright had dismissed Jones's suit in April, ruling that she had not presented sufficient evidence to sustain a sexual harassment claim against Clinton. Wrote Judge Wright:

> While the alleged incident in the hotel, if true, was certainly boorish and offensive, the Court has already found that the Governor's alleged conduct does not constitute sexual assault. This is thus not one of those exceptional cases in which a single incident of sexual harassment . . . was deemed sufficient to state a claim of hostile work environment sexual harassment.

President Clinton learned of Judge Wright's decision while in Africa to meet with the leaders of several nations there. He lit up a cigar in celebration. But as the summer solstice began to settle over Washington, even longer days of scandal, embarrassment, and political retreat awaited the president upon his return home. In December, the House of Representatives, for the first time in 130 years and only the second time ever, voted to impeach a sitting president, here on charges of perjury and obstruction of justice relating to President Clinton's testimony about his relationship with Monica Lewinsky in the Paula Jones case. The tawdry sequence of events that began in the Excelsior Hotel seven years before cast a twilight over the Clinton presidency, one that not even his acquittal by the Senate in January and near-record job-approval ratings could overcome.

## Reference

Marannis, David. *First in His Class.* New York: Simon & Schuster, 1995.

---

performance of the powers and duties of the office; one of the sponsors of that Amendment stressed the importance of providing that "at all times" there be a President "who has complete control and will be able to perform" those duties. . . .

It does not follow, however, that separation of powers principles would be violated by allowing this action to proceed. The doctrine of separation of powers is concerned with the allocation of official power among the three co equal branches of our Government. The Framers "built into the tripartite Federal Government . . . a self executing safeguard against the encroachment or aggrandizement of one branch at the expense of the other." . . .

Of course the lines between the powers of the three branches are not always neatly defined. But in this case there is no suggestion that the Federal Judiciary is being asked to perform any function that might in some way be described as "executive." Respondent is merely asking the courts to exercise their core Article III jurisdiction to decide cases and controversies. Whatever the outcome of this case, there is no possibility that the decision will curtail the scope of the official powers of the Executive Branch. The litigation of questions that relate entirely to the unofficial conduct of the individual who happens to be the President poses no perceptible risk of misallocation of either judicial power or executive power.

Rather than arguing that the decision of the case will produce either an aggrandizement of judicial power or a narrowing of executive power, petitioner contends that—as a by product of an otherwise traditional exercise of judicial power—burdens will be placed on the President that will hamper the performance of his official duties. We have recognized that "[e]ven when a branch does not arrogate power to itself . . . the separation of powers doctrine requires that a branch not impair another in the performance of its constitutional duties." As a factual matter, petitioner contends that this particular case—as well as the potential additional litigation that an affirmance of the Court of Appeals judgment might spawn—may impose an unacceptable burden on the President's time and energy, and thereby impair the effective performance of his office.

Petitioner's predictive judgment finds little support in either history or the relatively narrow compass of the issues raised in this particular case. As we have already noted, in the more than 200 year history of the Republic, only three sitting Presidents have been subjected to suits for their private actions. If the past is any indicator, it seems unlikely that a deluge of such litigation will ever engulf the Presidency. As for the case at hand, if properly managed by the District Court, it appears to us highly unlikely to occupy any substantial amount of petitioner's time. . . .

In sum, "[i]t is settled law that the separation of powers doctrine does not bar every exercise of jurisdiction over the President of the United States." If the Judiciary may severely burden the Executive Branch by reviewing the legality of the President's official conduct, and if it may direct appropriate process to the President himself, it must follow that the federal courts have power to determine the legality of his unofficial conduct. The burden on the President's time and energy that is a mere by product of such review surely cannot be considered as onerous as the direct burden imposed by judicial review and the occasional invalidation of his official actions. We therefore hold that the doctrine of separation of powers does not require federal courts to stay all private actions against the President until he leaves office.

The reasons for rejecting such a categorical rule apply as well to a rule that would require a stay "in all but the most exceptional cases." Indeed, if the Framers of the Constitution had thought it necessary to protect the President from the burdens of private litigation, we think it far more likely that they would have adopted a categorical rule than a rule that required the President to litigate the question whether a specific case belonged in the "exceptional case" subcategory. In all events, the question whether a specific case should receive exceptional treatment is more appropriately the subject of the exercise of judicial discretion than an interpretation of the Constitution. . . .

We add a final comment on two matters that are discussed at length in the briefs: the risk that our decision will generate a large volume of politically motivated harassing and frivolous litigation, and the danger that national security concerns might prevent the President from explaining a legitimate need for a continuance.

We are not persuaded that either of these risks is serious. Most frivolous and vexatious litigation is terminated at the pleading stage or on summary judgment, with little if any personal involvement by the defendant. Moreover, the availability of sanctions provides a significant deterrent to litigation directed at the President in his unofficial capacity for purposes of political gain or harassment. History indicates that the likelihood that a significant number of such cases will be filed is remote. Although scheduling problems may arise, there is no reason to assume that the

District Courts will be either unable to accommodate the President's needs or unfaithful to the tradition—especially in matters involving national security—of giving "the utmost deference to Presidential responsibilities." Several Presidents, including petitioner, have given testimony without jeopardizing the Nation's security. In short, we have confidence in the ability of our federal judges to deal with both of these concerns.

If Congress deems it appropriate to afford the President stronger protection, it may respond with appropriate legislation. Congress has enacted more than one statute providing for the deferral of civil litigation to accommodate important public interests. . . . If the Constitution embodied the rule that the President advocates, Congress, of course, could not repeal it. But our holding today raises no barrier to a [legislative] response to these concerns.

▼▲▼

## Executive Privilege

"Executive privilege" as a description of the president's self-proclaimed right to withhold information from Congress, the courts, and the public did not enter the American judicial lexicon until 1958, when Justice Stanley Reed used the phrase to describe the federal government's justification for refusing to turn over documents requested by a private corporation That case, *Kaiser Aluminum & Chemical Corp.* v. *United States* (1958) never reached the Supreme Court—Justice Reed in his role as a circuit judge presided over this lower court case by designation. Soon, however, executive privilege became a more familiar term through its frequent invocation by presidents from Eisenhower to Clinton to defend limiting or withholding altogether information requested by Congress and the courts.[90] Even before *Kaiser Aluminum*, though, the Court had confronted the issue of executive privilege, although not by name, when it ruled in two separate cases that the constitutional basis for such a presidential claim existed when the materials in question involved sensitive national security issues. The Court also concluded that the courts were an appropriate forum to determine whether the executive branch had asserted a valid claim.[91]

But the idea that the president should be entitled to such a privilege dates back to George Washington, who, as we discussed in Chapter 4, asserted that presidents could withhold sensitive materials that "would injure the public." Washington was responding to the request for material from a congressional committee investigating a botched 1791 military operation led by Major General Arthur St. Clair in the Northwest Territories.[92] It is important to note that President Washington, despite his claim to executive privilege, released all the documents requested by Congress. A similar confrontation between Washington and Congress came in 1796 when the president refused to allow the House to see papers related to his administration's negotiation of the Jay Treaty with France. While this decision is often cited as one based on executive privilege, Washington based his refusal on what he believed was the House's lack of constitutional power to demand these documents. Still, cases such as these, which have involved almost every American president since Washington, came to form what has been called the "constitutional myth" of executive privilege.[93]

Whether imagined or real, executive privilege did not undergo its first comprehensive examination by the Court until *United States* v. *Nixon* (1974), a decision of such constitutional and political import that it is difficult to know where and how to begin to describe its total impact.[94] Few cases in the history of American constitutional development have so tested the capacity of the nation's political and legal processes to absorb multiple points of pressure as *Nixon,* as it grew out of the Watergate scandal and led directly to President Nixon's resignation in August 1974. The following SIDEBAR offers a glimpse into this pivotal moment in American politics when the nation's perception of the presidency and the Court's understanding of presidential power changed forever. For now, it is important to understand the two key holdings in Chief Justice Warren Burger's opinion for a unanimous Court: (1) that executive privilege is not a myth, but a valid constitutional doctrine with appropriate uses, and (2) that the assertion of such a claim must yield to the demonstrated, specific need for evidence in criminal trials.

Some scholars have suggested that *Nixon,* even for all its gravity, still left the president with a sweeping claim to executive privilege, one that far outweighed most potential requests for materials related to congressional and prosecutorial inquiries. A similar criticism has been leveled against the Court's decision in the *Pentagon Papers* case. By establishing a right of the executive

branch to impose prior restraints on the dissemination of information by the news media, the Court gave judicial sanction to a power that had previously been a constitutional abstraction.[95] Do you believe such criticism is on the mark? Or does such criticism miss the larger significance of these cases in that the Court ruled that presidential discretion is subject to judicial review when that discretion intrudes upon the constitutional rights of other parties?

Fear that the Court would defer to executive claims of privilege in less extraordinary circumstances was quelled somewhat three years later in *Nixon* v. *Administrator of General Services* (1977). There the Court ruled that a federal law authorizing the General Services Administration to hold President Nixon's White House papers and determine what portions of them were suitable for transfer to the National Archives, where they would be accessible to the public, did not intrude upon executive privilege. Nixon claimed that executive privilege allowed him to examine the papers first and make any subsequent decision about returning them to the archives. The Court, in a 7-2 decision, emphatically rejected the former president's request, reiterating the ruling in the historic Nixon tapes case. Executive privilege was not absolute, and the public's right to information that did not threaten the confidentiality of presidential communication superceded any such opposite claim by the president. Chief Justice Burger dissented, as did Justice Rehnquist.

The Court had another brief encounter with executive privilege during July 1998, when President Clinton claimed that Secret Service agents subpoenaed by federal special prosecutors were protected by a "protective function" form of executive privilege from offering possibly damaging testimony about the president's then-alleged extramarital affair with a White House intern. Chief Justice Rehnquist, sitting while the Court was in summer recess, affirmed a federal appeals court's decision rejecting this novel interpretation of executive privilege, one that had never been previously recognized by a federal court. The president's subsequent admission to an "improper relationship" with his former employee strongly hinted that his assertion of the protective-function privilege was driven more by a political and personal interest in avoiding embarrassment than by constitutional precedent. Executive privilege is still defined by *Nixon* in that it is reserved for the most serious claims of national security.

# United States v. Nixon

418 U.S. 683 (1974)

The facts and background are set out in the accompanying SIDEBAR.

The Court's decision was unanimous. Chief Justice Burger delivered the opinion of the Court. Justice Rehnquist, who served as an assistant attorney general in the Nixon administration from 1969 to 1971, did not participate.

In the course of the Watergate investigation, President Richard Nixon refused to turn over documents and tapes to Special Prosecutor Leon Jaworski. Jaworski replaced Archibald Cox after the Saturday Night Massacre. After repeated attempts to force the president to turn over the materials, Jaworski appealed to the Supreme Court. The Court granted certiorari on an expedited basis.

▼▲▼

Mr. Chief Justice Burger delivered the opinion of the Court.

[W]e [now] turn to the claim that the subpoena should be quashed because it demands "confidential conversations between a President and his close advisors that it would be inconsistent with the public interest to produce." The first contention is a broad claim that the separation of powers doctrine precludes judicial review of a President's claim of privilege. The second contention is that, if he does not prevail on the claim of absolute privilege, the court should hold as a matter of constitutional law that the privilege prevails over the subpoena *duces tecum.*

In the performance of assigned constitutional duties, each branch of the Government must initially interpret the Constitution, and the interpretation of its powers by any branch is due great respect from the others. The President's counsel, as we have noted, reads the Constitution as providing an absolute privilege of confidentiality for all Presidential communications. Many decisions of this Court, however, have unequivocally reaffirmed the holding of *Marbury* v. *Madison*, (1803), that "[i]t is emphatically the province and duty of the judicial department to say what the law is."

No holding of the Court has defined the scope of judicial power specifically relating to the enforcement of a subpoena for confidential Presidential communications for use in a criminal prosecution, but other exercises of power by the Executive Branch and the Legislative Branch have been found invalid as in conflict with the Constitution. *Powell* v. *McCormack* (1969); *Youngstown Sheet & Tube Co.* v. *Sawyer* (1952). In a series of cases, the Court interpreted the explicit immunity conferred by express provisions of the Constitution on Members of the House and Senate by the Speech or Debate Clause. *Gravel* v. *United States* (1972); *United States* v. *Johnson* (1966). Since this Court has consistently exercised the power to construe and delineate claims arising under express powers, it must follow that the Court has authority to interpret claims with respect to powers alleged to derive from enumerated powers.

Our system of government, "requires that federal courts on occasion interpret the Constitution in a manner at variance with the construction given the document by another branch." *Powell* v. *McCormack*. And in *Baker* v. *Carr* (1961), the Court stated:

> Deciding whether a matter has in any measure been committed by the Constitution to another branch of government, or whether the action of that branch exceeds whatever authority has been committed, is itself a delicate exercise in constitutional interpretation, and is a responsibility of this Court as ultimate interpreter of the Constitution.

Notwithstanding the deference each branch must accord the others, the "judicial Power of the United States" vested in the federal courts by Article III, Section 1, of the Constitution can no more be shared with the Executive Branch than the Chief Executive, for example, can share with the Judiciary the veto power, or the Congress share with the Judiciary the power to override a Presidential veto. Any other conclusion would be contrary to the basic concept of separation of powers and the checks and balances that flow from the scheme of a tripartite government. *Federalist* 47. We therefore reaffirm that it is the province and duty of this Court "to say what the law is" with respect to the claim of privilege presented in this case.

In support of his claim of absolute privilege, the President's counsel urges two grounds, one of which is common to all governments and one of which is peculiar to our system of separation of powers. The first ground is the valid need for protection of communications between high Government officials and those who advise and assist them in the performance of their manifold duties; the importance of this confidentiality is too plain to require further discussion. Human experience teaches that those who expect public dissemination of their remarks may well temper candor with a concern for appearances and for

## UNITED STATES V. NIXON

### *"I Hereby Resign the Office of President of the United States"*

On July 13, 1973, Alexander Butterfield, the director of the Federal Aviation Agency, walked into Room G-334 of the New Senate Office Building, quietly took his place at the witness table, and began politely to answer questions from Senate Watergate Committee investigator Don Sanders. Before moving to the FAA, Butterfield had served as the president's daily scheduler and principal deputy to Nixon White House Chief of Staff H. R. (Bob) Haldeman. What Butterfield may have known about his superiors' role in the Watergate break-in and subsequent cover-up, not his thoughts on air safety and traffic patterns, was the topic that interested Senate investigators in closed session that morning.

The atmosphere in the hearing room soon took on an abrupt shift. Shortly into his questioning, Sanders calmly asked his witness the most important question of the Senate's Watergate investigation. The answer would ultimately result in the chain of legal maneuvering that culminated in the resignation of President Richard Nixon on August 9, 1974: "Do you know of any basis for the implication in [White House counsel John] Dean's testimony that conversations in the president's office are recorded?" Butterfield paused, not for dramatic effect, but because he knew his answer would end the White House's thus far successful effort to stonewall Congress's inquiries into the president's most closely guarded personal materials on his alleged involvement in the scandal. Calmly, he replied:

> I was hoping you fellows wouldn't ask me about that. I've wondered what I would say. I'm concerned about the effect my answer will have on national security and international affairs. But I suppose I have to assume that this is a formal official interview in the same vein as if I were being questioned in open session under oath. . . . Well . . . yes, there's a recording system in the president's office.
>
> There is a tape in each of the President's offices. It is kept by the Secret Service, and only four other men know about it.

Three days later, Butterfield dropped his bombshell before a national televised open session of the com-mittee when investigator (and future Republican senator from Tennessee) Fred Thompson asked Butterfield whether he was aware of any "listening devices in the Oval Office of the President?" "Yes," came Butterfield's reply. "I was aware of listening devices; yes, sir."

Butterfield's testimony threw the White House into panic. Haldeman, along with President Nixon's domestic advisor, John Erhlichman, knew the most about the president's taping system, but even that wasn't very much. Besides, they had resigned in April along with Dean and Attorney General Richard Kleindienst as part of a White House effort to show that it was just as surprised and appalled as the public was about the Watergate scandal. The tapes had been boxed and stored in an obscure Executive Office Building stairwell, with little thought given to their organization and contents. But fearful that the tapes might reveal something that other White House aides and surely the president wouldn't want Congress to hear, new Chief of Staff Alexander Haig ordered Maj. Gen. John Bennett to organize and catalog them. More than a thousand boxes of tapes were later placed in three guarded vaults. Opening a vault required the presence of a Secret Service agent.

Butterfield's revelation, combined with earlier testimony from John Dean that implicated numerous high-level officials in the Watergate scandal, led

Archibald Cox, the special prosecutor appointed by Attorney General–designate Elliot Richardson in May 1973, to request President Nixon to turn over the tapes. Cox wanted to determine their value as evidence in the prosecutions being brought against various Nixon administration aides. When Nixon refused on executive privilege grounds, Cox sought a federal court order compelling the president to release the tapes. After an extended battle in the courts, which Cox won on every round, Nixon agreed to release summarized transcripts of the tapes to the Watergate Special Prosecution Force. Cox refused the offer and demanded the raw tapes and documents for his and his staff's perusal. Infuriated by Cox's persistence and independence, Nixon ordered Acting Attorney General Robert Bork to fire the special prosecutor.

Cox's successor, Leon Jaworski, a Texas Democrat, wasted no time in picking up the investigation. The new special prosecutor subpoenaed the president to turn over all "tapes and other electronic and/or mechanical recordings or reproductions, and any memoranda, papers, transcripts and other writings" that contained sixty-four conversations about the Watergate break-in and cover-up. The cover-up was reportedly conceived in Nixon's Executive Office Building suite, the presidential retreat at Camp David, and the White House residence. Again, Nixon refused. He did agree, however, to issue about twenty edited tapes for Jaworski's review. These tapes soon became famous for the phrase "expletive deleted" that appeared throughout the transcripts. One tape included an eighteen-and-one-half-minute drop-off that made it appear as if someone had doctored the original recording.

Jaworski then filed another motion in April 1974 in federal court, where Judge John J. Sirica reviewed the case for a month before ordering the president to comply with the special prosecutor's order. Nixon continued his now-familiar pattern of resistance, claiming that the tapes were protected by executive privilege. But to avoid a criminal contempt charge, Nixon sought review in the D.C.

circuit court of appeals. Jaworski intervened and sought immediate review by the Supreme Court, which agreed to hear the case in early July, after its regular term had ended. By then, President Nixon had few defenders left in Congress and enjoyed almost no support from the public. As the Court prepared to hear *United States* v. *Nixon*, the House Judiciary Committee began to prepare for possible impeachment hearings against the president. Among the young, reform-minded lawyers that staffed the special Watergate subcommittee was former first lady Hillary Rodham Clinton. Twenty years later, Clinton became the target of a congressional investigation for her possible role in the Whitewater real estate scandal.

On the morning of July 8, 1974, the Court heard an extraordinary three-hour session of oral

**Supreme Court of the United States**
**Washington, D. C. 20543**

CHAMBERS OF
JUSTICE WILLIAM O. DOUGLAS

July 12, 1974

Dear Chief:

I have Lewis' revision of his views on the Executive Privilege under a covering letter of July 12th addressed to you. I don't think it is necessary to reach the decision of whether this is based on the Constitution. The office of the President as I read the Constitution is to execute the laws faithfully. A conspiracy to violate the laws or a conspiracy to protect people who have violated the law cannot be brought under Article 2 of the Constitution. We have here, according to the allegations, a conspiracy. The Grand Jury has found that the President was a co-conspirator and the District Judge has found that the conversations relating to the Watergate affair with the President and his aids were both relevant and presumably admissible in the criminal trials pending. What he will discover when he actually gets the tapes and examines them we do not know, but on the basis of the showing so far, conversations relating to law violations are impossible to bring within the scope of Article 2 obligations

The Chief Justice                    William O. Douglas

cc:  The Conference

arguments. On July 24 the Court handed down its decision ordering President Nixon to comply with Judge Sirica's earlier ruling on behalf of Jaworski's request for the tapes. A crowd had begun to assemble around 1:00 A.M. on the morning the Court was scheduled to issue its opinion. A *Washington Post* reporter described the scene this way:

> They were a patient crowd, those men, women and children, pleasant and good natured. They bore no signs or political placards: they were not there to demonstrate. The only sign that they were witnesses to an extraordinary event came shortly before 11:00 A.M. Across the street on the Capitol lawn, two men, dressed in black suits and wearing rubber masks of Henry Kissinger and Mr. Nixon, unfurled a large white banner. In bold, black, upper case letters the banner spelling out the words [from a released tape transcript]: "I DON'T GIVE A SH— WHAT HAPPENS. I WANT YOU ALL TO STONEWALL IT. LET THEM PLEAD THE FIFTH AMENDMENT. COVER UP OR ANYTHING ELSE THAT WILL SAVE THE PLAN. THAT'S THE WHOLE POINT"—Richard M. Nixon, March 22, 1973.

Within a week, the White House began to turn over to Judge Sirica the tapes Archibald Cox had first requested more than a year earlier. Included in one tape was a conversation between Nixon and Haldeman about "the problem area," with Haldeman saying "the FBI is not under control" and suggesting that the CIA should be told to order the FBI to "stay the hell out of this." Haldeman then said, "And the proposal would be that Erhlichman and I call them [CIA officials] in," to which Nixon replied, "All right, fine." Judge Sirica reviewed this damning tape on August 6, which convinced him of Nixon's guilt in the Watergate cover-up. Hundreds of boxes of tape were then shipped to Congress for review. With the House Judiciary Committee having already voted in favor of four articles of impeachment, President Nixon resigned three days later to avoid a certain conviction by the Senate.

Judge Sirica later reflected upon his crucial role in the Nixon tapes case as he watched the president give his farewell address in a nationally televised August 8 address:

> I watched that departure on television. I had been disgusted by the evidence of his role in the cover-up. I was appalled by his lying. But I couldn't help feeling sorry for him as he left, having lost the very thing he had spent most of his life trying to win, the presidency of the United States. I felt sorry for him, but I was also relieved to see him go.

## References

Johnson, Haynes. "Supreme Court Drama Shapes Mood of the City," *Washington Post,* July 25, 1974.

Lukas, Anthony J. *Nightmare: The Underside of the Nixon Years.* New York: Viking Press, 1976.

Sirica, John J. *To Set the Record Straight.* New York: W. W. Norton, 1979.

their own interests to the detriment of the decisionmaking process. Whatever the nature of the privilege of confidentiality of Presidential communications in the exercise of Art. II powers, the privilege can be said to derive from the supremacy of each branch within its own assigned area of constitutional duties. Certain powers and privileges flow from the nature of enumerated powers; the protection of the confidentiality of Presidential communications has similar constitutional underpinnings.

The second ground asserted by the President's counsel in support of the claim of absolute privilege rests on the doctrine of separation of powers. Here it is argued that the independence of the Executive Branch within its own sphere, insulates a President from a judicial subpoena in an ongoing criminal prosecution, and thereby protects confidential Presidential communications.

However, neither the doctrine of separation of powers nor the need for confidentiality of high-level communications, without more, can sustain an absolute, unqualified Presidential privilege of immunity from judicial process under all circumstances. The President's need for complete candor and objectivity from advisers calls for great deference from the courts. However, when the privilege depends solely on the broad, undifferentiated claim of public interest in the confidentiality of such conversations, a confrontation with other values arises. Absent a claim of need to protect military, diplomatic, or sensitive national security secrets, we find it difficult to accept the argument that even the very important interest in confidentiality of Presidential communications is significantly diminished by production of such material for *in camera* inspection with all the protection that a district court will be obliged to provide.

The impediment that an absolute, unqualified privilege would place in the way of the primary constitutional duty of the Judicial Branch to do justice in criminal prosecutions would plainly conflict with the function of the courts under Art. III. In designing the structure of our Government and dividing and allocating the sovereign power among three co-equal branches, the Framers of the Constitution sought to provide a comprehensive system, but the separate powers were not intended to operate with absolute independence. . . .

To read the Article II powers of the President as providing an absolute privilege as against a subpoena essential to enforcement of criminal statutes on no more than a generalized claim of the public interest in confidentiality of nonmilitary and nondiplomatic discussions would upset the constitutional balance of "a workable government" and gravely impair the role of the courts under Article III.

Since we conclude that the legitimate needs of the judicial process may outweigh Presidential privilege, it is necessary to resolve those competing interests in a manner that preserves the essential functions of each branch. The right and indeed the duty to resolve that question does not free the Judiciary from according high respect to the representations made on behalf of the President.

The expectation of a President to the confidentiality of his conversations and correspondence, like the claim of confidentiality of judicial deliberations, for example, has all the values to which we accord deference for the privacy of all citizens and, added to those values, is the necessity for protection of the public interest in candid, objective, and even blunt or harsh opinions in Presidential decision-making. A President and those who assist him must be free to explore alternatives in the process of shaping policies and making decisions, and to do so in a way many would be unwilling to express except privately. These are the considerations justifying a presumptive privilege for Presidential communications. The privilege is fundamental to the operation of Government, and inextricably rooted in the separation of powers under the Constitution. . . .

We agree with Mr. Chief Justice Marshall's observation, therefore, that "[i]n no case of his kind would a court be required to proceed against the president as against an ordinary individual."

But this presumptive privilege must be considered in light of our historic commitment to the rule of law. This is nowhere more profoundly manifest than, in our view, that "the twofold aim [of criminal justice] is that guilt shall not escape or innocence suffer." *Berger* v. *United States* (1935). We have elected to employ an adversary system of criminal justice in which the parties contest all issues before a court of law. The need to develop all relevant facts in the adversary system is both fundamental and comprehensive. The ends of criminal justice would be defeated if judgments were to be founded on a partial or speculative presentation of the facts. The very integrity of the judicial system and public confidence in the system depend on full disclosure of all the facts, within the framework of the rules of evidence. To ensure that justice is done, it is imperative to the function of courts that compulsory process be available for the production of evidence needed either by the prosecution or by the defense. . . .

The privileges referred to by the Court are designed to protect weighty and legitimate competing interests. Thus, the Fifth Amendment to the Constitution provides that no man "shall be compelled in any criminal case to be a witness against himself." And, generally, an attorney or a priest may not be required to disclose what has been revealed in professional confidence. These and other interests are recognized in law by privileges against forced disclosure, established in the Constitution, by statute, or at common law. Whatever their origins, these exceptions to the demand for every man's evidence are not lightly created nor expansively construed, for they are in derogation of the search for truth.

In this case, the President challenges a subpoena served on him as a third party requiring the production of materials for use in a criminal prosecution; he does so on the claim that he has a privilege against disclosure of confidential communications. He does not place his claim of privilege on the ground they are military or diplomatic secrets. As to these areas of Art. II duties, the courts have traditionally shown the utmost deference to Presidential responsibilities. . . .

No case of the Court, however, has extended this high degree of deference to a President's generalized interest in confidentiality. Nowhere in the Constitution, as we have noted earlier, is there any explicit reference to a privilege of confidentiality, yet to the extent this interest relates to the effective discharge of a President's powers, it is constitutionally based. . . .

In this case, we must weigh the importance of the general privilege of confidentiality of Presidential communications in performance of the President's responsibilities against the inroads of such a privilege on the fair administration of criminal justice. The interest in preserving confidentiality is weighty indeed, and entitled to great respect. However, we cannot conclude that advisers will be moved to temper the candor of their remarks by the infrequent occasions of disclosure because of the possibility that such conversations will be called for in the context of a criminal prosecution.

On the other hand, the allowance of the privilege to withhold evidence that is demonstrably relevant in a criminal trial would cut deeply into the guarantee of due process of law and gravely impair the basic function of the court. A President's acknowledged need for confidentiality in the communications of his office is general in nature, whereas the constitutional need for production of relevant evidence in a criminal proceeding is specific and central to the fair adjudication of a particular criminal case in the administration of justice. Without access to specific facts, a criminal prosecution may be totally frustrated. The President's broad interest in confidentiality of communications will not be vitiated by disclosure of a limited number of conversations preliminarily shown to have some bearing on the pending criminal cases.

We conclude that, when the ground for asserting privilege as to subpoenaed materials sought for use in a criminal trial is based only on the generalized interest in confidentiality, it cannot prevail over the fundamental demands of due process of law in the fair administration of criminal justice. The generalized assertion of privilege must yield to the demonstrated, specific need for evidence in a pending criminal trial.

*Affirmed.*

▼▲▼

## FOR FURTHER READING

Berger, Raoul. *Executive Privilege: A Constitutional Myth.* Cambridge, Mass.: Harvard University Press, 1974.

Bessette, Joseph and Jeffrey Tulis. *The Presidency in the Constitutional Order.* Baton Rouge: Louisiana State University Press, 1981.

Corwin, Edward S. *The President: Office and Powers,* 4th ed. New York: New York University Press, 1957.

Ely, John Hart. *War and Responsibility.* Princeton, N.J.: Princeton University Press, 1993.

Fisher, Louis. *Presidential War Power.* Lawrence: University Press of Kansas, 1995.

Greenstein, Fred. *Leadership in the Modern Presidency.* Cambridge, Mass.: Harvard University Press, 1988.

Harriger, Katy J. *Independent Justice: The Federal Special Prosecutor in American Politics.* Lawrence: University Press of Kansas, 1992.

Henkin, Louis. *Foreign Affairs and the Constitution.* New York: W. W. Norton, 1975.

Hofstadter, Richard. *The Progressive Movement, 1900–1915.* Englewood Cliffs, N.J.: Prentice-Hall, 1963.

Irons, Peter. *Justice at War: The Story of the Japanese American Internment Cases.* Berkeley, Calif.: University of California Press, 1993.

———. *The New Deal Lawyers.* Princeton, N.J.: Princeton University Press, 1982.

Marcus, Maeva. *Truman and the Steel Seizure Case.* Durham, N.C.: Duke University Press, 1994.

McKenzie, G. Calvin. *The Politics of Presidential Appointments.* New York: Free Press, 1981.

Neustadt, Richard E. *Presidential Power and the Modern Presidents.* New York: Free Press, 1990.

Rozell, Marc J. *Executive Privilege: The Dilemma of Secrecy and Democratic Accountability.* Baltimore: Johns Hopkins University Press, 1994.

Schlesinger, Arthur M., Jr. *The Imperial Presidency.* Boston: Houghton Mifflin, 1974.

Scigliano, Robert. *The Supreme Court and the Presidency.* New York: Macmillan, 1971.

Ungar, Sanford J. *The Papers and the Papers.* New York: Columbia University Press, 1972.

# 6 Congressional Power to Regulate Commerce and Promote the General Welfare

In February 1983, General Motors, the largest manufacturer and seller of automobiles in the United States, announced a historic agreement with Toyota, Japan's biggest auto maker, to enter into a joint production arrangement. These two companies would combine their industrial and marketing might to produce a subcompact car for sale in North American markets. American workers in California would make the new car, the Chevrolet Sprinter, but its design and advanced internal components—the engine, drive train, and computer control systems—would come from Japan. By the time it was built, the Sprinter would be almost indistinguishable from Toyota's best-selling subcompact car, the Corolla.[1]

Other American and Japanese automobile companies soon followed the General Motors–Toyota arrangement. Chrysler announced it would begin buying parts from Mitsubishi. Honda opened assembly plants in Ohio to produce its popular Accord model. Nissan opened a truck plant in Tennessee. General Motors entered into a separate agreement with Isuzu to purchase diesel engines from the Japanese automaker for General Motors trucks and cars assembled in the United States. This trend accelerated at an even more breathtaking clip during the 1990s, as the two leading German luxury car makers, Bavarian Motor Works (BMW) and Mercedes, opened assembly lines in South Carolina and Alabama, after an eager courtship, full of tax incentives and other favorable guarantees, by the leading business and political figures of those states.

Perhaps the ultimate symbol of the globalization of the automobile industry came in 1997, when the mid-size Toyota Camry became the best-selling car in the United States. And where was America's favorite car assembled? In Japan? No, in Georgetown, Kentucky, from parts manufactured in West Virginia, Indiana, and more than a dozen other countries. Toyota's success in the United States was not limited to the Camry. By 1998 more than 60 percent of all Toyota cars and trucks sold in the United States, including its luxury Lexus line and high-end sport utility vehicles, were manufactured in North America.

Economists and business analysts have offered numerous theories to explain the complex design, production, manufacturing, and marketing arrangements that are now standard operating procedure between and among the world's largest automobile companies. Whatever reason best explains the evolution of this once-parochial industry, this much is clear: attempting to label a Camry a Japanese car, a Chevrolet an American car, or a BMW a German car in the modern global economic marketplace describes nothing more than the geographic location of corporate headquarters.

What, then, accounts for the periodic Buy American campaigns that emerge in times of labor-management conflict, layoffs, or reports of trade imbalances in the automobile industry? What possible meaning can that appeal have in a market that is characterized by boundaries without borders? Indeed, is a Chevrolet made in Mexico more or less "American" than a Toyota made in Kentucky or a BMW built in Alabama? Behind the rhetoric and emotional appeal of a Buy American campaign—such efforts often feature well-produced television commercials that show tearful workers receiving their pink slips, on one side of the screen, while the other side shows a new plant under construction in some far-away land—lies this simple truth: It is very difficult to buy *anything,* much less a car, that is designed, made, shipped, sold, and serviced solely by Americans living and working in the United States.

The complex, interdependent character of modern production and distribution is not limited to foreign commerce. American-based companies by the score attempt to sell the image of their product as much as the product itself by identifying it with a region: bagels from New York, maple syrup from New England, Southern barbecue, exotic juices from Maine and Massachusetts, and bottled water from the hidden springs of Colorado. In truth, many of the ingredients or materials that go into these products come from other states, if not other countries. After all, how many oranges and pineapples are people in Maine plucking from their citrus trees during a New England winter?

Perhaps the Framers anticipated the seamless nature of foreign and domestic commerce in twenty-first-century America. Certainly, the desire to centralize the regulation of foreign and interstate commerce was front and center at the Constitutional Convention. And the dearth of Anti-Federalist opposition to the broad language of the Commerce Clause is evidence enough that the nation's system of commercial regulation was in dire straits and in need of drastic reform. That said, it is more likely that the Framers never imagined a world in which televisions, cellular telephones, personal computers, cars, food products, and aircraft bearing an American corporate imprint would be assembled with parts and labor from all over the globe.

Defining the meaning of foreign and domestic inter-state commerce and the scope of congressional power to regulate such activities has been, since the earliest days of the Republic, largely a judicial enterprise. Since its historic decisions under Chief Justice John Marshall, the Court's definition of commerce and the power of Congress to regulate it have had a profound impact on the social and economic development of American society. How the Court has interpreted the power of Congress to regulate commerce to promote both the interests of American business and the health, safety, and welfare of the broader population is the subject of this chapter.

## Congressional Commerce Power

By the time the Framers convened for the Constitutional Convention, the need to overhaul the nation's chaotic and piecemeal system of commercial regulation was so serious that it ranked, as Alexander Hamilton later wrote in *Federalist* 23, as one of the two "principle purposes to be answered by the Union." The first was "[t]he common defence of the members—the preservation of the public peace as well against internal convulsions as external attacks." The second was "the regulation of commerce with other nations and between the States—the superintendence of our intercourse, political and commercial, with foreign countries."[2] Even James Madison, whose commitment to constitutional nationalism was far less doctrinaire than Hamilton's, conceded in a letter to Thomas Jefferson prior to the convention that "[m]ost of our political evils may be traced to our commercial ones."[3] Neither Madison nor Hamilton ever doubted the need for the Constitution to correct the deficiencies of the Articles of Confederation by replacing its decentralized system of commercial regulation with a congressionally centered uniform body of law.

The ease with which the Framers agreed upon the language of the Commerce Clause and the near complete lack of Anti-Federalist opposition to it testified further to the consensus that existed among the delegates to vest broad regulatory control of commercial activity with Congress. Thus the language of Article 1, Section 8, granting Congress the power "to regulate Commerce with foreign Nations, and among the several States, and with the Indian Tribes" went to the states for ratification in 1787 as one of the least controversial provisions of the Constitution. Together with the Contract Clause, which barred the states from interfering with public and private contracts, the power of Congress to regulate commerce paved the road for the great wave of economic development that began to thrive upon ratification of the Constitution. For the first time since the birth of the Republic, the nation possessed a coherent system of economic and commercial regulation.

But the relative lack of conflict over the need to centralize the regulation of interstate and foreign commerce did not mean that the Framers agreed upon a precise constitutional definition of what such commerce was or the permissible scope of congressional power to regulate it. The Framers' decision to leave the contours of the Commerce Clause deliberately vague reflected the need to satisfy competing political constituencies that differed on the proper boundaries of federal and state power over commercial relations. Even in the wake of a relatively harmonious drafting process behind the Commerce Clause, firm lines were still not clearly drawn. Moreover, the Framers chose to phrase the great clauses of the Constitution, such as the Commerce Clause and the Contract Clause, in more general terms to allow the Court to give them meaning through the process of judicial review.[4]

In fairness, this analysis of the Framers' design for the Commerce Clause is more appropriate for the subsequent development of the law of *interstate* commerce, not the regulation of *foreign* commerce. Upon the Constitution's ratification, both interstate and foreign commerce increased at exponential rates, as Congress moved to relax the barriers to trade that had existed under the Articles of Confederation and create the large, transnational commercial republic envisioned by the Framers. Early congressional legislation, however, was directed at the regulation of foreign commerce, not commerce between and among the states. Laws establishing import duties, licensing requirements of vessels engaged in coastal trade, and regulations on foreign ships and cargoes were among the first acts of Congress under the Commerce Clause.

Federal power over foreign commerce has since been recognized as complete. In *Gibbons v. Ogden* (1824) (see Chapter 4), the Court gave judicial definition to what the Framers believed was implied by the very purpose of the Commerce Clause. This interpretation of the power of Congress to regulate foreign commerce has never faced a serious challenge. Powers available to Congress to regulate commerce between the United States and foreign nations include the power to set tariffs, establish boycotts and trade embargoes, enter international financial agreements, and participate in global banking. The Court has never wavered from Chief Justice John Marshall's authoritative declaration of congressional power as "full and complete" over foreign commerce established in *Gibbons*.

Congressional power to regulate interstate commerce, however, and the Court's interpretation of the substance

and scope of that power, has been an altogether different matter. As the first Congress moved to establish control over the foreign arena of commercial relations by promptly passing legislation, its approach to the regulation of interstate commerce reflected a more passive approach. States were no longer permitted to impose fees and other restrictions on companies and other business interests engaged in interstate commercial activities. Congress, wary to disturb the nation's budding and prosperous commercial economy, elected not to replace the old, discredited laws with a regulatory system of its own.

As with many of the other great constitutional questions of the day, the fragile consensus between the Federalists, such as Alexander Hamilton, John Adams, and John Marshall, and advocates of more decentralized government power, such as Thomas Jefferson, James Madison, and George Mason, on the need to establish congressional power over interstate commerce slowly unraveled. Theoretical differences over the political organization of commercial regulation took on a whole new light as they became real-world problems. In fact, evidence that the rapidly evolving financial and economic transition of the early Republic would place Hamiltonian nationalism and Jeffersonian federalism on a collision course was visible as early as 1791. That year, you will recall from our discussion of *McCulloch v. Maryland* (1819) in Chapter 4, President George Washington requested Hamilton and Jefferson to provide him with separate advisory opinions on the constitutionality of a congressional proposal to establish a national banking system.[5]

The result was two opinions of such clarity, intellectual force, and sense of purpose that each is considered a classic exposition of the philosophical ideas and political differences that divided the Federalists from the Democratic-Republican party of Jefferson and Madison. Hamilton and Jefferson offered two distinct theories of economic and political organization that formed the basis of the dueling constitutional theories of the Commerce Clause that confronted the Court in *Gibbons*.

Hamilton's conception of congressional power under the Commerce Clause was rooted in his well-articulated view of the Constitution as having established a *national* government with broad powers to legislate in the *national* interest. Just as the Necessary and Proper Clause prohibited the states from exercising legislative power that interfered with the authority of the national government made supreme by the Constitution, so too did the Commerce Clause intend to remove the artificial boundaries on commerce that existed between the states. Indeed, the phrasing of the Commerce Clause, that Congress shall have power "to regulate Commerce . . . among the several States," was intended to extend to Congress comprehensive power over all commerce conducted in the United States, regardless of where it originated or ended.

Jefferson's definition of congressional commerce power was much more contained. Whereas Hamilton's interpretation of the "among the several States" provision of the Commerce Clause was nationalistic, Jefferson's approach was territorial, rather than functional. Interstate commerce was just that—commerce between or among more than one state. If commerce remained confined to a single state, then was purely *intrastate* in nature and beyond the scope of congressional power. If commerce crossed the territorial boundaries of one state into another, then, and only then, did it become *interstate* and within the purview of Congress to regulate.

Although some scholars have argued that Congress, by the early nineteenth century, had begun to edge toward the nationalist interpretation of the Commerce Clause, the question of how far congressional power extended over interstate commerce was still an open question for the courts. *McCulloch* offered a crystalline vision of the Federalist conception of constitutional nationalism. But, because it did not raise a Commerce Clause question, *McCulloch* did not settle the growing confusion over the reach of congressional power to regulate interstate commercial activities.

The rise of the nascent commercial steamboat business in the early 1820s not only led to open economic warfare among the states but also gave the Court the chance to settle the question left open by *McCulloch* over the scope of congressional power to regulate commerce. As Robert Fulton and Robert Livingston's introduction of the commercial steamboat began to revolutionize interstate commerce, state legislatures were entering into various exclusive arrangements to grant monopolistic control to steamboat companies over the navigation of commercial waters within state boundaries. These charters placed prohibitive restrictions on the free

flow of interstate commerce, making it all but impossible for steamboats to carry on commerce outside of their home states. Powerful economic and political forces within the states had combined to place barriers to interstate commerce that conjured up memories of the disruptive era of commercial regulation under the Articles of Confederation.[6]

In his last truly great opinion for the Court, Chief Justice Marshall posed four major questions concerning the relationship between Congress and the regulation of interstate commerce: (1) What is commerce? (2) How far does the power of Congress extend over the states to regulate commerce? (3) Is the power of Congress to regulate commerce exclusive? and (4) Does the power of Congress to regulate commerce, and, more generally, to exercise its legislative powers, follow the model of Hamiltonian nationalism or Jeffersonian federalism?

Marshall's unanimous opinion for the Court addressed these questions. First, the chief justice offered an expansive interpretation of *commerce,* one that rejected the narrow Jeffersonian definition put forth by the supporters of the state-granted monopolies. Commerce, wrote Marshall, involves more than just buying and selling, or the interchange of commodities, or traffic. While commerce

> [u]ndoubtedly, is traffic . . . it is something more; it is intercourse. It describes the commercial intercourse between nations, and parts of nations, in all its branches, and is regulated by prescribing rules for carrying on that intercourse. The mind can scarcely conceive of a system for regulating commerce between nations, which shall exclude all laws concerning navigation, which shall be silent on the admission of the vessels of the one nation into the ports of the other, and be confined to prescribing rules for the conduct of individuals, in the actual employment of buying and selling, or of barter.
>
> The power over commerce, including navigation, was one of the primary objects for which the people . . . adopted their government, and must have been contemplated in forming it.[7]

Commerce, concluded Marshall, comprehended "every species of commercial intercourse between the United States and foreign nations."[8]

In addressing the second question, however, Marshall stopped short of granting Congress complete control over all commercial activities. As "[c]omprehensive as the word 'among' is, it may very properly be restricted to that commerce which concerns more states than one. . . . The completely internal commerce of a state, then, may be considered as reserved for the state itself." Congressional power, then, did not extend to "that commerce, which is completely internal, which is carried on between man and man in a state, or between different parts of the same state, and which does not extend to or affect the other states."[9]

Marshall's answer to the third question offered another important concession to the advocates of decentralized commerce power. Sensitive to the states' rights movement that had begun to emerge in the early 1820s and would reach its crescendo with the election of Andrew Jackson to the presidency in 1829, Marshall also held that states possessed a concurrent power to regulate commerce in the absence of federal laws. Laws intended to promote the safety and welfare of state and local communities were well within the reserved powers granted to the states by the Tenth Amendment. But states could not, Marshall emphasized, interfere in any way with federal regulation affecting interstate commerce. Still, in recognizing that states had legitimate interests in protecting the health, safety, and welfare of their citizens, Marshall opened the door for states to exercise what would later become known as their police power.

Marshall's astute political instincts did not, however, overwhelm the central theme of his *Gibbons* opinion: The Commerce Clause was intended to reflect the Federalist nationalism of its most powerful and articulate exponent, Alexander Hamilton. Thus, Congress must be given the broadest deference possible to regulate commerce. Any other interpretation of the Commerce Clause "would cripple the government, and render it unequal to the objects for which it is declared to be instituted."[10] In a sense the chief justice treated the power of Congress to regulate commerce as a political question, leaving to it and not the courts the final word to determine the restraints on the exercise of its power in this regard.[11]

Before John Marshall died in 1835, the Court handed down two other decisions of great import for the constitutional development of Commerce Clause doctrine. In *Brown* v. *Maryland* (1827), the Court ruled that states could not levy taxes on imported goods as long as the goods remained in their original package. For the Court, the chief justice wrote that states could tax imported goods once they became "mixed up with the mass of property in the country." Until then, however, goods in their original package were the subject of federal, not state, commercial regulation. The Court's opinion in *Brown* was expansive, so much so that it prohibited state taxation of all foreign *and* interstate commerce that met the threshold test of Marshall's "original package" doctrine.

In *Willson* v. *Black Bird Creek Marsh Co.* (1829), the Court resisted the chance to extend the scope of congressional commerce power over the navigable waters between states. The Court rejected the argument of several commercial vessel operators that Delaware's decision to authorize a dam to exclude water from a navigable marsh infringed upon their rights under the federal Coasting Act of 1793, the statute also at issue in *Gibbons*. Here, Marshall gave greater definition to the loophole he left for the state regulation of commerce in *Gibbons*. In more explicit terms, Marshall held that, in the absence of federal regulation, states were permitted to exercise their police powers to promote the state's legitimate commercial and welfare interests.

For all of Marshall's reputation as the consummate nationalist, his deliberate decision not to centralize all commercial regulatory power in the federal government in *Gibbons,* and later in *Brown,* demonstrated a sensitive ear to the new political environment of the late 1820s. The states' rights–centered political platform of the Democratic-Republicans had finally found in Andrew Jackson the charismatic leader to take its cause to the White House. In 1829, Jackson captured the presidency and immediately sought to restructure the balance of power between the national government and the states. His most famous confrontation with the residual forces of Federalist nationalism came in 1832, when he refused to recharter the Second National Bank of the United States. Jackson bluntly challenged John Marshall's decidedly nationalist interpretation of the Constitution, one that had all but eliminated the notion that the states were sovereign powers in a confederate constitutional arrangement.

The man who helped President Jackson write his veto message of the Second National Bank charter legislation was his Attorney General, Roger B. Taney. A Southerner and slaveholder descended from a prominent Maryland family, Taney was a committed soldier in the cause of Jacksonian democracy. Taney was integral to the planning and execution of Jackson's plan to attack the Marshall-built foundation of American constitutional law. Taney served the president's administration in two additional, crucial capacities: first as secretary of war and then as secretary of the treasury. As treasury secretary, Taney's most controversial decision came in 1833, when he refused to allow federal deposits into the national bank. Taney's action infuriated the Senate but enthralled the Jacksonians, whose power and influence around the nation continued to grow. In 1835, Taney received the ultimate reward for his determination to roll back the gravitational pull of Marshall's constitutional nationalism, when President Jackson appointed him to replace Justice Gabriel Duvall. After the Senate postponed Taney's confirmation, Jackson, well aware of the historical irony of the moment that chance had given him, renominated Taney just after Christmas to fill the seat left open by Chief Justice Marshall's death.

Fear that Taney would replace Marshall as chief justice and undo his constitutional legacy was widespread among Marshall's allies, and for good reason. On the Court, Taney immediately became an ardent advocate of the constitutional doctrine known as *dual federalism,* or the belief that states, as sovereign entities, possessed powers concurrent to and often exclusive of the national government. In fairness, Taney's federalism did not embrace the far more radical, even anarchistic theories of John C. Calhoun, the former vice president and senator from South Carolina. Calhoun's intractable support for slavery and the economic interests of the agrarian-based Southern economy led him to formulate his doctrine of nullification. Nullification was originally conceived as a means to counter the open discussion of secession among the Southern states in the late 1820s. Calhoun argued that the Constitution, securing as it did the sovereign rights of the states, permitted the concurrent majorities of the Northern and Southern states in Congress to follow or reject federal legislation. To express its objection to a federal law, a state was permitted to call a convention and decide whether it was an unconstitutional usurpation of sovereign state power. If the convention judged the law as such, it then became

null and void within the state. Failure of the other states to respect a dissenting state's decision to nullify a law later became grounds for secession.[12]

Calhoun's theories and subsequent defense of Southern secession had no friend in either Jackson or Taney. In 1832, President Jackson ordered naval gunboats into the Charleston harbor to enforce a federal tariff that South Carolina had nullified in a hastily called state convention to consider secession. Calling the action "incompatible with the existence of the Union," Jackson was able to persuade South Carolina to drop its nullification provision after it worked out a compromise feature on tariff rates. Jackson's swift and decisive action demonstrated that, for all its commitment to states rights, his administration was still very much committed to the cause of the Republic.[13]

Likewise, to see the Court's first important decisions under Chief Justice Taney involving federalism and congressional commerce power as a distinct departure from the supreme position that Marshall had carved out for the national government ignores two important features of Marshall's commerce clause jurisprudence. First, Marshall's opinion in *Gibbons* had deliberately left the door ajar for the states to exercise their commerce and police powers. Second, Marshall had declined, in *Willson,* to shut that door by holding that the states possessed concurrent power to regulate commerce in the absence of federal regulation. For sure, Taney, as chief justice, seized upon the opportunities Marshall had left and extended them to promote the doctrine of dual federalism. But Taney did not, at least at the outset, recharter the course of American constitutional law on a path that his Federalist predecessor had failed to anticipate. Furthermore, as if to confound the expectations of his worst critics, the Court under Taney solidified further the rights of the capitalist class created by the Marshall Court. In several important cases involving the Contract Clause, federal court jurisdiction, and national supremacy, the Taney Court affirmed and broadened the constitutional nationalism of John Marshall.[14]

Chief Justice Taney, buoyed by a Court that, by 1837, commanded a majority of justices appointed by Jackson and his Democratic party successor to the presidency, Martin Van Buren, diminished to a great degree Congress's power (on the federal-state continuum) to regulate commerce between the states. The Court's now

Democratic-based center of power was no mere accident of timing. In 1837, Congress had voted to expand the Court from six to nine members, giving President Van Buren an unprecedented chance to institutionalize the states' rights revolution in American constitutional development through the appointment of additional justices. This political windfall enabled Van Buren to create a tie-proof majority of Democratic appointees on the Court that could withstand a change in his party's electoral fortunes.

In *The License Cases* (1847), Chief Justice Taney broke clear from the shadow of the Marshall Court's nationalist interpretation of the Commerce Clause and offered the fullest expression to date of the new Court's philosophy of dual federalism. The Court produced nine opinions to deal with the questions raised by the case, which concerned the validity of three separate state tax laws on alcoholic beverages imported from other states. Their differences aside, the justices were able to agree that states were well within their police powers to impose taxes on interstate commerce to advance health, safety, and welfare objectives. Taxes levied for these purposes involved only an incidental effect on interstate commerce. Chief Justice Taney's opinion, in particular, offered a quantum leap in the power afforded to states under Marshall's opinion in *Gibbons*. States had a concurrent right to regulate commerce in the absence of federal regulation, and they also retained the power "inherent in every sovereignty" to "govern men and things within its dominion."[15] This language would have made Chief Justice Marshall wince.

The Taney Court (1836–1864) articulated firm spheres of influence in which national and state power over commercial activities were exclusive. It successfully reintroduced the notion of state sovereignty, rather than merely state police power, to the language of post-Marshall constitutional jurisprudence. Taney's emphasis on local control of commercial and property matters was motivated by several factors. These included the need to return to states and localities the right to regulate commercial interests and property rights claims in the public interest, a suspicion of large national corporations and the potential for economic disruption that a national "free trade" zone posed for regional interests, and, tragically, a passionate desire to protect Southern slavery from Northern opposition in Congress. The latter concern motivated Taney's entrance into the slavery question in *Dred Scott v. Sandford* (1857), a temptation of politics that stained for decades the near-reverential regard in which constitutional scholars now hold his influence on American constitutional development and accomplishments as chief justice.[16]

Justice Felix Frankfurter later commented that the Taney Court's "enduring contribution" to the evolution of American law was "the workable adjustment of the theoretical distribution of authority between two governments for a single people."[17] Dual federalism may well have been the most lasting impression left by the Taney Court upon constitutional development, as it did not improve upon or even change the definition of commerce created by the Marshall Court. For the Taney Court, all that mattered was *where* commerce was conducted. And that was either across or within state lines. Serious thought about *what* commerce was, as opposed to where it took place, did not become a matter of national importance, and thus an issue for the Court, until after the Civil War. Political changes brought about by the defeat of the South, not the least of which was the collapse of its political and economic infrastructure, and the arrival of the Industrial Revolution ushered in a new, more aggressive role for congressional oversight of commerce.

In 1887, Congress enacted its first major legislation intended to regulate the most powerful new economic and social creation of the Industrial Revolution: the concentration of power in a small number of great corporate "trusts" that, free from government regulation, had acquired monopolistic control over nearly all the key transportation and manufacturing sectors of the United States. Some of the most famous names in American business, such as Rockefeller, Carnegie, Mellon, Morgan, Kuhn, and Loeb, built their fortunes in the late 1800s, assisted in no small part by a Court willing to uphold their claims that the Constitution prohibited legislative interference with the free enterprise system. This battle between the Court and the legislatures, the fledgling American labor unions and the large corporations for whom they worked, and the reform-minded Progressive movement and business lobbyists would continue until well into the New Deal of President Franklin Roosevelt.

The Interstate Commerce Act of 1887, a comprehensive effort by Congress to bring order and greater market competition to the nation's railroads, was designed to meet the challenges that the new industrial era posed to the American constitutional order. The law did not attempt to seize control of the nation's railroad carriers, which were corporate subsidiaries of the financial empires of the Wall Street investment firms of J. P. Morgan and Kuhn, Loeb & Co. Instead, the act sought to regulate railroad rates and determine the rules of competition. In a sense, Congress had followed the administrative role that Woodrow Wilson, then a professor at Princeton University, had deemed essential for it in light of the nation's changing economic and political infrastructure. "Even if our government is not to follow the lead of the governments of Europe in buying or building telegraph and railroad lines," Wilson wrote, "no one can doubt that in some way it must take itself master of masterful corporations."[18]

Wilson's comments offered a very important insight into the coming conflict between the Court and the business interests it was determined to protect and the forces of Progressive reform. The Progressives believed that Congress and the state legislatures should have the power to protect the public interest from the social and economic consequences of industrialism. Economic markets and the rules that governed them were not, as the great corporations maintained, the ordained outcome of the Constitution. They were the product of deliberate choices made by the political process. Government had no obligation to ignore social and economic problems when it believed that legislation was needed to address them. Theodore Roosevelt later summarized this view in his first presidential address to Congress in 1901, much of which was taken up with the problem of regulating the great trusts of the day:

> It is no limitation upon property rights or freedom of contract to require that when men receive from government the privilege of doing business under corporate form, which frees them from individual responsibility, and enables them to call into their enterprises the capital of the public, they shall do so upon absolutely truthful representations as to the value of the property in which the capital is to be invested. Corporations engaged in interstate commerce should be regulated if they are found to exercise a license working to the public injury. It should be as much the aim of those who seek for social betterment to rid the

business world of crimes of cunning as to rid the entire body politic of crimes of violence. Great corporations exist only because they are created and safeguarded by our institutions; and it is therefore our right and our duty to see that they work in harmony with these institutions.[19]

Nonetheless, the social and economic welfare of the broader public was not the concern of Congress when it passed the Interstate Commerce Act of 1887. The same is true for the 1890 Sherman Antitrust Act, the federal government's first major effort to break up the large monopolistic corporations that restrained trade through unfair business practices. These laws were much closer in spirit to Jacksonian ideals than to the demand for social justice that animated the Progressive movement in the early 1900s. Their purpose was to create a more open and equitable environment in which more businesses could compete. The harsh consequences of the Industrial Revolution, such as the spread of fatal diseases created by the squalor of the rapidly growing industrial-based cities, unsafe working conditions in the factories, rising rates of infant mortality, child labor abuses, and domestic violence exacerbated by poverty and cramped living arrangements were not the concern of Congress. Fair competition was. And, in the mind of Congress, legislation intended to accomplish this objective was decidedly in the public interest.

By this time, however, the Court's jurisprudence had coalesced around the social and economic theories offered in support of a laissez-faire approach to business regulation. Enamored with the ideas of social theorists such as William Graham Sumner and Herbert Spencer, who believed that Charles Darwin's theories of natural selection and survival of the fittest were fully applicable to the nation's social and economic arrangements, the Court severely limited the reach of the 1887 and 1890 laws. The Court did not challenge the constitutional authority of Congress under the Commerce Clause to enact either statute, but did interpret the laws so that they possessed no real force. In several decisions involving lawsuits against the railroad trusts during the 1890s, the Court removed much of the 1887 law's punch by holding that the Commerce Clause did not authorize the Interstate Commerce Commission (ICC) to set rates. That power had always been implied from the ICC's power to rule that in-effect rates were unreasonable.

In *Interstate Commerce Commission v. Cincinnati, New Orleans, and Texas Pacific Railway Co.* (1897), the Court ruled that such action by the ICC violated the separation of powers because it involved the unconstitutional delegation of legislative power to an executive branch agency to set rates.[20]

But the decision that really set into stone the limits of the federal government to mount a vigorous campaign to reform the business practices of the nation's large corporations was *United States v. E.C. Knight Co.* (1895).[21] The Court, now composed of a solid majority of former corporate lawyers with strong ties to the industries that Congress had targeted for reform and devotees to the theories of laissez-faire economics and social Darwinism currently in vogue, used *E.C. Knight* to revisit the definition of interstate commerce set forth in *Gibbons. E.C. Knight* was both an antitrust case, as it involved the Justice Department's first major prosecution of a monopolistic trust under the 1890 Sherman law, and a testament from the Court about the wages of sin that government regulation posed for the entrepreneurial spirit of the time and the need to keep economic markets free from coercive legal schemes.

For an 8-1 Court, Chief Justice Melville Fuller, a prominent corporate appeals lawyer before President Grover Cleveland appointed him chief justice in 1888, declined to hold that the American Sugar Refining Co., a trust that controlled 98 percent of the market for all refined sugar in the United States, had violated the Sherman Act. Fuller reached this conclusion by noting that the antitrust law applied to interstate commerce, not manufacturing. Rather than view production as the touchstone of commercial activity and thus as an integral component of interstate commerce, Fuller concluded that congressional power to regulate commerce under the Sherman Act extended only to business practices that restrained actual trade, not production. Although Fuller's writing does not compare to Marshall's opinion in *Gibbons* for intellectual firepower, the distinction that Fuller drew between manufacturing and commerce in *E.C. Knight* made the decision one of profound importance in the development of Commerce Clause doctrine over the next forty years.

Some constitutional historians have suggested that the Court carved out such a narrow definition of interstate commerce in *E.C. Knight* so that the states could

better regulate the monopolistic business activities of the trusts. This view is based on the still-retained power of the states to regulate the manufacturing ventures of corporations chartered and based in other states that sought to do business inside their borders. Had the Court used *E.C. Knight* to combine production and distribution into a single definition of interstate commerce, the states would have been stripped of their powers to regulate manufacturing, still defined as *intrastate* commerce.[22]

But the states pursued the opposite path, enticing the large trusts to expand their presence in exchange for an implied promise not to break them up. Competition for corporate development was especially intense among the Southern states, still economically devastated from the Civil War. Smitten with the promise of favorable tax incentives, a low-wage, nonunionized labor force, and lax environmental regulation, several of the nation's largest trusts expanded operations from their established Northern industrial base into the former Confederacy.[23] Even states that later attempted to mitigate the social and economic consequences of their shortsighted embrace of unregulated industrial expansion were stymied by the Court's adoption around this time of a "liberty of contract" interpretation of the Due Process Clause of the Fourteenth Amendment. This doctrine prohibited states from interfering in the economic arrangements reached by two parties as long as the agreement was not contrary to public policy. Liberty of contract, its origins in the legal and social philosophies of the late nineteenth century, and its consequences for American constitutional development are discussed in Chapter 9. For now, it is important to note that the Court had added another crucial doctrinal weapon to restrain government regulation of business and commerce.

Nonetheless, the Court was not impervious to the need for Congress to address some of the more egregious problems caused by the monopolistic trusts, as decisions in two subsequent and important Commerce Clause cases demonstrated. In *The Shreveport Rate Case* (1914), the Court held that the Interstate Commerce Commission was authorized to set the rates of intrastate railroad travel when rates set by state transportation authorities impaired interstate commerce to a serious degree. Wrote Chief Justice Charles Evans Hughes:

"Whenever the interstate and intrastate carriers are so related that the government of the one involves the control of the other, it is Congress, and not the State, that is entitled to prescribe the final and dominant rule."[24]

The Court also restored some of the enforcement power it had stripped from the Sherman Act in *E.C. Knight*. In *Swift & Co.* v. *United States* (1905), the Court ruled that federal prosecutors were well within their power to prosecute the nation's largest meat packers, based in Chicago, for conspiring to fix prices and restrain the sale of cattle still confined to their stockyards. Justice Oliver Wendell Holmes rejected the mechanistic definition of interstate commerce put forth by the meat-packing trusts, which argued that the cattle stockyards did fall upon the continuum of interstate commerce because they had reached a temporary stopping point. Wrote Holmes:

> Commerce among the states is not a technical legal conception, but a practical one, drawn from the course of business. When cattle are sent for sale from a place in one State, with the expectation they will end their transit, after purchase, in another, and when in effect they do so, with only the interruption necessary to find a purchaser at the stock yards, and when this is a typical, constantly recurring course, the current thus existing is a current of commerce among the States, and the purchase of cattle is a part and incident of such commerce.[25]

The Chicago stockyards served as the setting for the Court's most important post-*Gibbons* exposition of the definition of interstate commerce until the constitutional revolution of 1937 completely revamped the scope of congressional commerce power. In *Stafford* v. *Wallace* (1923), the Court considered whether the Packers and Stockyard Act of 1921, passed by Congress after a series of inquiries into the business practices of the major beef and meat-packing companies revealed rampant fraud and price fixing, was an unconstitutional exercise of congressional commerce power. The 1921 law authorized the secretary of agriculture to regulate prices and oversee the business practices of the five largest meat-packing and distribution companies: Armour, Cudahy, Morris, Swift, and Wilson.

Chief Justice William H. Taft used *Stafford* to elucidate further the idea that the relationship between production and distribution in certain industries was uniform, thus making local activities part of a continuous *stream of commerce*. Note how the Court treated the meat-packing industry for the purpose of its Commerce Clause analysis: as a public utility in need of regulation. *Stafford* also stands up better than most of the Court's Commerce Clause decisions prior to 1937. In many ways, Taft's stream-of-commerce doctrine anticipates the approach of the Court after it embraced the New Deal.

The Court's willingness in *Swift* and *Stafford* to broaden the narrow definition it had given interstate commerce in *E.C. Knight* gave Congress much-desired power to exercise some control over the powerful corporate trusts that dominated the national economy. But this modest departure from laissez-faire principles did not occur because the social reformers of the Progressive movement had finally persuaded the Court to temper its use of judicial power to protect corporate America. True, Upton Sinclair had published *The Jungle* in 1906, his riveting, novelized account of the unsanitary conditions of butchering and packing in the Chicago slaughterhouses. *The Jungle* had a critical role in the congressional passage of the Pure Food and Drug Act soon afterward. And numerous other Progressive journalists and lawyers, such as Marie Van Vorst, John Spargo, and Robert Hunter, had offered exposés of their own on topics from child labor to the dire economic conditions of the laboring classes in the factories and fields.[26] Rather, the Court had followed the views of Theodore Roosevelt: Large corporations were an inevitable feature of the new industrial order and should be accepted. The key was to authorize government agencies to regulate industry's activities in the public interest and to encourage journalists to investigate and highlight corporate abuses. Many Progressives considered Roosevelt's views heretical. They earned him a stern rebuke in later books, articles, and public speeches by, among others, Louis Brandeis and Woodrow Wilson.[27]

Dividing the study of constitutional law into specific areas or periods sometimes helps to make sense of its development. Thus we often describe the period from the late 1890s through the late 1930s as an era of laissez-faire constitutionalism because of the firm line the Court took against social reform and economic regulation enacted by Congress and the state legislatures. The Court's repeated invocation of laissez-faire economic

*Conditions in meat-packing plants during the late 1800s and early 1900s were often unsanitary and unsafe, and became a prime target of Progressive movement reformers. Journalistic exposés and Upton Sinclair's novel,* The Jungle, *were quite influential in leading Congress to reform legislation such as the Food and Drug Act of 1906.*
Bettmann/CORBIS.

doctrines and social Darwinism as consistent with the Framers' vision of personal freedom was, more often than not, at odds with the forces of Progressive reform. But the Court also demonstrated its willingness to uphold the exercise of federal and state police power on behalf of economic and social welfare legislation to a degree that, for the sake of convenience, is often ignored.[28]

The Court's jurisprudential path in the era before it embraced the modern administrative welfare state created by the New Deal was one of legal uncertainty. It was an era in which the Court emerged as the nation's referee in the struggle between the dominant nineteenth-century philosophies of natural rights and laissez-faire and the Progressives' faith in the positive state as an instrument of reform. It was an era that tested the Court's adherence to the notion that certain rights existed as a natural condition prior to their creation by the Constitution and ought not to be disturbed. And it was an era that tested the countervailing view, exemplified by the New Deal, that social and economic arrangements were a creation of the political process and subject to modification. This tension culminated in a historic, explosive showdown between the Court and President Franklin Roosevelt, with the scope of congressional commerce power at the heart of this struggle. The result was nothing less than a renovation of the American legal culture.[29]

## United States v. E.C. Knight Co.
### 156 U.S. 1 (1895)

The Industrial Revolution concentrated economic power in the United States in an unprecedented manner. The most common tactic to build market share and control over a particular commodity that arrived with the industrial era was the creation of a trust. A trust was established by transferring large amounts of stock from several companies into a single corporation, thereby establishing joint operations and eliminating competition. The upshot was to make potential competitors corporate partners.

Trusts permeated all major industries by the late 1800s, with U.S. Steel, led by Andrew Carnegie, and Standard Oil, led by John Rockefeller, two of the more famous ones to emerge. By this time six companies held sway over the sugar-refining business, with American Sugar Refining Co. the largest and most powerful. In 1892, American Sugar acquired four of the remaining five sugar refineries, which together accounted for another 33 percent of the nation's refining capacity. One of those companies was the E.C. Knight Co.

In 1890, two years before the American Sugar Refining Co. deal, Congress passed the Sherman Anti-Trust Act, which made it illegal for businesses to contract, combine, or conspire to create a trust or monopoly for the purpose restraining trade or monopolizing interstate commerce. The United States unsuccessfully challenged the stock transaction in the lower federal courts.

The Court's decision was 8 to 1. Chief Justice Fuller delivered the opinion of the Court. Justice Harlan dissented.

▼▲▼

MR. CHIEF JUSTICE FULLER, after stating the case, delivered the opinion of the Court.

By the purchase of the stock of the four Philadelphia refineries, with shares of its own stock, the American Sugar Refining Company acquired nearly complete control of the manufacture of refined sugar within the United States. The bill charged that the contracts under which these purchases were made constituted combinations in restraint of trade, and that, in entering into them, the defendants combined and conspired to restrain the trade and commerce in refined sugar among the several States and with foreign nations, contrary to the act of Congress of July 2, 1890. . . .

The fundamental question is whether, conceding that the existence of a monopoly in manufacture is established by the evidence, that monopoly can be directly suppressed under the act of Congress in the mode attempted by this bill.

It cannot be denied that the power of a State to protect the lives, health, and property of its citizens, and to preserve good order and the public morals, "the power to govern men and things within the limits of its dominion," is a power originally and always belonging to the States, not surrendered by them to the general government nor directly restrained by the Constitution of the United States, and essentially exclusive. The relief of the citizens of each State from the burden of monopoly and the evils resulting from the restraint of trade among such citizens was left with the States to deal with, and this court has recognized their possession of that power even to the extent of holding that an employment or business carried on by private individuals, when it becomes a matter of such public interest and importance as to create a common charge or burden upon the citizen—in other words, when it becomes a practical monopoly to which the citizen is compelled to resort and by means of which a tribute can be exacted from the community—is subject to regulation by state legislative power. On the other hand, the power of Congress to regulate commerce among the several States is also exclusive. The Constitution does not provide that interstate commerce shall be free, but, by the grant of this exclusive power to regulate it, it was left free except as Congress might impose restraints. Therefore it has been determined that the failure of Congress to exercise this exclusive power in any case is an expression of its will that the subject shall be free from restrictions or impositions upon it by the several States, and if a law passed by a State in the exercise of its acknowledged powers comes into conflict with that will, the Congress and the State cannot occupy the position of equal opposing sovereignties, because the Constitution declares its supremacy and that of the laws passed in pursuance thereof, and that which is not supreme must yield to that which is supreme. "Commerce, undoubtedly, is traffic," said Chief Justice Marshall, "but it is something more; it is intercourse. It describes the commercial intercourse between nations and parts of nations in all its branches, and is regulated by prescribing rules for carrying on that intercourse." That which belongs to commerce is within the jurisdiction of the United States, but that which does not belong to commerce is within the jurisdiction of the police power of the State.

The argument is that the power to control the manufacture of refined sugar is a monopoly over a necessary of life, to the enjoyment of which by a large part of the population of the United States interstate commerce is indispensable, and that, therefore, the general government, in the exercise of the power to regulate commerce, may repress such monopoly directly and set aside the instruments which have created it. But this argument cannot be confined to necessaries of life merely, and must include all articles of general consumption. Doubtless the power to control the manufacture of a given thing involves in a certain sense the control of its disposition, but this is a secondary, and not the primary, sense, and although the exercise of that power may result in bringing the operation of commerce into play, it does not control it, and affects it only incidentally and indirectly. Commerce succeeds to manufacture, and is not a part of it. The power to regulate commerce is the power to prescribe the rule by which commerce shall be governed, and is a power independent of the power to suppress monopoly. But it may operate in repression of monopoly whenever that comes within the rules by which commerce is governed or whenever the transaction is itself a monopoly of commerce.

It is vital that the independence of the commercial power and of the police power, and the delimitation between them, however sometimes perplexing, should always be recognized and observed, for while the one furnishes the strongest bond of union, the other is essential to the preservation of the autonomy of the States, as required by our dual form of government, and acknowledged evils, however grave and urgent they may appear to be, had better be borne than the risk be run, in the effort to suppress them, of more serious consequences by resort to expedients of even doubtful constitutionality.

It will be perceived how far-reaching the proposition is that the power of dealing with a monopoly directly may be exercised by the general government whenever interstate or international commerce may be ultimately affected. The regulation of commerce applies to the subjects of commerce, and not to matters of internal police. Contracts to buy, sell, or exchange goods to be transported among the several States, the transportation and its instrumentalities, and articles bought, sold, or exchanged for the purposes of such transit among the States, or put in the way of transit, may be regulated, but this is because they form part of interstate trade or commerce. The fact that an article is manufactured for export to another State does not, of itself, make it an article of interstate commerce, and the intent of the manufacturer does not determine the time when the article or product passes from the control of the State and belongs to commerce. . . .

Contracts, combinations, or conspiracies to control domestic enterprise in manufacture, agriculture, mining, production in all its forms, or to raise or lower prices or wages might unquestionably tend to restrain external as well as domestic trade, but the restraint would be an indirect result, however inevitable and whatever its extent, and such result would not necessarily determine the object of the contract, combination, or conspiracy. . . .

It was in the light of well settled principles that the act of July 2, 1890, was framed. Congress did not attempt thereby to assert the power to deal with monopoly directly as such, or to limit and restrict the rights of corporations created by the States or the citizens of the States in the acquisition, control, or disposition of property, or to regulate or prescribe the price or prices at which such property or the products thereof should be sold, or to make criminal the acts of persons in the acquisition and control of property which the States of their residence or creation sanctioned or permitted. Aside from the provisions applicable where Congress might exercise municipal power, what the law struck at was combinations, contracts, and conspiracies to monopolize trade and commerce among the several States or with foreign nations; but the contracts and acts of the defendants related exclusively to the acquisition of the Philadelphia refineries and the business of sugar refining in Pennsylvania, and bore no direct relation to commerce between the States or with foreign nations. The object was manifestly private gain in the manufacture of the commodity, but not through the control of interstate or foreign commerce. It is true that the bill alleged that the products of these refineries were sold and distributed among the several States, and that all the companies were engaged in trade or commerce with the several States and with foreign nations; but this was no more than to say that trade and commerce served manufacture to fulfil its function. Sugar was refined for sale, and sales were probably made at Philadelphia for consumption, and undoubtedly for resale by the first purchasers throughout Pennsylvania and other States, and refined sugar was also forwarded by the companies to other States for sale. Nevertheless it does not follow that an attempt to monopolize, or the actual monopoly of, the manufacture was an attempt, whether executory or consummated, to monopolize commerce, even though, in order to dispose of the product, the instrumentality of commerce was necessarily invoked. There was nothing in the proofs to indicate any intention to put a restraint upon trade or commerce, and the fact, as we have seen, that trade or commerce might be indirectly affected was not enough to entitle complainants to a decree. The subject matter of the sale was shares of manufacturing stock, and the relief sought was the surrender of property which had already passed and the suppression of the alleged monopoly in manufacture by the restoration of the *status quo* before the transfers; yet the act of Congress only authorized the Circuit Courts to proceed by way of preventing and restraining violations of the act in respect of contracts, combinations, or conspiracies in restraint of interstate or international trade or commerce.

*Decree affirmed.*

Mr. Justice Harlan, dissenting.

The power of Congress covers and protects the absolute freedom of such intercourse and trade among the States as may or must succeed manufacture and precede transportation from the place of purchase. This would seem to be conceded, for the court in the present case expressly declare that, "*contracts to buy,* sell, or exchange goods *to be transported among the several States,* the transportation and its instrumentalities, and articles bought, sold, or exchanged for the purpose of such transit among the States, or put in the way of transit, *may be regulated,* but this is *because they form part of interstate trade or commerce.*" Here is a direct admission—one which the settled doctrines of this court justify—that contracts to buy and the purchasing of goods *to be transported from one State to another,* and transportation, with its instrumentalities, are all *parts* of interstate trade or commerce. Each part of such trade is then under the protection of Congress. And yet, by the opinion and judgment in this case, if I do not misapprehend them, Congress is without power to protect the commercial intercourse that such purchasing necessarily involves against the restraints and burdens arising from the existence of combinations that meet purchasers, from whatever State they come, with the threat—for it is nothing more nor less than a threat—that they *shall not* purchase what they desire to purchase, *except at the prices fixed by such combinations.* A citizen of Missouri has the right to go in person, or send orders, to Pennsylvania and New Jersey for the purpose of purchasing refined sugar. But of what value is that right if he is confronted in those States by a vast *combination* which absolutely controls the price of that article by reason of its having acquired all the sugar refineries in the United

States in order that they may fix prices in their own interest exclusively?

In my judgment, the citizens of the several States composing the Union are entitled, of right, to buy goods in the State where they are manufactured, or in any other State, without being confronted by an illegal combination whose business extends throughout the whole country, which by the law everywhere is an enemy to the public interests, and which prevents such buying, except at prices arbitrarily fixed by it. I insist that the free course of trade among the States cannot coexist with such combinations. When I speak of trade, I mean the buying and selling of articles of every kind that are recognized articles of interstate commerce. Whatever improperly obstructs the free course of interstate intercourse and trade, as involved in the buying and selling of articles to be carried from one State to another, may be reached by Congress under its authority to regulate commerce among the States. The exercise of that authority so as to make trade among the States in all recognized articles of commerce absolutely free from unreasonable or illegal restrictions imposed by combinations is justified by an express grant of power to Congress, and would redound to the welfare of the whole country. I am unable to perceive that any such result would imperil the autonomy of the States, especially as that result cannot be attained through the action of any one State.

Undue restrictions or burdens upon the purchasing of goods, in the market for sale, to be transported to other States cannot be imposed even by a State without violating the freedom of commercial intercourse guaranteed by the Constitution. But if a State within whose limits the business of refining sugar is exclusively carried on may not constitutionally impose burdens upon purchases of sugar *to be transported to other States,* how comes it that combinations of corporations or individuals, within the same State, may not be prevented by the national government from putting unlawful restraints upon the purchasing of that article *to be carried from the State in which such purchases are made?* If the national power is competent to repress State action in restraint of interstate trade as it may be involved in purchases of refined sugar to be transported from one State to another State, surely it ought to be deemed sufficient to prevent unlawful restraints attempted to be imposed by combinations of corporations or individuals upon those identical purchases; otherwise, illegal combinations of corporations or individuals may—so far as national power and interstate commerce are concerned—do with impunity what no State can do.

▼▲▼

## Stafford v. Wallace
258 U.S. 495 (1922)

Stafford and Co. was a commercial meat company that arranged for and shipped cattle to distributors around the country. It sued Secretary of Agriculture Henry Wallace shortly after Congress, in 1921, passed the Packers and Stockyard Act. Additional facts and the background of this case are set out on pp. 302–303.

The Court's decision was 7 to 1. Chief Justice Taft delivered the opinion of the Court. Justice McReynolds dissented. Justice Day did not participate.

MR. CHIEF JUSTICE TAFT delivered the opinion of the Court.

The object to be secured by the act is the free and unburdened flow of live stock from the ranges and farms of the West and the Southwest through the great stockyards and slaughtering centers on the borders of that region, and thence in the form of meat products to the consuming cities of the country in the Middle West and East, or, still, as live stock, to the feeding places and fattening farms in the Middle West or East for further preparation for the market.

The chief evil feared is the monopoly of the packers, enabling them unduly and arbitrarily to lower prices to the shipper, who sells, and unduly and arbitrarily to increase the price to the consumer, who buys. Congress thought that the power to maintain this monopoly was aided by control of the stockyards. Another evil, which it sought to provide against by the act, was exorbitant charges, duplication of commissions, deceptive practices in respect of prices, in the passage of the live stock through the stockyards, all made possible by collusion between the stockyards management and the commission men, on the one hand, and the packers and dealers, on the other. Expenses incurred in the passage through the stockyards necessarily reduce the price received by the shipper, and increase the price to be paid by the consumer. If they be exorbitant or unreasonable, they are an undue burden on the commerce which the stockyards are intended to facilitate. Any unjust or deceptive practice or combination that unduly and directly enhances them is an unjust obstruction to that commerce. The shipper, whose live stock are being cared for and sold in the stockyards market, is ordinarily not present at the sale, but is far away in the West. He is wholly dependent on the commission men. The packers and their agents and the dealers, who are the buyers, are at the elbow of the commission men, and their relations are constant and close. The control that the packers have had in the stockyards by reason of ownership and constant use, the relation of landlord and tenant between the stockyards owner, on the one hand, and the commission men and the dealers, on the other, the power of assignment of pens and other facilities by that owner to commission men and dealers, all create a situation full of opportunity and temptation, to the prejudice of the absent shipper and owner in the neglect of the live stock, in the mala fides of the sale, in the exorbitant prices obtained, and in the unreasonableness of the charges for services rendered.

The stockyards are not a place of rest or final destination. Thousands of head of live stock arrive daily by carload and trainload lots, and must be promptly sold and disposed of and moved out, to give place to the constantly flowing traffic that presses behind. The stockyards are but a throat through which the current flows, and the transactions which occur therein are only incident to this current from the West to the East, and from one state to another. Such transactions cannot be separated from the movement to which they contribute and necessarily take on its character. The commission men are essential in making the sales, without which the flow of the current would be obstructed, and this, whether they are made to packers or dealers. The dealers are essential to the sales to the stock farmers and feeders. The sales are not in this aspect merely local transactions. They create a local change of title, it is true, but they do not stop the flow; they merely change the private interests in the subject of the current, not interfering with, but, on the contrary, being indispensable to, its continuity. The origin of the live stock is in the West; its ultimate destination, known to, and intended by, all engaged in the business, is in the Middle West and East, either as meat products or stock for feeding and fattening. This is the definite and well-understood course of business. The stockyards and the sales are necessary factors in the middle of this current of commerce.

The act, therefore, treats the various stockyards of the country as great national public utilities to promote the flow of commerce from the ranges and farms of the West to the consumers in the East. It assumes that they conduct a business affected by a public use of a national character and subject to national regulation. That it is a business within the power of regulation by legislative action needs no discussion. That has been settled since the case of *Munn v. Illinois* (1877) Nor is there any doubt that in the receipt of live stock by rail and in their delivery by rail the stockyards are an interstate commerce agency. The only question here is whether the business done in the stock-yards, between the receipt of the live stock in the yards and the shipment of them therefrom, is a part of interstate commerce, or is so associated with it as to bring it within the power of national regulation. . . .

As already noted, the word 'commerce,' when used in the act, is defined to be interstate and foreign commerce. Its provisions are carefully drawn to apply only to those practices and obstructions which in the judgment of Congress are likely to affect interstate commerce prejudicially. Thus construed and applied, we think the act clearly within Congressional power and valid.

## The Constitutional Revolution of 1937

In *The Common Law* (1880), Oliver Wendell Holmes wrote that the life of the law was not logic, but experience. Holmes's conception of the judicial function was one in which judges deferred to the reasonableness of legislation and did not substitute their personal policy preferences for those of the legislature. Appointed to the Court by Theodore Roosevelt in 1902, Holmes offered the clearest and most concise explanation of his judicial philosophy in his famous dissent in *Lochner* v. *New York* (1905) (see Chapter 9). There, wrote Holmes, legislatures should be free to express their wishes, "unless it can be said that a rational and fair man necessarily would admit that the statute proposed would infringe fundamental principles" rooted in societal traditions. In *Lochner,* Holmes would have sustained a New York law mandating maximum work hours for retail bakers. The Constitution did not, he wrote, embrace a particular economic theory that prohibited the kind of law enacted by the New York legislature.[30]

Holmes's view stood far from the mainstream jurisprudence of legal formalism that dominated the Court's approach to economic and property rights cases in the late nineteenth and early twentieth centuries. His was a lonely voice on the Court, one that found little sympathy among his colleagues until Louis Brandeis came aboard in 1918. Brandeis, the nation's most famous Progressive lawyer, also rejected the legal formalism of the Court but for altogether different reasons. Like Holmes, Brandeis viewed the law as an instrument of reform, not as a system of apolitical rules intended to protect the "natural" social and economic arrangements of the sta-

tus quo. Although Brandeis and Holmes were considered the Court's leading liberal lights in the pre–New Deal struggle, Brandeis, unlike Holmes, believed that judges had the obligation to sustain laws that were aimed toward the improvement of social and economic conditions because of what those laws tried to accomplish. If liberalism is the correct description of their judicial philosophies, then Holmes's approach is best understood as a procedural liberalism, whereas the concerns that animated Brandeis were substantive, identical to those that formed the basis of his pre-Court public interest activism.[31]

In 1925, Harlan Fiske Stone, who shared their general disdain for the Court's adherence to legal formalism, joined Holmes and Brandeis. Although appointed by President Calvin Coolidge, an economic conservative, Stone wasted no time in gravitating toward the orbit of Holmes and Brandeis. Although closer at first to the skepticism of Holmes, Stone became more and more drawn to the sociological jurisprudence of Brandeis. In fact, Justice Stone's opinion in *United States* v. *Carolene Products* (1938) is most often cited as the jurisprudential rationale for the Court's self-imposed decision to treat economic regulation with deference and elevate civil rights and liberties claims to special protection from the political branches.[32] Holmes, Brandeis, and Stone articulated a powerful alternative to the pre–New Deal Court's formalism, but their views remained, for the most part, confined to the dissenter's role.

The tension between these two distinct theories of constitutional law was evident as far back as *Lochner,* when Holmes first challenged the motives behind the Court's professed commitment to objective rules of constitutional interpretation. Visible as well were the legislative successes of the Progressive movement in Congress and state legislatures from coast to coast. Some of the most ambitious social reform legislation ever enacted—minimum wage, child labor, maximum work-hour laws—came in response to the social and economic inequities caused by mass industrialization. In general, however, the laissez-faire sympathies of the Court triumphed over the forces of Progressive reform. This clash of values—limited government vs. the positive state, legal formalism vs. sociological jurisprudence—was on prominent display in two important cases, *Hammer* v. *Dagenhart* (1918) and *Bailey* v. *Drexel*

*Furniture* (1922). For many scholars these cases offer a clear picture of the differences that existed within the Court and, separately, between the Court and political branches on the power of law as an instrument of social change.

## Prelude: The Child Labor Cases

In 1916, Congress enacted the Owen-Keating law, which prohibited the interstate transport of goods if, within the thirty days prior to the removal of the goods from its place of manufacture, the following conditions were not met: (1) no child under sixteen years old could be employed at a mine or quarry; (2) no children under fourteen years of age could be employed at a mill, cannery, workshop, factory, or manufacturing establishment; and (3) children between fourteen and sixteen who were eligible for employment could not work more than eight hours a day, six days a week, and could not work between the hours of 7 P.M. and 6 A.M.

For a decade prior to enactment of the Owen-Keating law, Progressive organizations, such as the National Consumers League (NCL) and the National Child Labor Committee (NCLC), had lobbied Congress for federal restrictions on child labor. At the same time, the federal government had launched several investigations of its own into the practices and problems associated with child labor. Mills, canneries, mines, and glass works came under special scrutiny by federal investigators for the physical danger such labor inflicted upon children. In the 1900 census, taken before serious efforts to reform child labor practices were underway, approximately 1,750,000 children between the ages of ten and fifteen were employed across the nation.[33]

Child labor was not unique to any particular region. Northern cities had relied on child labor even before the arrival of the Industrial Revolution, a matter that prompted modest reform laws like those of Connecticut and New Hampshire requiring employers to provide a basic education for their child employees. Child labor had always been part of the South's farm-based economy, but the more hazardous forms soon were prevalent in the large mines and textile mills that emerged after the Civil War as industrialism came to the region. Labor laws designed to protect children, however, did not follow. Southern manufacturers argued that children

would be better off in the long run if they learned a trade at an early age. Mill owners in particular claimed that young children offered a distinct advantage to their industry: Learning to spin a textile machine proficiently became more difficult, if not impossible, after the age of sixteen.[34]

In 1907 the United States Department of Labor launched a special investigation into the growing allegations brought by reform groups of abusive labor practices involving women and children. Two years later the federal government released a report detailing the dangerous conditions in which children were often required to work. Particularly revealing were the high death rates of children employed in the mining and glass industries and the lack of financial compensation and medical treatment for children who suffered workplace injuries or fatalities. The South came in for an especially harsh indictment in the Labor Department report. More out of embarrassment than anything else, several Southern states soon adopted laws placing restrictions on child labor. These laws, however, were seldom enforced, as the economic consequences were too severe.[35]

Progressive activists recognized that states dependent upon child labor would never mount a serious campaign to address the social pathologies created by its abuses. Even though the NCLC and the NCL knew that any congressional effort to regulate child labor would be challenged as unconstitutional, they persisted in their crusade in the hope that the courts would consider such legislation an exception to the general restraints on economic regulation then in vogue. Congress justified Owen-Keating as a valid exercise of its power to regulate interstate commerce. But because the law was aimed at labor *practices*, it was much closer, under the Court's interpretation of interstate commerce in *E.C. Knight,* to the *manufacturing* end of the continuum.

Their prediction was correct. Before the law could go into effect on its scheduled date of September 1, 1917, Roland Dagenhart, the father of two sons, twelve and fourteen, who worked in a Charlotte, North Carolina, cotton mill operated by the Fidelity Manufacturing Co., filed suit in federal court to have Owen-Keating declared an unconstitutional use of congressional commerce power. North Carolina was one of the most important textile-producing states in the nation and a major employer of children in manufacturing jobs. An

*Two little girls, both under seven years old, juggling care for their baby sister with their job shucking oysters.*
Photography Collections, University of Maryland, Baltimore County.

*A "carrying in" boy taking a brief break for the camera in an Alexandria, Virginia, glass factory.*
Photography Collections, University of Maryland, Baltimore County.

examination of fifty-three factories in 1918 found that 622 children under the age of fourteen were employed in manufacturing capacities. Of this number, 430 children were also in violation of North Carolina's unenforced child labor law. Ninety-one were under ten years old: forty-three were nine; twenty-eight were eight years old, and twenty were between the ages of five and seven.

Roland Dagenhart, on his factory salary of fifteen dollars per week, did not foot the legal bills in *Hammer v. Dagenhart* (1918). David Clarke, who headed the Executive Committee of Southern Cotton Manufacturers, a regional trade association that had vigorously lobbied against Owen-Keating, carefully selected the Dagenharts and their employer, Fidelity Manufacturing, after a careful screening process for potential litigants. Two elements were critical to Clarke's decision to use the Dagenharts. First, the younger Dagenharts were permitted to work under North Carolina law, but they would encounter restrictions under Owen-Keating that would limit their daily hours, or in the case of thirteen-year-old John, not allow him to work at all. Second, the judge who presided over the federal court that heard the Dagenharts' case, James Boyd, believed that child labor laws were unconstitutional. In every sense of the term, *Dagenhart* was a prime early example of "test case" litigation.[36]

The Dagenharts were never more than pawns in this high-stakes confrontation between a Congress determined to use its power to reform abusive child labor practices and the powerful industries that depended on cheap child labor. Interviewed later about the benefits he received from participating in the lawsuit, Reuben Dagenhart replied, "[w]hy, we got some automobile rides when them big lawyers from the North was down here. Oh yes, and they bought both of us a Coca-Cola! That's all we got out of it." Reuben and his brother, John, continued to work for Fidelity after the Court struck down the law as an unconstitutional exercise of congressional commerce power. For a dollar a day, Reuben worked from 6 A.M. to 7 P.M., and often evenings as well. Although he weighed barely sixty-five pounds, he often carried materials and boxes that weighed twice as much. John worked under similar conditions for less pay than Reuben did, as did their younger sister after she turned twelve.[37]

Constitutional scholars consider the Court's 5-4 decision in *Dagenhart* one its most notorious and ill justified.

For the Court, Justice William Day held that the legislative purpose behind the enactment of Owen-Keating was to prohibit, rather than regulate, child labor. Because, under *E.C. Knight,* labor fell under the definition of manufacturing and not commerce, Congress was without authority under the Commerce Clause to prohibit a matter that the Tenth Amendment reserved to the states. Justice Holmes's dissent alludes to that analysis and highlights several other problems with the Court's rationale in *Dagenhart.* Note how Holmes points out that the Court, by this time, had upheld the exercise of congressional power under the Commerce Clause to ban prostitution and lotteries. It also had upheld the Pure Food and Drugs Act of 1906 and, separately, the power of Congress under its taxing and spending authority to regulate the general welfare for purposes unrelated to revenue.[38] Is Holmes correct when he says that *Dagenhart* cannot be distinguished from other such cases?

Less than a year after the Court handed down *Dagenhart,* Congress passed the Child Labor Tax Law of 1919, which imposed a 10 percent excise tax on the annual net profits of businesses that employed children under the terms prohibited by the statute. Except for the absence of references to the power of Congress to regulate interstate commerce, the terms were identical to those contained in the Owen-Keating Act. Congress offered no illusion on its motives here, which were to circumvent the Court's holding in *Dagenhart* by resorting to its power under Article I, Section 8, to "lay and collect Taxes, Duties, Imposts and Excises, to pay the Debts and provide for the common Defence and general Welfare of the United States." In other words, the Child Labor Tax Law was intended to accomplish the same objective as the law declared unconstitutional in *Dagenhart* without having to resort to a constitutional amendment. Even as the Court defended the laissez-faire principles of American business against the assault of Progressive legislation, the justices upheld the power of Congress to use both its taxing and spending power and the Commerce Clause to exercise police power over noneconomic matters. In fact, the failure of Congress to advance a police power objective under the Commerce Clause has often led it, with success, to turn to its taxing and spending power, and vice versa.

In *Bailey v. Drexel Furniture Co.* (1922), a unanimous Court would have none of the constitutional gamesmanship of Congress and declared the Child Labor Tax Law unconstitutional.[39] Chief Justice William Taft concluded that Congress had sought to impose a direct tax for purposes unrelated to revenue collection and thus was beyond its authority under its taxing and spending authority to regulate child labor practices. The Court's 8-1 opinion, joined by three of the four dissenters in *Dagenhart,* including Holmes and Brandeis, distinguished *Drexel* for earlier decisions in which it upheld the exercise of such congressional power to promote a police power objective. What is it about Taft's analysis of the taxing and spending issue that led Holmes and Brandeis to join the Court's majority? Holmes is an especially curious case, considering his observation in dissent in *Northern Securities Co.* v. *United States* (1904) that he could see "no part of the conduct of life with which on similar principles Congress might not interfere" if one accepted the "the logic of the argument for the Government."[40] Holmes's views, moreover, had prevailed in an important taxing and spending case subsequent to *Dagenhart, United States* v. *Doremus* (1919) involving the constitutionality of federal excise taxes on narcotic drugs. Of *Doremus,* Holmes wrote to the esteemed federal appeals judge Learned Hand, "As to the [Drug Act case], (*between ourselves*) I am tickled at every case of that sort as they seem to me to confirm the ground of my dissent in the Child Labor [*Dagenhart*] case last term. . . . Also, I think the drug act cases rightly decided. In my opinion Congress may have what ulterior motives they please if the act passed in the immediate aspect is within their powers—though personally, were I a legislator I might think it dishonest to use powers in that way."[41]

In all likelihood, Holmes and Brandeis shared Taft's view that *Drexel* was a trumped-up effort to circumvent *Dagenhart* and rejected the tax statute for reasons that had as much to do with protecting the Court's power to resolve constitutional questions as it did with their own legal logic.[42] If Congress rejected the Court on the matter of constitutional interpretation, then Congress must pursue the proper remedial course of action: reversal by constitutional amendment. In 1924, Congress approved just such an amendment that would have given it the power to regulate and prohibit the employment of persons under eighteen years of age. By 1931 only six states had ratified the child labor amendment, but that number jumped to twenty-eight by 1938. By then, however,

momentum on behalf of the amendment topped out amid charges from opponents that it promoted socialism and communism.[43]

In 1938, Congress passed the Fair Labor Standards Act, a comprehensive employment practices law that regulated the hours and wages of employees in manufacturing jobs. On this attempt, however, Congress had every reason to believe that the Court would uphold the sweeping new federal law, even though it prohibited, and not merely regulated, several employment practices, child labor among them. By this time the Constitutional Revolution of 1937 had discredited the legal formalism of the pre–New Deal period that had prevailed in *E.C. Knight,* in *Dagenhart,* and in numerous other cases involving the Commerce Clause and the taxing and spending power of Congress. Dual federalism, the production/distribution rule, "liberty of contract"— all the tools used by the Court to defend the "neutral" state and the principles of economic laissez faire—were by then nothing more than reminders of a tumultuous period in American constitutional development. In 1941 the Court, in *United States* v. *Darby,* upheld the Fair Labor Standards Act as a reasonable exercise of congressional commerce power and, in the process, explicitly overruled *Dagenhart. Darby,* along with *Wickard* v. *Filburn* (1942), both of which are discussed below, completed the transformation of legal rights brought about by the Court's ratification of the New Deal.

---

## Hammer v. Dagenhart
### 247 U.S. 251 (1918)

The facts and background of this case are set out on pp. 309–312.

The Court's decision was 5 to 4. Justice Day delivered the opinion of the Court. Justice Holmes filed a dissent, which was joined by Justices McKenna, Brandeis, and Clarke.

▼▲▼

MR. JUSTICE DAY delivered the opinion of the Court.

The controlling question for decision is: is it within the authority of Congress in regulating commerce among the States to prohibit the transportation in interstate commerce of manufactured goods, the product of a factory in which, within thirty days prior to their removal therefrom, children under the age of fourteen have been employed or permitted to work, or children between the ages of fourteen and sixteen years have been employed or permitted to work more than eight hours in any day, or more than six days in any week, or after the hour of seven o'clock P.M. or before the hour of 6 o'clock A.M.?

The power essential to the passage of this act, the Government contends, is found in the commerce clause of the Constitution, which authorizes Congress to regulate commerce with foreign nations and among the States. . . .

[I]t is insisted that adjudged cases in this court establish the doctrine that the power to regulate given to Congress incidentally includes the authority to prohibit the movement of ordinary commodities, and therefore that the subject is not open for discussion. The cases demonstrate the contrary. They rest upon the character of the particular subjects dealt with, and the fact that the scope of governmental authority, state or national, possessed over them is such that the authority to prohibit is as to them but the exertion of the power to regulate.

The first of these cases is *Champion* v. *Ames*, the so-called *Lottery Case*, in which it was held that Congress might pass a law having the effect to keep the channels of commerce free from use in the transportation of tickets used in the promotion of lottery schemes. In *Hipolite Egg Co.* v. *United States*, 220 U.S. 45, this court sustained the power of Congress to pass the Pure Food and Drug Act, which prohibited the introduction into the States by means of interstate commerce of impure foods and drugs. In *Hoke* v. *United States*, this court sustained the constitutionality of the so-called "White Slave Traffic Act," whereby the transportation of a woman in interstate commerce for the purpose of prostitution was forbidden. . . .

In each of these instances, the use of interstate transportation was necessary to the accomplishment of harmful results. In other words, although the power over interstate transportation was to regulate, that could only be accomplished by prohibiting the use of the facilities of interstate commerce to effect the evil intended.

This element is wanting in the present case. The thing intended to be accomplished by this statute is the denial of the facilities of interstate commerce to those manufacturers in the States who employ children within the prohibited ages. The act, in its effect, does not regulate transportation among the States, but aims to standardize the ages at which children may be employed in mining and manufacturing within the States. The goods shipped are, of themselves, harmless. The act permits them to be freely shipped after thirty days from the time of their removal from the factory. When offered for shipment, and before transportation begins, the labor of their production is

over, and the mere fact that they were intended for interstate commerce transportation does not make their production subject to federal control under the commerce power. . . .

It is further contended that the authority of Congress may be exerted to control interstate commerce in the shipment of child-made goods because of the effect of the circulation of such goods in other States where the evil of this class of labor has been recognized by local legislation, and the right to thus employ child labor has been more rigorously restrained than in the State of production. In other words, that the unfair competition thus engendered may be controlled by closing the channels of interstate commerce to manufacturers in those States where the local laws do not meet what Congress deems to be the more just standard of other States.

There is no power vested in Congress to require the States to exercise their police power so as to prevent possible unfair competition. Many causes may cooperate to give one State, by reason of local laws or conditions, an economic advantage over others. The Commerce Clause was not intended to give to Congress a general authority to equalize such conditions. In some of the States, laws have been passed fixing minimum wages for women, in others, the local law regulates the hours of labor of women in various employments. Business done in such States may be at an economic disadvantage when compared with States which have no such regulations; surely, this fact does not give Congress the power to deny transportation in interstate commerce to those who carry on business where the hours of labor and the rate of compensation for women have not been fixed by a standard in use in other States and approved by Congress.

The grant of power to Congress over the subject of interstate commerce was to enable it to regulate such commerce, and not to give it authority to control the States in their exercise of the police power over local trade and manufacture.

The grant of authority over a purely federal matter was not intended to destroy the local power always existing and carefully reserved to the States in the Tenth Amendment to the Constitution. . . .

In interpreting the Constitution, it must never be forgotten that the Nation is made up of States to which are entrusted the powers of local government. And to them and to the people the powers not expressly delegated to the National Government are reserved. The power of the States to regulate their purely internal affairs by such laws as seem wise to the local authority is inherent, and has never been surrendered to the general government. To sustain this statute would not be, in our judgment, a recognition of the lawful exertion of congressional authority over interstate commerce, but would sanction an invasion by the federal power of the control of a matter purely local in its character, and over which no authority has been delegated to Congress in conferring the power to regulate commerce among the States. . . .

In our view, the necessary effect of this act is, by means of a prohibition against the movement in interstate commerce of ordinary commercial commodities, to regulate the hours of labor of children in factories and mines within the States, a purely state authority. Thus, the act in a twofold sense is repugnant to the Constitution. It not only transcends the authority delegated to Congress over commerce, but also exerts a power as to a purely local matter to which the federal authority does not extend. The far-reaching result of upholding the act cannot be more plainly indicated than by pointing out that, if Congress can thus regulate matters entrusted to local authority by prohibition of the movement of commodities in interstate commerce, all freedom of commerce will be at an end, and the power of the States over local matters may be eliminated, and, thus, our system of government be practically destroyed.

MR. JUSTICE HOLMES, dissenting.

The single question in this case is . . . whether the exercise of its otherwise constitutional power by Congress can be pronounced unconstitutional because of its possible reaction upon the conduct of the States in a matter upon which I have admitted that they are free from direct control. I should have thought that that matter had been disposed of so fully as to leave no room for doubt. I should have thought that the most conspicuous decisions of this Court had made it clear that the power to regulate commerce and other constitutional powers could not be cut down or qualified by the fact that it might interfere with the carrying out of the domestic policy of any State. . . .

The notion that prohibition is any less prohibition when applied to things now thought evil I do not understand. But if there is any matter upon which civilized countries have agreed—far more unanimously than they have with regard to intoxicants and some other matters over which this country is now emotionally aroused—it is the evil of premature and excessive child labor. I should have thought that, if we were to introduce our own moral conceptions where in my opinion they do not belong, this was preeminently a case for upholding the exercise of all its powers by the United States.

But I had thought that the propriety of the exercise of a power admitted to exist in some cases was for the consid-

eration of Congress alone, and that this Court always had disavowed the right to intrude its judgment upon questions of policy or morals. It is not for this Court to pronounce when prohibition is necessary to regulation—if it ever may be necessary—to say that it is permissible as against strong drink, but not as against the product of ruined lives.

The act does not meddle with anything belonging to the States. They may regulate their internal affairs and their domestic commerce as they like. But when they seek to send their products across the state line, they are no longer within their rights. If there were no Constitution and no Congress, their power to cross the line would depend upon their neighbors. Under the Constitution, such commerce belongs not to the States, but to Congress to regulate. It may carry out its views of public policy whatever indirect effect they may have upon the activities of the States. Instead of being encountered by a prohibitive tariff at her boundaries, the State encounters the public policy of the United States, which it is for Congress to express. The public policy of the United States is shaped with a view to the benefit of the nation as a whole. If, as has been the case within the memory of men still living, a State should take a different view of the propriety of sustaining a lottery from that which generally prevails, I cannot believe that the fact would require a different decision from that reached in *Champion* v. *Ames*. Yet, in that case, it would be said with quite as much force as in this that Congress was attempting to intermeddle with the State's domestic affairs. The national welfare, as understood by Congress, may require a different attitude within its sphere from that of some self-seeking State. It seems to me entirely constitutional for Congress to enforce its understanding by all the means at its command.

## Bailey v. Drexel Furniture Co.
### 259 U.S. 20 (1922)

The facts and background of this case are set out on pp. 310–312.

The decision was 8 to 1. Chief Justice Taft delivered the opinion of the Court. Justice Clarke dissented.

MR. CHIEF JUSTICE TAFT delivered the opinion of the Court.

This case presents the question of the constitutional validity of the Child Labor Tax Law. The plaintiff below, the

Drexel Furniture Company, is engaged in the manufacture of furniture in the Western District of North Carolina. On September 20, 1921, it received a notice from Bailey, United States Collector of Internal Revenue for the District, that it had been assessed $6,312.79 for having during the taxable year 1919 employed and permitted to work in its factory a boy under fourteen years of age, thus incurring the tax of ten percent on its net profits for that year. The Company paid the tax under protest, and after rejection of its claim for a refund, brought this suit. . . .

The law is attacked on the ground that it is a regulation of the employment of child labor in the States—an exclusively state function under the Federal Constitution and within the reservations of the Tenth Amendment. It is defended on the ground that it is a mere excise tax levied by the Congress of the United States under its broad power of taxation conferred by Section 8, Article I, of the Federal Constitution. We must construe the law and interpret the intent and meaning of Congress from the language of the act. The words are to be given their ordinary meaning unless the context shows that they are differently used. Does this law impose a tax with only that incidental restraint and regulation which a tax must inevitably involve? Or does it regulate by the use of the so-called tax as a penalty? If a tax, it is clearly an excise. If it were an excise on a commodity or other thing of value, we might not be permitted under previous decisions of this court to infer solely from its heavy burden that the act intends a prohibition, instead of a tax. But this act is more. It provides a heavy exaction for a departure from a detailed and specified course of conduct in business. That course of business is that employers shall employ in mines and quarries children of an age greater than sixteen years; in mills and factories, children of an age greater than fourteen years, and shall prevent children of less than sixteen years in mills and factories from working more than eight hours a day or six days in the week. If an employer departs from this prescribed course of business, he is to pay to the Government one-tenth of his entire net income in the business for a full year. The amount is not to be proportioned in any degree to the extent or frequency of the departures, but is to be paid by the employer in full measure whether he employs five hundred children for a year, or employs only one for a day. Moreover, if he does not know the child is within the named age limit, he is not to pay; that is to say, it is only where he knowingly departs from the prescribed course that payment is to be exacted. *Scienter* is associated with penalties, not with taxes. The employer's factory is to be subject to inspection at any time not only by the taxing officers of the Treasury, the Department normally charged with the collection of taxes, but also by the Secretary of Labor and his subordinates, whose normal function is the advancement and protection of the welfare of the workers. In the light of these features of the act, a court must be blind not to see that the so-called tax is imposed to stop the employment of children within the age limits prescribed. Its prohibitory and regulatory effect and purpose are palpable. All others can see and understand this. How can we properly shut our minds to it?

It is the high duty and function of this court in cases regularly brought to its bar to decline to recognize or enforce seeming laws of Congress, dealing with subjects not entrusted to Congress, but left or committed by the supreme law of the land to the control of the States. We cannot avoid the duty even though it require us to refuse to give effect to legislation designed to promote the highest good. The good sought in unconstitutional legislation is an insidious feature because it leads citizens and legislators of good purpose to promote it without thought of the serious breach it will make in the ark of our covenant or the harm which will come from breaking down recognized standards. In the maintenance of local self-government, on the one hand, and the national power, on the other, our country has been able to endure and prosper for near a century and a half.

Out of a proper respect for the acts of a coordinate branch of the Government, this court has gone far to sustain taxing acts as such, even though there has been ground for suspecting from the weight of the tax it was intended to destroy its subject. But, in the act before us, the presumption of validity cannot prevail, because the proof of the contrary is found on the very face of its provisions. Grant the validity of this law, and all that Congress would need to do, hereafter, in seeking to take over to its control anyone of the great number of subjects of public interest, jurisdiction of which the States have never parted with, and which are reserved to them by the Tenth Amendment, would be to enact a detailed measure of complete regulation of the subject and enforce it by a so-called tax upon departures from it. To give such magic to the word "tax" would be to break down all constitutional limitation of the powers of Congress and completely wipe out the sovereignty of the States.

The difference between a tax and a penalty is sometimes difficult to define, and yet the consequences of the distinction in the required method of their collection often are important. Where the sovereign enacting the law has power to impose both tax and penalty, the difference between revenue production and mere regulation may be immaterial, but not so when one sovereign can impose a tax only, and the power of regulation rests in another. Taxes are occasionally imposed in the discretion of the legislature on proper subjects with the primary motive of obtaining revenue from them and with the incidental motive of discouraging them by making their continuance onerous. They do not lose their character as taxes because of the incidental motive. But there comes a time in the extension of the penalizing features of the so-called tax when it loses its character as such and becomes a mere penalty with the characteristics of regulation and punishment. Such is the case in the law before us. Although Congress does not invalidate the contract of employment or expressly declare that the employment within the mentioned ages is illegal, it does exhibit its intent practically to achieve the latter result by adopting the criteria of wrongdoing and imposing its principal consequence on those who transgress its standard.

The case before us cannot be distinguished from that of *Hammer v. Dagenhart* (1918). Congress there enacted a law to prohibit transportation in interstate commerce of goods made at a factory in which there was employment of children within the same ages and for the same number of hours a day and days in a week as are penalized by the act in this case. . . .

In the case at the bar, Congress in the name of a tax which, on the face of the act, is a penalty seeks to do the same thing, and the effort must be equally futile.

The analogy of the *Dagenhart* Case is clear. The congressional power over interstate commerce is, within its proper scope, just as complete and unlimited as the congressional power to tax, and the legislative motive in its exercise is just as free from judicial suspicion and inquiry. Yet when Congress threatened to stop interstate commerce in ordinary and necessary commodities, unobjectionable as subjects of transportation, and to deny the same to the people of a State in order to coerce them into compliance with Congress' regulation of state concerns, the court said this was not, in fact, regulation of interstate commerce, but rather that of State concerns, and was invalid. So here, the so-called tax is a penalty to coerce people of a State to act as Congress wishes them to act in respect of a matter completely the business of the state government under the Federal Constitution.

For the reason given, we must hold the Child Labor Tax Law invalid, and the judgment of the District Court is
*Affirmed.*

▼▲▼

## When Worlds Collide: The Court, the New Deal, and the Commerce Clause

Prior to Franklin Roosevelt's election in 1932, the federal government "had been a remote authority with a limited range of activity. It operated the postal system, improved rivers and harbors, maintained armed forces on a scale fearsome only to banana republics, and performed other functions of which the average citizen was hardly aware."[44] That all changed with the arrival of the New Deal. In the first one hundred days of his presidency, Franklin Roosevelt signed over fifteen laws that vastly increased the power of the federal government to regulate the economic affairs of the nation. Laws such as the National Industrial Relations Act (NIRA), which established an unprecedented relationship between corporate trade associations and government agencies to establish economic controls on problem industries, and the Agricultural Adjustment Act, which created massive subsidies for staple farmers, were bold, ambitious, and unprecedented experiments in economic regulation. Congress also enacted numerous laws to assist the long-term unemployed and ventured, for the first time, into public power development and regional planning when it created the Tennessee Valley Authority.[45]

The New Deal legislative locomotive did not stop there. Over the next two years, Congress enacted one revolutionary measure after another. These included the National Labor Relations Act, which guaranteed labor unions the right to bargain collectively with their employers, the National Bituminous Coal Conservation Act, which imposed wage and price controls on the coal industry, and the Social Security Act, which created a complex system of retirement and death benefits. The elite brain trust of lawyers and policy planners brought to Washington by President Roosevelt to rejuvenate the nation's economic health knew full well that the ambitious legislative agenda of the New Deal amounted to nothing less than a frontal assault on the established constitutional order. By embracing an experimental, pragmatic approach to law that emphasized its instrumental qualities, the New Deal lawyers openly rejected the legal formalism of their laissez-faire adversaries. This clash of legal cultures all but invited the constitutional crisis that would be played out in full public view from 1934 to 1937.

Although the New Deal did create and legitimize the administrative welfare state, the movement contained a number of conflicting strands. The Roosevelt administration sought to promote greater economic democratization by aggressively enforcing antitrust laws and capping the profits of industries believed to operate in the public trust. But the New Deal also created state-protected monopolies and, as epitomized by the NIRA, authorized corporate trade associations to write industry codes and regulation. The New Deal brain trust identified certain "essential" industries, like agriculture and banking, and protected them from the adverse consequences of competition through price supports and subsidies. As you will see, some of this legislative innovation was too much even for the justices who embraced the legal assumptions of the New Deal. But the most important thread that connected these sometimes disparate strands remained intact, and that was the constitutional premise upon which the New Deal was based: Legal rights were a function of political choices and not, to paraphrase Justice Holmes, some "brooding omnipresence in the sky."[46]

Such a view was crystal clear in President Roosevelt's own description of the New Deal. Economic arrangements and their social consequences, he observed, were not accidental. Said Roosevelt: "We must lay hold of the fact that economic laws are not made by nature. They are made by human beings." And no president before Roosevelt dared to acknowledge that poverty was the result of an economic system created and maintained by the process of politics, rather than the outcome of some sort of predetermined, natural condition. This fundamental tenet of the New Deal was set forth in the preamble to the 1932 Norris-La Guardia Act: "Whereas under prevailing economic conditions, developed with the aid of governmental authority for owners of property to organize in the corporate and other forms of ownership association, the individual worker is actually helpless to exercise liberty of contract and to protect his freedom of labor, and thereby to obtain acceptable terms and conditions of employment. . . ."[47]

In other words, the New Deal punctured the myth of laissez faire as the natural economic order of the Constitution. Economic markets do not just exist; they are created by law, and it is the law that establishes who can do what to whom. Failure to abide by the estab-

lished legal rules of the economic marketplace permits aggrieved parties to turn to the courts. Not even the purest of laissez-faire economic arrangements can avoid this basic fact of political organization. Government, if so motivated, had the right to address the social and economic problems of the people it was entrusted to represent, to respond, in Holmes's phrase, to the "felt necessities" of the time. The Constitution should be flexible enough to accommodate this merger of pragmatism with legal principles. If such flexibility required the adoption of a method to decide cases that was more pragmatic than formal to support the New Deal's experimental approach to problem-solving, then so be it.[48]

But in January 1935 the Court issued the first of eight major decisions over the next sixteen-month period that decimated the New Deal. In *Panama Refining Co. v. Ryan* (1935), the Court, 8 to 1, struck down a key provision of the NIRA. This section authorized the president to prohibit the transportation in interstate commerce of oil or petroleum-related products that exceeded the legal limitations imposed by states to prop up oil prices. The Court ruled this delegation of congressional power to the executive branch was unconstitutional.[49] *Panama Refining Co.* was the first case in which the Court found a congressional statute to violate the nondelegation rule. Four months later a unanimous Court, in *Schechter Poultry Corp. v. United States* (1935), discussed in Chapter 4, invalidated the NIRA in its entirety on the same grounds. The Court also added that Congress had no power under the Commerce Clause to regulate what the justices deemed matters of intrastate commerce, here the establishment of various industry-prescribed codes to regulate the New York City poultry industry.[50] Chief Justice Charles Evans Hughes, by no means a doctrinaire conservative, rejected the federal government's argument that the codes applied to activities within the stream of commerce. The matters in question—minimum wage and maximum work hour rules, health regulations, and sanitation requirements—had no more than an incidental effect on interstate transactions. *Stafford,* underscored by the production/distribution rule of *E.C. Knight,* still carried the day.

The Roosevelt administration did not anticipate this double blow to the constitutional solar plexus of the New Deal. In 1934 the Court had handed the forces of Progressive reform two major victories that appeared to

## THE COURT-PACKING PLAN OF 1937

### *President Roosevelt Confronts the Nine Old Men*

From the 1890s until the Constitutional Revolution of 1937, the Court's defense of the economic interests of American business made it a consistent target of populist and progressive reformers. While the Court had upheld some modest limitations on unfair business practices and exploitative economic arrangements, it remained steadfast in its resistance to the welfare state, even after the Depression had become a cold and persistent fact of life. Franklin Roosevelt took office in January 1933 knowing full well that the Court might serve as the barricade against the legislative march of the New Deal. Still, he held out hope that a majority of justices might see the need to relax the Court's stand because of the economic and social chaos that gripped the nation.

The government lawyers charged with navigating this constitutional minefield did what they could to avoid a test case on the admittedly far-reaching and experimental New Deal legislative agenda. As a result, the Court did not rule on a New Deal statute until January 1935. Until then the justices, in *Home Building & Loan Association v. Blaisdell* (1934) and *Nebbia v. New York* (1934), gave the Roosevelt administration hope that they would not stand in the way of the New Deal. In each case the Court upheld state laws against economic rights claims. Leaving nothing to chance, talk began early among Roosevelt and his advisors about how to deal with the Court if, as they all believed, it changed its tune on the New Deal.

Roosevelt received no chance during his first term to make an appointment to the Court, even though the average age of the justices was seventy-two. By 1932 the Court had divided into two distinct blocs on the merits of economic regulation, which were buffeted in the middle by two key swing votes. The Court's conservatives were known as the "Four Horsemen," a term borrowed from the great sportswriter Ring Lardner's description of the legendary offensive backfield that powered the Notre Dame football team in the 1920s. To the Four Horsemen—George Sutherland, James McReynolds, Pierce Butler, and Willis Van Devanter—economic and property rights were absolute. Forming their liberal opposition were Louis Brandeis, Benjamin Cardozo, whom President Hoover had appointed in 1932 to replace the Progressive acolyte, Oliver Wendell Holmes, and Harlan Fiske Stone. Camped in the middle were moderates Owen Roberts and the chief justice, Charles Evans Hughes. Roberts, the more conservative of the two, had cast the key votes in *Blaisdell* and *Nebbia*. In *Nebbia*, Roberts had gone so far as to write, "This court from the early days affirmed that the power to promote the general welfare is inherent in government."

On January 7, 1935, the Court fired its first torpedo against the New Deal, scoring a direct hit in *Panama Refining Co. v. Ryan* by declaring the "hot oil" provisions of the NIRA unconstitutional. Even though the Roosevelt administration won several important cases over the next couple of months, the president, convinced the worst was yet to come, was still exploring drastic steps to curtail the Court's power over the New Deal. The need for the president's brain trust to develop a plan to curtail the Court's power over the New Deal accelerated later that May when the Court, divided 5 to 4, struck down the Railway Retirement Act of 1934. Justice Roberts cast the crucial fifth vote in *Railroad Retirement Board v. Alton Railroad Co.*, a pattern that continued until his defection to the Court's liberal wing in 1937.

Two weeks later the Court handed the Roosevelt administration three major defeats in a single day, one that later became known as "Black Monday." The most devastating of these rulings was *Schechter Poultry Corp.* v. *United States,* in which the Court declared the *entire* NIRA, the heart of the New Deal's industrial recovery program, unconstitutional. Roosevelt had remained publicly silent about the Court's opposition to the New Deal, but the impact of Black Monday was simply too much. Before a room full of reporters gathered to hear his reaction to *Schechter,* the president declared: "We have been relegated to the horse-and-buggy definition of interstate commerce." The president's comment appeared on the front page of every major newspaper in the country and fueled the slowly building public backlash. More and more, the public viewed the Court as the personal bodyguard of the rich and powerful business interests fortunate enough to escape the ravages of the Depression.

On orders from the Roosevelt administration, the Justice Department continued to examine the options available to weaken the Court's stranglehold over the New Deal. The most popular idea floating around at this point was the submission of a constitutional amendment that either diminished the Court's power or explicitly made the New Deal constitutional. Several influential advisors close to the president opposed this maneuver as an unwise alteration of the constitutional system. The most prominent of these dissenters were Felix Frankfurter and his "hot dogs," the nickname given to the handpicked attorneys and policy planners that the future Supreme Court justice had sent to Washington from his perch at the Harvard law school to staff the New Deal agencies. Something, however, was needed and needed soon as the Court, on January 6, 1936, declared the Agricultural Adjustment Act unconstitutional, a law second only in importance to the NIRA in the architecture of the New Deal design. The Court's decision in *United States* v. *Butler* (1936) stimulated even more public criticism than *Schechter Poultry* had. Letters poured into the White House demanding that some action be taken against the Court. Suggestions included mandatory retirement upon reaching the age of seventy, impeachment of anti–New Deal justices, and limits on years of service. A common theme in the criticism directed at the Court was that the justices were too old and out of touch with the Depression's toll upon the nation.

President Roosevelt had remained silent on the New Deal defeats since his post-*Schechter* press conference, letting the public make his case against the Court for him. Within the Roosevelt administration, however, Justice Stone's dissent in *Butler* had convinced the New Deal strategists that the problem was not the Constitution, but the Court. Furthermore, a constitutional amendment to deal with the problem had started to appear less and less attractive. Although the large pro–New Deal majorities in both the House and Senate would have given Roosevelt anything he wanted to diminish the Court's power, no guarantee was available that the states would follow suit. But more important was this simple fact: The administration wanted to address the nation's economic crisis now, not wait in limbo for the ratification process to run its course.

Before Roosevelt went public with his Court-packing plan in 1937, Congress introduced several other plans to curb the Court's power, most of which would have created judicial vacancies for the president to fill. Even former president Herbert Hoover was moved to call for a constitutional amendment to restore the power of the states as a result of the Court's intransigence to state measures on wage and price controls. The decision that prompted Hoover's comment, *Tipaldo* v. *New York* (1936), which invalidated a New York minimum wage law, came on the heels of several other split anti–New Deal decisions in the winter and spring of 1936. Justice Roberts provided the crucial fifth vote to the Four Horsemen in these cases, leaving the impression with the New Deal brain trust that his swing vote was now firmly ensconced with the Court's conservatives.

After *Tipaldo* the Roosevelt administration abandoned any hope of avoiding a direct confrontation with the Court. For the first time since his *Schechter* press conference, the president spoke out on the constitutional crisis created by the Court's resistance to the New Deal and various state reform measures. The Court, said Roosevelt, had created a "no-man's land" that prohibited the exercise of federal and state power on behalf of economic reform. After making his comments, Roosevelt left the public to judge the Court's decisions. During the presidential campaign of 1936,

"All the News That's
Fit to Print."

# The New York Times.

LATE CITY EDITION
Generally fair, slightly colder today.
Tomorrow fair with rising
temperature.
Temperature Yesterday—Max., 46; Min., 36

VOL. LXXXVI.....No. 28,900.

Entered as Second-Class Matter,
Postoffice, New York, N. Y.

NEW YORK, WEDNESDAY, MARCH 10, 1937.

P   TWO CENTS In New York
City.

THREE CENTS Elsewhere Except
Within 200 Miles.

FOUR CENTS Elsewhere Except
in 7th and 8th Postal Zones.

## CHILD LABOR BILL DIES IN ASSEMBLY; VOTE IS 102 TO 42

## CHRYSLER IS FIRM ON 'CLOSED SHOP'; PLANTS STILL HELD

Company Talk With Union Fails

### 'Stuck in Mud' Striker Insists Town Fix Road

By the Associated Press.

JOLIET, Ill., March 9.—Cheek-nipping cold harassed Frank Fe-ferlin today but he was too hot under the collar to quit the na-tion's only "stuck in the mud" strike.

For the second day he sat stead-fastly in his car—stalled in mire

## ARMS SHIP TRACED BY BETRAYAL HERE; SINKING IS DENIED

Mar Cantabrico's Route, Code

## ROOSEVELT ASKS THAT NATION TRUST HIM IN COURT MOVE; RESENTS 'PACKING' CHARGES

*President Roosevelt decried the Court's "horse and buggy" conception of interstate commerce after it struck down the constitutionality of the National Industrial Recovery Act, the heart of the early New Deal legislative agenda.*
© The New York Times.

Roosevelt remained silent on the Court, emphasizing instead the successes and, ever so slyly, the would-be successes of the New Deal.

In November 1936, Roosevelt achieved the greatest presidential electoral landslide in the history of two-party competition, winning forty-six of forty-eight states. Aware that the Court stood ready to rule on several important federal and state economic relief programs, Roosevelt stepped up the pace on possible solutions to the stalemate between the Court and the New Dealers. Buoyed by the election results and confident that Congress would offer him unconditional support, the president again ordered the Justice Department to explore possible countermeasures. In the interim, Judge William Denman, who had known the president since childhood, had lobbied Roosevelt to increase the number of federal judges. This route would not only ease the burden on the courts created by the endless stream of constitutional challenges to the New Deal but also allow the president to appoint more pro–New Deal judges.

Another suggestion came forth from Edward Corwin, a prominent constitutional scholar who taught at Princeton. Corwin had opened a dialogue with Attorney General Homer Cummings, who had contacted the professor after he had published an article suggesting that no federal judge be allowed to serve after seventy years of age. Corwin later passed along a suggestion to Cummings that came from one of his academic colleagues: that the president should have the power to appoint new justices for every sitting justice over seventy so that the younger members would always outnumber the older ones. Better yet

was the fact that neither idea required a constitutional amendment, since Congress retained the power to establish federal courts and appoint federal judges. Cummings knew that a similar idea had been offered in 1913 by President Wilson's attorney general, James McReynolds, now one of the Four Horsemen the New Dealers wanted off the Court. McReynolds had suggested that the president should be allowed to appoint one new federal judge for every judge who had reached seventy years of age and had ten years of service, with the younger judge's vote counting for more. His proposal did not include the Supreme Court.

Cummings combined the suggestions of Corwin and Denman and presented them as one plan to President Roosevelt on December 26, 1936. The president was delighted. He and Cummings agreed that the plan offered a legitimate proposal to reform the federal courts and would not be seen as an outright attack on the Court. Still, Roosevelt insisted on keeping the Court-packing plan absolutely confidential. Justice Department officials who had been requested to compile data on the courts' workload and personnel were not even told the purpose of their work. Such an approach was uncharacteristic of Roosevelt, who normally sought the counsel of numerous subordinates and aides when planning a bold political initiative. Even the speechwriters selected to help draft his address to the nation announcing the Court-packing plan were sworn to secrecy. Congress and his cabinet, save for Cummings, were kept in the dark. Political scientist Michael Nelson has noted that the Court-packing plan was the one major initiative undertaken by Roosevelt on behalf of the New Deal in which he did not bring his formidable political skills to bear in appropriate fashion.

President Roosevelt's Court-packing announcement on February 5, 1937, generated a massive outpouring of letters and telegrams to Congress and the White House both supporting and criticizing the initiative. The large majorities of New Deal Democrats in the House and Senate made passage of the president's plan, upon first blush, seem likely. Several prominent Democrats quickly came out in favor of the plan, but it soon became clear that the key selling point, the crowded docket-age connection, was a monumental blunder. On March 9, 1937, the president dropped the political facade and stated his true motives. The people who had reelected him in record numbers did not want the Court to block the economic reforms of the New Deal. Thus he was prepared to take any action to clear that hurdle. This time, reaction among Democratic legislators and the public was almost purely negative. Congressional opposition to the plan soon emerged with substantial force, even among the Democrats who were most closely allied with the president. Still, Roosevelt would not bend. And his usually flawless political instincts deserted him once again in the face of what was undoubtedly a losing battle, as the president found himself sparring with Democrats while Republicans sat on the sidelines in an amused silence.

Some critics suggested that Roosevelt had confused the election returns with a totalitarian mandate, a particularly stinging criticism as the shadow of Hitler and Mussolini continued to cast its darkness over Europe. Louis Brandeis, then eighty years old, was particularly offended by the president's implication that senior citizens were not capable of serving on the Court. He arranged through Senator Burton Wheeler (D–Mont.) to have Chief Justice Hughes write a letter to the Senate Judiciary Committee informing it that the Court was up to speed on its workload and did not need the president's help. Hughes's letter was quite diplomatic and even included statistics to prove his point. The implication, however, was clear: The Court believed the president's initiative was a clear violation of the constitutional arrangement of separation of powers and he had better back off.

On March 29 the Court handed down *West Coast Hotel* v. *Parrish,* a 5-4 decision that saw the chief justice and Justice Roberts join the Court's pro–New Deal wing, this time for good. The Constitutional Revolution of 1937 had begun, with Roberts's abandonment of the Four Horsemen quickly dubbed the "switch in time that saved nine." Scholars are still unsure what motivated Roberts to change his position. One common explanation, that Roberts was intimidated by the Court-packing plan, is a stretch. In December 1936, after the election but before Roosevelt's announcement of his plan, Roberts had voted in the *West Coast Hotel* conference to uphold the Washington State minimum wage law. Roberts never commented on his reasons for the 1937 switch. When later asked how judges make up or change their minds, Roberts responded: "Maybe the breakfast he had has something to do with it."

Roosevelt's closest advisors encouraged the president to abandon the Court-packing plan after the Court's turnaround. The president, undeterred, continued to press ahead. Roberts had jumped ship before, the president responded, and he would do it again. Aides pointed out that Roberts's decision to join *West Coast Hotel* was basically an admission that his decision in *Tipaldo* was wrong, since the two cases were indistinguishable. Still, Roosevelt insisted on going ahead. Justice Willis Van Devanter's announcement on May 18 that he would retire at the term's end did nothing to dissuade the president. In June and July the Senate again took up a modified Court-packing plan submitted by the administration, with Majority Leader Joseph Robinson (D–Ark.) pushing his colleagues to hand the president some sort of modest victory. Hugo Black, senator from Alabama, who supported the president's original initiative, also worked hard on behalf of the plan.

On July 14, Joseph Robinson was found dead on the floor of his small rented apartment in the Methodist Building, which was situated between the Capitol plaza and the Supreme Court, the victim of an apparent heart attack. The Court-packing plan's hopes died right along with him. On July 22 the full Senate returned the bill proposing the plan back to the judiciary committee, from which it never emerged. Roosevelt could claim that Congress never actually defeated his proposal, but no amount of double talk could overcome what was apparent to everyone else: The president had suffered a severe setback, and the Court-packing plan was dead in the water.

One by one, the remaining Four Horsemen resigned from the Court, leaving Roosevelt the chance to remake almost in its entirety the body that had once so frustrated him. By 1943 the president, re-elected to a third term in 1940, had appointed seven of the nine justices serving on the Court. Having lost the battle, Roosevelt won the war. The Court was now his for the ages.

## References

Irons, Peter H. *The New Deal Lawyers.* Princeton, N.J.: Princeton University Press, 1982.

Leuchtenburg, William E. *The Supreme Court Reborn: The Constitutional Revolution in the Age of Roosevelt.* New York: Oxford University Press, 1995.

Nelson, Michael. "The President and the Court: Reinterpreting the Court Packing Episode of 1937," *Political Science Quarterly* 103 (1988), pp. 267–293.

O'Brien, David M. *Storm Center: The Supreme Court in American Politics.* New York: W. W. Norton and Company, 1986.

signal a retreat from laissez-faire constitutionalism. In *Home Building and Loan Association* v. *Blaisdell,* discussed in Chapter 8, and *Nebbia* v. *New York,* discussed in Chapter 9, the Court upheld state-mandated controls on economic and property rights claims as legitimate exercises of the public interest. In both cases narrow majorities of the Court concluded that the economic calamities brought on by the Depression justified the exercise of proportionate government power to ameliorate them.

For the architects of the New Deal, however, the hope raised by *Blaisdell* and *Nebbia* was short-lived. After *Schechter Poultry* the Court's assault on the New Deal continued unabated. The justices divided along sharp ideological lines that produced a string of 5-4 or, depending upon the vote of Chief Justice Hughes, 6-3 decisions invalidating major statutes such as the Railroad Retirement Act, the Agricultural Adjustment Act, and the Bituminous Coal Conservation Act. The Court's decision in *Carter* v. *Carter Coal Co.* (1936), striking down the federal coal law as an unconstitutional exercise of congressional commerce power, led Roosevelt to pursue in earnest what his administration had discussed as far back as the *Schechter* decision: a constitutional or legislative solution to clear the Court's obstruction of the New Deal. In February 1937 the Roosevelt administration presented Congress with a bill to reorganize the federal courts, the upshot of which would permit Roosevelt to appoint six additional members to the

Supreme Court, expand the number of judges serving in the lower courts, and expedite the appeals process for congressional statutes declared unconstitutional. A month later, Roosevelt brought this drama to its crescendo when he used one of his "fireside chats," the name commentators gave to his folksy evening national radio broadcasts, to appeal directly to the public to support his plan. The accompanying SIDEBAR describes in more detail the politics and personalities involved in President Roosevelt's "Court packing" plan.

On March 29, 1937, just over two weeks after Roosevelt went public with his Court-packing plan, the Court stunned the administration, Congress, reform-minded state legislatures, Progressives-turned-New Dealers, and everyone else when it upheld, in *West Coast Hotel Co.* v. *Parrish,* a Washington State minimum wage law for women. *West Coast Hotel* involved a due process challenge under the Fourteenth Amendment, but the tone of this opinion offered a strong hint of what was to come in future cases involving federal and state economic regulation. *West Coast Hotel* receives much more extensive discussion in Chapter 9; for now, however, a brief perusal of the Court's rationale in *West Coast Hotel* helps to show just how radical it was. The Court did not invoke Justice Holmes's dissent in *Lochner* to defend a posture of judicial deference to legislative policymaking. Instead, the opinion of Chief Justice Hughes recalled the legal progressivism of Brandeis, who, after nearly two decades in dissent, finally saw his vision of the law triumph. A minimum wage law, wrote Hughes, is a reasonable step to curtail "the exploiting of workers at wages so low as to be insufficient to meet the bare cost of living." The legislature should be free to "direct its law-making power to correct the abuse which springs from selfish disregard of the public interest."[51]

Having rejected, in *West Coast Hotel*, the doctrine of "liberty of contract," the Court, two weeks later, unveiled its new blueprint for the Commerce Clause. In *National Labor Relations Board* v. *Jones & Laughlin Steel Corp.* (1937), the Court held that the National Labor Relations Act was a constitutional exercise of congressional commerce power, even though the challenged provision involved the regulation of unfair labor practices in steel *production* facilities. Under *E.C. Knight*, labor practices fell on the production end of the stream-of-commerce continuum and thus were not subject to federal regulation. *Jones & Laughlin* discarded the production/distribution rule of *E.C. Knight* and its corollary, the "direct" and "indirect" effect-on-commerce standard. Note also how the Court distinguished *Jones & Laughlin* from *Carter Coal*, decided just the term before. Do these cases really merit different analyses under the Commerce Clause, or do you believe the Court created a distinction without a difference as a means to defend the New Deal?

The spring of 1937, in the words of Assistant Attorney General Robert Jackson, a staunch New Dealer appointed by Roosevelt to the Court in 1941, saw the "Court on the march," on behalf of organized labor, farmers, bankruptcy relief, and the minimum-wage.[52] The Court's change of heart was no fluke, as the ratification of the New Deal continued undisturbed throughout the remainder of the 1936–1937 term. Over the next five years, fate continued to smile upon the already good fortune of President Roosevelt, as he was able to appoint eight new justices by 1943, all of whom were committed to the New Deal. By the time the Court decided *United States* v. *Darby* (1941), which overruled *Hammer* v. *Dagenhart*, and *Wickard* v. *Filburn* (1942), the most far-reaching Commerce Clause decision to date, the Court was no longer divided by narrow majorities. The opinions were unanimous and, as you will read, worlds apart in their reasoning from the laissez-faire principles of the pre–New Deal era.

## *Carter* v. *Carter Coal Co.*
### 298 U.S. 238 (1936)

Congress passed the Bituminous Coal Conservation Act of 1935 to replace the NIRA coal codes, which were struck down with the rest of the NIRA in the *Schechter* decision. The act sought to curb overproduction and the negative effects of injurious competition, particularly involving labor unrest and strikes. The act created local boards charged with setting minimum prices for coal and provided for collective bargaining. The scheme was to be paid for with a tax on the coal industry. Participation was voluntary, but participants received a rebate of 90 percent of the tax. James W. Carter and other shareholders brought suit in the Supreme Court of the District of Columbia asking the court to enjoin Carter Coal Company from complying with the provisions of the code. The court refused, and Carter appealed to the U.S. Supreme Court.

The Court's opinion was 5 to 4. Justice Sutherland delivered the opinion of the Court. Chief Justice Hughes dissented in part. Justice Cardozo, joined by Justices Brandeis and Stone, dissented.

▼▲▼

MR. JUSTICE SUTHERLAND delivered the opinion of the Court. The ruling and firmly established principle is that the powers which the general government may exercise are only those specifically enumerated in the Constitution and such implied powers as are necessary and proper to carry into effect the enumerated powers. Whether the end sought to be attained by an act of Congress is legitimate is wholly a matter of constitutional power, and not at all of legislative discretion. Legislative congressional discretion begins with the choice of means, and ends with the adoption of methods and details to carry the delegated powers into effect. The distinction between these two things—power and discretion—is not only very plain, but very important. For while the powers are rigidly limited to the enumerations of the Constitution, the means which may be employed to carry the powers into effect are not restricted, save that they must be appropriate, plainly adapted to the end, and not prohibited by, but consistent with, the letter and spirit of the Constitution. Thus, it may be said that, to a constitutional end, many ways are open, but to an end not within the terms of the Constitution, all ways are closed. . . .

The general rule with regard to the respective powers of the national and the state governments under the Constitution is not in doubt. The states were before the Constitution, and, consequently, their legislative powers antedated the Constitution. Those who framed and those who adopted that instrument meant to carve from the general mass of legislative powers then possessed by the states only such portions as it was thought wise to confer upon the federal government, and, in order that there should be no uncertainty in respect of what was taken and what was left, the national powers of legislation were not aggregated, but enumerated—with the result that what was not embraced by the enumeration remained vested in the states without change or impairment. Thus, "when it was found necessary to establish a national government for national purposes," this court said in *Munn* v. *Illinois* (1877), "a part of the powers of the States and of the people of the States was granted to the United States and the people of the United States." . . .

While the states are not sovereign in the true sense of that term, but only *quasi*-sovereign, yet, in respect of all powers reserved to them, they are supreme—"as independent of the general government as that government, within its sphere, is independent of the States." And since every addition to the national legislative power to some extent detracts from or invades the power of the states, it is of vital moment that, in order to preserve the fixed balance intended by the Constitution, the powers of the general government be not so extended as to embrace any not within the express terms of the several grants or the implications necessarily to be drawn therefrom. . . .

We have set forth the foregoing principles, because it seemed necessary to do so in order to demonstrate that the general purposes which the act recites, and which, therefore, unless the recitals be disregarded, Congress undertook to achieve, are beyond the power of Congress except so far, and only so far, as they may be realized by an exercise of some specific power granted by the Constitution. Proceeding by a process of elimination which it is not necessary to follow in detail, we shall find no grant of power which authorizes Congress to legislate in respect of these general purposes unless it be found in the commerce clause—and this we now consider.

Since the validity of the act depends upon whether it is a regulation of interstate commerce, the nature and extent of the power conferred upon Congress by the commerce clause becomes the determinative question in this branch of the case. The commerce clause vests in Congress the power—"To regulate Commerce with foreign Nations, and among the several States, and with the Indian Tribes." The function to be exercised is that of regulation. The thing to be regulated is the commerce described. In exercising the authority conferred by this clause of the Constitution, Congress is powerless to regulate anything which is not commerce, as it is powerless to do anything about commerce which is not regulation. We first inquire, then—What is commerce? The term, as this court many times has said, is one of extensive import. No all-embracing definition has ever been formulated. The question is to be approached both affirmatively and negatively—that is to say, from the points of view as to what it includes and what it excludes. . . .

As used in the Constitution, the word "commerce" is the equivalent of the phrase "intercourse for the purposes of trade," and includes transportation, purchase, sale, and exchange of commodities between the citizens of the different states. And the power to regulate commerce embraces the instruments by which commerce is carried on. "Commerce among the several States" was defined as comprehending, "traffic, intercourse, trade, navigation, communication, the transit of persons and the transmission of messages by telegraph—indeed, every species of commercial intercourse among the several States." . . .

That commodities produced or manufactured within a state are intended to be sold or transported outside the state does not render their production or manufacture subject to federal regulation under the commerce clause. . . .

We have seen that the word "commerce" is the equivalent of the phrase "intercourse for the purposes of trade." Plainly, the incidents leading up to and culminating in the mining of coal do not constitute such intercourse. The employment of men, the fixing of their wages, hours of labor and working conditions, the bargaining in respect of these things—whether carried on separately or collectively each and all constitute intercourse for the purposes of production, not of trade. The latter is a thing apart from the relation of employer and employee, which, in all producing occupations, is purely local in character. Extraction of coal from the mine is the aim and the completed result of local activities. Commerce in the coal mined is not brought into being by force of these activities, but by negotiations, agreements, and circumstances entirely apart from production. Mining brings the subject matter of commerce into existence. Commerce disposes of it.

A consideration of the foregoing, and of many cases which might be added to those already cited, renders inescapable the conclusion that the effect of the labor provisions of the act, including those in respect of minimum wages, wage agreements, collective bargaining, and the Labor Board and its powers, primarily falls upon production, and not upon commerce, and confirms the further resulting conclusion that production is a purely local activity. It follows that none of these essential antecedents of production constitutes a transaction in, or forms any part of, interstate commerce. Everything which moves in interstate commerce has had a local origin. Without local production somewhere, interstate commerce, as now carried on, would practically disappear. Nevertheless, the local character of mining, of manufacturing and of crop growing is a fact, and remains a fact, whatever may be done with the products. . . .

That the production of every commodity intended for interstate sale and transportation has some effect upon interstate commerce may be, if it has not already been, freely granted, and we are brought to the final and decisive inquiry, whether here that effect is direct, as the "preamble" recites, or indirect. The distinction is not formal, but substantial in the highest degree, as we pointed out in the *Schechter case*, "If the commerce clause were construed," we there said, "to reach all enterprises and transactions which could be said to have an indirect effect upon interstate commerce, the federal authority would embrace practically all the activities of the people, and the authority of the State over its domestic concerns would exist only by sufferance of the federal government. Indeed, on such a theory, even the development of the State's commercial facilities would be subject to federal control." It was also pointed out, that, "the distinction between direct and indirect effects of intrastate transactions upon interstate commerce must be recognized as a fundamental one, essential to the maintenance of our constitutional system."

Whether the effect of a given activity or condition is direct or indirect is not always easy to determine. The word "direct" implies that the activity or condition invoked or blamed shall operate proximately—not mediately, remotely, or collaterally—to produce the effect. It connotes the absence of an efficient intervening agency or condition. And the extent of the effect bears no logical relation to its character. The distinction between a direct and an indirect effect turns not upon the magnitude of either the cause or the effect, but entirely upon the manner in which the effect has been brought about. If the production by one man of a single ton of coal intended for interstate sale and shipment, and actually so sold and shipped, affects interstate commerce indirectly, the effect does not become direct by multiplying the tonnage, or increasing the number of men employed, or adding to the expense or complexities of the business, or by all combined. It is quite true that rules of law are sometimes qual-

ified by considerations of degree, as the government argues. But the matter of degree has no bearing upon the question here, since that question is not what is the extent of the local activity or condition, or the extent of the effect produced upon interstate commerce, but what is the relation between the activity or condition and the effect?

Much stress is put upon the evils which come from the struggle between employers and employees over the matter of wages, working conditions, the right of collective bargaining, etc., and the resulting strikes, curtailment and irregularity of production and effect on prices, and it is insisted that interstate commerce is greatly affected thereby. But, in addition to what has just been said, the conclusive answer is that the evils are all local evils over which the federal government has no legislative control. The relation of employer and employee is a local relation. At common law, it is one of the domestic relations. The wages are paid for the doing of local work. Working conditions are obviously local conditions. The employees are not engaged in or about commerce, but exclusively in producing a commodity. And the controversies and evils which it is the object of the act to regulate and minimize are local controversies and evils affecting local work undertaken to accomplish that local result. Such effect as they may have upon commerce, however extensive it may be, is secondary and indirect. An increase in the greatness of the effect adds to its importance. It does not alter its character.

The government's contentions in defense of the labor provisions are really disposed of adversely by our decision in the *Schechter* case. The only perceptible difference between that case and this is that, in the *Schechter* case, the federal power was asserted with respect to commodities which had come to rest after their interstate transportation, while here the case deals with commodities at rest before interstate commerce has begun. That difference is without significance. The federal regulatory power ceases when interstate commercial intercourse ends; and, correlatively, the power does not attach until interstate commercial intercourse begins. There is no basis in law or reason for applying different rules to the two situations. . . .

A reading of the entire opinion makes clear what we now declare, that the want of power on the part of the federal government is the same whether the wages, hours of service, and working conditions, and the bargaining about them, are related to production before interstate commerce has begun or to sale and distribution after it has ended.

▼▲▼

## National Labor Relations Board v. Jones & Laughlin Steel Corp.
### 301 U.S. 1 (1937)

The National Labor Relations Act (NLRA) was another response by Congress to the Court's decision in *Schechter Poultry*. Enacted in July 1935, the NLRA, better known as the Wagner Act, so named for Senator Robert Wagner (D–N.Y.), established the National Labor Relations Board (NLRB), which was designed to protect the rights of labor to organize collectively. The board also mediated disputes between organized labor and management. In *Schechter Poultry* the Court had invalidated the provisions of the NIRA establishing the original National Labor Board (NLB). This ruling was neither unexpected nor unwelcome news for Senator Wagner, who concluded while serving as chair of the NLB that it was an ineffective tool to protect labor rights. Eleven days before *Schechter Poultry* was decided, the Senate had approved the NLRA by an overwhelming majority. The Court's decision helped Wagner garner the political support he needed to speed passage of the law. President Roosevelt, unsympathetic to organized labor at this point, had opposed the NLRA, which he believed would unnecessarily antagonize the business community. Ironically, the Communist Party also opposed the Wagner Act, believing that it was little more than a bare bone to appease the American worker. Faced with broad congressional support, Roosevelt decided to drop his position and sign the legislation.

The NLRB had free reign to search for cases that would allow it to test the Wagner Act's constitutionality in court. It settled on a labor dispute between the Amalgamated Association of Iron & Tin Workers of America and Jones & Laughlin Steel, one the nation's largest steel manufacturers. The board filed several complaints on behalf of the union against Jones & Laughlin, which refused to address them. A subsequent lawsuit filed by the NLRB to obtain enforcement was unsuccessful. Between the time the Court accepted the NLRB's case in October 1936 against Jones & Laughlin and heard oral argument in February 1937, Roosevelt had been reelected by a landslide majority. Four days before the Court heard *Jones & Laughlin*, Roosevelt introduced his Court-packing plan to Congress. Little did he know that it would be unnecessary.

The Court's decision was 5 to 4. Chief Justice Hughes delivered the opinion of the Court. Justice McReynolds, joined by Justices Van Devanter, Sutherland, and Butler, dissented.

▼▲▼

Mr. Chief Justice Hughes delivered the opinion of the Court.

The facts as to the nature and scope of the business of the Jones & Laughlin Steel Corporation have been found by the Labor Board, and, so far as they are essential to the determination of this controversy, they are not in dispute. The Labor Board has found: the corporation is organized under the laws of Pennsylvania and has its principal office at Pittsburgh. It is engaged in the business of manufacturing iron and steel in plants situated in Pittsburgh and nearby Aliquippa, Pennsylvania. It manufactures and distributes a widely diversified line of steel and pig iron, being the fourth largest producer of steel in the United States. With its subsidiaries—nineteen in number—it is a completely integrated enterprise, owning and operating ore, coal and limestone properties, lake and river transportation facilities, and terminal railroads located at its manufacturing plants. It owns or controls mines in Michigan and Minnesota. It operates four ore steamships on the Great Lakes, used in the transportation of ore to its factories. It owns coal mines in Pennsylvania. It operates towboats and steam barges used in carrying coal to its factories. It owns limestone properties in various places in Pennsylvania and West Virginia. It owns the Monongahela connecting railroad which connects the plants of the Pittsburgh works and forms an interconnection with the Pennsylvania, New York Central, and Baltimore and Ohio Railroad systems. It owns the Aliquippa and Southern Railroad Company, which connects the Aliquippa works with the Pittsburgh and Lake Erie, part of the New York Central system. Much of its product is shipped to its warehouses in Chicago, Detroit, Cincinnati and Memphis—to the last two places by means of its own barges and transportation equipment. In Long Island City, New York, and in New Orleans, it operates structural steel fabricating shops in connection with the warehousing of semi-finished materials sent from its works. Through one of its wholly owned subsidiaries, it owns, leases and operates stores, warehouses and yards for the distribution of equipment and supplies for drilling and operating oil and gas wells and for pipelines, refineries, and pumping stations. It has sales offices in twenty cities in the United States and a wholly owned subsidiary which is devoted exclusively to distributing its product in Canada. Approximately 75 percent of its product is shipped out of Pennsylvania. . . .

To carry on the activities of the entire steel industry, 33,000 men mine ore, 44,000 men mine coal, 4,000 men quarry limestone, 16,000 men manufacture coke, 343,000 men manufacture steel, and 83,000 men transport its product. Respondent has about 10,000 employees in its Aliquippa plant, which is located in a community of about 30,000 persons. . . .

We turn to the questions of law which respondent urges in contesting the validity and application of the Act.

*First. The scope of the Act.*—The Act is challenged in its entirety as an attempt to regulate all industry, thus invading the reserved powers of the States over their local concerns. It is asserted that the references in the Act to interstate and foreign commerce are colorable, at best; that the Act is not a true regulation of such commerce or of matters which directly affect it, but, on the contrary, has the fundamental object of placing under the compulsory supervision of the federal government all industrial labor relations within the nation. . . .

If this conception of terms, intent, and consequent inseparability were sound, the Act would necessarily fall by reason of the limitation upon the federal power which inheres in the constitutional grant, as well as because of the explicit reservation of the Tenth Amendment. The authority of the federal government may not be pushed to such an extreme as to destroy the distinction, which the commerce clause itself establishes, between commerce "among the several States" and the internal concerns of a State. That distinction between what is national and what is local in the activities of commerce is vital to the maintenance of our federal system.

But we are not at liberty to deny effect to specific provisions, which Congress has constitutional power to enact, by superimposing upon them inferences from general legislative declarations of an ambiguous character, even if found in the same statute. The cardinal principle of statutory construction is to save, and not to destroy. We have repeatedly held that, as between two possible interpretations of a statute, by one of which it would be unconstitutional and by the other valid, our plain duty is to adopt that which will save the act. . . .

We think it clear that the National Labor Relations Act may be construed so as to operate within the sphere of constitutional authority. . . . The critical words of this provision, prescribing the limits of the Board's authority in dealing with the labor practices, are "affecting commerce." The Act specifically defines the "commerce" to which it refers:

The term "commerce" means trade, traffic, commerce, transportation, or communication among the several States, or between the District of Columbia or any Territory of the United States and any State or other Territory, or between any foreign country and any State, Territory, or the District of Columbia, or within the District of Columbia or any Territory, or between points in the same State but through any other State or any Territory or the District of Columbia or any foreign country.

There can be no question that the commerce thus contemplated by the Act (aside from that within a Territory or the District of Columbia) is interstate and foreign commerce in the constitutional sense. The Act also defines the term "affecting commerce":

The term "affecting commerce" means in commerce, or burdening or obstructing commerce or the free flow of commerce, or having led or tending to lead to a labor dispute burdening or obstructing commerce or the free flow of commerce.

This definition is one of exclusion as well as inclusion. The grant of authority to the Board does not purport to extend to the relationship between all industrial employees and employers. Its terms do not impose collective bargaining upon all industry regardless of effects upon interstate or foreign commerce. It purports to reach only what may be deemed to burden or obstruct that commerce, and, thus qualified, it must be construed as contemplating the exercise of control within constitutional bounds. It is a familiar principle that acts which directly burden or obstruct interstate or foreign commerce, or its free flow, are within the reach of the congressional power. Acts having that effect are not rendered immune because they grow out of labor disputes. Whether or not particular action does affect commerce in such a close and intimate fashion as to be subject to federal control, and hence to lie within the authority conferred upon the Board, is left by the statute to be determined as individual cases arise. We are thus to inquire whether, in the instant case, the constitutional boundary has been passed.

*Second. The fair labor practices in question.*—The unfair labor practices found by the Board are those defined in Section 8, subdivisions (1) and (3). These provide:

Sec. 8. It shall be an unfair labor practice for an employer—

(1) To interfere with, restrain, or coerce employees in the exercise of the rights guaranteed in section 7.

(3) By discrimination in regard to hire or tenure of employment or any term or condition of employment to

encourage or discourage membership in any labor organization . . .

Section 8, subdivision (1), refers to Section 7, which is as follows:

Sec. 7. Employees shall have the right to self-organization, to form, join, or assist labor organizations, to bargain collectively through representatives of their own choosing, and to engage in concerted activities, for the purpose of collective bargaining or other mutual aid or protection.

Thus, in its present application, the statute goes no further than to safeguard the right of employees to self-organization and to select representatives of their own choosing for collective bargaining or other mutual protection without restraint or coercion by their employer.

That is a fundamental right. Employees have as clear a right to organize and select their representatives for lawful purposes as the respondent has to organize its business and select its own officers and agents. Discrimination and coercion to prevent the free exercise of the right of employees to self-organization and representation is a proper subject for condemnation by competent legislative authority. Long ago we stated the reason for labor organizations. We said that they were organized out of the necessities of the situation; that a single employee was helpless in dealing with an employer; that he was dependent ordinarily on his daily wage for the maintenance of himself and family; that, if the employer refused to pay him the wages that he thought fair, he was nevertheless unable to leave the employ and resist arbitrary and unfair treatment; that union was essential to give laborers opportunity to deal on an equality with their employer. . . .

*Third. The application of the Act to employees engaged in production.—The principle involved.*—Respondent says that whatever may be said of employees engaged in interstate commerce, the industrial relations and activities in the manufacturing department of respondent's enterprise are not subject to federal regulation. The argument rests upon the proposition that manufacturing, in itself, is not commerce.

The Government distinguishes these cases. The various parts of respondent's enterprise are described as interdependent and as thus involving "a great movement of iron ore, coal and limestone along well defined paths to the steel mills, thence through them, and thence in the form of steel products into the consuming centers of the country—a definite and well understood course of business." It is urged that these activities constitute a "stream" or "flow" of commerce, of which the Aliquippa manufacturing plant is the focal point, and that industrial strife at that point would cripple the entire movement. Reference is made to our decision sustaining the Packers and Stockyards Act. . . .

Respondent contends that the instant case presents material distinctions. Respondent says that the Aliquippa plant is extensive in size and represents a large investment in buildings, machinery and equipment. The raw materials which are brought to the plant are delayed for long periods and, after being subjected to manufacturing processes, "are changed substantially as to character, utility and value." The finished products which emerge, "are to a large extent manufactured without reference to preexisting orders and contracts, and are entirely different from the raw materials which enter at the other end." Hence, respondent argues that, "If importation and exportation in interstate commerce do not singly transfer purely local activities into the field of congressional regulation, it should follow that their combination would not alter the local situation."

We do not find it necessary to determine whether these features of defendant's business dispose of the asserted analogy to the "stream of commerce" cases. The instances in which that metaphor has been used are but particular, and not exclusive, illustrations of the protective power which the Government invokes in support of the present Act. The congressional authority to protect interstate commerce from burdens and obstructions is not limited to transactions which can be deemed to be an essential part of a "flow" of interstate or foreign commerce. Burdens and obstructions may be due to injurious action springing from other sources. The fundamental principle is that the power to regulate commerce is the power to enact "all appropriate legislation" for "its protection and advancement"; to adopt measures "to promote its growth and insure its safety"; "to foster, protect, control and restrain." That power is plenary, and may be exerted to protect interstate commerce "no matter what the source of the dangers which threaten it."

Although activities may be intrastate in character when separately considered, if they have such a close and substantial relation to interstate commerce that their control is essential or appropriate to protect that commerce from burdens and obstructions, Congress cannot be denied the power to exercise that control. Undoubtedly the scope of this power must be considered in the light of our dual system of government, and may not be extended so as to embrace effects upon interstate commerce so indirect and remote that to embrace them, in view of our complex society, would effectually obliterate the distinction between what is national and what is local and create a completely centralized government. The question is necessarily one of degree. . . .

The close and intimate effect which brings the subject within the reach of federal power may be due to activities in relation to productive industry although the industry, when separately viewed, is local.

It is thus apparent that the fact that the employees here concerned were engaged in production is not determinative. The question remains as to the effect upon interstate commerce of the labor practice involved. In the *Schechter case*, we found that the effect there was so remote as to be beyond the federal power. To find "immediacy or directness" there was to find it "almost everywhere," a result inconsistent with the maintenance of our federal system. In the *Carter* case, the Court was of the opinion that the provisions of the statute relating to production were invalid upon several grounds—that there was improper delegation of legislative power, and that the requirements not only went beyond any sustainable measure of protection of interstate commerce, but were also inconsistent with due process. These cases are not controlling here.

*Fourth. Effects of the unfair labor practice in respondent's enterprise.*—Giving full weight to respondent's contention with respect to a break in the complete continuity of the "stream of commerce" by reason of respondent's manufacturing operations, the fact remains that the stoppage of those operations by industrial strife would have a most serious effect upon interstate commerce. In view of respondent's far-flung activities, it is idle to say that the effect would be indirect or remote. It is obvious that it would be immediate, and might be catastrophic. We are asked to shut our eyes to the plainest facts of our national life, and to deal with the question of direct and indirect effects in an intellectual vacuum. Because there may be but indirect and remote effects upon interstate commerce in connection with a host of local enterprises throughout the country, it does not follow that other industrial activities do not have such a close and intimate relation to interstate commerce as to make the presence of industrial strife a matter of the most urgent national concern. When industries organize themselves on a national scale, making their relation to interstate commerce the dominant factor in their activities, how can it be maintained that their industrial labor relations constitute a forbidden field into which Congress may not enter when it is necessary to protect interstate commerce from the paralyzing consequences of industrial war? We have often

said that interstate commerce itself is a practical conception. It is equally true that interferences with that commerce must be appraised by a judgment that does not ignore actual experience.

Experience has abundantly demonstrated that the recognition of the right of employees to self-organization and to have representatives of their own choosing for the purpose of collective bargaining is often an essential condition of industrial peace. Refusal to confer and negotiate has been one of the most prolific causes of strife. This is such an outstanding fact in the history of labor disturbances that it is a proper subject of judicial notice, and requires no citation of instances. . . .

The steel industry is one of the great basic industries of the United States, with ramifying activities affecting interstate commerce at every point. The Government aptly refers to the steel strike of 1919–1920, with its far-reaching consequences. The fact that there appears to have been no major disturbance in that industry in the more recent period did not dispose of the possibilities of future and like dangers to interstate commerce which Congress was entitled to foresee and to exercise its protective power to forestall. It is not necessary again to detail the facts as to respondent's enterprise. Instead of being beyond the pale, we think that it presents in a most striking way the close and intimate relation which a manufacturing industry may have to interstate commerce, and we have no doubt that Congress had constitutional authority to safeguard the right of respondent's employees to self-organization and freedom in the choice of representatives for collective bargaining.

▼▲▼

## *United States v. Darby*
### 312 U.S. 100 (1941)

Fred Darby, who owned and operated a sawmill business in Statesboro, Georgia, was indicted in 1939 for violating the Fair Labor Standards Act (FLSA) of 1938, a centerpiece of the New Deal legislative program. The FLSA established a minimum wage of twenty-five cents per hour, created a provision mandating overtime pay for any time worked beyond forty hours per week, and required employers to maintain records of their employees' wage and hour history. Companies that failed to comply with the FLSA were barred from engaging in interstate commerce.

Congress patterned the FLSA on the 1916 Owen-Keating child labor law, which the Court invalidated in *Hammer v. Dagenhart* (1918). The only difference between the 1916 and 1938 laws was political. By 1938 the Court had ratified the New Deal, and there was no going back.

The Court's decision was unanimous. Justice Stone delivered the opinion of the Court.

▼▲▼

MR. JUSTICE STONE delivered the opinion of the Court.

The two principal questions raised by the record in this case are, first, whether Congress has constitutional power to prohibit the shipment in interstate commerce of lumber manufactured by employees whose wages are less than a prescribed minimum or whose weekly hours of labor at that wage are greater than a prescribed maximum, and, second, whether it has power to prohibit the employment of workmen in the production of goods "for interstate commerce" at other than prescribed wages and hours. . . .

The Fair Labor Standards Act set up a comprehensive legislative scheme for preventing the shipment in interstate commerce of certain products and commodities produced in the United States under labor conditions as respects wages and hours which fail to conform to standards set up by the Act. Its purpose is to exclude from interstate commerce goods produced for the commerce and to prevent their production for interstate commerce under conditions detrimental to the maintenance of the minimum standards of living necessary for health and general wellbeing, and to prevent the use of interstate commerce as the means of competition in the distribution of goods so produced, and as the means of spreading and perpetuating such substandard labor conditions among the workers of the several states. . . .

*The prohibition of shipment of the proscribed goods in interstate commerce.*

. . . While manufacture is not, of itself, interstate commerce, the shipment of manufactured goods interstate is such commerce, and the prohibition of such shipment by Congress is indubitably a regulation of the commerce. The power to regulate commerce is the power "to prescribe the rule by which commerce is governed." *Gibbons v. Ogden* (1824). It extends not only to those regulations which aid, foster and protect the commerce, but embraces those which prohibit it. It is conceded that the power of Congress to prohibit transportation in interstate commerce includes noxious articles, stolen articles, kidnapped persons, and articles, such as intoxicating liquor or convict made goods, traffic in which is forbidden or restricted by the laws of the state of destination.

But it is said that the present prohibition falls within the scope of none of these categories; that, while the prohibition is nominally a regulation of the commerce, its motive or purpose is regulation of wages and hours of persons engaged in manufacture, the control of which has been reserved to the states and upon which Georgia and some of the states of destination have placed no restriction; that the effect of the present statute is not to exclude the proscribed articles from interstate commerce in aid of state regulation . . . but instead, under the guise of a regulation of interstate commerce, it undertakes to regulate wages and hours within the state contrary to the policy of the state which has elected to leave them unregulated. . . .

Such regulation is not a forbidden invasion of state power merely because either its motive or its consequence is to restrict the use of articles of commerce within the states of destination, and is not prohibited unless by other Constitutional provisions. It is no objection to the assertion of the power to regulate interstate commerce that its exercise is attended by the same incidents which attend the exercise of the police power of the states.

The motive and purpose of the present regulation are plainly to make effective the Congressional conception of public policy that interstate commerce should not be made the instrument of competition in the distribution of goods produced under substandard labor conditions, which competition is injurious to the commerce and to the states from and to which the commerce flows. The motive and purpose of a regulation of interstate commerce are matters for the legislative judgment upon the exercise of which the Constitution places no restriction, and over which the courts are given no control. Whatever their motive and purpose, regulations of commerce which do not infringe some constitutional prohibition are within the plenary power conferred on Congress by the Commerce Clause. Subject only to that limitation, presently to be considered, we conclude that the prohibition of the shipment interstate of goods produced under the forbidden substandard labor conditions is within the constitutional authority of Congress.

In the more than a century which has elapsed since the decision of *Gibbons v. Ogden*, these principles of constitutional interpretation have been so long and repeatedly recognized by this Court as applicable to the Commerce Clause that there would be little occasion for repeating them now were it not for the decision of this Court twenty-two years ago in *Hammer v. Dagenhart* (1918). In that case, it was held by a bare majority of the Court, over the powerful and now classic dissent of Mr. Justice Holmes setting forth the fundamental issues involved, that Congress was without power to exclude the products of child labor from interstate commerce. The reasoning and conclusion of the Court's opinion there cannot be reconciled with the conclusion which we have reached, that the power of Congress under the Commerce Clause is plenary to exclude any article from interstate commerce subject only to the specific prohibitions of the Constitution. . . .

The conclusion is inescapable that *Hammer v. Dagenhart* was a departure from the principles which have prevailed in the interpretation of the Commerce Clause both before and since the decision, and that such vitality, as a precedent, as it then had, has long since been exhausted. It should be, and now is, overruled.

*Validity of the wage and hour requirements.*

[The FLSA] require employers to conform to the wage and hour provisions with respect to all employees engaged in the production of goods for interstate commerce. As appellee's employees are not alleged to be "engaged in interstate commerce," the validity of the prohibition turns on the question whether the employment, under other than the prescribed labor standards, of employees engaged in the production of goods for interstate commerce is so related to the commerce, and so affects it, as to be within the reach of the power of Congress to regulate it.

To answer this question, we must at the outset determine whether the particular acts charged . . . constitute "production for commerce" within the meaning of the statute. As the Government seeks to apply the statute in the indictment, and as the court below construed the phrase "produced for interstate commerce," it embraces at least the case where an employer engaged, as is appellee, in the manufacture and shipment of goods in filling orders of extrastate customers, manufactures his product with the intent or expectation that, according to the normal course of his business, all or some part of it will be selected for shipment to those customers.

Without attempting to define the precise limits of the phrase, we think the acts alleged in the indictment are within the sweep of the statute. The obvious purpose of the Act was not only to prevent the interstate transportation of the proscribed product, but to stop the initial step toward transportation, production with the purpose of so transporting it. Congress was not unaware that most manufacturing businesses shipping their product in interstate commerce make it in their shops without reference to its ultimate destination, and then, after manufacture, select some of it for shipment interstate and some intrastate, according to the daily demands of their business, and that it would be practically impossible, without disrupting manufacturing businesses, to restrict the prohibited kind of production to the particular pieces of lumber, cloth, furniture or the like which later move in interstate, rather than intrastate, commerce.

The recognized need of drafting a workable statute and the well known circumstances in which it was to be applied are persuasive of the conclusion . . . that the "production for commerce" intended includes at least production of goods which, at the time of production, the employer, according to the normal course of his business, intends or expects to move in interstate commerce although, through the exigencies of the business, all of the goods may not thereafter actually enter interstate commerce.

There remains the question whether such restriction on the production of goods for commerce is a permissible exercise of the commerce power. The power of Congress over interstate commerce is not confined to the regulation of commerce among the states. It extends to those activities intrastate which so affect interstate commerce or the exercise of the power of Congress over it as to make regulation of them appropriate means to the attainment of a legitimate end, the exercise of the granted power of Congress to regulate interstate commerce. . . .

Our conclusion is unaffected by the Tenth Amendment, which provides: "The powers not delegated to the United States by the Constitution, nor prohibited by it to the States, are reserved to the States respectively, or to the people."

The amendment states but a truism that all is retained which has not been surrendered. There is nothing in the history of its adoption to suggest that it was more than declaratory of the relationship between the national and state governments as it had been established by the Constitution before the amendment, or that its purpose was other than to allay fears that the new national government might seek to exercise powers not granted, and that the states might not be able to exercise fully their reserved powers. . . .

The Act is sufficiently definite to meet constitutional demands. One who employs persons, without conforming to the prescribed wage and hour conditions, to work on goods which he ships or expects to ship across state lines is warned that he may be subject to the criminal penalties of the Act. No more is required.

*Reversed.*

▼▲▼

## *Wickard* v. *Filburn*
### 317 U.S. 111 (1942)

Buoyed by the Court's about-face on the Commerce Clause in *Jones & Laughlin,* Congress enacted a second Agricultural Adjustment Act (AAA) in 1938, fully confident that any legal effort to challenge it would fail. The original AAA was invalidated in *United States* v. *Butler* (1936), in which the Court ruled that Congress did not possess authority under its taxing and spending power to enact such a comprehensive measure over agricultural production. In *Mulford* v. *Smith* (1939), the Court upheld the constitutionality of the second AAA. Justice Owen Roberts, who authored the *Butler* opinion, wrote the majority opinion in *Mulford.*

In 1941, Congress amended the 1938 law to limit the amount of wheat that farmers could grow. Farmers who exceeded the AAA limits were fined on the basis of the number of excess bushels they grew. Congress's objective under the 1941 amendments was fundamental: to stabilize wheat prices by eliminating surpluses and shortfalls caused by fluctuations in supply and demand. That same year, Roscoe Filburn, a small dairy farmer in Montgomery County, Ohio, was fined $117.11 for exceeding his wheat quota. He challenged the AAA, as amended, as an unconstitutional use of congressional commerce power. Filburn's chief contention was that the wheat quota touched upon production and consumption, not interstate commerce

The Court's decision was unanimous. Justice Jackson delivered the opinion of the Court.

Mr. Justice Jackson delivered the opinion of the Court.

It is urged that, under the Commerce Clause of the Constitution, Article I, section 8, clause 3, Congress does not possess the power it has in this instance sought to exercise. The question would merit little consideration, since our decision in *United States* v. *Darby* (1941) sustaining the federal power to regulate production of goods for commerce, except for the fact that this Act extends federal regulation to production not intended in any part for commerce, but wholly for consumption on the farm. The Act includes a definition of "market" and its derivatives, so that, as related to wheat, in addition to its conventional meaning, it also means to dispose of, "by feeding (in any form) to poultry or livestock which, or the products of

which, are sold, bartered, or exchanged, or to be so disposed of." Hence, marketing quotas not only embrace all that may be sold without penalty, but also what may be consumed on the premises. . . .

Appellee says that this is a regulation of production and consumption of wheat. Such activities are, he urges, beyond the reach of Congressional power under the Commerce Clause, since they are local in character, and their effects upon interstate commerce are, at most, "indirect." In answer, the Government argues that the statute regulates neither production nor consumption, but only marketing, and, in the alternative, that, if the Act does go beyond the regulation of marketing, it is sustainable as a "necessary and proper" implementation of the power of Congress over interstate commerce.

The Government's concern lest the Act be held to be a regulation of production or consumption, rather than of marketing, is attributable to a few dicta and decisions of this Court which might be understood to lay it down that activities such as "production," "manufacturing," and "mining" are strictly "local" and, except in special circumstances which are not present here, cannot be regulated under the commerce power because their effects upon interstate commerce are, as matter of law, only "indirect." Even today, when this power has been held to have great latitude, there is no decision of this Court that such activities may be regulated where no part of the product is intended for interstate commerce or intermingled with the subjects thereof. We believe that a review of the course of decision under the Commerce Clause will make plain, however, that questions of the power of Congress are not to be decided by reference to any formula which would give controlling force to nomenclature such as "production" and "indirect" and foreclose consideration of the actual effects of the activity in question upon interstate commerce. . . .

For nearly a century, however, decisions of this Court under the Commerce Clause dealt rarely with questions of what Congress might do in the exercise of its granted power under the Clause, and almost entirely with the permissibility of state activity which it was claimed discriminated against or burdened interstate commerce. During this period, there was perhaps little occasion for the affirmative exercise of the commerce power, and the influence of the Clause on American life and law was a negative one, resulting almost wholly from its operation as a restraint upon the powers of the states. In discussion and decision, the point of reference, instead of being what was "necessary and proper" to the exercise by Congress of its granted power, was often some concept of sovereignty thought to be implicit in the status of statehood. Certain activities such as "production," "manufacturing," and "mining" were occasionally said to be within the province of state governments and beyond the power of Congress under the Commerce Clause.

It was not until 1887, with the enactment of the Interstate Commerce Act, that the interstate commerce power began to exert positive influence in American law and life. This first important federal resort to the commerce power was followed in 1890 by the Sherman Anti-Trust Act and, thereafter, mainly after 1903, by many others. These statutes ushered in new phases of adjudication, which required the Court to approach the interpretation of the Commerce Clause in the light of an actual exercise by Congress of its power thereunder.

When it first dealt with this new legislation, the Court adhered to its earlier pronouncements, and allowed but little scope to the power of Congress. . . .

[Justice Jackson then summarized the Court's gradual willingness to consider the economic effects of "production" considered to affect interstate commerce to be within the scope of congressional power.] Once an economic measure of the reach of the power granted to Congress in the Commerce Clause is accepted, questions of federal power cannot be decided simply by finding the activity in question to be "production," nor can consideration of its economic effects be foreclosed by calling them "indirect." The present Chief Justice has said in summary of the present state of the law:

> The commerce power is not confined in its exercise to the regulation of commerce among the states. It extends to those activities intrastate which so affect interstate commerce, or the exertion of the power of Congress over it, as to make regulation of them appropriate means to the attainment of a legitimate end, the effective execution of the granted power to regulate interstate commerce. . . . The power of Congress over interstate commerce is plenary and complete in itself, may be exercised to its utmost extent, and acknowledges no limitations other than are prescribed in the Constitution. . . . It follows that no form of state activity can constitutionally thwart the regulatory power granted by the commerce clause to Congress. Hence, the reach of that power extends to those intrastate activities which in a substantial way interfere with or obstruct the exercise of the granted power.

Whether the subject of the regulation in question was "production," "consumption," or "marketing" is, therefore, not material for purposes of deciding the question of federal power before us. That an activity is of local character may help in a doubtful case to determine whether Congress intended to reach it. The same consideration might help in determining whether, in the absence of Congressional action, it would be permissible for the state to exert its power on the subject matter, even though, in so doing, it to some degree affected interstate commerce. But even if appellee's activity be local, and though it may not be regarded as commerce, it may still, whatever its nature, be reached by Congress if it exerts a substantial economic effect on interstate commerce, and this irrespective of whether such effect is what might at some earlier time have been defined as "direct" or "indirect." . . .

The wheat industry has been a problem industry for some years. Largely as a result of increased foreign production and import restrictions, annual exports of wheat and flour from the United States during the ten-year period ending in 1940 averaged less than 10 percent of total production, while, during the 1920's, they averaged more than 25 percent. The decline in the export trade has left a large surplus in production which, in connection with an abnormally large supply of wheat and other grains in recent years, caused congestion in a number of markets; tied up railroad cars, and caused elevators in some instances to turn away grains, and railroads to institute embargoes to prevent further congestion. . . .

The maintenance by government regulation of a price for wheat undoubtedly can be accomplished as effectively by sustaining or increasing the demand as by limiting the supply. The effect of the statute before us is to restrict the amount which may be produced for market and the extent, as well, to which one may forestall resort to the market by producing to meet his own needs. That appellee's own contribution to the demand for wheat may be trivial by itself is not enough to remove him from the scope of federal regulation where, as here, his contribution, taken together with that of many others similarly situated, is far from trivial.

It is well established by decisions of this Court that the power to regulate commerce includes the power to regulate the prices at which commodities in that commerce are dealt in and practices affecting such prices. One of the primary purposes of the Act in question was to increase the market price of wheat, and, to that end, to limit the volume thereof that could affect the market. It can hardly be denied that a factor of such volume and variability as home-consumed wheat would have a substantial influence on price and market conditions. This may arise because being in marketable condition such wheat overhangs the market, and, if induced by rising prices, tends to flow into the market and check price increases. But if we assume that it is never marketed, it supplies a need of the man who grew it which would otherwise be reflected by purchases in the open market. Home-grown wheat in this sense competes with wheat in commerce. The stimulation of commerce is a use of the regulatory function quite as definitely as prohibitions or restrictions thereon. This record leaves us in no doubt that Congress may properly have considered that wheat consumed on the farm where grown, if wholly outside the scheme of regulation, would have a substantial effect in defeating and obstructing its purpose to stimulate trade therein at increased prices.

It is said, however, that this Act, forcing some farmers into the market to buy what they could provide for themselves, is an unfair promotion of the markets and prices of specializing wheat growers. It is of the essence of regulation that it lays a restraining hand on the self-interest of the regulated, and that advantages from the regulation commonly fall to others. The conflicts of economic interest between the regulated and those who advantage by it are wisely left under our system to resolution by the Congress under its more flexible and responsible legislative process. Such conflicts rarely lend themselves to judicial determination. And with the wisdom, workability, or fairness, of the plan of regulation, we have nothing to do.

▼▲▼

## The Power to Tax and Spend: Before and After the New Deal

Prior to the Constitutional Revolution of 1937, the Court placed tight limits congressional taxing power. Although the Court had approved some early federal tax laws designed to raise revenue as far back as 1796, the decision in *Pollock v. Farmer's Loan and Trust Co.* (1895) was more reflective of the Court's pre–New Deal approach to congressional taxation power.[53] In *Pollack* a 5-4 majority struck down the entire federal income tax system as violative of Congress's power under Article I, Section 9, even though the Court, in *Springer v. United States* (1881), had upheld a series of congressional income taxes levied during the Civil War to raise funds for the war effort.[54] Caught up in the spirit of the laissez-faire economic principles that animated its approach to constitutional interpretation, the Court, in *Pollock,* handcuffed Congress from engaging in any income tax measures until this decision was overturned, in 1913, by the Sixteenth Amendment. The amendment's lan-

guage, which provides that "Congress shall have power to lay and collect taxes on incomes, from whatever source derived, without apportionment among the several States, and without regard to any census or enumeration," was intended to restore the taxing and spending power of Congress to pre-*Pollock* levels.

Even more controversial prior to the New Deal than the power of Congress to impose income taxes was the scope of its power to tax for police power purposes. Earlier in this chapter we briefly mentioned an important taxing and spending case, *McCray v. United States* (1904), in which the Court upheld a federal law that placed a tax of ten cents per pound on colored oleomargarine. The law's purpose was to protect butter from competition from a similar-looking product by making the oleo too expensive to produce. Chief Justice Edward White wrote, "[t]he decisions of this Court lend no support whatever to the assumption that the judiciary may restrain the exercise of a lawful power on the assumption that a wrongful purpose or motive has caused the power to be exerted."[55] In *United States v. Doremus*, the Court upheld a federal excise tax clearly designed to eliminate the manufacture and sale of narcotic drugs. Justice William Day, writing for a 5-4 majority, held that the Harrison Narcotics Act of 1914 "may not be deemed unconstitutional because its effect may be to accomplish another purpose."[56]

As we saw earlier in this chapter, the Court, in *Bailey v. Drexel Furniture Co.* (1922), tightened the conditions under which Congress could impose a tax designed to promote an objective unrelated to revenue. Despite affirming the power of Congress to enforce a regulatory purpose through its taxing and spending power in *J.W. Hampton, Jr. & Co. v. United States* (1928), by the early 1930s the Court had begun to uphold restrictions on congressional taxing power as part of its general opposition to New Deal legislation. The dual federalism that characterized the Court's Commerce Clause decisions in the pre–New Deal period soon became interwoven with the justices' taxing and spending decisions. The confrontation between the Roosevelt administration and the Court over the power of Congress to tax and spend on behalf of the general welfare reached its boiling point in *United States v. Butler* (1936). In *Butler* the Court invalidated a touchstone of the New Deal legislative agenda, the Agricultural Adjustment Act.[57]

*Butler* is best remembered as the pinnacle of the Court's invocation of legal formalism to defend laissez-faire economic principles. Justice Owen Roberts offered a theory of judicial review that became a source of ridicule almost as soon as the ink on his opinion had dried. "When an act of Congress is appropriately challenged in the courts as not conforming to the constitutional mandate," wrote Roberts, "the judicial branch of the government has but one duty; to lay the article of the Constitution which is invoked beside the statute which is challenged and decide whether the latter squares with the former."[58] Does this approach to constitutional interpretation have a home in any of the theories we discussed in Chapter 2, or, with the political soldiers of the New Deal mounted on the Court's doorstep, was it simply an effort to forestall the inevitable?

*Steward Machine Co.* v. *Davis* (1937), handed down within weeks of *West Coast Hotel* and *Jones & Laughlin,* upheld the Social Security Act against a challenge brought by an Alabama manufacturer who argued that Congress lacked the authority to impose an excise tax on earnings and income to fund the law's various compensation programs. Note that while it did not overrule *Butler,* Justice Cardozo's opinion in *Steward Machine* made *Butler* just another museum piece, along with *Lochner, Drexel,* and *Carter Coal. Steward Machine* was a major step in discrediting the Court's embrace of dual federalism, which, since the late 1890s, had impeded the exercise of congressional power on behalf of national economic and social objectives. Since *Steward Machine,* the Court has not invalidated a single federal law challenged as violative of the congressional power to tax and spend. The post–New Deal case that best illustrates the Court's deference to congressional taxing and spending power is *South Dakota* v. *Dole* (1987). *Dole* involved a challenge to a federal law authorizing the secretary of transportation to withhold funds to states that failed to raise their minimum age to purchase and use alcoholic beverages to twenty-one.

The Constitutional Revolution of 1937 was a watershed in American constitutional development. No longer committed to the idea of the economic and social status quo as a natural condition independent of the political forces that created it, the Court recognized that all laws were a positive form of government action. This principle was true whether the law's purpose was to promote laissez-faire economic principles or, from the standpoint of social justice, constrain them. While the practical political consequences of the Court's transformation after 1937 continue to affect the ebb and flow of American politics, the notion that law is something made by people to accomplish specific goals and not a force of mysterious, apolitical origins has been its most significant and lasting legacy.

## *United States* v. *Butler*
### 297 U.S. 1 (1936)

John Steinbeck's novel *The Grapes of Wrath,* published in 1939, symbolized the plight of America's farmers during the Great Depression. Always at the mercy of Mother Nature, farmers now had to contend with an economy so barren that it could not support the nation's agricultural industry. Attempts to improve their lot by increasing production simply made matters worse. Often stuck with abundant supplies and few buyers, farmers by the score either had their land foreclosed by the banks that held their mortgages or packed their belongings and their families and abandoned their farms in search of better luck elsewhere.

The Agricultural Adjustment Act (AAA) of 1933 was the cornerstone of the Roosevelt administration's plan to rescue the American farmer. The law introduced a practice that is still common: government subsidies to maintain a balance between production, supply, and pricing. For example, the federal government would pay farmers not to grow their crops, such as corn or wheat, or produce their commodities, such as milk, beyond a certain amount. The subsidies allowed supplies to remain in line with demand while compensating farmers for their "lost" production.

An excise tax levied on firms that processed agricultural products funded the subsidies. To no one's surprise, the nation's major agribusiness firms loathed the AAA. In *Butler* several companies came together to challenge the AAA as an unconstitutional exercise of federal taxing and spending power.

The Court's decision was 6 to 3. Justice Roberts delivered the opinion of the Court. Justice Stone, joined by Justices Brandeis and Cardozo, dissented.

MR. JUSTICE ROBERTS delivered the opinion of the Court.

In this case, we must determine whether certain provisions of the Agricultural Adjustment Act, 1933, conflict with the Federal Constitution. . . .

The tax plays an indispensable part in the plan of regulation. As stated by the Agricultural Adjustment Administrator, it is "the heart of the law"; a means of "accomplishing one or both of two things intended to help farmers attain parity prices and purchasing power." A tax automatically goes into effect for a commodity when the Secretary of Agriculture determines that rental or benefit payments are to be made for reduction of production of that commodity. The tax is to cease when rental or benefit payments cease. The rate is fixed with the purpose of bringing about crop reduction and price-raising. It is to equal the difference between the "current average farm price" and "fair exchange value." It may be altered to such amount as will prevent accumulation of surplus stocks. If the Secretary finds the policy of the act will not be promoted by the levy of the tax for a given commodity, he may exempt it. The whole revenue from the levy is appropriated in aid of crop control; none of it is made available for general governmental use. The entire agricultural adjustment program embodied in Title I of the act is to become inoperative when, in the judgment of the President, the national economic emergency ends, and as to any commodity, he may terminate the provisions of the law if he finds them no longer requisite to carrying out the declared policy with respect to such commodity.

The statute not only avows an aim foreign to the procurement of revenue for the support of government, but, by its operation, shows the exaction laid upon processors to be the necessary means for the intended control of agricultural production. . . .

The Government asserts that, even if the respondents may question the propriety of the appropriation embodied in the statute, their attack must fail because Article I, § 8 of the Constitution authorizes the contemplated expenditure of the funds raised by the tax. This contention presents the great and the controlling question in the case. We approach its decision with a sense of our grave responsibility to render judgment in accordance with the principles established for the governance of all three branches of the Government.

There should be no misunderstanding as to the function of this court in such a case. It is sometimes said that the court assumes a power to overrule or control the action of the people's representatives. This is a misconception. The Constitution is the supreme law of the land ordained and established by the people. All legislation must conform to the principles it lays down. When an act

of Congress is appropriately challenged in the courts as not conforming to the constitutional mandate, the judicial branch of the Government has only one duty—to lay the article of the Constitution which is invoked beside the statute which is challenged and to decide whether the latter squares with the former. All the court does, or can do, is to announce its considered judgment upon the question. The only power it has, if such it may be called, is the power of judgment. This court neither approves nor condemns any legislative policy. Its delicate and difficult office is to ascertain and declare whether the legislation is in accordance with, or in contravention of, the provisions of the Constitution; and, having done that, its duty ends.

The question is not what power the Federal Government ought to have, but what powers, in fact, have been given by the people. It hardly seems necessary to reiterate that ours is a dual form of government; that in every state there are two governments—the state and the United States. Each State has all governmental powers save such as the people, by their Constitution, have conferred upon the United States, denied to the States, or reserved to themselves. The federal union is a government of delegated powers. It has only such as are expressly conferred upon it and such as are reasonably to be implied from those granted. In this respect, we differ radically from nations where all legislative power, without restriction or limitation, is vested in a parliament or other legislative body subject to no restrictions except the discretion of its members.

Article I, Section 8, of the Constitution vests sundry powers in the Congress. But two of its clauses have any bearing upon the validity of the statute under review.

The third clause endows the Congress with power "to regulate Commerce . . . among the several States." Despite a reference in its first section to a burden upon, and an obstruction of the normal currents of commerce, the act under review does not purport to regulate transactions in interstate or foreign commerce. Its stated purpose is the control of agricultural production, a purely local activity, in an effort to raise the prices paid the farmer. Indeed, the Government does not attempt to uphold the validity of the act on the basis of the commerce clause, which, for the purpose of the present case, may be put aside as irrelevant.

The clause thought to authorize the legislation—the first—confers upon the Congress power, "to lay and collect Taxes, Duties, Imposts and Excises, to pay the Debts and provide for the common Defence and general Welfare of the United States . . ." It is not contended that this provision grants power to regulate agricultural production upon the theory that such legislation would promote the general welfare. The Government concedes that the phrase "to provide for the general welfare" qualifies the power "to lay and collect taxes." The view that the clause grants power to provide for the general welfare, independently of the taxing power, has never been authoritatively accepted. Mr. Justice Story points out that, if it were adopted, "it is obvious that, under color of the generality of the words, to "provide for the common defence and general welfare," the government of the United States is, in reality, a government of general and unlimited powers, notwithstanding the subsequent enumeration of specific powers." The true construction undoubtedly is that the only thing granted is the power to tax for the purpose of providing funds for payment of the nation's debts and making provision for the general welfare.

Nevertheless the Government asserts that warrant is found in this clause for the adoption of the Agricultural Adjustment Act. The argument is that Congress may appropriate and authorize the spending of moneys for the "general welfare"; that the phrase should be liberally construed to cover anything conducive to national welfare; that decision as to what will promote such welfare rests with Congress alone, and the courts may not review its determination, and finally that the appropriation under attack was, in fact, for the general welfare of the United States.

The Congress is expressly empowered to lay taxes to provide for the general welfare. Funds in the Treasury as a result of taxation may be expended only through appropriation. (Article I, Section 9, clause 7.) They can never accomplish the objects for which they were collected unless the power to appropriate is as broad as the power to tax. The necessary implication from the terms of the grant is that the public funds may be appropriated "to provide for the general welfare of the United States." These words cannot be meaningless, else they would not have been used. The conclusion must be that they were intended to limit and define the granted power to raise and to expend money. How shall they be construed to effectuate the intent of the instrument?

Since the foundation of the Nation, sharp differences of opinion have persisted as to the true interpretation of the phrase. Madison asserted it amounted to no more than a reference to the other powers enumerated in the subsequent clauses of the same section; that, as the United States is a government of limited and enumerated powers, the grant of power to tax and spend for the general national welfare must be confined to the enumerated legislative fields committed to the Congress. In this view, the phrase is mere tautology, for taxation and appropriation are, or may be, necessary incidents of the exercise of any of the enumerated legislative powers. Hamilton, on the other hand, maintained the clause confers a power separate and distinct from those later enumerated, is not restricted in meaning by the grant of them, and Congress consequently has a substantive power to tax and to appropriate, limited only by the requirement that it shall be exercised to provide for the general welfare of the United States. Each contention has had the support of those whose views are entitled to weight. This court has noticed the question, but has never found it necessary to decide which is the true construction. Mr. Justice Story, in his Commentaries, espouses the Hamiltonian position. We shall not review the writings of public men and commentators or discuss the legislative practice. Study of all these leads us to conclude that the reading advocated by Mr. Justice Story is the correct one. While, therefore, the power to tax is not unlimited, its confines are set in the clause which confers it, and not in those of Section 8 which bestow and define the legislative powers of the Congress. It results that the power of Congress to authorize expenditure of public moneys for public purposes is not limited by the direct grants of legislative power found in the Constitution. . . .

If the taxing power may not be used as the instrument to enforce a regulation of matters of state concern with respect to which the Congress has no authority to interfere, may it, as in the present case, be employed to raise the money necessary to purchase a compliance which the Congress is powerless to command? The Government asserts that whatever might be said against the validity of the plan if compulsory, it is constitutionally sound because the end is accomplished by voluntary cooperation. There are two sufficient answers to the contention. The regulation is not, in fact, voluntary. The farmer, of course, may refuse to comply, but the price of such refusal is the loss of benefits. The amount offered is intended to be sufficient to exert pressure on him to agree to the proposed regulation. The power to confer or withhold unlimited benefits is the power to coerce or destroy. If the cotton grower elects not to accept the benefits, he will receive less for his crops; those who receive payments will be able to undersell him. The result may well be financial ruin. The coercive purpose and intent of the statute is not obscured by the fact that it has not been perfectly successful. . . . It is clear that the Department of Agriculture has properly described the plan as one to keep a noncooperating minority in line. This is coercion by economic pressure. The asserted power of choice is illusory. . . .

Congress has no power to enforce its commands on the farmer to the ends sought by the Agricultural Adjustment Act. It must follow that it may not indirectly accomplish those ends by taxing and spending to purchase compliance. The Constitution and the entire plan of our government negate any such use of the power to tax and to spend as the act undertakes to authorize. It does not help to declare that local conditions throughout the nation have created a situation of national concern, for this is but to say that, whenever there is a widespread similarity of local conditions, Congress may ignore constitutional limitations upon its own powers and usurp those reserved to the states. If, in lieu of compulsory regulation of subjects within the states' reserved jurisdiction, which is prohibited, the Congress could invoke the taxing and spending power as a means to accomplish the same end, clause 1 of Section 8 of Article I would become the instrument for total subversion of the governmental powers reserved to the individual states.

Mr. Justice Stone, dissenting.

I think the judgment should be reversed.

The present stress of widely held and strongly expressed differences of opinion of the wisdom of the Agricultural Adjustment Act makes it important, in the interest of clear thinking and sound result, to emphasize at the outset certain propositions which should have controlling influence in determining the validity of the Act. They are:

1. The power of courts to declare a statute unconstitutional is subject to two guiding principles of decision which ought never to be absent from judicial consciousness. One is that courts are concerned only with the power to enact statutes, not with their wisdom. The other is that, while unconstitutional exercise of power by the executive and legislative branches of the government is subject to judicial restraint, the only check upon our own exercise of power is our own sense of self-restraint. For the removal of unwise laws from the statute books appeal lies not to the courts, but to the ballot and to the processes of democratic government.

2. The constitutional power of Congress to levy an excise tax upon the processing of agricultural products is not questioned. The present levy is held invalid not for any want of power in Congress to lay such a tax to defray public expenditures, including those for the general welfare, but because the use to which its proceeds are put is disapproved.

3. As the present depressed state of agriculture is nationwide in its extent and effects, there is no basis for saying that the expenditure of public money in aid of farmers is not within the specifically granted power of Congress to levy taxes to "provide for the . . . general welfare." The opinion of the Court does not declare otherwise. . . .

That the governmental power of the purse is a great one is not now for the first time announced. Every student of the history of government and economics is aware of its magnitude and of its existence in every civilized government. Both were well understood by the framers of the Constitution when they sanctioned the grant of the spending power to the federal government, and both were recognized by Hamilton and Story, whose views of the spending power as standing on a parity with the other powers specifically granted have hitherto been generally accepted.

The suggestion that it must now be curtailed by judicial fiat because it may be abused by unwise use hardly rises to the dignity of argument. So may judicial power be abused. The power to tax and spend is not without constitutional restraints. One restriction is that the purpose must be truly national. Another is that it may not be used to coerce action left to state control. Another is the conscience and patriotism of Congress and the Executive. "It must be remembered that legislators are the ultimate guardians of the liberties and welfare of the people in quite as great a degree as the courts."

A tortured construction of the Constitution is not to be justified by recourse to extreme examples of reckless congressional spending which might occur if courts could not prevent—expenditures which, even if they could be thought to effect any national purpose, would be possible only by action of a legislature lost to all sense of public responsibility. Such suppositions are addressed to the mind accustomed to believe that it is the business of courts to sit in judgment on the wisdom of legislative action. Courts are not the only agency of government that must be assumed to have capacity to govern. Congress and the courts both unhappily may falter or be mistaken in the performance of their constitutional duty. But interpretation of our great charter of government which proceeds on any assumption that the responsibility for the preservation of our institutions is the exclusive concern of any one of the three branches of government, or that it alone can save them from destruction is far more likely, in the long run, "to obliterate the constituent members" of "an indestructible union of indestructible states" than the frank recognition that language, even of a constitution, may mean what it says: that the power to tax and spend includes the power to relieve a nationwide economic maladjustment by conditional gifts of money.

Mr. Justice Brandeis and Mr. Justice Cardozo join in this opinion.

▼▲▼

## Steward Machine Co. v. Davis
### 301 U.S. 548 (1937)

The Social Security Act (SSA) of 1935 created the foundation of the modern American welfare state. Although the nation's commitment to government-funded services has increased exponentially since the New Deal, it was the SSA that established federal guarantees for retirement benefits, death benefits for survivors, aid to dependent children in poor families, and assistance to disabled persons. Many of these programs have taken on a life of their own; some, such as the program to aid dependent children, have been replaced by federal block grants in which the states administer their own programs. Social Security is still a contentious political issue, with its alleged survival or demise a central issue in presidential elections. Since the rise of the American Association of Retired Persons (AARP) as a powerful political lobby in the 1980s, few bother to question the constitutionality of Social Security. This was not always the case.

Funds for the Social Security program were raised by imposing an excise tax on companies with eight or more employees. Tax rates were determined by the total wages paid out by the employer. But if an employer chose to make a contribution to its state unemployment compensation fund, approved by the United States Treasury Department, the company was eligible to receive a tax credit of up to 90 percent of its tax obligations. Steward Machine Co., an Alabama corporation that manufactured coal equipment, paid a $46.14 tax into the Social Security fund and then promptly sued to collect a refund. It claimed the SSA was an unconstitutional exercise of congressional taxing and spending power. The lower federal courts rejected Steward Machine Co.'s contention. United States Solicitor General Stanley Reed, whom President Roosevelt later appointed to the Court in 1938 as a reward for his service during the New Deal, petitioned the Court to hear *Steward Machine Co.* to resolve the constitutionality of the Social Security law.

The Court's decision was 5 to 4. Justice Cardozo delivered the opinion of the Court. Justice McReynolds dissented. Justice Sutherland, joined by Justice Van Devanter, also dissented.

▼▲▼

MR. JUSTICE CARDOZO delivered the opinion of the Court.

The validity of the tax imposed by the Social Security Act on employers of eight or more is here to be determined. . . .

The assault on the statute proceeds on an extended front. Its assailants take the ground that the tax is not an excise; that it is not uniform throughout the United States as excises are required to be; that its exceptions are so many and arbitrary as to violate the Fifth Amendment; that its purpose was not revenue, but an unlawful invasion of the reserved powers of the states; and that the states in submitting to it have yielded to coercion and have abandoned governmental functions which they are not permitted to surrender.

The objections will be considered seriatim with such further explanation as may be necessary to make their meaning clear.

First: The tax, which is described in the statute as an excise, is laid with uniformity throughout the United States as a duty, an impost, or an excise upon the relation of employment. . . .

The subject-matter of taxation open to the power of the Congress is as comprehensive as that open to the power of the states, though the method of apportionment may at times be different. 'The Congress shall have Power to lay and collect Taxes, Duties, Imposts and Excises.' Article 1, Section 8. If the tax is a direct one, it shall be apportioned according to the census or enumeration. If it is a duty, impost, or excise, it shall be uniform throughout the United States. Together, these classes include every form of tax appropriate to sovereignty.

Whether the tax is to be classified as an 'excise' is in truth not of critical importance. . . . The statute books of the states are strewn with illustrations of taxes laid on occupations pursued of common right. We find no basis for a holding that the power in that regard which belongs by accepted practice to the Legislatures of the states, has been denied by the Constitution to the Congress of the nation.

Second: The excise is not invalid under the provisions of the Fifth Amendment by force of its exemptions. The statute does not apply, as we have seen, to employers of less then eight. It does not apply to agricultural labor, or domestic service in a private home or to some other classes of less importance. Petitioner contends that the effect of these restrictions is an arbitrary discrimination vitiating the tax.

The classifications and exemptions directed by the statute now in controversy have support in considerations of policy and practical convenience that cannot be condemned as arbitrary. . . .

The act of Congress is therefore valid, so far at least as its system of exemptions is concerned, and this though we assume that discrimination, if gross enough, is equivalent to confiscation and subject under the Fifth Amendment to challenge and annulment.

Third: The excise is not void as involving the coercion of the states in contravention of the Tenth Amendment or of restrictions implicit in our federal form of government.

The proceeds of the excise when collected are paid into the Treasury at Washington, and thereafter are subject to appropriation like public moneys generally. No presumption can be indulged that they will be misapplied or wasted. Even if they were collected in the hope or expectation that some other and collateral good would be furthered as an incident, that without more would not make the act invalid. This indeed is hardly questioned. The case for the petitioner is built on the contention that here an ulterior aim is wrought into the very structure of the act, and what is even more important that the aim is not only ulterior, but essentially unlawful. In particular, the 90 per cent. credit is relied upon as supporting that conclusion. But before the statute succumbs to an assault upon these lines, two propositions must be made out by the assailant. There must be a showing in the first place that separated from the credit the revenue provisions are incapable of standing by themselves. There must be a showing in the second place that the tax and the credit in combination are weapons of coercion, destroying or impairing the autonomy of the states. The truth of each proposition being essential to the success of the assault, we pass for convenience to a consideration of the second, without pausing to inquire whether there has been a demonstration of the first.

To draw the line intelligently between duress and inducement, there is need to remind ourselves of facts as to the problem of unemployment that are now matters of common knowledge. *West Coast Hotel Co.* v. *Parrish* (1937). The relevant statistics are gathered in the brief of counsel for the government. Of the many available figures a few only will be mentioned. During the years 1929 to 1936, when the country was passing through a cyclical depression, the number of the unemployed mounted to unprecedented heights. Often the average was more than 10 million; at times a peak was attained of 16 million or more. Disaster to the breadwinner meant disaster to dependents. Accordingly the roll of the unemployed, itself formidable enough, was only a partial roll of the destitute or needy. The fact developed quickly that the states were unable to give the requisite relief. The problem had become national in area and dimensions. There was need

of help from the nation if the people were not to starve. It is too late today for the argument to be heard with tolerance that in a crisis so extreme the use of the moneys of the nation to relieve the unemployed and their dependents is a use for any purpose narrower than the promotion of the general welfare. The nation responded to the call of the distressed. Between January 1, 1933, and July 1, 1936, the states (according to statistics submitted by the government) incurred obligations of $689,291,802 for emergency relief; local subdivisions an additional $775,675,366. In the same period the obligations for emergency relief incurred by the national government were $ 2,929,307,125, or twice the obligations of states and local agencies combined. According to the President's budget message for the fiscal year 1938, the national government expended for public works and unemployment relief for the three fiscal years 1934, 1935, and 1936, the stupendous total of $8,681,000,000. The parens patriae has many reasons—fiscal and economic as well as social and moral—for planning to mitigate disasters that bring these burdens in their train.

In the presence of this urgent need for some remedial expedient, the question is to be answered whether the expedient adopted has overlept the bounds of power. The assailants of the statute say that its dominant end and aim is to drive the state Legislatures under the whip of economic pressure into the enactment of unemployment compensation laws at the bidding of the central government. Supporters of the statute say that its operation is not constraint, but the creation of a larger freedom, the states and the nation joining in a co-operative endeavor to avert a common evil. Before Congress acted, unemployment compensation insurance was still, for the most part, a project and no more. . . .

The Social Security Act is an attempt to find a method by which all these public agencies may work together to a common end. Every dollar of the new taxes will continue in all likelihood to be used and needed by the nation as long as states are unwilling, whether through timidity or for other motives, to do what can be done at home. At least the inference is permissible that Congress so believed, though retaining undiminished freedom to spend the money as it pleased. On the other hand, fulfillment of the home duty will be lightened and encouraged by crediting the taxpayer upon his account with the Treasury of the nation to the extent that his contributions under the laws of the locality have simplified or diminished the problem of relief and the probable demand upon the resources of the fisc. Duplicated taxes, or burdens that approach them are recognized hardships that government, state or national, may properly avoid. If Congress believed that the general welfare would better be promoted by relief through local units than by the system then in vogue, the co-operating localities ought not in all fairness to pay a second time.

Who then is coerced through the operation of this statute? Not the taxpayer. He pays in fulfillment of the mandate of the local legislature. Not the state. Even now she does not offer a suggestion that in passing the unemployment law she was affected by duress. For all that appears, she is satisfied with her choice, and would be sorely disappointed if it were now to be annulled. The difficulty with the petitioner's contention is that it confuses motive with coercion. 'Every tax is in some measure regulatory. To some extent it interposes an economic impediment to the activity taxed as compared with others not taxed.' In like manner every rebate from a tax when conditioned upon conduct is in some measure a temptation. But to hold that motive or temptation is equivalent to coercion is to plunge the law in endless difficulties. The outcome of such a doctrine is the acceptance of a philosophical determinism by which choice becomes impossible. Till now the law has been guided by a robust common sense which assumes the freedom of the will as a working hypothesis in the solution of its problems. . . .

In ruling as we do, we leave many questions open. We do not say that a tax is valid, when imposed by act of Congress, if it is laid upon the condition that a state may escape its operation through the adoption of a statute unrelated in subject-matter to activities fairly within the scope of national policy and power. No such question is before us.

Separate opinion of Mr. Justice McReynolds (dissenting).

That portion of the Social Security legislation here under consideration, I think, exceeds the power granted to Congress. It unduly interferes with the orderly government of the state by her own people and otherwise offends the Federal Constitution. . . .

The doctrine thus announced and often repeated, I had supposed was firmly established. Apparently the states remained really free to exercise governmental powers, not delegated or prohibited, without interference by the federal government through threats of punitive measures or offers of seductive favors. Unfortunately, the decision just announced opens the way for practical annihilation of this theory; and no cloud of words or ostentatious parade of irrelevant statistics should be permitted to obscure that fact. . . .

No defense is offered for the legislation under review upon the basis of emergency. The hypothesis is that here-

after it will continuously benefit unemployed members of a class. Forever, so far as we can see, the states are expected to function under federal direction concerning an internal matter. By the sanction of this adventure, the door is open for progressive inauguration of others of like kind under which it can hardly be expected that the states will retain genuine independence of action. And without independent states a Federal Union as contemplated by the Constitution becomes impossible.

## South Dakota v. Dole
### 483 U.S. 203 (1987)

Shortly into his first term, an adamant President Reagan demanded that Congress raise the minimum drinking age to twenty-one as a means to curb alcohol-related automobile injuries and fatalities. In 1984, Congress responded by amending the Surface Transportation and Assistance Act to permit the Department of Transportation to withhold federal highway funds from states that did not raise their minimum drinking age. Most states complied with the new law rather than lose much-prized federal highway money.

South Dakota, however, refused to go along, claiming that the Tenth and Twenty-first Amendments barred Congress from regulating the sale and consumption of alcoholic beverages. Under South Dakota law, nineteen year olds were permitted to buy beer with a 3.2 percent alcohol content or lower. Twenty-one was the minimum age to purchase and consume alcohol with an alcohol content of 5.0 percent or greater. South Dakota sued Transportation Secretary Elizabeth Dole, who later sought—unsuccessfully—the Republican presidential nomination in 2000. The lower federal courts rejected South Dakota's contention.

The Court's decision was 7 to 2. Chief Justice Rehnquist delivered the opinion of the Court. Justices Brennan and O'Connor dissented.

Chief Justice Rehnquist delivered the opinion of the Court.

The Constitution empowers Congress to, "lay and collect Taxes, Duties, Imposts, and Excises, to pay the Debts and provide for the common Defence and general Welfare of the United States." Article I, Section 8, clause 1. Incident to this power, Congress may attach conditions on the receipt of federal funds, and has repeatedly employed the power, "to further broad policy objectives by conditioning receipt of federal moneys upon compliance by the recipient with federal statutory and administrative directives." The breadth of this power was made clear in *United States* v. *Butler* (1936), where the Court, resolving a longstanding debate over the scope of the Spending Clause, determined that, "the power of Congress to authorize expenditure of public moneys for public purposes is not limited by the direct grants of legislative power found in the Constitution." Thus, objectives not thought to be within Article I's "enumerated legislative fields," may nevertheless be attained through the use of the spending power and the conditional grant of federal funds.

The spending power is of course not unlimited, but is instead subject to several general restrictions articulated in our cases. The first of these limitations is derived from the language of the Constitution itself: the exercise of the spending power must be in pursuit of "the general welfare." *United States* v. *Butler* (1936). In considering whether a particular expenditure is intended to serve general public purposes, courts should defer substantially to the judgment of Congress. Second, we have required that, if Congress desires to condition the States' receipt of federal funds, it "must do so unambiguously . . enabl[ing] the States to exercise their choice knowingly, cognizant of the consequences of their participation." Third, our cases have suggested (without significant elaboration) that conditions on federal grants might be illegitimate if they are unrelated "to the federal interest in particular national projects or programs." Finally, we have noted that other constitutional provisions may provide an independent bar to the conditional grant of federal funds.

South Dakota does not seriously claim that Section 158 is inconsistent with any of the first three restrictions mentioned above. We can readily conclude that the provision is designed to serve the general welfare, especially in light of the fact that "the concept of welfare or the opposite is shaped by Congress . . ." Congress found that the differing drinking ages in the States created particular incentives for young persons to combine their desire to drink with their ability to drive, and that this interstate problem required a national solution. The means it chose to address this dangerous situation were reasonably calculated to advance the general welfare. The conditions upon which States receive the funds, moreover, could not be more clearly stated by Congress. And the State itself, rather than challenging the germaneness of the condition to federal purposes, admits that it "has never contended that the congressional action was . . . unrelated

to a national concern in the absence of the Twenty-first Amendment." Indeed, the condition imposed by Congress is directly related to one of the main purposes for which highway funds are expended—safe interstate travel. This goal of the interstate highway system had been frustrated by varying drinking ages among the States. A Presidential commission appointed to study alcohol-related accidents and fatalities on the Nation's highways concluded that the lack of uniformity in the States' drinking ages created "an incentive to drink and drive" because "young persons commut[e] to border States where the drinking age is lower." Presidential Commission on Drunk Driving, Final Report (1983). By enacting Section 158, Congress conditioned the receipt of federal funds in a way reasonably calculated to address this particular impediment to a purpose for which the funds are expended.

The remaining question about the validity of Section 158—and the basic point of disagreement between the parties—is whether the Twenty-first Amendment constitutes an "independent constitutional bar" to the conditional grant of federal funds. Petitioner, relying on its view that the Twenty-first Amendment prohibits *direct* regulation of drinking ages by Congress, asserts that, "Congress may not use the spending power to regulate that which it is prohibited from regulating directly under the Twenty-first Amendment." But our cases show that this "independent constitutional bar" limitation on the spending power is not of the kind petitioner suggests. *United States* v. *Butler* (1936), for example, established that the constitutional limitations on Congress when exercising its spending power are less exacting than those on its authority to regulate directly. . . .

These cases establish that the "independent constitutional bar" limitation on the spending power is not, as petitioner suggests, a prohibition on the indirect achievement of objectives which Congress is not empowered to achieve directly. Instead, we think that the language in our earlier opinions stands for the unexceptionable proposition that the power may not be used to induce the States to engage in activities that would themselves be unconstitutional. Thus, for example, a grant of federal funds conditioned on invidiously discriminatory state action or the infliction of cruel and unusual punishment would be an illegitimate exercise of the Congress' broad spending power. But no such claim can be or is made here. Were South Dakota to succumb to the blandishments offered by Congress and raise its drinking age to 21, the State's action in so doing would not violate the constitutional rights of anyone.

Our decisions have recognized that, in some circumstances, the financial inducement offered by Congress might be so coercive as to pass the point at which "pressure turns into compulsion." *Steward Machine Co. v. Davis* (1937). Here, however, Congress has directed only that a State desiring to establish a minimum drinking age lower than 21 lose a relatively small percentage of certain federal highway funds. Petitioner contends that the coercive nature of this program is evident from the degree of success it has achieved. We cannot conclude, however, that a conditional grant of federal money of this sort is unconstitutional simply by reason of its success in achieving the congressional objective. . . .

Here Congress has offered relatively mild encouragement to the States to enact higher minimum drinking ages than they would otherwise choose. But the enactment of such laws remains the prerogative of the States not merely in theory, but in fact. Even if Congress might lack the power to impose a national minimum drinking age directly, we conclude that encouragement to state action found in Section 158 is a valid use of the spending power. Accordingly, the judgment of the Court of Appeals is

*Affirmed.*

## The Commerce Clause as an Instrument of Social Reform

Police power, or the power of government to promote health and social welfare objectives through legislation, is most often considered the constitutional responsibility of the states. The constitutional and political basis for reserving broad police power to the states is discussed in Chapter 7. But even our limited discussion of this important function has made clear that several constitutional sources of such power authorize the national government to promote concerns related to the general welfare, or so the Supreme Court has said.

Although the Court had ruled as far back as the 1830s that communities possessed a police power to promote health and social welfare objectives, it did not recognize a similar power on behalf of the federal government until 1903. In *Champion v. Ames*, the Court held that Congress could use its commerce power in expansive terms to guard the "people of the United States against the 'widespread pestilence of lotteries.'" In *Stone v. Mississippi* (1880), the Court ruled that the Con-

tract Clause, the subject of Chapter 8, did not act as a barrier to a state decision to rescind a charter it had granted to a local business to own and operate a lottery. *Ames* offers a similar line of reasoning to justify state interference with the economic marketplace. Considering the narrow interpretation the Court was giving to congressional commerce power in cases that dealt more explicitly with "pure" commercial activities, the decision was a surprise. How does *Ames* compare with the Court's decision in *Hammer v. Dagenhart*? Congressional motives in both cases were the same—to outlaw a social evil. Is there an explanation independent of legal logic for the Court's decision in *Dagenhart* to distinguish *Ames* rather than follow it?

The Constitutional Revolution of 1937 enabled Congress to extend its police power on behalf of social reform as never before. Congress's use of the Commerce Clause to eradicate racial discrimination provides the most striking example of the degree to which the Court now defers to the legislative branch. In *Heart of Atlanta Motel v. United States* (1964) and *Katzenbach v. McClung* (1964), the Court upheld the Civil Rights Act of 1964, which barred discrimination in public accommodations by employers of fifteen persons or more and by institutions receiving federal funds. The Court ruled that the law was a valid exercise of congressional commerce power, even though the relationship of interstate commerce to the racially exclusionary policies at issue was tangential.[59] The SIDEBAR on these two cases offers more background on the groundswell of opposition to the 1964 civil rights law among small business owners such as the Heart of Atlanta Motel and Ollies' Barbecue, the small Birmingham restaurant that brought suit in *Katzenbach*. It also paints a much broader picture of the pervasiveness of racial discrimination in the pre–civil rights era South.

Numerous commentators have suggested that Congress, rather than relying on the Commerce Clause, should have used its power under Section 5 of the Fourteenth Amendment to enforce the nondiscrimination guarantee of the 1964 law. Justice William Douglas, concurring in *Heart of Atlanta*, took this position. Douglas wrote that his reluctance to join the Court's opinion "was not due to any conviction that Congress lacks power to regulate commerce in the interests of human rights. It is rather my belief that the right of people to be free of state action that discriminates against them because of race . . . 'occupies a more protected position in our constitutional system than does the movement of cattle, fruit, steel and coal across state lines.'"[60] Congress, however, was hamstrung by one of the Court's early post-Reconstruction decisions, *The Civil Rights Cases of 1883,* from using its amendment-enforcing power under Section 5.[61]

In that case an 8-1 Court invalidated an 1875 civil rights law that sought to guarantee African Americans full and equal rights in public accommodations. The Court ruled that "civil rights, such as are guaranteed by the Constitution, against State aggression, cannot be impaired by the wrongful acts of individuals, unsupported by State authority in the shape of laws, customs, or judicial or executive proceedings. The wrongful act of an individual, unsupported by any such authority, is simply a private wrong," one that Congress is powerless to prohibit under Section 5 of the Fourteenth Amendment.[62] Justice Joseph Bradley, who wrote the Court's opinion, did suggest in *dicta* that "Congress, in the exercise of its power to regulate commerce amongst the several states, might or might not pass a law regulating rights in public conveyances passing from one state to another." But even if Congress feigned any interest in pursuing an aggressive civil rights agenda on behalf of African Americans, the Court's adoption of the dual federalist doctrine and the rise of Jim Crow in the South would have rendered any such legislation meaningless.

Beginning in *Shelley* v. *Kraemer* (1948), the Court expanded the concept of state-imposed discrimination to include private conduct undertaken under the color, or approval, of state law. Nonetheless, the Court continued to distinguish the restrictive covenants in real estate transactions struck down in *Shelley* from access to public accommodations and fair employment practices in the private sector. Review the cases discussed in Chapter 4's section on the power of Congress to enforce constitutional amendments before you read *Heart of Atlanta Motel* and *McClung.* Is Justice Douglas right? Also, consider the implications of the 1937 constitutional revolution on the distinction between state and private action that continues to carry over from the *Civil Rights Cases.* Because the economic marketplace is the creation of law and not, as we have discussed, a natural condition, is congressional enforcement of federal civil rights laws more appropriately found in Section 5 of the Fourteenth Amendment than in the Commerce Clause?

## *Champion* v. *Ames*
### 188 U.S. 321 (1903)

By the late 1800s a nationwide movement to ban lotteries had pushed most states to enact antilottery laws. The Court, in *Stone* v. *Mississippi* (1880) (see Chapter 8), ruled that the Contract Clause did not prohibit states from banning lotteries, even if that meant terminating a previously granted corporate charter to permit such activity. Such action, the Court ruled, was well within the police powers of the state to promote the general welfare.

Consistent with this sentiment, Congress enacted a law in 1895 making it a crime for anyone to bring lottery tickets into the United States, place them in interstate commerce, or send them through the post office. In 1899, Charles Champion and several of his associates were indicted in federal district court for allegedly arranging for lottery tickets printed in Paraguay to be shipped from Texas to California. Champion was subsequently arrested by U.S. Marshall John Ames. Champion challenged the antilottery law as beyond the scope of congressional commerce power, arguing that such regulation was a matter for the states.

The Court's decision was 5 to 4. Justice Harlan delivered the opinion of the Court. Chief Justice Fuller, joined by Justices Brewer, Shiras, and Peckam, dissented.

MR. JUSTICE HARLAN delivered the opinion of the Court.

What is [the commerce] power? It is the power to regulate; that is, to prescribe the rule by which commerce is to be governed. This by which commerce is to be governed. This power, like all others vested in Congress, is complete in itself, may be exercised to its utmost extent, and acknowledges no limitations, other than are prescribed in the Constitution. These are expressed in plain terms, and do not affect the questions which arise in this case, or which have been discussed at the bar. If, as has always been understood, the sovereignty of Congress, though limited to specific objects, is plenary as to those objects, the power over commerce with foreign nations, and among the several states, is vested in Congress as absolutely as it would be in a single government, having in its constitution the same restrictions on the exercise of the power as are found in the Constitution of the United States. . . .

[P]rior adjudications . . . show that commerce among the states embraces navigation, intercourse, communication, traffic, the transit of persons, and the transmission of messages by telegraph. They also show that the power to regulate commerce among the several states is vested in Congress as absolutely as it would be in a single government, having in its constitution the same restrictions on the exercise of the power as are found in the Constitution of the United States; that such power is plenary, complete in itself, and may be exerted by Congress to its utmost extent, subject only to such limitations as the Constitution imposes upon the exercise of the powers granted by it; and that in determining the character of the regulations to be adopted Congress has a large discretion which is not to be controlled by the courts, simply because, in their opinion, such regulations may not be the best or most effective that could be employed.

We come, then, to inquire whether there is any solid foundation upon which to rest the contention that Congress may not regulate the carrying of lottery tickets from one state to another, at least by corporations or companies whose business it is, for hire, to carry tangible property from one state to another.

It was said in argument that lottery tickets are not of any real or substantial value in themselves, and therefore are not subjects of commerce. If that were conceded to be the only legal test as to what are to be deemed subjects of the commerce that may be regulated by Congress, we cannot accept as accurate the broad statement that such tickets are of no value. Upon their face they showed that the lottery company offered a large capital prize, to be paid to the holder of the ticket winning the prize at the drawing advertised to be held at Asuncion, Paraguay. Money was placed on deposit in different banks in the United States to be applied by the agents representing the lottery company to the prompt payment of prizes. These tickets were the subject of traffic; they could have been sold; and the holder was assured that the company would pay to him the amount of the prize drawn. That the holder might not have been able to enforce his claim in the courts of any country making the drawing of lotteries illegal, and forbidding the circulation of lottery tickets, did not change the fact that the tickets issued by the foreign company represented so much money payable to the person holding them and who might draw the prizes affixed to them. Even if a holder did not draw a prize, the tickets, before the drawing, had a money value in the market among those who chose to sell or buy lottery tickets. . . .

We are of opinion that lottery tickets are subjects of traffic, and therefore are subjects of commerce, and the regulation of the carriage of such tickets from state to state, at least by independent carriers, is a regulation of commerce among the several states. . . .

We have said that the carrying from state to state of lottery tickets constitutes interstate commerce, and that the regulation of such commerce is within the power of Congress under the Constitution. Are we prepared to say that a provision which is, in effect, a prohibition of the carriage of such articles from state to state is not a fit or appropriate mode for the regulation of that particular kind of commerce? If lottery traffic, carried on through interstate commerce, is a matter of which Congress may take cognizance and over which its power may be exerted, can it be possible that it must tolerate the traffic, and simply regulate the manner in which it may be carried on? Or may not Congress, for the protection of the people of all the states, and under the power to regulate interstate commerce, devise such means, within the scope of the Constitution, and not prohibited by it, as will drive that traffic out of commerce among the states? . . .

If a state, when considering legislation for the suppression of lotteries within its own limits, may properly take into view the evils that inhere in the raising of money, in that mode, why may not Congress, invested with the power to regulate commerce among the several states, provide that such commerce shall not be polluted by the carrying of lottery tickets from one state to another?

In this connection it must not be forgotten that the power of Congress to regulate commerce among the states is plenary, is complete in itself, and is subject to no limitations except such as may be found in the Constitution. What provision in that instrument can be regarded as limiting the exercise of the power granted? What clause can be cited which, in any degree, countenances the suggestion that one may, of right, carry or cause to be carried from one state to another that which will harm the public morals? We cannot think of any clause of that instrument that could possibly be invoked by those who assert their right to send lottery tickets from state to state except the one providing that no person shall be deprived of his liberty without due process of law. We have said that the liberty protected by the Constitution embraces the right to be free in the enjoyment of one's faculties; 'to be free to use them in all lawful ways; to live and work where he will; to earn his livelihood by any lawful calling; to pursue any livelihood or avocation, and for that purpose to enter into all contracts which may be proper.' But surely it will not be said to be a part of anyone's liberty, as recognized by the supreme law of the land, that he shall be allowed to introduce into commerce among the states an element that will be confessedly injurious to the public morals.

If it be said that the act of 1894 is inconsistent with the 10th Amendment, reserving to the states respectively, or to the people, the powers not delegated to the United States, the answer is that the power to regulate commerce among the states has been expressly delegated to Congress.

Besides, Congress, by that act, does not assume to interfere with traffic or commerce in lottery tickets carried on exclusively within the limits of any state, but has in view only commerce of that kind among the several states. It has not assumed to interfere with the completely internal affairs of any state, and has only legislated in respect of a matter which concerns the people of the United States. As a state may, for the purpose of guarding the morals of its own people, forbid all sales of lottery tickets within its limits, so Congress, for the purpose of guarding the people of the United States against the 'widespread pestilence of lotteries' and to protect the commerce which concerns all the states, may prohibit the carrying of lottery tickets from one state to another. In legislating upon the subject of the traffic in lottery tickets, as carried on through interstate commerce, Congress only supplemented the action of those states—perhaps all of them—which, for the protection of the public morals, prohibit the drawing of lotteries, as well as the sale or circulation of lottery tickets, within their respective limits. . . .

If what is done by Congress is manifestly in excess of the powers granted to it, then upon the courts will rest the duty of adjudging that its action is neither legal nor binding upon the people. But if what Congress does is within the limits of its power, and is simply unwise or injurious, the remedy is that suggested by Chief Justice Marshall in *Gibbons* v. *Ogden*, when he said: 'The wisdom and the discretion of Congress, their identity with the people, and the influence which their constituents possess at elections, are, in this, as in many other instances, as that, for example, of declaring war, the sole restraints on which they have relied, to secure them from its abuse. They are the restraints on which the people must often rely solely, in all representative governments.'

The judgment is affirmed.

Mr. CHIEF JUSTICE FULLER, with whom concur Mr. JUSTICE BREWER, Mr. JUSTICE SHIRAS, and Mr. JUSTICE PECKHAM, dissenting.

The case before us does not involve in fact the circulation of advertisements and the question of the abridgment of the freedom of the press; nor does it involve the importation of lottery matter, or its transmission by the mails. It is conceded that the lottery tickets in question, though purporting to be issued by a lottery company of Paraguay, were printed in the United States, and were not imported into the United States from any foreign country.

The naked question is whether the prohibition by Congress of the carriage of lottery tickets from one state to another by means other than the mails is within the powers vested in that body by the Constitution of the United States. That the purpose of Congress in this enactment was the suppression of lotteries cannot reasonably be denied. That purpose is avowed in the title of the act, and is its natural and reasonable effect, and by that its validity must be tested.

The power of the state to impose restraints and burdens on persons and property in conservation and promotion of the public health, good order, and prosperity is a power originally and always belonging to the states, not surrendered by them to the general government, nor directly restrained by the Constitution of the United States, and essentially exclusive, and the suppression of lotteries as a harmful business falls within this power, commonly called, of police.

It is urged, however, that because Congress is empowered to regulate commerce between the several states, it, therefore, may suppress lotteries by prohibiting the carriage of lottery matter. Congress may, indeed, make all laws necessary and proper for carrying the powers granted to it into execution, and doubtless an act prohibiting the carriage of lottery matter would be necessary and proper to the execution of a power to suppress lotteries; but that power belongs to the states and not to Congress. To hold that Congress has general police power would be to hold that it may accomplish objects not intrusted to the general government, and to defeat the operation of the 10th Amendment, declaring that 'the powers not delegated to the United States by the Constitution, nor prohibited by it to the states, are reserved to the states respectively, or to the people.' . . .

The power to prohibit the transportation of diseased animals and infected goods over railroads or on steamboats is an entirely different thing, for they would be in themselves injurious to the transaction of interstate commerce, and, moreover, are essentially commercial in their nature. And the exclusion of diseased persons rests on different ground, for nobody would pretend that persons could be kept off the trains because they were going from one state to another to engage in the lottery business. However enticing that business may be, we do not understand these pieces of paper themselves can communicate bad principles by contact. . . .

I regard this decision as inconsistent with the views of the framers of the Constitution, and of Marshall, its great expounder. Our form of government may remain notwithstanding legislation or decision, but, as long ago observed, it is with governments, as with religions: the form may survive the substance of the faith.

Many observers of American political history credit President Lyndon Johnson as the person most responsible for the passage of the Civil Rights Act of 1964. Johnson, a Texas Democrat steeped in New Deal politics, took his legendary reputation as a congressional dealmaker and arm-twister to the White House in November 1963, when, as John F. Kennedy's vice president, he succeeded the assassinated young president. Since taking office in January 1961, the Kennedy administration had butted heads with the Southern leadership in the House and Senate over the passage of a comprehensive civil rights law. Needing their votes for his domestic and foreign policy initiatives, Kennedy could not afford to alienate key Southern support. Until June 1963 the need to guarantee civil rights protection for African Americans was mostly talk and little else.

Several key events shook the ground underneath the nation's conscience that summer. In June, Justice Department lawyer Nicholas Katzenbach, with the full support of the Kennedy administration, successfully confronted the governor of Alabama, George Wallace, on the University of Alabama's Montgomery campus over the admission of two black students. In August several hundred thousand civil rights supporters staged a peaceful rally on the Mall in Washington, D.C., the day ending with Martin Luther King Jr. giving his moving and well-remembered "I Have a Dream" speech. By September the mood in the South had turned uglier and more defensive, with the tragic bombing of the Sixteenth Street Baptist Church in Birmingham the most piercing of the violent moments that lay on the horizon. President Kennedy was genuinely moved by the unwavering commitment of the protesters' dedication to nonviolent social change and outraged by the sheer cruelty of events such as the Sixteenth Street bombing. Shortly before his death, the president introduced what became the Civil Rights Act of 1964, the first major piece of federal civil rights legislation since Reconstruction.

Johnson lobbied tirelessly on behalf of the 1964 law, insisting that the nation owed its fallen young president a fitting tribute to the principles for which he stood. Assisted by a broad coalition of labor unions, religious groups, and civil rights organizations, Johnson secured the votes for the law's passage. Richard Russell, a staunch segregationist from Georgia, one of Johnson's oldest friends in the Senate, opposed the bill but had to express admiration for his former colleague's work, remarking that the president put so much pressure on everybody that there was never a doubt about the bill's passage.

Shortly after the law went into effect Moreton Rolleston, owner of the 216-room Heart of Atlanta Motel in downtown Atlanta, filed suit in federal court seeking to have the public accommodations provision of the 1964 act declared unconstitutional. The court rejected his request and ordered him to comply with the law.

One hundred and fifty miles west, Ollie's Barbecue, a family-owned restaurant in Birmingham, also challenged the public accommodations provision of the 1964 law. Ollie McClung Sr. argued in federal court that the law was unconstitutional; he was successful. The United States appealed.

## *Heart of Atlanta Motel* v. *United States*
### 379 U.S. 241 (1964)

Additional facts and background for *Heart of Atlanta Motel* and *Katzenbach* are set out in the accompanying SIDEBAR. The Court's decision in each case was unanimous. Justice Clark delivered the opinion of the Court. Justices Black, Douglas, and Goldberg filed separate concurring opinions.

▼▲▼

MR. JUSTICE CLARK delivered the opinion of the Court.

Congress first evidenced its interest in civil rights legislation in the Civil Rights or Enforcement Act of April 9, 1866. There followed four Acts, with a fifth, the Civil Rights Act of March 1, 1875, culminating the series. In 1883, this Court struck down the public accommodations sections of the 1875 Act in the *Civil Rights Cases* (1883). No major legislation in this field had been enacted by Congress for 82 years when the Civil Rights Act of 1957 became law. It was followed by the Civil Rights Act of 1960. Three years later, on June 19, 1963, the late President Kennedy called for civil rights legislation in a message to Congress to which he attached a proposed bill. Its stated purpose was

> to promote the general welfare by eliminating discrimination based on race, color, religion, or national origin in . . . public accommodations through the exercise by Congress of the powers conferred upon it . . . to enforce the provisions of the fourteenth and fifteenth amendments to regulate commerce among the several States, and to make laws necessary and proper to execute the powers conferred upon it by the Constitution.

. . . The Act as finally adopted was most comprehensive, undertaking to prevent, through peaceful and voluntary settlement, discrimination in voting as well as in places of accommodation and public facilities, federally secured programs, and in employment. Since Title II is the only portion under attack here, we confine our consideration to those public accommodation provisions.

This Title . . . provides that: "All persons shall be entitled to the full and equal enjoyment of the goods, services, facilities, privileges, advantages, and accommodations of any place of public accommodation, as defined in this section, without discrimination or segregation on the ground of race, color, religion, or national origin." . . .

It is admitted that the operation of the motel brings it within the provisions . . . of the Act, and that appellant refused to provide lodging for transient Negroes because of their race or color, and that it intends to continue that policy unless restrained.

The sole question posed is, therefore, the constitutionality of the Civil Rights Act of 1964 as applied to these facts. The legislative history of the Act indicates that Congress based the Act on Section 5 and the Equal Protection Clause of the Fourteenth Amendment, as well as its power to regulate interstate commerce under Article I, Section 8, clause 3, of the Constitution.

The Senate Commerce Committee made it quite clear that the fundamental object of Title II was to vindicate "the deprivation of personal dignity that surely accompanies denials of equal access to public establishments." At the same time, however, it noted that such an objective has been and could be readily achieved "by congressional action based on the commerce power of the Constitution." Our study of the legislative record, made in the light of prior cases, has brought us to the conclusion that Congress possessed ample power in this regard, and we have therefore not considered the other grounds relied upon. This is not to say that the remaining authority upon which it acted was not adequate, a question upon which we do not pass, but merely that, since the commerce power is sufficient for our decision here, we have considered it alone. . . .

## The *Civil Rights Cases* (1883) and their Application

In light of our ground for decision, it might be well at the outset to discuss the *Civil Rights Cases*, which declared provisions of the Civil Rights Act of 1875 unconstitutional. We think that decision inapposite and without precedential value in determining the constitutionality of the present Act. Unlike Title II of the present legislation, the 1875 Act broadly proscribed discrimination in "inns, public conveyances on land or water, theaters, and other places of public amusement," without limiting the categories of affected businesses to those impinging upon interstate commerce. In contrast, the applicability of Title II is carefully limited to enterprises having a direct and substantial relation to the interstate flow of goods and people, except where state action is involved. Further, the fact that certain kinds of businesses may not in 1875 have been sufficiently involved in interstate commerce to warrant bringing them within the ambit of the commerce power is not necessarily dispositive of the same question today. Our populace had not reached its present mobility, nor were facilities, goods and services circulating as readily in interstate commerce as they are today. Although the principles which we apply today are those first formulated by Chief Justice Marshall in *Gibbons v. Ogden* (1824), the conditions of transportation and commerce have changed dramatically, and we must apply those principles to the present state of commerce. The sheer increase in volume of interstate traffic alone would give discriminatory practices which inhibit travel a far larger impact upon the Nation's commerce than such practices had on the economy of another day. Finally, there is language in the *Civil Rights Cases* which indicates that the Court did not fully consider whether the 1875 Act could be sustained as an exercise of the commerce power. . . .

Since the commerce power was not relied on by the Government and was without support in the record, it is understandable that the Court narrowed its inquiry and excluded the Commerce Clause as a possible source of power. In any event, it is clear that such a limitation renders the opinion devoid of authority for the proposition that the Commerce Clause gives no power to Congress to regulate discriminatory practices now found substantially to affect interstate commerce. We therefore conclude that the *Civil Rights Cases* have no relevance to the basis of decision here, where the Act explicitly relies upon the commerce power and where the record is filled with testimony of obstructions and restraints resulting from the discriminations found to be existing. We now pass to that phase of the case.

## The Basis of Congressional Action

While the Act, as adopted, carried no congressional findings, the record of its passage through each house is replete with evidence of the burdens that discrimination by race or color places upon interstate commerce. This testimony included the fact that our people have become increasingly mobile, with millions of people of all races traveling from State to State; that Negroes in particular have been the subject of discrimination in transient accommodations, having to travel great distances to secure the same; that often they have been unable to obtain accommodations, and have had to call upon friends to put them up overnight, and that these conditions had become so acute as to require the listing of available lodging for Negroes in a special guidebook which was itself "dramatic testimony to the difficulties" Negroes encounter in travel. These exclusionary practices were found to be nationwide, the Under Secretary of Commerce testifying that there is "no question that this discrimination in the North still exists to a large degree" and in the West and Midwest as well. This testimony indicated a qualitative, as well as quantitative, effect on interstate travel by Negroes. The former was the obvious impairment of the Negro traveler's pleasure and convenience that resulted when he continually was uncertain of finding lodging. As for the latter, there was evidence that this uncertainty stemming from racial discrimination had the effect of discouraging travel on the part of a substantial portion of the Negro community. This was the conclusion not only of the Under Secretary of Commerce, but also of the Administrator of the Federal Aviation Agency, who wrote the Chairman of the Senate Commerce Committee that it was his, "belief that air commerce is adversely affected by the denial to a substantial segment of the traveling public of adequate and desegregated public accommodations." We shall not burden this opinion with further details, since the voluminous testimony presents overwhelming evidence that discrimination by hotels and motels impedes interstate travel.

## The Power of Congress Over Interstate Travel

The power of Congress to deal with these obstructions depends on the meaning of the Commerce Clause. . . .

In short, the determinative test of the exercise of power by the Congress under the Commerce Clause is simply whether the activity sought to be regulated is "commerce which concerns more States than one" and has a real and substantial relation to the national interest. Let us now turn to this facet of the problem. . . .

The same interest in protecting interstate commerce which led Congress to deal with segregation in interstate carriers and the white slave traffic has prompted it to extend the exercise of its power to gambling; to criminal enterprises; to deceptive practices in the sale of products; to fraudulent security transactions; to misbranding of drugs; to wages and hours; to members of labor unions; to crop control; to discrimination against shippers; to the protection of small business from injurious price-cutting; to resale price maintenance; to professional football; and to racial discrimination by owners and managers of terminal restaurants.

That Congress was legislating against moral wrongs in many of these areas rendered its enactments no less valid. In framing Title II of this Act, Congress was also dealing with what it considered a moral problem. But that fact does not detract from the overwhelming evidence of the disruptive effect that racial discrimination has had on commercial intercourse. It was this burden which empowered Congress to enact appropriate legislation, and, given this basis for the exercise of its power, Congress was not restricted by the fact that the particular obstruction to interstate commerce with which it was dealing was also deemed a moral and social wrong. . . .

[T]he power of Congress to promote interstate commerce also includes the power to regulate the local incidents thereof, including local activities in both the States of origin and destination, which might have a substantial and harmful effect upon that commerce. One need only examine the evidence which we have discussed above to see that Congress may—as it has—prohibit racial discrimination by motels serving travelers, however "local" their operations may appear.

Nor does the Act deprive appellant of liberty or property under the Fifth Amendment. The commerce power invoked here by the Congress is a specific and plenary one authorized by the Constitution itself. The only questions are: (1) whether Congress had a rational basis for finding that racial discrimination by motels affected commerce, and (2) if it had such a basis, whether the means it selected to eliminate that evil are reasonable and appropriate. If they are, appellant has no "right" to select its guests as it sees fit, free from governmental regulation.

There is nothing novel about such legislation. Thirty-two States now have it on their books either by statute or executive order, and many cities provide such regulation. Some of these Acts go back four-score years. It has been repeatedly held by this Court that such laws do not violate the Due Process Clause of the Fourteenth Amendment. Perhaps the first such holding was in the *Civil Rights Cases* themselves, where Mr. Justice Bradley for the Court inferentially found that innkeepers, "by the laws of all the States, so far as we are aware, are bound, to the extent of their facilities, to furnish proper accommodation to all unobjectionable persons who in good faith apply for them." . . .

We find no merit in the remainder of appellant's contentions, including that of "involuntary servitude." As we have seen, 32 States prohibit racial discrimination in public accommodations. These laws but codify the common law innkeeper rule, which long predated the Thirteenth Amendment. It is difficult to believe that the Amendment was intended to abrogate this principle. Indeed, the opinion of the Court in the Civil Rights Cases is to the contrary as we have seen, it having noted with approval the laws of "all the States" prohibiting discrimination. We could not say that the requirements of the Act in this regard are in any way "akin to African slavery." *Butler v. Perry* (1916).

We therefore conclude that the action of the Congress in the adoption of the Act as applied here to a motel which concededly serves interstate travelers is within the power granted it by the Commerce Clause of the Constitution, as interpreted by this Court for 140 years. It may be argued that Congress could have pursued other methods to eliminate the obstructions it found in interstate commerce caused by racial discrimination. But this is a matter of policy that rests entirely with the Congress, not with the courts. How obstructions in commerce may be removed— what means are to be employed—is within the sound and exclusive discretion of the Congress. It is subject only to one caveat—that the means chosen by it must be reasonably adapted to the end permitted by the Constitution. We cannot say that its choice here was not so adapted. The Constitution requires no more.

*Affirmed.*

MR. JUSTICE DOUGLAS, concurring.

Though I join the Court's opinions, I am somewhat reluctant here . . . to rest solely on the Commerce Clause. My reluctance is not due to any conviction that Congress lacks power to regulate commerce in the interests of human rights. It is, rather, my belief [in] the right of people to be free of state action that discriminates against them because of race. . . .

Hence, I would prefer to rest on the assertion of legislative power contained in Section 5 of the Fourteenth Amendment, which states: "The Congress shall have power to enforce, by appropriate legislation, the provi-

sions of this article"—a power which the Court concedes was exercised at least in part in this Act.

A decision based on the Fourteenth Amendment would have a more settling effect, making unnecessary litigation over whether a particular restaurant or inn is within the commerce definitions of the Act or whether a particular customer is an interstate traveler. Under my construction, the Act would apply to all customers in all the enumerated places of public accommodation. And that construction would put an end to all obstructionist strategies, and finally close one door on a bitter chapter in American history.

▼▲▼

## *Katzenbach* v. *McClung*
### 379 U.S. 294 (1964)

MR. JUSTICE CLARK delivered the opinion of the Court.

This case was argued with *Heart of Atlanta Motel* v. *United States*, in which we upheld the constitutional validity of Title II of the Civil Rights Act of 1964 against an attack by hotels, motels, and like establishments. This complaint attacks the constitutionality of the Act as applied to a restaurant. . . .

In the 12 months preceding the passage of the Act, the restaurant purchased locally approximately $150,000 worth of food, $69,683 or 46% of which was meat that it bought from a local supplier who had procured it from outside the State. The District Court expressly found that a substantial portion of the food served in the restaurant had moved in interstate commerce. The restaurant has refused to serve Negroes in its dining accommodations since its original opening in 1927, and, since July 2, 1964, it has been operating in violation of the Act. . . .

Ollie's Barbecue admits that it is covered by [the] provisions of the Act. The Government makes no contention that the discrimination at the restaurant was supported by the State of Alabama. There is no claim that interstate travelers frequented the restaurant. The sole question, therefore, narrows down to whether Title II, as applied to a restaurant annually receiving about $70,000 worth of food which has moved in commerce, is a valid exercise of the power of Congress. The Government has contended that Congress had ample basis upon which to find that racial discrimination at restaurants which receive from out of state a substantial portion of the food served does, in fact, impose commercial burdens of national magnitude upon interstate commerce. The appellees' major argument is directed to this premise. They urge that no such basis existed. It is to that question that we now turn.

## The Congressional Hearings

As we noted in *Heart of Atlanta Motel*, both Houses of Congress conducted prolonged hearings on the Act. And, as we said there, while no formal findings were made, which, of course, are not necessary, it is well that we make mention of the testimony at these hearings the better to understand the problem before Congress and determine whether the Act is a reasonable and appropriate means toward its solution. The record is replete with testimony of the burdens placed on interstate commerce by racial discrimination in restaurants. A comparison of per capita spending by Negroes in restaurants, theaters, and like establishments indicated less spending, after discounting income differences, in areas where discrimination is widely practiced. This condition, which was especially aggravated in the South, was attributed in the testimony of the Under Secretary of Commerce to racial segregation. This diminutive spending springing from a refusal to serve Negroes and their total loss as customers has, regardless of the absence of direct evidence, a close connection to interstate commerce. The fewer customers a restaurant enjoys, the less food it sells, and consequently the less it buys. In addition, the Attorney General testified that this type of discrimination imposed "an artificial restriction on the market," and interfered with the flow of merchandise. In addition, there were many references to discriminatory situations causing wide unrest and having a depressant effect on general business conditions in the respective communities.

Moreover, there was an impressive array of testimony that discrimination in restaurants had a direct and highly restrictive effect upon interstate travel by Negroes. This resulted, it was said, because discriminatory practices prevent Negroes from buying prepared food served on the premises while on a trip, except in isolated and unkempt restaurants and under most unsatisfactory and often unpleasant conditions. This obviously discourages travel and obstructs interstate commerce, for one can hardly travel without eating. Likewise, it was said that discrimination deterred professional as well as skilled people from moving into areas where such practices occurred, and thereby caused industry to be reluctant to establish there.

We believe that this testimony afforded ample basis for the conclusion that established restaurants in such areas sold less interstate goods because of the discrimination, that interstate travel was obstructed directly by it, that business in general suffered, and that many new businesses refrained from establishing there as a result of it. Hence, the District Court was in error in concluding that there was no connection between discrimination and the movement of interstate commerce. The court's conclusion that such a connection is outside "common experience" flies in the face of stubborn fact. . . .

We noted in *Heart of Atlanta Motel* that a number of witnesses attested to the fact that racial discrimination was not merely a state or regional problem, but was one of nationwide scope. Against this background, we must conclude that, while the focus of the legislation was on the individual restaurant's relation to interstate commerce, Congress appropriately considered the importance of that connection with the knowledge that the discrimination was but, "representative of many others throughout the country, the total incidence of which, if left unchecked, may well become far-reaching in its harm to commerce." . . .

Article I, Section 8, clause 3, confers upon Congress the power "[t]o regulate Commerce . . . among the several States" and Clause 18 of the same Article grants it the power "[t]o make all Laws which shall be necessary and proper for carrying into Execution the foregoing Powers . . ." This grant, as we have pointed out in *Heart of Atlanta Motel*, "extends to those activities intrastate which so affect interstate commerce, or the exertion of the power of Congress over it, as to make regulation of them appropriate means to the attainment of a legitimate end, the effective execution of the granted power to regulate interstate commerce." Much is said about a restaurant business being local, but, "even if appellee's activity be local, and though it may not be regarded as commerce, it may still, whatever its nature, be reached by Congress if it exerts a substantial economic effect on interstate commerce . . ." The activities that are beyond the reach of Congress are, "those which are completely within a particular State, which do not affect other States, and with which it is not necessary to interfere, for the purpose of executing some of the general powers of the government." This rule is as good today as it was when Chief Justice Marshall laid it down almost a century and a half ago.

This Court has held time and again that this power extends to activities of retail establishments, including restaurants, which directly or indirectly burden or obstruct interstate commerce. We have detailed the cases in *Heart of Atlanta Motel*, and will not repeat them here.

Nor are the cases holding that interstate commerce ends when goods come to rest in the State of destination

## HEART OF ATLANTA MOTEL V. UNITED STATES AND KATZENBACH V. McCLUNG

### *"We Reserve the Right to Refuse Service to Anyone"*

Situated just off the Green Springs Highway on Eighth Avenue South in Birmingham, Alabama, Ollie's Barbecue has been serving what it boasts as the "world's best barbecue" to locals and passers-by for more than fifty years. So well-known is this little barbecue stand that anyone unfortunate enough not to live in Birmingham can order its secret sauce and have it delivered anywhere in the world. Before 1964, however, the heavenly aroma of Ollie's barbecue ribs, chicken, and pork sandwiches was familiar only to residents of what was then a segregated African American corner of Birmingham. But residents of that neighborhood were prohibited by law from sitting down to lunch or dinner at Ollie's until the Court's decision in *Katzenbach v. McClung,* which upheld the ban on racial discrimination in public accommodations enacted by Congress in the Civil Rights Act of 1964.

Like so many other restaurants in the South, Ollie's prohibited African Americans from sitting down to a meal but permitted them to order their food from a take-out window in the back. Ollie's also honored the Jim Crow tradition of employing African Americans in low-paying custodial and kitchen jobs, a practice that kept them mostly invisible to Ollie's white customers. In the pre–civil rights era, such practices extended beyond restaurants to all public accommodations in the South, down to the smallest, most remote public water fountain.

Even as the rest of the nation began to allow African Americans to enter professions once cordoned off for whites only, the South refused to allow even the smallest exception to its system of racial exclusion. Even in the worlds of sports and entertainment, the two most visible areas in which racial barriers had slowly given way to the public's demand for excellence, African Americans were treated as subordinate and separate in the South, no matter how prominent and successful they were. In the early 1960s the crowds who gathered to watch integrated professional and collegiate sports, shout and scream as The Beatles invaded the South, and swoon and dance to the great African American singing groups of Motown did so separated by concrete barriers, ropes, and stairs.

Even for African Americans who had felt the sting of racial discrimination in the North, the law and custom of Jim Crow was especially humiliating. In 1964 the St. Louis Cardinals, who would win the World Series that October, counted more black players than any team in professional baseball and was considered a model in terms of racial composition and attitudes. The Cardinals had not, as the journalist David Halberstam has recounted, always been that way. In 1947 the Cardinals had considered striking if the Brooklyn Dodgers put Jackie Robinson, the first black player to break the color barrier in the big leagues, on the field. Before the Milwaukee Braves moved to Atlanta in 1965, St. Louis was considered the most Southern city in baseball and, for a time, the most segregated as well. It was the city that black players least liked visiting and playing in. The fan base of the Cardinals set the tone for the team's segregationist policies. KMOX, the radio station that broadcast Cardinal games, beamed its signal as far south as Memphis, Birmingham, and Jackson, Mississippi. In the mid-1950s young white men often traveled to St. Louis for the weekend to catch the Saturday and Sunday Cardinal games. As such, Cardinal management was careful not to offend the racial prejudices of its fans.

By the late 1950s the Cardinals, under the new ownership of Budweiser beer magnate Augustus Busch, had begun an earnest effort to sign black players. The first year that Busch visited spring training, he was stunned to find his team without a single black player. "How can it be the great American game if blacks can't play?" Busch asked. Besides, said Busch, "we sell beer to everyone." In other words, racial discrimination was bad for business.

Spring training was held in Florida, a state that abided by Jim Crow. In 1961, Bill White, the Cardinals' All-Star first baseman, challenged the long-standing practice of the St. Petersburg business community's annual whites-only breakfast welcoming visiting ballplayers. White informed several reporters of the black players' anger at being excluded from the breakfast, as well as their resentment at being forced to stay as boarders with African American families while their white teammates stayed in the best local hotels. Busch made clear his own dissatisfaction with the whites-only breakfast. A combination of bad publicity generated by news stories and pressure brought by Busch persuaded the business group to change its policy.

Getting the hotels to change their policies was a more difficult task, as Florida law authorized segregation. Busch convinced a friend to buy a hotel located near an interstate highway, and the players and their families stayed there. For the first time as far as anyone in St. Petersburg could remember, it was possible to walk past a hotel and see black and white children swimming in the pool, with their parents nearby relaxing and enjoying each other's company in desegregated public place. Such sights would become more common after the Court's decisions in *Katzenbach* and *Heart of Atlanta Motel*.

Professional sports was not the only place that tested the mettle of the South's entrenched racism. Popular music, and jazz music in particular, helped to start the erosion of racial prejudice as far back as the 1920s. Drawn to a radical new music form that counted an astounding black trumpet player from New Orleans, Louis Armstrong, and Bix Beiderbecke,

an equally prodigious white cornet player from Davenport, Iowa, among its foremost exponents, whites and blacks moved freely in the world they constructed for themselves. For the public, however, the idea of white band leaders—the most popular big bands before World War II were led by Benny Goodman, Tommy Dorsey, and Glenn Miller—putting

*Student demonstrators attempting to integrate an all-white lunch counter in Nashville meet a hostile reception from segregationists.*
AP/Wide World Photos.

black and white musicians on stage together was a very foreign concept and was met with great resistance in the South. A former trumpet player in Benny Goodman's band recalled what happened when the band leader hired the pianist Teddy Wilson, the first black musician to work in an all-white band:

Benny [was] very interested in money. But he cut off almost half the country for Teddy Wilson. He didn't want to travel in the South with the band, so he cut off a large part of his income. I've heard him stand up, even in the New Yorker, the first time we went in there. We had . . . five or six black guys. And I remember the manager saying, "I don't want these black guys coming in through the lobby and through the restaurant. In fact, I don't even want them here." And Benny said, "Well, I'm sorry. This is my band. If you don't want them in the band then screw yourself. We're walking out." So he said, "Well, they'll have to go through the kitchen." Benny said, "They do not go through the kitchen." Then he said, "All of the musicians go through the kitchen." And Benny said, "None of the musicians go through the kitchen." "Well, then, they can't wear their uniforms when they come." "All right, they won't wear their uniforms."

Harry James was another popular white band leader of the 1940s. A former member described a regular occurrence after James hired Willie Smith, a black saxophonist:

Advanced word would get to these southern cities that Harry James had a mixed band; there was one negro in the band. The sheriff would come up and say, "You can't go on with a mixed band." And Harry would say, "All right, point out the one that mixes it." They couldn't tell.

Not even Duke Ellington, whose contribution to twentieth century American music is unsurpassed, was immune from the stranglehold of Jim Crow. Ellington was a regal presence who refused to indulge racial prejudice when he traveled in the South. Because he and most of the members of his band were barred from the exclusive, all-white hotels where they often played, Ellington used to rent private railroad cars and stay in them. Explained Ellington:

In our music we have been talking for a long time about what it is to be a Negro in this country. And we've never let ourselves be put into a position of being treated with disrespect. From 1934 to 1936 we went touring deep into the South, without the benefit

of Federal judges, and we commanded respect. We didn't travel by bus. Instead, we had two Pullman cars and a 70-foot baggage car. We parked them in each station, and lived in them. We had our own water, food, electricity, and sanitary facilities. The natives would come by and say, "What's that?"

Well, we'd say, "that's the way the President travels."

The Court's decisions in *Katzenbach* and *Heart of Atlanta Motel* brought to a close the legal era of Jim Crow and opened the door for a new level of social integration. For sure, the transition was not smooth and was hampered early on by mutual suspicion. But even as Ollie McClung Sr. would profess his shock at the Court's decision upholding Title II, he and his son, Ollie Jr., announced that "as law-abiding Americans, we feel we must bow to this edict." Two hours after *Katzenbach* was announced, Ollie's served its first walk-in black customers.

Black couples were more reluctant to line up for a room at the Heart of Atlanta Motel, but that was due more to its rates—the highest in Atlanta—than to any overt effort to discourage African American patronage. Moreton Rolleston, who owned the motel, had argued before the Court that the public accommodations law was a form of indentured servitude and thus violated his rights under the Thirteenth Amendment. Even he, however, took a philosophical view of the future after learning that he had lost his case. "With my grandchildren," mused Rolleston, "there won't be any problems at all. They won't even know there were any."

## References

Crow, Bill. *Jazz Anecdotes*. New York: Oxford University Press, 1990.

Halberstam, David. *October 1964*. New York: Villard Books, 1994.

---

apposite here. That line of cases has been applied with reference to state taxation or regulation, but not in the field of federal regulation.

The appellees contend that Congress has arbitrarily created a conclusive presumption that all restaurants meeting the criteria set out in the Act "affect commerce."

Stated another way, they object to the omission of a provision for a case-by-case determination—judicial or administrative—that racial discrimination in a particular restaurant affects commerce.

But Congress' action in framing this Act was not unprecedented. In *United States* v. *Darby* (1941), this

Court held constitutional the Fair Labor Standards Act of 1938. There, Congress determined that the payment of substandard wages to employees engaged in the production of goods for commerce, while not itself commerce, so inhibited it as to be subject to federal regulation. The appellees in that case argued, as do the appellees here, that the Act was invalid because it included no provision for an independent inquiry regarding the effect on commerce of substandard wages in a particular business. But the Court rejected the argument, observing that: "[S]ometimes Congress itself has said that a particular activity affects the commerce, as it did in the present Act, the Safety Appliance Act, and the Railway Labor Act. In passing on the validity of legislation of the class last mentioned the only function of courts is to determine whether the particular activity regulated or prohibited is within the reach of the federal power."

Here, as there, Congress has determined for itself that refusals of service to Negroes have imposed burdens both upon the interstate flow of food and upon the movement of products generally. Of course, the mere fact that Congress has said when particular activity shall be deemed to affect commerce does not preclude further examination by this Court. But where we find that the legislators, in light of the facts and testimony before them, have a rational basis for finding a chosen regulatory scheme necessary to the protection of commerce, our investigation is at an end. The only remaining question—one answered in the affirmative by the court below—is whether the particular restaurant either serves or offers to serve interstate travelers or serves food a substantial portion of which has moved in interstate commerce. . . .

The power of Congress in this field is broad and sweeping; where it keeps within its sphere and violates no express constitutional limitation it has been the rule of this Court, going back almost to the founding days of the Republic, not to interfere. The Civil Rights Act of 1964, as here applied, we find to be plainly appropriate in the resolution of what the Congress found to be a national commercial problem of the first magnitude. We find it in no violation of any express limitations of the Constitution and we therefore declare it valid.

▼▲▼

Begining in 1995 the Court signaled that it might be willing to reconsider the latitude it afforded to Congress to promote police power objectives. In *United States v. Lopez* (1995), a badly divided Court invalidated a federal law under the Commerce Clause for just the second time since the 1937 revolution. *Lopez* stunned students

of the Court and constitutional law, as there was nothing to indicate that Congress, in making it a federal offense to possess a firearm on or within one thousand feet of a public, private, or parochial school, had exceeded its commerce power beyond that defined in *Wickard, Heart of Atlanta Motel,* or *McClung.* The SIDE-BAR on *Lopez* describes the political forces at work behind the passage of the Gun-Free School Zones Act of 1990, as well as the members of Congress and various organizations that filed friend-of-the-court briefs in support of and opposition to the act.

In *United States v. Morrison* (2000), the Court, again by a single vote, struck down the Violence Against Women Act, enacted by Congress in 1994 to provide the victims of rape and sexual assault a federal right to sue for civil damages. Do Chief Justice Rehnquist's opinions in *Lopez* and *Morrison* offer a persuasive critique of the Court's post-1937 Commerce Clause jurisprudence? Is the Constitutional Revolution of 1937, as Justice Clarence Thomas suggested in his *Lopez* concurrence, in need of review and reconsideration, at least as it pertains to the Court's willingness to defer to the congressional exercise of power to promote health and social welfare concerns?

## *United States v. Lopez*
### 514 U.S. 549 (1995)

The facts and background of this case are set out in the accompanying SIDEBAR.

The Court's decision was 5 to 4. Chief Justice Rehnquist delivered the opinion of the Court. Justice Kennedy, joined by Justice O'Connor, filed a concurring opinion. Justice Thomas also filed a concurring opinion. Justices Stevens and Souter filed separate dissenting opinions. Justice Breyer, joined by Justices Stevens, Souter, and Ginsberg, also dissented.

▼▲▼

CHIEF JUSTICE REHNQUIST delivered the opinion of the Court. We start with first principles. The Constitution creates a Federal Government of enumerated powers. As James Madison wrote, "[t]he powers delegated by the proposed Constitution to the federal government are few and defined. Those which are to remain in the State governments are numerous and indefinite." *Federalist* 45. . . .

For nearly a century thereafter, the Court's Commerce Clause decisions dealt but rarely with the extent of Congress' power, and almost entirely with the Commerce Clause as a limit on state legislation that discriminated against interstate commerce. Under this line of precedent, the Court held that certain categories of activity such as "production," "manufacturing," and "mining" were within the province of state governments, and thus were beyond the power of Congress under the Commerce Clause. . . .

[I]n the watershed case of *NLRB* v. *Jones & Laughlin Steel Corp.* (1937), the Court upheld the National Labor Relations Act against a Commerce Clause challenge, and in the process, departed from the distinction between "direct" and "indirect" effects on interstate commerce. The Court held that intrastate activities that, "have such a close and substantial relation to interstate commerce that their control is essential or appropriate to protect that commerce from burdens and obstructions," are within Congress' power to regulate. . . .

[The chief justice summarized the holdings in *United States v. Darby* (1941) and *Wickard v. Filburn* (1942).] But even these modern-era precedents which have expanded congressional power under the Commerce Clause confirm that this power is subject to outer limits. In *Jones & Laughlin Steel*, the Court warned that the scope of the interstate commerce power, "must be considered in the light of our dual system of government and may not be extended so as to embrace effects upon interstate commerce so indirect and remote that to embrace them, in view of our complex society, would effectually obliterate the distinction between what is national and what is local and create a completely centralized government." Since that time, the Court has heeded that warning and undertaken to decide whether a rational basis existed for concluding that a regulated activity sufficiently affected interstate commerce. . . .

[W]e have identified three broad categories of activity that Congress may regulate under its commerce power. First, Congress may regulate the use of the channels of interstate commerce. Second, Congress is empowered to regulate and protect the instrumentalities of interstate commerce, or persons or things in interstate commerce, even though the threat may come only from intrastate activities. Finally, Congress' commerce authority includes the power to regulate those activities having a substantial relation to interstate commerce, those activities that substantially affect interstate commerce.

Within this final category, admittedly, our case law has not been clear whether an activity must "affect" or "substantially affect" interstate commerce in order to be within

Congress' power to regulate it under the Commerce Clause. We conclude, consistent with the great weight of our case law, that the proper test requires an analysis of whether the regulated activity "substantially affects" interstate commerce.

We now turn to consider the power of Congress, in the light of this framework, to enact 922(q). The first two categories of authority may be quickly disposed of: 922(q) is not a regulation of the use of the channels of interstate commerce, nor is it an attempt to prohibit the interstate transportation of a commodity through the channels of commerce; nor can 922(q) be justified as a regulation by which Congress has sought to protect an instrumentality of interstate commerce or a thing in interstate commerce. Thus, if 922(q) is to be sustained, it must be under the third category as a regulation of an activity that substantially affects interstate commerce.

First, we have upheld a wide variety of congressional Acts regulating intrastate economic activity where we have concluded that the activity substantially affected interstate commerce. Examples include the regulation of intrastate coal mining, intrastate extortionate credit transactions, restaurants utilizing substantial interstate supplies, inns and hotels catering to interstate guests, and production and consumption of home-grown wheat, *Wickard* (1942). These examples are by no means exhaustive, but the pattern is clear. Where economic activity substantially affects interstate commerce, legislation regulating that activity will be sustained.

The Government's essential contention, *in fine*, is that we may determine here that 922(q) is valid because possession of a firearm in a local school zone does indeed substantially affect interstate commerce. The Government argues that possession of a firearm in a school zone may result in violent crime and that violent crime can be expected to affect the functioning of the national economy in two ways. First, the costs of violent crime are substantial, and, through the mechanism of insurance, those costs are spread throughout the population. Second, violent crime reduces the willingness of individuals to travel to areas within the country that are perceived to be unsafe. The Government also argues that the presence of guns in schools poses a substantial threat to the educational process by threatening the learning environment. A handicapped educational process, in turn, will result in a less productive citizenry. That, in turn, would have an adverse effect on the Nation's economic wellbeing. As a result, the Government argues that Congress could rationally have concluded that 922(q) substantially affects interstate commerce. We pause to consider the implications of the Government's arguments. The Government admits, under its "costs of crime" reasoning, that Congress could regulate not only all violent crime, but all activities that might lead to violent crime, regardless of how tenuously they relate to interstate commerce. Similarly, under the Government's "national productivity" reasoning, Congress could regulate any activity that it found was related to the economic productivity of individual citizens: family law (including marriage, divorce, and child custody), for example. Under the theories that the Government presents in support of 922(q), it is difficult to perceive any limitation on federal power, even in areas such as criminal law enforcement or education where States historically have been sovereign. Thus, if we were to accept the Government's arguments, we are hard-pressed to posit any activity by an individual that Congress is without power to regulate.

JUSTICE THOMAS, concurring.

The Court today properly concludes that the Commerce Clause does not grant Congress the authority to prohibit gun possession within 1,000 feet of a school, as it attempted to do in the Gun-Free School Zones Act of 1990. Although I join the majority, I write separately to observe that our case law has drifted far from the original understanding of the Commerce Clause. In a future case, we ought to temper our Commerce Clause jurisprudence in a manner that both makes sense of our more recent case law and is more faithful to the original understanding of that Clause. . . .

In an appropriate case, I believe that we must further reconsider our "substantial effects" test with an eye toward constructing a standard that reflects the text and history of the Commerce Clause without totally rejecting our more recent Commerce Clause jurisprudence. . . .

At the time the original Constitution was ratified, "commerce" consisted of selling, buying, and bartering, as well as transporting for these purposes. This understanding finds support in the etymology of the word, which literally means "with merchandise." In fact, when Federalists and Anti-Federalists discussed the Commerce Clause during the ratification period, they often used trade (in its selling/bartering sense) and commerce interchangeably.

As one would expect, the term "commerce" was used in contradistinction to productive activities such as manufacturing and agriculture. Alexander Hamilton, for example, repeatedly treated commerce, agriculture, and manufacturing as three separate endeavors. *Federalist* 36.

Moreover, interjecting a modern sense of commerce into the Constitution generates significant textual and structural problems. For example, one cannot replace "commerce" with a different type of enterprise, such as manufacturing. When a manufacturer produces a car, assembly cannot take place "with a foreign nation" or "with the Indian Tribes." Parts may come from different States or other nations and hence may have been in the flow of commerce at one time, but manufacturing takes place at a discrete site. Agriculture and manufacturing involve the production of goods; commerce encompasses traffic in such articles. . . .

The Constitution not only uses the word "commerce" in a narrower sense than our case law might suggest, it also does not support the proposition that Congress has authority over all activities that "substantially affect" interstate commerce. The Commerce Clause does not state that Congress may "regulate matters that substantially affect commerce with foreign Nations, and among the several States, and with the Indian Tribes." In contrast, the Constitution itself temporarily prohibited amendments that would "affect" Congress' lack of authority to prohibit or restrict the slave trade or to enact unproportioned direct taxation. Clearly, the Framers could have drafted a Constitution that contained a "substantially affects interstate commerce" clause had that been their objective. . . .

Put simply, much if not all of Art. I, section 8 would be surplusage if Congress had been given authority over matters that substantially affect interstate commerce. An interpretation of clause 3 that makes the rest of section 8 superfluous simply cannot be correct. Yet this Court's Commerce Clause jurisprudence has endorsed just such an interpretation: the power we have accorded Congress has swallowed.

Indeed, if a "substantial effects" test can be appended to the Commerce Clause, why not to every other power of the Federal Government? There is no reason for singling out the Commerce Clause for special treatment. Accordingly, Congress could regulate all matters that "substantially affect" the Army and Navy, bankruptcies, tax collection, expenditures, and so on. In that case, the clauses of section 8 all mutually overlap, something we can assume the Founding Fathers never intended.

Our construction of the scope of congressional authority has the additional problem of coming close to turning the Tenth Amendment on its head. Our case law could be read to reserve to the United States all powers not expressly *prohibited* by the Constitution. Taken together, these fundamental textual problems should at the very least, convince us that the "substantial effects" test should be reexamined. . . .

The comments of Hamilton and others about federal power reflected the well known truth that the new

## UNITED STATES V. LOPEZ

### *So Much for Show and Tell*

On the morning of March 10, 1992, Alfonso Lopez Jr., an eighteen-year-old senior at Thomas A. Edison High School in San Antonio, Texas, was summoned to the principal's office. A call to visit the principal in the middle of the morning is rarely issued to bestow a good citizenship award, and Lopez's invitation was no exception. He had good reason to be nervous. Even though Lopez carried a C average and had never been disciplined at Edison, this morning was the first time he had ever carried a gun to school.

When confronted by the principal, Lopez admitted that he was carrying a weapon. He opened his jacket and pulled a .38 caliber Smith and Wesson handgun from the waistband of his jeans, gave it to school authorities, and then reached into his pockets and pulled out five rounds of ammunition. When asked why he had chosen to carry a gun to school, Lopez responded that he had done so "for protection."

Lopez's response was curious, since violence had never been a serious issue at Thomas A. Edison High School. Although the San Antonio school district had expelled eleven students during the 1993–1994 academic year for firearm possession on school grounds, none attended Edison. Most students at Edison were aware of only one school gang, and it confined its public acts to public graffiti. Edison had no security guards or metal detectors and received no more than routine patrols from the police.

Lopez was arrested and charged under Texas state law with the felony possession of a handgun. Upon further questioning, Lopez told police that someone had given him forty dollars to deliver the gun to another student for use in a gang war. Authorities decided to drop the state charges against Lopez and prosecute him under a new gun possession law passed by Congress in 1990: the Gun-Free School Zones Act. The law made it a federal offense "for any individual to knowingly possess a firearm at a place that the indi-

vidual knows, or had reasonable cause to believe is a school zone." It defined a school zone as "in, or on the grounds of, a public, parochial or private school," or "within a distance of one thousand feet from the grounds of a public, private or parochial school."

Lopez pleaded guilty to the federal charge, but his attorney, John Carter of the San Antonio public defender's office, decided to argue in federal court that the Gun-Free School Zones Act was an unconstitutional exercise of congressional commerce power. He was unsuccessful. On appeal, however, a unanimous three-judge panel for the United States Court of Appeals for the Fifth Circuit ruled that the law was unconstitutional, holding that Congress had failed to connect the banning of guns in school zones to either the history or the comments that accompanied the act. The circuit court's ruling was momentous. Since the constitutional revolution of 1937, the lower federal courts had rarely invalidated the exercise of congressional commerce power. Stunned by this development, the United States Department of Justice appealed to the Supreme Court, which had not declared a federal law unconstitutional under the Commerce Clause since 1936.

That *Lopez* was no routine Commerce Clause case was evident as soon as the United States Court of Appeals for the Fifth Circuit agreed to hear the appeal on the constitutional question. Dozens of friend-of-the-court briefs poured in from public interest organizations; federal, state, and local law-enforcement associations; two state attorneys general; child welfare groups; public school officials; sixteen U.S. senators; and thirty-four members of the House of Representatives in support of the Gun-Free School Zones Act. Lopez received amicus support from the Pacific Legal Foundation, which had long argued against the exercise of broad federal power at the expense of the states. A broad coalition of state and local government groups also came to Lopez's defense, including the National Governor's Association, the National Conference of State Legislatures, and the National League of Cities. By and large, state governments viewed the 1990 law as a gross congressional usurpation of their state legislative responsibilities.

Perhaps the most adamant defender of the Gun-Free School Zones Act was its original sponsor, Senator Herbert Kohl (D–Wisc.). Since coming to the Senate in 1986, Kohl has led the fight for tougher gun-control measures, stiffer sentences for repeat criminal offenders, enhanced penalties for "hate crimes," and greater federal expenditures on police training and general crime prevention measures. On the importance of tough criminal laws, Kohl has said, "The first responsibility of the government is to keep our people safe. It's that simple." The amicus brief filed by Kohl and the forty-nine members of Congress in defense of the 1990 law noted that Congress does not have to provide a specific link to the Constitution or the Commerce Clause to exercise its federal police powers, a view that, until *Lopez*, was consistent with the Court's own since 1937.

The states of Ohio and New York and the District of Columbia made a similar argument in their joint brief. Although they argued that firearms in schools were directly related to interstate commerce, they also noted that Congress did not have to state its justification each time it passed legislation. Crime control, the brief pointed out, had reached the point where federal and state authorities needed to cooperate, rather than get into shouting matches and turf wars over proper jurisdiction. Public interest groups, such as the Center to Prevent Handgun Violence and Children Now, argued that handgun violence had a direct impact on school safety, which affected the quality of education and thus the long-term economic opportunities of high school students. All these concerns fell within the Court's prior definition of interstate commerce.

Not a single law-enforcement association sided with Lopez, even though *amici* on his behalf argued that criminal law and education were the two areas of law and public policy most properly reserved to the states. Groups such as the Fraternal Order of Police, the National Organization of Black Police Enforcement Executives, the International Association of Chiefs of Police, and the Federal Law Enforcement Officers Association, to name just some of the law-enforcement agencies that supported the Gun-Free School Zones Act of 1990, do sometimes differ on important criminal justice matters. But on gun-control and possession issues they rarely disagree on the need for tough measures and have long argued for more integrated and comprehensive policies to promote federal and state concerns in crime control.

The common theme in the arguments of the United States and its supporting *amici,* that Congress did not need to demonstrate a substantial relationship between the legislative objective of the 1990 gun possession law and its interstate commerce power, may well have led to the Court's abrupt departure from the principles that have animated its post-1937 Commerce Clause jurisprudence. Alfonso Lopez's original lawyer, John Carter, continued to press his argument—his first before the Court—that Congress had exceeded its authority to regulate interstate commerce when it passed the law. Although his position drew tough questions from several of the justices, Carter knew that a slim majority of the Court favored recalibrating the scales of federalism in favor of the states. For Carter and his supporting *amici,* keeping the argument centered on the failure of Congress to make a persuasive connection between the exercise of its commerce power and its need to regulate firearm possession was a successful strategy.

Alfonso Lopez Jr. may have had nothing more in mind than a dangerous game of show and tell when he carried his concealed Smith and Wesson handgun to school. As it ended, this C student offered something more substantial to share with more advanced students of law and politics: that, even in the post-1937 era of American constitutional development, some limits still exist on the scope of congressional power under the Commerce Clause.

### References

Cohen, Karen J. "Kohl Files Brief for Gun-Free School Zone," *Wisconsin State Journal,* June 2, 1994.

Hansen, Dennis. "Making It a Federal Crime to Possess a Firearm Near Local Schools: Did Congress Exceed Its Commerce Clause Authority?" *Preview of United States Supreme Court Cases,* October 24, 1994.

Government would have only the limited and enumerated powers found in the Constitution. Agriculture and manufacture, since they were not surrendered to the Federal Government, were state concerns. Even before the passage of the Tenth Amendment, it was apparent that Congress would possess only those powers "herein granted" by the rest of the Constitution.

Where the Constitution was meant to grant federal authority over an activity substantially affecting interstate commerce, the Constitution contains an enumerated power over that particular activity. Indeed, the Framers knew that many of the other enumerated powers in §8 dealt with matters that substantially affected interstate commerce. Madison, for instance, spoke of the bankruptcy power as being "intimately connected with the regulation of commerce." *Federalist* 42. Likewise, Hamilton urged that "[i]f we mean to be a commercial people or even to be secure on our Atlantic side, we must endeavour as soon as possible to have a navy." *Federalist* 24.

I am aware of no cases prior to the New Deal that characterized the power flowing from the Commerce Clause as sweepingly as does our substantial effects test. My review of the case law indicates that the substantial effects test is but an innovation of the 20th century. . . . Apart from its recent vintage and its corresponding lack of any grounding in the original understanding of the Constitution, the substantial effects test suffers from the further flaw that it appears to grant Congress a police power over the Nation. When asked at oral argument if there were *any* limits to the Commerce Clause, the Government was at a loss for words. Likewise, the principal dissent insists that there are limits, but it cannot muster even one example. Indeed, the dissent implicitly concedes that its reading has no limits when it criticizes the Court for "threaten[ing] legal uncertainty in an area of law that . . . seemed reasonably well settled." The one advantage of the dissent's standard is certainty: it is certain that, under its analysis, everything may be regulated under the guise of the Commerce Clause.

This . . . discussion of the original understanding and our first century and a half of case law does not necessarily require a wholesale abandonment of our more recent opinions. It simply reveals that our substantial effects test is far removed from both the Constitution and from our early case law and that the Court's opinion should not be viewed as "radical" or another "wrong turn" that must be corrected in the future. The analysis also suggests that we ought to temper our Commerce Clause jurisprudence.

At an appropriate juncture, I think we must modify our Commerce Clause jurisprudence. Today, it is easy enough to say that the Clause certainly does not empower Congress to ban gun possession within 1,000 feet of a school.

JUSTICE BREYER, with whom JUSTICE STEVENS, JUSTICE SOUTER, and JUSTICE GINSBURG join, dissenting.

In my view, the statute falls well within the scope of the commerce power as this Court has understood that power over the last half-century.

In reaching this conclusion, I apply three basic principles of Commerce Clause interpretation. First, the power to "regulate Commerce . . . among the several States," encompasses the power to regulate local activities insofar as they significantly affect interstate commerce. As the majority points out, the Court, in describing how much of an effect the Clause requires, sometimes has used the word "substantial" and sometimes has not. And, as the majority also recognizes in quoting Justice Cardozo, the question of degree (how *much* effect) requires an estimate of the "size" of the effect that no verbal formulation can capture with precision. I use the word "significant" because the word "substantial" implies a somewhat narrower power than recent precedent suggests. But, to speak of "substantial effect" rather than "significant effect" would make no difference in this case.

Second, in determining whether a local activity will likely have a significant effect upon interstate commerce, a court must consider, not the effect of an individual act (a single instance of gun possession), but rather the cumulative effect of all similar instances (*i.e.*, the effect of all guns possessed in or near schools).

Third, the Constitution requires us to judge the connection between a regulated activity and interstate commerce, not directly, but at one remove. Courts must give Congress a degree of leeway in determining the existence of a significant factual connection between the regulated activity and interstate commerce—both because the Constitution delegates the commerce power directly to Congress and because the determination requires an empirical judgment of a kind that a legislature is more likely than a court to make with accuracy. The traditional words "rational basis" capture this leeway. Thus, the specific question before us, as the Court recognizes, is not whether the "regulated activity sufficiently affected interstate commerce," but, rather, whether Congress could have had "*a rational basis*" for so concluding.

Applying these principles to the case at hand, we must ask whether Congress could have had a *rational basis* for finding a significant (or substantial) connection between gun-related school violence and interstate commerce. Or, to put the question in the language of the *explicit* finding that Congress made when it amended this law in 1994: could Congress rationally have found that "violent crime in school zones," through its effect on the "quality of education," significantly (or substantially) affects "interstate" or "foreign commerce"? As long as one views the commerce connection, not as a "technical legal conception," but as "a practical one," the answer to this question must be yes. Numerous reports and studies—generated both inside and outside government—make clear that Congress could reasonably have found the empirical connection that its law, implicitly or explicitly, asserts.

For one thing, reports, hearings, and other readily available literature make clear that the problem of guns in and around schools is widespread and extremely serious. These materials report, for example, that four percent of American high school students (and six percent of inner-city high school students) carry a gun to school at least occasionally, that 12 percent of urban high school students have had guns fired at them, that 20 percent of those students have been threatened with guns, and that, in any 6-month period, several hundred thousand schoolchildren are victims of violent crimes in or near their schools. And, they report that this widespread violence in schools throughout the Nation significantly interferes with the quality of education in those schools. Based on reports such as these, Congress obviously could have thought that guns and learning are mutually exclusive. And, Congress could therefore have found a substantial educational problem—teachers unable to teach, students unable to learn—and concluded that guns near schools contribute substantially to the size and scope of that problem.

To hold this statute constitutional is not to "obliterate" the "distinction of what is national and what is local," nor is it to hold that the Commerce Clause permits the Federal Government to "regulate any activity that it found was related to the economic productivity of individual citizens," to regulate "marriage, divorce, and child custody," or to regulate any and all aspects of education. For one thing, this statute is aimed at curbing a particularly acute threat to the educational process—the possession (and use) of life-threatening firearms in, or near, the classroom. The empirical evidence that I have discussed above unmistakably documents the special way in which guns and education are incompatible. This Court has previously recognized the singularly disruptive potential on interstate commerce that acts of violence may have. For another thing, the immediacy of the connection between education and the national economic wellbeing is documented by scholars and accepted by society at large in a way and to a degree that may not hold true for other social institutions. It must

surely be the rare case, then, that a statute strikes at conduct that (when considered in the abstract) seems so removed from commerce, but which (practically speaking) has so significant an impact upon commerce.

In sum, a holding that the particular statute before us falls within the commerce power would not expand the scope of that Clause. Rather, it simply would apply preexisting law to changing economic circumstances. *HOAM* v. *U.S.* (1964). It would recognize that, in today's economic world, gun-related violence near the classroom makes a significant difference to our economic, as well as our social, wellbeing. In accordance with well-accepted precedent, such a holding would permit Congress "to act in terms of economic . . . realities," would interpret the commerce power as "an affirmative power commensurate with the national needs," and would acknowledge that the "commerce clause does not operate so as to render the nation powerless to defend itself against economic forces that Congress decrees inimical or destructive of the national economy."

▼▲▼

## *United States* v. *Morrison*
### No. 99-05
### ___ U.S. ___ (2000)

In August 1994, Christy Brzonkala left her Fairfax County, Virginia, home in suburban Washington, D.C., to begin her freshman year at Virginia Tech. Shortly after the fall semester began in September, Brzonkala met varsity football players Antonio Morrison and James Crawford at a party. Brzonkala later alleged that Morrison and Crawford gang-raped her sometime that evening, and then told school officials that Morrison's final words to her had been, "You better not have any . . . diseases." Other witnesses later told school officials that they had heard Morrison boasting of his sexual conquests in campus dining facilities, announcing that he "like[d] to get girls drunk" and then sexually dominate them.

Brzonkala filed a complaint with Virginia Tech authorities under the university's sexual assault policy. Morrison claimed that he had had consensual sex with Brzonkala, even though he acknowledged that she had twice told him "no." The school found insufficient evidence against Crawford, but found Morrison guilty of sexual assault and suspended him for two semesters. A second hearing resulted in Morrison's guilty verdict remaining unchanged, but his offense was changed from "sexual assault" to "using abusive language." Morrison appealed again, and in August 1995 the university provost set aside Morrison's sentence, ruling that it was "excessive when compared with other cases where there has been a finding of violation of the Abusive Conduct Policy." By this time, Brzonkala had dropped out of school, having fallen into clinical depression. She read about Morrison's reinstatement in the newspaper, after which she decided to file suit in federal court under the 1994 Violence Against Women Act, passed by wide margins in the House and Senate.

Brzonkala's decision to sue under the 1994 law allowed the numerous organized interests that supported and opposed the law to enter the battle over its constitutionality. The New York City–based National Organization for Women (NOW) Legal Defense Fund represented Christy Brzonkala in court, while the Washington, D.C.–based Center for Individual Rights represented Antonio Morrison. Since the early 1970s, NOW, founded by feminist pioneer Betty Friedan in the mid-1960s, had litigated numerous cases involving sex discrimination and abortion rights. The Center for Individual Rights, a conservative public interest law firm, was a more recent entrant into the litigation arena, but had nonetheless achieved notable success, winning several cases before the Court during the 1990s involving affirmative action, First Amendment freedoms and the reach of congressional power.

The Court's decision was 5 to 4. Chief Justice Rehnquist delivered the opinion of the Court. Justice Thomas filed a concurring opinion. Justice Souter, joined by Justices Breyer, Ginsburg, and Stevens, dissented. Justice Breyer also dissented, and was joined by Justice Stevens and, in part, by Justices Ginsburg and Souter.

"There were no winners in this thing," a Virginia Tech spokesperson later said. "Two students have become poster children in ways they never could have imagined. One never finished college. The other is lost in the woods. Virginia Tech was maligned and mischaracterized. And a law that was supposed to help women has been declared unconstitutional."

CHIEF JUSTICE REHNQUIST delivered the opinion of the Court.

Due respect for the decisions of a coordinate branch of Government demands that we invalidate a congressional enactment only upon a plain showing that Congress has exceeded its constitutional bounds. With this presumption of constitutionality in mind, we turn to the question whether §13981 falls within Congress' power under Article I, Section 8, of the Constitution. . . .

As we discussed at length in *Lopez*, our interpretation of the Commerce Clause has changed as our Nation has developed. We need not repeat that detailed review of the Commerce Clause's history here; it suffices to say that, in the years since *NLRB* v. *Jones & Laughlin Steel Corp* (1937), Congress has had considerably greater latitude in regulating conduct and transactions under the Commerce Clause than our previous case law permitted. *Lopez* emphasized, however, that even under our modern, expansive interpretation of the Commerce Clause, Congress' regulatory authority is not without effective bounds.

As we observed in *Lopez*, modern Commerce Clause jurisprudence has "identified three broad categories of activity that Congress may regulate under its commerce power." "First, Congress may regulate the use of the channels of interstate commerce. Second, Congress is empowered to regulate and protect the instrumentalities of interstate commerce, or persons or things in interstate commerce, even though the threat may come only from intrastate activities." Finally, Congress' commerce authority includes the power to regulate those activities having a substantial relation to interstate commerce, . . . *i. e*, those activities that substantially affect interstate commerce."

Petitioners do not contend that these cases fall within either of the first two of these categories of Commerce Clause regulation. They seek to sustain §13981 as a regulation of activity that substantially affects interstate commerce. Given §13981's focus on gender-motivated violence wherever it occurs (rather than violence directed at the instrumentalities of interstate commerce, interstate markets, or things or persons in interstate commerce), we agree that this is the proper inquiry.

Since *Lopez* most recently canvassed and clarified our case law governing this third category of Commerce Clause regulation, it provides the proper framework for conducting the required analysis of §13981. In *Lopez*, we held that the Gun-Free School Zones Act of 1990, which made it a federal crime to knowingly possess a firearm in a school zone, exceeded Congress' authority under the Commerce Clause. Several significant considerations contributed to our decision.

First, we observed that [the 1990 gun law] was "a criminal statute that by its terms has nothing to do with 'commerce' or any sort of economic enterprise, however broadly one might define those terms." Reviewing our case law, we noted that "we have upheld a wide variety of congressional Acts regulating intrastate economic activity where we have concluded that the activity substantially affected interstate commerce." Although we cited only a few examples, including *Wickard* v. *Filburn* (1942); *Katzenbach* v. *McClung* (1964); and *Heart of Atlanta Motel* (1964), we stated that the pattern of analysis is clear. "Where economic activity substantially affects interstate commerce, legislation regulating that activity will be sustained."

Both petitioners and Justice Souter's dissent downplay the role that the economic nature of the regulated activity plays in our Commerce Clause analysis. But a fair reading of *Lopez* shows that the noneconomic, criminal nature of the conduct at issue was central to our decision in that case. . . .

The second consideration that we found important in analyzing [the 1990 gun law] was that the statute contained "no express jurisdictional element which might limit its reach to a discrete set of firearm possessions that additionally have an explicit connection with or effect on interstate commerce." Such a jurisdictional element may establish that the enactment is in pursuance of Congress' regulation of interstate commerce.

Third, we noted that neither [the 1990 gun law] "'nor its legislative history contain[s] express congressional findings regarding the effects upon interstate commerce of gun possession in a school zone.'" While "Congress normally is not required to make formal findings as to the substantial burdens that an activity has on interstate commerce," the existence of such findings may "enable us to evaluate the legislative judgment that the activity in question substantially affect[s] interstate commerce, even though no such substantial effect [is] visible to the naked eye."

Finally, our decision in *Lopez* rested in part on the fact that the link between gun possession and a substantial effect on interstate commerce was attenuated. The United States argued that the possession of guns may lead to violent crime, and that violent crime "can be expected to affect the functioning of the national economy in two ways. First, the costs of violent crime are substantial, and, through the mechanism of insurance, those costs are spread throughout the population. Second, violent crime reduces the willingness of individuals to travel to areas within the country that are perceived to be unsafe." The Government also argued that the presence of guns at schools poses a threat to the educational process, which in turn threatens to produce a less efficient and productive workforce, which will negatively affect national productivity and thus interstate commerce. . . .

With these principles underlying our Commerce Clause jurisprudence as reference points, the proper resolution of the present cases is clear. Gender-motivated crimes of violence are not, in any sense of the phrase, economic activity. While we need not adopt a categorical rule against aggregating the effects of any noneconomic activity in order to decide these cases, thus far in our Nation's history our cases have upheld Commerce Clause regulation of intrastate activity only where that activity is economic in nature.

Like the Gun-Free School Zones Act at issue in *Lopez*, §13981 contains no jurisdictional element establishing that the federal cause of action is in pursuance of Congress' power to regulate interstate commerce. Although *Lopez* makes clear that such a jurisdictional element would lend support to the argument that §13981 is sufficiently tied to interstate commerce, Congress elected to cast §13981's remedy over a wider, and more purely intrastate, body of violent crime.

In contrast with the lack of congressional findings that we faced in *Lopez*, §13981 *is* supported by numerous findings regarding the serious impact that gender-motivated violence has on victims and their families. But the existence of congressional findings is not sufficient, by itself, to sustain the constitutionality of Commerce Clause legislation. As we stated in *Lopez*, "'[S]imply because Congress may conclude that a particular activity substantially affects interstate commerce does not necessarily make it so.'" Rather, "'[w]hether particular operations affect interstate commerce sufficiently to come under the constitutional power of Congress to regulate them is ultimately a judicial rather than a legislative question, and can be settled finally only by this Court.'" In these cases, Congress' findings are substantially weakened by the fact that they rely so heavily on a method of reasoning that we have already rejected as unworkable if we are to maintain the Constitution's enumeration of powers. Congress found that gender-motivated violence affects interstate commerce "by deterring potential victims from traveling interstate, from engaging in employment in interstate business, and from transacting with business, and in places involved in interstate commerce; . . . by diminishing national productivity, increasing medical and other costs, and decreasing the supply of and the demand for interstate products."

Given these findings and petitioners' arguments, the concern that we expressed in *Lopez* that Congress might use the Commerce Clause to completely obliterate the Constitution's distinction between national and local authority seems well founded. The reasoning that petitioners advance seeks to follow the but-for causal chain from the initial occurrence of violent crime (the suppression of which has always been the prime object of the

States' police power) to every attenuated effect upon interstate commerce. If accepted, petitioners' reasoning would allow Congress to regulate any crime as long as the nationwide, aggregated impact of that crime has substantial effects on employment, production, transit, or consumption. Indeed, if Congress may regulate gender-motivated violence, it would be able to regulate murder or any other type of violence since gender-motivated violence, as a subset of all violent crime, is certain to have lesser economic impacts than the larger class of which it is a part. . . .

We accordingly reject the argument that Congress may regulate noneconomic, violent criminal conduct based solely on that conduct's aggregate effect on interstate commerce. The Constitution requires a distinction between what is truly national and what is truly local. In recognizing this fact we preserve one of the few principles that has been consistent since the Clause was adopted. The regulation and punishment of intrastate violence that is not directed at the instrumentalities, channels, or goods involved in interstate commerce has always been the province of the States. Indeed, we can think of no better example of the police power, which the Founders denied the National Government and reposed in the States, than the suppression of violent crime and vindication of its victims. . . .

Petitioner Brzonkala's complaint alleges that she was the victim of a brutal assault. But Congress' effort in §13981 to provide a federal civil remedy can[not] be sustained . . . under the Commerce Clause. . . . If the allegations here are true, no civilized system of justice could fail to provide her a remedy for the conduct of respondent Morrison. But under our federal system that remedy must be provided by the Commonwealth of Virginia, and not by the United States. The judgment of the Court of Appeals is *Affirmed.*

JUSTICE SOUTER, with whom JUSTICE STEVENS, JUSTICE GINSBURG, and JUSTICE BREYER join, dissenting.

The Court says both that it leaves Commerce Clause precedent undisturbed and that the Civil Rights Remedy of the Violence Against Women Act of 1994, 42 U.S.C. §13981 exceeds Congress's power under that Clause. I find the claims irreconcilable and respectfully dissent.

Our cases, which remain at least nominally undisturbed, stand for the following propositions. Congress has the power to legislate with regard to activity that, in the aggregate, has a substantial effect on interstate commerce. The fact of such a substantial effect is not an issue for the courts in the first instance, *ibid.,* but for the

Congress, whose institutional capacity for gathering evidence and taking testimony far exceeds ours. By passing legislation, Congress indicates its conclusion, whether explicitly or not, that facts support its exercise of the commerce power. The business of the courts is to review the congressional assessment, not for soundness but simply for the rationality of concluding that a jurisdictional basis exists in fact. See *ibid.* Any explicit findings that Congress chooses to make, though not dispositive of the question of rationality, may advance judicial review by identifying factual authority on which Congress relied. Applying those propositions in these cases can lead to only one conclusion.

One obvious difference from *United States* v. *Lopez* is the mountain of data assembled by Congress, here showing the effects of violence against women on interstate commerce. Passage of the Act in 1994 was preceded by four years of hearings, which included testimony from physicians and law professors; from survivors of rape and domestic violence; and from representatives of state law enforcement and private business. The record includes reports on gender bias from task forces in 21 States, and we have the benefit of specific factual findings in the eight separate Reports issued by Congress and its committees over the long course leading to enactment. With respect to domestic violence, Congress received evidence for the following findings:

"Three out of four American women will be victims of violent crimes sometime during their life." H. R. Rep. No. 103—395 p. 25 (1993)

"Violence is the leading cause of injuries to women ages 15 to 44. . . ." S. Rep. No. 103—138, p. 38 (1993)

"[A]s many as 50 percent of homeless women and children are fleeing domestic violence." S. Rep. No. 101—545, p. 37 (1990)

"Since 1974, the assault rate against women has outstripped the rate for men by at least twice for some age groups and far more for others." S. Rep. No. 101— 545, at 30

"[B]attering 'is the single largest cause of injury to women in the United States.'" S. Rep. No. 101—545, at 37.

"An estimated 4 million American women are battered each year by their husbands or partners." H. R. Rep. No. 103—395, at 26.

"Over 1 million women in the United States seek medical assistance each year for injuries sustained [from] their husbands or other partners." S. Rep. No. 101— 545, at 37.

"Between 2,000 and 4,000 women die every year from [domestic] abuse." S. Rep. No. 101—545, at 36.

"[A]rrest rates may be as low as 1 for every 100 domestic assaults." S. Rep. No. 101—545, at 38. . . .

"[E]stimates suggest that we spend $5 to $10 billion a year on health care, criminal justice, and other social costs of domestic violence." S. Rep. No. 103— 138, at 41.

The evidence as to rape was similarly extensive, supporting these conclusions:

"[The incidence of] rape rose four times as fast as the total national crime rate over the past 10 years." S. Rep. No. 101—545, at 30.

"According to one study, close to half a million girls now in high school will be raped before they graduate." S. Rep. No. 101—545, at 31.

"[One hundred twenty-five thousand] college women can expect to be raped during this—or any—year." S. Rep. No. 101—545, at 43. . . .

"[Forty-one] percent of judges surveyed believed that juries give sexual assault victims less credibility than other crime victims." S. Rep. No. 102—197, at 47.

"Less than 1 percent of all [rape] victims have collected damages." S. Rep. No. 102—197, at 44. . . .

"Almost one-quarter of convicted rapists never go to prison and another quarter received sentences in local jails where the average sentence is 11 months." S. Rep. No. 103—138, at 38.

"[A]lmost 50 percent of rape victims lose their jobs or are forced to quit because of the crime's severity." S. Rep. No. 102—197, at 53. . . .

Congress thereby explicitly stated the predicate for the exercise of its Commerce Clause power. Is its conclusion irrational in view of the data amassed? True, the methodology of particular studies may be challenged, and some of the figures arrived at may be disputed. But the sufficiency of the evidence before Congress to provide a rational basis for the finding cannot seriously be questioned.

Indeed, the legislative record here is far more voluminous than the record compiled by Congress and found sufficient in two prior cases upholding Title II of the Civil Rights Act of 1964 against Commerce Clause challenges. In *Heart of Atlanta Motel* and *Katzenbach*, the Court referred to evidence showing the consequences of racial discrimination by motels and restaurants on interstate commerce. Congress had relied on compelling anecdotal reports that individual instances of segregation cost thousands to millions of dollars. Congress also had evidence that the average black family spent substantially less than the average white family in the same income range on public accommodations, and that discrimination accounted for much of the difference.

While Congress did not, to my knowledge, calculate aggregate dollar values for the nationwide effects of racial discrimination in 1964, in 1994 it did rely on evidence of the harms caused by domestic violence and sexual assault, citing annual costs of $3 billion in 1990. Equally important, though, gender-based violence in the 1990's was shown to operate in a manner similar to racial discrimination in the 1960's in reducing the mobility of employees and their production and consumption of goods shipped in interstate commerce. Like racial discrimination, "[g]enderbased violence bars its most likely targets—women—from full partic[ipation] in the national economy."

If the analogy to the Civil Rights Act of 1964 is not plain enough, one can always look back a bit further. In *Wickard*, we upheld the application of the Agricultural Adjustment Act to the planting and consumption of homegrown wheat. The effect on interstate commerce in that case followed from the possibility that wheat grown at home for personal consumption could either be drawn into the market by rising prices, or relieve its grower of any need to purchase wheat in the market. The Commerce Clause predicate was simply the effect of the production of wheat for home consumption on supply and demand in interstate commerce. Supply and demand for goods in interstate commerce will also be affected by the deaths of 2,000 to 4,000 women annually at the hands of domestic abusers, and by the reduction in the work force by the 100,000 or more rape victims who lose their jobs each year or are forced to quit. Violence against women may be found to affect interstate commerce and affect it substantially.

The Act would have passed muster at any time between *Wickard* in 1942 and *Lopez* in 1995, a period in which the law enjoyed a stable understanding that congressional power under the Commerce Clause, complemented by the authority of the Necessary and Proper Clause, Art. I. §8 cl. 18, extended to all activity that, when aggregated, has a substantial effect on interstate commerce. As already noted, this understanding was secure even against the turmoil at the passage of the Civil Rights Act of 1964, in the aftermath of which the Court not only reaffirmed the cumulative effects and rational basis features of the substantial effects test, but declined to limit the commerce power through a formal distinction between legislation focused on "commerce" and statutes addressing "moral and social wrong[s]."

The fact that the Act does not pass muster before the Court today is therefore proof, to a degree that *Lopez* was not, that the Court's nominal adherence to the substantial effects test is merely that. Although a new jurisprudence has not emerged with any distinctness, it is clear that some congressional conclusions about obviously substantial, cumulative effects on commerce are being assigned lesser values than the once-stable doctrine would assign them. These devaluations are accomplished not by any express repudiation of the substantial effects test or its application through the aggregation of individual conduct, but by supplanting rational basis scrutiny with a new criterion of review. . . .

This new characterization of substantial effects has no support in our cases (the self-fulfilling prophecies of *Lopez* aside), least of all those the majority cites. Perhaps this explains why the majority is not content to rest on its cited precedent but claims a textual justification for moving toward its new system of congressional deference subject to selective discounts. Thus it purports to rely on the sensible and traditional understanding that the listing in the Constitution of some powers implies the exclusion of others unmentioned. The majority stresses that Art. I, Section 8, enumerates the powers of Congress, including the commerce power, an enumeration implying the exclusion of powers not enumerated. It follows, for the majority, not only that there must be some limits to "commerce," but that some particular subjects arguably within the commerce power can be identified in advance as excluded, on the basis of characteristics other than their commercial effects. Such exclusions come into sight when the activity regulated is not itself commercial or when the States have traditionally addressed it in the exercise of the general police power, conferred under the state constitutions but never extended to Congress under the Constitution of the Nation.

The premise that the enumeration of powers implies that other powers are withheld is sound; the conclusion that some particular categories of subject matter are therefore presumptively beyond the reach of the commerce power is, however, a *non sequitur*. From the fact that Art. I, Section 8., Clause 3, grants an authority limited to regulating commerce, it follows only that Congress may claim no authority under that section to address any subject that does not affect commerce. It does not at all follow that an activity affecting commerce nonetheless falls outside the commerce power, depending on the specific character of the activity, or the authority of a State to regulate it along with Congress. My disagreement with the majority is not, however, confined to logic, for history has shown that categorical exclusions have proven as unworkable in practice as they are unsupportable in theory.

Obviously, it would not be inconsistent with the text of the Commerce Clause itself to declare "noncommercial" primary activity beyond or presumptively beyond the scope of the commerce power. That variant of categorical approach is not, however, the sole textually permissible way of defining the scope of the Commerce Clause, and any such neat limitation would at least be suspect in the light of the final sentence of Article I, Section 8, authorizing Congress to make "all Laws . . . necessary and proper" to give effect to its enumerated powers such as commerce. Accordingly, for significant periods of our history, the Court has defined the commerce power as plenary, unsusceptible to categorical exclusions, and this was the view expressed throughout the latter part of the 20th century in the substantial effects test. These two conceptions of the commerce power, plenary and categorically limited, are in fact old rivals, and today's revival of their competition summons up familiar history, a brief reprise of which may be helpful in posing what I take to be the key question going to the legitimacy of the majority's decision to breathe new life into the approach of categorical limitation. . . .

Since adherence to these formalistically contrived confines of commerce power in large measure provoked the judicial crisis of 1937, one might reasonably have doubted that Members of this Court would ever again toy with a return to the days before *NLRB* v. *Jones & Laughlin Steel Corp.*, which brought the earlier and nearly disastrous experiment to an end. And yet today's decision can only be seen as a step toward recapturing the prior mistakes.

## FOR FURTHER READING

Brandeis, Louis. *Other People's Money.* New York: Frederick A. Stokes Co., 1914.

Cortner, Richard C. *The Supreme Court and the Second Bill of Rights: The Fourteenth Amendment and the Nationalization of Civil Liberties.* Madison: University of Wisconsin Press, 1981.

Egerton, John. *Speak Now against the Day: The Generation before the Civil Rights Movement in the South.* New York: Alfred A. Knopf, 1994.

Frankfurter, Felix. *The Commerce Clause under Marshall, Taney and Waite.* Chapel Hill: University of North Carolina Press, 1960.

Hine, Louis. *Louis Hine: Photographs of Child Labor in the New South,* John R. Kemp, ed. Jackson: University Press of Mississippi, 1986.

Hofstadter, Richard. *The Progressive Movement, 1900–1915.* Englewood Cliffs, N.J.: Prentice-Hall, 1963.

Hunter, Robert. *Poverty.* New York: Macmillan, 1904.

Irons, Peter H. *The New Deal Lawyers.* Princeton, N.J.: Princeton University Press, 1982.

Leuchtenburg, William E. *The Supreme Court Reborn: The Constitutional Revolution in the Age of Roosevelt.* New York: Oxford University Press, 1995.

Spargo, John. *The Bitter Cry of the Children.* New York: Macmillan, 1906.

Strum, Philipa. *Brandeis: Beyond Progressivism.* Lawrence: University Press of Kansas, 1993.

Van Vorst, Marie. *The Woman Who Toils: Being the Experiences of Two Gentlewomen as Factory Girls.* New York: Doubleday, 1903.

Wilson, Woodrow. *The New Freedom.* New York: Doubleday, Page & Company, 1913.

# Powers Reserved to the States

On June 11, 1963, Deputy Attorney General Nicholas Katzenbach, accompanied by Army Reserve Officer Zacharich Weaver and U.S. Marshall Peyton Norville, escorted Vivian Malone and James Hood to the Foster Auditorium on the University of Alabama's campus, where they planned to register for classes. The idea that two students should need federal supervision to register for their classes might seem strange now, but 1963 was no ordinary time, in Alabama or anywhere else, and Malone and Hood were no ordinary students. Since 1955, African American students had attempted to integrate the segregated University of Alabama. After the NAACP's historic win in *Brown v. Board of Education* (1954), Thurgood Marshall, its chief counsel, persuaded a federal court to admit Autherine Lucy, a twenty-five-year-old black woman, to the university. Lucy started classes in February 1956 but was expelled three days later for causing "mayhem" and "violence." Until Malone and Hood braved the ninety-five-degree heat on that Tuscaloosa morning seven years later, no African American had attempted to confront the university's segregationist policies.

Standing before the schoolhouse door was Governor George Wallace, who, in his inaugural address six months before, had proclaimed the immortal lines, "segregation now, segregation tomorrow, segregation forever." Katzenbach, Weaver, and Norville strode toward Wallace, with Malone and Hood a few steps behind. Like a traffic cop, Wallace raised his left hand to stop them. Katzenbach stepped forward, as much to get out of the sun as to counter Wallace's dramatic gesture, and pulled out a proclamation issued by President John F.

Kennedy calling for the admission of Malone and Hood: "I have come to ask you for unequivocal assurance that you or anyone under your control will not bar these students." Wallace replied, "No." Katzenbach handed the president's proclamation to Wallace, who took it and said nothing.

After a brief exchange between the two men, Wallace pulled out a speech and placed it on the podium in front of him. After a five-minute denunciation of the "central government" and an exposition on the "sovereignty of states" in the American constitutional system, Wallace concluded his remarks by saying, "I stand before you today in place of thousands of other Alabamians whose presence would have confronted you had I been derelict and neglected to fulfill the responsibilities of my office." He declared the action of the central government (he seldom called it "federal" in official statements) to be an "unwelcomed, unwanted, unwarranted, and force-induced intrusion upon the campus of the University of Alabama." He closed with a proclamation of his own: "I . . . hereby denounce and forbid this illegal and unwarranted action by the central government."

Wallace then turned around and walked back into Foster Auditorium. Katzenbach shouted to Wallace: "I take it from the statement that you are going to stand in the door and that you are not going to carry out the orders of the court, and that you are going to resist us in doing so. Is that so?" Wallace tersely responded, "I stand by my statement."

Katzenbach reported the events to the president and Attorney General Robert Kennedy. By 1:30 that afternoon, the president had signed an order authorizing the

Pentagon to nationalize the Alabama National Guard, which had flanked Wallace as he stood in the schoolhouse door. Two hours later, General Henry V. Graham stood before Wallace, who had returned to the Foster entrance. With Katzenbach, Malone, and Hood standing behind him and four sergeants bringing up the rear, Graham, after exchanging salutes with Wallace, said: "It is my sad duty to ask you to step aside, on order of the President of the United States." Wallace gave a brief speech denouncing federal interference and the "trend towards military dictatorship" in the United States." He gathered his aides and walked quickly to the motorcade waiting to take him back to the governor's mansion. Peace would not come to the University of Alabama's Tuscaloosa campus for a long while. James Hood withdrew soon after his admission. Somehow, Vivian Malone thrived for her remaining two years at the university, maintaining excellent grades and a busy social life. When she graduated in June 1965, ten additional black students were enrolled on the Tuscaloosa campus.

Years after the June 1963 theatrics, James Hood refused to see George Wallace's stand against integration as racially motivated. All the governor was trying do, Hood claimed, was to outline a defense of the legitimate power of the states in one of the most important elements of the American constitutional design: the federal structure that disperses and diffuses power between the national, state, and local governments.[1] The call for states' rights is often associated with some of the darker moments in the American experiment with constitutional federalism: the *Dred Scott v. Sandford* (1857) decision, the Civil War, the "dual federalism" of the Court that restricted the power of Congress and state legislatures to enact social legislation prior to the Constitutional Revolution of 1937, and most recently, the South's resistance to the Court's desegregation decisions and the civil rights movement's demands for equality during the 1950s and 1960s. In all fairness these episodes often obscure the real and genuine questions about the proper distribution of power between levels of government, questions whose answers have a great impact on the operation of the governmental process.

Moreover, advocates of greater state power have not always been with the forces of the political reactionaries. The Progressive movement that gained force in the late nineteenth and early twentieth centuries insisted that states should retain the power to experiment with solutions to the economic and social ills associated with modern industrialism. Justice Louis Brandeis, who never wavered in his belief that states should have the

*Deputy United States Attorney General Nicholas Katzenbach (far right) expresses his frustration with Alabama Governor George C. Wallace (left), who stood in the door of the registrar's office at the University of Alabama rather than admit two black students. After Wallace left, federal marshals later escorted Vivian Malone and James Hood into the university to begin classes.*
AP/Wide World Photos.

right to design legislative solutions to their problems, once penned, "It is one of the happy incidents of the federal system that a single courageous State may, if its citizens choose, serve as a laboratory; and try novel social and economic experiments without risk to the rest of the country."[2] Indeed, the states have sometimes preceded the federal government on important matters of policy innovation that are now taken for granted: minimum wage and maximum hour legislation, environmental protection, and occupational health and safety requirements, to offer just a few examples. Even today, state law sometimes exceeds federal constitutional and legislative guarantees. Examples include the rights of criminal defendants, abortion rights, civil rights for gays and lesbians, wildlife and environmental protection, and some First Amendment freedoms.

The purpose of this chapter is to explore the constitutional foundation of American federalism and its development. We first examine the theoretical framework of the American federal structure and the unique dispersion of national and state power under the Constitution. We then consider the constitutional provision most prominent in the debate over the distribution of power between the national government and the states, the Tenth Amendment, which states, "The powers not delegated to the United States by the Constitution, nor prohibited by it to the States, are reserved to the States respectively, or to the people." That discussion is followed by an examination of the substance and scope of the powers retained by the states in several areas: general police power, commerce power, congressional power to preempt state laws, and finally, environmental regulation.

## The Constitutional Foundation of Federalism

In *Federalist* 39, Madison attempted to sooth the suspicions of the Constitution's opponents on the issue of the distribution of power between the national government and the states by emphasizing the federal nature of its form. Wrote Madison:

> In its foundation, it is federal, not national; in the sources from which the ordinary powers of the government are drawn, it is partly federal and partly national; in the opera-

tion of these powers, it is national, not federal; in the extent of them, again, it is federal, not national; and, finally in the authoritative mode of introducing amendments, it is neither wholly federal nor wholly national.[3]

Madison used the word *federal* as the Anti-Federalists used it, going to great length to demonstrate that the proposed Constitution was a "compound" of federal and national features. He also took special care to note that its federal features recognized the states "as states"— e.g., ratification of the Constitution by state conventions, election of senators by states, ratification of amendments by states, and limiting the central government to "certain enumerated objects" and thereby leaving "supremacy" with respect to other objects in the state governments. Its national features treat America as if were one state—e.g., the election of representatives by districts of equal population, and the "'operation' of the government on individual citizens."[4]

*The Federalist* is, on the whole, unsympathetic to the significance of the states, but it does offer one important argument on behalf of their place in the political system. The new American federalism, as defined by the Federalists, offered the innovation of a fluid political structure that permitted the states to retain power and control over local matters while ceding the central functions of union to the national government. The states, although no longer sovereign in their respective spheres, served as checks against potential tyrannical acts by the national government. Under the Constitution the division of power between levels of government guards the rights of the people in the states just as the separation of powers in the national government allows each branch to protect its specified constitutional prerogatives. In *Federalist* 51, Madison referred to this arrangement as a "double security [that] arises to the rights of the people. The different governments will control each other, at the same time that each will be controlled by itself."[5]

Neither the Federalists nor the Anti-Federalists were so ideologically doctrinaire or naive in their politics to preclude some place for the states and the national government in their respective philosophies. The Federalists understood that reducing the states to nothing more than administrative functionaries was an unfathomable proposition. Besides, with the notable exception of Alexander Hamilton, no such sentiment existed among the Constitution's most prominent Federalist supporters. To broaden their base of support, the Federalists offered the new federalism and embraced it long before the Anti-Federalists did. Their differences emerged along the ambiguous fault line that separated national responsibilities from those of the states. Of the two groups, the Federalists held a more fluid understanding of the constitutional division of power. It emphasized the need for nationalism first and state power second, whereas the Anti-Federalists argued that the Constitution created separate and distinct sovereign spheres of power.

The merits of their respective arguments aside, the political tactics of the Federalists were far superior to the Anti-Federalists. The Federalists, not the Anti-Federalists, defined the terms of debate and placed their opponents in an airtight logical box that offered no escape hatch. As political theorist Herbert J. Storing has commented, "The Anti-Federalists could not consistently hold to the doctrine of state supremacy because they admitted it would lead to anarchy among the states. They could not accept national supremacy because they thought it would lead to centralized tyranny. To avoid both extremes [was] the somewhat dubious promise of the new federalism: to provide, somehow, for a government in which neither the whole nor the parts [was] supreme."[6] For the national and state spheres of power to avoid conflict under the new federalism would require a clear and exact constitutional partition of their responsibilities. Madison, of course, refused to offer this concession during the Constitutional Convention and campaigned in *Federalist* 39 for a "mixture" of powers that was neither "wholly national or wholly federal." Clearly, though, his vision of federalism erred on the side of nationalism. This situation left the Anti-Federalists in a profound dilemma, one that James Monroe summarized in a pamphlet he prepared for the ratification debates, but which was never distributed:

> To mark the precise point at which the powers of the general government shall cease, and that from whence those of the states shall commence, to poise them in such manner as to prevent either destroying the other, will require the utmost force of human wisdom and ingenuity. No possible ground of variance or even interference should be left, for there would the conflict commence, that might prove fatal to both.[7]

The Federalists' vision of the new federalism triumphed and was soon cemented into the foundation of American constitutional law, as the Court's early decisions in *Marbury v. Madison* (1803) (see Chapter 3), *Martin v. Hunter's Lessee* (1816) (see Chapter 3), *McCullough v. Maryland* (1819) (see Chapter 4), and *Gibbons v. Ogden* (1824) (see Chapter 4) made clear. But the Marshall Court's forceful vision of constitutional nationalism did not extinguish the strong reservoir of support that existed for a more diffuse, state-centered interpretation of the new American federalism. Indeed, as pointed out in our earlier discussion of congressional power, Thomas Jefferson and James Madison, who cut loose from his Federalist moorings in the late 1790s, emerged as the most persistent and scathing critics of the Hamiltonian blueprint of American constitutionalism.

In 1798, Madison and Jefferson, infuriated by the congressional passage earlier that year of the Alien and Sedition Acts, which made criticism of the United States government a crime, authored the Virginia and Kentucky Resolutions. Emphasizing the "sovereign and independent" power of the states to nullify federal laws that they believed were unconstitutional, the Virginia and Kentucky Resolutions offered an extreme assertion of states' rights. They ultimately commanded little support among the Federalists' opponents. Still, the bracing language of the Virginia and Kentucky Resolutions served as a potent reminder that consensus over the distribution points of power in the new American federalism, even after the ratification of the Constitution, was not settled.[8]

In truth, neither Madison nor Jefferson subscribed to the substance of the Virginia and Kentucky Resolutions. Madison, for one, considered his authorship of the Virginia Resolution an embarrassment, and regretted the contribution it made to his reputation among his enemies as someone who was too mutable on important matters of political principle.[9] As president (1801–1809), Jefferson trimmed the edges of the Federalist system, but did not lacerate it. This development came about in large part because many of the system's most vital parts were too well entrenched to welcome serious reform. But Jefferson also decided to leave much of the Federalist architecture undisturbed, even if it bore the signature of his archrival, Alexander Hamilton.[10]

For the most part, such strong rhetoric on behalf of the dual sovereignty of the national and state governments in the new American federalism was nothing more than a tactic to score political points against the Federalists' strong-armed tactics against their opponents. For others, however, the notion of the states as independent sovereignties was a deadly serious issue. Even without the restrictive language to limit the implied powers of the national government, the Tenth Amendment provided a textual basis for striking down federal legislation as an invasion of the sovereign constitutional prerogatives of the states. Especially after the Democratic Party came to power with the election of Andrew Jackson in 1828 and the ascension of the Taney Court, the Tenth Amendment, not withstanding the constitutional legacy of John Marshall, became a supremacy clause of its own for the states.

From this period in American constitutional development emerged the doctrine known as *dual federalism,* or the belief that the states, as sovereign entities, possessed powers concurrent to and often exclusive of the national government. Dual federalism, which permeated nearly every aspect of the Court's jurisprudence until the Constitutional Revolution of 1937, sharply limited the power of Congress to regulate commerce, impose taxes, and spend on behalf of the national welfare. The Court, under the dual federalist doctrine, refused to extend the protections of the Bill of Rights to the states. Jackson and Chief Justice Taney did much to recalibrate the relationship of the states to the national government. Until Taney's disastrous decision to have the Court attempt to "settle" the slavery question in *Dred Scott,* however, neither the chief justice nor the president embraced the notion that the Tenth Amendment authorized the states to nullify the constitutional prerogatives of the national government.[11] The most articulate and passionate defender of that position was South Carolina senator, John C. Calhoun, who also served as Jackson's vice president.

The basis for Calhoun's theory of nullification and state secession was discussed in Chapter 6, so here it merits only a brief review. Calhoun developed his theory as an alternative to answer the open discussion of secession among the Southern states that emerged in the late 1820s. He argued that the division of power between the national government and the states created by the Constitution permitted concurrent majorities of the Northern and Southern states in Congress to follow or reject federal legislation. If a majority within a state decided that a federal law usurped sovereign state power, the law became null and void within the borders of the state. Some commentators have interpreted Calhoun's arguments, which were undoubtedly centered around the desire to protect slavery, as a simple call for majority rights in a political system predicated upon majority rule. But Calhoun's defense of sectional and territorial rights was mostly concerned with the protection of minority privilege, rather than rights. He wanted the minority to have an equal, not merely proportionate, voice with the majority in making public policy. Such a position is incompatible with the principle of national sovereignty enshrined in the Constitution.[12]

*The Federalist*'s account of the role of the states in holding the line against the potential tyranny of the national government has been cited as often as the Tenth Amendment as the theoretical basis for the doctrines of nullification and secession. However, no such basis exists in either *The Federalist* or the Tenth Amendment for such an interpretation of the right of the states to take such action. First, neither nullification nor secession is permitted by the Constitution. They are, in fact, acts of revolution that will be properly met with resistance by the government of the United States. Second, as Hamilton argued in *Federalist* 9 and Madison later argued in *Federalist* 46, resistance to the national government must unite the states in a common cause. Revolution cannot succeed if the states do not share a "general alarm" against an oppressive national government. The Constitution intended to protect the right of the states to revolution as it was understood in 1776, not 1861.[13]

The South's defeat in the Civil War meant triumph for the constitutional principle of national sovereignty. The power of the national government increased dramatically during the war, as evidenced by the 1863 enactment of the nation's first comprehensive draft law. It made all male citizens between the ages of twenty and forty-five, as well as immigrants who declared their intentions to become citizens, eligible for military service. An even more radical extension of national power came when President Abraham Lincoln, on January 1,

*John C. Calhoun, the prominent secessionist leader, served as vice president under Andrew Jackson and as a United States senator from South Carolina. Calhoun argued that states could secede from the Union if the national government interfered with their sovereign rights.*

North Wind Picture Archive.

1863, issued the Emancipation Proclamation, which freed all persons held as slaves in those states still in rebellion against the Union. Lincoln's decision to free the slaves represented a dramatic change of heart. In August 1862 he had written to a friend, "My paramount object in this struggle is to save the Union, and is not either to save or to destroy slavery. If I could save the Union freeing any slave, I would do it; if I could save it by freeing all the slaves, I would do it; and if I could save it by freeing some and leaving others alone, I would also do that."[14]

Over time, it became apparent that the South had no interest in conciliatory gestures from the North. Offers to provide financial compensation to the Southern states that released their slaves were refused, and Lincoln soon adopted the emancipation issue as a tool of war. Lincoln confided to his advisors that his decision to issue the Emancipation Proclamation might otherwise be unconstitutional if he had not defended it on the grounds of military necessity. After *Dred Scott,* Lincoln and other defenders of the Union did not trust the Court to sustain the national government's actions in a time of war. "[M]uch of the trouble in which we are involved may be attributed to the fact that we had a pro-slavery judiciary," declared Representative W. McKee Dunn (R–Ind.). Prominent abolitionist Wendell Phillips denounced the Court and Chief Justice Taney as secessionist at heart: "God help the [N]egro if he hangs on Roger B. Taney for his liberty."[15]

Lincoln's most controversial wartime uses of executive power did not come before the Court until after the war's conclusion in 1865. By then, Lincoln had appointed five new justices to the Supreme Court, Noah Swayne, David Davis, Samuel Miller, Stephen J. Field, and Salmon P. Chase, all of whom had firm Republican, antislavery pedigrees. These new appointments shifted the political and geographic balance of the Court from Southern and Democratic to Northern and Republican. Lincoln's selection of Chase in 1864 to replace Chief Justice Taney, "more than any other appointment, symbolized the shift in power and attitude that the Republicans sought."[16]

The Republican ascendance did not mean, however, that the Court was prepared to strip the states of their powers. In fact, by 1883, after it ruled in the *Civil Rights Cases* that Congress had no authority under the Fourteenth Amendment to forbid racial discrimination in public accommodations, the Court had returned a great deal of power to the states on a wide range of policy questions. In *The Slaughterhouse Cases* (1873), discussed in Chapter 9, the Court emasculated the Privileges and Immunities Clause of the Fourteenth Amendment and did much to revive the Taney Court's notion of dual citizenship by holding that the most basic civil rights and liberties were to be protected by the states. In another, often overlooked decision, *United States* v. *Cruikshank*

(1876), the Court held that "no rights can be acquired under the Constitution or laws of the United States, except such as the government of the United States has the authority to grant or secure."[17] *Cruikshank* involved criminal charges brought against several whites who had been convicted of conspiring to oppress, threaten, injure, and intimidate African Americans to prevent them from exercising their rights to assemble and bear arms in their defense. The Court, relying on Chief Justice John Marshall's 1833 opinion in *Barron* v. *Baltimore,* held that the substantive protections of the Bill of Rights did not apply to the states, even if that meant that one group of citizens must suffer a deprivation of their fundamental civil rights.

Legal scholar Michael Curtis has commented of this period: "The view of the federal system espoused in the *Slaughterhouse Cases* was reaffirmed and extended in *Cruikshank.* It [had] becom[e] judicial orthodoxy . . . . [T]he federalism of 1866 was at the least a federalism where states stayed in their particular orbits, orbits carefully marked by the guidelines of the federal Bill of Rights. *Cruikshank* went beyond the state action question to free states from the constitutional constraints of the Bill of Rights."[18] By the late nineteenth century, the Court, had so restricted the commerce power of Congress, whether to promote a police power objective or economic fairness, as to render it toothless. States were responsible for the regulation of such important aspects of commerce as fair labor standards, production, and all those considered intrastate in nature. In turn, however, the Court ceded little police power to the states, on the grounds that laws regulating these very matters were illegitimate forms of interference with the natural forces of the economic market.

Dual federalism dominated the Court's understanding of the American federal structure until the Constitutional Revolution of 1937, when the Court embraced the New Deal and, as we discussed in Chapter 6, the idea that Congress was supreme over the states in key matters of public policy. Dual federalism was replaced by *cooperative federalism,* which is characterized by a much more fluid relationship between national and state authority and a federal arrangement in which the states serve primarily as agents to implement federal programs. Until the late 1990s, the Court, with only an occasional departure, deferred to Congress on almost all important cases challenging the post–New Deal division of power between the national government and the states. The Tenth Amendment, as you will see below, may now be well on course for a much more important place in the contemporary arrangement of the American federal structure.

## The Tenth Amendment

The Constitutional Revolution of 1937 indicated that the Court is not immune from the demands of politics. Indeed, precisely these sentiments were sprinkled throughout such cases as *Jones & Laughlin, Darby,* and *Wickard* v. *Filburn* (1942), which together suggested that the Court had exorcised the Tenth Amendment from the Constitution. Public opinion and electoral returns had made clear that the New Deal was what the people wanted, and the Court was no longer prepared to stand as a barrier against these gale-force winds of political change. By the early 1970s, however, enthusiasm within the Court for the far reaches of the New Deal welfare state had begun to wane. Nowhere was the desire to return power to the states greater than among the new justices appointed to the Court by President Richard Nixon, a conservative Republican whose successful 1968 campaign platform included a promise to return key governmental functions to the states.

Between 1968 and 1972, Nixon appointed four justices whose views on federalism stood at odds with the prevailing sentiment of successive Court majorities since 1937. His appointees, Warren E. Burger, who succeeded Earl Warren as chief justice in 1969, Harry Blackmun, Lewis F. Powell, and William H. Rehnquist were not cut from identical swaths of ideological cloth. In the beginning they did coalesce around a common belief that the Court had allowed Congress to intrude on functions that were state and local in their constitutional design.[19] In *National League of Cities* v. *Usery* (1976), these four justices, joined by Potter Stewart, came together to strike down an exercise of congressional power under the Commerce Clause for the first time since the constitutional revolution.[20] Since his appointment to the bench by President Dwight D. Eisenhower in 1958, Justice Stewart had carefully navigated a key strategic point between the Court's often bitterly divided liberal and conservative pluralities.

In *National League of Cities,* however, Chief Justice Burger provided the crucial vote. In conference, the Court had divided 5 to 4 to uphold the congressional statute at issue, the Fair Labor Standards Act (FLSA) of 1938. The law, upheld in *Darby,* established, among other things, a minimum wage scale that included employees of the federal government but excluded those at the state and local level. In 1974, Congress amended the law to include these employees. Justice Stevens, speaking for a majority that included the chief justice and Justices Brennan, Rehnquist, and White, dismissed the minority's argument that the FLSA intruded upon state sovereignty: "Congress always does things that impinge on state sovereignty. I don't think the requirement of minimum wages is that intrusive on state sovereignty." Justice Powell disagreed, claiming that he "would draw an equal protection analogy to say that the implications of federalism require strict scrutiny of federal legislation that is a direct impingement on state personnel practices." Federal regulation of such practices had to be justified by a compelling public necessity. Otherwise, states should be free to engage in activities that only they could perform.[21]

Burger's decision to defect to the Stewart, Powell, Blackmun, and Rehnquist wing came when Stewart pointed out that unless the Court's most important pre–*National League of Cities* case on this question, *Maryland v. Wirtz* (1968), was overturned, it would be necessary to uphold the 1974 FLSA amendments. In *Wirtz* the Court held that an earlier amendment to the FLSA extending federal wage and hour requirements to employees of state-operated schools and hospitals was a valid exercise of congressional commerce power.[22] Chief Justice Burger, who had balked at disturbing *Wirtz,* was persuaded by Stewart's argument and joined the original four *National League of Cities* dissenters to make a new majority.[23] Of far greater significance, however, was Burger's decision to assign the opinion to Rehnquist, by far the Court's most committed advocate on behalf of greater state power in the design of the American federal system.

Soon after Rehnquist joined the Court, it became clear that he did not subscribe to the Court's post-1937 understanding of the distribution of power between the national government and the states. Far more so than any of his colleagues at the time, Rehnquist was willing to shift power away from the national government to the states. In several dissents prior to *National League of Cities,* he had begun to revive the pre–New Deal era of dual federalism discredited in *Darby* and *Wickard v. Filburn.* Political scientist Sue Davis has commented that federalism occupies the highest position in Justice Rehnquist's hierarchy of constitutional values. His commitment extends beyond disputes between Congress and the states over economic regulation to the operation of the federal and state court systems and the state exercise of police power.[24]

Rehnquist made the most of his newfound position in the majority to produce an opinion that treated the Constitutional Revolution of 1937 as little more than an aberration. In handing Congress its first defeat under the Commerce Clause since the constitutional crisis of the New Deal, the chief justice wrote that "[w]e have repeatedly recognized that there are attributes of sovereignty attaching to every state government which may not be impaired by Congress."[25] Several commentators noted that Rehnquist's opinion in *National League of Cities* marked the Court's most explicit embrace of state sovereignty as a concurrent constitutional doctrine since the heyday of dual federalism. What about the substance of Rehnquist's opinion made it so controversial?

*National League of Cities* provided a moment of high drama, suggesting that the Court was prepared to revisit the fundamental principles of the 1937 revolution. But the dissenters in that case, recognizing its potential implications, refused to allow it to become settled precedent. Justice Brennan, who had been the most forceful dissenter in *National League of Cities,* began a concerted effort to woo Justice Harry Blackmun away from the original majority. After *National League of Cities* was decided, it soon became apparent that Blackmun, not Burger, was the most likely defector. Brennan had secured Blackmun's vote in *EEOC v. Wyoming* (1983), which upheld a state game warden's claim that the federal Age Discrimination Act protected him from such discrimination. Sensing that Justice Blackmun had fallen into the hands of the *National League of Cities* dissenters,

Chief Justice Burger assigned Blackmun the opinion in *Garcia v. San Antonio Metropolitan Transit Authority* (1985). That move blew up in the chief justice's face. Blackmun switched his vote and joined the *National League of Cities* dissenters to overrule Rehnquist's ambitious 1976 opinion.

*Garcia* was argued during the 1983–1984 term but was scheduled for reargument after the Court was unable to produce a majority opinion. One reason attributed to the Court's delay in handing down *Garcia* is that Chief Justice Burger wanted more time to pull Blackmun into the majority that included him, Rehnquist, Powell, and Sandra Day O'Connor. Justice O'Connor, the first woman to serve on the Court, had been appointed in 1981 by President Reagan, a supporter of the *National League of Cities* decision, to replace Stewart. Blackmun had written his colleagues after the original *Garcia* argument to say that he was prepared "to come down on the side of reversal. I have been able to find no principled way in which to affirm." After reviewing Blackmun's draft opinion, Burger responded, "At this stage—almost mid-June— a thirty-page opinion coming out contrary to the Conference vote on a very important issue placed those who may dissent in a very difficult position. I think we should set the case for reargument." Burger's written comments came after Blackmun had switched from his original conference vote, which was to strike down the wage and overtime provisions of the FLSA as they applied to employees of the San Antonio mass transit system.[26]

*Garcia* was reargued at the outset of the 1984–1985 term, but even a second round failed to shake Blackmun from his decision to abandon *National League of Cities*. Blackmun knew that Burger had assigned him the opinion because he was, in the chief justice's words, the "least persuaded" to strike down the contested FLSA provisions.[27] Brennan rewarded Blackmun's switch with the majority opinion in *Garcia*, which cast aside the *National League of Cities* precedent. That decision might well tell us more about the delicate nature of opinion assignment and case management within the Court than about federalism.[28] Nonetheless, *Garcia*'s consequences for the federal relationship were momentous, restoring it to where it was before *National League of Cities*.

But the notion that the Tenth Amendment had, after *Garcia*, once again gone dormant proved to be wrong. In *New York v. United States* (1992), the Court invalidated a provision of the Low-Level Radioactive Waste Policy Amendments Act of 1985. The law required states to accept responsibility for and dispose of all radioactive wastes generated within their borders. By this time the Court's sympathies had again shifted to the states. *New York* gave Sandra Day O'Connor, whose views on the excesses of national power were shared by post–*National League of Cities* appointees Antonin Scalia (replacing Burger), Clarence Thomas (replacing Marshall), Anthony Kennedy (replacing Powell), and initially, David Souter (replacing Brennan), her first opportunity to present a forthright statement of her views on federalism.[29] Writing for a 6-3 majority, with Rehnquist the only holdover from *National League of Cities,* Justice O'Connor claimed that the law infringed "upon the core of state sovereignty reserved by the Tenth Amendment."[30] O'Connor's opinion stopped short of revisiting *Garcia,* which several parties appearing as *amici* had requested of the Court, but did make a strong case on behalf of the right of the states to retain independence from the national government.

The Tenth Amendment's renewal continued in *Printz v. United States* (1997), in which the Court, by 5-4 majority, struck down the sections of the Brady Handgun Violence Prevention Act of 1993 requiring state and local law-enforcement officials to carry out background checks on prospective handgun purchases. It is more popularly known as the "Brady Bill," so named for James Brady, a former press secretary to President Ronald Reagan, who was shot in March 1981 during an assassination attempt on the president in front of a Washington, D.C., hotel. The law mandated the most extensive federal restrictions to date on the sale and purchase of handguns. Our SIDEBAR offers more detail on the massive lobbying effort surrounding the Brady Bill. For now, note the tone of Justice Scalia's opinion in *Printz* and the similarities that it bears to O'Connor's opinion in *New York.* Together, what do these opinions say about the status of *Garcia*? Is there a consistent principle that now animates the Court's understanding of the Tenth Amendment? Or is the Court influenced, as some theories of constitutional interpretation suggest, by the politics that dominate the particular moment?

# National League of Cities v. Usery
## 426 U.S. 833 (1976)

In 1974, Congress amended the Fair Labor Standards Act of 1938 (FLSA) to bring virtually all state and local government employees under its minimum wage and overtime provisions. Several associations representing state and municipal governments, including the National League of Cities and the National Governors' Conference, filed suit in federal court claiming that the action was unconstitutional. The essence of their complaint against the FLSA was that it extended a federal requirement to the states without the financial support to carry it out. Such a requirement, quite common in the American federal structure, is more commonly referred to among policymakers as an "unfunded mandate."

The Court's decision was 5 to 4. Chief Justice Rehnquist announced the opinion of the Court. Justice Blackmun filed a concurrence. Justice Brennan, joined by Justices White and Marshall, dissented. Justice Stevens filed a separate dissenting opinion.

▼▲▼

MR. JUSTICE REHNQUIST delivered the opinion of the Court.

This Court has never doubted that there are limits upon the power of Congress to override state sovereignty, even when exercising its otherwise plenary powers to tax or to regulate commerce which are conferred by Article I of the Constitution. In *Wirtz*, for example, the Court took care to assure the appellants that it had "ample power to prevent . . . 'the utter destruction of the State as a sovereign political entity,'" which they feared. Appellee Secretary in this case, both in his brief and upon oral argument, has agreed that our federal system of government imposes definite limits upon the authority of Congress to regulate the activities of the States as States by means of the commerce power. In *Fry*, the Court recognized that an express declaration of this limitation is found in the Tenth Amendment:

> While the Tenth Amendment has been characterized as a "truism," stating merely that "all is retained which has not been surrendered," *United States v. Darby* (1941), it is not without significance. The Amendment expressly declares the constitutional policy that Congress may not exercise power in a fashion that impairs the States' integrity or their ability to function effectively in a federal system. . . .

. . . One undoubted attribute of state sovereignty is the States' power to determine the wages which shall be paid to those whom they employ in order to carry out their governmental functions, what hours those persons will work, and what compensation will be provided where these employees may be called upon to work overtime. The question we must resolve here, then, is whether these determinations are "'functions essential to separate and independent existence,'" so that Congress may not abrogate the States' otherwise plenary authority to make them. . . .

Judged solely in terms of increased costs in dollars, these allegations show a significant impact on the functioning of the governmental bodies involved. The Metropolitan Government of Nashville and Davidson County, Tenn. for example, asserted that the Act will increase its costs of providing essential police and fire protection, without any increase in service or in current salary levels, by $938,000 per year. Cape Girardeau, Mo., estimated that its annual budget for fire protection may have to be increased by anywhere from $250,000 to $400,000 over the current figure of $350,000. The State of Arizona alleged that the annual additional expenditures which will be required if it is to continue to provide essential state services may total $2.5 million. The State of California, which must devote significant portions of its budget to fire suppression endeavors, estimated that application of the Act to its employment practices will necessitate an increase in its budget of between $8 million and $16 million.

Increased costs are not, of course, the only adverse effects which compliance with the Act will visit upon state and local governments, and, in turn, upon the citizens who depend upon those governments. In its complaint in intervention, for example, California asserted that it could not comply with the overtime costs (approximately $750,000 per year) which the Act required to be paid to California Highway Patrol cadets during their academy training program. California reported that it had thus been forced to reduce its academy training program from 2,080 hours to only 960 hours, a compromise undoubtedly of substantial importance to those whose safety and welfare may depend upon the preparedness of the California Highway Patrol. . . .

Quite apart from the substantial costs imposed upon the States and their political subdivisions, the Act displaces state policies regarding the manner in which they will structure delivery of those governmental services which their citizens require. The Act, speaking directly to the States *qua* States, requires that they shall pay all but an extremely limited minority of their employees the minimum wage rate currently chosen by Congress. It may well be that, as a matter of economic policy, it would be desirable that States, just as private employers, comply with these minimum wage requirements. But it cannot be gainsaid that the federal requirement directly supplant the considered policy choice of the States' elected officials and administrator as to how they wish to structure pay scale in state employment. The State might wish to employ persons with little or no training, or those who wish to work on a casual basis, or those who, for some other reason, do not possess minimum employment requirements, and pay them less than the federally prescribed minimum wage. It may wish to offer part-time or summer employment to teenagers at a figure less than the minimum wage, and, if unable to do so, may decline to offer such employment at all. But the Act would forbid such choice by the States. The only "discretion" left to them under the Act is either to attempt to increase their revenue to meet the additional financial burden imposed upon them by paying Congressionally prescribed wages to their existing complement of employees or to reduce that complement to a number which can be paid the federal minimum wage without increasing revenue.

This dilemma presented by the minimum wage restriction may seem not immediately different from that faced by private employers, who have long been covered by the Act and who must find ways to increase their gross income if they are to pay higher wages while maintaining current earnings. The difference, however, is that a State is not merely a factor in the "shifting economic arrangements" of the private sector of the economy, but is itself a coordinate element in the system established by the Framers for governing our Federal Union.

The degree to which the FLSA amendments would interfere with traditional aspects of state sovereignty can be seen even more clearly upon examining the overtime requirements of the Act. The general effect of these provisions is to require the States to pay their employees at premium rates whenever their work exceeds a specified number of hours in a given period. The asserted reason for these provisions is to provide a financial disincentive upon using employees beyond the work period deemed appropriate by Congress. . . . We do not doubt that this may be a salutary result, and that it has a sufficiently rational relationship to commerce to validate the application of the overtime provisions to private employers. But, like the minimum wage provisions, the vice of the Act as sought to be applied here is that it directly penalizes the States for choosing to hire governmental employees on terms different from those which Congress has sought to impose. . . .

Our examination of the effect of the 1974 amendments, as sought to be extended to the States and their political subdivisions, satisfies us that both the minimum wage and the maximum hour provisions will impermissibly interfere with the integral governmental functions of these bodies. We earlier noted some disagreement between the parties regarding the precise effect the amendments will have in application. We do not believe particularized assessments of actual impact are crucial to resolution of the issue presented, however. For even if we accept appellee's assessments concerning the impact of the amendments, their application will nonetheless significantly alter or displace the States' abilities to structure employer employee relationships in such areas as fire prevention, police protection, sanitation, public health, and parks and recreation. These activities are typical of those performed by state and local governments in discharging their dual functions of administering the public law and furnishing public services. Indeed, it is functions such as these which governments are created to provide, services such as these which the States have traditionally afforded their citizens. If Congress may withdraw from the States the authority to make those fundamental employment decisions upon which their systems for performance of these functions must rest, we think there would be little left of the States' "'separate and independent existence.'" Thus, even if appellants may have overestimated the effect which the Act will have upon their current levels and patterns of governmental activity, the dispositive factor is that Congress has attempted to exercise its Commerce Clause authority to prescribe minimum wages and maximum hours to be paid by the States in their capacities as sovereign governments. In so doing, Congress has sought to wield its power in a fashion that would impair the States' "ability to function effectively in a federal system." This exercise of congressional authority does not comport with the federal system of government embodied in the Constitution. We hold that, insofar as the challenged amendments operate to directly displace the States' freedom to structure integral operations in areas of traditional governmental functions, they are not within the authority granted Congress by Article I, Section 8, clause 3.

One final matter requires our attention. Appellee has vigorously urged that we cannot, consistently with the Court's decisions in *Maryland* v. *Wirtz* (1968), rule against him here. It is important to examine this contention so that it will be clear what we hold today, and what we do not. . . .

With respect to the Court's decision in *Wirtz*, we reach a different conclusion. Both appellee and the District

Court thought that decision required rejection of appellants' claims. Appellants, in turn, advance several arguments by which they seek to distinguish the facts before the Court in *Wirtz* from those presented by the 1974 amendments to the Act. There are undoubtedly factual distinctions between the two situations, but, in view of the conclusions expressed earlier in this opinion, we do not believe the reasoning in *Wirtz* may any longer be regarded as authoritative. . . .

[W]e have reaffirmed today that the States, as States, stand on a quite different footing from an individual or a corporation when challenging the exercise of Congress' power to regulate commerce. We think the dicta from *United States v. California* simply wrong. Congress may not exercise that power so as to force directly upon the States its choices as to how essential decisions regarding the conduct of integral governmental functions are to be made. We agree that such assertions of power, if unchecked, would indeed, as Mr. Justice Douglas cautioned in his dissent in *Wirtz,* allow "the National Government [to] devour the essentials of state sovereignty," and would therefore transgress the bounds of the authority granted Congress under the Commerce Clause. While there are obvious differences between the schools and hospitals involved in *Wirtz,* and the fire and police departments affected here, each provides an integral portion of those governmental services which the States and their political subdivisions have traditionally afforded their citizens. We are therefore persuaded that *Wirtz* must be overruled.

The judgment of the District Court is accordingly reversed, and the cases are remanded for further proceedings consistent with this opinion.

*So ordered.*

MR. JUSTICE BLACKMUN, concurring.

The Court's opinion and the dissents indicate the importance and significance of this litigation as it bears upon the relationship between the Federal Government and our States. Although I am not untroubled by certain possible implications of the Court's opinion—some of them suggested by the dissents—I do not read the opinion so despairingly as does my Brother BRENNAN. In my view, the result with respect to the statute under challenge here is necessarily correct. I may misinterpret the Court's opinion, but it seems to me that it adopts a balancing approach, and does not outlaw federal power in areas such as environmental protection, where the federal interest is demonstrably greater and where state facility compliance with imposed federal standards would be essential. With

this understanding on my part of the Court's opinion, I join it.

MR. JUSTICE BRENNAN, with whom MR. JUSTICE WHITE and MR. JUSTICE MARSHALL join, dissenting.

The Court concedes, as of course it must, that Congress enacted the 1974 amendments pursuant to its exclusive power under Article I, Section 8, clause 3, of the Constitution "[t]o regulate Commerce . . . among the several States." It must therefore be surprising that my Brethren should choose this bicentennial year of our independence to repudiate principles governing judicial interpretation of our Constitution settled since the time of Mr. Chief Justice John Marshall, discarding his postulate that the Constitution contemplates that restraints upon exercise by Congress of its plenary commerce power lie in the political process, and not in the judicial process. . . . My Brethren do not successfully obscure today's patent usurpation of the role reserved for the political process by their purported discovery in the Constitution of a restraint derived from sovereignty of the States on Congress' exercise of the commerce power. Mr. Chief Justice Marshall recognized that limitations "prescribed in the constitution," *Gibbons v. Ogden,* restrain Congress' exercise of the power. Thus, laws within the commerce power may not infringe individual liberties protected by the First Amendment, the Fifth Amendment, or the Sixth Amendment. But there is no restraint based on state sovereignty requiring or permitting judicial enforcement anywhere expressed in the Constitution; our decisions over the last century and a half have explicitly rejected the existence of any such restraint on the commerce power. . . .

The reliance of my Brethren upon the Tenth Amendment as "an express declaration of [a state sovereignty] limitation," not only suggests that they overrule governing decisions of this Court that address this question but must astound scholars of the Constitution. For not only early decisions, *Gibbons v. Ogden* (1824) and *Martin v. Hunter's Lessee* (1816), hold that nothing in the Tenth Amendment constitutes a limitation on congressional exercise of powers delegated by the Constitution to Congress. Rather, as the Tenth Amendment's significance was more recently summarized:

> The amendment states but a truism that all is retained which has not been surrendered. *There is nothing in the history of its adoption to suggest that it was more than declaratory of the relationship between the national and state governments as it had been established by the Constitution before the amendment, or that its purpose*

was other than to allay fears that the new national government might seek to exercise powers not granted, and that the states might not be able to exercise fully their reserved powers. . . .

Today's repudiation of this unbroken line of precedent that firmly reject my Brethren's ill-conceived abstraction can only be regarded as a transparent cover or invalidating a congressional judgment with which they disagree. The only analysis even remotely resembling that adopted today is found in a line of opinions dealing with the Commerce Clause and the Tenth Amendment that ultimately provoked a constitutional crisis for the Court in the 1930's. We tend to forget that the Court invalidated legislation during the Great Depression not solely under the Due Process Clause, but also and primarily under the Commerce Clause and the Tenth Amendment. It may have been the eventual abandonment of that overly restrictive construction of the commerce power that spelled defeat for the Court packing plan, and preserved the integrity of this institution, but my Brethren today are transparently trying to cut back on that recognition of the scope of the commerce power. My Brethren's approach to this case is not far different from the dissenting opinions in the cases that averted the crisis. . . .

Judicial restraint in this area merely recognizes that the political branches of our Government are structured to protect the interests of the States, as well as the Nation as a whole, and that the States are fully able to protect their own interests in the premises. Congress is constituted of representatives in both the Senate and House elected from the States. Decisions upon the extent of federal intervention under the Commerce Clause into the affairs of the States are in that sense decisions of the States themselves. Judicial redistribution of powers granted the National Government by the terms of the Constitution violates the fundamental tenet of our federalism that the extent of federal intervention into the States' affairs in the exercise of delegated powers shall be determined by the States' exercise of political power through their representatives in Congress. There is no reason whatever to suppose that in enacting the 1974 amendments Congress, even if it might extensively obliterate state sovereignty by fully exercising its plenary power respecting commerce, had any purpose to do so.

Surely the presumption must be to the contrary. Any realistic assessment of our federal political system, dominated as it is by representatives of the people elected from the States, yields the conclusion that it is highly unlikely that those representatives will ever be motivated to disregard totally the concerns of these States. Certainly

this was the premise upon which the Constitution, as authoritatively explicated in *Gibbons* v. *Ogden*, was founded. Indeed, though the States are represented in the National Government, national interests are not similarly represented in the States' political processes. Perhaps my Brethren's concern with the Judiciary's role in preserving federalism might better focus on whether Congress, not the States, is in greater need of this Court's protection.

A sense of the enormous impact of States' political power is gained by brief reference to the federal budget. The largest estimate by any of the appellants of the cost impact of the 1974 amendments—$1 billion—pales in comparison with the financial assistance the States receive from the Federal Government. In fiscal 1977, the President's proposed budget recommends $60.5 billion in federal assistance to the States, exclusive of loans. Appellants complain of the impact of the amended FLSA on police and fire departments, but the 1977 budget contemplates outlays for law enforcement assistance of $716 million. Concern is also expressed about the diminished ability to hire students in the summer if States must pay them a minimum wage, but the Federal Government's "summer youth program" provides $400 million for 670,000 jobs. Given this demonstrated ability to obtain funds from the Federal Government for needed state services, there is little doubt that the States' influence in the political process is adequate to safeguard their sovereignty. . . .

We are left then with a catastrophic judicial body blow at Congress' power under the Commerce Clause. Even if Congress may nevertheless accomplish its objectives—for example, by conditioning grants of federal funds upon compliance with federal minimum wage and overtime standards—there is an ominous portent of disruption of our constitutional structure implicit in today's mischievous decision. I dissent.

MR. JUSTICE STEVENS, dissenting.

The Court holds that the Federal Government may not interfere with a sovereign State's inherent right to pay a substandard wage to the janitor at the state capitol. The principle on which the holding rests is difficult to perceive.

The Federal Government may, I believe, require the State to act impartially when it hires or fires the janitor, to withhold taxes from his paycheck, to observe safety regulations when he is performing his job, to forbid him from burning too much soft coal in the capitol furnace, from dumping untreated refuse in an adjacent waterway, from overloading a state-owned garbage truck, or from driving either the truck or the Governor's limousine over 55 miles an hour. Even though these and many other activities of the capitol janitor are activities of the State *qua* State, I have no doubt that they are subject to federal regulation.

I agree that it is unwise for the Federal Government to exercise its power in the ways described in the Court's opinion. For the proposition that regulation of the minimum price of a commodity—even labor—will increase the quantity consumed is not one that I can readily understand. That concern, however, applies with even greater force to the private sector of the economy where the exclusion of the marginally employable does the greatest harm and, in all events, merely reflects my views on a policy issue which has been firmly resolved by the branches of government having power to decide such questions. As far as the complexities of adjusting police and fire departments to this sort of federal control are concerned, I presume that appropriate tailor-made regulations would soon solve their most pressing problems. After all, the interests adversely affected by this legislation are not without political power.

My disagreement with the wisdom of this legislation may not, of course, affect my judgment with respect to its validity. On this issue, there is no dissent from the proposition that the Federal Government's power over the labor market is adequate to embrace these employees. Since I am unable to identify a limitation on that federal power that would not also invalidate federal regulation of state activities that I consider unquestionably permissible, I am persuaded that this statute is valid. Accordingly, with respect and a great deal of sympathy for the views expressed by the Court, I dissent from its constitutional holding.

▼▲▼

## Garcia v. San Antonio Metropolitan Transit Authority
### 469 U.S. 528 (1985)

After the Court's decision in *National League of Cities,* the United States Department of Labor began a systematic review of which functions of state and local governments could be subjected to enforcement under the Fair Labor Standards Act (FLSA). In 1979, the Labor Department concluded that state railroads remained within the scope of FLSA coverage. The San Antonio Metropolitan Transit Authority (SAMTA) challenged the application of the FLSA to the authority's local rail operations in federal court. The court permitted Joe Garcia, a SAMTA employee, and the

American Public Transit Association (APTA), the trade association representing local public transit authorities, to intervene in the litigation. Garcia wanted back pay based on the wage and overtime provisions he believed should apply to local rail employees through FLSA, whereas the APTA wanted the court to rule that local transit authorities were free to determine their own compensation structures.

The lower court ruled on behalf of SAMTA and the APTA, holding that states remained essentially "sovereign" in matters of public transportation. The *National League of Cities* dissenters, who had gradually been wooing Justice Blackmun into their camp, seized upon *Garcia* as a vehicle to reconsider the earlier decision.

The Court's decision was 5 to 4. Justice Blackmun delivered the opinion of the Court. Justice Rehnquist, whose great victory in *National League of Cities* withered just nine years later, filed a dissent. Justice Powell, who was joined by Justices Rehnquist and O'Connor and Chief Justice Burger, also dissented.

JUSTICE BLACKMUN delivered the opinion of the Court.

We revisit in these cases an issue raised in *National League of Cities* v. *Usery,* (1976). In that litigation, this Court, by a sharply divided vote, ruled that the Commerce Clause does not empower Congress to enforce the minimum wage and overtime provisions of the Fair Labor Standards Act (FLSA) against the States "in areas of traditional governmental functions." Although *National League of Cities* supplied some examples of "traditional governmental functions," it did not offer a general explanation of how a "traditional" function is to be distinguished from a "non-traditional" one. Since then, federal and state courts have struggled with the task, thus imposed, of identifying a traditional function for purposes of state immunity under the Commerce Clause.

In the present cases, a Federal District Court concluded that municipal ownership and operation of a mass transit system is a traditional governmental function and thus, under *National League of Cities,* is exempt from the obligations imposed by the FLSA. Faced with the identical question, three Federal Courts of Appeals and one state appellate court have reached the opposite conclusion.

Our examination of this "function" standard applied in these and other cases over the last eight years now persuades us that the attempt to draw the boundaries of state regulatory immunity in terms of "traditional governmental function" is not only unworkable but is also inconsistent with established principles of federalism and, indeed, with those very federalism principles on which *National League of Cities* purported to rest. That case, accordingly, is overruled. . . .

The central theme of *National League of Cities* was that the States occupy a special position in our constitutional system, and that the scope of Congress' authority under the Commerce Clause must reflect that position. Of course, the Commerce Clause, by its specific language, does not provide any special limitation on Congress' actions with respect to the States. It is equally true, however, that the text of the Constitution provides the beginning, rather than the final answer, to every inquiry into questions of federalism, for "[b]ehind the words of the constitutional provisions are postulates which limit and control." *National League of Cities* reflected the general conviction that the Constitution precludes "the National Government [from] devour[ing] the essentials of state sovereignty." In order to be faithful to the underlying federal premises of the Constitution, courts must look for the "postulates which limit and control."

What has proved problematic is not the perception that the Constitution's federal structure imposes limitations on the Commerce Clause, but rather the nature and content of those limitations. One approach to defining the limits on Congress' authority to regulate the States under the Commerce Clause is to identify certain underlying elements of political sovereignty that are deemed essential to the States' "separate and independent existence." This approach obviously underlay the Court's use of the "traditional governmental function" concept in *National League of Cities*. It also has led to the separate requirement that the challenged federal statute "address matters that are indisputably 'attribute[s] of state sovereignty.'" In *National League of Cities* itself, for example, the Court concluded that decisions by a State concerning the wages and hours of its employees are an "undoubted attribute of state sovereignty." The opinion did not explain what aspects of such decisions made them such an "undoubted attribute," and the Court since then has remarked on the uncertain scope of the concept. The point of the inquiry, however, has remained to single out particular features of a State's internal governance that are deemed to be intrinsic parts of state sovereignty. We doubt that courts ultimately can identify principled constitutional limitations on the scope of Congress' Commerce Clause powers over the States merely by relying on *a priori* definitions of state sovereignty. In part, this is because of the elusiveness of objective criteria for "fundamental" elements of state sovereignty, a problem we have witnessed in the search for

"traditional governmental functions." There is, however, a more fundamental reason: the sovereignty of the States is limited by the Constitution itself. A variety of sovereign powers, for example, are withdrawn from the States by Article I, Section 10. Section 8 of the same Article works an equally sharp contraction of state sovereignty by authorizing Congress to exercise a wide range of legislative powers and (in conjunction with the Supremacy Clause of Article VI) to displace contrary state legislation. By providing for final review of questions of federal law in this Court, Article III curtails the sovereign power of the States' judiciaries to make authoritative determinations of law. Finally, the developed application, through the Fourteenth Amendment, of the greater part of the Bill of Rights to the States limits the sovereign authority that States otherwise would possess to legislate with respect to their citizens and to conduct their own affairs.

The States unquestionably do "retai[n] a significant measure of sovereign authority." They do so, however, only to the extent that the Constitution has not divested them of their original powers and transferred those powers to the Federal Government. In the words of James Madison to the Members of the First Congress:

> Interference with the power of the States was no constitutional criterion of the power of Congress. If the power was not given, Congress could not exercise it; if given, they might exercise it, although it should interfere with the laws, or even the Constitution of the States.

. . . As a result, to say that the Constitution assumes the continued role of the States is to say little about the nature of that role. . . .

When we look for the States "residuary and inviolable sovereignty," *Federalist 39*, in the shape of the constitutional scheme, rather than in predetermined notions of sovereign power, a different measure of state sovereignty emerges. Apart from the limitation on federal authority inherent in the delegated nature of Congress' Article I powers, the principal means chosen by the Framers to ensure the role of the States in the federal system lies in the structure of the Federal Government itself. It is no novelty to observe that the composition of the Federal Government was designed in large part to protect the States from overreaching by Congress. The Framers thus gave the States a role in the selection both of the Executive and the Legislative Branches of the Federal Government. The States were vested with indirect influence over the House of Representatives and the Presidency by their control of electoral qualifications and their role in Presidential elections. They were given more direct influence in the Senate, where each State received equal representation and each Senator was to be selected by the legislature of his State. Article I, Section 3. The significance attached to the States' equal representation in the Senate is underscored by the prohibition of any constitutional amendment divesting a State of equal representation without the State's consent.

The extent to which the structure of the Federal Government itself was relied on to insulate the interests of the States is evident in the views of the Framers. . . . In short, the Framers chose to rely on a federal system in which special restraints on federal power over the States inhered principally in the workings of the National Government itself, rather than in discrete limitations on the objects of federal authority. State sovereign interests, then, are more properly protected by procedural safeguards inherent in the structure of the federal system than by judicially created limitations on federal power.

The effectiveness of the federal political process in preserving the States' interests is apparent even today in the course of federal legislation. On the one hand, the States have been able to direct a substantial proportion of federal revenues into their own treasuries in the form of general and program-specific grants in aid. The federal role in assisting state and local governments is a longstanding one; Congress provided federal land grants to finance state governments from the beginning of the Republic, and direct cash grants were awarded as early as 1887 under the Hatch Act. In the past quarter century alone, federal grants to States and localities have grown from $7 billion to $96 billion. As a result, federal grants now account for about one-fifth of state and local government expenditures. The States have obtained federal funding for such services as police and fire protection, education, public health and hospitals, parks and recreation, and sanitation. Moreover, at the same time that the States have exercised their influence to obtain federal support, they have been able to exempt themselves from a wide variety of obligations imposed by Congress under the Commerce Clause. For example, the Federal Power Act, the National Labor Relations Act, the Labor-Management Reporting and Disclosure Act, the Occupational Safety and Health Act, the Employee Retirement Income Security Act, and the Sherman Act all contain express or implied exemptions for States and their subdivisions. The fact that some federal statutes such as the FLSA extend general obligations to the States cannot obscure the extent to which the political position of the States in the federal system has served to minimize the burdens that the States bear under the Commerce Clause.

We realize that changes in the structure of the Federal Government have taken place since 1789, not the least of which has been the substitution of popular election of Senators by the adoption of the Seventeenth Amendment in 1913, and that these changes may work to alter the influence of the States in the federal political process. Nonetheless, against this background, we are convinced that the fundamental limitation that the constitutional scheme imposes on the Commerce Clause to protect the "States as States" is one of process, rather than one of result. Any substantive restraint on the exercise of Commerce Clause powers must find its justification in the procedural nature of this basic limitation, and it must be tailored to compensate for possible failings in the national political process, rather than to dictate a "sacred province of state autonomy." . . .

Of course, we continue to recognize that the States occupy a special and specific position in our constitutional system, and that the scope of Congress' authority under the Commerce Clause must reflect that position. But the principal and basic limit on the federal commerce power is that inherent in all congressional action—the built-in restraints that our system provides through state participation in federal governmental action. The political process ensures that laws that unduly burden the States will not be promulgated. In the factual setting of these cases, the internal safeguards of the political process have performed as intended. . . .

We do not lightly overrule recent precedent. We have not hesitated, however, when it has become apparent that a prior decision has departed from a proper understanding of congressional power under the Commerce Clause. *United States* v. *Darby* (1941). Due respect for the reach of congressional power within the federal system mandates that we do so now.

The judgment of the District Court is reversed, and these cases are remanded to that court for further proceedings consistent with this opinion.

*It is so ordered.*

JUSTICE O'CONNOR, with whom JUSTICE POWELL and JUSTICE REHNQUIST join, dissenting.

. . . In my view, federalism cannot be reduced to the weak "essence" distilled by the majority today. There is more to federalism than the nature of the constraints that can be imposed on the States in "the realm of authority left open to them by the Constitution." The central issue of federalism, of course, is whether any realm is left open to the States by the Constitution—whether any area remains in which a State may act free of federal interference. "The issue . . . is whether the federal system has any *legal* substance, any core of constitutional right that courts will enforce." The true "essence" of federalism is that the States, as States, have legitimate interests which the National Government is bound to respect even though its laws are supreme. If federalism so conceived and so carefully cultivated by the Framers of our Constitution is to remain meaningful, this Court cannot abdicate its constitutional responsibility to oversee the Federal Government's compliance with its duty to respect the legitimate interests of the States.

Due to the emergence of an integrated and industrialized national economy, this Court has been required to examine and review a breathtaking expansion of the powers of Congress. In doing so, the Court correctly perceived that the Framers of our Constitution intended Congress to have sufficient power to address national problems. But the Framers were not single-minded. The Constitution is animated by an array of intentions. Just as surely as the Framers envisioned a National Government capable of solving national problems, they also envisioned a republic whose vitality was assured by the diffusion of power not only among the branches of the Federal Government, but also between the Federal Government and the States. In the 18th century, these intentions did not conflict, because technology had not yet converted every local problem into a national one. A conflict has now emerged, and the Court today retreats rather than reconcile the Constitution's dual concerns for federalism and an effective commerce power.

We would do well to recall the constitutional basis for federalism and the development of the commerce power which has come to displace it. The text of the Constitution does not define the precise scope of state authority other than to specify, in the Tenth Amendment, that the powers not delegated to the United States by the Constitution are reserved to the States. In the view of the Framers, however, this did not leave state authority weak or defenseless; the powers delegated to the United States, after all, were "few and defined." . . .

The problems of federalism in an integrated national economy are capable of more responsible resolution than holding that the States as States retain no status apart from that which Congress chooses to let them retain. The proper resolution, I suggest, lies in weighing state autonomy as a factor in the balance when interpreting the means by which Congress can exercise its authority on the States as States. It is insufficient, in assessing the validity of congressional regulation of a State pursuant to the commerce power, to ask only whether the same regulation

would be valid if enforced against a private party. That reasoning, embodied in the majority opinion, is inconsistent with the spirit of our Constitution. It remains relevant that a State is being regulated, as *National League of Cities* and every recent case have recognized. Instead, the autonomy of a State is an essential component of federalism. If state autonomy is ignored in assessing the means by which Congress regulates matters affecting commerce, then federalism becomes irrelevant simply because the set of activities remaining beyond the reach of such a commerce power "may well be negligible."

It has been difficult for this Court to craft bright lines defining the scope of the state autonomy protected by *National League of Cities*. Such difficulty is to be expected whenever constitutional concerns as important as federalism and the effectiveness of the commerce power come into conflict. Regardless of the difficulty, it is and will remain the duty of this Court to reconcile these concerns in the final instance. That the Court shuns the task today by appealing to the "essence of federalism" can provide scant comfort to those who believe our federal system requires something more than a unitary, centralized government. I would not shirk the duty acknowledged by *National League of Cities*. . . .

## New York v. United States
### 505 U.S. 144 (1992)

Environmental politics made its first major leap in the social conscience of the nation in the early 1970s. In April 1970 the nation celebrated its first Earth Day, which became the equivalent of a national teach-in on environmental issues and encouraged political activism to force greater governmental oversight and management of the nation's air, land, and water resources. One area that came in for greater scrutiny was the nuclear power industry. By the late 1970s, Congress had become concerned about the disposal of low-level radioactive nuclear waste. When Congress began hearings on the matter, only three states, Nevada, South Carolina, and Washington, had disposal sites. None had any interest in receiving the nuclear waste of other states with disposal problems. The Low-Level Radioactive Waste Policy Act, enacted in 1980, attempted to address this problem by encouraging states to enter into regional compacts to dispose of their waste. The law made the states responsible for disposing of radioactive waste within their borders. The law, amended in 1985, mandated that the three states with disposal sites accept out-of-state waste until 1992, when Congress anticipated the regional arrangements would be completed.

Congress had inserted several incentives into the 1985 amendments, including the right of states with disposal sites to collect a surcharge on all waste they processed. States were permitted to raise their surcharges gradually, which Congress hoped would lead other states to develop their own disposal sites or enter into regional arrangements, the preferred solution. States that did not comply by 1996 could be refused access to out-of-state disposal sites, leaving them with the full responsibility for handling the waste.

New York State challenged the law as an unconstitutional use of federal commerce authority, saying specifically that it violated the Tenth Amendment. The lower federal courts upheld the law.

The Court's decision was 6 to 3. Justice O'Connor delivered the opinion of the Court. Justice White filed a separate opinion, concurring in part and dissenting in part, joined by Justices Blackmun and Stevens. Justice Stevens filed an opinion concurring in part and dissenting in part.

▼▲▼

JUSTICE O'CONNOR delivered the opinion of the Court.

We live in a world full of low level radioactive waste. Radioactive material is present in luminous watch dials, smoke alarms, measurement devices, medical fluids, research materials, and the protective gear and construction materials used by workers at nuclear power plants. Low level radioactive waste is generated by the Government, by hospitals, by research institutions, and by various industries. The waste must be isolated from humans for long periods of time, often for hundreds of years. Millions of cubic feet of low level radioactive waste must be disposed of each year.

Our Nation's first site for the land disposal of commercial low level radioactive waste opened in 1962 in Beatty, Nevada. Five more sites opened in the following decade: Maxey Flats, Kentucky (1963), West Valley, New York (1963), Hanford, Washington (1965), Sheffield, Illinois (1967), and Barnwell, South Carolina (1971). Between 1975 and 1978, the Illinois site closed because it was full, and water management problems caused the closure of the sites in Kentucky and New York. As a result, since 1979, only three disposal sites—those in Nevada, Washington, and South Carolina—have been in operation. Waste generated in the rest of the country must be shipped to one of these three sites for disposal.

In 1979, both the Washington and Nevada sites were forced to shut down temporarily, leaving South Carolina to shoulder the responsibility of storing low level radioactive waste produced in every part of the country. The Governor of South Carolina, understandably perturbed, ordered a 50% reduction in the quantity of waste accepted at the Barnwell site. The Governors of Washington and Nevada announced plans to shut their sites permanently.

Faced with the possibility that the Nation would be left with no disposal sites for low level radioactive waste, Congress responded by enacting the Low-Level Radioactive Waste Policy Act. Relying largely on a report submitted by the National Governors' Association, Congress declared a federal policy of holding each State "responsible for providing for the availability of capacity either within or outside the State for the disposal of low-level radioactive waste generated within its borders," and found that such waste could be disposed of "most safely and efficiently . . . on a regional basis." The 1980 Act authorized States to enter into regional compacts that, once ratified by Congress, would have the authority, beginning in 1986, to restrict the use of their disposal facilities to waste generated within member States. The 1980 Act included no penalties for States that failed to participate in this plan.

By 1985, only three approved regional compacts had operational disposal facilities; not surprisingly, these were the compacts formed around South Carolina, Nevada, and Washington, the three sited States. The following year, the 1980 Act would have given these three compacts the ability to exclude waste from nonmembers, and the remaining 31 States would have had no assured outlet for their low level radioactive waste. With this prospect looming, Congress once again took up the issue of waste disposal. The result was the legislation challenged here, the Low-Level Radioactive Waste Policy Amendments Act of 1985.

The 1985 Act was again based largely on a proposal submitted by the National Governors' Association. In broad outline, the Act embodies a compromise among the sited and unsited States. The sited States agreed to extend for seven years the period in which they would accept low level radioactive waste from other States. In exchange, the unsited States agreed to end their reliance on the sited States by 1992.

The mechanics of this compromise are intricate. The Act directs, "[e]ach State shall be responsible for providing, either by itself or in cooperation with other States, for the disposal of . . . low-level radioactive waste generated within the State," with the exception of certain waste generated by the Federal Government. The Act authorizes States to, "enter into such [interstate] compacts as may be necessary to provide for the establishment and operation of regional disposal facilities for low-level radioactive waste." For an additional seven years beyond the period contemplated by the 1980 Act, from the beginning of 1986 through the end of 1992, the three existing disposal sites "shall make disposal capacity available for low-level radioactive waste generated by any source," with certain exceptions . . . .

In 1788, in the course of explaining to the citizens of New York why the recently drafted Constitution provided for federal courts, Alexander Hamilton observed:

> The erection of a new government, whatever care or wisdom may distinguish the work, cannot fail to originate questions of intricacy and nicety; and these may, in a particular manner, be expected to flow from the the the establishment of a constitution founded upon the total or partial incorporation of a number of distinct sovereignties. *Federalist 82.*

Hamilton's prediction has proved quite accurate. While no one disputes the proposition that "[t]he Constitution created a Federal Government of limited powers," and while the Tenth Amendment makes explicit that, "[t]he powers not delegated to the United States by the Constitution, nor prohibited by it to the States, are reserved to the States respectively, or to the people," the task of ascertaining the constitutional line between federal and state power has given rise to many of the Court's most difficult and celebrated cases. At least as far back as *Martin v. Hunter's Lessee* (1816), the Court has resolved questions "of great importance and delicacy" in determining whether particular sovereign powers have been granted by the Constitution to the Federal Government or have been retained by the States.

These questions can be viewed in either of two ways. In some cases, the Court has inquired whether an Act of Congress is authorized by one of the powers delegated to Congress in Article I of the Constitution. In other cases, the Court has sought to determine whether an Act of Congress invades the province of state sovereignty reserved by the Tenth Amendment. In a case like this one, involving the division of authority between federal and state governments, the two inquiries are mirror images of each other. If a power is delegated to Congress in the Constitution, the Tenth Amendment expressly disclaims any reservation of that power to the States; if a power is an attribute of state sovereignty reserved by the Tenth Amendment, it is necessarily a power the Constitution has not conferred on Congress.

It is in this sense that the Tenth Amendment "states but a truism that all is retained which has not been surrendered." *United State v. Darby* (1941). . . .

Congress exercises its conferred powers subject to the limitations contained in the Constitution. Thus, for example, under the Commerce Clause, Congress may regulate publishers engaged in interstate commerce, but Congress is constrained in the exercise of that power by the First Amendment. The Tenth Amendment likewise restrains the power of Congress, but this limit is not derived from the text of the Tenth Amendment itself, which, as we have discussed, is essentially a tautology. Instead, the Tenth Amendment confirms that the power of the Federal Government is subject to limits that may, in a given instance, reserve power to the States. The Tenth Amendment thus directs us to determine, as in this case, whether an incident of state sovereignty is protected by a limitation on an Article I power. . . .

This framework has been sufficiently flexible over the past two centuries to allow for enormous changes in the nature of government. The Federal Government undertakes activities today that would have been unimaginable to the Framers in two senses; first, because the Framers would not have conceived that any government would conduct such activities; and second, because the Framers would not have believed that the Federal Government, rather than the States, would assume such responsibilities. Yet the powers conferred upon the Federal Government by the Constitution were phrased in language broad enough to allow for the expansion of the Federal Government's role. Among the provisions of the Constitution that have been particularly important in this regard, three concern us here.

First, the Constitution allocates to Congress the power "[t]o regulate Commerce . . . among the several States." . . . The volume of interstate commerce and the range of commonly accepted objects of government regulation have, however, expanded considerably in the last 200 years, and the regulatory authority of Congress has expanded along with them. As interstate commerce has become ubiquitous, activities once considered purely local have come to have effects on the national economy, and have accordingly come within the scope of Congress' commerce power.

Second, the Constitution authorizes Congress "to pay the Debts and provide for the . . . general Welfare of the United States." As conventional notions of the proper objects of government spending have changed over the years, so has the ability of Congress to "fix the terms on which it shall disburse federal money to the States." While the spending power is "subject to several general restrictions articulated in our cases," these restrictions have not been so severe as to prevent the regulatory authority of Congress from generally keeping up with the growth of the federal budget. . . .

Finally, the Constitution provides that, "the Laws of the United States . . . shall be the supreme Law of the Land . . . any Thing in the Constitution or Laws of any State to the Contrary notwithstanding." As the Federal Government's willingness to exercise power within the confines of the Constitution has grown, the authority of the States has correspondingly diminished to the extent that federal and state policies have conflicted. We have observed that the Supremacy Clause gives the Federal Government "a decided advantage in th[e] delicate balance" the Constitution strikes between State and Federal power.

The actual scope of the Federal Government's authority with respect to the States has changed over the years, therefore, but the constitutional structure underlying and limiting that authority has not. In the end, just as a cup may be half empty or half full, it makes no difference whether one views the question at issue in this case as one of ascertaining the limits of the power delegated to the Federal Government under the affirmative provisions of the Constitution or one of discerning the core of sovereignty retained by the States under the Tenth Amendment. Either way, we must determine whether any of the three challenged provisions of the Low-Level Radioactive Waste Policy Amendments Act of 1985 oversteps the boundary between federal and state authority. . . .

This litigation . . . concerns the circumstances under which Congress may use the States as implements of regulation; that is, whether Congress may direct or otherwise motivate the States to regulate in a particular field or a particular way. Our cases have established a few principles that guide our resolution of the issue.

As an initial matter, Congress may not simply, "commandee[r] the legislative processes of the States by directly compelling them to enact and enforce a federal regulatory program." *Hodel* v. *Virginia Surface Mining & Reclamation Assn., Inc.,* (1981). . . .

While Congress has substantial powers to govern the Nation directly, including in areas of intimate concern to the States, the Constitution has never been understood to confer upon Congress the ability to require the States to govern according to Congress' instructions. . . .

In providing for a stronger central government, therefore, the Framers explicitly chose a Constitution that confers upon Congress the power to regulate individuals, not States. As we have seen, the Court has consistently respected this choice. We have always understood that, even where Congress has the authority under the Constitution to pass laws requiring or prohibiting certain acts, it lacks the power directly to compel the States to require or prohibit those acts. The allocation of power contained in the Commerce Clause, for example, authorizes Congress to regulate interstate commerce directly; it does not authorize Congress to regulate state governments' regulation of interstate commerce.

This is not to say that Congress lacks the ability to encourage a State to regulate in a particular way, or that Congress may not hold out incentives to the States as a method of influencing a State's policy choices. Our cases have identified a variety of methods, short of outright coercion, by which Congress may urge a State to adopt a legislative program consistent with federal interests. Two of these methods are of particular relevance here.

First, under Congress' spending power, "Congress may attach conditions on the receipt of federal funds." *South Dakota* v. *Dole* (1987). Such conditions must (among other requirements) bear some relationship to the purpose of the federal spending; otherwise, of course, the spending power could render academic the Constitution's other grants and limits of federal authority. Where the recipient of federal funds is a State, as is not unusual today, the conditions attached to the funds by Congress may influence a State's legislative choices. *Dole* was one such case: the Court found no constitutional flaw in a federal statute directing the Secretary of Transportation to withhold federal highway funds from States failing to adopt Congress' choice of a minimum drinking age.

Second, where Congress has the authority to regulate private activity under the Commerce Clause, we have recognized Congress' power to offer States the choice of regulating that activity according to federal standards or having state law preempted by federal regulation. This arrangement, which has been termed "a program of cooperative federalism," is replicated in numerous federal statutory schemes. . . .

By either of these two methods, as by any other permissible method of encouraging a State to conform to federal policy choices, the residents of the State retain the ultimate decision as to whether or not the State will comply. If a State's citizens view federal policy as sufficiently contrary to local interests, they may elect to decline a federal grant. If state residents would prefer their government to devote its attention and resources to problems other than those deemed important by Congress, they may choose to have the Federal Government, rather than the State, bear the expense of a federally mandated regulatory program, and they may continue to supplement that program to the extent state law is not preempted. Where Congress encourages state regulation, rather than compelling it, state governments remain responsive to the local electorate's preferences; state officials remain accountable to the people.

By contrast, where the Federal Government compels States to regulate, the accountability of both state and federal officials is diminished. If the citizens of New York, for example, do not consider that making provision for the disposal of radioactive waste is in their best interest, they may elect state officials who share their view. That view can always be preempted under the Supremacy Clause if it is contrary to the national view, but, in such a case, it is the Federal Government that makes the decision in full view of the public, and it will be federal officials that suffer the consequences if the decision turns out to be detrimental or unpopular. But where the Federal Government directs the States to regulate, it may be state officials who will bear the brunt of public disapproval, while the federal officials who devised the regulatory program may remain insulated from the electoral ramifications of their decision. Accountability is thus diminished when, due to federal coercion, elected state officials cannot regulate in accordance with the views of the local electorate in matters not preempted by federal regulation.

With these principles in mind, we turn to the three challenged provisions of the Low-Level Radioactive Waste Policy Amendments Act of 1985. . . .

The first set of incentives works in three steps. First, Congress has authorized States with disposal sites to impose a surcharge on radioactive waste received from other States. Second, the Secretary of Energy collects a portion of this surcharge and places the money in an escrow account. Third, States achieving a series of milestones receive portions of this fund.

The first of these steps is an unexceptionable exercise of Congress' power to authorize the States to burden interstate commerce. . . . Whether or not the States would be permitted to burden the interstate transport of low level radioactive waste in the absence of Congress' approval, the States can clearly do so *with* Congress' approval, which is what the Act gives them.

The second step, the Secretary's collection of a percentage of the surcharge, is no more than a federal tax on interstate commerce, which petitioners do not claim to be an invalid exercise of either Congress' commerce or taxing power.

The third step is a conditional exercise of Congress' authority under the Spending Clause: Congress has placed conditions—the achievement of the milestones—on the receipt of federal funds. . . . The expenditure is for the general welfare. . . .

The Act's first set of incentives, in which Congress has conditioned grants to the States upon the States' attainment of a series of milestones, is thus well within the authority of Congress under the Commerce and Spending Clauses. Because the first set of incentives is supported by affirmative constitutional grants of power to Congress, it is not inconsistent with the Tenth Amendment.

In the second set of incentives, Congress has authorized States and regional compacts with disposal sites gradually to increase the cost of access to the sites, and then to deny access altogether, to radioactive waste generated in States that do not meet federal deadlines. As a simple regulation, this provision would be within the power of Congress to authorize the States to discriminate against interstate commerce. Where federal regulation of private activity is within the scope of the Commerce Clause, we have recognized the ability of Congress to offer states the choice of regulating that activity according to federal standards or having state law preempted by federal regulation. . . .

The Act's second set of incentives thus represents a conditional exercise of Congress' commerce power, along the lines of those we have held to be within Congress' authority. As a result, the second set of incentives does not intrude on the sovereignty reserved to the States by the Tenth Amendment.

The take title provision is of a different character. This third so-called "incentive" offers States, as an alternative to regulating pursuant to Congress' direction, the option of taking title to and possession of the low level radioactive waste generated within their borders and becoming liable for all damages waste generators suffer as a result of the States' failure to do so promptly. In this provision, Congress has crossed the line distinguishing encouragement from coercion. . . .

The take title provision appears to be unique. No other federal statute has been cited which offers a state government no option other than that of implementing legislation enacted by Congress. Whether one views the take title provision as lying outside Congress' enumerated powers or as infringing upon the core of state sovereignty reserved by the Tenth Amendment, the provision is inconsistent with the federal structure of our Government established by the Constitution. . . .

The United States proposes three alternative views of the constitutional line separating state and federal authority. . . .

First, the United States argues that the Constitution's prohibition of congressional directives to state governments can be overcome where the federal interest is sufficiently important to justify state submission. This argument contains a kernel of truth: in determining whether the Tenth Amendment limits the ability of Congress to subject state governments to generally applicable laws, the Court *has*, in some cases, stated that it will evaluate the strength of federal interests in light of the degree to which such laws would prevent the State from functioning as a sovereign; that is, the extent to which such generally applicable laws would impede a state government's responsibility to represent and be accountable to the citizens of the State. But whether or not a particularly strong federal interest enables Congress to bring state governments within the orbit of generally applicable *federal* regulation, no Member of the Court has ever suggested that such a federal interest would enable Congress to command a state government to enact *state* regulation. No matter how powerful the federal interest involved, the Constitution simply does not give Congress the authority to require the States to regulate. The Constitution instead gives Congress the authority to regulate matters directly, and to preempt contrary state regulation. Where a federal interest is sufficiently strong to cause Congress to legislate, it must do so directly; it may not conscript state governments as its agents.

Second, the United States argues that the Constitution does, in some circumstances, permit federal directives to state governments. Various cases are cited for this proposition, but none support it. Some of these cases discuss the well established power of Congress to pass laws enforceable in state courts. These cases involve no more than an application of the Supremacy Clause's provision that federal law "shall be the supreme Law of the Land," enforceable in every State. More to the point, all involve congressional regulation of individuals, not congressional requirements that States regulate. Federal statutes enforceable in state courts do, in a sense, direct state judges to enforce them, but this sort of federal "direction" of state judges is mandated by the text of the Supremacy Clause. No comparable constitutional provision authorizes Congress to command state legislatures to legislate. . . .

Third, the United States, supported by the three sited regional compacts as *amici*, argues that the Constitution envisions a role for Congress as an arbiter of interstate disputes. The United States observes that federal courts, and this Court in particular, have frequently resolved conflicts among States. Many of these disputes have involved the allocation of shared resources among the States, a category perhaps broad enough to encompass the allocation of scarce disposal space for radioactive waste. The United States suggests that, if the Court may resolve such interstate disputes, Congress can surely do the same under the Commerce Clause. . . .

Some truths are so basic that, like the air around us, they are easily overlooked. Much of the Constitution is concerned with setting forth the form of our government, and the courts have traditionally invalidated measures deviating from that form. The result may appear "formalistic" in a given case to partisans of the measure at issue, because such measures are typically the product of the era's perceived necessity. But the Constitution protects us from our own best intentions: it divides power among sovereigns and among branches of government precisely so that we may resist the temptation to concentrate power in one location as an expedient solution to the crisis of the day. The shortage of disposal sites for radioactive waste is a pressing national problem, but a judiciary that licensed extraconstitutional government with each issue of comparable gravity would, in the long run, be far worse.

States are not mere political subdivisions of the United States. State governments are neither regional offices nor administrative agencies of the Federal Government. The positions occupied by state officials appear nowhere on the Federal Government's most detailed organizational chart. The Constitution instead "leaves to the several States a residuary and inviolable sovereignty," *Federalist* 39, reserved explicitly to the States by the Tenth Amendment.

Whatever the outer limits of that sovereignty may be, one thing is clear: the Federal Government may not compel the States to enact or administer a federal regulatory program. The Constitution permits both the Federal Government and the States to enact legislation regarding the disposal of low level radioactive waste. The Constitution enables the Federal Government to preempt state regulation contrary to federal interests, and it permits the Federal Government to hold out incentives to the States as a means of encouraging them to adopt suggested regulatory schemes. It does not, however, authorize Congress simply to direct the States to provide for the disposal of the radioactive waste generated within their borders. While there may be many constitutional methods of achieving regional self-sufficiency in radioactive waste disposal, the method Congress has chosen is not one of them. The judgment of the Court of Appeals is accordingly affirmed in part and reversed in part.

JUSTICE STEVENS, concurring in part and dissenting in part.

The notion that Congress does not have the power to issue "a simple command to state governments to implement legislation enacted by Congress," is incorrect and unsound. There is no such limitation in the Constitution. The Tenth Amendment surely does not impose any limit on Congress' exercise of the powers delegated to it by Article I. Nor does the structure of the constitutional order or the values of federalism mandate such a formal rule. To the contrary, the Federal Government directs state governments in many realms. The Government regulates state-operated railroads, state school systems, state prisons, state elections, and a host of other state functions. Similarly, there can be no doubt that, in time of war, Congress could either draft soldiers itself or command the States to supply their quotas of troops. I see no reason why Congress may not also command the States to enforce federal water and air quality standards or federal standards for the disposition of low-level radioactive wastes.

The Constitution gives this Court the power to resolve controversies between the States. Long before Congress enacted pollution control legislation, this Court crafted a body of "'interstate common law,'" *Illinois* v. *City of Milwaukee* (1972), to govern disputes between States involving interstate waters. In such contexts, we have not hesitated to direct States to undertake specific actions. For example, we have, "impose[d] on States an affirmative duty to take reasonable steps to conserve and augment the water supply of an interstate stream." Thus, we unquestionably have the power to command an upstate stream that is polluting the waters of a downstream State to adopt appropriate regulations to implement a federal statutory command.

With respect to the problem presented by the case at hand, if litigation should develop between States that have joined a compact, we would surely have the power to grant relief in the form of specific enforcement of the take title provision. Indeed, even if the statute had never been passed, if one State's radioactive waste created a nuisance that harmed its neighbors, it seems clear that we would have had the power to command the offending State to take remedial action. If this Court has such authority, surely Congress has similar authority.

▼▲▼

## *Printz* v. *United States*
117 S. Ct. 2365 (1997)

Soon after the Brady Bill went into effect, two local sheriffs, Ray Printz of Ravalli County, Montana, and Richard Mack of Graham County, Arizona, with the support of the National Rifle Association (NRA), filed suit in federal court to have it declared unconstitutional. A critical element of the NRA's litigation strategy was to base its objection to the Brady Bill on federalism grounds. For some time the debate over gun-control laws, whether in Congress or the state legislatures, had centered on the precise nature of the Second Amendment's guarantees. Sensing that the public had grown wary of absolute guarantees to unrestricted gun purchases and ownership, the NRA shifted away from the "right to bear arms" question. It focused instead on whether Congress possessed the authority to order state and local authorities to carry out federal mandates without the funds and personnel to assist them.

The NRA's strategic shift to the Tenth Amendment was a direct response to the Court's decision in *United States* v. *Lopez* (1995) (see Chapter 6), in which the Court struck down the Gun-Free School Zones Act of 1990 as an unconstitutional exercise of congressional commerce power. The law banned the possession of certain firearms near school zones. *Lopez* marked the first time since the Constitutional Revolution of 1937 that the Court invalidated an act of Congress under the Commerce Clause. Sensing that a majority more sensitive to states' rights was emerging on the Court, the NRA decided to encourage the sheriffs' attorney, Stephen P. Halbrook, a well-respected advocate of gun rights, to emphasize the Tenth Amendment angle. Halbrook told the justices that the law placed an unreasonable burden on local law-enforcement officers, who could not be expected to comb every federal, state, and local record to determine whether a prospective gun buyer had a criminal record. Halbrook also raised the issue of "unfunded mandates" the Court had seized upon in *National League of Cities.*

Since it was formally the counsel of record, the NRA filed a separate friend-of-the-court brief setting out its legal argument. Eight states and several associations representing state and local governments also filed briefs in support of Sheriffs Printz and Mack. The United States was supported by more than a dozen law-enforcement and gun-control groups, most of which had lobbied Congress to enact the Brady Bill. Even more intriguing was the fact that thirteen states filed a joint brief urging the Court to uphold the federal background check requirement.

The Court's decision was 5 to 4. Justice Scalia delivered the opinion of the Court. Justices O'Connor and Thomas filed concurring opinions. Justice Stevens, joined by Justices Souter, Ginsburg, and Breyer, filed a dissenting opinion. Justice Souter filed a dissenting opinion. Justice Breyer, joined by Justice Stevens, also dissented.

The 5 to 4 majorities in *Lopez* and *Printz* were identical.

▼▲▼

JUSTICE SCALIA delivered the opinion of the Court.

The question presented in these cases is whether certain interim provisions of the Brady Handgun Violence Prevention Act, commanding state and local law enforcement officers to conduct background checks on prospective handgun purchasers and to perform certain related tasks, violate the Constitution. . . .

[T]he Brady Act purports to direct state law enforcement officers to participate, albeit only temporarily, in the administration of a federally enacted regulatory scheme. Regulated firearms dealers are required to forward Brady Forms not to a federal officer or employee, but to the chief legal enforcement officer (CLEO), whose obligation to accept those forms is implicit in the duty imposed upon them to make "reasonable efforts" within five days to determine whether the sales reflected in the forms are lawful. While the CLEOs are subjected to no federal requirement that they prevent the sales determined to be unlawful (it is perhaps assumed that their state law duties will require prevention or apprehension), they are empowered to grant, in effect, waivers of the federally prescribed 5-day waiting period for handgun purchases by notifying the gun dealers that they have no reason to believe the transactions would be illegal.

The petitioners here object to being pressed into federal service, and contend that congressional action compelling state officers to execute federal laws is unconstitutional. Because there is no constitutional text speaking to this precise question, the answer to the CLEOs' challenge must be sought in historical understanding and practice, in the structure of the Constitution, and in the jurisprudence of this Court. We treat those three sources, in that order, in this and the next two sections of this opinion. . . .

The Government points to a number of federal statutes enacted within the past few decades that require the participation of state or local officials in implementing federal regulatory schemes. Some of these are connected to federal funding measures, and can perhaps be more accurately described as conditions upon the grant of federal funding than as mandates to the States; others, which require only the provision of information to the Federal Government, do not involve the precise issue before us here, which is the forced participation of the States' executive in the actual administration of a federal program. We, of course, do not address these or other currently operative enactments that are not before us; it will be time enough to do so if and when their validity is challenged in a proper case. For deciding the issue before us here, they are of little relevance. Even assuming they represent assertion of the very same congressional power challenged here, they are of such recent vintage that they are no more probative than the statute before us of a constitutional tradition that lends meaning to the text. Their persuasive force is far outweighed by almost two centuries of apparent congressional avoidance of the practice. Compare *INS* v. *Chadha* (1983), in which the legislative veto, though enshrined in perhaps hundreds of federal statutes, most of which were enacted in the 1970's and the earliest of which was enacted in 1932, was nonetheless held unconstitutional.

[C]onstitutional practice . . . tends to negate the existence of the congressional power asserted here, but is not conclusive. We turn next to consideration of the structure of the Constitution, to see if we can discern among its "essential postulate[s]," a principle that controls the present cases.

It is incontestable that the Constitution established a system of "dual sovereignty." Although the States surrendered many of their powers to the new Federal Government, they retained "a residuary and inviolable sovereignty." This is reflected throughout the Constitution's text. . . . Residual state sovereignty was also implicit, of course, in the Constitution's conferral upon Congress of not all governmental powers, but only discrete, enumerated ones, which implication was rendered express by the Tenth Amendment's assertion that, "[t]he powers not delegated to the United States by the Constitution, nor prohibited by it to the States, are reserved to the States respectively, or to the people." . . .

This separation of the two spheres is one of the Constitution's structural protections of liberty.

Just as the separation and independence of the coordinate branches of the Federal Government serve to prevent the accumulation of excessive power in any one branch, a healthy balance of power between the States and the Federal Government will reduce the risk of tyranny and abuse from either front.

To quote Madison once again:

In the compound republic of America, the power surrendered by the people is first divided between two distinct governments, and then the portion allotted to each subdivided among distinct and separate departments. Hence, a double security arises to the rights of the people. The different governments will control each other at the same time that each will be controlled by itself.

*Federalist* 51. See also *Federalist* 28. The power of the Federal Government would be augmented immeasurably if it were able to impress into its service—and at no cost to itself—the police officers of the 50 States.

We have thus far discussed the effect that federal control of state officers would have upon the first element of the "double security" alluded to by Madison: the division of power between State and Federal Governments. It would also have an effect upon the second element: the separation and equilibration of powers between the three branches of the Federal Government itself. The Constitution does not leave to speculation who is to administer the laws enacted by Congress; the President, it says, "shall take Care that the Laws be faithfully executed," Article II, Section 3, personally and through officers whom he appoints (save for such inferior officers as Congress may authorize to be appointed by the "Courts of Law" or by "the Heads of Departments" who are themselves presidential appointees), Article II, Section 2. The Brady Act effectively transfers this responsibility to thousands of CLEOs in the 50 States, who are left to implement the program without meaningful Presidential control (if indeed meaningful Presidential control is possible without the power to appoint and remove). The insistence of the Framers upon unity in the Federal Executive—to insure both vigor and accountability—is well known. That unity would be shattered, and the power of the President would be subject to reduction, if Congress could act as effectively without the President as with him, by simply requiring state officers to execute its laws. . . .

When we were at last confronted squarely with a federal statute that unambiguously required the States to enact or administer a federal regulatory program, our decision should have come as no surprise. At issue in *New York* v. *United States*, were the so-called "take title" provisions of the Low-Level Radioactive Waste Policy Amendments Act of 1985, which required States either to enact legislation providing for the disposal of radioactive waste generated within their borders, or to take title to, and possession of the waste—effectively requiring the States either to legislate pursuant to Congress's directions or to implement an administrative solution. We concluded that Congress could constitutionally require the States to do neither. "The Federal Government," we held, "may not compel the States to enact or administer a federal regulatory program."

The Government contends that *New York* is distinguishable on the following ground: unlike the "take title" provisions invalidated there, the background check provision of the Brady Act does not require state legislative or executive officials to make policy, but instead issues a final directive to state CLEOs. It is permissible, the Government asserts, for Congress to command state or local officials to assist in the implementation of federal law so long as "Congress itself devises a clear legislative solution that regulates private conduct," and requires state or local officers to provide only "limited, nonpolicymaking help in enforcing that law." "[T]he constitutional line is crossed only when Congress compels the States to make law in their sovereign capacities."

The Government's distinction between "making" law and merely "enforcing" it, between "policymaking" and mere "implementation," is an interesting one. It is perhaps not meant to be the same as, but it is surely reminiscent of, the line that separates proper congressional conferral of Executive power from unconstitutional delegation of legislative authority for federal separation of powers purposes. This Court has not been notably successful in describing the latter line; indeed, some think we have abandoned the effort to do so. We are doubtful that the new line the Government proposes would be any more distinct. Executive action that has utterly no policymaking component is rare, particularly at an executive level as high as a jurisdiction's chief law enforcement officer. Is it really true that there is no policymaking involved in deciding, for example, what "reasonable efforts" shall be expended to conduct a background check? It may well satisfy the Act for a CLEO to direct that (a) no background checks will be conducted that divert personnel time from pending felony investigations, and (b) no background check will be permitted to consume more than one-half hour of an officer's time. But nothing in the Act *requires* a CLEO to be so parsimonious; diverting at least *some* felony investigation time, and permitting at least *some* background checks beyond one-half hour would certainly not be *unreasonable*. Is this decision whether to devote maximum "reasonable efforts" or minimum "reasonable efforts" not preeminently a matter of policy? It is quite impossible, in short, to draw the Government's proposed line at "no policymaking," and we would have to fall back upon a line of "not too much policymaking." How much is too much is not likely to be answered precisely, and an imprecise barrier against federal intrusion upon state authority is not likely to be an effective one.

Even assuming, moreover, that the Brady Act leaves no "policymaking" discretion with the States, we fail to see how that improves, rather than worsens, the intrusion upon state sovereignty. . . . It is an essential attribute of the States' retained sovereignty that they remain independent and autonomous within their proper sphere of authority. It is no more compatible with this independence and autonomy that their officers be "dragooned" into administering federal law, than it would be compatible with the independence and autonomy of the United States that its officers be impressed into service for the execution of state laws. . . .

The Government also maintains that requiring state officers to perform discrete, ministerial tasks specified by Congress does not violate the principle of *New York* because it does not diminish the accountability of state or federal officials. This argument fails even on its own terms. By forcing state governments to absorb the financial burden of implementing a federal regulatory program, Members of Congress can take credit for "solving" problems without having to ask their constituents to pay for the solutions with higher federal taxes. And even when the States are not forced to absorb the costs of implementing a federal program, they are still put in the position of taking the blame for its burdensomeness and for its defects. Under the present law, for example, it will be the CLEO and not some federal official who stands between the gun purchaser and immediate possession of his gun. And it will likely be the CLEO, not some federal official, who will be blamed for any error (even one in the designated federal database) that causes a purchaser to be mistakenly rejected. . . .

Finally, the Government puts forward a cluster of arguments that can be grouped under the heading, "The Brady Act serves very important purposes, is most efficiently administered by CLEOs during the interim period, and places a minimal and only temporary burden upon state officers." There is considerable disagreement over the extent of the burden, but we need not pause over that detail. Assuming *all* the mentioned factors were true, they might be relevant if we were evaluating whether the incidental application to the States of a federal law of general

applicability excessively interfered with the functioning of state governments. But where, as here, it is the whole *object* of the law to direct the functioning of the state executive, and hence to compromise the structural framework of dual sovereignty, such a "balancing" analysis is inappropriate. It is the very *principle* of separate state sovereignty that such a law offends, and no comparative assessment of the various interests can overcome that fundamental defect. . . .

We held in *New York* that Congress cannot compel the States to enact or enforce a federal regulatory program. Today we hold that Congress cannot circumvent that prohibition by conscripting the State's officers directly. The Federal Government may neither issue directives requiring the States to address particular problems, nor command the States' officers, or those of their political subdivisions, to administer or enforce a federal regulatory program. It matters not whether policymaking is involved, and no case-by-case weighing of the burdens or benefits is necessary; such commands are fundamentally incompatible with our constitutional system of dual sovereignty. Accordingly, the judgment of the Court of Appeals for the Ninth Circuit is reversed.

*It is so ordered.*

JUSTICE STEVENS, with whom JUSTICE SOUTER, JUSTICE GINSBURG, and JUSTICE BREYER join, dissenting.

When Congress exercises the powers delegated to it by the Constitution, it may impose affirmative obligations on executive and judicial officers of state and local governments as well as ordinary citizens. This conclusion is firmly supported by the text of the Constitution, the early history of the Nation, decisions of this Court, and a correct understanding of the basic structure of the Federal Government.

These cases do not implicate the more difficult questions associated with congressional coercion of state legislatures addressed in *New York* v. *United States* (1992). Nor need we consider the wisdom of relying on local officials, rather than federal agents, to carry out aspects of a federal program, or even the question whether such officials may be required to perform a federal function on a permanent basis. The question is whether Congress, acting on behalf of the people of the entire Nation, may require local law enforcement officers to perform certain duties during the interim needed for the development of a federal gun control program. It is remarkably similar to the question, heavily debated by the Framers of the Constitution, whether the Congress could require state agents to collect federal taxes. Or the question whether Congress

## PRINTZ V. UNITED STATES

### The Brady Bill

On November 30, 1993, President Clinton signed into law the Brady Handgun Violence Prevention Act, the most comprehensive piece of federal gun-control legislation in a quarter of a century. Among those sitting beside the president during the elaborate Rose Garden ceremony held on behalf of the Brady Bill, as the 1993 law is more popularly known, was the man for whom the legislation was named, former White House press secretary to President Ronald Reagan, Jim Brady. In March 1981, Brady suffered a gunshot wound to the head during an assassination attempt on President Reagan in front of a Washington hotel that left Brady paralyzed from the waist down. After extensive physical therapy to recover the use of his upper body and restore his speech, Brady and his wife, Sarah, joined forces with Handgun Control, Inc., the nation's largest gun-control group, to campaign for federal and state laws to combat gun violence. Congressional passage of the Brady Bill represented the culmination of seven years of intense lobbying on the part of gun-control proponents.

That Jim Brady would emerge as a national spokesperson for gun control and join forces with a Democratic president to urge passage of the federal law bearing his name is tinged with more than just a shade of irony. Brady was a lifelong Republican who had worked in a variety of political jobs, and his appointment as the press secretary to President Reagan was, by Brady's own account, the crown jewel of his career. Uninterested, at best, in the gun-control issue, Brady now worked for a president who was on record as opposing even minimal legislation to regulate the sale and purchase of guns. When the Brady Bill was introduced in Congress in 1987, Brady, although long having since delegated his day-to-day duties to his assistants, found himself in the unique position of opposing the administration for which he worked.

Soon after the Brady Bill was introduced, the National Rifle Association (NRA), the nation's largest and most powerful gun owners lobby, and one of the powerful interest groups in American politics, marshaled its considerable resources to campaign against the legislation. The NRA claimed that the five-day waiting period, necessary to perform the background check on prospective gun buyers, would hinder the rights of law-abiding gun owners and sportsmen and have no impact on the ability of criminals to purchase guns. As recently as the late 1970s, the NRA had supported a waiting period for gun purchases but had switched its position in accord with the much harder line it had taken against federal and state gun regulation. Despite a well-organized effort by Handgun Control, Inc., and several law-enforcement groups, the NRA was able to get Congress to kill the Brady Bill when it came up for its first vote in September 1988. The NRA estimated that it spent upward of $3 million on media and grass-roots organizing efforts.

Undeterred by the NRA's display of raw political power, Handgun Control, Inc., continued with its lobbying effort to have Congress enact minimal gun-control legislation, such as the Undetectable Firearms Act of 1988, which banned the manufacture of so-called plastic guns that are able to pass undetectable through airport security equipment. Handgun Control, Inc., also continued to piece together a coalition of law-enforcement professionals, the American Bar Association, doctors' groups, and public officials to demand the greater regulation of guns. Jim Brady also became more assertive, challenging Congress to put aside its fear of the NRA to pass comprehensive gun-control legislation. Addressing the Senate one afternoon after defeat of the original Brady Bill proposal, Brady issued as of then his most stern admonition to Congress: "Many members of Congress don't want to stand up for the Brady bill because of all the aggravation they'd get from the gun lobby," but "their aggravation is minimal compared to the aggravation I face every day . . . . I want action on the Brady bill."

Gun-control proponents received a powerful boost in March 1991, when Ronald Reagan, speaking to a medical group on the tenth anniversary of the assassination attempt on his life, endorsed the Brady Bill. The next day the *New York Times* published an op-ed article by the former president in which he repudiated his long-held opposition to the Brady legislation. Wrote Reagan: "And it's just plain common sense that there be a waiting period to allow local law enforcement officials to conduct background checks on those who wish to purchase handguns. . . . I support the Brady Bill and I urge Congress to enact it without further delay." President George Bush, also on record as opposing the Brady Bill, switched his position after some gentle persuasion from the man he had served for eight years as vice president.

By the time Congress began to move on the Brady Bill, Bill Clinton had captured the presidency. During the 1992 campaign, Clinton had endorsed without equivocation the Brady Bill and another passionately

held goal of the gun-control lobbies: a ban on the manufacture, sale, or possession of assault weapons. When Congress took up the Brady Bill again after President Clinton's inauguration, a furious battle commenced between the NRA and Handgun Control, Inc., and their respective allies in the House and Senate. The heart of the issue remained the five-day waiting period. The NRA opposed it, arguing instead that gun buyers should not have to wait to purchase guns. The gun-rights group favored an "instant check" system drawn from a national database under con-

*Secret Service agents react quickly to protect President Reagan after an assassination attempt. Jim Brady (feet in foreground) suffered a gunshot wound to the head.*
Bettmann/CORBIS.

struction by the Department of Justice. Gun-control supporters countered that the Justice Department's preparation of such a database would take years, giving convicted criminals an escape hatch from any kind of regulation. Instead, supporters argued, state and local law enforcement should carry the responsibility of controlling weapon purchases in their communities.

Despite an even more aggressive public lobbying campaign by the NRA and private threats to oppose the reelection of senators and representatives who supported the Brady Bill—the NRA bragged that it could drop fifteen thousand pieces of direct mail in an opponent's district overnight—more than three dozen House members and a dozen senators switched their earlier pro-NRA votes to support the 1993 version of the legislation. President Clinton signed the legislation, as he pledged he would, after the Thanksgiving recess.

The Brady Bill's passage over the intense opposition of the NRA allowed members, in the words of Rep. Charles E. Schumer (D–N.Y.), a strong supporter of the legislation, to "realiz[e] that there's life after voting against the NRA." That may have been—and still might be—true. But the NRA's success in *Printz*, a case it selected and funded to test the Court's growing sympathies toward greater state autonomy in the federal system, also demonstrates that a carefully crafted litigation campaign in a sympathetic judicial environment can bypass the popular will, no matter how deep the reservoir of support.

## References

Eakins, Keith R. and Samuel C. Patterson. "Congress and Gun Control," in John M. Bruce and Clyde Wilcox, eds., *The Changing Politics of Gun Control*. Baltimore: Rowman & Littlefield, 1998, pp. 45–73.

Spitzer, Robert J. *The Politics of Gun Control*. Chatham, N.J.: Chatham House Publishers, Inc., 1995.

could impress state judges into federal service to entertain and decide cases that they would prefer to ignore.

Indeed, since the ultimate issue is one of power, we must consider its implications in times of national emergency. Matters such as the enlistment of air raid wardens, the administration of a military draft, the mass inoculation of children to forestall an epidemic, or perhaps the threat of an international terrorist, may require a national response before federal personnel can be made available to respond. If the Constitution empowers Congress and the President to make an appropriate response, is there anything in the Tenth Amendment, "in historical understanding and practice, in the structure of the Constitution, [or] in the jurisprudence of this Court," that forbids the enlistment of state officers to make that response effective? More narrowly, what basis is there in any of those sources for concluding that it is the Members of this Court, rather than the elected representatives of the people, who should determine whether the Constitution contains the unwritten rule that the Court announces today?

Perhaps today's majority would suggest that no such emergency is presented by the facts of these cases. But such a suggestion is itself an expression of a policy judgment. And Congress' view of the matter is quite different from that implied by the Court today. . . .

There is not a clause, sentence, or paragraph in the entire text of the Constitution of the United States that supports the proposition that a local police officer can ignore a command contained in a statute enacted by Congress pursuant to an express delegation of power enumerated in Article I. . . .

Indeed, the historical materials strongly suggest that the Founders intended to enhance the capacity of the federal government by empowering it—as a part of the new authority to make demands directly on individual citizens—to act through local officials. Hamilton made clear that the new Constitution, "by extending the authority of the federal head to the individual citizens of the several States, will enable the government to employ the ordinary magistracy of each, in the execution of its laws." *Federalist* 27. Hamilton's meaning was unambiguous; the federal government was to have the power to demand that local officials implement national policy programs. As he went on to explain:

> It is easy to perceive that this will tend to destroy, in the common apprehension, all distinction between the sources from which [the state and federal governments] might proceed, and will give the federal government the same advantage for securing a due obedience to its authority which is enjoyed by the government of each State. . . .

[T]he Court advises us that the "prior jurisprudence of this Court" is the most conclusive support for its position.

That "prior jurisprudence" is *New York* v. *United States.* The case involved the validity of a federal statute that provided the States with three types of incentives to encourage them to dispose of radioactive wastes generated within their borders. The Court held that the first two sets of incentives were authorized by affirmative grants of power to Congress, and therefore "not inconsistent with the Tenth Amendment." That holding, of course, sheds no doubt on the validity of the Brady Act.

The third so-called "incentive" gave the States the option either of adopting regulations dictated by Congress or of taking title to and possession of the low level radioactive waste. The Court concluded that, because Congress had no power to compel the state governments to take title to the waste, the "option" really amounted to a simple command to the States to enact and enforce a federal regulatory program. . . .

The provision of the Brady Act that crosses the Court's newly defined constitutional threshold is more comparable to a statute requiring local police officers to report the identity of missing children to the Crime Control Center of the Department of Justice than to an offensive federal command to a sovereign state. If Congress believes that such a statute will benefit the people of the Nation, and serve the interests of cooperative federalism better than an enlarged federal bureaucracy, we should respect both its policy judgment and its appraisal of its constitutional power.

Accordingly, I respectfully dissent.

## General Police Power

Chapter 6 discussed the police power of Congress, or its authority under the Commerce Clause; the Necessary and Proper Clause; and Congress's taxing and spending power to promote general health, welfare, environmental, and safety interests through legislation. That power, while broad in scope, does carry limits, as the Court's opinion in *United States* v. *Lopez* (1995) and *United States* v. *Morrison* (2000) made clear. In *Lopez* the Court rejected the notion that Congress had an undefined power under Article I to enact laws that interfered with legitimate claims of state power even if the law demonstrated a recognized public interest. *Morrison* held that the Commerce Clause did not authorize Congress to establish a right for the victims of sexual assault to sue their attackers for civil damages in Federal court. In

*Lopez* and *Morrison*, the Court said that Congress must show some reasonable relationship between its legislative objective and the federal law.

By contrast, the Constitution left undisturbed the Framers' widespread assumption that states should retain their power to enact laws on behalf of the public interest. In fact, the Court acknowledged an explicit state police power as early as *Gibbons* v. *Ogden* (1824), discussed in Chapters 4 and 6. Even as Chief Justice Marshall was laying the groundwork for a sweeping congressional power to regulate interstate commerce, he conceded that the states possessed the power to "regulate its police, its domestic trade, and to govern its own citizens."[31]

Marshall's point in *Gibbons* was to suggest that the states could still exercise legislative power over commercial matters in the absence of contrary federal law. The greater significance of his *dicta*, however, was that even such an ardent constitutional nationalist understood that the states, more so than the national government, held certain exclusive powers to promote the welfare of its citizens. Police power, wrote Marshall, reached "that *mass of legislation which embraces everything within the territory of a state not surrendered to the general government*. . . . Inspection laws [dealing with state power to inspect items in interstate commercial transit], quarantine laws, health laws of every description, as well as laws for regulating the internal commerce of a state, and those which respect turnpike-roads, ferries, etc., are component parts of this mass."[32]

It was, however, under the leadership of Chief Justice Roger Taney, Marshall's successor, that the Court first established a firm definition of state police power. In *Charles River Bridge Co.* v. *Warren Bridge* (1837), discussed in Chapter 8, the Court ruled that a state was within its constitutional bounds to change the terms and conditions of a public charter to a private corporation if doing so served the public interest. Chief Justice Taney emphasized that no right under the Constitution was so inviolable that it prevented the states from exercising "power over their own internal police and improvement, which is so necessary to their well-being and prosperity."[33]

The Court's expansion of state police power under Roger Taney was part of its general thrust toward dual federalism, a development that reflected a conscious effort to maintain the Court's legitimacy in a time when the states had begun to question out loud the excesses of Marshall's constitutional nationalism.[34] Political sensitivities aside, the Court also recognized that state police power was the single instrument through which government could address the problems that pressed the public interest. Congress had neither the resources nor the tested constitutional powers to do so. The development of state police power under Taney enabled the states to experiment with solutions to public policy problems that the national government would not face until the end of the nineteenth century.[35]

The Court has generally taken a deferential attitude toward the exercise of state police power. Unless the state has exercised its power in a manner that interferes with national prerogatives, such as interstate commercial regulation, or rights considered "fundamental" in their nature, such as First Amendment freedoms, the Court has required states to demonstrate no more than a reasonable relationship between the proposed rule and the public policy objective. *Jacobson* v. *Massachusetts* (1905) represents an excellent statement of the Court's position on the constitutional exercise of state police power. *Jacobson* involved a challenge to a Massachusetts law requiring the immunization of its residents against smallpox. Compare *Jacobson* with *Champion* v. *Ames* (1903) and *McCray* v. *United States* (1904) (see Chapter 6) in which the Court upheld the exercise of federal police power. What differences exist in the responsibilities of the federal and state governments to justify their respective exercises of police power?

## Jacobson v. Massachusetts
### 197 U.S. 11 (1905)

A Massachusetts law gave local boards of health the authority to order mandatory vaccinations if, in their opinion, it was necessary to promote public health. In 1902 the Cambridge Board of Health adopted a regulation mandating the vaccination of all persons for smallpox. Henning Jacobson refused, on the grounds that such vaccinations were not effective and in fact encouraged the spread of disease throughout the body. He was found guilty and fined five dollars. The Massachusetts Supreme Court affirmed.

The Court's decision was 7 to 2. Justice Harlan delivered the opinion of the Court. Justices Brewer and Peckam filed dissenting opinions.

▼▲▼

MR. JUSTICE HARLAN delivered the opinion of the Court.

. . . Is the statute . . . inconsistent with the liberty which the Constitution of the United States secures to every person against deprivation by the State?

The authority of the State to enact this statute is to be referred to [as] the police power—a power which the State did not surrender when becoming a member of the Union under the Constitution. Although this court has refrained from any attempt to define the limits of that power, yet it has distinctly recognized the authority of a State to enact quarantine laws and "health laws of every description"; indeed, all laws that relate to matters completely within its territory and which do not, by their necessary operation, affect the people of other States. According to settled principles, the police power of a State must be held to embrace, at least, such reasonable regulations established directly by legislative enactment as will protect the public health and the public safety. It is equally true that the State may invest local bodies called into existence for purposes of local administration with authority in some appropriate way to safeguard the public health and the public safety. The mode or manner in which those results are to be accomplished is within the discretion of the State, subject, of course, so far as Federal power is concerned, only to the condition that no rule prescribed by a State, nor any regulation adopted by a local governmental agency acting under the sanction of state legislation, shall contravene the Constitution of the United States or infringe any right granted or secured by that instrument. A local enactment or regulation, even if based on the acknowledged police powers of a State, must always yield in case of conflict with the exercise by the General Government of any power it possesses under the Constitution, or with any right which that instrument gives or secures.

We come, then, to inquire whether any right given or secured by the Constitution is invaded by the statute as interpreted by the state court. The defendant insists that his liberty is invaded when the State subjects him to fine or imprisonment for neglecting or refusing to submit to vaccination; that a compulsory vaccination law is unreasonable, arbitrary and oppressive, and, therefore, hostile to the inherent right of every freeman to care for his own body and health in such way as to him seems best, and that the execution of such a law against one who objects to vaccination, no matter for what reason, is nothing short of an assault upon his person. But the liberty secured by the Constitution of the United States to every person within its jurisdiction does not import an absolute right in each person to be, at all times and in all circumstances, wholly freed from restraint. There are manifold restraints to which every person is necessarily subject for the common good. On any other basis, organized society could not exist with safety to its members. Society based on the rule that each one is a law unto himself would soon be confronted with disorder and anarchy. Real liberty for all could not exist under the operation of a principle which recognizes the right of each individual person to use his own, whether in respect of his person or his property, regardless of the injury that may be done to others. This court has more than once recognized it as a fundamental principle that

> persons and property are subjected to all kinds of restraints and burdens, in order to secure the general comfort, health, and prosperity of the State, of the perfect right of the legislature to do which no question ever was, or upon acknowledged general principles ever can be, made so far as natural persons are concerned. . . .

Applying these principles to the present case, it is to be observed that the legislature of Massachusetts required the inhabitants of a city or town to be vaccinated only when, in the opinion of the Board of Health, that was necessary for the public health or the public safety. The authority to determine for all what ought to be done in such an emergency must have been lodged somewhere or in some body, and surely it was appropriate for the legislature to refer that question, in the first instance, to a Board of Health, composed of persons residing in the locality affected and appointed, presumably, because of their fitness to determine such questions. To invest such a body with authority over such matters was not an unusual nor an unreasonable or arbitrary requirement. Upon the principle of self-defense, of paramount necessity, a community has the right to protect itself against an epidemic of disease which threatens the safety of its members. It is to be observed that, when the regulation in question was adopted, smallpox, according to the recitals in the regulation adopted by the Board of Health, was prevalent to some extent in the city of Cambridge, and the disease was increasing. If such was the situation—and nothing is asserted or appears in the record to the contrary—if we are to attach any value whatever to the knowledge which, it is safe to affirm, is common to all civilized peoples touching smallpox and the methods most usually employed to

eradicate that disease, it cannot be adjudged that the present regulation of the Board of Health was not necessary in order to protect the public health and secure the public safety. Smallpox being prevalent and increasing at Cambridge, the court would usurp the functions of another branch of government if it adjudged, as matter of law, that the mode adopted under the sanction of the State, to protect the people at large was arbitrary and not justified by the necessities of the case. We say necessities of the case because it might be that an acknowledged power of a local community to protect itself against an epidemic threatening the safety of all, might be exercised in particular circumstances and in reference to particular persons in such an arbitrary, unreasonable manner, or might go so far beyond what was reasonably required for the safety of the public, as to authorize or compel the courts to interfere for the protection of such persons. . . . The liberty secured by the Fourteenth Amendment, this court has said, consists, in part, in the right of a person "to live and work where he will," *Allgeyer* v. *Louisiana* (1897) and yet he may be compelled, by force if need be, against his will and without regard to his personal wishes or his pecuniary interests, or even his religious or political convictions, to take his place in the ranks of the army of his country and risk the chance of being shot down in its defense. It is not, therefore, true that the power of the public to guard itself against imminent danger depends in every case involving the control of one's body upon his willingness to submit to reasonable regulations established by the constituted authorities, under the sanction of the State, for the purpose of protecting the public collectively against such danger. . . .

Looking at the propositions embodied in the defendant's rejected offers of proof, it is clear that they are more formidable by their number than by their inherent value. Those offers, in the main, seem to have had no purpose except to state the general theory of those of the medical profession who attach little or no value to vaccination as a means of preventing the spread of smallpox, or who think that vaccination causes other diseases of the body. What everybody knows, the court must know, and therefore the state court judicially knew, as this court knows, that an opposite theory accords with the common belief and is maintained by high medical authority. We must assume that, when the statute in question was passed, the legislature of Massachusetts was not unaware of these opposing theories, and was compelled, of necessity, to choose between them. It was not compelled to commit a matter involving the public health and safety to the final decision of a court or jury. It is no part of the function of a court or a jury to determine which one of two modes was likely to be the most effective for the protection of the public against disease. That was for the legislative department to determine in the light of all the information it had or could obtain. It could not properly abdicate its function to guard the public health and safety. The state legislature proceeded upon the theory which recognized vaccination as at least an effective, if not the best, known way in which to meet and suppress the evils of a smallpox epidemic that imperiled an entire population. Upon what sound principles as to the relations existing between the different departments of government can the court review this action of the legislature? If there is any such power in the judiciary to review legislative action in respect of a matter affecting the general welfare, it can only be when that which the legislature has done comes within the rule that,

> if a statute purporting to have been enacted to protect the public health, the public morals, or the public safety has no real or substantial relation to those objects, or is, beyond all question, a plain, palpable invasion of rights secured by the fundamental law, it is the duty of the courts to so adjudge, and thereby give effect to the Constitution. . . .

Whatever may be thought of the expediency of this statute, it cannot be affirmed to be, beyond question, in palpable conflict with the Constitution. Nor, in view of the methods employed to stamp out the disease of smallpox, can anyone confidently assert that the means prescribed by the State to that end has no real or substantial relation to the protection of the public health and the public safety. Such an assertion would not be consistent with the experience of this and other countries whose authorities have dealt with the disease of smallpox. And the principle of vaccination as a means to prevent the spread of smallpox has been enforced in many States by statutes making the vaccination of children a condition of their right to enter or remain in public schools. . . .

We are not prepared to hold that a minority, residing or remaining in any city or town where smallpox is prevalent, and enjoying the general protection afforded by an organized local government, may thus defy the will of its constituted authorities, acting in good faith for all, under the legislative sanction of the State. If such be the privilege of a minority, then a like privilege would belong to each individual of the community, and the spectacle would be presented of the welfare and safety of an entire population being subordinated to the notions of a single individual who chooses to remain a part of that population. We are unwilling to hold it to be an element in the liberty secured by the Constitution of the United States that one person, or a minority of persons, residing in any community and enjoying the benefits of its local government, should have the power thus to dominate the majority when supported in their action by the authority of the State. While this court should guard with firmness every right appertaining to life, liberty or property as secured to the individual by the Supreme Law of the Land, it is of the last importance that it should not invade the domain of local authority except when it is plainly necessary to do so in order to enforce that law. The safety and the health of the people of Massachusetts are, in the first instance, for that Commonwealth to guard and protect. They are matters that do not ordinarily concern the National Government. So far as they can be reached by any government, they depend, primarily, upon such action as the State in its wisdom may take, and we do not perceive that this legislation has invaded any right secured by the Federal Constitution.

▼▲▼

## State Commerce Power

In *Gibbons*, Chief Justice Marshall also recognized that congressional power to regulate interstate commerce did not reach activities that were "completely internal . . . of a State." Power over such commerce, wrote Marshall, "may be considered as reserved for the State itself."[36] Marshall's opinion in *Gibbons* has been justly celebrated as one of his best and most enduring. It is a forceful statement of constitutional nationalism and the supreme authority of Congress to manage the nation's commercial affairs. But *Gibbons* also reflects the chief justice's acute political instincts. As much as prominent states' rights advocates like Thomas Jefferson were horrified by *Gibbons*'s broad definition of interstate commerce and Marshall's bold assertion of congressional power to regulate it, "no watchful guardian of states' rights could contend that Marshall had erected constitutional barriers to all state commercial regulation."[37] In other words, Marshall's formulation of congressional power to regulate interstate commerce was exclusive, but left open the possibility that states were free to impose rules on commercial activities that took place within their borders.

The Court struggled for nearly three decades to articulate a theory that gave definition to Marshall's *dicta* in

*Gibbons.* The Taney Court's difficulties in defining the respective spheres of national and state power to regulate commerce stemmed in large part from the partition that had formed between the North and South over slavery. By 1837 the abolition movement had taken hold in the Northern states; Southern secession had moved from John C. Calhoun's abstract consideration to a viable political movement. If the Court did not scale down the reach of congressional commerce power, the real possibility existed that Congress could define the slaves as articles of interstate commerce and thus outlaw slavery as an institution.

The five Southern Democrats who now formed the Court's majority were aware of these dangers. Accordingly, the Taney Court began to transfer, on a gradual basis, power from Congress to the states to regulate commercial activities. It did this by narrowing Marshall's definition of interstate commerce without disturbing the core holding of *Gibbons.*[38] The fruit of this labor came in *Cooley v. Board of Wardens* (1852), which is still the Court's most important statement on the respective boundaries of national and state commerce power. *Cooley* is also one of the most important contributions of the Taney Court to American constitutional development.

*Cooley* remains the leading case on state commerce power because it effectively reconciled several competing theories that, since *Gibbons,* had floated in and around the Court's decisions commingling commerce and federalism. By *Cooley,* three such theories had come to dominate debate within the Court. The first, suggested by Justice William Johnson in his concurring opinion in *Gibbons,* argued that the Commerce Clause acted as a negative on state commerce power. That is, states were prohibited from regulating commerce even in the absence of federal regulation. Such was the exclusiveness of congressional commerce power that even the exercise of state police power was prohibited if it touched upon the flow of interstate commerce.

Not even Marshall went to those lengths to defend congressional power in such comprehensive terms, even though he had framed the power to regulate interstate commerce in *Gibbons* as "exclusive." Marshall viewed national and state commerce power as *mutually exclusive:* Congress had exclusive authority over interstate commercial activities, and the states retained the

right to regulate commerce that fell within their borders. That view was best expressed by Marshall's *dicta* in *Gibbons* and was the closest the Court came to an animating principle on the subject until Justice Benjamin Curtis set out what scholars have called the doctrine of "selective exclusiveness" in *Cooley.*

Justice Curtis's opinion for a 7-2 Court has been called the "yes, and no" solution to the problem of commercial regulation. One prominent scholar has written, "To the question whether the power of Congress is exclusive, Mr. Justice Curtis took a great step forward by answering, 'Yes, and no.' This is the wisest initial answer to give to many questions that embrace such a variety and diversity of issues that no single answer can possibly be suitable for all."[39]

Although *Cooley* did not embrace the more popular theory among states' rights advocates that a *concurrent,* or simultaneous, power to regulate commerce existed between the national government and the states, Curtis's opinion fell well within the confines of the Taney Court's dual federalist philosophy. By acknowledging that the states retained constitutional prerogatives against federal regulation, the Court enabled the Southern states to retain a powerful instrument against possible Northern efforts to abolish slavery by engaging the interstate commerce power of Congress. Moreover, *Cooley* did not disturb an important 1837 decision, *New York v. Miln.* There, the Court upheld a state law that permitted port authorities to inspect ships for undesirable passengers. It expressly authorized searches for "paupers, vagabonds, and possibly convicts, as it is to guard against the physical pestilence which may arise from unsound and infectious articles imported, or from a ship, the crew of which may be laboring under an infectious disease."[40] Justice Philip Barbour, a Virginian sympathetic to the protection of Southern slavery, held that New York's law was a valid exercise of state police power because it was directed toward persons, not articles of commerce. The Court's decision outraged Marshall's foremost intellectual protégé on the Court, Joseph Story. In a vociferous dissent, Story recalled from a personal conversation with the late chief justice that Marshall considered the New York law distinctly at odds with the principles established in *Gibbons.*

Later courts considered *Miln* extreme even by the dual federalist standards of the Taney Court. A century later it was effectively overruled.[41] *Cooley,* however, has remained in force, surviving even the dramatic changes to the federal system brought about by the Constitutional Revolution of 1937. Cooley's great strength is that it offered an eloquent statement of indefiniteness.[42] Congress and the states retained the independent power to regulate commerce, with the courts resolving disputes between the parties over their regulatory spheres on a case-by-case basis. This pragmatism offered a useful political solution to the sectional crisis pulling the Union apart in the 1850s, even if only temporarily, but did nothing to create a bright-line rule that future Courts could apply with any degree of certainty or regularity.

*Maine v. Taylor* (1986) offers an excellent example of the delicate, ever-shifting line the Court has navigated to remain true to the selective inclusiveness doctrine of *Cooley. Taylor* turns on the issue of how far states may extend their police power without discriminating against the commercial interests of other states. *Taylor,* in some ways, wrestles with a dilemma that goes all the way back to Chief Justice Marshall's opinion in *Gibbons.* Does the Court in *Taylor* remain true to Marshall's vision of congressional power?

## *Cooley v. Board of Wardens*
### 53 U.S. 299 (1851)

In 1803 the Pennsylvania legislature enacted a comprehensive law regulating the use of its ports. It included a provision that required any ship entering or leaving a Philadelphia harbor to employ local pilots. Any vessel operator who refused to use local pilots was subject to a fine. All fines received went into a fund for retired pilots, their dependents, and "distressed" members of their families. The law included three exceptions to the local pilot rule: ships of less than seventy-five tons, ships sailing to and from ports on the Delaware River, and coal ships that traveled to and from Pennsylvania.

Aaron Cooley owned two ships that used the Port of Philadelphia without employing a local pilot. He was prosecuted and fined by the local Board of Wardens that oversaw the operations of the Philadelphia port. Cooley appealed his fine, claiming that a 1789 law enacted by Congress permitting state and local authorities to regulate

commerce in the absence of a contrary federal law superceded the Pennsylvania law. Because Congress had not acted to regulate local ports, Cooley's argument was less about the state's power to *regulate* commerce than it was about the power to *tax* commerce. At bottom, the facts and context of the case turned on one central question: In the absence of congressional action, do states retain the power to regulate those features of interstate commerce that are local in nature?

The Court's decision was 8 to 1. Justice Curtis delivered the opinion of the Court. Justice Daniel wrote a concurring opinion. Justice McLean dissented.

▼▲▼

Mr. Justice Curtis delivered the opinion of the Court.

That the power to regulate commerce includes the regulation of navigation we consider settled. And when we look to the nature of the service performed by pilots, to the relations which that service and its compensations bear to navigation between the several states and between the ports of the United States and foreign countries, we are brought to the conclusion that the regulation of the qualifications of pilots, of the modes and times of offering and rendering their services, of the responsibilities which shall rest upon them, of the powers they shall possess, of the compensation they may demand, and of the penalties by which their rights and duties may be enforced, do constitute regulations of navigation, and consequently of commerce, within the just meaning of this clause of the Constitution. . . .

It becomes necessary therefore to consider whether this law of Pennsylvania, being a regulation of commerce, is valid.

The act of Congress of the 7th of August, 1789, section 4, is as follows:

That all pilots in the bays, inlets, rivers, harbors, and ports of the United States shall continue to be regulated in conformity with the existing laws of the states, respectively, wherein such pilots may be, or with such laws as the states may respectively hereafter enact for the purpose, until further legislative provision shall be made by Congress.

If the law of Pennsylvania now in question had been in existence at the date of this act of Congress, we might hold it to have been adopted by Congress, and thus made a law of the United States, and so valid. Because this act does, in effect, give the force of an act of Congress, to the then existing state laws on this subject, so long as they should continue unrepealed by the state which enacted them.

But the law on which these actions are founded was not enacted till 1803. What effect then can be attributed to so much of the act of 1789 as declares that pilots shall continue to be regulated in conformity, "with such laws as the states may respectively hereafter enact for the purpose until further legislative provision shall be made by Congress?"

If the states were divested of the power to legislate on this subject by the grant of the commercial power to Congress, it is plain this act could not confer upon them power thus to legislate. If the Constitution excluded the states from making any law regulating commerce, certainly Congress cannot re-grant, or in any manner re-convey to the states that power. And yet this act of 1789 gives its sanction only to laws enacted by the states. This necessarily implies a constitutional power to legislate, for only a rule created by the sovereign power of a state acting in its legislative capacity can be deemed a law enacted by a state, and if the state has so limited its sovereign power that it no longer extends to a particular subject, manifestly it cannot, in any proper sense, be said to enact laws thereon. Entertaining these views, we are brought directly and unavoidably to the consideration of the question whether the grant of the commercial power to Congress did *per se* deprive the states of all power to regulate pilots. This question has never been decided by this court, nor, in our judgment, has any case depending upon all the considerations which must govern this one come before this court. The grant of commercial power to Congress does not contain any terms which expressly exclude the states from exercising an authority over its subject matter. If they are excluded, it must be because the nature of the power thus granted to Congress requires that a similar authority should not exist in the states. If it were conceded, on the one side, that the nature of this power, like that to legislate for the District of Columbia, is absolutely and totally repugnant to the existence of similar power in the states, probably no one would deny that the grant of the power to Congress as effectually and perfectly excludes the states from all future legislation on the subject as if express words had been used to exclude them. And, on the other hand, if it were admitted that the existence of this power in Congress, like the power of taxation, is compatible with the existence of a similar power in the states, then it would be in conformity with the contemporary exposition of the Constitution and with the judicial construction given from time to time by this court, after the most deliberate consideration, to hold that the mere grant

of such a power to Congress did not imply a prohibition on the states to exercise the same power, that it is not the mere existence of such a power, but its exercise by Congress, which may be incompatible with the exercise of the same power by the states, and that the states may legislate in the absence of congressional regulations.

The diversities of opinion, therefore, which have existed on this subject have arisen from the different views taken of the nature of this power. But when the nature of a power like this is spoken of, when it is said that the nature of the power requires that it should be exercised exclusively by Congress, it must be intended to refer to the subjects of that power, and to say they are of such a nature as to require exclusive legislation by Congress. Now the power to regulate commerce embraces a vast field containing not only many but exceedingly various subjects quite unlike in their nature, some imperatively demanding a single uniform rule operating equally on the commerce of the United States in every port and some, like the subject now in question, as imperatively demanding that diversity which alone can meet the local necessities of navigation.

Either absolutely to affirm or deny that the nature of this power requires exclusive legislation by Congress is to lose sight of the nature of the subjects of this power and to assert concerning all of them what is really applicable but to a part. Whatever subjects of this power are in their nature national, or admit only of one uniform system or plan of regulation, may justly be said to be of such a nature as to require exclusive legislation by Congress. That this cannot be affirmed of laws for the regulation of pilots and pilotage is plain. The act of 1789 contains a clear and authoritative declaration by the first Congress that the nature of this subject is such that, until Congress should find it necessary to exert its power, it should be left to the legislation of the states, that it is local and not national, that it is likely to be the best provided for not by one system or plan of regulations, but by as many as the legislative discretion of the several states should deem applicable to the local peculiarities of the ports within their limits.

Viewed in this light, so much of this act of 1789 as declares that pilots shall continue to be regulated "by such laws as the states may respectively hereafter enact for that purpose," instead of being held to be inoperative as an attempt to confer on the states a power to legislate of which the Constitution had deprived them, is allowed an appropriate and important signification. It manifests the understanding of Congress, at the outset of the government, that the nature of this subject is not such as to require its exclusive legislation. The practice of the states and of the national government has been in conformity with this declaration from the origin of the national government to this time, and the nature of the subject, when examined, is such as to leave no doubt of the superior fitness and propriety, not to say the absolute necessity, of different systems of regulation, drawn from local knowledge and experience and conformed to local wants. How then can we say that, by the mere grant of power to regulate commerce, the states are deprived of all the power to legislate on this subject because, from the nature of the power, the legislation of Congress must be exclusive. This would be to affirm that the nature of the power is, in any case, something different from the nature of the subject to which, in such case, the power extends, and that the nature of the power necessarily demands, in all cases, exclusive legislation by Congress, while the nature of one of the subjects of that power not only does not require such exclusive legislation, but may be best provided for by many different systems enacted by the states, in conformity with the circumstances of the ports within their limits.

It is the opinion of a majority of the court that the mere grant to Congress of the power to regulate commerce did not deprive the states of power to regulate pilots, and that, although Congress has legislated on this subject, its legislation manifests an intention, with a single exception, not to regulate this subject, but to leave its regulation to the several states. To these precise questions, which are all we are called on to decide, this opinion must be understood to be confined. It does not extend to the question what other subjects, under the commercial power are within the exclusive control of Congress, or may be regulated by the states in the absence of all congressional legislation, nor to the general question how far any regulation of a subject by Congress may be deemed to operate as an exclusion of all legislation by the states upon the same subject. We decide the precise questions before us, upon what we deem sound principles, applicable to this particular subject in the state in which the legislation of Congress has left it. We go no further. . . .

We are of opinion that this state law was enacted by virtue of a power residing in the state to legislate; that it is not in conflict with any law of Congress; that it does not interfere with any system which Congress has established by making regulations, or by intentionally leaving individuals to their own unrestricted action; that this law is therefore valid, and the judgment of the Supreme Court of Pennsylvania in each case must be affirmed.

▼▲▼

## Maine v. Taylor
### 477 U.S. 131 (1986)

The Maine legislature enacted a law prohibiting the importation of "golden shiners," popular live bait used in sport fishing. Maine's main concern was to protect local fish species from the parasites of out-of-state fish. In 1981, Congress had enacted a law called the Lacey Act, making it a federal crime for anyone to ship any fish or wildlife into a state in violation of a state law.

Robert J. Taylor owned a bait business in Maine. He arranged to have 158,000 live golden shiners delivered to him from outside the state. The shipment was seized before it crossed the Maine border, and Taylor was later indicted in federal court for violating the 1981 congressional law. The court rejected Taylor's argument that Congress had exceeded its interstate commerce power in enacting the Lacey Act. An appeals court reversed.

The Court's decision was 8 to 1. Justice Blackmun delivered the opinion of the Court. Justice Stevens dissented.

▼▲▼

JUSTICE BLACKMUN delivered the opinion of the Court.

Once again, a little fish has caused a commotion. The fish in this case is the golden shiner, a species of minnow commonly used as live bait in sport fishing. . . .

In determining whether a State has overstepped its role in regulating interstate commerce, this Court has distinguished between state statutes that burden interstate transactions only incidentally and those that affirmatively discriminate against such transactions. While statutes in the first group violate the Commerce Clause only if the burdens they impose on interstate trade are "clearly excessive in relation to the putative local benefits," statutes in the second group are subject to more demanding scrutiny. The Court explained in *Hughes* v. *Oklahoma* (1979), that once a state law is shown to discriminate against interstate commerce "either on its face or in practical effect," the burden falls on the State to demonstrate both that the statute "serves a legitimate local purpose" and that this purpose could not be served as well by available nondiscriminatory means. . . .

No matter how one describes the abstract issue whether "alternative means could promote this local purpose as well without discriminating against interstate commerce," *Hughes v. Oklahoma*, the more specific question whether scientifically accepted techniques exist for the sampling and inspection of live baitfish is one of fact, and the District Court's finding that such techniques have not been devised cannot be characterized as clearly erroneous. Indeed, the record probably could not support a contrary finding. Two prosecution witnesses testified to the lack of such procedures, and appellee's expert conceded the point, although he disagreed about the need for such tests. That Maine has allowed the importation of other freshwater fish after inspection hardly demonstrates that the District Court clearly erred in crediting the corroborated and uncontradicted expert testimony that standardized inspection techniques had not yet been developed for baitfish. This is particularly so because the text of the permit statute suggests that it was designed specifically to regulate importation of salmonids, for which, the experts testified, testing procedures had been developed. . . .

Nor do we think that much doubt is cast on the legitimacy of Maine's purposes by what the Court of Appeals took to be signs of protectionist intent. Shielding in-state industries from out-of-state competition is almost never a legitimate local purpose, and state laws that amount to "simple economic protectionism" consequently have been subject to a "virtually *per se* rule of invalidity." *Philadelphia v. New Jersey* (1978). But there is little reason in this case to believe that the legitimate justifications the State has put forward for its statute are merely a sham or a "*post hoc* rationalization." . . .

The Commerce Clause significantly limits the ability of States and localities to regulate or otherwise burden the flow of interstate commerce, but it does not elevate free trade above all other values. As long as a State does not needlessly obstruct interstate trade or attempt to "place itself in a position of economic isolation," it retains broad regulatory authority to protect the health and safety of its citizens and the integrity of its natural resources. The evidence in this case amply supports the District Court's findings that Maine's ban on the importation of live baitfish serves legitimate local purposes that could not adequately be served by available nondiscriminatory alternatives. This is not a case of arbitrary discrimination against interstate commerce; the record suggests that Maine has legitimate reasons, "apart from their origin, to treat [out-of-state baitfish] differently." The judgment of the Court of Appeals setting aside appellee's conviction is therefore reversed.

*It is so ordered.*

JUSTICE STEVENS, dissenting.

There is something fishy about this case. Maine is the only State in the Union that blatantly discriminates against out-of-state baitfish by flatly prohibiting their importation. Although golden shiners are already present and thriving in Maine (and, perhaps not coincidentally, the subject of a flourishing domestic industry), Maine excludes golden shiners grown and harvested (and, perhaps not coincidentally, sold) in other States. This kind of stark discrimination against out-of-state articles of commerce requires rigorous justification by the discriminating State. . . .

This is not to derogate the State's interest in ecological purity. But the invocation of environmental protection or public health has never been thought to confer some kind of special dispensation from the general principle of nondiscrimination in interstate commerce.

A different view, that the ordinance is valid simply because it professes to be a health measure, would mean that the Commerce Clause of itself imposes no restraints on state action other than those laid down by the Due Process Clause, save for the rare instance where a state artlessly discloses an avowed purpose to discriminate against interstate goods.

If Maine wishes to rely on its interest in ecological preservation, it must show that interest, and the infeasibility of other alternatives, with far greater specificity. Otherwise, it must further that asserted interest in a manner far less offensive to the notions of comity and cooperation that underlie the Commerce Clause.

▼▲▼

## Federal Preemption

The previous discussion of congressional and state commerce power illustrates the tension that exists within the complex architecture of American federalism over the control of commercial activities. But conflict between the national government and the states is not limited to commercial legislation. Although Congress and the states have concurrent interests in a number of policy areas, ranging from environmental regulation to education to health care, they also often find themselves at odds over their respective authority to regulate in these and many other policy areas. The power of Congress to supersede state laws that conflict with a national policy interest is known as the *doctrine of federal preemption.*

Since the Constitutional Revolution of 1937, the Court has granted broad authority to Congress to legislate on matters once reserved to the states. In earlier chapters, we discussed how the Court altered the distribution of power within the American federal system by holding that social and economic problems once considered state and local in nature were now, in fact, national in scope (child labor, minimum wage, and workplace safety laws, for example). In other cases, the Court threw out the existing definition of a constitutional provision and replaced it with one more sympathetic to the exercise of national power (the Commerce Clause is the most obvious example here). Yet, as our earlier discussion of state commerce power demonstrates, states still enjoy some leeway in making laws that brush up against but do not enter the domain of federal legislative power.

The clearest articulation of the Court's position on the federal preemption doctrine comes in *Pennsylvania v. Nelson* (1956), a case that carried with it a political subtext of no small consequence.[43] Decided at the height of the Cold War, *Nelson* involved the state of Pennsylvania's decision to prosecute a high-profile Communist Party member for violating a state sedition law that made it a crime to advocate the overthrow of the United States government by force or violence. For a 6-3 Court, Chief Justice Earl Warren struck down a Pennsylvania sedition law on the grounds that Congress, through a "pervasive" body of federal law, already occupied the field of sedition. More important, the chief justice outlined a three-part test that continues to form the basis of the doctrine of federal preemption.

*Nelson* also marked a pivotal turning point in the Court's approach to cases involving internal security matters and the rights of political dissenters. The Court's decision cast immediate doubt on forty-two other state sedition laws and prompted the House of Representatives to introduce legislation that offered a modification of Chief Justice Warren's criteria for federal preemption. In 1958 and 1959 the House passed legislation in which states retained the right to legislate on matters of federal interest as long as Congress did not specifically preempt state power in a given field. Neither proposal made it past the Senate. Still, under *Nelson,* states could prosecute sedition against themselves, but not against the government of the United States. Over the next decade,

however, the Court, in *Dombrowski v. Pfister* (1965) and *Brandenburg v. Ohio* (1969), broadened the rights of political dissenters to the point where state sedition laws, no longer really enforced anyway, stood on the shakiest of constitutional ground.

One of the questions left open by the Court's ruling in *Nelson* was the extent to which Congress must specify its intent to preempt state regulation in a given policy area. *Cipollone v. Liggett Group* (1992) offers a splendid example of the way in which complex and controversial public policy issues often find their way into the courts for resolution. *Cipollone* involved a face-off between the family of a deceased cigarette smoker and the company that manufactured the cigarettes she smoked for more than forty years. Our SIDEBAR on *Cipollone* offers more background on the legal and political battles between the tobacco companies and the government over the need to warn consumers of the health risks involved in smoking. Does *Cipollone* suggest that federal preemption cases, in the Court's view, are better decided on a case-by-case basis rather than with broad theoretical brushstrokes?

## *Pennsylvania v. Nelson*
### 350 U.S. 497 (1956)

Freedom of speech and association are two of the most jealously guarded principles in the culture of American law and politics. But just as the history of political speech in the United States is replete with examples of the lonely dissenter bucking the tide of majority opinion to shine the light on truth, another long-standing, although less talked about, American tradition is the legal suppression of "subversive" and "seditious" speech. Seven years after the Bill of Rights was ratified, Congress enacted the Alien and Sedition Acts of 1798, one of the most notorious legacies of the Federalists. The Alien law lengthened the residence requirement to establish American citizenship, a move designed to punish the recent influx of French into the United States. It also authorized the president to deport "aliens" and their supporters who engaged in secret activities against the government. The sedition law punished any American citizen who engaged in "false, scandalous and malicious" speech against the United States. Passed to protect the threadbare support for President John Adams against the increasingly vocal Democratic-Republican opposition led by Thomas Jefferson, the law was used by prosecutors to round up numerous critics of the incumbent Federalist administration. The environment created by the Alien and Sedition Acts foreshadowed the red scare of the 1920s and the McCarthy era of the late 1940s and early 1950s. Jefferson hated the 1798 law, and one of his first acts as president, having won the 1800 election, was to announce that it was a dead letter.

This less noble tradition in the history of American free speech continued until well into the twentieth century. In 1919 the Supreme Court, in *Schenck v. United States,* held that Congress was free to outlaw any speech or related conduct that posed a "clear and present" danger. The rise of Soviet Russia and the perceived threat that Communism posed to the domestic security of the nation, much more so than fear aroused by Nazi Germany, led Congress and several states to impose restrictions on political dissent throughout the 1920s and 1930s. After World War II, as the Cold War atmosphere entered the social and political undercurrent of American life, the states, following Congress, began requiring state employees to sign loyalty oaths professing their allegiance to the state and the United States. Failure to comply with antisubversion laws meant the loss of one's job, jail time, or both.

In 1939, Pennsylvania passed a sedition law that made it illegal to engage in any activity intended to bring about violence against it or the United States. So severe was the Pennsylvania law that its penalties exceeded the leading federal antisubversion law, the Smith Act, passed a year later. In 1950 a witness called to testify before the House Un-American Activities committee (HUAC) (see Chapter 4, pp. 133–137, for more on HUAC) identified Steve Nelson as a Communist. Pennsylvania prosecuted Nelson, who found no takers among civil liberties lawyers or anyone else to represent him and thus went forward without counsel. He was convicted and sentenced to twenty years in prison.

On appeal, Nelson claimed that Congress had preempted the field of subversion and thus his conviction under the Pennsylvania law was unconstitutional. The Pennsylvania Supreme Court agreed and reversed the trial court.

The Court's decision was 6 to 3. Chief Justice Warren delivered the opinion of the Court. Justice Reed, joined by Justices Burton and Minton, filed a dissenting opinion.

▼▲▼

MR. CHIEF JUSTICE WARREN delivered the opinion of the Court.

[A]ll that is before us for review, is [whether] the Smith Act of 1940, as amended in 1948, which prohibits the knowing advocacy of the overthrow of the Government of the United States by force and violence, supersedes the enforceability of the Pennsylvania Sedition Act, which proscribes the same conduct.

It should be said at the outset that the decision in this case does not affect the right of States to enforce their sedition laws at times when the Federal Government has not occupied the field and is not protecting the entire country from seditious conduct. The distinction between the two situations was clearly recognized by the court below. Nor does it limit the jurisdiction of the States where the Constitution and Congress have specifically given them concurrent jurisdiction, as was done under the Eighteenth Amendment and the Volstead Act. Neither does it limit the right of the State to protect itself at any time against sabotage or attempted violence of all kinds. Nor does it prevent the State from prosecuting where the same act constitutes both a federal offense and a state offense under the police power. . . .

Where, as in the instant case, Congress has not stated specifically whether a federal statute has occupied a field in which the States are otherwise free to legislate, different criteria have furnished touchstones for decision. Thus,

[t]his Court, in considering the validity of state laws in the light of . . . federal laws touching the same subject, has made use of the following expressions: conflicting; contrary to; occupying the field; repugnance; difference; irreconcilability; inconsistency; violation; curtailment, and interference. But none of these expressions provides an infallible constitutional test or an exclusive constitutional yardstick. In the final analysis, there can be no one crystal clear distinctly marked formula.

In this case, we think that each of several tests of supersession is met.

*First,* "[t]he scheme of federal regulation [is] so pervasive as to make reasonable the inference that Congress left no room for the States to supplement it." The Congress determined in 1940 that it was necessary for it to reenter the field of anti-subversive legislation, which had been abandoned by it in 1921. In that year, it enacted the Smith Act, which proscribes advocacy of the overthrow of any government—federal, state or local—by force and violence and organization of and knowing membership in a group which so advocates. Conspiracy to commit any of these acts is punishable under the general criminal conspiracy provisions in 18 U.S.C. § [section] 371. The Internal Security Act of 1950 is aimed more directly at Communist organizations. It distinguishes between "Communist action organizations" and "Communist front organizations," requiring such organizations to register and to file annual reports with the Attorney General giving complete details as to their officers and funds. Members of Communist action organizations who have not been registered by their organization must register as individuals. Failure to register in accordance with the requirements of Sections 786–787 is punishable by a fine of not more than $10,000 for an offending organization and by a fine of not more than $10,000 or imprisonment for not more than five years or both for an individual offender—each day of failure to register constituting a separate offense. And the Act imposes certain sanctions upon both "action" and "front" organizations and their members. The Communist Control Act of 1954 declares, "that the Communist Party of the United States, although purportedly a political party, is, in fact, an instrumentality of a conspiracy to overthrow the Government of the United States," and that, "its role as the agency of a hostile foreign power renders its existence a clear present and continuing danger to the security of the United States." It also contains a legislative finding that the Communist Party is a "Communist action organization" within the meaning of the Internal Security Act of 1950, and provides that "knowing" members of the Communist Party are "subject to all the provisions and penalties" of that Act. It furthermore sets up a new classification of "Communist-infiltrated organizations," and provides for the imposition of sanctions against them.

We examine these Acts only to determine the congressional plan. Looking to all of them in the aggregate, the conclusion is inescapable that Congress has intended to occupy the field of sedition. Taken as a whole, they evince a congressional plan which makes it reasonable to determine that no room has been left for the States to supplement it. Therefore, a state sedition statute is superseded regardless of whether it purports to supplement the federal law. . . .

*Second,* the federal statutes, "touch a field in which the federal interest is so dominant that the federal system [must] be assumed to preclude enforcement of state laws on the same subject." Congress has devised an all-embracing program for resistance to the various forms of totalitarian aggression. Our external defenses have been strengthened, and a plan to protect against internal subversion has been made by it. It has appropriated vast sums, not only for our own protection, but also to strengthen freedom throughout the world. It has charged the Federal Bureau of Investigation and the Central Intelligence Agency with responsibility for intelligence concerning Communist seditious activities against our Government, and has denominated such activities as part of a world conspiracy. It accordingly proscribed sedition against all government in the nation—national, state and local. Congress declared that these steps were taken, "to provide for the common defense, to preserve the sovereignty of the United States as an independent nation, and to guarantee to each State a republican form of government. . . . " Congress having thus treated seditious conduct as a matter of vital national concern, it is in no sense a local enforcement problem. . . .

*Third,* enforcement of state sedition acts presents a serious danger of conflict with the administration of the federal program. Since 1939, in order to avoid a hampering of uniform enforcement of its program by sporadic local prosecutions, the Federal Government has urged local authorities not to intervene in such matters, but to turn over to the federal authorities immediately and unevaluated all information concerning subversive activities. . . .

In his brief, the Solicitor General states that forty-two States plus Alaska and Hawaii have statutes which, in some form, prohibit advocacy of the violent overthrow of established government. These statutes are entitled anti-sedition statutes, criminal anarchy laws, criminal syndicalist laws, etc. Although all of them are primarily directed against the overthrow of the United States Government, they are in no sense uniform. And our attention has not been called to any case where the prosecution has been successfully directed against an attempt to destroy state or local government. Some of these Acts are studiously drawn, and purport to protect fundamental rights by appropriate definitions, standards of proof, and orderly procedures in keeping with the avowed congressional purpose "to protect freedom from those who would destroy it, without infringing upon the freedom of all our people." Others are vague, and are almost wholly without such safeguards. Some even purport to punish mere membership in subversive organizations, which the federal statutes do not punish where federal registration requirements have been fulfilled. . . . Since we find that Congress has occupied the field to the exclusion of parallel state legislation, that the dominant interest of the Federal Government precludes state intervention, and that administration of state Acts would conflict with the operation of the federal plan, we are convinced that the decision of the Supreme Court of Pennsylvania is unassailable.

We are not unmindful of the risk of compounding punishments which would be created by finding concurrent state power. In our view of the case, we do not reach the question whether double or multiple punishment for the same overt acts directed against the United States has constitutional sanction. Without compelling indication to the contrary, we will not assume that Congress intended to permit the possibility of double punishment. The judgment of the Supreme Court of Pennsylvania is

*Affirmed.*

## Cipollone v. Liggett Group, Inc.

505 U.S. 504 (1992)

The facts and background of this case are set out in the accompanying SIDEBAR.

The Court divided 4 to 3 to 2. Justice Stevens announced the judgment of the Court. Justice Blackmun, joined by Justices Kennedy and Souter, wrote a separate opinion concurring in part and dissenting in part. Justice Scalia, joined by Justice Thomas, dissented.

JUSTICE STEVENS delivered the opinion of the Court.

Article VI of the Constitution provides that the laws of the United States, "shall be the supreme Law of the Land; . . . any Thing in the Constitution or Laws of any state to the Contrary notwithstanding." Thus, since our decision in *McCulloch v. Maryland* (1819), it has been settled that state law that conflicts with federal law is "without effect." Consideration of issues arising under the Supremacy Clause, "start[s] with the assumption that the historic police powers of the States [are] not to be superseded by . . . Federal Act unless that [is] the clear and manifest purpose of Congress." Accordingly, "'[t]he purpose of Congress is the ultimate touchstone'" of preemption analysis.

Congress' intent may be "explicitly stated in the statute's language or implicitly contained in its structure and purpose." In the absence of an express congressional command, state law is preempted if that law actually conflicts with federal law, or if federal law so thoroughly occupies a legislative field "'as to make reasonable the inference that Congress left no room for the States to supplement it.'" . . .

When Congress has considered the issue of preemption and has included in the enacted legislation a provision explicitly addressing that issue, and when that provision provides a "reliable indicium of congressional intent with respect to state authority," "there is no need to infer congressional intent to preempt state laws from the substantive provisions" of the legislation. Such reasoning is a variant of the familiar principle of expression *unius est exclusio alterius:* Congress' enactment of a provision defining the preemptive reach of a statute implies that matters beyond that reach are not preempted. In this case, the other provisions of the 1965 and 1969 Acts offer no cause to look beyond Section 5 of each Act. Therefore, we need only identify the domain expressly preempted by each of those sections. As the 1965 and 1969 provisions differ substantially, we consider each in turn.

In the 1965 preemption provision regarding advertising, Congress spoke precisely and narrowly: "No *statement* relating to smoking and health shall be required *in the advertising* of [properly labeled] cigarettes." Section 5(a) used the same phrase ("No *statement* relating to smoking and health") with regard to cigarette labeling. As Section 5(a) made clear, that phrase referred to the sort of warning provided for in Section 4, which set forth *verbatim* the warning Congress determined to be appropriate. Thus, on their face, these provisions merely prohibited state and federal rulemaking bodies from mandating particular cautionary statements on cigarette labels or in cigarette advertisements.

Beyond the precise words of these provisions, this reading is appropriate for several reasons. First, as discussed above, we must construe these provisions in light of the presumption against the preemption of state police power regulations. This presumption reinforces the appropriateness of a narrow reading of Section 5. Second, the warning required in Section 4 does not, by its own effect, foreclose additional obligations imposed under state law. That Congress requires a particular warning label does not automatically preempt a regulatory field. Third, there is no general, inherent conflict between federal preemption of state warning requirements and the continued vitality of state common law damages actions. For example, in the Comprehensive Smokeless Tobacco Health Education Act of 1986, Congress expressly preempted State or local imposition of a "statement relating to the use of smokeless tobacco products and health" but, at the same time, preserved state law damages actions based on those products. All of these considerations indicate that Section 5 is best read as having superseded only positive enactments by legislatures or administrative agencies that mandate particular warning labels.

This reading comports with the 1965 Act's statement of purpose, which expressed an intent to avoid "diverse, nonuniform, and confusing labeling and advertising

# CIPOLLONE V. LIGGETT GROUP, INC.

## *Where There's Smoke, There's . . . a Lawsuit*

Enthralled with the movies since her childhood, sixteen-year-old Rose Cipollone wanted nothing more than to emulate the glamorous, tough-girl image of the great female movie stars of her generation, such as Bette Davis, Joan Crawford, and Lauren Bacall. So in 1942 Rose began to smoke cigarettes because it made her feel cool, glamorous, and grown-up, just like her screen idols. By her twentieth birthday, Cipollone was a pack-a-day smoker, a habit she would maintain almost until her death in 1984 from cancer complications in her lungs, adrenal glands, liver, and brain. As a young woman, did Rose Cipollone ever worry about the health risks of smoking? Why, no, never. "Tobacco companies wouldn't do anything that was really going to kill you," she once said. Cigarette makers did little to dispel that perception prior to 1964, when the surgeon general issued a report that offered the first comprehensive findings on the hazards of smoking. In fact, magazine and television advertisements from the 1950s emphasized the safeness of smoking. Slogans such as "just what the doctor ordered" and "good for you" often accompanied cigarette advertisements to reassure consumers that theirs was a benign choice.

In 1981, Rose Cipollone discovered that she had contracted a malignant tumor in her right lung. Doctors removed the upper lobe of her lung. Still, she continued to smoke. A year later, the cancer returned. This time, her entire right lung was removed. Convinced that the manufacturer of Cipollone's favorite brands of cigarettes had withheld important research from the public on direct links between cigarette smoking and cancer, Rose and her family filed suit against the Liggett Group in 1983. Relying upon New Jersey personal injury law, the Cipollones offered five separate theories of recovery for damages caused by cigarette smoking:

1. *Design Defect:* This claim, which was not considered by the Supreme Court, alleged that the manufacturer's cigarettes were defective because Liggett had not used a safer alternative design.
2. *Failure to Warn:* This claim alleged that the product was defective because the manufacturer did not provide adequate warnings of the health consequences of cigarette smoking.

3. *Breach of Express Warranty:* This complaint alleged that the manufacturer had warranted that its products did not present any significant health consequences.
4. *Fradulent Misrepresentation:* This claim was based on the manufacturer's alleged efforts to neutralize the impact of the warnings mandated by federal law and on Liggett's failure to act on its knowledge of medical and scientific data indicating the health hazards of cigarettes.
5. *Conspiracy to Defraud:* The plaintiffs alleged that the major tobacco companies conspired to deprive the public of known medical and scientific data.

Liggett contended that the Cipollones could not proceed with a damage claim under New Jersey law because congressional legislation had preempted the right of states to hold tobacco companies liable for harm associated with cigarette smoking. In 1965, Congress enacted the Federal Cigarette and Advertising Act, which required all cigarette packages to carry the now-famous warning label, CAUTION: CIGA-RETTE SMOKING MAY BE HAZARDOUS TO YOUR HEALTH, in a conspicuous place. In 1969, Congress amended the label to read, WARNING: THE SUR-GEON GENERAL HAS DETERMINED THAT CIGA-RETTE SMOKING IS DANGEROUS TO YOUR HEALTH. A year later, Congress banned all cigarette advertising from radio and television.

In 1984, Congress approved its most stringent cigarette-labeling requirements to date. The Compre-hensive Smoking Education Act added four new labels to the mix, mandated their periodic rotation on the sides of cigarette packages, and required them to be 50 per-cent larger than previous labels. The warnings stated:

(1) SURGEON GENERAL'S WARNING: SMOK-ING BY PREGNANT WOMEN MAY RESULT IN FETAL INJURY, PREMATURE BIRTH, AND LOW BIRTH WEIGHT.

(2) SURGEON GENERAL'S WARNING: QUITTING SMOKING NOW GREATLY REDUCES SERI-OUS RISKS TO YOUR HEALTH.

(3) SURGEON GENERAL'S WARNING: SMOKING CAUSES LUNG CANCER, HEART DISEASE, EMPHYSEMA, AND MAY COMPLICATE PREG-NANCY.

(4) SURGEON GENERAL'S WARNING: CIGA-RETTE SMOKE CONTAINS CARBON MON-OXIDE.

In 1983, Rose Cipollone's case against the Liggett Group commenced in federal court. The litigation lasted close to ten years; generated almost $200 mil-lion in lawyers' fees; and continued even after Rose Cipollone, and later her husband, Antonio, died (their son, Thomas, continued the litigation). The key turn-ing point in the case came after Claude Martin, a busi-ness school professor and expert witness on behalf of Liggett, testified that advertising and public relations have very little effect on a consumer's decision to smoke. Martin testified that tobacco companies spend millions of dollars on advertising because they are afraid not to and because they want to persuade smokers to switch brands.

During Martin's cross-examination, Judge Stanley Sarokin, who had presided over previous tobacco liti-gation, asked the witness, "If a cigarette manufacturer

*Bette Davis was a smart, sassy, and beautiful actress who rose to fame in Hollywood during the 1930s and 1940s. Like many film starlets of the time, Davis is featured here smok-ing a cigarette in a movie industry promotional poster.* Culver Pictures.

put out an ad showing an attractive young woman in a tennis outfit in a nice setting, or put an ad showing a funeral for that woman and said, 'Smoking kills,' you mean that second ad would not have an impact upon the information environment?" Peter Bleakly, one of the attorneys representing Philip Morris, a tobacco company and codefendant in the case, approached the bench and told Judge Sarokin, "A jury is inevitably going to come to the conclusion that Your Honor has very strongly held views on this subject, and I think it is extremely prejudicial and I must object."

The United States Court of Appeals for the Third Circuit decided to remove Judge Sarokin after he again criticized the tobacco industry, this time accusing cigarette companies of concealing medical information on the health hazards of smoking. The Third Circuit cited one particular passage in a ruling by Judge Sarokin allowing the Cipollones' lawyers to access internal tobacco company documents. Wrote Sarokin:

> In light of the current controversy surrounding breast implants, one wonders when all industries will recognize their obligation to voluntarily disclose risks from the use of their products. All too often in the choice between the physical health of consumers and the financial well-being of business, concealment is chosen over disclosure, sales over safety, and money over morality. Who are these persons who knowingly and secretly decide to put the buying public at risk solely for the purpose of making profits and who believe that illness and death of consumers is an appropriate cost of their own prosperity!

Judge Sarokin, however, was not removed until the initial phrase of the Cipollone trial was over and the jury had ordered Liggett to pay the family $400,000 in damages. The damages were awarded based on the Cipollones' pre-1966 claims against the Liggett Group for failing to manufacture a safe cigarette. The jury,

however, found the tobacco industry innocent of fraud and of conspiring to misrepresent health risks. The key constitutional ruling came after the Liggett Group had appealed to the Third Circuit, which threw out the jury verdict. The appeals court also held all lawsuits seeking damages for smoking based on deceptive advertising and failure to warn after the 1966 effective dates of the 1965 Cigarette Labeling and Advertising Act were preempted by federal law. It ordered a new trial. By then, Thomas Cipollone had had enough, even after the Supreme Court overturned the Third Circuit's decisions and ruled that tobacco liability lawsuits could go forward under state law.

Rose Cipollone spent the better part of her smoking life in search of the perfect cigarette, one that was mild, pleasant, and above all, safe. That journey led her from Chesterfields, Liggett's famous filterless cigarette, to L&Ms, which featured the "miracle tip" (one that Liggett promoted in its television commercials as registering "SAFE" on a special machine), to Virginia Slims, the first cigarette marketed exclusively to women, and finally, to Parliaments, which were marketed as the safest cigarettes to date because of their low tar and nicotine content and special "recessed" filter. Rose eventually learned the hardest lesson of all: that despite the tobacco industry's claims, there is no safe cigarette. But her successful decision to challenge the advertising and marketing practices of the industry put the tobacco companies on notice that its immunity from liability was now, like the glamorous ads of 1940s cigarette-smoking Hollywood starlets, a thing of the past.

---

*regulations* with respect to any relationship between smoking and health." Read against the backdrop of regulatory activity undertaken by state legislatures and federal agencies in response to the Surgeon General's report, the term "regulation" most naturally refers to positive enactments by those bodies, not to common law damages actions. . . .

For these reasons, we conclude that Section 5 of the 1965 Act only preempted state and federal rulemaking

bodies from mandating particular cautionary statements, and did not preempt state law damages actions. . . .

[The Court then turned to consider each of the damage claims brought by Cipollone.]

### Failure to Warn

. . . In this case, petitioner offered two closely related theories concerning the failure to warn: first, that respondents "were negligent in the manner [that] they tested, researched, sold, promoted, and advertised" their cigarettes; and second, that respondents failed to provide "adequate warnings of the health consequences of cigarette smoking."

Petitioner's claims are preempted to the extent that they rely on a state law "requirement or prohibition . . . with respect to . . . advertising or promotion." Thus, insofar as claims under either failure to warn theory require a showing that respondents' post-1969 advertising or promotions should have included additional, or more clearly stated, warnings, those claims are preempted. The Act does not, however, preempt petitioner's claims that rely solely on respondents' testing or research practices or other actions unrelated to advertising or promotion.

## Breach of Express Warranty

Petitioner's claim for breach of an express warranty arises under [a New Jersey statute], which provides:

> Any affirmation of fact or promise made by the seller to the buyer which relates to the goods and becomes part of the basis of the bargain creates an express warranty that the goods shall conform to the affirmation or promise.

Petitioner's evidence of an express warranty consists largely of statements made in respondents' advertising. . . . [T]he appropriate inquiry is not whether a claim challenges the "propriety" of advertising and promotion, but whether the claim would require the imposition under state law of a requirement or prohibition based on smoking and health with respect to advertising or promotion. . . .

That the terms of the warranty may have been set forth in advertisements, rather than in separate documents, is irrelevant to the preemption issue (though possibly not to the state law issue of whether the alleged warranty is valid and enforceable), because, although the breach of warranty claim is made "with respect to advertising," it does not rest on a duty imposed under state law. Accordingly, to the extent that petitioner has a viable claim for breach of express warranties made by respondents, that claim is not preempted by the 1969 Act.

## Fraudulent Misrepresentation

Petitioner alleges two theories of fraudulent misrepresentation. First, petitioner alleges that respondents, through their advertising, neutralized the effect of federally mandated warning labels. Such a claim is predicated on a state law prohibition against statements in advertising and pro-

motional materials that tend to minimize the health hazards associated with smoking. Such a *prohibition*, however, is merely the converse of a state law *requirement* that warnings be included in advertising and promotional materials. Section 5(b) of the 1969 Act preempts both requirements and prohibitions; it therefore supersedes petitioner's first fraudulent misrepresentation theory. . . .

Petitioner's second theory, as construed by the District Court, alleges intentional fraud and misrepresentation both by "false representation of a material fact [and by] conceal[ment of] a material fact." The predicate of this claim is a state law duty not to make false statements of material fact or to conceal such facts. Our preemption analysis requires us to determine whether such a duty is the sort of requirement or prohibition proscribed by Section 5(b).

Section 5(b) preempts only the imposition of state law obligations "with respect to the advertising or promotion" of cigarettes. Petitioner's claims that respondents concealed material facts are therefore not preempted insofar as those claims rely on a state law duty to disclose such facts through channels of communication other than advertising or promotion. Thus, for example, if state law obliged respondents to disclose material facts about smoking and health to an administrative agency, Section 5(b) would not preempt a state law claim based on a failure to fulfill that obligation.

Moreover, petitioner's fraudulent misrepresentation claims that do arise with respect to advertising and promotions (most notably claims based on allegedly false statements of material fact made in advertisements) are not preempted by Section 5(b). Such claims are not predicated on a duty "based on smoking and health," but rather on a more general obligation—the duty not to deceive. This understanding of fraud by intentional misstatement is appropriate for several reasons. First, in the 1969 Act, Congress offered no sign that it wished to insulate cigarette manufacturers from longstanding rules governing fraud. To the contrary, both the 1965 and the 1969 Acts explicitly reserved the FTC's authority to identify and punish deceptive advertising practices—an authority that the FTC had long exercised and continues to exercise. . . .

Moreover, this reading of "based on smoking and health" is wholly consistent with the purposes of the 1969 Act. State law prohibitions on false statements of material fact do not create "diverse, nonuniform, and confusing" standards. Unlike state law obligations concerning the warning necessary to render a product "reasonably safe," state law proscriptions on intentional fraud rely only on a single, uniform standard: falsity. Thus, we conclude that the phrase "based on smoking and health," fairly but narrowly construed, does not encompass the more general duty not to make fraudulent statements. Accordingly, petitioner's claim based on allegedly fraudulent statements made in respondents' advertisements are not preempted by Section 5(b) of the 1969 Act.

## Conspiracy to Misrepresent or Conceal Material Facts

Petitioner's final claim alleges a conspiracy among respondents to misrepresent or conceal material facts concerning the health hazards of smoking. The predicate duty underlying this claim is a duty not to conspire to commit fraud. For the reasons stated in our analysis of petitioner's intentional fraud claim, this duty is not preempted by Section 5(b), for it is not a prohibition "based on smoking and health" as that phrase is properly construed. Accordingly, we conclude that the 1969 Act does not preempt petitioner's conspiracy claim.

To summarize our holding: the 1965 Act did not preempt state law damages actions; the 1969 Act preempts petitioner's claims based on a failure to warn and the neutralization of federally mandated warnings to the extent that those claims rely on omissions or inclusions in respondents' advertising or promotions; the 1969 Act does not preempt petitioner's claims based on express warranty, intentional fraud and misrepresentation, or conspiracy.

The judgment of the Court of Appeals is accordingly reversed in part and affirmed in part, and the case is remanded for further proceedings consistent with this opinion.

*It is so ordered.*

## Environmental Regulation

Since the dawn of the Industrial Revolution, the Court has recognized the power of the states to regulate land use, promote clean air and water, and protect natural resources. As the growth of the nation's industrial economy ushered in new problems in sanitation, waste disposal, pollution, and land development, the Court found itself drawn into an increasing number of disputes between the private and public sectors over the scope of state power to regulate the environment. In *Georgia* v. *Tennessee Copper Co.* (1907), the Court ruled that it was a "fair and reasonable demand on the part of the sovereign that the air over its territory should not be polluted on a great scale."[44] The state of Georgia had sued a Tennessee copper manufacturer to prevent it from dumping sulphurous fumes across its border that were killing vegetation. The Court upheld a lower court ruling ordering the Tennessee Copper Co. to cease its practices.

Until about 1970 environmental regulation, with the exception of public land management, remained largely a state enterprise. Starting with the passage of the Clear Air Act of 1963, however, Washington began to prod the states to set pollution abatement standards and to formulate implementation directives based on federal guidelines. Perhaps the most important moment in the transformation of the national environmental agenda came in the spring of 1970. On April 20, 1970, hundreds of thousands of people gathered on the Mall in Washington and around the country to celebrate Earth Day, which consisted of a nationwide teach-in on the dangers that an unattended environment posed for the nation's economic and public health. Congress, sensing a powerful and attractive political issue, eagerly embraced the environmental cause, and enacted an ambitious agenda of legislation designed to prevent environmental degradation.[45] Among the landmark pieces of federal environmental legislation in place by the end of the 1970s were the amended Clean Air Acts of 1970, 1972, and 1977; the National Environmental Policy Act of 1969; the enactment of "Superfund" legislation to mandate the cleanup of toxic waste sites; and the Clean Water Act of 1972.

Because environmental regulation has taken on a more complex quality, Congress and the states have, for the most part, worked cooperatively to coordinate their respective policy objectives. The Court has ruled that states are free to enact environmental laws of their own, as long as they do not conflict with congressional objectives. In the field of environmental regulation, as elsewhere, the Court has applied the doctrine of federal preemption to strike a balance between the respective interests of Congress and the states to exercise their commerce and police powers.[46]

The Court, as political scientist Lettie McSpadden has commented, has played an increasingly important role in setting the substance of environmental policy. Since the early 1970s, environmental groups, business interests, and government agencies have resorted to litigation to defend or attack environmental policies. Organizations such as the Sierra Club, the Natural Resources Defense Fund, the Environmental Defense Fund, and the National Audubon Society have used lawsuits to ensure vigorous enforcement of these new congressional mandates. Industries affected by environmental regulation responded by developing litigation capacities to defend their business practices. Government agencies responsible for enforcing environmental policies have found themselves on both sides of the issues, alternately defending their current enforcement of a law or suing another government agency over failing to adhere to the law's mandate.[47]

The Court's treatment of substantive and procedural issues posed by modern environmental regulation is illustrated well in two cases, *City of Philadelphia v. State of New Jersey* (1978) and *Oregon Waste Systems v. Department of Environmental Quality of the State of Oregon* (1994). Solid and toxic waste disposal is one of the major concerns in contemporary environmental policy. At issue in these two cases is the power of the national and state governments to use their regulatory authority to create incentives to comply with environmental mandates. Put more simply, few states have either the interest or incentive to dispose of another state's garbage. What are the similarities and differences in the Court's opinions in *City of Philadelphia* and *Oregon Waste Systems*? Note Chief Justice Rehnquist's dissent in *Oregon Waste Systems*, in which he laments the "dwindling options to the States as they contend with the environmental, health, safety, and political challenges posed by the problem of waste disposal in modern society." Is waste disposal a national problem that properly limits state efforts to deter the use of their landfills by other states? Are states justified in setting limits on the use of their landfill resources to promote their own environmental concerns?

## City of Philadelphia v. State of New Jersey
### 437 U.S. 617 (1978)

A 1973 New Jersey law prohibited the importation of most solid or liquid waste from outside the state. Several private landfill owners in New Jersey had agreements with a number of cities in other states, including Philadelphia,

for waste disposal. The owners brought suit in state court against New Jersey, challenging the constitutionality of the statute. The trial court declared the law unconstitutional. The New Jersey Supreme Court reversed. Philadelphia and the other plaintiffs appealed to the U.S. Supreme Court.

The Court's decision was 7 to 2. Justice Stewart announced the opinion of the Court. Justice Rehnquist, joined by Chief Justice Burger, filed a dissent.

▼▲▼

MR. JUSTICE STEWART delivered the opinion of the Court.

A New Jersey law prohibits the importation of most "solid or liquid waste which originated or was collected outside the territorial limits of the State. . . . " In this case, we are required to decide whether this statutory prohibition violates the Commerce Clause of the United States Constitution.

The . . . provision in question provides:

No person shall bring into this State any solid or liquid waste which originated or was collected outside the territorial limits of the State, except garbage to be fed to swine in the State of New Jersey, until the commissioner [of the State Department of Environmental Protection] shall determine that such action can be permitted without endangering the public health, safety and welfare and has promulgated regulations permitting and regulating the treatment and disposal of such waste in this State.

. . . Although the Constitution gives Congress the power to regulate commerce among the States, many subjects of potential federal regulation under that power inevitably escape congressional attention "because of their local character and their number and diversity." *South Carolina State Highway Dept. v. Barnwell Bros., Inc.* (1938). In the absence of federal legislation, these subjects are open to control by the States so long as they act within the restraints imposed by the Commerce Clause itself. The bounds of these restraints appear nowhere in the words of the Commerce Clause, but have emerged gradually in the decisions of this Court giving effect to its basic purpose. . . .

The opinions of the Court through the years have reflected an alertness to the evils of "economic isolation" and protectionism, while at the same time recognizing that incidental burdens on interstate commerce may be unavoidable when a State legislates to safeguard the health and safety of its people. Thus, where simple economic protectionism is effected by state legislation, a virtually *per se* rule of invalidity has been erected. The clearest example of such legislation is a law that overtly blocks the flow of interstate commerce at a State's borders. But where other legislative objectives are credibly advanced and there is no patent discrimination against interstate trade, the Court has adopted a much more flexible approach . . . .

The crucial inquiry, therefore, must be directed to determining whether ch. 363 is basically a protectionist measure, or whether it can fairly be viewed as a law directed to legitimate local concerns, with effects upon interstate commerce that are only incidental. . . .

[I]t does not matter whether the ultimate aim of ch. 363 is to reduce the waste disposal costs of New Jersey residents or to save remaining open lands from pollution, for we assume New Jersey has every right to protect its residents' pocketbooks, as well as their environment. And it may be assumed as well that New Jersey may pursue those ends by slowing the flow of all waste into the State's remaining landfills, even though interstate commerce may incidentally be affected. But whatever New Jersey's ultimate purpose, it may not be accomplished by discriminating against articles of commerce coming from outside the State unless there is some reason, apart from their origin, to treat them differently. Both on its face and in its plain effect, ch. 363 violates this principle of nondiscrimination.

The Court has consistently found parochial legislation of this kind to be constitutionally invalid, whether the ultimate aim of the legislation was to assure a steady supply of milk by erecting barriers to allegedly ruinous outside competition, or to create jobs by keeping industry within the State, or to preserve the State's financial resources from depletion by fencing out indigent immigrants. In each of these cases, a presumably legitimate goal was sought to be achieved by the illegitimate means of isolating the State from the national economy.

Also relevant here are the Court's decisions holding that a State may not accord its own inhabitants a preferred right of access over consumers in other States to natural resources located within its borders. These cases stand for the basic principle that a, "State is without power to prevent privately owned articles of trade from being shipped and sold in interstate commerce on the ground that they are required to satisfy local demands or because they are needed by the people of the State."

The New Jersey law at issue in this case falls squarely within the area that the Commerce Clause puts off limits to state regulation. On its face, it imposes on out-of-state commercial interests the full burden of conserving the State's remaining landfill space. It is true that, in our previous cases, the scarce natural resource was itself the article of commerce, whereas here the scarce resource and the article of commerce are distinct. But that difference is without consequence. In both instances, the State has overtly moved to slow or freeze the flow of commerce for protectionist reasons. It does not matter that the State has shut the article of commerce inside the State in one case, and outside the State in the other. What is crucial is the attempt by one State to isolate itself from a problem common to many by erecting a barrier against the movement of interstate trade.

The appellees argue that not all laws which facially discriminate against out-of-state commerce are forbidden protectionist regulations. In particular, they point to quarantine laws, which this Court has repeatedly upheld even though they appear to single out interstate commerce for special treatment. In the appellees' view, ch. 363 is analogous to such health-protective measures, since it reduces the exposure of New Jersey residents to the allegedly harmful effects of landfill sites.

It is true that certain quarantine laws have not been considered forbidden protectionist measures, even though they were directed against out-of-state commerce. But those quarantine laws banned the importation of articles such as diseased livestock that required destruction as soon as possible because their very movement risked contagion and other evils. Those laws thus did not discriminate against interstate commerce as such, but simply prevented traffic in noxious articles, whatever their origin.

The New Jersey statute is not such a quarantine law. There has been no claim here that the very movement of waste into or through New Jersey endangers health, or that waste must be disposed of as soon and as close to its point of generation as possible. The harms caused by waste are said to arise after its disposal in landfill sites, and, at that point, as New Jersey concedes, there is no basis to distinguish out-of-state waste from domestic waste. If one is inherently harmful, so is the other. Yet New Jersey has banned the former, while leaving its landfill sites open to the latter. The New Jersey law blocks the importation of waste in an obvious effort to saddle those outside the State with the entire burden of slowing the flow of refuse into New Jersey's remaining landfill sites. That legislative effort is clearly impermissible under the Commerce Clause of the Constitution.

Today, cities in Pennsylvania and New York find it expedient or necessary to send their waste into New Jersey for disposal, and New Jersey claims the right to close its borders to such traffic. Tomorrow, cities in New Jersey may find it expedient or necessary to send their waste into Pennsylvania or New York for disposal, and those States might then claim the right to close their borders. The Commerce Clause will protect New Jersey in the future, just as it protects her neighbors now, from efforts by one State to isolate itself in the stream of interstate commerce from a problem shared by all. The judgment is

Reversed.

## Oregon Waste Systems, Inc. v. Department of Environmental Quality of Oregon
### 511 U.S. 93 (1994)

Oregon imposed a $2.50 per ton surcharge on the instate disposal of solid waste generated in other states and an $0.85 per ton fee on the disposal of waste generated within Oregon. Revenues raised by the surcharge were slated for use by the Oregon Department of Environmental Quality to administer the state's policies for dealing with solid waste. Oregon Waste Systems transported solid waste from Washington State to Oregon. The company brought suit against the Department of Environmental Quality, challenging both the administrative rule setting the out-of-state fee and the law that permitted the Oregon court of appeals to enforce it.

The court rejected the challenge, and the State Supreme Court affirmed. Oregon Waste Systems then appealed to the Supreme Court.

The Court's decision was 7 to 2. Justice Thomas delivered the opinion of the Court. Chief Justice Rehnquist, joined by Justice Blackmun, filed a concurring opinion.

▼▲▼

JUSTICE THOMAS delivered the opinion of the Court.

The Commerce Clause provides that "[t]he Congress shall have Power . . . [t]o regulate Commerce . . . among the several States." Though phrased as a grant of regulatory power to Congress, the Clause has long been understood to have a "negative" aspect that denies the States the power unjustifiably to discriminate against or burden the interstate flow of articles of commerce. The Framers granted Congress plenary authority over interstate commerce in, "the conviction that, in order to succeed, the new Union would have to avoid the tendencies toward economic Balkanization that had plagued relations among the Colonies and later among the States under the Articles of Confederation." "This principle that our economic unit is the Nation, which alone has the gamut of powers necessary to control of the economy, . . . has as its corollary that the states are not separable economic units."

Consistent with these principles, we have held that the first step in analyzing any law subject to judicial scrutiny under the negative Commerce Clause is to determine whether it "regulates evenhandedly with only 'incidental' effects on interstate commerce, or discriminates against interstate commerce." As we use the term here, "discrimination" simply means differential treatment of in-state and out-of-state economic interests that benefits the former and burdens the latter. If a restriction on commerce is discriminatory, it is virtually *per se* invalid. By contrast, nondiscriminatory regulations that have only incidental effects on interstate commerce are valid unless "the burden imposed on such commerce is clearly excessive in relation to the putative local benefits." *Pike* v. *Bruce Church, Inc.* (1970). . . .

Because the Oregon surcharge is discriminatory, the virtually *per se* rule of invalidity provides the proper legal standard here, not the *Pike* balancing test. As a result, the surcharge must be invalidated unless respondents can "sho[w] that it advances a legitimate local purpose that cannot be adequately served by reasonable nondiscriminatory alternatives." Our cases require that justifications for discriminatory restrictions on commerce pass the "strictest scrutiny." The State's burden of justification is so heavy that "facial discrimination by itself may be a fatal defect."

At the outset, we note two justifications that respondents have *not* presented. No claim has been made that the disposal of waste from other States imposes higher costs on Oregon and its political subdivisions than the disposal of in-state waste. Also, respondents have not offered any safety or health reason unique to nonhazardous waste from other States for discouraging the flow of such waste into Oregon. Consequently, respondents must come forward with other legitimate reasons to subject waste from other States to a higher charge than is levied against waste from Oregon.

Respondents offer two such reasons, each of which we address below.

Respondents' principal defense of the higher surcharge on out-of-state waste is that it is a "compensatory tax" necessary to make shippers of such waste pay their "fair share" of the costs imposed on Oregon by the disposal of their waste in the State. In *Chemical Waste*, we noted the possibility that such an argument might justify a discriminatory surcharge or tax on out-of-state waste. In making that observation, we implicitly recognized the settled principle that interstate commerce may be made to "'pay its way.'" "It was not the purpose of the commerce clause to relieve those engaged in interstate commerce from their just share of state tax burden[s]." Nevertheless, one of the central purposes of the Clause was to prevent States from "exacting *more* than a just share" from interstate commerce. . . .

To justify a charge on interstate commerce as a compensatory tax, a State must, as a threshold matter, "identif[y] . . . the [intrastate tax] burden for which the State is attempting to compensate." Once that burden has been identified, the tax on interstate commerce must be shown roughly to approximate—but not exceed—the amount of the tax on intrastate commerce. Finally, the events on which the interstate and intrastate taxes are imposed must be "substantially equivalent"; that is, they must be sufficiently similar in substance to serve as mutually exclusive "prox[ies]" for each other. As Justice Cardozo explained for the Court in *Henneford*, under a truly compensatory tax scheme, "the stranger from afar is subject to no greater burdens as a consequence of ownership than the dweller within the gates. The one pays upon one activity or incident, and the other upon another, but the sum is the same when the reckoning is closed."

Although it is often no mean feat to determine whether a challenged tax is a compensatory tax, we have little difficulty concluding that the Oregon surcharge is not such a tax. Oregon does not impose a specific charge of at least $2.25 per ton on shippers of waste generated in Oregon, for which the out-of-state surcharge might be considered compensatory. In fact, the only analogous charge on the disposal of Oregon waste is $0.85 per ton, approximately one-third of the amount imposed on waste from other States. Respondents' failure to identify a specific charge on intrastate commerce equal to or exceeding the surcharge is fatal to their claim.

Respondents argue that, despite the absence of a specific $2.25 per ton charge on in-state waste, intrastate commerce does pay its share of the costs underlying the surcharge through general taxation. Whether or not that is true is difficult to determine, as "[general] tax payments are received for the general purposes of the [government], and are, upon proper receipt, lost in the general revenues." Even assuming, however, that various other means of general taxation, such as income taxes, could serve as an identifiable intrastate burden roughly equivalent to the out-of-state surcharge, respondents' compensatory tax argument fails because the in-state and out-of-state levies are not imposed on substantially equivalent events. . . .

Respondents' final argument is that Oregon has an interest in spreading the costs of the in-state disposal of Oregon waste to all Oregonians. That is, because all citizens of Oregon benefit from the proper in-state disposal of waste from Oregon, respondents claim it is only proper for Oregon to require them to bear more of the costs of disposing of such waste in the State through a higher general tax burden. At the same time, however, Oregon citizens should not be required to bear the costs of disposing of out-of-state waste, respondents claim. The necessary result of that limited cost-shifting is to require shippers of out-of-state waste to bear the full costs of in-state disposal, but to permit shippers of Oregon waste to bear less than the full cost.

We fail to perceive any distinction between respondents' contention and a claim that the State has an interest in reducing the costs of handling in-state waste. Our cases condemn as illegitimate, however, any governmental interest that is not "unrelated to economic protectionism," and regulating interstate commerce in such a way as to give those who handle domestic articles of commerce a cost advantage over their competitors handling similar items produced elsewhere constitutes such protectionism. To give controlling effect to respondents' characterization of Oregon's tax scheme as seemingly benign cost-spreading would require us to overlook the fact that the scheme necessarily incorporates a protectionist objective as well.

Respondents counter that if Oregon is engaged in any form of protectionism, it is "resource protectionism," not economic protectionism. It is true that by discouraging the flow of out-of-state waste into Oregon landfills, the higher surcharge on waste from other States conserves more space in those landfills for waste generated in Oregon. Recharacterizing the surcharge as resource protectionism hardly advances respondents' cause, however. Even assuming that landfill space is a "natural resource," "a State may not accord its own inhabitants a preferred right of access over consumers in other States to natural resources located within its borders." . . .

We recognize that the States have broad discretion to configure their systems of taxation as they deem appropriate. All we intimate here is that their discretion in this regard, as in all others, is bounded by any relevant limitations of the Federal Constitution, in this case the negative Commerce Clause. Because respondents have offered no legitimate reason to subject waste generated in other States to a discriminatory surcharge approximately three times as high as that imposed on waste generated in Oregon, the surcharge is facially invalid under the negative Commerce Clause. Accordingly, the judgment of the Oregon Supreme Court is reversed, and the cases are remanded for further proceedings not inconsistent with this opinion.

*It is so ordered.*

▼▲▼

# FOR FURTHER READING

Carson, Rachel. *Silent Spring.* New York: Houghton Mifflin, 1994.

Corwin, Edward S. *The Commerce Power Versus States' Rights.* Princeton, N.J.: Princeton University Press, 1936.

Elazar, Daniel J. *American Federalism: A View from the States.* New York: Harper & Row, 1984.

Fehrenbacher, Don E. *Slavery, Law & Politics: The Dred Scott Case in Historical Perspective.* New York: Oxford University Press, 1981.

Schmidhauser, John R. *The Supreme Court as Final Arbiter in Federal-State Relations, 1789–1957.* Chapel Hill: University of North Carolina Press, 1958.

Shaiko, Ronald G. *Voices and Echoes for the Environment: Public Interest Representation in the 1990s and Beyond.* New York: Columbia University Press, 1999.

Shapiro, David L. *Federalism: A Dialogue.* Evanston, Ill.: Northwestern University Press, 1995.

Walker, David B. *The Rebirth of Federalism.* Chatham, N.J.: Chatham House, 1994.

# 8  The Contract Clause

An oral contract, so goes the old expression, is not worth the paper it is written on. If promises made between two or more parties were bound by nothing more than a simple handshake, the vast space that contract law occupies in the legal profession could disappear tomorrow. But civil societies learned long ago that consensual agreements between two or more parties were most often honored when they were written and honored in accordance with the rule of law. Indeed, the idea that individuals have the right to enter into enforceable written contracts represents one of the most basic principles of the Anglo-American legal tradition.

That the Constitution was intended to protect market-based economies of public and private scale and to secure the rights of individuals to acquire and profit from private property are principles so fundamental to its foundation that they were considered inherent in the rights of man prior to the formation of the nation.[1] Alexander Hamilton asserted as much when he wrote in *Federalist* 1 that the Constitution would provide "additional security to the preservation of . . . liberty, and . . . property."[2] The emphasis Hamilton placed on the symbiotic relationship between liberty and property expressed the deep-rooted consensus among the Framers for the doctrine of "vested rights," or the belief that individuals possess a "natural" right to own and benefit from property that no civil government could uproot.

In *Federalist* 10, James Madison devoted much of his explanation of the "numerous advantages offered by a well-constructed union" to the protection conferred by the Constitution upon property owners. Equating the right to acquire property with the "original" rights of man, Madison explained that the "first object" of constitutional government was to protect the unequal abilities of men to acquire and possess private property. So urgent was the need to protect property rights from the masses in the state legislatures that it became the formulating principle that individual rights placed limits on the exercise of majority power. The Framers' decision to create a constitutional right to private property and protect it from democratic revision had numerous consequences on the distribution of political influence and social standing in the early Republic. Madison and numerous other Framers understood and accepted this result as consistent with the theory of natural rights popular at the time.[3] Wrote Madison:

> The latent causes of faction are thus sown into the nature of man; and we see them everywhere brought into different degrees of activity, according to the different circumstances of civil society. A different zeal for opinions concerning religion, concerning government, and many other points, as well of speculation as of practice . . . have, in turn divided mankind into parties, inflamed them with mutual animosity, and rendered them much more disposed to vex and oppress each other than to cooperate for the common good. . . .
>
> But the most common and durable source of factions has been the various and unequal distribution of property.[4]

Rather than attempt to control the differences created by the unequal possession of property by placing constraints on what he believed was an inherent right, Madison argued that "the regulation of these various and interfering interests forms the principal task of modern legislation."[5] The Contract Clause, found in Article 1, Section 10 of the Constitution, which states that "No State shall . . . pass any . . . Law impairing the Obligation of Contracts," was one of several important provisions designed by the Framers to protect and encourage private land ownership and economic development. Anti-Federalist opponents of the Constitution also embraced the "vested rights" doctrine. Their concern was geared toward what level of government should possess the power to encourage and regulate economic growth, not the inherent power of government to do so.[6] This question continued to divide the nation even after the ratification of the Constitution and formed much of the basis for early litigation on the Contract Clause.

The Court's use of the Contract Clause to promote the Federalists' vision of an extended commercial republic reached its zenith under Chief Justice John Marshall. The Contract Clause receded as a major area of litigation by the late 1800s, but the Court was not prepared to abandon its traditional concern for ownership and property rights. Instead, the Court turned to alternative provisions of the Constitution, such as the Due Process Clause of the Fourteenth Amendment, to expand the ownership rights and political autonomy of large national corporations. This dramatic shift in the organization and distribution of labor and capital had profound social and economic consequences.

In response to the Industrial Revolution, which began shortly after the Civil War, state legislatures began to use their police power on a wide scale to enact protective environmental, health, workplace, and other social welfare measures. Businesses affected by such laws, on the other hand, argued that they interfered with the vested rights that came with the ownership of capital. The purpose of legislation should be to remove the impediments to the economic liberties to which all persons were entitled, although persons in this case really meant corporations and small business owners. Before the Industrial Revolution, the Court had upheld laws that advanced a public interest as long as it bore a reasonable relationship to the general health and welfare, even if such legislation impeded ownership rights. But from the late 1800s until the Constitutional Revolution of 1937, the Court stood fast as a near-unconditional ally of American business practices,

regardless of the social and economic dislocation they caused nationwide. After 1937 the Court returned to the requirement that states need demonstrate only a reasonable purpose behind an economic regulation regardless of whether the constitutional challenge originated from the Contract Clause, the Due Process Clause, or the Commerce Clause. The Court has not since deviated from that position.

The cases and materials in this chapter examine a period in American constitutional development that had a substantial and far-reaching impact on the transformation of the nation's economic order. The Contract Clause was a pivotal instrument in the nation's gradual evolution from several agrarian-based regional economies in the early Republic to the national economies of scale that arrived with mass industrialization. The Contract Clause is now, for the most part, considered a dormant provision of the Constitution. At one time, however, it occupied a central place in the Court's vision of the appropriate constitutional relationship between private rights and the public interest.

## Federalist Principles and the Economic Nationalism of John Marshall

How fundamental did the Framers consider the right to enter into contracts free from undue state interference? During the Constitutional Convention, James Madison argued that "[p]roviding more effectually for the security of private rights and the steady dispensation of justice within the states" was a "necessity." Protecting private rights from the "evils" posed by unrestrained state power was "perhaps [more] than anything else" what motivated the call for the Convention.[7] Later, in *Federalist* 44, Madison wrote, "[L]aws impairing the obligation of contracts, are contrary to the first principles of the social compact and to every principle of sound legislation . . . [v]ery properly, therefore, have the convention added this constitutional bulwark in favor of personal security and private rights."[8] This argument was part of Madison's defense of the Constitution's federal structure, which, by design, limited the extent to which states could regulate their economies. Furthermore, wrote Madison:

> The sober people of America are weary of the fluctuating policy which has directed the public councils. They have

seen with regret and indignation that sudden changes and legislative interferences, in cases affecting personal rights, become jobs in the hands of enterprising and influential speculators, and snares to the more industrious and less informed part of the community. They have seen, too, that one legislative interference is but the first link of a long chain of repetitions, every subsequent interference being naturally produced by the effects of the preceding.[9]

The historical record is clear on the Framers' view of the Contract Clause as an important general protection against the sort of "legislative interference" experienced in post–Revolutionary War America. Under the Articles of Confederation, states could and often did pass laws that provided relief to debtors, created currencies that threatened property values, and overturned state court decisions that permitted loan and property foreclosures. The Contract Clause was intended to reverse the fortunes of those who often suffered at the hands of legislation protective of debtors, namely, the landed classes. But the language agreed upon at the Constitutional Convention stated only a general principle and did not answer the more specific questions concerning that clause's scope and application.

Did the Contract Clause restrict the power of states to impair contracts strictly between private parties, or did the clause also include contracts between state and local governments and private parties? The best evidence suggests that the Framers intended for the Contract Clause to include all contracts, whether public or private. Initial drafts of the Contract Clause made reference to "private" contracts, but this adjective was later dropped.[10] Even if a clear assessment of the Framers' intent were possible, it was inevitable that the Supreme Court, a generation removed from the Convention, would have to create and refine constitutional precepts from the unwritten, abstract doctrine of vested rights.

*Fletcher* v. *Peck* (1810) marked not only the Court's first authoritative interpretation of the Contract Clause but also the second of Chief Justice John Marshall's great decisions to expand national power through the exercise of judicial review.[11] The Court's unanimous opinion in *Fletcher* ruled that states were bound in their contractual obligations just the same as private parties, a "momentous" decision that gave real constitutional definition to the scope and substance of the Contract

Clause. Notice that Chief Justice Marshall never mentions the Contract Clause per se in his opinion, writing that Georgia was "restrained, *either* by general principles, which are common to our free institutions, or by the particular provisions of the Constitution."[12] Marshall also used *Fletcher* to affirm the Court's power to declare state laws unconstitutional, flexing its muscle in this regard well before its more explicit affirmation of judicial review in *Hunter* v. *Martin's Lessee* (1816).[13] The SIDEBAR on *Fletcher* offers a detailed account of the great "Yazoo" land swindle that resulted in this litigation.

*Fletcher* appeared to marginalize the Court's decision in *Calder* v. *Bull* (1798), which held that the prohibition on ex post facto laws in Article 1, Section 10, did not extend to civil law.[14] In *Calder*, Justice James Iredell wrote, "Some of the most necessary and important acts of legislation are . . . founded upon the principle, that private rights must yield to public exigencies."[15] Marshall's opinion in *Fletcher* offered no such concession to either the ex post facto laws or the Contract Clause. Instead, Marshall used *Fletcher* to create the constitutional floor on which Marshall built the Court's next great Contract Clause decision, *Dartmouth College* v. *Woodward* (1819).[16]

In 1769, King George III conveyed to the trustees of Dartmouth College, for a period of perpetuity, absolute control over the institution's governance. In 1816, New Hampshire's first Republican governor, William Plumer, with the support of Thomas Jefferson, persuaded the state legislature, also now Republican, to revoke the royal charter that had created Dartmouth. The effect of this law, which expanded the size of the board of trustees, authorized the governor to fill its vacancies, and created an oversight board to review its decisions on finance and personnel, was to turn an almost 150-year-old private college into a state school. Governor Plumer, before and after his election, had railed against Dartmouth's British origins, claiming that it was based upon "principles congenial to monarchy."

In correspondence, Jefferson had indicated his delight with Plumer's characterization of Dartmouth. Jefferson congratulated the governor for his steadfast adherence to republican principle and condemnation of the college's supporters as "lawyers and priests" who believed "the earth belongs to the dead, and not to the living." It was no coincidence that Dartmouth's board of trustees consisted predominantly of once-powerful, old-line Federalists. Dartmouth argued that the legislature's action amounted to a violation of the college's rights as a chartered, private corporation to conduct its internal affairs.[17]

For a 5-1 Court, Chief Justice Marshall held that the charter granted by King George III was tantamount to a contract and thus protected from revocation by the Contract Clause. Marshall rested his decision in considerable part on his conclusion that Dartmouth was a private college. Had Dartmouth been a public corporation, the question of whether the state possessed the power to rescind or alter its charter would have been altogether different. The Court had said as much in *New Jersey v. Wilson* (1815). Even as the Court acknowledged that the Contract Clause did not permit legislatures to revoke tax exemptions created for private entities, it held that states could revise the contractual obligations of civic institutions performing public functions.[18]

But the real innovative qualities of Marshall's *Dartmouth College* opinion lie with its conclusion that private corporations are entitled to the protections of the Contract Clause. Marshall left no doubt that the vested rights doctrine and the constitutional protection afforded it included corporations as well as individuals. The chief justice was sensitive to the increasing role of private corporations in the economic development of the nation. As a staunch supporter of business-oriented economic nationalism, he was determined to provide them with maximum freedom. Public corporations, which were once thought to reflect modes of political organization—counties and cities, for example—had assumed new, more functional responsibilities such as providing transportation, building roads, and maintaining sewage facilities.

Prior to *Dartmouth College*, the Court had ruled, in *Terrett v. Taylor* (1815), that public corporations of either form were within the power of state legislatures to regulate and control, whereas private corporations, consistent with the "principles of natural justice," were to receive much greater protection against legislative interference.[19] *Dartmouth College* erased the earlier distinction created in *Terrett* between private and public corporations and held that both deserved protection from state interference.

In less than a decade, the Court had integrated the doctrine of vested rights into the Constitution via the Contract Clause. After *Dartmouth College*, however, the Court began to retreat from the near-absolutist principles it had developed to limit state interference with public and private contracts. In *Ogden v. Saunders* (1827), a divided Court held that a law releasing debtors from a future contractual commitment to purchase property did not violate the Contract Clause.[20] *Saunders* signaled that internal forces within the Court were at work to reconsider the extent of its earlier Contract Clause decisions, as the direction of its next major such decision, *Charles River Bridge Co. v. Warren Bridge Co.* (1837), made clear. *Saunders* also merits more than a footnote in the annals of constitutional development: The decision marked the first and last time that Chief Justice Marshall dissented on an important question of constitutional law.[21]

## Fletcher v. Peck

### 10 U.S. 87 (1810)

The facts and background of this case are set out in the accompanying SIDEBAR.

The Court's decision was 6 to 1. Chief Justice Marshall delivered the opinion of the Court. Justice Johnson dissented.

▼▲▼

MR. CHIEF JUSTICE MARSHALL delivered the opinion of the Court.

The pleadings being now amended, this cause comes on again to be heard on sundry demurrers, and on a special verdict.

The suit was instituted on several covenants contained in a deed made by John Peck, the defendant in error, conveying to Robert Fletcher, the plaintiff in error, certain lands which were part of a large purchase made by James Gunn and others, in the year 1795, from the State of Georgia, the contract for which was made in the form of a bill passed by the Legislature of that State.

The first count in the declaration set forth a breach in the second covenant contained in the deed. The covenant is, "that the Legislature of the State of Georgia, at the time of passing the act of sale aforesaid, had good right to sell and dispose of the same in manner pointed out by the said act." The breach assigned is that the Legislature had no power to sell.

The plea in bar sets forth the Constitution of the State of Georgia, and avers that the lands sold by the defendant to the plaintiff were within that State. It then sets forth the granting act, and avers the power of the Legislature to sell and dispose of the premises as pointed out by the act.

To this plea the plaintiff below demurred, and the defendant joined in demurrer.

That the Legislature of Georgia, unless restrained by its own Constitution, possesses the power of disposing of the unappropriated lands within its own limits, in such manner as its own judgment shall dictate, is a proposition not to be controverted. The only question, then, presented by this demurrer, for the consideration of the Court is this: did the then Constitution of the State of Georgia prohibit the Legislature to dispose of the lands which were the subject of this contract in the manner stipulated by the contract?

The question whether a law be void for its repugnancy to the Constitution is, at all times, a question of much delicacy, which ought seldom, if ever, to be decided in the affirmative in a doubtful case. The court, when impelled by duty to render such a judgment, would be unworthy of its station could it be unmindful of the solemn obligations which that station imposes. But it is not on slight implication and vague conjecture that the Legislature is to be pronounced to have transcended its powers, and its acts to be considered as void. The opposition between the Constitution and the law should be such that the judge feels a clear and strong conviction of their incompatibility with each other.

In this case, the court can perceive no such opposition. In the Constitution of Georgia, adopted in the year 1789, the court can perceive no restriction on the legislative power which inhibits the passage of the Act of 1795. The court cannot say that, in passing that Act, the Legislature has transcended its powers and violated the Constitution. In overruling the demurrer, therefore, to the first plea, the Circuit Court committed no error.

The third covenant is that all the title which the State of Georgia ever had in the premises had been legally conveyed to John Peck, the grantor. . . .

The lands in controversy vested absolutely in James Gunn and others, the original grantees, by the conveyance of the Governor, made in pursuance of an act of assembly to which the Legislature was fully competent. Being thus in full possession of the legal estate, they, for a valuable consideration, conveyed portions of the land to those who were willing to purchase. If the original transaction was infected with fraud, these purchasers did not participate in it, and had no notice of it. They were innocent. Yet the Legislature of Georgia has involved them in the fate of the first parties to the transaction, and, if the act be valid, has annihilated their rights also.

The Legislature of Georgia was a party to this transaction, and for a party to pronounce its own deed invalid, whatever cause may be assigned for its invalidity, must be considered as a mere act of power which must find its vindication in a train of reasoning not often heard in courts of justice. . . .

If a suit be brought to set aside a conveyance obtained by fraud, and the fraud be clearly proved, the conveyance will be set aside as between the parties, but the rights of third persons who are purchasers without notice, for a valuable consideration, cannot be disregarded. Titles, which, according to every legal test, are perfect are acquired with that confidence which is inspired by the opinion that the purchaser is safe. If there be any concealed defect, arising from the conduct of those who had held the property long before he acquired it, of which he had no notice, that concealed defect cannot be set up against him. He has paid his money for a title good at law; he is innocent, whatever may be the guilt of others, and equity will not subject him to the penalties attached to that guilt. All titles would be insecure, and the intercourse between man and man would be very seriously obstructed if this principle be overturned. . . .

If the Legislature felt itself absolved from those rules of property which are common to all the citizens of the United States, and from those principles of equity which are acknowledged in all our courts, its act is to be supported by its power alone, and the same power may devest any other individual of his lands if it shall be the will of the Legislature so to exert it.

It is not intended to speak with disrespect of the Legislature of Georgia, or of its acts. Far from it. The question is a general question, and is treated as one. For although such powerful objections to a legislative grant as are alleged against this may not again exist, yet the principle on which alone this rescinding act is to be supported may be applied to every case to which it shall be the will of any legislature to apply it. The principle is this: that a legislature may, by its own act, devest the vested estate of any man whatever, for reasons which shall, by itself, be deemed sufficient. . . .

Is the power of the Legislature competent to the annihilation of such title, and to a resumption of the property thus held?

The principle asserted is that one Legislature is competent to repeal any act which a former legislature was competent to pass, and that one legislature cannot abridge the powers of a succeeding legislature.

The correctness of this principle, so far as respects general legislation, can never be controverted. But if an act be done under a law, a succeeding legislature cannot undo it. The past cannot be recalled by the most absolute power. Conveyances have been made, those conveyances have vested legal estate, and, if those estates may be seized by the sovereign authority, still that they originally vested is a fact, and cannot cease to be a fact.

When, then, a law is in its nature a contract, when absolute rights have vested under that contract, a repeal of the law cannot devest those rights; and the act of annulling them, if legitimate, is rendered so by a power applicable to the case of every individual in the community.

It may well be doubted whether the nature of society and of government does not prescribe some limits to the legislative power; and, if any be prescribed, where are they to be found if the property of an individual, fairly and honestly acquired, may be seized without compensation?

To the Legislature all legislative power is granted, but the question whether the act of transferring the property of an individual to the public be in the nature of the legislative power is well worthy of serious reflection.

It is the peculiar province of the legislature to prescribe general rules for the government of society; the application of those rules to individuals in society would seem to be the duty of other departments. How far the power of giving the law may involve every other power, in cases where the Constitution is silent, never has been, and perhaps never can be, definitely stated.

The validity of this rescinding act, then, might well be doubted, were Georgia a single sovereign power. But Georgia cannot be viewed as a single, unconnected, sovereign power, on whose legislature no other restrictions are imposed than may be found in its own Constitution. She is a part of a large empire; she is a member of the American Union; and that Union has a Constitution the supremacy of which all acknowledge, and which imposes limits to the legislatures of the several States which none claim a right to pass. The Constitution of the United States declares that no State shall pass any bill of attainder, ex post facto law, or law impairing the obligation of contracts.

Does the case now under consideration come within this prohibitory section of the Constitution?

In considering this very interesting question, we immediately ask ourselves what is a contract? Is a grant a contract?

A contract is a compact between two or more parties, and is either executory or executed. An executory contract is one in which a party binds himself to do, or not to do, a particular thing; such was the law under which the conveyance was made by the Governor. A contract executed is one in which the object of contract is performed, and this, says Blackstone, differs in nothing from a grant. The contract between Georgia and the purchasers was executed by the grant. A contract executed, as well as one which is executory, contains obligations binding on the parties. A grant, in its own nature, amounts to an extinguishment of the right of the grantor, and implies a contract not to reassert that right. A party is therefore always estopped by his own grant.

Since, then, in fact, a grant is a contract executed, the obligation of which still continues, and since the Constitution uses the general term "contract" without distinguishing between those which are executory and those which are executed, it must be construed to comprehend the latter as well as the former. A law annulling conveyances between individuals, and declaring that the grantors should stand seized of their former estates, notwithstanding those grants, would be as repugnant to the Constitution as a law discharging the vendors of property from the obligation of executing their contracts by conveyances. It would be strange if a contract to convey was secured by the Constitution, while an absolute conveyance remained unprotected.

If, under a fair construction of the Constitution, grants are comprehended under the term "contracts," is a grant from the State excluded from the operation of the provision? Is the clause to be considered as inhibiting the State from impairing the obligation of contracts between two individuals, but as excluding from that inhibition contracts made with itself?

The words themselves contain no such distinction. They are general, and are applicable to contracts of every description. If contracts made with the State are to be exempted from their operation, the exception must arise from the character of the contracting party, not from the words which are employed.

Whatever respect might have been felt for the State sovereignties, it is not to be disguised that the framers of the Constitution viewed with some apprehension [10 U.S. 138] the violent acts which might grow out of the feelings of the moment, and that the people of the United States, in adopting that instrument, have manifested a

## FLETCHER V. PECK

### *The Great Yazoo Land Caper*

Tales of corruption and greed in politics usually elicit nothing more than a lazy yawn from most citizens. After all, goes the common refrain, don't they *all* do it? Rarely is there a pause to think about just what exactly the "it" is that all politicians are apparently doing. Still, one can hardly blame a public cynical about the trustworthiness of its elected officials. Rarely a week goes by that some politician, from the president of the United States on down, is not being accused, investigated, indicted, tried, or convicted of some criminal offense. Even more common than alleged criminal or civil misbehavior are news stories that paint politicians as captive to powerful "special interests," usually wealthy corporate or individual campaign donors who expect favors in return. These stories usually end with demands for reform or bits of quoted populist wisdom from an "average" American, who wonders who will stick up for the little people. Little does anything change, however.

But even a generation that has come of political age in the post-Watergate era and endured the endless media coverage of President Clinton's affair with former White House intern, Monica Lewinsky, would have been stunned by the events surrounding the great Yazoo land fraud of 1795, one of the all-time great political scandals in American history. Bribery, nepotism, unethical business practices, and conflicts of interest involving some of the great American statesmen of the day—in other words, all the elements necessary for great political theater—were on display in the Yazoo scandal. Because the scandal was, at bottom, a political one, the job of resolving the economic and political forces in competition with each other ultimately fell to the Court. The result was *Fletcher* v. *Peck*, Chief Justice John Marshall's first great Contract Clause opinion and one of the Court's most important early statements on the limits of government power to interfere with the contractual arrangements between two parties.

The Yazoo scandal got its name from the great Yazoo River and surrounding land, encompassing much of what is now northern Mississippi. This region was the object of intensely competitive land speculation in the late 1700s. Three Indian tribes once inhabited this land, along with most of what is now Alabama. The area belonged to Georgia and was described on maps as the Georgia Western territory. Land speculation was to the late 1700s and early 1800s what high-stakes financial and stock transactions are to most Americans today: an enticing way to make a lot of money with a small investment, assuming, of course, that the gamble pays off. So popular was land speculation among the financial entrepreneurs of the time that it led one English visitor to declare in 1802: "Were I to characterize the United States, it should be by the appellation of the *land of speculation.*"

By the 1780s, Georgia had emerged as the magnet for land speculators looking to make a quick fortune. The first reason for this development was that Georgia possessed an inordinate amount of western lands.

Unlike other states holding western territories, such as Connecticut, New York, Virginia, and Massachusetts, Georgia decided not to cede its land titles to the United States. Georgia's territories stretched from west of the Chattahoochee River, then the state's western boundary with Alabama, to the Mississippi River and south from what is now Tennessee to western Spanish Florida, located in the state's panhandle. The other reason was that Georgia's land authorities played fast and loose with their properties, either giving outright large parcels of land to speculators in return for kickbacks or selling the land at such undervalued prices that a tidy profit was all but certain.

Georgia's first effort to promote speculation in the Yazoo lands came in 1789, when the state legislature agreed to sell almost 16 million acres to three land companies organized expressly for this transaction, one of which was headed by Patrick Henry. The deal fell apart when Spain, which claimed the land south of the Yazoo River, encouraged a confederation of Indian tribes to attack the frontier settlements there to discourage future colonization. President Washington also issued a stern warning to land speculators not to violate the rights of the Indian tribes in the Yazoo region retained under their treaties with the federal government.

Stalled for the moment, land speculators regrouped and reorganized, waiting for the right confluence of politics and economics to reopen opportunities in the Yazoo lands. In 1795 the Georgia legislature passed a bill permitting state authorities to sell 35 million acres of land to four land companies for the grand total of $500,000, or less than 1.5 cents per acre. Controlled by speculators primarily from Georgia and Pennsylvania, the land companies boasted as investors some of the nation's most well-known political figures. These

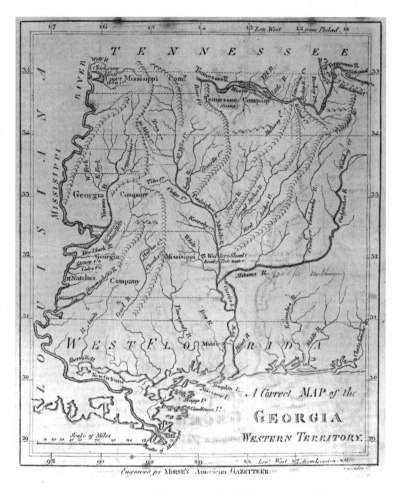

*A map of the Yazoo lands, which were part of the western territories of Georgia until the early 1800s.*
Courtesy of the Trustees of the Boston Public Library.

included Supreme Court Justice James Wilson; two members of Congress, Thomas Carnes and Robert Goodloe Harper; two senators, James Gunn and Robert Morris; and a host of individuals prominent in state and local politics. In geographic terms, Georgia divested itself of two-thirds of the land it held west of the Chattahoochee. All told, the Georgia Mississippi Co., the Tennessee Co., the Georgia Co., and the Upper Mississippi Co. snagged the greatest deal in real estate history.

Too good to be true? Seems that it was, as word slowly leaked out to the people of Georgia that their representatives either held substantial shares in the lands they sold for next to nothing or had been bribed outright in exchange for their vote. Led by one of Georgia's most colorful and well-known populists, James Jackson, anti-Yazoo forces organized a state-wide campaign to force the legislature to rescind the 1795 sale. After a series of public hearings and grand jury investigations on the sale of the Yazoo lands turned up incontrovertible evidence of the corrupt relationship between the land companies and state legislators, Georgians expressed their outrage by replacing virtually the entire state legislature in 1796.

The new legislature wasted no time in going after the Yazoo land companies. It passed the Georgia Repeal Act of 1796, which rescinded the sale of the lands and, in a measure of pure spite, authorized the destruction of all the records of the Yazoo transaction. But the legislature's most controversial action, and the one that resulted in the litigation that led to *Fletcher,* was its refusal to return the $500,000 payment the four Yazoo land companies had made under the 1795 law.

As a result, Georgia was now in control of all the Yazoo lands *and* the money of the despised land companies. In the interim, however, several of the original purchasers had already sold shares of their acreage to other willing investors, many of whom were blissfully unaware of how the sellers had obtained their land. Robert Fletcher was one such individual who found himself on the ropes after Georgia repealed the 1795 Yazoo sale. Although a seasoned speculator, Fletcher had no ties to the trail of deceit behind the Yazoo deal when he bought fifteen thousand acres of land from John Peck in January 1795. Peck, a director of the New England Mississippi Land Co., owned 600,000 acres of Yazoo lands, which he had purchased from John Gunn, a major mover behind the original Yazoo deal. After Georgia passed the Repeal Act of 1796, Fletcher was stripped of his property and his money. Claiming that the Contract Clause barred a state from annulling a private contract between two parties, Fletcher filed suit in federal court to have the Georgia Repeal Act declared unconstitutional.

Fletcher's lawsuit was unusual because it was collusive; that is, it was brought in conjunction with John Peck to receive a judicial determination on the status of the Yazoo lands. If a court ruled that Fletcher was entitled to his land, then Peck would get to keep the proceeds of his sale. Collusive suits are now prohibited under the Court's own reading of the Constitution's Article III requirement that a case or controversy must be present for a lawsuit to go forward in federal court. In other words, an adversarial relationship must exist between the parties.

Quite aware of the importance of the constitutional question presented in the case, Chief Justice John Marshall chose to address the substantive legal questions in *Fletcher* v. *Peck* rather than dismiss the case on procedural grounds. The political and legal entanglement of the Yazoo land deal was not unfamiliar to Marshall. While serving Virginia in the House of Representatives before his ascension to the Court, Marshall had voted for an amendment sponsored by Georgia senator and chief Yazooist James Gunn that provided compensation to speculators whose land was seized by the Georgia Repeal Act. His opinion in *Fletcher* navigated a fine line between the need to resolve a major Contract Clause question and his knowledge of the "impure motives" and "corruption" involved in the Yazoo sale.

Presidents Adams, Jefferson, and Madison each tried to negotiate a settlement between Congress, the land companies, populist reformers, and the third parties whose claims converged on the axis of money, power, and politics that centered on the Yazoo lands. Finally, in 1814, Congress indemnified all the Yazoo landholders by authorizing a $5-million buyout of their claims, laying to rest, with a political solution, what had been from the start a political problem.

## References

Hall, Kermit L., William M. Wiecek, and Paul Finkelman. *American Legal History: Cases and Materials.* New York: Oxford University Press, 1991.

McGrath, C. Peter. *Yazoo: Law and Politics in the New Republic.* Providence, R.I.: Brown University Press, 1966.

determination to shield themselves and their property from the effects of those sudden and strong passions to which men are exposed. The restrictions on the legislative power of the States are obviously founded in this sentiment, and the Constitution of the United States contains what may be deemed a bill of rights for the people of each State. . . .

It is, then, the unanimous opinion of the Court that, in this case, the estate having passed into the hands of a purchaser for a valuable consideration, without notice, the State of Georgia was restrained, either by general principles which are common to our free institutions or by the particular provisions of the Constitution of the United States, from passing a law whereby the estate of the plaintiff in the premises so purchased could be constitutionally and legally impaired and rendered null and void.

## Trustees of Dartmouth College v. Woodward

### 17 U.S. 518 (1819)

In 1769, King George III granted a charter establishing Dartmouth College in Hanover, New Hampshire, one the original thirteen colonies. The charter created a twelve-member board of trustees with full governing authority over the college. The board also was authorized to fill any vacancies by appointing its own successors. In 1816 the New Hampshire legislature amended the Dartmouth charter to expand the size of its board of trustees to twenty-one, and gave the governor the power to appoint new members. The law also established a board of overseers, whose members the governor appointed. The board of overseers had veto power over any decision made by the board of trustees. As a final measure the state now assumed control of Dartmouth.

The origins of the 1816 law were decidedly political. Dartmouth's second president, John Wheelcock, ran into the consistent problems with the board of trustees, which was dominated by Federalist party activists. Some have argued that Wheelcock's problems were self-inflicted, since he only came to the job by virtue of his father, Eleazar Wheelcock, who served as Dartmouth's first president. To protect himself, John Wheelcock formed an alliance with the Jeffersonian Republicans who had ascended to power in the state legislature.

The old trustees refused to recognize the law. As the two sides in this political battle continued to feud, the college, renamed Dartmouth University under the 1816 law, went into a tailspin, as faculty, students, and staff found themselves caught in the middle. The old trustees were unsuccessful in the state courts. Ever determined, the trustees appealed to the Supreme Court, which agreed to hear the case. Still, the trustees needed a break, and, fortunately for them, they got one. Daniel Webster, a graduate of the Dartmouth class of 1801 and one of the nation's preeminent lawyers, agreed to represent them.

In those days lawyers were not limited to the half-hour per side to make their case, as is the rule now. They could take as long as they wanted, and the more gifted orators, such as Webster, often did. Webster spent four hours in oral argument before the Court, concluding with one of his most famous passages:

> Sir, you may destroy this little institution. It is weak. It is in your hands! I know it is one of the lesser lights in the literary horizon of the country. You may put it out. But if you do so, you must carry though your work. You must extinguish, one after another, all those great lights of science, which, for more than a century, have thrown their radiance over our land.
>
> It is, Sir, as I have said, a small college and yet, there are those who love it. . . .

The decision was 6 to 1. Chief Justice Marshall delivered the opinion of the Court. Justices Washington and Story filed concurring opinions. Justice Duvall dissented.

MR. CHIEF JUSTICE MARSHALL delivered the opinion of the Court.

It can require no argument to prove that the circumstances of this case constitute a contract. An application is made to the Crown for a charter to incorporate a religious and literary institution. In the application, it is stated that large contributions have been made for the object, which will be conferred on the corporation as soon as it shall be created. The charter is granted, and on its faith the property is conveyed. Surely, in this transaction, every ingredient of a complete and legitimate contract is to be found. The points for consideration are, 1. Is this contract protected by the Constitution of the United States? 2. Is it impaired by the acts under which the defendant holds?

1. [I]t has been argued that the word "contract," in its broadest sense, would comprehend the political relations

between the government and its citizens, would extend to offices held within a State, for State purposes, and to many of those laws concerning civil institutions, which must change with circumstances and be modified by ordinary legislation, which deeply concern the public, and which, to preserve good government, the public judgment must control. That even marriage is a contract, and its obligations are affected by the laws respecting divorces. That the clause in the Constitution, if construed in its greatest latitude, would prohibit these laws. Taken in its broad, unlimited sense, the clause would be an unprofitable and vexatious interference with the internal concerns of a State, would unnecessarily and unwisely embarrass its legislation, and render immutable those civil institutions, which are established for purposes of internal government, and which, to subserve those purposes, ought to vary with varying circumstances. That, as the framers of the Constitution could never have intended to insert in that instrument a provision so unnecessary, so mischievous, and so repugnant to its general spirit, the term "contract" must be understood in a more limited sense. That it must be understood as intended to guard against a power of at least doubtful utility, the abuse of which had been extensively felt, and to restrain the legislature in future from violating the right to property. . . .

The parties in this case differ less on general principles, less on the true construction of the Constitution in the abstract, than on the application of those principles to this case and on the true construction of the charter of 1769. This is the point on which the cause essentially depends. If the act of incorporation be a grant of political power, if it create a civil institution, to be employed in the administration of the government, or if the funds of the college be public property, or if the State of New Hampshire, as a government, be alone interested in its transactions, the subject is one in which the legislature of the State may act according to its own judgment, unrestrained by any limitation of its power imposed by the Constitution of the United States.

Dartmouth College is an eleemosynary institution incorporated for the purpose of perpetuating the application of the bounty of the donors to the specified objects of that bounty; that its Trustees or Governors were originally named by the founder and invested with the power of perpetuating themselves; that they are not public officers, nor is it a civil institution, participating in the administration of government, but a charity school or a seminary of education incorporated for the preservation of its property and the perpetual application of that property to the objects of its creation. . . .

This is plainly a contract to which the donors, the Trustees, and the Crown (to whose rights and obligations New Hampshire succeeds) were the original parties. It is a contract made on a valuable consideration. It is a contract for the security and disposition of property. It is a contract on the faith of which real and personal estate has been conveyed to the corporation. It is, then, a contract within the letter of the Constitution, and within its spirit also, unless the fact that the property is invested by the donors in Trustees for the promotion of religion and education, for the benefit of persons who are perpetually changing, though the objects remain the same, shall create a particular exception taking this case out of the prohibition contained in the Constitution.

It is more than possible that the preservation of rights of this description was not particularly in the view of the framers of the Constitution when the clause under consideration was introduced into that instrument. It is probable that interferences of more frequent occurrence, to which the temptation was stronger, and of which the mischief was more extensive, constituted the great motive for imposing this restriction on the State legislatures. But although a particular and a rare case may not, in itself, be of sufficient magnitude to induce a rule, yet it must be governed by the rule, when established, unless some plain and strong reason for excluding it can be given. It is not enough to say that this particular case was not in the mind of the convention when the article was framed, nor of the American people when it was adopted. It is necessary to go further and to say that, had this particular case been suggested, the language would have been so varied as to exclude it, or it would have been made a special exception. The case, being within the words of the rule, must be within its operation likewise, unless there be something in the literal construction so obviously absurd or mischievous or repugnant to the general spirit of the instrument as to justify those who expound the Constitution in making it an exception. . . .

The opinion of the Court, after mature deliberation, is that this is a contract the obligation of which cannot be impaired without violating the Constitution of the United States. This opinion appears to us to be equally supported by reason and by the former decisions of this Court.

2. We next proceed to the inquiry whether its obligation has been impaired by those acts of the Legislature of New Hampshire to which the special verdict refers.

From the review of this charter which has been taken, it appears that the whole power of governing the College, of appointing and removing tutors, of fixing their salaries, of directing the course of study to be pursued by the students, and of filling up vacancies created in their own body, was vested in the Trustees. On the part of the Crown, it was expressly stipulated that this corporation thus constituted should continue forever, and that the number of Trustees should forever consist of twelve, and no more. By this contract, the Crown was bound, and could have made no violent alteration in its essential terms without impairing its obligation.

The founders of the College contracted not merely for the perpetual application of the funds which they gave, to the objects for which those funds were given; they contracted also to secure that application by the constitution of the corporation. They contracted for a system which should, so far as human foresight can provide, retain forever the government of the literary institution they had formed in the hands of persons approved by themselves. This system is totally changed. The charter of 1769 exists no longer. It is reorganized, and reorganized in such a manner as to convert a literary institution, moulded according to the will of its founders, and placed under the control of private literary men, into a machine entirely subservient to the will of government. This may be for the advantage of this College in particular, and may be for the advantage of literature in general, but it is not according to the will of the donors, and is subversive of that contract on the faith of which their property was given.

It results from this opinion that the acts of the Legislature of New Hampshire are repugnant to the Constitution of the United States. [R]eversed.

▼▲▼

## Jacksonian Democracy Comes to the Court: States' Rights and Dual Federalism

In the decision in *Charles River Bridge,* the Court clearly showed that it was prepared to pursue a new and different path on the Contract Clause. Under Chief Justice Roger Taney, the Court would depart from the Marshall Court's tightly knit noose around the power of state legislatures to regulate economic and business transactions. *Charles River Bridge* involved a dispute between two companies over the construction of a bridge over the Charles River, which runs between Boston and Cambridge. The Massachusetts legislature had authorized the Charles River Bridge Co. in 1785 to build such a bridge and charge a toll for ferry travel, a percentage of which was to be paid to Harvard College. In 1832 the legislature authorized the Warren Bridge Co. to build a

another bridge over the Charles River, approximately three hundred yards from the site of the original bridge, even though the legislature had extended the Charles River Bridge Co.'s corporate charter in 1792 for an additional seventy years.

Moreover, the legislature had decided not to charge a toll for the use of the new bridge. Charles River Bridge Co. claimed that Massachusetts had violated the terms of its earlier contract, which implied exclusive control to operate a bridge over the Charles. The dispute, as framed by the parties, also made *Charles River Bridge* an important test of state power to discourage monopolies. In fact, constitutional historian Charles Warren regards *Charles River Bridge,* along with *Gibbons* v. *Ogden* (1824), the most important of John Marshall's great Commerce Clause decisions, as two of the seminal antitrust cases decided by the Court in the nineteenth century.[22]

A 5-2 Court rejected Charles River Bridge Co.'s position that its corporate charter implied an exclusive right to operate a bridge. The Court's opinion reflected the views of its new chief justice and former Treasury secretary, Roger B. Taney, appointed by President Andrew Jackson to replace John Marshall, who died in 1835. Chief Justice Taney, in the first of several influential opinions that would leave a firm imprint on American constitutional development, held that states were well within their police powers to enact regulations on behalf of the public interest, even if these rules, in the strictest sense, upset private contractual arrangements. "The object and end of all government," wrote Taney, "is to promote the happiness and prosperity of the community by which it is established; and it can never be assumed, that the government intended to diminish its power of accomplishing the end for which it was created . . . [t]he state police power . . . would be of no great value, if by implications and presumptions, it was disarmed of the powers necessary to accomplish the ends of its creation and the functions it was designed to perform transferred into the hands of privileged corporations."[23]

What would Marshall have thought of Taney's decision? Here was Andrew Jackson's long-time political confidant implementing his philosophy of states' rights through judicial review. Marshall, the consummate Federalist and economic nationalist, had brilliantly handcrafted the still-newborn provisions of the Constitution to advance the interests of the large, commercial republic envisioned by founding statesmen such as Hamilton, Madison, and John Adams through the very same means. Indeed, could language such as Taney's in *Charles River Bridge,* "We cannot deal thus with the rights reserved to the States, and by legal intendments . . . take away from them any portion of that power over their own internal police and improvement, which is so necessary to their well-being and improvement," ever have flowed from Marshall's quill?

But the 1830s were no longer Marshall's time. Economic depression, social disorder, and the political dissatisfaction that accompanied such problems had emerged to a greater degree than ever before. Legislative responses by the states to address these concerns had become more common. Rather than set aside such efforts as inconsistent with the vested rights doctrine that Marshall had codified into constitutional law, the Court under Chief Justice Taney and Jackson's four other appointees was prepared to return power to the states. Consistent with the principles of Jacksonian democracy, the Court believed the states were better tuned to the health and welfare needs of their people than the national government.

Economic nationalism, which Marshall had done so much to encourage through his judicial opinions, reached its constitutional high-water mark by the time of Taney's ascent to the Court. In its place was the Jackson-Taney doctrine of *dual federalism,* which emphasized the political and economic independence of the states from national obligations. This conception of the constitutional structure of American federalism was precisely the antithesis of the constitutional vision Marshall had for the Court during his thirty-four years as chief justice. Even the great Daniel Webster, the senior senator from Massachusetts who represented the Charles River Bridge Co., was unable to muster his legendary powers of oration and legal scholarship to persuade the Court that legislative interests should remain subservient to the doctrine of vested rights. Such an argument had proven successful when Webster represented Dartmouth College in 1819. But, as Webster discovered, Federalist economics and Jacksonian democracy did not mix. *Charles River Bridge* demonstrated that the Court under Roger Taney was firmly allied with the latter.

## Charles River Bridge Co. v. Warren Bridge Co.
### 36 U.S. 420 (1837)

The facts and background of this case are set out on pp. 431–432.

Daniel Webster once again came to the defense of the principles of Federalist economic nationalism. Although the Charles River Bridge Co. lost in the Massachusetts courts, Webster had every reason to believe that his appeal to the United States Supreme Court would succeed. When the Court agreed to hear the case in 1831, John Marshall still commanded the Court's center chair. To Webster's chagrin, the Court was unable to reach a decision after the initial argument and set the case for reargument in 1833. The justices remained divided, and the Court slated the case for a third set of oral arguments in 1837. By then the last bastion of Federalist power, the federal judiciary, had receded into the mists. Constitutional law would soon reflect the states' rights orientation of Andrew Jackson, whose election in 1828 had offered a telling indication that the days of the Federalist ascendancy were over. Symbolic of the seismic shift that loomed in American constitutional development was the replacement of Chief Justice Marshall, who died in 1835, with Roger Taney. Of Taney's appointment, Webster is said to have remarked, "The Constitution is gone."

The Constitution ultimately survived, in spite of Chief Justice Taney's opinion in *Dred Scott* v. *Sandford* (1857), but the Charles River Bridge did not. By 1900 the final pieces of the famous old bridge were hauled away. In its place the Boston Transit Commission authorized the construction of the Charlestown Bridge, built with steel and stone, which still stands.

The Court's decision was 5 to 2. Chief Justice Taney announced the decision of the Court. Justice McLean delivered an opinion claiming the Court had no jurisdiction to hear the case. Justice Story, joined by Justice Thompson, dissented.

▼▲▼

CHIEF JUSTICE TANEY delivered the opinion of the Court.

A good deal of evidence has been offered, to show the nature and extent of the ferry right granted to the college, and also to show the rights claimed by the proprietors of the bridge, at different times by virtue of their charter, and the opinions entertained by committees of the Legislature and others upon that subject. . . .

The plaintiffs in error insist . . . the Legislature had not the power to establish another ferry on the same line of travel, because it would infringe the rights of the college, and that these rights, upon the erection of the bridge in the place of the ferry under the charter of 1785, were transferred to, and became vested in "The Proprietors of the Charles River Bridge," and that under, and by virtue of this transfer of the ferry right, the rights of the bridge company were as exclusive in that line of travel as the rights of the ferry . . . that the Legislature would not authorize another bridge, and especially, a free one, by the side of this, and placed in the same line of travel, whereby the franchise granted to the "Proprietors of the Charles River Bridge" should be rendered of no value . . . and that the law authorizing the erection of the Warren Bridge in 1828 impairs the obligation of one or both of these contracts. . . .

[T]he object and end of all government is to promote the happiness and prosperity of the community by which it is established, and it can never be assumed that the government intended to diminish its power of accomplishing the end for which it was created. And in a country like ours, free, active and enterprising, continually advancing in numbers and wealth, new channels of communication are daily found necessary, both for travel and trade, and are essential to the comfort, convenience and prosperity of the people. A State ought never to be presumed to surrender this power, because, like the taxing power, the whole community have an interest in preserving it undiminished. And when a corporation alleges that a State has surrendered, for seventy years, its power of improvement and public accommodation in a great and important line of travel, along which a vast number of its citizens must daily pass, the community have a right to insist, in the language of this Court, above quoted, "that its abandonment ought not to be presumed in a case in which the deliberate purpose of the State to abandon it does not appear." The continued existence of a government would be of no great value if, by implications and presumptions, it was disarmed of the powers necessary to accomplish the ends of its creation, and the functions it was designed to perform transferred to the hands of privileged corporations. The rule of construction announced by the Court was not confined to the taxing power, nor is it so limited in the opinion delivered. On the contrary, it was distinctly placed on the ground that the interests of the community were concerned in preserving undiminished the power then in

question, and whenever any power of the State is said to be surrendered or diminished, whether it be the taxing power or any other affecting the public interest, the same principle applies, and the rule of construction must be the same. No one will question that the interests of the great body of the people of the state would, in this instance be affected by the surrender of this great line of travel to a single corporation, with the right to exact toll and exclude competition for seventy years. While the rights of private property are sacredly guarded, we must not forget that the community also have rights, and that the happiness and wellbeing of every citizen depends on their faithful preservation.

Adopting the rule of construction above stated as the settled one, we proceed to apply it to the charter of 1785, to the proprietors of the Charles River Bridge. This act of incorporation is in the usual form, and the privileges such as are commonly given to corporations of that kind. It confers on them the ordinary faculties of a corporation for the purpose of building the bridge, and establishes certain rates of toll which the company are authorized to take; this is the whole grant. There is no exclusive privilege given to them over the waters of Charles River, above or below their bridge, no right to erect another bridge themselves, nor to prevent other persons from erecting one, no engagement from the State that another shall not be erected, and no undertaking not to sanction competition, nor to make improvements that may diminish the amount of its income. Upon all these subjects the charter is silent, and nothing is said in it about a line of travel, so much insisted on in the argument, in which they are to have exclusive privileges. No words are used from which an intention to grant any of these rights can be inferred. If the plaintiff is entitled to them, it must be implied, simply, from the nature of the grant, and cannot be inferred from the words by which the grant is made.

The relative position of the Warren Bridge has already been described. It does not interrupt the passage over the Charles River Bridge, nor make the way to it, or from it, less convenient. None of the faculties or franchises granted to that corporation has been revoked by the Legislature, and its right to take the tolls granted by the charter remains unaltered. In short, all the franchises and rights of property enumerated in the charter and there mentioned to have been granted to it remain unimpaired. But its income is destroyed by the Warren Bridge, which, being free, draws off the passengers and property which would have gone over it and renders their franchise of no value. This is the gist of the complainant, for it is not pretended that the erection of the Warren Bridge would have

*The Massachusetts legislature's decision to permit the construction of the Warren Bridge after having once granted an exclusive charter to the Charles River Bridge Company to operate its own bridge touched off a major controversy over the government's obligation to protect property rights while promoting the public interest.*
Culver Pictures.

done them any injury, or in any degree affected their right of property, if it had not diminished the amount of their tolls. In order, then, to entitle themselves to relief, it is necessary to show that the Legislature contracted not to do the act of which they complain, and that they impaired, or, in other words, violated, that contract by the erection of the Warren Bridge.

The inquiry, then, is does the charter contain such a contract on the part of the state? Is there any such stipulation to be found in that instrument? It must be admitted on all hands that there is none—no words that even relate to another bridge, or to the diminution of their tolls, or to the line of travel. If a contract on that subject can be gathered from the charter, it must be by implication, and cannot be found in the words used. Can such an agreement be implied? . . .

Indeed, the practice and usage of almost every State in the Union old enough to have commenced the work of internal improvement is opposed to the doctrine contended for on the part of the plaintiffs in error. Turnpike roads have been made in succession, on the same line of travel, the later ones interfering materially with the profits of the first. These corporations have, in some instances, been utterly ruined by the introduction of newer and better modes of transportation and traveling. In some cases, railroads have rendered the turnpike roads on the same line of travel so entirely useless that the franchise of the turnpike corporation is not worth preserving. Yet in none of these cases have the corporation supposed that their privileges were invaded, or any contract violated on the part of the state. Amid the multitude of cases which have occurred, and have been daily occurring, for the last forty or fifty years, this is the first instance in which such an implied contract has been contended for and this Court called upon to infer it from an ordinary act of incorporation containing nothing more than the usual stipulations and provisions to be found in every such law. The absence of any such controversy, when there must have been so many occasions to give rise to it, proves that neither states nor individuals nor corporations ever imagined that such a contract could be implied from such charters. It shows that the men who voted for these laws never imagined that they were forming such a contract, and if we maintain that they have made it, we must create it by a legal fiction, in opposition to the truth of the fact and the obvious intention of the party. We cannot deal thus with the rights reserved to the states, and, by legal intendments and mere technical reasoning, take away from them any portion of that power over their own internal police and improvement, which is so necessary to their wellbeing and prosperity. . . .

[Affirmed]

JUSTICE STORY, dissenting. . . .

I maintain that, upon the principles of common reason and legal interpretation, the present grant carries with it a necessary implication that the Legislature shall do no act to destroy or essentially to impair the franchise, that (as one of the learned judges of the State court expressed it) there is an implied agreement that the State will not grant another bridge between Boston and Charlestown, so near as to draw away the custom from the old one, and (as another learned judge expressed it) that there is an implied agreement of the State to grant the undisturbed use of the bridge and its tolls so far as respects any acts of its own or of any persons acting under its authority. In other words, the State impliedly contracts not to resume its grant or to do any act to the prejudice or destruction of its grant. I maintain that there is no authority or principle established in relation to the construction of Crown grants, or legislative grants, which does not concede and justify this doctrine. . . . I maintain that a different doctrine is utterly repugnant to all the principles of the common law, applicable to all franchises of a like nature, and that we must overturn some of the best securities of the rights of property before it can be established. I maintain that the common law is the birthright of every citizen of Massachusetts, and that he holds the title deeds of his property, corporeal and incorporeal, under it. I maintain that, under the principles of the common law, there exists no more right in the Legislature of Massachusetts to erect the Warren Bridge, to the ruin of the franchise of the Charles River Bridge, than exists to transfer the latter to the former, or to authorize the former to demolish the latter. If the Legislature does not mean in its grant to give any exclusive rights, let it say so expressly, directly, and in terms admitting of no misconstruction. The grantees will then take at their peril, and must abide the results of their overweening confidence, indiscretion, and zeal.

My judgment is formed upon the terms of the grant, its nature and objects, its designs and duties; and, in its interpretation, I seek for no new principles, but I apply such as are as old as the very rudiments of the common law.

▼▲▼

# The Contract Clause Confronts the Industrial Revolution

The Court's diminishing enthusiasm for the earlier protection afforded contractual rights against state regulation continued into the late nineteenth and early twentieth century. Litigation brought under the Contract Clause, however, did not abate even with the Court's slow but eventual abandonment of the vested rights doctrine as inherent protection against public interest legislation. In his influential book, *The Contract Clause and the Constitution*, political scientist Benjamin Wright noted that almost 40 percent of all cases to come before the federal courts before 1889 were brought under the Contract Clause.[24]

Decisions such as *Stone* v. *Mississippi* (1880), in which a unanimous Court held Mississippi's right to amend its constitution to invalidate a contractual agreement between the state and a private corporation if the business agreed upon was determined to be detrimental to the public's health and welfare, reflected the Court's new willingness to permit states to protect the public interest at the expense of contractual rights. How *Stone* differed from earlier Contract Clause cases was in Mississippi's decision to criminalize a business enterprise that was once legal—in this case, the sale of lottery tickets. Note that the cases discussed and excerpted through *Stone* involve disputes over state power to alter economic arrangements or discourage business monopolies. If the Court had eased the Marshall-era restrictions on state legislation to curtail perceived corporate and business abuses of the public trust, then in retrospect *Stone*'s outcome would have been a foregone conclusion.

Contract Clause law at the end of the nineteenth century no longer bore the imprint of John Marshall, but of Roger Taney. Had Taney not also authored the Court's infamous and reckless decision in *Dred Scott* v. *Sandford* (1857), which classified African Americans as persons "unworthy" of citizenship and disenfranchised them from constitutional recognition and protection, he might well be remembered as a progressive jurist.[25] He did, after all, create the constitutional opening for state laws enacted throughout the Progressive Era and Great Depression to address the problems caused by unregulated corporate power.

The Court continued to weaken the Contract Clause's protection against state impairment of private and public contracts into the early twentieth century. Perhaps the decision that best crystallized the Court's transformation in this area from an emphasis on economic liberties to state police power on behalf of the public good came in *Home Building & Loan Association* v. *Blaisdell* (1934).[26] There, the Court, in a 5-4 decision, upheld the constitutionality of the Minnesota Mortgage Moratorium Act, a Great Depression–era response to allow mortgage extensions to homeowners who had fallen behind in their payments. The Minnesota legislature acknowledged that the Moratorium Act impaired the contractual rights of mortgage companies. But the legislature also contended that extraordinary circumstances justified what it acknowledged was a far-reaching but nonetheless constitutional use of its police power.

Minnesota was not alone in enacting a mortgage moratorium law. By the time *Blaisdell* was decided, numerous states had enacted laws since the Great Depression began in 1929 to enable homeowners experiencing undue hardship to retain their mortgages. *Blaisdell* confirmed what most constitutional scholars had suspected for sometime: The Court now considered the Contract Clause an anachronism of American constitutional law, a bygone relic of an economic and political era that had long since faded from public consciousness.

## *Home Building & Loan Association* v. *Blaisdell*
### 290 U.S. 398 (1934)

During the Great Depression, Minnesota, like so many others across the country, declared a state of emergency and began taking extraordinary steps to deal with the economic and social problems the crisis had created. One of the saddest and most prevalent consequences of the Depression was the number of people who lost their homes because of their inability to meet their mortgage payments. In 1934 the Minnesota legislature sought to offset the fears of homeowners by enacting the Mortgage Moratorium Act. The law permitted homeowners behind in their payments to petition a state court for an extension to work out a payment plan with the lenders who held title to their homes. The rate was usually tied to their current

assets and tried to strike a reasonable halfway point between a lender's need to receive payment and the homeowner's ability to pay.

John and Rosella Blaisdell had asked for and received a two-year extension from a state court to work out a payment plan with their lender, the Home Building & Loan Association. They were ordered to pay forty dollars per month on the mortgage of their Minneapolis home. Home Building & Loan claimed that the moratorium law violated the Contract Clause by impairing an existing contract between the company and the Blaisdells.

The Great Depression represented one of the most serious threats ever to the social stability of the United States. Middle- and working-class Americans began to question the ability of a market-based economy rooted in private property to weather future shocks to its system. Radical politics became a much more visible presence, especially in the nation's nascent organized labor movement. For the first time, a Communist Party, encouraged by the Soviet Union, emerged as a political force in the United States. Labor unions, which had emerged as an important constituency in President Franklin D. Roosevelt's New Deal coalition, became a prime target for Communist organizers, as did other groups on the margins of American life. Roosevelt, possessed of peerless political instincts, understood perhaps better than any other national politician that capitalism could survive only if the nation accepted fundamental changes in the relationship between government and the private sector. The New Deal acknowledged what even the Framers had in the 1780s—that private property and a market-based economy, both conscious creations of law, could survive only if they managed to serve the public interest as well.

For more on the Depression, see the accompanying SIDEBAR.

The Court's decision was 5 to 4. Chief Justice Hughes delivered the opinion of the Court. Justice Sutherland, joined by Justices Van Devanter, McReynolds, and Butler, dissented.

MR. CHIEF JUSTICE HUGHES delivered the opinion of the Court.

In determining whether the provision for this temporary and conditional relief exceeds the power of the State by reason of the clause in the Federal Constitution prohibiting impairment of the obligations of contracts, we must consider the relation of emergency to constitutional power, the historical setting of the contract clause, the development of the jurisprudence of this Court in the construction of that clause, and the principles of construction which we may consider to be established.

Emergency does not create power. Emergency does not increase granted power or remove or diminish the restrictions imposed upon power granted or reserved. The Constitution was adopted in a period of grave emergency. Its grants of power to the Federal Government and its limitations of the power of the States were determined in the light of emergency, and they are not altered by emergency. What power was thus granted and what limitations were thus imposed are questions which have always been, and always will be, the subject of close examination under our constitutional system.

While emergency does not create power, emergency may furnish the occasion for the exercise of power. . . . The constitutional question presented in the light of an emergency is whether the power possessed embraces the particular exercise of it in response to particular conditions. Thus, the war power of the Federal Government is not created by the emergency of war, but it is a power given to meet that emergency. It is a power to wage war successfully, and thus it permits the harnessing of the entire energies of the people in a supreme cooperative effort to preserve the nation. But even the war power does not remove constitutional limitations safeguarding essential liberties. When the provisions of the Constitution, in grant or restriction, are specific, so particularized as not to admit of construction, no question is presented. But where constitutional grants and limitations of power are set forth in general clauses, which afford a broad outline, the process of construction is essential to fill in the details. That is true of the contract clause. The necessity of construction is not obviated by the fact that the contract clause is associated in the same section with other and more specific prohibitions. Even the grouping of subjects in the same clause may not require the same application to each of the subjects, regardless of differences in their nature.

In the construction of the contract clause, the debates in the Constitutional Convention are of little aid. But the reasons which led to the adoption of that clause, and of the other prohibitions of Section 10 of Article I, are not left in doubt, and have frequently been described with eloquent emphasis. The widespread distress following the revolutionary period, and the plight of debtors, had called forth in the States an ignoble array of legislative schemes for the defeat of creditors and the invasion of contractual obligations. Legislative interferences had been so numerous and extreme that the confidence essential to prosperous trade had been undermined and the utter destruction of credit was threatened. "The sober people of America" were convinced that some "thorough reform" was needed which would "inspire a general prudence and industry, and give a regular course to the business of society." *Federalist* 44. It was necessary to interpose the restraining power of a central authority in order to secure the foundations even of "private faith." The occasion and general purpose of the contract clause are summed up in the terse statement of Chief Justice Marshall in *Ogden v. Saunders* (1827), "The power of changing the relative situation of debtor and creditor, of interfering with contracts, a power which comes home to every man, touches the interest of all, and controls the conduct of every individual in those things which he supposes to be proper for his own exclusive management, had been used to such an excess by the state legislatures, as to break in upon the ordinary intercourse of society, and destroy all confidence between man and man. This mischief had become so great, so alarming, as not only to impair commercial intercourse and threaten the existence of credit, but to sap the morals of the people and destroy the sanctity of private faith. To guard against the continuance of the evil was an object of deep interest with all the truly wise, as well as the virtuous, of this great community, and was on of the important benefits expected from a reform of the government."

But full recognition of the occasion and general purpose of the clause does not suffice to fix its precise scope. Nor does an examination of the details of prior legislation in the States yield criteria which can be considered controlling. To ascertain the scope of the constitutional prohibition, we examine the course of judicial decisions in its application. These put it beyond question that the prohibition is not an absolute one, and is not to be read with literal exactness, like a mathematical formula. . . .

It is manifest from this review of our decisions that there has been a growing appreciation of public needs and of the necessity of finding ground for a rational compromise between individual rights and public welfare. The settlement and consequent contraction of the public domain, the pressure of a constantly increasing density of population, the interrelation of the activities of our people and the complexity of our economic interests, have inevitably led to an increased use of the organization of society in order to protect the very bases of individual opportunity. Where, in earlier days, it was thought that only the concerns of individuals or of classes were involved, and that those of the State itself were touched only remotely, it has later been found that the fundamental interests of the State are directly affected, and that the question is no longer merely that of one party to a contract as against another, but of the use of reasonable means to safeguard the economic structure upon which the good of all depends.

It is no answer to say that this public need was not apprehended a century ago, or to insist that what the provision of the Constitution meant to the vision of that day it must mean to the vision of our time. If, by the statement that what the Constitution meant at the time of its adoption it means today, it is intended to say that the great clauses of the Constitution must be confined to the interpretation which the framers, with the conditions and outlook of their time, would have placed upon them, the statement carries its own refutation. It was to guard against such a narrow conception that Chief Justice Marshall uttered the memorable warning—"We must never forget that it is a constitution we are expounding"—"a constitution intended to endure for ages to come, and, consequently, to be adapted to the various crises of human affairs." When we are dealing with the words of the Constitution, said this Court in *Missouri* v. *Holland* (1920), "we must realize that they have called into life a being the development of which could not have been foreseen completely by the most gifted of its begetters. . . . The case before us must be considered in the light of our whole experience, and not merely in that of what was said a hundred years ago."

Nor is it helpful to attempt to draw a fine distinction between the intended meaning of the words of the Constitution and their intended application. When we consider the contract clause and the decisions which have expounded it in harmony with the essential reserved power of the States to protect the security of their peoples, we find no warrant for the conclusion that the clause has been warped by these decisions from its proper significance, or that the founders of our Government would have interpreted the clause differently had they had occasion to assume that responsibility in the conditions of the later day. The vast body of law which has been developed was unknown to the fathers, but it is believed to have preserved the essential content and the spirit of the Constitution. With a growing recognition of public needs and the relation of individual right to public security, the court has sought to prevent the perversion of the clause through its use as an instrument to throttle the capacity of the States to protect their fundamental interests. This development is a growth from the seeds which the fathers planted. It is

a development forecast by the prophetic words of Justice Johnson in *Ogden* v. *Saunders*. And the germs of the later decisions are found in the early cases of the Charles River Bridge and the West River Bridge, supra, which upheld the public right against strong insistence upon the contract clause. The principle of this development is, as we have seen, that the reservation of the reasonable exercise of the protective power of the State is read into all contracts, and there is no greater reason for refusing to apply this principle to Minnesota mortgages than to New York leases.

Applying the criteria established by our decisions we conclude:

1. An emergency existed in Minnesota which furnished a proper occasion for the exercise of the reserved power of the State to protect the vital interests of the community. The declarations of the existence of this emergency by the legislature and by the Supreme Court of Minnesota cannot be regarded as a subterfuge, or as lacking in adequate basis. The finding of the legislature and state court has support in the facts of which we take judicial notice.

2. The legislation was addressed to a legitimate end, that is, the legislation was not for the mere advantage of particular individuals, but for the protection of a basic interest of society.

3. In view of the nature of the contracts in question—mortgages of unquestionable validity—the relief afforded and justified by the emergency, in order not to contravene the constitutional provision, could only be of a character appropriate to that emergency, and could be granted only upon reasonable conditions.

4. The conditions upon which the period of redemption is extended do not appear to be unreasonable. The initial extension of the time of redemption for thirty days from the approval of the Act was obviously to give a reasonable opportunity for the authorized application to the court. As already noted, the integrity of the mortgage indebtedness is not impaired; interest continues to run; the validity of the sale and the right of a mortgagee-purchaser to title or to obtain a deficiency judgment if the mortgagor fails to redeem within the extended period are maintained, and the conditions of redemption, if redemption there be, stand as they were under the prior law. . . .

If it be determined, as it must be, that the contract clause is not an absolute and utterly unqualified restriction of the State's protective power, this legislation is clearly so reasonable as to be within the legislative competency.

5. The legislation is temporary in operation. It is limited to the exigency which called it forth. While the postponement of the period of redemption from the foreclosure sale is to May 1, 1935, that period may be reduced by the order of the court under the statute, in case of a change in circumstances, and the operation of the statute itself could not validly outlast the emergency or be so extended as virtually to destroy the contracts.

We are of the opinion that the Minnesota statute, as here applied, does not violate the contract clause of the Federal Constitution. Whether the legislation is wise or unwise as a matter of policy is a question with which we are not concerned.

The judgment of the Supreme Court of Minnesota is affirmed.

Judgment affirmed.

MR. JUSTICE SUTHERLAND, dissenting.

Few questions of greater moment than that just decided have been submitted for judicial inquiry during this generation. He simply closes his eyes to the necessary implications of the decision who fails to see in it the potentiality of future gradual but ever-advancing encroachments upon the sanctity of private and public contracts. The effect of the Minnesota legislation, though serious enough in itself, is of trivial significance compared with the far more serious and dangerous inroads upon the limitations of the Constitution which are almost certain to ensue as a consequence naturally following any step beyond the boundaries fixed by that instrument. And those of us who are thus apprehensive of the effect of this decision would, in a matter so important, be neglectful of our duty should we fail to spread upon the permanent records of the court the reasons which move us to the opposite view.

A provision of the Constitution, it is hardly necessary to say, does not admit of two distinctly opposite interpretations. It does not mean one thing at one time and an entirely different thing at another time. If the contract impairment clause, when framed and adopted, meant that the terms of a contract for the payment of money could not be altered in invitum by a state statute enacted for the relief of hardly pressed debtors to the end and with the effect of postponing payment or enforcement during and because of an economic or financial emergency, it is but to state the obvious to say that it means the same now. This view, at once so rational in its application to the written word and so necessary to the stability of constitutional principles, though from time to time challenged, has never, unless recently, been put within the realm of doubt by the

decisions of this court. The true rule was forcefully declared in *Ex parte Milligan* (1866), in the face of circumstances of national peril and public unrest and disturbance far greater than any that exist today. In that great case, this court said that the provisions of the Constitution there under consideration had been expressed by our ancestors in such plain English words that it would seem the ingenuity of man could not evade them, but that, after the lapse of more than seventy years, they were sought to be avoided. "Those great and good men," the court said, "foresaw that troublous times would arise when rulers and people would become restive under restraint, and seek, by sharp and decisive measures, to accomplish ends deemed just and proper, and that the principles of constitutional liberty would be in peril unless established by irrepealable law. The history of the world had taught them that what was done in the past might be attempted in the future." And then, in words the power and truth of which have become increasingly evident with the lapse of time, there was laid down the rule without which the Constitution would cease to be the "supreme law of the land," binding equally upon governments and governed at all times and under all circumstances, and become a mere collection of political maxims to be adhered to or disregarded according to the prevailing sentiment or the legislative and judicial opinion in respect of the supposed necessities of the hour. . . .

The whole aim of construction, as applied to a provision of the Constitution, is to discover the meaning, to ascertain and give effect to the intent, of its framers and the people who adopted it. The necessities which gave rise to the provision, the controversies which preceded, as well as the conflicts of opinion which were settled by its adoption, are matters to be considered to enable us to arrive at a correct result. The history of the times, the state of things existing when the provision was framed and adopted, should be looked to in order to ascertain the mischief and the remedy. As nearly as possible, we should place ourselves in the condition of those who framed and adopted it. And if the meaning be at all doubtful, the doubt should be resolved, wherever reasonably possible to do so, in a way to forward the evident purpose with which the provision was adopted.

An application of these principles to the question under review removes any doubt, if otherwise there would be any, that the contract impairment clause denies to the several states the power to mitigate hard consequences resulting to debtors from financial or economic exigencies by an impairment of the obligation of contracts of indebtedness. A candid consideration of the history and circumstances which led up to and accompanied the framing and

## HOME BUILDING & LOAN ASSOCIATION V. BLAISDELL

### *The Limits of Charity*

To restore the confidence of the banking community shattered by the October 1929 stock market crash, Rome C. Stephenson, the vice president of the American Bankers Association, told a meeting of bankers and financiers gathered in downtown Cleveland almost a year to the day later that there was no need to panic. Business was about to improve as more Americans came to understand the crash of the stock market bore no relationship to the nation's general economic health:

> The depression of the stock market impressed the general public with the idea that it would depress general business. Because of a psychological consequence, it did, but it should not have. There are 120,000,000 persons in the country and at the maximum not more than 10,000,000 were involved in the stock-market transactions. The remaining 110,000,000 suffered no loss.

It was true enough that most Americans suffered no losses in the stock market. But such a view of the economic depression rapidly overtaking the country was shortsighted. It neglected to include the record level of unemployment that worsened by the day, shops and factories closing by the score, and most ominously, the hundreds of banks that were failing and taking with them millions of dollars in uninsured deposits. Confidence in the nation's economy plummeted even further by the end of November 1930, when 256 banks failed in a single month. The worst was yet to come, however, when the United States Bank, with deposits of more than $200 million, collapsed two weeks later, making it the largest such bank failure to date. It contributed to the rapidly deteriorating economy, a free fall with no apparent end in sight. The atmosphere, for most Americans, was one of pure, unadulterated fear.

Fear was the right word to describe the nation's collective mood. By the end of 1931, more than 3,600 banks with deposits of $2.5 billion had failed. Unemployment had reached 8 million and would hit 12 million a few months later. More than fifty thousand businesses, failing at record rates, had gone under. The value of all farm property had declined from $57.7 billion in 1929 to $51.8 billion in 1931, and the approximately 450,000 corporations still in business had a combined deficit greater than $5.5 billion.

Such economic devastation had no precedent in American history. The impact of the Depression on the most anonymous and smallest of human lives was visible at every turn. Men who earned comfortable middle-class incomes were forced to turn to street peddling; panhandling; and, more often than anyone would care to admit, petty crime. Women took in laundry and boarders to offset their husband's loss of income, and children left school in record numbers to scrounge up any money in any way they could.

Despite the comments of some unaffected by the Depression that the homeless families living in the streets were simply indolent or too stupid to adapt to the fast-paced industrial economy of the day, the social pathologies that had seeped in nationwide could not be so easily explained away. The deprivation grew day by day, week by week, and with such indiscriminate speed that it touched, at some point, just about every single American. For the lucky few who escaped the wrath of the Depression's clutches, just seeing a neighbor's furniture and worldly belongings stacked up on the sidewalk with nowhere to go was reminder enough that such a fate could have easily visited them.

Still, said President Herbert Hoover in December 1931, "no one is going hungry and no one need go hungry or cold." Fewer and fewer close observers of the Depression's impact agreed with Hoover by this point. Wrote one social critic of the period: "We saw the city at its worst. One vivid, gruesome moment of those dark days we shall never forget. We saw a crowd of some fifty men fighting over a barrel of garbage which had been set outside the back door of a restaurant. American citizens fighting for scraps of food like animals!" Journalist Edmund Wilson offered an even more stark and frightening assessment of the depths to which the human condition had fallen during the Depression. Coming across an abandoned building that stunk of garbage, urine, and excrement but was nonetheless populated with black families, Wilson described it as:

> [S]even stories, thick with dark windows, caged in a dingy mess of fire-escapes like mattress-springs on a junk-heap, hunched up, hunchback-proportioned, jam-crammed in its dumbness and darkness with miserable wriggling life. . . . There is darkness in the hundred cells: the tenants cannot pay for light; and cold: the heating system no longer works. . . . And now, since it is no good for anything else, its owner has turned it over to the Negroes, who flock into tight-packed apartments and get along there as best they can.

Desperation did not discriminate on the basis of geography or race. In the Appalachian Mountains, another journalist recounted a story of a young schoolgirl who, looking pale and tired, was told to go home and get something to eat. "I can't," the girl replied. "It's my sister's turn to eat."

Factories and stores across the nation were boarded up and abandoned in record numbers, often

*Shantytowns such as this one outside Seattle dotted the urban landscape during the Great Depression. They were referred to as "Hoovervilles," an unflattering reference to Herbert Hoover, who was president at the time the stock market crashed in October 1929.*
Bettmann/CORBIS.

in the dead of night to reduce the possibilities of riots and looting. Stealing to survive was becoming more common as the Depression intensified. With nowhere to turn, the newly unemployed, often with their families in tow, began to wander aimlessly from town to town in search of work. Reported the *New York Times* of America's new vagabond class: "Expectant mothers, sick babies, young childless couples, grim-faced middle-aged dislodged from lifetime jobs—on they go, an index of insecurity, in a country used to the unexpected. We think of the nomads of the desert—now we have the nomads of the depression."

Hundreds of thousands of people were on the move by 1932, with stolen rides in railroad boxcars the preferred mode of transport. Southern Pacific Railroad estimated that it once threw 683,000 transients off its cars in a single year, with almost one-third of them unaccompanied adolescents. "Tramps," as the kids were called to distinguish them from their adult "hobo" counterparts, often traveled in gangs to ensure their own safety and that of the considerable number of teenage girls among them. "Girls in box cars," wrote Thomas Minehan, a sociologist who had joined the transients to study their habits, "are not entirely at the mercy of any man on the road whatever their relations with the boys may be. In the event of loneliness or illness, the boys and girls have friends to comfort and care for them."

The homeless who chose to remain in their cities and towns were often forced to sleep in flophouses infested with vermin and rodents. Such a luxury came when they could scrape together the fifteen cents that a mattress on a flophouse floor commonly cost. More often, the new homeless turned to park benches, alleys, doorways, packing crates, abandoned refrigerators, construction sites, and city dumps for a place to sleep.

Ambition and industriousness among the homeless surfaced in the form of the makeshift shanty towns that began to pop up on the outskirts of cities and towns large enough to have outskirts. Shacks were pieced together from scraps of wood and cardboard, fence posts, and anything else that could guard them from the elements of the season. Large bonfires were often lit in the center of these villages; the fires provided warmth during the day and a gathering place for residents to commiserate with each other over the hopelessness of their fate. They were called "Hoovervilles," no term of endearment from the hundreds of thousands of people who occupied them during the Depression.

Laws such as the Minnesota Mortgage Moratorium Act upheld by the Supreme Court in *Blaisdell* were a recognition that President Hoover's deeply held faith in the virtues of self-reliance and rugged individualism were profoundly misplaced. Even the Court, which had rarely deviated from its laissez-faire interpretation of the Constitution's economic liberties even as the Depression worsened, conceded that not all government intervention was misguided social engineering. Of course, the Court, after *Blaisdell*, soon returned to the "liberty of contract" doctrine, setting the stage for its confrontation with the New Deal of President Franklin Roosevelt. For a moment, though, the Court demonstrated that it, too, understood what an unfortunate number of middle-class Americans had learned from their Depression experience: Even the most heartfelt and well-intended charity had its limits.

## Reference

The narrative account of the Depression, including quotations, is adopted from T. H. Watkins, *The Great Depression: America in the 1930s* (Boston: Back Bay Books, 1993).

---

adoption of this clause will demonstrate conclusively that it was framed and adopted with the specific and studied purpose of preventing legislation designed to relieve debtors especially in time of financial distress. Indeed, it is not probable that any other purpose was definitely in the minds of those who composed the framers' convention or the ratifying state conventions which followed, although the restriction has been given a wider application upon principles clearly stated by Chief Justice Marshall in the Dartmouth College Case (1819). . . .

The Minnesota statute either impairs the obligation of contracts or it does not. If it does not, the occasion to which it relates becomes immaterial, since then the passage of the statute is the exercise of a normal, unrestricted, state power, and requires no special occasion to render it effective. If it does, the emergency no more furnishes a proper occasion for its exercise than if the emergency were nonexistent. And so, while, in form, the suggested distinction seems to put us forward in a straight line, in reality, it simply carries us back in a circle, like bewildered travelers lost in a wood, to the point where we parted company with the view of the state court.

If what has now been said is sound, as I think it is, we come to what really is the vital question in the case: does the Minnesota statute constitute an impairment of the obligation of the contract now under review? . . .

It is quite true also that "the reservation of essential attributes of sovereign power is also read into contracts," and that the legislature cannot "bargain away the public health or the public morals." General statutes to put an end to lotteries, the sale or manufacture of intoxicating liquors, the maintenance of nuisances, to protect the public safety, etc., although they have the indirect effect of absolutely destroying private contracts previously made in contemplation of a continuance of the state of affairs then in existence but subsequently prohibited, have been uniformly upheld as not violating the contract impairment clause. The distinction between legislation of that character and the Minnesota statute, however, is readily observable. . . .

A statute which materially delays enforcement of the mortgagee's contractual right of ownership and possession does not modify the remedy merely; it destroys, for the period of delay, all remedy so far as the enforcement of that right is concerned. The phrase, "obligation of a contract," in the constitutional sense, imports a legal duty to perform the specified obligation of that contract, not to substitute and perform, against the will of one of the parties, a different, albeit equally valuable, obligation. And a state, under the contract impairment clause, has no more power to accomplish such a substitution than has one of the parties to the contract against the will of the other. It cannot do so either by acting directly upon the contract or by bringing about the result under the guise of a statute in form acting only upon the remedy. If it could, the efficacy of the constitutional restriction would, in large measure, be made to disappear. As this court has well said, whatever tends to postpone or retard the enforcement of a contract, to that extent weakens the obligation. . . . .

I quite agree with the opinion of the court that whether the legislation under review is wise or unwise is a matter with which we have nothing to do. Whether it is likely to work well or work ill presents a question entirely irrelevant to the issue. The only legitimate inquiry we can make is whether it is constitutional. If it is not, its virtues, if it have any, cannot save it; if it is, its faults cannot be invoked to accomplish its destruction. If the provisions of the Constitution be not upheld when they pinch, as well as when they comfort, they may as well be abandoned. Being unable to reach any other conclusion than that the Minnesota statute infringes the constitutional restriction under review, I have no choice but to say so.

▼▲▼

## The Demise of the Contract Clause

Since *Blaisdell,* the Court has not viewed the Contract Clause as an impediment to the power of states to use their police power, even if such regulation compromises or nullifies contracts between private parties or contracts entered into by the state. In *City of El Paso* v. *Simmons* (1965), the Court extended *Blaisdell's* central holding by ruling that the exigencies that motivated Minnesota to enact its mortgage relief bill were not required for the state to defend the annulment of a contractual arrangement with a private party.[27] All that mattered was whether a state law was directed toward the betterment of public welfare.

*Simmons* involved, in plain and simple terms, an effort by the Texas legislature to change the terms of a bad land deal by canceling contracts that the state had entered into to sell land to private parties. Enacted in 1876, the Texas law encouraged the sale of public lands to private corporations and land speculators. When Texas realized the much of the land it had sold turned out to have astronomical value, particularly the land housing oil and mineral fields, the state changed the conditions of many of its original agreements.

In an 8–1 opinion, the Court held that El Paso was not required to sell back land under a default provision added to the original state law in 1941. In dissent, Justice Black commented that the Court's decision was inconsistent with Madison's intentions in *Federalist 44* for the Contract Clause. In Black's view the core purpose of the Contract Clause was to protect contractual agreements from the "fluctuating policy" of the legislatures. Wrote Black, "I . . . cannot agree that constitutional law is simply a matter of what the Justices of this Court decide is not harmful for the country, and therefore is 'reasonable.'" What do you think of Black's comment in his *Simmons* dissent charging that the Court creates constitutional law as a response to what it senses are the social and political needs of the nation?

Some commentators have suggested that two Contract Clause cases the Court has decided since *Simmons* indicate that interest in elevated constitutional protection for contractual rights might be undergoing a renaissance of sorts. Time has proven that a shortsighted prediction. In *United States Trust Co. of New York v. New Jersey* (1977), a 4-3 Court held that the New York and New Jersey legislatures could not concurrently repeal an existing agreement between their respective states to subsidize their public transportation systems from revenue generated by bonds issued by the New York Port Authority.[28]

During the Energy Crisis of the 1970s, a period that produced block-long gasoline lines, lowered thermostats, and a president who wore a cardigan sweater to emphasize that national sacrifice began at the top, New York and New Jersey invoked their respective police powers as the basis for repealing their long-standing transportation agreement. Each state argued that its interest in mass transportation, energy conservation, and environmental protection justified the decision to reinvest public funds in those public concerns rather than compensate private creditors. The Court not only rejected that argument but also held that when a law impaired a state's contractual obligations to private parties the law must be "reasonable and necessary" and advance an "important public purpose" to survive a Contract Clause challenge. The Court determined that *United States Trust Co.* did not involve the exigent circumstances of *Blaisdell*, thus narrowing the scope of state police power to invalidate a contract between public and private parties.

The Court surprised students of Contract Clause doctrine a year later in *Allied Structural Steel Co. v. Spannaus* (1978), in which it held that state laws that impaired a contract between private parties were entitled to heightened judicial scrutiny as well. This opinion appeared to depart from the standard established in *Blaisdell*.[29] The Minnesota Pension Benefits Protection Act of 1974 required companies that moved or terminated their business in Minnesota to offer pension payouts to all employees who lost their jobs, even those who did not meet the requirements for vesture in their respective pension plans. With Justice Potter Stewart writing for a 6-3 majority, the Court held that, while the Contract Clause had "receded into comparative desuetude" with the rise of property and contract claims brought under the Constitution's Due Process Clauses, states were not permitted to impose "severe" impair-

ments on contractual agreements between private parties under a less strict standard of review. "Minimal alteration of contractual obligations may end the inquiry at its first stage," wrote Stewart, but "[s]evere impairment, on the other hand, will push the inquiry to a careful examination of the nature and purpose of the state legislation."[30] The Court was careful throughout its opinion to distinguish the factual circumstances in *Allied Steel* from those in *Blaisdell*. As it had in *United States Trust*, the Court emphasized the absence of exigent circumstances to warrant such severe interference with contractual obligations.

But two cases decided since then suggest that *U.S. Trusts* and *Allied Steel* were aberrations in the Court's modern Contract Clause jurisprudence. In *Energy Reserves Group v. Kansas Power & Light Co.* (1983) and *Exxon Corp. v. Eagerton* (1983), two separate and unanimous Courts rejected Contract Clause claims directed toward state impairment of contracts between private parties.[31] Both cases witnessed the return of the Court to the approach of *Blaisdell* and *Simmons*.

In *Energy Reserves Group*, Justice Blackmun offered a three-step approach to Contract Clause claims derived from the Court's earlier decisions. First, has state law operated as a substantial burden on a contractual relationship? Second, has the state articulated a significant and legitimate purpose in support of the contested regulation? There, Blackmun noted that it was not necessary for the state to link the public purpose behind the law to exigent circumstances. Third, has the adjustment brought about by the law been done under reasonable conditions that are related to the state-identified public purpose? The Court applied Blackmun's approach to reach a far different result than in *United States Trust* or *Allied Steel*.

In *Eagerton* the Court did not even bother with the three-part test that Blackmun used in *Energy Reserves Group*. For the Court, Justice Marshall held that an Alabama law that prohibited oil and gas companies from passing on to consumers costs associated with a severance tax did not violate the Contract Clause. The Court held that the "pass through" prohibition of the Alabama law imposed a generally applicable rule of conduct designed to advance a "broad societal interest." This law was not different from the decisions of numerous state legislatures in earlier cases to limit or ban alcohol, restrict lotteries, or apply environmental controls.

*Energy Reserves Group* and *Eagerton*, not *United States Trust* and *Allied Steel*, form the foundation of the Court's current Contract Clause jurisprudence. The Court's sole Contract Clause decision of import since then, *Keystone Bituminous Coal Association v. DeBenedictis* (1987), followed the approach established in *Blaisdell*.[32] Refusal to restore the Federalist-era emphasis on vested rights and private property to the Contract Clause has disappointed many conservative and libertarian constitutional scholars. Many argue that the Constitution creates no analytical distinction between economic rights and the personal freedoms the Court has ruled are "fundamental," such as freedom of speech, religion, and assembly. Richard Epstein, perhaps the most insistent advocate of greater judicial protection for economic and property rights, has argued that the "distinction between interference with the agreement itself and the taking of its subject matter" is irrelevant. Government acts that compromise or abolish altogether private contractual arrangements are never justified as tools of social and economic betterment. Private companies whose resources are "taken" for the public good are still entitled to compensation.[33]

The Court, for now, appears to have returned to the approach established prior to *United States Trust* and *Allied Steel*. Still, Epstein's questions are worth consideration and debate. Does the Constitution, in fact, make explicit reference to some individual rights (speech, equality, religious freedom) as deserving greater protection than others (economic and property)? Is the public interest in low energy prices or competitive construction contracts more compelling than prohibiting hate speech or pornography? How you develop your own thoughts on the Contract Clause will serve you well when you confront the issues raised in the Court's treatment of other economic and property rights claims brought under the Due Process and Takings Clauses, the subjects of Chapter 9 and 10, respectively.

## City of El Paso v. Simmons
### 379 U.S. 497 (1965)

To raise revenue for a public school system and to encourage settlement, Texas began offering public land for sale in 1876. Purchasers could buy property for a down payment of 25 percent of the sale price, plus 3 percent interest per year. State forfeiture laws permitted Texas to reclaim sold land if a purchaser missed a payment. A purchaser lost title to the land unless the purchaser paid the interest before a third party bought the land. In 1941 the Texas legislature amended the original law to limit reinstatement rights to five years after the initial forfeiture.

Greenberry Simmons bought land under the program. In 1947 he forfeited his property to the state. In 1952, Simmons filed for reinstatement, offering to make full restitution of back interest. His missed the five-year cut off point by two days, so the state denied his petition. Three years later, Texas sold the land to El Paso, one of its fast-growing cities. Simmons filed suit in a lower federal court to recover his forfeited land. He was unsuccessful, but an appeals court reversed.

The Court's decision was 8 to 1. Justice White delivered the opinion of the Court. Justice Black's dissent offers another excellent example of his literalist approach to constitutional interpretation.

▼▲▼

MR. JUSTICE WHITE delivered the opinion of the Court.

The City seeks to bring this case within the long line of cases recognizing a distinction between contract obligation and remedy and permitting a modification of the remedy as long as there is no substantial impairment of the value of the obligation. . . .

We do not pause to chart again the dividing line under federal law between "remedy" and "obligation," or to determine the extent to which this line is controlled by state court decisions, decisions often rendered in contexts not involving Contract Clause considerations. For it is not every modification of a contractual promise that impairs the obligation of contract under federal law, any more than it is every alteration of existing remedies that violates the Contract Clause. *Stone v. Mississippi* (1881). Assuming the provision for reinstatement after default to be part of the State's obligation, we do not think its modification by a five-year statute of repose contravenes the Contract Clause.

The decisions "put it beyond question that the prohibition is not an absolute one, and is not to be read with literal exactness, like a mathematical formula," as Chief Justice Hughes said in *Home Building & Loan Assn. v. Blaisdell* (1934). The Blaisdell opinion, which amounted to a comprehensive restatement of the principles underlying the application of the Contract Clause, makes it quite clear that "[n]ot only is the constitutional provision qualified by the measure of control which the state retains over remedial processes, but the state also continues to possess authority to safeguard the vital interests of its people. It does not matter that legislation appropriate to that end "has the result of modifying or abrogating contracts already in effect." *Stephenson v. Binford*. Not only are existing laws read into contracts in order to fix obligations as between the parties, but the reservation of essential attributes of sovereign power is also read into contracts as a postulate of the legal order. . . . This principle of harmonizing the constitutional prohibition with the necessary residuum of state power has had progressive recognition in the decisions of this Court." Moreover, the "economic interests of the state may justify the exercise of its continuing and dominant protective power notwithstanding interference with contracts." The State has the "sovereign right . . . to protect the . . . general welfare of the people. . . . Once we are in this domain of the reserve power of a State, we must respect the "wide discretion on the part of the legislature in determining what is and what is not necessary." . . .

Of course, the power of a State to modify or affect the obligation of contract is not without limit. "[W]hatever is reserved of state power must be consistent with the fair intent of the constitutional limitation of that power. The reserved power cannot be construed so as to destroy the limitation, nor is the limitation to be construed to destroy the reserved power in its essential aspects. They must be construed in harmony with each other. This principle precludes a construction which would permit the state to adopt as its policy the repudiation of debts or the destruction of contracts or the denial of means to enforce them." *Blaisdell*. But we think the objects of the Texas statute make abundantly clear that it impairs no protected right under the Contract Clause. . . .

The State's policy of quick resale of forfeited lands did not prove entirely successful; forfeiting purchasers who repurchased the lands again defaulted, and other purchasers bought without any intention of complying with their contracts unless mineral wealth was discovered. The market for land contracted during the depression. These developments, hardly to be expected or foreseen, operated to confer considerable advantages on the purchaser and his successors, and a costly and difficult burden on the State. This Court's decisions have never given a law which imposes unforeseen advantages or burdens on a contracting party constitutional immunity against change. Laws which restrict a party to those gains reasonably to be expected from the contract are not subject to attack under the Contract Clause, notwithstanding that they technically alter an obligation of a contract. The five-year limitation allows defaulting purchasers with a bona fide

interest in their lands a reasonable time to reinstate. It does not, and need not, allow defaulting purchasers with a speculative interest in the discovery of minerals to remain in endless default while retaining a cloud on title. . . .

The program adopted at the turn of the century for the sale, settlement, forfeiture, and reinstatement of land was not wholly effectual to serve the objectives of the State's land program many decades later. Settlement was no longer the objective, but revenues for the school fund, efficient utilization of public lands, and compliance with contracts of sale remained viable and important goals, as did the policy of relieving purchasers from the hardships of temporary adversity. Given these objectives and the impediments posed to their fulfillment by timeless reinstatement rights, a statute of repose was quite clearly necessary. The measure taken to induce defaulting purchasers to comply with their contracts, requiring payment of interest in arrears within five years, was a mild one indeed, hardly burdensome to the purchaser who wanted to adhere to his contract of purchase, but nonetheless an important one to the State's interest. The Contract Clause does not forbid such a measure.

Mr. Justice Black, dissenting.

I have previously had a number of occasions to dissent from judgments of this Court balancing away the First Amendment's unequivocally guaranteed rights of free speech, press, assembly and petition. In this case, I am compelled to dissent from the Court's balancing away the plain guarantee of Art. 1, §10, that "No State shall . . . pass any . . . Law impairing the Obligation of Contracts . . . ," a balancing which results in the State of Texas' taking a man's private property for public use without compensation in violation of the equally plain guarantee of the Fifth Amendment, made applicable to the States by the Fourteenth, that " . . . private property [shall not] be taken for public use, without just compensation." The respondent, Simmons, is the loser, and the treasury of the State of Texas the ultimate beneficiary, of the Court's action. . . .

[This case] for me, is just another example of the delusiveness of calling "balancing" a "test." With its deprecatory view of the equities on the side of Simmons and other claimants and its remarkable sympathy for the State, the Court, through its balancing process, states the case in a way inevitably destined to bypass the Contract Clause and let Texas break its solemn obligation. As the Court's opinion demonstrates, constitutional adjudication under the balancing method becomes simply a matter of this Court's deciding for itself which result in a particular case seems in the circumstances the more acceptable governmental policy, and then stating the facts in such a way that the considerations in the balance lead to the result. Even if I believed that we, as Justices of this Court, had the authority to rely on our judgment of what is best for the country, instead of trying to interpret the language and purpose of our written Constitution, I would not agree that Texas should be permitted to do what it has done here. But, more importantly, I most certainly cannot agree that constitutional law is simply a matter of what the Justices of this Court decide is not harmful for the country, and therefore is "reasonable." *Ferguson v. Skrupa* (1963). James Madison said that the Contract Clause was intended to protect people from the "fluctuating policy" of the legislature. *Federalist* 44. Today's majority holds that people are not protected from the fluctuating policy of the legislature so long as the legislature acts in accordance with the fluctuating policy of this Court.

▼▲▼

# United States Trust Co. of New York v. New Jersey
### 431 U.S. 1 (1977)

The interdependent nature of the commercial economies of New York and New Jersey extends back to the earliest days of the Republic. In fact, the Court's first great decision on congressional power to regulate interstate commerce, *Gibbons v. Ogden* (1824), stemmed from a conflict over waterway rights for commercial steamboat operators. In *Gibbons* the Court ruled that states could not erect barriers to prevent companies from engaging in interstate commerce. *Gibbons* is justly recognized as one of the Court's most important decisions, as it gave life to the Federalist blueprint for a large, extended commercial republic in which parochial interests gave way to economic nationalism. Interstate compacts in which states agree to cooperate on transportation, energy, and construction projects are quite common, especially in regions with fluid economies, such as those of New York and New Jersey, which are linked by mass transportation.

In 1921, New York and New Jersey agreed to establish the Port Authority of New York to regulate commercial transportation between the two states. Although its name suggested otherwise, the Port Authority was privately funded. The agreement did, however, permit the investors to issue bonds against future revenues. *United States Trust Co.* stemmed from a conflict involving a 1962 agreement

reached by New York and New Jersey limiting the Port Authority's ability to subsidize its newly acquired commuter rail line, the Hudson & Manhattan railroad, with revenues earmarked for its bond issues. That agreement was modified in 1974, when the states, as part of a response to deal with the energy crisis brought about by the oil embargo instituted by the Arab nations, agreed to repeal the 1962 provision so that the Port Authority could use its revenues to subsidize the rail line. United States Trust Co. of New York, which held bonds affected by the 1974 decision, sued New Jersey, claiming that the state's action impaired the company's original contract with the Port Authority under the 1962 agreement. The state responded that its action was a valid exercise of state police power to deal with an emergency condition.

The Court's decision was 4 to 3. Justice Blackmun delivered the opinion of the Court. Chief Justice Burger concurred. Justice Brennan filed a dissent joined by Justices White and Marshall. Justices Powell and Stewart did not participate.

▼▲▼

MR. JUSTICE BLACKMUN delivered the opinion of the Court.

At the time the Constitution was adopted, and for nearly a century thereafter, the Contract Clause was one of the few express limitations on state power. The many decisions of this Court involving the Contract Clause are evidence of its important place in our constitutional jurisprudence. Over the last century, however, the Fourteenth Amendment has assumed a far larger place in constitutional adjudication concerning the States. We feel that the present role of the Contract Clause is largely illuminated by two of this Court's decisions. In each, legislation was sustained despite a claim that it had impaired the obligations of contracts.

*Home Building & Loan Assn.* v. *Blaisdell* (1934), is regarded as the leading case in the modern era of Contract Clause interpretation. At issue was the Minnesota Mortgage Moratorium Law, enacted in 1933, during the depth of the Depression and when that State was under severe economic stress, and appeared to have no effective alternative. The statute was a temporary measure that allowed judicial extension of the time for redemption; a mortgagor who remained in possession during the extension period was required to pay a reasonable income or rental value to the mortgagee. A closely divided Court, in an opinion by Mr. Chief Justice Hughes, observed that "emergency may furnish the occasion for the exercise of power," and that the "constitutional question presented in the light of an emergency is whether the power possessed embraces the particular exercise of it in response to particular conditions." It noted that the debates in the Constitutional Convention were of little aid in the construction of the Contract Clause, but that the general purpose of the Clause was clear: to encourage trade and credit by promoting confidence in the stability of contractual obligations. Nevertheless, a State "continues to possess authority to safeguard the vital interests of its people. . . . This principle of harmonizing the constitutional prohibition with the necessary residuum of state power has had progressive recognition in the decisions of this Court." The great clauses of the Constitution are to be considered in the light of our whole experience, and not merely as they would be interpreted by its Framers in the conditions and with the outlook of their time.

This Court's most recent Contract Clause decision is *El Paso* v. *Simmons* (1965). That case concerned a 1941 Texas statute that limited to a 5-year period the reinstatement rights of an interest-defaulting purchaser of land from the State. For many years prior to the enactment of that statute, such a defaulting purchaser, under Texas law, could have reinstated his claim to the land upon written request and payment of delinquent interest, unless rights of third parties had intervened. This Court held that "it is not every modification of a contractual promise that impairs the obligation of contract under federal law." It observed that the State "has the 'sovereign right . . . to protect the . . . general welfare of the people'" and "'we must respect the wide discretion on the part of the legislature in determining what is and what is not necessary.'" The Court recognized that "the power of a State to modify or affect the obligation of contract is not without limit," but held that "the objects of the Texas statute make abundantly clear that it impairs no protected right under the Contract Clause."

Both of these cases eschewed a rigid application of the Contract Clause to invalidate state legislation. Yet neither indicated that the Contract Clause was without meaning in modern constitutional jurisprudence, or that its limitation on state power was illusory. Whether or not the protection of contract rights comports with current views of wise public policy, the Contract Clause remains a part of our written Constitution. We therefore must attempt to apply that constitutional provision to the instant case with due respect for its purpose and the prior decisions of this Court. . . .

Mass transportation, energy conservation, and environmental protection are goals that are important, and of legitimate public concern. Appellees contend that these goals are so important that any harm to bondholders from repeal of the 1962 covenant is greatly outweighed by the public benefit. We do not accept this invitation to engage in a utilitarian comparison of public benefit and private loss. Contrary to Mr. Justice Black's fear, expressed in sole dissent in *El Paso* v. *Simmons*, the Court has not "balanced away" the limitation on state action imposed by the Contract Clause. Thus, a State cannot refuse to meet its legitimate financial obligations simply because it would prefer to spend the money to promote the public good, rather than the private welfare of its creditors. We can only sustain the repeal of the 1962 covenant if that impairment was both reasonable and necessary to serve the admittedly important purposes claimed by the State.

The more specific justification offered for the repeal of the 1962 covenant was the States' plan for encouraging users of private automobiles to shift to public transportation. The States intended to discourage private automobile use by raising bridge and tunnel tolls and to use the extra revenue from those tolls to subsidize improved commuter railroad service. Appellees contend that repeal of the 1962 covenant was necessary to implement this plan because the new mass transit facilities could not possibly be self-supporting and the covenant's "permitted deficits" level had already been exceeded. We reject this justification because the repeal was neither necessary to achievement of the plan nor reasonable in light of the circumstances.

The determination of necessity can be considered on two levels. First, it cannot be said that total repeal of the covenant was essential; a less drastic modification would have permitted the contemplated plan without entirely removing the covenant's limitations on the use of Port Authority revenues and reserves to subsidize commuter railroads. Second, without modifying the covenant at all, the States could have adopted alternative means of achieving their twin goals of discouraging automobile use and improving mass transit. Appellees contend, however, that choosing among these alternatives is a matter for legislative discretion. But a State is not completely free to consider impairing the obligations of its own contracts on a par with other policy alternatives. Similarly, a State is not free to impose a drastic impairment when an evident and more moderate course would serve its purposes equally well. In *El Paso* v. *Simmons*, the imposition of a five-year statute of limitations on what was previously a perpetual right of redemption was regarded by this Court as "quite clearly necessary" to achieve the State's vital interest in the orderly administration of its school lands program. In the instant case, the State has failed to demonstrate that repeal of the 1962 covenant was similarly necessary.

We also cannot conclude that repeal of the covenant was reasonable in light of the surrounding circumstances. In this regard, a comparison with *El Paso v. Simmons*, again is instructive. There a 19th century statute had effects that were unforeseen and unintended by the legislature when originally adopted. As a result, speculators were placed in a position to obtain windfall benefits. The Court held that adoption of a statute of limitation was a reasonable means to "restrict a party to those gains reasonably to be expected from the contract" when it was adopted.

By contrast, in the instant case the need for mass transportation in the New York metropolitan area was not a new development, and the likelihood that publicly owned commuter railroads would produce substantial deficits was well known. As early as 1922, over a half century ago, there were pressures to involve the Port Authority in mass transit. It was with full knowledge of these concerns that the 1962 covenant was adopted. Indeed, the covenant was specifically intended to protect the pledged revenues and reserves against the possibility that such concerns would lead the Port Authority into greater involvement in deficit mass transit.

During the 12-year period between adoption of the covenant and its repeal, public perception of the importance of mass transit undoubtedly grew because of increased general concern with environmental protection and energy conservation. But these concerns were not unknown in 1962, and the subsequent changes were of degree, and not of kind. We cannot say that these changes caused the covenant to have a substantially different impact in 1974 than when it was adopted in 1962. And we cannot conclude that the repeal was reasonable in the light of changed circumstances.

We therefore hold that the Contract Clause of the United States Constitution prohibits the retroactive repeal of the 1962 covenant. The judgment of the Supreme Court of New Jersey is reversed.

MR. JUSTICE BRENNAN, with whom MR. JUSTICE WHITE and MR. JUSTICE MARSHALL join, dissenting.

Decisions of this Court for at least a century have construed the Contract Clause largely to be powerless in binding a State to contracts limiting the authority of successor legislatures to enact laws in furtherance of the health, safety, and similar collective interests of the polity. In short, those decisions established the principle that lawful exercises of a State's police powers stand paramount

to private rights held under contract. Today's decision, in invalidating the New Jersey Legislature's 1974 repeal of its predecessor's 1962 covenant, rejects this previous understanding and remolds the Contract Clause into a potent instrument for overseeing important policy determinations of the state legislature. At the same time, by creating a constitutional safe haven for property rights embodied in a contract, the decision substantially distorts modern constitutional jurisprudence governing regulation of private economic interests. I might understand, though I could not accept, this revival of the Contract Clause were it in accordance with some coherent and constructive view of public policy. But elevation of the Clause to the status of regulator of the municipal bond market at the heavy price of frustration of sound legislative policymaking is as demonstrably unwise as it is unnecessary. The justification for today's decision, therefore, remains a mystery to me. . . .

I would not want to be read as suggesting that the States should blithely proceed down the path of repudiating their obligations, financial or otherwise. Their credibility in the credit market obviously is highly dependent on exercising their vast lawmaking powers with self-restraint and discipline, and I, for one, have little doubt that few, if any, jurisdictions would choose to use their authority "so foolish[ly] as to kill a goose that lays golden eggs for them." But in the final analysis, there is no reason to doubt that appellant's financial welfare is being adequately policed by the political processes and the bond marketplace itself. The role to be played by the Constitution is, at most, a limited one. For this Court should have learned long ago that the Constitution—be it through the Contract or Due Process Clause—can actively intrude into such economic and policy matters only if my Brethren are prepared to bear enormous institutional and social costs. Because I consider the potential dangers of such judicial interference to be intolerable, I dissent.

▼▲▼

## Allied Structural Steel Co. v. Spannaus
### 438 U.S. 234 (1978)

Allied Structural Steel Co. was an Illinois corporation that maintained a small office in Minnesota with thirty employees. In 1963 the company adopted a retirement plan entitling employees to receive a pension if they satisfied certain conditions of length of service and age. Those who left Allied Steel before the date at which they became vested in the retirement plan, whether voluntarily or through termination, did not receive a pension. Unlike most retirement plans today, which feature a combination of employer and employee contribution, Allied Steel was the sole contributor to its plan. It could amend the plan for any reason at any time.

To protect corporate employees from such arbitrary actions, the Minnesota legislature enacted in 1974 the Private Pension Benefit Protection Act. Among the law's features was a provision subjecting companies that closed down their offices in Minnesota to a "pension fund charge." The penalty went to fund full pensions for employees who had been with the same company for ten or more years.

In July 1974, Allied Steel began closing its Minnesota office, a decision that had been planned well before the legislature enacted the pension protection law. Nine dismissed employees with more than ten years of service had failed to meet the company's retirement plan. Minnesota assessed Allied Steel $185,000 to fund their pensions. The company brought suit against the state, claiming that its action violated the Contract Clause. A lower federal court rejected Allied Steel's argument, a decision that was affirmed on appeal.

The Court's decision was 5 to 3. Justice Stewart delivered the opinion of the Court. Justice Brennan, joined by Justices White and Marshall, dissented. Justice Blackmun took no part in the consideration of this case.

▼▲▼

MR. JUSTICE STEWART delivered the opinion of the Court.

There can be no question of the impact of the Minnesota Private Pension Benefits Protection Act upon the company's contractual relationships with its employees. The Act substantially altered those relationships by superimposing pension obligations upon the company conspicuously beyond those that it had voluntarily agreed to undertake. But it does not inexorably follow that the Act, as applied to the company, violates the Contract Clause of the Constitution. . . .

Although it was perhaps the strongest single constitutional check on state legislation during our early years as a Nation, the Contract Clause receded into comparative desuetude with the adoption of the Fourteenth Amendment, and particularly with the development of the large body of jurisprudence under the Due Process Clause of that Amendment in modern constitutional history. None-

theless, the Contract Clause remains part of the Constitution. It is not a dead letter. . . .

First of all, it is to be accepted as a commonplace that the Contract Clause does not operate to obliterate the police power of the States. "It is the settled law of this court that the interdiction of statutes impairing the obligation of contracts does not prevent the State from exercising such powers as are vested in it for the promotion of the common weal, or are necessary for the general good of the public, though contracts previously entered into between individuals may thereby be affected. This power, which in its various ramifications is known as the police power, is an exercise of the sovereign right of the Government to protect the lives, health, morals, comfort and general welfare of the people, and is paramount to any rights under contracts between individuals." . . .

If the Contract Clause is to retain any meaning at all . . . it must be understood to impose some limits upon the power of a State to abridge existing contractual relationships, even in the exercise of its otherwise legitimate police power. The existence and nature of those limits were clearly indicated in a series of cases in this Court arising from the efforts of the States to deal with the unprecedented emergencies brought on by the severe economic depression of the early 1930's.

In *Home Building & Loan Assn.* v. *Blaisdell*, (1934) the Court upheld against a Contract Clause attack a mortgage moratorium law that Minnesota had enacted to provide relief for homeowners threatened with foreclosure. Although the legislation conflicted directly with lenders' contractual foreclosure rights, the Court there acknowledged that, despite the Contract Clause, the States retain residual authority to enact laws "to safeguard the vital interests of [their] people." In upholding the state mortgage moratorium law, the Court found five factors significant. First, the state legislature had declared in the Act itself that an emergency need for the protection of homeowners existed. Second, the state law was enacted to protect a basic societal interest, not a favored group. Third, the relief was appropriately tailored to the emergency that it was designed to meet. Fourth, the imposed conditions were reasonable. And, finally, the legislation was limited to the duration of the emergency.

The *Blaisdell* opinion thus clearly implied that, if the Minnesota moratorium legislation had not possessed the characteristics attributed to it by the Court, it would have been invalid under the Contract Clause of the Constitution. . . .

In applying these principles to the present case, the first inquiry must be whether the state law has, in fact, operated as a substantial impairment of a contractual relationship. The severity of the impairment measures the height of the hurdle the state legislation must clear. Minimal alteration of contractual obligations may end the inquiry at its first stage. Severe impairment, on the other hand, will push the inquiry to a careful examination of the nature and purpose of the state legislation.

The severity of an impairment of contractual obligations can be measured by the factors that reflect the high value the Framers placed on the protection of private contracts. Contracts enable individuals to order their personal and business affairs according to their particular needs and interests. Once arranged, those rights and obligations are binding under the law, and the parties are entitled to rely on them.

Here, the company's contracts of employment with its employees included as a fringe benefit or additional form of compensation, the pension plan. The company's maximum obligation was to set aside each year an amount based on the plan's requirements for vesting. The plan satisfied the current federal income tax code and was subject to no other legislative requirements. And, of course, the company was free to amend or terminate the pension plan at any time. The company thus had no reason to anticipate that its employees' pension rights could become vested except in accordance with the terms of the plan. It relied heavily, and reasonably, on this legitimate contractual expectation in calculating its annual contributions to the pension fund.

The effect of Minnesota's Private Pension Benefits Protection Act on this contractual obligation was severe. The company was required in 1974 to have made its contributions throughout the pre-1974 life of its plan as if employees' pension rights had vested after 10 years, instead of vesting in accord with the terms of the plan. Thus, a basic term of the pension contract—one on which the company had relied for 10 years—was substantially modified. The result was that, although the company's past contributions were adequate when made, they were not adequate when computed under the 10-year statutory vesting requirement. The Act thus forced a current recalculation of the past 10 years' contributions based on the new, unanticipated 10-year vesting requirement.

Not only did the state law thus retroactively modify the compensation that the company had agreed to pay its employees from 1963 to 1974, but also it did so by changing the company's obligations in an area where the element of reliance was vital—the funding of a pension plan. . . .

Moreover, the retroactive state-imposed vesting requirement was applied only to those employers who terminated their pension plans or who, like the company, closed their Minnesota offices. The company was thus forced to make all the retroactive changes in its contractual obligations at one time. By simply proceeding to close its office in Minnesota, a move that had been planned before the passage of the Act, the company was assessed an immediate pension funding charge of approximately $185,000.

Thus, the statute in question here nullifies express terms of the company's contractual obligations and imposes a completely unexpected liability in potentially disabling amounts. . . . Yet there is no showing in the record before us that this severe disruption of contractual expectations was necessary to meet an important general social problem. The presumption favoring "legislative judgment as to the necessity and reasonableness of a particular measure," simply cannot stand in this case. . . .

[W]hether or not the legislation was aimed largely at a single employer, it clearly has an extremely narrow focus. It applies only to private employers who have at least 100 employees, at least one of whom works in Minnesota, and who have established voluntary private pension plans, qualified under 401 of the Internal Revenue Code. And it applies only when such an employer closes his Minnesota office or terminates his pension plan. Thus, this law can hardly be characterized, like the law at issue in the *Blaisdell* case, as one enacted to protect a broad societal interest, rather than a narrow class.

Moreover, in at least one other important respect, the Act does not resemble the mortgage moratorium legislation whose constitutionality was upheld in the *Blaisdell* case. This legislation, imposing a sudden, totally unanticipated, and substantial retroactive obligation upon the company to its employees, was not enacted to deal with a situation remotely approaching the broad and desperate emergency economic conditions of the early 1930's—conditions of which the Court in *Blaisdell* took judicial notice.

Entering a field it had never before sought to regulate, the Minnesota Legislature grossly distorted the company's existing contractual relationships with its employees by superimposing retroactive obligations upon the company substantially beyond the terms of its employment contracts. And that burden was imposed upon the company only because it closed its office in the State.

This Minnesota law simply does not possess the attributes of those state laws that, in the past, have survived challenge under the Contract Clause of the Constitution.

The law was not even purportedly enacted to deal with a broad, generalized economic or social problem. It did not operate in an area already subject to state regulation at the time the company's contractual obligations were originally undertaken, but invaded an area never before subject to regulation by the State. It did not effect simply a temporary alteration of the contractual relationships of those within its coverage, but worked a severe, permanent, and immediate change in those relationships—irrevocably and retroactively. And its narrow aim was leveled not at every Minnesota employer, not even at every Minnesota employer who left the State, but only at those who had, in the past, been sufficiently enlightened as voluntarily to agree to establish pension plans for their employees.

[W]e . . . hold that, if the Contract Clause means anything at all, it means that Minnesota could not constitutionally do what it tried to do to the company in this case.

MR. JUSTICE BRENNAN, with whom MR. JUSTICE WHITE and MR. JUSTICE MARSHALL join, dissenting.

In cases involving state legislation affecting private contracts, this Court's decisions over the past half century, consistently with both the constitutional text and its original understanding, have interpreted the Contract Clause as prohibiting state legislative Acts which, "[w]ith studied indifference to the interests of the [contracting party] or to his appropriate protection," effectively diminished or nullified the obligation due him under the terms of a contract. But the Contract Clause has not, during this period, been applied to state legislation that, while creating new duties, in nowise diminished the efficacy of any contractual obligation owed the constitutional claimant. The constitutionality of such legislation has, rather, been determined solely by reference to other provisions of the Constitution, e.g., the Due Process Clause, insofar as they operate to protect existing economic values.

Today's decision greatly expands the reach of the Clause. The Minnesota Private Pension Benefits Protection Act (Act) does not abrogate or dilute any obligation due a party to a private contract; rather, like all positive social legislation, the Act imposes new, additional obligations on a particular class of persons. In my view, any constitutional infirmity in the law must therefore derive not from the Contract Clause, but from the Due Process Clause of the Fourteenth Amendment. I perceive nothing in the Act that works a denial of due process, and therefore I dissent.

The primary question in this case is whether the Contract Clause is violated by state legislation enacted to protect employees covered by a pension plan by requiring an employer to make outlays—which, although not in this case, will largely be offset against future savings—to provide terminated employees with the equivalent of benefits reasonably to be expected under the plan. The Act does not relieve either the employer or his employees of any existing contract obligation. Rather, the Act simply creates an additional, supplemental duty of the employer, no different in kind from myriad duties created by a wide variety of legislative measures which defeat settled expectations but which have nonetheless been sustained by this Court. For this reason, the Minnesota Act, in my view, does not implicate the Contract Clause in any way. The basic fallacy of today's decision is its mistaken view that the Contract Clause protects all contract-based expectations, including that of an employer that his obligations to his employees will not be legislatively enlarged beyond those explicitly provided in his pension plan.

Historically, it is crystal clear that the Contract Clause was not intended to embody a broad constitutional policy of protecting all reliance interests grounded in private contracts. It was made part of the Constitution to remedy a particular social evil—the state legislative practice of enacting laws to relieve individuals of their obligations under certain contracts—and thus was intended to prohibit States from adopting "as [their] policy the repudiation of debts or the destruction of contracts or the denial of means to enforce them." But the Framers never contemplated that the Clause would limit the legislative power of States to enact laws creating duties that might burden some individuals in order to benefit others.

Today's conversion of the Contract Clause into a limitation on the power of States to enact laws that impose duties additional to obligations assumed under private contracts must inevitably produce results difficult to square with any rational conception of a constitutional order. Under the Court's opinion, any law that may be characterized as "superimposing" new obligations on those provided for by contract is to be regarded as creating "sudden, substantial, and unanticipated burdens" and then to be subjected to the most exacting scrutiny. The validity of such a law will turn upon whether judges see it as a law that deals with a generalized social problem, whether it is temporary (as few will be) or permanent, whether it operates in an area previously subject to regulation, and, finally, whether its duties apply to a broad class of persons. The necessary consequence of the extreme malleability of these rather vague criteria is to vest judges with broad subjective discretion to protect property interests that happen to appeal to them. . . .

The Act is an attempt to remedy a serious social problem: the utter frustration of an employee's expectations that can occur when he is terminated because his employer closes down his place of work. The burden on his employer is surely far less harsh than that saddled upon coal operators by the federal statute. Too, a large part of the employer's outlay that the Act requires will be offset against future savings. To this extent, the Act merely prevents the employer from obtaining a windfall, an effect which would immunize this aspect of the statutory requirement from attack even under the more stringent standards the Court reads into the Contract Clause. *El Paso* v. *Simmons* (1965). To the extent the Act does more than prevent a windfall, it is simply implementing a reasonable legislative judgment that the expectation interests of employees of more than 10 years' service in the receipt of a pension but who, as an actuarial matter, would not satisfy the vesting requirements of the pension plan, should not be frustrated by the generally unforeseen contingency of a plant's closing. . . .

Significantly, also, the Minnesota Act, unlike the federal statute upheld in Turner Elkhorn Mining, is not wholly retrospective in its operation. The Act requires an outlay from an employer like appellant only if after the enactment date of the Act (thus when it may give full consideration to the economic consequences of its decision) the employer decides to close its plant.

In sum, in my view, the Contract Clause has no applicability whatsoever to the Act, and because I conclude the Act is consistent with the only relevant constitutional restriction—the Due Process Clause—I would affirm the judgment of the District Court.

▼▲▼

## Energy Reserves Group v. Kansas Power & Light

### 459 U.S. 400 (1983)

Kansas Power & Light Company (KPL), a public utility, had a contract with Energy Reserves Group, Inc. (ERG) to purchase wellhead and residue gas from a certain gas field. The agreement provided that if a governmental authority fixes a price for any natural gas at a rate higher than the price specified in the contract, the contract price shall be increased to the higher level. It also gave ERG the option to reconsider the contract price once every two years. The companies agreed that the sole purpose of the price escalator clause is to compensate ERG for "anticipated" increases in its operating costs and for the value of its gas.

Another provision in the contract also provided that "[n]either party shall be held in default for failure to perform hereunder if such failure is due to compliance with" any "relevant present and future state and federal laws."

In 1978, Congress enacted the Natural Gas Policy Act. The act set a gradually increasing ceiling price for newly produced natural gas. It also extended federal price regulation to the intrastate gas market. The act further authorized states to set a maximum price that did not conflict with the federal regulation for natural gas.

In accord with the federal law, the Kansas legislature imposed price controls on its intrastate gas market when, in 1979, it enacted the Kansas Natural Gas Price Protection Act. ERG notified KPL that, consistent with the governmental price escalator clauses, ERG would escalate the price of its natural gas. KPL then decided to terminate the contract rather than pay the new price. After ERG insisted that KPL could not terminate the agreement, KPL filed suit in state court seeking a release from the contract. The court agreed with KPL that the Kansas price controls act did not violate the Contract Clause.

The Court's decision was unanimous. Justice Blackmun delivered the opinion of the Court. Justice Powell, joined by Chief Justice Burger and Justice Rehnquist, filed a concurring opinion.

JUSTICE BLACKMUN delivered the opinion of the Court.

This case concerns the regulation by the State of Kansas of the price of natural gas sold at wellhead in the intrastate market. It presents a federal Contract Clause issue and a statutory issue. . . .

ERG raises both statutory and constitutional issues in challenging the ruling of the Kansas Supreme Court. The constitutional issue is whether the Kansas Act impairs ERG's contracts with KPL in violation of the Contract Clause. The statutory issue is whether the federal enactment of §105 triggered the governmental price escalator clause. As to the latter issue, if §105's enactment did have that effect, ERG was entitled to a price increase on December 1, 1978. If not, ERG could rely only on the price redetermination clause for any increase. That clause could not be exercised until November, 1979. The statutory issue thus controls the timing of any increase. The constitutional issue, on the other hand, affects the price that ERG may claim under either clause. If ERG prevails, the price may be escalated to the §102 ceiling; if ERG does not prevail, the price may be escalated only to the §109 ceiling. We consider the Contract Clause issue first.

Although the language of the Contract Clause is facially absolute, its prohibition must be accommodated to the inherent police power of the State "to safeguard the vital interests of its people." *Home Bldg. & Loan Assn. v. Blaisdell* (1934). In *Blaisdell,* the Court approved a Minnesota mortgage moratorium statute, even though the statute retroactively impaired contract rights. The Court balanced the language of the Contract Clause against the State's interest in exercising its police power, and concluded that the statute was justified.

The Court in two recent cases has addressed Contract Clause claims. In *United States Trust Co. v. New Jersey* (1977), the Court held that New Jersey could not retroactively alter a statutory bond covenant relied upon by bond purchasers. One year later, in *Allied Structural Steel Co. v. Spannaus* (1978), the Court invalidated a Minnesota statute that required an employer who closed its office in the State to pay a "pension funding charge" if its pension fund at the time was insufficient to provide full benefits for all employees with at least 10 years' seniority. Although the legal issues and facts in these two cases differ in certain ways, they clarify the appropriate Contract Clause standard.

The threshold inquiry is "whether the state law has, in fact, operated as a substantial impairment of a contractual relationship." The severity of the impairment is said to increase the level of scrutiny to which the legislation will be subjected. Total destruction of contractual expectations is not necessary for a finding of substantial impairment. On the other hand, state regulation that restricts a party to gains it reasonably expected from the contract does not necessarily constitute a substantial impairment. In determining the extent of the impairment, we are to consider whether the industry the complaining party has entered has been regulated in the past. . . .

If the state regulation constitutes a substantial impairment, the State, in justification, must have a significant and legitimate public purpose behind the regulation, such as the remedying of a broad and general social or economic problem. Furthermore, since *Blaisdell,* the Court has indicated that the public purpose need not be addressed to an emergency or temporary situation. One legitimate state interest is the elimination of unforeseen windfall profits. The requirement of a legitimate public purpose guarantees that the State is exercising its police power, rather than providing a benefit to special interests.

Once a legitimate public purpose has been identified, the next inquiry is whether the adjustment of "the rights and responsibilities of contracting parties [is based] upon reasonable conditions and [is] of a character appropriate to the public purpose justifying [the legislation's] adoption." Unless the State itself is a contracting party, "[a]s is customary in reviewing [459 U.S. 413] economic and social regulation, . . . courts properly defer to legislative judgment as to the necessity and reasonableness of a particular measure."

It is in this context that the indefinite escalator clauses at issue here are to be viewed. In drafting each of the contracts, the parties included a statement of intent, which made clear that the escalator clause was designed to guarantee price increases consistent with anticipated increases in the value of ERG's gas. While it is not entirely inconceivable that ERG in September, 1975, anticipated the deregulation of gas prices introduced by the Act in 1978, we think this is highly unlikely, and we read the statement of intent to refer to nothing more than changes in value resulting from changes in the federal regulator's "just and reasonable" rates. In exchange for these anticipated increases, KPL agreed to accept gas from the Spivey-Grabs field for the lifetime of that field. Thus, at the time of the execution of the contracts, ERG did not expect to receive deregulated prices. The very existence of the governmental price escalator clause and the price redetermination clause indicates that the contracts were structured against the background of regulated gas prices. If deregulation had not occurred, the contracts undoubtedly would have called for a much smaller price increase than that provided by the Kansas Act's adoption of the §109 ceiling.

Moreover, the contracts expressly recognize the existence of extensive regulation by providing that any contractual terms are subject to relevant present and future state and federal law. This latter provision could be interpreted to incorporate all future state price regulation, and thus dispose of the Contract Clause claim. Regardless of whether this interpretation is correct, the provision does suggest that ERG knew its contractual rights were subject to alteration by state price regulation. Price regulation existed and was foreseeable as the type of law that would alter contract obligations. Reading the Contract Clause as ERG does would mean that indefinite price escalator clauses could exempt ERG from any regulatory limitation of prices whatsoever. Such a result cannot be permitted. In short, ERG's reasonable expectations have not been impaired by the Kansas Act.

To the extent, if any, the Kansas Act impairs ERG's contractual interests, the Kansas Act rests on, and is prompted by, significant and legitimate state interests.

Kansas has exercised its police power to protect consumers from the escalation of natural gas prices caused by deregulation. The State reasonably could find that higher gas prices have caused and will cause hardship among those who use gas heat but must exist on limited fixed incomes. . . .

The regulation of energy production and use is a matter of national concern. Congress set out on a new path with the Natural Gas Policy Act of 1978. In pursuing this path, Congress explicitly envisioned that the States would regulate intrastate markets in accordance with the overall national policy. The Kansas Natural Gas Price Protection Act is one State's effort to balance the need to provide incentives for the production of gas against the need to protect consumers from hardships brought on by deregulation of a traditionally regulated commodity. We see no constitutional or statutory infirmity in Kansas' attempt.

▼▲▼

## FOR FURTHER READING

Ackerman, Bruce. *Private Property and the Constitution.* New Haven, Conn.: Yale University Press, 1977.

Beard, Charles A. *An Economic Interpretation of the Constitution of the United States.* New York: Macmillan, 1913.

Clinton, Robert Lowery. *Marbury v. Madison and Judicial Review.* Lawrence: University Press of Kansas, 1989.

Epstein, Richard A. *Takings: Private Property and the Power of Eminent Domain.* Cambridge, Mass.: Harvard University Press, 1985.

Garraty, John A., ed. *Quarrels That Have Shaped the Constitution.* New York: Harper & Row, 1987.

Horwitz, Morton. *The Transformation of American Law, 1780–1860.* Cambridge, Mass.: Harvard University Press, 1977.

McGrath, C. Peter. *Yazoo: Law and Politics in the New Republic.* Providence, R.I.: Brown University Press, 1966.

Nedelsky, Jennifer. *Private Property and the Limits of American Constitutionalism.* Chicago: University of Chicago Press, 1990.

Sittes, Francis N. *Private Interest and Public Gain: The Dartmouth College Case.* Amherst: University of Massachusetts Press, 1972.

Wright, Benjamin F. *The Contract Clause of the Constitution.* Cambridge, Mass.: Harvard University Press, 1938.

# Rights, Rules, and the Economic Marketplace

In April 1993, fourteen-year-old Tommy McCoy landed just about the best summer job for which any young baseball fan living in Savannah, Georgia, could have hoped—batboy for the Savannah Cardinals, the class A minor league team of the Atlanta Braves. Every afternoon or evening the Cardinals played at home, Tommy's job was to organize the bats, stock them carefully in the dugout, and retrieve them from home plate after each player's turn at bat. Best of all, Tommy got to wear the Cardinal uniform and hang out with players who might one day make the major leagues.

But in May the Cardinals were forced to fire Tommy after an investigator for the United States Department of Labor informed team officials that fourteen year olds were not permitted to work past 7 P.M. on school nights. Cardinal management, players, coaches, and fans were heartsick over Tommy's fate. Facing a stiff fine for violating federal child labor laws, the team had no real choice other than to let him go. Even Tommy's teachers submitted copies of his grade reports to Labor Department investigators to show what a good, well-behaved student he was at school. Tough, responded the Labor Department. The law is the law.

Secretary of Labor Robert B. Reich had no idea who Tommy McCoy was or the fate that had befallen him until several weeks later. When Reich turned on his television one June morning to catch the news, he heard that the Savannah Cardinals were planning a "Save Tommy's Job Night." The purpose was to attract attention to what the entire city believed was the clearest example of bone-headed, bureaucratic decision making it had ever seen. Horrified by the negative public re-

sponse the story would stir up if it made the evening news programs, Reich immediately convened a meeting of his senior staff responsible for the enforcement of child labor laws. He wanted an explanation of what he also believed was a silly decision. Reich informed his staff he wanted Tommy reinstated.

"You can't back down," replied his staff, which then went on to tell him of the potential consequences of allowing Tommy to work on school nights. Vendors would exploit young kids to sell peanuts and popcorn; stadiums would hire fourteen-year-old janitors; and parking lots would use kids to collect money. And all of this would take place past 7 P.M. on school nights.

What about an exemption for batboys and batgirls? suggested Reich.

Silence.

Reich decided to make the decision himself. "We'll tell the Savannah team that they can keep Tommy. We'll change the regulation to allow batboys and -girls. I want to put out a press release right *now,* saying that the application of child labor laws to batboys is *silly.*"

But as Reich made his decision, a network news program had already begun to air the story. The secretary ordered his assistant to call one of the show's producers on the air to inform the network that the department had reversed its earlier ruling. Two minutes into the reporter's story of Tommy's firing at the hands of federal bureaucrats, the anchor chimed in to announce the tale's happy ending: Tommy would be permitted to go back to work. The Cardinals changed the night's scheduled events from "Save Tommy's Job Night" to "We Saved Tommy's Job Night."

Reich knew his staff was not pleased with his decision, in no small part because, in his own words, he "caved in" to the media attention given the story. He did so, however, because he believed the public was right to be outraged over the bureaucrats' lack of common sense. The public is not always right, Reich later commented, and there are times and places for taking stands on principle. But the case of Tommy the batboy was not it.[1]

Prior to the Constitutional Revolution of 1937, such a face-off between the federal government and business owners over work rules for children would have been unthinkable, as the Court refused to uphold legislation that, in its view, interfered in the private contractual arrangements between employers and employees. The Progressive Era reform movement had persuaded the states to enact child labor, minimum wage, maximum work hour, and occupational safety laws directed toward the employment practices of American business. Nonetheless, the Court struck down these laws in serial fashion during the forty-year period between 1897 and 1937 on the grounds that such rules violated an employer's "liberty of contract," a right derived from the Due Process Clause of the Fourteenth Amendment.

How did the Court conclude that such a fundamental right to control economic arrangements existed? Simple. It took the provision of the Fourteenth Amendment prohibiting the deprivation of life, liberty, or property without due process of law and fused it with an interpretation of the Constitution holding that such rights were "absolute" in the minds of the Framers. Most scholars now consider the liberty of contract era an aberration in American constitutional development, a judicial invention influenced by the economic and social philosophies created to defend the Gilded Age era of American capitalism that emerged after the Industrial Revolution. This assessment is more than fair, as the Court has not invalidated a federal or state law on liberty of contract grounds since 1937.

This chapter examines one of the most controversial periods in American constitutional development, one in which the Court crafted a series of rulings that profoundly altered the relationship between the rights and rules governing entrance into the economic marketplace. How the Court made the principles of "laissez faire" economics into a constitutional mandate after the Civil War and then, with the Constitutional Revolution of 1937, rejected them in favor of the New Deal offers an important lesson in how the interplay of social and economic forces influences the development of law. This transition in legal thought represented a monumental shift in the Court's views on the relationship between law, economics, and the social order. No longer did the Court accept the assumption that laissez-faire economics was a natural condition of a preexisting political order. Instead, the justices embraced the view that ownership rights were a product of law. As such, rules setting the boundaries of economic relationships were the product of political choices and not merely the reflection of a natural condition.[2]

The cases and materials in this chapter also illuminate how the Court's determination to embrace laissez faire as a constitutional requirement led to other critical developments in the law. These include the creation of legal rules that justified everything from racial segregation to the different standards that applied to men and women in the workplace. The Court's deliberate decision in 1937 to abandon the economic and social choices of a previous generation represented more than a simple repudiation of the liberty of contract doctrine. That decision ushered in an entirely new understanding of the relationship between law and society, one with which the Court continues to struggle in an effort to balance the complex forces that contribute to the linear progress of constitutional law.

## Due Process and Entrepreneurial Rights: The Strange But True Story of "Liberty of Contract"

The Court's gradual departure from Marshall-era absolutism on the Contract Clause to the more deferential stance toward public interest–oriented state regulation of contractual rights that began under Roger Taney in the 1830s did not mean that the Court was prepared to abandon the interests of the propertied classes. In retrospect, one can argue that the Taney Court's embrace of state regulation was not driven by a concern for the judicial correction of social and economic inequities. Rather, it was part of a larger effort to replace the Marshall Court's emphasis on Federalist constitutional nationalism with the Jacksonian principles of states' rights and dual federalism. *Dred Scott* v. *Sandford* (1857), of course, later obscured the Taney Court's great achievement: the development of a well-respected constitutional jurisprudence of nation-state equilibrium, one largely in sync with the political moment. Some scholars, however, have argued that *Dred Scott* should not be seen as an exception in the Taney Court's judicial legacy. In this view expansion of state police power to regulate economic development was a tolerable byproduct of Taney's broader desire "to protect state interests and institutions, and preeminently the institution of slavery" from congressional intrusion.[3]

Constitutional protection for economic growth did not receive short shrift under Taney. Although it did not have the nationalist bent of John Marshall's Supreme Court, the Taney Court did not leave Congress powerless to manage commercial development on a national scale. Its Commerce Clause decisions demonstrated that the Taney Court held no illusions about the direction of the American political economy. By the 1850s whatever vision remained of the Jefferson-Jacksonian agrarian ideal had been subsumed by a thriving, national mercantilist economy. The Taney Court wanted states to have as much say in this economic transformation as possible. Moreover, it did not want national legislative power to reach a point that would permit Congress to abolish slavery. Such was the basis for Roger Taney's emphasis on state power in the American constitutional structure.

But the Civil War, Reconstruction, and the addition of the Thirteenth, Fourteenth, and Fifteenth Amendments to the Constitution appeared to nullify the dual federalism developed by the Taney Court on behalf of state power. The constitutional balance between national and state power, the issue that had so occupied the Marshall and Taney Courts, appeared settled for the moment. Prior to the Civil War, the Court had addressed all other questions of constitutional law within this central context. Now the Court confronted a different America, one that faced a new set of social, economic, and political challenges.

Were the old rules created by the Marshall and Taney Courts now obsolete? How would the destruction of the Southern economy affect the social and economic organization of that region? How much discretion would states receive under the restrictions placed on them by the Fourteenth Amendment to exercise their police power in the public interest? How much control would Congress and the Court have over state legislation in the wake of the nation's rebirth? What specific guarantees did the majestic phrases of the Fourteenth Amendment afford to the former slaves and general population?

The Marshall and Taney Courts defined the political tenor of their times. Now, although absent a chief justice as dominant as either of these men, the Court would continue to perform this function. The Court's pervasive imprint on American social and economic development in the late-nineteenth and early-twentieth centuries led directly to the nation's first major post–Civil War constitutional crisis, when the Court and President Franklin Roosevelt locked swords over the New Deal. Economic liberties again assumed a central place in the Court's vision of the constitutional order. This time, however, the Court's concern was not with whether national or state power was the appropriate constitutional source of regulation; it was with whether the Constitution permitted *any* regulation of economic and contractual liberties. Curiously enough, the answer to that question did not rest with the Anglo-American legal tradition, but with the speculative theories of an obscure British evolutionary scientist.

## Charles Darwin Meets Constitutional Law

No student of American constitutional law could have possibly expected that the 1859 publication of Charles Darwin's *The Origin of Species* would provide the intellectual undercurrent for the Supreme Court's conscious decision in the late nineteenth century to incorporate laissez-faire economics into the Due Process Clause of the Fourteenth Amendment.[4] Nor could any constitutional scholar have predicted what a profound impact the scholarship of another Englishman, the sociologist Herbert Spencer, would have on the Court's new defense of the Fourteenth Amendment right to liberty of contract. Spencer, in his most influential work, *Social Statics* (1851), sought to synthesize the evolutionary principles later popularized by Darwin with the arithmetical principles of British economist Thomas Malthus to support a sociological defense of economic individualism.[5] Darwin, in fact, credited Yale sociologist William Graham

Sumner for the famous phrase most often associated with Darwinism: "the survival of the fittest."

In 1883, Sumner, with the publication of *What Social Classes Owe to Each Other,* became the first high-profile American intellectual to blow the notes of the social Darwinian trumpet in a clear, unmistakable tone.[6] Sumner's singular accomplishment, in historian Richard Hofstadter's view, was to merge "the three great traditions of western capitalist culture: the Protestant ethic, the doctrines of classical economics, and Darwinian natural selection" into a unified theory of social organization. This fusion of ideas perfectly complemented the impulses that dominated the social and economic forces behind the Industrial Revolution. In particular, one cannot overestimate the influence of Darwinism on the economic and political elites that came to power during the post–Industrial Revolution era. Darwinism added the weight of "scientific evidence" to the popular Gilded Age belief that "all attempts to reform social processes were efforts to remedy the irredeemable, that they interfered with the wisdom of nature, and that they could lead only to degeneration."[7]

Sumner, more than Darwin and Spencer, directed his work toward the American social and political condition. Darwin's chief concern was to explain the evolution of plant and animal species, not to provide the United States Supreme Court with incontrovertible scientific evidence to justify a legal jurisprudence rooted in laissez-faire economics. Meanwhile, Spencer focused on a "comprehensive world-view, uniting under one generalization everything in nature from protozoa to politics."[8]

Unlike Darwin and Spencer, Sumner did not seek to remake the world. Instead, he used his teaching position at Yale to write and lecture on the natural evolution of industrial societies into economic oligarchies and the evil of political interference with the natural social and economic order brought about by this evolution. Sumner also decried the "wasteful" efforts of both government and private charity to protect the weak or promote social welfare. Natural evolution of the social and economic order would eliminate the weak in favor of a productive industrial class.

Interference with this natural progression of society through protective legislation, wrote Sumner, would ultimately "destroy the finest efforts of the wise and industrious, and are dead weight on the society in its struggle to realize any better things."[9] Life was what it was. And the sooner that one accepted his or her place in the evolutionary process, the better. As Sumner put it, "Everyone is a child of his age and cannot get out of it."[10] Sumner's confidence in Darwinian natural selection analogies to explain the current social and economic structure was unshakable. To tinker with the forces of social determinism was to tinker with evolution itself, something over which individuals, no matter what their motivation, were powerless. Government should protect the natural order, not destroy it.

Supported by Darwin's universal explanation of adaptation and survival, the Court seized upon the social theories of Spencer and Sumner. It was eager to find a constitutional home to protect the freedom of contract, a right it claimed was derived from the laws of nature. Constitutional law's alliance with social Darwinism, as well as the strains within the Court, is best expressed in the Court's signature decision of this period, *Lochner v. New York* (1905). In *Lochner* the Court struck down a New York state maximum work hour law, holding that "the freedom of master and employe[e] to contract with each other . . . cannot be prohibited or interfered with" without violating the liberty provision of the Due Process Clause.[11]

In dissent, Justice Oliver Wendell Holmes wrote, "[T]he Fourteenth Amendment does not enact Mr. Herbert Spencer's *Social Statics.*"[12] Holmes was not concerned with whether Spencer was right and, in fact, had privately complemented Spencer's work. In general, Holmes was quite comfortable with laissez-faire economics and the "survival of the fittest" principles that animated this theory. He distrusted social reformers, to whom he referred as do-gooders. Little doubt exists, in fact, that Holmes would have voted against most, if not all, of the Progressive reform legislation.[13]

What raised Holmes's judicial hackles was the application of so-called scientific principles to questions of legal jurisprudence. Distrustful of absolutes and doubtful of natural law's "certainties," Holmes was a firm believer in *legal positivism,* or laws enacted by people through the deliberative nature of the legislative process.[14] The Constitution, wrote Holmes in *Lochner,* was not "intended to embody a particular economic theory, whether of paternalism and the organic relationship of the citizen to the State or of laissez faire." If legislatures wanted to enact a law on behalf of the general welfare, the Constitution posed no barrier. Holmes, in language that later formed the basis of the Court's post–*Lochner* era jurisprudence on economic regulation, said all that was required of such legislation was a rational basis for its enactment.[15]

## The Progressive Response

*Lochner* represented more than just the Court's clearest and most articulate opinion to date in defense of the liberty of contract guarantee. In striking down a centerpiece of the Progressive agenda, the Court positioned itself solidly against a social movement that had begun to emerge as a force in American politics. Perhaps it is mere coincidence that the decision in which the Court first announced its support for the liberty of contract theory of the Due Process Clause, *Allgeyer* v. *Louisiana* (1897), came around the same time that Progressive politics began to flourish in cities and states throughout the nation. As one historian has described the rise of Progressivism:

> What had happened, as a great many men of good will saw it at the beginning of the Progressive era, was that in the extraordinary outburst of productive energy of the last few decades, the nation had not developed in any corresponding degree the means of meeting human needs or controlling or reforming the manifold evils that come with any such rapid physical change. The Progressive movement, then, may be looked upon as an attempt to develop the moral will, the intellectual insight and the political and administrative agencies to remedy the accumulated evils and negligences of a period of industrial growth.[16]

Economic absolutism and social determinism had no place in Progressivism. Presidents Theodore Roosevelt (1905–1913) and Woodrow Wilson (1913–1921); Robert M. La Follette, who served as governor of Wisconsin and then as U.S. senator from that state; Upton Sinclair, author of *The Jungle;* Louis Brandeis, who revolutionized the practice of public interest law in his work with the National Consumers' League prior to serving on the Supreme Court; Herbert Croly, author of *The Promise of American Life;* journalist Walter Lippman; social activist and Hull-House founder Jane Addams; and women's rights leader Florence Kelly were among the more prominent individuals associated with the Progressive movement.

The diverse composition of the Progressive movement naturally led to internal disagreements over which aspects of American public and economic life were most in need of reform. Still, the Progressives shared a fundamental belief that activist government was essential to social progress and the general improvement of the human condition. Civic alertness, brought about through strong political leadership and the public exposure of corporate excesses, would result in pressure for legislative reform. Legislative initiatives would result in laws to protect men, women, and children in the workplace, improve the environment, reign in corporate monopolies, and alleviate poverty. Liberal reform through the democratic process offered the best hope to redeem the crass materialism and indifference to human needs that characterized the political and business atmosphere that prospered in post–industrial America.[17]

From 1897, when *Allgeyer* was decided, until 1937, when the Court reversed course in *West Coast Hotel Co.* v. *Parrish,* the entrepreneurial, antigovernment conception of American constitutionalism butted heads with the reform-minded, regulation-oriented impulses of the Progressive movement in one case after another. This period, as you will see, became a transforming interval in American constitutional development, one in which the Court's creation and self-imposed rejection of the liberty of contract theory represents just one story line. Another was the successful challenge directed at legal formalism by proponents of a method of constitutional interpretation that incorporated sociological and historical reasoning and analysis.

Such gifted and influential jurists as Holmes, Brandeis, Benjamin Cardozo, and Harlan Fiske Stone were instrumental in the demise of *Lochner* and the rise, in its place, of a liberal, sociological-oriented jurisprudence. Whether coming from the pen of one of Holmes's great dissents; from Cardozo, who commented in his well-regarded book, *The Nature of the Judicial Process,* that "[t]he great tides and currents which engulf the rest of mankind do not turn aside in their course, and pass the judges idly by"; or from Stone, who, in *United States* v. *Carolene Products* (1938) wrote an opinion for the constitutional ages when he held that economic regulation was not presumptively unconstitutional, but laws that fell within "a specific prohibition of the Constitution," such as those of the Bill of Rights, should receive "exacting judicial scrutiny," the Court's direction after the Constitutional Revolution of 1937 was clear: Courts could not and should not approach the economic and social problems raised in modern litigation independent of their causes and consequences. Legal formalism as a vibrant constitutional doctrine, which dominated both the bench and the bar in American jurisprudence after the Civil War, died when the Court, in *West Coast Hotel*, validated the constitutional foundation of the modern welfare state created by the New Deal.[18]

Litigation as an instrument of social and political reform, as opposed to a vehicle for the implementation of the "vested rights" doctrine and corporate advantage, also emerged during the Progressive Era. The National Consumers' League (NCL), which women's rights activists formed in the 1890s to publicize and counter the poor working conditions and wages of female employees, turned to the courts to defend the constitutionality of the protective laws for which it had successfully lobbied in state legislatures. Litigation now provided the reform movement with an additional weapon in its arsenal for political and social change. In *Muller v. Oregon* (1908), which involved a liberty of contract challenge to an Oregon law that prohibited women from working more than ten hours per day in professional laundries, the NCL submitted an innovative amicus curiae brief emphasizing factual data rather than legal arguments to document the ill effects of long hours on women's health.

NCL general secretary Florence Kelley, a former law student with ties to other consumer and women's rights organizations in the Progressive movement, approached Louis Brandeis to defend the Oregon law before the Supreme Court. By this time, Brandeis had secured a reputation through his labor law practice as one the nation's foremost legal minds. It was in *Muller* that Brandeis made his most significant contribution to the practice of public interest law—the "Brandeis Brief," or the use of social science data to support legal arguments. This approach to legal argument became a staple in the litigation strategies of the next generation of the liberal reform movement.[19] Our SIDEBAR on *Muller* describes in greater detail Florence Kelley's key role in bringing the NCL to the forefront of the Progressive movement.

Still, the question remains: How did the battle over the meaning and application of the Due Process Clause of the Fourteenth Amendment come to this? How did language designed to enforce the constitutional rights of African Americans after the Civil War and create universal citizenship under the Constitution of the United States come to mean that business enterprises must be protected from the ill-conceived efforts of the political process to meddle with the natural evolution of the American social and economic order? Before we turn to the Court's opinions that provide the cinematic scope of the rise and fall of the liberty of contract theory of the Due Process Clause, we must first retrace our steps to the Court's initial interpretation of the Fourteenth Amendment after its ratification in 1870.

### The *Slaughterhouse Cases* and the Judicial Nullification of the Fourteenth Amendment

Given the choice, what are the odds that we would associate the tortuous path of the Due Process Clause of the Fourteenth Amendment from its enactment through *West Coast Hotel* with the decision of the Louisiana legislature in 1869 to award a single corporation monopolistic control over the slaughter of livestock? Consider, for a moment, the three core provisions of the Fourteenth Amendment: "No state shall make or enforce any law which shall abridge the privileges or immunities of citizens of the United States . . . nor deprive any person of life, liberty, or property, without due process of law . . . [or] the equal protection of the laws." Perhaps the most obvious purpose and intent of the Reconstruction-era Congress was to overturn *Dred Scott* and establish full citizenship (including all associated privileges, immunities, and civil rights) for African Americans, regardless of their previous condition.

After that, what was the Fourteenth Amendment designed to accomplish? Did the restraints on state power reflect a congressional concern to make the guarantees of the Bill of Rights applicable to the states? Was the Fourteenth Amendment written for African Americans, as a constitutional reparation for their enslavement and the injustices bestowed upon them by *Dred Scott*, or for all citizens of the United States, in a statement of the new nation-state relationship in post–Civil War America?

*A New Orleans slaughterhouse in the 1870s. The Court's decision in the* Slaughterhouse Cases *(1873) severely limited the power of the federal government to enforce the Fourteenth Amendment, and set the stage for a judicial counterrevolution ultimately resulting in the doctrine of "liberty of contract."*
Courtesy of the Louisiana State Museum.

Good questions, all. But it does seem strange, upon first glance, that the Court would use a case involving a dispute between New Orleans butchers over the "right" to compete for a share of the slaughterhouse market to give its first full-blown judicial construction to the Fourteenth Amendment. Even more bizarre was the Court's reliance on what one constitutional scholar has called the "Negro rights" theory of the Fourteenth Amendment to uphold the exercise of state legislative power to regulate an economic question that had absolutely nothing to do with African Americans.[20] The Court was asked to decide whether the Louisiana statute, in sealing off competition in the slaughterhouse market, abridged the "privileges and immunities" of independent butchers because it denied them, in effect, the right to engage in their economic livelihood.

Before moving on to *Butchers' Benevolent Association v. Crescent City Livestock Landing & Slaughterhouse Co.*

(1873), better known as the *Slaughterhouse Cases*, consider these questions: If not for the Fourteenth Amendment, enacted in 1868, would the aggrieved butchers have even brought this case? Recall from Chapter 8 that the Court, prior to the Civil War, had steered its Contract Clause decisions in a direction much more amenable to legislative dominance in economic matters. Do constitutional amendments provide creative litigants—and creative justices—the chance to reconsider outdated rules or to simply create new constitutional rights?

The *Slaughterhouse Cases* raise all these questions and more. Justice Samuel F. Miller's majority opinion in the *Slaughterhouse Cases* did not entertain the "economic rights" theory of the Due Process Clause advanced by the New Orleans butchers. His opinion, one the most criticized, yet pivotal in American constitutional development, was devoted to the scope of the procedural safeguards created by the Fourteenth Amendment and their application to alleged state violations of constitutional rights.

The dissents of Justices Stephen Field and Joseph Bradley, however, made clear that the seeds of such a reading of the Due Process Clause already had begun to germinate. It would take almost twenty-five years for the liberty of contract theory to fully emerge in the Court's conception of the substantive guarantees created by the Due Process Clause. During this period important changes were at work in the Court's interpretation of the Equal Protection Clause as well. Upon closer examination, more than a tangential relationship exists between the theoretical foundation established for the Due Process Clause in the *Slaughterhouse Cases* and the judicial creation of the "separate but equal doctrine" enshrined in *Plessy* v. *Ferguson* (1896).[21]

The *Slaughterhouse Cases* left an indelible mark upon constitutional law and development, one that affected the course of the Fourteenth Amendment's interpretation and application for generations to come. How so? First, Justice Miller found that "the most cursory" glance at the Civil War amendments revealed a "unity of purpose, when taken in connection with the history of the times." That purpose was to protect the rights of African Americans from their former oppressors.[22] Such a construction of the Fourteenth Amendment set aside the argument of whether it was intended to protect the "fundamental" rights of all citizens, without regard to race, as state residents from state legislative intrusion. It was not. The Privileges and Immunities Clause protected only a narrow band of rights and privileges, such as the right to protection on the high seas and the right to interstate travel, since these were requisites of national citizenship. Fundamental rights of the nature associated with protection from the national government were not transferable to the states.

Second, the Court used the *Slaughterhouse Cases* to affirm its 1833 decision in *Barron* v. *Baltimore,* which held that the Bill of Rights restrained national, not state, power as it affected fundamental rights claims. The Court thus refused the chance to embrace the Fourteenth Amendment as an instrument intended to extend the protections of the Bill of Rights to the states. Justice Miller's construction of the Privileges and Immunities Clause runs counter to the intent of the Radical Republicans who dominated the proceedings over the Fourteenth Amendment. They believed that the Privileges

and Immunities Clause embraced the fundamental rights of *national* citizenship that the states could not abridge. Seen in this light, Justice Miller inverted the entire design of the Fourteenth Amendment.[23]

Also difficult to square is the Court's simultaneous nullification of the Privileges and Immunities Clause and affirmation of *Barron* with its conclusion that the Fourteenth Amendment was, above all, intended to extend the Constitution's protections to African Americans. In Justice Miller's opinion the Fourteenth Amendment did not require the states to respect core constitutional guarantees as conditions of national citizenship. Applied to the Equal Protection Clause, this interpretation left no constraints on the states to create a new, albeit "separate" standard of citizenship for blacks. The Fourteenth Amendment, as Justice Miller wrote, had "nothing to do" with state enforcement of the Constitution's fundamental rights guarantees. If that was true, Justice Steven Field wrote in dissent, then the Fourteenth Amendment was a "vain and idle enactment, which accomplished nothing and most unnecessarily excited Congress and the people upon its passage."[24]

The Court's narrow interpretation of the Fourteenth Amendment laid the groundwork for a series of decisions that devastated all the possibilities that Reconstruction might have held for African American equality.[25] Two cases stand out. In *United States* v. *Cruikshank* (1876), a case borne out of the Colfax massacre, the bloodiest race-motivated killing and lynching spree of the Reconstruction era, the Court held that the responsibility for prosecuting criminal acts rested with state and local authorities, not the national government. This decision, rooted in the Court's pre–Civil War conception of federalism, rendered the Enforcement Act of 1870, designed to provide federal remedies for conspiracies intended to deprive individuals of their civil rights, without force. The Court said, in effect, that the Fourteenth Amendment did not confer upon Congress, the language of Section 5 aside, the power to protect blacks or provide legal remedies for constitutional violations as citizens of their respective states.

In 1883 the Court, in a decision that consolidated several challenges to the Civil Rights Act of 1875, ruled that Congress had no power under the Fourteenth Amendment to enforce the Equal Protection Clause outside of direct state action. The law prohibited racial discrimination in public accommodations. In the *Slaughterhouse*

*Cases,* Justice Bradley, dissenting, had written that "the mischief to be remedied" by the Fourteenth Amendment "was not merely slavery and its . . . consequences; but that spirit of insubordination and disloyalty . . . and (allow) every citizen . . . the full enjoyment of every right and privilege belonging to a freedman, without fear of violence or molestation."[26] Ten years later, now writing for the *Civil Rights Cases* majority, Bradley held that the Fourteenth Amendment did not confer upon Congress the power to "create a code of municipal law for the regulation of private rights."[27]

Discrimination might well be wrong, offered Justice Bradley, but it is a "private wrong," one that the government is powerless to eradicate. The Fourteenth Amendment provides a guarantee against wrongful acts "sanctioned in some way by the State"; it does not, however, prohibit the exercise of such acts when carried out in private. Justice Bradley, who had argued in his dissent in the *Slaughterhouse Cases* that the Fourteenth Amendment was foremost a constitutional provision to protect African Americans, had completely reversed himself.

Given the line of logic from the *Slaughterhouse Cases* through *Cruikshank* to the *Civil Rights Cases,* the Court's decision in *Plessy* should not come as a surprise. Here is what the Court said:

- The Privileges and Immunities Clause does not recognize the transfer of national rights to the states. Responsibility for the substantive content of fundamental rights and their enforcement belongs to the states (*Slaughterhouse Cases*).

- The Fourteenth Amendment does not authorize the national government to enforce congressional laws intended to protect the civil rights of African Americans. The protection of citizens in the states is the business of state and local government (*Cruikshank*).

- Section 5 of the Fourteenth Amendment, which gives Congress the power to enforce the Privileges and Immunities, Due Process, and Equal Protection Clauses, does not confer upon African Americans the right to use public accommodations. Such rights are *private* in nature (*Civil Rights Cases*).

By this logic, discrimination against blacks in hotels, restaurants, and theaters did not reflect second-class citizenship. Such policies were a mirror of private customs, which were independent of state authority. In the *Civil Rights Cases,* the Court distinguished between the rights afforded to persons as public and private citizens, thus extending state independence from the Bill of Rights that the inverted federalism of the *Slaughterhouse Cases* and *Cruikshank* had created. But because the Court had said that African Americans were dependent upon the states for the recognition and enforcement of their fundamental rights, and that such rights were limited to their capacities as public citizens, what possible route was left for the Court to travel in *Plessy* but to validate the "separate but equal" doctrine?

So how did a case that laid the foundation for a racial caste system in the United States manage to become a manifesto for the liberty of contract interpretation of the Due Process Clause, one that reigned supreme from 1897 to 1937? Constitutional scholars most often point to the dissents of Justice Field and Justice Bradley as the foundation upon which this theory was constructed. First, let us consider Justice Field's dissent:

What, then, are the privileges and immunities which are secured against abridgements by state legislation?

The privileges and immunities designated are those which of right belong to the citizens of all free governments. Clearly among these must be placed the right to pursue a lawful employment in a lawful manner, without other restraint than such as equally affects all persons. . . .

This equality of right . . . is the distinguishing privilege of citizens of the United States. To them everywhere, all pursuits, all professions, all avocations are open without other restrictions than such as are imposed equally upon all others of the same age, sex and condition. *The state may prescribe such regulations . . . as will promote the public health, secure the good order and advance the general prosperity of society, but when once prescribed, the pursuit or calling must be free to be followed by every citizen who is within the conditions designated, and will conform to the regulations. This is the fundamental idea upon which our institutions rest, and unless adhered to in the legislation of the country our government will be a Republic only in name.* The Fourteenth Amendment, in my judgement, makes it essential to the validity of the legislation of every state that this equality of right should be respected.[28]

So that no one would misunderstand where he was prepared to take the Fourteenth Amendment, Justice Field, in a footnote toward the end of his dissent, alluded to Adam Smith's theory of labor value. Field observed that legislative interference with the "natural" terms of labor, as the foundation of property, constituted a "manifest encroachment upon the just liberty both of the workman and those who might be disposed to employ him."[29] Political scientist Paul Kens has commented that Justice Field's unswerving commitment to contract and property rights as the core of American constitutional value was such that it was "as if he had laid a page of the *U.S. Supreme Court Reporter* over *Social Statics* and traced Herbert Spencer's first principle."[30]

Justice Field's dissent is paradoxical, for he argues that the Privileges and Immunities Clause did in fact alter the federal relationship and prohibit the states from trespassing upon fundamental rights. But he emphasized that the most important of those rights were economic, not social and political, as the Radical Republicans had argued during the ratification debates over the Fourteenth Amendment. Although it left no doubt about how he read its substantive guarantees, Justice Field's dissent did not make clear where those rights received their specific protection in the Fourteenth Amendment. It was Justice Bradley who gave that construction its ultimate home—the Due Process Clause.

Justice Bradley concurred with Justice Field that the Court had missed the mark in its interpretation of the Privileges and Immunities Clause. To remedy this mistake, Bradley linked Justice Field's concern for economic rights to the historical concern of the Due Process Clause. In American constitutional law, due process centers on the notion that government is required to respect "fundamental fairness" when it wants to deprive persons of their rights and liberties. Fundamental fairness traditionally is considered the right to advance notice and the right to contest the government's claim in court. Justice Bradley offered a different take:

> In my view, a law which prohibits a large class of citizens from adopting a lawful employment, or from following a lawful employment previously adopted, does deprive them of liberty as well as property, without due process of law. Their right of choice is a portion of their liberty; their occupation is their property. Such a law also deprives those citizens of the equal protection of the laws, contrary to the last clause of the section.[31]

In other words, liberty and property operate in tandem. To deny one is to deny the other. The only way to protect these rights against arbitrary assault, which Justice Bradley equated with the exercise of police power through the legislative process, was to accept the economic principles of laissez faire as an article of constitutional faith. With Justice Bradley's dissent, the jurisprudence of "substantive" due process, or the recognition of "values not explicitly designated for special protection by the Constitution, yet values which government may not impinge upon without meeting an unusually high standard of justification," was born.[32]

Clever as his articulation of a Due Process Clause–based liberty of contract theory was, Justice Bradley did not develop it by himself. He had help from the lawyer who argued on behalf of the aggrieved New Orleans butchers, John A. Campbell. Campbell drew heavily upon legal theorist Thomas M. Cooley's seminal book on the centrality of property rights in American constitutional law, *Constitutional Limitations,* published in 1868, the same year the Fourteenth Amendment was ratified.[33] Political scientist Benjamin R. Twiss has noted that Cooley's book, published "almost as a direct counter to the appearance a year earlier of Karl Marx's *Das Kapital,*" emerged as the most influential legal text in the creation of nineteenth-century laissez-faire constitutional doctrine.[34]

Cooley's great contribution to the liberty of contract doctrine later embraced by the Court came in his comprehensive articulation of the "substantive" due process principle into a unified theory that prohibited state interference with property and contract rights. He believed that the private basis of American society was based on the laissez-faire premise that government existed to protect property, not compete with or regulate it. Judicial review, which Cooley did not question as a component of judicial power, existed to enforce the "constitutional limitations" on legislative power. In some sense Cooley's argument on behalf of substantive due process does not seem that different from those advanced in defense of the "vested rights" doctrine that shaped the constitutional development of the Contract Clause under John Marshall. Protection for private property animates both theories.

A more careful examination offers another result. Substantive due process is rooted in the constitutional phrase of the same name, whereas the doctrine of vested rights is derived from natural rights principles external to the text of the Constitution. Cooley argued that extra-constitutional justifications for the protection of private property were unnecessary. The Constitution provided a textual source in the Due Process Clause. That provision alone created absolute protection against interference with property and contract rights. On this latter point Cooley went beyond anything Marshall had ever envisioned for the Contract Clause to include the right to enter into prospective agreements without government interference, as well as respect the enforcement of existing contracts. *Constitutional Limitations* was almost singularly responsible for the transformation of the procedural guarantees of the Due Process Clause as it applied to personal rights to a substantive principle that protected property rights.[35]

Cooley's theories on the Due Process Clause could not have found a worthier courtroom advocate than John Campbell. A former Supreme Court justice (1853–1861) who served until Alabama, his home state, seceded from the Union, Campbell was regarded as one of the nation's premier lawyers, renowned especially for his scholarly approach to legal advocacy. Although he did not prevail, Campbell's argument on behalf of his clients' right to pursue their economic livelihood is considered one of the great moments in Supreme Court advocacy. Campbell began his argument by stating what he believed was the purpose behind the ratification of the Privileges and Immunities Clause: to place the states under the oversight and the restraining and enforcing hand of Congress.

From that point forward, Campbell turned to the substantive rights created by the Fourteenth Amendment, much of which was gleaned straight from *Constitutional Limitations*. Liberty, argued Campbell, was constitutionally defined as "the power of determining, by his own choice, his own conduct; to have no master, no overseer put over him; to be able to employ himself without constraint of law or owner; (and) social right to combine his faculties with those of others, to profit by the combination." Campbell's liberty of contract theory was bound to the Privileges and Immunities Clause, whereas Cooley had placed it within substantive rights created under the due process guarantee.[36] Constitutional location aside, Campbell's argument in the

*Slaughterhouse Cases* marked the successful transition of *Constitutional Limitations* from an academic exercise in the nation's law schools to the intellectual justification cited by state and federal courts for striking down economic legislation in the late nineteenth and early twentieth centuries.

## The Slaughterhouse Cases (The Butchers' Benevolent Association of New Orleans v. The Crescent City Live-Stock Landing and Slaughter-House Company)
### 83 U.S. 36 (1873)

In 1869 the Louisiana legislature created the Crescent City Livestock Landing and Slaughterhouse Company and granted it an exclusive twenty-five-year franchise over the slaughter of all livestock in the state's largest and oldest city, New Orleans, located on the Mississippi River near the Gulf Coast. The state claimed that the law, which also covered the parishes around New Orleans, was necessary to contain the further pollution of the Mississippi. After the Civil War southern Louisiana had experienced an outbreak of cholera and other diseases, a development that the state believed was directly related to the region's slaughterhouse industries.

Smaller butchers did not see the law as a civic-minded response to a public health and environmental crisis. They saw it as a political payoff to well-connected and powerful financial backers of state legislators. Worse, the butchers had to contend with the effects of monopoly. Forced to pay exorbitant prices to use the Crescent City slaughterhouse, their profits suffered. Quite simply, the butchers believed the state had deprived them of their now constitutionally protected right to earn a living without undue state interference. To bolster their financial and political power, the independent butchers created their own trade group, the Butchers' Benevolent Association, and filed suit against Crescent City to have the monopoly overturned. The association lost in the state courts before the Supreme Court agreed to hear the case.

The Court's decision was 5 to 4. Justice Miller delivered the opinion of the Court. Justices Bradley, Field, and Swayne filed separate dissents.

▼▲▼

MR. JUSTICE MILLER delivered the opinion of the Court.

The power here exercised by the legislature of Louisiana is, in its essential nature, one which has been, up to the present period in the constitutional history of this country, always conceded to belong to the States, however it may *now* be questioned in some of its details. . . .

This power is, and must be from its very nature, incapable of any very exact definition or limitation. Upon it depends the security of social order, the life and health of the citizen, the comfort of an existence in a thickly populated community, the enjoyment of private social life, and the beneficial use of property. . . .

The regulation of the place and manner of conducting the slaughtering of animals, and the business of butchering within a city, and the inspection of the animals to be killed for meat, and of the meat afterwards, are among the most necessary and frequent exercises of this power. It is not, therefore, needed that we should seek for a comprehensive definition, but rather look for the proper source of its exercise. . . .

It may, therefore, be considered as established that the authority of the legislature of Louisiana to pass the present statute is ample unless some restraint in the exercise of that power be found in the constitution of that State or in the amendments to the Constitution of the United States, adopted since the date of the decisions we have already cited.

The plaintiffs in error, accepting this issue, allege that the statute is a violation of the Constitution of the United States in these several particulars:

- That it creates an involuntary servitude forbidden by the thirteenth article of amendment;
- That it abridges the privileges and immunities of citizens of the United States;
- That it denies to the plaintiffs the equal protection of the laws; and,
- That it deprives them of their property without due process of law, contrary to the provisions of the first section of the fourteenth article of amendment.

This court is thus called upon for the first time to give construction to these articles. . . .

The most cursory glance at these articles discloses a unity of purpose, when taken in connection with the history of the times, which cannot fail to have an important bearing on any question of doubt concerning their true meaning. Nor can such doubts, when any reasonably exist, be safely and rationally solved without a reference to that history, for in it is found the occasion and the necessity for recurring again to the great source of power in this country, the people of the States, for additional guarantees of human rights, additional powers to the Federal government; additional restraints upon those of the States. Fortunately, that history is fresh within the memory of us all, and its leading features, as they bear upon the matter before us, free from doubt. The institution of African slavery, as it existed in about half the States of the Union, and the contests pervading the public mind for many years between those who desired its curtailment and ultimate extinction and those who desired additional safeguards for its security and perpetuation, culminated in the effort, on the part of most of the States in which slavery existed, to separate from the Federal government and to resist its authority. This constituted the war of the rebellion, and whatever auxiliary causes may have contributed to bring about this war, undoubtedly the overshadowing and efficient cause was African slavery. . . .

These circumstances, whatever of falsehood or misconception may have been mingled with their presentation, forced upon the statesmen who had conducted the Federal government in safety through the crisis of the rebellion, and who supposed that, by the thirteenth article of amendment, they had secured the result of their labors, the conviction that something more was necessary in the way of constitutional protection to the unfortunate race who had suffered so much. They accordingly passed through Congress the proposition for the fourteenth amendment, and they declined to treat as restored to their full participation in the government of the Union the States which had been in insurrection until they ratified that article by a formal vote of their legislative bodies.

Before we proceed to examine more critically the provisions of this amendment, on which the plaintiffs in error rely, let us complete and dismiss the history of the recent amendments, as that history relates to the general purpose which pervades them all. A few years' experience satisfied the thoughtful men who had been the authors of the other two amendments that, notwithstanding the restraints of those articles on the States and the laws passed under the additional powers granted to Congress, these were inadequate for the protection of life, liberty, and property, without which freedom to the slave was no boon. They were in all those States denied the right of suffrage. The laws were administered by the white man alone. It was urged that a race of men distinctively marked, as was the negro, living in the midst of another and dominant race, could never be fully secured in their person and their property without the right of suffrage. . . .

We repeat, then, in the light of this recapitulation of events, almost too recent to be called history, but which are familiar to us all, and on the most casual examination of the language of these amendments, no one can fail to be impressed with the one pervading purpose found in them all, lying at the foundation of each, and without which none of them would have been even suggested; we mean the freedom of the slave race, the security and firm establishment of that freedom, and the protection of the newly made freeman and citizen from the oppressions of those who had formerly exercised unlimited dominion over him. It is true that only the fifteenth amendment, in terms, mentions the negro by speaking of his color and his slavery. But it is just as true that each of the other articles was addressed to the grievances of that race, and designed to remedy them as the fifteenth.

We do not say that no one else but the negro can share in this protection. Both the language and spirit of these articles are to have their fair and just weight in any question of construction. Undoubtedly while negro slavery alone was in the mind of the Congress which proposed the thirteenth article, it forbids any other kind of slavery, now or hereafter. . . . But what we do say, and what we wish to be understood, is that, in any fair and just construction of any section or phrase of these amendments, it is necessary to look to the purpose which we have said was the pervading spirit of them all, the evil which they were designed to remedy, and the process of continued addition to the Constitution, until that purpose was supposed to be accomplished as far as constitutional law can accomplish it. . . .

The next observation is more important in view of the arguments of counsel in the present case. It is that the distinction between citizenship of the United States and citizenship of a State is clearly recognized and established. Not only may a man be a citizen of the United States without being a citizen of a State, but an important element is necessary to convert the former into the latter. He must reside within the State to make him a citizen of it, but it is only necessary that he should be born or naturalized in the United States to be a citizen of the Union.

It is quite clear, then, that there is a citizenship of the United States, and a citizenship of a State, which are distinct from each other, and which depend upon different characteristics or circumstances in the individual.

We think this distinction and its explicit recognition in this amendment of great weight in this argument, because the next paragraph of this same section, which is the one mainly relied on by the plaintiffs in error, speaks only of privileges and immunities of citizens of the United States, and does not speak of those of citizens of the several States. The argument, however, in favor of the plaintiffs rests wholly on the assumption that the citizenship is the same, and the privileges and immunities guaranteed by the clause are the same.

The language is, "No State shall make or enforce any law which shall abridge the privileges or immunities of citizens of *the United States.*" It is a little remarkable, if this clause was intended as a protection to the citizen of a State against the legislative power of his own State, that the word citizen of the State should be left out when it is so carefully used, and used in contradistinction to citizens of the United States in the very sentence which precedes it. It is too clear for argument that the change in phraseology was adopted understandingly and, with a purpose.

Of the privileges and immunities of the citizen of the United States, and of the privileges and immunities of the citizen of the State, and what they respectively are, we will presently consider; but we wish to state here that it is only the former which are placed by this clause under the protection of the Federal Constitution, and that the latter, whatever they may be, are not intended to have any additional protection by this paragraph of the amendment. . . .

The argument has not been much pressed in these cases that the defendant's charter deprives the plaintiffs of their property without due process of law, or that it denies to them the equal protection of the law. The first of these paragraphs has been in the Constitution since the adoption of the fifth amendment, as a restraint upon the Federal power. It is also to be found in some form of expression in the constitutions of nearly all the States as a restraint upon the power of the States. This law, then, has practically been the same as it now is during the existence of the government, except so far as the present amendment may place the restraining power over the States in this matter in the hands of the Federal government.

We are not without judicial interpretation, therefore, both State and National, of the meaning of this clause. And it is sufficient to say that under no construction of that provision that we have ever seen, or any that we deem admissible, can the restraint imposed by the State of Louisiana upon the exercise of their trade by the butchers of New Orleans be held to be a deprivation of property within the meaning of that provision.

"Nor shall any State deny to any person within its jurisdiction the equal protection of the laws." In the light of the history of these amendments, and the pervading purpose of them, which we have already discussed, it is not difficult to give a meaning to this clause. The existence of laws in the States where the newly emancipated negroes resided, which discriminated with gross injustice and hardship against them as a class, was the evil to be remedied by this clause, and by it such laws are forbidden.

If, however, the States did not conform their laws to its requirements, then by the fifth section of the article of amendment Congress was authorized to enforce it by suitable legislation. We doubt very much whether any action of a State not directed by way of discrimination against the negroes as a class, or on account of their race, will ever be held to come within the purview of this provision. It is so clearly a provision for that race and that emergency that a strong case would be necessary for its application to any other. But as it is a State that is to be dealt with, and not alone the validity of its laws, we may safely leave that matter until Congress shall have exercised its power, or some case of State oppression, by denial of equal justice in its courts, shall have claimed a decision at our hands. We find no such case in the one before us, and do not deem it necessary to go over the argument again, as it may have relation to this particular clause of the amendment.

In the early history of the organization of the government, its statesmen seem to have divided on the line which should separate the powers of the National government from those of the State governments, and though this line has never been very well defined in public opinion, such a division has continued from that day to this.

[W]e do not see in [the Thirteenth, Fourteenth and Fifteenth] Amendments any purpose to destroy the main features of the general system. Under the pressure of all the excited feeling growing out of the war, our statesmen have still believed that the existence of the State with powers for domestic and local government, including the regulation of civil rights, the rights of person and of property was essential to the perfect working of our complex form of government, though they have thought proper to impose additional limitations on the States, and to confer additional power on that of the Nation.

But whatever fluctuations may be seen in the history of public opinion on this subject during the period of our national existence, we think it will be found that this court, so far as its functions required, has always held with a steady and an even hand the balance between State and Federal power, and we trust that such may continue to be the history of its relation to that subject so long as it shall have duties to perform which demand of it a construction of the Constitution or of any of its parts.

Mr. Justice Field, dissenting.

I am unable to agree with the majority of the court in these cases, and will proceed to state the reasons of my dissent from their judgment. . . .

The act of Louisiana presents the naked case, unaccompanied by any public considerations, where a right to pursue a lawful and necessary calling, previously enjoyed by every citizen, and in connection with which a thousand persons were daily employed, is taken away and vested exclusively for twenty-five years, for an extensive district and a large population, in a single corporation, or its exercise is for that period restricted to the establishments of the corporation, and there allowed only upon onerous conditions. . . .

The question presented is, therefore, one of the gravest importance not merely to the parties here, but to the whole country. It is nothing less than the question whether the recent amendments to the Federal Constitution protect the citizens of the United States against the deprivation of their common rights by State legislation. In my judgment, the fourteenth amendment does afford such protection, and was so intended by the Congress which framed and the States which adopted it.

The counsel for the plaintiffs in error have contended with great force that the act in question is also inhibited by the thirteenth amendment.

That amendment prohibits slavery and involuntary servitude, except as a punishment for crime, but I have not supposed it was susceptible of a construction which would cover the enactment in question. I have been so accustomed to regard it as intended to meet that form of slavery which had previously prevailed in this country, and to which the recent civil war owed its existence, that I was not prepared, nor am I yet, to give to it the extent and force ascribed by counsel. Still it is evidence that the language of the amendment is not used in a restrictive sense. It is not confined to African slavery alone. It is general and universal in its application. Slavery of white men as well as of black men is prohibited, and not merely slavery in the strict sense of the term, but involuntary servitude in every form. . . .

It is not necessary, however, as I have said, to rest my objections to the act in question upon the terms and meaning of the thirteenth amendment. The provisions of the fourteenth amendment, which is properly a supplement to the thirteenth, cover, in my judgment, the case before us, and inhibit any legislation which confers special and exclusive privileges like these under consideration. The amendment was adopted to obviate objections which had been raised and pressed with great force to the validity of the Civil Rights Act, and to place the common rights of American citizens under the protection of the National government. It first declares that, "all persons born or naturalized in the United States, and subject to the jurisdiction thereof, are citizens of the United States and of the State wherein they reside." It then declares that, "no State shall make or enforce any law which shall abridge the privileges or immunities of citizens of the United States, nor shall any State deprive any person of life, liberty, or property, without due process of law, nor deny to any person within its jurisdiction the equal protection of the laws." . . .

The first clause of the fourteenth amendment changes this whole subject, and removes it from the region of discussion and doubt. It recognizes in express terms, if it does not create, citizens of the United States, and it makes their citizenship dependent upon the place of their birth, or the fact of their adoption, and not upon the constitution or laws of any State or the condition of their ancestry. A citizen of a State is now only a citizen of the United States residing in that State. The fundamental rights, privileges, and immunities which belong to him as a free man and a free citizen now belong to him as a citizen of the United States, and are not dependent upon his citizenship of any State. The exercise of these rights and privileges, and the degree of enjoyment received from such exercise, are always more or less affected by the condition and the local institutions of the State, or city, or town where he resides. They are thus affected in a State by the wisdom of its laws, the ability of its officers, the efficiency of its magistrates, the education and morals of its people, and by many other considerations. This is a result which follows from the constitution of society, and can never be avoided, but in no other way can they be affected by the action of the State, or by the residence of the citizen therein. They do not derive their existence from its legislation, and cannot be destroyed by its power. . . .

The terms "privileges" and "immunities" are not new in the amendment; they were in the Constitution before the amendment was adopted. They are found in the second section of the fourth article, which declares that "the citizens of each State shall be entitled to all privileges and immunities of citizens in the several States," and they have been the subject of frequent consideration in judicial decisions. . . .

The privileges and immunities designated are those which of right belong to the citizens of all free governments. Clearly among these must be placed the right to pursue a lawful employment in a lawful manner, without other restraint than such as equally affects all persons. . . .

[G]rants of exclusive privileges, such as is made by the act in question, are opposed to the whole theory of free government, and it requires no aid from any bill of rights to render them void. That only is a free government, in the American sense of the term, under which the inalienable right of every citizen to pursue his happiness is unrestrained, except by just, equal, and impartial laws.

I am authorized by the CHIEF JUSTICE, MR. JUSTICE SWAYNE, and MR. JUSTICE BRADLEY to state that they concur with me in this dissenting opinion.

MR. JUSTICE BRADLEY, also dissenting.

First. Is it one of the rights and privileges of a citizen of the United States to pursue such civil employment as he may choose to adopt, subject to such reasonable regulations as may be prescribed by law?

Secondly. Is a monopoly, or exclusive right, given to one person to the exclusion of all others, to keep slaughterhouses, in a district of nearly twelve hundred square miles, for the supply of meat for a large city, a reasonable regulation of that employment which the legislature has a right to impose? . . .

In my view, a law which prohibits a large class of citizens from adopting a lawful employment, or from following a lawful employment previously adopted, does deprive them of liberty as well as property, without due process of law. Their right of choice is a portion of their liberty; their occupation is their property. Such a law also deprives those citizens of the equal protection of the laws, contrary to the last clause of the section.

The constitutional question is distinctly raised in these cases; the constitutional right is expressly claimed; it was violated by State law, which was sustained by the State court, and we are called upon in a legitimate and proper way to afford redress. Our jurisdiction and our duty are plain and imperative.

It is futile to argue that none but persons of the African race are intended to be benefited by this amendment. They may have been the primary cause of the amendment, but its language is general, embracing all citizens, and I think it was purposely so expressed.

The mischief to be remedied was not merely slavery and its incidents and consequences, but that spirit of insubordination and disloyalty to the National government which had troubled the country for so many years in some of the States, and that intolerance of free speech and free discussion which often rendered life and property insecure, and led to much unequal legislation. The amendment was an attempt to give voice to the strong National yearning for that time and that condition of things, in which American citizenship should be a sure guaranty of safety, and in which every citizen of the United States might stand erect on every portion of its soil, in the full enjoyment of every right and privilege belonging to a freeman, without fear of violence or molestation.

▼▲▼

## Laissez Faire Comes to the Constitution

Despite an unprecedented wave of liberty of contract litigation that invoked the Cooley-Campbell-Bradley conception of the Due Process Clause, Justice Miller's interpretation of the Fourteenth Amendment remained in place. Justice Miller later expressed a combination of irritation and astonishment that anyone would press such a version of the Due Process Clause as falling within the American constitutional tradition:

> It is not a little remarkable, that while [due process] has been in the Constitution . . . for nearly a century . . . its powers ha[d] rarely been invoked in the judicial forum . . . But while it has been a part of the Constitution, as a restraint upon the power of the States, only a very few years, the docket of this court is crowded with cases in which we are asked to hold that State courts and State legislatures have deprived their own citizens of life, liberty or property without due process of law. There is here abundant evidence that there exists some strange misconception of the scope of this provision as found in the Fourteenth Amendment.[37]

Indeed, Justice Miller had done his part to discourage a receptive forum for substantive due process claims brought under the Fourteenth Amendment. In *Munn v. Illinois* (1877), he was part of a 7-2 majority, which included *Slaughterhouse* dissenters Joseph Bradley and Noah H. Swayne, that repelled such a challenge to an Illinois law capping the charges that grain storage companies could impose on their customers. *Munn* symbolized the tension that existed between the powerful Chicago storage companies that controlled the distribution of grain to the East Coast and the farmers who depended on the grain elevators for storage of their grain. Later organized into a more concerted social movement, the "Grangers," as they were better known, were able, with the support of the Chicago Board of Trade, to persuade the state legislature to regulate the often-corrupt and generally price-gouging business practices of the grain companies. The Grangers were successful in having laws enacted that set maximum freight and passenger rates in the railroad transport of grain and regulated the storage rates in the grain warehouses.

The Court found that the grain companies engaged in a *business that directly affected the public interest* (BAPI).

"Property does become clothed with a public interest when used in a manner to make it of public consequence, and affect the community at large," wrote Chief Justice Morrison R. Waite, a moderate Republican appointed by President Ulysses Grant (who never embraced laissez-faire constitutionalism). But Chief Justice Waite's opinion was more subtle than this statement makes it, without context, appear. Waite wrote in *Munn* that, "[f]or protection against abuses by legislatures, the people must resort to the polls, not the courts." But did he also suggest that some forms of economic regulation might be less reasonable than others on substantive grounds and thus suspect under the Due Process Clause?[38]

*Munn* established under the Due Process Clause what the Taney Court established under the Contract Clause in *Charles River Bridge:* State legislatures were free to regulate business to promote public interests related to health, welfare, and safety. For two decades after it decided *Munn,* the Court continued to uphold economic regulation as a valid exercise of state police power against what historian C. Peter McGrath has called the "Patrons of Capital."[39] But signals that the Court was prepared to depart from the principles it established in the *Slaughterhouse Cases* and *Munn* were evident as early as 1886. In *Santa Clara County v. Southern Pacific Railroad* (1886), the Court held that corporations were "persons" entitled to all appropriate protection under the Fourteenth Amendment. The same term, the Court, in an opinion by Chief Justice Waite, held in *Stone v. Farmers' Loan and Trust Co.* (1886), a Mississippi railroad rate case, that states could not impose regulatory burdens that reduced the value of private property to a level considered the equivalent of a "taking" under the Due Process Clause.[40]

Perhaps the clearest indication that the Court was prepared to set down a marker on behalf of the liberty of contract doctrine came during the next term in *Mugler v. Kansas* (1887). There, the Court turned back a substantive due process challenge to a state prohibition law that banned the manufacture and sale of liquor, but not beer and wine. But in language that later served as a seamless transition point to *Allgeyer,* Justice John M. Harlan, appointed to the Court to replace David Davis, a member of the *Slaughterhouse* and *Munn* majorities, wrote:

The Courts are not bound by mere forms. *They are at liberty—indeed are under a solemn duty—to look at the substance of things, whenever they enter upon the inquiry whether the legislature has transcended the limits of its authority.* If, therefore, a statute purporting to have been enacted to protect the public health, the public morals, or the public safety, has no real or substantial relation to those objects, or is a palpable invasion of rights secured by fundamental law, it is the duty of the courts to so adjudge, and thereby give affect to the Constitution.[41]

In other words, the Court held that laws claiming to advance a public interest of the sort described in *Munn* but that in fact burdened business practices with no discernible public benefit could and would be declared unconstitutional on substantive due process grounds.

Justice Harlan's announcement in *Mugler* that the Court would evaluate subsequent economic regulation on substantive grounds received a more complete articulation in *Chicago, Milwaukee and St. Paul Railway Co.* v. *Minnesota* (1890), which involved a challenge to the constitutionality of an 1887 Minnesota railroad rate law. In striking down the law, Justice Samuel Blatchford, another post-*Munn* appointee, wrote that the "reasonableness" of legislation in such cases involves

a question for judicial investigation, requiring due process of law for its determination. If the company is deprived of the power of charging reasonable rates for the use of its property, and such deprivation takes place in the absence of an investigation by judicial machinery, it is deprived of the lawful use of its property, and thus, in substance and effect of the property itself, without due process of law. . . .[42]

By this time a critical mass within the Court had turned the corner on substantive due process. Gone were seven of the justices who decided *Munn*. Appointed in their place were property-minded Republicans with social backgrounds and economic sympathies drawn from the entrepreneurial class, most of whom had more than passing ties to the great corporations and railroads that had emerged after the Civil War. After 1890 they were joined by conservative Democrats with similar associations.[43] Steeped in the theories of Darwin, Spencer, and Sumner and determined to bring them to legal life, the Court after *Mugler* had taken on a radically new ideological predisposition. The question

was now when, not if, the Court would inscribe constitutional nexus between social Darwinism and the laissez-faire legal theories articulated in Cooley's *Constitutional Limitations* into constitutional law.

Seven years after *Chicago, Milwaukee and St. Paul Railway Co.*, the Court, in *Allgeyer v. Louisiana*, demonstrated that it was prepared to go the distance on substantive due process. Justice Rufus W. Peckham, who later wrote the Court's opinion in *Lochner*, held that the "liberty mentioned" in the Due Process Clause went beyond the right of unfair physical restraint. It embraced "the right of the citizen to be free in the enjoyment of all his faculties; to be free to use them in all lawful ways . . . to earn his livelihood by any lawful calling . . . [and] . . . enter into all contracts which may be proper, necessary and essential to his carrying out to a successful conclusion the purposes above mentioned."[44] With those words, the deed was done. The *Slaughterhouse* dissents of Field, for whom *Allgeyer,* handed down during his final days on the Court, was the culmination of his judicial career, and Bradley, who was the first justice to tie together the constitutional phrase "due process" with economic absolutism, had become law of the land.

## Munn v. Illinois
### 94 U.S. 113 (1876)

Ira Munn was a principal partner in Munn & Scott, a prosperous grain elevator business in Chicago. After the Civil War, Chicago quickly emerged as the nation's central distribution point for farm commodities. Local regulation over the grain companies was minimal. Businessmen such as Munn exploited this environment by charging high fees to farmers who needed to store grain and by agreeing to fix prices to spread the wealth and protect each elevator company's respective market share. By 1858 just thirteen companies controlled the storage of more than 4 million bushels of grain at any given time.

In the late 1860s angry farmers organized a political revolt, soon known as the Granger movement, against the Chicago grain operators and persuaded the Illinois legislature, in 1871, with the full support of the Chicago Board of Trade, to regulate the pricing policies of the grain elevator companies. The Grangers had the support of Chicago's leading newspaper, the *Chicago Tribune*, whose editor, Joseph Medill, loathed the grain companies. Medill ran several devastating exposés on the corrupt business practices of Munn & Scott and the other companies that led the Board of Trade, in December 1872, to expel Munn & Scott. Munn lost his fortune in a fraction of the time it took to build it; he soon passed into bankruptcy and oblivion, remembered only for the Supreme Court decision that bears his name.

The Court's decision was 7 to 2. Chief Justice Waite delivered the opinion of the Court. Justice Field, joined by Justice Strong, dissented.

▼▲▼

Mr. Chief Justice Waite delivered the opinion of the Court.

The question to be determined in this case is whether the general assembly of Illinois can, under the limitations upon the legislative power of the States imposed by the Constitution of the United States, fix by law the maximum of charges for the storage of grain in warehouses at Chicago and other places in the State having not less than one hundred thousand inhabitants, "in which grain is stored in bulk, and in which the grain of different owners is mixed together, or in which grain is stored in such a manner that the identity of different lots or parcels cannot be accurately preserved." . . .

Every statute is presumed to be constitutional. The courts ought not to declare one to be unconstitutional unless it is clearly so. If there is doubt, the expressed will of the legislature should be sustained.

The Constitution contains no definition of the word "deprive," as used in the Fourteenth Amendment. To determine its signification, therefore, it is necessary to ascertain the effect which usage has given it, when employed in the same or a like connection. . . .

[I]t is apparent that, down to the time of the adoption of the Fourteenth Amendment, it was not supposed that statutes regulating the use, or even the price of the use, of private property necessarily deprived an owner of his property without due process of law. Under some circumstances they may, but not under all. The amendment does not change the law in this particular; it simply prevents the States from doing that which will operate as such a deprivation.

This brings us to inquire as to the principles upon which this power of regulation rests, in order that we may determine what is within and what without its operative effect. Looking, then, to the common law, from whence came the right which the Constitution protects, we find that, when

private property is "affected with a public interest, it ceases to be *juris privati* only." . . . Property does become clothed with a public interest when used in a manner to make it of public consequence and affect the community at large. When, therefore, one devotes his property to a use in which the public has an interest, he, in effect, grants to the public an interest in that use, and must submit to be controlled by the public for the common good, to the extent of the interest he has thus created. He may withdraw his grant by discontinuing the use, but, so long as he maintains the use, he must submit to the control. . . .

The quantity [of grain] received in Chicago has made it the greatest grain market in the world. This business has created a demand for means by which the immense quantity of grain can be handled or stored, and these have been found in grain warehouses, which are commonly called elevators, because the grain is elevated from the boat or car, by machinery operated by steam, into the bins prepared for its reception, and elevated from the bins, by a like process, into the vessel or car which is to carry it on. . . . In this way, the largest traffic between the citizens of the country north and west of Chicago and the citizens of the country lying on the Atlantic coast north of Washington is in grain which passes through the elevators of Chicago. It has been found impossible to preserve each owner's grain separate, and this has given rise to a system of inspection and grading by which the grain of different owners is mixed, and receipts issued for the number of bushels which are negotiable, and redeemable in like kind, upon demand. This mode of conducting the business was inaugurated more than twenty years ago, and has grown to immense proportions. The railways have found it impracticable to own such elevators, and public policy forbids the transaction of such business by the carrier; the ownership has, therefore, been by private individuals, who have embarked their capital and devoted their industry to such business as a private pursuit. . . .

Under such circumstances, it is difficult to see why, if the common carrier, or the miller, or the ferryman, or the innkeeper . . . or the baker, or the cartman, or the hackney-coachman, pursues a public employment and exercises "a sort of public office," these plaintiffs . . . do not. They stand, to use again the language of their counsel, in the very "gateway of commerce," and take toll from all who pass. Their business most certainly "tends to a common charge, and is become a thing of public interest and use." . . . Certainly, if any business can be clothed "with a public interest, and cease to be *juris privati* only," this has been. It may not be made so by the operation of the Constitution of Illinois or this statute, but it is by the facts. . . .

It matters not in this case that these plaintiffs in error had built their warehouses and established their business before the regulations complained of were adopted. What they did was from the beginning subject to the power of the body politic to require them to conform to such regulations as might be established by the proper authorities for the common good. They entered upon their business and provided themselves with the means to carry it on subject to this condition. If they did not wish to submit themselves to such interference, they should not have clothed the public with an interest in their concerns. The same principle applies to them that does to the proprietor of a hackney-carriage, and as to him it has never been supposed that he was exempt from regulating statutes or ordinances because he had purchased his horses and carriage and established his business before the statute or the ordinance was adopted.

It is insisted, however, that the owner of property is entitled to a reasonable compensation for its use, even though it be clothed with a public interest, and that what is reasonable is a judicial, and not a legislative, question.

As has already been shown, the practice has been otherwise. . . .

*Judgment affirmed.*

Mr. Justice Field, dissenting.

I am compelled to dissent from the decision of the court in this case, and from the reasons upon which that decision is founded. The principle upon which the opinion of the majority proceeds is, in my judgment, subversive of the rights of private property, heretofore believed to be protected by constitutional guaranties against legislative interference, and is in conflict with the authorities cited in its support.

The defendants had constructed their warehouse and elevator in 1862 with their own means, upon ground leased by them for that purpose, and, from that time until the filing of the information against them, had transacted the business of receiving and storing grain for hire. The rates of storage charged by them were annually established by arrangement with the owners of different elevators in Chicago, and were published in the month of January. In 1870, the State of Illinois adopted a new constitution, and, by it, "all elevators or storehouses where grain or other property is stored for a compensation, whether the property stored be kept separate or not, are declared to be public warehouses."

. . . The question presented, therefore, is one of the greatest importance—whether it is within the competency of a State to fix the compensation which an individual may receive for the use of his own property in his private business and for his services in connection with it. . . .

The legislation was, among other grounds, assailed in the State court as being in conflict with that provision of the State Constitution which declares that no person shall be deprived of life, liberty, or property without due process of law, and with that provision of the Fourteenth Amendment of the Federal Constitution which imposes a similar restriction upon the action of the State. In this court, the legislation was also assailed on the same ground. But it would seem from its opinion that the court holds that property loses something of its private character when employed in such a way as to be generally useful. The doctrine declared is that property "becomes clothed with a public interest when used in a manner to make it of public consequence and affect the community at large," and, from such clothing, the right of the legislature is deduced to control the use of the property and to determine the compensation which the owner may receive for it. . . .

If this be sound law, if there be no protection, either in the principles upon which our republican government is founded or in the prohibitions of the Constitution against such invasion of private rights, all property and all business in the State are held at the mercy of a majority of its legislature. The public has no greater interest in the use of buildings for the storage of grain than it has in the use of buildings for the residences of families, nor, indeed, anything like so great an interest, and, according to the doctrine announced, the legislature may fix the rent of all tenements used for residences, without reference to the cost of their erection. If the owner does not like the rates prescribed, he may cease renting his houses. . . .

By the term "liberty," as used in the provision, something more is meant than mere freedom from physical restraint or the bounds of a prison. It means freedom to go where one may choose, and to act in such manner, not inconsistent with the equal rights of others, as his judgment may dictate for the promotion of his happiness—that is, to pursue such callings and avocations as may be most suitable to develop his capacities and give to them their highest enjoyment.

The same liberal construction which is required for the protection of life and liberty, in all particulars in which life and liberty are of any value, should be applied to the protection of private property. If the legislature of a State, under pretence of providing for the public good, or for any other reason, can determine, against the consent of the owner, the uses to which private property shall be devoted, or the prices which the owner shall receive for its uses, it can deprive him of the property as completely as by a special act for its confiscation or destruction. If, for instance, the owner is prohibited from using his building for the purposes for which it was designed, it is of little consequence that he is permitted to retain the title and possession; or, if he is compelled to take as compensation for its use less than the expenses to which he is subjected by its ownership, he is, for all practical purposes, deprived of the property as effectually as if the legislature had ordered his forcible dispossession. If it be admitted that the legislature has any control over the compensation, the extent of that compensation becomes a mere matter of legislative discretion. The amount fixed will operate as a partial destruction of the value of the property, if it fall below the amount which the owner would obtain by contract, and, practically, as a complete destruction if it be less than the cost of retaining its possession. There is, indeed, no protection of any value under the constitutional provision which does not extend to the use and income of the property, as well as to its title and possession. . . .

I am of opinion that the judgment of the Supreme Court of Illinois should be reversed.

▼▲▼

## Allgeyer v. State of Louisiana
### 165 U.S. 578 (1897)

Continuing its zeal to protect the public interest through state-established monopolies, the Louisiana legislature enacted an 1894 law that barred any of its citizens and corporations from doing business with any out-of-state marine insurance companies. The state claimed that the law's purpose was to protect Louisiana consumers from fraudulent business practices by shady, carpetbagging Northern insurance companies. Local companies that needed to buy insurance believed the real reason could be found in the cozy relationship between the Louisiana insurance industry and its patrons in the legislature. The context of this case is very similar to the *Slaughterhouse Cases*.

E. Allgeyer and Co. deliberately violated the law soon after its passage. The company's lawyers offered the very same arguments that John Campbell, the lawyer for the Butchers' Benevolent Association, had almost twenty-five years before in the *Slaughterhouse Cases*. Louisiana prevailed in the state courts. Events in the Supreme Court, however, would take a very different and crucial turn.

The Court's decision was 9 to 0. Justice Peckham delivered the unanimous opinion of the Court.

MR. JUSTICE PECKHAM, after stating the facts, delivered the opinion of the Court.

There is no doubt of the power of the state to prohibit foreign insurance companies from doing business within its limits. The state can impose such conditions as it pleases upon the doing of any business by those companies within its borders, and unless the conditions be complied with the prohibition may be absolute. . . .

A conditional prohibition in regard to foreign insurance companies doing business within the state of Louisiana is to be found in article 236 of the constitution of that state, which reads as follows: "No foreign corporation shall do any business in this state without having one or more known places of business and an authorized agent or agents in the state upon whom process may be served."

In the course of the opinion delivered in this case by the supreme court of Louisiana that court said:

> The open policy in this case is conceded to be a New York contract; hence the special insurance effected on the cotton complained of here was a New York contract.
>
> The question presented is the simple proposition whether under the act a party while in the state can insure property in Louisiana in a foreign insurance company, which has not complied with the laws of the state, under an open policy, the special contract of insurance and the open policy being contracts made and entered into beyond the limits of the state. . . .

The general contract contained in the open policy, as well as the special insurance upon each shipment of goods of which notice is given to the insurance company, being contracts made in New York and valid there, the state of Louisiana claims notwithstanding such facts that the defendants have violated the act of 1894, by doing an act in that state to effect for themselves insurance on their property then in that state in a marine insurance company which had not complied in all respects with the laws of that state, and that such violation consisted in the act of mailing a letter or sending a telegram to the insurance company in New York describing the cotton upon which the defendants desired the insurance under the open marine policy to attach. It is claimed on the part of the state that its legislature had the power to provide that such an act should be illegal, and to subject the offender to the penalties provided in the statute. . . .

It is natural that the state court should have remarked that there is in this "statute an apparent interference with the liberty of defendants in restricting their rights to place insurance on property of their own whenever and in what company they desired." Such interference is not only apparent, but it is real, and we do not think that it is justified for the purpose of upholding what the state says is its policy with regard to foreign insurance companies which had not complied with the laws of the state for doing business within its limits. In this case the company did no business within the state, and the contracts were not therein made.

The supreme court of Louisiana says that the act of writing within that state the letter of notification was an act therein done to effect an insurance on property then in the state, in a marine insurance company which had not complied with its laws, and such act was therefore prohibited by the statute. As so construed, we think the statute is a violation of the fourteenth amendment of the federal constitution, in that it deprives the defendants of their liberty without due process of law. The statute which forbids such act does not become due process of law, because it is inconsistent with the provisions of the constitution of the Union. The 'liberty' mentioned in that amendment means, not only the right of the citizen to be free from the mere physical restraint of his person, as by incarceration, but the term is deemed to embrace the right of the citizen to be free in the enjoyment of all his faculties; to be free to use them in all lawful ways; to live and work where he will; to earn his livelihood by any lawful calling; to pursue any livelihood or avocation; and for that purpose to enter into all contracts which may be proper, necessary, and essential to his carrying out to a successful conclusion the purposes above mentioned.

It was said by Mr. Justice Bradley, in *Butchers' Union Slaughterhouse Co.* v. *Crescent City Live-Stock Landing Co.* [the *Slaughterhouse Cases* (1873)], in the course of his concurring opinion in that case, that "the right to follow any of the common occupations of life is an inalienable right. It was formulated as such under the phrase 'pursuit of happiness' in the Declaration of Independence, which commenced with the fundamental proposition that 'all men are created equal; that they are endowed by their Creator with certain inalienable rights; that among these are life, liberty, and the pursuit of happiness.' This right is a large ingredient in the civil liberty of the citizen." It is true that these remarks were made in regard to questions of monopoly, but they well describe the rights which are covered by the word 'liberty,' as contained in the fourteenth amendment.

[I]n *Powell v. Pennsylvania*, Mr. Justice Harlan, in stating the opinion of the court, said: "The main proposition advanced by the defendant is that his enjoyment upon terms of equality with all others in similar circumstances of the privilege of pursuing an ordinary calling or trade, and of acquiring, holding, and selling property, is an essential part of his rights of liberty and property, as guarantied by the fourteenth amendment. The court assents to this general proposition as embodying a sound principle of constitutional law." It was there held, however, that the legislation under consideration in that case did not violate any of the constitutional rights of the plaintiff in error.

The foregoing extracts have been made for the purpose of showing what general definitions have been given in regard to the meaning of the word 'liberty' as used in the amendment, but we do not intend to hold that in no such case can the state exercise its police power. When and how far such power may be legitimately exercised with regard to these subjects must be left for determination to each case as it arises.

Has not a citizen of a state, under the provisions of the federal constitution above mentioned, a right to contract outside of the state for insurance on his property, a right of which state legislation cannot deprive him? . . .

To deprive the citizen of such a right as herein described without due process of law is illegal. Such a statute as this in question is not due process of law, because it prohibits an act which under the federal constitution the defendants had a right to perform. This does not interfere in any way with the acknowledged right of the state to enact such legislation in the legitimate exercise of its police or other powers as to it may seem proper. In the exercise of such right, however, care must be taken not to infringe upon those other rights of the citizen which are protected by the federal constitution.

In the privilege of pursuing an ordinary calling or trade, and of acquiring, holding, and selling property, must be embraced the right to make all proper contracts in relation thereto; and although it may be conceded that this right to contract in relation to persons or property or to do business within the jurisdiction of the state may be regulated, and sometimes prohibited, when the contracts or business conflict with the policy of the state as contained in its statutes, yet the power does not and cannot extend to prohibiting a citizen from making contracts of the nature involved in this case outside of the limits and jurisdiction of the state, and which are also to be performed outside of such jurisdiction; nor can the state legally prohibit its citizens from doing such an act as writing this letter of notification, even though the property which is the subject of the insurance may at the time when such insurance attaches be within the limits of the state. The mere fact that a citizen may be within the limits of a particular state does not prevent his making a contract outside its limits while he himself remains within it. . . .

For these reasons we think the statute in question was a violation of the federal constitution, and afforded no justification for the judgment awarded by that court against the plaintiffs in error. That judgment must therefore be reversed, and the case remanded to the supreme court of Louisiana for further proceedings not inconsistent with his opinion.

▼▲▼

## The Rise and Fall of *Lochner:* Social Darwinism Recedes; the Positive State Emerges

*Lochner* was decided around the same time that the "literature of exposure" on the business practices of the nation's corporations, railroads, and trusts was began to appear in national magazines, journals, and books. For example, in 1902 Ida M. Tarbell, a respected biographer of popular works on Abraham Lincoln and Napoleon Bonaparte, published an expose in *McClure's* magazine on the ruthless and often unethical business practices of the Rockefeller family in building the Standard Oil Co. In 1903, Marie Van Vorst, a New York socialite active in reform causes, published *The Woman Who Toils: Being the Experiences of Two Gentlewomen as Factory Girls.* The book, which included a preface from President Theodore Roosevelt, was an account of Van Vorst's secret expedition as a "working girl" in the New York garment industry. Robert Hunter, in 1904, published his book, *Poverty,* in which he argued that more than 10 million Americans lived in poverty, even as the nation's large businesses and stock markets prospered. And in 1906, twenty-eight-year-old journalist Upton Sinclair published *The Jungle,* a stark and graphic novelized account of the Chicago slaughterhouse industry and the horrible conditions in which its workers toiled.

Perhaps more than any other single factor, *The Jungle* was responsible for a federal law passed that same year, the Pure Food and Drug Act, which mandated new health and safety standards for the meat-packing business and numerous others.[45] It was just this kind of careful, investigative journalism and academic research

that Louis Brandeis would draw upon for his brief in *Muller.* Problems such as these had always been associated with market capitalism. During corporate America's Gilded Age infatuation with social Darwinism and laissez-faire economics, these problems had gotten much, much worse.

Justice Peckham's opinion in *Lochner* has received more attention from students of American constitutional development than his liberty of contract pronouncement in *Allgeyer.* What substantive difference in his analysis of the Fourteenth Amendment claims in the two cases justifies naming the economic substantive due process era after *Lochner* and not *Allgeyer?* Several reasons explain *Lochner's* status as the Due Process Clause decision that defined the liberty of contract era.

First, *Lochner* involved a challenge to a maximum work hour law, one that most people could agree bore a reasonable relationship to public health. *Allgeyer,* on the other hand, involved a challenge to an obscure economic regulation—whether insurance companies could issue marine insurance to businesses that had not fully complied with Louisiana law—that did not appear to fall within the *Munn-Mugler* BAPI requirement for the judicial evaluation of legislative reasonableness. Whether Justice Harlan's opinion in *Mugler* was, in retrospect, a correct reading of the Due Process Clause is not important to illustrate this point. That the *Lochner* Court felt no obligation to use the "public interest" rule to analyze legislation that was not enacted in bad faith or without evidence to support its reasonableness indicated the limited reach of such a standard. The SIDEBAR offers a more detailed account of the working conditions that led to the laws challenged in *Lochner.*

Moreover, *Lochner* also encouraged businesses to dispute just about every piece of state economic regulation as violative of their liberty of contract, no matter how fundamental or long-standing their association with basic government functions had been. Even the use of standard weights and measures in agricultural and commercial transactions was challenged as a due process violation.[46] Second, *Lochner* resulted in Justice Holmes's classic dissent, which offered the first clear statement of his judicial philosophy. Third, the Court's refusal to recognize the substantive reasonableness of the New York regulation—numerous studies had documented the health hazards of the baking profession—led Justice

Harlan, a member of the unanimous *Allgeyer* Court and judicial supporter of the liberty of contract doctrine, to dissent. Even in the face of strong evidence, the Court had refused to adhere to the public health exception it, and Harlan specifically, had articulated in *Mugler.* Is Harlan's criticism, that the Court erroneously viewed *Lochner* as an example of burdensome class legislation rather than a valid public health regulation, valid?

*Lochner* did not foreclose the constitutional status of economic legislation. Of particular note, of course, was the Court's unanimous 1908 decision in *Muller* to uphold Oregon's maximum work hour law for professional laundresses. Given what the Court had just said in *Lochner,* the obvious question is this: What in the world would inspire the Court to uphold, without dissent, a maximum work hour law for women when it had just struck down almost identical legislation designed to protect the health of New York bakers? Constitutional scholars and historians of the Progressive Era have, in general, approached this question from three perspectives.

First, and least popular, is the idea that *Lochner,* as a matter of constitutional law, has been treated out of proportion to its actual significance. From 1897, when *Allgeyer* was decided, to 1911, the Court upheld all but 3 of the 560 "social justice" laws challenged on due process and equal protection grounds.[47] Some scholars have also suggested that *Lochner* never encouraged the frontal assault on progressive economic reform that its detractors have argued. Instead, the ruling sought to protect small business owners and independent contractors from a social movement enamored with "class" legislation. Such class warfare was inconsistent with what the Court believed were the core principles of the American economic tradition.[48]

The second, and more conventional, sentiment on *Muller* is that it represented the continuation of the Court's paternal strain on matters of constitutional law affecting women, especially laws designed to "protect" them from public health risks or the perils of business, politics, and the professions. In *Minor* v. *Happersett* (1875), the Court ruled that that states were not required under the Fourteenth Amendment to extend the vote to women.[49] In *Bradwell* v. *Illinois* (1873), the Court, on the same day the *Slaughterhouse Cases* were handed down, ruled that states were permitted to exclude women from the legal profession. The Court reasoned that "[m]an is, or should be, woman's protector and defender. The natural and proper timidity and delicacy which belongs to the female sex evidently unfits it for many of the occupations of civil life . . . [the] destiny and mission of woman are to fulfill the noble and benign offices of wife and mother."[50] Some feminist scholars have argued that *Muller* did nothing more than offer the judicial affirmation of the inferior social and political status of women.[51]

But *Muller* is perhaps best understood in a third way: through the contribution of Louis Brandeis both to the practice of reform-oriented public interest law and the rise of "sociological jurisprudence" that triumphed after *Lochner*'s demise. Political scientist Philipa Strum has noted that Brandeis pursued *Muller* from three angles. Although he believed, as a personal matter, that liberty of contract was nonsense, Brandeis did not contest *Lochner* as constitutional law. Instead, Brandeis believed that lawyers defending protective legislation should emphasize "factual" evidence of the social harm being prevented rather than criticize prevailing conceptions of legal theory. This approach might better persuade the Court to see such cases as within the public interest domain of state police power. Second, Brandeis understood rather than contested the shift that occurred in *Lochner:* Public interest initiatives carried out under legislative authority were no longer presumed to be constitutional. Substantial proof was needed to defend the legislature's encroachment of liberty of contract. Third, compared with laws that simply stated a general purpose, public health statutes that amassed specific evidence to support the relationship between their means and ends stood a better chance of surviving constitutional review.

On this last point, Brandeis reminded the Court that *Lochner* permitted exceptions to liberty of contract in the name of health, safety, morals, or the general welfare. No one deserved the protection of paternal government more than American women did. He demonstrated how the Oregon law accomplished that objective with almost one hundred pages of factual data, compared with two pages of legal argumentation.[52] Which perspective on *Lochner* do you believe best explains the Court's decision in *Muller?*

# Lochner v. New York
## 198 U.S. 45 (1905)

In 1897 the New York legislature enacted a law setting the maximum hours that bakers could work at ten per day and sixty hours per week. Joseph Lochner, who owned and operated the Lochner Bakery in Utica, located in upstate New York, was fined $50, a hefty sum in the early 1900s, for breaking the law. He challenged the New York Bakeshop Act as a violation of his liberty of contract rights under the Due Process Clause of the Fourteenth Amendment. He was unsuccessful in the New York state courts. The Supreme Court, of course, was another matter, as Joseph Lochner's name soon became synonymous with an entire era of American constitutional development.

The Court's decision was 5 to 4. Justice Peckham delivered the opinion of the Court. Justice Harlan, joined by Justices White and Day, dissented. Justice Holmes also dissented.

▼▲▼

Mr. Justice Peckham, after making the foregoing statement of the facts, delivered the opinion of the Court.

The mandate of the statute that "no employee shall be required or permitted to work," is the substantial equivalent of an enactment that "no employee shall contract or agree to work," more than ten hours per day, and, as there is no provision for special emergencies, the statute is mandatory in all cases. It is not an act merely fixing the number of hours which shall constitute a legal day's work, but an absolute prohibition upon the employer's permitting, under any circumstances, more than ten hours' work to be done in his establishment. The employee may desire to earn the extra money which would arise from his working more than the prescribed time, but this statute forbids the employer from permitting the employee to earn it.

The statute necessarily interferes with the right of contract between the employer and employees concerning the number of hours in which the latter may labor in the bakery of the employer. The general right to make a contract in relation to his business is part of the liberty of the individual protected by the Fourteenth Amendment of the Federal Constitution. *Allgeyer v. Louisiana* (1897). Under that provision, no State can deprive any person of life, liberty or property without due process of law. The right to purchase or to sell labor is part of the liberty protected by this amendment unless there are circumstances which

exclude the right. There are, however, certain powers, existing in the sovereignty of each State in the Union, somewhat vaguely termed police powers, the exact description and limitation of which have not been attempted by the courts. Those powers, broadly stated and without, at present, any attempt at a more specific limitation, relate to the safety, health, morals and general welfare of the public. Both property and liberty are held on such reasonable conditions as may be imposed by the governing power of the State in the exercise of those powers, and with such conditions the Fourteenth Amendment was not designed to interfere.

The State therefore has power to prevent the individual from making certain kinds of contracts, and, in regard to them, the Federal Constitution offers no protection. If the contract be one which the State, in the legitimate exercise of its police power, has the right to prohibit, it is not prevented from prohibiting it by the Fourteenth Amendment. Contracts in violation of a statute, either of the Federal or state government, or a contract to let one's property for immoral purposes, or to do any other unlawful act, could obtain no protection from the Federal Constitution as coming under the liberty of person or of free contract. Therefore, when the State, by its legislature, in the assumed exercise of its police powers, has passed an act which seriously limits the right to labor or the right of contract in regard to their means of livelihood between persons who are *sui juris* (both employer and employee), it becomes of great importance to determine which shall prevail—the right of the individual to labor for such time as he may choose or the right of the State to prevent the individual from laboring or from entering into any contract to labor beyond a certain time prescribed by the State.

This court has recognized the existence and upheld the exercise of the police powers of the States in many cases which might fairly be considered as border ones, and it has, in the course of its determination of questions regarding the asserted invalidity of such statutes on the ground of their violation of the rights secured by the Federal Constitution, been guided by rules of a very liberal nature, the application of which has resulted, in numerous instances, in upholding the validity of state statutes thus assailed. Among the later cases where the state law has been upheld by this court is that of *Holden v. Hardy* (1898). . . .

The latest case decided by this court involving the police power is that of *Jacobson v. Massachusetts* (1905). It related to compulsory vaccination, and the law was held valid as a proper exercise of the police powers with reference to the public health. It was stated in the opinion that it was a case, "of an adult who, for aught that appears, was himself in perfect health and a fit subject for vaccination, and yet, while remaining in the community, refused to obey the statute and the regulation adopted in execution of its provisions for the protection of the public health and the public safety, confessedly endangered by the presence of a dangerous disease." That case is also far from covering the one now before the court. . . .

It must, of course, be conceded that there is a limit to the valid exercise of the police power by the State. There is no dispute concerning this general proposition. Otherwise the Fourteenth Amendment would have no efficacy, and the legislatures of the States would have unbounded power, and it would be enough to say that any piece of legislation was enacted to conserve the morals, the health or the safety of the people; such legislation would be valid no matter how absolutely without foundation the claim might be. The claim of the police power would be a mere pretext—become another and delusive name for the supreme sovereignty of the State to be exercised free from constitutional restraint. This is not contended for. In every case that comes before this court, therefore, where legislation of this character is concerned and where the protection of the Federal Constitution is sought, the question necessarily arises: is this a fair, reasonable and appropriate exercise of the police power of the State, or is it an unreasonable, unnecessary and arbitrary interference with the right of the individual to his personal liberty or to enter into those contracts in relation to labor which may seem to him appropriate or necessary for the support of himself and his family? Of course, the liberty of contract relating to labor includes both parties to it. The one has as much right to purchase as the other to sell labor.

This is not a question of substituting the judgment of the court for that of the legislature. If the act be within the power of the State, it is valid although the judgment of the court might be totally opposed to the enactment of such a law. But the question would still remain: is it within the police power of the State?, and that question must be answered by the court.

The question whether this act is valid as a labor law, pure and simple, may be dismissed in a few words. There is no reasonable ground for interfering with the liberty of person or the right of free contract by determining the hours of labor in the occupation of a baker. There is no contention that bakers as a class are not equal in intelligence and capacity to men in other trades or manual occupations, or that they are able to assert their rights and care for themselves without the protecting arm of the State, interfering with their independence of judgment and of action. They are in no sense wards of the State. Viewed in

the light of a purely labor law, with no reference whatever to the question of health, we think that a law like the one before us involves neither the safety, the morals, nor the welfare of the public, and that the interest of the public is not in the slightest degree affected by such an act. The law must be upheld, if at all, as a law pertaining to the health of the individual engaged in the occupation of a baker. It does not affect any other portion of the public than those who are engaged in that occupation. Clean and wholesome bread does not depend upon whether the baker works but ten hours per day or only sixty hours a week. The limitation of the hours of labor does not come within the police power on that ground.

It is a question of which of two powers or rights shall prevail—the power of the State to legislate or the right of the individual to liberty of person and freedom of contract. The mere assertion that the subject relates though but in a remote degree to the public health does not necessarily render the enactment valid. The act must have a more direct relation, as a means to an end, and the end itself must be appropriate and legitimate, before an act can be held to be valid which interferes with the general right of an individual to be free in his person and in his power to contract in relation to his own labor. . . .

We think the limit of the police power has been reached and passed in this case. There is, in our judgment, no reasonable foundation for holding this to be necessary or appropriate as a health law to safeguard the public health or the health of the individuals who are following the trade of a baker. If this statute be valid, and if, therefore, a proper case is made out in which to deny the right of an individual, *sui juris,* as employer or employee, to make contracts for the labor of the latter under the protection of the provisions of the Federal Constitution, there would seem to be no length to which legislation of this nature might not go. The case differs widely, as we have already stated, from the expressions of this court in regard to laws of this nature . . . We think that there can be no fair doubt that the trade of a baker, in and of itself, is not an unhealthy one to that degree which would authorize the legislature to interfere with the right to labor, and with the right of free contract on the part of the individual, either as employer or employee. In looking through statistics regarding all trades and occupations, it may be true that the trade of a baker does not appear to be as healthy as some other trades, and is also vastly more healthy than still others. To the common understanding, the trade of a baker has never been regarded as an unhealthy one. Very likely, physicians would not recommend the exercise of that or of any other trade as a remedy for ill health. Some occupations are more healthy than others, but we think there are none which might not come under the power of the legislature to supervise and control the hours of working therein if the mere fact that the occupation is not absolutely and perfectly healthy is to confer that right upon the legislative department of the Government. It might be safely affirmed that almost all occupations more or less affect the health. There must be more than the mere fact of the possible existence of some small amount of unhealthiness to warrant legislative interference with liberty. It is unfortunately true that labor, even in any department, may possibly carry with it the seeds of unhealthiness. But are we all, on that account, at the mercy of legislative majorities? A printer, a tinsmith, a locksmith, a carpenter, a cabinetmaker, a dry goods clerk, a bank's, a lawyer's or a physician's clerk, or a clerk in almost any kind of business, would all come under the power of the legislature on this assumption. No trade, no occupation, no mode of earning one's living could escape this all-pervading power, and the acts of the legislature in limiting the hours of labor in all employments would be valid although such limitation might seriously cripple the ability of the laborer to support himself and his family. In our large cities there are many buildings into which the sun penetrates for but a short time in each day, and these buildings are occupied by people carrying on the business of bankers, brokers, lawyers, real estate, and many other kinds of business, aided by many clerks, messengers, and other employs. Upon the assumption of the validity of this act under review, it is not possible to say that an act prohibiting lawyers' or bank clerks, or others from contracting to labor for their employers more than eight hours a day would be invalid. It might be said that it is unhealthy to work more than that number of hours in an apartment lighted by artificial light during the working hours of the day; that the occupation of the bank clerk, the lawyer's clerk, the real estate clerk, or the broker's clerk in such offices is therefore unhealthy, and the legislature, in its paternal wisdom, must therefore have the right to legislate on the subject of, and to limit the hours for, such labor, and, if it exercises that power and its validity be questioned, it is sufficient to say it has reference to the public health; it has reference to the health of the employees condemned to labor day after day in buildings where the sun never shines; it is a health law, and therefore it is valid, and cannot be questioned by the courts.

It was . . . urged on the argument that restricting the hours of labor in the case of bakers was valid because it tended to cleanliness on the part of the workers, as a man was more apt to be cleanly when not overworked, and, if

cleanly, then his "output" was also more likely to be so. What has already been said applies with equal force to this contention. We do not admit the reasoning to be sufficient to justify the claimed right of such interference. The State in that case would assume the position of a supervisor, or *pater familias*, over every act of the individual, and its right of governmental interference with his hours of labor, his hours of exercise, the character thereof, and the extent to which it shall be carried would be recognized and upheld. In our judgment, it is not possible, in fact, to discover the connection between the number of hours a baker may work in the bakery and the healthful quality of the bread made by the workman. The connection, if any exists, is too shadowy and thin to build any argument for the interference of the legislature. If the man works ten hours a day, it is all right, but if ten and a half or eleven, his health is in danger and his bread may be unhealthful, and, therefore, he shall not be permitted to do it. This, we think, is unreasonable, and entirely arbitrary. When assertions such as we have adverted to become necessary in order to give, if possible, a plausible foundation for the contention that the law is a "health law," it gives rise to at least a suspicion that there was some other motive dominating the legislature than the purpose to subserve the public health or welfare. . . .

This interference on the part of the legislatures of the several States with the ordinary trades and occupations of the people seems to be on the increase. . . .

It is impossible for us to shut our eyes to the fact that many of the laws of this character, while passed under what is claimed to be the police power for the purpose of protecting the public health or welfare, are, in reality, passed from other motives. We are justified in saying so when, from the character of the law and the subject upon which it legislates, it is apparent that the public health or welfare bears but the most remote relation to the law. The purpose of a statute must be determined from the natural and legal effect of the language employed, and whether it is or is not repugnant to the Constitution of the United States must be determined from the natural effect of such statutes when put into operation, and not from their proclaimed purpose.

It is manifest to us that the limitation of the hours of labor as provided for in this section of the statute under which the indictment was found, and the plaintiff in error convicted, has no such direct relation to, and no such substantial effect upon, the health of the employee as to justify us in regarding the section as really a health law. It seems to us that the real object and purpose were simply to regulate the hours of labor between the master and his

## *LOCHNER V. NEW YORK*

### *Flour Power*

Although you might be familiar with the phrase "you sound like a broken record," the odds are that you have never heard a broken record nor would you know what one sounded like if you did. Compact discs made vinyl records obsolete by the late 1980s. Getting up to move the record needle or to turn the record over makes about as much sense to you as leaving the couch to change the television channel.

Likewise, if you told someone in late-nineteenth- or early-twentieth-century America that you were heading down to the supermarket for a loaf of bread, he or she would look at you with the same bewildered expression that you gave the person who uttered the broken-record phrase. In 1900, three-fourths of all the bread consumed in the United States was baked at home. Bread that was purchased outside the home was not made in large, mass-scale production factories, but in small bakeries that were most often housed in the basements of tenement buildings. Freshly baked bread was then delivered to specialized retail bakeries or small grocers for sale or, for a small fee, directly upstairs to tenement dwellers.

As the baking industry grew in proportion to the rapid industrialization and urbanization of small towns and large cities throughout the United States, two separate branches developed. One, known as the cracker industry, produced nonperishable staples such as hardbread, crackers, and hardtack. These products, which were designed for long cross-country or overseas trips, were well suited to mass production and wholesale distribution. By 1898 the nation's four largest "cracker trusts" consolidated to form the National Biscuit Co. This merger gave one corporation a 70 percent market share of the cracker business. The National Biscuit Co., which easily assumed near-monopoly control of this branch of the baking industry, was exactly the type of corporation that became the target of Theodore Roosevelt's "trust busting" campaign when he became president in 1901.

The work environment of small-time, fresh bread bakers like Joseph Lochner was totally different from the cracker industry's. Major trusts in the fresh bread business did not form until after 1910, and the first large holding company did not emerge until 1922. The gradual consolidation of the fresh bread industry by the late 1920s would result in antitrust suits. But before then, and specifically between 1897 and 1905, when New York bakers were contesting the state's Bakeshop Act, countless small baking businesses supplied fresh bread to retailers.

How small were these bakeries? In 1899, 78 percent employed four or fewer people. How sophisticated were their methods of production? Not very. In contrast to the cracker industry, the baking of fresh bread remained a labor-intensive craft. Power machines, such as molding machines, dough rounders, and mixers, were introduced between 1880 and 1905. But their cost was often prohibitive to small bakers. In 1899 only 10 percent of fresh bread bakeries used these elaborate new inventions.

All that it took to enter the fresh bread business was an oven and sufficient space in which to prepare and bake bread. Because small-time bakers had no power to negotiate the cost of their supplies, and because of the highly perishable nature of their product, they were forced to turn to other areas to limit their costs. Almost without exception, these bakers occupied the cellars and basements of the ubiquitous tenement buildings that housed the waves of immigrants streaming into America in the late 1800s and early 1900s. Conditions in these facilities were simply horrendous. Drainage pipes, which were often made of brick and clay, often leaked, giving off a foul smell that was not easily masked. Floors, which consisted of wood, dirt, or, on rare occasion, concrete, were usually saturated with water, as were the unfinished walls and low ceilings, some of which were not even five and a half feet high.

Lighting, even in the daytime, also was extremely poor. The few openings to the outside often consisted of horizontal grates, which provided as little ventilation as they did light. Exhaust fans to blow out the flour dust and gas fumes of the ovens were nonexistent. These problems of locale did not even take into account the sanitation practices of the bakers. In one exposé after another that described the filth and squalor of the cellar bakeries, the bakers themselves were often described as filthy and unkempt. One report noted that when moving heavy dough, bakers often carried it against their sweaty torsos, and that knives used for slitting loaves of bread were carried in the bakers' mouths. It was not uncommon, moreover, for bakers to use dough that had been dropped on the floor or had touched the permeable pipes that carried raw sewage.

Progressives viewed the general conditions of the baking industry as a case study for the need for reform legislation to protect workers against the harsh consequences of unregulated capitalism. Of primary concern, however, was a terrible new disease called consumption, which had emerged with the rise of industrialization. Consumption is often thought of as the nineteenth-century name for tuberculosis, a disease that affects the lungs, but back then it actually described much more than just respiratory illnesses. Although little was known about how consumption originated or how to treat it, few disputed the severity of the disease. Consumption was the greatest killer disease of its time, the nineteenth-century equivalent of cancer in the twentieth.

Medical research differed as to whether consumption and tuberculosis were hereditary or bacterial and contagious. Upon an outbreak of tuberculosis in New York City in the early 1900s, where 87 percent of the baking industry was located as late as 1912, the commissioner of health implemented a program to require all such occurrences of the disease to be reported to public health authorities. This program, however, met considerable resistance and was not implemented until 1907, two years after *Lochner* was decided.

Even though doctors came to associate consumption and tuberculosis with environmental conditions such as those found in the cellar bakeries of New York City, containment of the spread of disease was not the primary motivation behind the original effort to enact the Bakeshop Act. Disease simply accelerated the Progressives' contention that industrialization had brought with it public health hazards that were not always immediately visible. The arduous and irregular hours that bakers were required to work—around-the-clock shifts two or three times a week, stretches of twelve-hour days without time off, and the assignment of day and night shifts without regard to rest and sleep—drove the early reform efforts. In 1881, when New York bakers first went on strike, their demand was for a twelve-hour day. Given that most bakers worked a minimum of six (but often seven) days a week, this request amounted to a reduced workweek of 72 to 84 hours.

Such long hours, combined with the conditions in which they were required to labor, led bakers to complain that a balanced family life was impossible. Not until later, after *Lochner,* did even the experienced, journeymen bakers begin to comprehend the role that their dismal working conditions played in their often-chronic poor health. Consumption was, as tuberculosis is, a debilitating disease that slowly wears down its victims. Fatigue, as the world would later learn, was one of the early symptoms of this disease. But in 1897, when the New York bakeshop law was passed, the primary issue for bakers was the length of their workday.

Justice Oliver Wendell Holmes began his famous dissent in *Lochner* by noting that the case was "decided upon an economic theory which a large part of the country does not entertain." No other description more accurately captured the sentiments of one small segment of a nation coming to grips with the social and economic dislocation caused by the rapid industrialization of its workforce. Modern bakeries glisten with stainless steel and operate under a comprehensive set of federal and state regulations designed to promote health and safety in the workplace. In early-twentieth-century America, however, even modest reform such as that encompassed by the New York Bakeshop Act was considered an infringement of an employer's constitutional right to extract labor in whatever fashion possible. Bakeries are no longer permitted to make bread like great-grandma used to—and for good reason.

## Reference

Kens, Paul. *Judicial Power and Reform Politics: The Anatomy of Lochner v. New York.* Lawrence: University Press of Kansas, 1990, pp. 6–13.

---

employees (all being men *sui juris*) in a private business, not dangerous in any degree to morals or in any real and substantial degree to the health of the employees. Under such circumstances, the freedom of master and employee to contract with each other in relation to their employment, and in defining the same, cannot be prohibited or interfered with without violating the Federal Constitution.

Mr. Justice Harlan, with whom Mr. Justice White and Mr. Justice Day concurred, dissenting.

While this court has not attempted to mark the precise boundaries of what is called the police power of the State, the existence of the power has been uniformly recognized, both by the Federal and state courts.

All the cases agree that this power extends at least to the protection of the lives, the health, and the safety of the public against the injurious exercise by any citizen of his own rights. . . .

Speaking generally, the State, in the exercise of its powers, may not unduly interfere with the right of the citizen to enter into contracts that may be necessary and essential in the enjoyment of the inherent rights belonging to everyone, among which rights is the right, "to be free in the enjoyment of all his faculties; to be free to use them in all lawful ways; to live and work where he will; to earn his livelihood by any lawful calling; to pursue any livelihood or avocation." This was declared in *Allgeyer* v. *Louisiana*. But, in the same case, it was conceded that the right to contract in relation to persons and property or to do business within a State may be "regulated, and sometimes prohibited, when the contracts or business conflict with the policy of the State as contained in its statutes." . . .

I take it to be firmly established that what is called the liberty of contract may, within certain limits, be subjected to regulations designed and calculated to promote the general welfare or to guard the public health, the public morals or the public safety. Granting then that there is a liberty of contract which cannot be violated even under the sanction of direct legislative enactment, but assuming, as according to settled law we may assume, that such liberty of contract is subject to such regulations as the State may reasonably prescribe for the common good and the wellbeing of society, what are the conditions under which the judiciary may declare such regulations to be in excess of legislative authority and void? Upon this point there is no room for dispute, for the rule is universal that a legislative enactment, Federal or state, is never to be disregarded or held invalid unless it be, beyond question, plainly and palpably in excess of legislative power. . . . If there be doubt as to the validity of the statute, that doubt must therefore be resolved in favor of its validity, and the courts must keep their hands off, leaving the legislature to meet the responsibility for unwise legislation. If the end which the legislature seeks to accomplish be one to which its power extends, and if the means employed to that end, although not the wisest or best, are yet not plainly and palpably unauthorized by law, then the court cannot interfere. In other words, when the validity of a statute is questioned, the burden of proof, so to speak, is upon those who assert it to be unconstitutional.

Let these principles be applied to the present case. By the statute in question, it is provided that, "No employee shall be required or permitted to work in a biscuit, bread or cake bakery or confectionery establishment more than sixty hours in any one week, or more than ten hours in any one day, unless for the purpose of making a shorter work day on the last day of the week; nor more hours in any one week than will make an average of ten hours per day for the number of days during such week in which such employee shall work."

It is plain that this statute was enacted in order to protect the physical wellbeing of those who work in bakery and confectionery establishments. It may be that the statute had its origin, in part, in the belief that employers and employees in such establishments were not upon an equal footing, and that the necessities of the latter often compelled them to submit to such exactions as unduly taxed their strength. Be this as it may, the statute must be taken as expressing the belief of the people of New York that, as a general rule, and in the case of the average man, labor in excess of sixty hours during a week in such establishments may endanger the health of those who thus labor. Whether or not this be wise legislation it is not the province of the court to inquire. Under our systems of government, the courts are not concerned with the wisdom or policy of legislation. So that, in determining the question of power to interfere with liberty of contract, the court may inquire whether the means devised by the State are germane to an end which may be lawfully accomplished and have a real or substantial relation to the protection of health, as involved in the daily work of the persons, male and female, engaged in bakery and confectionery establishments. But when this inquiry is entered upon, I find it impossible, in view of common experience, to say that there is here no real or substantial relation between the means employed by the State and the end sought to be accomplished by its legislation. . . . It must be remembered that this statute does not apply to all kinds of business. It applies only to work in bakery and confectionery establishments, in which, as all know, the air constantly breathed by workmen is not as pure and healthful as that to be found in some other establishments or out of doors. . . .

I do not stop to consider whether any particular view of this economic question presents the sounder theory. What the precise facts are it may be difficult to say. It is enough for the determination of this case, and it is enough for this court to know, that the question is one about which there is room for debate and for an honest difference of opinion. There are many reasons of a weighty, substantial character, based upon the experience of mankind, in support of the theory that, all things considered, more than ten hours' steady work each day, from week to week, in a bakery or confectionery establishment, may endanger the health, and shorten the lives of the workmen, thereby diminishing their physical and mental capacity to serve the State, and to provide for those dependent upon them.

If such reasons exist, that ought to be the end of this case, for the State is not amenable to the judiciary in respect of its legislative enactments unless such enactments are plainly, palpably, beyond all question, inconsistent with the Constitution of the United States. We are not to presume that the State of New York has acted in bad faith. Nor can we assume that its legislature acted without due deliberation, or that it did not determine this question upon the fullest attainable information, and for the common good. We cannot say that the State has acted without reason, nor ought we to proceed upon the theory that its action is a mere sham. Our duty, I submit, is to sustain the statute as not being in conflict with the Federal Constitution for the reason—and such is an all-sufficient reason—it is not shown to be plainly and palpably inconsistent with that instrument. Let the State alone in the management of its purely domestic affairs so long as it does not appear beyond all question that it has violated the Federal Constitution. This view necessarily results from the principle that the health and safety of the people of a State are primarily for the State to guard and protect.

MR. JUSTICE HOLMES, dissenting.

This case is decided upon an economic theory which a large part of the country does not entertain. If it were a question whether I agreed with that theory, I should desire to study it further and long before making up my mind. But I do not conceive that to be my duty, because I strongly believe that my agreement or disagreement has nothing to do with the right of a majority to embody their opinions in law. It is settled by various decisions of this court that state constitutions and state laws may regulate life in many ways which we, as legislators, might think as injudicious, or, if you like, as tyrannical, as this, and which, equally with this, interfere with the liberty to contract. Sunday laws and usury laws are ancient examples. A more modern one is the prohibition of lotteries. The liberty of the citizen to do as he likes so long as he does not interfere with the liberty of others to do the same, which has been a shibboleth for some well known writers, is interfered with by school laws, by the Post Office, by every state or municipal institution which takes his money for purposes thought desirable, whether he likes it or not. The Fourteenth Amendment does not enact Mr. Herbert Spencer's *Social Statics*. The other day, we sustained the Massachusetts vaccination law. *Jacobson* v. *Massachusetts*. United States and state statutes and decisions cutting down the liberty to contract by way of combination are familiar to this court. Two years ago, we upheld the prohibition of sales of stock on margins or for future delivery in the constitution of California. *Otis* v. *Parker*. The decision sustaining an eight hour law for miners is still recent. *Holden* v. *Hardy*. Some of these laws embody convictions or prejudices which judges are likely to share. Some may not. But a constitution is not intended to embody a particular economic theory, whether of paternalism and the organic relation of the citizen to the State or of *laissez faire*. It is made for people of fundamentally differing views, and the accident of our finding certain opinions natural and familiar or novel and even shocking ought not to conclude our judgment upon the question whether statutes embodying them conflict with the Constitution of the United States.

General propositions do not decide concrete cases. The decision will depend on a judgment or intuition more subtle than any articulate major premise. But I think that the proposition just stated, if it is accepted, will carry us far toward the end. Every opinion tends to become a law. I think that the word liberty in the Fourteenth Amendment is perverted when it is held to prevent the natural outcome of a dominant opinion, unless it can be said that a rational and fair man necessarily would admit that the statute proposed would infringe fundamental principles as they have been understood by the traditions of our people and our law. It does not need research to show that no such sweeping condemnation can be passed upon the statute before us. A reasonable man might think it a proper measure on the score of health. Men whom I certainly could not pronounce unreasonable would uphold it as a first installment of a general regulation of the hours of work. Whether in the latter aspect it would be open to the charge of inequality I think it unnecessary to discuss.

▼▲▼

## Muller v. State of Oregon
### 208 U.S. 412 (1908)

The facts and background of this case are set out in the accompanying SIDEBAR.

The Court's decision was unanimous. Justice Brewer delivered the opinion of the Court.

MR. JUSTICE BREWER delivered the opinion of the Court.

The single question is the constitutionality of the statute under which the defendant was convicted so far as it affects the work of a female in a laundry. That it does not conflict with any provisions of the state constitution is set-

tled by the decision of the Supreme Court of the State. The contentions of the defendant, now plaintiff in error, are thus stated in his brief:

1. Because the statute attempts to prevent persons *sui juris* from making their own contracts, and thus violates the provisions of the Fourteenth Amendment. . . .
2. Because the statute does not apply equally to all persons similarly situated, and is class legislation.
3. The statute is not a valid exercise of the police power. The kinds of work prescribed are not unlawful, nor are they declared to be immoral or dangerous to the public health; nor can such a law be sustained on the ground that it is designed to protect women on account of their sex. There is no necessary or reasonable connection between the limitation prescribed by the act and the public health, safety, or welfare.

It is the law of Oregon that women, whether married or single, have equal contractual and personal rights with men. . . .

It thus appears that, putting to one side the elective franchise, in the matter of personal and contractual rights, they stand on the same plane as the other sex. Their rights in these respects can no more be infringed than the equal rights of their brothers. We held in *Lochner* v. *New York* (1905), that a law providing that no laborer shall be required or permitted to work in bakeries more than sixty hours in a week or ten hours in a day was not, as to men, a legitimate exercise of the police power of the State, but an unreasonable, unnecessary, and arbitrary interference with the right and liberty of the individual to contract in relation to his labor, and, as such, was in conflict with, and void under, the Federal Constitution. That decision is invoked by plaintiff in error as decisive of the question before us. But this assumes that the difference between the sexes does not justify a different rule respecting a restriction of the hours of labor.

In patent cases, counsel are apt to open the argument with a discussion of the state of the art. It may not be amiss, in the present case, before examining the constitutional question, to notice the course of legislation, as well as expressions of opinion from other than judicial sources. In the brief filed by Mr. Louis D. Brandeis for the defendant in error is a very copious collection of all these matters, an epitome of which is found in the margin.*

The legislation and opinions referred to in the margin may not be, technically speaking, authorities, and in them is little or no discussion of the constitutional question presented to us for determination, yet they are significant of a widespread belief that woman's physical structure, and the functions she performs in consequence thereof, justify special legislation restricting or qualifying the conditions under which she should be permitted to toil. Constitutional questions, it is true, are not settled by even a consensus of present public opinion, for it is the peculiar value of a written constitution that it places in unchanging form limitations upon legislative action, and thus gives a permanence and stability to popular government which otherwise would be lacking. At the same time, when a question of fact is debated and debatable, and the extent to which a special constitutional limitation goes is affected by the truth in respect to that fact, a widespread and long-continued belief concerning it is worthy of consideration. We take judicial cognizance of all matters of general knowledge.

It is undoubtedly true, as more than once declared by this Court, that the general right to contract in relation to one's business is part of the liberty of the individual, protected by the Fourteenth Amendment to the Federal Constitution; yet it is equally well settled that this liberty is not absolute, and extending to all contracts, and that a State may, without conflicting with the provisions of the Fourteenth Amendment, restrict in many respects the individual's power of contract.

That woman's physical structure and the performance of maternal functions place her at a disadvantage in the struggle for subsistence is obvious. This is especially true when the burdens of motherhood are upon her. Even when they are not, by abundant testimony of the medical fraternity, continuance for a long time on her feet at work, repeating this from day to day, tends to injurious effects upon the body, and, as healthy mothers are essential to vigorous offspring, the physical wellbeing of woman becomes an object of public interest and care in order to preserve the strength and vigor of the race.

Still again, history discloses the fact that woman has always been dependent upon man. He established his control at the outset by superior physical strength, and this control in various forms, with diminishing intensity, has continued to the present. As minors, though not to the same extent, she has been looked upon in the courts as needing especial care that her rights may be preserved. Education was long denied her, and while now the doors of the schoolroom are opened and her opportunities for acquiring knowledge are great, yet, even with that and the consequent increase of capacity for business affairs, it is still true that, in the struggle for subsistence, she is not an equal competitor with her brother. Though limitations upon personal and contractual rights may be removed by legislation, there is that in her disposition and habits of life which will operate against a full assertion of those rights. She will still be where some legislation to protect her seems necessary to secure a real equality of right. Doubtless there are individual exceptions, and there are many respects in which she has an advantage over him; but, looking at it from the viewpoint of the effort to maintain an independent position in life, she is not upon an equality. Differentiated by these matters from the other sex, she is properly placed in a class by herself, and legislation designed for her protection may be sustained even when like legislation is not necessary for men, and could not be sustained. It is impossible to close one's eyes to the fact that she still looks to her brother, and depends upon him. Even though all restrictions on political, personal, and contractual rights were taken away, and she stood, so far as statutes are concerned, upon an absolutely equal plane with him, it would still be true that she is so constituted that she will rest upon and look to him for protection; that her physical structure and a proper discharge of her maternal functions—having in view not merely her own health, but the wellbeing of the race—justify legislation to protect her from the greed, as well as the passion, of man. The limitations which this statute places upon her contractual powers, upon her right to agree with her employer as to the time she shall labor, are not imposed solely for her benefit, but also largely for the benefit of all. Many words cannot make this plainer. The two sexes differ in structure of body, in the functions to be performed by each, in the amount of physical strength, in the capacity for long-continued labor, particularly when done standing, the influence of vigorous health upon the future wellbeing of the race, the self-reliance which enables one to assert full rights, and in the capacity to maintain the struggle for subsistence. This difference justifies a difference in legislation, and upholds that which is designed to compensate for some of the burdens which rest upon her.

We have not referred in this discussion to the denial of the elective franchise in the State of Oregon, for, while that may disclose a lack of political equality in all things with her brother, that is not of itself decisive. The reason runs deeper, and rests in the inherent difference between the two sexes and in the different functions in life which they perform.

For these reasons, and without questioning in any respect the decision in *Lochner v. New York,* we are of the opinion that it cannot be adjudged that the act in question is in conflict with the Federal Constitution so far as it respects the work of a female in a laundry, and the judgment of the Supreme Court of Oregon is affirmed.

## MULLER V. STATE OF OREGON

### *Florence Kelley and the National Consumer's League*

In an era when American women were not expected to do much more than to marry well and care for children, Florence Kelley stood apart for her determination to raise their economic and political profile. Born in 1859, Kelley was the only daughter of the prominent Philadelphia entrepreneur and politician William D. (Pig-Iron) Kelley, who encouraged her to pursue a formal education and later supported her lifelong interest in reforming the living and working conditions of the poor. Kelley's interest in the relationship between political power and economic class was evident from her early studies at Cornell University, but not until her arrival at the University of Zurich did her political activism fully emerge. There she embraced socialism; discussed Frederich Engels's manifesto, *The Working Class in England in 1844,* with fellow radicals; and was briefly married to a Russian revolutionary.

After the collapse of her marriage, Kelley returned to the United States, where she immediately aligned herself with the nascent Progressive movement. In 1889, at the request of the United States Commerce and Labor Department, Kelley engaged in a comprehensive study of women's rights activist Jane Addams's Hull-House, a Chicago settlement house designed to provide low-cost refuge for immigrants and other working poor who toiled in the local factories. Kelley's admittedly crude statistical studies of the deplorable working and living conditions of factory workers were brought to life by her vivid narrative that described the impact of industrial capitalism on family life, public health, and the environment.

Kelley's report struck a raw nerve with the public. The Illinois legislature launched an immediate inquiry into state and local factory conditions to follow up on Kelley's findings. A special legislative committee later reported that hundreds of Illinois factories were inadequate on several counts, ranging from poor or nonexistent ventilation to unsanitary waste disposal facilities. The culmination of these efforts was Illinois's first law regulating working conditions in factories.

In recognition of her expertise and critical early research, the state of Illinois appointed Kelley as its chief inspector of factories. Her mandate was to investigate whether factories were in compliance with the state's new building and sanitation codes and to enforce anti-sweatshop legislation on behalf of women and children. Kelley's hope that Illinois might charter the path of progressive reform of the nation's industrial economy soon withered as she encountered persistent uninterest on the part of the state to enforce the new codes. Her experience led her to conclude that any meaningful legal enforcement of progressive legislation would have to come from outside the public sector, which she believed was still indentured to the wishes of the state's powerful business interests.

To understand better the nature of law and its relationship to the political process, Kelley left her government post and entered Northwestern University law school, graduating in 1895. After graduation, Kelley moved to New York City, where she became the first executive secretary of the National Consumer's League (NCL), an organization created to consolidate the efforts of the numerous associations around the country dedicated to the reform of working conditions for women in low-paying factory and retail jobs. Under Kelley's leadership, the NCL organized successful public campaigns to educate consumers about the exploitation of "shop girls," the nickname of the time given to women who worked in the factories and stores. NCL efforts included a "Shop Early" campaign, which was designed to encourage consumers to make their Christmas-season purchases soon after Thanksgiving to allow factory and shop women to spend more time with their families as the holidays drew

*This turn-of-the-century Chicago street bustles with street vendors and busy sidewalks. Such scenes conjure up images of a simpler time, but in fact local urban markets were dirty, exposed to disease, and often the site of abusive labor practices. They were a frequent target of Progressive reform groups.*
Chicago Historical Society, neg. # DN 068691; Photographer: Chicago Daily News.

closer, and the publication of a "White List," a monthly report urging consumers to boycott retail establishments where unfair employment practices existed. Kelley was also responsible for persuading local health boards to adopt the Consumer's League label, a cloth swatch that was stitched onto factory products. The label indicated that the state factory law had been obeyed and that "all goods [were] made on the premises; overtime [was] not worked; [and] children under sixteen years of age [were] not employed."

Guided by Kelley's extraordinary leadership skills and principled politics, the NCL became a persistent and forceful advocate of protective labor legislation for women and children. By 1905 the NCL had sixty-four local chapters scattered throughout the country. Although it never claimed more than a few thousand members, the NCL counted some of the Progressive movement's most elite and respected activists among its membership, such as Josephine Goldmark; her sister, Alice Goldmark Brandeis, the wife of Louis

Brandeis; and Jane Addams. 1905 was also the year the Supreme Court decided *Lochner v. New York,* which overturned a maximum work hour law on the grounds that it violated the liberty of contract rights of employers. Kelley immediately recognized that the Court's decision placed the hard-won foundation of Progressive legislation in danger of judicial demolition. So when the NCL learned that the Court had agreed to hear the appeal of Kurt Muller, who owned the Grand Laundry in Portland, Oregon, its leadership was determined to defend the statute it had been instrumental in passing. Muller had been convicted of violating a state law setting a maximum ten-hour work day for "female laundresses."

After Joseph H. Choate, the former United States ambassador to Great Britain, turned down the NCL's initial overture to take the case—he considered it appropriate that a "big husky Irishwoman should . . . work more than ten hours a day in a laundry if her employer so desired"— Kelley and Goldmark decided to approach Louis Brandeis, who by this time had earned his well-deserved reputation as the most effective legal advocate in the Progressive reform movement. Goldmark, who was the NCL's lead researcher on the relationship between public health and poor working conditions, made the initial overture to Brandeis. Kelley believed that more than just Goldmark's common expertise with Brandeis on labor reform would improve the NCL's chance of securing his services—Brandeis was, after all, her brother-in-law.

Brandeis agreed to defend the Oregon statute, but insisted that the state must give him complete control over the case. If the NCL limited its involvement in *Muller* to amicus curiae, Brandeis would not be permitted to participate in oral argument or develop the legal strategy to defend the law. That latter point was crucial, insisted Brandeis, because he planned to integrate the NCL's statistical data about the effects of long working hours on women into his legal argument. Brandeis knew that the use of social science data to support his constitutional argument was risky, as it had never been employed before as a litigation strategy. Although left unsaid, Brandeis also knew his prestige would give the novel approach in *Muller* a level of credibility that Oregon's state lawyers could not hope to match.

Oregon was pleased to meet Brandeis's demands. As Brandeis set to work on the legal argument, Kelley and Goldmark began collecting data on the substance and scope of laws that limited women's work hours in other states and in Europe, as well as statistical evidence that tied women's health to the amount of hours they were required to work. Kelley and Goldmark produced a mountain of data that offered persuasive empirical evidence that long hours in labor-intensive jobs adversely affected the health of women. Brandeis did not use all the research compiled by Kelley and Goldmark in his brief, but he was impressed enough by their findings to arrange for their publication in book form. Credited to Josephine Goldmark, who had done the brunt of the research for the *Muller* brief, *Fatigue and Efficiency* was published by the Russell Sage Foundation in 1912.

Brandeis emphasized two points in his legal argument. The first was that liberty of contract gave way when the state could demonstrate that an industry's employment practices posed a genuine health risk to employees. Second, and somewhat controversial

*Florence Kelley was a pioneering activist on behalf of the rights of women and children in the workplace. Her research on working conditions was crucial in Louis Brandeis's successful argument in* Muller v. Oregon *(1908) upholding a maximum work day for women.*
Bettmann/CORBIS.

within the feminist leadership of the NCL, was that women, as the "weaker" sex, were in need of special protections that men were not. Whether Brandeis genuinely believed this is still open to debate; he did, however, believe it was essential to make this point so as to distinguish the Oregon law from the legislation struck down by the Court in *Lochner*.

Between the lines, Brandeis's point was clear—natural selection was fine for men, but not for women.

Because of their singular role in bearing children, any physical harm that came to women because of their working conditions would be passed on to future generations. Thus society at large, argued Brandeis, would suffer if women were not adequately protected.

Brandeis's strategic gamble paid off. In fact, Brandeis's brief on behalf of the Oregon law so impressed Justice David Brewer that, in his opinion for the unanimous Court, he paid direct tribute to Brandeis by name: "It may not be amiss, in the present case, before examining the constitutional question, to notice the course of legislation as well as the expressions on opinion from other than judicial sources. In the brief filed by Mr. Louis D. Brandeis . . is a very copious collection of all these matters, an epitome of which is found in the margin." *Muller's* impact was immediate and profound, as several states enacted laws based on their belief that the inevitable court challenges to them could be defended by the approach pioneered by Brandeis. By 1915, Brandeis, supported by the ongoing research of the NCL, successfully defended protective legislation for women enacted in more than half a dozen states.

*Muller* added to Brandeis's already formidable public reputation but did little to turn the spotlight on Kelley, who recognized early on that litigation held the potential to broaden the potential of Progressive Era reform. In an age when women were dependent on the paternal comfort of the male-dominated worlds of politics and law to secure protection from the harsh environment created by the Industrial Revolution, Florence Kelley should be remembered as a pivotal activist on behalf of women, children, and the working poor. Her determination and innovative vision forever changed the social organization of labor and work in the United States.

### References

Paulson, Ross Evans. *Liberty, Equality and Justice: Civil Rights, Women's Rights, and the Regulation of Business, 1865–1932*. Durham, N.C.: Duke University Press, 1997.

Sklar, Kathryn Kish. *Florence Kelley and the Nation's Work: The Rise of Women's Political Culture, 1830–1900*. New Haven, Conn.: Yale University Press, 1995.

Strum, Philipa. *Louis D. Brandeis: Justice for the People*. New York: Schocken Books, 1984.

---

* The following legislation of the states imposes restriction in some form or another upon the hours of labor that may be required of women: Massachusetts; Rhode Island; Louisiana; Connecticut; Maine; New Hampshire; Maryland; Virginia; Pennsylvania; New York; Nebraska; Washington; Colorado; New Jersey; Oklahoma; North Dakota; South Dakota; Wisconsin; South Carolina. . . .

Then follow extracts from over ninety reports of committees, bureaus of statistics, commissioners of hygiene, inspectors of factories, both in this country and in Europe, to the effect that long hours of labor are dangerous for women, primarily because of their special physical organization. The matter is discussed in these reports in different aspects, but all agree as to the danger. It would, of course, take too much space to give these reports in detail. Following them are extracts from similar reports discussing the general benefits of short hours from an economic aspect of the question. In many of these reports, individual instances are given tending to support the general conclusion. Perhaps the general scope and character of all these reports may be summed up in what an inspector for

Hanover says: "The reasons for the reduction of the working day to ten hours—(a) the physical organization of women, (b) her maternal functions, (c) the rearing and education of the children, (d) the maintenance of the home— are all so important and so far-reaching that the need for such reduction need hardly be discussed."

▼▲▼

---

Evidence that Brandeis had scored a direct hit in *Muller* against the liberty of contract doctrine came in *Bunting v. Oregon* (1917). In *Bunting* the Court, 5-3, upheld a maximum work hour law, with overtime provisions, for all workers in the flour industry. Justice Joseph McKenna must have heard echoes of Brandeis's *Muller* argument in his head as he wrote for the Court. Wrote McKenna: "The contention [on behalf of the flour industry] that the law, even regarded as regulating hours of service, is not either necessary or useful for the preservation of the health of employees in mills, factories and manufacturing establishments. The record contains no facts to support the contention and against it is the judgement of the legislature . . . [it] cannot be held, as a matter of law, that the legislative requirement is unreasonable or arbitrary."[53]

Notice that Justice McKenna rests the burden of proof in this case with industry, not the legislature. His opinion also emphasized that the plaintiffs had failed to provide *factual* evidence to support the argument that the maximum work hour law was unrelated to the public interest. Now take the logic of *Bunting* an additional step and consider this question: Are *Lochner* and *Bunting* reconcilable? Some constitutional scholars have argued that *Bunting* marked the de facto overturning of *Lochner,* since the factual settings in the two cases hardly differed. But to see this turn of events in such narrow terms misses the significance of *Lochner* and overstates *Bunting.* *Bunting* and *Muller* were decided in accordance with *Lochner's* requirements to uphold a public health or interest exception to the liberty of contract doctrine. The legislature, in each case, had simply met the burden that *Lochner* required. Liberty of contract remained alive and well, indeed in better health than ever before, even after *Bunting.* The Court's 1923 decision in *Adkins* v. *Children's Hospital,* invalidating a minimum wage law passed by Congress to cover female hospital employees in the District of Columbia, affirmed the vitality of liberty of contract doctrine.

In *Adkins* liberty of contract advocates reached their constitutional mountaintop. Despite a wealth of sociological data amassed in support of the minimum wage law's health and welfare benefits for women, the Court, more conservative than ever before with the entrenchment of the Four Horsemen and the return of Justice McKenna to the fold, struck down the law.[54] To quell any doubt that the Court had gone soft on substantive due process, Justice George Sutherland made it evident that the voices inside his head were those of Spencer and Sumner, not of his colleague, Louis Brandeis. "The statute now under consideration," wrote Sutherland:

> is simply and exclusively a price-fixing law, confined to adult women . . . who are legally as capable of contracting for themselves as men. It forbids parties having lawful capacity—under penalties as to the employer—to freely contract with one another in respect of the price for which one shall render service to the other in a purely private employment. . . .

The feature of this statute which, perhaps more than any other, puts upon it the stamp of invalidity is that it exacts from the employer an arbitrary payment for a purpose and upon a basis having no causal connection with his business, or the contract, or the work the employee engages to do. The declared basis . . . is not the value of the service rendered, but the extraneous circumstance that the employee needs to get a prescribed sum of money to insure *her* subsistence, health, and morals.[55]

An astonished Holmes countered in dissent:

> To me . . . the power of Congress [to establish a minimum wage] seems absolutely free from doubt. The end—to remove conditions leading to ill health, immorality, and the deterioration of the race—no one would deny to be within the scope of constitutional legislation. When so many intelligent persons, who have studied the matter more than any of us can, have thought that the means are effective and are worth the price, it seems to me impossible to deny that the belief reasonably may be held by reasonable men. . . .
>
> [Our] earlier decisions [on due process] began with our memory, and went no farther than an unpretentious assertion of the liberty to follow the ordinary callings. Later that innocuous generality was expanded into the dogma, Liberty of Contract. Contract is not specially mentioned in the text that we have to construe. It is merely an example of doing what you want to do, embodied in the word "liberty." But pretty much all law consists in forbidding men to some things they want to do, and contract is no more exempt from law than other acts.[56]

Even Chief Justice William H. Taft, a conservative stalwart in economic regulation cases, dissented. The Court's entire line of substantive due process jurisprudence since *Lochner,* in fact, appeared to bewilder him:

> It is impossible for me to reconcile the *Bunting Case* and the *Lochner Case* and I have always supposed that the *Lochner Case* was thus overruled *sub silentio* [without saying so]. Yet the opinion of the Court herein in support of its conclusion quotes from the opinion in the *Lochner Case* as one which has been sometimes distinguished but never overruled. Certainly there was no attempt to distinguish it in the *Bunting Case.*[57]

Nonetheless, the Court used *Adkins* to revitalize the liberty of contract doctrine for another run through the

Roaring 1920s, oblivious to the Progressive movement's campaign to publicize the consequences of unbridled capitalism in economic terms and combat them through legislation. It also ignored the ever-increasing number of states and localities enacting legislation that protected union organization, established minimum wages, created occupational safety and health rules, and required consumer-disclosure notices.[58] Indeed, the interpretation the Court had given the constitutional phrase "due process" seemed to affirm, rather than question, the thesis of Progressive historian Charles Beard's controversial 1913 book, *An Economic Interpretation of the Constitution of the United States.* Beard argued that the Framers created the Constitution to advance and protect the economic and commercial interests of the propertied classes.[59]

Not even the stock market crash in October 1929 and the arrival of the Great Depression could shake the Court's commitment to the constitutional protection of laissez-faire economics. The nation's economic collapse had even encouraged President Herbert Hoover, a market-oriented conservative, to expand the scope of the welfare state beyond all previous borders, even those recommended by the Progressives. The nation, however, was not persuaded that President Hoover's initiatives were sufficient to tame the Great Depression. In 1932, with the promise of a "New Deal" for America, Franklin Delano Roosevelt handily defeated Hoover. With liberty of contract still entrenched in the Court and the promise of unprecedented legislative experimentation to renew the economy on the horizon, the battle lines were drawn for the last hurrah of economic laissez faire.

If, to paraphrase Justice Holmes, a large part of the country did not believe that the Fourteenth Amendment enacted Herbert Spencer's *Social Statics* when *Lochner* was decided, the 1932 elections indicated that number had increased exponentially. In January 1933 the nation's industrial production had dropped to 50 percent of its pre–October 1929 levels, 12 million people were unemployed, and bread lines and soup kitchens were commonplace. Bank failures, with uninsured deposits, drained life savings overnight. Labor unrest had become more prevalent and increasingly violent. Roosevelt responded in kind to the nation's fears and hopes with a barrage of legislation designed to stabilize the economy and provide an undercurrent of support to the economically ravaged. Numerous states followed Roosevelt's examples, instituting economic controls of their own. These ranged from minimum wage laws to price supports to farmers to debt forgiveness, with many more programs in between.

Thus, when the Court, in *Nebbia v. New York* (1934), upheld a New York law that created a state control board to set minimum and maximum prices on milk, the decision suggested that liberty of contract might well be scheduled for retirement. In *Nebbia,* the first major state-level economic substantive due process case of the New Deal period, Justice Owen Roberts broadened the conditions that justified state economic regulation of business beyond the "public interest" requirement created in *Munn.* Roberts wrote, "There is no closed class or category of business affected with a public interest."[60] *Nebbia* and *Home Building & Loan Assn. v. Blaisdell* (1934), the important Contract Clause case (see Chapter 8) in which the Court upheld Minnesota's right to offer mortgage relief to farmers on the grounds that state police power included the authority to respond to emergencies, were examples of state laws that satisfied the BAPI rule. For a moment it appeared that the Court had grasped the significance of the New Deal and was prepared to reconsider judicial supervision of economic policy questions.

But in January 1935 the Court embarked on a series of decisions, you will recall from Chapter 6, that halted the New Deal in its tracks. Until the Court's about-face in 1937, it rejected one major Roosevelt initiative after another. The Court was no more sympathetic to state legislation designed to address the consequences of the Depression. Most telling in the economic substantive due process area was *Morehead v. New York ex rel. Tipaldo* (1936). There, the Court ruled that New York's minimum wage law for women violated the Due Process Clause, a decision that appeared to marginalize the constitutional significance of *Nebbia.*[61] As a matter of constitutional law, *Tipaldo* is hard to understand because the legislative record behind the enactment of the New York law met the Court's requirement in *Adkins*—that the minimum wage must be tied to the economic value of the labor.

Justice Roberts, who wrote the *Tipaldo* opinion, was not present for *Adkins.* Nor did Roberts appear to have read it very closely, for he announced that "the state is without power by any form of legislation to prohibit, change or nullify contracts between employers and adult women workers as to the amount of wages to be paid."[62] Justice Stone, who had come to the Court in 1925 and had quickly taken his place alongside, first, Brandeis and Holmes, and later, Benjamin Cardozo, summarized the stalemate between the Court and the New Deal reformers after the conclusion of the 1935 term:

> Our latest exploit was a holding by a divided vote that there was no power in a state to regulate minimum wages for women. Since the court last week said that this could not be done by the national government, as the matter was local, and it is said that it cannot be done by local government even though it is local, we have tied Uncle Sam up in a hard knot.[63]

It took another substantive due process challenge to a minimum wage law, this time one that covered minors as well as women, to sound the retreat from the *Lochner* era. Justice Roberts, who had just written the Court's opinion in *Tipaldo*, joined Chief Justice Hughes, a dissenter in that case, and the Stone-Brandeis-Cardozo triumvirate to form the 5-4 majority that ended the *Lochner* era of liberty of contract and rendered economic substantive due process from a vibrant constitutional doctrine to a constitutional artifact. Here, as in *NLRB* v. *Jones & Laughlin* (1937) and *Steward Machine Co.* v. *Davis* (1937), which together formed a burial ground for dual federalism, Justice Roberts provided the critical fifth vote to hand Roosevelt the Court's constitutional go-ahead for the New Deal. Given our discussion of Roosevelt's Court-packing plan in Chapter 6, is it fair to say that Roberts, in particular, was stirred to abandon his position in *Tipaldo*, as the New York and Washington state laws were essentially the same? Or was it Roosevelt's landslide victory in 1936, which included every state but Maine and Vermont, that set the course of events in motion toward the Constitutional Revolution of 1937?[64]

*West Coast Hotel* brought the curtain down on the *Lochner* era once and for all. Is there any doubt that Chief Justice Hughes, who had wavered between the judicial liberalism of Brandeis, Cardozo, and Stone and the economic absolutism of the Four Horsemen prior to that crucial spring of 1937, was determined to put the past to rest? When Hughes wrote that "[t]he Constitution does not speak of freedom of contract. It speaks of liberty and prohibits the deprivation of liberty without due process of law . . . [and] [t]his essential limitation of liberty in general governs freedom of contract in particular," it was as if *Lochner* had never existed.[65]

Far more typical of the Court's modern approach to such claims is *Ferguson* v. *Skrupa* (1963), where it unanimously rejected a Due Process Clause challenge to a Kansas law requiring debt adjusters to receive a state-issued license to enter that profession. Indeed, the voices of Darwin, Cooley, Spencer, and Sumner were distant echoes of another time, one that political forces, economic change, and social transformation eclipsed long ago.

---

## *Nebbia* v. *New York*
### 291 U.S. 502 (1934)

Leo Nebbia owned a grocery store in Rochester, New York. He was convicted in 1933 of violating a state law enacted earlier that year setting price limits on the sale of milk products in all cities, towns, and villages with populations of one thousand or more, with the sole exception of the New York City metropolitan area. The law, which set the minimum price for a quart of milk at nine cents, was a response to the collapse of the state's dairy industry, which affected more people in New York than in any other state.

Like many small business owners, Nebbia was well aware that the Supreme Court did not look kindly on state laws that interfered with the right of buyers and sellers to engage in "voluntary" transactions. In *Adkins* v. *Children's Hospital* (1923), Justice Holmes had referred to the idea that such economic arrangements, whether between buyers and sellers or employers and employees, were, in fact, voluntary as the "dogma, liberty of contract." Leo Nebbia disagreed, believing that he was free to sell his products for whatever price best served his business interests. Upon his conviction for selling two quarts of milk and a loaf of bread to Jedo Del Signore for eighteen cents, Nebbia was arrested. After losing consecutive rounds in the New York state courts on his liberty contract challenge to the New York milk control law, Nebbia appealed to the Supreme Court.

The Court's decision was 5 to 4. Justice Roberts delivered the opinion of the Court. Justice McReynolds, joined by Justices Van Devanter, Sutherland, and Butler, dissented.

▼▲▼

MR. JUSTICE ROBERTS delivered the opinion of the Court.

The question for decision is whether the Federal Constitution prohibits a state from so fixing the selling price of milk. We first inquire as to the occasion for the legislation, and its history.

During 1932, the prices received by farmers for milk were much below the cost of production. The decline in prices during 1931 and 1932 was much greater than that of prices generally. The situation of the families of dairy producers had become desperate, and called for state aid similar to that afforded the unemployed, if conditions should not improve.

On March 10, 1932, the senate and assembly resolved: "That a joint Legislative committee is hereby created . . . to investigate the causes of the decline of the price of milk to producers and the resultant effect of the low prices upon the dairy industry and the future supply of milk to the cities of the State; to investigate the cost of distribution of milk and its relation to prices paid to milk producers, to the end that the consumer may be assured of an adequate supply of milk at a reasonable price, both to producer and consumer."

The committee organized May 6, 1932, and its activities lasted nearly a year. It held 13 public hearings at which 254 witnesses testified and 2,350 typewritten pages of testimony were taken. Numerous exhibits were submitted. Under its direction, an extensive research program was prosecuted by experts and official bodies and employees of the state and municipalities, which resulted in the assembling of much pertinent information. Detailed reports were received from over 100 distributors of milk, and these were collated, and the information obtained analyzed. As a result of the study of this material, a report covering 473 closely printed pages, embracing the conclusions and recommendations of the committee, was presented to the legislature April 10, 1933. This document included detailed findings, with copious references to the supporting evidence; appendices outlining the nature and results of prior investigations of the milk industry of the state, briefs upon the legal questions involved, and forms of bills recommended for passage. The conscientious effort and thoroughness exhibited by the report lend weight to the committee's conclusions.

In part, those conclusions are:

Milk is an essential item of diet. It cannot long be stored. It is an excellent medium for growth of bacteria. These facts necessitate safeguards in its production and handling for human consumption which greatly increase the cost of the business. Failure of producers to receive a reasonable return for their labor and investment over an extended period threaten a relaxation of vigilance against contamination.

The production and distribution of milk is a paramount industry of the state, and largely affects the health and prosperity of its people. Dairying yields fully one-half of the total income from all farm products. Dairy farm investment amounts to approximately $1,000,000,000. Curtailment or destruction of the dairy industry would cause a serious economic loss to the people of the state.

In addition to the general price decline, other causes for the low price of milk include: a periodic increase in the number of cows and in milk production; the prevalence of unfair and destructive trade practices in the distribution of milk, leading to a demoralization of prices in the metropolitan area and other markets, and the failure of transportation and distribution charges to be reduced in proportion to the reduction in retail prices for milk and cream.

The fluid milk industry is affected by factors of instability peculiar to itself which call for special methods of control. Under the best practicable adjustment of supply to demand, the industry must carry a surplus of about 20 percent, because milk, an essential food, must be available as demanded by consumers every day in the year, and demand and supply vary from day to day and according to the season; but milk is perishable, and cannot be stored. Close adjustment of supply to demand is hindered by several factors difficult to control. Thus, surplus milk presents a serious problem, as the prices which can be realized for it for other uses are much less than those obtainable for milk sold for consumption in fluid form or as cream. A satisfactory stabilization of prices for fluid milk requires that the burden of surplus milk be shared equally by all producers and all distributors in the milkshed. So long as the surplus burden is unequally distributed, the pressure to market surplus milk in fluid form will be a serious disturbing factor. The fact that the larger distributors find it necessary to carry large quantities of surplus milk, while the smaller distributors do not, leads to price-cutting and other forms of destructive competition. Smaller distributors, who take no responsibility for the surplus, by purchasing their milk at the blended prices (*i.e.*, an average between the price paid the producer for milk for sale as fluid milk, and the lower surplus milk price paid by the larger organizations) can undersell the larger distributors. Indulgence in this price-cutting often compels the larger dealer to cut the price, to his own and the producer's detriment.

Various remedies were suggested, amongst them united action by producers, the fixing of minimum prices for milk and cream by state authority, and the imposition of certain graded taxes on milk dealers proportioned so as to equalize the cost of milk and cream to all dealers, and so remove the cause of price-cutting. . . .

Under our form of government, the use of property and the making of contracts are normally matters of private, and not of public, concern. The general rule is that both shall be free of governmental interference. But neither property rights nor contract rights are absolute, for government cannot exist if the citizen may at will use his property to the detriment of his fellows, or exercise his freedom of contract to work them harm. Equally fundamental with the private right is that of the public to regulate it in the common interest. As Chief Justice Marshall said, speaking specifically of inspection laws, such laws form, "a portion of that immense mass of legislation which embraces every thing within the territory of a State . . . , all which can be most advantageously exercised by the States themselves. Inspection laws, quarantine laws, health laws of every description, as well as laws for regulating the internal commerce of a State . . . are component parts of this mass." . . .

Thus has this court, from the early days, affirmed that the power to promote the general welfare is inherent in government. Touching the matters committed to it by the Constitution, the United States possesses the power, as do the states in their sovereign capacity touching all subjects jurisdiction of which is not surrendered to the federal government. . . . These correlative rights, that of the citizen to exercise exclusive dominion over property and freely to contract about his affairs and that of the state to regulate the use of property and the conduct of business, are always in collision. No exercise of the private right can be imagined which will not in some respect, however slight, affect the public; no exercise of the legislative prerogative to regulate the conduct of the citizen which will not to some extent abridge his liberty or affect his property. But, subject only to constitutional restraint, the private right must yield to the public need.

The Fifth Amendment, in the field of federal activity, and the Fourteenth, as respects state action, do not prohibit governmental regulation for the public welfare. They merely condition the exertion of the admitted power by securing that the end shall be accomplished by methods consistent with due process. And the guaranty of due process, as has often been held, demands only that the law shall not be unreasonable, arbitrary or capricious, and that the means selected shall have a real and substantial relation to the object sought to be attained. It results that a regulation valid for one sort of business, or in given circumstances, may be invalid for another sort or for the same business under other circumstances, because the reasonableness of each regulation depends upon the relevant facts. . . .

The court has repeatedly sustained curtailment of enjoyment of private property in the public interest. The owner's rights may be subordinated to the needs of other private owners whose pursuits are vital to the paramount interests of the community. The state may control the use of property in various ways; may prohibit advertising billboards except of a prescribed size and location, or their use for certain kinds of advertising; may in certain circumstances authorize encroachments by party walls in cities; may fix the height of buildings, the character of materials, and methods of construction, the adjoining area which must be left open, and may exclude from residential sections offensive trades, industries and structures likely injuriously to affect the public health or safety; or may establish zones within which certain types of buildings or businesses are permitted and others excluded. And although the Fourteenth Amendment extends protection to aliens as well as citizens, a state may for adequate reasons of policy exclude aliens altogether from the use and occupancy of land.

Laws passed for the suppression of immorality, in the interest of health, to secure fair trade practices, and to safeguard the interests of depositors in banks, have been found consistent with due process. These measures not only affected the use of private property, but also interfered with the right of private contract. Other instances are numerous where valid regulation has restricted the right of contract, while less directly affecting property rights.

The Constitution does not guarantee the unrestricted privilege to engage in a business or to conduct it as one pleases. . . .

The milk industry in New York has been the subject of longstanding and drastic regulation in the public interest. The legislative investigation of 1932 was persuasive of the fact that, for this and other reasons, unrestricted competition aggravated existing evils, and the normal law of supply and demand was insufficient to correct maladjustments detrimental to the community. The inquiry disclosed destructive and demoralizing competitive conditions and unfair trade practices which resulted in retail price-cutting and reduced the income of the farmer below the cost of production. We do not understand the appellant to deny that, in these circumstances, the legislature might reasonably consider further regulation and control desirable for protection of the industry and the consuming public. That body believed conditions could be improved by preventing destructive price-cutting by stores which, due to the flood of surplus milk, were able to buy at much lower prices than the larger distributors and to sell without incurring the delivery costs of the latter. In the order of which complaint is made, the Milk Control Board fixed a price of ten cents per quart for sales by a distributor to a consumer, and nine cents by a store to a consumer, thus recognizing the lower costs of the store and endeavoring to establish a differential which would be just to both. In the light of the facts, the order appears not to be unreasonable or arbitrary, or without relation to the purpose to prevent ruthless competition from destroying the wholesale price structure on which the farmer depends for his livelihood, and the community for an assured supply of milk.

But we are told that, because the law essays to control prices, it denies due process. Notwithstanding the admitted power to correct existing economic ills by appropriate regulation of business, even though an indirect result may be a restriction of the freedom of contract or a modification of charges for services or the price of commodities, the appellant urges that direct fixation of prices is a type of regulation absolutely forbidden. His position is that the Fourteenth Amendment requires us to hold the challenged statute void for this reason alone. The argument runs that the public control of rates or prices is *per se* unreasonable and unconstitutional, save as applied to businesses affected with a public interest; that a business so affected is one in which property is devoted to an enterprise of a sort which the public itself might appropriately undertake, or one whose owner relies on a public grant or franchise for the right to conduct the business, or in which he is bound to serve all who apply; in short, such as is commonly called a public utility; or a business in its nature a monopoly. The milk industry, it is said, possesses none of these characteristics, and, therefore, not being affected with a public interest, its charges may not be controlled by the state. Upon the soundness of this contention the appellant's case against the statute depends.

We may as well say at once that the dairy industry is not, in the accepted sense of the phrase, a public utility. We think the appellant is also right in asserting that there is in this case no suggestion of any monopoly or monopolistic practice. It goes without saying that those engaged in the business are in no way dependent upon public grants or franchises for the privilege of conducting their activities. But if, as must be conceded, the industry is subject to regulation in the public interest, what constitutional principle bars the state from correcting existing maladjustments by legislation touching prices? We think there is no such principle. The due process clause makes no mention of sales or of prices any more than it speaks of business or contracts or buildings or other incidents of property. The thought seems nevertheless to have persisted that there is something peculiarly sacrosanct about the price one

may charge for what he makes or sells, and that, however able to regulate other elements of manufacture or trade, with incidental effect upon price, the state is incapable of directly controlling the price itself. This view was negatived many years ago. . . .

It is clear that there is no closed class or category of businesses affected with a public interest, and the function of courts in the application of the Fifth and Fourteenth Amendments is to determine in each case whether circumstances vindicate the challenged regulation as a reasonable exertion of governmental authority or condemn it as arbitrary or discriminatory. The phrase "affected with a public interest" can, in the nature of things, mean no more than that an industry, for adequate reason, is subject to control for the public good. In several of the decisions of this court wherein the expressions "affected with a public interest" and "clothed with a public use" have been brought forward as the criteria of the validity of price control, it has been admitted that they are not susceptible of definition and form an unsatisfactory test of the constitutionality of legislation directed at business practices or prices. These decisions must rest, finally, upon the basis that the requirements of due process were not met, because the laws were found arbitrary in their operation and effect. But there can be no doubt that, upon proper occasion and by appropriate measures, the state may regulate a business in any of its aspects, including the prices to be charged for the products or commodities it sells.

So far as the requirement of due process is concerned, and in the absence of other constitutional restriction, a state is free to adopt whatever economic policy may reasonably be deemed to promote public welfare, and to enforce that policy by legislation adapted to its purpose. The courts are without authority either to declare such policy or, when it is declared by the legislature, to override it. If the laws passed are seen to have a reasonable relation to a proper legislative purpose, and are neither arbitrary nor discriminatory, the requirements of due process are satisfied, and judicial determination to that effect renders a court *functus officio*. "Whether the free operation of the normal laws of competition is a wise and wholesome rule for trade and commerce is an economic question which this court need not consider or determine." And it is equally clear that, if the legislative policy be to curb unrestrained and harmful competition by measures which are not arbitrary or discriminatory, it does not lie with the courts to determine that the rule is unwise. With the wisdom of the policy adopted, with the adequacy or practicability of the law enacted to forward it, the courts are both incompetent and unauthorized to deal. The course of decision in this court exhibits a firm adherence to these principles. Times without number, we have said that the legislature is primarily the judge of the necessity of such an enactment, that every possible presumption is in favor of its validity, and that, though the court may hold views inconsistent with the wisdom of the law, it may not be annulled unless palpably in excess of legislative power. . . .

Tested by these considerations, we find no basis in the due process clause of the Fourteenth Amendment for condemning the provisions of the Agriculture and Markets Law here drawn into question.

## *West Coast Hotel* v. *Parrish*
### 300 U.S. 379 (1937)

In 1913, the Washington state legislature enacted a law making it "unlawful to employ women or minors . . . under conditions detrimental to their health or morals; and . . . to employ women workers in any industry . . . at wages which are not adequate for their maintenance." A commission created by the law established a salary of $14.50 per week for women employed as chambermaids in Washington's hospitality industry. In the summer of 1933, Elsie Parrish went to work for the Cascadian Hotel, owned by the West Coast Hotel Company, in Wenatchee, Washington, a resort community and home to some of the Pacific Northwest's lushest apple orchards. So beautiful was the region that the Works Progress Administration, a major New Deal innovation of the Roosevelt administration, included Wenatchee in its guide to national vacation spots.

In May 1935, Parrish, who had married since she began working at the Cascadian, was fired. She asked the hotel for $216.19 in back pay, an amount she was owed under the 1913 minimum wage law. Cascadian management offered to settle with her for seventeen dollars. Parrish refused and sued the hotel in state court. She lost at trial, but the Washington Supreme Court reversed, holding that *Adkins* v. *Children's Hospital* (1923), which invalidated a *congressional* minimum wage law, did not affect the right of states to enact such laws of their own. West Coast Hotel appealed, hoping that the United States Supreme Court would consider *Adkins* controlling. In the interim, Elsie Parrish was dealt a serious blow when the Court ruled, in *Moorhead* v. *Tipaldo* (1936), that a near-identical New York

minimum wage law for women and children violated the liberty of contract rights of employers. *Tipaldo* convinced even the National Consumers' League, which had persuaded the Court to uphold a maximum work hour law for women in *Muller* v. *Oregon* (1908), that Parrish's case was hopeless. She was on her own.

After *Tipaldo* employers nationwide were free to set wages as low as they pleased, and many did, well aware that women and children, forced into the labor force by the Depression as never before, would take whatever work they could get. One feminist group, the National Woman's Party, praised the Court's decision, insisting that women would never achieve equal rights with men as long as they insisted on being covered by protective legislation. "It is hair-raising to consider how very close women in America came to being ruled inferior citizens," wrote one member of the group to Justice George Sutherland, who wrote the Court's *Tipaldo* opinion. That view was a clear exception to the opinions of most other women's rights groups on the minimum wage issue. In *Tipaldo*, wrote the historian Mary Beard to Chief Justice Harlan Fiske Stone, the Court "play[ed] into the hands of the rawest capitalists."[66]

The Court's decision was 5 to 4. Chief Justice Hughes delivered the opinion of the Court. Justice Sutherland, joined by Justices Van Devanter, McReynolds, and Butler, dissented.

MR. CHIEF JUSTICE HUGHES delivered the opinion of the Court.

This case presents the question of the constitutional validity of the minimum wage law of the State of Washington. . . .

The appellant conducts a hotel. The appellee, Elsie Parrish, was employed as a chambermaid and (with her husband) brought this suit to recover the difference between the wages paid her and the minimum wage fixed pursuant to the state law. The minimum wage was $14.50 per week of 48 hours. The appellant challenged the act as repugnant to the due process clause of the Fourteenth Amendment of the Constitution of the United States.

The appellant relies upon the decision of this Court in *Adkins* v. *Children's Hospital*, which held invalid the District of Columbia Minimum Wage Act, which was attacked under the due process clause of the Fifth Amendment. On the argument at bar, counsel for the appellees attempted to distinguish the Adkins case upon the ground that the appellee was employed in a hotel, and that the business of an innkeeper was affected with a public interest. That effort at distinction is obviously futile, as it appears that, in one of the cases ruled by the Adkins opinion, the employee was a woman employed as an elevator operator in a hotel.

The recent case of *Morehead* v. *New York ex rel. Tipaldo* (1936), came here on certiorari to the New York court, which had held the New York minimum wage act for women to be invalid. A minority of this Court thought that the New York statute was distinguishable in a material feature from that involved in the Adkins case, and, that for that and other reasons, the New York statute should be sustained. But the Court of Appeals of New York had said that it found no material difference between the two statutes, and this Court held that the "meaning of the statute" as fixed by the decision of the state court "must be accepted here as if the meaning had been specifically expressed in the enactment." That view led the affirmance by this Court of the judgment in the Morehead case, as the Court considered that the only question before it was whether the Adkins case was distinguishable, and that reconsideration of that decision had not been sought. Upon that point, the Court said:

> The petition for the writ sought review upon the ground that this case [*Morehead*] is distinguishable from that one [*Adkins*]. No application has been made for reconsideration of the constitutional question there decided. The validity of the principles upon which that decision rests is not challenged. This court confines itself to the ground upon which the writ was asked or granted. . . . Here, the review granted was no broader than that sought by the petitioner. . . . He is not entitled, and does not ask, to be heard upon the question whether the *Adkins* case should be overruled. He maintains that it may be distinguished on the ground that the statutes are vitally dissimilar.

We think that the question which was not deemed to be open in the Morehead case is open and is necessarily presented here. . . . We are of the opinion that this ruling of the state court demands on our part a reexamination of the *Adkins* case. The importance of the question, in which many States having similar laws are concerned, the close division by which the decision in the Adkins case was reached, and the economic conditions which have supervened, and in the light of which the reasonableness of the exercise of the protective power of the State must be considered, make it not only appropriate, but we think imperative, that, in deciding the present case, the subject should receive fresh consideration. . . .

The principle which must control our decision is not in doubt. The constitutional provision invoked is the due process clause of the Fourteenth Amendment, governing the States, as the due process clause invoked in the Adkins case governed Congress. In each case, the violation alleged by those attacking minimum wage regulation for women is deprivation of freedom of contract. What is this freedom? The Constitution does not speak of freedom of contract. It speaks of liberty and prohibits the deprivation of liberty without due process of law. In prohibiting that deprivation, the Constitution does not recognize an absolute and uncontrollable liberty. Liberty in each of its phases has its history and connotation. But the liberty safeguarded is liberty in a social organization which requires the protection of law against the evils which menace the health, safety, morals and welfare of the people. Liberty under the Constitution is thus necessarily subject to the restraints of due process, and regulation which is reasonable in relation to its subject and is adopted in the interests of the community is due process. This essential limitation of liberty in general governs freedom of contract in particular. . . .

This power under the Constitution to restrict freedom of contract has had many illustrations. That it may be exercised in the public interest with respect to contracts between employer and employee is undeniable. . . . In dealing with the relation of employer and employed, the legislature has necessarily a wide field of discretion in order that there may be suitable protection of health and safety, and that peace and good order may be promoted through regulations designed to insure wholesome conditions of work and freedom from oppression. . . .

We think that the decision in the Adkins case was a departure from the true application of the principles governing the regulation by the State of the relation of employer and employed. . . . In *Nebbia* v. *New York* (1934), dealing with the New York statute providing for minimum prices for milk, the general subject of the regulation of the use of private property and of the making of private contracts received an exhaustive examination, and we again declared that, if such laws, "have a reasonable relation to a proper legislative purpose, and are neither arbitrary nor discriminatory, the requirements of due process are satisfied"; that, "with the wisdom of the policy adopted, with the adequacy or practicability of the law enacted to forward it, the courts are both incompetent and unauthorized to deal"; that, "times without number, we have said that the legislature is primarily the judge of the necessity of such an enactment, that every possible presumption is in favor of its validity, and that, though the court may hold views inconsistent with the wisdom of the law, it may not be annulled unless palpably in excess of legislative power."

With full recognition of the earnestness and vigor which characterize the prevailing opinion in the Adkins case, we find it impossible to reconcile that ruling with these well considered declarations. What can be closer to the public interest than the health of women and their protection from unscrupulous and overreaching employers? And if the protection of women is a legitimate end of the exercise of state power, how can it be said that the requirement of the payment of a minimum wage fairly fixed in order to meet the very necessities of existence is not an admissible means to that end? The legislature of the State was clearly entitled to consider the situation of women in employment, the fact that they are in the class receiving the least pay, that their bargaining power is relatively weak, and that they are the ready victims of those who would take advantage of their necessitous circumstances. The legislature was entitled to adopt measures to reduce the evils of the "sweating system," the exploiting of workers at wages so low as to be insufficient to meet the bare cost of living, thus making their very helplessness the occasion of a most injurious competition. The legislature had the right to consider that its minimum wage requirements would be an important aid in carrying out its policy of protection. The adoption of similar requirements by many States evidences a deepseated conviction both as to the presence of the evil and as to the means adapted to check it. Legislative response to that conviction cannot be regarded as arbitrary or capricious, and that is all we have to decide. Even if the wisdom of the policy be regarded as debatable and its effects uncertain, still the legislature is entitled to its judgment.

There is an additional and compelling consideration which recent economic experience has brought into a strong light. The exploitation of a class of workers who are in an unequal position with respect to bargaining power, and are thus relatively defenceless against the denial of a living wage, is not only detrimental to their health and wellbeing, but casts a direct burden for their support upon the community. What these workers lose in wages, the taxpayers are called upon to pay. The bare cost of living must be met. We may take judicial notice of the unparalleled demands for relief which arose during the recent period of depression and still continue to an alarming extent despite the degree of economic recovery which has been achieved. It is unnecessary to cite official statistics to establish what is of common knowledge through the length and breadth of the land. While, in the instant case, no factual brief has been presented, there is no reason to doubt that the State of Washington has encountered the same social problem that is present elsewhere.

The community is not bound to provide what is, in effect, a subsidy for unconscionable employers. The community may direct its lawmaking power to correct the abuse which springs from their selfish disregard of the public interest. . . .

Our conclusion is that the case of *Adkins* v. *Children's Hospital*, supra, should be, and it is, overruled.

MR. JUSTICE SUTHERLAND, dissenting:

MR. JUSTICE VAN DEVANTER, MR. JUSTICE MCREYNOLDS, MR. JUSTICE BUTLER and I think the judgment of the court below should be reversed.

Under our form of government, where the written Constitution, by its own terms, is the supreme law, some agency, of necessity, must have the power to say the final word as to the validity of a statute assailed as unconstitutional. The Constitution makes it clear that the power has been intrusted to this court when the question arises in a controversy within its jurisdiction, and, so long as the power remains there, its exercise cannot be avoided without betrayal of the trust. . . .

It is urged that the question involved should now receive fresh consideration, among other reasons, because of "the economic conditions which have supervened"; but the meaning of the Constitution does not change with the ebb and flow of economic events. We frequently are told in more general words that the Constitution must be construed in the light of the present. If by that it is meant that the Constitution is made up of living words that apply to every new condition which they include, the statement is quite true. But to say, if that be intended, that the words of the Constitution mean today what they did not mean when written—that is, that they do not apply to a situation now to which they would have applied then—is to rob that instrument of the essential element which continues it in force as the people have made it until they, and not their official agents, have made it otherwise. . . .

If the Constitution, intelligently and reasonably construed in the light of these principles, stands in the way of desirable legislation, the blame must rest upon that instrument, and not upon the court for enforcing it according to its terms. The remedy in that situation—and the only true remedy—is to amend the Constitution. Judge Cooley, in the first volume of his *Constitutional Limitations*, very clearly pointed out that much of the benefit expected from written constitutions would be lost if their provisions were to be bent to circumstances or modified by public opinion. He pointed out that the common law, unlike a constitution, was subject to modification by public sentiment and action which the courts might recognize, but that: a court or legislature which should allow a change in public sentiment to influence it in giving to a written constitution a construction not warranted by the intention of its founders would be justly chargeable with reckless disregard of official oath and public duty, and if its course could become a precedent, these instruments would be of little avail.... What a court is to do, therefore, is to declare the law as written, leaving it to the people themselves to make such changes as new circumstances may require. The meaning of the constitution is fixed when it is adopted, and it is not different at any subsequent time when a court has occasion to pass upon it. . . .

In support of minimum wage legislation it has been urged, on the one hand, that great benefits will result in favor of underpaid labor, and, on the other hand, that the danger of such legislation is that the minimum will tend to become the maximum, and thus bring down the earnings of the more efficient toward the level of the less efficient employees. But with these speculations we have nothing to do. We are concerned only with the question of constitutionality.

## Ferguson v. Skrupa
### 372 U.S. 726 (1963)

In 1961 the Kansas legislature enacted a law prohibiting the practice of "debt adjustment." Debt adjustment is a practice that requires a debtor to make payments on money owed to an adjuster, who then distributes the money among various creditors. The law exempted attorneys, who were permitted to engage in debt adjustment as "incident to the lawful practice of law." Skrupa ran a business offering people credit advice. He challenged the law using the old liberty of contract argument that prevailed prior to *West Coast Hotel*.

Justice Black's closing line, "Whether the legislature takes for its textbook Adam Smith, Herbert Spencer, Lord Keynes, or some other is no concern of ours," is often cited as the Court's final eulogy to *Lochner*-era economic substantive due process. One question here is worth considering, however, and it involves a philosopher traditionally considered the least funny of the Marx brothers. Suppose the Kansas legislature had taken Karl Marx for its textbook. Would the Court remain so deferential to the wishes of the legislature?

The Court's decision was unanimous. Justice Black delivered the opinion of the Court. Justice Harlan filed a concurring statement.

MR. JUSTICE BLACK delivered the opinion of the Court.

In this case . . . , we are asked to review the judgment of a three-judge District Court enjoining, as being in violation of the Due Process Clause of the Fourteenth Amendment, a Kansas statute making it a misdemeanor for any person to engage "in the business of debt adjusting" except as an incident to "the lawful practice of law in this state." The statute defines "debt adjusting" as, "the making of a contract, express, or implied with a particular debtor whereby the debtor agrees to pay a certain amount of money periodically to the person engaged in the debt adjusting business who shall for a consideration distribute the same among certain specified creditors in accordance with a plan agreed upon." . . .

Under the system of government created by our Constitution, it is up to legislatures, not courts, to decide on the wisdom and utility of legislation. There was a time when the Due Process Clause was used by this Court to strike down laws which were thought unreasonable, that is, unwise or incompatible with some particular economic or social philosophy. In this manner, the Due Process Clause was used, for example, to nullify laws prescribing maximum hours for work in bakeries, *Lochner* v. *New York* (1905), outlawing "yellow dog" contracts, *Coppage* v. *Kansas* (1915), setting minimum wages for women, *Adkins* v. *Children's Hospital* (1923), and fixing the weight of loaves of bread, *Jay Burns Baking Co.* v. *Bryan*, (1924). This intrusion by the judiciary into the realm of legislative value judgments was strongly objected to at the time, particularly by Mr. Justice Holmes and Mr. Justice Brandeis. Dissenting from the Court's invalidating a state statute which regulated the resale price of theatre and other tickets, Mr. Justice Holmes said, "I think the proper course is to recognize that a state Legislature can do whatever it sees fit to do unless it is restrained by some express prohibition in the Constitution of the United States or of the State, and that Courts should be careful not to extend such prohibitions beyond their obvious meaning by reading into them conceptions of public policy that the particular Court may happen to entertain." And, in an earlier case, he had emphasized that, "The criterion of constitutionality is not whether we believe the law to be for the public good."

The doctrine that prevailed in *Lochner, Coppage, Adkins, Burns,* and like cases—that due process authorizes courts to hold laws unconstitutional when they believe the legislature has acted unwisely—has long since been discarded. We have returned to the original constitutional proposition that courts do not substitute their social and economic beliefs for the judgment of legislative bodies, who are elected to pass laws. . . .

We conclude that the Kansas Legislature was free to decide for itself that legislation was needed to deal with the business of debt adjusting. Unquestionably, there are arguments showing that the business of debt adjusting has social utility, but such arguments are properly addressed to the legislature, not to us. We refuse to sit as a "super-legislature to weigh the wisdom of legislation," and we emphatically refuse to go back to the time when courts used the Due Process Clause "to strike down state laws, regulatory of business and industrial conditions, because they may be unwise, improvident, or out of harmony with a particular school of thought." Nor are we able or willing to draw lines by calling a law "prohibitory" or "regulatory." Whether the legislature takes for its textbook Adam Smith, Herbert Spencer, Lord Keynes, or some other is no concern of ours. The Kansas debt adjusting statute may be wise or unwise. But relief, if any be needed, lies not with us, but with the body constituted to pass laws for the State of Kansas.

▼▲▼

## Epilogue: Privacy, Personal Autonomy, and the Revival of Substantive Due Process

The Court's abandonment of the liberty of contract doctrine after the Constitutional Revolution of 1937 did not mean that it forever discarded substantive due process analysis. The action simply meant that the Court no longer considered ownership rights one of the fundamental liberties protected by the Due Process Clause of the Fourteenth Amendment. In *West Coast Hotel* the Court offered clear reasons how and why it reached this conclusion. Its decision to embrace the New Deal welfare state represented a clear break from the property and contract-centered emphasis in the American constitutional tradition. For this reason, the rise and fall of the *Lochner* era deserves the attention of contemporary students of American constitutional law.[67]

Often the *Lochner* era and substantive due process are discussed in terms that make them seem almost interchangeable. But the notion that the *Lochner* era represented a distortion of the basic premise behind the due process guarantee—the right to fundamental fairness in the event that government threatens to deprive a citizen of a constitutional right—is a misconception. Not long after the Court decided that the Due Process Clause protected Joseph Lochner's right to work his bakers as he pleased, it ruled that the same provision permitted parents to establish and send their children to private parochial schools.[68] The same year the Court struck down the Washington, D.C., minimum wage law in *Adkins* on liberty of contract grounds, the Court held that Nebraska could not prohibit a public school teacher from reading a German-language book and using parts of it for class instruction. The right to "acquire useful knowledge . . . and generally to enjoy privileges, essential to the orderly pursuit of free men," said the Court, was among the liberties protected by the Due Process Clause.[69]

Indeed, the Court brushed up against the most familiar of modern substantive due process claims, those involving the right of privacy, long before it decided that access to birth control, the right to abortion, and the right to refuse unwanted medical treatment were among the liberties protected by the Due Process Clause. In 1927 the Court, in *Buck* v. *Bell*, ruled that a Virginia law mandating the sterilization of persons confined to mental institutions was within the scope of state police power. It rejected the claim of Carrie Buck, an eighteen year old who tested as a nine year old on the Binet-Simon I.Q. test, the leading such test of the day, that compulsory sterilization violated her "bodily integrity," a basic liberty protected by the Due Process Clause. Writing for an 8-1 Court, Justice Holmes noted that Carrie, whose mother had been incarcerated, had already given birth to one retarded child. "It is better for all the world," wrote Holmes, "if instead of waiting to execute degenerate offspring for crime, or to let them starve for the imbecility, society can prevent those who are manifestly unfit from continuing their kind. The principle that sustains compulsory vaccination is broad enough to cover cutting the Fallopian tubes. . . . . Three generations of imbeciles are enough."[70]

By modern standards, this is an astonishing statement, especially coming from Holmes, justly considered one of the greatest figures in American law and perhaps the finest literary stylist to serve on the Court. But it quite accurately reflected Holmes's own sentiments on the human condition and, as strange as it might seem now, elite opinion more generally. The Progressive movement endorsed eugenic sterilization, which saw the practice as a means to improve the human race. For Holmes, however, the issue in *Buck v. Bell* (1927) was not his own distaste for the lesser lights of society, but rather the idea that Carrie Buck had some abstract right to bodily integrity anchored in the Constitution that protected her against a law such as Virginia's. Holmes rejected Carrie's claim that the Due Process Clause of the Fourteenth Amendment afforded her such a right, just as he had argued as far back as 1905 in *Locher* that the same constitutional provision did not include a fundamental right to "liberty of contract" protecting business owners from government regulation intended to promote the public welfare. Virginia's law was informed by the very best science of the day and procedural guarantees had been scrupulously followed. That was all that mattered to Holmes. After *Buck*, numerous states enacted laws modeled on Virginia's. Between 1922 and 1972, when it repealed its law, Virginia sterilized approximately 8,300 people, many of whom were never informed of the procedure.

In 1942 the Court set out an entirely new course for the future of substantive due process analysis when it ruled, in *Skinner v. Oklahoma*, that a state could not compel the sterilization of "habitual criminals."[71] The Court did not overturn *Buck*; but Justice Douglas's unanimous opinion was extremely critical of the Court's opinion. In extraordinary language, given the Court's firm renouncement of *Lochner*-era economic due process just five years before, Justice Douglas wrote that a far more essential matter of personal liberty was at stake in *Skinner*:

> We are dealing here with legislation which involves one of the basic civil rights of man. Marriage and procreation are *fundamental* to the very existence and survival of the race. The power to sterilize, if exercised, may have subtle, far-reaching and devastating effects. In evil or reckless hands it can cause races or types which are inimical to the dominant group to wither and disappear. There is no redemption for the individual whom the law touches. Any experiment which the State conducts is to his irreparable injury. He is forever deprived of a *basic liberty*.[72]

*Skinner* remained the sole exception to the Court's rejection of substantive due process until 1965, when it ruled that a state law barring married couples from receiving information about and obtaining contraceptives violated the Due Process Clause. In *Griswold v. Connecticut*, Justice Douglas, returning to the same themes that animated his opinion in *Skinner*, wrote that the marital relationship fell "within a zone of privacy created by several fundamental constitutional guarantees." Douglas did not link this privacy right with any specific provision of the Constitution, a failing that, in the eyes of *Griswold*'s critics, undermined the integrity of the Court's opinion. Douglas wrote that this privacy right was secured by the "penumbras" that "emanated" from the specific guarantees of the Bill of Rights. The right of married couples to make decisions about procreation and contraception was a basic human liberty protected from government intrusion.[73] Seven years later the Court, in *Eisenstadt v. Baird* (1972), extended *Griswold* to include unmarried couples.[74]

*Griswold* and *Eisenstadt* laid the foundation for the Court's most controversial post-*Lochner* decision involving substantive due process analysis, *Roe v. Wade* (1973), the landmark case establishing the right of women to abortion. Between *Griswold* and *Roe* the Court handed down an important decision involving substantive due process rights that bore only a tangential relationship to contraception and abortion rights. In *Loving v. Virginia* (1967), the Court ruled that Virginia's ban on interracial marriage violated the freedom to marry. No state had the right to restrict such a basic right on the basis of race. *Loving* synthesized substantive due process (the right to marry) and equal protection (racial discrimination) claims to create a "fundamental" right that relied upon the Court's interpretation of rights protected by societal tradition rather than an explicit constitutional guarantee.[75]

In *Roe* the Court returned to the concept of privacy as personal autonomy established in Griswold. Writing for a 7-2 Court, Justice Harry A. Blackmun held that "this right of privacy, whether it be founded in the 14th Amendment's concept of personal liberty [as] we feel it is . . . [or elsewhere] is broad enough to encompass a woman's decision whether or not to terminate her pregnancy." Such a right was not absolute; like the state's interest in compulsory vaccination or in sterilization, the right to "bodily integrity" must be weighed against "important state interests in regulation."[76]

Justice Blackmun's opinion's referred to the Court's previous decisions recognizing fundamental rights not mentioned in the Constitution, so long as such rights were "implicit within the concept of ordered liberty."

This reliance on tradition, however, to validate the right to abortion was questioned by Justice Potter Stewart. Concurring, Stewart offered a more candid assessment of the Court's decision to recognize such a right:

> In 1963, this Court, in *Ferguson v. Skrupa,* purported to sound the death knell for the doctrine of substantive due process. Barely two years later, in *Griswold* . . . , the Court held a Connecticut birth control law unconstitutional. In view of what had been so recently said in *Skrupa,* the Court's opinion in *Griswold* understandably did its best to avoid reliance on the Due Process Clause. [I]t was clear to me then, and it is equally clear to me now, that the *Griswold* decision can be rationally understood only as a holding that the Connecticut statute substantively invaded the "liberty" that is protected by the Due Process Clause of the Fourteenth Amendment. *As so understood Griswold stands as one in a long line of pre-Skrupa cases decided under the doctrine of substantive due process, and I now accept it as such.*[77]

Justice Blackmun's opinion in *Roe* created an immense controversy. State legislatures, some of which had begun to reform their abortion laws during the late 1960s, were by and large not prepared to extend the right to abortion as far as the Court did. Supporters argued that the nation's criminal abortion laws were relics of prevailing attitudes of the practice during the nineteenth century and were in need of a clean sweep off the books that only the Court could provide.[78] Critics responded by saying the Court had returned to the discredited days of *Lochner:* If "liberty" encompassed the right to abortion, a different Court majority could just as easily revive absolute contract and property rights as fundamental liberties protected by the Due Process Clause. After all, the right to abortion and birth control had no standing in the nation's tradition of rights "implicit in the concept of ordered liberty."[79] In fact, property, and the right to acquire and profit from it, was a central tenet—perhaps *the* central value—of the American constitutional tradition until the Constitutional Revolution of 1937.[80]

Criticized and defended with an intensity unmatched by any other case in American constitutional law, *Roe* nonetheless remains good law. After a contentious twenty-year period of litigation, the Court reaffirmed the central holding of *Roe* in *Planned Parenthood v. Casey* (1992), even as it gave the states wider latitude to discourage abortion through regulation. *Casey* was remarkable for the Court's candor in addressing the political nature of the abortion issue. Supporters and opponents of *Roe*—more than one hundred organizations filed amicus curiae briefs in *Casey*—put the same demand before the Court: Either overrule or affirm the 1973 decision, but do not let the matter continue to hang in the balance. The Court offered a complex explanation for its decision to affirm *Roe;* but above all, it held that a "woman's right to terminate her pregnancy before viability . . . is a rule of law and a component of liberty we cannot renounce."[81]

But the Court's most recent decision involving privacy and personal autonomy offers firm notice that, at least for now, it is not prepared to take substantive claims to liberty under the Due Process Clause beyond the right to abortion. In *Washington v. Glucksburg* (1997), the Court rejected an argument by a group of Washington State physicians that among the Fourteenth Amendment's substantive liberties was a right to physician-assisted suicide. Chief Justice Rehnquist's opinion for a unanimous Court offers an insightful comparison of its approach to substantive due process analysis in the post-*Lochner* era. His opinion never questions the legitimacy of substantive claims to liberty, noting the Due Process Clause "guarantees more than fair process, and . . . protect[ion] against physical restraint. [I]t also provides heightened protection against government interference with certain fundamental rights and liberty interests."[82]

The Court also emphasized the role of tradition in deciding whether the right to physician-assisted suicide deserved any place in the realm of protected liberties involving privacy. Here, as opposed to *Roe* and *Casey,* the Court concluded that it could not recognize a right to die because it was not rooted in societal tradition. But neither the right to abortion, the right to interracial marriage, nor the right of unmarried persons to purchase and use contraception held a place in societal tradition when the Court decided that each was protected by the Due Process Clause.[83] In fact, the Court's line of substantive due process decisions involving privacy and autonomy is more notable for going *against* the consensus of law and social values prevalent at the time.

How then do we explain the apparent contradiction between the Court's conception of substantive due process before and after the Constitutional Revolution of 1937? If one sees no difference between an asserted right to liberty of contract and the right to abortion, then the Court's rejection of *Lochner* and embrace of *Roe* is difficult to explain. But, as supporters of the Court's modern privacy doctrine suggest, if wholly different state interests are involved in promoting workplace safety and in limiting reproductive freedom, then the differences between the two cases are more readily understood. Rejection of the economic, social, and political status quo was the fundamental legacy of the Court's acceptance of the New Deal.

The continuing debate over the Court's role in defining and protecting liberties outside the specific protections of the Bill of Rights offers a clear illustration of how intertwined the Court's conception of the proper relationship between political power and individual rights is with the pulse of social and political change. The Court's decisions in *Lochner, West Coast Hotel, Roe, Casey,* and *Glucksberg* are proof positive that the justices, to paraphrase Justice Cardozo, are not immune from the great tides and currents that constantly reshape the values of American society and its political institutions.

## *Washington v. Glucksberg*
### 521 S.Ct. 702 (1997)

*Cruzan* gave the "right to die" issue a major public profile. Certainly, the idea that families faced difficult decisions over whether to continue life support for their loved ones was not new. A grasp of the legal issues involved in making such a decision, however, was foreign for many people. *Cruzan* clarified the difference between "substituted judgement," that is, making a decision in lieu of formal consent, and the right of a designated family member or friend to authorize an attending physician to remove life-supporting medical treatment. "Living wills"—a legal document in which, for example, a husband grants permission to his wife and/or children to end medical treatment—became much more popular after *Cruzan*.

By the early 1990s another issue emerged alongside the right to withdraw life support, although in much more controversial light: physician-assisted suicide. Jack Kevorkian, a Michigan physician, began making news after he disclosed to reporters that he had "assisted" several terminally ill patients with suicide. His methods were crude, but his news appeal rested more with his unapologetic attitude toward assisted suicide. Kevorkian believed that his mission was a humanitarian one. He was simply

putting people out of their misery—cancer patients and sufferers of other terminal diseases, for example—not murdering them. Kevorkian's fame reached its zenith in 1999 after nationally broadcasting the assisted suicide of a patient with Lou Gehrig's disease. The doctor was convicted of murder in Michigan, the first successful prosecution of Kevorkian since he began his national crusade.

Kevorkian's dramatics obscured a larger debate still taking place in many legislatures around the nation: Does the Constitution permit a "right to die"? In Washington State the legislature passed a "natural death law" permitting physicians, with consent, to withdraw life-supporting sustenance and medical treatment but specifically barred physicians from prescribing drugs or taking any other action to hasten death. Harold Glucksberg and several physicians challenged the law as a violation of the Due Process Clause of the Fourteenth Amendment.

CHIEF JUSTICE REHNQUIST delivered the opinion of the Court.

The question presented in this case is whether Washington's prohibition against "caus[ing]" or "aid[ing]" a suicide offends the Fourteenth Amendment to the United States Constitution. We hold that it does not. . . .

We begin, as we do in all due process cases, by examining our Nation's history, legal traditions, and practices. In almost every State—indeed, in almost every western democracy—it is a crime to assist a suicide. The States' assisted suicide bans are not innovations. Rather, they are longstanding expressions of the States' commitment to the protection and preservation of all human life. . . . Moreover, the majority of States in this country have laws imposing criminal penalties on one who assists another to commit suicide. Indeed, opposition to and condemnation of suicide—and, therefore, of assisting suicide—are consistent and enduring themes of our philosophical, legal, and cultural heritages. More specifically, for over 700 years, the Anglo American common law tradition has punished or otherwise disapproved of both suicide and assisting suicide. . . .

Though deeply rooted, the States' assisted suicide bans have in recent years been reexamined and, generally, reaffirmed. Because of advances in medicine and technology, Americans today are increasingly likely to die in institutions, from chronic illnesses. Public concern and democratic action are therefore sharply focused on how best to protect dignity and independence at the end of life, with the result that there have been many significant changes in state laws and in the attitudes these laws reflect. Many States, for example, now permit "living wills," surrogate health care decisionmaking, and the withdrawal or refusal of life sustaining medical treatment. At the same time, however, voters and legislators continue for the most part to reaffirm their States' prohibitions on assisting suicide.

The Washington statute at issue in this case was enacted in 1975 as part of a revision of that State's criminal code. Four years later, Washington passed its Natural Death Act, which specifically stated that the "withholding or withdrawal of life sustaining treatment . . . shall not, for any purpose, constitute a suicide" and that "[n]othing in this chapter shall be construed to condone, authorize, or approve mercy killing . . . ." In 1991, Washington voters rejected a ballot initiative which, had it passed, would have permitted a form of physician assisted suicide. Washington then added a provision to the Natural Death Act expressly excluding physician assisted suicide . . . .

[O]ur laws have consistently condemned, and continue to prohibit, assisting suicide. Despite changes in medical technology and notwithstanding an increased emphasis on the importance of end of life decisionmaking, we have not retreated from this prohibition. Against this backdrop of history, tradition, and practice, we now turn to respondents' constitutional claim.

The Due Process Clause guarantees more than fair process, and the "liberty" it protects includes more than the absence of physical restraint. The Clause also provides heightened protection against government interference with certain fundamental rights and liberty interests. In a long line of cases, we have held that, in addition to the specific freedoms protected by the Bill of Rights, the "liberty" specially protected by the Due Process Clause includes the rights to marry, to have children, to direct the education and upbringing of one's children, to marital privacy, to use contraception, to bodily integrity, *Rochin* v. *California,* and to abortion, *Casey.* We have also assumed, and strongly suggested [in *Cruzan*], that the Due Process Clause protects the traditional right to refuse unwanted lifesaving medical treatment.

But we "ha[ve] always been reluctant to expand the concept of substantive due process because guideposts for responsible decisionmaking in this unchartered area are scarce and open ended." By extending constitutional protection to an asserted right or liberty interest, we, to a great extent, place the matter outside the arena of public debate and legislative action. We must therefore "exercise the utmost care whenever we are asked to break new ground in this field," lest the liberty protected by the Due Process Clause be subtly transformed into the policy preferences of the members of this Court.

Our established method of substantive due process analysis has two primary features: First, we have regularly observed that the Due Process Clause specially protects those fundamental rights and liberties which are, objectively, "deeply rooted in this Nation's history and tradition, and "implicit in the concept of ordered liberty," such that "neither liberty nor justice would exist if they were sacrificed," *Palko* v. *Connecticut* (1937). Second, we have required in substantive due process cases a "careful description" of the asserted fundamental liberty interest. Our Nation's history, legal traditions, and practices thus provide the crucial "guideposts for responsible decisionmaking that direct and restrain our exposition of the Due Process Clause. As we stated recently in *Flores,* the Fourteenth Amendment "forbids the government to infringe . . . 'fundamental' liberty interests at all, no matter what process is provided, unless the infringement is narrowly tailored to serve a compelling state interest." . . .

We now inquire whether this asserted right has any place in our Nation's traditions. Here, as discussed above, we are confronted with a consistent and almost universal tradition that has long rejected the asserted right, and continues explicitly to reject it today, even for terminally ill, mentally competent adults. To hold for respondents, we would have to reverse centuries of legal doctrine and practice, and strike down the considered policy choice of almost every State.

Respondents contend, however, that the liberty interest they assert is consistent with this Court's substantive due process line of cases, if not with this Nation's history and practice. Pointing to *Casey* and *Cruzan,* respondents read our jurisprudence in this area as reflecting a general tradition of "self sovereignty," and as teaching that the "liberty" protected by the Due Process Clause includes "basic and intimate exercises of personal autonomy." According to respondents, our liberty jurisprudence, and the broad, individualistic principles it reflects, protects the "liberty of competent, terminally ill adults to make end of life decisions free of undue government interference." The question presented in this case, however, is whether the protections of the Due Process Clause include a right to commit suicide with another's assistance. With this "careful description" of respondents' claim in mind, we turn to *Casey* and *Cruzan.* . . .

The right assumed in *Cruzan,* however, was not simply deduced from abstract concepts of personal autonomy. Given the common law rule that forced medication was a battery, and the long legal tradition protecting the decision to refuse unwanted medical treatment, our assumption was entirely consistent with this Nation's history and constitutional traditions. The decision to commit suicide with the assistance of another may be just as personal and profound as the decision to refuse unwanted medical treatment, but it has never enjoyed similar legal protection. Indeed, the two acts are widely and reasonably regarded as quite distinct. In Cruzan itself, we recognized that most States outlawed assisted suicide—and even more do today—and we certainly gave no intimation that the right to refuse unwanted medical treatment could be somehow transmuted into a right to assistance in committing suicide. . . .

The history of the law's treatment of assisted suicide in this country has been and continues to be one of the rejection of nearly all efforts to permit it. That being the case, our decisions lead us to conclude that the asserted "right" to assistance in committing suicide is not a fundamental liberty interest protected by the Due Process Clause. The Constitution also requires, however, that Washington's assisted suicide ban be rationally related to legitimate government interests. This requirement is unquestionably met here. As the court below recognized, Washington's assisted suicide ban implicates a number of state interests.

First, Washington has an "unqualified interest in the preservation of human life." The State's prohibition on assisted suicide, like all homicide laws, both reflects and advances its commitment to this interest. . . .

The State also has an interest in protecting the integrity and ethics of the medical profession. [T]he American Medical Association, like many other medical and physicians' groups, has concluded that "[p]hysician assisted suicide is fundamentally incompatible with the physician's role as healer." And physician assisted suicide could, it is argued, undermine the trust that is essential to the doctor patient relationship by blurring the time honored line between healing and harming. . . .

Next, the State has an interest in protecting vulnerable groups—including the poor, the elderly, and disabled persons—from abuse, neglect, and mistakes. . . . If physician assisted suicide were permitted, many might resort to it to spare their families the substantial financial burden of end of life health care costs. . . .

Throughout the Nation, Americans are engaged in an earnest and profound debate about the morality, legality, and practicality of physician assisted suicide. Our holding permits this debate to continue, as it should in a democratic society.

It is so ordered.

▼▲▼

## FOR FURTHER READING

Abraham, Henry J. *Justices, Presidents and Senators: A History of the U.S. Supreme Court Appointments from Washington to Clinton.* Baltimore: Rowman & Littlefield, 1999.

Amar, Akhil Reed. *The Bill of Rights: Creation and Reconstruction.* New Haven, Conn.: Yale University Press, 1998.

Beard, Charles A. *An Economic Interpretation of the Constitution of the United States.* New York: Macmillan, Inc., 1913.

Cardozo, Benjamin. *The Nature of the Judicial Process.* New Haven, Conn.: Yale University Press, 1921.

Corwin, Edward. "The Doctrine of Due Process of Law Before the Civil War," *Harvard Law Review* 24 (1911), pp. 366–394.

Curtis, Michael Kent. *No State Shall Abridge: The Fourteenth Amendment and the Bill of Rights.* Durham, N.C.: Duke University Press, 1986.

Foner, Eric. *Reconstruction: America's Unfinished Revolution, 1863–1877.* New York: Harper & Row, 1989.

Gillman, Howard. *The Constitution Besieged: The Rise and Demise of Lochner Era Police Powers Jurisprudence.* Durham, N.C.: Duke University Press, 1993.

Hofstadter, Richard. *The Age of Reform: From Bryan to F.D.R.* New York: Vintage Books, 1955.

——. *Social Darwinism in American Thought.* Boston: Beacon Press, 1955.

——. *The Progressive Movement, 1900–1915.* Englewood Cliffs, N.J.: Prentice-Hall, 1963.

Holmes, Stephen and Cass R. Sunstein. *The Cost of Rights: Why Liberty Depends on Taxes.* New York: W. W. Norton, 1999.

Kens, Paul. *Judicial Power and Reform Politics: The Anatomy of Lochner v. New York.* Lawrence: University Press of Kansas, 1989.

Keynes, Edward. *Liberty, Property and Privacy: Toward a Jurisprudence of Substantive Due Process.* University Park, Penn.: Pennsylvania State University Press, 1996.

Shamir, Ronen. *Managing Legal Uncertainty: Elite Lawyers in the New Deal.* Durham, N.C.: Duke University Press, 1995.

Spencer, Herbert. *Social Statics.* New York: D. Appleton & Co., 1864.

Strum, Phillipa. *Louis D. Brandeis: Justice for the People.* Cambridge, Mass.: Harvard University Press, 1984.

Sumner, William Graham. *What Social Classes Owe to Each Other.* New York: Harper & Bros., 1883.

Sunstein, Cass R. *Free Markets and Social Justice.* New York: Oxford University Press, 1997.

Twiss, Benjamin R. *Lawyers and the Constitution: How Laissez-Faire Came to the Supreme Court.* Princeton, N.J.: Princeton University Press, 1942.

# 10 Takings

Moments after Brian Bea asked his girlfriend, Jody Lathrop, to marry him, he turned and motioned toward the picturesque Columbia River Gorge situated on the Oregon-Washington state border. "Someday we're going to be over there and have a beautiful house," he said. "We're going to raise our kids there." Jody must have agreed. She said yes.

Brian's parents wanted to help their son and his new wife fulfill their dream. They gave the newlyweds fifteen acres of homestead property that had been in the family since the 1850s, when the federal government granted Brian's great-grandfather six hundred acres of gorge property on the Washington side. When he went to apply for a building permit, Brian learned that state regulations required a minimum of twenty acres to build in the area. He saved enough money to buy the additional five acres from an uncle four years after his parents' initial gift.

Brian's next step was to apply for a building permit. He was successful, but the county attached thirty-three conditions to the construction, including limiting the house to one story with a loft and requiring a daylight basement. Brimming with excitement, the Beas went to work, with Brian serving as the general contractor. It was then, according to the Columbia River Gorge Commission, the bistate agency that oversees land use in the gorge area, that Brian began to violate the conditions of the building permit.

By June 1998 the Beas had spent more than $250,000 on their self-described "dream house." Then, in late July, Brian received a phone call from the gorge commission to see whether he was following the permit's guidelines.

A hearing held later that November found that the Beas had violated the scenic codes of the permit by building the house on a site that visually overwhelmed its surroundings, by building it higher than twenty-five feet, and by clearing trees and vegetation that would have hidden the house from view. The commission ordered the Beas to stop building their house. They could either move it or tear it down. Either way, the Beas' dream house was not going to interfere with the natural view of the Columbia River Gorge. The Beas were entitled to a view of the gorge. But they could not, as Kevin Gorman, the director of the nonprofit Friends of the Columbia Gorge, put it, "*be* the view."

The Beas spent $60,000 in legal fees before the Pacific Legal Foundation, a conservative public interest law firm, agreed to take their case for nothing. Founded in 1973 by former members of California Governor Ronald Reagan's administration and supported by the California Chamber of Commerce to combat growing environmental and land-use regulation, lawyers for the Pacific Legal Foundation asserted that Washington's conduct was "outrageous" and must be fought tooth and nail. The Beas and the Pacific Legal Foundation shared the same outrage: How could the government make Brian tear down his house *after* he had started building? For Brian, the lawsuit was about getting his dream house back. For the Pacific Legal Foundation, Brian's case was an opportunity to establish a precedent protecting property owners from such "heavy handed" government action. It was a perfect match.

The Beas lost in court, but their case generated nationwide publicity. If they were going to lose, at least

Brian Bea, standing in front of his unfinished "dream house."
The Columbia River Gorge, situated along the Oregon-
Washington border, is in the background.
Robbie McClaran/SABA.

they drew attention to an issue important to them and the property rights groups that supported their lawsuit. It added a human dimension to an issue that is often clouded in abstraction and obscure academic debates. The Beas' loss ensured that more cases like theirs would make their up the judicial ladder.

Does the Constitution permit government to seize private property in the name of the public interest? If so, must the government compensate individuals whose property is taken? How much compensation is fair? What rights do property owners have to develop their property as they see fit? Questions such as these, and more, lie at the heart of our subject this chapter, the Takings Clause.

## Understanding the Takings Clause

The Constitutional Revolution of 1937 amounted to a Court-created earthquake that shook the foundation of American constitutional law. The Court's ratification of the New Deal confirmed the wisdom of Justice Holmes's observation in his *Lochner* dissent that the Constitution did not embrace any particular economic theory. After 1937 the Constitution no longer prohibited Congress and the states from altering the social and economic sta-

tus quo, as long as legislation bore a reasonable relationship to the public interest. The constitutional status of ownership rights, the relationship between labor and capital, and the distribution of wealth were now recognized as the result of political preferences expressed through law.

Underneath the surface changes in governance brought about by the New Deal was a seismic shift in the place of property rights in the constitutional order. Prior to 1937 the Court had used judicial review to protect the notion of property rights as natural or inherent to citizenship. Political scientist Jennifer Nedelsky has commented that Chief Justice John Marshall laid the foundation for the judicial expression of this view in *Marbury v. Madison* (1803). By placing the structure of government in the category of law, Marshall gave the Court authority to decide conflicts over the Constitution. Because the Constitution was fundamental law, the Court's responsibility was to apply legal rules to disputes over matters of law. Judicial review was distinct from politics in that the former was an "objective" means to articulate and defend the principles of the Constitution.[1]

In reality, the cases before the Marshall Court were intensely political in nature, and the Court's decisions were far more consistent with the Federalists' vision of a large, commercial republic and the importance they attached to property rights than any straightforward application of neutral legal principles. Prior to *Marbury,* the Court, in *Calder v. Bull* (1798), had acknowledged that property rights were a societal creation and thus *"always* subject to the rules prescribed by *positive* law."[2] After 1937 the Court rejected the notion that constitutional values were fixed, immutable, and off-limits from the political process. It now understood the regulation of contractual rights, the ownership of private property, and commercial activities as a means to regulate conflicting social and economic interests, not as a body of rules rooted in nature.[3]

This casebook has emphasized how materials and sources beyond the Constitution are used to interpret its meaning. The importance of external sources was certainly evident throughout the era of economic substantive due process, the subject of Chapter 9. To validate its "liberty of contract" theory of the Fourteenth Amendment, the Court drew upon the economic theories of

Adam Smith, the scientific structure of Charles Darwin, the models of socioeconomic organization advanced by Herbert Spencer and William Graham Sumner, and the legal theories of Thomas Cooley. The Court's rejection of the *Lochner*-era approach to ownership rights did not mean that external materials were no longer relevant to its interpretation of the Constitution. If anything, the Court was more explicit about its awareness of the social and political dynamics at work in American society. But its embrace of the New Deal required the Court to turn elsewhere for constitutional principles.

Perhaps the foremost influence from outside the law on the Court's post-1937 approach to constitutional jurisprudence was John Dewey, a philosopher and psychologist who rose to prominence during the Progressive Era. Dewey was best known for his advocacy of educational and political reform, but his ideas influenced just about every facet of American public life until his death in 1952. Justice Holmes once said of Dewey that he wrote and spoke as God would have "had He been inarticulate but keenly desirous to tell you how it was."[4]

Dewey's major philosophical contribution to American legal jurisprudence was the idea of "pragmatism," a system of thought based on the belief that the scientific method offered "a method of moral and political diagnosis and prognosis" through which to advance the possibilities of the human condition. That philosophy was best expressed in his enormously influential book, *The Public and Its Problems* (1927). Dewey wrote that "the doctrine of the individual in possession of antecedent political rights," or natural rights prior to the creation of civil society, was a philosophical fiction to advance a particular model of social and economic organization. Rights and privileges did not reveal themselves in natural or preordained fashion. They were identified by the members of those societies with political power and protected by law.[5]

Dewey, along with William James, another influential Progressive Era philosopher, also believed that the progress of political societies depended on the resources and capabilities of the human intellect. Pragmatism sought to take advantage of the experimental nature of American democracy by allowing legislatures to experiment with solutions to social and economic problems. Dewey frowned upon hard and fast ideological assumptions, particularly when they were passed off as funda-

mental law and thus not open to change. In particular, Dewey rejected the idea that individuals were assigned to a particular station in life by the laws of nature. Individuals, like societies, were capable of progress through the right balance of government support and private cooperation.[6]

Dewey's imprint was all over the Constitutional Revolution of 1937. The Court drew upon the ideas of Dewey when it gave the go-ahead for the New Deal to proceed in *West Coast Hotel* v. *Parrish* (1937) (see Chapter 9) and *N.L.R.B* v. *Jones & Laughlin Steel* (1937) (see Chapter 6). In place of the "dogma, Liberty of Contract," to borrow Justice Holmes's phrase from *Adkins* v. *Children's Hospital* (1923), the Court said that the people, acting through their elected representatives, should be allowed to alter, abolish, or create new legal categories. In doing so, the Court acknowledged that it was as much an institution of governance as it was a court of law, removed from the realm of politics.

Pragmatism is a central element of the Court's Takings Clause jurisprudence. Unlike the other provisions of the Constitution that have been used to protect property and contract rights, the Takings Clause sets out *conditional* rights. In contrast to the Contract Clause, which says that "[n]o state shall . . . pass any . . . Law impairing the Obligation of Contracts," and thus places an *absolute* constraint on government power, the Takings Clause states that "private property [shall not] be taken for public use, without just compensation." The Framers intended for Congress to retain the power of *eminent domain,* or the right of government to appropriate private property for the public good. The Takings Clause required that the government provide just compensation, based on the fair market value of the seized property, to the owner.

Litigation under the Takings Clause has centered on three major questions: When does government "take" private property? What is public use? and What is just compensation? We shall examine these provisions of the Takings Clause in turn.

### When Does Government "Take" Private Property?

The Takings Clause is triggered when the government seizes private property in the name of public use, thus transferring the exclusive possession of ownership rights. Government may only "take" property for public use; if the government cannot demonstrate the public purpose of its decision to appropriate private property, then it has not met the threshold required by the Takings Clause. Few contest the power of government to condemn or assume the physical control of private property under the Takings Clause. Such power is considered inherent in the concept of eminent domain. Courts of law have rarely contested the government's power to seize physical control of private property in the name of public use, as the lack of judicial precedent in this area attests. In fact, the Supreme Court, in *Chicago, B & Q.R. Co.* v. *Chicago* (1897), made the Takings Clause, before any other provision of the Bill of Rights, applicable to the states through the Fourteenth Amendment.[7]

Less obvious and more difficult to define is when government action that affects property rights constitutes a Takings Clause violation. Since 1922 the Court has answered that a "regulatory" taking occurs when an economic regulation makes it impossible for owners to use their property for the purposes for which it was intended. In *Pennsylvania Coal Co.* v. *Mahon* (1922), the Court ruled that government regulation eliminating the entire worth of private property constituted a taking, just as the actual seizure of private land would. *Mahon* involved a coal company that had deeded the surface-level interest but retained the right to mine coal underneath the land. After the deal the Pennsylvania legislature passed the Kohler Act, which prohibited mining under any surface-level property that could cause damage to the owner, even though the buyers of the surface interest had waived all their rights to any damage that might occur in connection with mining activities. Justice Holmes held that private "property may be regulated to a certain extent, [but] if regulation goes too far it will be recognized as a taking," for which compensation must be paid.[8] Whether Holmes was right on the law was less important than his uncharacteristic failure to articulate a clear judicial standard. Even though Holmes had given initial judicial expression to the idea that government can take property without actually physically possessing it, exactly when property owners were entitled to compensation remained unclear. His opinion offered property owners no specific calculus of costs and benefits to assess the impact of a regulatory taking.

Since the Constitutional Revolution of 1937, the Court has adhered to Justice Stone's famous Footnote Four in *United States* v. *Carolene Products* (1938) in cases involving economic regulation. In *Caroline Products* the Court ruled that economic regulation need only advance a reasonable legislative objective, thus giving legislatures broad latitude to regulate the economy and private property in the public interest. Justice Stone, having all but withdrawn the Court from serious scrutiny of cases involving economic regulation, wrote that

[t]here may be narrower scope of operation of the presumption of constitutionality when legislation appears on its face to be within a specific prohibition of the Constitution, such as those of the first ten Amendments, which are deemed equally specific when held to embraced with the Fourteenth.

It is unneccessary to consider now whether legislation which restricts those political processes which can ordinarily be expected to bring about repeal of undesirable legislation, is to be subjected to more exacting judicial scrutiny under the general prohibitions of the Fourteenth Amendment than are most other types of legislation. . . .

Nor need we enquire whether similar considerations enter into the review of statutes directed at particular religious, national or racial minorities; whether prejudice against discrete and insular minorities may be a special condition, which tends seriously to curtail the operation of those political processes ordinarily to be relied upon to protect minorities, and which may call for a correspondingly more searching judicial inquiry.

Since *Carolene Products* the Court has required property owners bringing claims under the Takings Clause to demonstrate that (1) government regulation has rendered their property worthless and (2) the contested rule bears no legitimate relationship to the stated public interest or use. Unlike, for example, free speech or the right to abortion, property rights are not considered among the preferred rights entitled to "more searching judicial inquiry." This development does not mean, however, that since *Carolene Products* support for greater protection for property rights has been without its advocates. Many of the most compelling arguments on behalf of treating property rights as preferred rights will be discussed later in this chapter.

On occasion the Court has recognized that regulatory action can amount to a taking and thus require the government to provide just compensation. In *United*

*States* v. *Causby* (1946), the Court ruled that the consequences of the federal government's decision to build an airfield near a private farm qualified as a Takings Clause violation. Continuous takeoffs and landings from the airfield had disastrous health effects on the farm's chicken population to the point that it depleted the worth of an entire commercial enterprise. More often than not, though, the Court has treated the Takings Clause as a grant of government power to seize property, not as a limitation. *Penn Central Transportation Co.* v. *New York* (1978) illustrates this position well.

Cities often enact rules to protect historic buildings, entire neighborhoods, or commercial areas to promote their aesthetic value, encourage local patronage, and attract tourists. Older cities with rich histories, such as Boston, New York, San Francisco, Savannah, Charleston, Williamsburg, Philadelphia, Chicago, and Concord, New Hampshire, have state and local boards that exist solely for the purpose of identifying historic sites and protecting them through landmarking ordinances. Such laws, for example, usually require owners to retain their property in accord with certain aesthetic standards and to limit commercial development on or near the area. Sometimes the government will offer special benefits to owners who are subject to historic preservation laws, such as rent adjustments or development incentives for additional properties.

In 1967, New York City, pursuant to a local landmark law enacted two years before, designated its Grand Central Terminal as a historic site. The following year the Penn Central Transportation Co., which owned the terminal, presented two plans to build an office tower over the landmarked facade, each of which involved a minimum of fifty-five stories and adjustments to the original facade. The Landmark Preservation Commission of New York City denied Penn Central the right to erect the structures over the historic terminal. Penn Central argued that the commission's action amounted to a taking because it prohibited development of the only place (the airspace above the terminal) in which the company could effectively utilize its property.

The Court, in an opinion that offers a splendid example of the *Carolene Products* footnote applied to economic rights claims, rejected Penn Central's argument. In no uncertain terms, a 6-3 Court dismissed each claim brought by Penn Central in succession. Writing for the Court, Justice Brennan first ruled that owners could not

establish a "'taking' simply by showing that they heretofore had believed was available for development is quite simply untenable." Justice Brennan next rejected Penn Central's claim that it had established a "taking" because the historic preservation law's application to the terminal site significantly diminished its value. According to Justice Brennan, Penn Central's position

appears to be that the only means of ensuring that selected owners are not singled out to endure financial hardship for no reason is to hold that any restriction imposed on individual landmarks pursuant to the New York City scheme is a "taking" requiring the payment of "just compensation." Agreement with this argument would, of course, invalidate not just New York City's law, but all comparable landmark legislation in the Nation. We find no merit in it.[9]

Justice Brennan also dismissed Penn Central's last claim, that the commission's decision to landmark Grand Central Terminal was arbitrary and subjective, since it involved, in the company's words, a matter of taste. Because the law applied to thirty-one historic districts and more than four hundred buildings, many of which were proximate to the terminal, Justice Brennan concluded that the commission's decision had been reasonable and substantially related to its promotion of the general welfare through historic preservation. Noting that Penn Central had relied on *Mahon* to frame its Takings Clause claim, Justice Brennan also pointed out the difference between government regulation that affects the *existing* use of property and that which would affect the *future,* unrelated use of the property.

But the expansive notion of eminent domain offered by Justice Brennan's *Penn Central* opinion did not discourage subsequent Takings Clause litigation. In fact, Justice Brennan's willingness to acknowledge that the Court, "[q]uite simply, has been unable to develop any 'set formula' for determining when 'justice and fairness' require that economic injuries caused by public action be compensated by the government, rather than remain disproportionately concentrated on a few persons." It also acknowledged that its inquiries into the Takings Clause had been "essentially *ad hoc*."[10] Justice Brennan's confession in *Penn Central* that the Court had failed to produce a coherent approach to the Takings Clause enabled a more conservative Court, ten years later, to make it more difficult for government to seize private property on behalf of ownership rights in such cases.

## Penn Central Transportation Co. v. New York
### 438 U.S. 104 (1978)

The facts and background of this case are set out on pp. 511–512.

The Court's decision was 6 to 3. Justice Brennan delivered the opinion of the Court. Justice Rehnquist, joined by Chief Justice Burger and Justice Stevens, dissented.

MR. JUSTICE BRENNAN delivered the opinion of the Court.

The question presented is whether a city may, as part of a comprehensive program to preserve historic landmarks and historic districts, place restrictions on the development of individual historic landmarks—in addition to those imposed by applicable zoning ordinances—without effecting a "taking" requiring the payment of "just compensation." Specifically, we must decide whether the application of New York City's Landmarks Preservation Law to the parcel of land occupied by Grand Central Terminal has "taken" its owners' property in violation of the Fifth and Fourteenth Amendments.

Over the past 50 years, all 50 States and over 500 municipalities have enacted laws to encourage or require the preservation of buildings and areas with historic or aesthetic importance. These nationwide legislative efforts have been precipitated by two concerns. The first is recognition that, in recent years, large numbers of historic structures, landmarks, and areas have been destroyed without adequate consideration of either the values represented therein or the possibility of preserving the destroyed properties for use in economically productive ways. The second is a widely shared belief that structures with special historic, cultural, or architectural significance enhance the quality of life for all. Not only do these buildings and their workmanship represent the lessons of the past and embody precious features of our heritage, they serve as examples of quality for today. "[H]istoric conservation is but one aspect of the much larger problem, basically an environmental one, of enhancing—or perhaps developing for the first time—the quality of life for people." . . .

Before considering appellants' specific contentions, it will be useful to review the factors that have shaped the jurisprudence of the Fifth Amendment injunction "nor shall private property be taken for public use, without just compensation." The question of what constitutes a "taking" for purposes of the Fifth Amendment has proved to be a problem of considerable difficulty. While this Court has recognized that the "Fifth Amendment's guarantee . . . [is] designed to bar Government from forcing some people alone to bear public burdens which, in all fairness and justice, should be borne by the public as a whole," this Court, quite simply, has been unable to develop any "set formula" for determining when "justice and fairness" require that economic injuries caused by public action be compensated by the government, rather than remain disproportionately concentrated on a few persons.

In engaging in these essentially *ad hoc,* factual inquiries, the Court's decisions have identified several factors that have particular significance. The economic impact of the regulation on the claimant and, particularly, the extent to which the regulation has interfered with distinct investment-backed expectations are, of course, relevant considerations. So, too, is the character of the governmental action. A "taking" may more readily be found when the interference with property can be characterized as a physical invasion by government, than when interference arises from some public program adjusting the benefits and burdens of economic life to promote the common good. . . .

More importantly for the present case, in instances in which a state tribunal reasonably concluded that "the health, safety, morals, or general welfare" would be promoted by prohibiting particular contemplated uses of land, this Court has upheld land use regulations that destroyed or adversely affected recognized real property interests. Zoning laws are, of course, the classic example, which have been viewed as permissible governmental action even when prohibiting the most beneficial use of the property.

Zoning laws generally do not affect existing uses of real property, but "taking" challenges have also been held to be without merit in a wide variety of situations when the challenged governmental actions prohibited a beneficial use to which individual parcels had previously been devoted, and thus caused substantial individualized harm.

*Pennsylvania Coal Co. v. Mahon* (1922), is the leading case for the proposition that a state statute that substantially furthers important public policies may so frustrate distinct investment-backed expectations as to amount to a "taking." There the claimant had sold the surface rights to particular parcels of property, but expressly reserved the right to remove the coal thereunder. A Pennsylvania statute, enacted after the transactions, forbade any mining of coal that caused the subsidence of any house, unless the house was the property of the owner of the underlying coal and was more than 150 feet from the improved property of another. Because the statute made it commercially impracticable to mine the coal, and thus had nearly the same effect as the complete destruction of rights claimant had reserved from the owners of the surface land, the Court held that the statute was invalid as effecting a "taking" without just compensation.

Finally, government actions that may be characterized as acquisitions of resources to permit or facilitate uniquely public functions have often been held to constitute "takings." *Causby* is illustrative. In holding that direct overflights above the claimant's land, that destroyed the present use of the land as a chicken farm, constituted a "taking," *Causby* emphasized that Government had not "merely destroyed property [but was] using a part of it for the flight of its planes."

In contending that the New York City law has "taken" their property in violation of the Fifth and Fourteenth Amendments, appellants make a series of arguments, which, while tailored to the facts of this case, essentially urge that any substantial restriction imposed pursuant to a landmark law must be accompanied by just compensation if it is to be constitutional. Before considering these, we emphasize what is not in dispute. Because this Court has recognized, in a number of settings, that States and cities may enact land use restrictions or controls to enhance the quality of life by preserving the character and desirable aesthetic features of a city, . . . appellants do not contest that New York City's objective of preserving structures and areas with special historic, architectural, or cultural significance is an entirely permissible governmental goal. They also do not dispute that the restrictions imposed on its parcel are appropriate means of securing the purposes of the New York City law. Finally, appellants do not challenge any of the specific factual premises of the decision below. They accept for present purposes both that the parcel of land occupied by Grand Central Terminal must, in its present state, be regarded as capable of earning a reasonable return and that the transferable development rights afforded appellants by virtue of the Terminal's designation as a landmark are valuable, even if not as valuable as the rights to construct above the Terminal. In appellants' view, none of these factors derogate from their claim that New York City's law has effected a "taking."

They first observe that the airspace above the Terminal is a valuable property interest, citing *United States* v. *Causby*. They urge that the Landmarks Law has deprived them of any gainful use of their "air rights" above the Terminal and that, irrespective of the value of the remainder of their parcel, the city has "taken" their right to this superjacent airspace, thus entitling them to "just compensation" measured by the fair market value of these air rights.

Apart from our own disagreement with appellants' characterization of the effect of the New York City law, the submission that appellants may establish a "taking" simply by showing that they have been denied the ability to exploit a property interest that they heretofore had believed was available for development is quite simply untenable. Were this the rule, this Court would have erred not only in upholding laws restricting the development of air rights, but also in approving those prohibiting both the subjacent, development of particular parcels. "Taking" jurisprudence does not divide a single parcel into discrete segments and attempt to determine whether rights in a particular segment have been entirely abrogated. In deciding whether a particular governmental action had effected a taking, this Court focuses rather both on the character of the action and on the nature and extent of the interference with rights in the parcel as a whole—here, the city tax block designated as the "landmark site."

Secondly, appellants, focusing on the character and impact of the New York City law, argue that it effects a "taking" because its operation has significantly diminished the value of the Terminal site. Appellants concede that the decisions sustaining other land use regulations, which, like the New York City law, are reasonably related to the promotion of the general welfare, uniformly reject the proposition that diminution in property value, standing alone, can establish a "taking," and that the "taking" issue in these contexts is resolved by focusing on the uses the regulations permit. Appellants, moreover, also do not dispute that a showing of diminution in property value would not establish a "taking" if the restriction had been imposed as a result of historic district legislation, but appellants argue that New York City's regulation of individual landmarks is fundamentally different from zoning or from historic district legislation because the controls imposed by New York City's law apply only to individuals who own selected properties.

Stated baldly, appellants' position appears to be that the only means of ensuring that selected owners are not singled out to endure financial hardship for no reason is to hold that any restriction imposed on individual landmarks pursuant to the New York City scheme is a "taking" requiring the payment of "just compensation." Agreement with this argument would, of course, invalidate not just New York City's law, but all comparable landmark legislation in the Nation. We find no merit in it.

Equally without merit is the related argument that the decision to designate a structure as a landmark "is inevitably arbitrary, or at least subjective, because it is basically a matter of taste," thus unavoidably singling out individual landowners for disparate and unfair treatment. The argument has a particularly hollow ring in this case. For appellants not only did not seek judicial review of either the designation or of the denials of the certificates of appropriateness and of no exterior effect, but do not even now suggest that the Commission's decisions concerning the Terminal were in any sense arbitrary or unprincipled. But, in any event, a landmark owner has a right to judicial review of any Commission decision, and, quite simply, there is no basis whatsoever for a conclusion that courts will have any greater difficulty identifying arbitrary or discriminatory action in the context of landmark regulation than in the context of classic zoning or indeed in any other context.

Next, appellants observe that New York City's law differs from zoning laws and historic district ordinances in that the Landmarks Law does not impose identical or similar restrictions on all structures located in particular physical communities. It follows, they argue, that New York City's law is inherently incapable of producing the fair and equitable distribution of benefits and burdens of governmental action which is characteristic of zoning laws and historic district legislation and which, they maintain, is a constitutional requirement if "just compensation" is not to be afforded. It is, of course, true that the Landmarks Law has a more severe impact on some landowners than on others, but that, in itself, does not mean that the law effects a "taking." Legislation designed to promote the general welfare commonly burdens some more than others.

In any event, appellants' repeated suggestions that they are solely burdened and unbenefited is factually inaccurate. This contention overlooks the fact that the New York City law applies to vast numbers of structures in the city in addition to the Terminal—all the structures contained in the 31 historic districts and over 400 individual landmarks, many of which are close to the Terminal. Unless we are to reject the judgment of the New York City Council that the preservation of landmarks benefits all New York citizens and all structures, both economically and by improving the quality of life in the city as a whole—which we are unwilling to do—we cannot conclude that the owners of the Terminal have in no sense been benefited by the Landmarks Law. . . .

[T]he New York City law does not interfere in any way with the present uses of the Terminal. Its designation as a landmark not only permits, but contemplates, that appellants may continue to use the property precisely as it has been used for the past 65 years: as a railroad terminal containing office space and concessions. So the law does not interfere with what must be regarded as Penn Central's primary expectation concerning the use of the parcel. More importantly, on this record, we must regard the New York City law as permitting Penn Central not only to profit from the Terminal but also to obtain a "reasonable return" on its investment.

Appellants, moreover, exaggerate the effect of the law on their ability to make use of the air rights above the Terminal in two respects. First, it simply cannot be maintained, on this record, that appellants have been prohibited from occupying any portion of the airspace above the Terminal. While the Commission's actions in denying applications to construct an office building in excess of 50 stories above the Terminal may indicate that it will refuse to issue a certificate of appropriateness for any comparably sized structure, nothing the Commission has said or done suggests an intention to prohibit any construction above the Terminal. The Commission's report emphasized that whether any construction would be allowed depended upon whether the proposed addition "would harmonize in scale, material, and character with [the Terminal]." Since appellants have not sought approval for the construction of a smaller structure, we do not know that appellants will be denied any use of any portion of the airspace above the Terminal. . . .

On this record, we conclude that the application of New York City's Landmarks Law has not effected a "taking" of appellants' property. The restrictions imposed are substantially related to the promotion of the general welfare, and not only permit reasonable beneficial use of the landmark site, but also afford appellants opportunities further to enhance not only the Terminal site proper but also other properties.

*Affirmed.*

MR. JUSTICE REHNQUIST, with whom THE CHIEF JUSTICE and MR. JUSTICE STEVENS join, dissenting.

Of the over one million buildings and structures in the city of New York, appellees have singled out 400 for designation as official landmarks. The owner of a Building might initially be pleased that his property has been chosen by a distinguished committee of architects, historians, and city planners for such a singular distinction. But he may well discover, as appellant Penn Central Transportation Co. did here, that the landmark designation imposes upon him a substantial cost, with little or no offsetting benefit except for the honor of the designation. The question in this case is whether the cost associated with the city of New York's desire to preserve a limited number of "landmarks" within its borders must be borne by all of its taxpayers, or whether it can, instead, be imposed entirely on the owners of the individual properties.

Only in the most superficial sense of the word can this case be said to involve "zoning." Typical zoning restrictions

# LEWIS POWELL AND THE CHAMBER OF COMMERCE

## *"The American Economic System Is Under Broad Attack"*

Public interest litigation experienced a boom in the 1960s and early 1970s. Encouraged by the success of the NAACP in bringing down school segregation in the South, organizations representing groups at a similar disadvantage in the political process, such as religious minorities, women, and political dissenters, turned to the courts to advance their public policy objectives. More often than not, these great constitutional victories invalidated laws that denied them basic rights, or established rights in cases when legislatures had remained silent on pressing matters of individual rights. During this period the Supreme Court rewrote the law of criminal due process rights, invalidated school prayer and Bible reading practices in public schools, established a right to privacy that laid the foundation for the constitutional right to abortion, ruled that the Equal Protection Clause banned sex-based discrimination, and held that school busing to achieve racial integration in the public schools was in some cases required by the Constitution.

Liberal, reform-oriented groups dominated the litigation environment. They met little or no opposition in the courts from defenders of the status quo. In some cases, such as school segregation, no one was willing to take up the cause. By and large, however, conservative organizations were simply caught flat-footed. Accustomed to success in Congress and the state legislatures, few conservative organizations possessed the skill, knowledge, and sophistication to take on liberal public interest groups in the courts. In fact, few such organizations even existed in the 1960s and early 1970s to defend conservative constitutional causes.

That all changed, however, after the consumer advocacy and environmental movements, two high-profile social movements of the 1960s, succeeded in puncturing the dominance of economic regulation by corporate and business interests. The consumer movement persuaded Congress to enact legislation forcing major American corporations and entire industries to tighten the safety standards of such commonplace products as cars, foods, and children's toys. It was headed by a young lawyer, Ralph Nader, who achieved almost overnight fame with the publication of *Unsafe at Any Speed* in 1965, which singled out a popular General Motors (GM) car, the Corvair, as unsafe to drive. Nader testified before Congress that GM had covered up evidence of the Corvair's unreliability and hired spies to steal his research and discredit his findings. A successful lawsuit against GM left Nader with a cash settlement of $250,000. With this money he started the Center for the Study of Responsive Law in 1969, to complement the efforts of his education and lobbying group, Public Citizen, Inc. So popular was Nader with college students and newly minted law school graduates that they came to work for him in droves, often for little or no money. They were nicknamed "Nader's Raiders."

In 1971, Charles Reich, a Yale law professor and a former clerk to Justice Black, published *The Greening of America.* Subtitled *How the Youth Generation Is Trying to Make America Livable,* Reich warned of disastrous environmental consequences for America if major corporations were not held in check by tough government regulation. He encouraged students to use education, litigation, and living by example to improve environmental quality. Public support for greater environmental awareness was already in place by the time Reich published his call to environmental arms; on April 22, 1970, the nation had celebrated its first Earth Day. Its wide popularity forced Congress to sit up and take notice. The result was a flurry of environmental regulation, including the nation's first comprehensive clean air and water laws, strict controls on pesticides and fungicides, and laws mandating the cleanup of toxic wastes.

The success of the consumer and environmental movements hit the American business community like a bolt of lightning. In 1971 the largest and most powerful association representing small businesses and large corporations alike, the United States Chamber of Commerce, was so concerned by this unprecedented wave of economic regulation that it commissioned the former president of the American Bar Association, Lewis F. Powell Jr., to conduct an analysis on the problems its members faced and how to overcome them. Powell was perhaps the nation's most highly regarded attorney in private practice. In 1969, Powell had been President Nixon's first choice to serve on the Court after the Senate had rejected the nominations of Clement Haynsworth and G. Harrold Carswell. The president wanted a white southerner with a business-oriented background, but one who would not raise the eyebrows of civil rights groups.

Powell certainly fit the bill. A partner in an elite Richmond law firm, Powell had an exemplary record of public service. He had counseled the Richmond schools throughout their desegregation efforts, working behind the scenes to encourage gradual compliance, and served on President Lyndon Johnson's Crime Commission and Nixon's Blue Ribbon Defense Panel. Powell had also served as the president of the American College of Trial Lawyers. But Powell declined Nixon's offer. Powell did so because of his age, sixty-two, and because he did not want to go through the confirmation process and risk public embarrassment. In January 1972, President Nixon called on Powell again. This time, after a gentle lobbying campaign by friends and high-level administration officials, Powell accepted.

Shortly before Powell was confirmed—without incident—he released his confidential memo to the Chamber of Commerce. Titled "Attack on the American Free Enterprise System," Powell wrote that "no

thoughtful person can question that the American economic system is under attack" by a powerful tide of liberal forces. Fingering Nader and Reich specifically, Powell commented that liberals had succeeded in equating greater economic regulation with the "public interest." An effective response would require more than just encouraging a few individual law firms

Lewis Powell (right), then president of the American Bar Association, presenting an award to Justice Potter Stewart. Powell later became a key "swing" vote in many important cases during his fifteen years on the Court.
Collection of the Supreme Court of the United States.

to get involved; it would require the chamber to support scholars and speakers to get the message of business out. Powell also encouraged the chamber to encourage its members to create and fund conservative "public interest" groups to litigate and contest the consumer and environmental groups in court.

Powell's memo captured the mood of the chamber's members and conservative public officials who felt handcuffed by liberal legislation. It was widely distributed across the nation. One place where Powell's recommendations caught immediate fire was in California. Governor Ronald Reagan had lobbied successfully for changes in the state's welfare system but had been blocked in the courts by civil rights groups. An aide to Governor Reagan, Ronald Zubrun, and the lawyer who defended the welfare changes in court, Raymond Momboisse, admired the work of their enemies enough to create, with the support of the California Chamber of Commerce, the Pacific Legal Foundation (PLF) in 1973. The PLF soon developed a litigation agenda that focused on regional environmental, property, and consumer regulation. Sensing that it needed to go national, its founders recruited additional lawyers to study the most feasible option. In 1975, the National Legal Center for the Public Interest was started to serve as an umbrella organization and clearinghouse on information and litigation strategy for conservative public interest firms similar to the PLF. More than twenty-five years later, its board of directors reads like a Who's Who of the American business and legal communities.

The conservative public interest law movement is now a significant force in Supreme Court litigation involving economic regulation. Conservative organizations also litigate in state courts and in lower federal courts. Groups formed as a direct outgrowth of the Powell memo, such as the PLF, the Mountain States Legal Foundation, and the Southeastern Legal Foundation, have been joined by the Landmark Legal Foundation, the Center for Individual Rights, Defenders of Property Rights, and the Washington Legal Foundation. In some cases they provide direct sponsorship to plaintiffs in economic regulation cases; more often, these groups submit friend-of-the-court briefs encouraging the court to adopt their favored positions. Almost all these groups maintain an office in Washington, D.C., to offer testimony and other information to Congress when it takes up environmental, consumer, and general business regulation affecting property interests.

The growth of the conservative public interest law movement has fundamentally reordered the dynamics of litigation involving economic regulation. Once the domain of liberal groups favoring expansive consumer, environmental, and economic regulation, the litigation environment on these and related questions is more open, plural, and confrontational than ever before. This renaissance over the debate over the place of property rights in the constitutional order owes much to the vision of Lewis Powell before his ascent to the Supreme Court.

---

may, it is true, so limit the prospective uses of a piece of property as to diminish the value of that property in the abstract because it may not be used for the forbidden purposes. But any such abstract decrease in value will more than likely be at least partially offset by an increase in value which flows from similar restrictions as to use on neighboring properties. All property owners in a designated area are placed under the same restrictions, not only for the benefit of the municipality as a whole, but also for the common benefit of one another. In the words of Mr. Justice Holmes, speaking for the Court in *Pennsylvania Coal Co.* v. *Mahon*, (1922), there is "an average reciprocity of advantage."

Where a relatively few individual buildings, all separated from one another, are singled out and treated differently from surrounding buildings, no such reciprocity exists. The cost to the property owner which results from the imposition of restrictions applicable only to his property and not that of his neighbors may be substantial—in this case, several million dollars—with no comparable reciprocal benefits. And the cost associated with landmark legislation is likely to be of a completely different order of magnitude than that which results from the imposition of normal zoning restrictions. Unlike the regime affected by the latter, the landowner is not simply prohibited from using his property for certain purposes, while allowed to use it for all other purposes. Under the historic landmark preservation scheme adopted by New York, the property owner is under an affirmative duty to preserve his property as a landmark at his own expense. To suggest that, because traditional zoning results in some limitation of use of the property zoned, the New York City landmark preservation scheme should likewise be upheld, represents the ultimate in treating as alike things which are different. The rubric of "zoning" has not yet sufficed to avoid the well established proposition that the Fifth Amendment bars the "Government from forcing some people alone to bear public burdens which, in all fairness and justice, should be borne by the public as a whole." . . .

The Fifth Amendment provides in part: "nor shall private property be taken for public use, without just compensation." In a very literal sense, the actions of appellees violated this constitutional prohibition. Before the city of New York declared Grand Central Terminal to be a landmark, Penn Central could have used its "air rights" over the Terminal to build a multistory office building, at an apparent value of several million dollars per year. Today, the Terminal cannot be modified in any form, including the erection of additional stories, without the permission of the Landmark Preservation Commission, a permission which appellants, despite good faith attempts, have so far been unable to obtain. Because the Taking Clause of the Fifth Amendment has not always been read literally, however, the constitutionality of appellees' actions requires a closer scrutiny of this Court's interpretation of the three key words in the Taking Clause—"property," "taken," and "just compensation."

Appellees do not dispute that valuable property rights have been destroyed. And the Court has frequently emphasized that the term "property" as used in the Taking Clause includes the entire "group of rights inhering in the citizen's [ownership]." The term is not used in the "vulgar and untechnical sense of the physical thing with respect to which the citizen exercises rights recognized by law. [Instead, it] . . . denote[s] the *group of rights* inhering in the citizen's relation to the physical thing, as *the right to possess, use and dispose of it.* . . . The constitutional provision is addressed to *every sort of interest* the citizen may possess."

While neighboring landowners are free to use their land and "air rights" in any way consistent with the broad boundaries of New York zoning, Penn Central, absent the permission of appellees, must forever maintain its property in its present state. The property has been thus subjected to a nonconsensual servitude not borne by any neighboring or similar properties.

Appellees have thus destroyed—in a literal sense, "taken"—substantial property rights of Penn Central. While the term "taken" might have been narrowly interpreted to include only physical seizures of property rights, "the construction of the phrase has not been so narrow. The courts have held that the deprivation of the former owner, rather than the accretion of a right or interest to the sovereign, constitutes the taking."

Over 50 years ago, Mr. Justice Holmes, speaking for the Court, warned that the courts were "in danger of forgetting that a strong public desire to improve the public condition is not enough to warrant achieving the desire by a shorter cut than the constitutional way of paying for the change. *Pennsylvania Coal Co. v. Mahon,* (1922) The Court's opinion in this case demonstrates that the danger thus foreseen has not abated. The city of New York is in a precarious financial state, and some may believe that the costs of landmark preservation will be more easily borne by corporations such as Penn Central than the overburdened individual taxpayers of New York. But these concerns do not allow us to ignore past precedents construing the Eminent Domain Clause to the end that the desire to improve the public condition is, indeed, achieved by a shorter cut than the constitutional way of paying for the change.

▼▲▼

For some time prior to *Nollan v. California Coastal Commission* (1987), a small but influential cadre of scholars and conservative public interest law firms had argued that Justice Stone's *Carolene Product's* footnote had arbitrarily and without justification reduced the constitutional status of property rights. Bernard H. Siegan, in *Economic Liberties and the Constitution* (1980), has argued that Footnote Four is "a statement of philosophy about the role of the Court that had no basis in the original intention of the Framers." In this view the Court used *West Coast Hotel, Jones & Laughlin Steel,* and subsequent pro–New Deal decisions to advance the political interests of President Roosevelt and its own idea of what the Constitution means. Had the Court's true concern been to reconcile the modern political economy with the Framers' intent, the Court would have left *Lochner* intact and by extension the preferred position of economic and ownership rights claims.[11]

Other provocative arguments have been advanced suggesting that judges cannot draw constitutional distinctions between economic and personal rights. In this view the Court's self-imposed decision not to include property and ownership rights among the fundamental freedoms deserving of special protection from government intrusion cannot be justified on the basis of the language, logic, or intent of the Constitution. The Framers' concern for property rights led them to create a government of limited, enumerated powers, one that could not deprive individuals of their most fundamental rights. In contrast to legal realist notion that economic markets and property rights are a function of political decision making, many modern advocates of greater protection for property rights consider them inherent in citizenship. Such rights exist prior to the formation of political societies, which merely provide formal protection for rights considered natural and prepolitical.[12]

*Dollan* did not take protection for property rights nearly that far, but it did up the ante for government by making it show more than just a "reasonable" basis for the exercise of its power of eminent domain. Writing for a sharply divided 5-4 Court, Justice Scalia commented that prior Takings Clause decisions had failed to produce a coherent standard upon which to analyze land-use regulation that affected economically viable private property. Sensing an opening, Scalia held that the government had to demonstrate a "rough proportionality" between the seizure of property and the public use for which it was intended. Arguably, Justice Scalia was no more successful in creating a recognizable standard for a Takings Clause violation than Justice Brennan had been in *Penn Central* or Justice Holmes in *Mahon*. But *Nollan* did encourage many property rights groups to litigate or support cases that challenged existing notions of land-use regulation and the government's obligation to property owners.

## Nollan v. California Coastal Commission
### 483 U.S. 825 (1987)

James and Marilyn Nollan, along with several others, owned beach-front lots that were located between two popular public beaches in Ventura County, California. The Nollans wanted to replace an old summer rental bungalow with a new beach house. The California Coastal Commission agreed to allow the Nollans to build the house but, as a condition of their building permit, required them to build a walking path between the two public beaches and then sell it back to the government. Private property that is transferred in a such a manner for public use is called an easement.

The Nollans contested the easement, claiming that it deprived them of valuable property and thus constituted a taking under the Fifth Amendment. They were successful in state trial court, but the California Supreme Court sided with the coastal commission.

The Court's decision was 5 to 4. Justice Scalia delivered the opinion of the Court. Justices Brennan, Blackmun, and Stevens each filed dissents.

JUSTICE SCALIA delivered the opinion of the Court.

. . . We have long recognized that land use regulation does not effect a taking if it "substantially advance[s] legitimate state interests" and does not "den[y] an owner economically viable use of his land." Our cases have not elaborated on the standards for determining what constitutes a "legitimate state interest" or what type of connection between the regulation and the state interest satisfies the requirement that the former "substantially advance" the latter. They have made clear, however, that a broad range of governmental purposes and regulations satisfies these requirements. The Commission argues that among these permissible purposes are protecting the public's ability to see the beach, assisting the public in overcoming the "psychological barrier" to using the beach created by a developed shorefront, and preventing congestion on the public beaches. We assume, without deciding, that this is so—in which case, the Commission unquestionably would be able to deny the Nollans their permit outright if their new house (alone, or by reason of the cumulative impact produced in conjunction with other construction) would substantially impede these purposes, unless the denial would interfere so drastically with the Nollans' use of their property as to constitute a taking.

The Commission argues that a permit condition that serves the same legitimate police power purpose as a refusal to issue the permit should not be found to be a taking if the refusal to issue the permit would not constitute a taking. We agree. Thus, if the Commission attached to the permit some condition that would have protected the public's ability to see the beach notwithstanding construction of the new house—for example, a height limitation, a width restriction, or a ban on fences—so long as the Commission could have exercised its police power (as we have assumed it could) to forbid construction of the house altogether, imposition of the condition would also be constitutional. Moreover (and here we come closer to the facts of the present case), the condition would be constitutional even if it consisted of the requirement that the Nollans provide a viewing spot on their property for passersby with whose sighting of the ocean their new house would interfere. Although such a requirement, constituting a permanent grant of continuous access to the property, would have to be considered a taking if it were not attached to a development permit, the Commission's assumed power to forbid construction of the house in order to protect the public's view of the beach must surely include the power to condition construction upon some concession by the owner, even a concession of property rights, that serves the same end. If a prohibition designed to accomplish that purpose would be a legitimate exercise of the police power, rather than a taking, it would be strange to conclude that providing the owner an alternative to that prohibition which accomplishes the same purpose is not.

The evident constitutional propriety disappears, however, if the condition substituted for the prohibition utterly fails to further the end advanced as the justification for the prohibition. When that essential nexus is eliminated, the situation becomes the same as if California law forbade shouting fire in a crowded theater, but granted dispensations to those willing to contribute $100 to the state treasury. While a ban on shouting fire can be a core exercise of the State's police power to protect the public safety, and can thus meet even our stringent standards for regulation of speech, adding the unrelated condition alters the purpose to one which, while it may be legitimate, is inadequate to sustain the ban. Therefore, even though, in a sense, requiring a $100 tax contribution in order to shout fire is a lesser restriction on speech than an outright ban, it would not pass constitutional muster. Similarly here, the lack of nexus between the condition and the original purpose of the building restriction converts that purpose to something other than what it was. The purpose then becomes, quite simply, the obtaining of an easement to serve some valid governmental purpose, but without payment of compensation. Whatever may be the outer limits of "legitimate state interests" in the takings and land use context, this is not one of them. In short, unless the permit condition serves the same governmental purpose as the development ban, the building restriction is not a valid regulation of land use, but "an out-and-out plan of extortion." . . .

The Commission claims that it concedes as much, and that we may sustain the condition at issue here by finding that it is reasonably related to the public need or burden that the Nollans' new house creates or to which it contributes. We can accept, for purposes of discussion, the Commission's proposed test as to how close a "fit" between the condition and the burden is required, because we find that this case does not meet even the most untailored standards. The Commission's principal contention to the contrary essentially turns on a play on the word "access." The Nollans' new house, the Commission found, will interfere with "visual access" to the beach. That in turn (along with other shorefront development) will

interfere with the desire of people who drive past the Nollans' house to use the beach, thus creating a "psychological barrier" to "access." The Nollans' new house will also, by a process not altogether clear from the Commission's opinion but presumably potent enough to more than offset the effects of the psychological barrier, increase the use of the public beaches, thus creating the need for more "access." These burdens on "access" would be alleviated by a requirement that the Nollans provide "lateral access" to the beach.

Rewriting the argument to eliminate the play on words makes clear that there is nothing to it. It is quite impossible to understand how a requirement that people already on the public beaches be able to walk across the Nollans' property reduces any obstacles to viewing the beach created by the new house. It is also impossible to understand how it lowers any "psychological barrier" to using the public beaches, or how it helps to remedy any additional congestion on them caused by construction of the Nollans' new house. We therefore find that the Commission's imposition of the permit condition cannot be treated as an exercise of its land use power for any of these purposes. Our conclusion on this point is consistent with the approach taken by every other court that has considered the question, with the exception of the California state courts.

*Reversed.*

JUSTICE BRENNAN, with whom JUSTICE MARSHALL joins, dissenting.

The Court's conclusion that the permit condition imposed on appellants is unreasonable cannot withstand analysis. First, the Court demands a degree of exactitude that is inconsistent with our standard for reviewing the rationality of a State's exercise of its police power for the welfare of its citizens. Second, even if the nature of the public access condition imposed must be identical to the precise burden on access created by appellants, this requirement is plainly satisfied.

There can be no dispute that the police power of the States encompasses the authority to impose conditions on private development. It is also by now commonplace that this Court's review of the rationality of a State's exercise of its police power demands only that the State *"could rationally have decided"* that the measure adopted might achieve the State's objective. In this case, California has employed its police power in order to condition development upon preservation of public access to the ocean and tidelands. The Coastal Commission, if it had so chosen, could have denied the Nollans' request for a development permit, since the property would have remained economically viable without the requested new development. Instead, the State sought to accommodate the Nollans' desire for new development, on the condition that the development not diminish the overall amount of public access to the coastline. Appellants' proposed development would reduce public access by restricting visual access to the beach, by contributing to an increased need for community facilities, and by moving private development closer to public beach property. The Commission sought to offset this diminution in access, and thereby preserve the overall balance of access, by requesting a deed restriction that would ensure "lateral" access: the right of the public to pass and repass along the dry sand parallel to the shoreline in order to reach the tidelands and the ocean. In the expert opinion of the Coastal Commission, development conditioned on such a restriction would fairly attend to both public and private interests.

Imposition of the permit condition in this case represents the State's reasonable exercise of its police power. The Coastal Commission has drawn on its expertise to preserve the balance between private development and public access by requiring that any project that intensifies development on the increasingly crowded California coast must be offset by gains in public access. Under the normal standard for review of the police power, this provision is eminently reasonable. Even accepting the Court's novel insistence on a precise *quid pro quo* of burdens and benefits, there is a reasonable relationship between the public benefit and the burden created by appellants' development. The movement of development closer to the ocean creates the prospect of encroachment on public tidelands, because of fluctuation in the mean high-tide line. The deed restriction ensures that disputes about the boundary between private and public property will not deter the public from exercising its right to have access to the sea.

Furthermore, consideration of the Commission's action under traditional takings analysis underscores the absence of any viable takings claim. The deed restriction permits the public only to pass and repass along a narrow strip of beach, a few feet closer to a seawall at the periphery of appellants' property. Appellants almost surely have enjoyed an increase in the value of their property even with the restriction, because they have been allowed to build a significantly larger new home with garage on their lot. Finally, appellants can claim the disruption of no expectation interest, both because they have no right to exclude the public under state law and because, even if they did, they had full advance notice that new develop-

ment along the coast is conditioned on provisions for continued public access to the ocean. . . .

I dissent.

*Lucas* v. *South Carolina Coastal Council* (1992) and *Dolan* v. *Tigard* (1994) are examples of how the Court can create or alter the environment for litigation. Sensing a new willingness on the Court's part to reconsider its approach to the Takings Clause, more than a dozen conservative public interest law firms filed friend-of-the-court briefs in *Lucas*, encouraging the Court to extend the "rough proportionality" standard it created in *Nollan*. Twenty state attorneys general met the conservative challenge, arguing that an extension of *Nollan* would wreak havoc on state land-use, zoning, and planning policies. Several business and environmental groups also filed briefs in *Lucas*. This pattern repeated itself in *Dolan*. The SIDEBAR on *Lucas* and *Dolan* offers greater detail on the legal mobilization of groups in these two cases.

## *Lucas* v. *South Carolina Coastal Council*
### 505 U.S. 1003 (1992)

The facts and background of this case are set out in the accompanying SIDEBAR.

The Court's decision was 6 to 3. Justice Scalia delivered the opinion of the Court. Justices Blackmun and Stevens filed separate dissents. Justice Souter filed a separate statement claiming that the Court should not have granted a writ of certiorari to hear the case.

JUSTICE SCALIA delivered the opinion of the Court.

Prior to Justice Holmes' exposition in *Pennsylvania Coal Co.* v. *Mahon* (1922), it was generally thought that the Takings Clause reached only a "direct appropriation" of property, or the functional equivalent of a "practical ouster of [the owner's] possession." Justice Holmes recognized in *Mahon*, however, that, if the protection against physical appropriations of private property was to be meaningfully enforced, the government's power to redefine the range of interests included in the ownership of property was necessarily constrained by constitutional limits. If, instead, the uses of private property were subject to unbridled, uncompensated qualification under the police power, "the natural tendency of human nature [would be] to extend the qualification more and more until at last private property disappear[ed]." These considerations gave birth in that case to the oft-cited maxim that, "while property may be regulated to a certain extent, if regulation goes too far, it will be recognized as a taking."

Nevertheless, our decision in *Mahon* offered little insight into when, and under what circumstances, a given regulation would be seen as going "too far" for purposes of the Fifth Amendment. In 70-odd years of succeeding "regulatory takings" jurisprudence, we have generally eschewed any "'set formula'" for determining how far is too far, preferring to "engag[e] in . . . essentially *ad hoc*, factual inquiries," *Penn Central Transportation Co. v. New York City* (1978). We have, however, described at least two discrete categories of regulatory action as compensable without case-specific inquiry into the public interest advanced in support of the restraint. The first encompasses regulations that compel the property owner to suffer a physical "invasion" of his property. In general (at least with regard to permanent invasions), no matter how minute the intrusion, and no matter how weighty the public purpose behind it, we have required compensation. . . .

The second situation in which we have found categorical treatment appropriate is where regulation denies all economically beneficial or productive use of land. As we have said on numerous occasions, the Fifth Amendment is violated when land use regulation "does not substantially advance legitimate state interests *or denies an owner economically viable use of his land.*"

We have never set forth the justification for this rule. Perhaps it is simply, as Justice Brennan suggested, that total deprivation of beneficial use is, from the landowner's point of view, the equivalent of a physical appropriation. And the *functional* basis for permitting the government, by regulation, to affect property values without compensation—that "Government hardly could go on if, to some extent, values incident to property could not be diminished without paying for every such change in the general law,"—does not apply to the relatively rare situations where the government has deprived a landowner of all economically beneficial uses.

On the other side of the balance, affirmatively supporting a compensation requirement, is the fact that regulations that leave the owner of land without economically beneficial or productive options for its use—typically, as here, by requiring land to be left substantially in its natural

state—carry with them a heightened risk that private property is being pressed into some form of public service under the guise of mitigating serious public harm. . . .

We think, in short, that there are good reasons for our frequently expressed belief that, when the owner of real property has been called upon to sacrifice *all* economically beneficial uses in the name of the common good, that is, to leave his property economically idle, he has suffered a taking.

The trial court found Lucas' two beachfront lots to have been rendered valueless by respondent's enforcement of the coastal-zone construction ban. Under Lucas' theory of the case, which rested upon our "no economically viable use" statements, that finding entitled him to compensation. Lucas believed it unnecessary to take issue with either the purposes behind the Beachfront Management Act or the means chosen by the South Carolina Legislature to effectuate those purposes. The South Carolina Supreme Court, however, thought otherwise. In its view, the Beachfront Management Act was no ordinary enactment, but involved an exercise of South Carolina's "police powers" to mitigate the harm to the public interest that petitioner's use of his land might occasion. By neglecting to dispute the findings enumerated in the Act or otherwise to challenge the legislature's purposes, petitioner "concede[d] that the beach/dune area of South Carolina's shores is an extremely valuable public resource; that the erection of new construction, *inter alia*, contributes to the erosion and destruction of this public resource; and that discouraging new construction in close proximity to the beach/dune area is necessary to prevent a great public harm." In the court's view, these concessions brought petitioner's challenge within a long line of this Court's cases sustaining against Due Process and Takings Clause challenges the State's use of its "police powers" to enjoin a property owner from activities akin to public nuisances.

It is correct that many of our prior opinions have suggested that "harmful or noxious uses" of property may be proscribed by government regulation without the requirement of compensation. For a number of reasons, however, we think the South Carolina Supreme Court was too quick to conclude that that principle decides the present case. The "harmful or noxious uses" principle was the Court's early attempt to describe in theoretical terms why government may, consistent with the Takings Clause, affect property values by regulation without incurring an obligation to compensate—a reality we nowadays acknowledge explicitly with respect to the full scope of the State's police power. . . .

The transition from our early focus on control of "noxious" uses to our contemporary understanding of the broad realm within which government may regulate without compensation was an easy one, since the distinction between "harm-preventing" and "benefit-conferring" regulation is often in the eye of the beholder. It is quite possible, for example, to describe in *either* fashion the ecological, economic, and aesthetic concerns that inspired the South Carolina legislature in the present case. One could say that imposing a servitude on Lucas' land is necessary in order to prevent his use of it from "harming" South Carolina's ecological resources; or, instead, in order to achieve the "benefits" of an ecological preserve. . . . Whether Lucas' construction of single-family residences on his parcels should be described as bringing "harm" to South Carolina's adjacent ecological resources thus depends principally upon whether the describer believes that the State's use interest in nurturing those resources is so important that *any* competing adjacent use must yield.

When it is understood that "prevention of harmful use" was merely our early formulation of the police power justification necessary to sustain (without compensation) any regulatory diminution in value; and that the distinction between regulation that "prevents harmful use" and that which "confers benefits" is difficult, if not impossible, to discern on an objective, value-free basis; it becomes self-evident that noxious-use logic cannot serve as a touchstone to distinguish regulatory "takings"—which require compensation—from regulatory deprivations that do not require compensation. *A fortiori,* the legislature's recitation of a noxious-use justification cannot be the basis for departing from our categorical rule that total regulatory takings must be compensated. . . .

Where the State seeks to sustain regulation that deprives land of all economically beneficial use, we think it may resist compensation only if the logically antecedent inquiry into the nature of the owner's estate shows that the proscribed use interests were not part of his title to begin with. This accords, we think, with our "takings" jurisprudence, which has traditionally been guided by the understandings of our citizens regarding the content of, and the State's power over, the "bundle of rights" that they acquire when they obtain title to property. It seems to us that the property owner necessarily expects the uses of his property to be restricted, from time to time, by various measures newly enacted by the State in legitimate exercise of its police powers; "[a]s long recognized, some values are enjoyed under an implied limitation, and must yield to the police power." And in the case of personal property, by reason of the State's traditionally high degree of control over commercial dealings, he ought to be aware of the possibility that new regulation might even render his property economically worthless (at least if the property's only economically productive use is sale or manufacture for sale). In the case of land, however, we think the notion pressed by the Council that title is somehow held subject to the "implied limitation" that the State may subsequently eliminate all economically valuable use is inconsistent with the historical compact recorded in the Takings Clause that has become part of our constitutional culture.

Where "permanent physical occupation" of land is concerned, we have refused to allow the government to decree it anew (without compensation), no matter how weighty the asserted "public interests" involved, though we assuredly *would* permit the government to assert a permanent easement that was a preexisting limitation upon the landowner's title. We believe similar treatment must be accorded confiscatory regulations, *i.e.,* regulations that prohibit all economically beneficial use of land: any limitation so severe cannot be newly legislated or decreed (without compensation), but must inhere in the title itself, in the restrictions that background principles of the State's law of property and nuisance already place upon land ownership. A law or decree with such an effect must, in other words, do no more than duplicate the result that could have been achieved in the courts—by adjacent landowners (or other uniquely affected persons) under the State's law of private nuisance, or by the State under its complementary power to abate nuisances that affect the public generally, or otherwise.

On this analysis, the owner of a lakebed, for example, would not be entitled to compensation when he is denied the requisite permit to engage in a landfilling operation that would have the effect of flooding others' land. Nor the corporate owner of a nuclear generating plant, when it is directed to remove all improvements from its land upon discovery that the plant sits astride an earthquake fault. Such regulatory action may well have the effect of eliminating the land's only economically productive use, but it does not proscribe a productive use that was previously permissible under relevant property and nuisance principles. The use of these properties for what are now expressly prohibited purposes was *always* unlawful, and (subject to other constitutional limitations) it was open to the State at any point to make the implication of those background principles of nuisance and property law explicit. In light of our traditional resort to "existing rules or understandings that stem from an independent source such as state law" to define the range of interests that qualify for protection as "property" under the Fifth (and Fourteenth) amendments, this recognition that the Takings Clause does not require compensation when an owner is barred from putting land to a use that is proscribed by those "existing rules or understandings" is surely unexceptional. When, however, a regulation that declares "off limits" all economically productive or beneficial uses of land goes beyond what the relevant background principles would dictate, compensation must be paid to sustain it.

The "total taking" inquiry we require today will ordinarily entail (as the application of state nuisance law ordinarily entails) analysis of, among other things, the degree of harm to public lands and resources, or adjacent private property, posed by the claimant's proposed activities, the social value of the claimant's activities and their suitability to the locality in question, and the relative ease with which the alleged harm can be avoided through measures taken by the claimant and the government (or adjacent private landowners) alike. The fact that a particular use has long been engaged in by similarly situated owners ordinarily imports a lack of any common law prohibition (though changed circumstances or new knowledge may make what was previously permissible no longer so. So also does the fact that other landowners, similarly situated, are permitted to continue the use denied to the claimant.

It seems unlikely that common law principles would have prevented the erection of any habitable or productive improvements on petitioner's land; they rarely support prohibition of the "essential use" of land. The question, however, is one of state law to be dealt with on remand. We emphasize that, to win its case, South Carolina must do more than proffer the legislature's declaration that the uses Lucas desires are inconsistent with the public interest, or the conclusory assertion that they violate a common law maxim such as *sic utere tuo ut alienum non laedas*. As we have said, a "State, by *ipse dixit*, may not transform private property into public property without compensation. . . . " Instead, as it would be required to do if it sought to restrain Lucas in a common law action for public nuisance, South Carolina must identify background principles of nuisance and property law that prohibit the uses he now intends in the circumstances in which the property is presently found. Only on this showing can the State fairly claim that, in proscribing all such beneficial uses, the Beachfront Management Act is taking nothing.

The judgement is reversed.

JUSTICE BLACKMUN, dissenting.

Today the Court launches a missile to kill a mouse.

The State of South Carolina prohibited petitioner Lucas from building a permanent structure on his property from 1988 to 1990. Relying on an unreviewed (and implausible) state trial court finding that this restriction left Lucas' property valueless, this Court granted review to determine whether compensation must be paid in cases where the State prohibits all economic use of real estate. According to the Court, such an occasion never has arisen in any of our prior cases, and the Court imagines that it will arise "relatively rarely" or only in "extraordinary circumstances." Almost certainly, it did not happen in this case.

Nonetheless, the Court presses on to decide the issue, and as it does, it ignores its jurisdictional limits, remakes its traditional rules of review, and creates simultaneously a new categorical rule and an exception (neither of which is rooted in our prior case law, common law, or common sense). I protest not only the Court's decision, but each step taken to reach it. More fundamentally, I question the Court's wisdom in issuing sweeping new rules to decide such a narrow case. Surely, as Justice Kennedy demonstrates, the Court could have reached the result it wanted without inflicting this damage upon our Takings Clause jurisprudence. . . .

In short, I find no clear and accepted "historical compact" or "understanding of our citizens" justifying the Court's new taking doctrine. Instead, the Court seems to treat history as a grab-bag of principles, to be adopted where they support the Court's theory and ignored where they do not. If the Court decided that the early common law provides the background principles for interpreting the Taking Clause, then regulation, as opposed to physical confiscation, would not be compensable. If the Court decided that the law of a later period provides the background principles, then regulation might be compensable, but the Court would have to confront the fact that legislatures regularly determined which uses were prohibited, independent of the common law, and independent of whether the uses were lawful when the owner purchased. What makes the Court's analysis unworkable is its attempt to package the law of two incompatible eras and peddle it as historical fact.

The Court makes sweeping and, in my view, misguided and unsupported changes in our taking doctrine. While it limits these changes to the most narrow subset of government regulation—those that eliminate all economic value from land—these changes go far beyond what is necessary to secure petitioner Lucas' private benefit. One hopes they do not go beyond the narrow confines the Court assigns them to today.

I dissent.

▼▲▼

# *Dolan v. City of Tigard*
## 512 U.S. 374 (1994)

In accordance with a 1973 Oregon law that required localities to develop land-use programs consistent with state environmental objectives, Tigard, a suburb of Portland, decided to build a pedestrian and bicycle trail. Tigard passed a separate law that required that all new businesses opening along the trail to set aside part of their property for the trail.

Florence and John Dolan owned a plumbing and electrical supply store in downtown Tigard. They wanted to build an addition to their original store and pave their gravel parking lot. The local planning commission agreed to let the Dolans add their building space but required them to convert part of their land to public green space. The commission also required the Dolans to set aside a fifteen-foot strip of land for the pedestrian and bicycle trail. The Dolans claimed the commission's requirements amounted to a taking, since they were offered no compensation for their land. The commission claimed that the trail would actually increase the Dolans' business by offering additional access to their store.

Additional material on the Dolans' case is set out in the accompanying SIDEBAR.

The Court's decision was 5 to 4. Chief Justice Rehnquist delivered the opinion of the Court. Justices Souter, joined by Justices Blackmun and Ginsburg, filed a dissent. Justice Stevens wrote a separate dissent.

▼▲▼

CHIEF JUSTICE REHNQUIST delivered the opinion of the Court.

One of the principal purposes of the Takings Clause is "to bar Government from forcing some people alone to bear public burdens which, in all fairness and justice, should be borne by the public as a whole." *Armstrong* v. *United States,* (1960). Without question, had the city simply required petitioner to dedicate a strip of land along Fanno Creek for public use, rather than conditioning the grant of her permit to redevelop her property on such a dedication, a taking would have occurred. Such public access would deprive petitioner of the right to exclude others, "one of the most essential sticks in the bundle of rights that are commonly characterized as property."

On the other side of the ledger, the authority of state and local governments to engage in land use planning has been sustained against constitutional challenge as long ago as our decision in *Euclid* v. *Ambler Realty Co.,* (1926). "Government hardly could go on if to some extent values incident to property could not be diminished without paying for every such change in the general law." *Pennsylvania Coal Co.* v. *Mahon,* (1922). A land use regulation does not effect a taking if it "substantially advance[s] legitimate state interests" and does not "den[y] an owner economically viable use of his land." *Agins* v. *Tiburon,* (1980).

The sort of land use regulations discussed in the cases just cited, however, differ in two relevant particulars from the present case. First, they involved essentially legislative determinations classifying entire areas of the city, whereas here, the city made an adjudicative decision to condition petitioner's application for a building permit on an individual parcel. Second, the conditions imposed were not simply a limitation on the use petitioner might make of her own parcel, but a requirement that she deed portions of the property to the city. In *Nollan, supra,* we held that governmental authority to exact such a condition was circumscribed by the Fifth and Fourteenth Amendments. Under the well settled doctrine of "unconstitutional conditions," the government may not require a person to give up a constitutional right—here the right to receive just compensation when property is taken for a public use—in exchange for a discretionary benefit conferred by the government where the property sought has little or no relationship to the benefit.

Petitioner contends that the city has forced her to choose between the building permit and her right under the Fifth Amendment to just compensation for the public easements. Petitioner does not quarrel with the city's authority to exact some forms of dedication as a condition for the grant of a building permit, but challenges the showing made by the city to justify these exactions. She argues that the city has identified "no special benefits" conferred on her, and has not identified any "special quantifiable burdens" created by her new store that would justify the particular dedications required from her which are not required from the public at large.

In evaluating petitioner's claim, we must first determine whether the "essential nexus" exists between the "legitimate state interest" and the permit condition exacted by the city. If we find that a nexus exists, we must then decide the required degree of connection between the exactions and the projected impact of the proposed development. We were not required to reach this question in *Nollan,* because we concluded that the connection did not meet even the loosest standard. Here, however, we must decide this question. . . .

Undoubtedly, the prevention of flooding along Fanno Creek and the reduction of traffic congestion in the Central Business District qualify as the type of legitimate public purposes we have upheld. It seems equally obvious that a nexus exists between preventing flooding along Fanno Creek and limiting development within the creek's 100-year floodplain. Petitioner proposes to double the size of her retail store and to pave her now-gravel parking lot, thereby expanding the impervious surface on the property and increasing the amount of stormwater run-off into Fanno Creek. . . .

The same may be said for the city's attempt to reduce traffic congestion by providing for alternative means of transportation. In theory, a pedestrian/bicycle pathway provides a useful alternative means of transportation for workers and shoppers: "Pedestrians and bicyclists occupying dedicated spaces for walking and/or bicycling . . . remove potential vehicles from streets, resulting in an overall improvement in total transportation system flow."

The second part of our analysis requires us to determine whether the degree of the exactions demanded by the city's permit conditions bear the required relationship to the projected impact of petitioner's proposed development. Here the Oregon Supreme Court deferred to what it termed the "city's unchallenged factual findings" supporting the dedication conditions and found them to be reasonably related to the impact of the expansion of petitioner's business.

The city required that petitioner dedicate "to the city as Greenway all portions of the site that fall within the existing 100-year floodplain [of Fanno Creek] . . . and all property 15 feet above [the floodplain] boundary." In addition, the city demanded that the retail store be designed so as not to intrude into the greenway area. The city relies on the Commission's rather tentative findings that increased stormwater flow from petitioner's property "can only add to the public need to manage the [floodplain] for drainage purposes" to support its conclusion that the "requirement of dedication of the floodplain area on the site is related to the applicant's plan to intensify development on the site."

The city made the following specific findings relevant to the pedestrian/bicycle pathway: "In addition, the proposed expanded use of this site is anticipated to generate additional vehicular traffic thereby increasing congestion on nearby collector and arterial streets. Creation of a convenient, safe pedestrian/bicycle pathway system as an alternative means of transportation could offset some of the traffic demand on these nearby streets and lessen the increase in traffic congestion."

The question for us is whether these findings are constitutionally sufficient to justify the conditions imposed by the city on petitioner's building permit. Since state courts have been dealing with this question a good deal longer than we have, we turn to representative decisions made by them. . . .

It is axiomatic that increasing the amount of impervious surface will increase the quantity and rate of stormwater flow from petitioner's property. Therefore, keeping the floodplain open and free from development would likely confine the pressures on Fanno Creek created by petitioner's development. In fact, because petitioner's property lies within the Central Business District, the Community Development Code already required that petitioner leave 15% of it as open space and the undeveloped floodplain would have nearly satisfied that requirement. But the city demanded more—it not only wanted petitioner not to build in the floodplain, but it also wanted petitioner's property along Fanno Creek for its Greenway system. The city has never said why a public greenway, as opposed to a private one, was required in the interest of flood control.

The difference to petitioner, of course, is the loss of her ability to exclude others. As we have noted, this right to exclude others is "one of the most essential sticks in the bundle of rights that are commonly characterized as property." It is difficult to see why recreational visitors trampling along petitioner's floodplain easement are sufficiently related to the city's legitimate interest in reducing flooding problems along Fanno Creek, and the city has not attempted to make any individualized determination to support this part of its request. . . .

If petitioner's proposed development had somehow encroached on existing greenway space in the city, it would have been reasonable to require petitioner to provide some alternative greenway space for the public either on her property or elsewhere. But that is not the case here. We conclude that the findings upon which the city relies do not show the required reasonable relationship between the floodplain easement and the petitioner's proposed new building.

With respect to the pedestrian/bicycle pathway, we have no doubt that the city was correct in finding that the larger retail sales facility proposed by petitioner will increase traffic on the streets of the Central Business District. The city estimates that the proposed development would generate roughly 435 additional trips per day. Dedications for streets, sidewalks, and other public ways are generally reasonable exactions to avoid excessive congestion from a proposed property use. But, on the record before us, the city has not met its burden of demonstrating

## DOLAN V. CITY OF *TIGARD* AND *LUCAS* V. SOUTH CAROLINA COASTAL COUNCIL

*"Keep Your Laws Off My Sidewalks"*

> In every civilized society property rights must be carefully safeguarded;
> human rights and property rights are fundamentally . . . identical.
> —Theodore Roosevelt

In the final moments of the 1992 presidential election campaign, President George Bush, down in the polls, suddenly shifted gears away from his emphasis on education, job training, and government-supported growth strategies to reinvigorate the American economy and from his challenger, Arkansas Governor Bill Clinton. Having already referred to Clinton as "that clown," Bush now turned his attention to Al Gore, Clinton's vice-presidential nominee. Gore had just published *Earth in the Balance* (1992), a serious examination of the causes and possible solutions to the dangers confronting the global environment. Bush singled out Gore, whom he derided as the "Ozone Man," as representative of "environmental extremists" who cared more about the birds and trees than about good jobs for average Americans.

Bush's attack on Gore did nothing to boost the president's candidacy, but it did highlight the growing impatience of many corporations and industry trade associations with federal and state environmental policies. After the Court's decision in *Nollan v. California Coastal Commission* (1987), advocates for greater protection for property rights delved into litigation involving land use, zoning, and residential development, more confident than before that the courts would apply the Takings Clause to constrain government regulation. *Nollan* also stimulated a movement of grassroots activists and business groups to spur public awareness and legislative action to limit environmental controls. It called itself the "wise use" movement, a term it appropriated from Gifford Pinchot, the first head of the United States Forest Service. In 1910, Pinchot called for a national forestry policy based on the wise use of America's trees and minerals.

That triggered a long-simmering feud between Pinchot and John Muir, the founder of the Sierra Club. Muir viewed the wilderness as the spiritual center of the world and believed that government policies should value the wilderness for its own sake. The compromise was to combine national forests managed for resource extraction with wilderness areas managed for recreation. This solution, more or less, has remained federal policy.

The wise use movement that emerged in the late 1980s and early 1990s did not, however, share the moderate conservationism of Pinchot. Its founders selected the term because it was ambiguous, suggested sympathy with environmental protection, and fit neatly into newspaper headlines. Said Ron Arnold, one of its leaders, "Facts don't matter; in politics perception is reality." Funding for wise use groups has come from timber, mining, and chemical companies. In turn, they have claimed that the well-documented hole in the ozone layer does not exist, that airborne chemicals in the air and water are not harmful, much less cancer causing, and that trees will not grow properly unless forests are clear-cut.

*Lucas* gave the wise use movement another critical boost. In holding that South Carolina had violated the Takings Clause by rendering David Lucas's recently purchased beach-front residential lots worthless through a zoning regulation designed to protect the shoreline against erosion, the Court encouraged wise use groups to seek legislative reform in Congress and the states. *Lucas* did not give the wise use groups everything they wanted. Justice Scalia's opinion for the Court still held that the state had committed a taking if a regulatory action or seizure rendered private property *absolutely worthless.* But, by holding that states must show a more exact relationship between government regulation and the public interest, the Court did demonstrate that *Nollan* was no aberration and that future Takings Clause cases might go even further in protecting property owners.

By the end of 1992, a loose coalition of conservative public interest law firms and wise use groups had introduced takings legislation in twenty-seven states. Features of the legislation varied from state to state, depending on geography and the natural resources at issue (mining, coastal lands, forestry, wetlands, and so on). But the common theme was a lower "trigger point" for government's devaluation of property for a takings violation to occur. Rather than render a $975,000 investment worthless, as South Carolina had done in *Lucas,* states would commit a takings violation if they devalued land by 50 percent. In *Lucas,* South Carolina ended up purchasing the lots it "took" from David Lucas for $425,000 each, as well as paying him $725,000 to cover interest, attorneys' fees, and courts costs to settle the case. The state ultimately sold the land to a developer for $785,000 to recover its expenses. States might think twice before they acted if they knew the financial consequences.

Only three states, Arizona, Delaware, and Utah, enacted takings legislation into law by the time the Court decided *Dolan.* Two other states, Idaho and Wyoming, passed takings laws; in each case the governor vetoed them. But the Court's decision in *Dolan* jump started another round of legislative maneuverings in the states as well as in Congress. This time property rights groups were able to enact laws in more than a dozen more states within two years after *Dolan.* They were less successful in Congress, which held well-publicized hearings on federal takings policies but refused to enact legislation.

Florence and John Dolan actually received concerted interest group support in their challenge to the City of Tigard's land-use regulations. The Oregonians in Action Legal Center, the litigation arm of Oregonians in Action, a property rights lobbying organization that receives support from individuals and corporations, sponsored the Dolans' case from the moment it entered state trial court. Four years after the Court's decision, Tigard ended up settling with Florence Dolan—John died in the intervening period—for

Background
Doland Case
Cases of Interest
Articles
Litigation Report
Background
Join

# OREGONIANS IN ACTION
## Legal Center

### CITY OF TIGARD WILL PAY DOLANS $1.5 MILLION IN BIKEPATH "TAKINGS" CASE

**Tigard, OR** . . . Three and a half years ago, national attention was focussed on a precedent-setting U.S. Supreme Court decision on property rights. In Dolan v. City of Tigard (1994), the court struck down the city's effort to use its permitting power to force the Dolan family to give up part of their land for a public bikepath which, the Dolans contended, had no connection with the expansion of their A Boy Plumbing store.

But the case didn't end there. The high court allowed the city to try to establish that the bikepath condition was "roughly proportional" to the impact of the plumbing store expansion.

Finally, after long, costly city proceedings and protracted court litigation, the City of Tigard agreed this week to settle the case by paying the Dolan family $1,500,000 for a bikepath the city could have purchased eight years ago for about $14,000. At the time of settlement, the Dolans were in the midst of a jury trial seeking compensation for the unconstitutional "taking" of their land.

The Dolans were represented in their successful appeal to the U.S. Supreme Court by attorneys for Oregonians In Action Legal Center, a nonprofit organization that provides legal services without charge in property rights cases.

In the subsequent trial court proceedings, the Dolans were represented by John Shonkwiler, a Tigard land use attorney, and Joe Willis and Jill Gelineau, with the Portland based law firm, Schwabe, Williamson & Wyatt.

Bill Moshofsky, President of Oregonians In Action Legal Center, said "We are very pleased that the Dolans are finally getting significant compensation for what they suffered and expended over the past seven years, and that their long delayed building expansion can proceed unfettered by unconstitutional exactions."

"It's been a valiant struggle and they deserve a big round of applause for their perseverance and dedication to property rights protection."

"Also, we believe this settlement will help send a strong message to cities and counties everywhere that they must comply with the U.S. Supreme Court's decision. Much too often, cities and counties have been flaunting the high court's decision by using their permitting powers to `extort' land, rights of way, money or other concessions.

Copyright © 1998 by Oregonians In Action. All rights reserved. Send comments to Oregonians In Action..

HOME | Oregonians In Action
OIA Legal Center | OIA Education Center
OIA Political Action Committee | OIA-Ballot Measure PAC
Legislative News | Current Legal Cases
Looking Forward Magazine
Land-Use Forum | Library | Media List | Legislator List

Copyright © 1998 by Oregonians In Action. All rights reserved. Send comments to Oregonians In Action..

*Oregonians in Action, which represented the Dolans in their lawsuit against Tigard, Oregon, typifies the sophistication of litigating groups—full Web site, grassroots support, and effective public relations.*
Reprinted by permission of Oregonians in Action.

$1.4 million, plus $100,000 in attorneys' fees. The settlement also gave Mrs. Dolan the right to build a new store. In addition, a commemorative plaque of the Court's decision was erected on the pedestrian and bicycle path taken from the Dolans.

*Dolan* and *Lucas* attracted considerable amicus participation. Environmental protection groups such as the National Audubon Society, National Trust for Historic Preservation, and National Planning Association and more than a dozen state and local governments submitted briefs in support of Tigard's land-use policies. The Dolans received support from regional and national wise use groups and conservative public interest firms, whose briefs emphasized greater latitude for private development and right to compensation for taken property. Several briefs also encouraged the Court to modify the triggering point for a taking from absolute worthlessness to anywhere from 75 to 50 percent.

The legislative arena is no longer the primary battleground where standards are developed on the proper balance between public needs and private property rights. Since *Nollan* the courts have become ground zero in this resurgent, highly contested debate. Organizations from across the ideological divide have adapted their legal and political capabilities in accord with the flow of power between the courts and the legislative process, giving Takings Clause litigation a new and robust political flavor.

---

that the additional number of vehicle and bicycle trips generated by the petitioner's development reasonably relate to the city's requirement for a dedication of the pedestrian/bicycle pathway easement. The city simply found that the creation of the pathway "could offset some of the traffic demand . . . and lessen the increase in traffic congestion." . . .

No precise mathematical calculation is required, but the city must make some effort to quantify its findings in support of the dedication for the pedestrian/bicycle pathway beyond the conclusory statement that it could offset some of the traffic demand generated.

Cities have long engaged in the commendable task of land use planning, made necessary by increasing urbanization particularly in metropolitan areas such as Portland. The city's goals of reducing flooding hazards and traffic congestion, and providing for public greenways, are laudable, but there are outer limits to how this may be done.

The judgment of the Supreme Court of Oregon is reversed.

▼▲▼

## What Is Public Use?

The answer here is both simple and subtle. When government seizes the physical control of private property under the Takings Clause, the property must be put to public use, as is the case when government exercises a "regulatory taking," as in the case of environmental regulation. In the most traditional sense, eminent domain involves the seizure of property to create or expand government services. Road construction, affordable public housing, sewage repair, and schools are considered among these basic government functions. Property "taken" under such auspices is certain to be put to public use. Environmental regulation, historic preservation, and zoning requirements are all examples in which the government has exercised its regulatory powers for the purpose of putting private property to public use. Consider *Nollan, Lucas,* and *Dolan:* The issue in each case was whether the devaluation of private property entitled the owners to government compensation, not whether the asserted regulatory objectives put the properties so affected to public use.

Does the power of eminent domain permit the government to seize private property and then sell it to private companies if the sale of such property is designed to advance a public interest? This novel conception of the public use requirement was precisely the question the Court faced in *Hawaii Housing Authority* v. *Midkiff* (1984).[13] Writing for a unanimous Court, Justice Sandra Day O'Connor held that Hawaii's authority under its Land Reform Act of 1967 to compel the owners of residential lots to sell their properties to the government did not violate the public use requirement of the Takings Clause. The state, in turn, then sold the property back to private purchasers at more reasonable prices.

The Hawaii legislature had determined that such a seizure and resale of private property was the best tool available to break up the tightly held control of residential real estate. Even justices who would later form the core of the *Nollan, Lucas,* and *Dolan* majorities agreed. Why? How did the facts in *Midkiff* persuade the more property rights minded justices to side with the government?

---

# Hawaii Housing Authority v. Midkiff
## 467 U.S. 229 (1984)

In 1967 the Hawaii legislature enacted the Land Reform Act, authorizing the state to condemn tracts of residential property. The law was a response to a long tradition of concentrated land ownership that reached back to the islands' original settlement by Polynesian feudal barons. Even after the United States admitted Hawaii into the Union in 1959, this pattern continued, with ownership divided almost evenly between the federal government and fewer than one hundred private owners.

Frank Midkiff led an ownership group that held title to a large piece of property on Oahu, the most commercially developed of Hawaii's islands and home to its largest city, Honolulu. After his property was seized under the 1967 law, Midkiff refused to accept the state's price for his land. He filed suit in federal court, claiming that the Hawaiian law violated the Takings Clause by seizing his property without just compensation. The lower court agreed, but the United States Court of Appeals for the Ninth Circuit reversed.

The Court's decision was unanimous. Justice O'Connor delivered the opinion of the Court. Justice Marshall did not participate.

▼▲▼

JUSTICE O'CONNOR delivered the opinion of the Court.

The Fifth Amendment of the United States Constitution provides, in pertinent part, that "private property [shall not] be taken for public use, without just compensation." These cases present the question whether the Public Use Clause of that Amendment, made applicable to the States through the Fourteenth Amendment, prohibits the State of Hawaii from taking, with just compensation, title in real property from lessors and transferring it to lessees in order to reduce the concentration of ownership of fees simple in the State. We conclude that it does not. . . .

The starting point for our analysis of the Act's constitutionality is the Court's decision in *Berman v. Parker* (1954).

In *Berman,* the Court held constitutional the District of Columbia Redevelopment Act of 1945. That Act provided both for the comprehensive use of the eminent domain power to redevelop slum areas and for the possible sale or lease of the condemned lands to private interests. . . .

The Court explicitly recognized the breadth of the principle it was announcing, noting: "Once the object is within the authority of Congress, the right to realize it through the exercise of eminent domain is clear. For the power of eminent domain is merely the means to the end. . . . Once the object is within the authority of Congress, the means by which it will be attained is also for Congress to determine. Here one of the means chosen is the use of private enterprise for redevelopment of the area. Appellants argue that this makes the project a taking from one businessman for the benefit of another businessman. But the means of executing the project are for Congress and Congress alone to determine, once the public purpose has been established." The "public use" requirement is thus coterminous with the scope of a sovereign's police powers.

There is, of course, a role for courts to play in reviewing a legislature's judgment of what constitutes a public use, even when the eminent domain power is equated with the police power. But the Court in *Berman* made clear that it is "an extremely narrow" one. . . .

In short, the Court has made clear that it will not substitute its judgment for a legislature's judgment as to what constitutes a public use "unless the use be palpably without reasonable foundation."

To be sure, the Court's cases have repeatedly stated that "one person's property may not be taken for the benefit of another private person without a justifying public purpose, even though compensation be paid." . . . But where the exercise of the eminent domain power is rationally related to a conceivable public purpose, the Court has never held a compensated taking to be proscribed by the Public Use Clause.

On this basis, we have no trouble concluding that the Hawaii Act is constitutional. The people of Hawaii have attempted, much as the settlers of the original 13 Colonies did, to reduce the perceived social and economic evils of a land oligopoly traceable to their monarchs. The land oligopoly has, according to the Hawaii Legislature, created artificial deterrents to the normal functioning of the State's residential land market and forced thousands of individual homeowners to lease, rather than buy, the land underneath their homes. Regulating oligopoly and the evils associated with it is a classic exercise of a State's police powers. We cannot disapprove of Hawaii's exercise of this power.

Nor can we condemn as irrational the Act's approach to correcting the land oligopoly problem. The Act presumes that, when a sufficiently large number of persons declare that they are willing but unable to buy lots at fair prices, the land market is malfunctioning. When such a malfunction is signaled, the Act authorizes HHA to condemn lots in the relevant tract. The Act limits the number of lots any one tenant can purchase, and authorizes HHA to use public funds to ensure that the market dilution goals will be achieved. This is a comprehensive and rational approach to identifying and correcting market failure.

Of course, this Act, like any other, may not be successful in achieving its intended goals. But "whether *in fact* the provision will accomplish its objectives is not the question: the [constitutional requirement] is satisfied if . . . the . . . [state] Legislature *rationally could have believed* that the [Act] would promote its objective. When the legislature's purpose is legitimate and its means are not irrational, our cases make clear that empirical debates over the wisdom of takings—no less than debates over the wisdom of other kinds of socioeconomic legislation—are not to be carried out in the federal courts. Redistribution of fees simple to correct deficiencies in the market determined by the state legislature to be attributable to land oligopoly is a rational exercise of the eminent domain power. Therefore, the Hawaii statute must pass the scrutiny of the Public Use Clause.

The mere fact that property taken outright by eminent domain is transferred in the first instance to private beneficiaries does not condemn that taking as having only a private purpose. The Court long ago rejected any literal requirement that condemned property be put into use for the general public. As the unique way titles were held in Hawaii skewed the land market, exercise of the power of eminent domain was justified. The Act advances its purposes without the State's taking actual possession of the land. In such cases, government does not itself have to use property to legitimate the taking; it is only the taking's purpose, and not its mechanics, that must pass scrutiny under the Public Use Clause.

Similarly, the fact that a state legislature, and not the Congress, made the public use determination does not mean that judicial deference is less appropriate. Judicial deference is required because, in our system of government, legislatures are better able to assess what public purposes should be advanced by an exercise of the taking power. State legislatures are as capable as Congress of making such determinations within their respective spheres of authority. Thus, if a legislature, state or federal, determines there are substantial reasons for an exercise of the taking power, courts must defer to its determination that the taking will serve a public use.

The State of Hawaii has never denied that the Constitution forbids even a compensated taking of property when executed for no reason other than to confer a private benefit on a particular private party. A purely private taking could not withstand the scrutiny of the public use requirement; it would serve no legitimate purpose of government, and would thus be void. But no purely private taking is involved in these cases. The Hawaii Legislature enacted its Land Reform Act not to benefit a particular class of identifiable individuals, but to attack certain perceived evils of concentrated property ownership in Hawaii—a legitimate public purpose.

▼▲▼

*Midkiff* reinforced a 1954 decision, *Berman* v. *Parker*, in which the Court upheld a congressional statute that created a public-private partnership to encourage urban renewal and development in Washington, D.C. There, a unanimous Court held that the power of eminent domain permitted the state to require private entities to assist in the promotion of the public interest. Wrote Justice Douglas:

> For the power of eminent domain is merely the means to an end. Once the object is within the authority of Congress, the means by which it will be attained is also for Congress to determine. Here one of the means chosen is the use of private enterprise for redevelopment of the area. Appellants argue that this makes the project a taking from one businessman for the benefit of another businessman. But the means of executing the project are for Congress and Congress alone to determine, once the public purpose has been established. The public end may be as well or better served through an agency of private enterprise than through a department of government. . . .
>
> We cannot say that public ownership is the sole method of promoting the public purposes of community redevelopment projects.[14]

Together *Berman* and *Midkiff* authorize legislative bodies to delegate partial or full responsibility for the promotion of the public use provision of the Takings Clause to private companies. Government action may not, however, allow a private company to gain financially as a result. Even in the wake of *Lucas* and *Dolan*, the Court remains quite deferential to legislative definitions of public use.

## What Is Just Compensation?

The Court has defined just compensation for property owners as "what a willing buyer would pay in cash to a willing seller at the time of the taking."[15] In *Bauman* v. *Ross* (1897), the Court held that a market-based determination of just compensation can be adjusted by the courts if the owner receives a benefit disproportionate to the public's actual use of the property.[16] As for the matter of fairness in determining just compensation, the Court has ruled that "[a]ll that is essential is that in some appropriate way, before some properly constituted tribunal, inquiry shall be made as to the amount of compensation, and when this has been provided there is that due process of law which is required by the Federal Constitution."[17]

## Property Rights as Fundamental Rights?

Legal scholar Richard A. Epstein, one of the foremost (and most controversial) advocates of greater constitutional protection for property rights, has argued that the Takings Clause and the Free Speech Clause protect very similar values. Free speech is necessary so that individuals can develop their full potential and enjoy a realm of personal freedom in which they are free to act upon their thoughts. Free speech also contributes to equality by allowing individuals to voice their opinions free of government control or favoritism. Property serves much the same function, as it permits individuals a degree of independence and chance for self-improvement they would not have if the state monopolized the ownership of property or could seize it at will.[18]

Epstein has suggested that property rights receive a level of protection from the courts akin to free speech rights. He has drawn five analogies between the Takings and Free Speech Clauses that are worthy of analysis:[19]

- What is the asserted interest in protecting free speech or property rights? It could be unpopular speech, or beach-front property the government wishes to seize for a public purpose.

- What is the alleged constitutional harm? Did the government ban speech based on its content? Did the government "take" property without reason or fail to offer just compensation?

- What is the government's justification for limiting a constitutional right? Could it be to preserve order or to eliminate the market for child pornography? Could it be the historic preservation of a building or land site?

- What remedies are available to compensate the individual for the violation of a constitutional right? The remedy could be the issuance of a parade permit, an injunction against the government seizure of property, or the payment of just compensation to an owner.

- When does government have constitutional permission to limit otherwise fundamental rights? In both cases, when does the government satisfy a compelling public purpose?

Returning property rights to a preferred place among the personal freedoms now considered off-limits from the political branches carries with it an assumption that such rights are natural and central to the American constitutional order. Until the Constitutional Revolution of 1937, the Court largely subscribed to this view. Some scholars argue that societies reserve the right to change the centrality of certain rights in response to societal needs. The New Deal remains the preeminent example of how America fundamentally altered the distribution of economic power and social status in America without changing the Constitution. Property rights advocates have argued that such a transformation is permissible only through constitutional amendment. Indeed, Epstein has argued that massive reforms on the order of the New Deal are unconstitutional. The Constitution, rooted in the principle of limited government and based on enumerated powers, is simply not elastic enough to permit that kind of change. Moreover, the disintegration of property rights flies in the face of the Framers.[20] These are interesting arguments, applied to an interesting problem, with no obvious answer. With numerous groups poised to argue on behalf of greater protection for property rights, the last word on the Takings Clause is still to come.

## FOR FURTHER READING

Ackerman, Bruce. *Private Property and the Constitution.* New Haven, Conn.: Yale University Press, 1977.

Ely, James W., Jr. *The Guardian of Every Other Right: A Constitutional History of Property Rights.* New York: Oxford University Press, 1992.

Epstein, Richard A. *Takings: Private Property and the Power of Eminent Domain.* Cambridge, Mass.: Harvard University Press, 1985.

Meltz, Robert, Dwight H. Merriam, and Richard M. Frank. *The Takings Issue: Constitutional Limits on Land-Use Control and Environmental Regulation.* Washington, D.C.: Island Press, 1999.

Nedelsky, Jennifer. *Private Property and the Limits of American Constitutionalism.* Chicago: University of Chicago Press, 1990.

Paul, Ellen Frankel. *Liberty, Property, and the Foundations of the American Constitution.* Albany: State University of New York Press, 1988.

Siegan, Bernard H. *Economic Liberties and the Constitution.* Chicago: University of Chicago Press, 1980.

Sunstein, Cass R. *Free Markets and Social Justice.* New York: Oxford University Press, 1997.

# The Constitution of the United States

We the People of the United States, in Order to form a more perfect Union, establish Justice, insure domestic Tranquility, provide for the common defence, promote the general Welfare, and secure the Blessings of Liberty to ourselves and our Posterity, do ordain and establish this Constitution for the United States of America.

## Article I.

**Section 1.** All legislative Powers herein granted shall be vested in a Congress of the United States, which shall consist of a Senate and House of Representatives.

**Section 2.** The House of Representatives shall be composed of Members chosen every second Year by the People of the several States, and the Electors in each State shall have the Qualifications requisite for Electors of the most numerous Branch of the State Legislature.

No person shall be a Representative who shall not have attained to the age of twenty five Years, and been seven Years a Citizen of the United States, and who shall not, when elected, be an Inhabitant of that State in which he shall be chosen.

*Representatives and direct Taxes shall be apportioned among the several States which may be included within this Union, according to their respective Numbers, which shall be determined by adding to the whole Number of free Persons, including those bound to Service for a Term of Years, and excluding Indians not taxed, three fifths of all other Persons.*[1] The actual Enumeration shall be made within three Years after the first Meeting of the Congress of the United States, and within every subsequent Term of ten Years, in such Manner as they shall by Law direct. The Number of Representatives shall not exceed one for every thirty Thousand, but each State shall have at Least one Representative; and until such enumeration shall be made, the State of New Hampshire shall be entitled to chuse three, Massachusetts eight, Rhode-Island and Providence Plantations one, Connecticut five, New-York six, New Jersey four, Pennsylvania eight, Delaware one, Maryland six, Virginia ten, North Carolina five, South Carolina five, and Georgia three.

When vacancies happen in the Representation from any State, the Executive Authority thereof shall issue Writs of Election to fill such Vacancies.

The House of Representatives shall chuse their Speaker and other Officers; and shall have the sole Power of Impeachment.

**Section 3.** The Senate of the United States shall be composed of two Senators from each State, *chosen by the Legislature thereof,*[2] for six Years; and each Senator shall have one Vote.

Immediately after they shall be assembled in Consequence of the first Election, they shall be divided as equally as may be into three Classes. The Seats of the Senators of the first class shall be vacated at the Expiration of the second Year, of the second Class at the Expiration of the fourth Year, and of the third Class at the Expiration of the sixth Year, so that one third may be chosen every second Year; *and if Vacancies happen by Resignation, or otherwise, during the Recess of the Legislature of any State, the Executive thereof may make temporary Appointments until the next Meeting of the Legislature, which shall then fill such Vacancies.*[3]

No Person shall be a Senator who shall not have attained to the Age of thirty Years, and been nine Years a Citizen of the United States, and who shall not, when elected, be an Inhabitant of that State for which he shall be chosen.

The Vice President of the United States shall be President of the Senate, but shall have no Vote, unless they be equally divided.

The Senate shall chuse their other Officers, and also a President pro tempore, in the Absence of the Vice President, or when he shall exercise the Office of President of the United States.

The Senate shall have the sold Power to try all Impeachments. When sitting for that Purpose, they shall

---

*Note:* Those portions set in italic type have been superseded or changed by later amendments.
[1] Changed by the Fourteenth Amendment, Section 2.

[2] Changed by the Seventeenth Amendment.
[3] Changed by the Seventeenth Amendment.

be on Oath or Affirmation. When the President of the United States is tried the Chief Justice shall preside: And no Person shall be convicted without the Concurrence of two thirds of the Members present.

Judgment in Cases of Impeachment shall not extend further than to removal from Office, and disqualification to hold and enjoy any Office of honor, Trust or Profit under the United States: but the Party convicted shall nevertheless be liable and subject to Indictment, Trial, Judgment and Punishment, according to Law.

**Section 4.**   The Times, Places and Manner of holding Elections for Senators and Representatives, shall be prescribed in each State by the Legislature thereof; but the Congress may at any time by Law make or alter such Regulations, except as to the Places of chusing Senators.

The Congress shall assemble at least once in every Year, and such Meeting shall be on the *first Monday in December, unless they shall by Law appoint a different Day.*[4]

**Section 5.**   Each House shall be the Judge of the Elections, Returns and Qualifications of its own Members, and a Majority of each shall constitute a Quorum to do Business; but a smaller number may adjourn from day to day, and may be authorized to compel the Attendance of absent Members, in such Manner, and under such Penalties as each House may provide.

Each House may determine the Rules of its Proceedings, punish its Members for disorderly Behaviour, and, with the Concurrence of two thirds, expel a Member.

Each House shall keep a Journal of its Proceedings, and from time to time publish the same, excepting such Parts as may in their Judgment require Secrecy; and the Yeas and Nays of the Members of either House on any question shall, at the Desire of one fifth of those Present, be entered on the Journal.

Neither House, during the Session of Congress, shall, without the Consent of the other, adjourn for more than three days, nor to any other Place than that in which the two Houses shall be sitting.

**Section 6.**   The Senators and Representatives shall receive a Compensation for their Services, to be ascertained by Law, and paid out of the Treasury of the United States. They shall in all Cases, except Treason, Felony and Breach of the Peace, be privileged from Arrest during their Attendance at the Session of their respective Houses, and in going to and returning from the same; and for any Speech or Debate in either House, they shall not be questioned in any other Place.

No Senator or Representative shall, during the Time for which he was elected, be appointed to any civil Office under the Authority of the United States, which shall have been created, or the Emoluments whereof shall have been encreased during such time; and no Person holding any Office under the United States, shall be a Member of either House during his Continuance in Office.

**Section 7.**   All Bills for raising Revenue shall originate in the House of Representatives; but the Senate may propose or concur with Amendments as on other Bills.

Every Bill which shall have passed the House of Representatives and the Senate, shall, before it become a Law, be presented to the President of the United States; If he approve he shall sign it, but if not he shall return it, with Objections to that House in which it shall have originated, who shall enter the Objections at large on their Journal, and proceed to reconsider it. If after such Reconsideration two thirds of that House shall agree to pass the Bill, it shall be sent, together with the Objections, to the other House, by which it shall likewise be reconsidered, and if approved by two thirds of that House, it shall become a Law. But in all such Cases the Votes of both Houses shall be determined by yeas and Nays, and the Names of the Persons voting for and against the Bill shall be entered on the Journal of each House respectively. If any Bill shall not be returned by the President within ten days (Sundays excepted) after it shall have been presented to him, the Same shall be a Law, in like Manner, as if he had signed it, unless the Congress by their Adjournment prevent its Return, in which Case it shall not be a Law.

Every Order, Resolution, or Vote to which the Concurrence of the Senate and House of Representatives may be necessary (except on a question of Adjournment) shall be presented to the President of the United States; and before the Same shall take Effect, shall be approved by him, or being disapproved by him, shall be repassed by two thirds of the Senate and House of Representatives, according to the Rules and Limitations prescribed in the Case of a Bill.

**Section 8.**   The Congress shall have Power To lay and Collect Taxes, Duties, Imposts and Excises, to pay the Debts and provide for the common Defence and general Welfare of the United States; but all Duties, Imposts and Excises shall be uniform throughout the United States.

To borrow Money on the credit of the United States;

To regulate Commerce with foreign Nations, and among the several States, and with the Indian Tribes;

---

[4] Changed by the Twentieth Amendment, Section 2.

To establish an uniform Rule of Naturalization, and uniform Laws on the subject of Bankruptcies throughout the United States;

To coin Money, regulate the Value thereof, and of foreign Coin, and fix the Standard of Weights and Measures;

To provide for the Punishment of counterfeiting the Securities and current Coin of the United States;

To establish Post Offices and post Roads;

To promote the Progress of Science and useful Arts, by securing for limited Times to Authors and Inventors the exclusive Right to their respective Writings and Discoveries;

To constitute Tribunals inferior to the Supreme Court;

To define and punish Piracies and Felonies committed on the high Seas, and Offences against the Law of Nations;

To declare War, grant Letters of Marque and Reprisal, and make Rules concerning Captures on Land and Water;

To raise and support Armies, but no Appropriation of Money to that Use shall be for a longer Term than two Years;

To provide and maintain a Navy;

To make Rules for the Government and Regulation of the land and naval Forces;

To provide for calling forth the Militia to execute the Laws of the Union, suppress Insurrections and repel Invasions;

To provide for organizing, arming, and disciplining, the Militia, and for governing such Part of them as may be employed in the Service of the United States, reserving to the States respectively, the Appointment of the Officers, and the Authority of training the Militia according to the discipline prescribed by Congress;

To exercise exclusive Legislation in all Cases whatsoever, over such District (not exceeding ten Miles square) as may, by Cession of Particular States, and the Acceptance of Congress, become the Seat of the Government of the United States, and to exercise like Authority over all Places purchased by the Consent of the Legislature of the State in which the Same shall be, for the Erection of Forts, Magazines, Arsenals, dock-Yards and other needful Buildings;—And

To make all Laws which shall be necessary and proper for carrying into Execution the foregoing Powers, and all other Powers vested by this Constitution in the Government of the United States, or in any Department or Officer thereof.

**Section 9.** The Migration or Importation of such Persons as any of the States now existing shall think proper to admit, shall not be prohibited by the Congress prior to the Year one thousand eight hundred and eight, but a Tax or duty may be imposed on such Importation, not exceeding ten dollars for each Person.

The Privilege of the Writ of Habeas Corpus shall not be suspended, unless when in Cases of Rebellion or Invasion the public Safety may require it.

No bill of Attainder or ex post facto Law shall be passed.

No Capitation, or other direct, Tax shall be laid, *unless in Proportion to the Census or Enumeration herein before directed to be taken.*[5]

No Tax or Duty shall be laid on Articles exported from any State.

No Preference shall be given by any Regulation of Commerce or Revenue to the Ports of one State over those of another; nor shall Vessels bound to, or from, one State, be obliged to enter, clear or pay Duties in another.

No Money shall be drawn from the Treasury, but in Consequence of Appropriations made by Law; and a regular Statement and Account of the Receipts and Expenditures of all public Money shall be published from time to time.

No Title of Nobility shall be granted by the United States: And no Person holding any Office of Profit or Trust under them, shall, without the Consent of the Congress, accept of any present, Emolument, Office, or Title, of any kind whatever, from any King, Prince, or foreign State.

**Section 10.** No State shall enter into any Treaty, Alliance, or Confederation; grant Letters of Marque and Reprisal; coin Money; emit Bills of Credit; make any Thing but gold and silver Coin a Tender in Payment of Debts; pass any Bill of Attainder, ex post facto Law, or Law impairing the Obligation of Contracts, or grant any Title of Nobility.

No State shall, without the Consent of Congress, lay any Imposts or Duties on Imports or Exports, except what may be absolutely necessary for executing its inspection Laws; and the net Produce of all Duties and Imposts, laid by any State on Imports or Exports, shall be for the Use of the Treasury of the United States; and all such Laws shall be subject to the Revision and Controul of the Congress.

No State shall, without the Consent of Congress, lay any Duty of Tonnage, keep Troops, or Ships of War in time of Peace, enter into any Agreement or Compact

---

[5] Changed by the Sixteenth Amendment.

with another State, or with a foreign Power, or engage in War, unless actually invaded, or in such imminent Danger as will not admit of delay.

## Article II.

**Section 1.**   The executive Power shall be vested in a President of the United States of America. He shall hold his Office during the Term of four Years, and, together with the Vice President, chosen for the same Term, be elected, as follows

Each State shall appoint, in such Manner as the Legislature thereof may direct, a Number of Electors, equal to the whole Number of Senators and Representatives to which the State may be entitled in the Congress: but no Senator or Representative, or Person holding an Office of Trust or Profit under the United States, shall be appointed an Elector.

*The Electors shall meet in their respective States, and vote by Ballot for two Persons, of whom one at least shall not be an Inhabitant of the same State with themselves. And they shall make a List of all the Persons voted for, and of the Number of Votes for each; which List they shall sign and certify, and transmit sealed to the Seat of the Government of the United States, directed to the President of the Senate. The President of the Senate shall, in the Presence of the Senate and House of Representatives, open all the Certificates, and the Votes shall then be counted. The Person having the greatest Number of Votes shall be the President, if such Number be a Majority of the whole Number of Electors appointed; and if there be more than one who have such Majority, and have an equal Number of Votes, then the House of Representatives shall immediately chuse by Ballot one of them for President; and if no Person have a Majority, then from the five highest on the List said House shall in like Manner chuse the President. But in chusing the President, the Votes shall be taken by States, the Representation from each State having one Vote; a quorum for this Purpose shall consist of a Member or Members from two thirds of the States, and a Majority of all the States shall be necessary to a Choice. In every Case, after the Choice of the President, the Person having the greatest Number of Votes of the Electors shall be the Vice President. But if there should remain two or more who have equal Votes, the Senate shall chuse from them by Ballot the Vice President.*[6]

The Congress may determine the Time of chusing the Electors, and the Day on which they shall give their Votes, which Day shall be the same throughout the United States.

No Person except a natural born Citizen, or a Citizen of the United States, at the time of the Adoption of this Constitution, shall be eligible to the Office of President; neither shall any person be eligible to that Office who shall not have attained to the Age of thirty five Years, and been fourteen Years a Resident within the United States.

*In Case of the Removal of the President from Office, or of his Death, Resignation, or Inability to discharge the Powers and Duties of the said Office, the Same shall devolve on the Vice President, and the Congress may by Law provide for the Case of Removal, Death, Resignation or Inability, both of the President and Vice President, declaring what Officer shall then act as President, and such Officer shall act accordingly, until the Disability be removed, or a President shall be elected.*[7]

The President shall, at stated Times, receive for his Services, a Compensation, which shall neither be increased nor diminished during the Period for which he shall have been elected, and he shall not receive within that Period any other Emolument from the United States, or any of them.

Before he enter on the Execution of his Office, he shall take the following Oath or Affirmation:—"I do solemnly swear (or affirm) that I will faithfully execute the Office of President of the United States, and will to the best of my Ability preserve, protect and defend the Constitution of the United States."

**Section 2.**   The President shall be Commander in Chief of the Army and Navy of the United States, and of the Militia of the several States, when called into the actual Service of the United States; he may require the Opinion, in writing, of the principal Officer in each of the executive Departments, upon any Subject relating to the Duties of their respective Offices, and he shall have Power to grant Reprieves and Pardons for Offences against the United States, except in Cases of Impeachment.

He shall have Power, by and with the Advice and Consent of the Senate, to make Treaties, provided two thirds of the Senators present concur; and he shall nominate, and by and with the Advice and Consent of the Senate, shall appoint Ambassadors, other public Ministers and Consuls, Judges of the supreme Court, and all other Officers of the United States, whose Appoint-

---

[6] Superseded by the Twelfth Amendment.

[7] Modified by the Twenty-fifth Amendment.

ments are not herein otherwise provided for, and which shall be established by Law: but the Congress may by Law vest the Appointment of such inferior Officers, as they think proper, in the President alone, in the Courts of Law, or in the Heads of Departments.

The President shall have Power to fill up all Vacancies that may happen during the Recess of the Senate, by granting Commissions which shall expire at the End of their new Session.

**Section 3.**   He shall from time to time give to the Congress Information of the State of the Union, and recommend to their Consideration such Measures as he shall judge necessary and expedient; he may, on extraordinary Occasions, convene both Houses, or either of them, and in Case of Disagreement between them, with Respect to the Time of Adjournment, he may adjourn them to such Time as he shall think proper; he shall receive Ambassadors and other public Ministers; he shall take Care that the Laws be faithfully executed, and shall Commission all the Officers of the United States.

**Section 4.**   The President, Vice President and all civil Officers of the United States, shall be removed from Office on Impeachment for, and Conviction of, Treason, Bribery, or other high Crimes and Misdemeanors.

## Article III.

**Section 1.**   The judicial Power of the United States, shall be vested in one supreme Court, and in such inferior Courts as the Congress may from time to time ordain and establish. The Judges, both of the supreme and inferior Courts, shall hold their Offices during good Behaviour, and shall, at stated Times, receive for their Services, a Compensation, which shall not be diminished during their Continuance in Office.

**Section 2.**   The judicial Power shall extend to all Cases, in Law and Equity, arising under this Constitution, the Laws of the United States, and Treaties made, or which shall be made, under their Authority;—to all Cases affecting Ambassadors, other public Ministers and Consuls;—to all Cases of admiralty and maritime Jurisdiction;—to Controversies to which the United States shall be a Party;—to Controversies between two or more States;—*between a State and Citizens of another State*;[8]—between Citizens of different States;—between

Citizens of the same State claiming Lands under Grants of different States, and between a State, or the Citizens thereof, and foreign States, Citizens or Subjects.

In all Cases affecting Ambassadors, other public Ministers and Consuls, and those in which a State shall be Party, the supreme Court shall have original Jurisdiction. In all the other Cases before mentioned, the supreme Court shall have appellate Jurisdiction, both as to Law and Fact, with such Exceptions, and under such Regulations as the Congress shall make.

The Trial of all Crimes, except in Cases of Impeachment, shall be by Jury; and such Trial shall be held in the State where the said Crimes shall have been committed; but when not committed within any State, the Trial shall be at such Place or Places as the Congress may by Law have directed.

**Section 3.**   Treason against the United States, shall consist only in levying War against them, or in adhering to their Enemies, giving them Aid and Comfort. No Person shall be convicted of Treason unless on the Testimony of two Witnesses to the same overt Act, or on Confession in open Court.

The Congress shall have Power to declare the Punishment of Treason, but no Attainder of Treason shall work Corruption of Blood, or Forfeiture except during the Life of the Person attainted.

## Article IV.

**Section 1.**   Full Faith and Credit shall be given in each State to the public Acts, Records, and judicial Proceedings of every other State. And the Congress may by general Laws prescribe the Manner in which such Acts, Records and Proceedings shall be proved, and the Effect thereof.

**Section 2.**   The Citizens of each State shall be entitled to all Privileges and Immunities of Citizens in the several States.

A person charged in any State with Treason, Felony, or other Crime, who shall flee from Justice, and be found in another State, shall on Demand of the executive Authority of the State from which he fled, be delivered up, to be removed to the State having Jurisdiction of the Crime.

*No Person held to Service or Labour in one State, under the Laws thereof, escaping into another, shall, in Consequence of any Law or Regulation therein, be discharged from*

---

[8] Modified by the Eleventh Amendment.

*such Service or Labour, but shall be delivered up on Claim of the Party to whom such Service or Labour may be due.*[9]

**Section 3.**  New States may be admitted by the Congress into this Union; but no new State shall be formed or erected within the Jurisdiction of any other State; nor any State be formed by the Junction of two or more States, or Parts of States, without the Consent of the Legislatures of the States concerned as well as of the Congress.

The Congress shall have Power to dispose of and make all needful Rules and Regulations respecting the Territory or other Property belonging to the United States; and nothing in this Constitution shall be so construed as to Prejudice any Claims of the United States, or of any particular State.

**Section 4.**  The United States shall guarantee to every State in this Union a Republican Form of Government, and shall protect each of them against Invasion; and on Application of the Legislature, or of the Executive (when the Legislature cannot be convened) against domestic Violence.

## Article V.

The Congress, whenever two thirds of both Houses shall deem it necessary, shall propose Amendments to this Constitution, or, on the Application of the Legislatures of two thirds of the several States, shall call a Convention for proposing Amendments, which, in either Case, shall be valid to all Intents and Purposes, as Part of this Constitution, when ratified by the Legislatures of three fourths of the several States, or by Conventions in three fourths thereof, as the one or the other Mode of Ratification may be proposed by the Congress; Provided that no Amendment which may be made prior to the Year One thousand eight hundred and eight shall in any Manner after the first and fourth Clauses in the Ninth Section of the first Article; and that no State, without its Consent, shall be deprived of its equal Suffrage in the Senate.

## Article VI.

All Debts contracted and Engagements entered into, before the Adoption of this Constitution, shall be as valid against the United States under this Constitution, as under the Confederation.

[9] Changed by the Thirteenth Amendment.

This Constitution, and the Laws of the United States which shall be made in Pursuance thereof; and all Treaties made, or which shall be made, under the Authority of the United States, shall be the Supreme Law of the Land; and the Judges in every State shall be bound thereby, any Thing in the Constitution or Laws of any State to the Contrary notwithstanding.

The Senators and Representatives before mentioned, and the Members of the several State Legislatures, and all executive and judicial Officers, both of the United States and of the several States, shall be bound by Oath or Affirmation, to support this Constitution; but no religious Test shall ever be required as a Qualification to any Office or public Trust under the United States.

## Article VII.

The Ratification of the Conventions of nine States, shall be sufficient for the Establishment of this Constitution between the States so ratifying the Same.

Done in Convention by the Unanimous Consent of the States present the Seventeenth Day of September in the Year of our Lord one thousand seven hundred and Eighty seven and of the Independence of the United States of America the Twelfth In witness whereof We have hereunto subscribed our Names,

G°.ASHINGTON—*Presid.*[t]
*and deputy from Virginia*

| | |
|---|---|
| *New Hampshire* | John Langdon<br>Nicholas Gilman |
| *Massachusetts* | Nathaniel Gorham<br>Rufus King |
| *New Jersey* | Wil: Livingston<br>David Brearley<br>W.ᴹ Paterson<br>Jona: Dayton |
| *Pennsylvania* | B Franklin<br>Thomas Mifflin<br>Rob.ᵀ Morris<br>Geo. Clymer<br>Tho.ˢ FitzSimons<br>Jared Ingersoll<br>James Wilson<br>Gouv Morris |

| Connecticut | { | W.<sup>M</sup> SAM.<sup>L</sup> JOHNSON |
|---|---|---|
| | | ROGER SHERMAN |

Connecticut    { W<sup>M</sup> SAM<sup>L</sup> JOHNSON
               { ROGER SHERMAN

New York       ALEXANDER HAMILTON

Maryland       { JAMES M<sup>C</sup>HENRY
               { DAN OF S<sup>T</sup> THO<sup>S</sup> JENIFER
               { DAN<sup>L</sup> CARROLL

Virginia       { JOHN BLAIR—
               { JAMES MADISON JR.

North Carolina { W<sup>M</sup> BLOUNT
               { RICH<sup>D</sup> DOBBS SPAIGHT
               { HU WILLIAMSON

South Carolina { J. RUTLEDGE
               { CHARLES COTESWORTHY PINCKNEY
               { CHARLES PINCKNEY
               { PIERCE BUTLER

Delaware       { GEO: READ
               { GUNNING BEDFORD jun
               { JOHN DICKINSON
               { RICHARD BASSETT
               { JACO: BROOM

Georgia        { WILLIAM FEW
               { ABR BALDWIN

[The first ten amendments, known as the "Bill of Rights," were ratified in 1791.]

## Amendment I (1791)

Congress shall make no law respecting an establishment of religion, or prohibiting the free exercise thereof, or abridging the freedom of speech, or of the press; or the right of the people peaceably to assemble, and to petition the Government for a redress of grievances.

## Amendment II (1791)

A well regulated Militia, being necessary to the security of a free State, the right of the people to keep and bear Arms, shall not be infringed.

## Amendment III (1791)

No Soldier shall, in time of peace be quartered in any house without the consent of the Owner, nor in time of war, but in a manner to be prescribed by law.

## Amendment IV (1791)

The right of the people to be secure in their persons, houses, papers, and effects, against unreasonable searches and seizures, shall not be violated, and no Warrants shall issue, but upon probable cause, supported by Oath or affirmation, and particularly describing the place to be searched, and the persons or things to be seized.

## Amendment V (1791)

No person shall be held to answer for a capital, or otherwise infamous crime, unless on a presentment or indictment of a Grand Jury, except in cases arising in the land or naval forces, or in the Militia, when in actual service in time of War or public danger; nor shall any person be subject for the same offence to be twice put in jeopardy of life or limb; nor shall be compelled in any criminal case to be a witness against himself, nor be deprived of life, liberty, or property, without due process of law, nor shall private property be taken for public use, without just compensation.

## Amendment VI (1791)

In all criminal prosecutions, the accused shall enjoy the right to a speedy and public trial, by an impartial jury of the State and district wherein the crime shall have been committed, which district shall have been previously ascertained by law, and to be informed of the nature and cause of the accusation; to be confronted with the witnesses against him; to have compulsory process for obtaining witnesses in his favor, and to have the Assistance of Counsel for his defence.

## Amendment VII (1791)

In Suits at common law, where the value in controversy shall exceed twenty dollars, the right of trial by jury shall be preserved, and no fact tried by a jury, shall be otherwise reexamined in any Court of the United States, than according to the rules of the common law.

## Amendment VIII (1791)

Excessive bail shall not be required, nor excessive fines imposed, nor cruel and unusual punishments inflicted.

## Amendment IX (1791)

The enumeration in the Constitution, of certain rights, shall not be construed to deny or disparage others retained by the people.

## Amendment X (1791)

The powers not delegated to the United States by the Constitution, nor prohibited by it to the States, are reserved to the States respectively, or to the people.

## Amendment XI (1795)

The Judicial power of the United States shall not be construed to extend to any suit in law or equity, commenced or prosecuted against one of the United States by Citizens of another state, or by Citizens or Subjects of any Foreign State.

## Amendment XII (1804)

The Electors shall meet in their respective states and vote by ballot for President and Vice President, one of whom, at least, shall not be an inhabitant of the same state with themselves; they shall name in their ballots the person voted for as President, and in distinct ballots the person voted for as Vice President, and they shall make distinct lists of all persons voted for as President, and of all persons voted for as Vice President, and of the number of votes for each, which lists they shall sign and certify, and transmit sealed to the seat of government of the United States, directed to the President of the Senate;—The President of the Senate shall, in the presence of the Senate and House of Representatives, open all the certificates and the votes shall then be counted;—The person having the greatest number of votes for President, shall be the President, if such number be a majority of the whole number of Electors appointed; and if no person have such majority, then from the persons having the highest numbers not exceeding three on the list of those voted for as President, the House of Representatives shall choose immediately, by ballot, the President. But in choosing the President, the votes shall be taken by states, the representation from each state having one vote; a quorum for this purpose shall consist of a member or members from two-thirds of the states, and a majority of all the states shall be necessary to a choice. *And if the House of Representatives shall not choose a President whenever the right of choice shall devolve upon them, before the fourth day of March next following, then the Vice President shall act as President, as in the case of the death or other constitutional disability of the President.*—[10] The person having the greatest number of votes as Vice President, shall be the Vice President, if such number be a majority of the whole number of Electors appointed, and if no person have a majority, then from the two highest numbers on the list, the Senate shall choose the Vice President; a quorum for the purpose shall consist of two-thirds of the whole number of Senators, and a majority of the whole number shall be necessary to a choice. But no person constitutionally ineligible to the office of President shall be eligible to that of Vice President of the United States.

## Amendment XIII (1865)

**Section 1.** Neither slavery nor involuntary servitude, except as a punishment for crime whereof the party shall have been duly convicted, shall exist within the United States, or any place subject to their jurisdiction.

**Section 2.** Congress shall have power to enforce this article by appropriate legislation.

## Amendment XIV (1868)

**Section 1.** All persons born or naturalized in the United States and subject to the jurisdiction thereof, are citizens of the United States and of the State wherein they reside. No State shall make or enforce any law which shall abridge the privileges or immunities of citizens of the United States; nor shall any State deprive any person of life, liberty, or property, without due process of law; nor deny to any person within its jurisdiction the equal protection of the laws.

**Section 2.** Representatives shall be apportioned among the several States according to their respective numbers, counting the whole number of persons in each State, excluding Indians not taxed. But when the right to vote at any election for the choice of electors for

[10] Changed by the Twentieth Amendment, Section 3.

President and Vice President of the United States, Representatives in Congress, the Executive and Judicial officers of a State, or the members of the Legislature thereof, is denied to any of the male inhabitants of such State, being *twenty-one*[11] years of age and citizens of the United States, or in any way abridged, except for participation in rebellion, or other crime, the basis of representation therein shall be reduced in the proportion which the number of such male citizens shall bear to the whole number of male citizens twenty-one years of age in such State.

**Section 3.**   No person shall be a Senator or Representative in Congress, or elector of President and Vice President, or hold any office, civil or military, under the United States, or under any State, who, having previously taken an oath, as a member of Congress, or as an officer of the United States, or as a member of any State legislature, or as an executive or judicial officer of any State, to support the Constitution of the United States, shall have engaged in insurrection or rebellion against the same, or given aid or comfort to the enemies thereof. But Congress may by a vote of two-thirds of each House, remove such disability.

**Section 4.**   The validity of the public debt of the United States, authorized by law, including debts incurred for payment of pensions and bounties for services in suppressing insurrection or rebellion, shall not be questioned. But neither the United States nor any State shall assume or pay any debt or obligation incurred in aid of insurrection or rebellion against the United States, or any claim for the loss or emancipation of any slave; but all such debts, obligations and claims shall be held illegal and void.

**Section 5.**   The Congress shall have power to enforce, by appropriate legislation, the provisions of this article.

## Amendment XV (1870)

**Section 1.**   The right of citizens of the United States to vote shall not be denied or abridged by the United States or by any State on account of race, color, or previous condition of servitude.

**Section 2.**   The Congress shall have power to enforce this article by appropriate legislation.

[11] Changed by the Twenty-sixth Amendment.

## Amendment XVI (1913)

The Congress shall have power to lay and collect taxes on incomes, from whatever source derived, without apportionment among the several States, and without regard to any census or enumeration.

## Amendment XVII (1913)

The Senate of the United States shall be composed of two Senators from each State, elected by the people thereof, for six years; and each Senator shall have one vote. The electors in each State shall have the qualifications requisite for electors of the most numerous branch of the State legislatures.

When vacancies happen in the representation of any State in the Senate, the executive authority of such State shall issue writs of election to fill such vacancies: Provided, That the legislature of any State may empower the executive thereof to make temporary appointments until the people fill the vacancies by election as the legislature may direct.

This amendment shall not be so construed as to affect the election or term of any Senator chosen before it becomes valid as part of the Constitution.

## Amendment XVIII (1919)

**Section 1.**   *After one year from the ratification of this article the manufacture, sale, or transportation of intoxicating liquors within, the importation thereof into, or the exportation thereof from the United States and all territory subject to the jurisdiction thereof for beverage purposes is hereby prohibited.*

**Section 2.**   *The Congress and the several States shall have concurrent power to enforce this article by appropriate legislation.*

**Section 3.**   *This article shall be inoperative unless it shall have been ratified as an amendment to the Constitution by the legislatures of the several States, as provided in the Constitution, within seven years from the date of the submission hereof to the States by the Congress.*[12]

## Amendment XIX (1920)

The right of citizens of the United States to vote shall not be denied or abridged by the United States or by any State on account of sex.

[12] Repealed by the Twenty-first Amendment.

Congress shall have power to enforce this article by appropriate legislation.

## Amendment XX (1933)

**Section 1.** The terms of the President and Vice President shall end at noon on the 20th day of January, and the terms of Senators and Representatives at noon on the 3d day of January, of the years in which such terms would have ended if this article had not been ratified; and the terms of their successors shall then begin.

**Section 2.** The Congress shall assemble at least once in every year, and such meeting shall begin at noon on the 3d day of January, unless they shall by law appoint a different day.

**Section 3.** If, at the time fixed for the beginning of the term of the President, the President elect shall have died, the Vice President elect shall become President. If a President shall not have been chosen before the time fixed for the beginning of his term, or if the President elect shall have failed to qualify, then the Vice President elect shall act as President until a President shall have qualified; and the Congress may by law provide for the case wherein neither a President elect nor a Vice President elect shall have qualified, declaring who shall then act as President, or the manner in which one who is to act shall be selected, and such person shall act accordingly until a President or Vice President shall have qualified.

**Section 4.** The Congress may by law provide for the case of the death of any of the persons from whom the House of Representatives may choose a President whenever the right of choice shall have devolved upon them, and for the case of the death of any of the persons from whom the Senate may choose a Vice President whenever the right of choice shall have devolved upon them.

**Section 5.** Sections 1 and 2 shall take effect on the 15th day of October following the ratification of this article.

**Section 6.** This article shall be inoperative unless it shall have been ratified as an amendment to the Constitution by the legislatures of three-fourths of the several States within seven years from the date of its submission.

## Amendment XXI (1933)

**Section 1.** The eighteenth article of amendment to the Constitution of the United States is hereby repealed.

**Section 2.** The transportation or importation into any State, Territory, or possession of the United States for delivery or use therein of intoxicating liquors, in violation of the laws thereof, is hereby prohibited.

**Section 3.** This article shall be inoperative unless it shall have been ratified as an amendment to the Constitution by conventions in the several States, as provided in the Constitution, within seven years from the date of submission hereof to the States by the Congress.

## Amendment XXII (1951)

**Section 1.** No person shall be elected to the office of the President more than twice, and no person who has held the office of President, or acted as President, for more than two years of a term to which some other person was elected President shall be elected to the office of President more than once. But this Article shall not apply to any person holding the office of President when this Article was proposed by the Congress, and shall not prevent any person who may be holding the office of President, or acting as President, during the term within which this Article becomes operative from holding the office of President or acting as President during the remainder of such term.

**Section 2.** This Article shall be inoperative unless it shall have been ratified as an amendment to the Constitution by the legislatures of three-fourths of the several States within seven years from the date of its submission to the States by the Congress.

## Amendment XXIII (1961)

**Section 1.** The District constituting the seat of Government of the United States shall appoint in such manner as the Congress may direct:

A number of electors of President and Vice President equal to the whole number of Senators and Representatives in Congress to which the District would be entitled if it were a State, but in no event more than the least populous State; they shall be in addition to those appointed by the States, but they shall be considered, for the purposes of the election of President and Vice President, to be electors appointed by a State; and they shall meet in the District and perform such duties as provided by the twelfth article of amendment.

**Section 2.** The Congress shall have power to enforce this article by appropriate legislation.

## Amendment XXIV (1964)

**Section 1.** The right of citizens of the United States to vote in any primary or other election for President or Vice President, for electors for President or Vice President, or for Senator or Representative in Congress, shall not be denied or abridged by the United States or any State by reason of failure to pay any poll tax or other tax.

**Section 2.** The Congress shall have the power to enforce this article by appropriate legislation.

## Amendment XXV (1967)

**Section 1.** In case of the removal of the President from office or of his death or resignation, the Vice President shall become President.

**Section 2.** Whenever there is a vacancy in the office of the Vice President, the President shall nominate a Vice President who shall take office upon confirmation by a majority vote of both Houses of Congress.

**Section 3.** Whenever the President transmits to the President pro tempore of the Senate and the Speaker of the House of Representatives his written declaration that he is unable to discharge the powers and duties of his office, and until he transmits to them a written declaration to the contrary, such powers and duties shall be discharged by the Vice President as Acting President.

**Section 4.** Whenever the Vice President and a majority of either the principal officers of the executive departments or of such other body as Congress may by law provide, transmit to the President pro tempore of the Senate and the Speaker of the House of Representatives their written declaration that the President is unable to discharge the powers and duties of his office, the Vice President shall immediately assume the powers and duties of the office as Acting President.

Thereafter, when the President transmits to the President pro tempore of the Senate and the Speaker of the House of Representatives his written declaration that no inability exists, he shall resume the powers and duties of his office unless the Vice President and a majority of either the principal officers of the executive department[s] or of such other body as Congress may by law provide, transmit within four days to the President pro tempore of the Senate and the Speaker of the House of Representatives their written declaration that the President is unable to discharge the powers and duties of his office. Thereupon Congress shall decide the issue, assembling within forty-eight hours for that purpose if not in session. If the Congress, within twenty-one days after receipt of the latter written declaration, or, if Congress is not in session, within twenty-one days after Congress is required to assemble, determines by two-thirds vote of both Houses that the President is unable to discharge the powers and duties of his office, the Vice President shall continue to discharge the same as Acting President; otherwise, the President shall resume the powers and duties of his office.

## Amendment XXVI (1971)

**Section 1.** The right of citizens of the United States, who are eighteen years of age or older, to vote shall not be denied or abridged by the United States or by any State on account of age.

**Section 2.** The Congress shall have power to enforce this article by appropriate legislation.

## Amendment XXVII (1992)

No law varying the compensation for the services of the Senators and Representatives shall take effect, until an election of Representatives shall have intervened.

# Appendix 2

## How to Brief a Supreme Court Case

A case brief is a simple summary of the facts, questions, resolution, and holding of a Supreme Court decision. In many ways a brief serves a function similar to an outline of a short story or a book—it provides you with the essentials of the cast of characters, the story line, what happened along the way, the significance of the outcome, and how it fits into the larger picture. I encourage my students to brief the cases for three reasons:

1. It allows them to organize their notes and materials for class discussion in a much more effective way than thumbing through pages of notes and highlighted case opinions, saving time and encouraging better student preparation and participation.
2. It gives students the chance to build a filing system that will serve them well at exam time.
3. It permits the instructor to point out to students the important parts of the case they may have missed, underemphasized, or overstated.

### An Example:

### Lochner v. People of State of New York
### 198 U.S. 45 (1905)

*Facts:* In 1897 the New York legislature passed a law setting the maximum hours that bakers could work at ten per day and sixty per week. Joseph Lochner, who owned and operated the Lochner Bakery in Utica, located in upstate New York, was fined $50 for breaking the law. He challenged the New York Bakeshop Act as a violation of his "liberty of contract" rights under the Due Process Clause of the Fourteenth Amendment. He was unsuccessful in the New York courts and appealed to the United States Supreme Court.

*Legal Question:* Did the New York Bakeshop Act represent a valid exercise of police power to regulate the health and welfare of bakers?

*Decision:* By a 5-4 vote, the Court struck down the law.

*Majority Opinion:* Justice Peckham:

1. The New York law interferes with the right of contract between employers and employees concerning the number of hours bakers may work. The Court previously held in *Allgeyer v. Louisiana* (1897) that the right to liberty and property under the Fourteenth Amendment is absolute and may not be abridged except for the most compelling public health, safety, and welfare reasons.
2. No significant safety, moral, welfare, or public interest is affected by the New York law. Clean and wholesome bread does not depend on the number of hours per day or week a baker works. Any law infringing on the contract rights between employer and employee must have a more direct relationship to the public interest or the status of the employee.
3. The mere assertion of a public health interest does not necessarily render a law valid. Documentation must accompany any such legislation.

*Dissenting Opinion:* Justice Harlan:

1. Even recognizing the right to liberty of contract, the New York law represents valid public welfare legislation and should be upheld as such.

*Dissenting Opinion:* Justice Holmes:

1. The Constitution does not embody a particular economic theory. The New York law was a valid exercise of state police power to protect the health and welfare of bakers, not a violation of a fundamental liberty of contract right.
2. A judge's personal views on proper economic theory have nothing to do with the right of the majority to embody its opinions in law. The word *liberty* is perverted when the Fourteenth Amendment is interpreted to prevent the natural outcome of dominant opinion in a way that a rational person would consider fair and reasonable.
3. The New York law represents a reasonable measure to regulate health. Reasonable people can also inter-

pret the law as a proper means to regulate more generally the hours and conditions of work.

*General Significance:*

- *Lochner* became synonymous with the period of American constitutional development between the early 1900s and the late 1930s. During this time the Court used the liberty of contract theory to invalidate state efforts to enact wage, hour, workplace, and public health legislation.

- Justice Holmes's dissent is considered his greatest, both for its contribution to legal theory and the role of the courts in the American constitutional system.

## Internet Guide to Legal Research

Several excellent law and law-related research sites are available on the Internet. The sites listed offer great variety and are easy to locate. Two notes of caution:

1. Do not confuse pulling material off the Web with "real" research. Research is what you extract and find from the materials you have located. Cutting and pasting material without understanding its significance and how it supports your research inquiry is not research.

2. There is no substitute for actually reading—several times, if necessary—the case(s) you are trying to learn more about. Technology is a great asset in the learning process but cannot do the hard thinking for you.

The author welcomes additional suggestions for research sites and other Internet resources not mentioned here. Please contact the author at either: ivers@american.edu or through the *American Constitutional Law* Web site (www.college.hmco.com).

### General

**http://www.supremecourtus.gov**
The official site of the Supreme Court of the United States.

**http://www.findlaw.com/casecode/supreme.html**
Search by citation, party name, or full text for U.S. Supreme Court cases since 1983. Also provides links to a wealth of legal databases.

**http://supct.law.cornell.edu/supct/**
The Legal Information Institute offers all Supreme Court opinions issued since May 1990. In addition, this site has more than 580 of the Court's most important decisions dating back to 1793. This site also provides the Court calendar, the schedule of oral arguments, and a glossary of legal terms.

**http://www.fedworld.gov/supcourt/index.htm**
The site contains the full text of U.S. Supreme Court decisions from 1937 to 1975. You can search each case by using a keyword.

**http://www.washingtonpost.com/wp-srv/national/longterm/supcourt/supcourt.htm**
Use this site to access the Supreme Court docket, as well as the history and summary of major cases in the past few years.

**http://www.supremecourthistory.org**
The Supreme Court Historical Society is devoted to expanding public awareness of the Supreme Court's history and heritage.

**http://oyez.nwu.edu**
Oyez, Oyez, Oyez multimedia database: A searchable database of solicited cases, including summaries of both written decisions and oral arguments in audio biographies of every Supreme Court justice with links to their opinions and a virtual tour of the Supreme Court.

**http://www.courttv.com/legaldocs**
Court TV Law Center Library: This site has Supreme Court news and decisions, biographies of Supreme Court justices, a legal glossary, and a guide to the federal courts. This site categorizes cases according to topic such as business cases, civil rights cases, cyber law, government documents, and miscellaneous cases.

**http://www.americanlawyer.com**
The *American Lawyer* is a monthly journal that covers topics of general interest to practicing lawyers. The journal also offers criticism, book reviews, Supreme Court coverage, and first-person essays by lawyers on the work they do.

**http://www.legaltimes.com**
The *Legal Times* is a weekly newspaper offering general coverage of the legal profession, including important litigation, legal developments, personality profiles and many other features. The Web site offers daily coverage of breaking news stories of interest to lawyers and students on a state-by-state basis.

**http://www.cato.org**
The Cato Institute's Center for Constitutional Studies publishes daily articles on legal issues from a libertarian perspective.

**http://www.lawhost.com/suprctsrch.html**
A search engine for full text display of Supreme Court cases going back to 1893. Browse by year, U.S. Reports, or volume number or search by citation or case title.

**http://www.clubs.psu.edu/SCTSociety/links.htm**
This site not only includes important links to Supreme Court cases but also provides the link to state supreme courts as well as international courts. Furthermore, use this site to find out more about current constitutional issues.

**http://www.usc.edu/dept/law-lib/legal/topiclst.html**
This menu provides links to a variety of legal resources available on the Internet including federal and state statutes and case law, government information, and publications. Resources have been arranged by subject. This index is a service of the USC Law Library.

**http://www.westgroup.com/products/westlaw/**
Westlaw is an online legal research service that provides legal and business information drawn from more than 10,000 databases. You can access federal and state statutes and court cases, federal regulations, citation information, public records, news, business, and financial information.

**http://www.jmls.edu/Library/Journals.html**
A full text search of law journals on the Internet. Many links as well as individual journals regarding various aspects of the law. Look here for journals on gender issues, constitutional law, and civil law.

## Constitutional Law

**http://www.lectlaw.com/tcon.htm**
This site provides specific articles and issues related to the Bill of Rights and various other constitutional issues.

**http://www.law.indiana.edu/law/v-lib/**
Search a variety of articles written on constitutional law issues. This site also provides articles in other areas of the law such as civil, business, and criminal law.

**http://www.law.cornell.edu/topics/first_amendment.html**
First Amendment Law—Overview of First Amendment, which includes historic and more recent decisions. View U.S. court of appeals decisions regarding freedom of religion, press, and speech.

**http://www.fedlaw.gsa.gov/legal31.htm**
This site links you to the circuit appeals courts and searchable databases of their opinions.

**http://jurist.law.pitt.edu/ol_artcl.htm**
Online articles about constitutional law that give the current status of constitutional law today.

## Civil Rights Law

**http://www.ljx.com/practice/civilrights/index.html**
This site has news, case law, legal memos, statutes, and resources on civil rights issues from *Law Journal Extra!*

**http://www.law.cornell.edu/topics/civil_rights.html**
Overview of federal civil rights and discrimination law. Includes recent court decisions and text of civil rights statutes.

**http://www.eeoc.gov/qs-employees.html**
Outlines employee rights, equal opportunity laws, sexual harassment, discrimination, and the federal complaint process.

**http://fedlaw.gsa.gov:80/legal6.htm**
Fedlaw highlights civil liberties, civil rights, equal opportunity, and discrimination laws compiled by the General Services Administration.

**http://www.usdoj.gov/crt/crt-home.html**
This site is put together by the Civil Rights division of the Department of Justice and displays recent articles, speeches, special issues, and particular cases on the topic.

## U.S. Code

**http://www4.law.cornell.edu/uscode**
This legal information institute allows you to access parts of U.S. Code. You can search by title or refer to the table of popular names. If you know the title and section of the code you are looking for, you can search that way as well.

## Civil Rights and Liberties: Gender Issues

**http://www.law.cam.ac.uk/ESSAYS/SCHOL.HTM**
Legal essays indexed by subject. The list of subjects includes gender and the law, civil liberties, and procedures and constitutional law.

**http://www.aclu.org:80/issues/women/hmwo.html**
The American Civil Liberties Union provides recent developments in women's rights and links to other useful sites.

**http://dol.gov:80/dol/wb/**
U.S. Labor Department Women's Bureau publications. Includes statistics and data applicable to gender issues, searchable by region. Link to other sites and learn about recent developments.

**http://now.org:80/issues/economic/eratext.html**
The National Organization for Women provides information on the history of the Equal Protection Amendment and related articles.

**http://www.feminist.org/**
The Feminist Majority provides an updated account of current issues that are affecting women.

## Directory of Law Libraries Across the Country

**http://library.wcl.american.edu**
American University—Washington College of Law—includes information about the library and the entire catalog online.

**http://pappas-ntl.bu.edu/pappas.htm**
Boston University—Pappas Law Library

**http://lawwww.cwru.edu/cwrulaw/library/libinfo.html**
Case Western Reserve University Law Library

**http://clelaw.lib.oh.us/**
Cleveland Law Library Association—contains the law library catalog, Cuyahoga County, Ohio, court and agency information, research guides, and legal information services.

**http://users.ccnet.com/~ccllib/**
Contra Costa County Law Library

**http://www.lawschool.cornell.edu/lawlibrary/**
Cornell Law Library

**http://www.bcpl.gov.bc.ca/ell/**
Electronic Law Library—British Columbia, Canada—links to online legal information for British Columbians.

**http://www.law.emory.edu/LAW/law.html**
Emory University—Hugh F. MacMillan Law Library

**http://www.gmu.edu/departments/law/library/index.html**
George Mason University School of Law Library

**http://www.ll.georgetown.edu/**
Georgetown University Law Library—extensive source of legal information on the Internet.

**http://www.co.hennepin.mn.us/lawlibrary/lawlib.htm**
Hennepin County Law Library—library information and links to legal information.

**http://www.jenkinslaw.org/**
Jenkins Law Library—the county law library for the city and county of Philadelphia.

**http://lcweb2.loc.gov/glin/lawhome.html**
Law Library of Congress

**http://lawsocnsw.asn.au/resources/library/**
Law Society of New South Wales Library

**http://lalaw.lib.ca.us/**
Los Angeles County Law Library

**http://www.maricopa.gov/lawlibrary/**
Maricopa County Superior Court Law Library

**http://www.lawlib.state.md.us/**
Maryland State Law Library

**http://library.law.mercer.edu/**
Mercer University—Furman Smith Law Library

**http://www.osu.edu/units/law/law3.htm**
Michael E. Moritz Law Library—Ohio State University College of Law

**http://www.courts.state.mn.us/library/**
Minnesota State Law Library—includes an archive of Minnesota appellate court opinions, library information, and other legal research content and links.

**http://www.library.nwu.edu/law/**
Northwestern University Law Library

**http://wwwl.sdcll.org**
San Diego County Public Law Library—provides legal research and reference books for attorneys, lawyers, judges, and citizens. Automated legal research and access services available.

**http://pw1.netcom.com/~smcll/smcll.htm**
San Mateo County Law Library

**http://www.socialaw.com/**
Social Law Library—Boston, Massachusetts—private, not-for-profit institution serving the research needs of the practicing and the judiciary in Massachusetts.

**http://www.aallnet.org/chapter/scall/**
Southern California Association of Law Libraries (SCALL)

**http://www.siu.edu/offices/lawlib/**
Southern Illinois University School of Law Library

**http://www.stanford.edu/group/law/library/index.html**
Stanford University—Robert Crown Law Library

**http://www.lawlibrary.state.mt.us**
State Law Library of Montana

**http://www.sclqld.org.au**
Supreme Court Library of Queensland—contains information on legal research.

**http://www.sll.courts.state.tx.us/**
Texas State Law Library—provides access to basic sources of legal information for citizens and state entities.

**http://www.law.berkeley.edu/library/index.shtml**
University of California at Berkeley—Boalt Hall Library

**http://lawlibrary.ucdavis.edu/**
University of California at Davis

**http://www.lib.uchicago.edu/LibInfo/Law/**
University of Chicago—D'Angelo Law Library

**http://stripe.colorado.edu/~lawlib/Home.html**
University of Colorado Law Library

**http://www.lawlib.uh.edu/Libraries/**
University of Houston Law Libraries

**http://www.law.miami.edu/library/**
University of Miami Law School Library

**http://www.olemiss.edu/depts/law_library_school/libndex.html**
University of Mississippi—Law Library

**http://library.usask.ca/law/**
University of Saskatchewan Law Library—with links to internal resources and to electronic legal material in numerous Canadian, American, and international legal sites.

**http://www.usc.edu/dept/law-lib/**
University of Southern California—Law Center and Law Library

**http://www.law.usyd.edu.au/~library/**
University of Sydney Law Library

**http://www.law.utexas.edu/**
University of Texas at Austin—Tarlton Law Library

**http://lib.law.washington.edu**
University of Washington Gallagher Law Library

**http://www.vermontlaw.edu/library/library.htm**
Vermont Law School—Cornell Library

**http://www.droit.umontreal.ca/doc/biblio/en/index.html**
Virtual Canadian Law Library

**http://198.187.0.226/courts/lawlib/home.htm**
Washington State Law Library

**http://elsinore.cis.yale.edu/lawweb/lawlib.htm**
Yale Law School—Lillian Goldman Library

# Notes

## Chapter 1

1. Kermit L. Hall, *The Magic Mirror: Law in American History* (New York: Oxford University Press, 1989), pp. 4–8.
2. Alexander Hamilton, John Jay, and James Madison, *The Federalist Papers,* Clinton Rossiter, ed. (New York: Mentor Books, 1961), p. 301. (All references from here on are taken from this edition.)
3. Ibid.
4. Ibid., p. 322.
5. *Federalist 1,* p. 33 (emphasis added).
6. Quoted in Hall, *The Magic Mirror,* p. 67.
7. Michael Kammen, *A Machine That Would Go of Itself: The Constitution in American Culture* (New York: Vintage Books, 1987), pp. 1–39.
8. "Essays of 'Brutus' to the Citizens of the State of New-York," in Michael Kammen, ed. *Origins of the American Constitution* (New York: Penguin Books, 1986), pp. 304–305.
9. Herbert J. Storing, *What the Anti-Federalists Were For* (Chicago: University of Chicago Press, 1981), p. 24.
10. *Federalist 23,* p. 157.
11. Storing, *What the Anti-Federalists Were For,* p. 29.
12. Ibid.
13. *Federalist 44,* p. 284.
14. Ibid., p. 47.
15. David F. Epstein, *The Political Theory of the Federalist* (Chicago: University of Chicago Press, 1984).
16. *Federalist 47,* p. 301 (emphasis added).
17. Epstein, *Political Theory of the Federalist,* p. 127.
18. John Locke, *Second Treatise of Government,* chapter 11, section 136, pp. 405–406.
19. Epstein, *Political Theory of the Federalist,* pp. 126–130.
20. *Federalist 51,* p. 322 (emphasis added).
21. Quoted in Storing, *What the Anti-Federalists Were For,* p. 34.
22. *Federalist 39,* p. 246.
23. Ibid., pp. 244–245.
24. *Federalist 51,* p. 322.
25. Catherine Drinker Bowen, *Miracle at Philadelphia* (New York: Little, Brown, 1986), p. 243.
26. Quoted in Storing, *What the Anti-Federalists Were For,* pp. 64–65.
27. Ibid., p. 66.
28. *Federalist 84,* p. 515.
29. Quoted in Storing, *What the Anti-Federalists Were For,* p. 66.
30. In Chapter 2 I discuss in greater depth what "natural law" is and the place that some legal and political theorists see for natural law in constitutional interpretation.
31. Quoted in Storing, *What the Anti-Federalists Were For,* p. 70
32. Thomas Jefferson, *The Papers of Thomas Jefferson,* vol. 12, Julian Boyd, ed. (Princeton, N.J.: Princeton University Press, 1950) p. 440.
33. Richard C. Cortner, "Strategies and Tactics in Litigants in Constitutional Cases," *Journal of Public Law* 17 (1968) pp. 287–307.
34. George L. Watson and John A. Stookey, *Shaping America: The Politics of Supreme Court Appointments* (New York: Harper-Collins, 1995).
35. *NAACP v. Button,* 371 U.S. 415 (1963), at 429–430.

## Chapter 2

1. Mark Hertsgaard, *A Day in the Life: The Music and Artistry of the Beatles* (New York: Delacorte Press, 1995), p. 58.
2. Jack N. Rakove, *Original Meanings: Politics and Ideas in the Making of the Constitution* (New York: Alfred A. Knopf, 1997), pp. 3–22.
3. Thomas L. Pangle, *The Spirit of Modern Republicanism* (Chicago: University of Chicago Press, 1988), pp. 1–12.
4. Thomas L. Pangle, "The Philosophic Understandings of Human Nature Informing the Constitution," in *Confronting the Constitution,* Allan Bloom, ed. (Washington, D.C.: American Enterprise Institute, 1990), p. 9.
5. Harry H. Wellington, *Interpreting the Constitution* (New Haven, Conn.: Yale University Press, 1990), pp. 54–55.
6. For an effective discussion of this literature, see Lee Epstein and Jack Knight, *The Choices Justices Make* (Washington, D.C.: Congressional Quarterly, 1997); Jeffrey A. Segal and Harold J. Spaeth, *The Supreme Court and the Attitudinal Model* (New York: Cambridge University Press, 1993); and the pioneering work in this area, C. Herman Pritchett, "Divisions of Opinion Among Justices of the U.S. Supreme Court, 1939–41," *American Political Science Review* 35 (1941), pp. 890–898.
7. Cass R. Sunstein, *The Partial Constitution* (Cambridge, Mass.: Harvard University Press, 1993), p. 119.
8. Robert H. Bork, *The Tempting of America: The Political Seduction of the Law* (New York: The Free Press, 1990).
9. For a rich and even-handed treatment of the Bork nomination, see Ethan Bronner, *Battle for Justice* (New York: W. W. Norton, 1989).
10. George L. Watson and John A. Stookey, *Shaping America, The Politics of Supreme Court Appointments* (New York: Harper-Collins, 1995); John Anthony Maltese, *The Selling of Supreme Court Nominees* (Baltimore: Johns Hopkins University Press, 1998).
11. Edwin Meese III, "Address Before the American Bar Association," Washington, D.C., July 12, 1985.
12. William J. Brennan, "Address to the Text and Teaching Symposium," Georgetown University, Washington, D.C., October 12, 1985 (emphasis added).
13. Judge Bork took Justice Brennan directly to task as one the offenders of "liberal constitutional revisionism" in *The Tempting of America,* pp. 219–220.
14. Maltese, *Selling of Supreme Court Nominees,* pp. 137–138.
15. For a discussion of Judge Bork's difficulties before the Senate Judiciary Committee with *Brown* and *Roe,* see Bronner, *Battle for Justice,* pp. 231–232, 292–293. Judge Bork's criticism of *Roe* was much harsher than his criticism of *Brown,* which he called a "great and correct decision, but . . . in all candor . . . supported by a very weak opinion." See Bork, *The Tempting of America,* pp. 74–84. *Roe,* on the other hand, was "itself,

an unconstitutional decision, a serious and wholly unjustifiable judicial usurpation of state legislative authority." Testimony of Robert H. Bork, *Hearings on a Bill to Provide That Human Life Shall Be Deemed to Exist from Conception,* J-97-16, April, May, June 1981, p. 310.

16. Bork, *The Tempting of America,* pp. 159–166.

17. Ibid., pp. 147, 165, 166.

18. Michael Kammen, *The Origins of the American Constitution* (New York: Penguin Books, 1986), pp. 90–93.

19. James H. Hutson, "The Creation of the Constitution: The Integrity of the Documentary Record," *Texas Law Review* 65 (1986): 1–39, p. 2.

20. Bork, *The Tempting of America,* p. 176.

21. Sunstein, *The Partial Constitution,* p. 99.

22. H. Jefferson Powell, "The Original Understanding of Original Intent," *Harvard Law Review* 98 (1985): 885–948, p. 948.

23. Sunstein, *The Partial Constitution,* p. 107.

24. *Ferguson* v. *Skrupa,* 372 U.S. 726 (1963), at 732.

25. Tinsley E. Yarbrough, *Mr. Justice Black and His Critics* (Durham, N.C.: Duke University Press, 1988), pp. 39–40.

26. *Youngstown Sheet & Tube Co.* v. *Sawyer,* 343 U.S. 579, 587-89 (1952).

27. Leonard W. Levy, *The Emergence of a Free Press* (New York: Oxford University Press, 1985). When this book was published under its original title, *Legacy of Suppression: Freedom of Speech and Press in Early American History* (Cambridge, Mass.: Harvard University Press), in 1960, Justice Black remarked that "it raised disquieting questions about the constitutional future of the United States. [It] seems to be part of a well organized, carefully planned advocacy of a philosophy which reduces all of the Constitution's affirmations and prohibitions to a rather lowly standard of reasonableness as determined by judges. Whether this is good for a country or not, I am unable to persuade myself up to now that it is what our Constitution meant." The latter quote is taken from Roger K. Newman, *Hugo Black* (New York: Pantheon Books, 1994), p. 498.

28. Hugo L. Black, *A Constitutional Faith* (New York: Alfred A. Knopf, 1969), pp. 45–46.

29. Bork, *The Tempting of America,* pp. 333–336.

30. Robert Hale, "Coercion and Distribution in a Supposedly Non-Coercive State," *Political Science Quarterly* 38 (1923), pp. 470–494; Morris Cohen, "Property and Sovereignty," *Cornell Law Quarterly* 13 (1927), pp. 8–30.

31. Oliver Wendell Holmes Jr., *The Common Law,* 2nd. ed., Mark DeWolfe Howe, ed. (Cambridge, Mass.: Harvard University Press, 1963).

32. Ibid., p. 5.

33. "The Place of Justice Holmes in American Legal Thought," in Robert W. Gordon, ed., *The Legacy of Oliver Wendell Holmes, Jr.* (Stanford, Calif.: Stanford University Press, 1992), p. 63.

34. Philipa Strum, *Louis D. Brandeis: Justice for the People* (New York: Schoken, 1984), p. 337.

35. 208 U.S. 412 (1908).

36. Herbert Wechsler, "Toward Neutral Principles of Constitutional Law," *Harvard Law Review* 73 (1959), pp. 1–35.

37. Richard Kluger, *Simple Justice* (New York: Alfred A. Knopf, 1976).

38. Ronald Kahn, *The Supreme Court and Constitutional Theory, 1953–1993* (Lawrence: University Press of Kansas, 1994), pp. 87–89.

39. John Hart Ely, *Democracy and Distrust* (Cambridge, Mass.: Harvard University Press, 1980), pp. 181, 11–41.

40. Wellington, *Interpreting the Constitution,* p. 67.

41. Ely, *Democracy and Distrust,* pp. 11–14.

42. Sunstein, *The Partial Constitution,* pp. 104–105.

43. See, for example, Laurence Tribe, "The Puzzling Persistence of Process Based Constitutional Theories," *Yale Law Journal* 89 (1980), pp. 1063–1080; Tribe, *American Constitutional Law,* 2nd ed. (Mineola, Minn.: Foundation Press, 1988); Ronald Dworkin, *Law's Empire* (Cambridge, Mass.: Harvard University Press, 1986); and Dworkin, *Taking Rights Seriously* (Cambridge, Mass.: Harvard University Press, 1977).

44. Ronald Dworkin, *A Matter of Principle* (Cambridge, Mass.: Harvard University Press, 1985).

45. John H. Garvey, *What Are Freedoms For?* (Cambridge, Mass.: Harvard University Press, 1996).

46. Sunstein, *The Partial Constitution,* pp. 25–37.

47. Forrest McDonald, *Novus Ordo Seclorum: The Intellectual Origins of the Constitution* (Lawrence: University Press of Kansas, 1985), pp. 57–60.

48. Edward S. Corwin, "The 'Higher Law' Background of American Constitutional Law," *Harvard Law Review* 42 (1928), pp. 149–185, 365–409.

49. Benjamin F. Wright, *American Interpretations of Natural Law* (Cambridge, Mass.: Harvard University Press, 1931), pp. 339–340.

50. 60 U.S. 393 (1857).

51. 83 U.S. 130 (1872), at 141.

52. 163 U.S. 537 (1896), at 544.

53. Garry Wills, *Inventing America* (Garden City, N.Y.: Doubleday, 1978), p. xiii.

54. These are discussed and criticized in Bork, *The Tempting of America,* pp. 209–210. Bork opposes the use of natural law theories in constitutional interpretation.

55. Ely, *Democracy and Distrust,* p. 49.

56. Erwin Chemerinsky, "Foreword: The Vanishing Constitution," *Harvard Law Review* 103 (1989): 43–104, p. 104.

## *Chapter 3*

1. Marvin Miller, *A Whole Different Ballgame* (New York: Simon & Schuster, 1991); John Heylar, *Lords of the Realm* (New York: Villard Books, 1994); Geoffrey C. Ward and Ken Burns, *Baseball: An Illustrated History* (New York: Alfred A. Knopf, 1994).

2. *Federal Baseball Club* v. *The National League,* 259 U.S. 200 (1922).

3. *Toolson* v. *New York Yankees,* 346 U.S. 356 (1953).

4. Quoted in Miller, *A Whole Different Ballgame,* pp. 190–191.

5. *Flood* v. *Kuhn,* 407 U.S. 258 (1972).

6. Ibid., at 292.

7. Alexander Hamilton, John Jay, and James Madison, *The Federalist Papers,* Clinton Rossiter, ed. (New York: Mentor Books, 1961), p. 465.

8. Alexander M. Bickel, *The Least Dangerous Branch* (New Haven, Conn.: Yale University Press, 1961), p. 1.

9. Quoted in Herbert J. Storing, *What the Anti-Federalists Were For* (Chicago: University of Chicago, 1981), p. 50.

10. *Federalist* 47, pp. 300–301.

11. *Federalist* 78, p. 465.

12. Alfred H. Kelly, Winfred A. Harbison, and Herman Belz, *The American Constitution: Its Origins and Development* (New York: W. W. Norton, 1991), pp. 159–160.

13. Susan R. Burgess, *Contest for Constitutional Authority* (Lawrence: University Press of Kansas, 1992); Louis Fisher, *Constitutional Dialogues* (Princeton, N.J.: Princeton University Press, 1988).

14. Bickel, *The Least Dangerous Branch*, p. 1; Christopher Wolfe, *The Rise of Modern Judicial Review* (New York: Basic Books, 1986), pp. 17–37.

15. *Brown v. Allen*, 344 U.S. 443 (1953), at 540.

16. Kelly, Harbison, and Belz, *The American Constitution*, pp. 157–159.

17. Kermit L. Hall, *The Magic Mirror* (New York: Oxford University Press, 1989), pp. 71–72.

18. Kelly, Harbison, and Belz, *The American Constitution*, pp. 157–158.

19. Edward Keynes and Randall K. Miller, *The Court v. Congress* (Durham, N.C.: Duke University Press, 1989), p. 309.

20. Felix Frankfurter and James M. Landis, *The Business of the Supreme Court: A Study in the Federal Judicial System* (New York: Macmillan, 1928), pp. 1–14.

21. Virginia and Massachusetts received additional district courts in order to hear additional cases from Kentucky, then part of Virginia, and Maine, then part of Massachusetts.

22. Hall, *Magic Mirror*, p. 75.

23. *Federalist* 78, p. 469.

24. 2 Dall. 419 (1793), at 457.

25. Ibid., at 471.

26. E.g., *Ware v. Hylton*, 3 Dall. 199 (1796), in which the Court held that states could not pass laws that impeded the terms and conditions of treaties established between the United States and foreign countries.

27. In 1891, Congress eliminated circuit riding for good and authorized the president to appoint judges to serve on the appeals courts but left in place the three-judge panel requirement.

28. 1 Cranch 137 (1803), at 177, 178, 180 (emphasis in original).

29. Robert A. Burt, *The Constitution in Conflict* (Cambridge, Mass.: Harvard University Press, 1992), pp. 105–132.

30. *Federalist* 78, pp. 466, 468.

31. 1 Cranch, at 177–178.

32. Benjamin F. Wright, *The Growth of American Constitutional Law* (New York: Holt, 1942), pp. 15–16.

33. In 1914, Congress enacted legislation that further expanded the Court's jurisdiction over cases arising from state courts. The Judiciary Act of 1914 authorized the Court to issue writs of certiorari, or orders that required a lower court to send up a case for appellate review, in cases where state courts had upheld, and not just denied, a federal claim or right.

34. 6 Wheat. 264 (1821), at 414.

35. Quoted in Charles Warren, *The Supreme Court in United States History* (Boston: Little, Brown, 1935), vol. 1., p. 265.

36. Ibid., p. 562.

37. E.g., *McCullough v. Maryland*, 4 Wheat. 316 (1819); *Gibbons v. Ogden*, 9 Wheat. 1 (1824).

38. Ibid., pp. 192, 211–233.

39. Wolfe, *The Rise of Modern of Judicial Review*, p. 95.

40. 358 U.S. 1 (1958), at 18.

41. Burt, *The Constitution in Conflict*, pp. 287–288.

42. In *Smith*, Justice Scalia, who wrote the Court's much-criticized opinion, noted that the "compelling interest" test at issue was "familiar from other fields." Indeed it is, as the compelling interest test is the jurisprudential standard in cases involving civil rights and liberties claims.

43. Joan Biskupic, "Supreme Court Overturns Religious Practice Statute," *Washington Post*, June 26, 1997, p. 1. The quotation is from Douglas Laycock, a University of Texas law professor who was instrumental in the drafting and passage of the Religious Freedom Restoration Act of 1993.

44. Linda Greenhouse, "Supreme Court Quashes Law Expanding Religious Rights," *New York Times*, June 26, 1997, p. 1.

45. The remainder of our discussion of congressional power over federal court jurisdiction is adapted from Keynes and Miller, *The Court v. Congress*, pp. 2–25.

46. 7 Wall 506 (1869), at 514, 515.

47. *Ex parte Yerger*, 8 Wall. 85 (1869), at 104.

48. For a detailed examination of the legislative proposals designed to eliminate the Court's jurisdiction in school prayer, abortion, and school desegregation cases, see Keynes and Miller, *The Court v. Congress*, pp. 174–312.

49. E.g., Robert K. Carr, *The Supreme Court and Judicial Review* (New York: Farrar & Rinehart, 1942); Fisher, *Constitutional Dialogues*; and Keynes and Miller, *The Court v. Congress*.

50. *Flast v. Cohen*, 392 U.S. 83 (1968), at 95.

51. Quoted in Bickel, *The Least Dangerous Branch*, p. 114.

52. 219 U.S. 346 (1911), at 362.

53. *Wallace v. Jaffree*, 472 U.S. 38 (1985), at 76–77.

54. Ibid., at 62.

55. 159 U.S. 651 (1895), at 653.

56. Bernard Schwartz, *The Ascent of Pragmatism: The Burger Court in Action* (Reading, Mass.: Addison-Wesley, 1990), pp. 45–46.

57. *DeFunis v. Odegard*, 416 U.S. 312 (1974), at 350.

58. *Roe v. Wade*, 410 U.S. 113 (1973), at 125.

59. 262 U.S. 447 (1923), at 488.

60. *United States v. Richardson*, 418 U.S. 166 (1974); *Schlesinger v. Reservists Committee to Stop the War*, 418 U.S. 208 (1974).

61. *Valley Forge Christian College v. Americans United for Separation of Church and State*, 454 U.S. 464 (1982); *Lujan v. Defenders of Wildlife*, 504 U.S. 555 (1992).

62. *Marbury*, 1 Cranch 137 (1803), at 170.

63. E.g., *Foster v. Neilson*, 2 Pet. 253 (1829); *United States v. Curtiss-Wright Export Corporation*, 299 U.S. 304 (1936); *Goldwater v. Carter*, 444 U.S. 996 (1979).

64. E.g., *Nixon v. United States*, 506 U.S. 224 (1993).

65. 7 How. 1 (1849), at 42.

66. 328 U.S. 549 (1946), at 553–554.

67. *Wesberry v. Sanders*, 376 U.S. 1 (1964); *Reynolds v. Sims*, 377 U.S. 533 (1963).

68. *Davis v. Bandemer*, 478 U.S. 109 (1986).

69. 495 U.S. 33 (1990).

70. 506 U.S. 224 (1993).

## Chapter 4

1. *McGrain* v. *Daugherty*, 273 U.S. 135 (1927), at 174.

2. Haynes Johnson, *Sleepwalking through History: America in the Reagan Years* (New York: W. W. Norton, 1991).

3. Max Farrand, ed., *The Records of the Federal Convention of 1787* (New Haven, Conn.: Yale University Press, 1911), vol. 3, p. 133.

4. Alexander Hamilton, "The Plan of Alexander Hamilton," in Michael Kammen, ed. *The Origins of the American Constitution* (New York: Penguin Books, 1986), pp. 36–38.

5. *Nixon* v. *United States*, 506 U.S. 228 (1993).

6. *I.N.S.* v. *Chadha*, 462 U.S. 919 (1983).

7. Ronald Dworkin, "Unenumerated Rights: Whether and How Roe Should Be Overruled," in Geoffrey R. Stone, Richard A. Epstein and Cass R. Sunstein, eds., *The Bill of Rights in the Modern State* (Chicago: University of Chicago Press, 1991), pp. 381–432.

8. *Church of Lukumi Babalu Aye* v. *City of Hialeah*, 508 U.S. 570 (1993); *Texas* v. *Johnson*, 491 U.S. 397 (1989); *Ake* v. *Oklahoma*, 470 U.S. 68 (1985).

9. Dworkin, "Unenumerated Rights," pp. 387–389.

10. Quoted in Alfred H. Kelly, Winfred A. Harbison, and Herman Belz, *The American Constitution: Its Origins and Development* (New York: W. W. Norton, 1991), p. 127.

11. Ibid., pp. 125–128.

12. Marshall Smelser, *The Democratic Republic* (New York: Harper & Row, 1968), pp. 230–232.

13. Bray Hammond, "The Bank Cases," in John A. Garraty, ed. *Quarrels That Have Shaped the Constitution* (New York: Harper & Row, 1987), pp. 37–38.

14. *McCulloch* v. *Maryland*, 4 Wheat. 316 (1819), at 421.

15. Ibid., at 431.

16. E.g., *The Legal Tender Cases*, 110 U.S. 421 (1884); *Katzenbach* v. *Morgan*, 384 U.S. 641 (1966).

17. Quoted in Charles Warren, *The Supreme Court in United States History* (Boston: Little, Brown, 1926), vol. 1, p. 597.

18. Alexander Hamilton, John Jay, and James Madison, *The Federalist Papers,* Clinton Rossiter, ed.  (New York: Mentor Books, 1961). Madison devoted *Federalist 42* to the Commerce Clause. Hamilton had addressed the need for national authority over commerce in *Federalist 22*, which was devoted to a more general condemnation of the Articles of Confederation.

19. McCloskey, *The American Supreme Court,* p. 45.

20. George Dangerfield, "The Steamboat Case," in *Quarrels That Have Shaped the Constitution,* John A. Garraty, ed. (New York: Harper & Row, 1987), pp. 57–69.

21. *Gibbons* v. *Ogden,* 9 Wheat. 1 (1824), at 196–197.

22. Ibid, at 194.

23. Quoted in Warren, *The Supreme Court in United States History,* vol. 1, pp. 620–621.

24. *Gibbons,* 9 Wheat., at 194.

25. Joan Biskupic and Elder Witt, *The Supreme Court & the Powers of the American Government* (Washington, D.C.: Congressional Quarterly, 1997), p. 140.

26. Quoted in John C. Miller, *The Federalist Era, 1789–1801* (New York: Harper & Row, 1960), p. 147.

27. Marc J. Rozell, *Executive Privilege: The Dilemma of Secrecy and Democratic Accountability* (Baltimore: Johns Hopkins University Press, 1994), pp. 32–35, 9.

28. Ibid., pp. 35–36.

29. Woodrow Wilson, *Congressional Government* (Boston: Houghton Mifflin, 1885), p. 303.

30. *Anderson* v. *Dunn,* 6 Wheat. 204 (1821), at 228.

31. *McGrain,* 273 U.S. at 173 (1927).

32. Ross Evans Paulson, *Liberty, Equality and Justice: Civil Rights, Women's Rights, and the Regulation of Business, 1865–1932* (Durham, N.C.: Duke University Press, 1997), pp. 178–203.

33. Walter Goodman, *The Committee: The Extraordinary Career of the House Committee on Un-American Activities* (New York: Farrar, Straus & Giroux, 1968), pp. 6–8.

34. Ibid., p. 12.

35. Ibid., p. 49.

36. Ibid., p. 55.

37. William L. O'Neill, *American High: The Years of Confidence, 1945–1960* (New York: The Free Press, 1986), pp. 141–142.

38. Ellen W. Schrecker, *No Ivory Tower: McCarthyism and the Universities* (New York: Oxford University Press, 1986), p. 9.

39. Richard H. Rovere, *Senator Joe McCarthy* (New York: Harper Books, 1959), pp. 125–126.

40. O'Neill, *American High,* p. 159.

41. Rovere, *Senator Joe McCarthy,* pp. 205–229.

42. Victor S. Navasky, *Naming Names* (New York: Viking Press, 1980), pp. 199–222.

43. O'Neill, *American High,* pp. 160–162.

44. *Dennis* v. *United States,* 341 U.S. 494 (1951).

45. 354 U.S. 178 (1957).

46. 360 U.S. 109 (1959).

47. Ibid., at 137.

48. Edward Keynes and Randall Miller, *The Court* v. *Congress: Prayer, Busing, and Abortion* (Durham, N.C.: Duke University Press, 1989), pp. 168–171.

49. 372 U.S. 539 (1963), at 554.

50. E.g., *Deutch* v. *United States,* 367 U.S. 4546 (1961); *Russell* v. *United States,* 369 U.S. 749 (1962); *Yellin* v. *United States,* 374 U.S. 109 (1963).

51. Rodney A. Smolla, *Free Speech in an Open Society* (New York: Alfred A. Knopf, 1992), pp. 110, 116 (emphasis in original).

52. Eric Foner, *Reconstruction: America's Unfinished Revolution, 1863–1877* (New York: Harper & Row, 1988), p. 446.

53. Ibid., pp. 556–557.

54. John Hope Franklin, *Reconstruction after the Civil War* (Chicago: University of Chicago Press, 1994), pp. 189–210, 215.

55. *The Civil Rights Cases of 1883,* 109 U.S. 3 (1883), at 17.

56. Ibid., at 19.

57. Gerald Gunther, *Constitutional Law,* 12th ed. (Westbury, N.Y.: Foundation Press, 1991), p. 888.

58. 334 U.S. 1 (1948).

59. 392 U.S. 409 (1968), at 424, 443.

60. 427 U.S. 160 (1976).

61. David Lublin, *The Paradox of Representation* (Princeton, N.J.: Princeton University Press, 1997), p. 18.

62. E.g., Jesse H. Choper, "Congressional Power to Expand Judicial Definitions of the Substantive Terms of the Civil War Amendments," *Minnesota Law Review* 67 (1982), pp. 299–341; William Cohen, "Congressional Power to Interpret Due Process and Equal Protection," *Stanford Law Review* 27 (1975), pp. 603–620.

63. 491 U.S. 164 (1989).

64. David G. Savage, *Turning Right: The Making of the Rehnquist Supreme Court* (New York: John Wiley & Sons, 1992), pp. 188–192, 221–222.

65. 521 U.S. 507 (1997), at 533.

66. Richard Neustadt, *Presidential Power and the Modern Presidents* (New York: The Free Press, 1990), pp. 29.

67. *Federalist 47*, pp. 301, 302–303. Quotation is taken from Montesquieu, *The Spirit of the Laws.*

68. Sotirios A. Barber, *The Constitution and the Delegation of Congressional Power* (Chicago: University of Chicago Press, 1975), pp. 11–51, 108.

69. 10 Wheat. 1 (1825), at 43.

70. Alfred H. Kelly, Winfred A. Harbison, and Herman Belz, *The American Constitution: Its Origin and Development* (New York: W. W. Norton, 1991), pp. 471–474.

71. Barbara Hinkson Craig, *Chadha: The Story of an Epic Constitutional Struggle* (New York: Oxford University Press, 1988), pp. 50–52.

72. Louis Fisher, *Constitutional Dialogues: Interpretation as a Political Process* (Princeton, N.J.: Princeton University Press, 1988), pp. 224–225.

73. 462 U.S. 919 (1983), at 951, 959.

74. Fisher, "The Legislative Veto: Invalidated, It Survives," *Law and Contemporary Problems* 56 (1993), pp. 273–292; Fisher, *Constitutional Dialogues,* pp. 224–229.

75. Craig, *Chadha,* pp. 53–56.

76. Quoted in Karen O'Connor and Larry J. Sabato, *American Government: Continuity and Change* (Boston: Allyn & Bacon, 1997), p. 299.

77. Biskupic and Witt, *The Supreme Court and the Powers of American Government,* p. 149.

78. Bernard Schwartz, *Super Chief: Earl Warren and His Supreme Court* (New York: New York University Press, 1983), pp. 757–759.

79. 115 U.S. 1842 (1995).

80. Lincoln J. Connolly, "Mowing Down a Grass Roots Movement but Protecting the Crabgrass: Congressional Term Limits Are Unconstitutional," *University of Miami Law Review* 50 (1996), pp. 678–705.

81. Dennis Thompson, *Ethics in Congress* (Washington, D.C.: The Brookings Institution, 1995).

82. 166 U.S. 661 (1897), at 669–670.

83. 103 U.S. 168 at 204.

## Chapter 5

1. This vignette is drawn from Richard E. Neustadt, *Presidential Power and the Modern Presidents* (New York: Free Press, 1990), p. 10 (emphasis in original).

2. Ibid., pp. 11, 28.

3. Ibid., pp. 32–35.

4. Arthur M. Schlesinger Jr., *The Imperial Presidency* (Boston: Houghton Mifflin, 1974); Fred Greenstein, *Leadership in the Modern Presidency* (Cambridge, Mass.: Harvard University Press, 1988); Richard Rose, *The Postmodern President* (Chatham, N.J.: Chatham House, 1988).

5. 272 U.S. 52 (1926), at 117.

6. Quoted in Karen O'Connor and Larry J. Sabato, *American Government: Continuity and Change* (Boston: Allyn and Bacon, 1997), p. 313.

7. *Federalist 73*, pp. 422–423. Quotation of Madison is taken from Louis Fisher, *Constitutional Conflicts between Congress and the President* (Princeton, N.J.: Princeton University Press, 1985), p. 144.

8. *Federalist 47*, p. 302.

9. Fisher, *Constitutional Conflicts,* pp. 140–141.

10. 19 Howard 393 (1857).

11. Edward S. Corwin, *The President: Office and Powers,* 4th ed. (New York: New York University Press, 1957), p. 3.

12. Richard Hofstadter, *The Progressive Movement* (Englewood Cliffs, N.J.: Prentice-Hall, 1963), pp. 3–15, 141–144.

13. Theodore Roosevelt, *An Autobiography* (New York: Macmillan, 1920), p. 406 (emphasis added).

14. Indeed, few academic political scientists—Wilson later taught at Princeton—have had the opportunity to turn theory into practice on such a spectacular scale.

15. Samuel Eliot Morrison, Henry Steele Commager, and William E. Leuchtenberg, *The Growth of the American Republic,* vol. 2 (New York: Oxford University Press, 1969).

16. William E. Leuchtenburg, "Franklin D. Roosevelt: The First Modern President," in Fred I. Greenstein, ed., *Leadership in the Modern Presidency* (Cambridge, Mass.: Harvard University Press, 1988), pp. 7–41.

17. *Federalist 70*, pp. 423–424.

18. Richard Rose, *The Postmodern President* (Chatham, N.J.: Chatham House, 1988), p. 20.

19. John Locke, *Two Treatises of Government,* Thomas I. Cook, ed. (New York: Free Press, 1974).

20. Quoted in Rose, *The Postmodern President,* p. 50.

21. Ibid., p. 20.

22. Ibid.

23. William H. Taft, *Our Chief Magistrate and His Powers* (New York: Columbia University Press, 1916), pp. 139–140.

24. Joseph Bessette and Jeffrey Tulis, *The Presidency in the Constitutional Order* (Baton Rouge: Louisiana State University Press, 1981).

25. *In re Neagle,* 135 U.S. 1 (1890), at 64.

26. Francis E. Rourke, *Bureaucracy, Politics and Public Policy* (Boston: Little, Brown, 1988).

27. G. Calvin McKenzie, *The Politics of Presidential Appointments* (New York: The Free Press, 1981).

28. 487 U.S. 654 (1988).

29. Katy J. Harriger, *Independent Justice: The Federal Special Prosecutor in American Politics* (Lawrence: University Press of Kansas, 1992), p. 41.

30. Cass R. Sunstein, "Unchecked and Unbalanced: Why the Independent Counsel Act Must Go," *The American Prospect* 38 (May–June 1998), pp. 20–27.

31. *Federalist 77*, p. 459

32. Alfred H. Kelly, Winfred A. Harbison, and Herman Belz, *The Constitution: Its Origins and Development,* vol. 1 (New York: W. W. Norton, 1997), pp. 120–121.

33. C. Herman Pritchett, *Constitutional Law of the Federal System* (Englewood Cliffs, N.J.: Prentice-Hall, 1984), pp. 292–293.

34. 272 U.S. 52 (1926).

35. 295 U.S. 602 (1935).

36. Donald L. Robinson, "Presidential Prerogative and the Spirit of American Constitutionalism," in *The Constitution and the Conduct of American Foreign Policy,* David Gray Adler and Larry N. George, eds.

(Lawrence: University Press of Kansas, 1996), pp. 114–115.

37. Ibid., pp. 115–116.

38. Quoted in Fisher, *Constitutional Conflicts*, p. 288.

39. Robinson, "Presidential Prerogative," pp. 117–118.

40. Quoted in Biskupic and Witt, *The Supreme Court and the Powers of American Government*, p. 173.

41. Dean Alfange Jr., "The Quasi-War and Presidential Warmaking," in *The Constitution and the Conduct of American Foreign Policy*, pp. 274–281.

42. 4 Dall. 36 (1800); 1 Cranch 1 (1801).

43. Francis D. Wormuth, "The Vietnam War: The President vs. the Constitution," in Richard A. Falk, ed., *The Vietnam War and International Law* (Princeton, N.J.: Princeton University Press, 1969). According to the State Department, the United States had engaged in 125 limited wars without congressional authorization as of 1967. The State Department's official publication on this matter, "Armed Actions Taken by the United States without a Declaration of War, 1798–1967," U.S. Department of State, Research Project 806A (August 1967), was part of a larger effort by the Johnson administration to defend the constitutionality of America's role in Vietnam.

44. 22 Black 635 (1863).

45. Ibid., at 698.

46. This quotation from Senator James A. Mayard (D–Del.) is taken from David Herbert Donald, *Lincoln* (New York: Simon & Schuster, 1995), p. 380.

47. Kelly, Harbison, and Belz, *The American Constitution*, p. 298.

48. 4 Wall 2 (1866).

49. This and the discussion of *Milligan* that follows is taken from Allan Nevins, "The Case of the Copperhead Conspirator," in John A. Garraty, ed., *Quarrels That Have Shaped the Constitution* (New York: Harper & Row, 1987), pp. 101–118.

50. Ibid., p. 111.

51. *Milligan*, 4 Wall at 120–121, 126–127.

52. Corwin, *The President*, pp. 272, 502.

53. 249 U.S. 47 (1919); 249 U.S. 211 (1919); 250 U.S. 616 (1919).

54. Rodney K. Smolla, *Free Speech in an Open Society* (New York: Oxford University Press, 1992), p. 101.

55. President Wilson issued an executive order in 1921 commuting Debs's prison sentence to time served. However, his citizenship was never restored.

56. Quoted in Biskupic and Witt, *The Supreme Court and American Government*, p. 178.

57. Peter G. Irons, *The Courage of Their Convictions* (New York: The Free Press, 1988), pp. 39–49.

58. 320 U.S. 81 (1943), at 98.

59. Irons, *Courage of Their Convictions*, pp. 45–46.

60. 323 U.S. 214 (1944).

61. Ibid., at 248, 242, 233.

62. Bennett M. Rich, *The Presidents and Civil Disorder* (Washington, D.C.: Brookings Institution, 1941), pp. 177–183.

63. Louis Fisher, *Presidential War Power* (Lawrence: University Press of Kansas, 1995), pp. 84–91.

64. Ibid., pp. 101–103.

65. John Hart Ely, *War and Responsibility* (Princeton, N.J.: Princeton University Press, 1993), p. ix.

66. Fisher, *Presidential War Power*, pp. 123–128.

67. Sanford J. Ungar, *The Papers and the Papers* (New York: Columbia University Press, 1972), pp. 36–37.

68. Ibid., pp. 83–84.

69. 403 U.S. 713 (1971).

70. In *Snepp v. United States* (1980), the Court ruled that a Central Intelligence Agency rule, derived in part from congressional requirements, prohibiting former officers from publishing information about its operations without prior permission was a valid exercise of government power to safeguard national security interests.

71. George C. Herring, *America's Longest War: The United States and Vietnam* (New York: John Wiley & Sons, 1979), pp. 252–256.

72. Edward Keynes, "The War Powers Resolution and the Persian Gulf War," in *The Constitution and the Conduct of American Foreign Policy*, pp. 241–242.

73. 453 U.S. 654 (1981).

74. This statement was first made by John Marshall while still serving in Congress as a House member from Virginia in 1799 to support President John Adams's extradition of a fugitive under the Jay

Treaty. Quoted in Corwin, *The President*, pp. 177–178.

75. Louis Henkin, *Foreign Affairs and the Constitution* (New York: W. W. Norton, 1972), pp. 18–19, 297.

76. For further comment on this point, see Robert A. Divine, "The Case of the Smuggled Bombers," in *Quarrels That Have Shaped the Constitution*, pp. 253–265.

77. *Federalist 70*, p. 427.

78. E.g., *United States v. Belmont*, 301 U.S. 324 (1937); and *United States v. Pink*, 315 U.S. 203 (1942).

79. Pritchett, *Constitutional Law of the Federal System*, p. 316.

80. *Federalist 51*, p. 322.

81. Raoul Berger, *Executive Privilege: A Constitutonal Myth* (Cambridge, Mass.: Harvard University Press, 1974), p. 306.

82. 4 Wall 475 (1867).

83. Eric Foner, *Reconstruction: America's Unfinished Revolution, 1863–1877* (New York: Harper & Row, 1988), pp. 290–291.

84. 6 Wall 40 (1868).

85. 7 Wall 506 (1869).

86. John Hope Franklin, *Reconstruction after the Civil War*, 2nd ed. (Chicago: University of Chicago Press, 1994), p. 73.

87. 7 Wall at 498.

88. 457 U.S. 731 (1982), at 751–753.

89. Ibid., at 759.

90. 157 F. Supp. 937 (Ct. Cl. 1958). For a description of the rise of executive privilege claims since the Eisenhower presidency, see Marc J. Rozell, *Executive Privilege: The Dilemma of Secrecy and Accountability* (Baltimore: Johns Hopkins University Press, 1994).

91. *Chicago & Southern Airlines v. Waterman S.S. Co.*, 333 U.S. 103 (1948); and *United States v. Reynolds*, 345 U.S. 1 (1953).

92. Quoted in John C. Miller, *The Federalist Era, 1789–1801* (New York: Harper & Row, 1960), p. 147.

93. Berger, *Executive Privilege*, pp. 163–208.

94. 418 U.S. 683 (1974).

95. Bernard Schwartz, *The Ascent of Pragmatism: The Burger Court in Action* (Reading, Mass.: Addison-Wesley, 1990), pp. 81–87; Ungar, *The Papers and the Papers*, pp. 301–307.

## *Chapter 6*

1. I borrow this example, in part, from Robert B. Reich, *The Resurgent Liberal*

*and Other Unfashionable Prophecies* (New York: Vintage Books, 1991), pp. 166–173.

2. *Federalist* 23, p. 153.

3. Quoted in Charles Warren, *The Supreme Court in United States History,* vol. 1 (Boston: Little, Brown, 1926), p. 597.

4. Robert G. McCloskey, *The American Supreme Court,* 2nd ed. (Chicago: University of Chicago Press, 1994), p. 78.

5. 4 Wheat. 316 (1819).

6. Alfred H. Kelly, Winfred A. Harbison, and Herman Belz, *The American Constitution: Its Origins and Development,* vol. 1 (New York: W. W. Norton, 1991), pp. 194–195.

7. 9 Wheat. 1 (1824), at 189–190.

8. Ibid., at 193.

9. Ibid., at 194–95.

10. Ibid., at 188.

11. Kelly, Harbison, and Belz, *The American Constitution,* p. 196.

12. For the fullest expression of Calhoun's nullification theory, see John C. Calhoun, *A Disquisition on Government,* Richard K. Cralle, ed. (New York: P. Smith, 1963).

13. C. Herman Pritchett, *Constitutional Law of the Federal System* (Englewood Cliffs, N.J.: Prentice-Hall, 1984), pp. 56–57.

14. *Charles River Bridge v. Warren Bridge,* 11 Peters 420 (1837); *United States v. King,* 7 Howard 833 (1849); *Swift v. Tyson,* 16 Peters 1 (1842).

15. 46 U.S. 504 (1847).

16. Bernard Schwartz, *A History of the Supreme Court* (New York: Oxford University Press, 1993), pp. 69–104.

17. Felix Frankfurter, *The Commerce Clause under Marshall, Taney and Waite* (Chapel Hill: University of North Carolina Press, 1960), p. 46.

18. Woodrow Wilson, "The Study of Administration," *Political Science Quarterly* 2 (1887): 197–222, at 201.

19. Quoted in Richard Hofstadter, *The Progressive Movement, 1900–1915* (Englewood Cliffs, N.J.: Prentice-Hall, 1963), p. 143.

20. 167 U.S. 479 (1897).

21. 156 U.S. 1 (1895).

22. Kelly, Harbison, and Belz, *The American Constitution,* pp. 379–380.

23. For further discussion on the industrialization of the post-Reconstruction South and its long-term social and economic impact, see John Egerton, *Speak Now Against the Day: The Generation Before the Civil Rights Movement in the South* (New York: Alfred A. Knopf, 1994).

24. 234 U.S. 342 (1914), at 352.

25. 96 U.S 375 (1905), at 398–399.

26. Marie Van Vorst, *The Woman Who Toils: Being the Experiences of Two Gentlewomen as Factory Girls* (New York: Doubleday 1903); John Spargo, *The Bitter Cry of the Children* (New York: Macmillan, 1906); Robert Hunter, *Poverty* (New York: Macmillan, 1904).

27. Louis Brandeis, *Other People's Money* (New York: Frederick A. Stokes Co., 1914); Woodrow Wilson, *The New Freedom* (New York: Doubleday, Page & Company, 1913).

28. See, for example, Paul Kens, *Judicial Power and Reform Politics: The Anatomy of Lochner v. New York* (Lawrence: University Press of Kansas, 1989); Howard Gillman, *The Constitution Besieged: The Rise and Demise of Lochner Era Police Powers Jurisprudence* (Durham, N.C.: Duke University Press, 1993).

29. Cass Sunstein, *The Partial Constitution* (Cambridge, Mass.: Harvard University Press, 1993), p. 42.

30. 198 U.S. 45 (1905), at 76, 75.

31. Philipa Strum, *Brandeis: Beyond Progressivism* (Lawrence: University Press of Kansas, 1993).

32. 304 U.S. 144 (1938).

33. Alec Fyfe, *Child Labour* (Cambridge, Mass.: Polity Press, 1989), p. 58.

34. Grace Abbott, *The Child and the State* (Chicago: University of Chicago Press, 1938), p. 462.

35. Ibid., pp. 268, 359.

36. Stephen B. Wood, *Constitutional Politics in the Progressive Era: Child Labor and the Law* (Chicago: University of Chicago Press, 1968).

37. Ibid., pp. 55–56.

38. *Hoke v. United States,* 227 U.S. 308 (1913) (upholding the Mann Act prohibiting the transportation of women across state lines for "immoral" purposes); *Champion v. Ames,* 188 U.S. 256 (1903) (also known as the *Lottery Case,* discussed later in this chapter); *McCray v. United States,* 195 U.S. 27 (1904) (also known as the *Oleomargarine Case,* upholding under its power to tax and spend the power of Congress to impose a tax intended to penalize the purchase of falsely labeled foods); and *Hipolite Egg Co. v. United States,* 220 U.S. 45 (1911) (upholding under the Commerce Clause a ban on the sale of certain impure foods).

39. 259 U.S. 20 (1922).

40. 193 U.S. 197 (1904).

41. Quoted in Gerald Gunther, *Constitutional Law,* 12th ed. (Westbury, N.Y.: Foundation Press, 1991), p. 180.

42. Strum, *Brandeis,* p. 192, fn. 52.

43. Louis Hine, *Louis Hine: Photographs of Child Labor in the New South,* John R. Kemp, ed. (Jackson: University Press of Mississippi, 1986), p. 11.

44. V. O. Key, *The Responsible Electorate* (Cambridge, Mass.: Harvard University Press, 1966), p. 31.

45. Quoted in William E. Leuchtenburg, *The Supreme Court Reborn: The Constitutional Revolution in the Age of Roosevelt* (New York: Oxford University Press, 1995), p. 213.

46. Sunstein, *The Partial Constitution,* p. 57.

47. Ibid., p. 58.

48. On the importance of philosophical pragmatism in the Court's rejection of pre–New Deal legal formalism, see Gary J. Jacobsohn, *Pragmatism, Statesmanship and the Supreme Court* (Ithaca, N.Y.: Cornell University Press, 1977).

49. 293 U.S. 388 (1935).

50. 295 U.S. 495 (1935).

51. 300 U.S. 379 (1937), at 399–400.

52. Robert H. Jackson, *The Struggle for Judicial Supremacy* (New York: Alfred A. Knopf, 1941), p. 213.

53. *Hylton v. United States,* 3 Dall. 171 (1796) (ruling that Article I, Section 9, barred only capitation and land taxes as direct forms of taxation); 158 U.S. 601 (1895).

54. 102 U.S. 586 (1881).

55. 195 U.S. 27 (1904), at 56.

56. 249 U.S. 86 (1919), at 94.

57. 297 U.S. 1 (1936).

58. Ibid., at 62.

59. 379 U.S. 241 (1964); 379 U.S. 264 (1964).

60. 379 U.S. 241, at 279, quoting *Edwards v. California,* 314 U.S. 160 (1941).

61. 109 U.S. 3 (1883).

62. Ibid., at 17.

## Chapter 7

1. This account of Governor Wallace's stand-in the schoolhouse door, including all quotations, is taken from E. Culpepper

Clark, *The Schoolhouse Door: Segregation's Last Stand at the University of Alabama* (New York: Oxford University Press, 1993), pp. 225–237, 254.

2. *New State Ice Co. v. Liebmann,* 285 U.S. 262 (1932), at 311.

3. *Federalist* 39, p. 246.

4. David F. Epstein, *The Political Theory of the Federalist* (Chicago: University of Chicago Press, 1984), p. 51.

5. *Federalist* 51, p. 323.

6. Herbert J. Storing, *What the Anti-Federalists Were For* (Chicago: University of Chicago Press, 1981), p. 33.

7. Quoted in ibid., p. 34.

8. Dumas Malone, *Jefferson and the Ordeal of Liberty* (Boston: Little, Brown, 1962).

9. Richard K. Matthews, *If Men Were Angels: James Madison and the Heartless Empire of Reason* (Lawrence: University Press of Kansas, 1995), p. 20.

10. Richard Hofstadter, *The American Political Tradition* (New York: Random House, 1948), pp. 18–44.

11. Alfred H. Kelly, Winfred A. Harbison, and Herman Belz, *The American Constituion: Its Origins and Development* (New York: W. W. Norton, 1997), pp. 118–119.

12. Hofstadter, *American Political Tradition,* p. 91.

13. Epstein, *Political Theory of the Federalist,* pp. 55–56

14. Quoted in Melvin I. Urofsky, *A March of Liberty: A Constitutional History of the United States* (New York: Alfred A. Knopf, 1988), p. 418.

15. Ibid., p. 420.

16. Ibid., pp. 411–412

17. 15.92 U.S. 542 (1876), at 551.

18. Michael Kent Curtis, *No State Shall Abridge: The Fourteenth Amendment and the Bill of Rights* (Durham, N.C.: Duke University Press, 1994), p. 179.

19. Vincent Blasi, "The Rootless Activism of the Burger Court," in Vincent Blasi, ed., *The Burger Court: The Counterrevolution That Wasn't* (New Haven, Conn.: Yale University Press, 1983), pp. 198–217.

20. 426 U.S. 833 (1976).

21. Conference discussion taken from Bernard Schwartz, *The Ascent of Pragmatism: The Burger Court in Action* (Boston: Addison-Wesley, 1990), p. 101.

22. 392 U.S. 183 (1968).

23. Schwartz, *The Ascent of Pragmatism,* pp. 101–102.

24. Sue Davis, "Justice Rehnquist: Right-Wing Ideologue or Majoritarian Democrat," in Charles M. Lamb and Stephen C. Halpern, eds., *The Burger Court: Political and Judicial Profiles* (Bloomington: University of Indiana Press, 1991), pp. 315, 321–323, 334.

25. *National League of Cities,* 426 U.S. at 845.

26. Phillip J. Cooper, *Battles on the Bench: Conflict Inside the Supreme Court* (Lawrence: University Press of Kansas, 1995), p. 97.

27. Schwartz, *The Ascent of Pragmatism,* p. 105.

28. Ibid., p. 110.

29. Appointed by President George Bush in 1990, Justice Souter began to move away from the Court's conservative orbit by the end of the 1991–1992 term, with his most spectacular defections coming in *Planned Parenthood* v. *Casey,* which upheld *Roe* v. *Wade,* and *Lee* v. *Wiseman,* which invalidated a high school commencement prayer. Justices Kennedy and O'Connor joined with Souter to provide the key swing votes in *Planned Parenthood* and *Wiseman,* a development that led some commentators to conclude that they were now the command and control center on the Court. Kennedy's and O'Connor's move to the middle proved short-lived. For Souter, it served as a weigh station on the path to his transformation into perhaps the Court's most articulate liberal voice. For more on Justice Souter's evolution on the Court, see David J. Garrow, "Justice Souter Emerges," *New York Times Magazine,* September 25, 1994.

30. 505 U.S. 144 (1992), at 177.

31. *Gibbons* v. *Ogden,* 9 Wheat. 1, at 208.

32. Ibid., at 203 (emphasis supplied).

33. 11 Pet. 420 (1837), at 552.

34. Robert G. McCloskey, *The American Supreme Court* (Chicago: University of Chicago Press, 1960), pp. 56–59.

35. Alpheus T. Mason and William M. Beaney, *The Supreme Court in a Free Society* (Englewood Cliffs, N.J.: Prentice-Hall, 1959), p. 82.

36. 9 Wheat. 1 (1824), at 242.

37. McCloskey, *The American Supreme Court,* p. 46.

38. Kelly, Harbison, and Belz, *The American Constitution,* pp. 230–231.

39. Thomas Reed Powell, *Vagaries and Varieties in Constitutional Interpretation* (New York: AMS Press, 1967), p. 152.

40. 11 Peters 102 (1837), at 132–133.

41. *Edwards* v. *California,* 314 U.S. 160 (1941) (striking down a California law that made it a misdemeanor knowingly to transport an indigent into the state).

42. Carl B. Swisher, *History of the Supreme Court of the United States, Vol. V: The Taney Period 1836–64* (New York: Macmillan, 1941), p. 407.

43. 350 U.S. 497 (1956).

44. 206 U.S. 230 (1907), at 238.

45. For an excellent general overview on the development of federal environmental regulation, see Michael E. Kraft and Norman J. Vig, "Environmental Policy from the 1970s to the 1990s: An Overview," in Norman J. Vig and Michael E. Kraft, eds., *Environmental Policy in the 1990s,* 3rd ed. (Washington, D.C.: Congressional Quarterly Press, 1997), pp. 1–30.

46. For a summary of the Court's application of the preemption doctrine to environmental protection cases, see Joan Biskupic and Elder Witt, *The Supreme Court and the Powers of American Government* (Washington, D.C.: Congressional Quarterly Press, 1997), p. 303.

47. Lettie McSpadden, "Environmental Policy in the Courts," in Norman J. Vig and Michael E. Kraft, eds., *Environmental Policy in the 1990s,* 3rd. ed. (Washington, D.C.: Congressional Quarterly, 1997), pp. 168–186.

## *Chapter 8*

1. Alfred H. Kelly, Winfred A. Harbison, and Herman Belz, *The American Constitution: Its Origins and Development* (New York: W. W. Norton, 1997), pp. 186–188.

2. *Federalist* 1, p. 36.

3. Jennifer Nedelsky, *Private Property and the Limits of American Constitutionalism* (Chicago: University of Chicago Press, 1990). The "preoccupation" for the protection of private property and how it influenced the choices of the Framers in framing the Constitution is the core thesis of Nedelsky's book.

4. *Federalist* 10, p. 79.

5. Ibid.

6. Kelly, Harbison, and Belz, *The American Constitution*, p. 187.

7. Quoted in Alpheus T. Mason and Donald Grier Stephenson Jr., *American Constitutional Law: Introductory Essays and Selected Cases* (Upper Saddle River, N.J.: Prentice-Hall, 1996), p. 295.

8. *Federalist* 44, p. 282.

9. Ibid., p. 283.

10. Robert Lowry Clinton, *Marbury v. Madison and Judicial Review* (Lawrence: University Press of Kansas, 1989), pp. 143–145.

11. 6 Cranch 87 (1810).

12. Ibid., at 139.

13. Robert G. McCloskey, *The American Supreme Court* (Chicago: University of Chicago Press, 1994), pp. 32–34.

14. 3 Dallas 386 (1798).

15. Ibid., at 400.

16. 4 Wheaton 518 (1819).

17. For an excellent and lively account of the political machinations behind the battle over Dartmouth College, see Richard N. Current, "The Dartmouth College Case," in John A. Garraty, ed., *Quarrels That Have Shaped the Constitution* (New York: Harper Torchbooks, 1987), pp. 21–35.

18. 7 Cranch 164 (1812).

19. 9 Cranch 43 (1815).

20. 12 Wheat. 213 (1827).

21. 11 Peters 420 (1837).

22. Henry F. Graff, "The Charles River Bridge Case," in *Quarrels That Have Shaped the Constitution*, pp. 71–85.

23. 36 U.S. 420 (1837), at 547–548.

24. Benjamin Wright, *The Contract Clause of the Constitution* (Cambridge, Mass.: Harvard University Press, 1938). For an assessment of Wright's influence on Contract Clause scholarship, see Clinton, *Marbury v. Madison*, pp. 150–160.

25. 19 Howard 393 (1857).

26. 290 U.S. 398 (1934).

27. 379 U.S. 497 (1965).

28. 431 U.S. 1 (1977).

29. 438 U.S. 234 (1978).

30. Ibid., at 241, 245.

31. 459 U.S. 176 (1983); 462 U.S. 176 (1983).

32. 480 U.S. 470 (1987).

33. Richard A. Epstein, *Takings: Private Property and the Power of Eminent Domain* (Cambridge, Mass.: Harvard University Press, 1985), p. 92.

## Chapter 9

1. Vignette, including quotations, is taken from Robert B. Reich, *Locked in the Cabinet* (New York: Alfred A. Knopf, 1997), pp. 113–116.

2. Cass R. Sunstein, *The Partial Constitution* (Cambridge, Mass.: Harvard University Press, 1993), pp. 40–42.

3. Alfred H. Kelly, Winfred A. Harbison, and Herman Belz, *The American Constitution: Its Origins and Development*, vol. 1 (New York: W. W. Norton, 1991), p. 240.

4. Charles Darwin, *The Origin of Species* (London: J. Murray, 1859).

5. Herbert Spencer, *Social Statics* (New York: D. Appleton & Co., 1864).

6. William Graham Sumner, *What Social Classes Owe to Each Other* (New York: Harper & Bros., 1883).

7. Richard Hofstadter, *Social Darwinism in American Thought* (Boston: Beacon Press, 1955), p. 51.

8. Ibid., p. 31.

9. Sumner, *Social Classes*, p. 19.

10. Sumner, "The Absurd Effort to Remake the World Over," in Stow Persons, ed., *Social Darwinism: Selected Essays of William Graham Sumner* (Englewood Cliffs, N.J.: Prentice-Hall, 1963), p. 179.

11. 198 U.S. 45 (1905).

12. Ibid., at 75.

13. Mark DeWolfe Howe, ed., *Holmes-Pollock Letters*, vol. 1 (Cambridge, Mass.: Harvard University Press, 1941), pp. 57–58.

14. Harold J. Laski, "The Political Philosophy of Mr. Justice Holmes," *Yale Law Journal* 40 (1931), p. 683; Francis Biddle, *Mr. Justice Holmes* (New York: Charles Scribner's Sons, 1943).

15. 198 U.S. 45 at 76.

16. Richard Hofstadter, *The Progressive Movement, 1900–1915* (Englewood Cliffs, N.J.: Prentice-Hall, 1963), pp. 2–3.

17. Ibid., pp. 6–15.

18. Oliver Wendell Holmes, *The Common Law* (Cambridge, Mass.: Harvard University Press, 1897); Benjamin Cardozo, *The Nature of the Judicial Process* (New Haven, Conn.: Yale University Press, 1921), p. 168; *United States v. Carolene Products*, 304 U.S. 144 (1938).

19. Karen O'Connor, *Women's Organizations' Use of the Courts* (Lexington, Mass.: D.C. Heath and Co., 1980), pp. 65–75.

20. Michael Kent Curtis, *No State Shall Abridge: The Fourteenth Amendment and the Bill of Rights* (Durham, N.C.: Duke University Press, 1986).

21. 163 U.S. 537 (1896).

22. *Slaughterhouse Cases*, 83 U.S. 36 (1873).

23. Curtis, *No State Shall Abridge*, pp. 175–176.

24. Eric Foner, *Reconstruction: America's Unfinished Revolution* (New York: Harper & Row, 1989), p. 529.

25. Ibid., p. 530.

26. *Slaughterhouse Cases*, 83 U.S. at 123.

27. *The Civil Rights Cases*, 109 U.S. 3 (1883), at 17.

28. *Slaughterhouse Cases*, 83 U.S. at 96, 97, 109–110. (emphasis added).

29. Ibid., at 110, fn. 14.

30. Paul Kens, *Judicial Power and Reform Politics: The Anatomy of Lochner v. New York* (Lawrence: University Press of Kansas, 1989), p. 105.

31. *Slaughterhouse Cases*, 83 U.S. at 122.

32. Gerald Gunther, *Constitutional Law*, 12th ed. (Westbury, N.Y.: Foundation Press, 1991), p. 432.

33. Thomas M. Cooley, *Constitutional Limitations* (Boston: Little, Brown, 1868).

34. Benjamin R. Twiss, *Lawyers and the Constitution: How Lassiez-Faire Came to the Supreme Court* (Princeton, N.J.: Princeton University Press, 1942), p. 18.

35. Ibid, pp. 26–27.

36. Ibid., pp. 50–51.

37. 96 U.S. 97 (1878).

38. 94 U.S. 113 (1876).

39. For a thorough description of the historical and political setting of the *Granger* case, see C. Peter Magrath, "The Case of the Unscrupulous Warehouseman," in John A. Garraty, ed., *Quarrels That Shaped the Constitution* (New York: Harper & Row, 1987), pp. 119–138.

40. Recall that six years earlier, in *Stone v. Mississippi* (1880), the Court rejected a Contract Clause challenge to a Mississippi law banning lotteries, holding it was a reasonable exercise of state police power in the public interest.

41. 123 U.S. 623 (1887), at 661 (emphasis added).

42. 134 U.S. 418 (1890), at 458.

43. Kelly, Harrison, and Belz, *The American Constitution,* p. 393.

44. 165 U.S. 578 (1897).

45. Hofstadter, *The Progressive Movement,* pp. 28–33.

46. Kens, *Judicial Power and Reform Politics,* p. 142.

47. Charles Warren, "The Progressiveness of the United States Supreme Court," *Columbia Law Review* 13 (1913), pp. 294–295.

48. Of particular interest here are Howard Gillman, *The Constitution Besieged: The Rise and Demise of Lochner Era Police Powers Jurisprudence* (Durham, N.C.: Duke University Press, 1993) and Melvin I. Urofsky, "Myth and Reality: The Supreme Court and Protective Legislation in the Progressive Era: A Reevaluation," *Yearbook of the Supreme Court Historical Society* (1983), pp. 53–72.

49. 21 Wall 162 (1875).

50. 16 Wall 130 (1873).

51. Theda Skocpol, *Protecting Soldiers and Mothers: The Political Origins of Social Policy in the United States* (Cambridge, Mass.: Harvard University Press, 1992).

52. Philipa Strum, *Louis D. Brandeis: Justice for the People* (Cambridge, Mass.: Harvard University Press, 1984), pp. 119–124.

53. 243 U.S. 426 (1917), at 438.

54. 261 U.S. 525 (1923).

55. Ibid., at 553–558 (emphasis added).

56. Ibid., at 567–568.

57. Ibid., at 564.

58. Richard Hofstadter, *The Age of Reform: From Bryan to F.D.R.* (New York: Vintage Books, 1955).

59. Charles A. Beard, *An Economic Interpretation of the Constitution of the United States* (New York: The Free Press, 1986).

60. *Nebbia* v. *New York,* 291 U.S. 502 (1934).

61. 298 U.S. 587 (1936).

62. Ibid., at 611.

63. Quoted in Alpheus T. Mason, *Harlan Fiske Stone: Pillar of the Law* (New York: Viking Press, 1956), p. 426.

64. Walter F. Murphy, James E. Fleming, and Sotrios A. Barber, *American Constitutional Interpretation* (Westbury, N.Y.: Foundation Press, 1995), pp. 1078–1079.

65. 300 U.S. 379 (1937), at 391–392.

66. William E. Leuchtenburg, "The Case of the Wenatchee Chamberbaid," in John A. Garraty, ed., *Quarrels That Shaped the Constitution* (New York: Harper & Row, 1987), pp. 266–284.

67. Jennifer Nedelsky, *Private Property and the Limits of American Constitutionalism* (Chicago: University of Chicago Press, 1990), pp. 228–230.

68. *Pierce* v. *Society of Sisters,* 268 U.S. 510 (1925).

69. *Meyer* v. *Nebraska,* 262 U.S. 390 (1923), at 399.

70. 274 U.S. 200 (1927), at 207.

71. 316 U.S. 535 (1942).

72. Ibid., at 541 (emphasis added).

73. 381 U.S. 479 (1965), at 484–486.

74. 405 U.S. 438 (1972).

75. 388 U.S. 1 (1967).

76. 410 U.S. 113 (1973).

77. Ibid., at 167–168 (emphasis added).

78. James C. Mohr, *Abortion in America* (New York: Oxford University Press, 1978).

79. A particularly trenchant criticism of *Roe* is offered by John Hart Ely, "The Wages of Crying Wolf: A Comment on *Roe* v. *Wade,*" 82 *Yale Law Journal* 920 (1973).

80. Nedelsky, *Private Property,* especially pp. 203–231.

81. 505 U.S. 833 (1992), at 871.

82. 521 U.S. 702 (1997), at 719.

83. Cass R. Sunstein, *One Case at a Time: Judicial Minimalism and the Supreme Court* (Cambridge, Mass.: Harvard University Press, 1999), pp. 84–88.

## Chapter 10

1. Jennifer Nedelsky, *Private Property and the Limits of American Constitutionalism* (Chicago: University of Chicago Press, 1990), pp. 196–197.

2. 3 Dall 386 (1798) (emphasis in original).

3. Nedelsky, *Private Property,* pp. 196–198.

4. Quoted in David A. Hollinger and Charles Capper, *The American Intellectual Tradition,* vol. 2, 2nd ed. (New York: Oxford University Press, 1993), p. 165.

5. Excerpted from Thomas A. Alexander and Harry A. Hickman, eds., *The Essential Dewey: Ethics, Logic, Psychology* (Bloomington: Indiana University Press, 1998).

6. John Dewey, *The Influence of Darwin on Philosophy and Other Essays in Contemporary Thought* (New York: Holt, 1910), pp. 1–19.

7. 166 U.S. 226 (1897).

8. 260 U.S. 393 (1922), at 415.

9. 438 U.S. 104 (1978), at 132.

10. Ibid., at 124.

11. Bernard Siegan, *Economic Liberties and the Constitution* (Chicago: University of Chicago Press, 1980), pp. 110–125, 188–189.

12. Richard A. Epstein, *Takings: Private Property and the Power of Eminent Domain* (Cambridge, Mass.: Harvard University Press, 1985), pp. 331–334.

13. 467 U.S. 229 (1984).

14. 348 U.S. 26 (1954), at 33.

15. *United States* v. *564.54 Acres of Land,* 441 U.S. 506 (1979).

16. 167 U.S. 648 (1897).

17. *Backus* v. *Fort Street Union Depot Co.,* 169 U.S. 557 (1898).

18. Epstein, *Takings,* pp. 136–140.

19. Richard A. Epstein, "The Politics of Distrust," in Richard A. Epstein, Geoffrey Stone, and Cass R. Sunstein, eds., *The Bill of Rights and the Modern State* (Chicago: University of Chicago Press, 1991), pp. 41–89.

20. Epstein, *Takings,* pp. 136–140.

***a fortiori*** By even greater force of logic; even more so <if a 14-year-old child cannot sign a binding contract, then, *a fortiori*, a 13 year old cannot>.

**ad hoc** Formed for a particular purpose <the board created an ad hoc committee to discuss funding for the new arena>.

**adjudicate** To rule upon judicially.

**advisory opinion** A nonbinding statement by a court of its interpretation of the law on a matter submitted for that purpose.

**affirm** 1. To confirm (a judgment) on appeal. 2. To solemnly declare, rather than swear under oath.

***amicus curiae*** (Latin "friend of the court") A person who is not a party to a lawsuit but who petitions the court or is requested by the court to file a brief in the action because that person has a strong interest in the subject matter.

**appeal** To seek review (from a lower court's decision) by a higher court <petitioner appeals the conviction>.

**appellant** A party who appeals a lower court's decision, usually seeking reversal of that decision.

**appellee** A party against whom an appeal is taken and whose role is to respond to that appeal, usually seeking affirmance of that lower court's decision.

***arguendo*** (Latin "in arguing") 1. For the sake of argument (assuming *arguendo* that discovery procedures were correctly followed, the court still cannot grant the defendant's motion to dismiss). 2. During the course of argument.

**bill of attainder** A legislative act that inflicts punishment on named individuals or members of an easily ascertainable group without a judicial trial. The U.S. Constitution forbids Congress and the states from passing bills of attainder.

**Black Codes** 1. Antebellum state laws enacted to regulate the institution of slavery. 2. Laws enacted shortly after the Civil War in the former Confederate states to restrict the liberties of the newly freed slaves as a way to ensure a supply of inexpensive agricultural labor and to maintain white supremacy.

**brief** A written statement setting out the legal contentions of a party in litigation, especially on appeal; a document prepared by council as the basis for arguing a case, consisting of legal and factual arguments and the authorities in support of them.

**case** A proceeding, action, suit, or controversy at law or in equity.

***certiorari*, writ of** (Latin "to be more fully informed") An extraordinary writ issued by an appellate court, at its discretion, directing a lower court to deliver the record in the case for review.

**civil law** The law of civil or private rights, as opposed to criminal law or administrative law.

**class action** A lawsuit in which a single person or a small group of people represents the interests of a larger group. Requirements under federal law for maintaining a class action are (1) the class must be so large that individual suits would be impracticable, (2) there must be legal or factual questions common to the class, (3) the claims or defenses of the representative parties must be typical of those of the class, and (4) the representative parties must adequately protect the interests of the class.

**color of law** The appearance or semblance, without the substance, of legal right. The term usually implies a misuse of power made possible because the wrongdoer is clothed with the authority of the state. State action is synonymous with color of law in the context of federal civil rights statutes or criminal law.

**comity** Courtesy among political entities (as nations, states, or courts of different jurisdiction), involving especially mutual recognition of legislative, executive, and judicial acts.

**common law** The body of law derived from judicial decisions, rather than from statutes or constitutions.

**concurring opinion** A separate written opinion explaining such a vote.

**consent decree** A court decree that all parties agree to. Also termed consent order.

**contempt** Conduct that defies the authority or dignity of a court or legislature. Such conduct interferes with the administration of justice and is punishable, usually by fine or imprisonment.

**criminal law** The body of law defining offenses against the community at large, regulating how suspects are investigated, charged, and tried, and establishing punishment for convicted offenders.

**declaratory judgment** A court's final determination of the rights and obligations of the parties in a case.

**de facto** (Latin "in point of fact") 1. Actual; existing in fact; having effect, even though not formally or legally recognized.

**de jure** (Latin "as a matter of law") Existing by right or according to law.

**dicta** A statement of opinion or belief considered authoritative because of the dignity of the person making it.

**dissenting opinion**  A judicial opinion disagreeing with that of the majority of the same court, given by one or more members of the court.

**docket**  A brief entry describing the proceedings and filings in a court case.

**due process**  The conduct of legal proceedings according to established rules and principles for the protection and enforcement of private rights, including notice and the right to a fair hearing before a tribunal with the power to decide the case.

**enjoin**  1. To legally prohibit or restrain by injunction (the company was enjoined from selling its stock). 2. To prescribe, mandate, or strongly encourage.

**equity**  The recourse to principles of justice to correct or supplement the law as applied to particular circumstances.

**error, writ of**  A writ issued by an appellate court directing a lower court to deliver the record in the case for review.

***ex parte***  On or from one party only, usually without notice to or argument from the adverse party (the judge conducted the hearing *ex parte*).

**grand jury**  A body of people who are chosen to sit permanently for at least a month—sometimes a year—and who, in *ex parte* proceedings, decide whether to issue indictments. If the grand jury decides that evidence is strong enough to hold a suspect for trial, it returns a bill of indictment charging the suspect with a specific crime.

**habeas corpus**  (Latin "that you have the body") A writ employed to bring a person before a court, most frequently to ensure that the party's imprisonment or detention is not illegal.

**immunity**  An exemption from a duty, liability, or service of process; especially, such exemption granted to a public official.

***in camera***  1. In the judge's private chambers. 2. In the courtroom with all spectators excluded. 3. (Of judicial action) taken when court is not in session. Also termed in reference to the opinion of one judge.

***in forma pauperis***  (Latin "in the manner of a pauper") In the manner of an indigent who is permitted to disregard filing fees and court costs <when suing, a poor person is generally entitled to proceed *in forma pauperis*>.

***infra***  (Latin "below") Later in this text. *Infra* is used as a citational signal to refer to a later-cited authority. In medieval Latin, *infra* also acquired the sense "within."

**inter alia**  Among other things.

**ipso facto**  (Latin "by the fact itself") By the very nature of the situation.

**litigant**  A party to a lawsuit.

**mandamus, writ of**  (Latin "we command") A writ issued by a superior court to compel a lower court or a government officer to perform mandatory or purely ministerial duties correctly.

**moot**  Having no practical significance; hypothetical or academic.

**motion**  A written or oral application requesting a court to make a specified ruling or order.

**obiter dicta (see dicta)**  (Latin "something said on passing") A judicial comment made during the course of delivering a judicial opinion, but one that is unnecessary to the decision in the case and therefore not precedential.

***per curiam***  By the court as a whole.

***per se***  1. Of, in, or by itself; standing alone, without reference to additional facts. 2. As a matter of law.

**petit jury**  A jury (usually consisting of twelve persons) summoned and empaneled in the trial of a specific case.

**petitioner**  A party who presents a petition to a court or other official body, especially when seeking relief on appeal.

**plaintiff**  The party who brings a civil suit in a court of law.

**plenary**  Full; complete; to be attended by all members or participants.

**plurality opinion**  An appellate opinion without enough judges' votes to constitute a majority, but having received the greatest number of votes of any of the opinions filed.

**recuse**  To remove (oneself) as a judge in a particular case because of prejudice or conflict of interest.

**remand**  To send (a case or claim) back to the court or tribunal from which it came for some further action <the appellate court reversed the trial court's opinion and remanded the case for new trial>.

**respondent**  The party against whom an appeal is taken.

**reverse**  An appellate court's overturning of a lower court's decision.

***seriatim***  One after another; in a series; successively.

***stare decisis***  (Latin "to stand by things decided") The doctrine of precedent, under which it is necessary for a court to follow earlier judicial decisions when the same points arise again in litigation.

**state action**  Official government action, especially, in constitutional law, an intrusion on a person's rights (especially civil rights) either by a governmental entity or by a private requirement that can be enforced only by governmental action.

**statute**  A law passed by a legislative body.

**stay**  The postponement or halting of a proceeding, judgment, or the like.

***sub silento*** Under silence; without notice being taken; without being expressly mentioned.

**subpoena** (Latin "under penalty") A writ commanding a person to appear before a court or other tribunal, subject to a penalty for failing to comply.

**subpoena *duces tecum*** A subpoena ordering the witness to appear and to bring specified documents or records.

**summary judgment** A judgment granted on a claim about which there is no genuine issue of material fact and upon which the movant is entitled to prevail as a matter of law. This procedural device allows the speedy disposition of a controversy without the need for trial.

***supra*** (Latin "above") Earlier in this text; used as a citational signal to refer to a previously cited authority.

**tort** A civil wrong for which a remedy may be obtained, usually in the form of damages; as breach of a duty that the law imposes on everyone in the same relation to one another as those involved in a given transaction.

**trespass** An unlawful act committed against the person or property of another.

**vacate** To nullify or cancel; make void; invalidate.

**writ** A written court order, in the name of a state or other competent legal authority, commanding the addressee to do or refrain from doing some specified act.

implied powers of Congress
  commerce regulation and, 323
  defined, 112–113
  national bank and, 118
implied powers of the executive, 5
import taxes, 297
independent counsel. *See also* special
    prosecutors
  appointment of, 221–227
  control over, 223–224, 226–227
  creation of, 218
  jurisdiction of, 222
  role of, 221–227
  separation of powers and, 226–227
Independent Counsel, Office of, 222–224
Independent Counsel Act of 1994, 218–219
Industrial Revolution
  commerce regulation and, 299–300
  Contract Clause and, 435–436
  monopolies and, 304
  police power and, 421
  public health hazards of, 483–484
  social welfare and, 300
inferior officers
  appointment of, 219, 221–227
  Congressional approval of, 222–224
  defined, 221–222
  removal of, 228–233
insurance industry regulation, 475–477
"intelligible principle" test, 173
interest groups. *See also* political influence
  conservative public interest law
    movement, 517–518
  litigation process and, 82–85
  role of, 12
Internal Security Act, 408
International Claims Settlement Act of 1949,
  269
International Emergency Economic Powers
  Act (EEPA), 267–270
international treaties. *See* treaties
Internet guide to legal research, 548–551
interracial marriage, 503–504
interstate commerce. *See also* commerce;
  commerce regulation
  Contract Clause and, 447
  defined, 295
  environmental regulation and, 390
  expansion of government regulation
    under, 386, 387
  federal regulation of, 295, 300–302
  flow of, 417–418
  gun control and, 359
  "horse-and-buggy" definition of, 319, 320
  interpretation of, 305, 324, 327–329

legislative regulation of, 116–117, 124,
  125–128
lottery ticket transport as, 345–347
minimum drinking age and, 342
public accommodations regulation,
  347–350
racial discrimination in, 343, 350–351,
  354–355
regulation of, 116–117, 124, 125–128,
  169–172, 296, 301, 313, 317,
  347–350, 386, 387, 400–405
state laws discriminating against, 404
state power over, 402–405
state regulation of, 301, 400–405
"substantial effects" test, 356, 357, 360,
  362–363, 365–366
taxes on, 299
violence against women, 362–366
Interstate Commerce Act, 169, 299–300,
  333
Interstate Commerce Commission (ICC)
  constitutionality of, 301–302
  establishment of, 300
interstate compacts, 447
interstate travel, 349–350
intrastate commerce regulation, 296, 301,
  317, 333
investigation power of Congress, 128–150
  authority for, 131–133
  controversy over use of, 129–130
  historical roots of, 128–129
  limits on, 138
involuntary servitude, 469
Iran, 267–270
Iran-Contra scandal, 109–110, 218, 221
Iran hostage crisis, 243–244, 267–270
Iraq, 243

Jackson, Andrew, 220, 297
  on commerce regulation, 297–298
  dual federalism doctrine, 372
  states' rights and, 432
Jackson, Robert H. (Justice), 41, 227, 240,
  323
  on emergency power, 241
  on executive immunity, 281
  *Korematsu v. United States,* 251, 254–255
  *United States v. Butler,* 332–334
  *Youngstown Sheet & Tube Co. v. Sawyer,*
  257–259
Jacksonian democracy, 298
  Contract Clause and, 431–432
  influence of, 457–458
Jaffree, Ishmael, 19, 21
James, Henry, 354

James, William, 23, 510
Japanese Americans
  apology to, 254
  attitudes toward, 252
  as national security threat, 248, 252
  racial discrimination against, 239–240
  World War II evacuation of, 239–240,
  247–255
Jaworski, Leon, 287, 289
Jay, John (Justice), 3, 6, 74, 268
  *Chisholm v. Georgia,* 46
Jay Treaty, 129, 236, 266
  executive privilege and, 286
  president's negotiation of, 272
Jefferson, Thomas, 10, 12, 18, 19, 20, 32,
  214
  adverseness and, 74
  Alien and Sedition Act and, 407
  budgetary discretion, 190
  on commerce, 117
  on congressional commerce power, 296
  on Contract Clause, 422–423
  on executive immunity, 281
  executive prerogative used by, 235–236
  on federal judiciary, 46
  on interstate commerce, 295, 400
  judicial review and, 49–50
  *Marbury v. Madison* and, 48, 50
  on Necessary and Proper Clause, 114
  on Speech and Debate Clause, 205
  on states' rights, 371
  Yazoo land scandal and, 428
Jehovah's Witnesses, 240
Johnson, Andrew, 72–73, 220, 238
  Reconstruction Act and, 275–276
Johnson, Lyndon, 82, 157, 216, 517
  civil rights legislation, 347
  emergency power, 242
  on responsibilities of the president, 281
Jones, Paula, 277
  sexual harassment case, 218, 282
Jones & Laughlin Steel, 326
judges
  appointments, 13
  impeachment of, 105–107
judicial branch. *See also* federal judiciary
  establishment of, 41–44
  role of, 41–44
judicial federalism, 42
judicial independence, 42, 44–46
judicial power, 37–108
  affirmative power *vs.,* 70–72
  Article III and, 5
  defined in *Marbury v. Madison,* 53, 55
  Hamilton's description of, 2

# Case Index

Note: cases in boldface type are excerpted in this text.